MW01618150

Nineteenth-Century Art in the Norton Simon Museum

Volume I

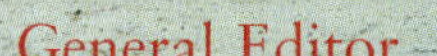

General Editor

Sara Campbell

Technical Notes by

Susan Sayre Batton

Joseph Fronek

Rosamond Westmoreland

Published for

The Norton Simon Art Foundation

by

Yale University Press New Haven and London

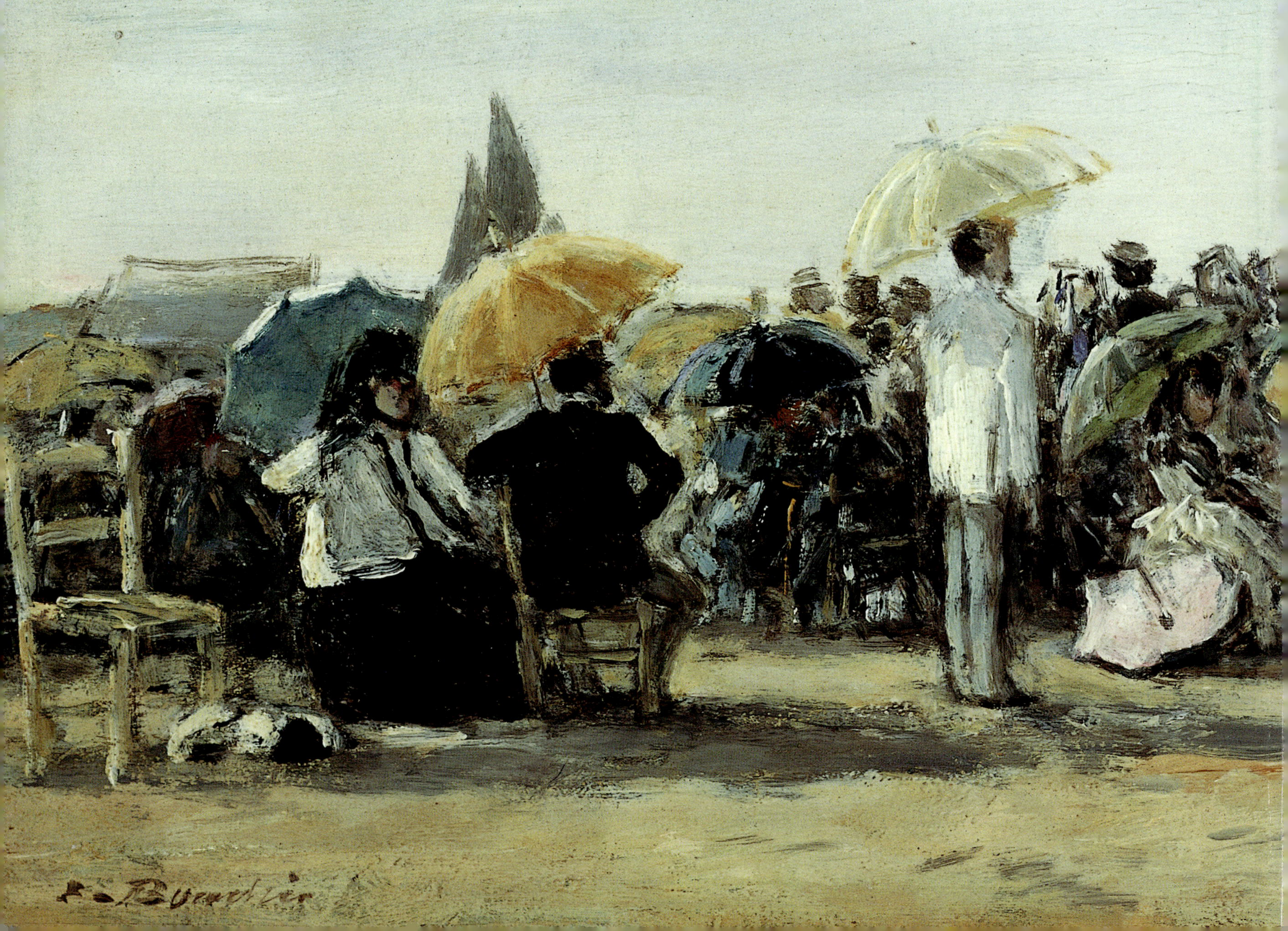

Nineteenth-Century Art in the Norton Simon Museum

Volume I

Richard R. Brettell and Stephen F. Eisenman

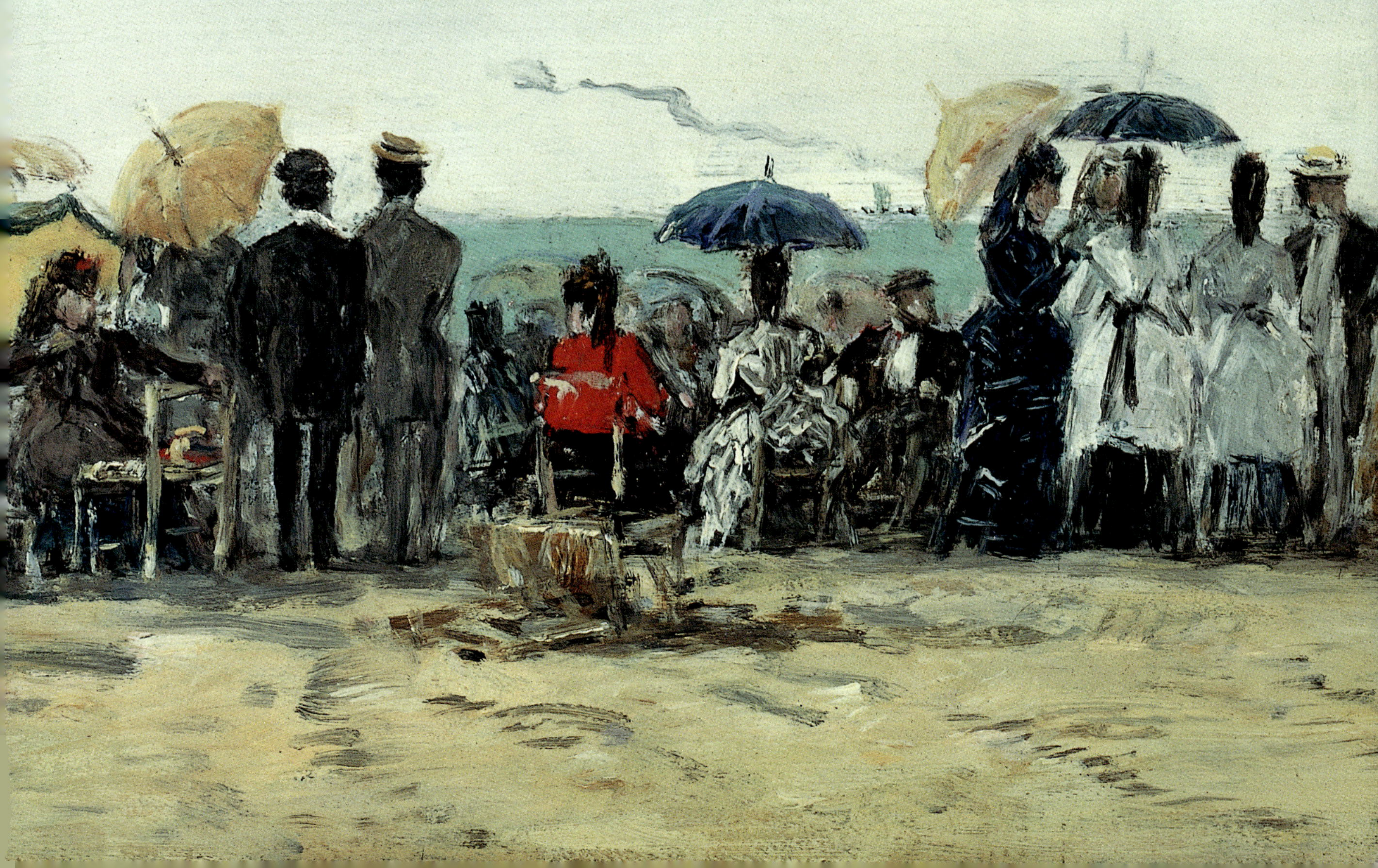

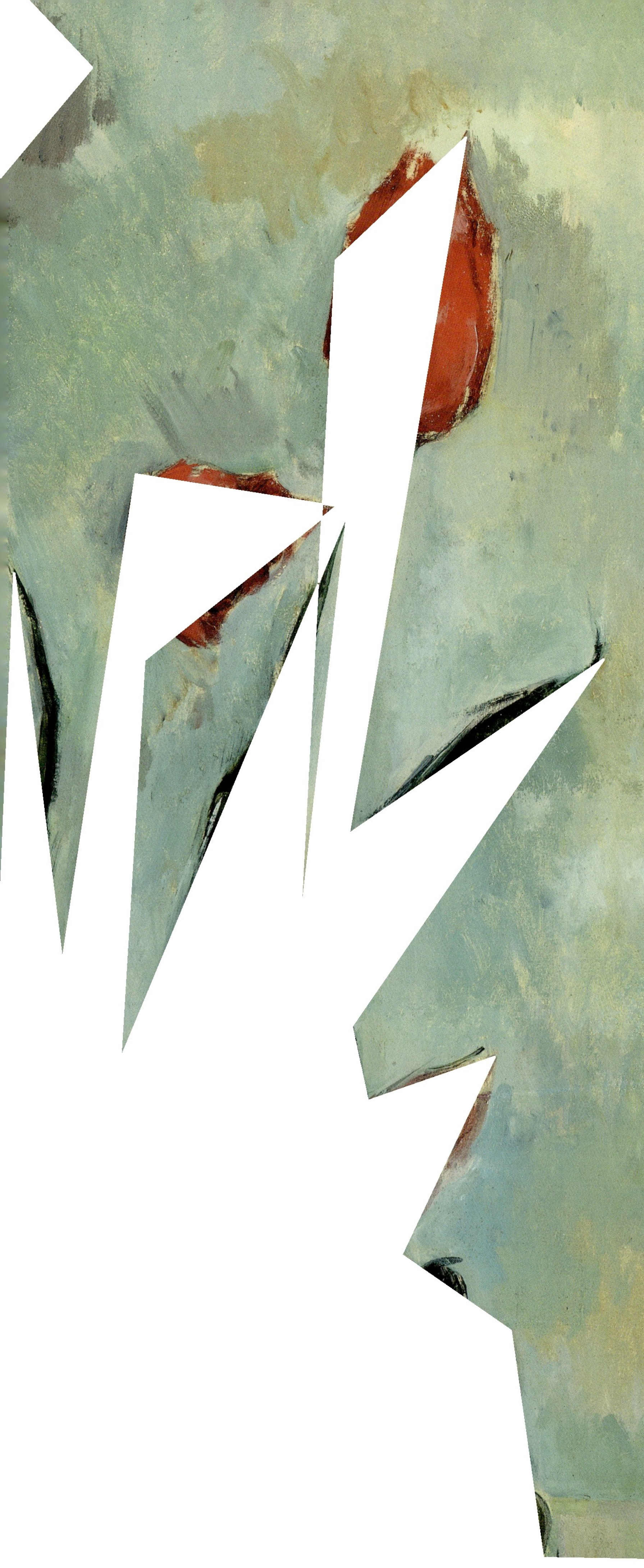

Edited by Fronia Simpson
Designed by Gillian Malpass
Printed in Singapore

Library of Congress Cataloging in Publication Data

Brettell, Richard R.
Nineteenth century paintings in the Norton Simon Museum / Richard R. Brettell and Stephen Eisenman.
p. cm.
Includes bibliographical references.
ISBN 0-300-12101-6 (cl : alk. paper)
1. Painting, European–19th century–Catalogs.
2. Painting–California–Pasadena–Catalogs.
3. Norton Simon Museum (Pasadena, Calif.)–Catalogs.
I. Eisenman, Stephen. II. Title.
III. Title: 19th century paintings in the Norton Simon Museum.
ND457.B698 2006
708.194′93–DC22
2006018168

A catalogue record is available for this book from the British Library

Pages ii–iii Louis-Eugène Boudin, *Beach at Trouville* (detail of cat. 53)

This page Paul Cézanne, *Tulips in a Vase* (detail of cat. 82)

Contents

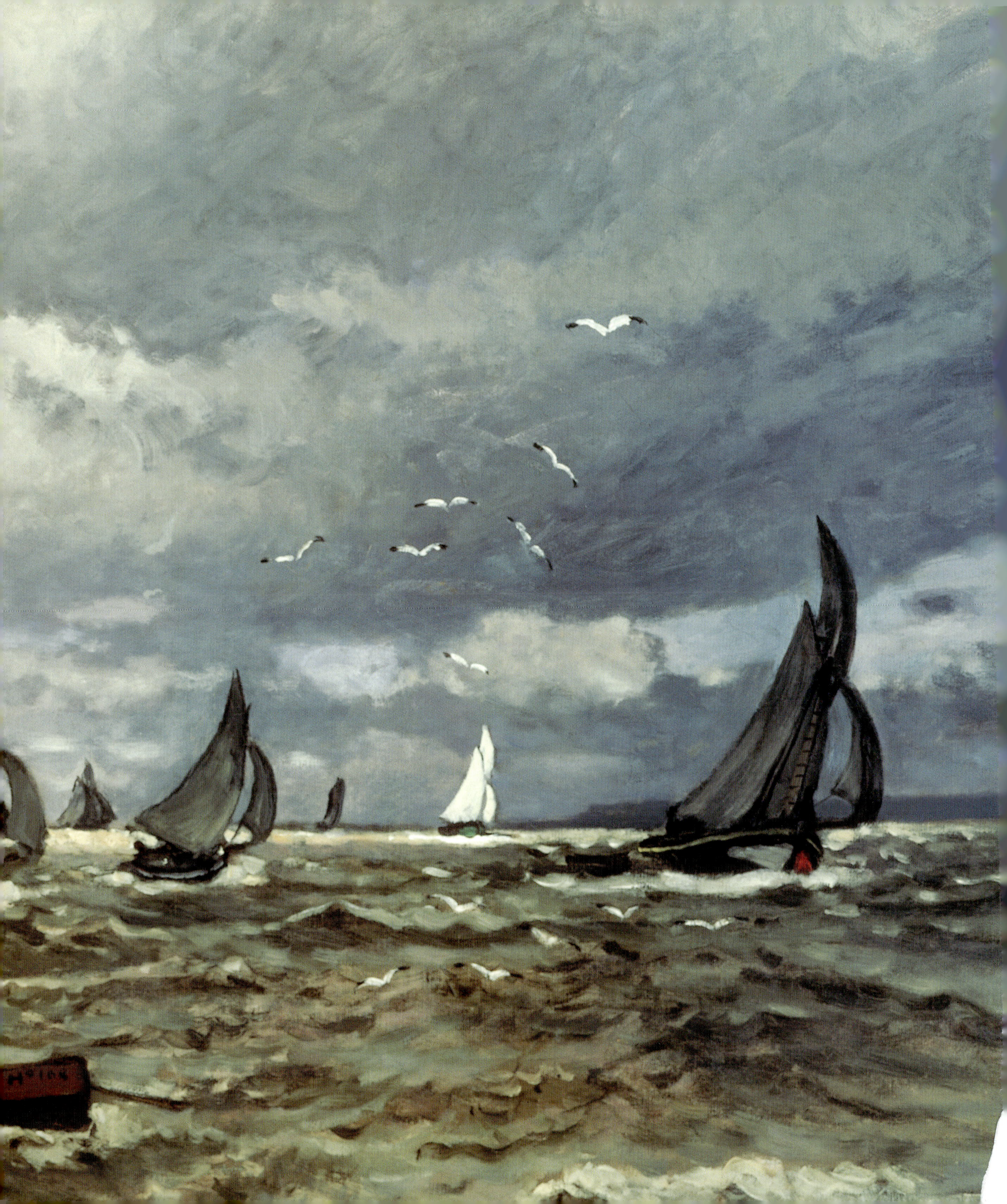

Foreword

Norton Simon (1907–1993) was a successful entrepreneur and industrialist who initially made his reputation collecting companies.[1] Yet it is as a brilliant and astute collector of artworks that he is internationally known today. His interest in art began in 1954 at the relatively late age of forty-seven. Although his first purchases were unexceptional, Simon quickly gained the knowledge and eye to make astute and sometimes daring acquisitions—and equally daring deaccessions.[2] Over the next thirty years he amassed one of the world's greatest private art collections, encompassing European art from before the Renaissance through the twentieth century. Just as noteworthy are the extensive holdings of Asian art, consisting of hundreds of artworks from the Indian subcontinent, the Himalayas, and Southeast Asia, assembled in little more than a decade, from 1971 until 1983. By the early 1970s Simon had accumulated more than four thousand artworks that he lent to museums throughout the world, and in 1974 he assumed control of the financially troubled Pasadena Museum of Modern Art. The Norton Simon Museum took its present name in 1975 and now is the repository for artworks from both the former Pasadena Museum and the Norton Simon collections.[3]

This book catalogues the nineteenth-century art that today is housed in the Norton Simon Museum. However, since a good deal of twentieth-century scholarship devoted to art of the previous century starts with the arts around the time of the French Revolution, this catalogue begins with the last decade of the eighteenth century, with the works of both the Spanish artist Francisco Goya and his contemporaries in France. It continues through the sequence of major art movements into the early years of the twentieth century with works by Édouard Vuillard, Pierre Bonnard, and the Pont-Aven painters around Paul Gauguin. The Introduction treats the collection in terms of its gradual formation as a contribution to the history of taste and collecting and also brings needed attention to some of the hundreds of works from the same period of the history of art once owned by Mr. Simon, which he sold or traded for others. Knowledge of this lost collection is essential for a real understanding both of the taste of Norton Simon and of his manipulations of an art market he perhaps knew better than any other twentieth-century collector.

The Norton Simon Art Foundation is ambitiously engaged in producing collection catalogues covering the major holdings at the Norton Simon Museum. The present book marks the fifth in our series, following a catalogue of the Blue Four Collection and three volumes on aspects of our Asian collection.[4] This volume is the first of two examining nineteenth-century artworks

facing page Claude Monet, *Mouth of the Seine, Honfleur* (detail of cat. 84)

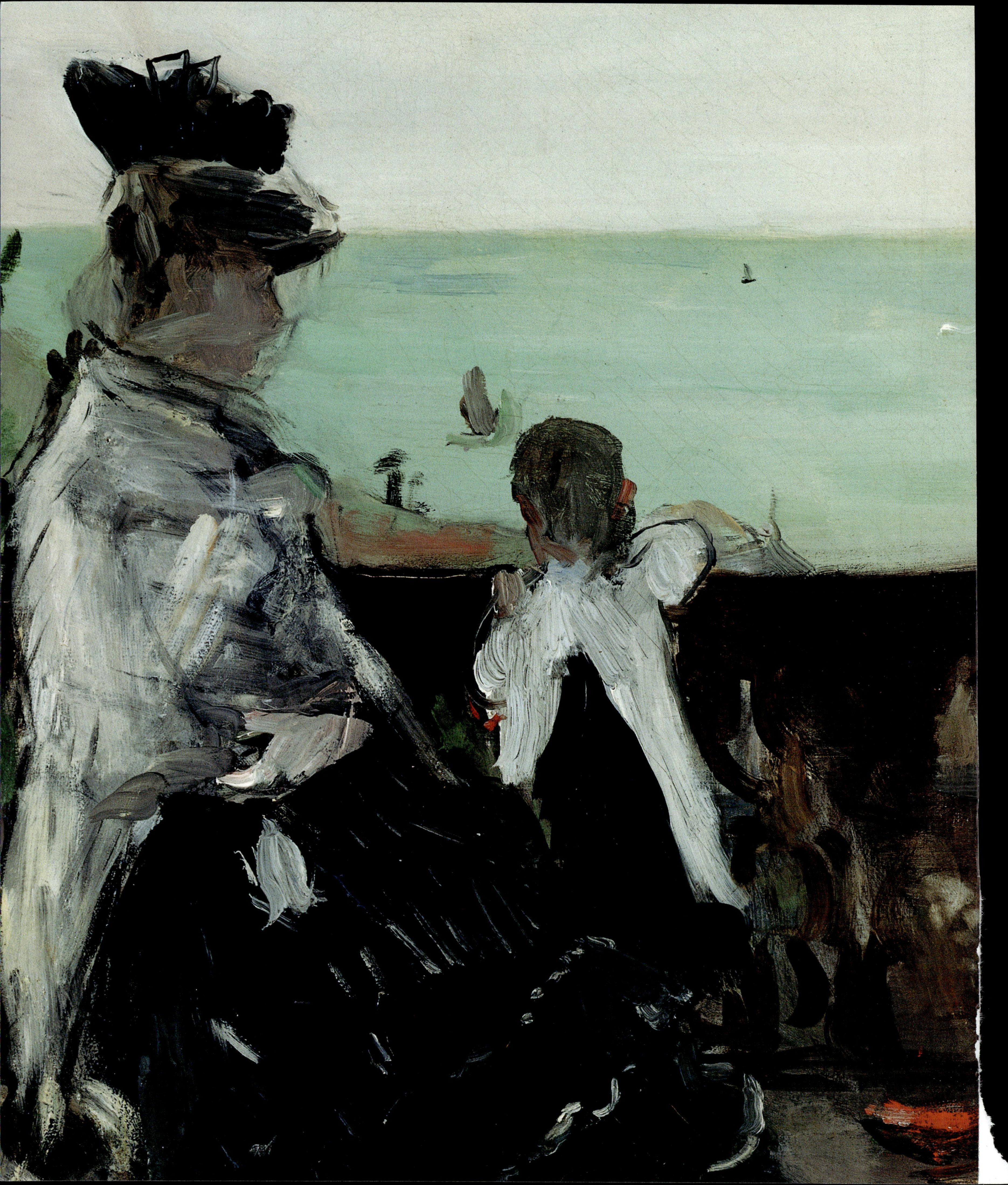

collected by Mr. Simon. It excludes works by Edgar Degas, an artist who is in fact well represented in the collections by 103 paintings, works on paper, and sculpture, and who will be the subject of a second volume.[5] It is a pleasure to acknowledge my thanks to the Board of Trustees of the Norton Simon Art Foundation and President Walter W. Timoshuk for their foresight and generosity in supporting this ambitious enterprise.

One of the many privileges one encounters in working with this extraordinary collection for more than thirty-five years is the opportunity to meet and collaborate with some of the museum world's most renowned art historians. I am extremely grateful to the scholars Richard R. Brettell, Margaret McDermott Distinguished Professor of Art and Aesthetics at the University of Texas at Dallas, and Northwestern University Professor of Art History Stephen F. Eisenman, for assuming the enormous task of writing about our nineteenth-century collection. Their diligence, accessibility, and generosity made this entire project a delight. It is a pleasure to thank Susan Sayre Batton, John Childs, Joseph Fronek, and Rosamond Westmoreland for their technical examinations of the artworks, and Jeannine Clarion for her transcriptions and translations of the artists' letters. Fronia W. Simpson's astute editing and counsel helped us achieve a publication worthy of this magnificent collection. This catalogue has benefited from the ideas and advice of Carol Togneri. My thanks also to Giselle Arteaga-Johnson, Frances Bowles, Andrea Clark, Lisa Griffin, Nicole Hungerford, Casie Kesterson, Gillian Malpass, James Mayner, Brian Regan, Jenna Siman, John Sudolcan, and Gloria Williams for their assistance, support, insightful observations, and tireless good humor.

Sara Campbell
Senior Curator and General Editor
Norton Simon Museum

facing page Berthe Morisot, *In a Villa at the Seaside* (detail of cat. 94)

1 At the time of Simon's retirement from his corporation in 1969, Norton Simon Inc. was a major consumer products conglomerate that included, among other companies, Hunt-Wesson Foods, Inc., Canada Dry Corporation, Glass Containers Corporation, United Can Company, and McCall Corporation.

2 Many of Mr. Simon's deaccessions of nineteenth-century art are noted in the introduction to this catalogue.

3 The four collections on display at the Museum are those of The Norton Simon Foundation, the Norton Simon Art Foundation, the Jennifer Jones Simon Art Trust, and the Norton Simon Museum. The ownership of each work in this catalogue is noted in its entry.

4 The previous publications are Vivian Endicott Barnett, *The Blue Four Collection at the Norton Simon Museum*, New Haven, 2002; Pratapaditya Pal, *Asian Art at the Norton Simon Museum*. vol. 1, *Art from the Indian Subcontinent*, New Haven, 2003, vol. 2, *Art from the Himalayas and China*, New Haven, 2003, and vol. 3, *Art from Sri Lanka and Southeast Asia*, New Haven, 2004.

5 The catalogue of the Edgar Degas collection is being co-authored by Richard Kendall, who will write about the paintings, drawings, and graphics, and this writer, who will catalogue the sculpture.

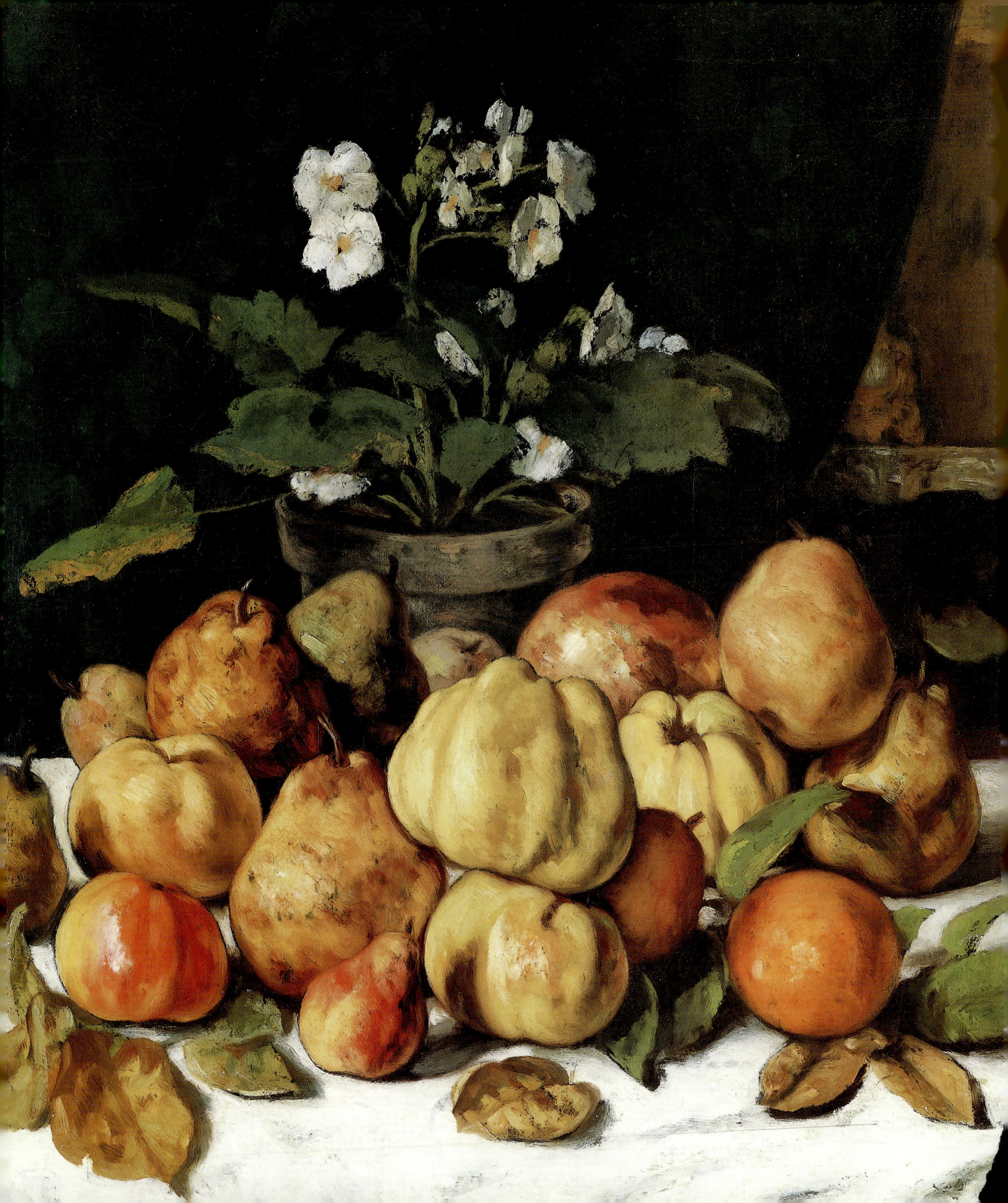

INTRODUCTION

The Value of Collecting
Norton Simon and Nineteenth-Century Art

FORTUNATELY FOR THE HISTORIAN OF TASTE AND COLLECTING, Norton Simon kept very good files. Even before he created the museum that bears his name, he employed a professional staff to compile meticulous records of the provenance, publication, exhibition, and conservation history of each work he owned. Today, these records are among the most complete of any museum in the United States and are the basis of the present catalogue and this essay. What the documents reveal at once is that Simon was unafraid of the truth of collecting. He carefully preserved information about prices paid, appraisals, and the dissenting opinions of scholars concerning attribution, quality, or condition. In this, he is probably unique among important capitalist collectors in providing a paper trail of his interactions with a complex web of dealers, art historians and connoisseurs, museum professionals, conservators, family members, and personal friends. This essay can only hint at the full story of the development of Norton Simon's taste and knowledge about art and will focus on the formation (and partial dispersal) of his large and important collection of nineteenth-century art.

As far as we know, Norton Simon bought his first works of art on 22 December 1954 from the Dalzell Hatfield Gallery in Los Angeles, with which he maintained a long relationship even after he had begun to buy paintings from world-famous dealers like Wildenstein & Co., Thomas Agnew & Sons, M. Knoedler & Company, Duveen Brothers, or Paul Rosenberg & Co. The two were a small, unambitious canvas called *Bass Section* by the American Regionalist painter Dan Lutz for $300, and his first serious picture for $16,000. Two years later, this painting, *Andrée in Blue* of 1916–1918 by Pierre-Auguste Renoir (fig. 1), was among the first works donated by Simon (in this case anonymously) to a public institution, Pomona College Art Gallery.[1] Like many financially savvy collectors, he obtained a new, higher evaluation of the work before he gave it, presumably to obtain the maximum tax benefit from his gift. It was Wildenstein in New York who provided the appraisal,[2] and it would be to Wildenstein that Simon would most frequently turn in subsequent years when he wished to buy the best available artworks to improve and augment his rapidly growing collection. Indeed, he had already acquired from that firm, in March 1955, a major painting by Paul Gauguin set in Pont-Aven, *Brittany Landscape with a Swineherd* (fig. 2), now in the collection of the Los Angeles County Museum of Art. He paid $60,000 for the Gauguin, which left his personal possession as part of his divorce settlement with his first wife, Lucille Ellis Simon, in 1970.

facing page Gustave Courbet, *Apples, Pears, and Primroses on a Table* (detail of cat. 46)

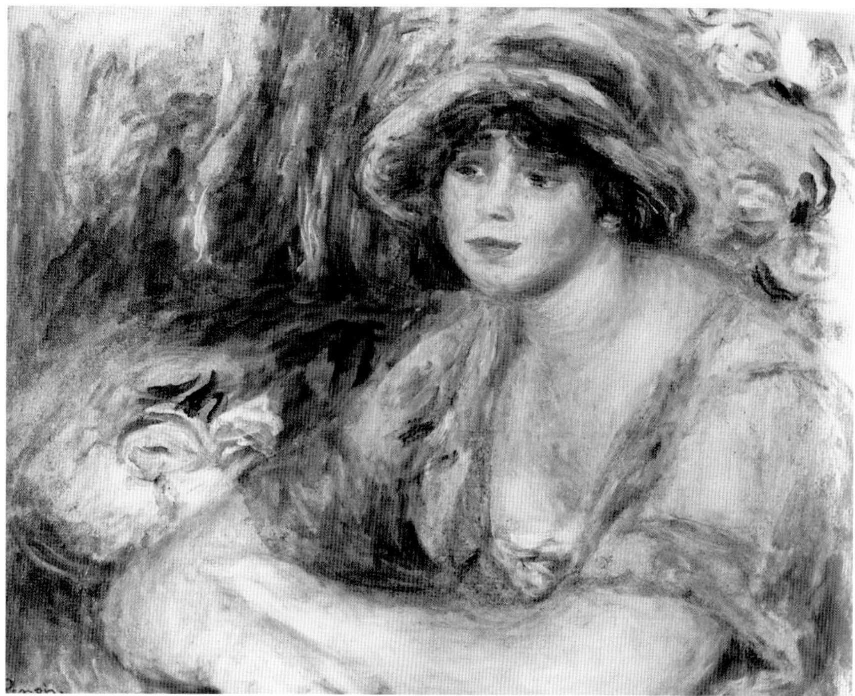

Fig. 1 Pierre-Auguste Renoir, *Andrée in Blue*, 1916–1918, oil on canvas, 15 ¾ × 19⅞ in. (40 × 50.5 cm), private collection

The information in the paragraph above, concerning acquisitions made in less than a year, reveals the outlines of the larger story of Norton Simon as a collector. Within just three months, his acquisitions had progressed from an attractive, minor work of provincial contemporary art to a major painting by one of the greatest modern masters. Yet neither of these works of art remains in the Norton Simon Museum, suggesting that in the course of his acquisitions he came to think of artworks not merely as part of a stable entity called a collection but as a commodity. Indeed, some of Simon's critics during his lifetime went so far as to maintain that he was essentially a collector-dealer, as interested in the deal as in what might be called the intrinsic value of art.

John Coplans was the most strident in expressing this view in a scathing 1975 article in *Artforum*, in which he accused Norton Simon of treating works of art "not as esthetic objects, but as securities, the equivalent of stocks and bonds, to be manipulated to produce profits in much the same manner as an art investment trust."[3] Coplans was not alone in this view, and there is considerable evidence in the files of the Norton Simon Museum to suggest he was at least partially right. But distinctions between types of collectors—some more, some less drawn to the commodity status of art—are difficult to make, and a careful study of major collectors who might also be called dealers has never been done. At the end of the nineteenth century, Bertha Potter Palmer manipulated markets for artists she favored, such as Claude Monet and Jean-Charles Cazin. More recently, Louis Manilow and Charles Saatchi bought works of contemporary art in order to sell them at a profit so that they might invest in less expensive works.

Yet walking through the galleries of the Norton Simon Museum, it is possible to forget all of the financial manipulations and consider instead the aesthetic and historic significance of the many major works by important artists, as well as the equally compelling works by compara-

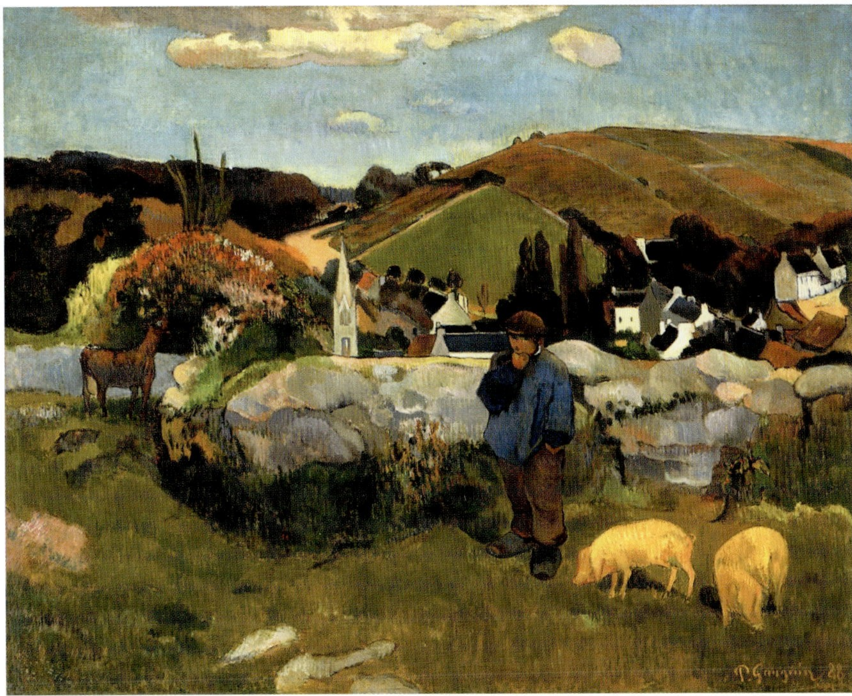

Fig. 2 Paul Gauguin, *Brittany Landscape with a Swineherd*, 1888, oil on canvas, $28\frac{3}{4} \times 36\frac{5}{8}$ in. (73.3 × 93.3 cm), Los Angeles County Museum of Art

tively minor ones. Whatever the motivations of modern collectors like Simon, they effectively stripped the commodity status from the works in their collection when they removed them from the marketplace and placed them in permanent, public trust. They have produced the potential for knowledge and pleasure where it did not exist before, however questionable the market maneuvers that brought it into being. and they have given over to an audience, varied in class and ethnic makeup, works that once belonged only to the rich and (mostly) the white. Impediments to the broad understanding of works of art remain strong, but the establishment of public museums at least makes that critical appreciation an open question.

Norton Simon was certainly not born to be an art collector, nor did he receive any serious formal education in the history and connoisseurship of art. His interest in art may in fact have originated with his first wife, Lucille Ellis, although one must remember that his sister, Marcia Weisman, became a formidable collector of contemporary art in her own right and that the competitive siblings clearly thought of art as an essential part of modern wealth (figs. 3 and 4). Several of Simon's friends and business associates collected art, and for most of these men and women, art meant "modern art," that is, painting and sculpture, mostly French, from the period around 1860 to the evolving present. This was an art that was profoundly secular and acquired through a network of private dealers and auction houses.

Norton Simon was also among a number of important collectors of his generation, like David Rockefeller and Nathan Cummings, who wanted to integrate art into the workplace, forming what today we would call a corporate collection. Photographs of Simon in his corporate office at Hunt Foods & Industries (fig. 5) always include works of art, several of which hang today in the Norton Simon Museum. For Simon, art was a part of life in all its manifestations, and its acquisition was a source of pleasure almost akin to the hunt in earlier landed societies. More-

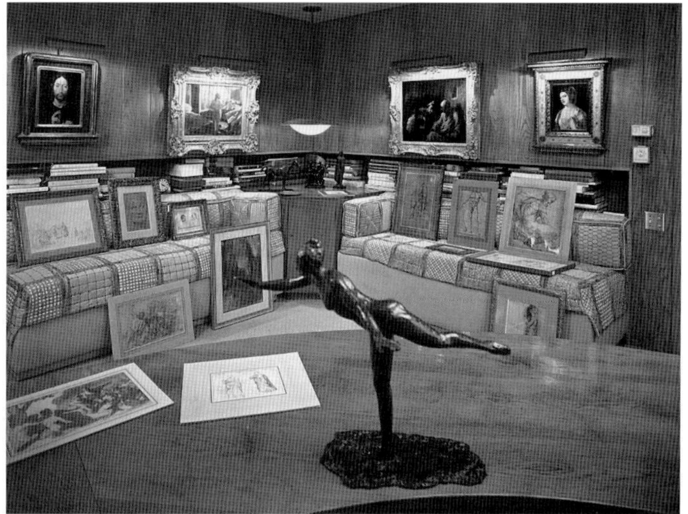

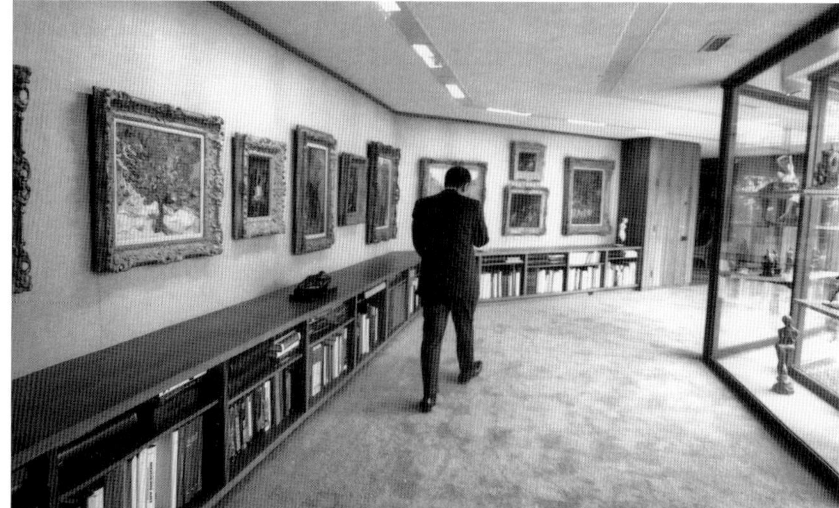

Fig. 3 (*above left*) Norton Simon's study, Los Angeles, c. 1964

Fig. 4 (*above right*) Norton Simon in his hallway gallery, April, 1970

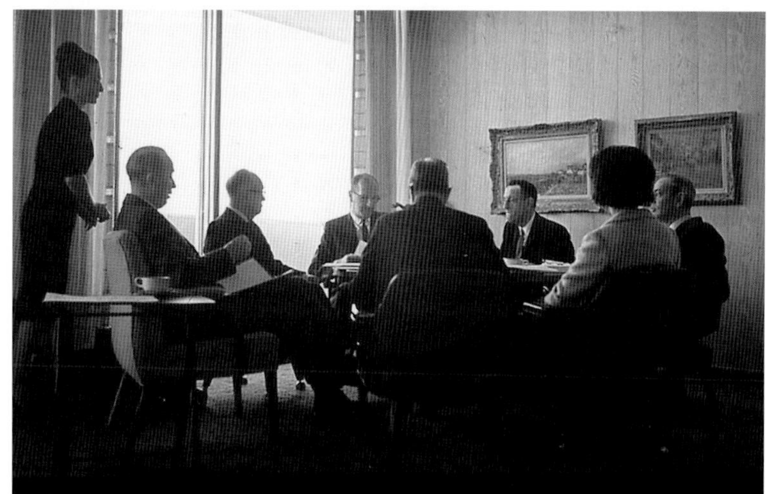

Fig. 5 Norton Simon (third from right) meeting with his senior staff at Hunt Foods & Industries, Fullerton, California, 1965

over, it was natural for him to apply to the arcane and highly private capitalist art market lessons he learned from other markets and other commodities. He also applied his formidable skills in business negotiation to the art market, thereby becoming as effective an art businessman as any dealer from whom he purchased or to whom he sold works of art.

All of Norton Simon's purchases in 1954 and 1955 were works of nineteenth- and twentieth-century art. It was not until May 1956 that he bought his first old master painting, the haunting portrait of Hendrickje Stoffels (fig. 6), then firmly ascribed to Rembrandt, and it was also Simon's first purchase from the legendary dealer Duveen Brothers. Again, the sheer ambition of Simon as a collector is clear, though for a staunch advocate of modern art it was not so great an aesthetic leap to acquire a seventeenth-century painting by an artist worshiped by virtually every great nineteenth- and twentieth-century painter as a progenitor of the modern sensibility. The thick museum file for this object also makes it clear that Simon, then still an inexperienced collector, negotiated formidably with the vastly practiced international art dealer, deciding to include in the evolving contract another work then ascribed to Rembrandt, called *The Jewish Philosopher*,[4] and to engage Richard F. Brown, the founding director of the Los Angeles County

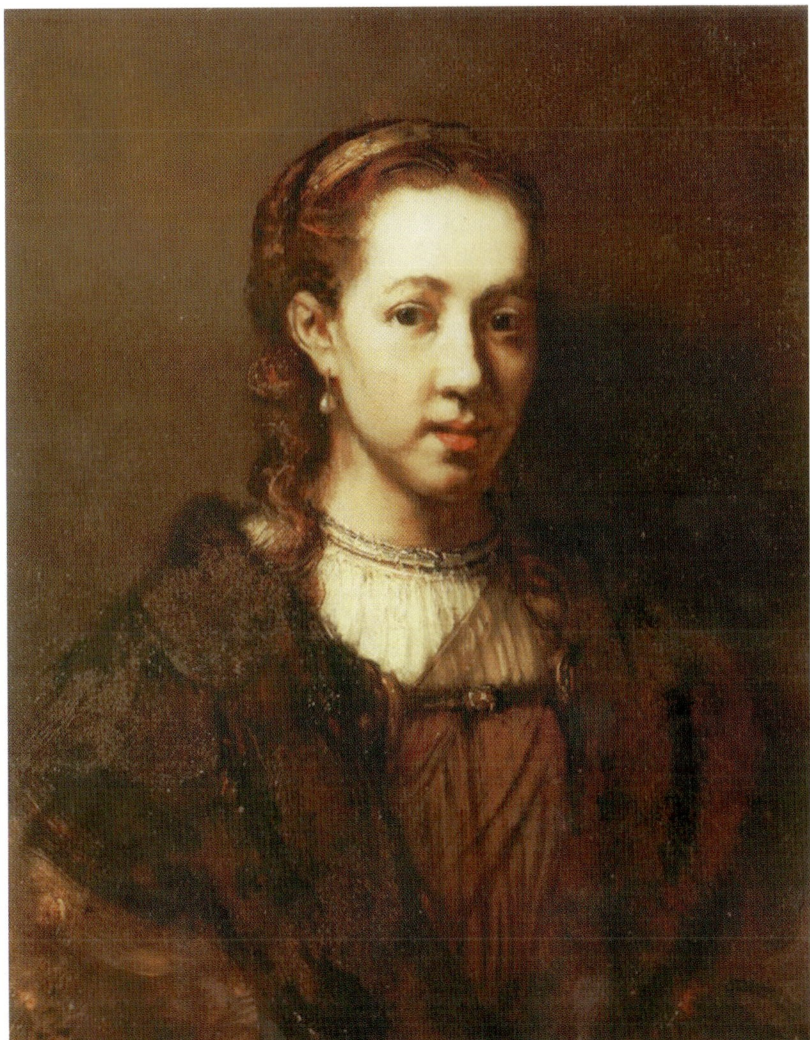

Fig. 6 Studio of Rembrandt Harmensz. van Rijn, *Portrait of a Lady, traditionally said to be Hendrickje Stoffels*, oil on canvas, 25¾ × 21¼ in. (65.5 × 54 cm), private collection

Museum of Art, as well as the Harvard scholar Seymour Slive and the conservator Billy Suhr, in what amounted to extensive private research on the paintings.

Far from simply writing a check for his Rembrandts, as most beginning collectors would, Simon used their acquisition to learn a good deal about questions of attribution, meaning, value, and condition in the old master market, which was then, as today, much more complicated than that for modern art. This very complexity regularly became for Simon an excuse to prolong negotiations and alter his offers as conditions changed and the opinions of others became available. In fact, his procedure in this early old master negotiation was no different from that employed today in professional art museums with expert staffs. Since at that time Simon had no such staff, he used outside scholars, connoisseurs, and dealers as his guides and his sounding boards, gaining from them a solid understanding of the intricate and often conflicted relationship between art history and the art market.

Norton Simon's practice of seeking expert advice was hardly unique to him: Bernard Berenson's work for Isabella Stewart Gardner in Boston at the beginning of the twentieth century is a well-known example of such a relationship. But we know of no modern collector who was more fearless than Norton Simon in tracking down scholars and museum professionals, many of whom actually disagreed with each other about the authenticity or art historical merits of the work of art in question. The very seriousness with which Norton Simon in 1956 approached the acquisition of the two works attributed to Rembrandt became the model for his later collecting of modern art. The same critical discernment, the same consideration of different and opposing scholarly viewpoints, was necessary for each endeavor. It is interesting to note that today the Norton Simon collections contain neither of the Rembrandt paintings. *Hendrickje Stoffels*, the more important of the two, remained in Simon's private collection until his divorce from Lucille Ellis Simon in 1970 and was recently sold at auction.[5] *The Jewish Philosopher* did not live up to Simon's expectations or to the high praise given the painting in a letter to Simon from Richard Brown.[6] Indeed, Simon soon learned that more scholars rejected the work as a Rembrandt than accepted it, and in 1959, just four years later, he sold it back to Duveen for the original purchase price—or, put more bluntly, Simon asked for his money back.

Simon's early deaccessioning of *The Jewish Philosopher* is worthy of a little more discussion. First of all, the practice was one aspect of what may be called the reciprocal relationship of collectors and dealers. Simon established long-term relationships with dealers who would sometimes buy back or trade for works purchased earlier in order to keep the trust and goodwill of their valuable client capable of spending sizeable sums in the future. Many important twentieth-century collectors and dealers maintained ongoing relations for precisely this reason. Yet, although Simon continued to purchase works from a group of dealers in Los Angeles, New York, London, and Paris, he was not actually very faithful to any of them. His patterns of collecting as revealed in the files show clearly that he bought works of art from anyone who had them and that he was not at all averse to playing dealers against each other if it would help him gain an advantage. It was his evolving knowledge of the inventories of many international dealers—information difficult to acquire personally, but more readily obtained with the help of a network of curators and scholars—that allowed him to negotiate increasingly advantageous prices and arrangements. Dealers often accepted smaller profit margins for their sales to Norton Simon in the expectation that larger profits would come later. Only a few actually found that to be true.

The other reason to highlight these early old master acquisitions is to demonstrate that just a little more than a year after he bought his first work of art, Simon was purchasing art in several different parts of the art market. From 1956 until his death in 1993, he bought and sold works of modern art in the course of developing a collection that spanned many cultures, periods, and media. He became a sophisticated connoisseur of European painting, drawing, printmaking, and sculpture—as well as the art of India and Southeast Asia—not by formally studying art history but by learning through reading, travelling, negotiating, buying, trading, and selling. While neither of the two works mentioned above thought to be by Rembrandt are currently attributed to him, the three paintings ascribed to the Dutch master now in the Norton Simon collections have all passed the scrutiny of the Rembrandt Research Project, proving that in this case at least, Simon's connoisseurship became sharper with time.[7]

Because Simon collected across the art market, he quickly learned that works of modern art—especially those within the established canon—were comparatively overvalued. Although he remained faithful to the project of collecting works by the best-known and most-admired modern masters, he did so in a much larger context. Rather than modeling himself on collectors like Chester Dale, Paul Mellon, Walter Annenberg, Nathan Cummings, and others whose entire collection was modern, Simon evolved into a collector more like Martin Reyerson, Sterling Clark, Albert Barnes, and Robert Lehman, who annexed modernism to the great traditions of old master painting. He quickly learned that he could buy many great prints and several great drawings by Rembrandt or Edgar Degas for the same price as a single painting. He also learned that, because of the increasing dominance of the modern market, old master paintings, particularly those with religious subjects, were comparatively inexpensive given their rarity and evident quality. These market lessons, again, were learned less through repeated visits to museums, though Simon did that too, than through observation of the markets themselves and the act of acquisition and negotiation.

It also must be remembered that Norton Simon formed his extraordinary collection of European art during a period in which many American art museums—as well as private collectors—were competing directly against him. The major American art museums all had designated acquisition funds—either from endowment or donated monies—and tremendous buying power during the period of accelerated corporate profits and low inflation from 1955 to 1975, when the bulk of Simon's collection was formed. Yet, in spite of the fact that he loved to create protracted and complex deals, Simon, as a private collector, could act relatively quickly, not being constrained by the cumbersome process of obtaining permission from committees and trustees. In Los Angeles, Simon quickly became a dominating force in the collecting world, even as the far wealthier J. Paul Getty continued to collect. In the late 1950s and 1960s he also began to involve himself with the staff of the Los Angeles County Museum of Art, particularly its able director, Richard F. Brown, who did not have at his own disposal the money of Norton Simon. Simon thus used the eye, knowledge, and connections of Brown to his own advantage.

It would be wrong, however, to characterize Norton Simon as a collector who used the staffs of only the local art museums of Los Angeles. His circle of advisors extended well beyond the decidedly provincial Los Angeles art world of the 1950s and 1960s. He routinely consulted art historians from Harvard, Princeton, the Institute of Fine Arts, Yale, the University of Pennsylvania, the University of North Carolina, and many other institutions, as well as California-based experts from either museums or universities. Many museum professionals outside California were eager to offer advice to Simon, hoping, perhaps, that gifts would follow. He also increasingly consulted European scholars and museum professionals, and came to hold a position of such eminence as a collector of European art that few other Americans could match him. This network of informal advisors was as large and important for Simon as the network of dealers from whom he bought works. Simon was unafraid to spend months—in several cases years—investigating a work of art before deciding to buy or sell. Several of these protracted examinations—like that involved in the acquisition of a painting by Pierre-Paul Prud'hon (cat. 6)—are detailed in the entries of this catalogue.

Another strategy Simon employed in his thinking about a particular acquisition was to ask a range of people with no knowledge of, or even interest in, art for their reaction to a work. Simon must have amazed his drivers, secretaries, and junior business associates by asking them what they thought of a painting by Hans Memling, Giovanni Battista Tiepolo, or Paul Cézanne. People who knew him well remember that he asked almost anyone who walked into his home or office when a work of art was being considered what she or he thought of the work. These reactions were useful to a man who, by the mid-1960s, was already thinking about his collection in public terms. The responses of people who knew nothing of the art world—ordinary working people, businessmen, and powerful colleagues alike—were therefore crucial to his assessment of the power of art, and his own reputation in a highly competitive capitalist society.

Nonetheless, in all the material left in the files of the Norton Simon Museum, there is very little direct evidence of Simon's own views of art or its acquisition. He communicated better orally than in writing, and in the cases in which he did record something, it is generally a scrawled directive to an assistant to do something, call someone, write a letter. These numerous short texts are essentially devoid of judgment or reflection, making it difficult for the historian to do more than surmise his motivations. On only one occasion—in one of three lengthy interviews given to a writer who in 1975 proposed to write a biography (it was never completed)—did Simon talk on the record about the act of acquisition. This unpublished interview, a typescript of which remains in the Norton Simon Museum curatorial files, records the reasoning behind his acquisition of Vincent van Gogh's extraordinary *Portrait of a Peasant (Patience Escalier)* (cat. 110), which was then hanging on approval in his home in the room in which the interview was conducted. Simon evidently felt comfortable in the situation, because he responded at some length to the following question: "What do you have to question and what do you have to know in order to be effective in terms of marching up to that van Gogh?" "And buying it?" Simon replied. "And buying it or not buying it," the interviewer added, and then continued: "It might be a terrible mistake to buy it. I don't know." Norton Simon's ruminations are worth publishing almost in their entirety:

facing page Vincent van Gogh, *Portrait of a Peasant (Patience Escalier)* (detail of cat. 110)

> Well, number one, I have to know and make a judgment on whether I feel it is financially wise in relationship to my own financial position or the Foundation's, obviously, and in rela-

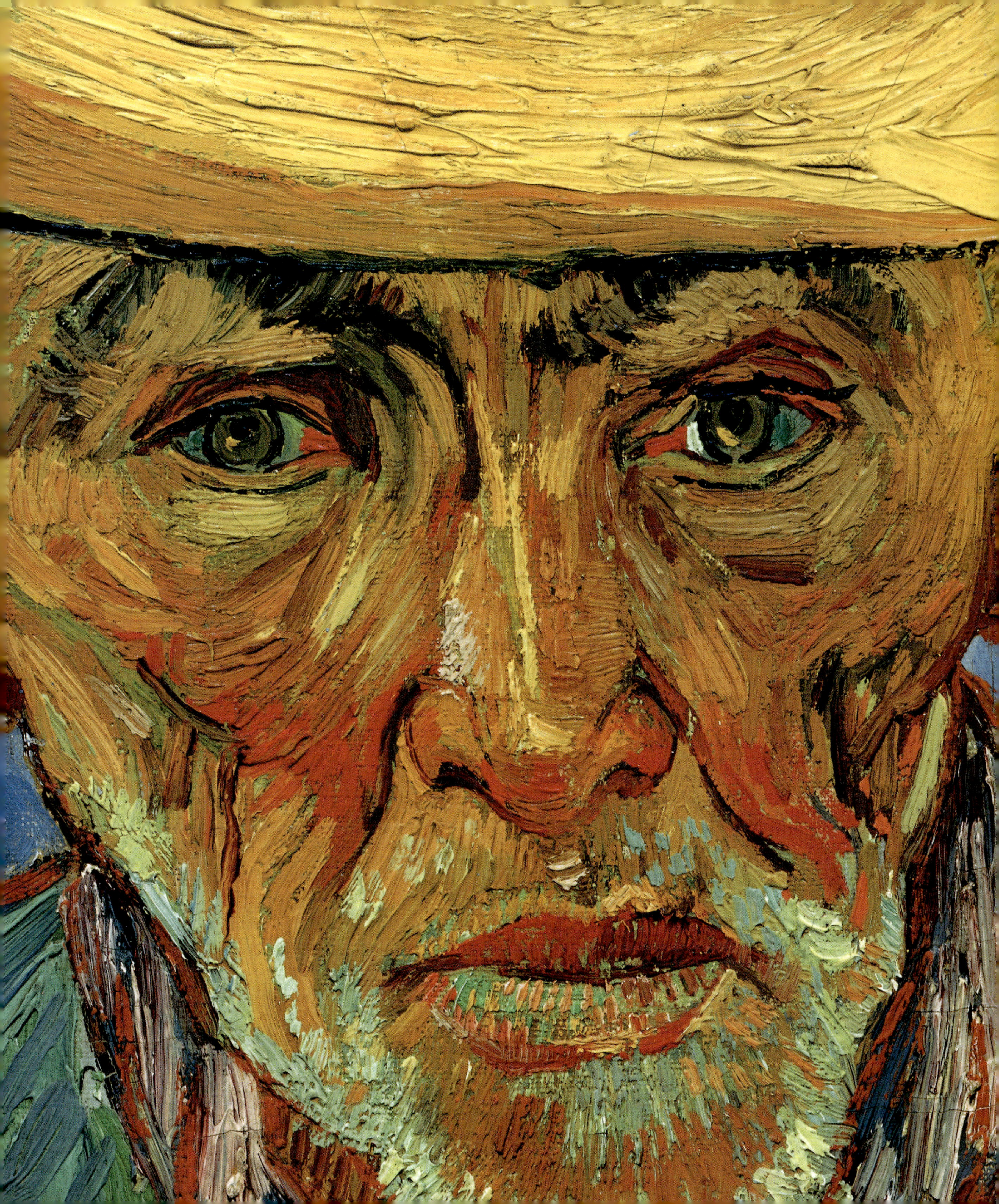

tionship to the times. And then, number two, I've got to compare that picture with other pictures because there are lots of pictures around to buy. And then you have to make a judgment as to what you think of the artist and the value relationship to other artists, how great a . . . work of art it is in the man's work, how great it is aesthetically—I wouldn't touch it if it weren't aesthetically great—that I know. But how great? Is it a crowd-pleaser in a museum or isn't it a crowd-pleaser? Sometimes a picture like this Braque here on the wall[8] is not a crowd-pleaser but is a gutsy, magnificent picture. But the fact is that there are gutsy, magnificent pictures that are crowd-pleasers too. And they cost a lot more money. So you've got a scale of weight that you go on, and measure it, and that's all. Then you have to take the whole thing and measure it against the economics of the time. I feel comfortable that it is a very fine work by van Gogh. Anything that I would have any question about as far as condition or authenticity, [in this case] I have nominal questions, but I would reassure myself in any event because I never would fail to do that—that's almost routine. But there's no worry [in the case of the van Gogh]. The worry about it being the top part of his work—whether that 10 percent, or 15 percent, or 18, or 12, or 7, I don't know.[9]

The interviewer then asks him why he is not concerned in this case about the authenticity of the van Gogh. "Seeing so many, and the source of it," Simon replied. "You mean a great copyist couldn't do that?" the interviewer asks. "I can't believe that they could come close," Simon said. "But I would never accept my own judgment on it. The history is also good—where it came from, but that could be deceptive too. Many of these things can be wrong. Same way on condition—you can be wrong on it." Simon then tells his interviewer that he does not bother checking the details related to the painting until he has essentially decided to acquire it, and that, in a day or two, he can verify the information and learn from experts their opinions. He explains what he means by saying, "I'd get it X-rayed and I'd get infra-red pictures of it and for the technical things like that. . . . I would look it up and see if it is referred to in any van Gogh letters and check that out, which I am quite sure it is. I wouldn't do much more, because the picture has too good a history and is too secure . . . the place that it ranks in his work I like people's judgment on . . . I would say the primary worry would be the economic conditions and the price of it in relationship to other paintings. The price of it in relationship with other paintings isn't as bad as the economic conditions—I would say that is primary."

Simon's lengthy ruminations about "the economic conditions" are perhaps the most revealing and tantalizing parts of the interview:

Well, if a recession gets tougher and a depression becomes a possibility, and money gets out in spite of inflation, [becoming] necessary for more necessary things than a work of art, if it's a foundation and I feel that income and securities might fall off, then I start saying, can I afford to tie the money up in pictures at this time unless it was unusually competitive in its price versus other works of art? Now I've got to watch out for my own subjectivity and bias—and I have a tremendous bias towards certain works by van Gogh, and little biases against other works of his. So I've got a bias for it and I've got to think, well it's an abstraction. What the hell, a painting is an abstraction. Inflation, deflation—some people say that inflation makes great pictures go up. That's a lot of nothing; it has nothing to do with it. It's a state of psychological being that makes gold worth whatever it is worth [at the moment]. Because it is not usable, it's just the fact that a lot of people are in it. [Also,] a lot of people believe in art. But they are both [gold and art] abstractions. How do you weigh that abstraction against economics? You always get more questioning out of abstractions, I think, in times of stress in the economics.

The next seven pages of the interview transcription constitute a lengthy and complex speculation on the concept of value. Simon discussed the art market versus the money market, the role that museums play in markets, the fact that art is in no way necessary for life, and what might be called the sheer evanescence of the deal. At times he is startlingly direct: "It's a painting, it's a precious object, it's a rare work by van Gogh, van Gogh's a good artist, great artist, there aren't going to be that many on the market where you're going to be able to buy a better one cheaper, there aren't many better ones, so it becomes difficult. There'll never be one like it. But then again its rarity, and how far do you go on rarity? It's still an abstraction."

What we learn from this interview is that Simon's imagination was restless, that he thought on several levels simultaneously, that he questioned virtually everything and everyone, and that aesthetic value was for him always part of a larger system of economic values and thus constantly subject to fluctuation and revision. We also learn that he was a ruthlessly self-critical and sometimes rigorous thinker, refusing to allow himself to be ruled by his own aesthetic passion ("my own subjectivity," as he called it), and that he generally tried harder to talk himself out of an acquisition of a work of art than into it. For a man who continuously bought and sold both art and companies throughout his working life, he was surprisingly never completely certain of the wisdom of any acquisition, because he always knew that economic conditions and new knowledge could change the value of anything. In lengthy passages of the interview he discussed the radical shifts over time in the value of particular works of art, generally, however, stressing the rise and underplaying the decline. Surely this sense of the general rise in the relative exchange value of works of art fueled his desire to pursue the art market with as much ardor as he did.

Norton Simon's complete acceptance of the fluidity of values—of a kind of economic relativity—created for him the conditions in which he could buy and sell works of art without feeling particularly attached to any one of them. This is not to say that he was immune to the aesthetic effects of works of art. But his tendency to self-doubt led him to question even his strongest responses. This psychological trait made him a truly great negotiator for the simple reason that he was always fully prepared to walk away from a deal. Simon knew that another day would bring another painting to his attention, renewing his restless search for the best. We also learn that each transaction—whether successful or not—was another notch in his belt as a collector, giving him more experience as both a connoisseur and a negotiator. Yet he never rested on his laurels, and his restless self-doubt is reflected in the Museum's files.

After the Norton Simon Museum opened to the public and his collection began to dominate its galleries, it was routinely visited by important dealers, scholars, and museum professionals. Simon himself rarely accompanied these men and women through the galleries, preferring to send members of the Museum staff, who took detailed notes of the opinions expressed on each work of art. Whether the visitor was the Louvre's Pierre Rosenberg, the Metropolitan's Everett Fahy, the dealer Edward Speelman, or the conservator Mario Modestini, the responses of these professionals were placed in the files, providing the historian of painting with an accumulation of diverse judgments. Simon would carefully review these notes before they were transcribed into the object's curatorial file, learning in this way of shifts in scholarly opinion that he would never have heard himself if he accompanied these distinguished visitors through the galleries. (Etiquette generally requires visitors in the company of a collector to praise rather than criticize his judgments.) These uncensored evaluations provided him with even more material for his continuing negotiations on future acquisitions and sales.[10]

As Norton Simon extended and refined his collection, he sold and traded many works of art, especially nineteenth-century European art, but he also acquired and generally sold important works of contemporary art. He owned works by Arshile Gorky, Hans Hofmann, Willem de Kooning, Jackson Pollock (a 1950 drip painting and a suite of prints), and Helen Frankenthaler (who seems to have taken him around to dealers in New York in 1955) as well as two important sculptures by David Smith, which are today in the Des Moines Art Center and the Eli Broad collection in Los Angeles. Simon also sold a major Rose Period nude by Pablo Picasso to the Kimbell Art Museum in Fort Worth (fig. 7), because, from the logic made clear in his interview quoted above, it had become too valuable relative to old master paintings, and he could not pass up the very generous offer made to him by the Kimbell's director Edmund Pillsbury Jr. To help his distraught staff come to terms with his decision, Simon asked them to weigh the relative values of the Picasso and various important old master paintings in the collection.[11] Again, Simon demonstrated a supreme relativism with regards to aesthetic value as well as a clear feeling that modern art, financially speaking, was overvalued compared to old master painting at that time. Simon also made attempts to form a small collection of antiquities, both Egyptian and Greco-Roman, but most of the numerous works from these collections were sold within his lifetime.

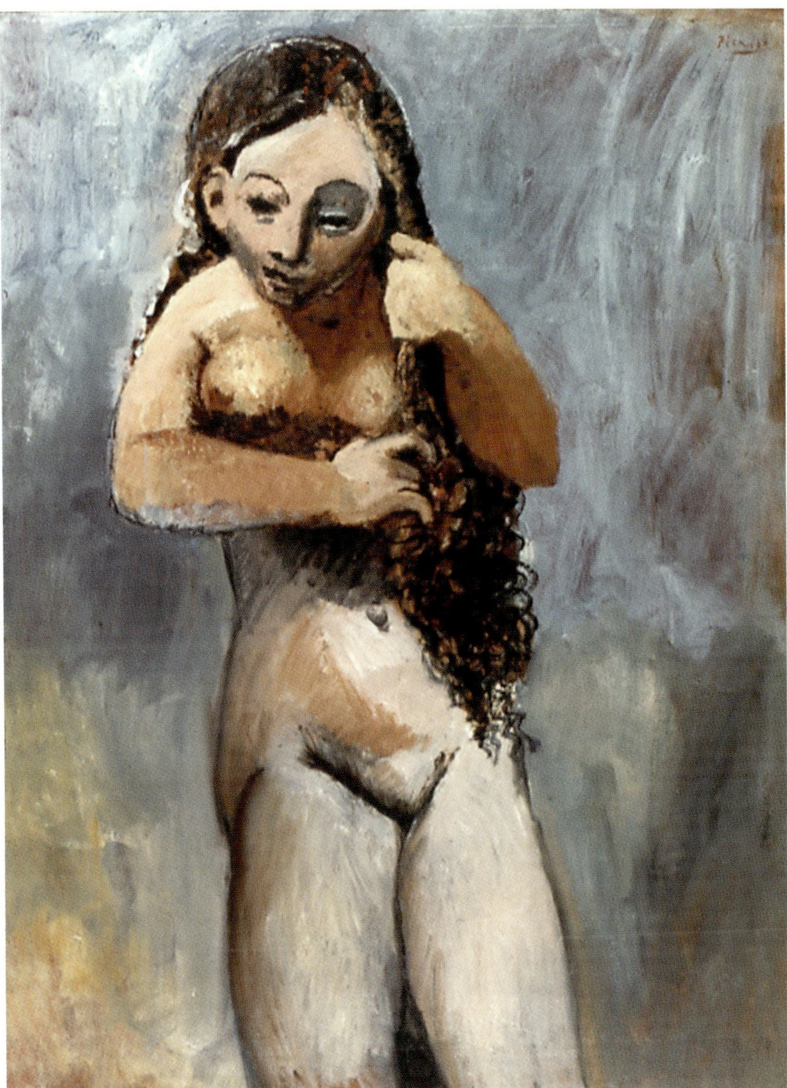

Fig. 7 Pablo Picasso, *Nude Combing her Hair*, 1906, oil on canvas, 41½ × 32 in. (105.4 × 81.3 cm), Kimbell Art Museum, Fort Worth

Simon's reevaluation of his collection began in earnest in 1970. In late 1969 he retired as head of Norton Simon Inc. and moved his personal office from Fullerton, California, to Los Angeles. While remaining active in many areas, he had more time to focus on his art collecting, and to reassess himself and his assets in sweeping terms. The results of this reassessment were four highly public auctions of large portions of the collection in 1971 and 1973.[12] The 1971 sales were spread over three days and included seventy-four works from the private collection of Norton Simon (5 May) and 233 lots of fine and decorative arts, mostly acquired from Duveen, from the collection of the Norton Simon Foundation, created in 1952 for diverse charitable purposes.

The private collection sale was almost exclusively devoted to modern art and included works by Degas, Claude Monet, Camille Pissarro, Renoir, van Gogh, Édouard Vuillard, Cézanne, Henri Matisse, Picasso, and Braque. The 1973 sale in particular included works of art of a quality consistent with others that today remain in the Museum. Indeed, the areas of Impressionism, Post-Impressionism, and Nabis would be considerably stronger today had Simon not pruned his collection. One principal area of loss was works on paper. Since the late 1950s Simon had worked

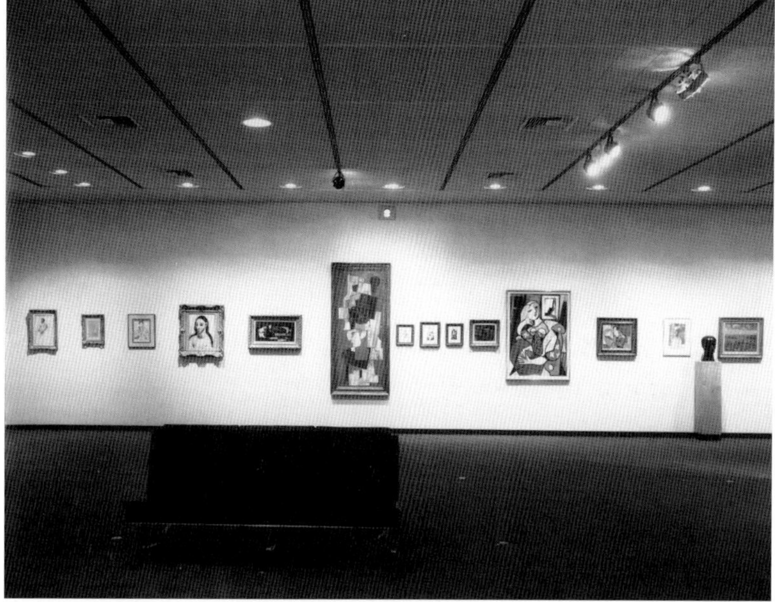

Fig. 8 Installation photograph: *A Selection from the Mr. and Mrs. Norton Simon Collection Honoring the College Art Association*, Los Angeles County Museum of Art, 18 January–7 March 1965

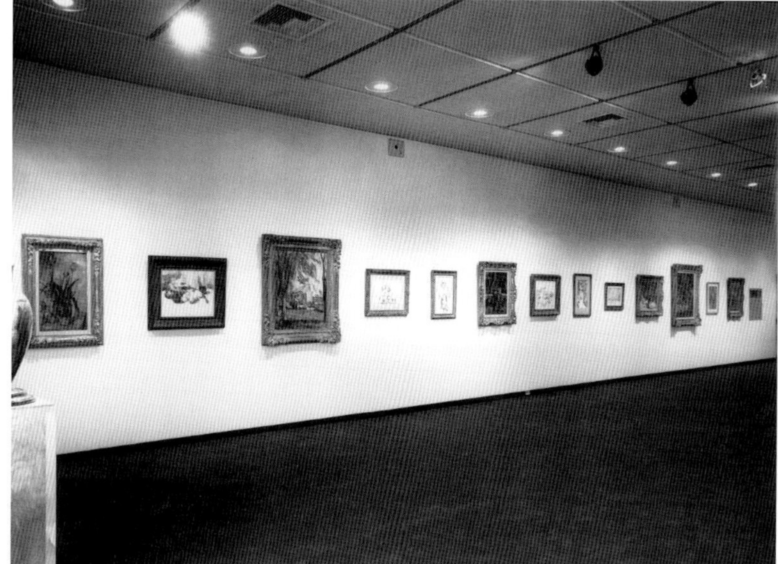

Fig. 9 Installation photograph: *A Selection from the Mr. and Mrs. Norton Simon Collection Honoring the College Art Association*, Los Angeles County Museum of Art, 18 January–7 March 1965

with many great dealers of European prints and drawings and learned a good deal about the highly specialized markets in European prints and drawings from William Schab, Robert Light, Rosenberg & Stiebel, Peter and Fritz Nathan, the Feilchenfeldts, and Eugene V. Thaw. From these sources, he formed a distinguished collection of old master and modern works on paper, only a fraction of which remains in the Museum. His holdings of prints by Goya were virtually definitive (he helped Pomona College acquire its important collection of prints by Goya). Indeed, the Norton Simon Museum still possesses one of the finest collections of Goya's graphic work in the world in spite of the fact that Simon may have sold more than he kept.[13]

As for nineteenth-century drawings, the various collections of Norton Simon included masterpieces by many major artists. A large selection of these works on paper was included in a 1965 exhibition, which had no accompanying publication, held at the Los Angeles County Museum

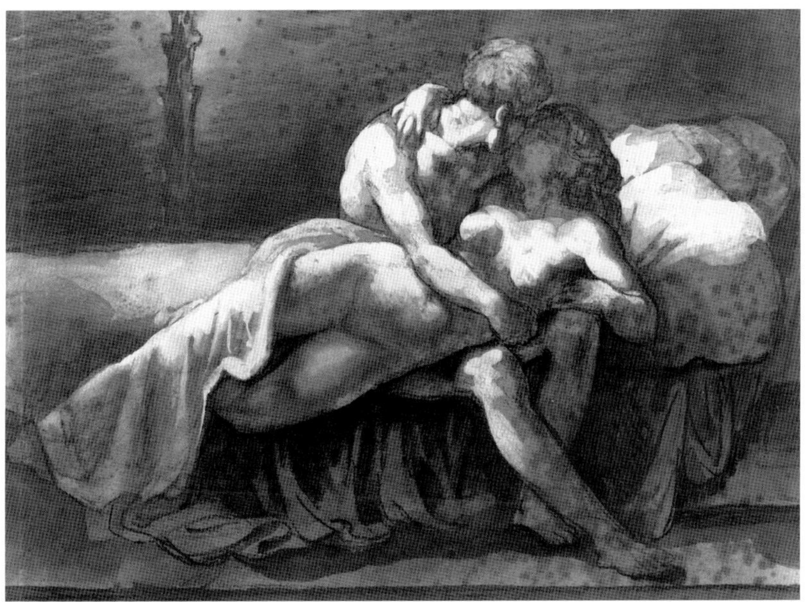

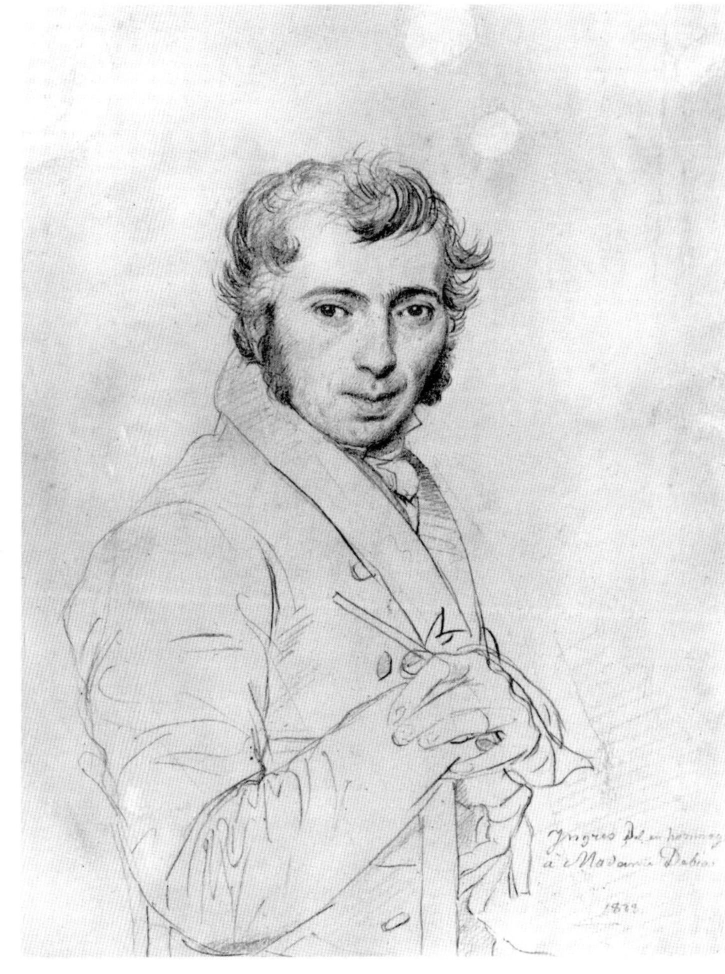

Fig. 10 (*above left*) Théodore Géricault, *The Kiss*, c. 1822, sepia and black chalk heightened with white on paper, 8 × 10$\frac{1}{2}$ in. (20.3 × 26.8 cm), Museo Thyssen-Bornemisza, Madrid

Fig. 11 (*above right*) Jean-Auguste-Dominique Ingres, *The Painter Prosper Debia*, graphite on paper, 8$\frac{3}{8}$ × $\frac{9}{16}$ in. (21.2 × 16.2 cm), private collection

of Art in conjunction with the annual meeting of the College Art Association. Photographs of this installation (figs. 8 and 9) show major drawings by many modern masters, and a careful study of the files in the Norton Simon Museum demonstrates that he could easily have mounted an exhibition of nineteenth-century European drawings that would include masterpieces by Jean-Auguste-Dominique Ingres, Eugène Delacroix, Théodore Géricault (fig. 10), Jean-François Millet, Honoré Daumier, Jean-Baptiste Camille Corot, Gustave Moreau, Constantin Guys, Édouard Manet, Degas, Pissarro, Georges Seurat, Odilon Redon, van Gogh, and Cézanne. Simon's collection also included several groups of drawings by artists of real importance to him. He owned as many as eight drawings by Ingres, including six graphite portraits (fig. 11),[14] one early compositional drawing of *Scipio and His Son with the Envoys of Antiochus*, and a sublime pencil and black chalk presentation drawing related to the great painting *Odalisque and Slave* in the Fogg Art Museum.[15] Simon also possessed a number of important drawings by Daumier as well as a superb group by Charles Baudelaire's favorite draftsman, Constantin Guys. Many of the finest of these sheets were sold at auction or through Simon's friend, the dealer Eugene Thaw.

Given the fact that the Norton Simon collections have so many works by Degas, it is perhaps surprising that Simon once owned even more, and that certain of the works he sold are of the highest quality. Perhaps the most fascinating subgroup consists of four monotypes of 1879 from

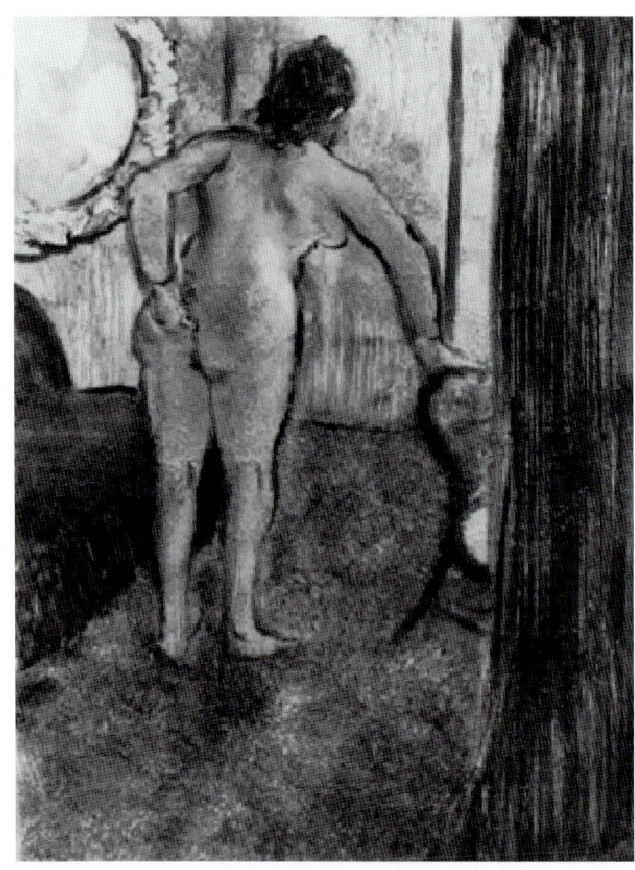

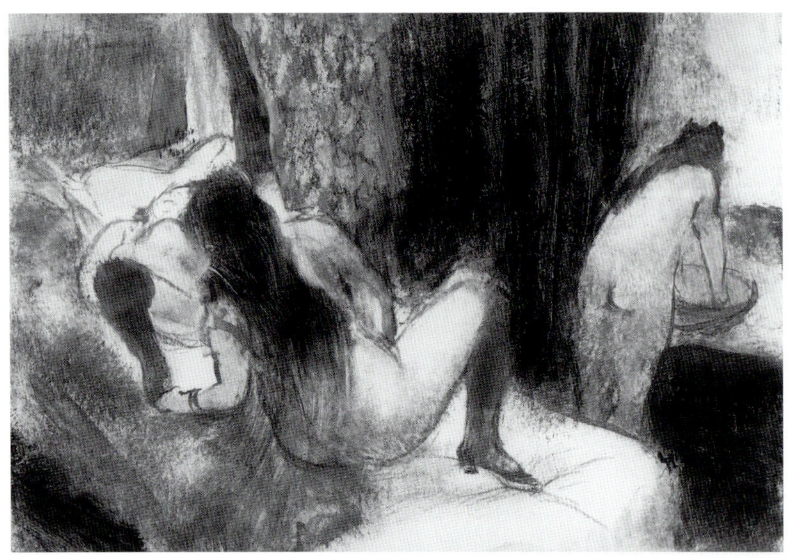

Fig. 12 (*above left*) Hilaire-Germain-Edgar Degas, *Nude Women*, c. 1879, pastel over monotype on paper, $5\frac{1}{2} \times 8$ in. (14×20.5 cm), private collection

Fig. 13 (*above right*) Hilaire-Germain-Edgar Degas, *Room in a Brothel*, c. 1879, monotype in black ink on paper, $8\frac{3}{4} \times 6\frac{1}{4}$ in. (22.2×15.9 cm), Stanford University Museum of Art, Stanford, Calif.

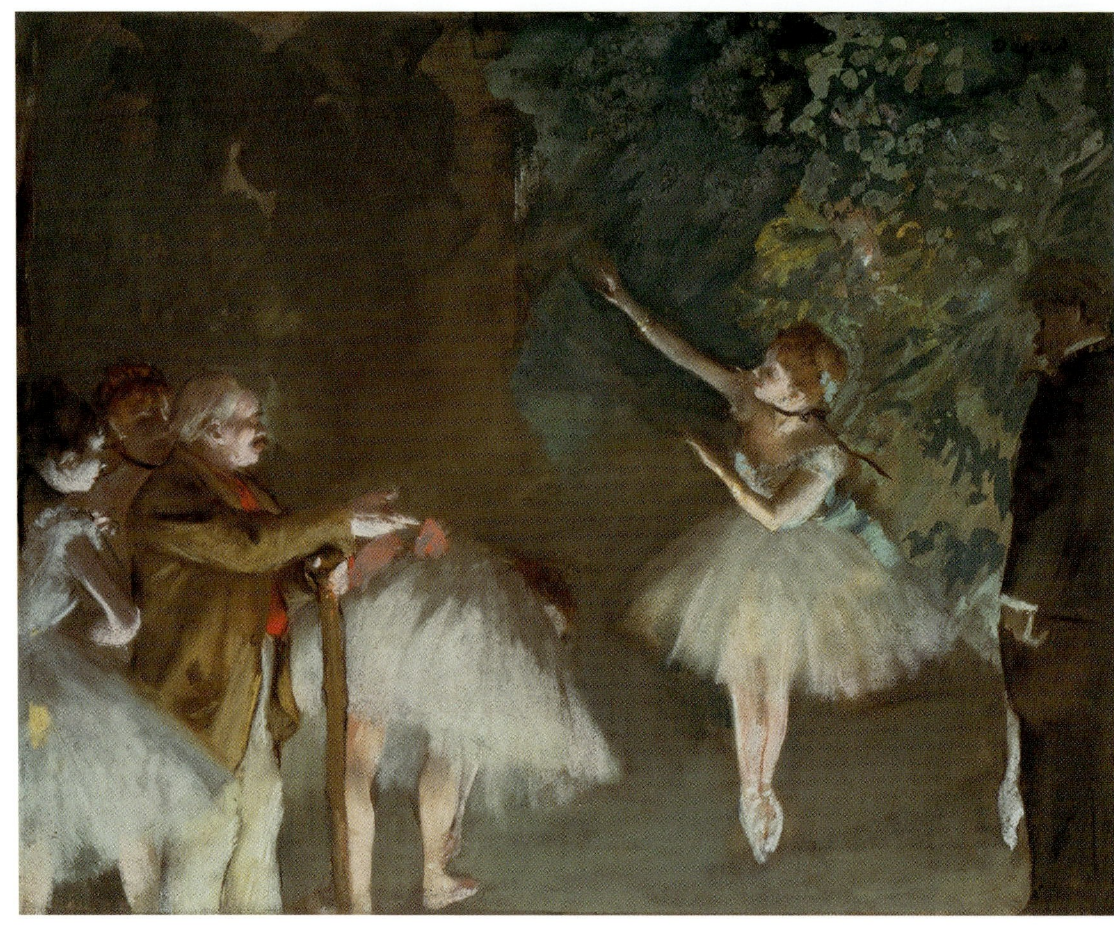

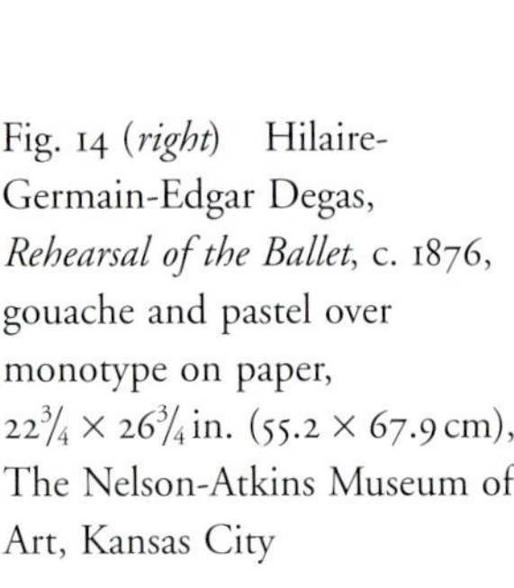

Fig. 14 (*right*) Hilaire-Germain-Edgar Degas, *Rehearsal of the Ballet*, c. 1876, gouache and pastel over monotype on paper, $22\frac{3}{4} \times 26\frac{3}{4}$ in. (55.2×67.9 cm), The Nelson-Atkins Museum of Art, Kansas City

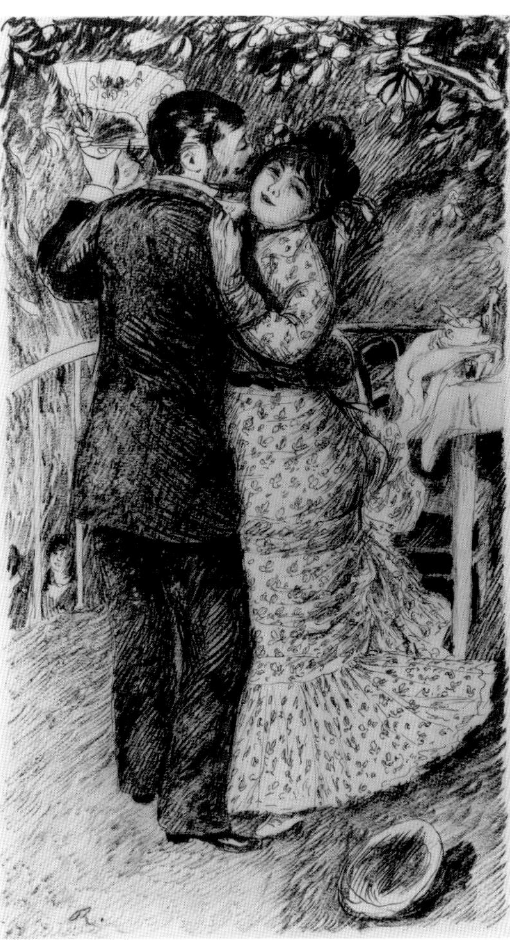

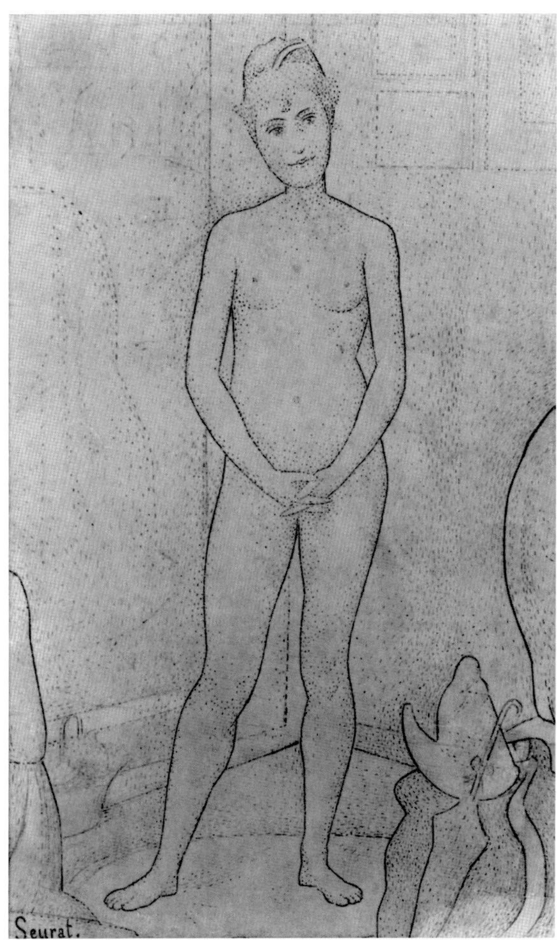

Fig. 15 (*right*) Pierre-Auguste Renoir, *Dance in the Country*, 1883, pen and brush and gray ink on paper, 18¾ × 11⅞ in. (47.6 × 30.2 cm), National Gallery of Art, Washington, D.C.

Fig. 16 (*far right*) Georges Seurat, *Study after "The Models"*, 1888, pen and brown ink over graphite on paper, 10⅜ × 6 5/16 in (26.4 × 16.1 cm), National Gallery of Art, Washington, D.C.

the artist's extraordinary group of representations in that medium of *maisons closes*, or regulated houses of prostitution. These works, never exhibited publicly in Degas's lifetime (figs. 12 and 13), have been much studied by art historians in the past three decades. Of all the works on paper by Degas that Simon sold the loss of one is most keenly felt. There are few works by Degas from the 1870s that are more important and poetic than *Rehearsal of the Ballet* (fig. 14). Simon elected to sell it because he had become worried about its condition and the possible necessity of treatment that could compromise its integrity. In retrospect, his caution was ill-advised.

Unlike many collectors of the graphic arts, Simon also possessed Impressionist drawings, and his collection of works on paper included important examples by Monet, Pissarro, and Renoir (fig. 15). Of the Post-Impressionist masters of graphic arts, Simon owned three important drawings by Seurat, including a signed exhibition drawing of the frontal nude now in the National Gallery of Art in Washington (fig. 16), four drawings by van Gogh,[16] and a group of pastels and drawings by Redon, of which the finest is *Trees* (fig. 17). He seems never to have owned a drawing or print by Gauguin, but he more than made up for these lacunae by purchasing three major pencil drawings and twelve watercolors by Cézanne. If installed together, this group would form a mini-retrospective of Cézanne's work on paper, ranging from an analytical self-portrait drawing of 1874–1875 to sublime watercolors from the last decade of his working life. Again, the group was formed one by one through time, so that Simon could compare one to the other and relate

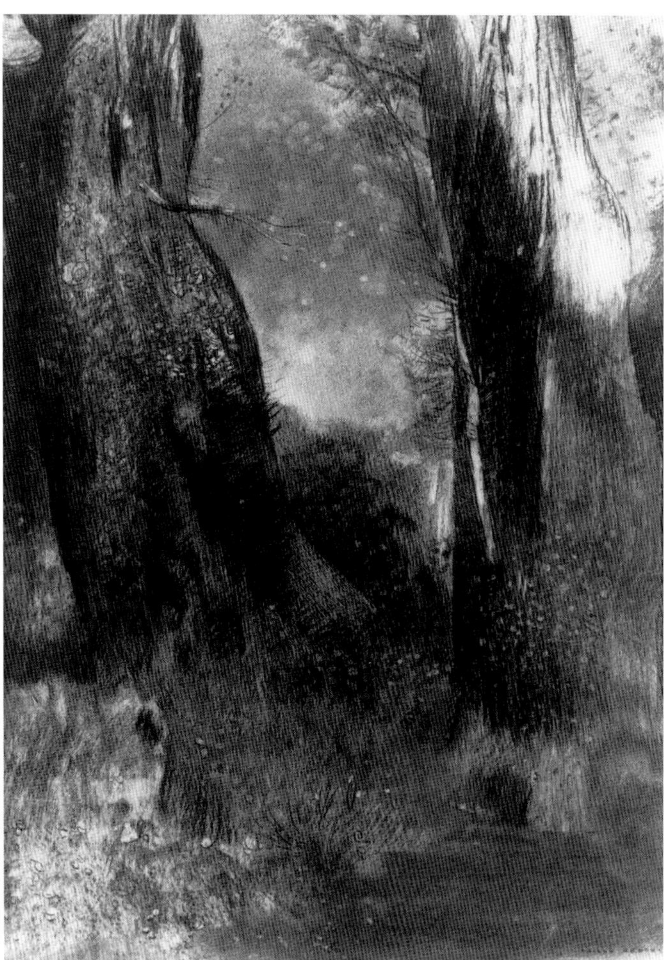

Fig. 17 Odilon Redon, *Trees*, 1890s, charcoal on paper, 19¾ × 14¾ in. (50.2 × 37.5 cm), The Museum of Fine Arts, Houston

works in his collection to famous drawings and watercolors he studied in books and museum collections. Perhaps the greatest of these are two watercolor still lifes, one of which was given by Eugene Thaw in 2002 to the Morgan Library (fig. 18) and the other acquired by the J. Paul Getty Museum in 1983 (fig. 19).

Walking through the Norton Simon Museum today, one does not keenly feel the lack of these works on paper, because they could be exhibited only rarely if still in the collections. When we move into the area of oil paintings on canvas and consider what could have been integrated into the collection, however, the absence of works is palpable. They would have at least doubled the Museum's holdings of Romantic, Realist, Impressionist, and Post-Impressionist works with paintings of the same or, in certain cases, greater quality than those that remain. Although his divorce and retirement played a role in Simon's decision to sell works from his collection, they were only part of a larger process of reassessment and deaccession that consumed him in the 1970s. He had come to know the great museum director John Walker, who, after retiring from his position at the National Gallery of Art, became convinced that southern California held more promise for the future of art collecting and museums than any other part of the country. In addition to joining the board of trustees of the Los Angeles County Museum of Art, Walker helped Norton Simon to appraise his collection in a systematic and thorough-going way. Walker

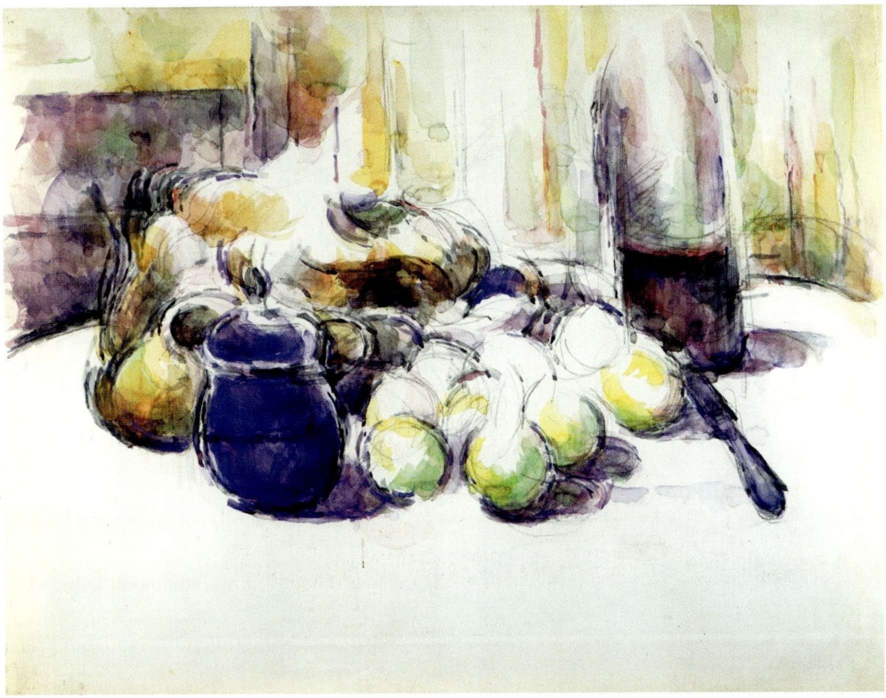

Fig. 18 Paul Cézanne, *Still Life with Pears and Apples, Covered Blue Jar, and a Bottle of Wine*, 1904–1906, watercolor over black chalk on paper, $18\frac{3}{4} \times 24\frac{15}{16}$ in. (47.6 × 61.7 cm), The Pierpont Morgan Library, New York

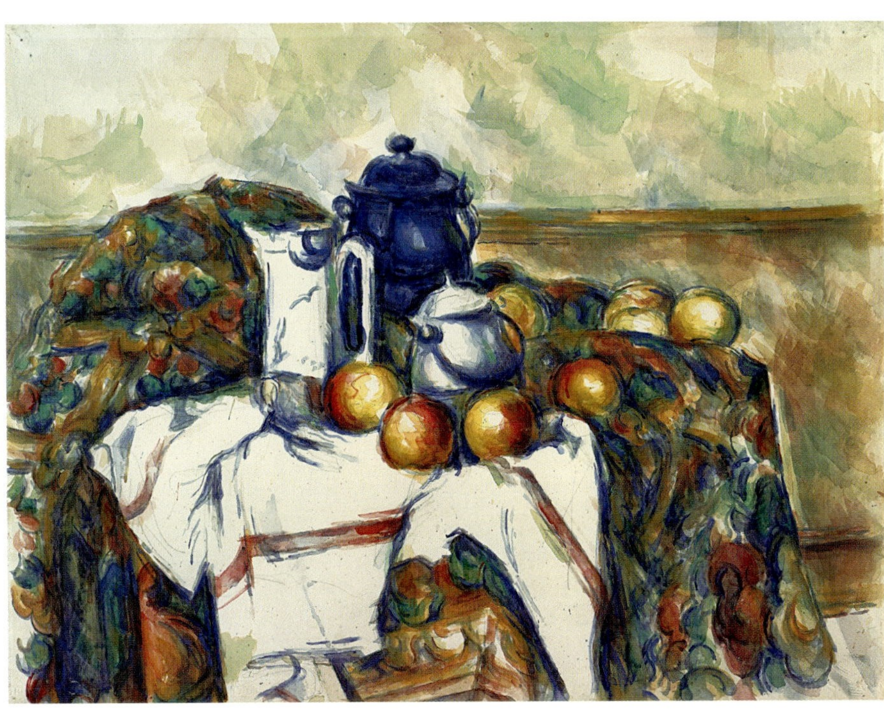

Fig. 19 Paul Cézanne, *Still Life with Blue Pot*, c. 1900–1906, watercolor and graphite on paper, $18\frac{7}{8} \times 24\frac{7}{8}$ in. (48 × 63.2 cm), The J. Paul Getty Museum, Los Angeles

sought the advice of experts and art historians while informing Simon of all deliberations. This procedure was so important for Simon that it pushed him to envision a long-term project of pruning and judiciously adding to his collections. This project, which continued for two decades, led to the sale of many works of nineteenth-century art, generally in favor of the purchase of old master paintings.

Although only a few works from the middle of the nineteenth century could be added to the current collection from the works that were sold, these are of the first quality. Unfortunately,

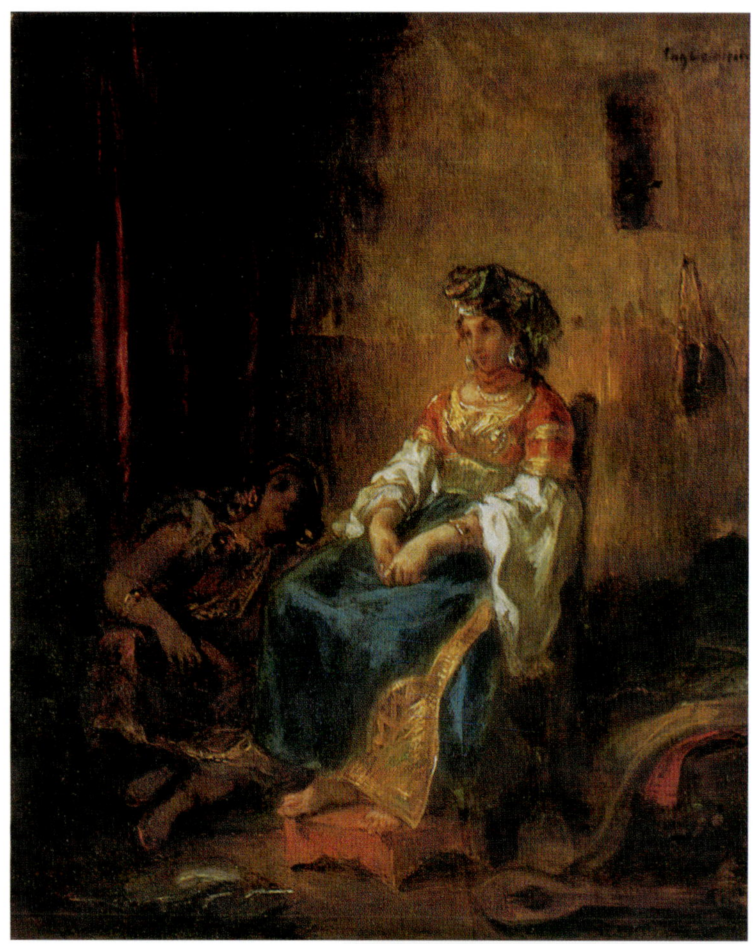

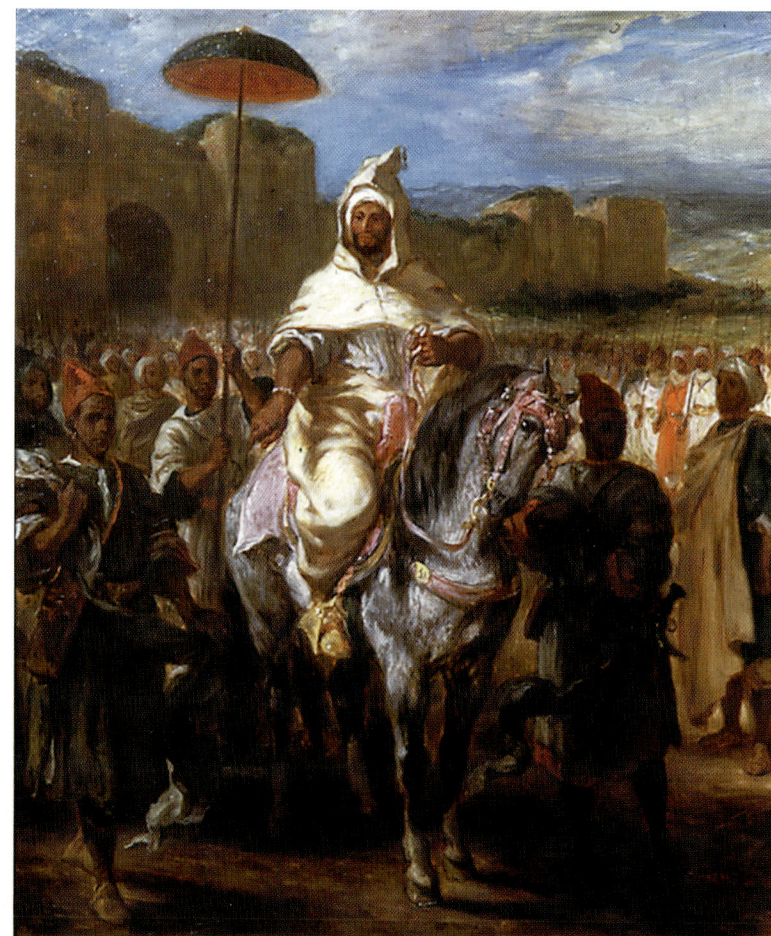

Fig. 20 (*above left*) Eugène Delacroix, *Jewish Bride of Tangier*, c. 1833, oil on canvas, $18\frac{1}{2} \times 15\frac{1}{2}$ in. (47×39.5 cm), private collection

Fig. 21 (*above right*) Eugène Delacroix, *Abd er Rahman, the Sultan of Morocco Reviewing His Guard*, 1856, oil on canvas, $25\frac{5}{8} \times 21\frac{9}{16}$ in. (65×54.7 cm), private collection

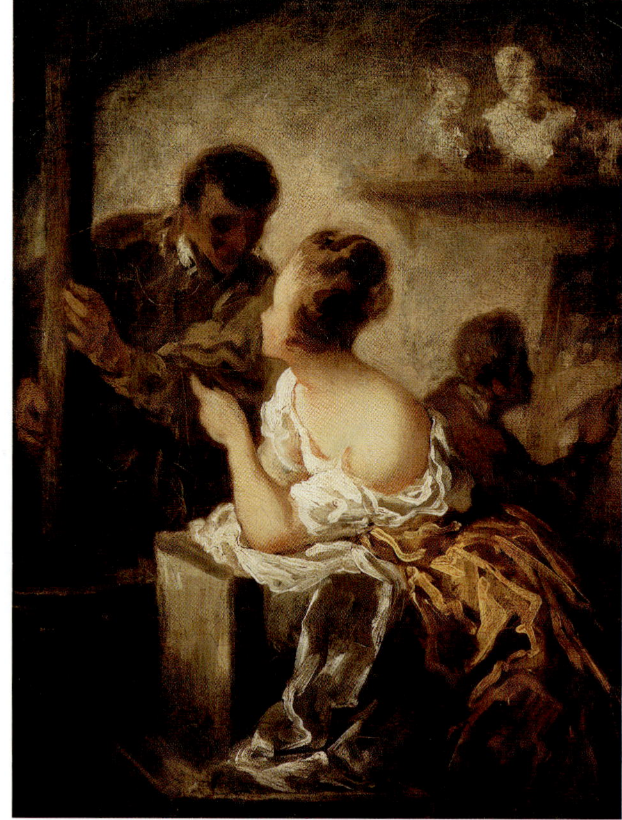

Fig. 22 (*right*) Honoré Daumier, *The Studio*, c. 1870, oil on canvas, $16 \times 12\frac{1}{2}$ in. (40.6×31.7 cm), The J. Paul Getty Museum, Los Angeles

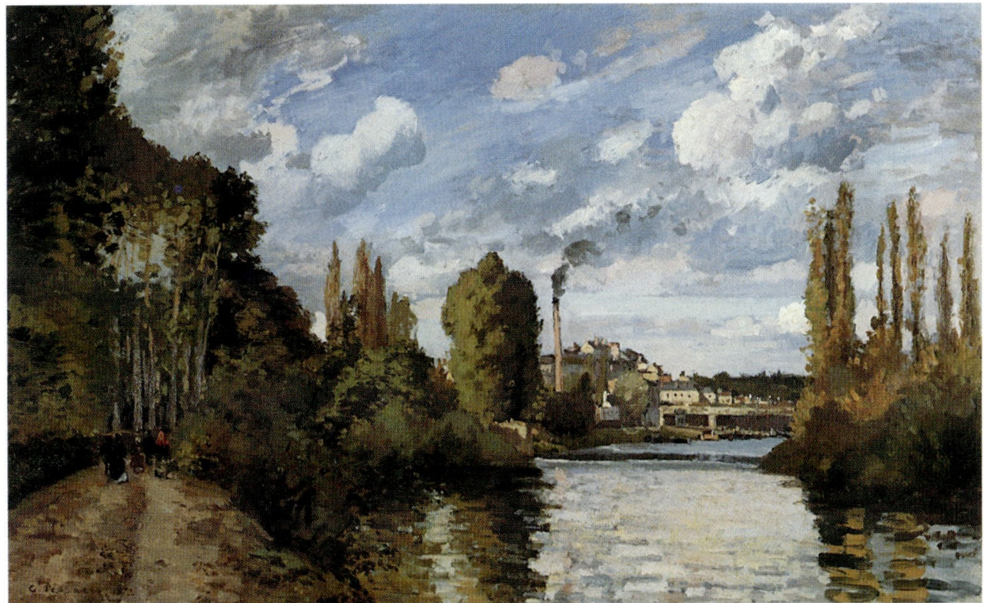

Fig. 23 Camille Pissarro, *Riverbanks in Pontoise*, 1872, oil on canvas, 21⅝ × 35⅞ in. (55 × 91 cm), private collection, Chicago

both of Simon's paintings by Eugène Delacroix, a superb small canvas from 1832 called *Jewish Bride of Tangier* (fig. 20) and the wondrous *Abd er Rahman, the Sultan of Morocco Reviewing His Guard*, a canvas of 1856 (fig. 21), succumbed to the vicissitudes of the art market (and possibly to undocumented expert advice). This means that one of the very greatest French artists of the nineteenth century—and the virtual artistic god of the young avant-garde painters so well represented in the collection—is unrepresented at the Norton Simon Museum, except by a minor and rarely exhibited set of lithographs. Simon also once owned wonderful paintings by Gustave Courbet, Théodore Rousseau, Paul Guigou, and Daumier. The great Guigou Salon painting of 1867 now in the Art Institute of Chicago was once in southern California (cat. 70, fig. 70a), and Daumier's magical *The Studio* has remained in the area, but in the collection of the J. Paul Getty Museum (fig. 22).

Although Simon retained major proto-Impressionist landscapes by Monet and Renoir from the 1860s as well as works by Jean-Baptiste Armand Guillaumin, Alfred Sisley, Pissarro, and Berthe Morisot from the next decade, he sold a small group of important paintings that would have added both depth and quality to this critical decade in the history of modern painting. Pissarro's *Riverbanks in Pontoise* of 1872 (fig. 23) and *Pontoise, Banks of the River* from the same year[17] would have been a perfect complement to the *Boulevard des Fossés* (cat. 63) still in the collections. Lucille Ellis Simon, who understood Pissarro very well, selected the larger picture as part of her divorce settlement. Simon sold the smaller one to Reid and Lefevre in 1982 for slightly more than twice what he had paid for it in 1968. In hindsight, he was wrong about this latter decision to sell if we think merely of Pissarro and Impressionism, but he was considering and buying other works of art by other artists in 1982 and applied his rigorously relativist logic to his own collection.

Other Impressionist paintings from the 1870s, the first true decade of the movement, also fell to Simon's personal asset management or to the great collector's relentless questioning of

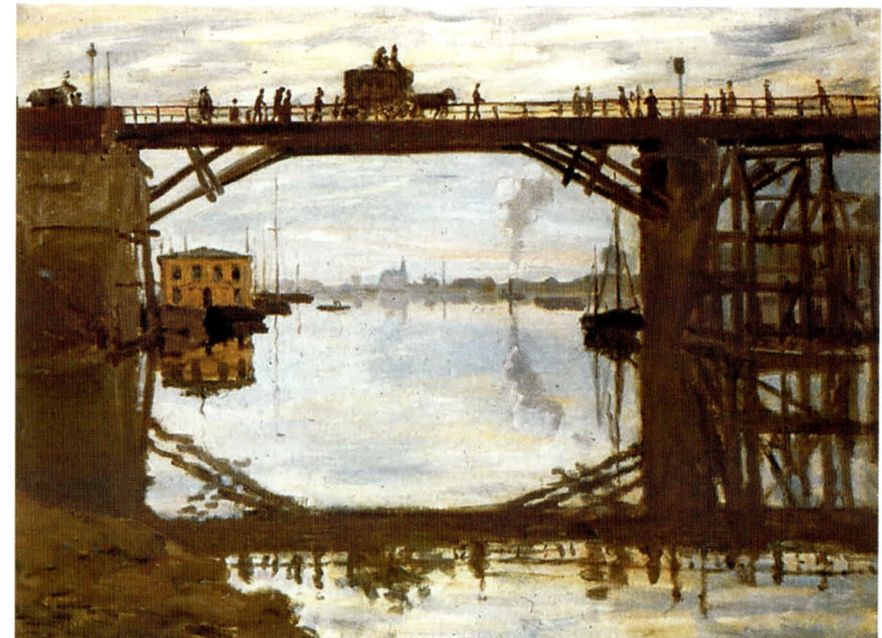

Fig. 24 Claude Monet, *The Wooden Bridge at Argenteuil*, 1872, oil on canvas, 21 × 28¾ in. (54 × 73 cm), Fondation Rau, Zurich

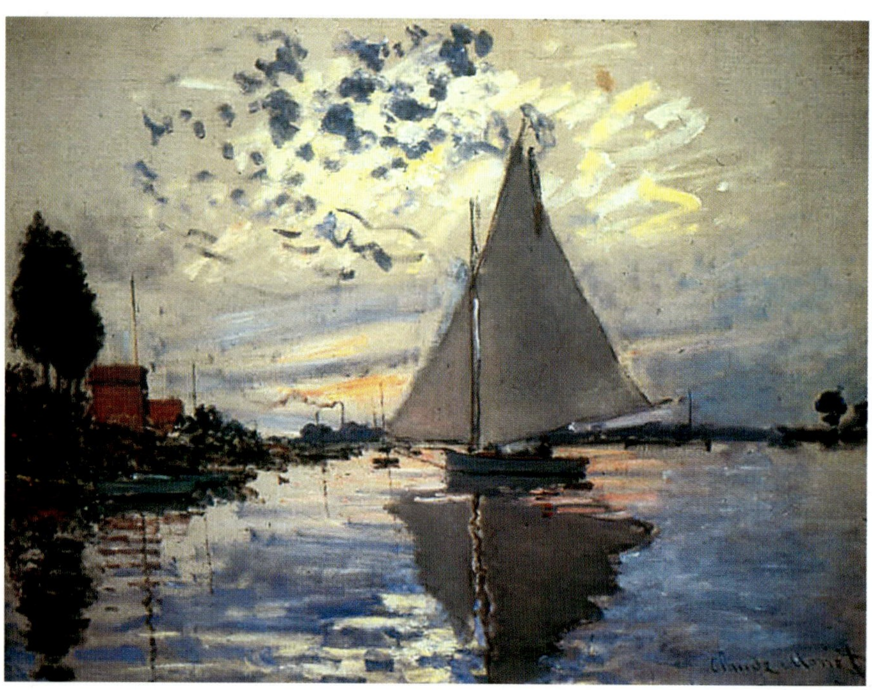

Fig. 25 Claude Monet, *Sailboat at Petit Gennevilliers*, 1874, oil on canvas, 21 × 28¾ in. (54 × 73 cm), private collection

monetary and aesthetic value. Monet's now-famous *The Wooden Bridge at Argenteuil* (fig. 24) is perhaps the single most poignant pictorial response to the Franco-Prussian War by an Impressionist painter, but it was sold by Simon for a very good profit,[18] and his sublime *Sailboat at Petit Gennevilliers* of 1874 (fig. 25) was chosen by Mrs. Simon in the divorce. And Simon's finest landscape by Sisley, *The Seine at Bougival* of 1873 (fig. 26), was sold to Eugene Thaw in 1972 for more than ten times its 1956 purchase price. So, too, a rare Pissarro floral still life bought at auction for $90,000 in 1968 was sold five years later, also at auction, for $150,000.[19] Had he retained this picture, it would have looked wonderful with the Renoir floral still life (cat. 90)

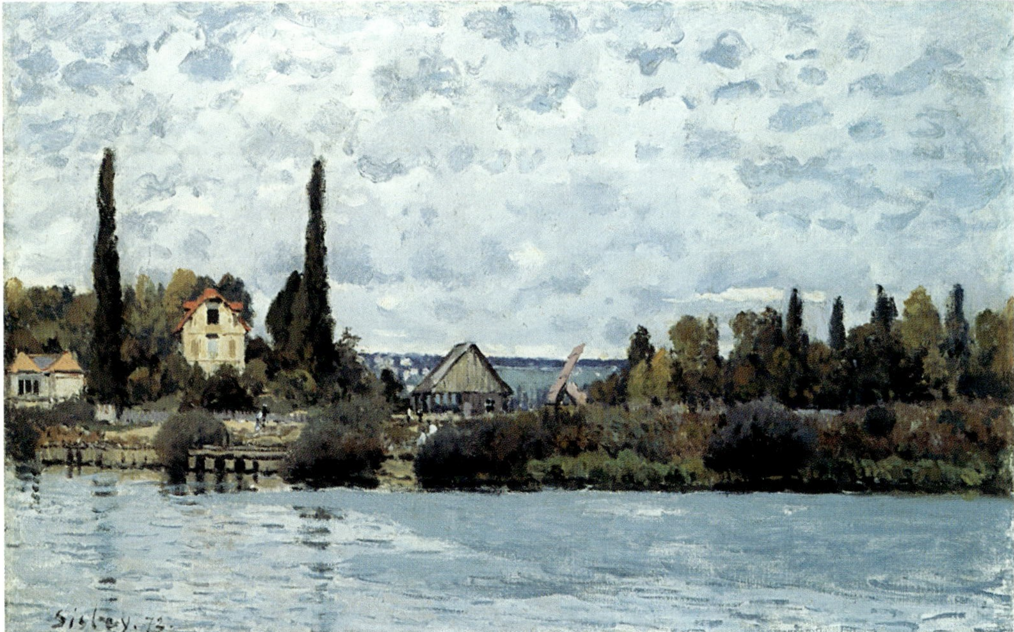

Fig. 26 Alfred Sisley, *The Seine at Bougival*, 1873, oil on canvas, 15¼ × 24½ in. (38.5 × 62 cm), private collection

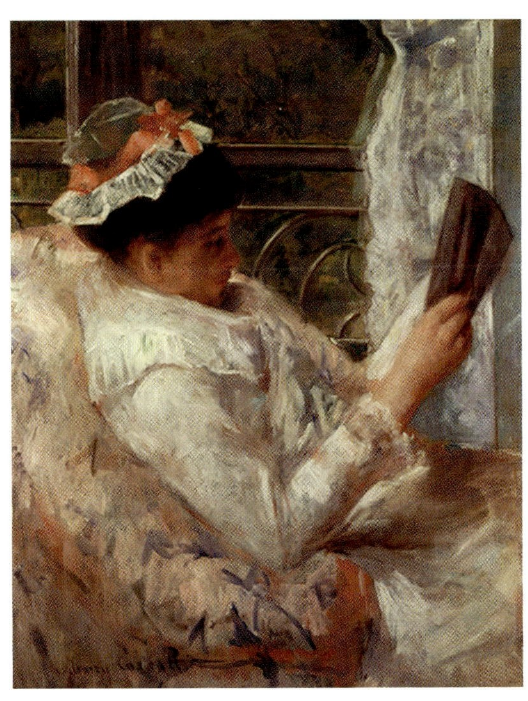

Fig. 27 Mary Cassatt, *Woman Reading*, 1878, oil on canvas, 31 × 24¾ in. (78.7 × 62.9 cm), location unknown

that he kept. But Simon was no more partial to the Impressionist Renoir than he was to Pissarro or Monet, selling two delightful small figure paintings, *Couple Reading* and *Jacques-Eugène Spuller*, the first for a modest gain, the second at a loss. Also, unfortunately, Mr. Simon's rigorous processes of reevaluation led him to sell Mary Cassatt's wonderful Impressionist genre scene from 1878, *Woman Reading* (fig. 27).

For Impressionist painting of the 1880s and 1890s, Norton Simon was equally hard-hearted in evaluating certain works. He sold one of Monet's views of Rouen cathedral (fig. 28) in 1982 for the then-impressive sum of $1,500,000, and four major works by Renoir from those two

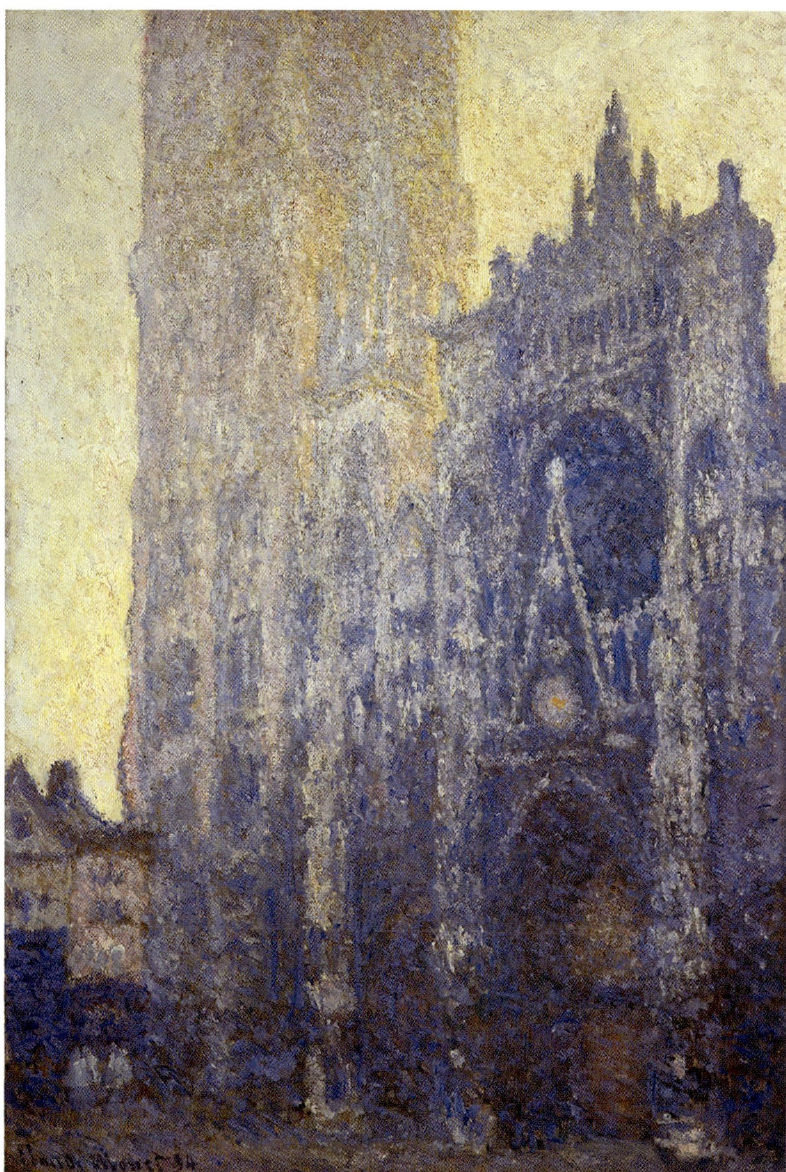

Fig. 28 Claude Monet, *Rouen Cathedral, the Tour d'Albane, Morning*, 1894, 41¾ × 29 in. (106 × 73.6 cm), Fondation Beyeler, Basel

decades, one acquired in 1965 and three in 1969, were sold in 1971, 1973, and 1982, the latter for more than double his investment. This painting, *Girl in a Yellow Hat* of 1886 (fig. 29), was bought from Wildenstein by Simon in 1969 for the comparatively high price of $425,000. Simon reportedly never liked the painting (and we are somewhat sympathetic to this view) and actually attempted to arrange its private sale for several years before finally selling it to Eugene Thaw in 1982 for $1,000,000. The collector also parted with two very important Parisian view paintings by Camille Pissarro, both of which would have rhymed brilliantly with the Italian urban view paintings of the eighteenth century that he retained. The earlier of the two, *Boulevard Montmartre, Mardi-Gras* of 1897,[20] is today in the Hammer Museum. The even more important *Place du Théâtre Français, Afternoon Sun in Winter* (fig. 30) was sold to Eugene Thaw in 1980 for more than triple the amount Simon paid for it sixteen years earlier and remains today in a private collection.

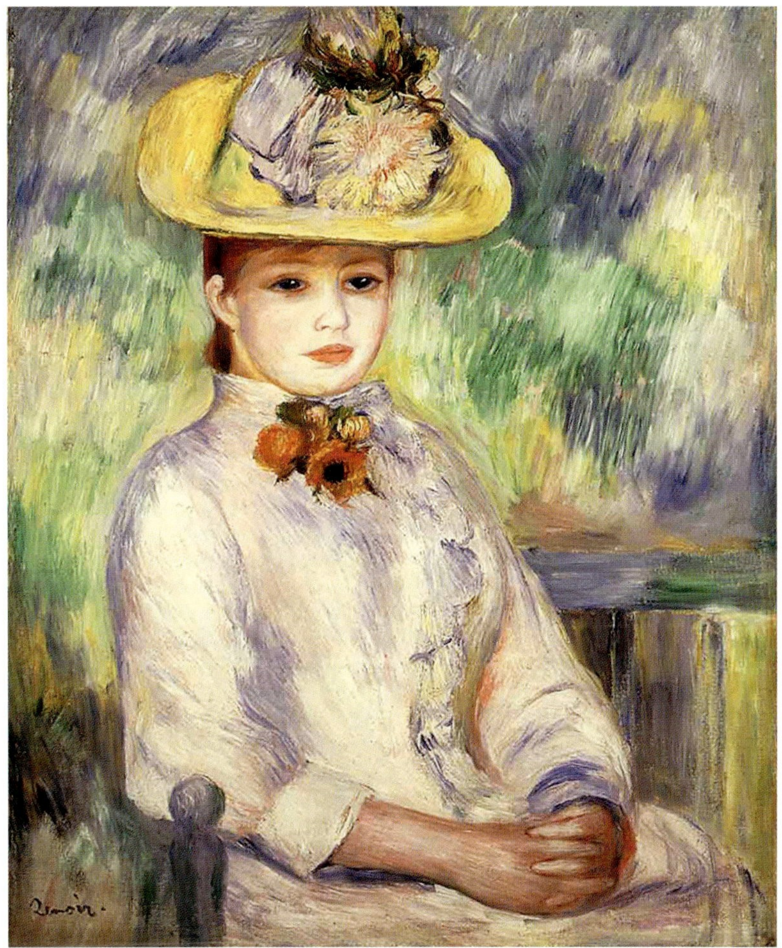

Fig. 29 Pierre-Auguste Renoir, *Girl in a Yellow Hat*, 1886, oil on canvas, 26¼ × 21⅝ in. (66.7 × 54.9 cm), location unknown

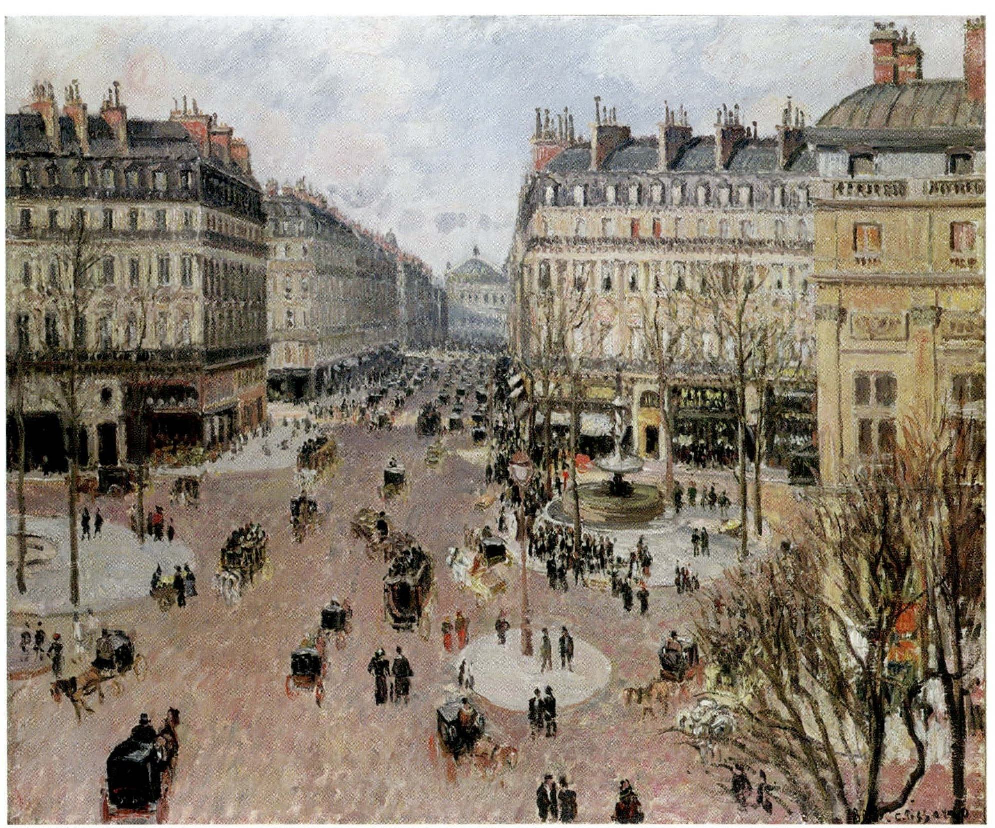

Fig. 30 Camille Pissarro, *Place du Théâtre Français, Afternoon Sun in Winter*, 1898, oil on canvas, 28¾ × 36¼ in. (73 × 92 cm), private collection

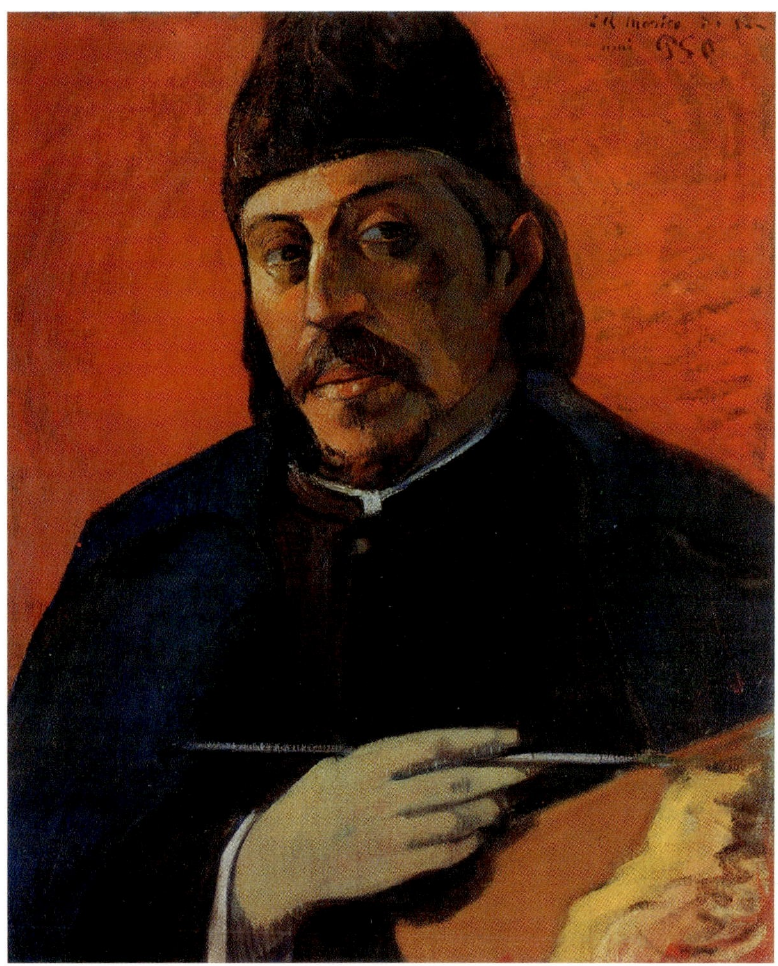

Fig. 31 Paul Gauguin, *Self-Portrait with a Palette*, 1893–1894, oil on canvas, 21½ × 18 in. (54.6 × 45.7 cm), private collection

These important paintings by Sisley, Pissarro, Renoir, Cassatt, and Monet would have enriched the Norton Simon Museum's representation of Impressionist painting immeasurably, not just numerically but also in terms of the range and depth of the movement. And, if this is true of Impressionism, his retention of the masterpieces of Post-Impressionist painting he sold would have had a similar effect on the permanent holdings of his museum in that area of the history of art. Oddly, the Norton Simon Museum has only one painting by Paul Gauguin (cat. 99), in spite of the fact that it has a virtually definitive collection of works by his followers in Pont-Aven. Already mentioned is the great Pont-Aven landscape of 1889 (fig. 2) now at the Los Angeles County Museum of Art, which almost cries out to move to Pasadena to be with its companions by Émile Bernard, Georges Lacombe, Jacob Meyer de Haan, and Paul Sérusier. Few people remember today that Simon also once owned one of Gauguin's greatest self-portraits, *Self-Portrait with a Palette*, from the first years of the 1890s (fig. 31), which he sold in 1971. Today, it is in a private collection in New York and has played crucial roles in many major exhibitions and books devoted to that artist. We also remember that Simon sold a major work van Gogh painted in Saint-Rémy in the 5 May 1971 sale of his personal collection, but the Los Angeles area is lucky that Armand Hammer bought it at the sale so that it remains in the city. Simon also sold several paintings by Cézanne, including two whose absence is regretted

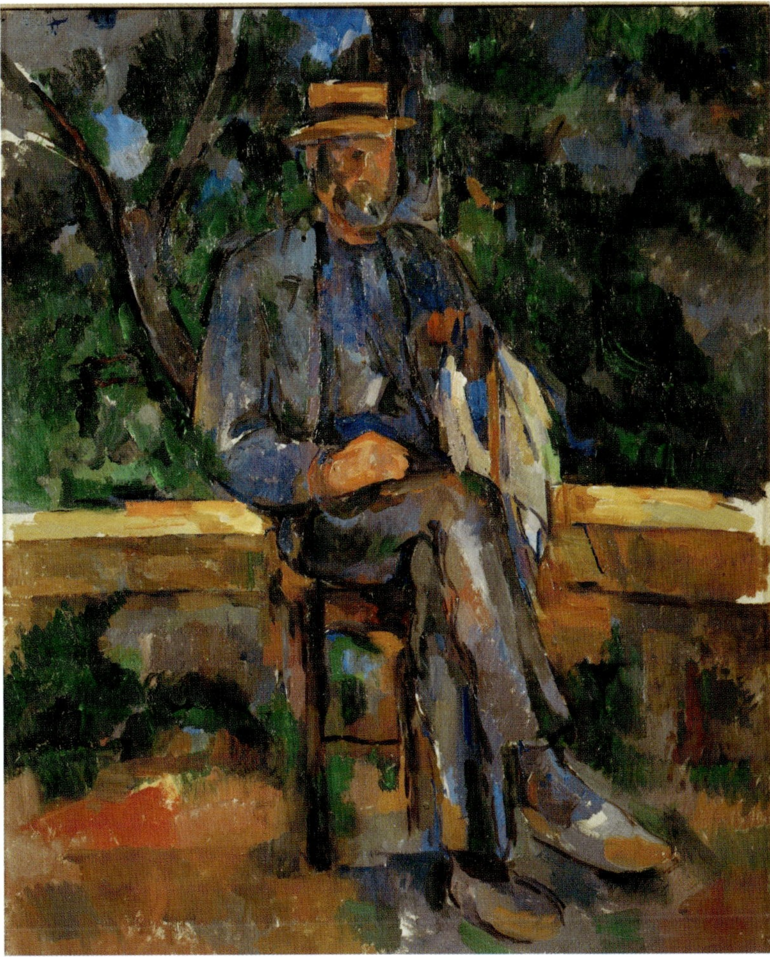

Fig. 32 Paul Cézanne, *Portrait of a Peasant*, c. 1901–1906, oil on canvas, $25\frac{5}{8} \times 21\frac{1}{4}$ in. (65×54 cm), Museo Thyssen-Bornemisza, Madrid

today, *Rock Quarries at Bibemus*[21] and *Portrait of a Peasant* (fig. 32), which was accompanied in the Norton Simon collection by a closely related watercolor of the painter's seated gardener, Vallier. Both these works would have added depth and superb quality to the Norton Simon collection of paintings by Cézanne.

It is perhaps worth mentioning a few early-twentieth-century paintings once owned by Mr. Simon that would have appeared in this catalogue had he retained ownership. The largest and, in certain ways, most important is Monet's *The Basin of Water Lilies, Giverny* (fig. 33), signed and dated 1919, sold by Mr. Simon from his personal collection in 1971 at a very slight profit. Few works of this scale and importance from Monet's last decade are both signed and dated, and, had Simon kept it, it would have been among the very greatest late works by this artist in a public collection in California. Equally unfortunate was Simon's decision in 1980 to sell his only painting by Edvard Munch, *Three Girls on a Bridge*. Purchased by him in 1963 for the comparatively modest sum of $130,000, it brought $2,000,000 when it was sold.[22] Perhaps its status as the sole painted work of Scandinavian modernism in the Museum prompted Simon to sell it. He also might have thought its monetary value was out of step with its aesthetic quality. And, as Munch's career was better studied in the 1970s, it became clear that the artist repeated many of his classic compositions several times, perhaps suggesting to Mr. Simon that Munch's achieve-

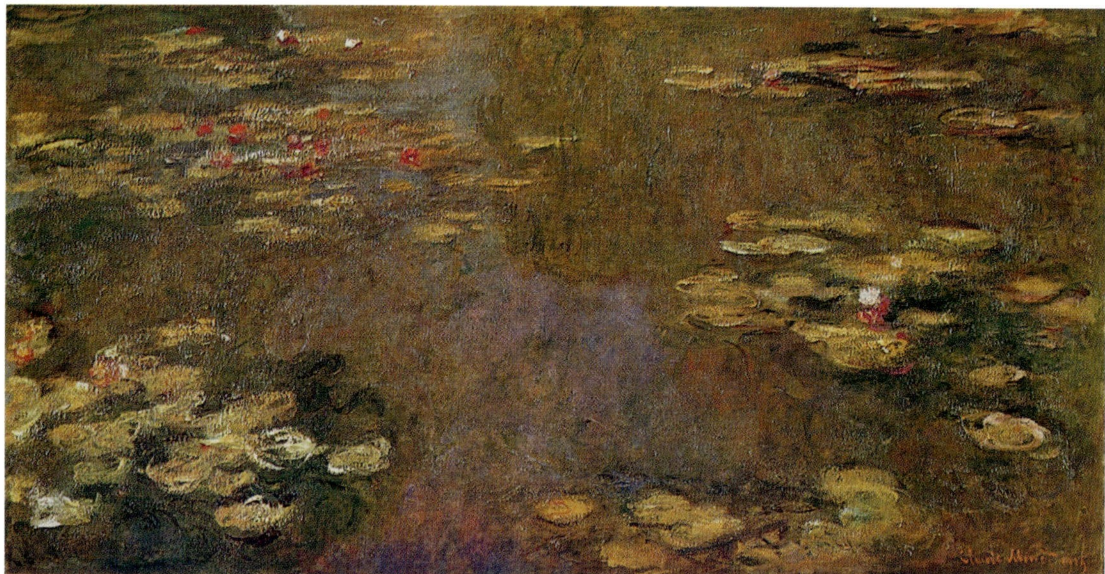

Fig. 33 Claude Monet, *The Basin of Water Lilies, Giverny,* 1919, oil on canvas, $39\frac{1}{2} \times 79$ in. (100.3×200.7 cm), private collection

ment as a pictorial inventor was at a lower level than that of artists like Cézanne, Matisse, or Picasso.[23] Simon also sold two superb paintings by the English artist Walter Sickert in the sale of 5 May 1971, which, had he retained them, would have been unique in a public collection in California.

Simon's sheer restlessness as a collector—and as a businessman—meant that he spent his life in a state of continuous reassessment—juggling in his mind paintings, companies, stocks, real estate, and other assets against prevailing conditions in the larger realms of politics and the economy. Like other successful businessmen, he tried his hand at politics, running unsuccessfully in the Republican Party primary for the United States Senate in 1970. The loss in the race (which he privately rejoiced), his retirement from his corporation, the dissolution of his first marriage, and the death of his son all occurred in a very short period. He was sixty-three years old, thankfully full of ferocious energy, and completely committed to his avocation of art collecting. Although he sold great works of art, several of which have been published here, he used this housecleaning as part of a greater momentum to broaden and improve his collection and to create a museum for it. The story of the negotiations that resulted in the Norton Simon Museum has been told many times and does not need rehearsal here. What is important, though, in the context of Simon's collection of modern art in the museum that bears his name is that it remains today a superb summary of what was an even greater collection. It is important to remember that had Simon simply confined himself to modern art, he would have resembled scores of collectors across Europe and America who specialize in that popular period in the history of Western art. He was too restless—and too ambitious—for that.

Not surprisingly, many of the finest works that were once included in Simon's collection are now in public institutions in Europe, Asia, and the United States. Visitors to the Thyssen-Bornemisza Collection in Madrid, the National Gallery of Australia, the National Gallery of Art in Washington, the Kimbell Art Museum in Fort Worth, the Morgan Library and the Metropolitan Museum of Art in New York, and many other institutions have no idea that certain works they see in those institutions once hung in the home or office of Norton Simon in California. Yet, because of the fortunate stewardship of collectors and museum professionals in southern California, a wonderful small group of works from Norton Simon's collection is at the Los Angeles County Museum of Art, the Armand Hammer Museum, and the J. Paul Getty Museum. Perhaps in future years still others will join them as an extended part of Norton Simon's legacy in southern California.

Richard R. Brettell

1 Pomona College sold the painting in 1973, using the proceeds to aid in the formation of its collection of graphic works by Francisco Goya.

2 Wildenstein provided an appraisal of $40,000.

3 Coplans, 1975, p. 45.

4 Bredius, 1936, no. 260.

5 New York, Christie's, 7 June 2002, no. 24.

6 Letter, 2 June 1956, Norton Simon Museum curatorial files.

7 The three paintings are *Portrait of a Bearded Man in a Wide-Brimmed Hat*, *Self-Portrait*, and *Portrait of a Boy in Fancy Costume, aka the Artist's Son, Titus*. *Portrait of a Bearded Man* was attributed to Rembrandt by the Rembrandt Research Project (Josua Bruyn, Bob Haak, S. H. Levie, P. J. J. van Thiel, and Ernst van de Wetering, *A Corpus of Rembrandt Paintings*, vol. 2, 1631–1634, The Hague, 1986, no. A86). *Self-Portrait* was initially rejected by the Rembrandt Research Project (vol. 3, 1635–1642, 1989, no. C97). Among those who now accept the painting, however, is Ernst van de Wetering, a member of the original group who currently directs the project and will include the Norton Simon painting as an autograph Rembrandt in a forthcoming volume of the corpus dedicated to Rembrandt's self-portraits. In 2001 and 2003 van de Wetering was able to perform a detailed technical examination of the work, a procedure not available to the original RRP team. *Portrait of a Boy in Fancy Costume* has not yet been published by the RRP but appears in van de Wetering's *Rembrandt: The Painter at Work*, Berkeley, 2000, p. 211.

8 Georges Braque, *Nude with Raised Arm*, 1926, on approval February 1975 from Paul Rosenberg & Co.; not purchased.

9 Norton Simon interview with Marshall Berges, recorded 23 February 1975; transcripts in the Norton Simon Museum curatorial files.

10 Most museums listen to the opinions of connoisseurs and historians of art, but few record them with such tenacity.

11 Sara Campbell, conversation with author, 6 August 2005.

12 New York, Parke-Bernet Galleries, 5, 7, and 8 May 1971, and New York, Sotheby Parke-Bernet, 2–4 May 1973.

13 At one time, according to Sara Campbell, he possessed more first-edition sets of Goya's suite of the *Tauromaquia* than any museum in the world.

14 Naef, 1977–1980, vol. 4, nos. 37–40, 202, vol. 5, no. 315.

15 The firm attribution to Ingres was questioned by Hans Naef, which contributed to Norton Simon's decision to sell it (letter, 13 December 1971, Norton Simon Museum curatorial files).

16 Cat. 106; and Faille, 1928, nos. 901, 1012, and 1545.

17 Pissarro and Venturi, 1939, vol. 1, no. 182.

18 London, Christie's, 30 November 1971, lot 24.

19 Pissarro and Venturi, 1939, vol. 1, no. 377, vol. 2, no. 378.

20 Pissarro and Venturi, 1939, vol. 1, no. 996.

21 Venturi, 1936, no. 777.

22 New York, Christie's, 10 December 1980, lot 201.

23 There are twelve paintings and several works on paper of this subject. Paintings can be found at the Kimbell Art Museum in Fort Worth, the Pushkin Museum of Fine Arts in Moscow, the Munch Museum and the National Gallery in Oslo, the Rasmus Meyers Foundation in Bergen, and the Wallraf-Richartz Museum in Cologne, as well as in several private collections.

following pages Vincent van Gogh, *The Mulberry Tree* (detail of cat. 112)

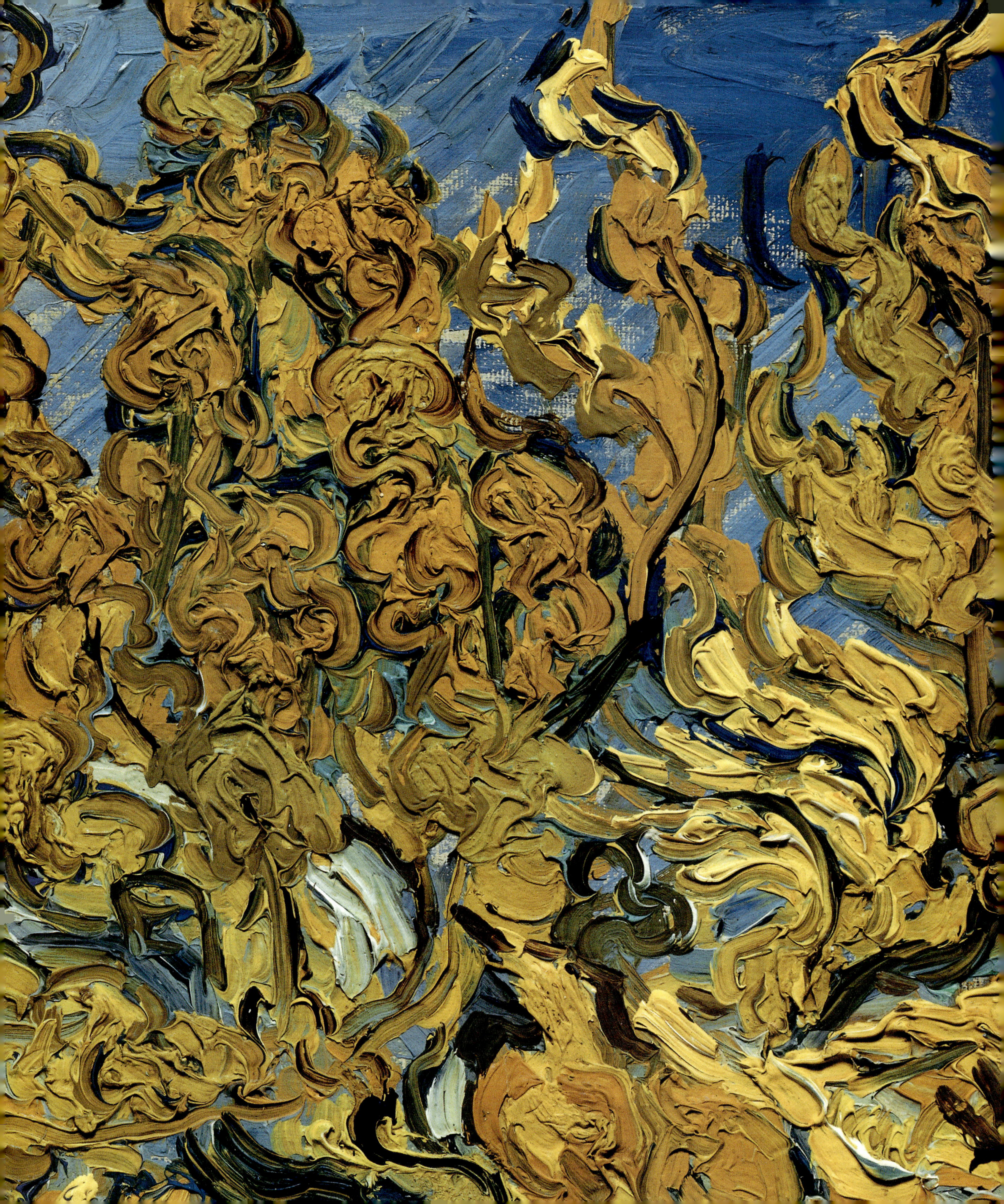

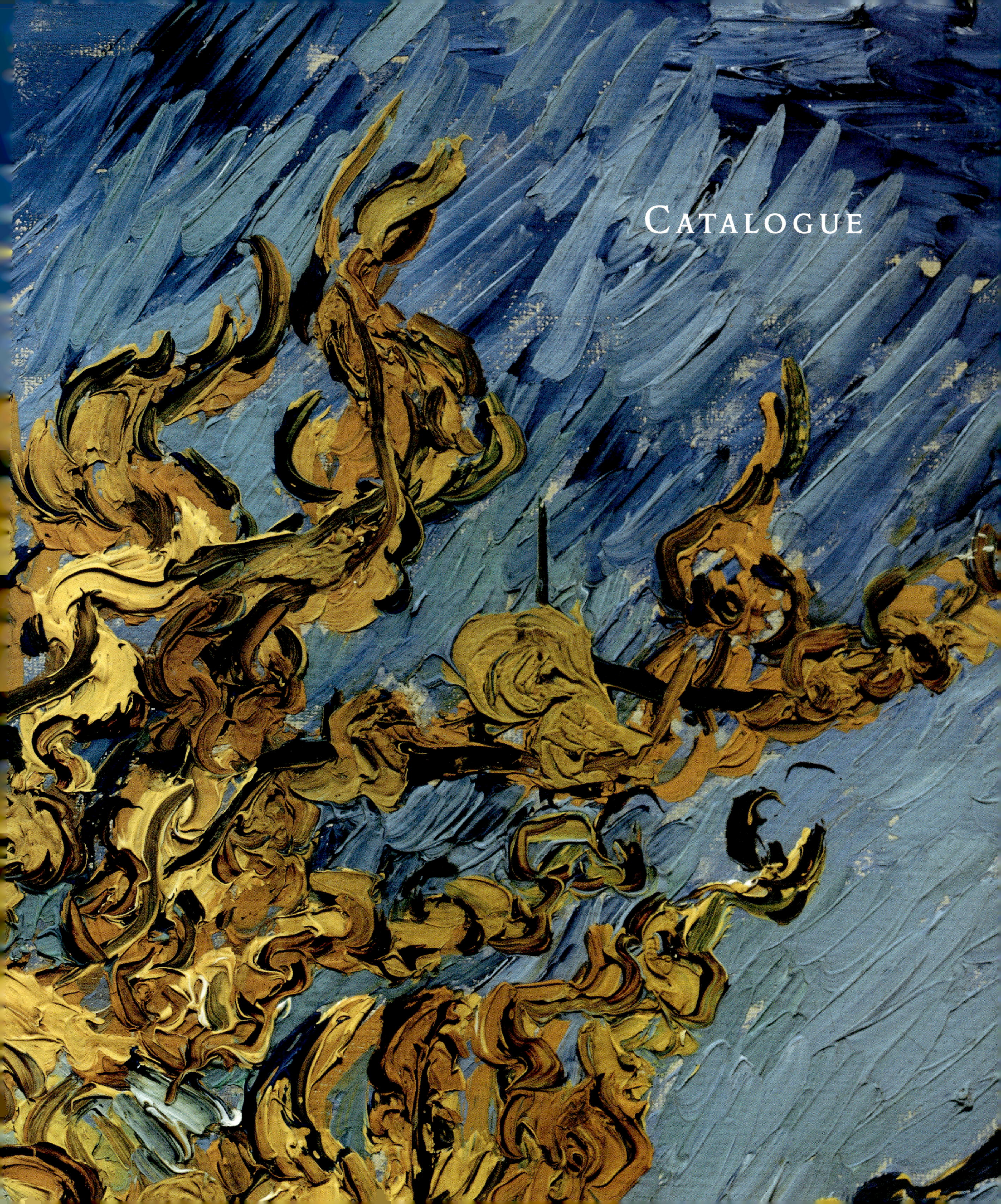

Catalogue

Note to the Reader

The catalogue essays were written collaboratively by Richard R. Brettell and Stephen F. Eisenman. The catalogue entries are arranged sequentially by the artist's birth date, and when there is more than one artwork by an artist, they are listed in chronological order. The Technical Notes summarizing the contents of examination reports of the paintings were prepared by Joseph Fronek, Senior Paintings Conservator and Head of Paintings Conservation, Los Angeles County Museum of Art (JF), and private conservator of paintings Rosamond Westmoreland (RW). John Childs, a conservator of furniture in private practice, assisted in writing the Technical Notes for the Bernard cupboard, cat. 128. The Technical Notes for the works on paper were prepared by Susan Sayre Batton, consulting paper conservator for the Norton Simon Museum from 1998–2005, and now Deputy Director of the Honolulu Academy of Art (SSB). The appropriate initials appear at the end of each Technical Note.

The citations for exhibitions and references have been abbreviated; full lists of each appear at the end of this catalogue. The Norton Simon Art Foundation owns a small collection of nineteenth-century artists' letters. Transcriptions and translations of the letters begin on page 515.

Alphabetical Listing of Artists with Catalogue Numbers

1

Francisco de Goya y Lucientes
Spanish, 1746–1828

She Is Bashful about Undressing (recto of cat. 2)
1796–1797

India ink on paper, sheet, 9 1/8 × 5 5/8 in. (23.2 × 14.2 cm); image, 7 5/8 × 5 in. (19.5 × 12.7 cm)
Inscribed upper right in brush: "79"; across bottom below image in pen: "Tiene cortedad de desnudarse, bayá estese V. quieto"
M.1974.4.2a

Provenance: William Matson Roth, San Francisco; [R. E. Lewis, Larkspur, Calif., sold 1974 to]; Norton Simon Art Foundation.

References: Sayre, 1964, no. 79, p. 29, fig. 22; Gassier, 1971, no. 437, pp. 160, 162, 175, ill., 389, 397; Gassier, 1973, no. B.79, pp. 47, 109, fig. 82, p. 134.

2

Francisco de Goya y Lucientes
Spanish, 1746–1828

Masquerades of Holy Week in the Year '94
(verso of cat. 1)
1796–1797

India ink on paper, sheet, 9 1/8 × 5 5/8 in. (23.2 × 14.2 cm); image, 7 5/8 × 5 in. (19.5 × 12.7 cm)
Inscribed upper left in brush, "80"; across bottom below image in brush: "Mascaras de semana santa del año de 94"
M.1974.4.2b

Provenance: William Matson Roth, San Francisco; [R. E. Lewis, Larkspur, Calif., sold 1974 to]; Norton Simon Art Foundation.

References: Sayre, 1964, no. 80, p. 29, fig. 23; Gassier, 1971, no. 438, pp. 118, ill., 119, 160, 162, 175, ill., 389, 397; Gassier, 1973, no. B.80, p. 110, fig. 83, p. 134; Wilson-Bareau, 1994, p. 316, fig. 218; Wilson-Bareau, 2001, pp. 18, 19, fig. 10.

Technical Notes: This drawing was bound in the sketchbook album known as the Madrid Album B, with seventy-four known drawings. Intact in 1860, the disbanding date is unknown. The drawing is on handmade laid paper, removed from an album. The recto right edge reveals a vertical trim line, indicating the gutter or binding edge of the sketchbook. Made of 100% cotton rag, the paper is supple and intact. A watermark was discovered in the 2000 conservation treatment, a fleur-de-lis in the lower right corner. The chain lines are spaced 2.65 cm apart, and the laid lines are approximately 1 mm apart, as revealed in transmitted light. The paper support is stable, but damaged through handling, water damage, adhesive residues, and contact with acidic materials. There are pronounced stains, especially on the verso, which bleed through to the recto in the lower center. Adhesive residues and darkening around the perimeter indicate a previous mounting to a secondary support. The verso top edge has composite elements, possible previous repairs or accretions, which are lighter than the rest of the sheet. Lower corners are skinned, thin, and have pinholes. Paper loss has weakened the corners. The primary medium is India ink. In the design layer, the recto consists of a darker, undiluted ink wash background, moving the figures into the foreground, with clear, consistent medium. The verso design exhibits a lighter mix of gray ink wash, without breaks or fading. The titles under the drawings were written in two different inks, the recto title created with pen and sepia ink, and the verso title created with a brush and an India ink wash similar to the drawing and numbers. The medium is stable and has not faded from exposure to light or previous treatment. The primary medium in the drawings is in good condition. The titles below the drawings contain damages, including water damage in the recto sepia ink over the second word with a tideline and abrasion on the verso title right side, as well as abrasion and surface soil obscuring the text. (SSB)

Francisco Goya's depictions of the Spanish *pueblo* (popular classes) expose his historic location between the past and the present. He was a man of the eighteenth century, the Rococo, and the ancien régime, but he was also an artist of the nineteenth century, Romanticism, and the epoch of political and industrial revolutions. His earliest independent designs for the Royal Tapestry Factory at Santa Barbara, which date from 1776, are lighthearted, picturesque, and mildly erotic, recalling compositions by the French artists François Boucher, J. B. Oudry, and Hubert Robert. They depict milkmaids, shepherds, happy peasants, and gentlemen and ladies from aristocratic courts in expansive, idealized landscapes. By the mid-1790s, however, Goya's representations of the *pueblo* are no longer Rococo or carefree. His men and women are often sober, endangered, or threatening, and his narrative scenarios ominous, violent, and even macabre. An age of carnival has given way to one of Lent, an epoch of picnics to one of inquisition, an era of peace to one of war. An art of idealism has given way to one of realism.

In 1796, on the cusp of the nineteenth century, Goya traveled to Sanlúcar de Barrameda in Andalusia, in the company of the beautiful and celebrated duchess of Alba. Later that year, while recovering from the relapse of a serious illness that four years before had left him deaf but

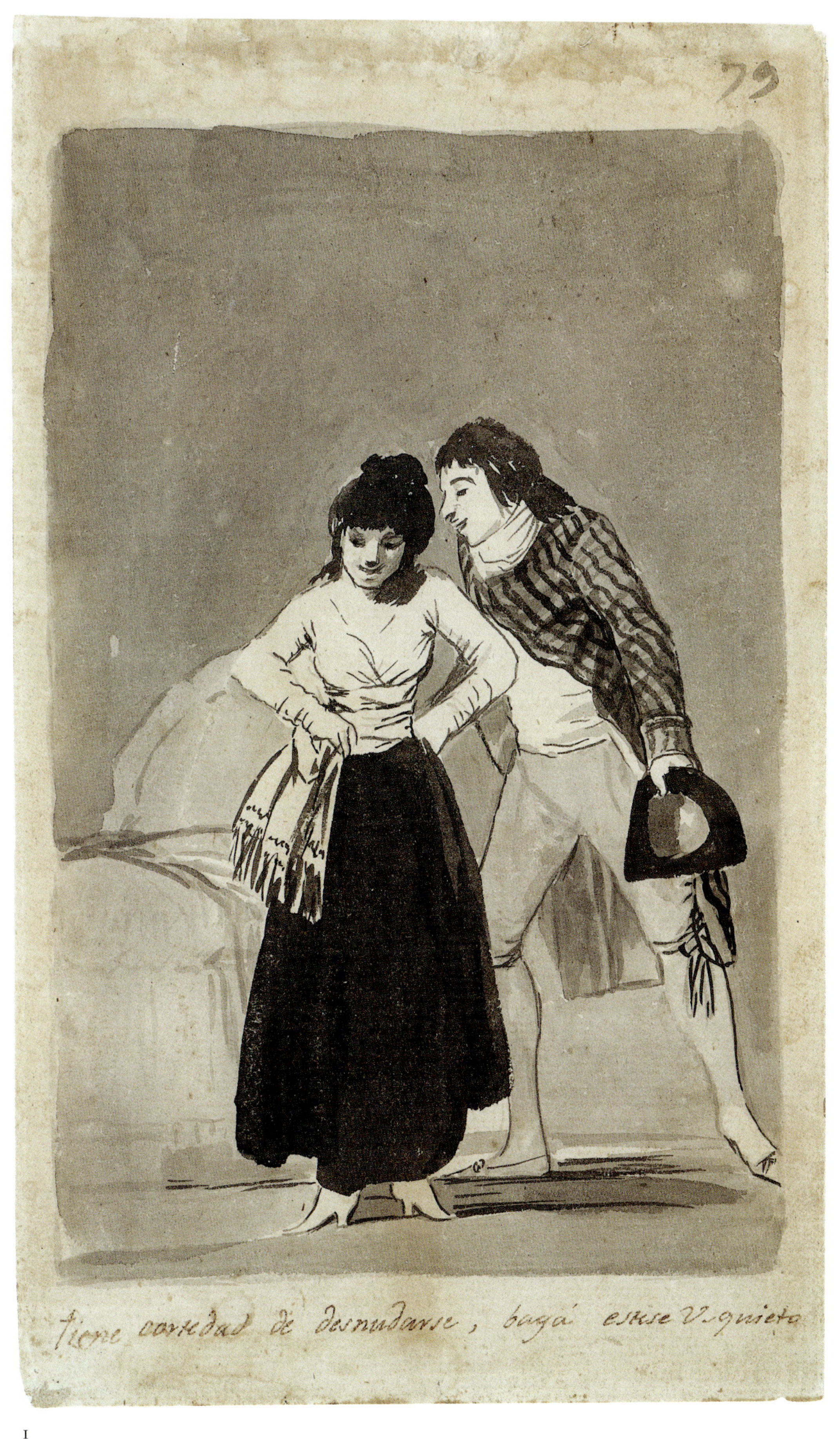

1

Fig. 1a Francisco de Goya y Lucientes, *Gallant Apraising a Maja with a Parasol on the Paseo*, 1796–1797, brush with India ink, retouched with brush and iron-gall ink, $8\frac{5}{8} \times 5\frac{1}{4}$ in. (22 × 13.4 cm), Kupferstichkabinett, Hamburger Kunsthalle

whose character remains a mystery, he went on his own to Seville and Cadiz. In one of these cities, he purchased two diaries or notebooks. The smaller of these books, now called Sanlúcar Album A, is filled with intimate or erotic drawings of women—possibly modeled on the body and comportment of the duchess. The second, larger book, called Madrid Album B, originally consisting of ninety-four drawings on forty-seven sheets (recto and verso; ten sheets are missing), is devoted to imaginative, comic, satiric, or grotesque subjects, often derived from popular legends and folklore, or to scenes from the everyday life of the *pueblo*, particularly the lower-class *majas* and *majos*. *Majas* (fem.) and *majos* (masc.) were the aristocracy of the Spanish street, the nobility of the gutter, who claimed to represent the *autentico ser*, or true essence of Castilian Spain. They wore easily identifiable clothes, spoke in unusual argot, and had ritualized behaviors and manners (often flamboyant and violent) that were aped by their betters among the "real" aristocrats. The drawings, now dispersed among many public and private collections, served as the basis for a projected series of etchings called *Sueños* (*Dreams*), later reconceived and realized as *Los Caprichos* (1799), perhaps the most important suite of prints in the history of art, and the work that launched a new phase in Goya's career.

The drawings in Madrid Album B were all made with brush and gray wash, heightened with black or brown ink, on fine, handmade Netherlandish paper measuring approximately 240 by 150 millimeters. Each is numbered at the upper right and—from the middle of the album to the end—captioned at the bottom with a title, ironic comment, or brief interpretation. These legends were probably inscribed by Goya himself, using brush and gray wash or pen and iron-gall ink. Most of the drawings are independent compositions; a few constitute complementary or contrasting pairs, or even brief narratives. The earliest drawings in the album continue themes from Album A: there is a *maja* and her procuress or *celestina* (no. 4, Kunsthalle, Hamburg), lovers sitting on a rock (no. 24, The Metropolitan Museum of Art, New York), and a young dandy providing his *maja* with the shelter of a parasol (no. 37, fig. 1a). Later drawings—those beginning with number 55r—take up the subjects of masquerade and corrupt priests and are darker and

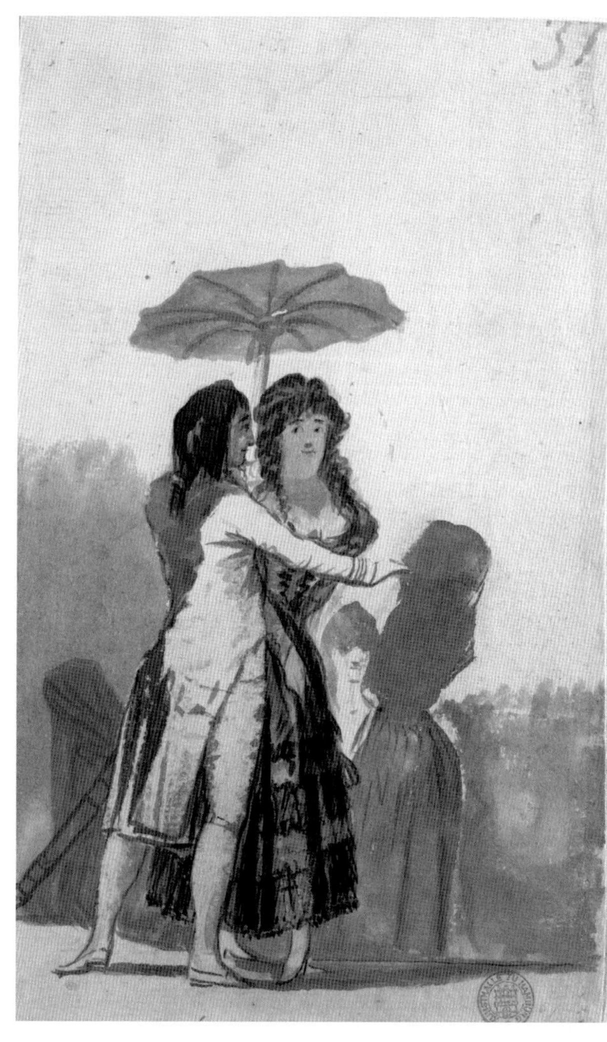

more portentous in mood. Some reprise carceral themes (nos. 84–85) first explored by Goya in 1793–1794, in his *Courtyard with Lunatics* (Meadows Museum, Dallas), one in a series of fourteen strange or fantastic cabinet paintings on tin, made in the immediate aftermath of the serious illness mentioned above. The two Norton Simon drawings, numbers 79 and 80 (recto and verso of a single sheet), fall near the end of Madrid Album B.

Drawing 79 is captioned with obvious irony, "Tiene cortedad de desnudarse, bayá estese V. quieto" (She is bashful about undressing. Go on, keep still, will you). A couple is shown standing together in the middle of a bedroom. The man's head and upper body are shown in profile with the rest of his torso and legs in three-quarter view, as he leans toward the young woman by his side. His legs are spread wide, and his jacket is unbuttoned to his collar, its blunt tail hanging between his legs. He holds a tricorn hat in his left hand, its concavity open to the spectator. A scarf or kerchief is wrapped high around his neck, in the fashion of certain dandies of the day, as portrayed by Goya in drawing 32 of Madrid Album B (Museo del Prado, Madrid). His female companion is turned toward the viewer, her left hand on her hip and her right hand beginning to unwind the fringed *faja* (sash) around her waist. She wears a tight blouse that reveals the shape of her bosom and a long, wide, dark skirt. She stands in high-heeled shoes with toes pointed outward, a sign that she is a prostitute. The broad, rounded forms at the lower left of the drawing appear to indicate the contours of a bed, with large pillows or a round headboard. The upper two-thirds of the background is covered with a dark gray wash, the lower portion, between the man's legs, a lighter tone, and alternating horizontal bands of gray wash mark the floor of the room. The room in which this liaison occurs is suited for nothing else but romance; no one can be bashful here.

Goya's composition was the basis for another drawing, *Sueño* 19 (fig. 1b), captioned "Las viejas se salen de risa pr.qe. saben qe. el no lleba un quarto" (The old women laugh themselves sick because they know he hasn't a bean). This in turn was the origin of *Capricho* 5, *Tal para qual* (*Two of a Kind*) (fig. 1c). The bed and pillows at the left of the Norton Simon drawing were transformed in these two subsequent works into the hunched backs of a pair of laughing old women. In addition, the disrobing woman in the present drawing was changed into a *maja* dressed in her *basquina* (black petticoat), *mantilla* (black lace shawl), and fan. The imagery and text of this *capricho* cast additional light on the Norton Simon drawing. The scene of bashful undressing must now be understood to refer to the man as well as the woman; he

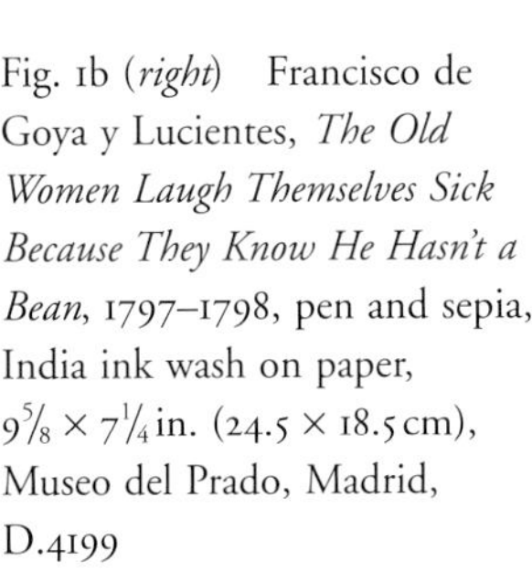

Fig. 1b (*right*) Francisco de Goya y Lucientes, *The Old Women Laugh Themselves Sick Because They Know He Hasn't a Bean*, 1797–1798, pen and sepia, India ink wash on paper, $9\frac{5}{8} \times 7\frac{1}{4}$ in. (24.5 × 18.5 cm), Museo del Prado, Madrid, D.4199

Fig. 1c (*far right*) Francisco de Goya y Lucientes, *Two of a Kind*, 1797–1798, plate 5 of *Los Caprichos*, etching, aquatint, and drypoint, plate, $8\frac{5}{8} \times 6$ in. (21.9 × 15.2 cm); sheet, $12 \times 7\frac{3}{4}$ in. (30.5 × 19.7 cm), Norton Simon Art Foundation

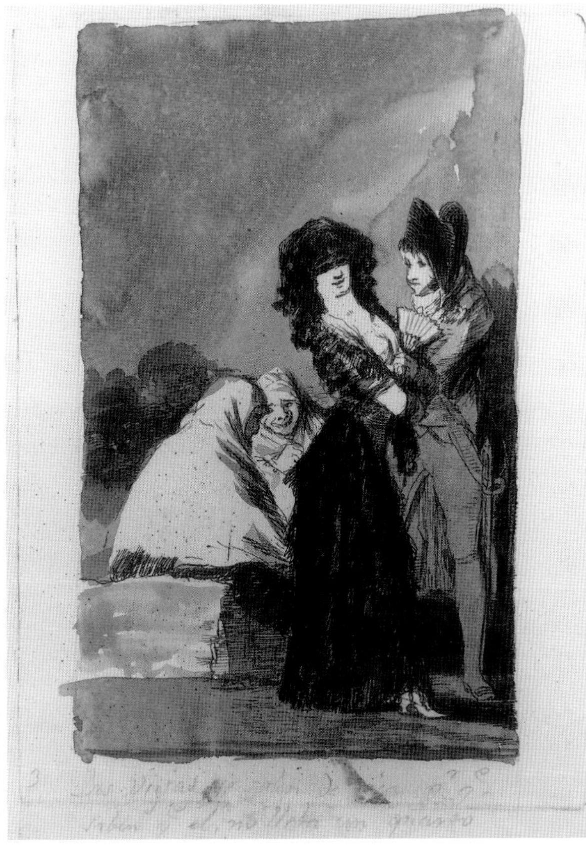

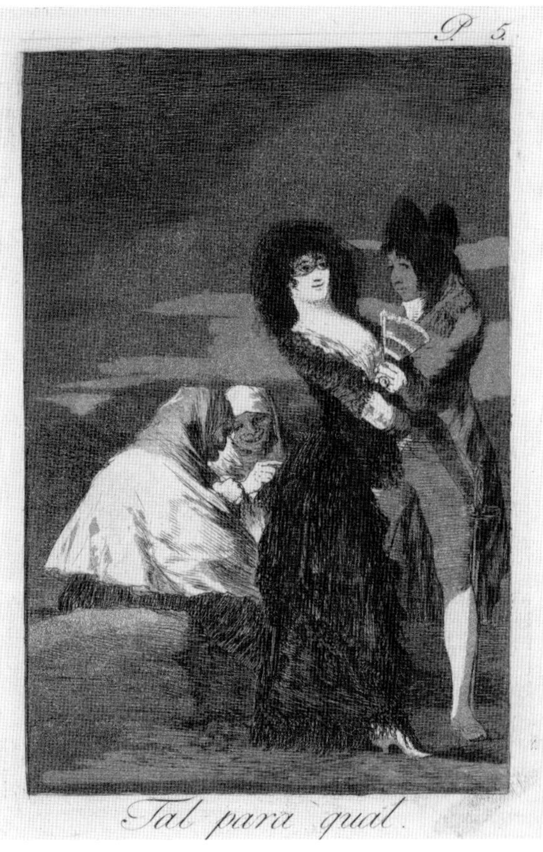

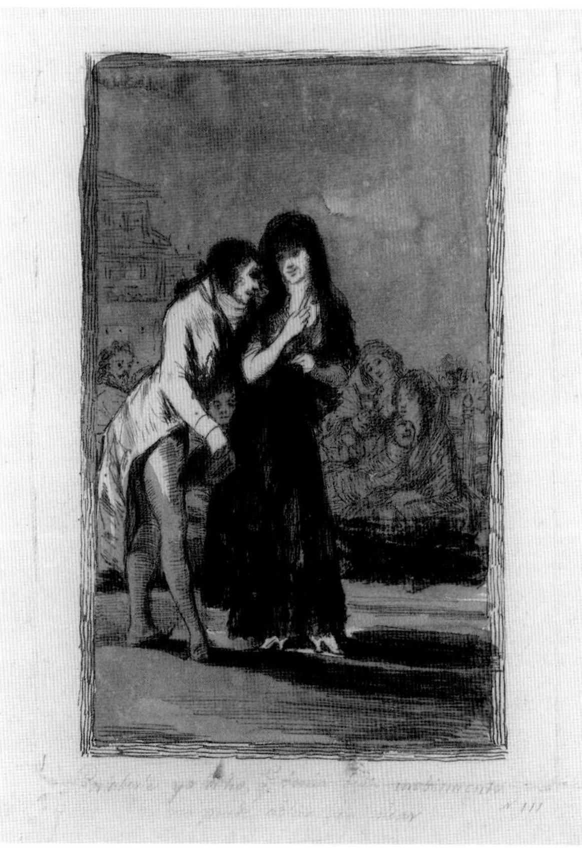

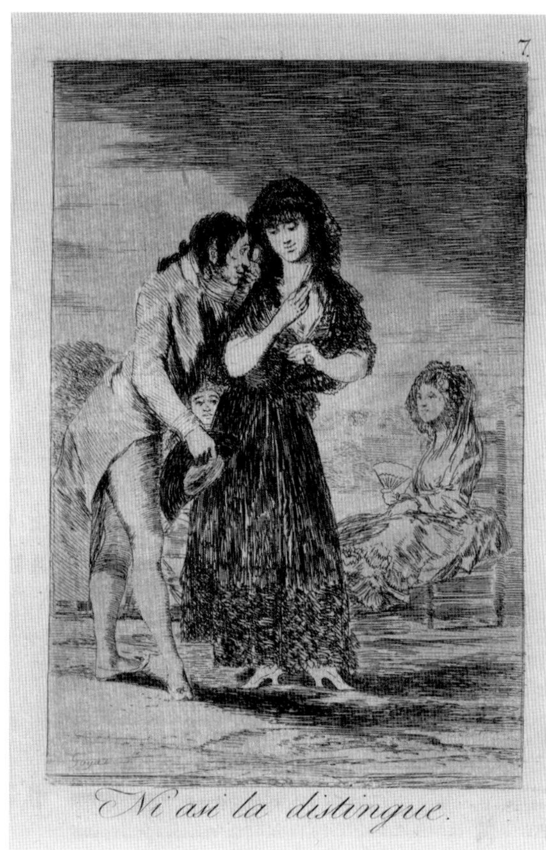

Fig. 1d (*right*) Francisco de Goya y Lucientes, *Because I Told Her That She Moved Gracefully, She Cannot Speak without Shaking Her Tail*, 1797–1798, pen and sepia, India ink wash on paper, $9\frac{5}{8} \times 7\frac{1}{4}$ in. (24.5 × 18.5 cm), Museo del Prado, Madrid, D. 4200

Fig. 1e (*far right*) Francisco de Goya y Lucientes, *Even Thus He Cannot Make Her Out*, 1797–1798, plate 7 of *Los Caprichos*, etching, aquatint, and drypoint, plate, $8\frac{5}{8} \times 6$ in. (21.9 × 15.2 cm); sheet, $12 \times 7\frac{3}{4}$ in. (30.5 × 19.7 cm), Norton Simon Art Foundation

will soon be stripped of his money, as she will be her clothes. They also are "two of a kind."

Finally, the Norton Simon composition also bears comparison to a drawing that falls earlier in Madrid Album B, number 19, though the position of the man and woman are reversed; the gentleman here is on the left, with his leg and body slightly in front of his companion. This drawing was the basis for *Sueño* number 21 (fig. 1d), which bears the legend "Por aberle yo dicho, qe tenia buen mobimiento / no puede abler sin colear" (Because I told her that she moved gracefully, she cannot speak without shaking her tail). And this drawing, once more in turn, was the model for *Capricho* 7, *Ni asi la distingue* (*Even Thus He Cannot Make Her Out*) (fig. 1e). This etching (with aquatint and drypoint) is further explained by an accompanying text that accompanied a full set of *Caprichos* now in the Museo del Prado, Madrid: "Como ha de distinguirla? Para conocer lo qe. ella es no basta el anteojo se necesita juicio y practica de mundo y esto es precisamente lo qe. le falta al pobre caballero" (How can he make her out? To know what she is, a monocle isn't enough; one needs judgment and worldly knowledge, and that is precisely what the poor gentleman lacks). The difference between the significance of this earlier ensemble of drawings and prints and the later group is clear: the former is gentle, the latter is incisive; the earlier is condescending, the latter is dismissive, almost angry. The verso of *She Is Bashful about Undressing* is considerably more disturbing.

Drawing number 80, the verso of number 79, *She Is Bashful about Undressing*, from Goya's Madrid Album B is captioned at the bottom "Mascaras de semana santa del año de 94" (Masquerades of Holy Week in the year '94). Aside from some obvious similarities of technique and style—the use of diluted and undiluted India ink and the dramatic use of contour and silhouette—the two drawings appear to have little in common, and it seems surprising they share a single piece of paper. In fact, however, both scenes—one depicting an assignation and the other a parade of Easter penitents—expose a common feature of late-eighteenth-century *pueblo* culture: its machismo and exhibitionism. The drawings also reveal the reformist zeal of this *illustrado* (enlightened) artist.

Masquerades of Holy Week in the Year '94 portrays a bare-backed flagellant or *penitente* with a tall, conical hat (*coroza*), holding a scourge in his right hand, and five other men. Three stand in the foreground in very close proximity; one, at left, wears a mask and tall hat and blows a bugle; another, at right, also wears a mask and

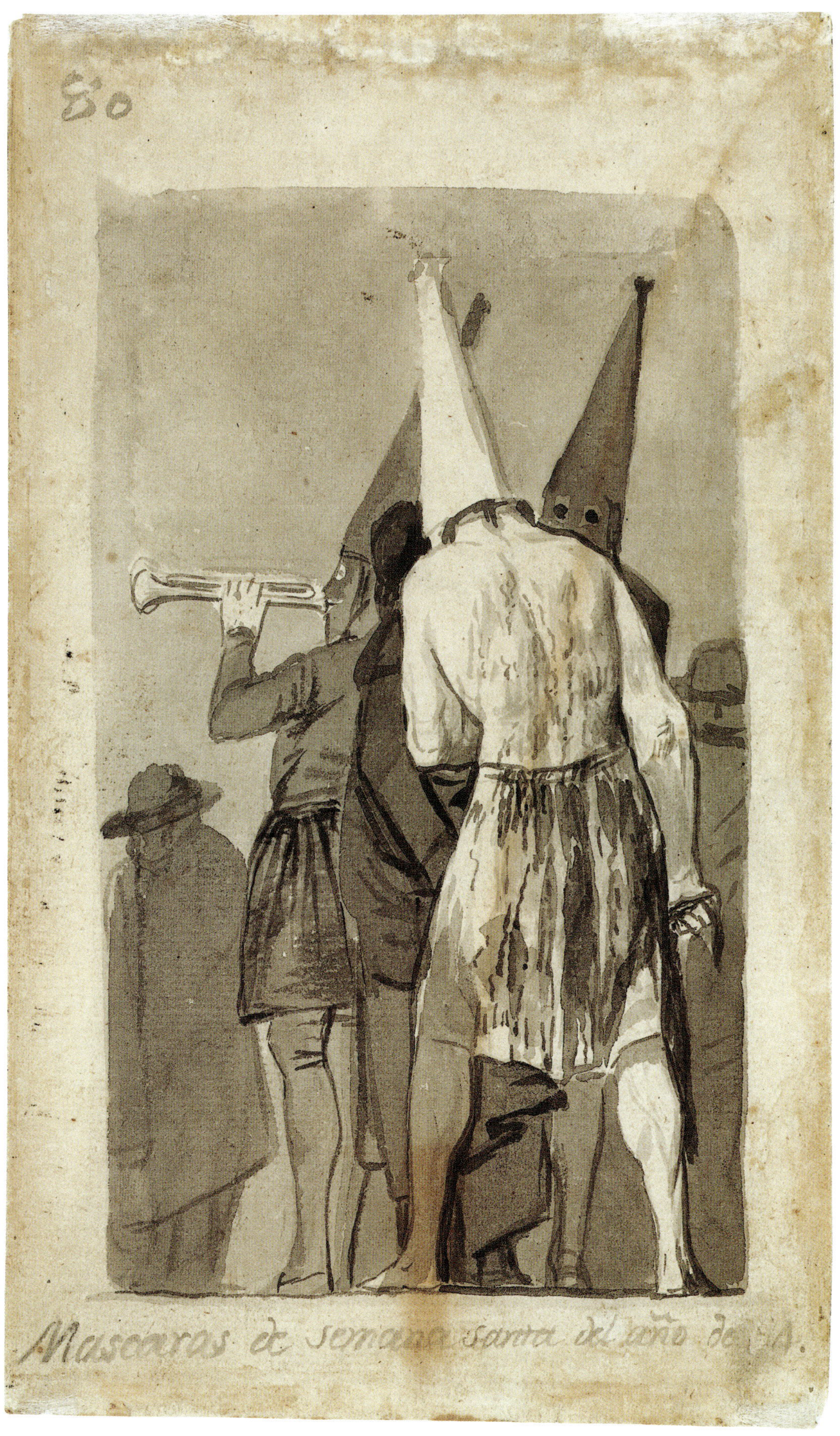

2

Fig. 2a Francisco de Goya y Lucientes, *Holy Week in Past Times in Spain*, c. 1825, black chalk on gray laid paper, $7^{9}/_{16} \times 5^{13}/_{16}$ in. (19.2 × 14.8 cm), National Gallery of Canada, Ottawa

pointed hat and gazes toward the right shoulder of the flagellant; the third is little more than a shrouded silhouette in front and to the left of the *penitente.* Two additional figures, more vaguely represented with cloaks over their hunched shoulders and rounded, broad-brimmed hats pulled down to their eyes, stand at the left and right margins of the drawing. The artist's low perspective renders the scene highly dramatic, even confrontational. We are at once part of the procession of *penitentes*—the man with bared back is brought nearly into the space of the spectator—and separate from it, because the figures are turned away and loom above us. We are spectators at a mysterious and frightful ritual.

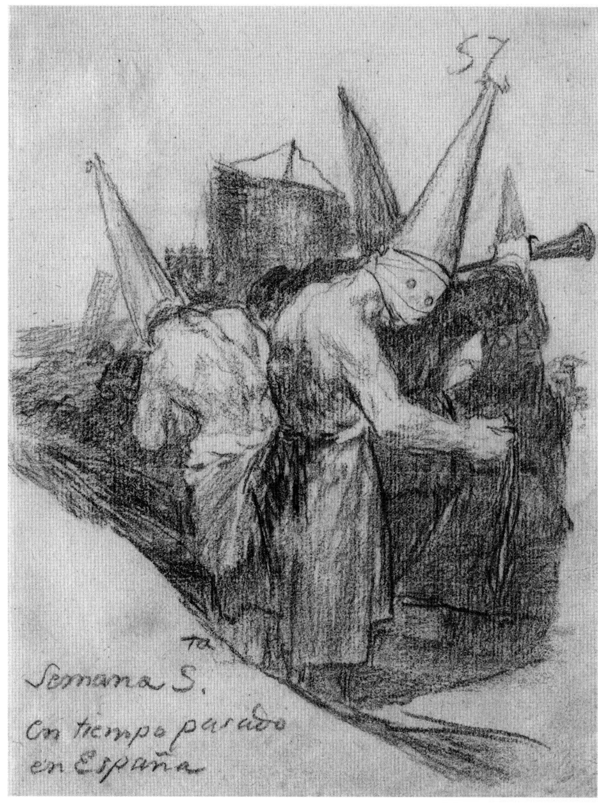

Goya's contemporaries would have easily recognized the subject of his drawing. It was the procession of flagellants that formerly took place during Holy Week (the last week of Lent) in every major city or parish in Spain. By Goya's day, the practice of public self-chastisement had been banned in many places, and contemporary accounts differ as to its persistence, or the frequency of its revival. Ten years after Goya's visit to Seville, Don Leucadio Doblado (José María Blanco y Crespo) provided an account of the procession of flagellants there, based on a mixture of observation, recollection, and storytelling:

> It is scarcely forty years since the disgusting exhibition of people streaming in their own blood was discontinued by an order of the Government. These *penitents* were generally from among the most debauched and abandoned of the lower classes. They appeared in white linen petticoats, pointed white caps and veils and a jacket of the same color, which exposed the naked shoulders to view. Having, previous to joining the procession, been scarified on the back, they beat themselves with a cat-o'-nine-tails, making the blood run down to the skirts of their garment. It may be easily conceived that religion had no share in these voluntary inflictions. There was a notion afloat that this act of penance had an excellent effect on the constitution; and while vanity was concerned in the applause which the most bloody flagellation obtained from the vulgar, a still stronger passion looked forward to the irresistible impression it produced on the strapping belles of the lower ranks.[1]

Doblado's description is significant in two respects. First, he remarks on the illicit character of the proceedings in 1806, and the previous forty years, suggesting that Goya's representation may have been contrived from imagination and anecdote, not actual observation. Indeed, the date inscribed on the drawing is 1794, fully two years before the artist bought the notebook from which the sheet was extracted. Perhaps the artist had simply heard that a penitents' procession took place in Seville or Cadiz two or so years earlier and wanted to try to give it form. Twenty-five years later, Goya was more explicit in his retrospection; he captioned another drawing of flagellants (fig. 2a) "Semana S.ta en tiempo pasado en Espana" (Holy week in past times in Spain).

Doblado's account is significant in an additional respect. He indicates that the bloody performance was not a manifestation of the sincere desire of pious young men to experience the sufferings of Christ on his way to

Fig. 2b Francisco de Goya y Lucientes, *A Procession of Penitents*, c. 1815, oil on canvas, $18\frac{1}{8} \times 28\frac{3}{4}$ in. (46×73 cm), Museo de la Real Academia de Bellas Artes de San Fernando, Madrid; © Scala / Art Resource, NY

Crucifixion, but instead was an ostentatious, even exhibitionist display of working-class bravado (what in Spanish is called *macho*), intended to impress young women of the same social class. Goya himself alludes to this likelihood by the caption he employed. He did not write simply "procession of penitents," but "masquerade [mascaras] of Holy Week," thereby alluding to an entirely separate carnival tradition (also outlawed by the government), and depicted by Goya in his famous *Burial of the Sardine* (Real Academia de Bellas Artes de San Fernando, Madrid). Describing the costumes worn by present-day, government-sanctioned "mock penitents," Doblado writes:

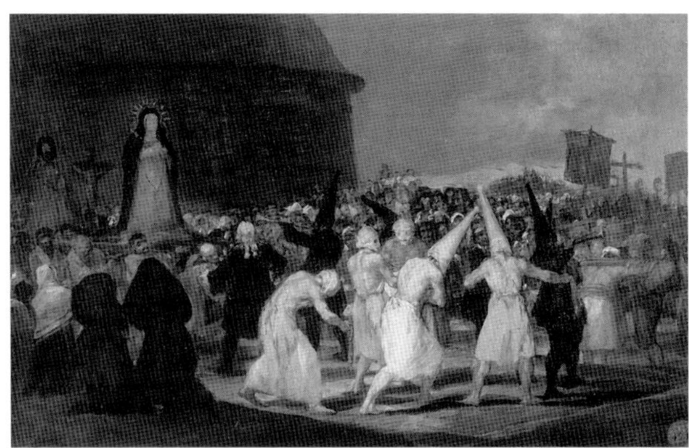

> The pleasure of appearing in a disguise, in a country where masquerades are not tolerated by the Government, is a great inducement to our young men for subscribing to this religious association. The disguise, it is true, does not in the least relax the rules of strict decorum which the ceremony requires; yet the mock penitents think themselves repaid for the fatigue and trouble of the night by the fresh impression which they expect to make on the already won hearts of their mistresses, who, by pre-concerted signals, are enabled to distinguish their lovers, in spite of the veils and the uniformity of the dresses.

In *Masquerades of Holy Week in the Year '94*, in other words, Goya has depicted a procession of Lenten penitents as a form of erotic or carnivalesque masquerade or erotic dress-up. The flagellants, like the young man and woman in the recto drawing, are actors in an ironic "scene of bashful undressing." All are engaged in an elaborate, public performance of *pueblo* sexuality, and all are at once mocked by Goya for their duplicity and applauded for their ingenuity in the face of national and class oppression.

Goya did not use his drawing of flagellants as a basis for any of his subsequent *Sueños* or *Caprichos.* He did, however, depict men wearing *corazos*—those symbols of iniquity and disgrace that remind us of dunce caps—in his many renderings of victims of the Inquisition, including *Caprichos* 23 and 24, and drawings 87–89 of the so-called Inquisition Album, probably made between 1808 and 1812. It was also at about this time, or perhaps a little later, that Goya united his interests in popular spectacle, religious extremism, and madness, producing four paintings, now in the Real Academia de Bellas Artes de San Fernando, on the subjects of a bullfight, a procession of penitents (fig. 2b), an Inquisition scene, and a madhouse.

1 Doblado, 1822, p. 291.

3

Francisco de Goya y Lucientes
Spanish, 1746–1828

Saint Jerome in Penitence
1798

Oil on canvas, $75\frac{1}{8} \times 45$ in. (190.8×114.3 cm)
F.1970.8

Provenance: Jesuit Mission, Province of Toledo, Spain. Manuel Vilches, Madrid, by 1917; Luis Vilches, Madrid, by 1923, still in 1951. [Stanley Moss and Co., Inc., New York]. [Schmid & Schmid Aktiengesellschaft für Kunsthandel, Vaduz, Liechtenstein, sold 22 January 1964 to]; [Marlborough-Gerson Gallery, New York/Galerie des Arts Anciens et Modernes, Schaan, Liechtenstein]; [Spencer A. Samuels and Co., Ltd., New York; by September 1969, sold 1970 to]; The Norton Simon Foundation.

Exhibitions: On loan, National Gallery of Art, Washington, D.C., 30 March 1970–February 1971; on loan, The Cleveland Museum of Art, March 1971–26 July 1973; on loan, Los Angeles, County Museum of Art, 27 July 1973–27 November 1974.

References: Ceán-Bermúdez, 1800, pp. 68–69; de Beruete y Moret, 1917, vol. 2, pp. 103–104, pl. 20; Mayer, 1923, no. 48, fig. 10; Longhi and Mayer, 1938, p. 18; Sánchez de Rivera y Moset, 1943, p. 73, pl. L; Sánchez Cantón, 1946, pp. 297–298; Sánchez Cantón, 1951, pp. 61, 136; Lurie, 1970, pp. 131, 140 n. 3, fig. 4; Gudiol, 1971, vol. 1, no. 181, vol. 2, figs. 279, 280 (detail); Gassier, 1971, no. 716, pp. 165, 191, ill.; Steadman, 1975, fig. 10; Young, 1976, p. 185, fig. B, color ill.; Young, 1978, no. 17, color ill.; de Salas, 1978, no. 314, p. 186, ill.; Cleveland, 1982, no. 216, fig. 216c; Sullivan, 1982, no. I.9, fig. 34; Covey, 1991, p. 49, pl. 11; Williams, 2003, no. 3, fig. 2.

Technical Notes: The support is a plain-weave, heavy, tightly woven fabric now lined with wax-resin to a slightly lighter-weight canvas. Original tacking edges exist on the top and bottom edges, and it appears that the painting was extended on the left and right sides with original tacking edges now overpainted. In addition, the top edge was extended by part of the original tacking edge. Ridges exist inside the extended edges. The ground, thick and pinkish in color, does not cover the original tacking edges. The arcs of shallow ridges and gouges that are visible on the surface in raking light may have to do with the ground application. There are large white and salmon-colored particles in the ground that give a gritty appearance to the surface of the picture. Some of these large particles have dislodged, leaving craters that are visible in the paint surface. The particles are probably lead soap inclusions. It is not apparent if the forms were first sketched in some way on the ground. The artist worked both wet in wet and wet over set paint over the entire canvas, leaving the marks of his brushes. The opaque dark brown background paint was applied in an open, brushy manner so that the light warm ground shows through to create an atmospheric space. In contrast, the red cloth consists of dense, solid paint. The flesh (especially the face) and the foreground have a quick, sketchy application of opaque pasty paint, and the crucifix and scourge are very loosely painted and simplified to their essentials. Along some contours and in modeling of the flesh the artist pulled a dark color over a light one in such a way as to create a fuzzy appearance that shimmers or appears unfocused. Along the back of the saint there is a "shadow" of the form of the figure that may represent some adjustment and reworking. In a few areas gouges and ridges unrelated to the ones mentioned above in that they are deeper and not so regular may have been made with the end of the brush, or perhaps these represent scraped areas that were subsequently repainted. In any case, original paint covers them. The condition of the picture is good. Fine to medium cracks run through the paint and ground layers. Lining flattened the paint to some degree. The shadow on the drape behind Saint Jerome's ankle has restoration toning. At the lower right in the rock area restoration in the form of an X repairs a damage that is about 4 inches long. After or during cleaning photos show loss along the right edge and a vertical loss about 2 inches long extending from Jerome's upper back into the background. The varnish, probably a synthetic that is flat and nonsaturating, fluoresces especially thickly along the left and top edges. Ultraviolet light shows drips and odd splotches around the figure in the surface coating. (JF)

The religious paintings of Francisco Goya, like those by many great artists associated with modernism, including his great admirer Édouard Manet, have never been considered central to his achievement. Although catalogued and discussed many times in the voluminous critical and historical literature devoted to Goya, they play only a cameo part in the public discourse around his oeuvre, which is decidedly secular. Indeed, Goya's oeuvre is tied more often to political radicalism and the Enlightenment than to the Catholic Church of his contemporary Spain. There are several reasons for this, but perhaps the most important is that there is only one major religious painting (a *Crucifixion* of 1780) by Goya in the single greatest collection of his work, that of the Museo del Prado in Madrid. (And, again in parallel, there are no major religious paintings by Manet in the Musée d'Orsay in Paris.) Indeed, many of Goya's religious works were painted in fresco or commissioned as altarpieces and remain in situ in churches throughout Spain, forcing the cultural tourist to work hard to find them. It is for this reason that the central masterpiece of Goya's religious painting outside Spain, the Norton Simon *Saint Jerome in Penitence*, is comparatively little known. Although prominently displayed since its

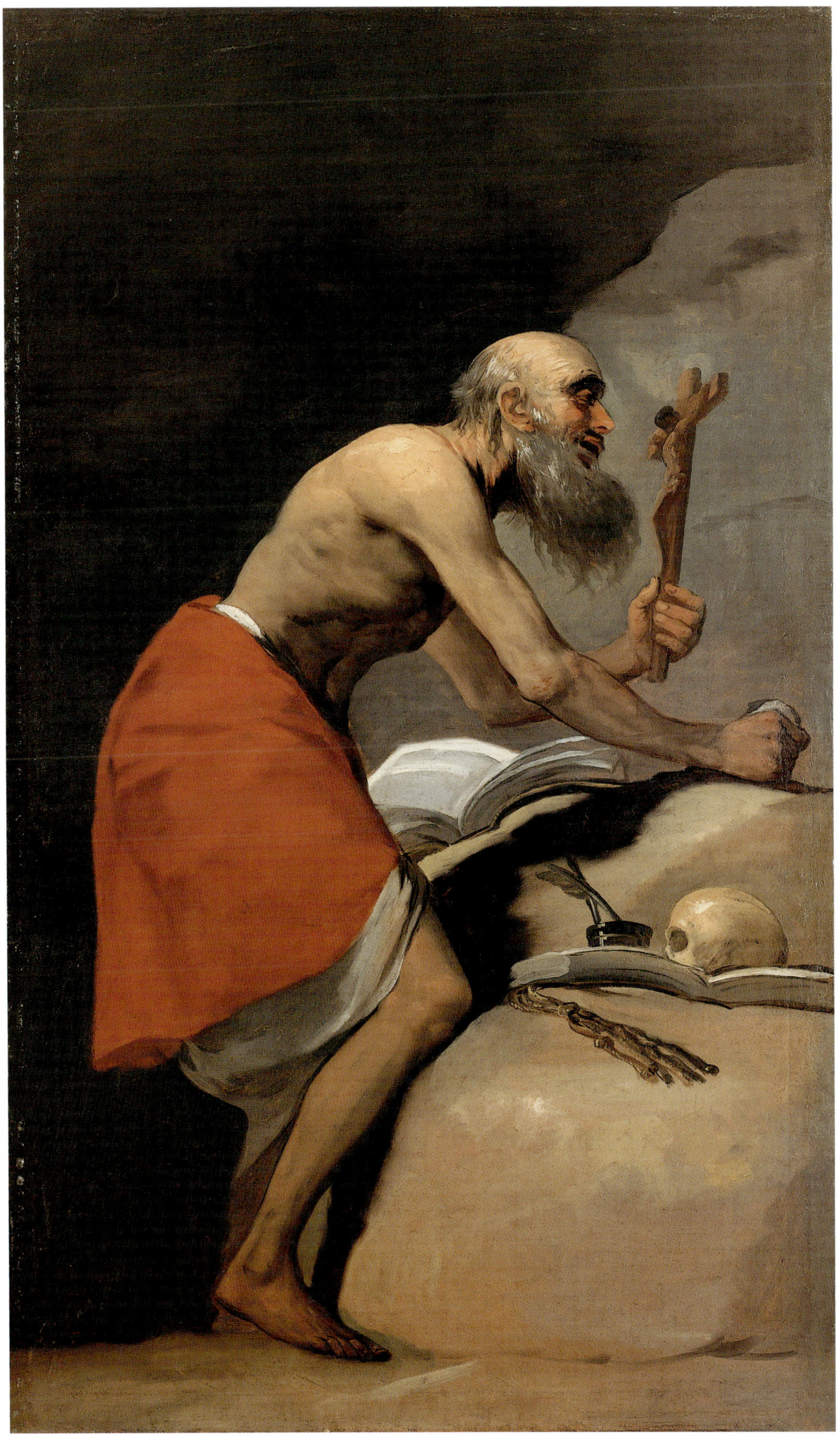

3

Fig. 3a (*right*) Francisco de Goya y Lucientes, *Saint Ambrose*, c. 1798, oil on canvas, $74\frac{3}{4} \times 44\frac{1}{2}$ in. (190 × 113 cm), The Cleveland Museum of Art, Leonard C. Hanna, Jr., Fund

Fig. 3b (*far right*) Francisco de Goya y Lucientes, *Saint Gregory the Great*, c. 1798, oil on canvas, $74\frac{7}{8} \times 45\frac{3}{8}$ in. (190.2 × 115.3 cm), Museo Romantico, Madrid

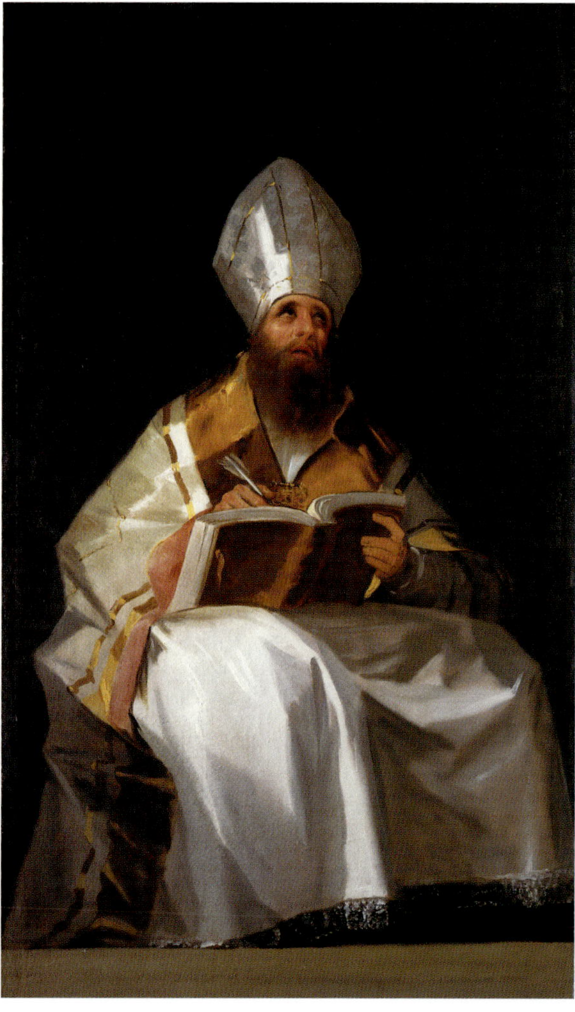

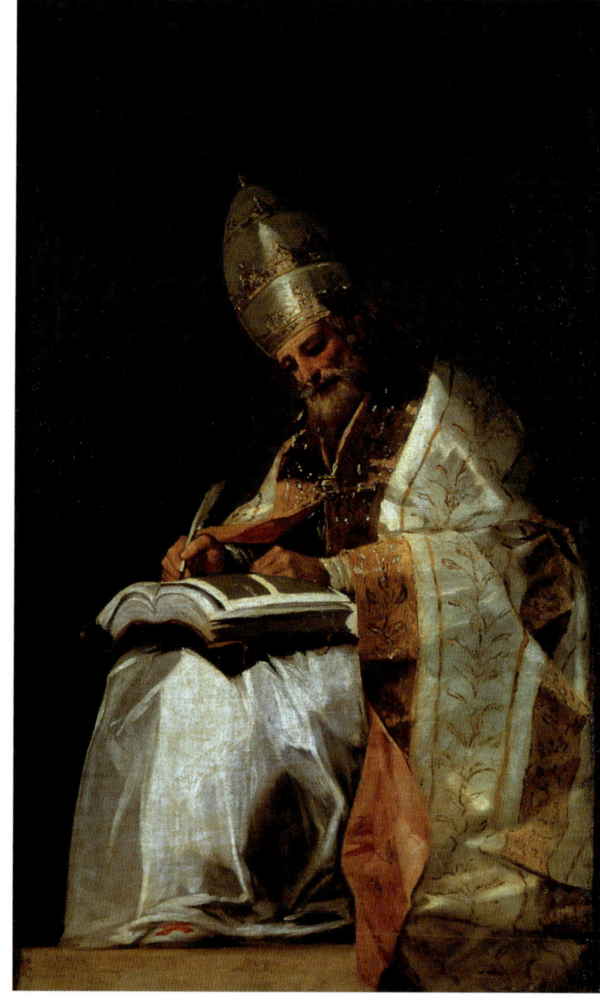

acquisition by Mr. Simon in 1970 and lent to the National Gallery of Art, the Cleveland Museum of Art, and the Los Angeles County Museum of Art before the creation of the Norton Simon Museum, it has not been included in any of the defining Goya exhibitions of the past three decades, nor has it been often reproduced or discussed in the Goya literature flourishing in Europe and America. Instead, visitors to Pasadena have seen it hung proudly as an easel picture in the galleries of the Norton Simon Museum, and art historians have reacted variously to it. In 1979 Agnes Mongan found it "strong" and "intensely painted," as did Walter Feilchenfeldt in 1985 and Hubert von Sonnenburg in 1984.[1] Yet Harold Wethey, while standing in front of it in 1979, remarked that there is "something odd about Goya's religious paintings," Michael Jaffe did not like the painting in 1982, and in 1985 Mario Modestini thought that it badly drawn and not by Goya.[2] This sampling from the curatorial files hardly gives one the confidence to claim its preeminence as a masterpiece central to the painter's oeuvre.

Yet few people who stand in front of it unaware of the varying opinions will disagree with Eric Young, who, in his monograph on Goya in 1978, said that "nowhere else in Goya's oeuvre has the intensity of religious fervor been conveyed more convincingly."[3] Jerome (not yet a saint) kneels partially against a smooth rock in a cave, staring fixedly at a sculpture representing the crucified Christ that he holds in his left hand. In his right hand, he clutches a stone with which he will beat himself to intensify the pain of his devotion. Wearing two layers of cloth around his naked torso (an intense red over a pale gray), he ignores two large books, each open and resting on small rocky shelves. An inkwell and a quill pen near the lower of the two books refer pictorially to Jerome's important role in translating the Hebrew Bible into Vulgate Latin, a task often interrupted by the future saint's devotion. A rope scourge with which to beat himself and a skull rest on the lower of the two books (that in which Jerome writes his translation from the Hebrew), reminding both Jerome and us of our mortality and exhorting us to work. Goya's Jerome occupies a

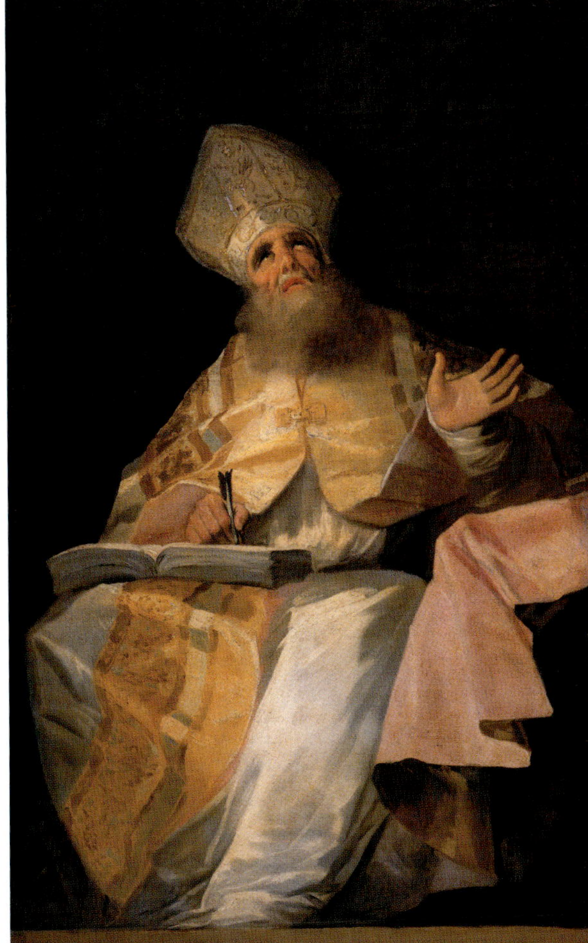

Fig. 3c Francisco de Goya y Lucientes, *Saint Augustine*, c. 1798, oil on canvas, 74⅞ × 45⅜ in. (190 × 115 cm), private collection, Madrid

diagonal place between the black void of the cave's interior and the strongly lit stones; his body casts an inky shadow across their rounded contours almost as if lit by a spotlight. The instability of his position is made all the more evident by Goya, who represents Jerome with only one thin leg, which is visually inadequate to support his torso. His eyelids, nose, cheeks, and lips are so intensely red that we fear he has just beaten his head. By contrast, Christ's miniature body is inert and imperturbable.

Virtually every scholar who has published the Norton Simon *Saint Jerome* has related it to three other paintings of almost identical dimensions, which collectively represent the so-called four fathers of the Latin Church, the others being Saint Ambrose (fig. 3a), Saint Gregory the Great (fig. 3b), and Saint Augustine (fig. 3c). While it is true that the published dimensions and orientation of the four paintings force a connection and while there are numerous other representations of the four saints in the history of Western art, the differences between the Norton Simon *Saint Jerome* and the other three paintings are marked, forcing one to question whether it belongs in the group. Where the other three represent the saints as bishops of the church, wearing heavy ecclesiastical robes and posed so as to face the viewer, Jerome is almost naked, shown in strict profile, and engaged in intense devotion. Indeed, were it not for similarities in the size of the canvases and the fact that Jerome was the fourth saint of the group, few would think to relate the *Jerome* to the other three paintings. Neither its style nor its provenance helps to explain its anomalous status. None of the saints has an eighteenth- or early-nineteenth-century provenance, and each has a separate history by the late nineteenth century. In the absence of a firmly documented early provenance, the first listing in the painting's provenance—Jesuit Mission, Province of Toledo—is at once suspect and fascinating, since none of the other paintings of the so-called series shares this.

The works have been variously dated in the Goya literature, with the recent consensus agreeing on the last years of the eighteenth century. Several scholars link the *Saint Jerome* and its companions to *Los Caprichos*, on which Goya worked from 1796 to 1798. Others suggest that the series was made after Goya's trip to Andalusia in 1796–1797, making much of the similarities in pose between the Norton Simon *Saint Jerome* and Pedro Torrigiano's polychrome terracotta figure of Saint Jerome now in the Museum of Fine Arts in Seville. Unfortunately, neither the pose nor the physical characteristics of Torrigiano's figure are close enough to Goya's *Saint Jerome* to make the comparison more than generic. Other scholars link the painting to Goya's third and greatest cycle of religious frescoes, those of San Antonio de la Florida, Madrid, executed with real speed by the painter in 1798. Indeed, some have speculated that the four fathers of the Latin Church were slated to be altarpieces in the four small chapels of that church, although there is no documentary evidence for this whatsoever. Even if Goya had begun the works for this purpose, it is clear that they were never installed in the Madrid church, and, perhaps because of their failure as a group, Goya transformed the *Saint Jerome* into an independent work. This supposition is partially borne out when one looks carefully at the painting's facture. Goya worked with large brushes, creating a series of strokes that run underneath the present figure of the saint and his attributes, suggesting that he may have started the painting differently with the saint garbed and posed in a manner similar to the other three, but that he completely reworked it. Indeed, the Cleveland canvas seems too aesthetically dependent on the other two to make sense as an individual work of art, while the Norton Simon *Saint Jerome* can survive alone, with no known ecclesiastical context. One thing is clear from physical examination—that the Norton Simon *Saint Jerome* was painted with a kind of rapid assurance of stroke that comes from the practice of fresco painting.

Although Mr. Simon had been offered the painting twice before finally purchasing it from the New York dealer Spencer Samuels in 1970, he was concerned enough about its condition that he insisted on having it cleaned and examined by the conservator of the Los Angeles County Museum before acquiring it in a complex trade. Whether his worries were genuine or connected to his brilliant bargaining strategies is unknown. Yet, not only did he buy himself time in the process of negotiation, but he learned that the painting is in surprisingly good condition for such a large canvas. Verbal suggestions that the background of the painting was extensively retouched by later hands proved unfounded, forcing us to accept as genuine such features as the saint's missing leg as well as the bravura brushwork of the torso and two books.

If this date of 1796–1798 can be accepted, it is tempting to think about the links between Goya himself and his middle-aged Saint Jerome. Goya was fifty-two years old in 1798—an advanced age in eighteenth-century Europe. Indeed, his Saint Jerome seems to be of a similar age, and Goya clearly identified with his almost fanatical devotion. The particularities of Jerome's features and the carefully observed qualities of his torso even suggest that Goya may have painted the figure from a model, although none of the other three canvases in the series has this quality. It is perhaps for this reason that the painting has an intense modernity that belies its conventional religious iconography. Indeed, it almost seems that the layers of representational tradition that had grown around the image of this often-painted saint were stripped away by Goya, who, using an elderly lower-class model, allowed us a seemingly unmediated chance to witness Jerome in the throes of real devotion, well before his ecclesiastical elevation to sainthood.

1 Memoranda dated 28 March 1979, 20 November 1985, and 4 May 1984, Norton Simon Museum curatorial files.

2 Memoranda dated 20 December 1979, 4 November 1982, and 16 September 1985, Norton Simon Museum curatorial files.

3 Young, 1978, no. 17.

4

Francisco de Goya y Lucientes
Spanish, 1746–1828

Martin Miguel de Goicoechea
1805

Oil on copper, roundel, $3\frac{1}{8}$ in. diameter (8 cm) (here reproduced larger than actual size
F.1978.3

Provenance: Alejandro Pidal y Mon (1847–1913), Madrid, by 1900. Clemente Altarriba, Paris. [Galerie René Drouet/Sylvia Blatas, Paris, sold 1978 to]; The Norton Simon Foundation.

Exhibitions: Madrid, 1900, no. 65; New York, 1974a, no. 37, color ill.; on loan, Seattle, Henry Gallery, University of Washington, 28 December 1978–10 July 1979; Madrid, 1993, no. 68, ill.

References: Mayer, 1924, no. 284; Lafuente Ferrari, 1947, pp. 37–38, 347, ill.; Soria, 1949, p. 4; Gudiol, 1971, vol. 1, no. 503, vol. 3, fig. 801; Gassier, 1971, no. 850, p. 200, ill.; de Angelis, 1974, no. 442, p. 118, ill.

Technical Notes: The portrait is executed directly on a round copperplate. All of the paint appears to be secure and well attached to the metal. Beneath the face there is a reddish brown underpainting, which is occasionally visible, for example, around the eyes. The face is painted in opaque flesh tones directly over this layer in very small brushstrokes, only slightly blended. The plum-colored coat appears to have been painted directly on the copper, and the white shirt was painted on top of the plum color, rendered with tiny lines in hatching strokes. The white collar and cravat have slightly thicker, more fluidly brushed paint. The background also was painted directly on the copper. At the boundary between the proper left shoulder and the background, the two colors merge. At the left of the support, the dark shadow and the background color also merge. Magnification with raking light reveals two systems of cracking: branched cracks in the paint film, related to drying; and fine, dense cracks in the brittle coating material. The crackle pattern as well as the orange fluoresce under ultraviolet light, suggesting that the coating is aged shellac. In an undocumented treatment, the coating was removed from most of the white areas and the lapels, but the remainder is strongly discolored. The coating over the face is quite thick. A small spot of retouching is at the left edge. (RW)

The name Goya is not generally associated with miniature painting, or limning, an art form that developed in England and France in the early sixteenth century. Whereas Goya was among the most innovative and original artists of his age, the practice of limning—like the art of manuscript illumination from which it arose—exhibited great stability of form and style. Moreover, while Goya was committed to a tradition of portraiture that expressed the individuality of his sitters as well as confirmed the artist's own autonomy, miniature portrait painters—from Nicholas Hilliard in the late sixteenth century to Richard Cosway in the late eighteenth—were primarily concerned with creating jewel-like and vivid keepsakes, suited to private contemplation and even loving devotion. Held in the hand, hung around the neck, placed on a makeup table or dresser, or hung on the wall of a boudoir or cabinet, miniatures are thus the veritable obverse of large-scale private or official portraits and history paintings, the genres that chiefly occupied Goya during his long and varied career. With rare exceptions, the best portraits in miniature are those that succeed in the reproduction of type and the expression of social station, not those that attempt truth-telling or the revelation of character. Goya's *Martin Miguel de Goicoechea* roundel is one of those exceptional miniatures.

Goya's sitter is shown bust length and in three-quarter view. He wears a yellow-brown, almost plum-colored jacket, with a white shirt, collar, and cravat. He is olive complexioned and black haired; his brows are heavy and dark and nearly meet between his eyes. Martin Miguel displays sideburns that extend down past his ears and the dark shadow of a day's beard on the chin and upper lip. His hair falls straight down on his forehead in irregularly clipped bangs and over his collar. His dark eyes are wide open and staring, and his lips are just slightly parted, as if he were on the point of opening them more fully to speak. There is a trace of red or pink at the bottom of his eyes, as if from tiredness, hard work, or sleeplessness. (The color here is partly a residue of the reddish brown underpaint, used beneath the face alone.) In some areas the miniature, which was executed on copper, is quite freely painted, especially around the shirt collar and cravat. In others, the paint handling is restrained and precise, particularly for the beard, eyes, and mouth. It is as if the portrait were crafted with a miniaturist's skill but at the same time endowed with the vitality of a Romantic history painter or portraitist. This combination of traits is unusual, and a comparison of Goya's portrait of Martin Miguel de Goicoechea (or his portraits of other members of the same family) with miniatures by his Spanish and

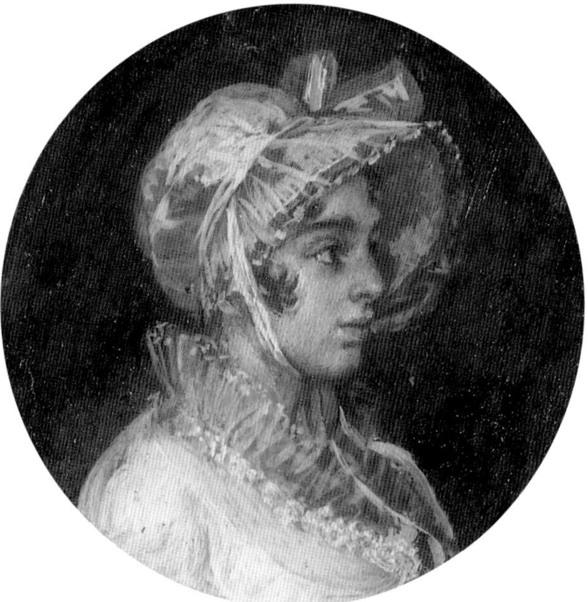

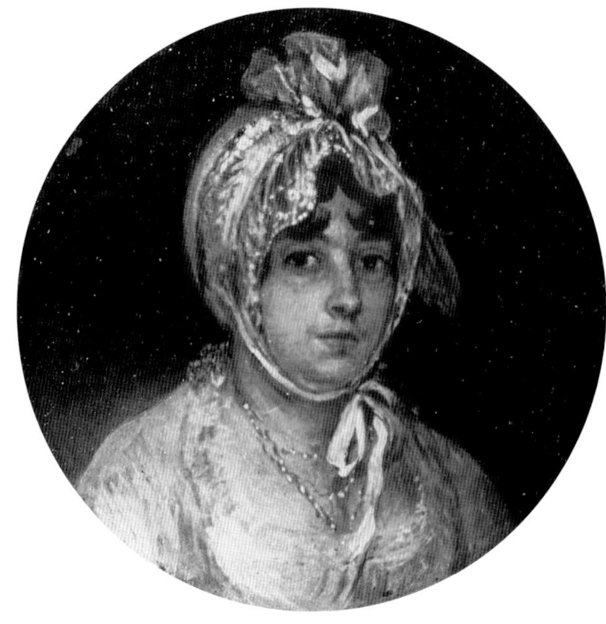

Fig. 4a (*above left*) Francisco de Goya y Lucientes, *Manuela Goicoechea*, 1805, oil on copper, roundel, 3 3/16 in. diameter (8.1 cm), Museo del Prado, Madrid

Fig. 4b (*above right*) Francisco de Goya y Lucientes, *Juana Galarza de Goicoechea*, 1805, oil on copper, roundel, 3 3/16 in. diameter (8.1 cm), Museo del Prado, Madrid; © Scala / Art Resource, NY

French contemporaries, such as François Ferrier or Firmin Massot, confirms the distinction.[1]

The circumstances of the Norton Simon miniature have been carefully explored by Juliet Wilson-Bareau and Manuela B. Mena Marques in their exhibition and catalogue devoted to the small paintings of Goya. Don Martin Miguel de Goicoechea and his wife, Dona Juana Galarza, were the parents of Gumersinda de Goicoechea y Galarza, who married the artist's beloved son Javier in 1805. The groom was twenty years old and the bride seventeen, and the artist, then fifty-nine, was apparently jubilant about the match. (Distress and disappointment would soon follow.) Perhaps in anticipation of the pending nuptials, and the linking of the two families, Goya painted six miniatures on copper of the principal members of the Goicoechea family, plus a seventh of his own son. It is not known whether the portrait group was intended as a gift to the couple or made simply in joyous commemoration of the event, but in either case, the pictures were dispersed early in their history. Two of the best of the group, in addition to the Norton Simon picture, are now in the Museo del Prado in Madrid; they are the portraits of Manuela Goicoechea and Juana Galarza de Goicoechea (figs. 4a and 4b). The former is animated, lighthearted, and decorative, with great emphasis given to the freely painted white bonnet, collar, and dress. The latter is clearly the pair to the Norton Simon miniature. Like her husband, Juana Galarza is seen in three-quarter view and offers us her direct gaze. Her expression is similarly intense, with great attention paid to her mouth, nose, and especially her eyes. Her left eye, set well back from the picture plane, is somewhat cold, thereby directing attention to the right eye, closer to, and parallel with the picture plane. In the portraits of husband and wife, the flesh is quite thick—almost viscous in texture—with brushstrokes clearly visible, revealing minute gaps in the paint, permitting a view of the copper below. Dona Juana Galarza's portrait, however, unlike that of her husband, reveals the artist's considerable interest in pattern, as in the treatment of the bonnet, lace, and long ribbon tied beneath her chin, with one ribbon end curling down to trail off just above her breasts. In this way, Goya has emphasized the intellectual capacities of the husband and the expressive, ornamental character of the wife. Even the great Goya was victim of the gender clichés of the age.

1 du Pasquier, Sturm, and Jean-Richard, 1995, pp. 188, 235.

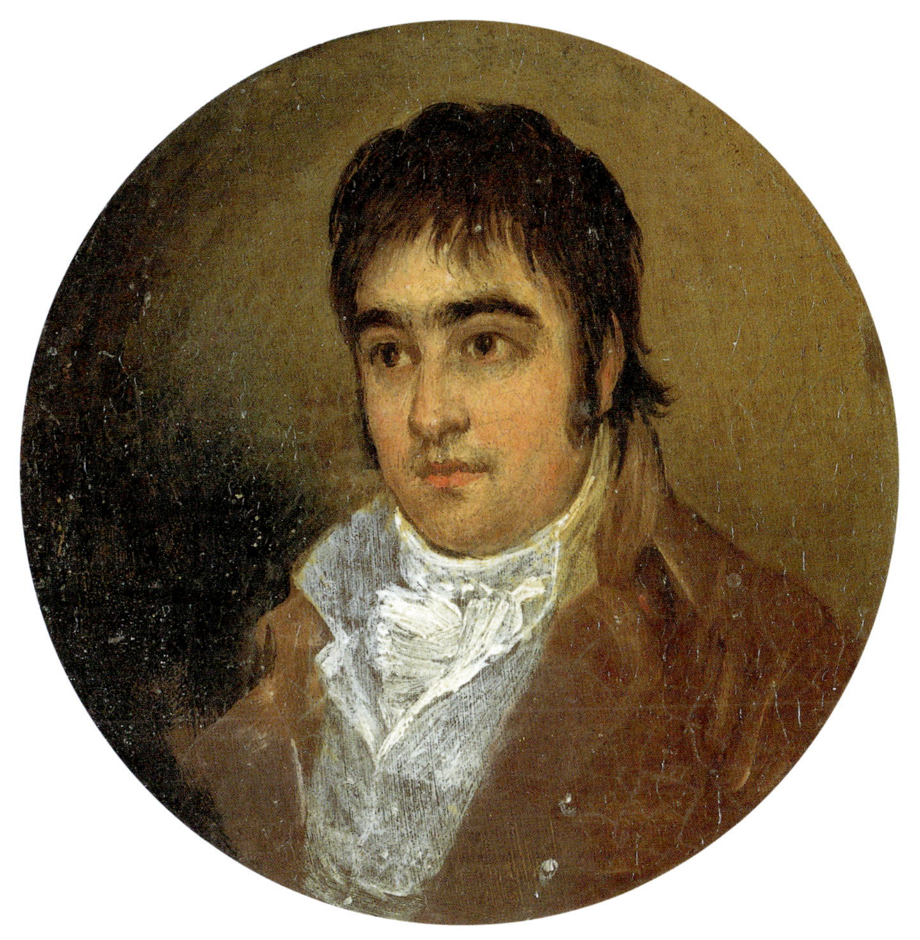

4

5

Francisco de Goya y Lucientes
Spanish, 1746–1828

Doña Francisca Vicenta Chollet y Caballero
1806

Oil on canvas, 40½ × 31⅞ in. (102.9 × 80.9 cm)
Signed, inscribed, and dated left side on back of sofa: "D.ª Fran.ca Vicenta Chollet y / cavallero. / por Goya, año 1806"
M.1981.7

Provenance: López Cepero, Seville. Groult, Paris. Harrison Williams (late husband of Countess Bismarck), New York, by 1928; by inheritance to Countess Bismarck, New York (sale, New York, Sotheby's, 10 July 1981, lot 122, to); Norton Simon Art Foundation.

Exhibitions: New York, 1928b, no. 13; New York, 1934b, no. 14, ill.; New York, 1943a, no. 77, ill.

References: De Beruete y Moret, 1922, p. 125; Mayer, 1924, no. 216; Desparmet Fitz-Gerald, 1928–1950, vol. 1, p. 27, vol. 2, no. 449, pl. 369; Sanchez Cantón, 1951, p. 80 n. 100; Gudiol, 1971, vol. 1, no. 524, vol. 4, fig. 829; Gassier, 1971, no. 853, p. 200, ill.; de Angelis, 1974, no. 450, ill.; de Salas, 1978, no. 412.

Technical Notes: The original is a plain, tight-weave, medium-weight canvas lined with an aqueous adhesive to a similar fabric. With tacking edges now removed, the original support is about ⅛ inch shy of 2 sides but slightly folded over the stretcher on the top and left edges. Although paint was cut and lost in some areas when the tacking edges were removed, the presence of cusping along each edge observed through careful inspection indicates that the painting retains its original format. The stretcher appears later in date than the painting. The ground contains large white particles that protrude through the upper paint layers and are visible to the unaided eye. Rather than being intended, these particles are probably lead soap that developed later owing to a reaction of the pigment and the oil binding medium. Goya's generally thin paint application ensures that the ground and underlayers play a part in the final appearance. Thin opaque layers of white and pink, as well as glazes such as the blue, depicting a cool shadow on the sitter's neck, create the face over an ocher underpainting that shows around the eyes and acts as a midtone. Goya probably laid in the figure with dark paint that shows in some shadows. The hair has a solid brown layer overpainted with black, and the couch has crimson glazes and opaque vermilion over a solid color of gray (couch back) or crimson (seat). But while layering creates optical colors in many cases, the painting appears directly done, and Doña Francisca's left hand shows masterful alla prima painting. The ornaments in the hair and dress were made with a stiff brush loaded with paint. Swiftly and simply accomplished, they give a special tactile quality. There is virtually no evidence on the surface of this painting that Goya made considerable changes. However, the X-ray shows that the sitter was earlier set in a three-quarter pose to her right and in her lap she may have held a book or some object other than a dog. The painting was cleaned and restored in 1981. Though somewhat overcleaned at earlier times, the painting reads rather well. Discreet retouching tones abrasions throughout the painting including the face and shows in ultraviolet light, especially in the face. A large crackle pattern with tiny losses along the cracks was set down with the lining. The black over the brown layer of the hair is much abraded. The surface coating appears to be a synthetic and fluoresces bluish green in ultraviolet light. Traces of an earlier yellowed varnish are visible. (JF)

Unlike most sitters in the history of Western easel painting, who are anonymous today, this placidly seated woman has a name. Neither a "Portrait of a Seated Woman" nor a "Woman with a Dog," she is Doña Francisca Vicenta Chollet y Caballero, and she was painted by Goya in 1806, when he was the most famous painter in Spain. At first glance, she seems confident in her task of posing for this great man. She wears a superb embroidered silk dress in the latest Parisian style and is liberally covered in jewelry. Her hair is dressed with beautifully arranged curls, and she holds her collared pug with perfectly fitted long silk gloves. Indeed, she sits in majesty on a gold-framed damask-covered sofa like a queen. Yet, she stares vacantly at us as she did at Goya, as if either fearful or suspicious. Clearly, Doña Chollet y Caballero had nothing of the confidence of Goya's other female sitters from the early nineteenth century. Señora Sabasa Garcia (fig. 5a) and Doña Isabel de Porcel (National Gallery, London) command the painter's pictorial field with such confidence that we forget they were there to be painted. Not so Doña Chollet y Caballero—and her psychological plight as a sitter brings us back to her identity.

Who, actually, was Doña Francisca Vicenta Chollet y Caballero? Nigel Glendinning, the most persistent recent student of Goya's sitters, had connected her to the family of the marqués Caballero, for whom Goya painted companion portraits only slightly larger than this one of the marqués and his wife in 1807.[1] Yet, she is too old to be their daughter, and the absence of a companion portrait of her husband makes it difficult for us to identify her as the marqués's married sister. Indeed, Spanish naming practices suggest that her mother was a Caballero and her father a man with the decidedly French name of Chollet. Glendinning, in an unpublished letter, identified the Chollet as a nineteenth-century medical family, but more archival work needs to be done

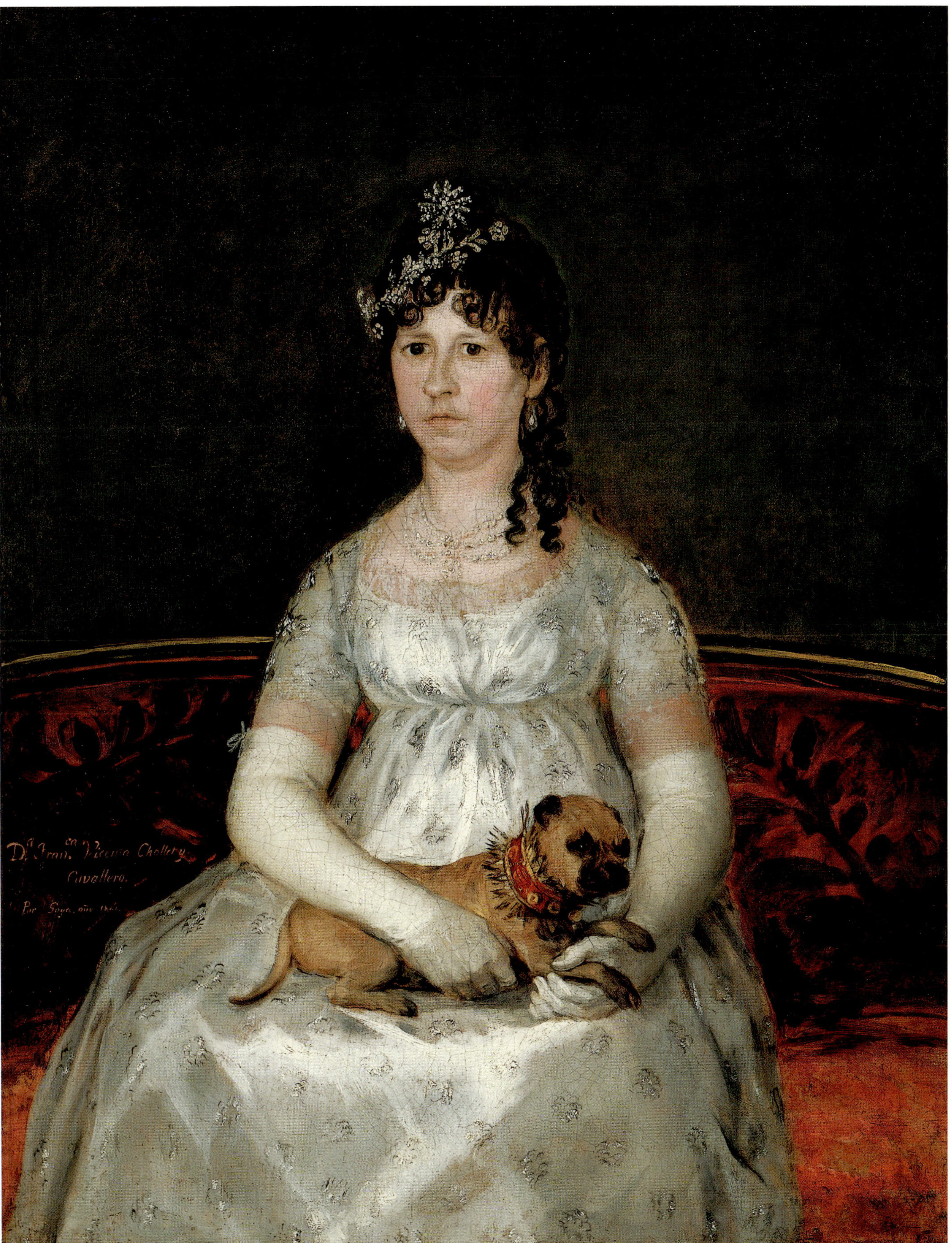

5

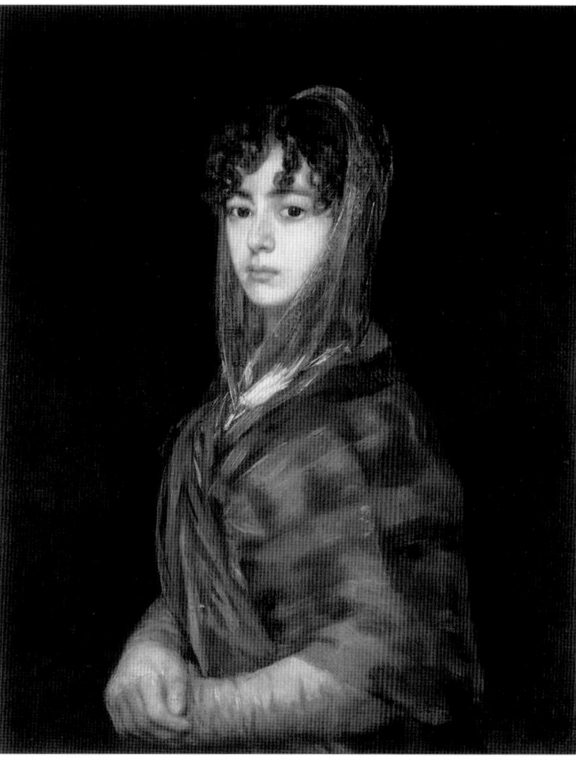

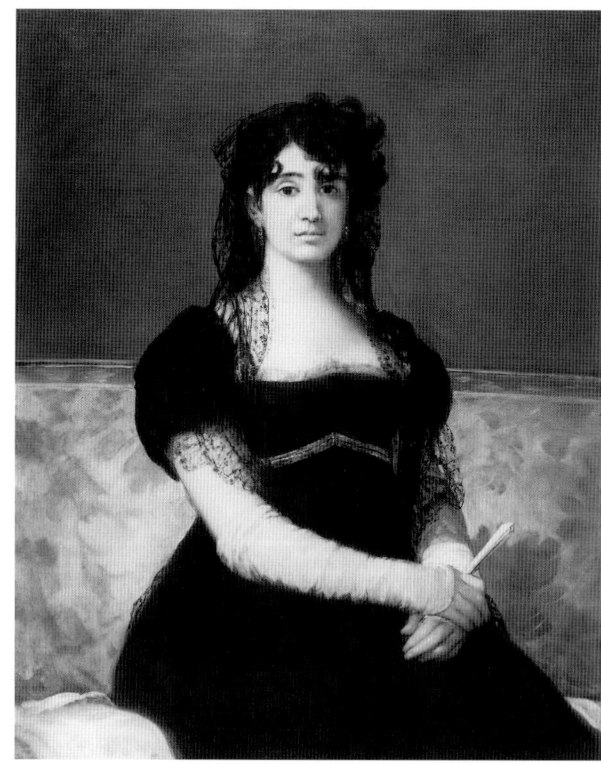

Fig. 5a (*right*) Francisco de Goya y Lucientes, *Señora Sabasa Garcia*, c. 1806–1811, oil on canvas, 28 × 22⅞ in. (71 × 58 cm), National Gallery of Art, Washington, Andrew W. Mellon Collection

Fig. 5b (*far right*) Francisco de Goya y Lucientes, *Antonia Zárate*, 1805–1806, oil on canvas, 40¾ × 32¼ in. (103.5 × 82 cm), National Gallery of Ireland, Dublin

to identify the family of this sitter more precisely.[2] Indeed, to be half French and half Spanish in 1806 was not yet as difficult as it became later in the decade, and we know from Goya's later work and his exile in Bordeaux that he himself was ambivalent about the French. All of this tells us that there is more to identity than a name, which, although precise, has not been traced with enough corroborating evidence to help us analyze Goya's wonderful portrait of this woman.

Many scholars have lamented the sitter's plainness, and some have found her downright ugly. The great conservator John Brealey damned the sitter with faint praise by remarking only about her "wonderful dog," while Michael Jaffé, when looking at the painting in 1982, observed that ugliness is "the essence of Goya," and in the same year Peter Ludwig called her a "prune."[3] Only Mario Modestini, who cleaned the painting before it came to the Norton Simon, gloried in the fact that she was "so beautifully provincial" that she was "afraid to pose for so great an artist."[4] Nonetheless, almost everyone else has looked past the sitter's plainness and marveled at Goya's superb mature technique. The technical analysis of the painting makes it clear that Goya was a complete master of his craft, using variously thick and viscous paints with several brushes to create wonderful illusions of translucency and sparkle in silk, thread, and faceted gemstone. And the delightful contrast between the perky pug and the stupefied woman gives the painting a psychological richness that is rare in conventional portraits.

Interestingly, Goya did not originally conceive of the painting with the pug, which he introduced after having tried a book or another inert object. He had already painted a much grander lady, the marchioness of Pontejos, walking in the landscape with her pug in a formal portrait of 1786 (National Gallery of Art, Washington, D.C.), and the pug surely provided him with a sense of immediacy in this otherwise conventional portrait of an untitled woman. In fact, he had painted another identically sized portrait of a woman seated on a similar damask sofa in 1805–1806 (fig. 5b). But in this latter portrait, the sitter was a famous actress, whose beauty, superb posture, practiced glance, and alertly positioned fan were ingredients enough. Antonia Zárate required no pug, but the poor Doña Francisca seems to have needed all the jewelry, the sequins, and the pets she could muster.

1 Gassier, 1971, nos. 860 (*Marquesa de Caballero*, private collection, Germany) and 861 (*Marqués de Caballero*, (Museum of Fine Arts, Budapest).
2 Letter dated 14 May 1993, Norton Simon Museum curatorial files.
3 Memoranda dated 29 January 1984, 4 November 1982, and 15 September 1982, the Norton Simon Museum curatorial files.
4 Memorandum dated 16 September 1985, the Norton Simon Museum curatorial files.

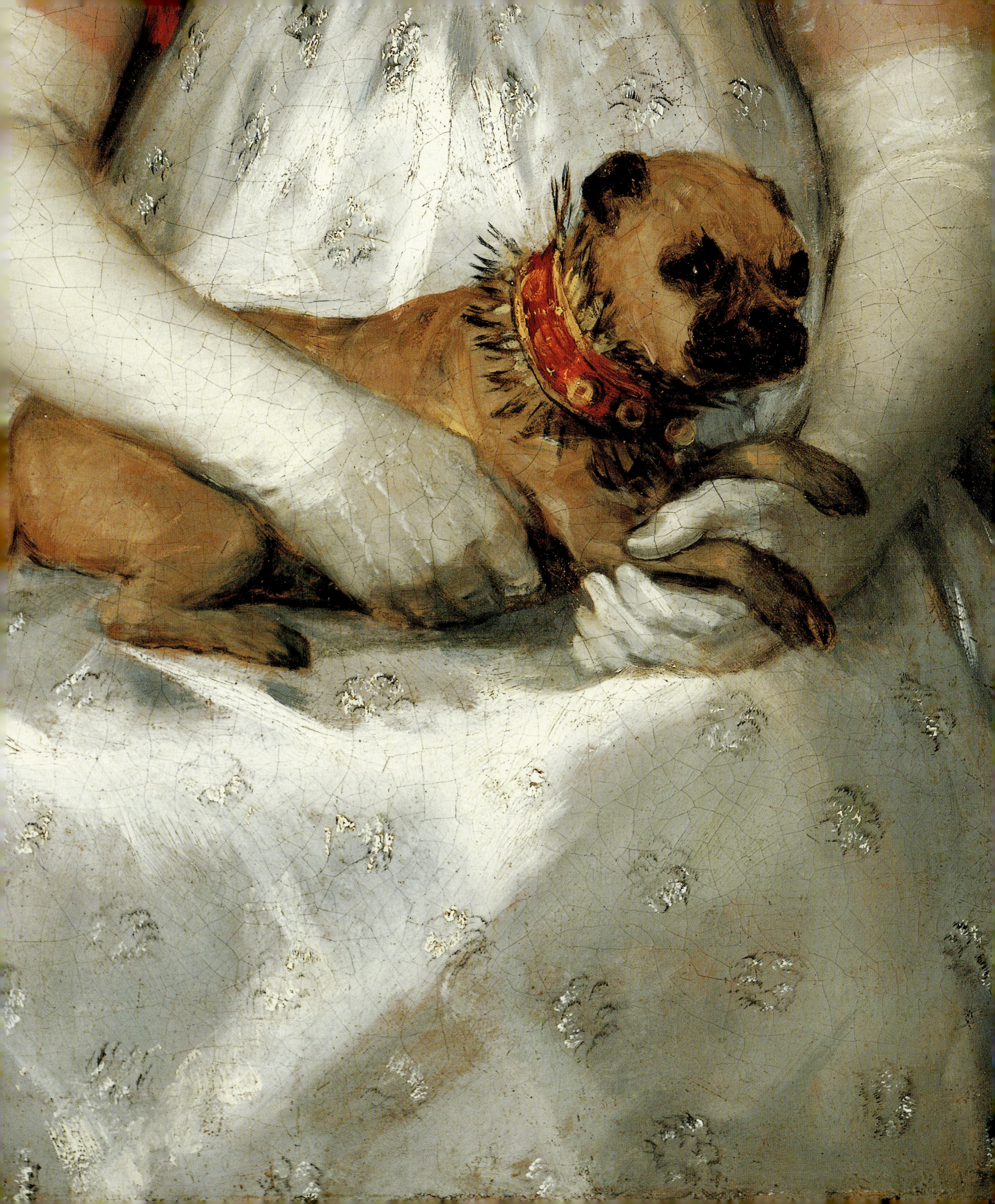

6

PIERRE-PAUL PRUD'HON (WITH CONSTANCE MAYER?) OR FOLLOWER
French, 1758–1823

The Abduction of Psyche by Zephyrus to the Palace of Eros
After 1808, probably before 1820

Oil on canvas, $39\frac{3}{4} \times 32\frac{1}{2}$ in. (101 × 82.5 cm)
M.1985.1

Fig. 6a Pierre-Paul Prud'hon, *The Abduction of Psyche*, 1808, oil on canvas, $76 \times 59\frac{1}{2}$ in. (193 × 151 cm), Musée du Louvre, Paris; photo: Erich Lessing / Art Resource, NY

PROVENANCE: Henry Camille Marcel (1854–1926), Paris, by 1923. ?[Dr. Fritz and Dr. Peter Nathan, Zurich, by April 1972, as *L'Enlèvement de Psyché par des amours*]. [Jan Milner, London, in partnership with Shepherd Gallery Associates, New York, 1978]. [French & Co., New York, 1979–1980]. (sale, New York, Sotheby's, 28 May 1981, lot 20, ill., to); [Paul Rosenberg & Co., New York, stock no. 2867–6577, sold 25 January 1985 to]; Norton Simon Art Foundation.

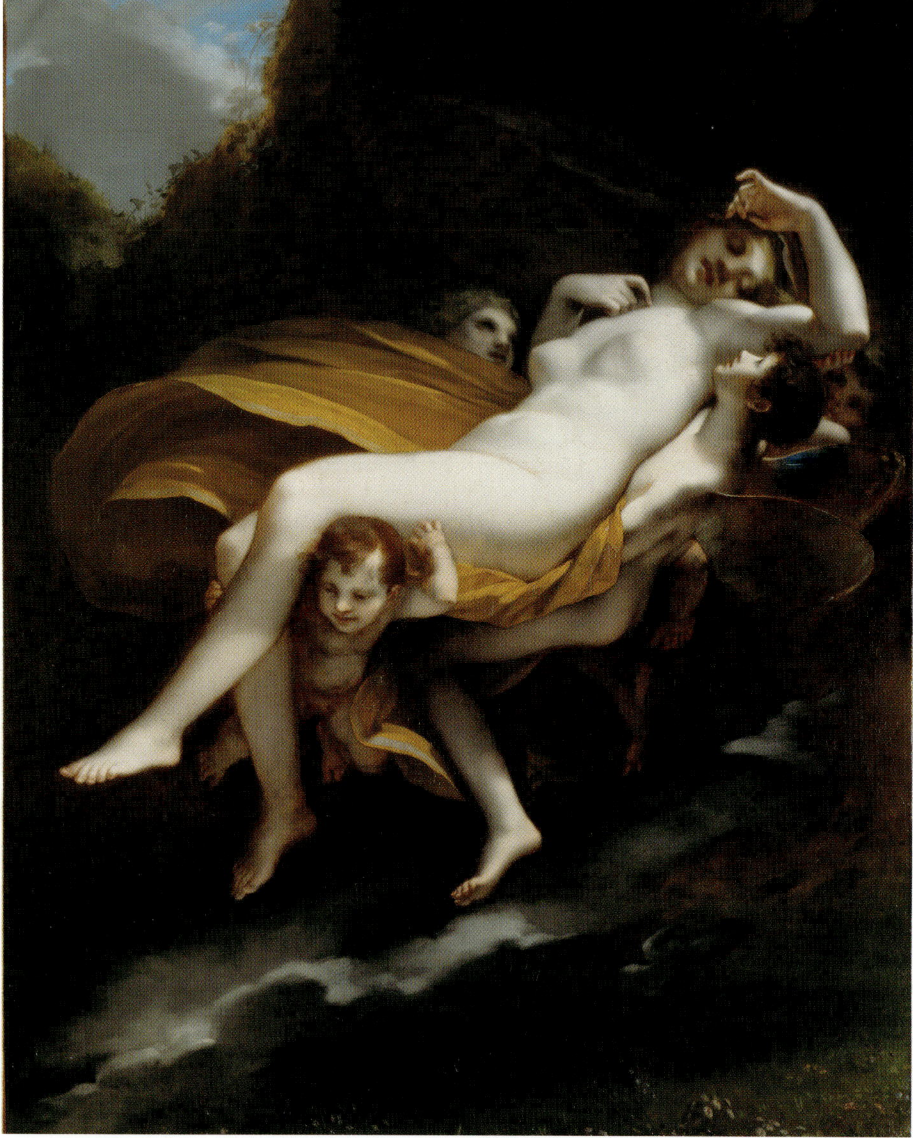

EXHIBITIONS: Prague, 1923, no. 6, ill.; Chapel Hill, 1978, no. 52.

REFERENCES: Guiffrey, 1924, under no. 147; Wintermute, 1989, under no. 24, p. 196, fig. 1; Laveissière, 1997, pp. 240, 241 nn. 4, 5; Guffey, 2001, pp. 133, 136, fig. 92, p. 250 n. 76.

TECHNICAL NOTES: The original support is a plain-weave canvas of undetermined weight. It has been wax-lined with the original edges unevenly cut. A vertical tear at center left, a circular damage at the lower left, and a long vertical tear at the upper left have been repaired by the lining. The smooth white ground covers the canvas weave entirely. A thin red-brown imprimatura was painted over the ground and is visible immediately to the left of Psyche's left forearm (between her wrist and her head) and also surrounding her ankles where the background paint does not completely cover it. Paint was applied in thin glazes as well as more opaque passages, but the transitional tones and glazes have been removed. In a previous restoration, cleaning of the figures of Zephyrus and Psyche was aggressive, and many contours and thinly painted passages are seriously abraded. Residues from uneven cleaning were left in the depressions of brush marking and are very disfiguring. The varnish has an uneven gloss and is quite thick. The painting's condition has been a subject of discussion for many years. No documentation reliably describes its previous state or treatment, but it is clear that the earlier restorations were poorly done. In its present condition, there is widespread abrasion and inappropriate retouching. A letter from the dealer refers to the use of bitumen as a cause of its problem, but this is probably in error.[1] Although the version in the Louvre clearly shows deep contraction cracks consistent with the use of bitumen, microscopic examination does not provide evidence of bitumen in this painting. (RW)

ANY REASONABLY KNOWLEDGEABLE student of French nineteenth-century painting relates this canvas instantly to the 1807–1808 painting by Prud'hon entitled *L'Enlèvement de Psyché* (*The Abduction of Psyche*, fig. 6a) and exhibited to great acclaim at the Salons of 1808 and 1814. This much is simple. Yet, in evaluating the painting's position in the history of Prud'hon's art, we are left with three choices: the Norton Simon painting is an autograph study or early version painted in Prud'hon's studio in preparation for the famous Salon painting; it is a reduced copy of the painting by Prud'hon for an unknown early collector; it is a copy of the painting made by another artist, most likely at the time of its exhibitions in 1808 or 1814. Proponents of the first theory point to the fact that the painting has pentimenti, especially in the drapery, and that it would easily have served as a midpoint between the smaller early study in

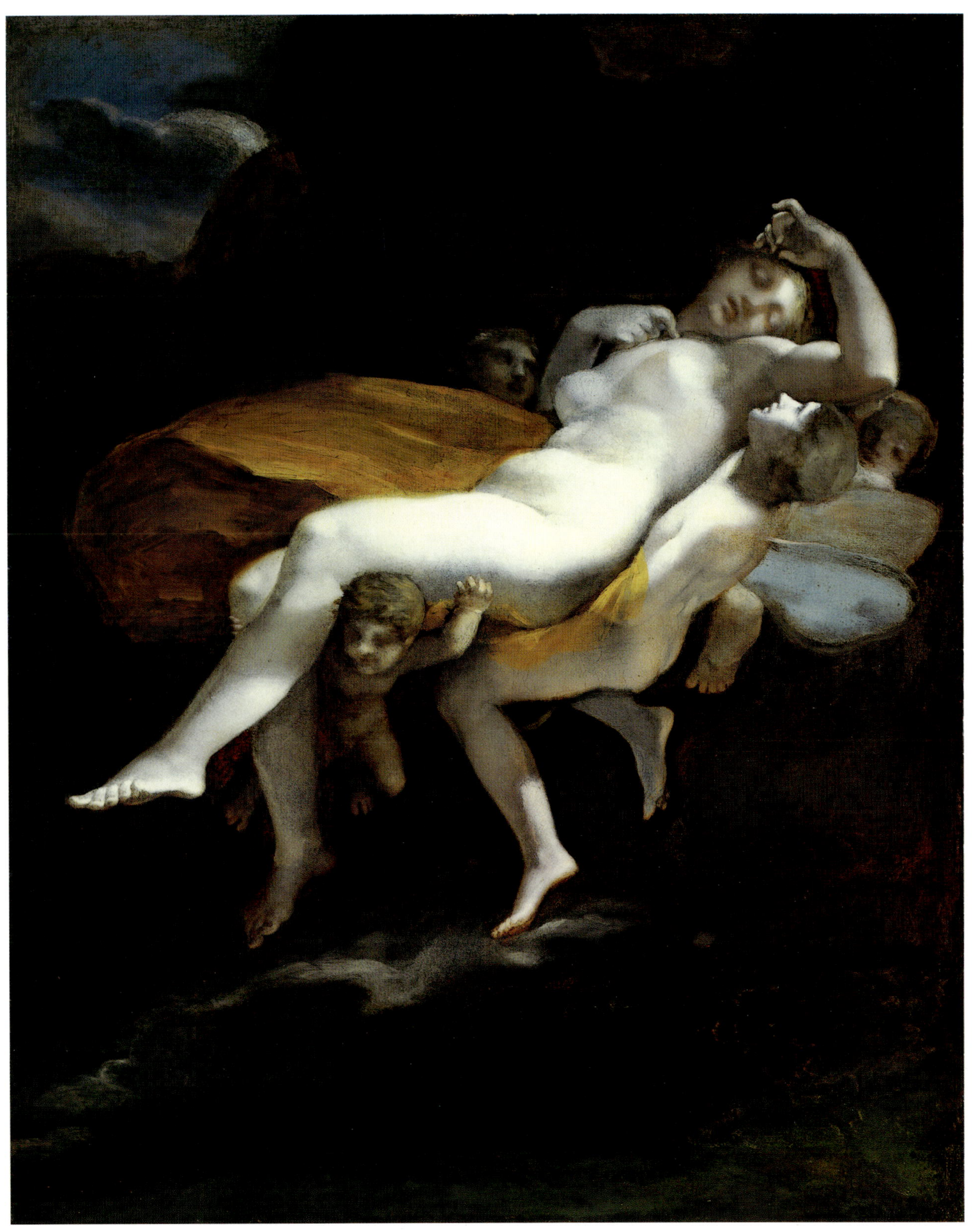
6

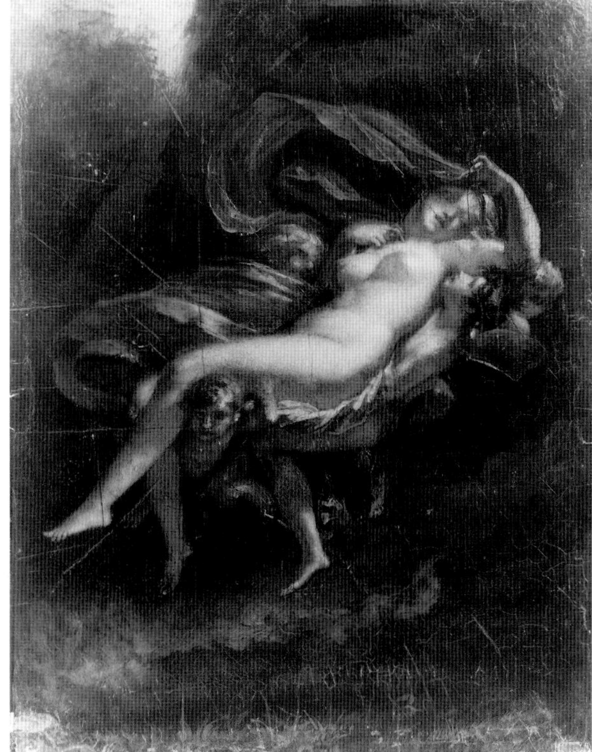

Fig. 6b Pierre-Paul Prud'hon?, *The Abduction of Psyche*, oil on canvas, 11¼ × 9⅟₁₆ in. (28.5 × 23 cm), Musée des Beaux-Arts, Chartres

Chartres (fig. 6b), whose authenticity has been questioned by Sylvain Laveissière,[2] and the final painting. Proponents of the second point to its sheer dependence on the Louvre version and, while recognizing its problems of condition, contend that it is of such high quality to rule out another artist. Few, of course, have had the courage to confront the third characterization of the work as a copy by another artist. There are many reasons for this timidity. First of all, much of the writing about the painting in the Museum's curatorial file stems from one of the numerous dealers who attempted to sell it after its reappearance on the market in 1972. And, after its acquisition by the Norton Simon Art Foundation in 1985, few scholars have questioned its authorship.

The place to begin is with the painting itself. All conservators who have worked on it or studied it characterize it as a damaged or compromised work of art. Andrea Rothe, then conservator at the J. Paul Getty Museum, wrote that it had been aggressively overcleaned—with the removal of what might have been either tinted varnish or glazes—in the area of the lights, while large segments of the darker portions of the canvas are essentially held together with old varnish.[3] This results in a situation in which the lights are lighter, the darks darker, and middle tones lost. Others have been less harsh, confining their discussion to the areas of pentimenti in the drapery of the figures, suggesting that the work is not a copy, but autograph. Still others have correctly stressed Prud'hon's penchant for technical experimentation (linked, in many cases, to the vaunted precedent of Leonardo and, to a lesser extent, Correggio, the most obvious models for Prud'hon's oeuvre). This latter position makes an assessment of the work as autograph easier: if it is in compromised condition, the reasoning goes, the more likely it is to be by the master himself rather than a technically workaday copy by a studio assistant or another artist. Yet, as we see from the technical report on the painting, many of the work's problems stem as much from overcleaning and improper conservation as from technical experimentation on the part of the artist himself. It has been the conservator, more than the painter, who was experimental. Nonetheless, after all of this is said, there is much to recommend the painting. It is not, in any obvious sense, slavish, as are many copies of famous works of art. Rather, its sfumato and its vaguely defined contours suggest that it was made either by Prud'hon or in his studio by an assistant. Laveissière goes so far as to suggest that it was a collaborative work, begun by Prud'hon himself, but worked on by his student, Constance Mayer.[4]

The first recorded owner of the painting was no less a figure in the French museum world than Henry Camille Marcel (1854–1926), an important art historian and the director of the Musées de France. The importance of Marcel for French art has, in some senses, been transferred to this work of art, which has for some become a Prud'hon simply because of its distinguished nineteenth-century owner. Yet when, we must ask, did Marcel acquire this object? There is one preparatory oil study for the painting in the Musée du Louvre listed in the death sale of Prud'hon, which all scholars except Laveissière identify as the sketch in Chartres. Where did Marcel acquire the Norton Simon work and why would an object in the collection of such a prominent man have had no provenance if it was indeed a sketch or an autograph copy made by the artist himself? Unfortunately, we know neither when Marcel acquired it (and from whom) or to whom he sold it. After all, he died in 1926, and the work is not recorded next until 1972. Still, its appearance during his lifetime in an exhibition in Prague in 1923 surely proves that he owned it.

Thus neither the work of art itself nor its documentary evidence enables us to reach a clear conclusion about either its position in the artist's career or its authorship. This forces a cataloguer to look carefully into the paper trail after the work appeared in Switzerland in 1972. What we learn is that the painting was offered for sale by a bewildering succession of dealers between its undocumented, but often asserted, initial appearance in Zurich with the Nathans in 1972 and its sale thirteen years later to Norton Simon. The file proves conclusively that it was offered to Simon three times—by the London dealer Jan Milner in partnership with the New York firm of Shepherd Galleries; by French and Company; and, finally, by Alexandre Rosenberg, from whom Mr. Simon finally purchased it, after Rosenberg himself had bought the painting at auction in New York. From this, we know that the work was considered problematic, and it is clear from the extensive correspondence in the Norton Simon Museum files that the collector bought it only after the price was lowered to the point at which he thought it worth the gamble.

What is particularly interesting is that Norton Simon was not interested in bidding for the work at auction, although he often bought works of art in this way. Indeed, unless he was an unidentified underbidder (which is unlikely), Simon and his colleagues were willing to wait to see what would happen to a work of art he had watched for nearly a decade, been formally offered twice, and had on approval in California well before the auction. In the event, Alexandre Rosenberg bought it and then (obviously with the full knowledge of Simon's earlier history with the painting) made a strong case both for its authenticity and for its position in Prud'hon's career as an autograph replica of the 1808 Salon painting. If anyone did his homework on the painting, Rosenberg did. His cogent three-paragraph essay with an attached condition report is the most intelligent document in the painting's considerable file (cited in full in n. 1, below).

Rosenberg's text was not the first full assessment of the painting; that can be found in a landmark exhibition catalogue produced by the Ackland Memorial Art Gallery at the University of North Carolina under the direction of John Minor Wisdom in 1978, when the painting was owned by Jan Milner and the Shepherd Gallery. The lengthy entry on the painting, though fully aware of the dangers, concludes that it is a preparatory painting made after the Chartres sketch and before the Louvre version. The Ackland catalogue places the work in the context of the eleven studies and four drawings directly related to the Louvre painting and recorded in Jean Guiffrey's magisterial 1924 book on Prud'hon.[5] Although these works are listed neither in the Ackland catalogue nor in Rosenberg's unpublished essay, they are included in an annotated updating of Guiffrey's list in the Museum files listing the ten directly related paintings, two indirectly related paintings, three directly related drawings, and four indirectly related drawings then known. From its age and position in the file, it is clear that this crucial list was used as evidence by Norton Simon before he bought the painting.

What do we learn from it? First of all, this, the so-called Marcel version, is listed as number two after the Louvre painting. Of the next group, five have dimensions that are so much smaller than either the Norton Simon (Marcel) or the Louvre version that they cannot ever have been mistaken for it. Of the eleven related studies, five have no dimensions, allowing us to conclude that any of these works might indeed be the same as works recorded with dimensions. Of these, the Alphonse Kann version was exhibited in St. Petersburg in 1912, another appeared in the Wery sale in Paris in 1848, another was shown in exhibition at Versailles in 1881 as being part of the collection of the comte de Perrigny, and the final one was included in an anonymous sale in December 1823 (the year of Prud'hon's death and after his own death sale, where another version was recorded). Of these, at least two sales—those of 1823 and 1848—and possibly the 1881 one are possible identifications of the Marcel work before the museum director acquired it. How wonderful it would be to create a putative provenance beginning "Anonymous collector (1823), Wery (until 1848), and comte de Perrigny (until 1881)." Yet, however much one wants provenance closure, more evidence is required. And none of these works appeared with any visual evidence or listed dimensions.

To reach a conclusion from this welter of material is challenging even to the seasoned scholar of French early-nineteenth-century painting. It is our sense that the work is unique in terms of scale and facture among those known to relate to Prud'hon's canvas in the Louvre.

However, uniqueness itself does not prove authenticity or suggest position within an artist's oeuvre. Interestingly, in the only case in Prud'hon's career in which an autograph sketch survives for an autograph painting—that of the so-called *Young Zephyr* in the Louvre—both works are of almost identical dimension, suggesting that Prud'hon worked the painting up at full scale before attempting the final canvas. It is tempting simply to go with Norton Simon and his major source, Alexandre Rosenberg, the only person he trusted to convince him of the authorship of this work. For Rosenberg, the Marcel version is an autograph reduction painted after the painting exhibited in the Salon—either in 1808 or 1814—for an unknown private client. Was it M. Wery, who owned a version until 1848? We need much more evidence to know.

What we can say with certainty is that the Norton Simon painting is as close as one can get in California to the sublime painting in the Louvre. Is it close enough to be by Prud'hon? Both its compromised condition and its probable placement for Prud'hon after the Salon painting make it difficult to interpret without lingering doubts that cannot now be assuaged. We must conclude, in the absence of even closer scholarly study, that it is hard to know whether Prud'hon painted it and, if so, when he did. Thus, we will take the optimistic course and place the master's name first as its probable artist.

1 Alexandre Rosenberg to Norton Simon, 16 June 1981, the Norton Simon Museum curatorial files:

"To the Salon of 1808, Prud'hon sent three entries: 'Vengeance and Justice pursuing Crime,' 'The Rape of Psyche,' and a portrait. Although the first won an official prize and the painter was rewarded with the Legion of Honor, the second became the most renowned of Prud'hon's paintings. Acquired by Mr. de Sommariva and now in the Louvre, this large picture was preceded by numerous drawn studies, at least two complete drawings in black and with chalks and a painted sketch now in the museum of Chartres. The present painting is a smaller repetition of the Salon entry, certainly painted by Prud'hon at the request of a collector.

"It differs from the large version in a number of features. The body of Psyche is slightly more inclined and set closer to the top of the picture, leaving less space above the main subject. The drapery has been simplified and the folds hanging below the body have been omitted altogether. The upper part of the background is different and has also been simplified. Most conspicuously, the veil billowing above the group of figures is absent.

"This absence has been wrongly imputed to the fact that the veil has been damaged at some time and completely painted out by a restorer. Such supposition rests on the faulty assumption that the smaller version should conform in all respects to the larger one. It is unrealistic to imagine that the veil, if ever painted, would have deteriorated in its entirety: had some damage occurred in that area, the restorer would have filled in the losses rather than obliterating it completely. In fact, what happened is surely that Prud'hon decided to omit the veil because it would have made the composition top-heavy as a result of the reduced size and the raised position of the figure within the format. Substantiation of this decision to introduce changes is brought by the similar suppression of the lower folds of the drapery in an area that is clearly exempt of any repainting, and by the addition at center top of a zone of lighter paint not in the Louvre example, destined to compensate for the dark uniformity of the upper background. X-rays of the area detect no traces of any remaining underpaint. It is to be noted that the present picture, as befits a reduction in size, is altogether painted more freely than the larger version, and it is certain that the veil never existed.

"*Condition*: All paintings by Prud'hon have suffered to a certain extent from aging, some disastrously. The reason is the liberal use of bitumen by the painter in the dark tones, a practice widespread at the time because unwisely recommended by the official schools. . . . In addition, Prud'hon is known to have invented a varnish which was intended by him to preserve the paint but did not live to his expectation. If anything, it made matters worse. Prud'hon's technique consisted in painting the entire surface of his canvas in neutral tones . . . then adding the color values and finishing with thin glazing to define the transitions. . . . The present picture is painted in this manner. Because the subject called for little chiaroscuro effects, fortunately, it has fared much better than most of Prud'hon's compositions, and it is probably the best preserved of all. When the ill-devised original varnish had to be removed, some small losses occurred in the background and in the immediate vicinity of the outline of some small sections of the figures, but without encroaching on any part of them. No vital element is affected. Occasionally, some of the transition glazing between dark and light have been locally thinned, but without impairing the integrity of the modeling and sculptural weight of the forms. The definition of the figures is substantially intact and the general condition can be termed satisfactory."

2 Laveissière, 1997, p. 241, n. 4.

3 Notes from an examination by Andrea Rothe 13 October 1983, the Norton Simon Museum curatorial files.

4 Laveissière, 1997, p. 240: "the picture, despite its quality, remains intriguing. It shows a loose handling that could be Constance Mayer's. It could also have been a collaborative effort, prepared by Prud'hon, roughed in by Mayer, and then reworked by the master. . . . If the picture was left unfinished at this point, it was probably because Prud'hon received a commission for a work in a larger format to be painted by him alone."

5 Guiffrey, 1924, nos. 146–151.

7

STUDIO OF PIERRE-PAUL PRUD'HON
French, 1758–1823

Study of a Male Nude
Black chalk on gray-blue paper, 24 × 18¼ in. (61 × 46.3 cm)

Inscribed along the right edge: "Br••t••l Vibrant [?] Cote [?] d [?]••l—T••l Estirrien [?]"
M.1975.22

PROVENANCE: [Paul Botte, Paris, sold November 1968 to]; Norton Simon, gift 1975 to; Norton Simon Art Foundation.

TECHNICAL NOTES The drawing is black chalk on thick blue artist's paper, which has been laid down on a larger secondary support sheet of blue paper at an unknown date. The work is hinged to an acid-free 4-ply rag board at the top corners. The drawing suffers from a significant tear in the center of the figure's left arm and torso and tears in the upper right and left corners. Because of these structural damages, the work was laid down on a sympathetic blue paper by a previous conservator. The drawing is relatively stable in this mount, and while there is some undulation in the sheet, it has remained more or less planar. The sheet contains brown spots near the figure's right groin and throughout the leg areas, a larger brown spot or mark to the left of the figure's right ribs, and smudges and marks all around the perimeter of the sheet. The entire lower half of the work is faded and severely diminished, and the medium is abraded along the left and right edges. A partial inscription remains along the right edge. (SSB)

THIS SHEET REPRESENTS a standing nude male youth in a heroic posture, striding forward and to the right, while looking back over his left shoulder. The head is fine and expressive, with large lips, a broad nose, and Roman-style curls over his brow and framing his face. The treatment of the body is much more approximate than the head. The raised right arm is awkward: the shoulder and arm appear to be parallel to the picture plane but they must extend diagonally back into space. Thus the arm feels weak, stunted like the right arm of Théodore Géricault's *Wounded Cuirassier* (Musée du Louvre, Paris). The sheet was clearly drawn from a model posed for use as a figure in a history painting.

The drawing was acquired by Norton Simon as a work by Pierre-Paul Prud'hon, but scholars have doubted this attribution, citing the weaknesses of the lower portion of the legs and left arm of the figure.[1] It is directly related to a sheet by Prud'hon in the Cabinet des Dessins in the Louvre (fig. 7a). There is no doubt about the authenticity or attribution of the sheet in the Louvre, which is somewhat smaller than the Norton Simon drawing, thus forcing speculation as to the authorship of the latter. Although it is known that Prud'hon had assistants in his atelier and that they occasionally worked with him from the same posed figure, this sheet seems more likely to be a studio copy of the Louvre drawing than an independent work made while Prud'hon himself worked from the same model.[2] The fact that the two sheets are unfinished in precisely analogous ways and that the angle of vision is identical prove that the author of this sheet made it not from life, but from art.

1 Correspondence, Norton Simon Museum curatorial files.
2 Brettell, 2002, no. 13, pp. 29–32.

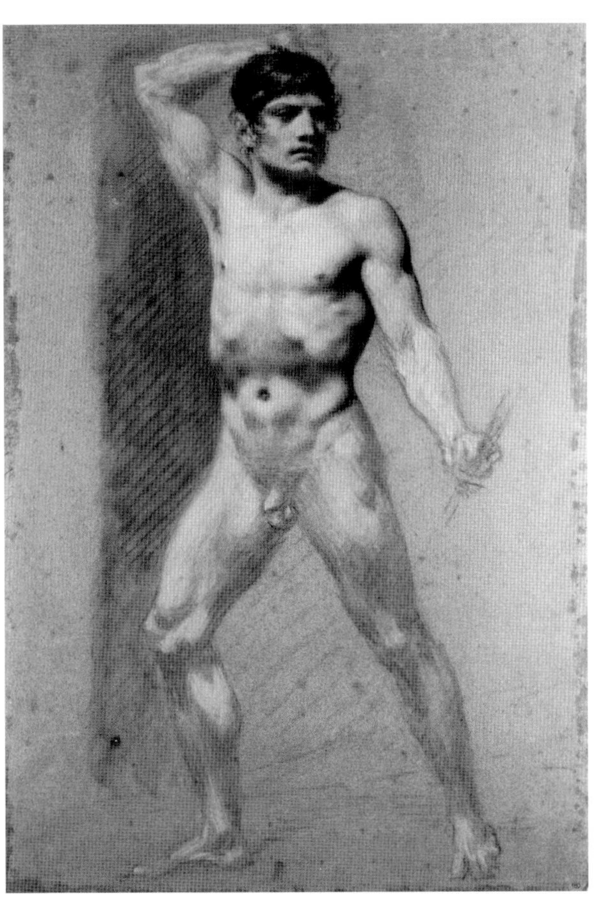

Fig. 7a Pierre-Paul Prud'hon, *Study of a Male Nude*, black and white chalk on paper, 23¼ × 11⅞ in. (59 × 30 cm), Musée du Louvre, Cabinet des Dessins, Paris; photo: Réunion des Musées Nationaux / Art Resource, NY

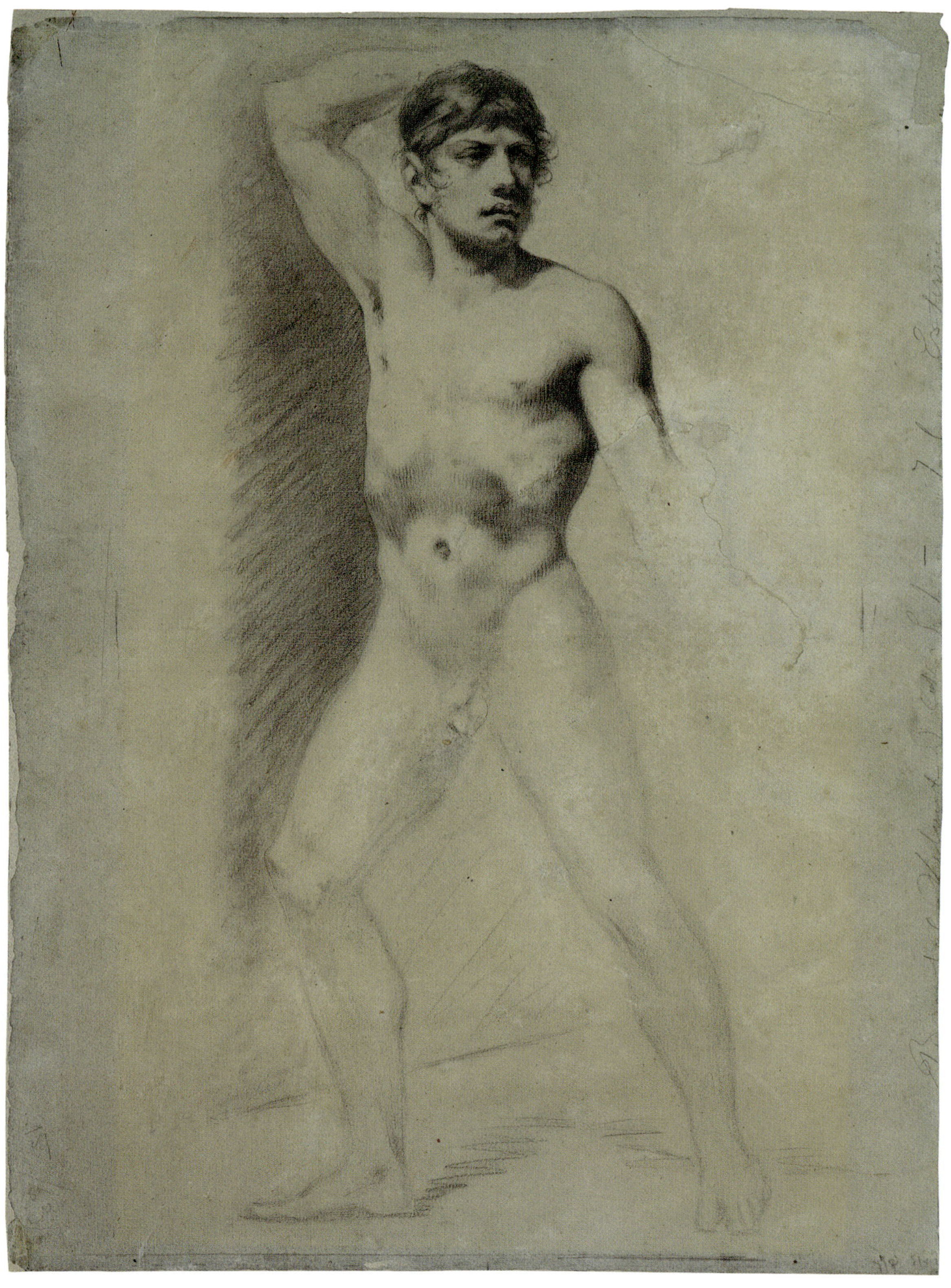

7

8

Marie-Geneviève Bouliar
French, 1762–1825

Self-Portrait
1790–1795

Oil on canvas, $21\frac{7}{8} \times 18\frac{1}{8}$ in. (55.5×46 cm)
M.1979.43

Provenance: Possibly [Gimpel] or [Sulzbach] (sale, Paris, Hôtel Drouot, 31 May 1919, lot 32, to; Mancuso[?]). [Édouard Jonas, Paris, in 1923]. Baronne Maurice Hottinguer (1872–1969), in 1926 and 1928. (sale, Paris, Palais Galliera, 7 April 1976, lot 18, ill., to); [Sylvia Blatas, Paris, buying for]; Norton Simon, gift 1979 to; Norton Simon Art Foundation.

Exhibition: Paris, 1926, no. 8, p. 27.

References: *La Renaissance*, 1923, p. 339; Oulmont, 1928, p. 56 n. 1; Harris and Nochlin, 1976, p. 202 n. 3.

Technical Notes: The support is a medium-weight, plain-weave fabric. It has a fairly thick white ground that nevertheless allows the canvas weave to show on the surface. The wax-resin lining to a similar fabric made the painting stiff and caused the weave to be visible on the surface. Tacking edges no longer exist, but the 5-part butt-join stretcher may be original. It is expected that the artist first laid in the design and shadows with a dark red-brown paint. Painting is direct wet in wet for each color but wet over dry, for example, with the shawl over the blouse. Paint layers are thin and therefore allow the ground to just peek through. The white has some impasto, but it is fairly low. Brush sizes seem to have ranged from about $\frac{1}{8}$- to $\frac{1}{4}$- inch wide. For the flesh, the medium tone was laid in and then gray shadow, pink, and the rusty red (of the nostrils). This is mostly painted wet into wet to a fairly high finish, but strokes of the brush can still be detected. Only one small change is evident at the top of the head. While the flesh is in good state, the background has been abraded and grossly overpainted. The varnish, probably synthetic, appears as greenish to blue streaks in ultraviolet light. It is dirty and a bit discolored. (JF)

Marie-Geneviève Bouliar is chiefly known for being among the small contingent of women artists exhibiting at the Paris Salon during the years just after the French Revolution and the liberalization of access rules in 1791. The others, now more famous than Bouliar, are Marguerite Gérard, Adélaïde Labille-Guiard, Élisabeth Vigée- Le Brun, and Constance Mayer. However, Bouliar was an accomplished history painter and a fine portraitist whose best works in the latter genre deserve to be seen beside those by her celebrated male contemporaries, Jacques-Louis David, Pierre-Narcisse Guérin, Anne-Louis Girodet-Trioson, and François Gérard.

Bouliar is alleged to have studied with several masters, among them Gabriel-François Doyen and Jean-Baptiste Greuze, and the attribution to the latter of what is undoubtedly a self-portrait by Bouliar in the National Gallery of Foreign Art in Sofia, Bulgaria, is indication of a certain similarity of their styles. But Bouliar's works are both less sentimental and less flamboyant than those of Greuze, and the now accepted view of her education—that she studied only with the portrait painter Joseph-Siffred Duplessis (1725–1802)—is likely to be correct. In the decade before the Revolution, Duplessis met with great success for portraits whose unflinching realism appealed to those French *philosophes* (and their aristocratic sponsors) who cherished and trumpeted their own virtue, patriotism, and matter-of-fact rationality. His portrait of Benjamin Franklin (renowned as a veritable Renaissance man at the court of Louis XV) shows the American patriot as he was: astute, stout, jowly, and plain. (The portrait is well known to Americans of a certain rank because it was later engraved on the hundred-dollar bill.) A work from Duplessis's studio (fig. 8a) depicts a handsome, heavy-set woman of early middle age with arched brows, upturned eyes, wide nostrils, and slender lips. The set of her mouth is uncannily like that in the Norton Simon *Self-Portrait* by

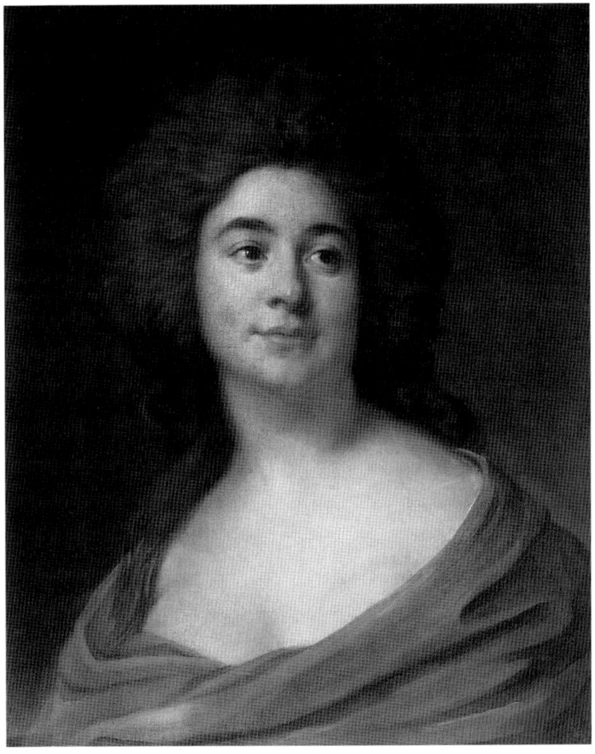

Fig. 8a Studio of Joseph-Siffrid Duplessis, *Portrait of a Woman*, c. 1785, oil on canvas, $24 \times 19\frac{3}{4}$ in. (61×50.2 cm), Fine Arts Museums of San Francisco, Bequest of M. H. de Young, 41.1.3

Fig. 8b Marie-Geneviève Bouliar, *Chevalier Alexandre-Marie Lenoir*, 1796, oil on canvas, Musée Carnavalet, Paris; © Bridgeman-Giraudon, Art Resource / NY

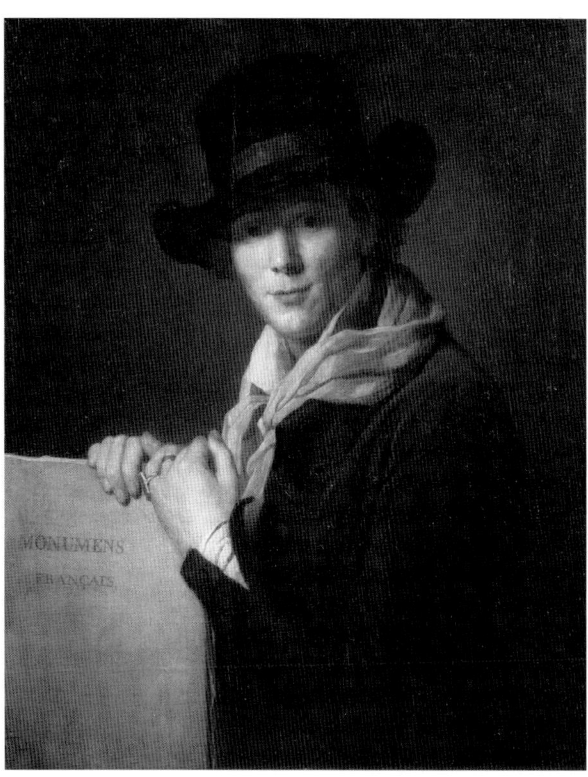

Bouliar and clinches the relationship of teacher and student. (In any case, Duplessis was specifically named as Bouliar's teacher in Salon *livrets* of 1796 and 1798.)

Bouliar's *Self-Portrait* reveals an attractive young woman who inclines her head slightly to her right, but faces us nearly completely frontally. Her dark blond hair is partly tied with a pink ribbon just above her forehead, and a gauzy shawl is tied in a knot at her bust. Her prominent brows, widely spaced eyes, long, straight nose, and small, pink, closed mouth give her a serious, even contemplative air, as does the softness of her gaze. The modeling of the flesh is achieved with small, but distinct, liquid strokes of pink, red, white, and gray. (Her nostrils are red, painted with a small brush.) Her bodice is yellow at the shoulder and ocher-colored in the shadows below. A thin, black-spotted tulle shawl is wrapped around her upper arms. At the left, behind the sitter's shoulder, is a chair, its back cushion upholstered with a crimson fabric fastened with brass tacks. Almost the entire dark background of the canvas has unfortunately been repainted. The lightness of tone just above the sitter's left shoulder, beside her hair, gives a sense of the original light tone and open, scumbled touch. The character of this original background may be gauged by comparison with the otherwise damaged *Self-Portrait* at the Musée des Beaux-Arts of Angers. There the brushy technique, developed most extensively by David in his great portraits of the 1790s, is clearly visible. Another version of the *Self-Portrait*, dated 1792, may be found at the Musée Magnin, Dijon. Still others have appeared on the New York and international art markets.[1]

Though Bouliar exhibited more than forty paintings and drawings at the Salon between 1791 and 1817, only about one-quarter of them are known today, and about half of these are self-portraits. Bouliar's known portraits and self-portraits, including the Norton Simon painting and the portrait of Chevalier Alexandre-Marie Lenoir (fig. 8b), are at once flattering and incisive, and expose a sure, modern sense of the relation between pictorial space and canvas surface. The Lenoir portrait, now taken to be the canonical record of the appearance of the celebrated painter, archaeologist, and founder of Musée National des Monuments Français—and easily Bouliar's best-known work—shows the artist's adaptation of a pictorial device first used by David two years earlier in his *The Death of Marat* (1793, Musées royaux des Beaux-Arts de Belgique, Brussels): an inscription placed on a flat surface—for David a wooden crate serving as a desk and for Bouliar a large book—that reads as identical with the picture surface itself. The Norton Simon *Self-Portrait* has no such ostentatious trick of art, but its subtle way with frontality, inclination of head, downcast eyes, and knotted shawl indicate the presence of an artist of sophistication and ambition.

1 See, for example, New York, Sotheby's, sale 6564, 19 May 1994, lot 92, where the figure seems just a bit older, though with identical pose and costume.

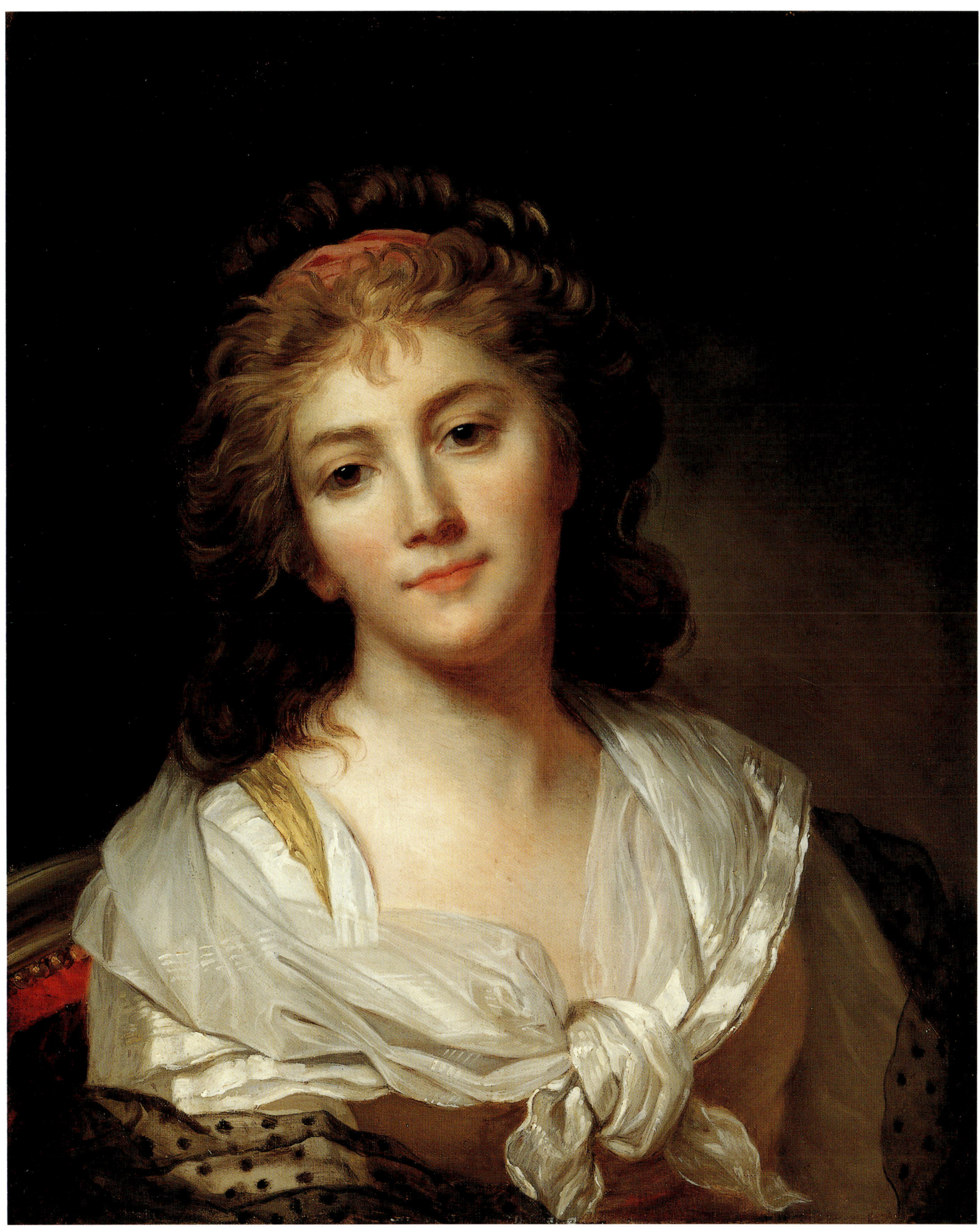

9

Louis Ducis
French, 1775–1847

Sappho Recalled to Life by the Charm of Music
c. 1811

Oil on canvas, $45\frac{3}{8} \times 57\frac{5}{8}$ in. (115.2 × 146.3 cm)
Signed and dated lower left: "DUCIS 1811[?]"
F.1983.10

Provenance: General Count Rapp, original commission, by 1812 (sale, Paris, 15 June 1830, lot 2, to); Plailly, Paris; [Artibus, Geneva, consigned by 10 January 1977 to]; [Heim Gallery Ltd., London, sold 1979 to]; Norton Simon, gift 1983 to; The Norton Simon Foundation.

Exhibitions: Paris, 1812, no. 327, as *Sapho*; London, 1978, no. 9, ill.

References: *Annales*, 1812, vol. 1, pp. 26–27, pl. 12; Fère, 1868, vol. 15, p. 7; Bellier de La Chavignerie and Avray, 1882, vol. 1, pp. 465–466; Beaumont, 1900, no. 25, p. 544; Daniels, 1977, p. 19, fig. 1, p. 18; Bordes, 2005, p. 210, fig. 71.

Technical Notes: The tight plain-weave canvas (medium-weight) has an off-white commercial priming. The design area has a substantial white ground layer that must contain lead white. The painting has an aqueous lining stretched on a newer stretcher, but the tacking edges are mostly preserved. An infrared examination shows extensive underdrawing directly on the ground, which the artist followed faithfully, with only minor deviations. In addition, some scoring in the lead ground and in paints can be found for the tiled floor and some of the furniture. The flesh is brought to a high finish using fine brushes, but the drapes show some brushstrokes. Primary and secondary colors mixed with white as well as earths and black can be found. Glazing creates colors such as the purple drape, which is a light blue layer overlaid with a thin glaze of a red lake and blue. The painting was cleaned in 1979 and varnished with acryloids. Its condition is good; there is some abrasion of glazes on the red robe at the right and possibly the green hanging drape. The latter seems to have been toned at a later date. (JF)

This superbly preserved and ambitious painting by the Neoclassical master Louis Ducis was among three paintings by the artist submitted to and accepted by the jury at the Salon of 1812. The painter had made an inauspicious debut at the Salon of 1802 with *Portrait of M. and Mme Cramayel* but received a first-class medal at the Salon of 1808 for a pair of mythological paintings concerned with the origin of the arts, *Dibutades* (from Pliny's *Natural History*) and *Orpheus* (from Ovid's *Metamorphoses*). Based on that success, Ducis's distinguished career was launched. Yet the unsettled times in the Napoleonic France of his youth meant that Ducis made his first trip to Italy, not when he was in his twenties, as was the norm for bright young French artists, but in his late thirties, in 1811. He seems not to have spent much if any time in the traditional city of French Neoclassicism, Rome, but was sent instead to Naples, where he had been commissioned to paint portraits of the queen and the princess royal. Although it is not so inscribed, the present painting is said to have been conceived and executed in Naples and submitted to the Salon on his return to Paris.

When it appeared at the Salon, the catalogue entry indicated that it had been painted on commission for General Jean Rapp, a distinguished Napoleonic military commander from Alsace. Records of the Rapp family—both the inventory of the Parisian house at the death of General Rapp in 1821 and the sale of the possessions of his widow in 1830—make it clear that the general (later a count) was the most important patron of Ducis in the years after 1810. This is no doubt because Ducis completed the large painting *Napoleon on the Terrace of St. Cloud* in that year (stolen from the Musée de l'Île de France, Sceaux). Favorably received at the Salon, the painting linked the young artist to the imperial court, of which Rapp was a prominent member. The inventory of Count Rapp's *hôtel particulière* at 23, rue Plumet in Paris indicates that the Norton Simon painting hung in the dining room with another pair of mythological paintings and a portrait of Napoleon, also by Ducis. Rapp's widow kept the painting along with other contemporary pictures, important furniture, and the general's extensive library and moved to another *hôtel*, at 18, rue Pigalle. The contents of this house were sold in 1830, and the present work, though listed in the catalogue as one of two paintings by Ducis, appears to have been bought in by the family, in whose possession it remained until its sale in 1977.

The subject of the painting is of particular interest, especially given the position of Ducis in Parisian literary society. The painter was the nephew of the celebrated playwright and poet Jean-François Ducis, as well as the brother-in-law of the then-famous Parisian tragic actor Talma, whose sister Anne-Euphrosine he married in 1810. Through these circles, Ducis undoubtedly encountered the tragedy *Sappho*, written by the woman playwright Constance de Pipelet, first staged in 1794 and frequently performed in Paris throughout the first decade of the nineteenth century. The play caused a kind of renaissance for the ancient poetess Sappho, whose image was painted by artists from Baron Gros and Jacques-Louis David (fig. 9a) to the young Anne-Louis Girodet (whose drawings of Sappho were published in engraved form

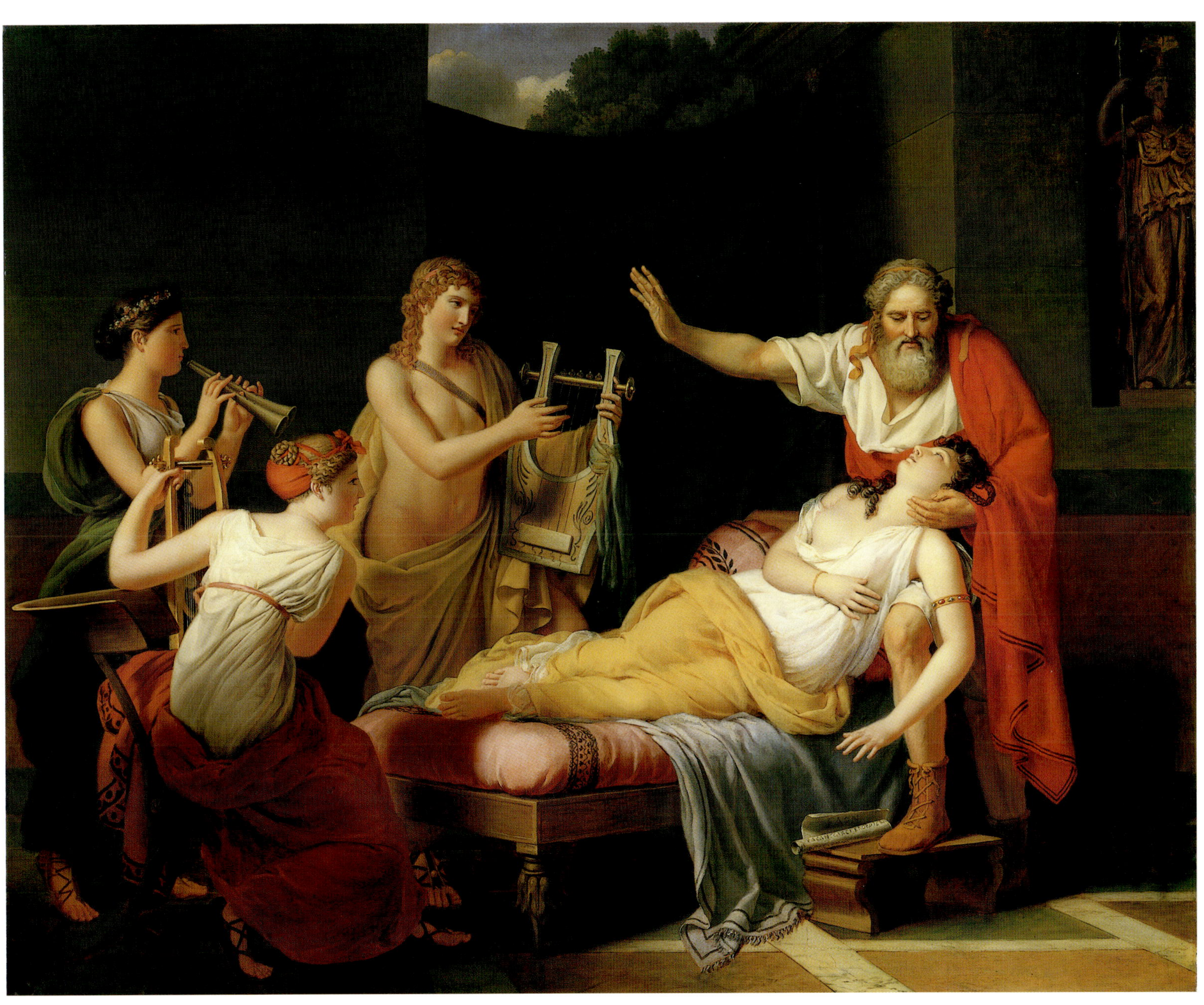

9

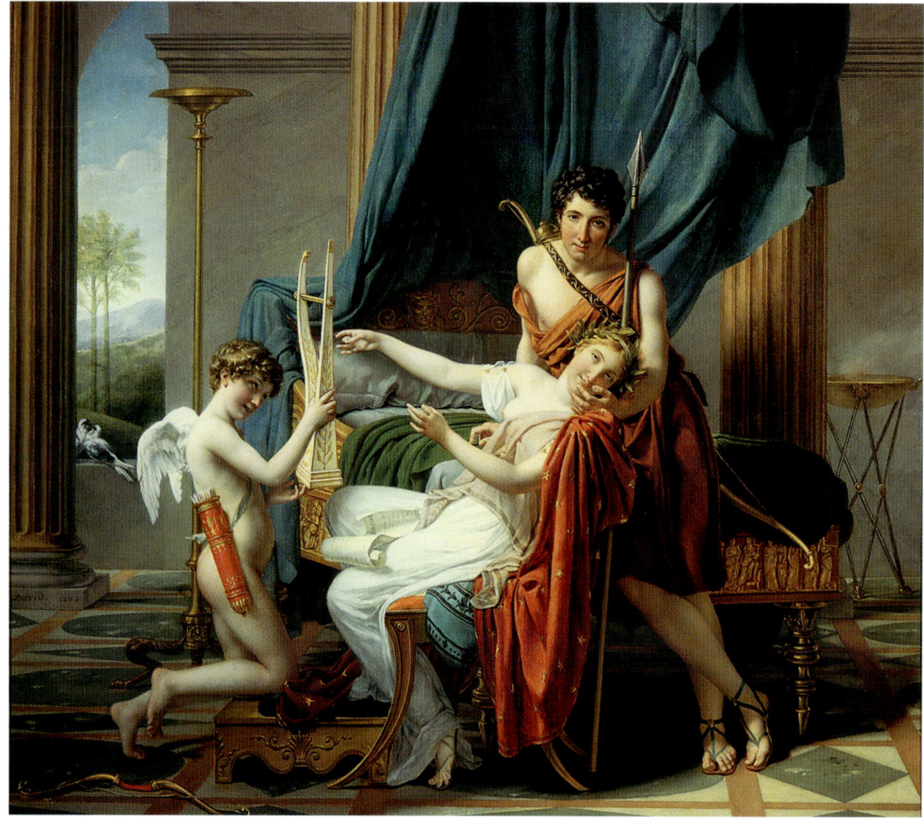

Fig. 9a Jacques-Louis David, *Sappho, Phaon, and Cupid*, 1809, Oil on canvas, $88\frac{5}{8} \times 103\frac{1}{4}$ in. (225 × 262 cm), State Hermitage Museum, St. Petersburg; photo: Scala / Art Resource, NY

only in 1829 and are not, hence, relevant to our enquiry). Ducis represented the Greek poetess in her place of retreat on Sicily, where she recovered from her historic abandonment by her male lover, Phaon, in whose arms she was represented by David three years earlier in a painting made on commission for the Russian Prince Youssoupoff. David's pupil, Ducis, responded directly to the master by creating a painting that can easily be read as a narrative sequel to David's earlier painting, known to Ducis both from his friendship with David and from the fact that the Russian prince lived in Paris between 1808 and 1811. Although David's work has not been linked to Pipelet's play, he surely knew it, most likely because the play actually began with the scene portrayed by the older artist, while Ducis chose to represent the poetess somewhat later in her dramatic abandonment. Pipelet placed this scene in the first act of her play, but Ducis adapted his work freely from at least two scenes in that act. Thus, this painting represents the highest intellectual ambitions of a Parisian artist, linking ancient and modern literature with the work of the greatest living French painter.

Surprisingly, no contemporary of Ducis made the link between the David and the Ducis paintings when the latter appeared in 1812. This is surely because David's late masterpiece had not received a favorable response when it appeared in 1809 and perhaps also because it had already left Paris for St. Petersburg in 1811. Although Ducis's painting is considerably smaller than that of David and has different proportions (more in keeping with David's earlier historical and literary canvases), there is no doubt that Ducis was paying homage to David. Indeed, the pictorial relation between the reclining Sappho and the older poet, Stesichorus, in Ducis's painting seems to have been prompted by David's seated Sappho and her standing lover, Phaon. Yet David forced the viewer into a confrontation with his painted subjects by composing his two principal figures so that they look directly out of the canvas. We are thus made witnesses to a pictorial re-creation of literary history shown at full scale. This break in the codes of representation (which anticipates the painting of Édouard Manet) was corrected by the more timid young Ducis, who borrows from earlier Davidian prototypes in which the characters are arranged in a closed tableau of reduced proportion with no reference to the contemporary viewer or our world. Instead, we watch three young musicians of both genders playing for Sappho in an attempt to wrest her from her profound melancholy.

The painting was selected by the painter Charles-Paul Landon for publication and illustration in the prestigious collection of successful paintings from the Salon of 1812 published in *Annales du musée*.[1] Ducis's submission (undoubtedly because his name comes early in the alphabet) was number 12 in the first volume, and a lengthy text describes the life of Sappho and the details of Ducis's interpretation of his subject. Landon seems not to have known Ducis's literary source (he called Stesichorus "the old man") and actually praised the painter for having chosen an unprecedented subject rather than one often used by painters for representation. He is, strictly speaking, correct, because no other French painter had depicted this particular scene from the life of the Greek lyric poet, allowing Ducis's painting to fill a narrative gap between David's and Gros's Sapphic scenes. Perhaps because the painting has its origins in Naples, it has a vividly southern quality in its hidden landscape and its brilliant colors. However, we are not allowed to be diverted from the heroine's melancholy by taking a visual walk in gorgeous Italy.

1 *Annales*, 1812, vol. 1, pp. 26–27, pl. 12.

10

Jérôme-Martin Langlois
French, 1779–1838

Self-Portrait
c. 1830

Oil on canvas, 25⅜ × 21½ in. (64.5 × 54.6 cm)
M.1977.14

Provenance: Family of the artist until 1970. [Établissement Rustique, Vaduz, Liechtenstein; consigned to]; [Heim Gallery, Ltd., London, sold 1977 to]; Norton Simon Art Foundation.

Technical Notes: The plain-weave canvas has been lined and the original tacking edges have been removed. Cusped threads are visible at the left side; small remaining portions of the top and bottom tacking edges confirm that the painting's dimensions have not changed. A 3-inch vertical tear at the lower right side is slightly opened and protrudes, and several small tears originate at the edges. These damages all protrude slightly. The thin cream-colored ground was smoothly applied. The background, coat, and hair were brushed directly over the ground with quick, sketchy strokes in thin, translucent paint, which may have been mixed with varnish. The dark coat has only a suggestion of the lapels and shoulder seam. The hair was also very loosely rendered in varied shades of brown. The fully realized face was painted in thicker, opaque paint. In general, the smoothly blended brushstrokes are invisible. Shadows are cool gray over reddish brown or gray over the flesh color. The thickest paint is the white highlighted area in the center of the forehead. The paint film has almost no cracks. However, there are numerous small losses throughout. Chemical abrasion has occurred around the proper right ear and hairline and in the shadow at that side of the face; the paint has been thinned directly in front of the ear, breaking the continuity of that shadow. Additional areas of abrasion are in the hair and face. In previous treatment, varnish was removed from over the face and cravat. The remainder of the varnish is moderately yellowed, with a noticeable bloom. Several retouched repairs have discolored or are otherwise conspicuous. Superficial abrasions and shallow scratches are found at all edges. (RW)

Jérôme-Martin Langlois was a pupil of Jacques-Louis David. As a young man, he overcame his father's objections to a career as a painter (his father was himself a miniaturist) by joining the atelier of the most renowned and rewarded artist in Napoleonic France. He earned the trust and patronage of his teacher by dutifully and skillfully helping with the big *machines, Napoleon Crossing the St. Bernard Pass* (1800, Châteaux de Versailles et de Trianon) and *Leonidas at Thermopylae* (1802–1814, Musée du Louvre, Paris), a work that occupied the studio, on and off, for more than a decade. In a sense, Langlois's career stopped there. Though he was awarded a Prix de Rome in 1809 and exhibited regularly at the Salon until his death in 1838,[1] Langlois never developed an independent career or personality of the kind achieved by the first generation of David pupils, Jean-Germain Drouais, Anne-Louis Girodet-Trioson, François Gérard, Philippe-Auguste Hennequin, and others. Throughout his career he made copies of paintings by David, including *Napoleon Crossing the St. Bernard Pass* and *The Death of Marat* (1793, Musées royaux des Beaux-Arts de Belgique, Brussels), and adapted for his own use the innovative compositions of the Davidians. His *Diana and Endymion*, for example,[2] was based on Girodet's celebrated *Endymion* (Musée du Louvre, Paris) but given a more Rococo feel by the inclusion of the huntress swathed in curling, vaporous garments and a mischievous putto who pulls back a cloth to reveal the naked, alluring male prey. His *Cassandre* (1810, Musée des Beaux-Arts, Chambéry) is essentially a historical *académie* (academic study of a male nude), derived from the work of the David pupils of the next generation—those known as the Primitives or Bearded Ones—such as Jean Broc. But once again, Langlois retreated from the most extreme and challenging elements of Davidian style, in this case embracing anecdote and pathos in place of the neo-Grec asperity and abstraction of Broc's *Death of Hyacinth in the Arms of Apollo* (1801, Musée des Beaux-Arts, Poitiers).

In 1819 Langlois was awarded a first-class medal at the Salon and five years later traveled to Brussels to paint a portrait of David (Musée du Louvre, Paris), in exile since the fall of Napoleon. The result is one of the best works of Langlois's career; the low vantage point and the upturned gaze of David's eyes are idealizing, but the depiction of the aged artist holding chalk in his right hand and a drawing in his left (it might be Paris and Helen), is otherwise unflinching. The placement of David's head somewhat forward on his shoulders suggests an artist who is stooped with age, and the famously disfigured cheek—represented in David's *Self-Portrait* (1793, Musée du Louvre, Paris) some thirty years before—is veritably the focus of the painting. Moreover, the style of the work, though clearly Neoclassical in inspiration, is contemporary in feeling, recalling the work of Louis-Léopold Boilly and other artists active during the Restoration regimes of Louis XVIII and Charles X.

However, when the time came for Langlois to paint his own portrait, he immediately—and with astonishing skill—reverted to Davidian type. The style of the portrait is that employed by his teacher approximately during the years 1790–1805, as in the *Self-Portrait* cited above and the *Portrait of Madame Trudaine* (c. 1792, Musée du

Louvre, Paris). The bust-length figure of the middle-aged painter extends nearly the full height of the canvas. He gazes directly out at the viewer, eyes wide open, lips parted, head turned slightly to the left. The shadow of his beard is visible around his jaws and upper lip, and the volume of his slackening cheeks and jaws are composed of varied tones of pink, gray, and yellow. His body is quarter-turned to the right, so that we are presented first with his left arm and shoulder. This body, however, is only very summarily sketched in and by itself does not persuade us that it possesses weight and volume. The background of the portrait reveals the expressive brushing and scumbling employed by David in the portraits cited above; both men may have employed the technique to heighten (by comparison) the verisimilitude and palpability of the figure and to lend it expression and animation. But to see this particular style of painting—and style of men's clothes—in a work made at the end of the Bourbon Restoration or the beginning of the July Monarchy, instead of one exhibited during the period of the Revolution or Directory, is at once to know that Langlois was engaged in a revivalist project. The political or ideological parameters of that project are not known, but Langlois may have been swept up in the wave of patriotism and Revolutionary nostalgia that was widespread during the first flush of excitement following the overthrow of the Bourbon monarch, Charles X. Louis-Philippe himself, the so-called Citizen-King, shared this enthusiasm for a time, employing Horace Vernet to decorate some rooms of the palace at Versailles with scenes of French victories at Friedland, Wagram, and Jena. It is entirely possible that Langlois's revival of Davidian painting may have been an effort to highlight his own heroic past and gain for himself a portion of this new, pro-Revolutionary patronage.

In the event, Langlois seems not to have secured any very significant commissions from Louis-Philippe in the years leading up to the artist's death. He did, however, receive a commission to paint a series of portraits of past and present *maréchals* of France, from the seventeenth-century *François-Annibal, duc d'Estrees* (c. 1835, quartier des Héronnières, Fontainebleau) to the Napoleonic *Michel Ney, prince de la Moskowa, duc d'Elchingen* (Châteaux de Versailles et de Trianon). These works are painted in a style of pure *juste milieu* eclecticism: the earlier figures in the series are depicted in a highly formal manner that recalls French and Flemish court painting of the early seventeenth century, such as by Frans Pourbus the Younger, court painter to Marie de Médici and Louis XIII in Paris. The portrait of Ney is painted in a Neoclassical style that David and Langlois together employed in 1800 in their *Napoleon Crossing the St. Bernard Pass.* Thus Langlois remained at the end of his life what he was at the beginning, a talented and resourceful student of David.

1 Langlois became a member of Académie des Beaux-Arts in April 1838 and died eight months later.

2 Private collection; engraved by Henri-Charles Müller, Musée du Louvre, Département des Arts Graphiques, Paris.

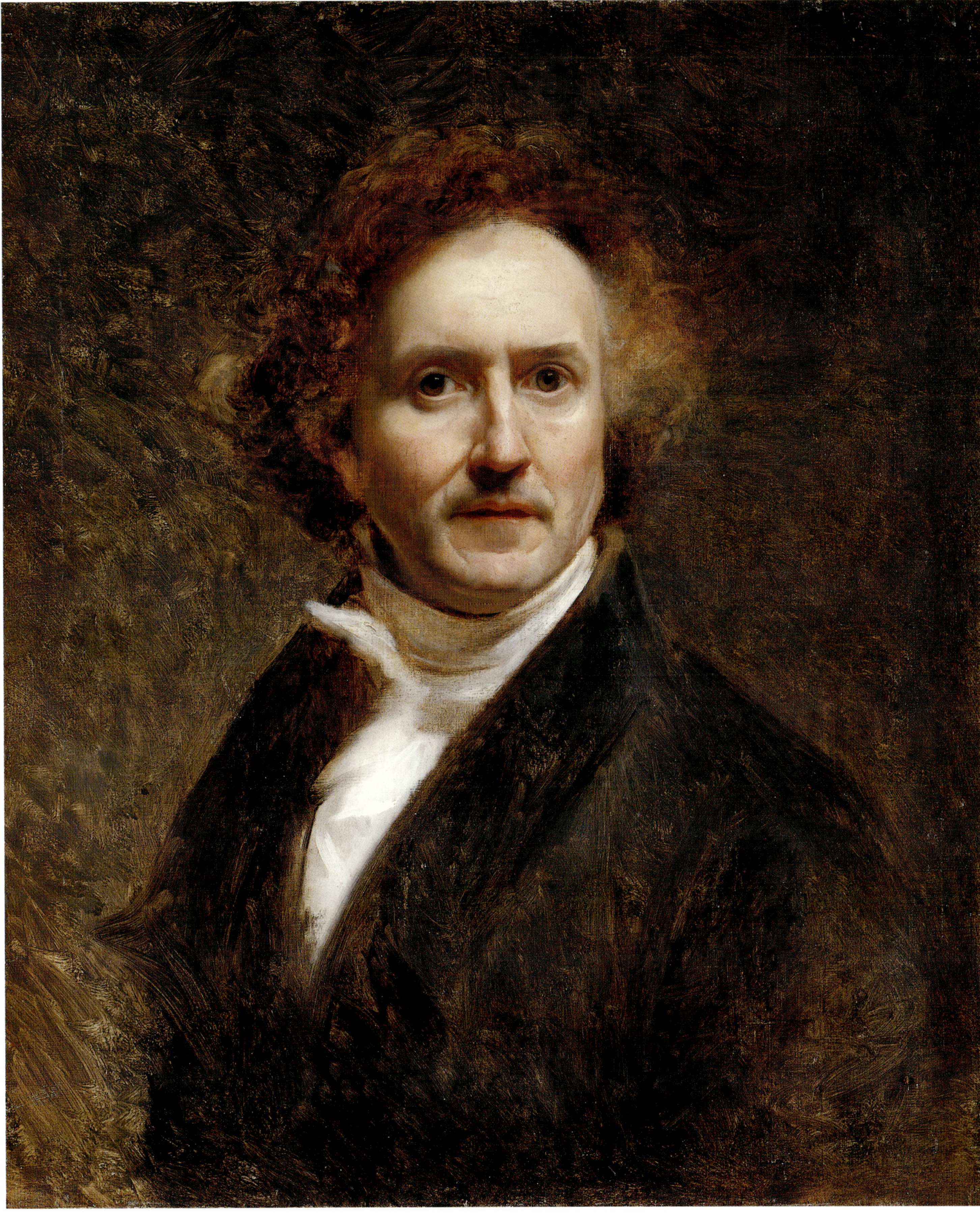

11

JEAN-AUGUSTE-DOMINIQUE INGRES
French, 1780–1867

Baron Joseph-Pierre Vialètes de Mortarieu
1805–1806

Oil on canvas, 24 1/8 × 19 3/4 in. (61.2 × 50.2 cm)
Signed lower left: "yngres."
F.1983.3

PROVENANCE: Baron Joseph Vialètes de Mortarieu (1768–1849), Montauban, by inheritance to; his heirs; sold c. 1905 (to a dealer in Biarritz, presumably); Delas, Biarritz, in 1929; private collection, France, by 1956; [Galerie Schmit, Paris/Sarec, S.A., Geneva, by 1979; sold December 1981, though E. V. Thaw, to]; The Norton Simon Foundation.

EXHIBITION: Montauban, 1862, no. 548.

REFERENCES: Delaborde, 1870, no. 159, p. 262; Lapauze, 1910, p. 150; Lapauze, 1911, pp. 41, 54, 47, ill.; Horticq, 1928, pp. III, 9; Alzard, 1950, p. 32 and n. 24; Schlenoff, 1956, p. 92 n. 3; G. Wildenstein, 1956, no. 39, fig. 24; Ternois, 1965, no. 91, p. 93; Méras, 1967, pp. 116, ill., 117, 121–122; Radius and Camesasca, 1968, no. 39, p. 90, ill.; Coural, 1985, p. 15; Vigne, 1995, p. 48, fig. 31; Tinterow and Conisbee, 1999, pp. 33–34, 43 nn. 32–34, 52, 56, 58, 69, 546, fig. 52; Bajou-Charpentreau, 1999, p. 62, fig. 33.

TECHNICAL NOTES: The support, a plain-weave canvas, has been glue-lined to a heavier, rather coarse-weave canvas. The original tacking edges were retained but trimmed slightly. The X-ray shows a 2 1/4-inch horizontal tear in the upper left quadrant. The purpose of lining most likely was to repair the tear at upper left and possibly to flatten the heavily cracked paint film. The smooth white ground is moderately thick, completely filling the canvas weave. The X-radiograph suggests that the ground layer may have some lead content. Some alteration to the surface texture has occurred, probably because of lining pressure. The rich paint was brushed on smoothly, with colors blended wet into wet, with a fine finish and delicate modeling. A thin red-brown underpainting defines the hair; dark curls were painted over it, with the underpainting intentionally left partially exposed; blue from the background was brought into the outline of the hair. No brush marking is visible except in the fluid white paint of the shirt and tie and the medals. The background, left and right, is painted with small hatching strokes done with a small brush. Shadows are thin and translucent, in warm red-brown tones, beside the nose, the proper left temple, and below the nose. Shadows on the lower part of the face and in the shirtfront are a delicate warm gray. The paint has widespread cracking, in a branched pattern, with edges that are slightly raised. Magnification shows numerous microscopic losses at the edges of cracks, exposing the white ground and the thinness of the paint. Small abrasions in the dark coat are evident; the last four letters of the signature have been thinned slightly. Ultraviolet light reveals retouching in the face and coat, which was done to cover cracks. Brushstrokes in the lower background are not consistent with those elsewhere in the painting, and an infrared photograph confirms that extensive repainting was done, although the soundness of the portrait itself was not compromised. (RW)

J.-A.-D. INGRES ENTERED the studio of Jacques-Louis David in 1797 and won the coveted Prix de Rome in 1801 with an ambitious history painting, *The Ambassadors of Agamemnon Visiting Achilles* (École des Beaux-Arts, Paris). With seeming effortlessness, the twenty-one-year-old artist from Montauban, a fortified town in southwestern France, some thirty miles north of Toulouse, had mastered the rhetoric of Davidian classicism: the arrangement of figures to maximize legibility while nevertheless enabling narrative complexity; the depiction of the ephebic, yet still muscular, male nude body as a sign of moral virtue and heroic self-restraint; and the confident marshaling of the costumes, hairstyles, furniture, and architecture of Greco-Roman antiquity. Having leaped to the first rank of Napoleonic history painters, Ingres then asserted his expertise as a painter of portraits, genre scenes, and female nudes. In time, he would excel at all these and become the most widely respected artist of his generation. However, in 1806, the newly crowned emperor disliked Ingres's *Napoleon on His Imperial Throne* (Musée de l'Armée, Paris)—perhaps for the sheer crassness of its projection of godlike power—and the young artist's career was for a moment checked. At this juncture, Ingres decided to accept the prize he had won five years earlier and take up residence in the French Academy in Rome. The succeeding fifteen years spent in Rome permitted him fully to develop his unique artistic personality as an arch-classicist, albeit one committed to an idiosyncratic blend of eroticism, political and religious orthodoxy, and formal perfectionism. This peculiar formula would be nurtured and sustained by Ingres until his death in 1867. It would also be emulated (minus the originality) by countless others who studied with him in his atelier and at the École des Beaux-Arts in Paris. By the late 1840s the school of Ingres was a buttress of the artistic establishment; it would come under assault by Eugène Delacroix and his followers and the small coterie of artists who represented the avant-garde.

Just before his departure for Rome in September 1806, Ingres painted the portrait of Joseph Vialètes de Mortarieu.[1] The future baron, scion of a wealthy, royalist, and yet reform-minded textile manufacturing family from

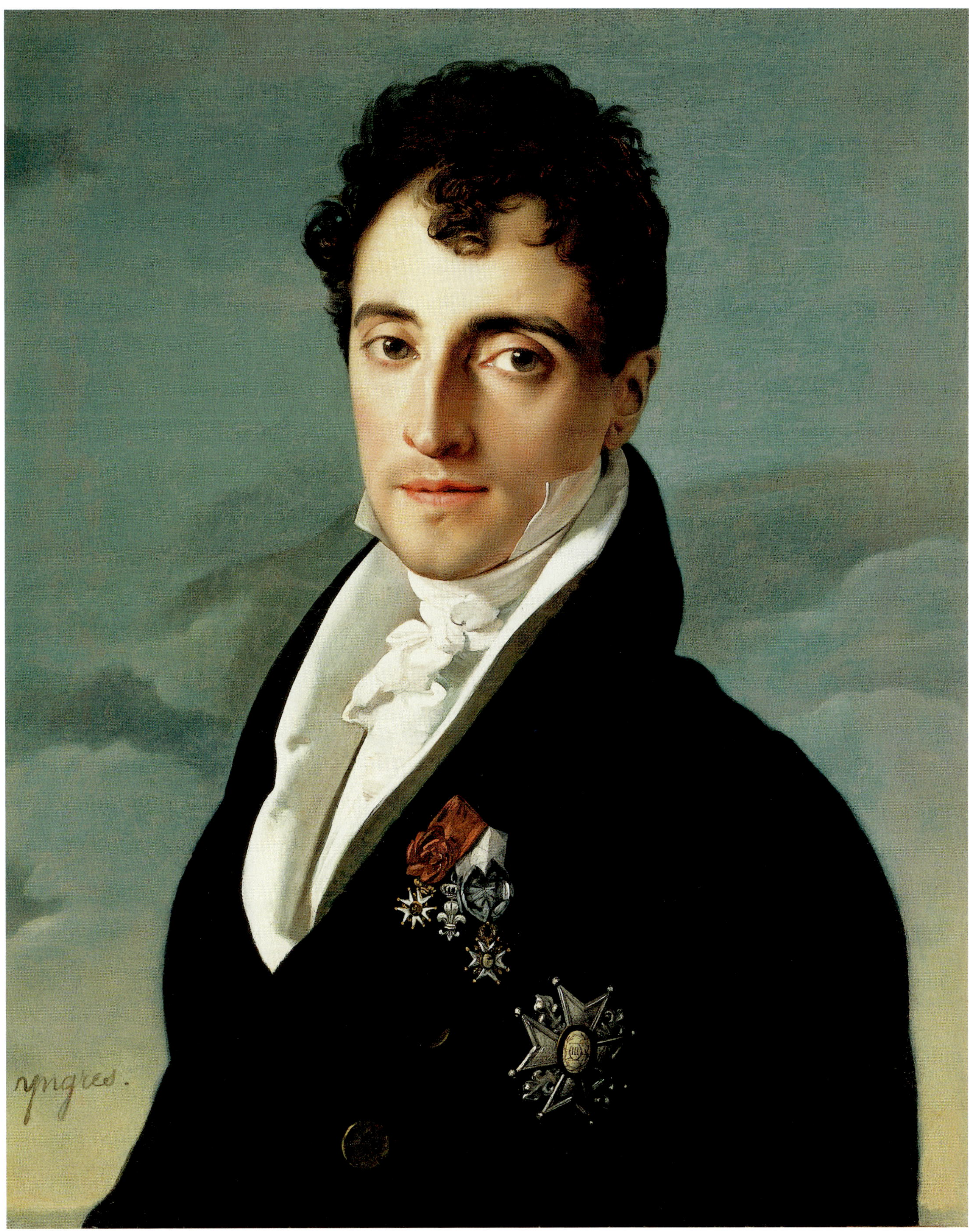

II

Montauban, was well known to Ingres. Born in 1768, de Mortarieu was successively president of the canton of Négrepelisse (1803) and mayor of Montauban (1806–1815) and a leading patron of the arts. His appointment as mayor may have been the reason he asked Ingres to paint his portrait. Ingres's father, also named Joseph, had been employed by the de Mortarieu family in the 1780s to design and carve stucco for the Hôtel Vialètes de Mortarieu on the rue de la Serre. It was thus only natural that the younger Ingres, already celebrated and soon to leave Paris to take up residence in Rome, should also be patronized.[2] Joseph Vialètes de Mortarieu's illustrious career would continue to intersect with that of Ingres for another four decades. In 1820 the former mayor of Montauban, now deputy in the Corps Législatif, arranged for Ingres to receive a commission to paint *The Vow of Louis XIII* for Montauban Cathedral. The work is one of Ingres's most ambitious and self-revealing; it depicts the seventeenth-century king in an act of adoration both to the Virgin Mary and to a work of art, since the pose of the former closely resembles that seen in Raphael's *Sistine Madonna* (Gemäldegalerie, Staatliche Kunstsammlungen, Dresden). In 1843 de Mortarieu (made baron in 1813) established the museum at Montauban, later the Musée Ingres, by his gift of sixty-four works, mostly from the seventeenth and eighteenth centuries, including some by François Boucher, Jean-Baptiste Greuze, and a number of minor Dutch artists. He did not include the portrait of himself by Ingres in the donation, retaining it for his family, but commissioned a copy by one Léon Combes to be placed in the museum. The baron died wealthy and much honored in 1849.

For his portrait of Joseph Vialètes de Mortarieu, Ingres employed the compact and emotionally concentrated bust-length format he developed during the years just before and after his move from Paris to Rome in 1806. It was also used in his *Portrait of the Artist's Father* (1804, Musée Ingres, Montauban), *A Member of the Belvèze-Foulon Family* (fig. 11a), and *Portrait of a Young Man, Nephew of the Actor Talma* (1806, Musée du Louvre, Paris). The type, derived from late Roman and Hellenistic sculpted busts and coins, was rarely used by Ingres's teacher David, who preferred half- and three-quarter-length portraits, but was common in works by French artists of the previous generation, principally Greuze. Ingres shows his sitter's face in three-quarter

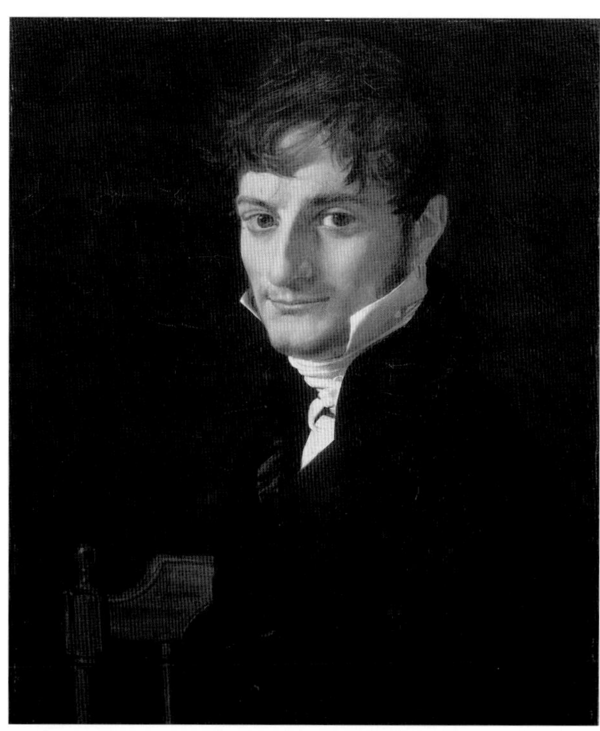

Fig. 11a Jean-Auguste-Dominique Ingres, *A Member of the Belvèze-Foulon Family*, 1805, oil on canvas, 21⅝ × 18 in. (55 × 45.7 cm), Musée Ingres, Montauban; © Bridgeman-Giraudon / Art Resource, NY

view, with his body placed at a diagonal, left shoulder closest to the spectator. De Mortarieu is depicted as a handsome man, somewhat younger than his actual age of thirty-eight, with an oblong face and square jaw, porcelain complexion, and only a faint shadow of beard on his chin and upper lip. He has a high forehead, on which a thick, curly lock of hair artfully falls.

The impression of physiognomic perfection is partly belied by the artist's treatment of the mouth, nose, and eyes. The slender, barely parted, pink lips are asymmetrical, the aquiline nose bends slightly to the sitter's left, the eyes just protrude, the left eye is larger than the right, and the left eyebrow is nearly twice as long as the right. The last-mentioned exaggeration might seem a function of perspective and foreshortening, but in fact is a matter of art alone: the larger eye and brow provide viewers a single focal point, permitting them more immediate access to the face and personality of the sitter.

De Mortarieu wears a starched white collar that extends up to the middle of his cheeks and a white cravat, resembling an orchid, that falls on his white shirtfront, which in turn is surrounded by the white

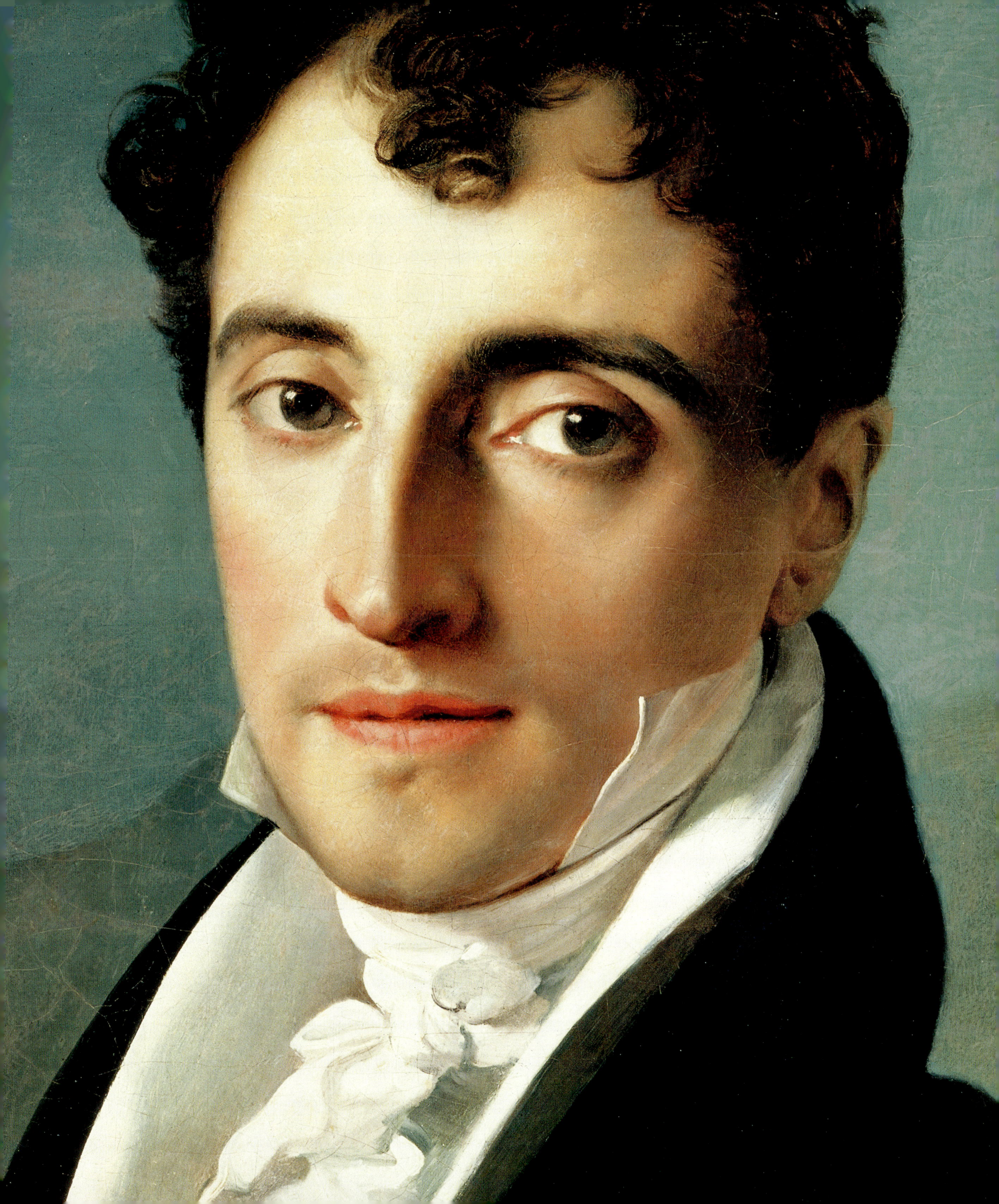

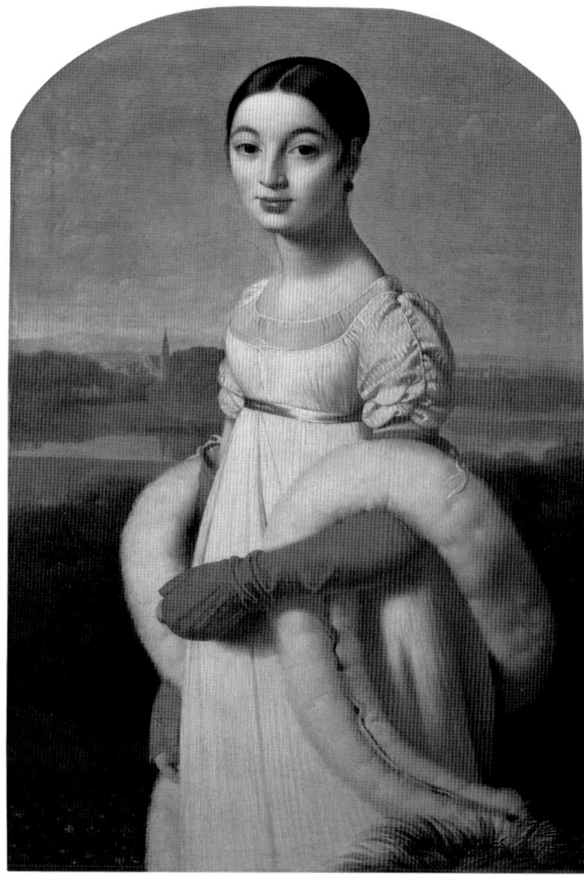

Fig. 11b Jean-Auguste-Dominique Ingres, *Mademoiselle Caroline Rivière*, 1805, oil on canvas, $39\frac{3}{8} \times 27\frac{1}{2}$ in. (100 × 70 cm), Musée du Louvre, Paris; photo: Erich Lessing / Art Resource, NY

collars of his waistcoat. This whole white-on-white contraption is surrounded by a blue-black coat with broad lapels against which are pinned four distinct medals. The gentleman's arms, cut off midlength by the lower edge of the picture, fall to his sides, his right just slightly raised, as if he were using it to establish his balance. Behind the figure are glimpses of blue sky broken by puffy, translucent yellow-white clouds. At lower left, the signature of the artist floats in the air, punctuated with a superfluous period.

The medals on Vialètes de Mortarieu's chest were painted years later than the rest of the picture, possibly by Ingres himself. The practice is not uncommon in the history of art, or in the work of Ingres. His *Portrait of the Marquis de Pastoret* (The Art Institute of Chicago) also contains a medal painted later than the rest of the portrait. The cross of the officer of the Legion of Honor, which hangs from a red ribbon at left, was awarded to the sitter only in 1815. The *Decoration de Lys*, with its prominent fleurs-de-lis was instituted during the period of Napoleon's first exile on the island of Elba in 1814, nearly a decade after the portrait was completed. And the award of medals designating knight and commander of the Spanish Order of Charles III—the two at right—were suspended between 1808 and 1814; given the date of the other medals, it appears likely that these, too, were painted well after the rest of the portrait was finished.

As noted above, the bust-length format of Ingres's de Mortarieu is found in several other of his portraits from this period, as well as earlier ones by Greuze. But the type goes back much further, at least to Botticelli and Raphael. The latter artist, whom Ingres esteemed above all others, used this format for his *Portrait of a Man* (c. 1502–1504, Liechtenstein Museum, Vienna), among other works. But Raphael also liked to set his figures—in religious paintings as well as portraits—against open skies. This airy and Romantic backdrop was used by the Renaissance artist in a number of pictures that were very familiar to Ingres, including *La Belle Jardinière* (1507, Musée du Louvre, Paris) and the *Madonna of the Goldfinch* (c. 1505–1506, Galleria degli Uffizi, Florence). Ingres used similar painted skies in the background of his portraits of Mademoiselle Caroline Rivière (fig. 11b) and *Madame Aymon* (also known as *La Belle Zélie*, 1806, Musée des Beaux-Arts, Rouen), as well as the present painting. The Rivière portraits (Ingres painted the father and mother in addition to the daughter), among the artist's very finest, may in fact have come about due to the intercession of the Vialètes de Mortarieu family.[3]

In his *Baron Joseph-Pierre Vialètes de Mortarieu* and other contemporary portraits, Ingres sought to extend the Davidian rhetoric first mastered five years before into the domain of contemporary portraiture. In these works, derived from Raphael and Greuze as well as David, the idealization of the human body is tempered by the inclusion of idiosyncrasies of anatomy and form so as create a new, hybrid person, neither classical nor entirely modern. De Mortarieu possesses the pride, serene comportment, and bon ton of an aristocrat who has never known of a French Revolution, yet also displays in his face the Romantic sensibility—heightened by the vivid summer sky in the background—of the modern man who knows the former world is gone and a new one beckons.

1 Delaborde, 1870, p. 262. In a set of notes compiled just before he left for Rome, Ingres listed the work as one of those recently completed.

2 Méras, 1967, p. 117.

3 Tinterow and Conisbee, 1999, p. 40.

12

Alexandre Abel de Pujol
French, 1785–1861

Portrait of a Magistrate
c. 1820

Oil on canvas, 39½ × 31⅞ in. (100.3 × 81 cm)
Signed lower left (on desk): "Abel de Pujol"
Numbered bottom right: "737"
M.1979.19.2

Provenance: [Artibus, Geneva, consigned by November 1978 to]; [Heim Gallery, London, sold 1979 to]; Norton Simon Art Foundation.

Exhibition: London, 1978, no. 15, ill.

Technical Notes: The support is a rather coarse, plain-weave canvas; it is unlined and tacked with its original tacks and hand-forged nails to the original stretcher. The canvas has been damaged by two tears: a right-angled tear at the lower center, at the bottom end of the rolled paper; and a diagonal tear at the lower left in the red robe. Both are repaired by patches glued to the reverse. The white ground is smooth and moderately thick, masking the canvas texture. A light golden-brown imprimatura covers the ground. The monochromatic background, painted in opaque paint with a smooth finish, was applied in multiple layers, wet into wet. A reserve left for the hair uses the imprimatura as the midtone, with black and gray strokes applied over it. In the face the imprimatura shapes the eye sockets and other shadowed parts. Flesh tones are painted with opaque, robust paint, as is the red cloak. The painting is well preserved despite some superficial losses. It has been selectively cleaned to reduce varnish in the flesh tones and all white areas, leaving a thick natural resin elsewhere. Retouching during two separate restorations includes an area on the left shoulder to cover cracks, a small amount of strengthening in the darks of the hair, small spots in the right sleeve and hand, and the diagonal tear at the lower left. The more recent retouching includes the tear at the lower center and contraction cracks at the left center background. The varnish is not significantly discolored, but differences in gloss are very distracting. (RW)

If one were to make an overall judgment about early-nineteenth-century French portraiture from this *Portrait of a Magistrate* by Alexandre Abel de Pujol, one would conclude that the genre was conservative, formulaic, and invariably idealizing. That view would be wrong—the works of Jacques-Louis David, J.-A.-D. Ingres, and Eugène Delacroix are cases in point—but Pujol's painting clearly suffers from an absence of verve. The painting is a stiff and sedate representation of a somewhat pompous man in late middle age. His advanced social and professional station—that of a judge or magistrate—may have determined his choice of painter and pose, but the modern viewer must lament the lack of personality and expression. Like the vast majority of surviving portraits from the period, this one represents an unidentified sitter. Efforts to determine his identity, based on what is probably the Salon catalogue number (737) pasted to the canvas in the lower right corner, have not so far been successful.

The identity of Abel de Pujol, however, is another matter. Born in 1785 as Alexandre-Denis Abel, he was the illegitimate son of an important artist and administrator, baron de la Grave, Pujol de Mortry, founder of the Academy of Painting and Sculpture in Valenciennes. Abel was admitted to David's studio as a scholarship student, won prizes at the Salons of 1806 and 1810, and received the coveted Prix de Rome in 1811. (This honor caused his father to recognize him and to give him his proper name.) Ill health caused him to return prematurely to France after only eight months in Rome (usually students remained at least two years), but Abel de Pujol immediately resumed his Salon career, winning the prize for history painting with his *Saint Stephen Preaching* in 1817 under the restored Bourbon regime of Louis XVIII.

For the next twenty-five years he worked as a successful painter of historical and religious subjects, executing ceiling paintings at the Louvre (*Egypt Saved by Joseph*, 1827) and frescoes for the chapel of St. Roch in the Church of St.-Sulpice in Paris. Yet Abel de Pujol's professional mainstay throughout much of his life was portraiture. The example here was obviously important enough either to the sitter or to the painter to demand a very high degree of finish and, perhaps, submission to a Salon. It is especially noteworthy today by virtue of its superb state of preservation. The canvas remains on its original stretcher; it has never been lined with glue, wax, or other adhesive; and its paint surface looks as fresh today as when the painting was made. The subtle gray tones beneath the skin, which invoke blood vessels and sagging musculature, are clearly visible and evocative of maturity and experience. That flesh, equally vivid in the treatment of the hands, is the best part of the picture. The portrait is in fact so perfectly preserved that we can observe Abel de Pujol making slight adjustments and alterations as he worked his brush across the surface of the canvas.

Although prominently signed "Abel de Pujol" on the magistrate's desk, the painting is neither inscribed nor dated. The sitter's costume, with its medals—a Maltese cross and a second, unidentified medallion—offers few clues in this regard: the uniforms and hats of French magistrates changed little in the nineteenth century, in spite of the rapid changes of government and political philosophy between 1806, when Pujol entered the scene, and 1861, when he departed it. However, the relatively painterly construction of this work, which recalls a tradition of color inaugurated by Peter Paul Rubens in the seventeenth century, suggests a date after 1820. A preparatory oil sketch of the same sitter—identical in format but approximately one-quarter the size of the finished picture—was recently auctioned in Paris.[1]

1 Paris, Drouot Richelieu, 28 June 2002, lot 172.

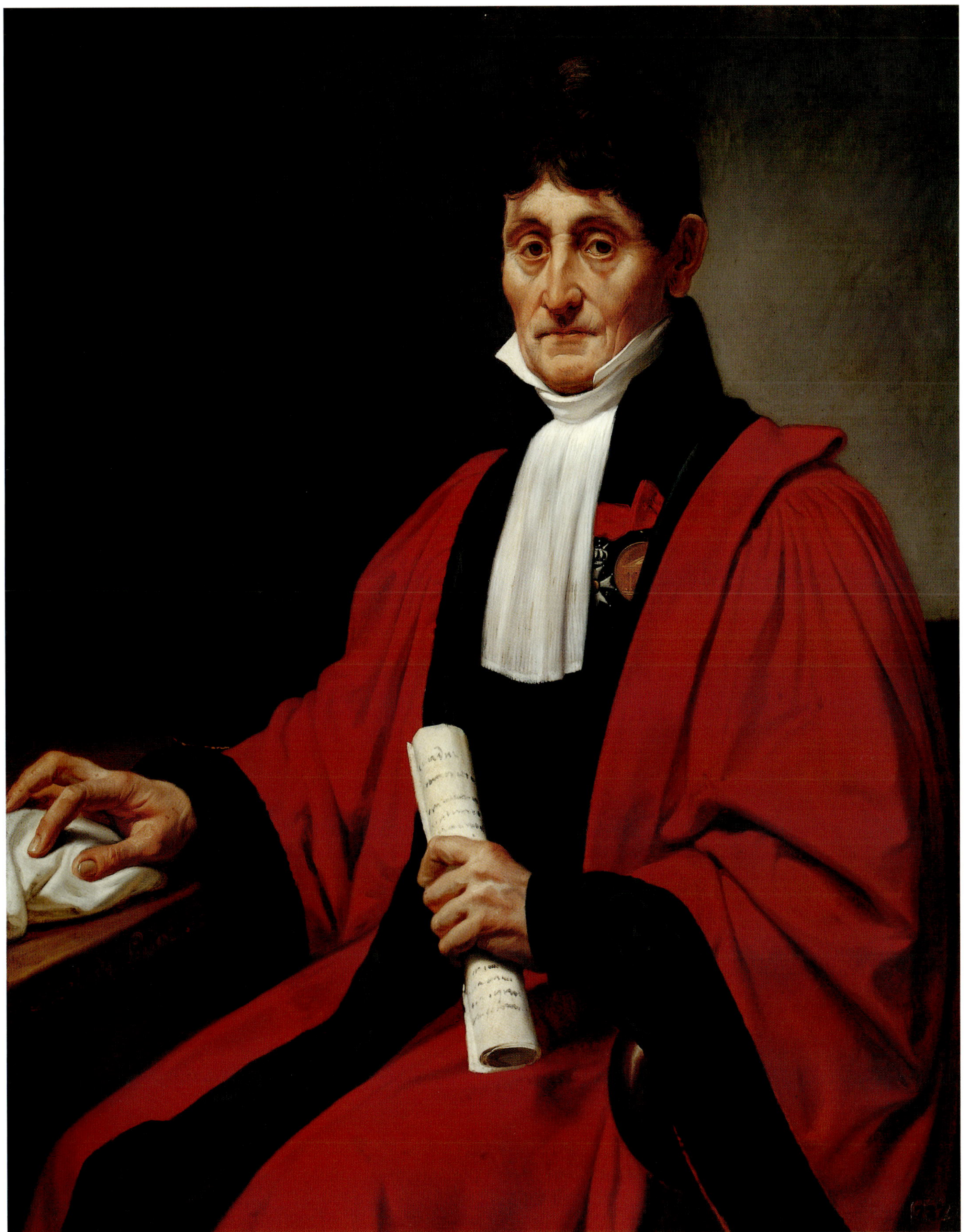

13

William Etty
English, 1787–1849

Study for "Leda and the Swan"
c. 1840

Oil on canvas, $16\frac{3}{4} \times 21$ in. (42.4×53.3 cm)
N.1964.14

Provenance: Sir Thomas Lawrence, P.R.A. (sale, London, Christie's, 19 June 1830, lot 341); Norton; Ralph Fletcher, Gloucester (sale, London, Christie's, 9 June 1838, lot 29, to); Artaria; G. T. Andrews (sale, London, Christie's, 31 May 1851, lot 82, to); Rogier; H. A. J. Munro of Novar; Percy Moore Turner, sold 1926 to; the earl of Sandwich, Hinchingbrooke; Amiya, countess of Sandwich (sale, London, Christie's, 20 November 1964, lot 54, to); [Thos. Agnew & Sons, London, on behalf of]; Norton Simon, bequest 1993 to; Jennifer Jones Simon Art Trust.

Exhibitions: London, 1934, no. 659, cat. no. 433, pl. CXXI; Manchester, 1934, no. 78; London, 1936b, no. 5; London, 1937b, no. 72; York, 1949, no. 1; London, 1955, no. 38.

References: Gaunt and Roe, 1943, p. 68, pl. 36; Farr, 1958, no. 68, pp. 62, 148, pl. 38a.

Technical Notes: The painting is on a heavy plain-weave fabric that has had its tacking edges removed. It is lined to a lighter-weight fabric with an aqueous adhesive. The 4-part keyable stretcher may or may not be original. A thick white ground does not quite fill the canvas weave. The artist laid out the design with dark brown paint. Leda is worked up to a high finish with carefully blended local colors, but highlights are thick and loosely applied. Most of the surrounding design is only partially worked up if at all. Paint is in good condition with few losses. The painting has a thin varnish that seems suitable. (JF)

Like the French artist J.-A.-D. Ingres, the young English painter William Etty was relentless in his desire to paint the nude female figure. Like the Frenchman too, he often clothed the figure in a diaphanous veil of allegory or history in order to have it both ways: he would at once gratify the prurience of male, heterosexual spectators and seize the proud mantle of the history painter. As his career advanced, however, the former practice almost wholly subsumed the latter ambition, and erotic desire triumphed over hypocrisy. By the mid-1830s Etty, who had been trained both at the Royal Academy of Arts in London (under Thomas Lawrence) and at the École des Beaux-Arts in Paris (under Jean-Baptiste Regnault), was producing explicit picture after explicit picture for a new clientele of merchants, manufacturers, and nobles who had little interest in classical subjects, or what the eighteenth-century English painter and pedagogue Joshua Reynolds called "the Grand Manner."

Many of Etty's works from the last two decades of his life, including *Study for a Magdalene* (c. 1845, Victoria and Albert Museum, London), *The Deluge* (fig. 13a), and the present picture purport to be preparations for larger works with religious, historical and mythological themes. A few others, such as *Female Nude in a Landscape* (c. 1830–1835, The J. Paul Getty Museum, Los Angeles), would appear to be studies for compositions derived from the Venetian painters Titian and Giorgione, who established the convention of placing fully nude, supine females in lush landscape settings. The high finish of the nude figures in all these works and the absence of any later, more definitive composition belie the idea that these are studies at all. They are instead finished paintings made marginally more respectable by association with historical subjects, and by an ostentatious display of *non finito.*

Study for "Leda and the Swan" depicts a robust, even muscular female nude in profile, nestled into a kind of curved mattress or cradle. Leda's head is inclined downward, her eyes are shaded, and her cheeks are flushed. Her hair is tied in a braid, though a thick lock covers her ear, and two broad, black wisps of either hair or ribbon flutter behind her head. Her legs are drawn up with knees parted and ankles crossed. Her right arm is casually slung across her left knee, and her extended left arm falls away from her body. To the left of the figure, a

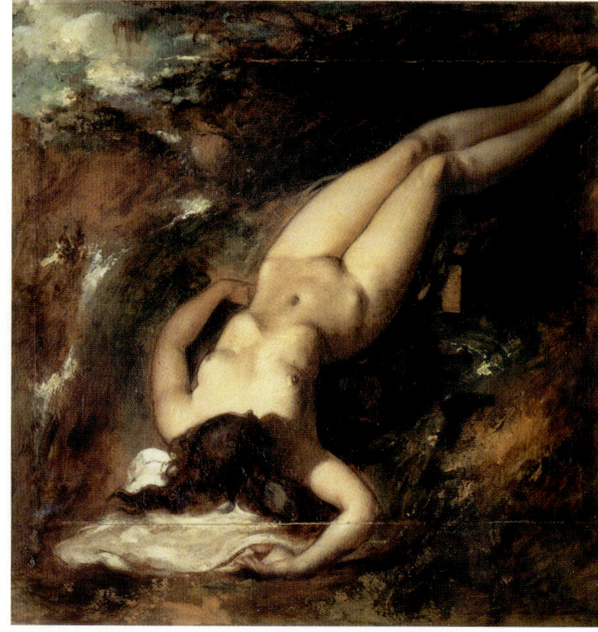

Fig. 13a William Etty, *The Deluge*, c. 1835–1845, oil on canvas, 25×27 in. (63.5×68.6 cm), Victoria and Albert Museum, London

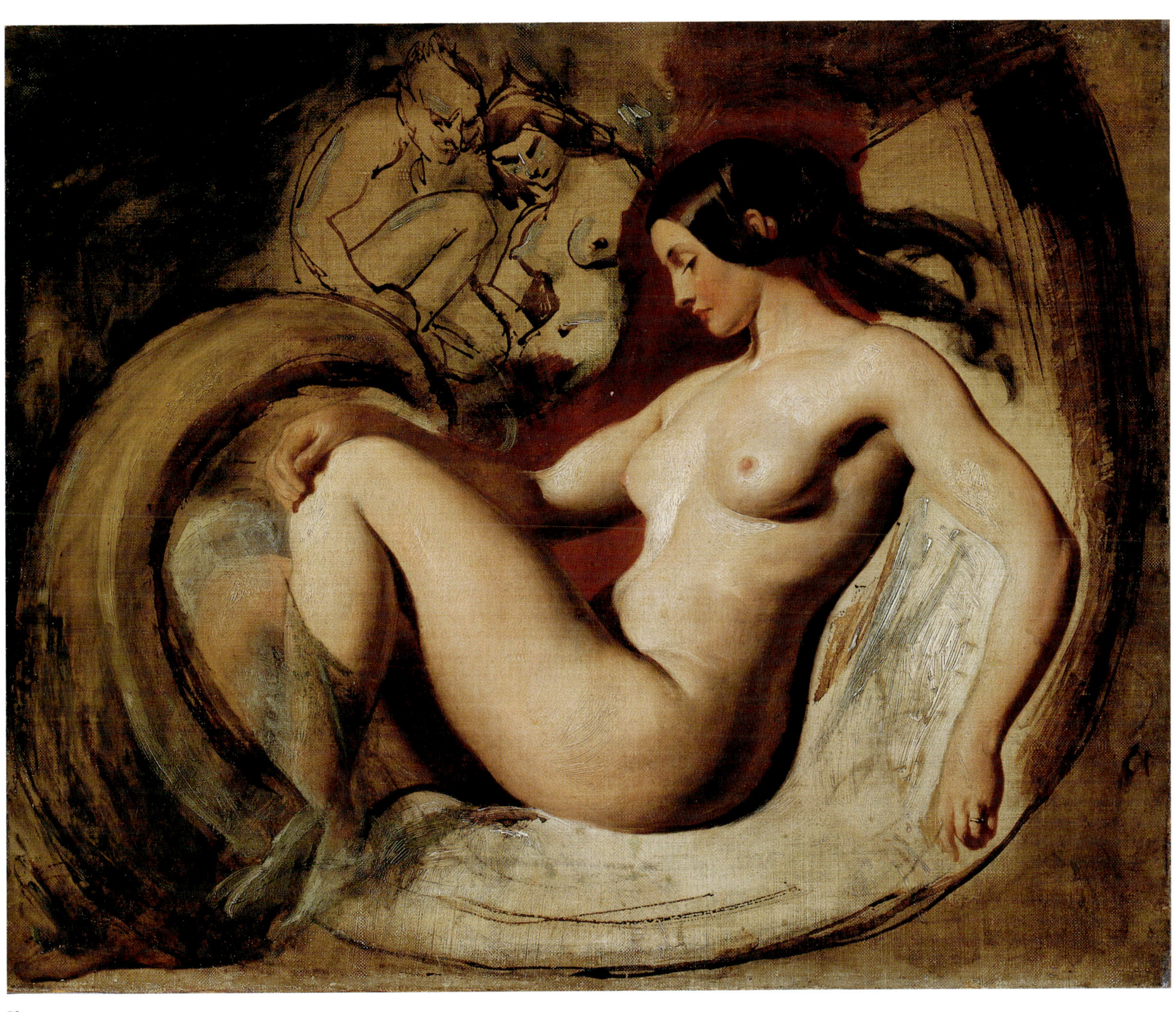

13

Fig. 13b After Michelangelo, *Leda and the Swan*, after 1530, oil on canvas, $41\frac{1}{2} \times 55\frac{1}{2}$ in. (105.4 × 141 cm), National Gallery, London; photo: Alinari / Art Resource, NY

great arching form, like the tail of a giant snake—though it must be meant to be the stylized head and neck of the swan—rises from near the nude's feet to the middle of her right forearm. Its tapered tip points downward, toward her opened thighs. Just above and to the left of the nude are the painted outlines of a pair of seated grotesque figures, one, at the left, with the pointed ears of a faun, and the other, at right, with the large breasts and swollen nipples of a witch. They leer at the nude and the unnatural coupling between god and mortal that will soon take place, or that has just concluded.

The figure is by far the most resolved part of the picture, with only the right leg and left calf and foot incomplete. Both feet are loosely sketched with gray-white paint, and at least three positions have been outlined. After the figure was nearly completed, a red background was added, giving greater relief to the head, right arm, and left leg. The grotesque figures above and the serpent-swan were similarly added after the figure was nearly finished. The upper left, lower right, and upper right corners of the painting might have been roughly brushed in by a later hand; they appear to exhibit a different application of paint: thin, directionless, and vague in color.

The subject of Leda and the Swan derives from Greek mythology and the Roman poet Ovid's *Metamorphoses*; the latter would certainly have been Etty's literary source, if he needed one. Many artists before Etty depicted the story of the mortal daughter of Thestius, wife of Tyndareus, raped by the god Zeus in the form of a swan. The best-known depictions are by Leonardo da Vinci, Michelangelo, Correggio, and François Boucher. Etty himself made a drawing of a female nude and a swan (c. 1830–1835, Courtauld Institute, London) some years before; its format, with a standing female figure in *contrapposto* pose gazing down with longing at a swan, is generally derived from Leonardo's famous composition, known from a copy by Cesare da Sesto owned by the earl of Pembroke, at Wilton House, Salisbury. Etty's painting, however, is more likely derived from the *Leda and the Swan* of Michelangelo (fig. 13b), again known from a copy, this time by an anonymous artist. The painting must have been well known to Etty, since it was donated by the duke of Northumberland to the National Gallery in London in 1838. Etty may have been intrigued by

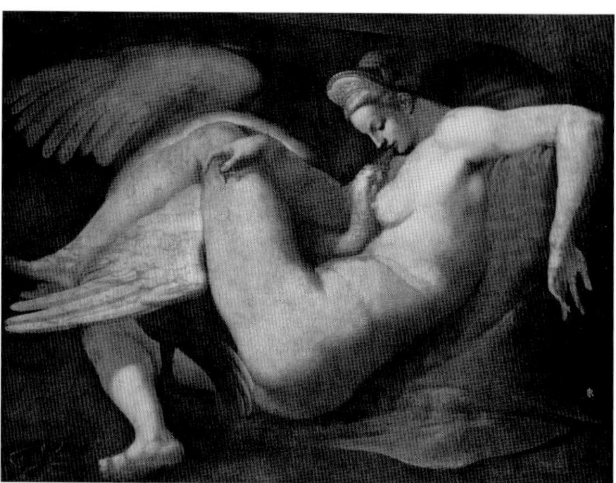

Giorgio Vasari's account of the Leda in the latter's *Lives*. There, the picture was described as the product of a great number of "designs and cartoons" and endowed with the "breath" of life.[1] Vasari added that the bulk of these studies had disappeared, and that the loss was "incalculable." The English painter may have felt challenged to produce his own study for a Leda and thus remedy, to some extent, the historic loss.

The greatest mystery presented by the painting is the identity of the grotesque figures above and to the left of the nude. They are certainly not the Dioscuri, Castor and Pollux, just hatched from the egg laid (improbably enough) by Leda after her impregnation by Zeus. Nor are they likely to be Helen and Clytemnestra, the former being the third offspring from the unholy pairing, and the latter being Leda's legitimate daughter from her marriage to Tyndareus. No doubt, each of these two women was indirectly or directly responsible for a litany of subsequent Greek horrors, but neither figure in Etty's painting can plausibly be "the face that launched a thousand ships." In all likelihood, the grotesque beings are mere caprices on the part of Etty, inspired by his reflection on the strange and brutal tale of a young woman raped by a superhuman bird. In any case, neither these figures, the swan-snake, nor the roughly painted-in background provides much distraction from the fevered nude that is the artist's preoccupation here and in dozens of similar, contemporaneous works.

1 Vasari, 1912–1915, vol. 9, p. 50.

14

Horace Vernet
French, 1789–1863

A Soldier on the Field of Battle
1818

Oil on canvas, $18^{1}/_{16} \times 21^{5}/_{8}$ in. (46 × 55 cm)
M.1977.26.3

Provenance: Louis-Philippe, duc d'Orléans, later king of the French, Château de Neuilly, by 1818[?]–1848. Private collection, England. [Établissement Rustique, Vaduz, Liechtenstein, consigned to]; [Heim Gallery, Ltd., London, sold 1977 to]; Norton Simon Art Foundation.

Exhibition: Paris, 1822, no. XIX, as *Un Grenadier sur le champ de bataille.*

References: Jouy and Jay, 1822, pp. 93–100; Vatout and Quénot, 1826, vol. 4, pp. 299–302; Réveil, 1828–1834, vol. 5, 1829, no. 359; Ruutz-Rees, 1880, p. 9; Dayot, 1898, pp. 127, 198–201; de Bona, 1900?, p. 281.

Technical Notes: The coarse plain-weave fabric has irregular size threads and is commercially prepared with a thick cream-colored ground. In the proprietary stamp on the reverse only "Bedot" is legible. The 5-part butt-join stretcher is original, but the painting was restretched at some later time. The commercial ground seeps through to the reverse and is visible since the painting remains unlined. A second lighter and thicker ground covers only the design area. The large-interval cracks are typical of this type of ground. Following academic practice, the scene was sketched with dark brown paint. The artist applied medium-rich paints directly but retained the dark underpainting to create shadows. The condition is very good, but there have been some scattered losses and abrasions, and in the central scene some colors are blanched. The thick varnish saturates the dark colors. In ultraviolet light an earlier, partially removed varnish fluoresces green. (JF)

In 1819 the French painter Horace Vernet exhibited some two dozen paintings at the Salon. They were a remarkably varied lot, attesting to the artist's virtuosity, self-confidence, and vaunting ambition. His submission included history paintings, portraits, genre scenes, marines, and a few works that combined history and genre, including *Molière consultant sa servante* (*Molière Consulting His Servant*) (location unknown) and *Un Grenadier français sur le champ de bataille* (*A French Grenadier on the Field of Battle*). The latter painting—too small and anecdotal to be a history painting and too historical to be a genre scene—was a great success, eliciting critical encomia and finding an immediate buyer, in fact, three buyers. The eminent duc d'Orléans, the future Louis-Philippe, king of France from 1830 to 1848, purchased the painting in 1818, even before its public exhibition, and a year later, two other versions of the picture were sold to a M. Lariboissière and the duc de Liancourt, each for the healthy sum of 1,500 francs. In that year, Vernet also sold to another artist the rights to make a painted copy of the *Grenadier* and to the engraver Aumont the rights to make an engraving of the work.

Vernet's *Soldier on the Field of Battle* depicts a *grenadier à pied*, or Napoleonic foot soldier, after a battle has ended. He may be recognized as such by his *habit veste*, a double-breasted Spencer jacket (here somewhat longer than usual) buttoned to the waist with rectangular lapels and short epaulets. Vernet's *grenadier* appears to have removed his gaiters and boots, permitting his ankles and wounded foot to be visible. In place of his usual musket and bayonet, he holds a shovel, the tool with which he had been burying some of the unnumbered dead of battle. The French *grenadiers* at Waterloo, led by Brigade Commanders Petit and Morvan, were first in the order of battle, and thousands of these foot soldiers must have fallen during the epochal hours of 18 June 1815. Vernet's soldier sits dejectedly on a mound of earth, surrounded by the shattered paraphernalia of battle and the detritus of death. His wounded right leg and bandaged foot are extended, and his left leg is bent to support his left elbow. He rests his head on his hand in the posture of the melancholic or bereaved, as represented by the artist's friend Théodore Géricault in his figure of the grieving father at the lower left of the contemporaneous *Raft of the Medusa* (1819, Musée du Louvre, Paris). There are also echoes here of other mourning figures from acclaimed French paintings of the recent past, including Pierre-Narcisse Guérin's *Return of Marius Sextus* (1799, Musée du Louvre, Paris) and Jacques-Louis David's *Lictors Returning to Brutus the Bodies of His Two Dead Sons* (1789, Musée du Louvre, Paris).

Vernet may also have been affected by Géricault's powerful and sympathetic representations of wounded Napoleonic soldiers, such as the lithograph *The Retreat from Russia* (1818) and the wash drawing of the same title (fig. 14a). Like Vernet's painting, the latter drawing depicts a wounded figure in the uniform of a *grenadier*, facing right and seated on a mound. It should be recalled that Vernet and Géricault belonged to the same community of liberals who championed the cause of the defeated emperor. Their studios were just doors apart on the rue des Martyrs in Montmartre, and they shared propinquity and friendship with such former Napoleonic officers and Waterloo veterans as Colonel Louis Bro.[1]

Fig. 14a (*right*) Théodore Géricault, *The Retreat from Russia*, c. 1814, watercolor on paper, $9\frac{7}{8} \times 8\frac{1}{4}$ in. (25 × 21 cm), Musée des Beaux-Arts, Rouen; © Réunion des Musées Nationaux / Art Resource, NY

Fig. 14b (*below*) Théodore Géricault, *Study of Severed Limbs*, 1818, oil on canvas, $21\frac{3}{8} \times 25\frac{1}{4}$ in. (54 × 64 cm), Musée Fabre, Montpellier

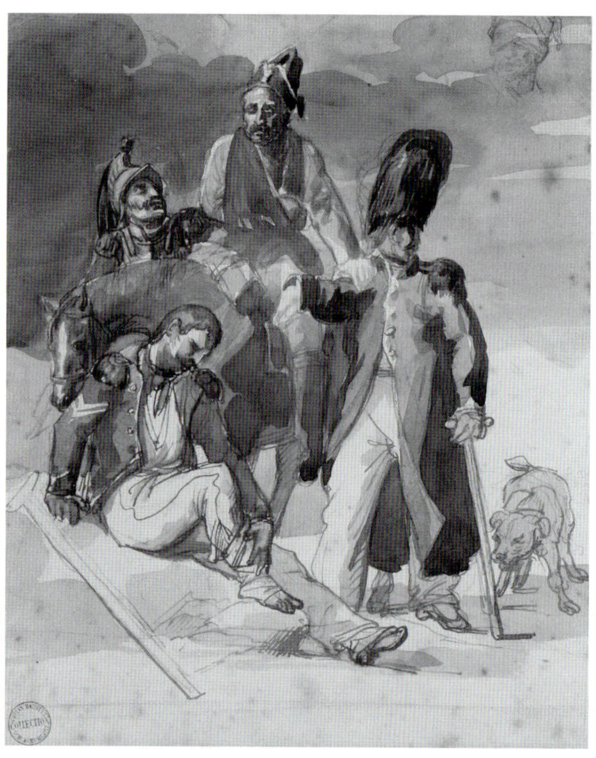

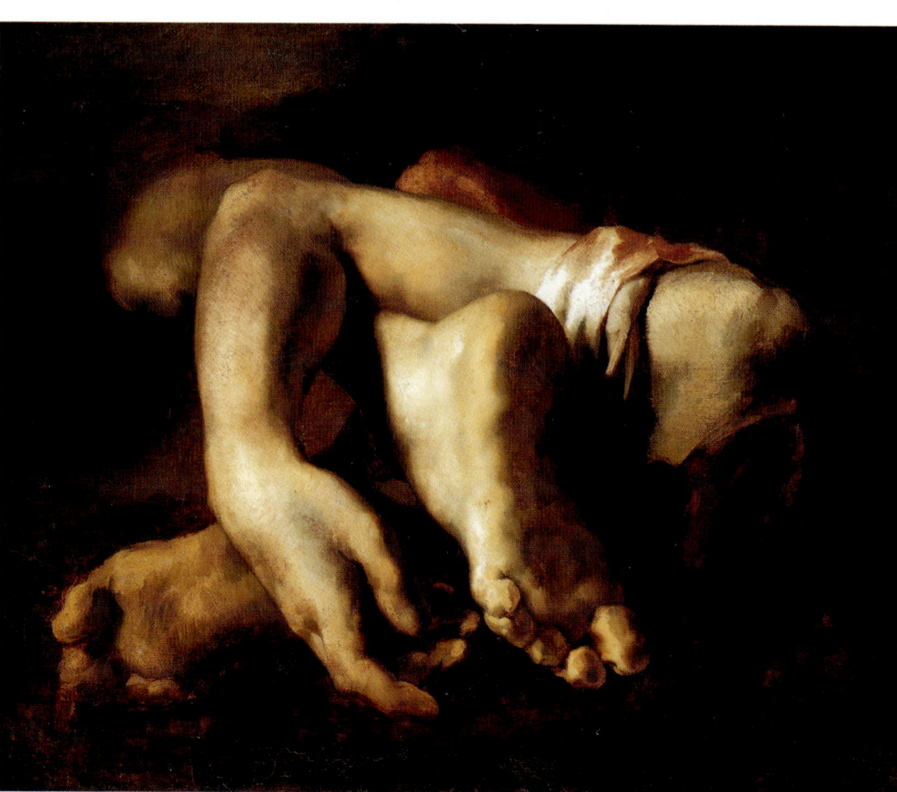

It is thus entirely likely that each artist saw the other's works in progress, exchanged ideas, and shared the same models. The dissected body parts—hands, legs, and heads—that Géricault famously brought to his studio in 1818 while at work on the *Raft*, and which were the subject of a series of macabre *natures mortes* (fig. 14b), may have been the basis for Vernet's own depiction of limbs in *A Soldier on the Field of Battle*. Vernet's interest in the morbid and funereal is also evident in a contemporaneous pencil and sepia wash drawing, similar in composition to the present picture, called *The Soldier's Grave* (The Wallace Collection, London).

There is no question that Vernet intended his painting to deeply touch the feelings of its audience. It is vividly colored with green grasses below and at right. Red, bloody wounds are visible on the foot and thigh of the principal soldier, corpses are shown sprawled in the background, and in the foreground, below the seated *grenadier*, is the partly buried body of another foot soldier that is visible by its knees, both hands, and head. The picture clearly mixes the elegiac and the grotesque, elements that would soon be the expressive basis of the Romantic dramas and novels of Victor Hugo. The redemptive image of the cross in the left background, however, claimed as a symbol by the restored Bourbon monarchy, diminished any incendiary effect the work otherwise might have had. (At this time, the mere public proclamation of the heroism of Napoleon could land the speaker in jail.) Pathos, alienation, horror, the sheer uselessness of carnage, and Christian redemption—these, rather than Napoleonic ardor and Revolutionary virtue—are the principal sentiments generated by Vernet's *Soldier on the Field of Battle*. The contemporary critic who praised Vernet's painting for its "grandeur and simplicity" and who claimed that "all eyes become moistened with tears when they fix upon this composition" likely grasped its ecumenical intent.[2]

Emboldened by his successes, Vernet in 1822 submitted to the Salon jury an ensemble of seven paintings certain to antagonize the Bourbon regime of Louis XVIII. These included the *Battle of Jemappes* (1819, National Gallery, London), depicting the Revolutionary General Dumouriez and his troops defeating the Austrians in 1892, the *Defense of the Gate of Clichy* (Musée du Louvre, Paris), a Napoleonic subject, and *A Soldier on the Field of*

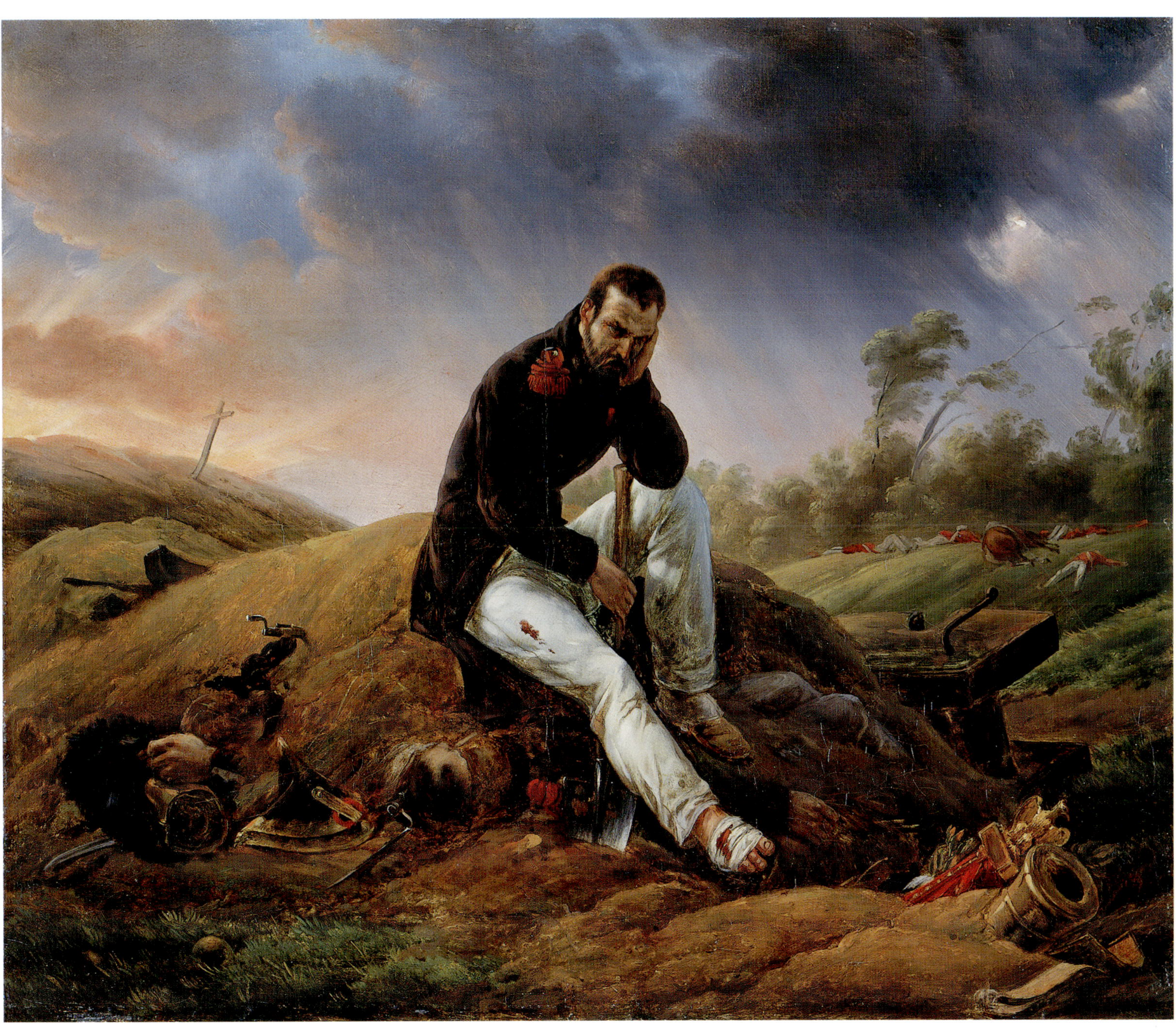

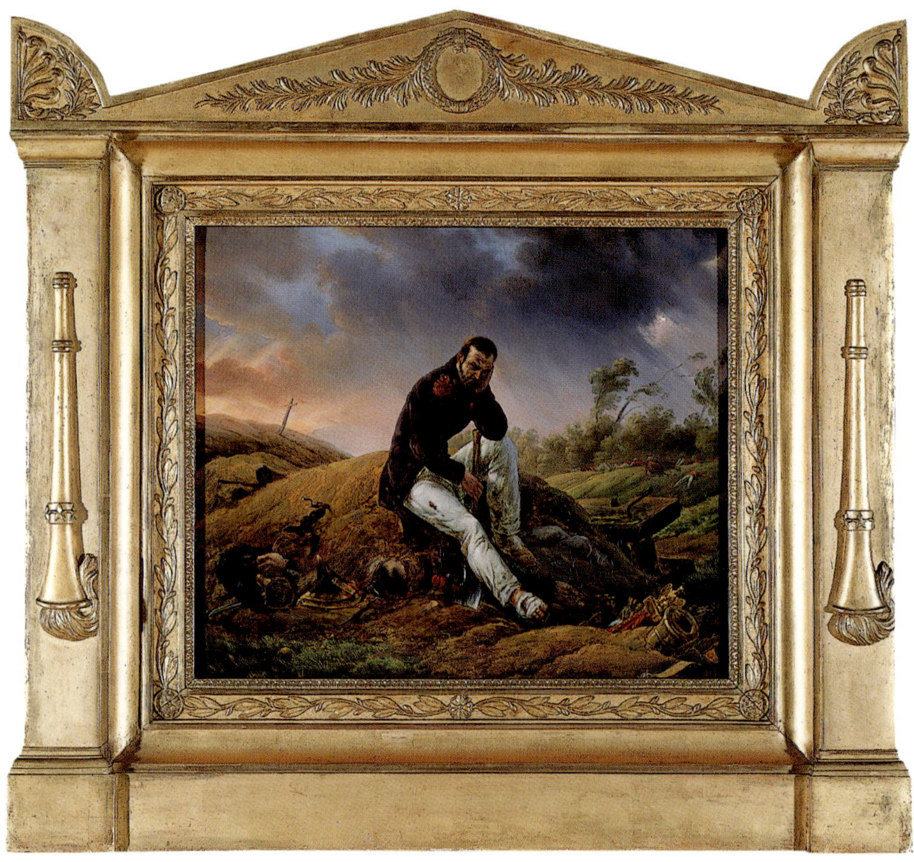

Fig. 14c Cat. 14, in its frame.

Battle. The jury rejected the seven, prompting Vernet to mount at his own studio a retrospective exhibition of forty-five works, including the offending pictures. This exhibition, perhaps the first Salon des Refusés in the history of art, was a genuine scandal and received considerable publicity. "Who can see it," wrote one critic, "without being brought to tears by the heartbreaking expression of this figure, and by the sight of the simple wooden cross which indicates the tomb of the soldiers of the Fatherland!"[3] "The sun is setting," wrote another, "and its last rays illumine the scene. The warrior, overcome with fatigue, after having buried his comrades and friends, gives a last sigh to his banners, a last thought to glory."[4]

Within a few years of his atelier exhibition, Vernet was embraced by the Bourbon king Charles X, and vice versa. He received numerous royal commissions, was made an officer of the Legion of Honor in 1825, and appointed director of the French Academy in Rome in 1828. In addition, the support Vernet had received from the duc d'Orléans in the late 1810s and 1820s ensured the painter's continued success when the duke became King Louis-Philippe after the July Revolution of 1830. For the remainder of his career, Vernet painted history pictures, Orientalist scenes, and portraits in an eclectic style, combining elements of Neoclassicism and Romanticism in a mélange that gratified *juste-milieu* sensibilities.

It is not clear which of the two surviving versions of *A Soldier on the Field of Battle* is in the Norton Simon Museum, although the caliber of the frame (fig. 14c) suggests that the picture was owned by a prestigious patron. Comparison of the present painting with old, lithographed and engraved copies of the version owned by the duc d'Orléans suggests that they may be the same, but the evidence is not conclusive. Documentation that accompanied another version of work as it passed through the art market in the mid-1980s indicates that it may be the picture formerly in the collection of the duke, but here too there are evident ambiguities. Ultimately, the precise provenance of the Norton Simon picture does not matter. Both it and the last-mentioned canvas are by Vernet, both attest at once to the impact of Géricault and the legacy of Napoleon, and both reveal the ambitions and talents of a celebrated artist eager to make his way in rapidly changing Restoration France.

1 Boime, 2004, p. 124.

2 *Lettres à David sur le Salon de 1819 par quelques élèves*, Paris, 1819, p. 103.

3 Jouy and Jay, 1822, p. 95.

4 Réveil, 1828–1834, vol. 5, 1829, no. 359.

15

Claude-Marie Dubufe
French, 1790–1864

Memories
1826–1827

Oil on canvas, oval, stretcher dimensions $36\frac{1}{4} \times 47$ in. (92.1×119.3 cm)
Signed lower left: "Dubufe"
N. 1978.07.1.2

Provenance: (Sale, Paris, Palais d'Orsay, 13 June 1978, lot 17, ill., as *L'Attente*, to); [Galerie Cailleux, Paris, on behalf of]; Norton Simon, bequest 1993 to; Jennifer Jones Simon Art Trust.

Exhibition: Paris, 1827, no. 1459, as *Le Souvenir.*

References: Lacambre, 1975, p. 404; Bréon, 1988, pp. 48, 68, 70, 66, ill.; Whiteley, 1996, p. 331.

Technical Notes: The original support, a fine, medium-weight, plain-weave fabric, is lined with wax-resin adhesive to a heavy, plain-weave canvas. It is tacked to a 6-part wood butt-join stretcher with crossbars and all 12 keys in place. The stretcher of crude manufacture was on the painting when lined in 1982. The artist painted the scene in an oval, leaving the corners with only the commercially applied cream-colored ground and some dabs of paint and sketching. Originally the center of each side had a shallow rectangular projection about 14 inches wide so that the shape of the canvas was cruciform. At some time the tacking edges on either side of the projections were turned out and the stretcher was given its rectangular shape. Academically painted, the design was laid in with a brownish color and then worked up with parallel strokes that remain visible, especially in the woman's arm. The numerous mixtures of flesh color painted wet in wet give the modeling. The red curtain was painted with a more fluid paint that does not show brushstrokes. First a midtone was laid in and then highlights and shadows, the latter using deep red mixed with black. Other than repositioning the gold chain, only minor adjustments exist. The condition is good but there are serious contraction cracks, especially in the central part of the picture, which were toned at various stages. While the artist may have toned some of those cracks, ultravliolet light reveals obvious later restorations of the contraction cracks as well as some minor damages. The painting was cleaned, lined, and varnished with Acryloid B72 in 1982. (JF)

16

Claude-Marie Dubufe
French, 1790–1864

Regrets
1826–1827

Oil on canvas, oval, stretcher dimensions $36\frac{1}{4} \times 46\frac{3}{4}$ in. (92.1×118.8 cm)
Signed lower right: "Dubufe"
N.1978.07.1.1

Provenance: (Sale, Paris, Palais d'Orsay, 13 June 1978, lot 17, ill., as *La Deception*, to); [Galerie Cailleux, Paris, on behalf of]; Norton Simon, bequest 1993 to; Jennifer Jones Simon Art Trust.

Exhibition: Paris, 1827, no. 1460.

References: Lacambre, 1975, p. 404; Bréon, 1988, pp. 48, 68, 70, 67, ill.; Whiteley, 1996, p. 331.

Technical Notes: The original support, a fine, medium-weight, plain-weave fabric, is lined with wax resin to a heavy, plain-weave canvas. It is tacked to a 6-part butt-join stretcher with crossbars and all 12 keys in place. The stretcher of crude manufacture was on the painting when lined in 1982. The artist painted the scene in an oval leaving the corners with only the commercially applied cream-colored ground and some dabs of paint and sketching. The center of each side originally had a shallow rectangular projection about 14 inches wide, giving the canvas a cruciform shape. However, at some time the tacking edges on either side of the projections were turned out and the stretcher was given its rectangular shape. Academically painted, the design was laid in with a brownish color and then worked up in some cases to a high finish as in the flesh. Numerous mixtures of flesh tones worked wet in wet with a fine brush helped to achieve the careful modeling. The condition is good but there are serious contraction cracks, especially in the central part of the picture that have been toned at various stages. In fact, it appears that the artist may have toned some of those cracks, but ultraviolet light reveals obvious later restorations of the contraction cracks as well as some minor damages. The painting was cleaned, lined, and varnished with Acryloid B72 in 1982. (JF)

Claude-Marie Dubufe was among the numerous late followers of Jacques-Louis David who navigated the troubled waters of French art in the decades following the master's death in 1825. Born in Paris into a distinguished diplomatic family, the nineteen-year-old Dubufe was on the verge of being sent on a diplomatic venture to America when he was identified by David as a promising painter. The young man remained in Paris and inaugurated a highly successful artistic career, exhibiting at the annual Salons from 1810 until the end of his life in

1864. This pair of paintings was submitted to the Salon of 1827, where they appear in the first supplement of the immense exhibition's catalogue. The year 1827 was crucial for Dubufe; he included not only this pair of moralizing erotic paintings but also ten other canvases, four overdoor paintings representing Egypt, Greece, Italy, and France for the Conseil d'État,[1] a religious painting, *Deliverance of Saint Peter*,[2] a pair of religious paintings devoted to Adam and Eve and Paradise Lost,[3] and three painted studies of sleep, awakening, and a head of an evangelist.[4] These demonstrated the range of his imagery, which encompassed religious, historical, and genre subjects.

Memories and *Regrets* represent a gorgeous dark-haired model dressed only in a filmy negligee and arranged full scale on a beautifully dressed bed in front of contrasting dark red curtains. The erotic allure of the model is beyond dispute, and the painting predicts in many ways the novels, plays, operas, and paintings of the Second Empire that deal forthrightly with high-class prostitution and its effect on contemporary society. The narrative cycle is not hard to decipher. A young woman looks into the eyes of her lover, represented in *Memories* by a painted miniature in a locket attached to a thick and very long gold chain that takes on the slithering characteristics of a snake. The quality of absorption in her pictorial devotion is complete, and the viewer is freed by Dubufe to examine without guilt her breasts, the tiny hairs on the nape of her neck, her plump hands, and her beauty marks. Yet, in the second picture, she clutches the miniature in her hand while looking heavenward with eyes red and wet from crying. She has been deserted by the very lover she strove to adore in the first painting and is completely alone. Dubufe seems to have noticed every small detail of her suffering, and the careful viewer of the painting can see that the almost imperceptible blue arteries in her breasts in *Memories* have become engorged in *Regrets* so that they mar the perfection of her skin. The two paintings seem almost to revive the erotic genre tradition perfected in the second half of the eighteenth century by Jean-Baptiste Greuze. Yet, Dubufe used the techniques of the Davidians to update these conventions.

This narrative pairing of states of desire and disappointment was relatively new in French painting in 1827, and Dubufe's gorgeously painted pair was immediately taken up by the popular press. Several copies survive, some by other hands, and numerous prints after the pairing were made in 1827 and 1828.[5] The great French writer Stendhal is even reported to have found copies of the pair in the hostels for foreigners in Rome.[6] Dubufe himself was an upstanding married man and father in 1827 when he painted these salacious paintings, and clearly the moralism of their narrative stance made it possible for the paintings to slip under the bar of official censorship or critical approbation. They were not, however, acquired by the State, and, despite their immense popularity in their time, there is no evidence, either physical or documentary, about their original ownership. They arrived in California only in 1978, and Norton Simon was their first recorded owner more than 150 years after they titillated French audiences at the Salon and in taverns and print collections throughout Europe in the years following that exhibition.

There are many areas in both paintings with craquelure that contrasts with that of the painting as a whole, suggesting that these are indeed Dubufe's original 1827 Salon paintings. These areas suggest that the artist made numerous small alterations of contour and color while working on the paintings, which, in spite of a rather crude wax lining and inpainting of the craquelure, have a surface vitality that makes it easy for us to understand why they alone among Dubufe's twelve submissions to the Salon of 1827 became famous. One almost wonders whether Édouard Manet had a copy of one of the prints in the late 1850s and early 1860s, when he investigated issues of modern morality and sexual desire with even greater élan.

1 Paris, 1827, p. 16 in the Salon catalogue, without numbers.

2 Paris, 1827, no. 550.

3 Nos. 1640–1641.

4 Nos. 1642–1644.

5 A pair is in the collection of the Norton Simon Art Foundation.

6 Bréon, 1988, p. 48.

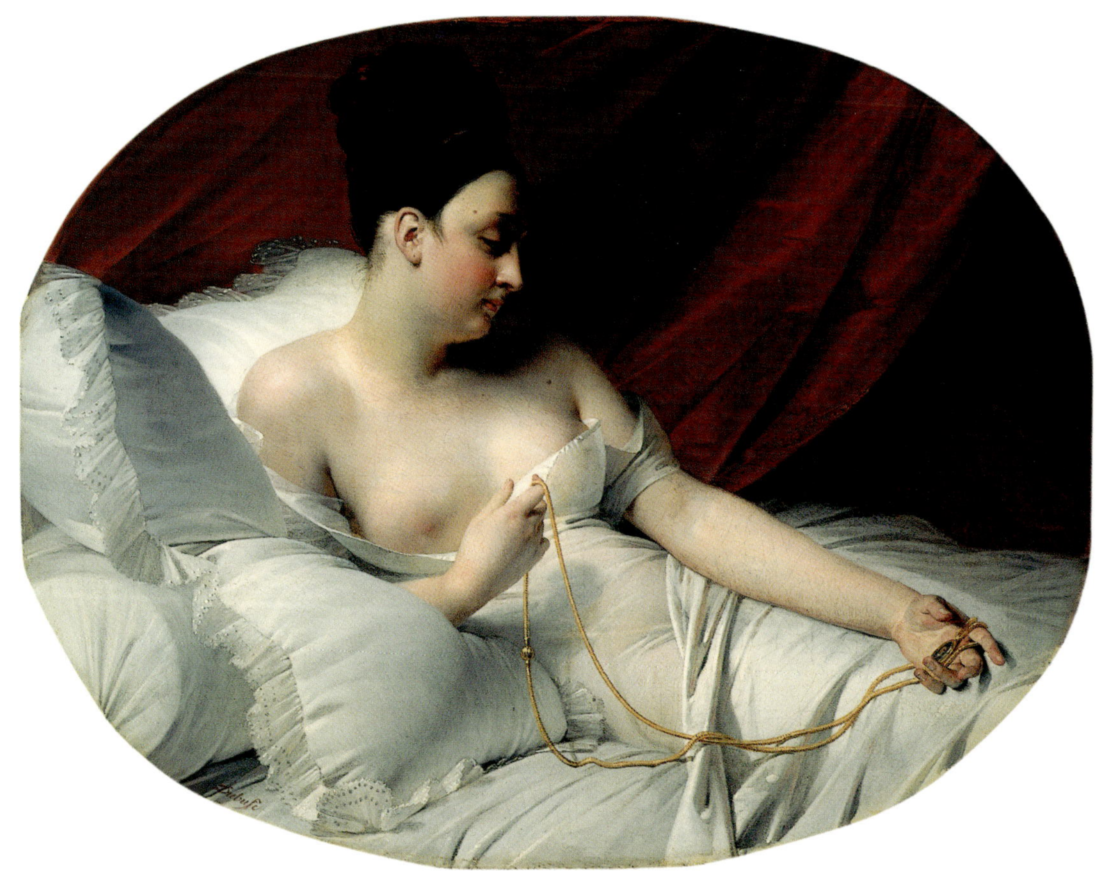

15

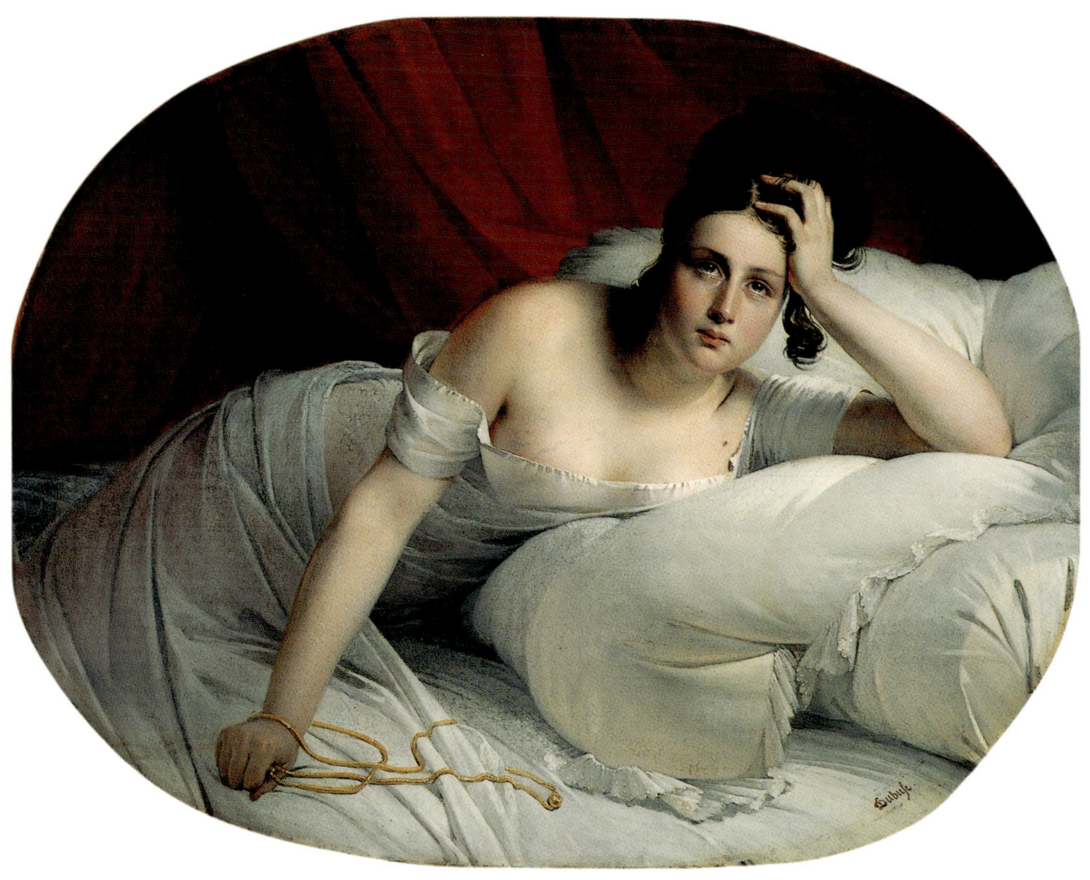

16

17

CLAUDE-MARIE DUBUFE
French, 1790–1864

Portrait of a Young Woman
c. 1843

Oil on canvas, 51⅛ × 38⅜ inches (129.8 × 97.3 cm)
Signed lower right: "Dubufe"
M.1977.13.2

PROVENANCE: Private collection, Paris; [Établissement Rustique, Vaduz, Liechtenstein; consigned to]; [Heim Gallery Ltd., London, sold 1977 to]; Norton Simon Art Foundation.

REFERENCE: Bréon, 1988, p. 118, ill.

TECHNICAL NOTES: The original plain-weave canvas is lined with an aqueous adhesive to fabric. Its tacking edges are partially removed. The canvas has a medium thick, off-white ground. The artist laid out the scene with dark red paint brushed in the areas of shadow, visible in the region of the eyes, for example. In the background the artist daubed on gray with a thick brush so that the brown underlayer shows, and he worked gray openly over a vermilion-colored layer. The texture of the dress fabric was achieved by the scumbling of gray over black. The face paint was worked wet into wet to create a fairly finished surface, and the individual hairs on the lady's head were picked out with a fine brush. The artist made some changes in the position of forms; these are especially visible with infrared. The hands were repositioned and the vase was moved from the right edge to its present location. These pentimentti were toned at some point to make them less visible, and some of this toning may even be by the artist. Contraction cracks in some areas may have been repainted by the artist, notably in the vertical center of the dress. A textural line runs along the left edge of the canvas, about 2 inches in, indicating that it may have been folded over at one time. This edge was almost completely repainted at a considerably later time. Ultraviolet light reveals numerous restorations in the face, possibly hiding surface abrasions. Nevertheless, the picture seems in fairly good state. The fine-to-medium crackle pattern is not disturbing. The varnish appears to be natural resin and relatively recent. (JF)

WHEN THIS PAINTING was first published in 1988, it was identified as a portrait of a "Young English Woman" and dated "about 1843."[1] Unfortunately, there is no evidence either to corroborate or to deny these two slight facts, and we have no idea who she is and when or where she sat for this elegant portrait. Such large portraits were relatively common among the upper-middle class in both Paris and London during the mid-nineteenth century, and, if one could not afford to sit for J.-A.-D. Ingres, his contemporary Claude-Marie Dubufe was an acceptable alternative. This attractive young woman is shown in a darkened interior with heavy furniture, three bound books, a Chinese porcelain vase with a gilded bronze base, a branch of small pink roses, and a vast red damask drapery. She is calm, beautifully modeled, and dressed entirely in black silk trimmed with lace. Her only jewelry is a heavy gold bracelet with a three-part attachment that dangles from her wrist. Her brown hair is superbly, but modestly, dressed and is painted with a care that even her hairdresser might admire. She is thus utterly correct and utterly unremarkable. Were she not in what must have been the black of mourning (has she lost her father, mother, or young husband?), we would take this to be a portrait advertising her availability for marriage, and, as if to prove this true, she seems to play with the wedding ring finger of her left hand. If ever a portrait was *juste milieu,* it is this one. It embodies the social, political, and artistic balance sought by most artists, writers, and ideologues during the regime of the Citizen King, Louis-Philippe (1830–1848).

The painting is in a fine state of preservation. It seems to have been painted confidently and without incident. The only changes that Dubufe made in the working process were to lower the contours of the red drapery to the right of the figure to give greater emphasis to the books and to adjust the positions of the hands and vase. Otherwise, Dubufe seems to have had few problems with this utterly unproblematic sitter. Was she English? If so, it would not be surprising, since Dubufe was one of the first generation of French painters who sent work for public exhibition in both London and New York in addition to his native Paris.

1 Bréon, 1988, p. 118.

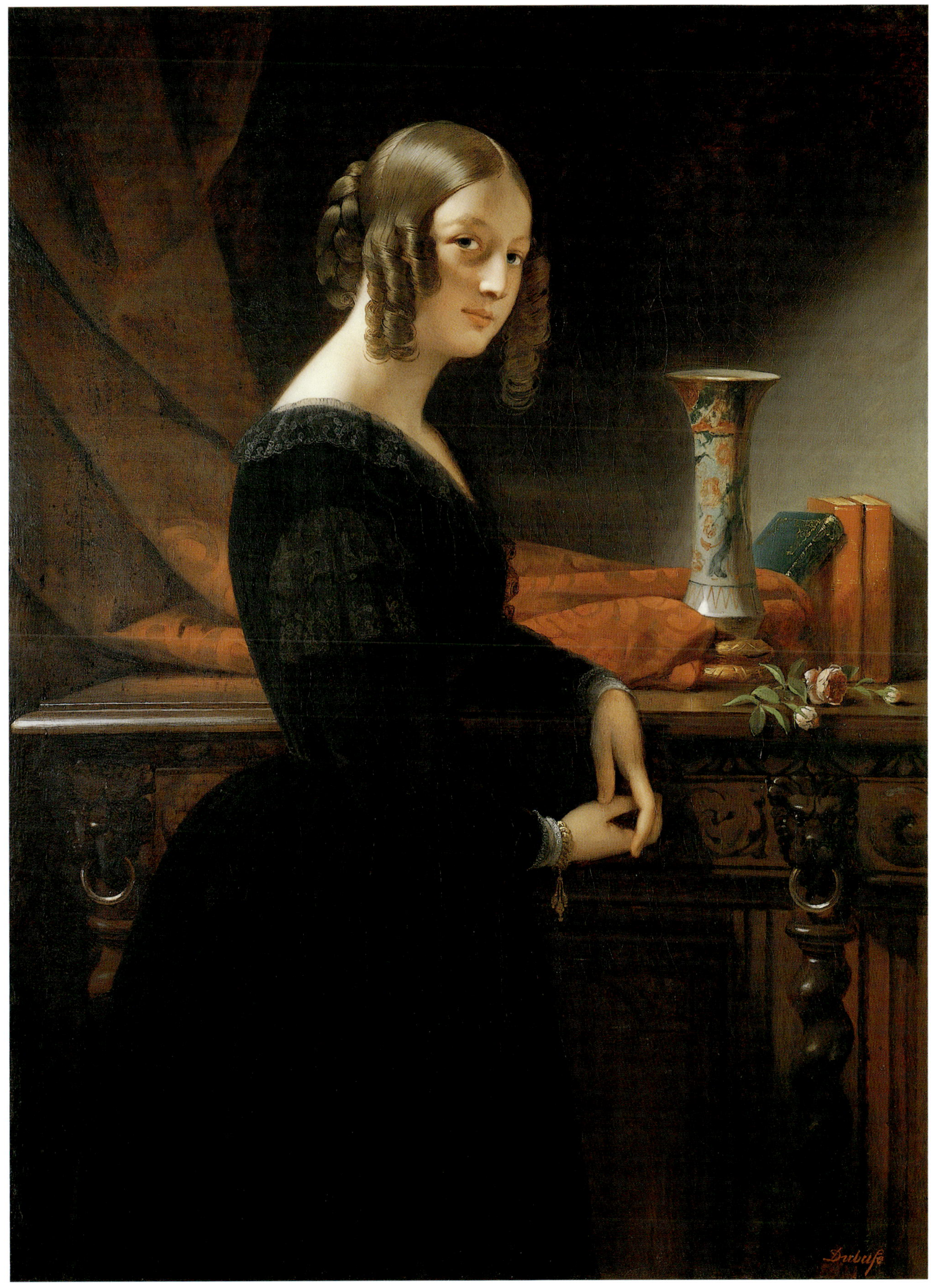

17

18

THÉODORE GÉRICAULT OR IMITATOR
French, 1791–1824

Head of a Horse
1808–1810 or 1820s

Oil on canvas, $23\frac{7}{8} \times 19\frac{1}{2}$ in. (60.7×49.5 cm)
P.1978.4

PROVENANCE: François Marcille (1790–d. 1856); Mme M. Georges Dortu, Le Vesinet, Paris. [Galerie Hector Brame, Paris, by 1957]. Pierre Dubaut, Paris, by 1959. (Anonymous sale, London, Sotheby's, 23 June 1965, lot 151, to); [Paul Kantor]. [A. C. Cooper, London, by 1974]; Mike Nichols, New York, gift 1978 to; Norton Simon Museum.

EXHIBITIONS: London, 1952, no. l; Winterthur, 1953, no. 42; Salisbury, 1957, no. 114.

REFERENCES: Eitner, 1959, p. 125 n. 18; Chiego, 1974, p. 252, fig. 47; Grunchec, 1976, pp. 397, fig. 3, 398; Grunchec and Thuillier, 1978, no. 8; Grunchec, 1982, pp. 6, 21; Bazin, 1989, vol. 3, pp. 12, 101, no. 586.

TECHNICAL NOTES: This rapidly painted study displays expressive brushwork, especially in the area of the horse's mane. Paints were built up wet in wet with little attempt at blending. Pasty brown tones and white create the horse's head, but thin medium-rich brown paint applied on top creates the shadows. The density of the ground prevents any interpretation of the X-ray other than to show some ambiguous changes. The original support, a medium-weight, coarse, open-weave fabric is lined to a similar fabric with an aqueous adhesive. No tacking edges remain, and the stretcher is recent. The medium-thick white ground that almost fills the canvas weave is visible along the edges of the horse's head. The condition of the horse's head itself is rather good except that the shadow on the neck seems to be toned possibly to hide abrasion of the thin brown shadow. The upper left and lower right areas of the painting have quite a lot of later toning that hides the condition of the original paint in those areas. The lining closed the crackle pattern, making it almost invisible. In ultraviolet light the thick, discolored varnish fluoresces a dense opaque green and may hide any restorations underneath. (JF)

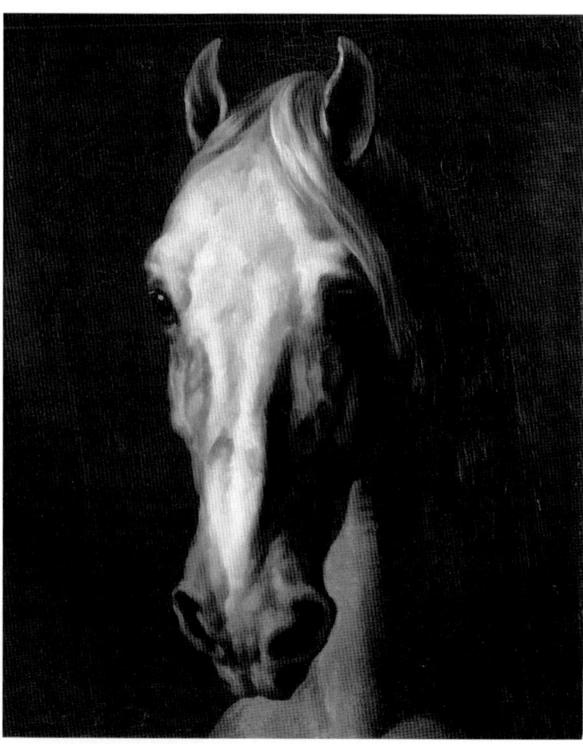

Fig. 18a (*above*) Carle Vernet, *Study of a Neapolitan Horse*, lithograph, Location unknown; Photo: Grunchec and Thuillier, 1978, no. 8-1

Fig. 18b (*right*) Théodore Géricault, *Head of a White Horse*, c. 1814–1815, oil on canvas, $25\frac{3}{4} \times 21\frac{1}{2}$ in. (65.5×54.5 cm), Musée du Louvre, Paris; photo: © Erich Lessing / Art Resource, NY

THE ESSENTIAL QUESTION to ask of this strongly Romantic depiction of the head of a horse is whether or not it is by the great French artist Théodore Géricault. Since at least 1952, it has been recognized as an oil rendering of an engraving by Debucourt after a painting by Carle Vernet entitled *Étude de cheval napolitain* (*Study of a Neapolitan Horse*, fig. 18a).[1] This derivation from a printed source with an early date has led most serious students of Géricault's work to accept the painting as an autograph, if immature, work by the master.[2] However, when compared with an autograph (but later) painting of an identical subject by Géricault in the Musée du Louvre (fig. 18b), the awkwardness and melodrama of the Norton Simon painting are clear,

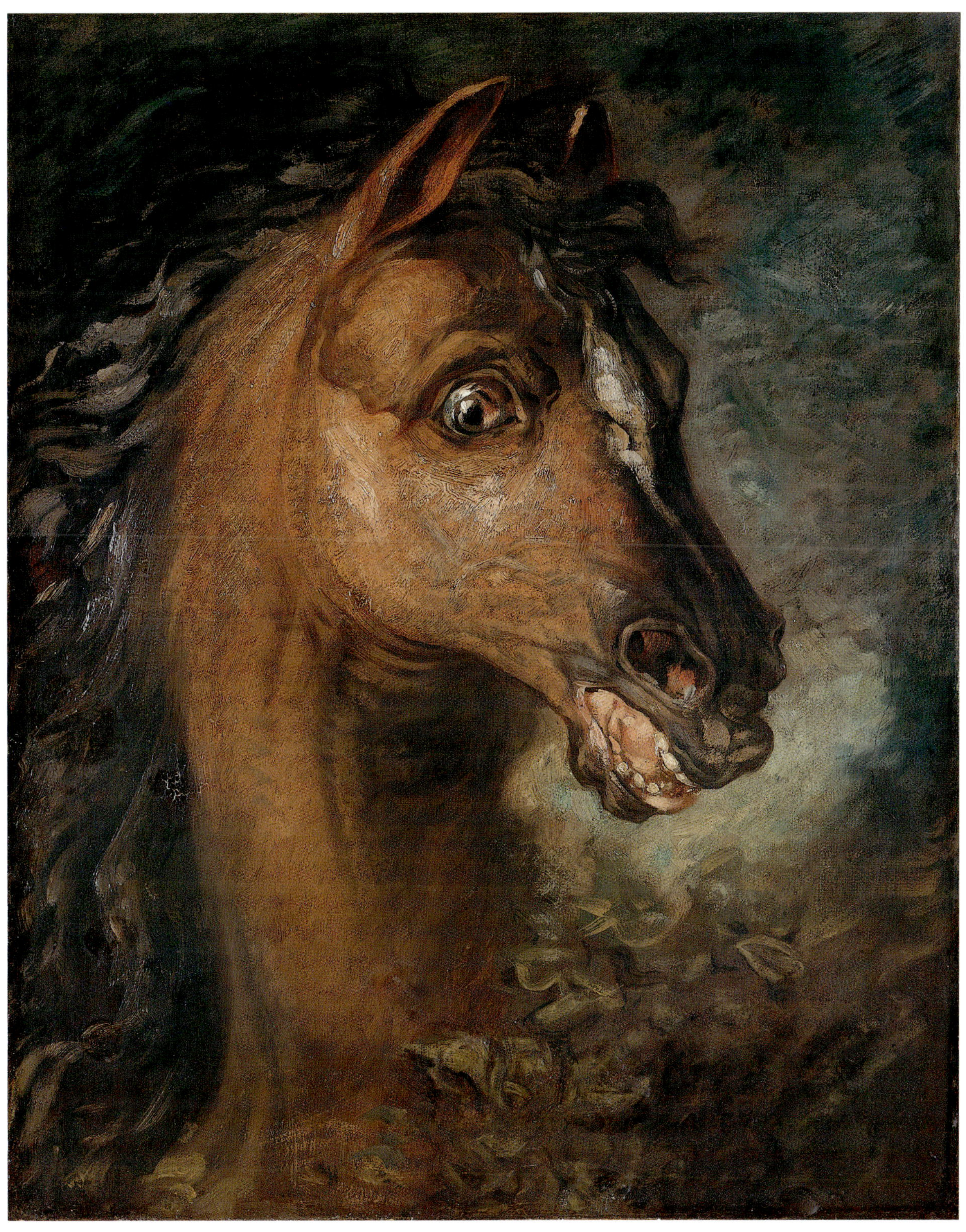

18

which makes the attribution to Géricault difficult to sustain.

The documentary evidence of the painting's provenance does not, unfortunately, confirm or refute the attribution. The publications of the sale of Géricault's studio in 1824 make it clear that this work could have been included in that sale under several categories—"3 chevaux bruns, trois études de chevaux, cheval maron, 2 têtes de cheval"—for example.[3] But there are many unattributed works surviving from the first half of the nineteenth century in France that could fit the titles equally well, and there is no unbroken evidentiary link between the inventory and the Norton Simon canvas. Indeed, the painting was relined and mounted on a new stretcher in the mid–twentieth century, removing any physical evidence of its early provenance. Philippe Grunchec in his catalogue of Géricault's paintings of 1978 refers to an inscription on the stretcher linking the work to the collector François Marcille, who was a contemporary of Géricault and died in 1856.[4] Yet no such inscription survives today, and that early provenance must remain in doubt, unless new, confirming evidence arises.

Géricault was only in his late teens in 1808–1810 when he worked under the direction of Carle Vernet. His surviving paintings of this period, as well as those made during the succeeding eleven months of study with the classicist Pierre-Narcisse Guérin, are few in number and mostly consist of copies of prints and earlier works of art—by Vernet, Titian, Rembrandt, Van Dyck, and Rubens. Thus, Géricault's mature style was not yet formed at the time *Head of a Horse* was presumably painted, rendering the attribution on stylistic grounds problematic. What is certain is that compared with his fellow students in the Vernet and Guérin studios, the young artist painted with unusual verve, earning him the nickname "cuisinier de Rubens."[5] His *Antique Chariot Race* (c. 1810, Musée des Beaux-Arts, Rouen), based on a lithograph by Vernet, contains thick, regular strokes of paint, similar to the zigzags of white on the neck of the horse in the present painting. Géricault's *Sleep of the Apostles* (c. 1811, private collection) and *Entombment of Christ* (c. 1812, Musée Cantonal des Beaux-Arts, Lausanne) are thickly painted and vividly colored, calling to mind the early Paul Cézanne more than any Neoclassical painters of Géricault's age. But even compared with these works, the Norton Simon painting is so fully Romantic in its conception and execution that it is difficult to accept unequivocally as a work of 1808–1810; the horse's head is defined with robust strokes of thick paint applied wet on wet to the canvas, anticipating the manner of Eugène Delacroix a decade or so later. For this reason, it is tempting to date this painting to the 1820s or after, rather than to the first decade of the century. *Head of a Horse* must therefore be placed beside other pictures of uncertain attribution to Géricault, including *Horse Attacked by a Lion* (Musée du Louvre, Paris), based on a print by R. Laurie after the famous painting by George Stubbs (and once owned by Delacroix), and *Head of a Horse* (Portland Art Museum, Oregon).

1 London, 1952, no. 1.

2 An exception is Albert Boime, an astute and critical scholar of the period who raised questions about its authorship on a visit to the Museum on 27 June 1979, one year after its gift to the Museum by the film director Mike Nichols. Information recorded in the Norton Simon Museum curatorial archives.

3 Eitner, 1959, p. 119.

4 Grunchec, 1978, no. 8, p. 87. Marcille, whose collection was famous for its Prud'hons and Chardins, also amassed a large number of pictures by Géricault, as did his two sons.

5 Eitner, 1971, p. 37.

19

Jean-Baptiste Camille Corot
French, 1796–1875

Farm Building at Bois-Guillaume, near Rouen
c. 1823–1824

Oil and pencil on paper, laid down on canvas, 10 × 13 in. (25.3 × 33 cm)
Stamped on stretcher with wax stamp: "Vente Corot"
N. 1976.18

Provenance: Corot estate (sale, Paris, Hôtel Drouot, 26 May 1875, lot 244, as *Aux environs de Rouen; chaumière*, bought in by); Jules Chamouillet (the artist's grandnephew). probably John Dix Coffin, (1885–1961) New York and Quebec, to; [Manhattan Gallery, New York, sold April 1964 to]; [Wildenstein & Co., New York, sold May 1964 to]; [Paul Brame]. (sale, London, Christie's, 6 April 1976, lot 9, to); Norton Simon, bequest 1993 to; Jennifer Jones Simon Art Trust.

References: Robaut, 1905, vol. 2, no. 12, ill.; Moreau-Nélaton, 1924, vol. 1, p. 11, fig. 9.

Technical Notes: The heavy cream-colored paper support carries white priming that goes to its very edges. There is a secondary support of a medium- to lightweight, open, and plain-weave fabric. The paper and fabric have the same dimensions, but it is impossible to say if the canvas was a later addition. The paper on canvas is lined with an aqueous adhesive to a second canvas. The last support is attached to a 4-part keyable stretcher. Opaque local color and thinner translucent paints entirely cover the ground. The sky was laid in first over a reddish color probably to give some vibrancy to the clouds (as one finds in seventeenth-century Dutch painting). Then the barn was solidly laid in with white paint and the trees were painted. The artist brushed in architectural details over the white paint of the barn and the red paint of the chimney. Some graphite drawing visible around the top of the barn indicates that it was laid in with simple drawing. The condition of the painting is rather good, but there are some restorations along the top of the barn and chimneys. In the tan foreground at lower left there is one larger restoration and at the lower right a restored tear. Though the greens, browns, fine details, and scumbles are fragile, they have only minimal abrasion. No record of cleaning (except for removal of surface dirt) is available. Under ultraviolet light yellow-green patches fluoresce; these must be remnants of an older natural resin. On the surface there is a later nonsaturating varnish that appears to be synthetic. (JF)

Listed as number twelve in Alfred Robaut's still-definitive catalogue of the paintings of Camille Corot, *Farm Building at Bois-Guillaume, near Rouen* is probably the earliest painting by Corot in the United States. Dated by Robaut with some authority to the years 1823–1824, the small painting on paper is evidence of Corot's early fascination with French rural architecture, an indication that, even before his first long trip to Italy in 1825–1828, he was beginning to turn away from the Italian imagery and classical ideals of his teacher-mentors, Jean-Victor Bertin and Achille-Etna Michallon. Indeed, this modest oil sketch prefigures Corot's eventual decision to become the first great French landscape painter who painted French, rather than Italian, landscape scenery, and the first important French landscape painter who privileged anonymous rural as well as religious and aristocratic architecture.

The building represented so faithfully by Corot is a Norman farm building. (The French word *chaumière* in the painting's earliest recorded title literally means a thatched farmhouse, but this building is so large that it was surely a combination dwelling, stable, and perhaps storage facility.) The building was part of an important property in the village of Bois-Guillaume near Rouen owned by one of Corot's father's friends, a M. Sennegon, who had served as the future painter's guardian while he was in boarding school in Rouen between 1807 and 1812. The year following Corot's return to his parents' home in Paris after the completion of his schooling, his older sister, Annette-Octavie, married M. Sennegon's son, Laurent-Denis, bringing the two families even closer. Corot was often to stay with the Sennegon family, and he painted sensitive portraits of his "Sennegon" sister and nieces in future years. Thus, this wonderful picture is only the very beginning of a lifelong pictorial study of the Sennegon family and its properties.

Its family associations suggest that this small and relatively humble painting of a rural building is a "landscape of sentiment," alive, that is, with personal associations. Yet, in painting it, Corot was making a study of French rural architecture as such, and there are several comparable paintings of anonymous rural buildings in Fontainebleau and Seine-Port from the years before his Italian study trip.[1] In making these patient studies of buildings with no architectural pretension, Corot was elevating their status in ways unknown in previous French painting. Although François Boucher, Jean-Honoré Fragonard, and even Antoine Watteau had represented such buildings, they always form part of a picturesque setting for figures, all of which are arranged to become part of an idealized pastoral. Corot treated this

Fig. 19a Jean-Baptiste Camille Corot, *Farm Building at Bois-Guillaume, near Rouen*, c. 1822–1824, oil on canvas, $9\frac{1}{2} \times 12\frac{5}{8}$ in. (24 × 32 cm), location unknown; photo: Robaut, 1905, no. 13

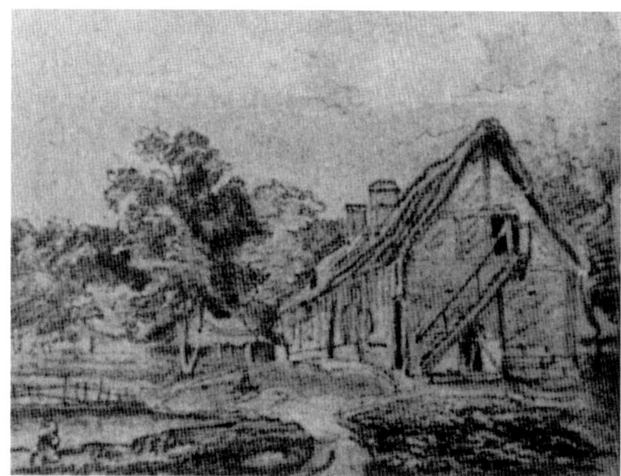

farm building with the same clarity and sober respect that he was to give to the Roman Forum or the Temple of the Sibyl in Tivoli in 1825–1826.

The building itself is of typically Norman half-timber construction and dates from the late seventeenth or eighteenth centuries. Its pair of chimneys is not identical, indicating that it was probably constructed in several phases. In fact, the building survives today and several photographs of it are in the curatorial files. Originally constructed as a stable, it was transformed into a farmhouse-stable in the eighteenth century and reconfigured completely for solely domestic purposes in 1937. The ample spaces for ventilation on the side facing Corot suggest that the entire second story of the building was used for storage of grain and foodstuffs. Corot was clearly fascinated with the interplay of strong side-light, probably at the end of the day, with the white and brown patterns of the building's facade. His decision not to include any figures indicates that, in his mind, the small painting was made as an architectural study, perhaps for future use in a more complex composition done in the studio. In fact, Robaut catalogues as number 13 the work that surely must be the second step in this process (fig. 19a). Yet, it is even smaller in dimension than the Norton Simon painting, suggesting that it was perhaps a compositional sketch for a larger picture that does not survive or was never attempted. In it, Corot set the building into a larger landscape setting with more space and paid greater attention to trees and paths. Robaut's summary sketch suggests that Corot added a pond in the left foreground, and a group of squiggles in the lower left corner must surely be the figure of a rural laundress. Fortunately, none of this picturesque incidence mars the Norton Simon painting, which almost seems the work of an Italian painter, discovering the rural architecture of Normandy for the first time and painting it as he would a farm in the Roman Campagna.

1 Robaut, 1905, nos. 18, 24, 27, and 29.

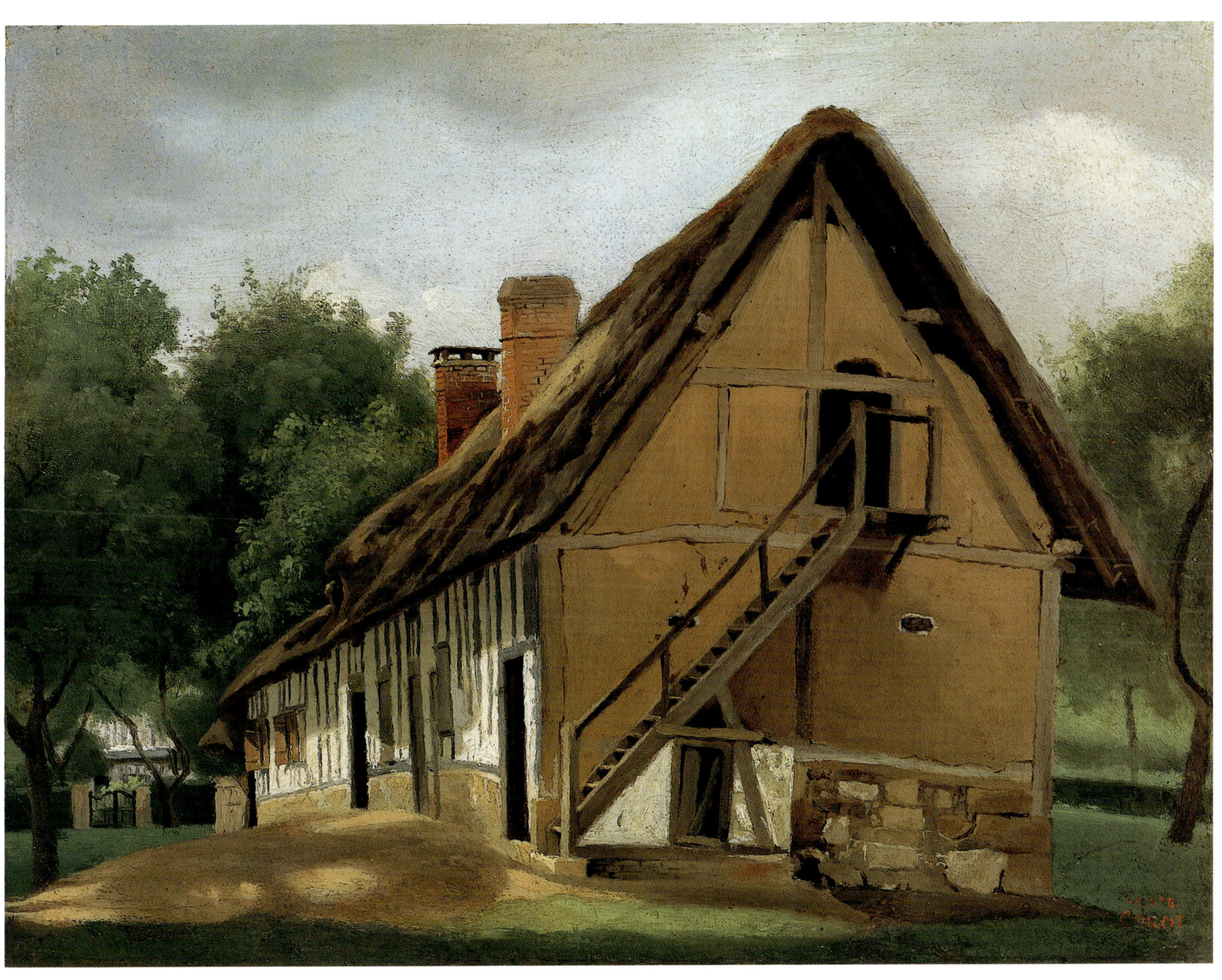

19

20

Jean-Baptiste Camille Corot
French, 1796–1875

View of Venice: The Piazzetta Seen from the Riva degli Schiavoni
1835–1845

Oil on canvas, $18\frac{3}{8} \times 27$ in. (46.7×68.6 cm)
Signed lower left: "C. Corot"
F.1973.27

Provenance: [Arnold & Tripp, Paris; 1898]. Van Wessen by 1905. Charles Deshayes. Baron Denys Cochin, by 1914. [Reid & Lefevre, Glasgow, stock no. 468/26; owned jointly with Knoedler, Paris, 1926]; [Reid & Lefevre, London; sold $\frac{1}{2}$ share July 1928 to]; [M. Knoedler & Co., New York, stock no. A274, as *Venise quai des Esclavons*; sold 1/2 share 31 January 1930 to]; [Reid & Lefevre, London, sold 1930 to]; [Galerie Raphaël Gérard, Paris]. [Dieterle & Cie, Paris; sold 14 May 1937, for Ff 257,000, to]; [Tedesco Frères, Paris, stock no. 13057, as *Venise, Vue du Quai des Esclavons*; sold 14 May 1937, for Ff 300,000, to]; Maurice Coutot (b. 1901), 21, blvd St. Germain, Paris. ?Private collection, Paris. Michaux, Paris. [Art Moderne la Gradelle, sold June 1970 to]; [Paul Rosenberg & Co., New York, stock no. 6408, sold 26 September 1973 to]; The Norton Simon Foundation.

Exhibitions: Paris, 1914b, no. 16; Amsterdam, 1928, no. 5, ill.; New York, 1928a, no. 2, ill.; Paris, 1934c; London, 1935, no. 5; Paris, 1936d, no. 6; London, 1936c, no. 11; on loan, Seattle, University of Washington, Henry Gallery, 26 September 1973–11 June 1974; San Francisco, 1974, no. 13, ill.; on loan, Toronto, Art Gallery of Ontario, 26 February–25 August 1981; Paris, 1996, no. 56, color ill.

References: Robaut, 1905, vol. 2, no. 323, pp. 114–115; Blanche, 1920, no. 4, p. 15, ill.; Manson, 1928, ill. (opp. p. 276); Meier-Graefe, 1930, p. 47, pl. XVI; Alpatov, 1961, p. 174, as *Matinée à Venise*; McCleery, 1974, p. 13; Roberts, 1976, pp. 877, 879, fig. 119; Brommer, 1981, p. 25; Seta, 1998, p. 391.

Technical Notes: The support is a fine, plain-weave canvas. The painting has been lined with the original tacking edges cut off. The surface reveals a microcondition of tiny bumps, which are visible in raking light, and probably issue in some way from the lining. The edges of the painting are completely covered with tape; however, the X-radiograph reveals a full second set of tacks beneath the visible ones. The white ground is smoothly applied. The paint is directly applied, often in a single layer, working wet into wet with controlled brushwork. It is quite thin in the sky; the rest of the painting has been brushed with rich, opaque paint. The clear light is described by shadows painted with opaque gray or mauve. Although the painting reads well, the paint has been altered by solvents. The sky is noticeably abraded. Not only was cleaning carried out unevenly, but some areas of the sky have been retouched and others not at all, leaving white thread tops visible. An area of the sky, just to the left of the Doge's Palace, has a very thin gray-yellow layer, but its origin is not clear; there may have been a thin second color, most of which has been removed. Magnification reveals broken or interrupted brushstrokes in darker colors. The flagpole, ships' rigging, lines, and flags at the lower left are abraded, and much of the foreground of the piazza has been noticeably thinned. Ultraviolet light reveals a long, narrow repair extending from the top right corner down approximately 7 inches. Retouching is scattered throughout the sky but much abrasion remains visible. The most recent surface coating is a slightly uneven application of synthetic resin, although small amounts of older varnishes remain. (RW)

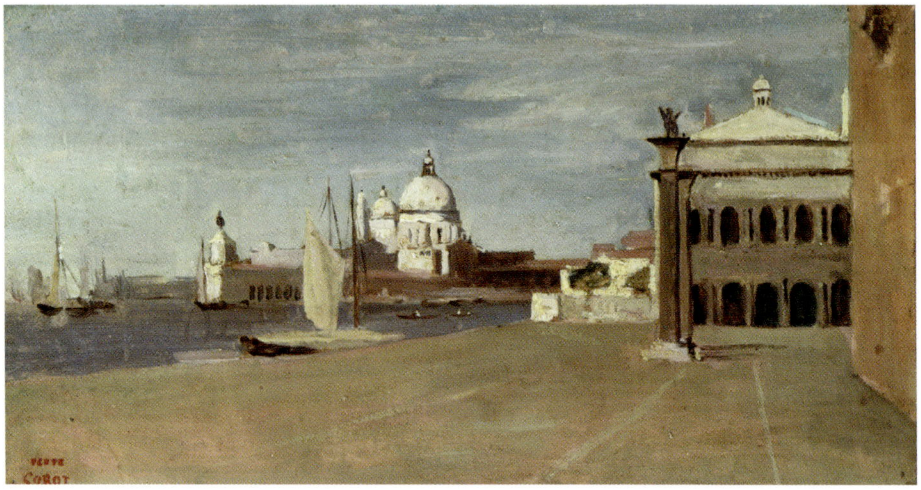

Fig. 20a Jean-Baptiste Camille Corot, *View of the Grand Canal, Venice, from the Riva degli Schiavoni*, 1828, oil on paper laid down on canvas, $8\frac{5}{8} \times 15\frac{3}{4}$ in. (22×40 cm), private collection; © Lefevre Fine Art Ltd., London

This extraordinarily accomplished and highly finished Venetian view painting, or *veduta*, has virtually no nineteenth-century provenance and no exhibition history before 1914. Thus, it occupies an unusual position as one of the most highly wrought of the Norton Simon paintings by Corot, but one with the least known about its significance in Corot's oeuvre and in the minds of his contemporaries. Yet, since its first publication in 1905 in the immense catalogue raisonné compiled by his friend Alfred Robaut, it has been seen as a masterpiece of Corot's career and been included in numerous exhibitions, culminating in the landmark 1996–1997 retrospective in the Grand Palais, the National Gallery of Canada, and the Metropolitan Museum of Art.

Robaut includes five versions[1] of this composition in his catalogue. The first (fig. 20a) is an oil sketch done on paper and later mounted to canvas, and dated to the very end of Corot's first trip to Venice in 1828. Then, the

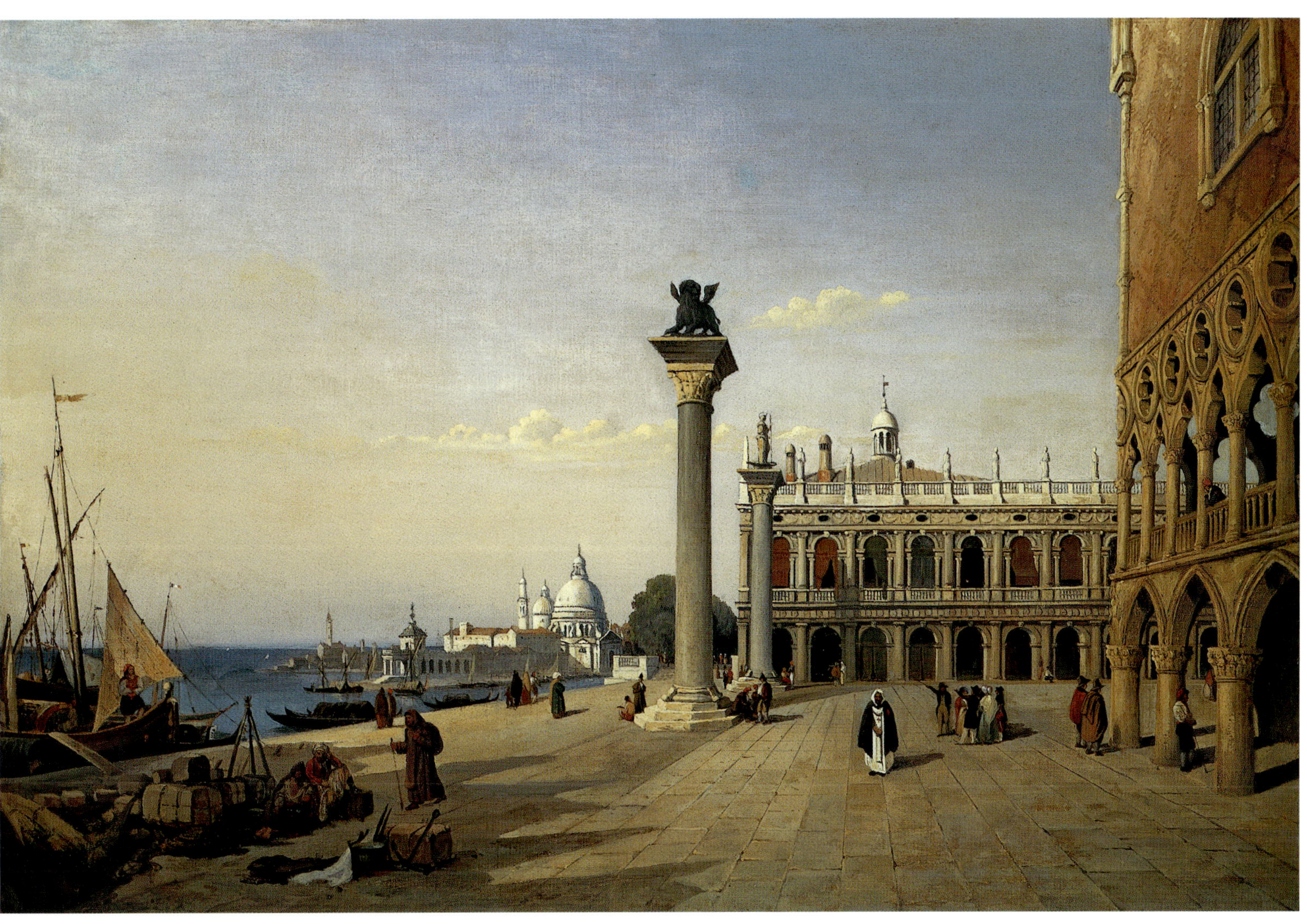

20

painter was so anxious to get back to his family after nearly three years in Italy that he left the city after just two or three days. He returned in 1834, on what he thought would be his final trip to Italy, though he was later to return to Rome and its environs in 1843. On the 1834 trip to Venice, he spent three weeks in the magical city, making additional studies of the Piazzetta and the quays similar to those he had already made in 1828. One of these, the view of the Piazzetta looking toward San Giorgio Maggiore with the Doge's Palace on the right, became his standard Venetian view, and, using the two sketches of 1828 and 1834 (fig. 20b) as his source, he painted three larger compositions, of which the Norton Simon version is generally acknowledged to be the finest. A very similar composition can be found in the National Gallery of Victoria (fig. 20c). Another version, now in a private collection, is grouped by Robaut among the others from 1834, although it is signed and, according to Robaut, dated 1845.[2] This later painting is, however, in no way stylistically dissimilar from the earlier group, suggesting that the Norton Simon painting, which is conventionally dated to 1834 or 1835, could be as much as a decade later. Unfortunately, no documentary evidence survives to give it a more precise date than 1835–1845.

Both the Melbourne and Pasadena canvases take their cues from the two oil sketches of 1828 and 1834. Of these, the latter is better known, because it has been conserved and published by the Pushkin Museum in Moscow (fig. 20b). The earlier of the two sketches—that of 1828 (fig. 20a)—has greater compositional affinities with the two larger and later versions in Pasadena and Melbourne because of its pervasive horizontality and its inclusion of a good deal of water on the left of the composition. Its absence of figures and its distanced vantage point also give it the air of an eighteenth-century *veduta*, while the Pushkin painting has a much more compressed space, a

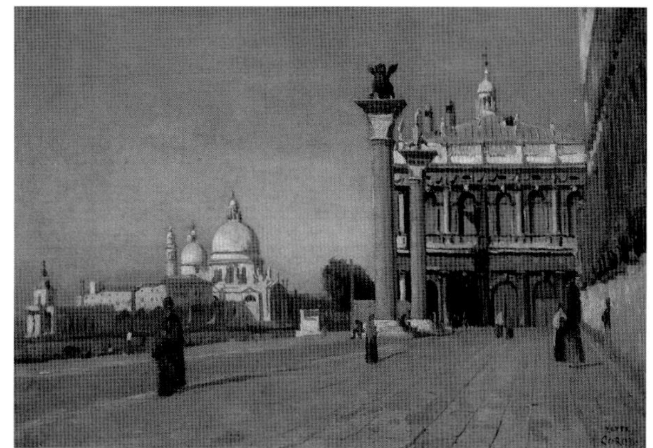

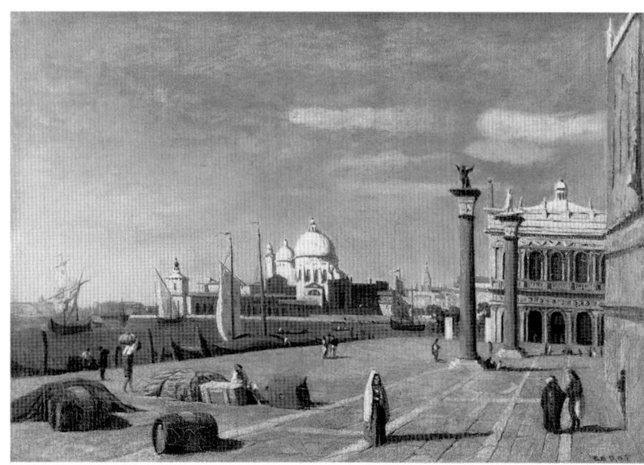

Fig. 20b (*right, top*) Jean-Baptiste Camille Corot, *Morning in Venice*, 1834, oil on canvas, $10\frac{5}{8} \times 15\frac{3}{8}$ in. (27×39 cm), Pushkin Museum of Fine Arts, Moscow; photo: Erich Lessing / Art Resource, NY

Fig. 20c (*right, bottom*) Jean-Baptiste Camille Corot, *View of the Quay of the Schiavoni, Venice*, oil on canvas, $18\frac{1}{8} \times 31\frac{1}{2}$ in. (46×80 cm), National Gallery of Victoria, Melbourne

ground-level vantage point, and figures that are at once prominent and proximate. These characteristics give it an immediacy completely lacking in the larger, more formal paintings, both of which were surely painted in Paris from the earlier sketches and from small drawings done on the spot.

Clearly, Corot was burdened by the precedent of the great eighteenth-century view painters, Canaletto, Guardi, and Bellotto, for his images of Venice cling closely to the idea of that great city they had already made canonical. The strength of the pictorial tradition goes a long way in explaining Corot's reluctance to stay very long in Venice and not to return there on his last Italian trip in 1843. Indeed, Corot resisted Venice's charms. This is perhaps because of the French painter's shyness and his dislike of interruptions when he worked. Venice had few open spaces where a painter could sketch without being bothered or without bothering others, and the picturesque small streets and canals that abound in the city were simply too full of people for Corot. Hence, all his views of Venice were painted from the large urban spaces around the Doge's Palace and S. Marco (he even painted one interior of the basilica). Corot never painted the city from the water, as John Singer Sargent and Claude Monet were to do, nor did he like painting from the windows of rented rooms, as many foreign artists in Italian cities did.

There is little doubt that Norton Simon was moved to buy this unusual painting by Corot because of the superb Venetian views by Canaletto and Guardi in his collection. It is at once instructive and important to rush from the European eighteenth-century galleries to the gallery devoted to mid-nineteenth-century French art to make the comparison. The Corot shares with the superb Canaletto a precision of execution and a marked clarity of composition, and it represents precisely the same part of the city. With the three Guardis, however, it shares nothing. The latter artist grayed his palette and evoked his human and architectural subjects with short, flickering strokes of paint, wanting the city to quiver with life. Corot preferred the static calm associated with Canaletto and his nephew Bellotto to the nervous style of Guardi. Yet, what is most apparent is the contrast between the humid, heavy atmosphere in the eighteenth-century *vedute* and the brilliant clarity of the light in Corot's later painting. Corot's Venice seems clean and dry—more like a northern than a southern European city. Before making too much of Corot's precedents, however, we must remember that his knowledge of works by the eighteenth-century Venetian view painters was limited. The Louvre's collections are paltry, and Corot never visited England, where the most important holdings of such paintings can be found. He did see important examples in Venice, and surely his visits to the Accademia were not infrequent in his longer three-week stay. Though even with that exposure, he had a generic rather than a profound sense of Canaletto's achievement as a painter. In making the Pasadena and Melbourne paintings, Corot chose to take on Canaletto directly, and although his foray into *veduta* painting was a success, it was not to be repeated.

Among the various commentators about the present painting, only one, Vincent Pomarède, has pointed out the deliberate oddities of Corot's figures.[3] Unlike the eighteenth-century view painters, who crowd their compositions with various Venetian types in eighteenth-century dress, Corot isolates certain of his figures and clumps others in groups that read as units. This attempt at separating and isolating the figures forces the viewer to move visually from one group or figure to another in a jumpy fashion. Their contrasts of position, scale, costume, color, and pose force us to ponder their locations and meanings rather than to accept them simply as staffage. To the left and right of the large column with the lion of Saint Mark are two monks. One, directly facing the viewer/painter, is wearing a white habit and a black cloak. His prominent cross makes it clear that he is a monk, relating him to his counterpart with a brown habit and cloak to the left of the column. This latter figure is walking toward a pile of packaged goods and luggage presided over by a pair of turbaned men identified by Pomarède as "Turks." Whatever their country of origin, they are clearly Middle Eastern, and, in this, they are all but unique among the staffage figures in Venetian *vedute*, which stress the "Europeanness" of the city. Corot seems to have been fascinated by the idea of Venice as a sea capital straddling two worlds—eastern and western Europe, and he placed Muslim traders in the same urban space as a group of northern European tourists with their cicerone, or tour guide, who points in the middle group to the lion of Saint Mark.

As in many other paintings by Corot, the fact that a centrally placed figure faces the viewer of the painting, almost as if acknowledging our presence, gives the work an odd awkwardness. In this cityscape abounding in ethnic difference, we as viewers are forced, in a way, to wonder about our own positions in the city. Whichever figure or group of figures we relate to—and surely it is the tourists with their guide—we do so with a sense of our otherness. Wherever we allow our eyes to wander, we are always in front of the monk with the white habit and black cloak, and, hence, we are always outside the city arrayed for us in the clear light of Corot. What is perhaps most fascinating about the figures with respect to each other and to a viewer contemporary to Corot is that, with the exception of the tourists in the middle distance, none of the figures is at all modern or bound to early-nineteenth-century time. In this, Corot presented the city to us very much as he did Rome—as a timeless place in which figures occupy roles and wear clothes that have no association with contemporary fashion.

It is interesting, in reading the superb curatorial file, to come across a strongly worded note from Ben Johnson, then the chief conservator at the Los Angeles County Museum of Art, who had examined the painting for Norton Simon in April 1973. Johnson doubted the attribution of the painting to Corot "in my bone marrow" and found it "cold and impersonal," requesting that Simon "recheck the provenance." In a sense, he was right, and he obviously knew Corot more fully from the later paintings common in American collections. There is a kind of dutiful quality to the painting and a real failure to convey the atmosphere and delightful decay of the maritime capital of western Europe in the Mediterranean. Others, in the end, did it better. One wonders, actually, whether this work was painted for a particular client, who admired the sketch on a visit to Corot's studio and commissioned a larger view with requirements that it have exact descriptions of the architecture and urban spaces. Corot painted almost every stone on the plaza and spent so much time with the architecture that we can understand why someone doubted its attribution. None of his views of Roman buildings comes even close to the almost neurotic linearity of this Venetian view. In this, he was undoubtedly thinking of Canaletto. Corot's painting is, however, convincingly signed in the lower left. It is a pity that Robaut recorded its earliest existence only when he found it in 1883, eight years after Corot's death. It will take an assiduous documentalist or scholar to begin to identify the owners of works by Corot in the 1840s, 1850s, and 1860s, before Robaut set to work. Surely this painting was acquired by someone in the late 1830s or, more likely, the 1840s. One suspects that knowledge of its earliest owner may help future scholars to understand its oddities as a Corot.

1 The five are Robaut, 1905, vol. 2, nos. 194 (fig. 20a, private collection); 318 (fig. 20b, Pushkin Museum of Fine Arts, Moscow); 321 (fig. 20c, National Gallery of Victoria, Melbourne); 322 (private collection), and 323 (cat. 20, The Norton Simon Foundation).

2 According to Robaut (1905, vol. 2, no. 322, p. 114), it was painted on commission in 1845 for M. Robert of Mantes.

3 Paris, 1996, p. 131.

21

JEAN-BAPTISTE CAMILLE COROT
French, 1796–1875

Site in Italy
1839

Oil on canvas, $21\frac{1}{4} \times 32$ in. (54 × 81.3 cm)
Signed and dated lower left: "Corot 18[3?]9"
F.1971.1.2

PROVENANCE: Mme Jessé, Versailles, 1876. Louis Sarlin, Paris, by 1910 (sale, Paris, Galerie Georges Petit, 2 March 1918, lot 8, ill., as *Lac d'Italie*, sale did not take place, sold en bloc to); Wilhelm Hansen, Copenhagen; [Georges Bernheim et Cie, Paris, by 1928]. ?[Paul Rosenberg, Paris]. Alphonse Kann (1868–1948), Saint-Germain-en-Laye. [Arthur Tooth & Sons, London, sold May 1963 to]; [E. V. Thaw & Co., New York, sold 8 July 1963 to]; Donald Ellis Simon, Los Angeles, gift 1971 to; The Norton Simon Foundation.

EXHIBITIONS: Paris, 1839, no. 403?; Paris, 1910b, no. 15; Paris, 1928c, no. 19; Los Angeles, 1965; on loan, Los Angeles, County Museum of Art, July 1970–May 1971; on loan, Minneapolis Institute of Arts, 21 May 1971–28 September 1972; San Francisco, 1973, no. 19.

REFERENCES: Robaut, 1905, vol. 2, no. 371, p. 137, ill.; Wissman, 1989, p. 47.

TECHNICAL NOTES: The support, a plain-weave canvas of fine to medium weight, was commercially primed with a thick cream-colored ground. The picture has been extended along each side by about $\frac{1}{8}$–$\frac{1}{4}$ inch with the original tacking edges. The painting is lined with an aqueous adhesive to fabric that backs only the design part of the painting. The tacking edges have an additional set of holes that may correspond to holes in the stretcher, which could suggest that this 5-part butt-joined stretcher is original. Corot set in the landscape with dark brown underpainting. The darker foliage and water were built up with steel blue, eggplant, and dark greens in direct strokes. The sky was laid in first with textured cream-white paint that was then painted with thin blue and alizarin nearer the horizon. The purplish clouds resulted from a thin blue layer over pink. The bright blue of the pond is probably ultramarine thinly applied over a white base, and the shrub to the left of that is a translucent layer of blue and alizarin crimson. Almost all colors appear to have some admixture of white, adhering to a statement made by the artist himself for a tonality referred to as *peinture blonde*.[1] The sky was painted around the trees; however, some foliage and the little tree at center left were painted over the sky color; light paint was dabbed in to show the sky peeking through the trees. A reserve was left for the central figure when the landscape was painted, but the other figure and the goats were painted on top of the landscape paint. The varnish, possibly synthetic, gives a fairly even semigloss to the surface. It is clear but does not really saturate the colors. The condition is good, but some large cracks in the sky would be disturbing had they not been toned. The upper left corner is restored. The lining flattened the paint to a small degree, and age, lining, and light abrasion have probably all contributed to greater contrast between the darks and lights. (JF)

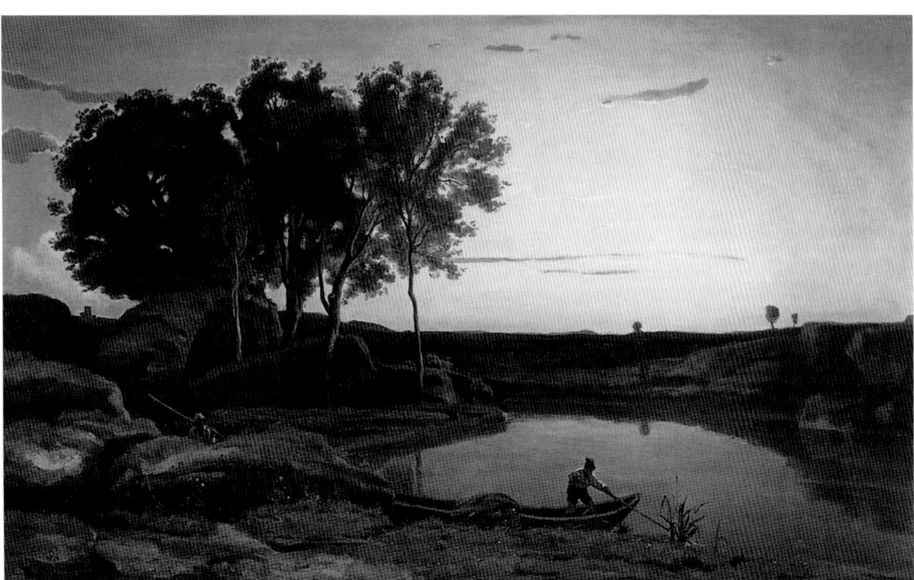

Fig. 21a Jean-Baptiste Camille Corot, *Landscape with Lake and Boatman*, 1839, oil on canvas, $24\frac{5}{8} \times 40\frac{1}{2}$ in. (62.5 × 102.9 cm), The J. Paul Getty Museum, Los Angeles; © The J. Paul Getty Museum

IF COROT WAS to become the greatest French landscape painter since Claude Lorrain, he had at the very least to acknowledge—and, in a sense, surpass—the achievement of his seventeenth-century predecessor. This he did in a series of ideal landscapes painted in the 1830s and 1840s in Paris, but using Italian motifs and compositional strategies derived from Claude. Among the finest of these is *Site in Italy*. This painting was acquired by a collector known only as Mme Jessé during Corot's lifetime (it was not included in the studio sales of 1875, after Corot's death), and it was in Mme Jessé's collection in 1876 when Alfred Robaut made a lively sketch of it for inclusion in his catalogue eventually published in 1905.

From its distinguished provenance (it was owned by the great Danish collector Wilhelm Hansen and by the French connoisseur Alphonse Kann) and from Robaut's account of its exhibition, it should be ranked among the handful of Claudian landscape paintings by Corot widely known in his lifetime. Robaut unhesitatingly identified the painting as having been the work of the same title included in the Salon of 1839 along with another landscape known as *Un Soir, paysage* (*Landscape with Lake and Boatman*) now in the J. Paul Getty Museum (fig. 21a). There had been no reason to doubt the identification of this painting as the 1839 Salon painting until the most assiduous student of Corot's Salon

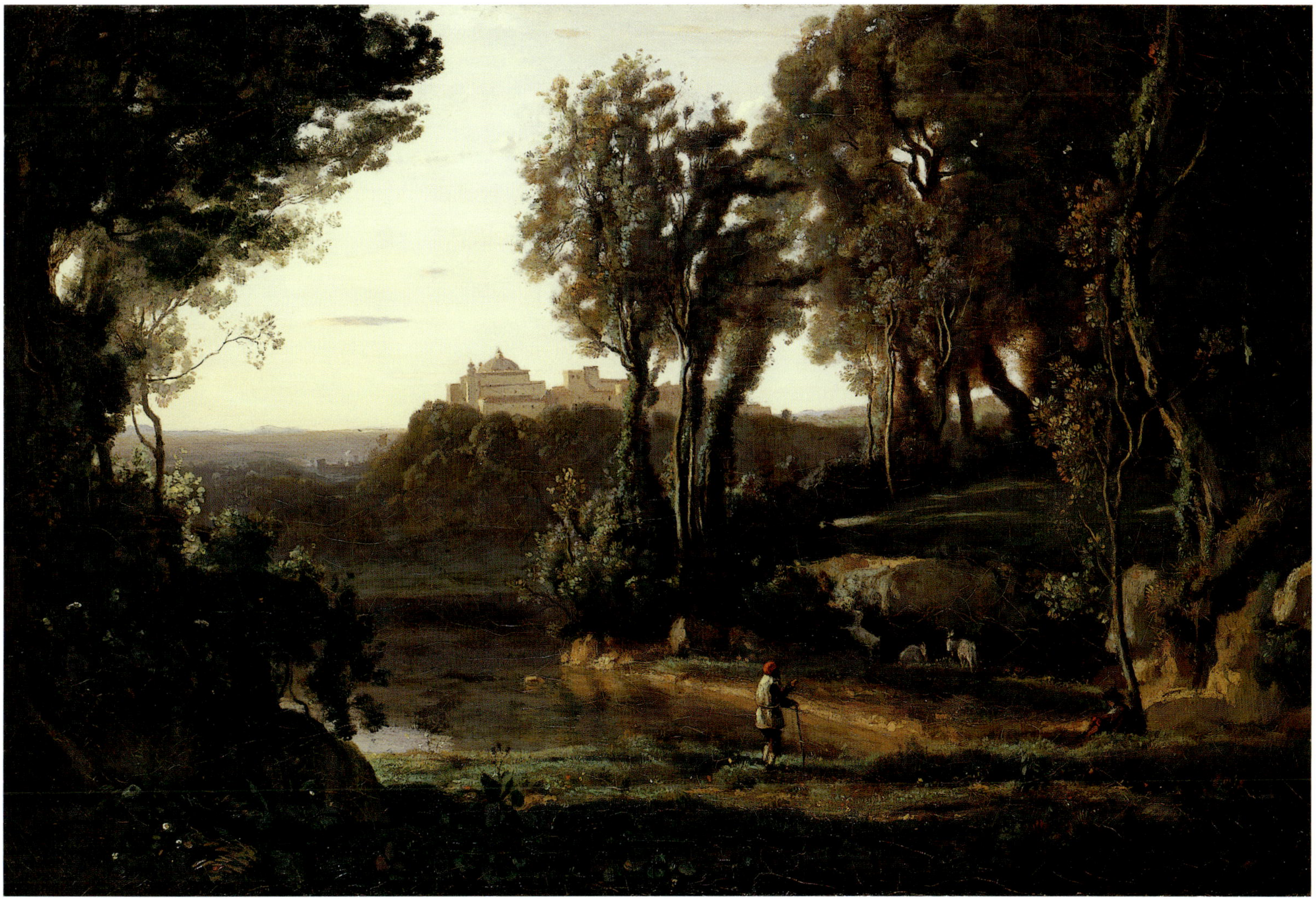

21

paintings, Fronia Wissman, identified another painting, also in the Getty Museum, *Site d'Italie, soleil levant* (*Italian Landscape, Sunrise*) (fig. 21b) as the likelier candidate for the Salon of 1839.[2]

Her reasoning is, in many senses, impeccable. The Getty sunrise landscape is virtually identical in dimension to the evening painting, and both are larger and hence, more ambitious than the Norton Simon painting. Also, the two paintings in the Getty, acquired as a pair by the museum, although with separate histories, are each signed and dated 1839. Robaut also recorded a signature and date of 1839 on the Norton Simon painting, but this has not been verified until a recent examination by Joseph Fronek in connection with the present catalogue. Indeed, the painting was signed in small off-white letters in the lower left and dated 1839.

Why would Robaut have said that the present painting was in the Salon of 1839 when it was not? Unfortunately, one can only surmise the answer. To begin with, he had no knowledge at that point of the Getty painting, which had been owned and sold by the duc d'Orléans, who purchased it in May 1839. This date is close enough to the Salon that Wissman concluded that the Orléans painting was purchased from the Salon, although the second work by Corot acquired just days later by the

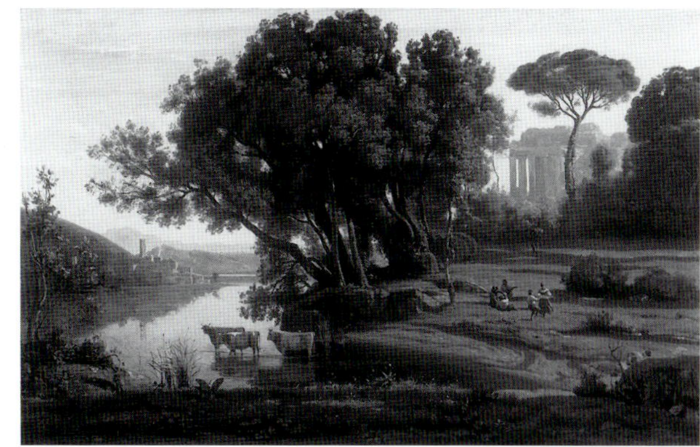

Fig. 21b Jean-Baptiste Camille Corot, *Italian Landscape, Sunrise,* 1839, oil on canvas, $25 \times 39\frac{7}{8}$ in. (63.5×101.3 cm), The J. Paul Getty Museum, Los Angeles; © The J. Paul Getty Museum

duke had been exhibited two years earlier, in the Salon of 1837. Wissman's second reason is that the Getty painting makes a Claudian pair with the evening picture, whose presence in the 1839 Salon has never been disputed.

Although all of this detail might seem irrelevant, it affects very much our interpretation of the Norton Simon painting. If Robaut, who was much too young to have actually seen the painting himself in the Salon of 1839, did have reliable information from someone who did, then we can confidently interpret this work as a Salon painting. Wissman's arguments, although not without reason, do not in fact prove that the Getty "pair" was exhibited as such in 1839. Indeed, artists often exhibited different kinds of paintings rather than submitting pairs, and it is odd that the duc d'Orléans, a sophisticated collector, would have bought one painting of a pair, if both were available and exhibited in the Salon. Also, none of the critics who reviewed the Salon linked the paintings. Théophile Thoré called them "two small landscapes" and lavished more attention on the evening picture, while Jules G. Janin spoke of them both and related the painting called "Site d'Italie" to the work of Nicolas Poussin, which would be much easier to do

Fig. 21c Claude Lorrain, *Pastoral Landscape*, 1639, oil on canvas, 20½ × 27⅛ in. (52 × 69 cm), Musée du Louvre, Paris; photo: H. Lewandowski; © Réunion des Musées Nationaux / Art Resource, NY

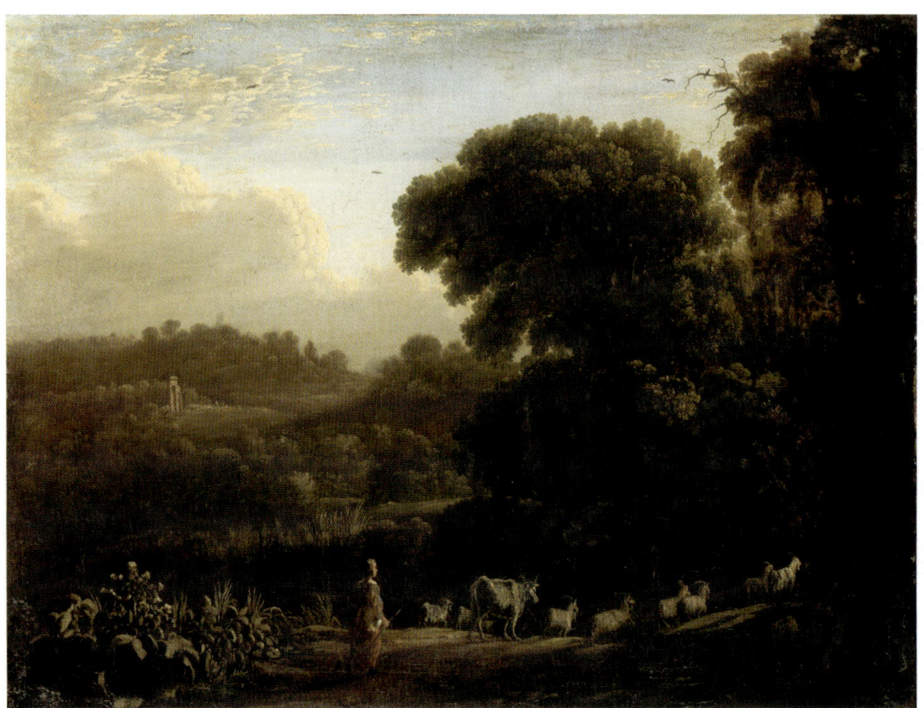

with the Norton Simon painting than with the Getty picture. Yet, he referred to *Site d'Italie* as a landscape with "a field burnt by the sun, a barren bush, some pigs, a shepherd in rags." And, although there is a shepherd in rags in the Norton Simon painting, none of the rest of the description fits either the Getty or the Simon painting. The Getty work is more burdened with the precedence of Claude Lorrain than any single painting in Corot's career, forcing Théophile Silvestre who wrote about it in 1853 to say that it recalled Claude too directly and allowing experts as recently as the 1950s even to question its attribution to Corot.

Unfortunately, we know nothing of the history of the painting in Pasadena before 1876, and we can only guess at Robaut's reasons for identifying it with the 1839 Salon. Yet, it is also impossible to prove that the Getty painting actually was the Salon painting, forcing us to accept provisionally Robaut's word because his opinion was arrived at earlier and was, thus, more likely to come from a reliable source. If the Norton Simon painting did not possess an effaced but legible signature and date (the *1* and the *8* are clear, the *9* is abraded, but most likely readable as a *9*, and the *3* is so severely abraded that a secure reading is not possible), one might want to place it earlier in the decade, when Corot seems to have struggled in his creation of Italianate landscapes in France and worked seriously to internalize the prototypes of Claude and Poussin. Others have argued that the Getty painting dates from the mid-1830s and that Corot dated it only when he sold it to the duc d'Orléans. The same could be said for the Norton Simon painting, but the identity of its first owner, unless it was a very young M. or Mme Jessé, is unknown.

What is fascinating in interpreting what seems to be an utterly Claudian painting by Corot is that it is not directly related to any particular painting or drawing by Claude. The pervasive horizontality of Corot's painting and its darkness make it as Poussiniste as Claudian, and its four groups of trees, one of which stands directly in front of the architectural subject, has no single parallel in Claude's oeuvre. One could link it to a painting in the Musée du Louvre, *Pastoral Landscape*, which had been in the collection of Louis XIV and was, hence, accessible to Corot throughout his life (fig. 21c). The two works, though of a similar size and pastoral subject, have very

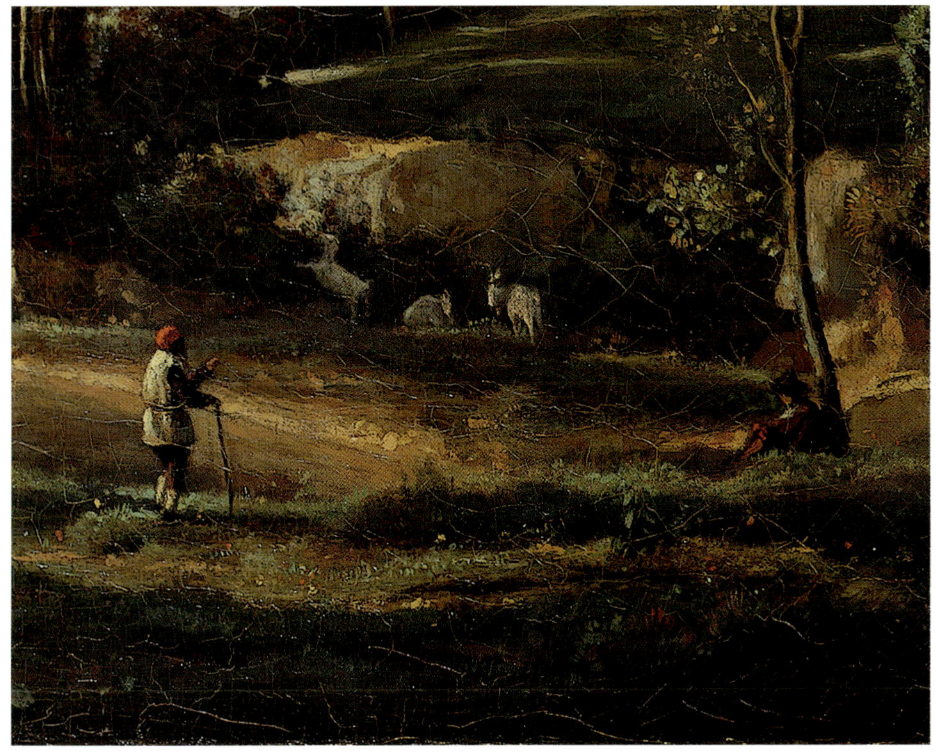

different compositions. Claude seems fascinated by the foreground and by the downward descent of a group of goats and a cow with their shepherdess. For Corot, the figures are fully in the middle ground, and the nineteenth-century painter made a much more complex study of trees than his source. In fact, no single work by Claude can explain the Corot, suggesting that the modern artist had so thoroughly subsumed his long-dead master that he could be Claudian without looking at any particular Claude.

For careful students of "the anxiety of influence," it is worth noting that the central shepherd in Corot's painting is actively engaged in conversation with a figure sitting at the base of a small tree to the right. This latter figure wears a cloak and a broad-brimmed hat just like the numerous figures of northerners common as staffage in the drawings and paintings of Claude, particularly those of the 1630s and early 1640s. What is he saying? Who is he? What century are we in?

1 Callen, 2000, pp. 86, 87.

2 Wissman, 1989, pp. 47–49.

22

Jean-Baptiste Camille Corot
French, 1796–1875

Rebecca at the Well
1838–1839

Oil on canvas, $19\frac{3}{4} \times 29\frac{1}{4}$ in. (50.2×74.3 cm)
Signed and dated lower right: "Corot. 1839"
Remnant of signature and date lower left: "ot/8"
F.1972.21

Provenance: Chailloux, 1883. Manzi, Paris; [Alphonse Portier, Paris, 1890]; Paul Gallimard, Paris; Jules Strauss (sale, Paris, Hôtel Drouot, 3 May 1902, lot 12, ill., for Ff 9,000, to); Nicolas Auguste Hazard to; Julie Pauline Hazard (d. 1919; sale, Paris, Galerie Georges Petit, 1–3 December 1919, lot 75, ill., for Ff 35,000 to); [Bernheim-Jeune et Cie, Paris, stock no. 21.800, sold 7 March 1923 to];[1] Burgeard. David David-Weill, Paris, by 1920[13] or 1936–1958; [Galerie Schmit, Paris, by 1971, sold 24 April 1972 to]; The Norton Simon Foundation.

Exhibitions: Basel, 1921, no. 20; Paris, 1928c, no. 20; Paris, 1936e, no. 36, pl. VI; Lyon, 1936, no. 29; Paris, 1971, no. 13, ill.; on loan, Phoenix, Art Museum, 25 July 1972–9 February 1973; San Francisco, 1973, no. 20, ill.; Paris, 1996, no. 71, ill.

References: Robaut, Carton 26, fol. 6; Robaut, 1905, vol. 2, no. 382, ill.; G. Bataille, 1929, p. 87, ill.; Moreau-Nélaton, 1924, vol. 2, p. 158, fig. 281; Fosca, 1928, p. 161, ill.; Meier-Graefe, 1930, p. 58; Faure, 1936, fig. 24; Fosca, 1958, fig. 30; "Exposicion Corot," 1971, p. 59; Toussaint, 1975, under no. 100; A. Zimmermann, 1986, pp. 91, 272 n. 145, no. 104, pl. 104; Exum, 1986, pp. 62–63 color ill.; Selz, 1988, p. 126, color ill.; Bätschmann, 1998, p. 313.

Technical Notes: The plain-weave canvas support has been lined with the original tacking edges removed. Adhesion between the two canvases appears to be uniformly strong. The painting is tacked to a 5-member stretcher, which is probably the original. Because the tacking edges are gone and the paint completely covers the canvas, the ground is exposed only where there are small paint losses at the right edge. The ground is white and presumed to be of medium thickness, as the canvas texture is masked. The painting was worked from the back (sky) forward; the blue sky was painted with horizontal strokes, in shades of blue mixed on the palette. Contours and colors in the foliage and the landscape are softened. Trees on the horizon are hastily applied little blobs of green paint. The paint is quite well preserved. A horizontal line of dark gray paint extends out to the side from the figure's left eye. Microscopic examination shows it extending very slightly over the dark brown line of her hair; it is bisected by a crack and appears to have the same character (particle size, color) as other gray paint strokes on the opposite side of the figure and in the distant landscape. No explanation presents itself; it appears there is no damage beneath it that might justify a retouch. Although lining has probably smoothed out the paint texture, it is still possible to see underlying brushstrokes at the left side of the painting, especially in the large gray rock, which are beneath and different from the visible image, suggesting that Corot had not completely worked out the composition at the beginning. The reworking is confirmed by the presence of an earlier signature, seen at bottom left on a gray rock where *ot* and *8* remain exposed, with the other letters and numbers covered by a stroke of dark brown paint. There is no information about earlier treatment; it seems probable, however, that the painting has been cleaned. The varnish is clear and uniform. (RW)

Corot had painted human figures from the time of his first trip to Italy, where he made small oil sketches on paper from hired models, to the end of his life. He tended not to exhibit these works, preferring to treat the human figure in private and encouraging critics and the public to think of him as a landscape painter by exhibiting mostly landscapes at the Salons. Yet, beginning in the mid-1830s, his Salon landscapes became larger and featured figures of increasing sophistication and scale. Indeed, certain of his landscapes contain midsize human figures so carefully painted that they become authoritative, like actors on a stage. It was not, however, until the last years of the 1830s that Corot painted a small

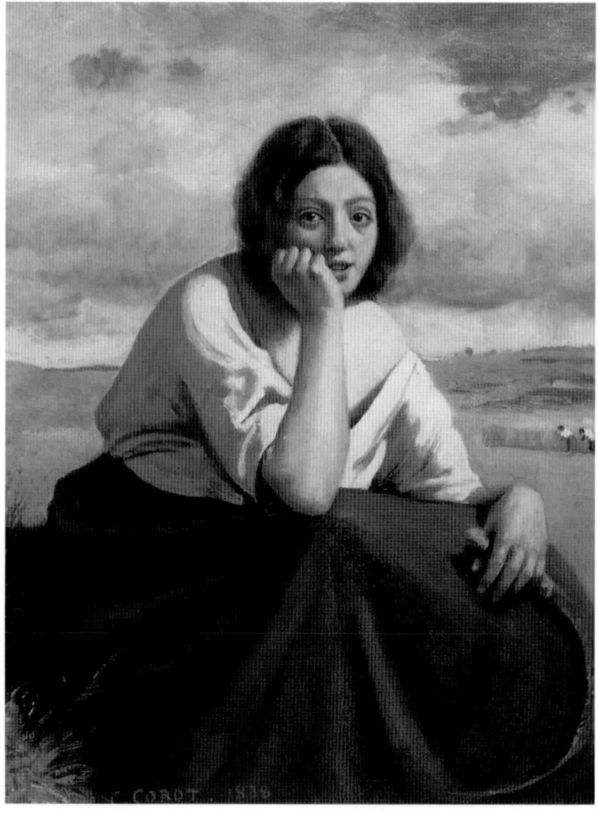

Fig. 22a Jean-Baptiste Camille Corot, *Reaper with a Sickle*, 1838, oil on canvas, $13\frac{7}{8} \times 10\frac{5}{8}$ in. (35.3×27 cm), Museum of Fine Arts, Boston, Bequest of William A. Coolidge; photograph © 2004 Museum of Fine Arts, Boston

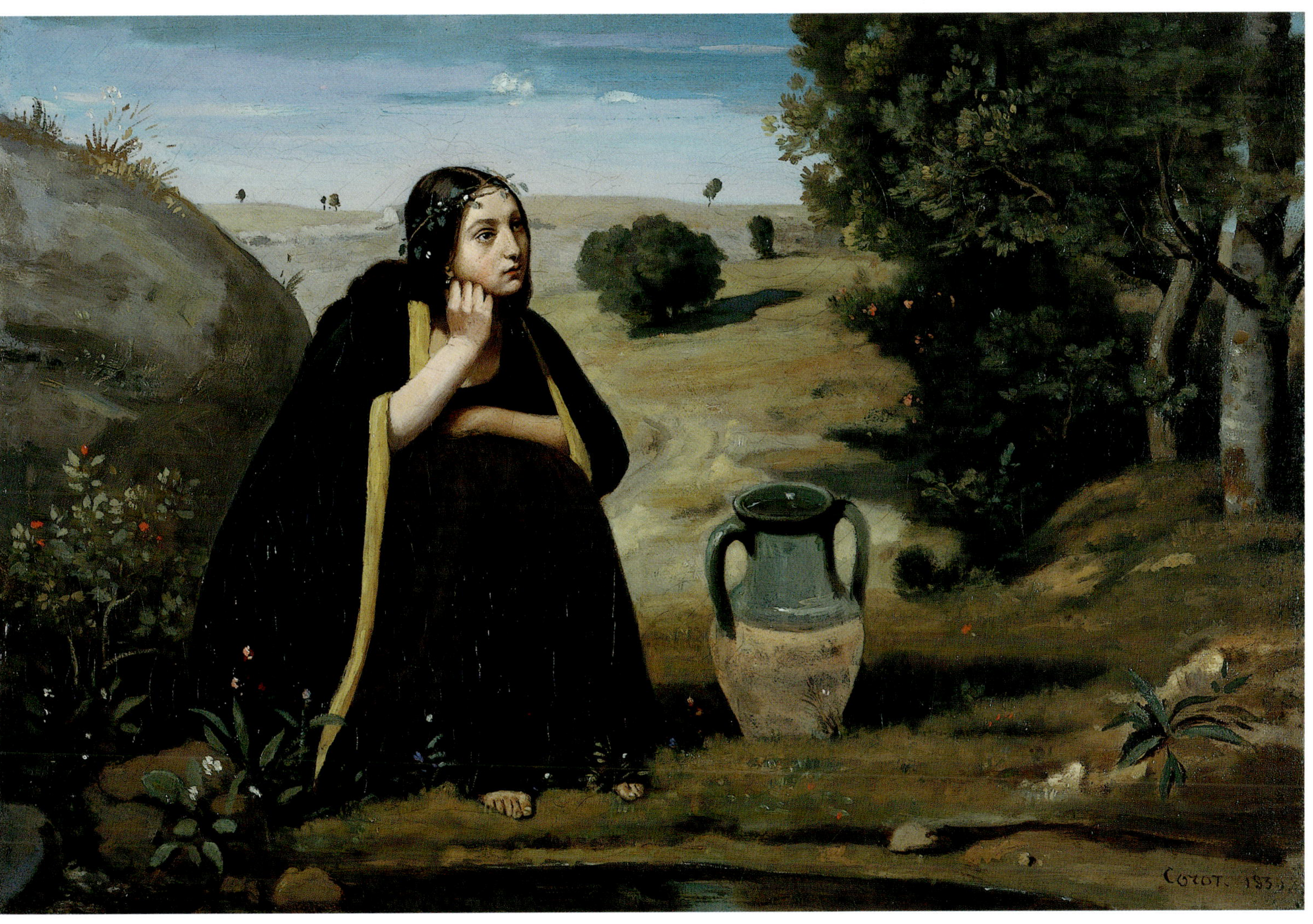

22

group of populated landscapes in which the figures absolutely dominate their setting. Perhaps the earliest and most important is *Rebecca at the Well.* Until the present publication, it was dated 1839, following the prominent signature and date in the lower right corner. However, a close examination of the painting made in connection with this catalogue revealed a signature and date of 1838, partially overpainted by Corot, who obviously felt uncomfortable with the painting and reworked it after its initial completion. It is fascinating, however, that he allowed enough of the earlier signature and date to remain visible after the second bout of painting in 1839 to let us know about the two periods of work. The earlier date places the painting in the same year as the small, enigmatic *Reaper with a Sickle* (fig. 22a) in the Museum of Fine Arts, Boston and two years before the enigmatic landscape with a monk in the Moreau-Nélaton collection at the Louvre.[3]

Although the Norton Simon painting has been known as *Rebecca at the Well* since its publication by Robaut in 1905, it has no exhibition history or provenance during Corot's lifetime, and, therefore, there is no proof that this identification is correct. Also, the painting has been relined, like most works by Corot (including all but one of the Norton Simon paintings), and no inscription in Corot's hand or early label can be seen on the back to confirm the subject. Yet, both Robaut and Moreau-Nélaton identify the painting unequivocally as Rebecca, and there is no reason, at this stage, to doubt them. The story of Rebecca is told in the Hebrew Bible and was most recently summarized by Michael Pantazzi.[4] Abraham's son Isaac needed a wife, and the father sent a trusted friend, Eliezer, to Mesopotamia (where Abraham had been born) to find an appropriate bride. As he approached the Mesopotamian city of Nahor, he came upon a spring and met there a young woman named

Rebecca. Rebecca happened to be Abraham's niece and, in a gesture of kindness, drew water from the spring for Eliezer and his camels. Eliezer, recognizing the providential quality of the meeting, gave Rebecca a ring and gold bracelets. Later, she married Isaac.

Pantazzi rightly pointed out the oddity of Corot's representation of Rebecca. She is alone at the spring, and there is not a hint of a nearby city or of Eliezer and his camels. Furthermore, her arms and fingers show no evidence of the golden bracelets and the ring mentioned in the Bible. In the isolation of Rebecca and the omission of the gifts she was to receive, Corot situates the action before the meeting with Eliezer. Rebecca is shown seated almost on the ground, her pose evocative of the Melancholia pose derived from Albrecht Dürer's famous engraving. Her hair is garlanded with flowers, and her head is raised slightly, while her wide-open eyes look outside the picture. Corot placed her hand very near her ear and emphasized by its light color her earlobe, on which he places an earring. Pantazzi seems to have decided that this represents the gift from Eliezer and thus concluded that Corot depicts the scene just after the meeting. However, it is likelier from the pose and glance of Rebecca (if she is Rebecca) that she is alone at the spring, having filled her jug, and that she hears or perhaps sees Eliezer and his camels approaching from the right. There is a sense of anticipation, even of doubt, in her demeanor, and it is possible that she has crouched down out of caution.

There are other cases in Western art and literature in which a young woman is shown alone at a spring, a stream, or in a forest clearing. In some, she is unaware of the existence of her viewers. In this instance, however, Corot suggests that she is aware of the presence of others and, thus, that she is not truly alone and has no notion of the consequences that will result from her encounter. She cannot be aware of the identity of the approaching man and has no reason to assume that he is a relative. Corot compressed the scene by electing to paint it on such a short and wide canvas. Indeed, if Rebecca were to stand up, she would not fit in the pictorial confines Corot created for her. Yet, at the same time, he stressed the vastness and emptiness of the space, suggesting, in so doing, that she has nowhere to escape. In the end, her calm and stable pose and the lack of tension in her body do not encourage us to read her as a fearful woman. Rather, she is accepting of her fate, listening and looking, and the viewer is placed in the position of Eliezer.

1 Information regarding Bernheim-Jeune transactions comes from Bernheim-Jeune archive and was provided by Guy-Patrice Dauberville in a letter dated 3 May 2002.

2 Bataille, 1920, lists the painting as in the David-Weill collection, which conflicts with the information from the Bernheim-Jeune archive.

3 Robaut, 1905, no. 375.

4 Tinterow, Pantazzi, and Pomarède, *Corot*, 1996, p. 174.

23

Jean-Baptiste Camille Corot
French, 1796–1875

The Cicada
1865–1875

Oil on panel, 18¼ × 14⅝ in. (46.4 × 37.2 cm)
Signed lower right: "Corot"
M.1975.13.1

Provenance: According to Robaut, "Vente X, 1877 for Ff 1,200 to Perreau"; Victor Desfossés by 1889 (sale, Paris, 26 April 1899, no. 18, for Ff 10,100, to); [Durand-Ruel et Cie, Paris and New York, sold 5 May 1926 to]; Carl Weeks, Des Moines, Iowa (sale, New York, Sotheby's, 26 October 1967, lot 18, to); Mr. and Mrs. Norton Simon, Los Angeles, in 1970 to; Lucille Ellis Simon, Los Angeles; [Paul Rosenberg & Co., New York; sold 14 August 1975 to]; Norton Simon Art Foundation.

Exhibitions: Paris, 1889, no. 19, as *Femme en rouge, jouant de la guitare*; Paris, 1895b, no. 65; New York, 1930, no. 32; Northampton, 1934, no. 16; Chicago, 1934, no. 173; Pittsburgh, 1936, no. 41; Chicago, 1937; New York, 1937b, no. 2; Chicago, 1940, no. 12; Los Angeles, 1943; Philadelphia, 1946, no. 58; Pomona, 1950; Omaha, 1951; Cedar Rapids, 1952, no. 1; Des Moines, 1955; New York, 1956c, no. 30; Chicago, 1960, no. 115; Paris, 1962c, no. 73, p. 169, ill.; on loan, Phoenix, Art Museum, 8 August–1 December 1975.

References: Robaut, 1905, vol. 3, no. 1566; Bernheim de Villers, 1930, no. 266; A. Zimmerman, 1986, p. 352, pl. 47.

Technical Notes: The small panel, which has been thinned and cradled in a traditional manner, may be oak; the grain is oriented vertically. It has a medium-thick white ground with a pebbly texture and a gray imprimatura. Paint is generally opaque local color directly applied wet in wet or wet over dry. However, the artist also used glazes and scumbles. For example, Corot painted a black underlayer for the dress that he scumbled with ocher, brown, gray, and red to give visual texture to the fabric, and for the shadows of the flesh he applied thin dark brown glazes over the brown underpainting. The girl was clearly set in first with thin dark brown paint that is visible in the shadows. Her outline was adjusted with the landscape paint but also with her own colors over the landscape. Raking light and X-ray expose a rounded chair back behind and to the right of the girl (figs. 23b and 23c). The outline of the figure was adjusted in many areas and there are numerous unclear changes in the placement of the hands and the mandolin. The condition of the painting is good. Contraction cracks are visible in a number of areas such as where the chair was painted out, as would be expected. The painting was cleaned in 1967. (JF)

La Cigale (*The Cicada*) was among the earliest published titles of this superb late study of a figure by Corot. It is among a group of nearly one hundred figure paintings made by Corot from the mid-1850s until his death in 1875, most probably in his Parisian studio, where he employed models and various costume elements to create illusory muses, mostly of a contemplative and occasionally a melancholic temperament. Usually, they sit or stand in static poses, either in interiors or imaginary landscape settings, holding simple props such as a book, a letter, a musical instrument, flowers, or a ceramic vessel. Rarely do they engage actively with these props; the books and letters, though available to them, remain mostly unread, the flowers unarranged, the instruments unplayed and silent. Whether they are waiting for inspiration, contemplating what they have already done, or simply sitting listlessly without thought is left up to the viewer.

It is customary in writing about these figure paintings to say that they were a private exercise of the famous, elderly painter, unknown to the public who clamored for his landscapes. Yet this is not at all true. While he preferred to send landscapes to the Salons, he did submit major figure paintings to the Salons of 1840, 1859, 1861, and 1869. The earliest three have imposing landscape backgrounds and an air of classical allegory. Only one, the enigmatic figure painting at the Salon of 1869, *A Woman Reading* (fig. 23a), is like the single-figure painting in the Norton Simon Museum. This superb painting received comparatively little attention in the critical press that year, and some of it was negative. Yet, we know that Corot's Parisian studio was open to many others—fellow painters, students, models, collectors, and friends—and, particularly after the appearance of *A Woman Reading* in 1869, private collectors began to purchase figure paintings by Corot with increasing regularity. In fact, it seems that they more or less ensured the continuing vitality of Corot's reputation in the last decade of his life, and an important group of them were selected for his memorial exhibition, hastily arranged at the École des Beaux-Arts just months after his death in 1875. Also, the presence of many of these works in the public sales after the death of the childless and unmarried painter guaranteed that every serious artist and collector in Paris came to know Corot as an important painter of the human figure, among the greatest in France at midcentury.

It is perhaps because of the narrow range of situations, models, compositions, and props employed by Corot in creating his figure paintings that his works are so deeply satisfying. Unlike Gustave Courbet or Édouard Manet,

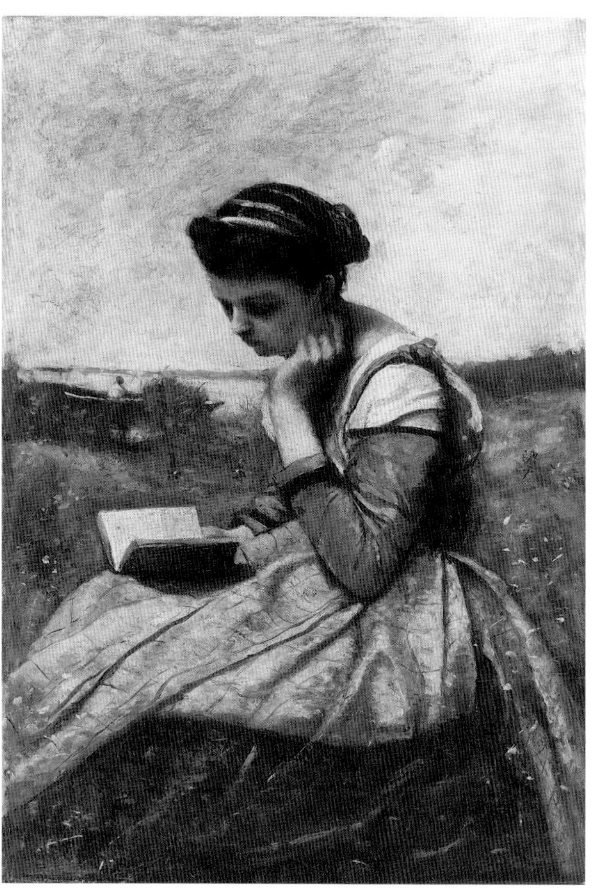

Fig. 23a Jean-Baptiste Camille Corot, *A Woman Reading*, 1869, oil on canvas, $21\frac{3}{8} \times 14\frac{3}{4}$ in. (54.3×37.5 cm), The Metropolitan Museum of Art, Gift of Louis Senff Cameron, in memory of Charles H. Senff, 1928

who placed figures in groups, often in plausible public settings in the city or the country, Corot preferred isolated figures in settings that are so simple and generic that neither competes with the other. Corot's viewers are not encouraged to think about social class, sexual relations, technological innovations, or even traditional iconography associated with Western figural allegories. His late figures are simply too vague and polyvalent to be called "Melancholia," "Rebecca at the Well," "The Penitent Magdalene," or any other historical or religious trope. In this way, his paintings are modern without being contemporary. Thus, Corot prepares the way for the figure paintings of Paul Cézanne, who, although he never seems to have owned a Corot figure painting, was enormously affected by them.

When analyzing an individual figure painting from Corot's late years, the mysteries of their meanings and contexts multiply. The present work has been known to Corot's admirers since its first documented appearance in the centennial exhibition organized by the French State at the Exposition Universelle of 1889. There, it was among forty-four paintings by Corot, including thirteen figure paintings—a veritable mini-retrospective—and it was given the banal descriptive title *Femme en rouge, jouant de la guitare* (*Woman in Red, Playing a Guitar*), in spite of the fact that the woman is neither exclusively in red nor playing a guitar. When the painting next entered the public sphere, in the great 1895 Corot exhibition organized at the centennial of his birth, it was called *La Cigale* (*The Cicada*), a title that is reiterated in the estate sale of the painting's first recorded owner, Victor Desfossés, in 1899. In that catalogue, it was given its longest descriptive analysis, in a paragraph worthy of full quotation.

> The Cicada. In the countryside, a seated young woman is seen almost in profile to the left; she is dressed in a black dress and a red bodice, the edges of which are drawn aside to reveal the white undershirt. Her two hands carry on her knees a mandolin, which her eyes caress with melancholy glances. In her black hair, two crossed ribbons hold a flower.[1]

The earliest history of the painting is not clear. Although certain sources assert that it was sold in Corot's estate sales in 1875, there is no listing in the catalogue that permits us to identify it, suggesting that perhaps Robaut was correct in placing it first in an 1877 sale called simply Vente X (at which it was sold to Perreau for Ff 1,200). If Robaut is correct—and confirmation will have to await a full study of French sale catalogues of 1877—it is likely that the painting was sold within Corot's lifetime, which explains its evidently authentic signature rather than the estate stamp placed on works that remained in the artist's studio at his death.

In the twentieth century, *The Cicada* fared well. It was purchased in 1926 by Mr. and Mrs. Carl Weeks from Des Moines, Iowa, and was kept in their vast Neo-Tudor estate called Salisbury House. As the exhibition history above makes clear, the Weekses were generous lenders. Their Corot appeared in one of the inaugural exhibitions of the Museum of Modern Art in 1930, at the *Century of Progress* exhibition at the Art Institute of Chicago, at the great Corot retrospectives in Philadelphia (1946) and

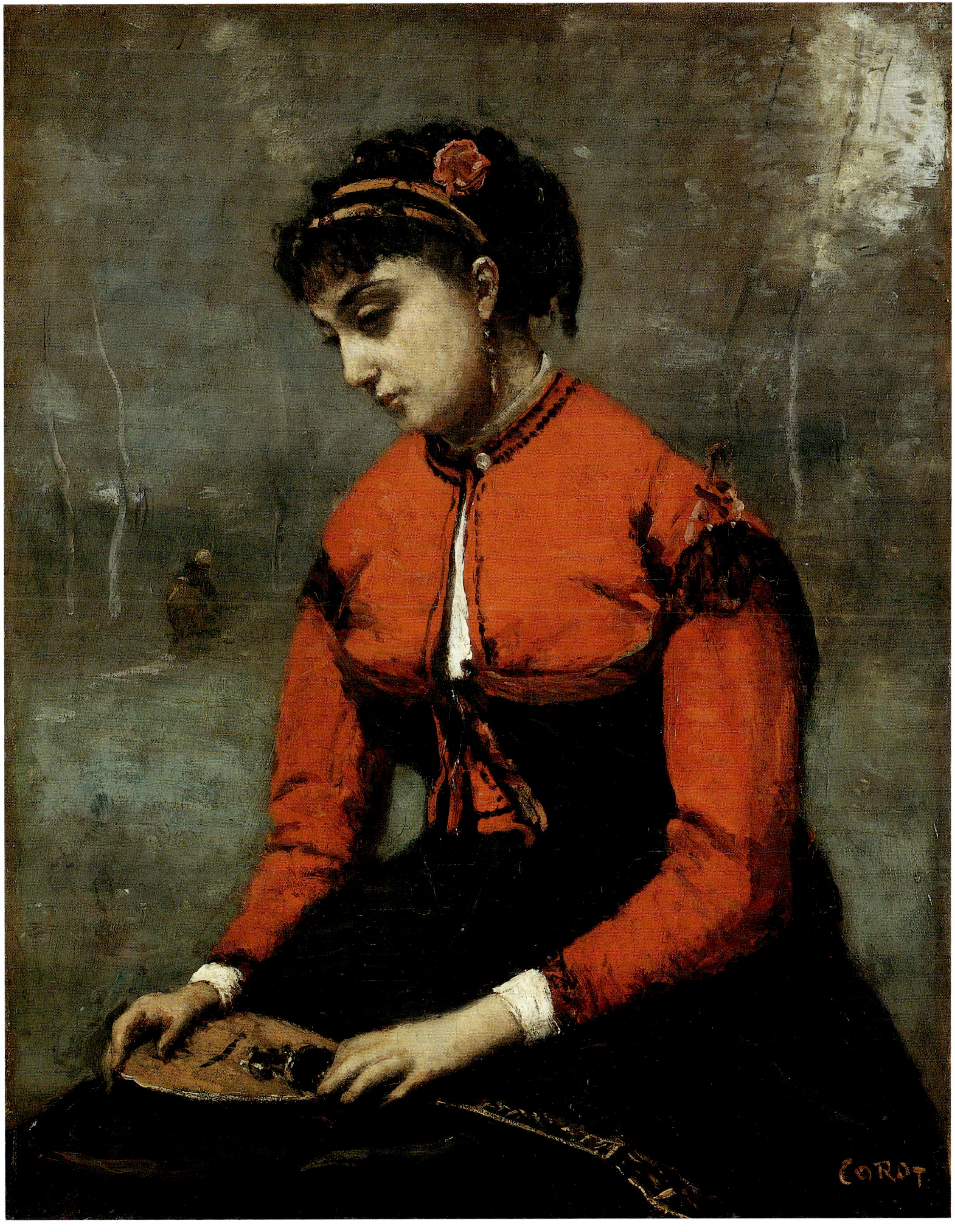

23

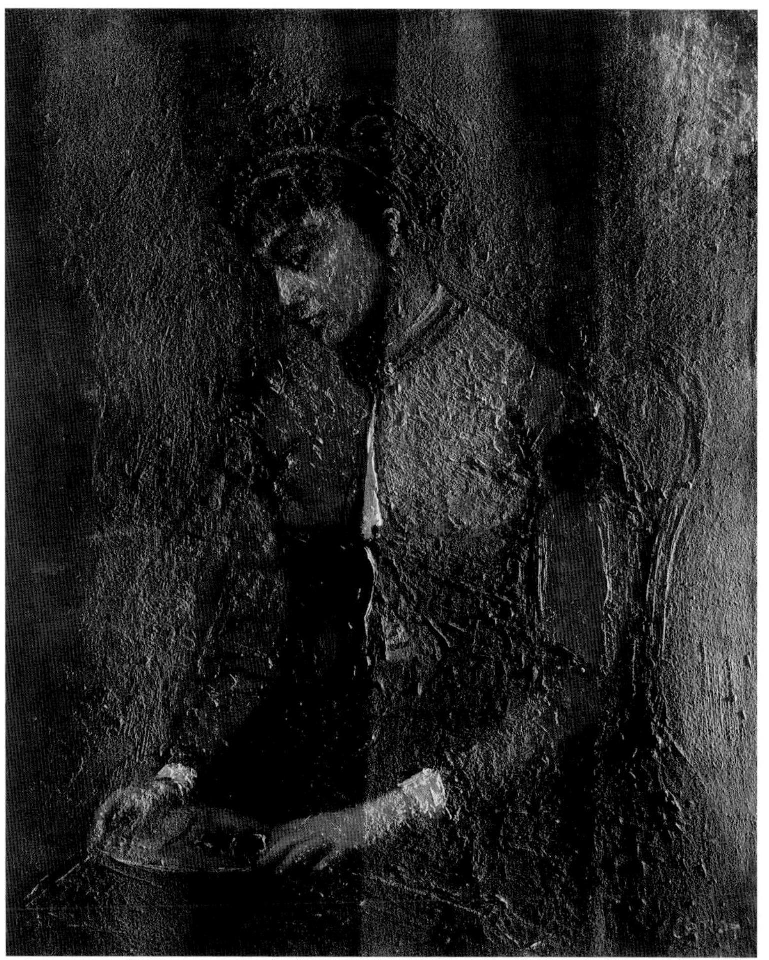

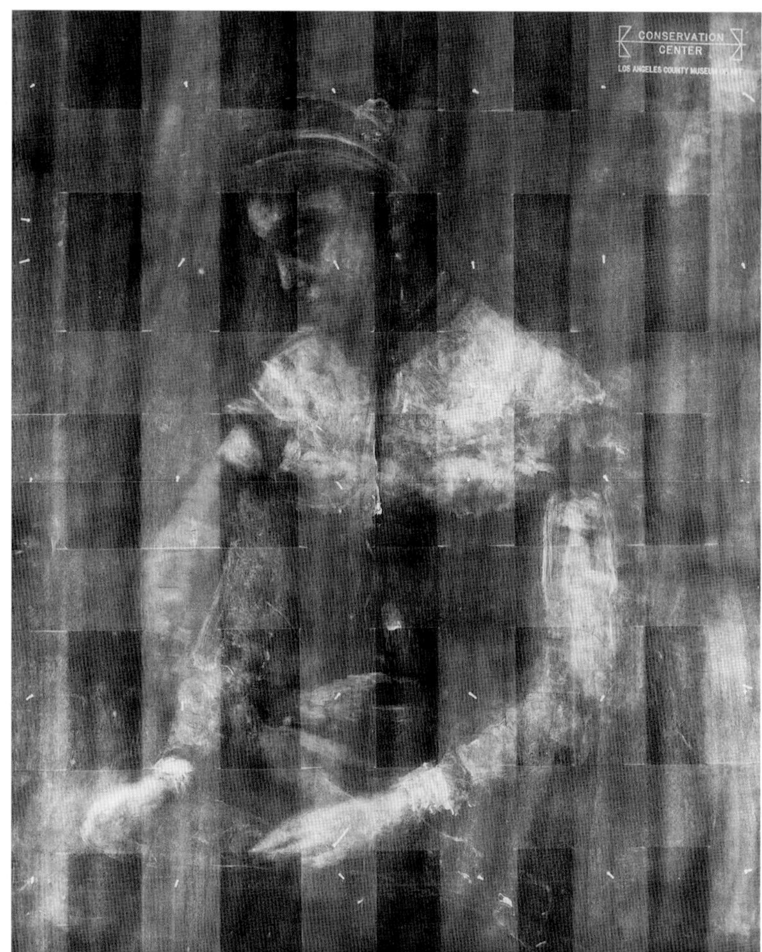

Fig. 23b (*above left*) Photograph of cat. 23 in raking light

Fig. 23c (*above right*) X-ray photograph of cat. 23

Chicago (1960), and in the most important exhibition of Corot's figural compositions ever mounted at the Musée du Louvre in 1962. When it sold at auction in New York in 1967, interest in the painting was so high that it set a world record price for the artist and, thus, had a profound effect on market levels for Corot's figure paintings.

Unlike the majority of Corot's figure paintings, *The Cicada* is painted on panel. For that reason, its surface is extraordinarily well preserved, making it possible to follow Corot's working method. In contrast to its placid and melancholic subject, surface examination (fig. 23b) and X-ray analysis (fig. 23c) make it clear that the painting is a veritable battleground of failed ideas and compositional and figural changes. Even a cursory examination of the photograph taken in raking light shows evidence of a chair to the right of the figure, on which she was sitting at an earlier stage in the composition, forcing us to remember that the woman was painted, not in a real landscape, but from a posed model in Corot's Parisian studio. It is even possible that Corot began the painting without an idea of the eventual landscape setting. And the X-ray reveals that she wore completely different costumes at various times in the history of the composition (previously she had a distinctly Italian cast, like that of many other costumed figures of the period), and that her hands were placed in as many as three different poses, being folded in at least two positions on her lap with a mandolin. Even the latter was added at a relatively late stage. All of these shifts force us to realize that the painting was made in at least three major campaigns, possibly separated by months or even years. Corot painted somewhat rarely on panel. Indeed, only six of the more than one hundred figural paintings included in Robaut's catalogue are so recorded, and even the size of this work is an anomaly in the artist's career—no other figure paintings share its dimensions.

Recent physical studies of Corot's late paintings record many similar instances of major changes made to compositions as well as various campaigns of work on a single canvas. This is surely because all of these works were painted in Corot's Parisian studio without pressure of time and he could abandon them and take them up again when his model returned or his mood shifted.

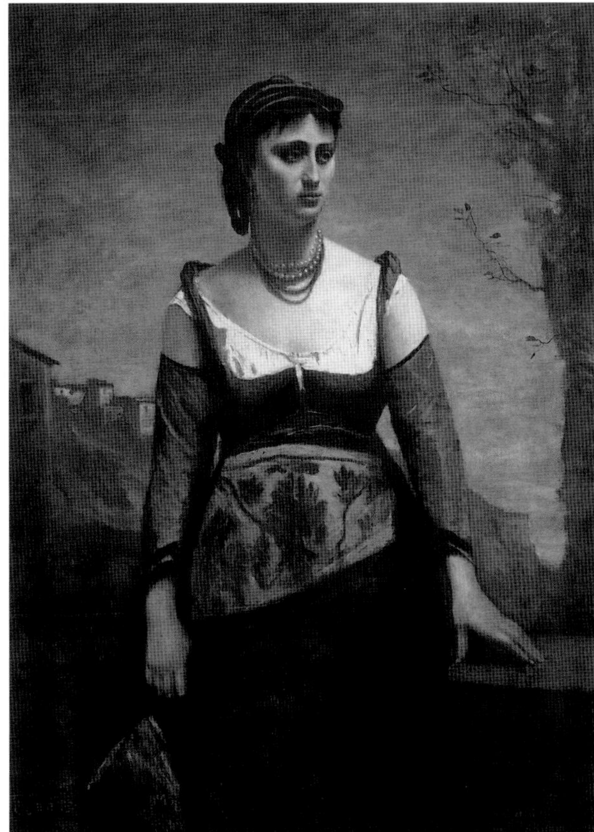

Fig. 23d Jean-Baptiste Camille Corot, *The Italian Agostina*, 1866, oil on canvas, $52\frac{1}{8} \times 38\frac{3}{8}$ in. (132.4 × 97.6 cm), National Gallery of Art, Washington, D.C., Chester Dale Collection

There has not been sufficient technical study of these works to make many comparative observations or even to speculate with any degree of precision on the identity of the model or even the dates of the work. For now, it is best to expand somewhat Robaut's date of 1868–1870 by pushing the beginning of work on the painting back at least to 1866, when Corot painted *The Italian Agostina* (fig. 23d). There is no reason to assign a terminus of 1870, making it wisest to be broadest and to settle on 1865–1875.

Perhaps the single most interesting aspect of this enigmatic painting is the French title, *La Cigale* (*The Cicada*). Cicadas are, of course, singing insects associated with hot climates—the south of France and certain parts of Italy. They are also featured in one of the most famous of the many French fables of La Fontaine, "La Cigale et les fournis" (The Cicada, or Grasshopper and the Ants), in which the *cigales* "chants toute l'été" (sing all summer). There is also a southern French popular song of uncertain origin that ends with the following pair of couplets: "Cigale, ma cigale / allons il faut chanter / Car les lauriers du bois / Sont déjà repousses" (Cicada, my cicada / Let's sing / For the laurels in the wood / Have already sprung).

Each of these verbal sources associates *La Cigale* with both singing and summer, and it is perhaps worth noting the presence of a painting with the same title in a sale of works by Corot's follower, Paul-Desiré Trouillebert, in 1893.[2] Yet, how silent Corot's woman is and how cool the landscape seems. Who, may we ask, is singing?

1 *Vente après decès Collection de M. Victor Desfossés*, Paris, 26 April 1899. The text reads in French: "La Cigale. Dans la campagne, une jeune femme assise est vue presque de profil à gauche; elle est vêtue d'une robe noire et d'un corsage rouge dont les bords écartés laissent voir la chemisette blanche. Les deux mains portent sur les genoux une mandoline que ses yeux caressent de regards mélancoliques. Dans ses cheveux noirs, deux rubans croisés retiennent une fleur."

2 Bénézit, 1966, vol. 8, p. 389.

24

Jean-Baptiste Camille Corot
French, 1796–1875

Thatched Cottage in Normandy
c. 1872

Oil on canvas, $17\frac{3}{4} \times 24\frac{1}{16}$ in. (45.1 × 61.2 cm)
Signed lower right: "Corot"
M.2002.01

Provenance: The artist; sold for Ff 2,000 to; Beugniet, Paris. Guibert, by at least 1875–at least 1878. John Saulnier, Bordeaux (sale, Paris, Hôtel Drouot, 5 June 1886, lot 22, ill., as *Paysage: Ferme normande. Environs d'Yport*, for Ff 18,000 to); Professor Dieulafoy (sale, Paris, Galerie Georges Petit, 21 June 1928, lot 5, ill., as *La Ferme normande aux trois commères*, to); [Paul Rosenberg, Paris]. Laulitier, Paris. Max Silberberg, Breslau, by 1930 (sale, Paris, Galerie Georges Petit, 9 June 1932, lot 15, ill., as *La Ferme normande aux trois commères*, for Ff 181,500 to); Mme Beredit (possibly meant to indicate the following); Mme Léon Berard. Sir Alfred Chester Beatty (1875–1968), London and Dublin, October 1936 (sale, London, Sotheby's, 4 May 1960, lot 50, as *La Ferme normande aux trois commères*, bought in); (sale, London, Sotheby's, 28 June 1967, lot 4, ill., as *La Ferme normande aux trois commères* [*Étretat ou Yport*] to); [Stephen Hahn Gallery, New York; sold 23 February 1968 to]; Norton Simon; bequest 1993 to; Jennifer Jones Simon Art Trust, gift 2002 to; Norton Simon Art Foundation.

Exhibitions: Paris, 1875, no. 168, as *La Chaumière*; Paris, 1878, no. 74; Paris, 1886, no. 53; Paris, 1936e, no. 101; Lyon, 1936, no. 102; on loan, Dublin, National Gallery of Ireland, November 1956–May 1957.

References: Robaut, 1905, vol. 3, no. 2059, ill.; Meier-Graefe, 1930, pl. 138; Scheffler, 1931, p. 8; Bazin, 1942, no. 113; Kennedy, 1987, pp. 48 n. 16, 50, App. 3.

Technical Notes: The very open plain-weave, light- to medium-weight fabric has only a strip lining; its original tacking edges still exist. Two canvas preparer's stamps can be read with the painting set vertically. The 5-part butt-join stretcher is probably original. Light blue-gray commercial priming covers the tacking edges. Since the ground does not fully fill the interstices of the canvas, hollowed half-spheres formed in the opaque paints at the interstices of the fabric. There may be a first lay-in of dark brown paint at least to set out the architecture and the general tree line. Then the painting must have proceeded quickly and directly with strokes of the pasty paints. In addition, rich translucent paints are present. For example, the shadows of the eaves of the roof were created with a rich brown over the cool ground, and the basic design of the line of trees was painted with a dark brown that allows the ground to visually interact. The lighter colors may also be glazed in some areas, with green for foliage, for example. The artist paid careful attention to color nuances; for instance, on the purple side of the house they range from dark brown just under the roof to light purple and light brown and then to dark purple. The form of the foreground figures was reserved when the landscape was painted but the other figures were painted on top. The X-ray suggests that the tall tree at left was rearranged. Remnants of a yellowed varnish are visible but no record of varnish removal is available. The newer varnish fluoresces greenish in ultraviolet light. The condition of the picture is very good with only slight abrasion and a scratch at the upper right. Some mechanical cracks developed in the sky, and fine contraction cracks are in the landscape. (JF)

Camille Corot fell ill in September 1869 and remained in Paris for the rest of the year. Perhaps as a consequence of this illness, he was one of many Frenchmen trapped in the city during the onset of the Franco-Prussian War and throughout the lengthy siege of the French capital by the German armies. He painted more or less continuously during this period of privation and remained in the capital for the entire year of 1870 and the first three months of 1871. Thus, the Franco-Prussian War and the ensuing Commune were the first political events that directly affected the orderly patterns of the elderly painter's life. Rather than working throughout the winter months in Paris in his studio on the rue de Paradis-Poissonnière and then planning lengthy trips and summer holidays from spring through early autumn, as was his custom, Corot spent almost two full years in Paris, and it is perhaps during this period that a large number of his figure paintings were begun and his earlier landscapes completed.

As if released from a kind of urban prison, Corot spent his first summer holiday of the 1870s in the northern French cities of Douai and Arras, returning for a few months at the end of 1871 and early 1872 to the capital before leaving again on one of the longest pictorial trips of his life. Despite his recent ill health and his age of nearly seventy-six, Corot left Paris in April 1872 and did not return until the very end of December or early January 1873. During this period of nearly nine months, Corot visited Beauvais, Ville-d'Avray, Fumay, Coubron, Douai, Arras, Rouen, Yport, Criqueboeuf, Étretat, Marcoussis, Port Marly, Luzancy, Argenteuil, Fontainebleau, Mantes, Bordeaux, Saint-Jean-de-Luz, and Biarritz in France and Irun, Fuenterrabia, and San Sebastian in Spain. Even reading the list is exhausting if one knows the difficulties of travel for an elderly artist with his luggage, paint supplies, and companions. Each place involved fresh visual stimulus and a new small society of friends, because Corot tended to travel to be with someone as much as to be in a particular landscape.

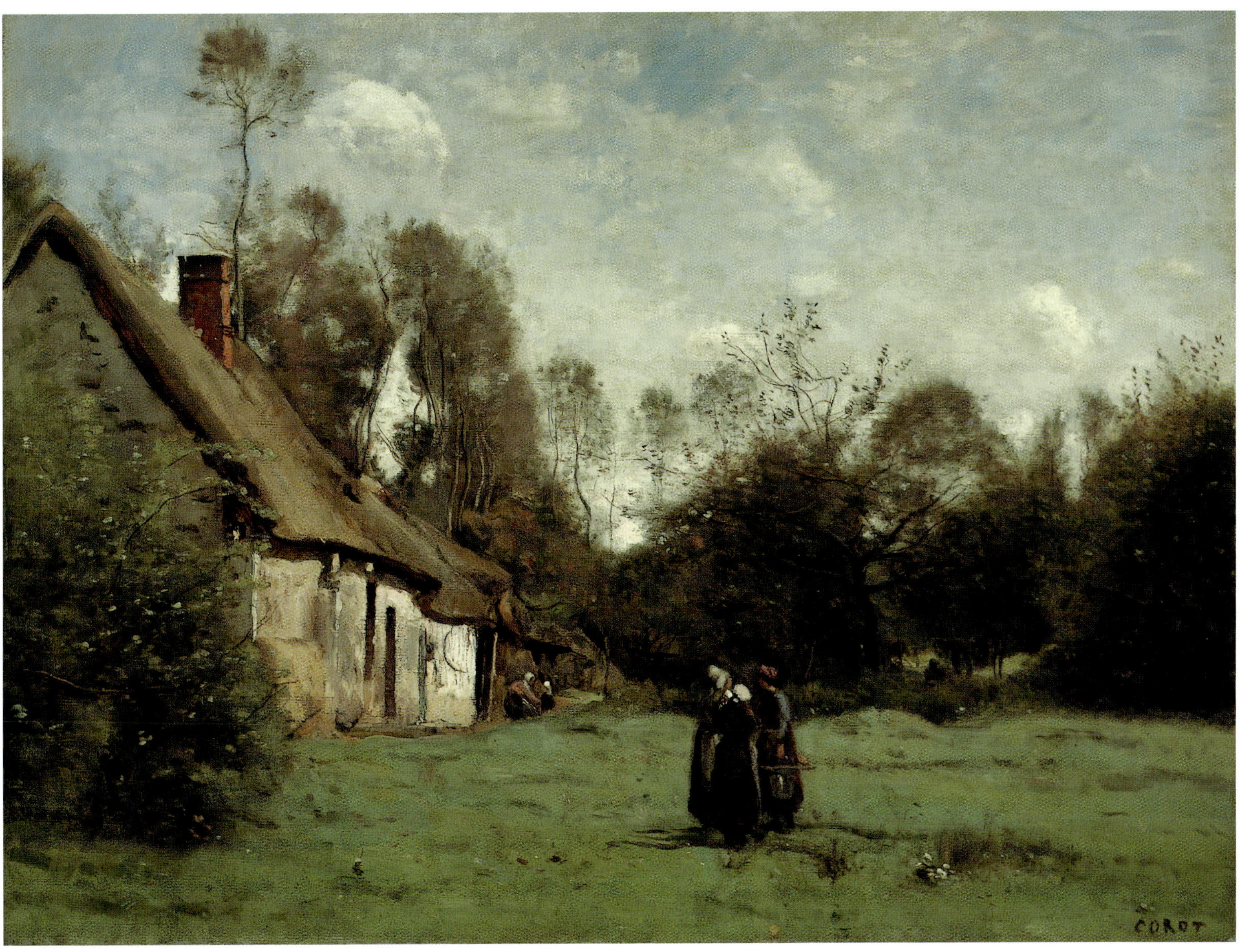

24

This delicious small rural landscape surely comes from that almost fugal period of travel. The word *fugue* is here used in the Freudian sense of fleeing trauma or disaster and has not often been applied to the study of landscape painting. Surely it applies to the aged Corot as much as it applies to the career of Claude Monet in the decade following the death of his first wife in 1879. Almost every form of trauma that could be imagined—ill health, war, internal insurrection, privations, and family worries—weighed on the mind of Corot, whose calm disposition and steady work habits surely suffered. He had even painted a rare representation of urban warfare, the two-night bombardment of Paris by the Germans on 9 and 10 September 1870, in the days following the event.[1] And, just as the sublimely peaceful landscapes of 1872 painted by Monet, Alfred Sisley, Pierre-Auguste Renoir, and Camille Pissarro can be read as part of a national healing process for the French, so too can Corot's landscapes of 1872. He traveled almost the length and breadth of his country that year, and wherever he went, he painted landscapes and topographical studies that represent what the French call *la longue durée*, the timeless "present" of French historical continuity. The anonymous building chosen by Corot could have been painted by a landscape painter any time from the late Middle Ages through the nineteenth century.

Like most paintings by Corot, this landscape has had many titles, each of which has a different effect on our interpretation of it. The first published title, in 1875, was *La Chaumière* (*The Thatched Cottage*), which is surely correct, but fails to help us place the work of art. The cottage is like those that are common throughout

Normandy, where Corot spent a good deal of his time on the 1872 journey. By 1886 the painting had become *Paysage: Ferme normande, environs d'Yport* (*Landscape, Norman Farm in the Region of Yport*). Surely the increased precision of the title comes from the fact that most of Corot's companions on that 1872 journey were very much alive in 1875, particularly his student and future cataloguer, Alfred Robaut, whose family came from Normandy and who witnessed Corot paint several works that summer. By the time that Robaut published his immense catalogue of Corot's work in 1905, the title was again changed to become *La Ferme normande aux trois commères (Étretat ou Yport)* (*The Norman Farm of the Three Gossiping Women [Étretat or Yport]*). Surely the lively title has some basis in fact, because Corot included three women chatting in the foreground, and Robaut must either have remembered this name or simply invented it to explain these three figures. He was a little indecisive about the place this time around, but Étretat and Yport are very near each other, and Corot could easily have viewed such an inland farm from either Norman fishing town.

We must remember, in all this welter of detail, that Corot himself actually avoided any precise topographical indicators in painting this small landscape. Instead, the farm buildings are typical rather than particular, participating in a broad vernacular tradition that had persisted for centuries in France. Indeed, Corot painted the new chalet of M. Dumesnil in Étretat almost as Monet had done in the late 1860s. Monet, the modern painter, avoided thatched cottages, which, for the elderly Corot, were a symbol of the continuity of what one calls *la France profonde.*

As Joseph Fronek has made clear in his analysis of this small painting, it is a technical marvel. In making the present painting, we know, for example, that Corot anticipated the three figures, leaving room for them as he painted their setting. This lends credence to Robaut's title, suggesting that, rather than adding figures where they were needed for scale and color, as Corot often did, he centered the composition on the figures, making them as important as the buildings and more important than the trees. A careful user of Robaut's crucially important catalogue raisonné will spot many photographs of paintings from the last decade of the painter's life that exist in two forms, A and B. These photographs record the state of the painting after it was initially completed in the field (A) and as it was retouched and reconsidered in the Parisian studio (B). A careful examination of the trees and background features of the Norton Simon landscape will reveal that Corot opened up the foliage to create a spatial recession absent in the initial composition. He also refined the particularly elegant contours of the large tree that rises above the cottage and the trunks of the row of neighboring trees. These small shifts prove that, even in creating a small landscape, Corot considered every element of the composition carefully and then reconsidered these decisions when he was in the studio, far from the strong influence of the landscape itself.

It is worth noting that this charming but "typical" late Corot landscape was selected by his friends for inclusion in the memorial exhibition held months after the painter's death three years after it was made. Hence, it must have held pride of place in the minds of his most sympathetic contemporaries. It was also chosen by the great German historian of modern art, Julius Meier-Graefe, for inclusion in his 1930 monograph on Corot, and there is little doubt that Meier-Graefe played some role in the decision of the German collector Max Silberberg to buy the painting. Corot's belief in the persistence of memory and in the ongoing strength of the French people was expressed profoundly in the group of landscapes he painted on his liberating trip of 1872. The Norton Simon painting is neither the largest nor the most original work from that trip. Perhaps for those reasons it speaks so clearly of the artist's intentions to soothe the unrest both of his nation and of himself.

1 Robaut, 1905, no. 2352.

25

Achille-Jacques-Jean-Marie Devéria
French, 1800–1857

Odalisque
c. 1830–1835

Oil on panel, 9 × 12½ in. (22.9 × 31.8 cm)
Signed lower left: "A. Devéria"
M.1967.6

Provenance: (Sale, New York, Parke-Bernet, 2 March 1967, lot 95, to); Norton Simon Art Foundation.

Exhibitions: Princeton, 1972, no. 19, ill.; San Francisco, 1974, no. 14, ill.; Malibu, 1996.

References: Steadman, 1973a, p. 10, ill.; Weisberg, 1978b, pp. 11, 12, 82, fig. 1; Croutier, 1989, p. 160, ill.; Michel, Prince of Greece, 1992, p. 90, ill.; DelPlato, 2002, pp. 75, 77, 124–125 and cover, color ill., fig. 3.9.

Technical Notes: The small painting was executed on a horizontally grained oval panel; the reverse is beveled around the perimeter. The smooth white ground is sufficiently thick to mask the wood grain almost completely. From the center of the left side, a horizontal crack extends inward for 1½ inches; it is slightly open, and it appears that some of the filling material has fallen out, while other tiny fills at the edges have not been retouched. The paint was directly applied over the white ground and manipulated with a delicacy similar to that seen in a miniature painted in watercolor. Shadows in the flesh tones are a thin, salmon color; the blanket beneath the figure's feet appears to be very dilute black paint evenly striated with a small stiff brush, then overpainted here and there with the decorative design. Most of the painting is a single layer; a rosy-colored underlayer is visible in the sky to the right of the balustrade. Tiny swirls of impasto provide decorative touches on the necklace, earrings, the teapot, and cup. The paint is well preserved overall except for two small paint losses in the white sleeve. Abrasion is minimal; the *D* in the signature is slightly thinned. The varnish is yellowed, brittle, and streaked. (RW)

Achille Devéria was a French painter, lithographer, curator, illustrator, and pornographer. Notwithstanding his varied and colorful résumé, he is not as well known as his brother Eugène, whose monumental painting *The Birth of Henri IV* (Musée du Louvre, Paris) was taken by many to be the epitome of the Romantic school when it was exhibited at the Paris Salon of 1827. Achille did, however, achieve his own brief renown as a history painter when he completed an impressive *Apotheosis of Saint Clotilde* for the choir ambulatory of St.-Roch, an important eighteenth-century church built from earlier designs by Jacques Lemercier on the rue St. Honoré in Paris. There, his painting was seen beside earlier altarpieces by Joseph-Marie Vien and Gabriel-François Doyen, and contemporary works by Théodore Chassériau, Victor Schnetz, Ary Scheffer, and the sculptor Auguste Préault. Devéria's many later illustrations after works by diverse authors may have served him as compensation for his failure to secure more commissions for large-scale history paintings. Devéria also designed stained-glass windows and was an outstanding colorist, a fact apparent from his brilliant costume designs for Molière's *Don Juan* (1847, Bibliothèque de la Comédie Française, Paris) and the present painting.

Devéria's *Odalisque* is an early example of Orientalism, a genre of painting that flourished in France from approximately the 1830s to the 1930s, though there were Romantic antecedents and postcolonial successors. The epoch is framed by two events: the invasion and conquest of Algeria (1830) and the *L'Exposition coloniale de Paris* (1931). The first ushered in a new international, and imperial, outlook, manifested in art and literature by a few masterpieces, such as Eugène Delacroix's *Women of Algiers* (1834) and Gustave Flaubert's *Salammbô* (1858), and by many lesser works. The second event marked the beginning of the end of public support for *la mission civilatrice*, the ideological justification for imperial aggression. Orientalist art and literature are marked by the tendency to portray non-European and non-white people (especially those from the Middle or Far East: the "Orient") as violent, decadent, indolent, and lacking the capacity for independent thought and action, in other words, as fit subjects for conquest. Women in particular are the receptacles of Orientalist fantasy; they are represented as hedonistic, hypersexual, and capricious. Few works of art are more dated today than Orientalist ones by Devéria, Eugène Fromentin, and Jean-Léon Gérôme.

Achille Devéria's painting is an early essay in the visual and ideological tropes that would quickly come to define Orientalism. It does not depict an actual Moroccan, Algerian, or other Arab or North African woman as she might have been seen in her native land, or in later Orientalist pictures where accurate ethnographic detail was prized. Indeed, it represents a confection of such a woman, contrived from stories, pictures, fantasies, and a model (or lover) posed in a studio. Here, a young, voluptuous woman, wearing vermilion drawstring pants and a peasant blouse opened to the waist, lies on an upholstered mattress, smoking a cigarette. Behind her is a verdant, walled garden with a fountain, orange trees, and a parrot. Beside her in the foreground are a coffeepot and

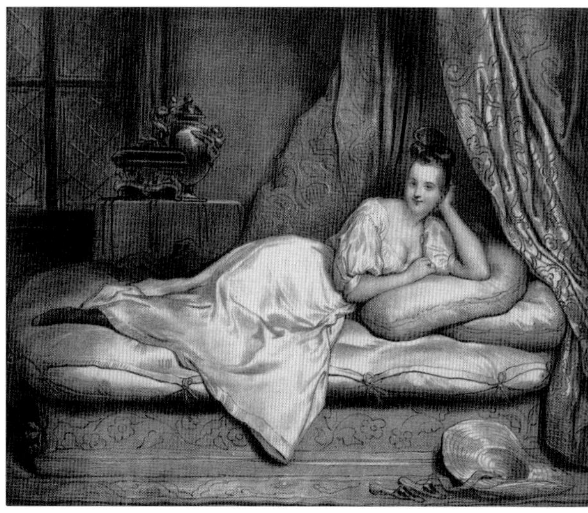

Fig. 25a Achille-Jacques-Jean-Marie Devéria, *Satisfaction*, 1830, lithograph, $8\frac{1}{2} \times 10$ in. (21.1×25.4 cm), Wake Forest University Print Collection; photo: Martine Sherrill

cup, a box for tobacco, and a pair of shoes. The enumerated details are formally combined to create an Orientalist totality. The mattress on which she reclines parallels both the picture surface before her and the wall behind her; the swelling oval shape of her pants is repeated by the oval shape of the wooden panel support; and the vermilion plumage of the parrot perched on the wall echoes the color of the slave, or harem woman's, pants. The parrot is a symbol particularly redolent of eroticism and the East. It is veritably a substitute for female sexual organs (and a symbol of women's chatter) and a sign of the phallus as well, as in Gustave Courbet's frank *Woman with a Parrot* (1866, The Metropolitan Museum of Art, New York).

The painting was apparently derived from several sources. J.-A.-D. Ingres's famous slave girl or *Odalisque* (1814, Musée du Louvre, Paris) is one touchstone for the artist, as no doubt were the several recumbent, nude, or Oriental figures in paintings by Delacroix, including the *Scenes of a Massacre at Chios* (1822), *Greece Expiring* (1824), and *Death of Sardanapalus* (1827). Devéria's own lithograph with the provocative title *Satisfaction* (fig. 25a) is another. It too depicts a young woman, in revealing décolletage, reclining on a bed placed parallel to the picture surface, with shoes discarded. The ease with which Devéria moved from contemporary to Oriental ambience indicates that his ambition in the Norton Simon *Odalisque* may in fact have been more narrowly erotic than exotic. The consumption of the cigarette suggests that the reclining woman, like the figure in the lithograph, has just concluded a sexual liaison and is now basking in the afterglow. Devéria made a number of explicitly pornographic as well as simply erotic prints, and sex was most of all his stock-in-trade. (See especially the twelve illustrations, made in collaboration with Pierre Grevedon, for Alfred de Musset's *Gamiani*, 1833.) The present painting nevertheless stands as an early moment in the history of Orientalist images of feminine passivity and indolence, and it would be followed by hundreds of others, culminating in the odalisques of Henri Matisse, made in Morocco in the 1920s.

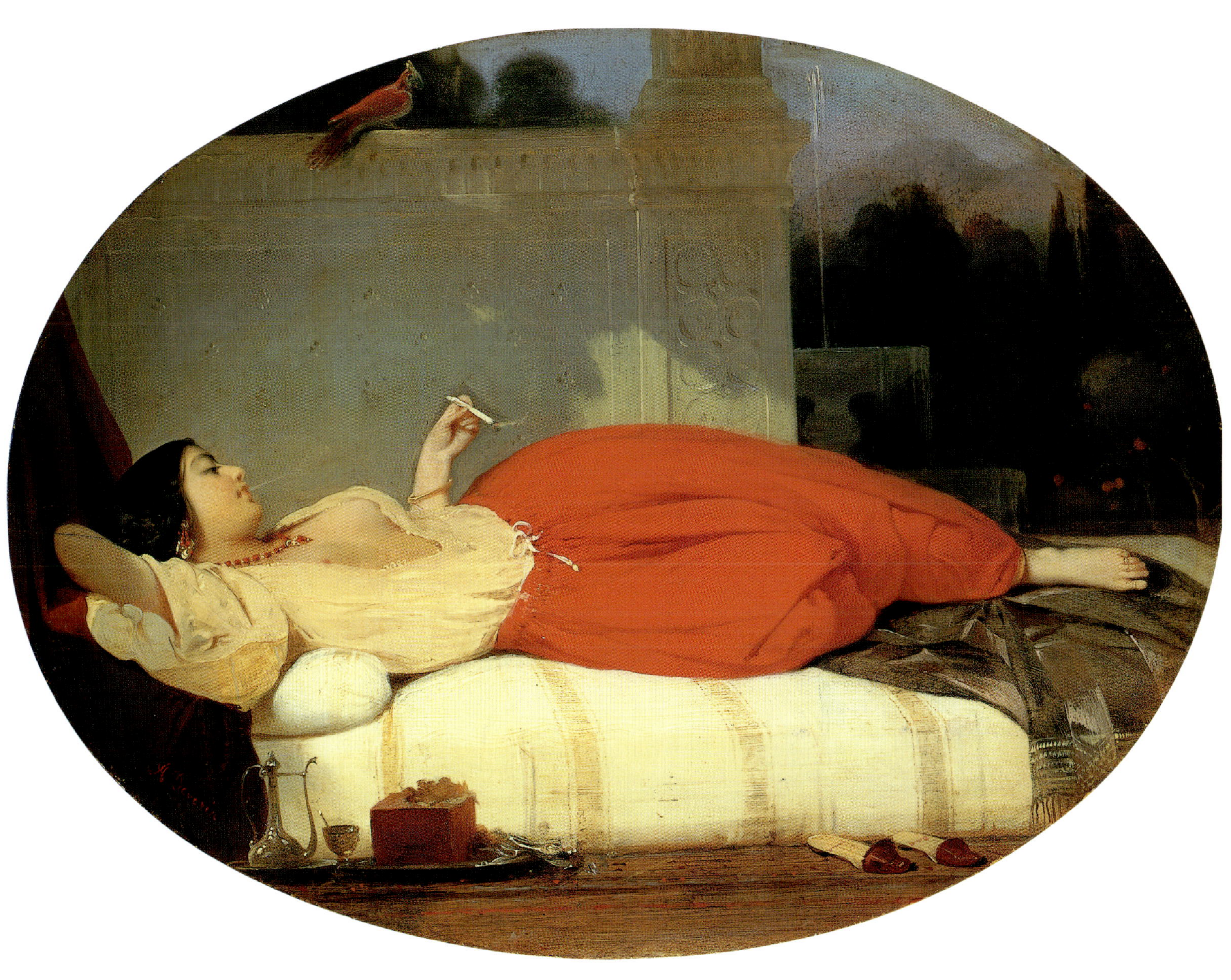

25

26

Achille-Jacques-Jean-Marie Devéria
French, 1800–1857

Young Woman with a Rose
1850

Oil on canvas, $33\frac{3}{4} \times 27\frac{1}{4}$ in. (85.7×69.2 cm)
Signed lower left: "AD"
Signed and dated on verso, lower left: "A. Devéria dep 1850"
F.1983.8

Provenance: Ambassador N. (sale, Paris, Hôtel Drouot, 10 March 1976, lot 45, ill., to); [Sylvia Blatas, Paris, buying for]; Norton Simon, gift 1983 to; The Norton Simon Foundation.

Technical Notes: The original support is a plain-weave canvas; it has been lined with the original edges retained. Selvedges are at both the left and right edges, which are extremely narrow. A horizontal tear in the proper right sleeve was well mended; there are a small repaired hole at the left bottom edge and additional minor losses at the bottom center in the red cushion. The signature and date of 1850 on the reverse of the original canvas were recorded in photographs before lining. The thin white ground was not commercially prepared. It was applied on the front surface only, and not on the tacking edges. A thin, light brown layer beneath the background paint can be seen with high magnification at the right edge, where bits of fractured paint reveal the paint strata. In the figure, faint graphite lines of preparatory drawing are visible in the folds of the white blouse, the fingers, and the rose. They may also be present in other parts of the painting, but darker paint obscures them. Paint was directly applied with smoothly blended brushwork. The major part of it is quite thin; only the flesh tones are opaque. The background monochrome layer is modified slightly by the brown tint below it. Losses from abrasion are rather widespread. The most noticeable areas are located in the eyes, the shadow to the right of the nose, the proper right ear, the bottom of the hair above the proper left shoulder, and the area surrounding the rosebud. Much of the abrasion has been left without retouching. The painting was treated in 1984. (RW)

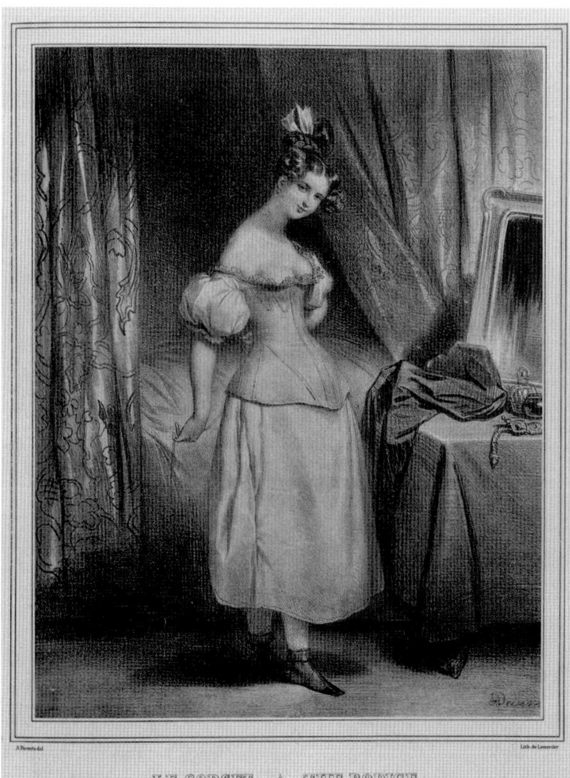

Fig. 26a Achille-Jacques-Jean-Marie Devéria, *The Corset*, engraved by Alfred Lemercier, lithograph, Stapleton Collection, UK

The bulk of Achille Devéria's energy and talents was dedicated to portrait painting and illustration, especially by means of the new medium of lithography. Often he combined these skills, as with his lithographs of the composer and pianist Franz Liszt (1832, Bibliothèque de l'Opéra, Paris), the economist and philosopher Jean-Baptiste Say (c. 1830, Bibliothèque nationale de France, Paris), and Théodore Géricault (1824, University of Michigan Museum of Art), in which the recently deceased artist is exotically attired in a turban that drapes across his neck and shoulders. Devéria's fashion plates, such as *Eleven O'Clock* (Musée Carnavalet, Paris) and *The Corset* (fig. 26a), are probably his most numerous works, and they exhibit precisely the combination of vapidity and eroticism that has defined the genre ever since: a young woman, standing before a mirror, casts a seductive glance over her shoulder, as she proudly displays her narrow waist and ample bust. Édouard Manet would both embrace and mock the format when he painted his *Nana* (1877, Kunsthalle, Hamburg).

Young Woman with a Rose was painted from a model, but it should not be considered a portrait. The modesty or reserve that was requisite for women's portraits in the middle of the nineteenth century is absent here. The half-length figure is instead shown with a blouse falling seductively off her shoulders. Her hands and arms rest on a large velvet pillow decorated with a tassel that hangs from a corner and extends out toward the viewer's space. A mauve cloak is draped around the young woman's right sleeve, across the pillow, and under her left hand and arm, ending in the lower right corner. Her head is inclined, and she wears a vague, Leonardesque smile. (The *Mona Lisa* as well as the *Donna Velata* [1513, Pitti Palace, Florence]) by Raphael are generally invoked here.) Her hair falls in ringlets, and she holds the stem of a rose between her index and middle finger. She may be about

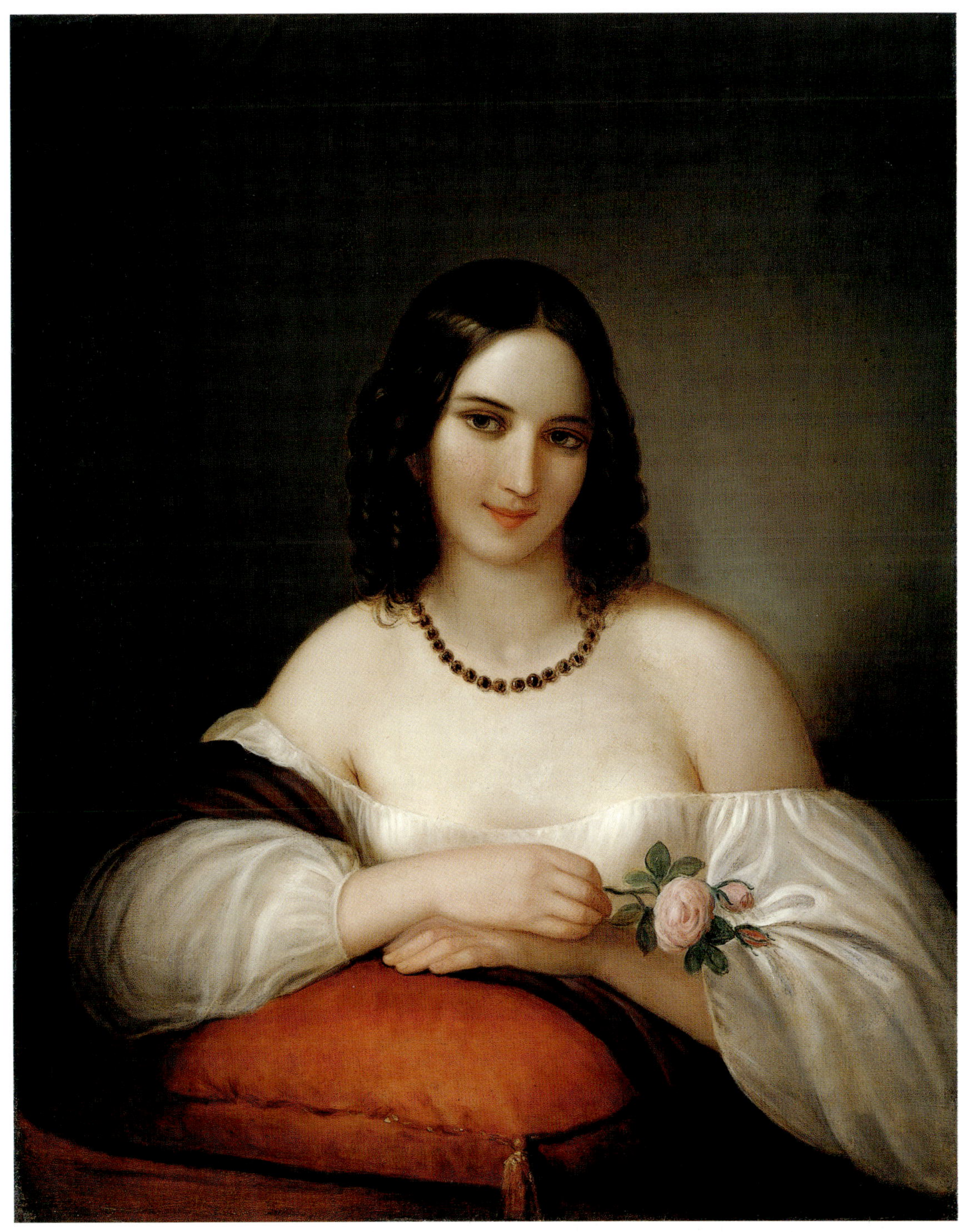

26

to drop the blossom, just as her blouse may soon fall from her arms. The flower, beads, and fancy pillow are gifts, we are meant to believe, and the model is a kept woman, or mistress.

It is easy to understand why Charles Baudelaire, the art critic and greatest poet of the age, so approved of Devéria. In his first *Salon* (1845), Baudelaire wrote that "All [Devéria's] sweetly sensual coquettes were idealizations of those women we see and desire every evening at the concert, vaudeville houses, operas, and grand salons."[1] For the poet concerned most of all with modern life, its allures, corruption, vitality, and dislocations, Devéria was the essential painter of modern femininity and masculine desire.

1 Baudelaire, 1975–1976, vol. 2, p. 365.

27

Circle of Eugène Delacroix, Possibly Richard Parkes Bonington
English, 1801–1828

The Crucifixion
c. 1825

Oil on canvas, $19\frac{3}{4} \times 25\frac{3}{4}$ in. (50.2×65.4 cm)
F.1965.1.006

Provenance: Patrick O'Connor (1909–1963), Dublin, sold 5 October 1960 to; [Duveen Bros., New York, as Delacroix, sold 1965 to]; The Norton Simon Foundation.

Reference: Possibly Dubuisson, 1924, no. 32, p. 167.

Technical Notes: According to information in the curatorial file, the painting was originally executed on panel and was removed from the wood support and transferred to canvas. Careful microscopic examination of the surface, however, leads to the conclusion that the original support was a plain-weave canvas. The original tacking edges have been removed and the paint layer has a composite support of gesso, muslin, and linen, which is tacked to a stretcher. Canvas-weave texture is visible throughout the surface, and it is especially recognizable in areas of abrasion, where white thread tops are revealed. Paint was fluidly brushed in a broad and confident handling. The central figures were painted in light-colored, opaque paint with much of the remaining composition painted in glazes. The use of bitumen for dark shadows is evident in the wide drying cracks typical of that substance. The paint overall is in fair condition. Damage from cleaning has caused widespread abrasion, which has partially removed facial features, as well as glazes and midtones. Flesh tones that contained white pigment in the painting mixture were more durable and are better preserved. Cracks in the paint layer are of many types, although most are a variant of contraction cracks; their abraded edges make them more noticeable. Coloring that may have been dramatic in the original state is compromised by partial cleaning and discolored varnish. (RW)

The oil sketch depicts the Crucifixion of Christ, perhaps the most common subject in all of European religious art. It shows Christ on the cross, brightly illuminated in the center of the canvas, between the two thieves, accompanied by a number of other easily identifiable figures: the Virgin Mary, supported by Mary, the mother of James; John the Evangelist, by Mary's side; Mary Magdalene, kneeling at the feet of Christ; a figure who may be Saint Longinus, the lance bearer, to the right of Christ; and a group of soldiers in the foreground, casting lots and arguing about dividing up Christ's seamless tunic. At the lower left, a shaft of light of unknown origin reveals the good thief whose cross has not yet been raised. At the upper right, half in darkness and half in light is the bad thief, tied to his cross and disfigured by an anguished expression. The sun and moon are both visible at the upper left, in accord with the standard iconography that darkness settled over the land at the time of the Crucifixion.

The format, subject, and elements of the style of the painting recall the oil sketches of the Flemish Baroque artists Peter Paul Rubens and Jacob Jordaens. For them both, oil sketches were a means whereby compositional, tonal, and color schemes could be quickly tested on a small format before commencing work on a large scale. These small paintings, usually on wood panels, could also be independent works of art and were cherished by collectors and connoisseurs—almost from the moment they were made—for their vitality and evident virtuosity. Certain details of the present picture may be associated with oil sketches and larger works by Rubens: the horse at the right of the Norton Simon picture derives from the one in Rubens's triptych *The Raising of the Cross*, made for the St.-Walburga Church of Antwerp, and now in the transept of Antwerp Cathedral.[1]

Several Rubens oil sketches, including the *Crucifixion* (Stichting Nicolaas Rockox, Antwerp) and *The Bearing of the Cross* (Akademie der Bildenden Künste, Vienna), contain details or compositional ideas repeated in the present work. The first shows the principal figures in poses approximately those in the Norton Simon work; the second exhibits a surging energy and expressive vehemence emulated by the artist of *The Crucifixion.*

However, neither Rubens nor Jordaens, nor anyone in their circle, made the present oil sketch. The Romantic intensity of the scene, the physiognomic exaggeration, the use of near complementary colors in the sky and elsewhere, and the overall fluidity of paint handling suggest that *The Crucifixion* was made by a follower of Eugène Delacroix, possibly Richard Parkes Bonington or someone in his circle. Delacroix was of course a great admirer of Rubens and was familiar with some of the specific works by the Flemish master cited above. *The Raising of the Cross* is one of the artist's best-known altarpieces, and an oil sketch of the composition was exhibited in the British Gallery in 1818. Delacroix himself used the painting as a source for his *Christ on the Cross* (Walters Art Museum, Baltimore) of 1846. Rubens's oil sketch of *The Crucifixion* is now believed to have been owned by Delacroix.[2]

But the Norton Simon painting does not bear the telltale brushwork and color of the great French master. The suggestion (first made by Duveen Bros.) that Bonington and not Delacroix was the author of the

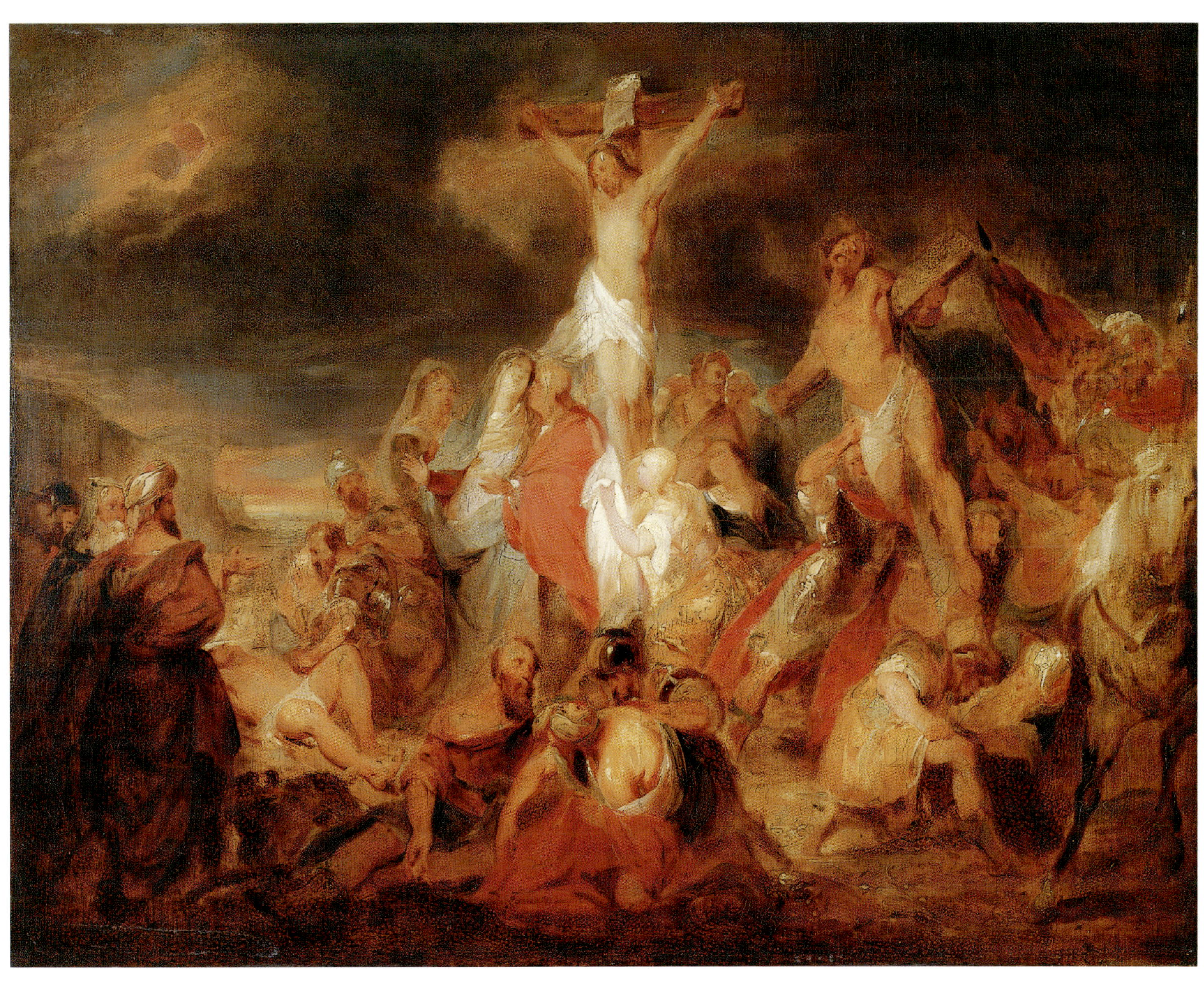

27

Norton Simon *Crucifixion* is plausible but, in the end, unconvincing. In 1820 Bonington studied in the Paris atelier of the Baron Antoine-Jean Gros and at the École des Beaux-Arts, and made the acquaintance of Delacroix at about the same time. The two young men soon became friends, exchanging ideas about the development of a modern style of drawing and painting based on the rapid and self-expressive handling of artistic media and strong contrasts of color. Between September 1825 and January 1826 the two shared a studio in Paris, but successive trips by Bonington to Italy and England—followed in 1828 by his early death from tuberculosis—ended the collaboration.

Bonington's figure style in such works as *The Earl of Surrey and the Fair Geraldine* and *François I and Marguerite de Navarre* (both c. 1826, Wallace Collection, London)—with elongated necks, twisted torsos, and exaggerated facial expressions—is similar to that seen in *The Crucifixion.* His lithographs in particular, such as *The Hanged Man—Escape from Argyle Castle* (c. 1825, Fine Arts Museums of San Francisco), exhibit a melodrama comparable to that found in *The Crucifixion.* But in none of these works did Bonington combine his figures in so integrated or fluid a manner as that seen in the present picture. Nor was he very often a painter of religious subjects. The 1829 sale catalogue of Bonington's works following his death lists a "Sketch of the Agony of Our Savior, on panel," whose present whereabouts are unknown.[3]

But the Norton Simon picture is decidedly not an "Agony" (which would represent Christ in the Garden of Gethsemane, accompanied by some of his disciples, with Jerusalem and some approaching soldiers, led by Judas, in the distance). Nor is the present work painted on panel. (Duveen's belief that *The Crucifixion* was transferred from panel has now been disproved.)

Given the absence of any provenance before 1960 and significant damage to the picture, a secure attribution may never be possible. The faces of most of the principal figures are abraded, there is widespread contraction of paint ("alligatoring") due to the use of a bitumen-derived brown pigment, and the thick layers of varnish have discolored. Nevertheless, there are moments of real power and pathos in the work—the open-jawed bad thief at right and combination of Mary, the Evangelist, and holy woman at the center—that indicate the presence of a considerable artistic talent. The accumulated evidence points to a follower of Delacroix and likely an artist working in the circle of Bonington, but this suggestion must for now remain conjectural.

1 Julius S. Held, *The Oil Sketches of Peter Paul Rubens: A Critical Catalogue*, Princeton, 1980, vol. 1, p. 479, vol. 2, pls. 343–344.

2 Held, vol. 1, p. 485; vol. 2, pl. 348.

3 Sotheby and Son, London, 29 June 1829, lot 32.

28

Michel Bouquet
French, 1807–1890

Woodland Scene with Hunters
c. 1865

Oil on canvas, $16\frac{1}{4} \times 22\frac{1}{2}$ in. (41.2×57.2 cm)
Signed lower left: "M. Bouquet"
F.1983.5

Provenance: Daniel Huntington; William Wilson Corcoran, gift 10 May 1869 to; Corcoran Gallery, Washington, D.C. (sale, New York, Sotheby, Parke-Bernet, 3 May 1979, lot 37, to); Norton Simon, gift 1983 to; The Norton Simon Foundation.

Exhibition: On loan, Washington, D.C., Renwick Gallery, 1971–1979.

References: Corcoran, 1915, no. 208; Corcoran, 1939, no. 29.

Technical Notes: The primary support is a lightweight, plain-weave canvas; it has been wax-lined with the original tacking edges cut off. A small, repaired hole is located at the lower right corner. A small vertical tear at the right bottom edge has also been repaired. The stretcher is a replacement. A smooth white ground covers the canvas, sufficiently thick to fill the canvas weave. Fissures in cracks in different areas reveal white, black, and reddish brown, which would indicate a fairly defined system of underpainting to lay out the composition. Clouds in the blue sky were painted with rich, opaque white paint. Trees were built up with dabs of opaque paint, some juxtaposed, some superimposed. Some white paint from the clouds and blue of the sky were brushed over the outer edges; a few additional branches and small leaves were painted in at the last. In the foreground, the earth was depicted with small, short overlapping strokes of opaque paint in closely related colors. A pentimento at the lower left, 5–6 inches from the left side and 4 inches from the bottom, seems to show an earlier image of a horse's four legs; it has been painted out, but paint covering the lower portion has become more transparent. Heat and pressure in lining have flattened the surface texture and also forced thicker dots of paint below the surface plane. In the sky, the white paint of the clouds has not adhered well to the underlying blue and has chipped off in peculiar-shaped losses. Clustered at the bottom left corner are several small unrepaired paint losses. Another area of small paint loss is located at the upper left. Varnish has been removed from the sky and clouds in a partial cleaning. The remainder of the painting has areas of natural resin varnish in uneven thicknesses; it has been reduced in some of the less-shadowed areas of the painting. The painting was last treated in 1979. (RW)

The French painter and decorator Michel Bouquet is not well known today, but he achieved a modest success in the middle of the nineteenth century with his landscapes and marines. He first exhibited at the French Salon in 1835 and was awarded medals for his submissions in 1847 and 1848. Later in his career, he decorated faience and made marine and landscape lithographs. During his long life, he appears to have traveled across Europe in search of motifs—from southern Italy to Scotland—and his compositions are both panoramic and narrative. He was similarly wide-ranging in his artistic borrowings. Though he studied with Théodore Gudin (an academically trained painter of historical seascapes), he looked back to the Dutch marines of Jan van Goyen and the van de Veldes, to the work of J. M. W. Turner, and to his contemporaries, the Romantic landscape painter and printmaker Paul Huet and the Barbizon artists Narcisse-Virgile Diaz de la Peña, Jules Dupré, and Théodore Rousseau. Bouquet's works are not often seen in museums today, though paintings and lithographs appear from time to time on the art market. A fine pastoral landscape by the artist, called *Breton Laundry* (c. 1875), which shows washerwomen near a stream, is in the collection of the Musée des Beaux-Arts de Quimper.

Woodland Scene with Hunters depicts hunters with their dogs and servants at rest in a forest clearing. The seated hunter in the middle foreground is listening to his servant, who is gesturing toward the young man in the middle ground at right who blows through a horn. At left, another rider approaches, accompanied by his servant. An enthusiastic dog in the left foreground seems to respond to the call to hunt. The landscape is formulaic and picturesque, with broken tree limbs at left and right directing the spectator's attention to the narrative center of the canvas, and great toppled oak trees in the center functioning as a stage for the main actors. Above the woodland scene, a break in the trees exposes a blue sky and white clouds, permitting light to illuminate the forest clearing.

Though the rugged landscape setting suggests the work of Rousseau and Diaz, and the subject matter the hunting pictures of Gustave Courbet, Bouquet's painting is very different from either Barbizon or Realist works. *Woodland Scene with Hunters* is both anecdotal and nostalgic; its figures are dressed in hunting garb from an earlier century, recalling the troubadour world of Sir Walter Scott, perhaps familiar to the artist from his teacher's Scottish pictures, including *Scottish Hunting Party* (exhibited at the Salon of 1849), and from his own travel to Scotland in 1850. The painting has also been

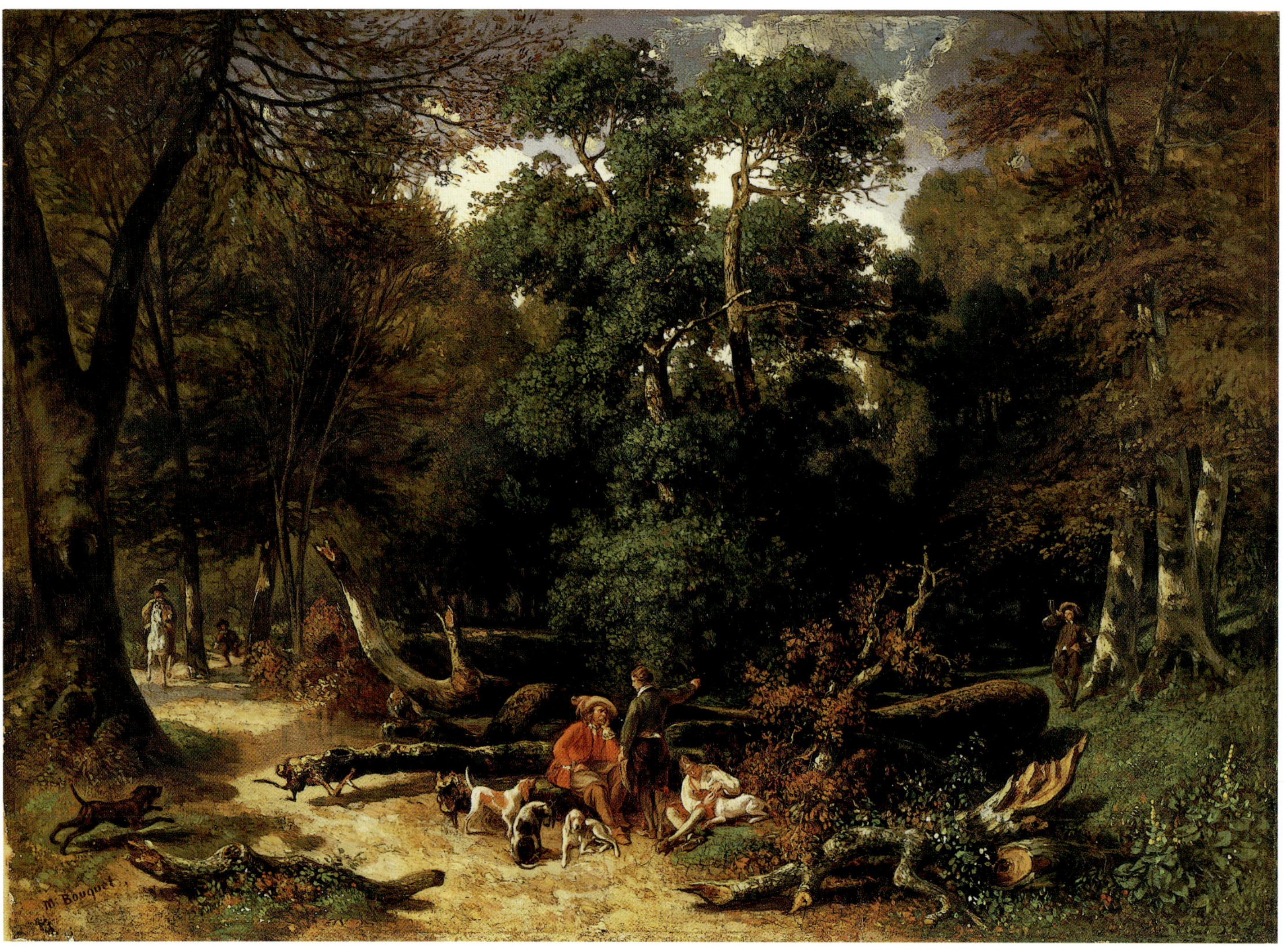

28

known, since 1939, by the title *Halt of the Hunters at Fontainebleau*, but there is no reason to believe the title is original to the work, or that the landscape is specifically based on observation and sketches made in the Forest of Fontainebleau.

Norton Simon acquired the picture in 1979 at a Sotheby's auction of works from the Corcoran Gallery of Art. According to gallery records, the picture had belonged to William Wilson Corcoran (1798–1888) himself, the wealthy banker and philanthropist who founded the museum—the first art museum in Washington, D.C.—in 1874. He acquired the landscape in 1869 for $300.00 from Daniel Huntington, the great painter of religious and historical landscapes, later renowned as one of the founders of the Metropolitan Museum of Art. Corcoran's educational mission, he stated, was to collect and display great works of European and American art "solely for the purpose of encouraging the American genius." It is not known what genius Corcoran believed might be kindled by the viewing of Bouquet's handsome and ingratiating picture. But it may have been the resemblance of the work to certain later Hudson River School landscapes—such as those by Alexander Wyant (himself deeply influenced by the Barbizon School)—that led to the purchase from Huntington and exhibition at the Corcoran Gallery.

29

Narcisse-Virgile Diaz de la Peña
French, 1807–1876

The Approaching Storm
1870

Oil on canvas, $33\frac{1}{4} \times 41\frac{5}{8}$ in. (84.4×105.6 cm)
Signed and dated lower left: "N. Diaz '70"
F.1983.9

Provenance: George I. Seney, New York (sale, New York, American Art Association, 11–13 February 1891, lot 294, for $3,100, to); Corcoran Gallery of Art, Washington, D.C. (sale, New York, Sotheby Parke-Bernet, 3 May 1979, lot 44, to); Norton Simon, gift 1983 to; The Norton Simon Foundation.

Exhibition: On loan, Washington, D.C., Renwick Gallery, 22 July 1971–1979 (?).

References: Corcoran, 1915, no. 85; Corcoran, 1939, no. 105; Bajou-Charpentreau, 1996, vol. 8, p. 860.

Technical Notes: The original support, a medium-weight fabric with a slightly open double-thread (basket) weave, is lined to fabric with a wax-resin adhesive. Tacking edges have been removed; the stretcher is later. The canvas carries a medium-thick cream-colored ground. Diaz reportedly used bitumen for the *ébauche* in his paintings and that seems likely in this case. After the *ébauche* (initial underpainting) the artist laid in the textured landscape with dark brown and green paints applied wet in wet leaving brushwork visible. He also skipped lean paint over dried paint, and light green and yellow are dabbed on the surface. Rocks and trees were painted over the initial lay-in of textured paint. To block in the large tree at this point he first applied a cream-colored paint for the trunk to set it off from the dark textured landscape. In the sky the X-ray shows a broad application of paint that must be the light blue or gray lay-in that is observable with magnification in some areas. Over this, the sky was worked up with darker and lighter blue. The tree line on the horizon was once higher, and this is visible in normal light and in the X-ray, which also shows some indistinct changes in the lower right part of the picture. A mastic varnish was removed in 1979. At the same time an acrylic coating was applied. The painting is in good condition with only some surface abrasions here and there. A medium crackle pattern is slightly lifted. Contraction cracks developed in a few areas but they are not disturbing. (JF)

Narcisse-Virgile Diaz de la Peña was a child of Spanish exile parents living in Bordeaux. Orphaned at the age of ten, he was raised by a Protestant minister and sent to work early as an apprentice colorist in a porcelain factory run by Arsène Gillet in Paris. This particular training, as Albert Boime has pointed out, was common among a number of future Barbizon artists, including Jules Dupré, Auguste Raffet, and Constant Troyon (the latter pair also worked for Gillet).[1] Nearly all the Barbizon artists—including Diaz, Camille Corot, Théodore Rousseau, Dupré, Alexandre Decamps, Paul Huet, Charles Jacque, Jean-François Millet, and Henri-Joseph Harpignies—were in fact tremendously productive, and most were adept at achieving what may be termed *effets*, that is, artistic affects or caprices. Diaz and Rousseau were perhaps the most brilliant in this regard, capturing transient effects of light and weather—roseate dawns and amber sunsets, shafts of light through parting storm clouds, and even the sudden illumination of a lightning strike—though they also had a solid understanding of geography, geology, meteorology, and rural labor.

Beyond his practical training as a decorator with Gillet, however, Diaz gained an appreciation for figure painting and *istoria*; as a young artist, he looked at works in the Musée du Louvre by Correggio, Jean-Honoré Fragonard and Pierre-Paul Prud'hon, and all three of these artists remained profoundly influential for him throughout his life, as seen in his small, erotic pictures such as *Venus and Two Cupids* (1847, National Gallery, London) and *Venus Disarming Cupid* (c. 1855, Wallace Collection, London). He also produced religious, historical, and Orientalist pictures, such as *The Lament of Jephthah's Daughter* and *Turkish Family* (both c. 1845, State Hermitage Museum, St. Petersburg), exhibiting them at the Salon during the 1830s and 1840s. Nevertheless, it was at Barbizon, the small town just north of the Forest of Fontainebleau, that Diaz created his best and most acclaimed works.

Beginning in 1835 he joined the other landscape painters at the inn of Père Ganne and shared with them his antagonism to metropolitan social constraints and academic norms, the latter represented by the classicizing landscapes of Pierre-Henri de Valenciennes and Jean-Charles-Joseph Rémond. He preferred works by the Dutch masters of the seventeenth century—Jacob van Ruisdael, Meindert Hobbema, Phillips Koninck, and Rembrandt—all of whom were being collected with avidity before midcentury by the artists themselves and the wider public. Diaz was particularly close to Rousseau and Dupré and, like them, rejected conventional notions

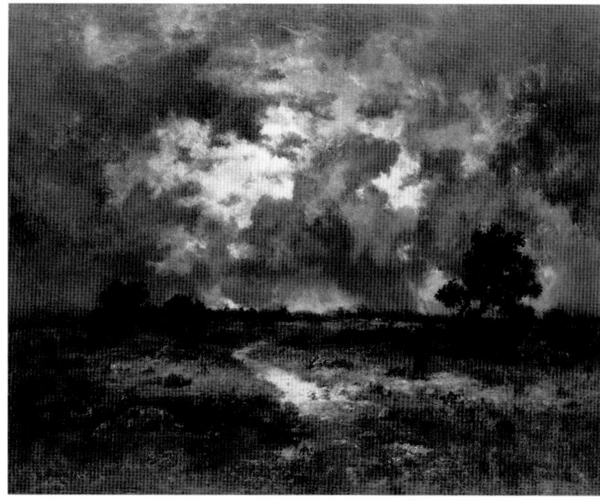

Fig. 29a Narcisse-Virgile Diaz de la Peña, *The Storm*, 1871, oil on panel, $24\frac{1}{4} \times 30\frac{1}{8}$ in. (61.5×76.5 cm), National Gallery, London

of finish; he therefore produced pictures that retained the quality of spontaneous sketches or improvisations *en plein air*. This animation and expressiveness, taken at the time to be an assertion of both personal and political freedom, is apparent from nearly the beginning of Diaz's career. It led one prominent writer of the 1840s, the art critic and radical, political activist Théophile Thoré, to embrace Rousseau and Diaz as expressive of the national yearning for liberty and equality.

The Approaching Storm was painted late in Diaz's career, when the Barbizon group was no longer seen as quite so insurgent. It is a depiction of a boulder-strewn landscape and turbulent sky. The scene is illuminated by light that pours through an opening in the storm clouds. A stunted tree stands isolated in the right middle ground, dwarfing a lone woman just to the left carrying a bundle in her arms. She is only a small part of the scene but she is important, reminding spectators that this is still France, a civilized place. There are other signs of culture and cultivation: in the distant background at upper right is a horizontal sliver of golden yellow, representing a field of grain. The illuminated clearing in the center of the picture may be part of a path that extends horizontally across the picture but is partly hidden by the large boulder in the left middle ground. A very similar, though smaller and much sketchier composition, painted on mahogany panel, is closely related to the present painting (fig. 29a).

More than other Barbizon painters, Diaz was a colorist. *The Approaching Storm* is intensely colored, dominated by blue-grays and dark greens, with a striking contrast of yellow and yellow-green in the tree at right. The cloudy, gun metal sky is parted in the middle to expose a patch of blue, the lower part of which is actually painted over the adjacent gray and white, lending it substance and relief. Orange and sienna are prominent in the left fore- and middle ground, creating strong, complementary contrasts with the surrounding greens and blues. The consequence of this marked emphasis on color is a strong sense of three-dimensionality, despite the absence of clear linear or even atmospheric perspective, and a pronounced visual drama, or visual affect. As in the roughly contemporaneous late landscapes of Gustave Courbet (see cats. 44 and 45), all parts of the depicted landscape retain visual interest, suggesting what might be called a democratic approach to pictorial composition.

1 Boime, 2004, p. 460.

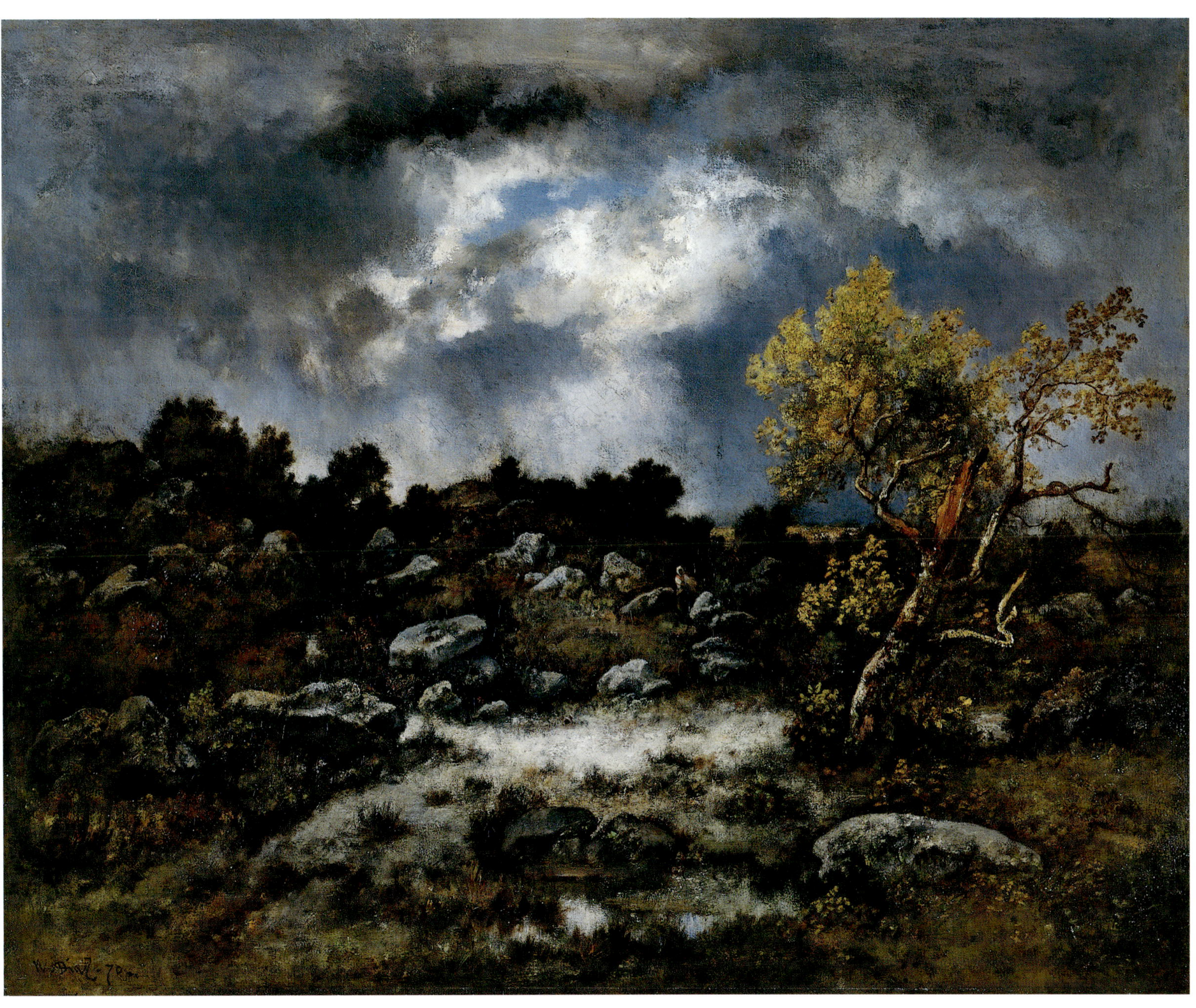

29

30

Honoré Daumier
French, 1808–1879

Study for "Saltimbanques Resting"
c. 1865–1866

Oil on panel, $11\frac{3}{4} \times 14\frac{3}{4}$ in. (29.8×37.5 cm)
M.1985.2

Provenance: Colonel Briggs, Grand Rapids, Mich., sold to; [Vose Gallery, Boston, sold 27 August 1923 to]; [M. Knoedler & Co., New York, sold 24 January 1924 to]; Philips Memorial Gallery, Washington, D.C., consigned 13 February 1940 to]; [M. Knoedler & Co., New York, sold 9 August 1940 to]; [Sam Salz, New York]; Erich Maria Remarque (1898–1970). [Sam Salz/19th and 20th Century Art, Inc., New York, sold 1957 to]; Robert Ellis Simon, Los Angeles, bequest 1969 to; The Norton Simon Foundation, transferred 1985 to; Norton Simon Art Foundation.

Exhibitions: Paris, 1908a; New York, 1943c, no. 4, ill., as *Mountebanks Resting*; Los Angeles, 1958, no. 220; Los Angeles, 1965; San Francisco, 1973, no. 17, ill.

References: Phillips, 1926, p. 94, pl. XIV; Fuchs, 1930, no. 300a, ill.; Phillips, 1931, pl. IX; Sterling, 1934, no. 35; Maison, 1968, no. II-43, pl. 196; Barzini and Mandel, 1971, no. 225.

Technical Notes: The horizontally grained panel is cradled; there are no splits or cracks. It was prepared with a white ground, which, although thick and possibly in two layers, still allows some of the wood's texture to remain visible in the more thinly painted parts. Daumier covered the ground with a red-brown scumble, which remains exposed at the left side of the background and in the neck of the Pierrot figure at the right. It is also visible in several small losses above the central figure. Fast brushstrokes of brownish green paint established a slightly structured background. The three figures were placed in front, and Daumier worked and reworked their placement and contours, as seen in raking light where the first brushwork was later painted over. The strongly lit white shirt on the figure at the right was painted with vigorous brushstrokes of opaque, rich paint directly over the red-brown underpainting; this figure also was adjusted with superimposed additions. The painting has sustained numerous small losses, and the haphazard treatment of nicks and scratches is quite distracting. For example, the head of the man at the center seems especially questionable. The varnish is thick, and there may be several layers. A matting agent has been added, and the lack of saturation minimizes the little damages across the surface. (RW)

31

Honoré Daumier
French, 1808–1879

Saltimbanques Resting
1870

Oil on canvas, $21\frac{1}{2} \times 25\frac{3}{4}$ in. (54.6×65.4 cm)
Signed lower left: "h. Daumier"
M.1976.6

Provenance: [Durand-Ruel, Paris]. Jean Joubert, Paris, by 1901, still in 1922. [Paul Rosenberg, Paris, stock nos. 1274 and 1151]. C. C. Stillman, by inheritance to; Dr. Ernest G. Stillman (sale, New York, American Art Association, 3 February 1927, lot 23, ill., as *Le Repos des saltimbanques*, to); [Paul Rosenberg, Paris]. Arthur Sachs, New York and Paris, by 1930, until at least 1939; [Wildenstein and Co., New York, sold 1955 to]; Norton Simon, gift 1976 to; Norton Simon Art Foundation.

Exhibitions: Paris, 1901b, no. 62; on loan, Cambridge, Mass., Harvard University, Fogg Art Museum, 1927; New York, 1930, no. 72, ill., as *Mountebanks Resting*; London, 1932, no. 330, pl. 410; New York, 1932a; New York, 1934a, no. 12; Paris, 1934d, no. 35; Paris, 1936b, no. 19, ill.; Los Angeles, 1958, no. 221; Los Angeles, 1965; San Francisco, 1973, no. 18, ill.

References: Geffroy, 1901 p. 20; Klossowski, 1908, no. 204, p. 51, ill.; Rosenthal, 1911, pp. 85–86, pl. XXXV; Soffici, 1921, p. 415, ill.; Phillips, 1922, pp. viii, 25, ill.; Escholier, 1923, ill. opp. p. 8; Fontainas, 1923, pl. 23; Klossowski, 1923, no. 204, pp. 84, 104, ill.; Sadleir, 1924, pp. 33–34, pl. 9; *Art News*, 1927, pp. 1, 10, ill.; Fontainas, 1927, pl. 5; Fuchs, 1927, no. 131, p. 51, pl. 131; Alexandre, 1928, p. 64, pl. 33; Meier-Graefe, 1929b, p. 21; Fuchs, 1930, no. 131, ill.; M. Sachs, 1939, p. 23, pl. 12; *Formes*, 1931, ill. opp. p. 185; *Art News*, 1932, p. 5, ill.; G. Wildenstein, 1932, pp. 25, ill., 54; Escholier, 1934, ill., following p. 40; Philadelphia, 1937, no. 8, ill.; Fleischmann, 1938, pl. 12; Lassaigne, 1938, p. 168, pl. 146; Bransten, 1944, p. 22, ill.; Georges-Michel, 1945, ill. opp. p. 33; Gauthier, 1950, pl. 57; Schweicher, 1953, no. 10, ill.; Adhémar, 1954, no. 160, pl. 160; R. Rey, 1965, p. 146, color ill. p. 147; Maison, 1968, vol. 1, no. 185, pl. 136; Barzini and Mandel, 1971, no. 224; Harper, 1981, no. 43, pp. 131–136; Eitner, 2000, pp. 189–190, fig. 1.

Technical Notes: The canvas support has been glue-lined with the tacking edges trimmed. X-radiography reveals several fairly minor damages to the original canvas: two short tears at the lower part of the far right side, a small hole at the bottom left corner, and a horizontal tear at the upper left, which falls at the inner edge of the stretcher bar. The keyed stretcher appears to be the original. The ground is sufficiently thick to fill the canvas weave. No methods of underdrawing were seen with magnification. The medium is characteristic of oil, with occasional use of black ink. The complex structure and multiple layers of paint indicate that it was worked and reworked. Many brushstrokes were rather dry, resulting in small gaps in paint that break the continuity of a stroke and reveal underlying colors. Other areas involve a subtraction of paint, as in scraping back or rubbing off. Black lines in the upper left background were drawn in ink on top of the oil paint, where it formed tiny unconnected droplets. Both opaque paint and thinner glazes were used, although many glazes are interrupted. Although Daumier's technique and materials were detrimental to the longevity and preservation of his work, and extensive restoration has often been the result, it appears in this painting that the scraped or abraded areas were largely his. Prior restoration may have been the cause of some abrasion, but the degree is not clear. The widely spaced cracks are deep but the paint structure is secure. Brush marking is faint, having been somewhat smoothed in lining and further obscured by thick varnish. The painting was superficially cleaned in 1986, when minor retouching of losses at the edges was also carried out. The varnish, a thick natural resin, is discolored.[1] (RW)

Honoré Daumier was the greatest French caricaturist of the nineteenth century. His work has influenced every succeeding generation of graphic satirists as well as many of the founding figures of modern art, including Edgar Degas, Henri de Toulouse-Lautrec, Paul Cézanne, Pablo Picasso, Georges Rouault, and Marc Chagall. His output was prodigious: between 1829 and 1875 he produced more than four thousand lithographs and wood engravings. These prints—first published in the satirical weeklies *La Silhouette* (1829–1830) and *La Caricature* (1830–1832), and then for more than forty years in the illustrated daily *Le Charivari*—represent the full pageant of public and private life during the July Monarchy (1830–1848), Second Republic (1848–1852), Second Empire (1852–1870), and early Third Republic. They expose the corruption of a monarch, the cupidity of the professional classes, the ignorance of country bumpkins, the blindness of the bourgeoisie, the pomposity of classical artists, the self-importance of Realist artists, the sufferings of the proletariat, and the necessity of social and political revolution. Daumier also depicted, at times, the vanity of resistance and the impossibility of revolution, thus revealing one thing more about this body of art: it provides a precise barometer of the state of French and European intellectual and press freedom.

In addition to his achievement as a caricaturist, Daumier was a highly experimental painter, draftsman, and sculptor. These aspects of his career, however, are not well known to the general public and are much debated among specialists. Though it is generally believed that his oil paintings number more than three hundred, the authorship of many works remains in doubt and their dating—with just a few exceptions—is the result of little more than informed guesswork. Apart from a dealer retrospective a few months before the artist's death, Daumier exhibited just six paintings during his lifetime. They are *Sketch for "The Republic"* (Musée d'Orsay, Paris), exhibited as part of a competition in 1848; *The Miller, His Son and the Ass* (Burrell Collection, Glasgow Art Gallery) shown at the Salon of 1849; *Nymphs Pursued by Satyrs* (Montreal Museum of Fine Arts) and *Don Quixote and Sancho Panza* (The Bridgestone Museum of Art, Tokyo) at the Salon of 1850–1851; *The Laundress* (Albright-Knox Art Gallery, Buffalo) at the Salon of 1861 and again that year at Martinet's gallery, along with *The Drinkers* (The Metropolitan Museum of Art, New York). Only one painting by Daumier is dated, *The Laundress* (186[3?], (The Metropolitan Museum of Art, New York), but the last numeral of the year is now indistinct, and in any case it reprises an undated, smaller composition shown at the Salon of 1861.

As if the problems of chronology were not vexing enough, there is the matter of attribution. The only retrospective exhibition in Daumier's lifetime was held at the Durand-Ruel gallery in 1878. On that occasion, ninety-four paintings were shown and, given the artist's participation, all of these may be presumed authentic. Attendance at the exhibition, however, was very low, and Daumier died a few months later, broke and forgotten by all except a few poets, collectors, and artists. (These latter include the surviving Barbizon painters and the Impressionists.) A decade later, the contents of his studio, dozens of "unfinished paintings and many sketches," Durand-Ruel wrote in his memoirs, were sold by the artist's widow for next to nothing to "contemptible speculators."[2] The dealer Ambroise Vollard described the removal of "a whole moving van full" of studies, and there can be no doubt that many of these unfinished works and painted sketches were later "completed" by hands other than Daumier's.[3] The rapid resurgence of Daumier's reputation after 1900 also assured a flourishing trade in outright forgeries.

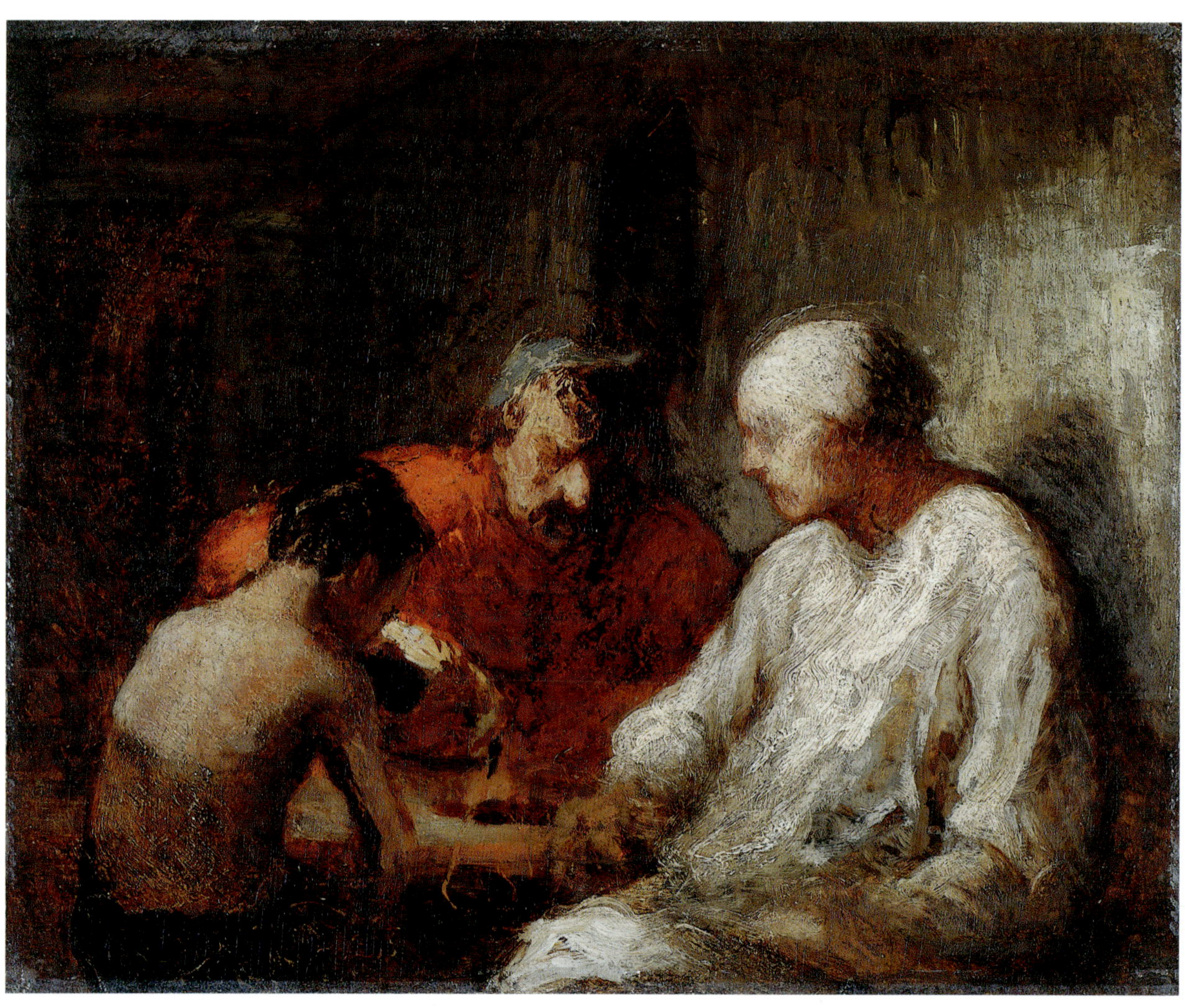

30

Despite these impediments, art historians have managed to establish a basic painting oeuvre and rudimentary chronology. *Saltimbanques Resting* and *Study for "Saltimbanques Resting"* were not exhibited in the 1878 exhibition at Durand-Ruel's but have long been recognized as works by Daumier. Like his other oil paintings of *saltimbanques*, for example, *A Sideshow* (private collection) and *The Strong Man* (fig. 31a), or watercolors, such as *The Sideshow* (British Museum, London) and *The Mountebanks Changing Place* (fig. 31b), the Norton Simon paintings are generally dated to the years 1864–1870. The clown in the center of the latter drawing appears to be the same model—seen from nearly the same point of view—as the central figure in the large, finished *Saltimbanques Resting*. The figure at the center of the *Study* looks quite different from this model; indeed, the little painting may have been made after, rather than before, the larger work. The right-hand figure, too, differs greatly from the larger painting. This Pierrot, lacking buttons, is painted in an expressive style that recalls Jean-Honoré Fragonard. His posture and costume, however, are sepulchral, probably derived from Rembrandt's painting and etching *The Raising of Lazarus* (c. 1630, Los Angeles County Museum of Art). An X-ray of the panel (fig. 31c) exposes a different painting beneath the surface, a ghostly ensemble of three heads, recalling Daumier's drawings and paintings of spectators in a theater.

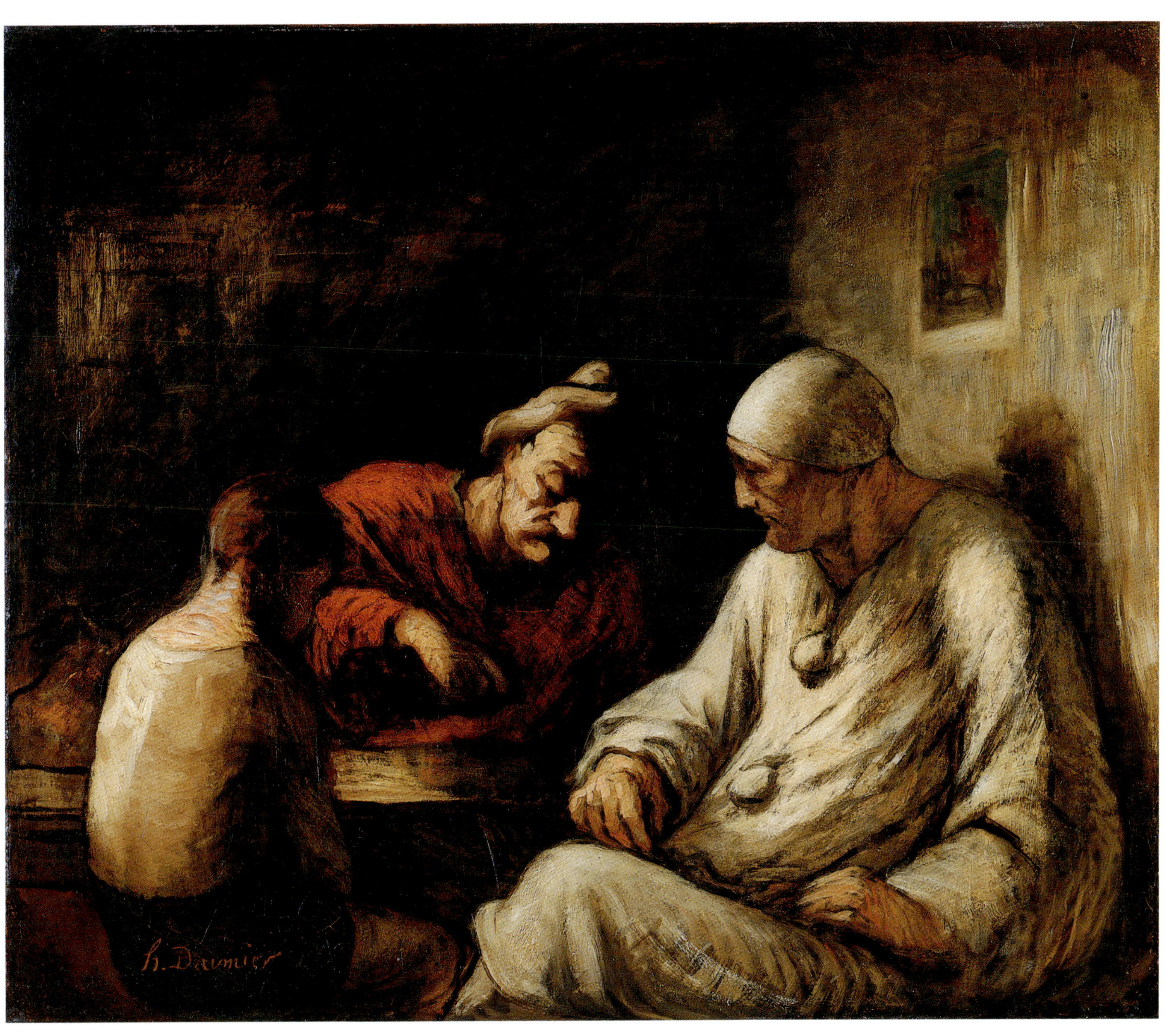

31

Fig. 31a Honoré Daumier, *The Strong Man*, c. 1865, oil on panel, $10\frac{5}{8} \times 13\frac{7}{8}$ in. (26.9×35.2 cm), The Phillips Collection, Washington, D.C.

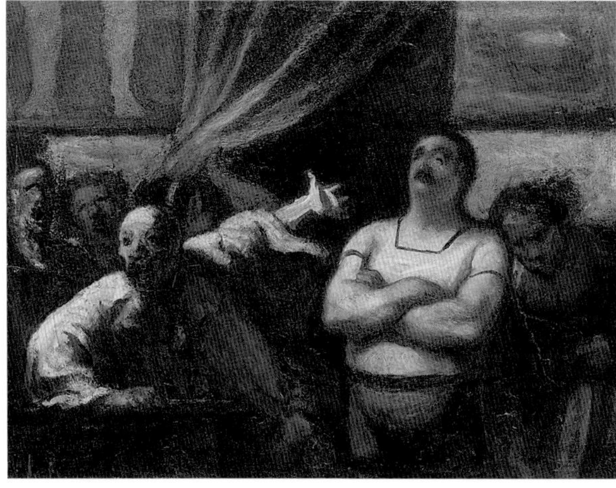

The subject of the two paintings—the popular, clownish performers called *saltimbanques*—is one that the artist depicted numerous times in prints, drawings, and paintings and was widely discussed in the Romantic literary circles in which Daumier moved. The artist's friend and supporter Jules Champfleury, for example, wrote sketches in the 1840s for the enormously popular Théâtre des Funambules on the boulevard du Crime and created roles for its star, Gaspard Deburau, universally known as Baptiste (he is familiar to American audiences from J.-L. Barrault's performance in the great 1943 film *Les Enfants du paradis*, directed by Marcel Carne). Charles Baudelaire poignantly discussed the sad lives of these acrobats and clowns in his "Le Vieux Saltimbanque" from the set of prose poems called *Le Spleen de Paris* (1861).[4] These contemporary references prove that the two Norton Simon paintings in fact represent "saltimbanques" rather than "mountebanks," as they have been called since Maison.[5] *Saltimbanques* are street performers, while the word *mountebank* applies to a huckster or medicine seller who exhorts the crowd while standing on a bench. Although both are performers, for the mountebank, performance is to result in a sale of spurious medicines, while for the *saltimbanque*, it is an end in itself. Daumier was also undoubtedly familiar with the itinerant street performers, sometimes called *paradistes*, who displayed their varied acrobatic and comic skills on street corners for the benefit of passersby and in exchange for a few pennies. These latter, impromptu entertainments were curbed by law in 1853 as part of the regulatory campaign of Napoleon III. Acrobats and clowns, freaks and strongmen, jugglers and organ grinders were considered threats to the moral and social order of newly Hausmannized, economically dynamic, Second Empire France. Though no less a revolutionary than Karl Marx judged beggars, peddlers, and petty thieves to be politically inert members of the *lumpenproletariat*, French police and bureaucrats, as the art historian T. J. Clark showed, believed them to be potential subversives.[6] Indeed, by the late 1850s and 1860s, *saltimbanques* were thin on the ground in Paris, and writers and artists began to mourn their disappearance. Victor Fournel wrote monographs about them in 1858 and 1863, at about the same time that Daumier began to draw and paint them in earnest.[7] His renderings have an air of nostalgia about them. The atmosphere is somber in *Saltimbanques Resting*, and the figures are bowed or bent—the opposite of the tension and erectness displayed by the actors during performances, as seen in *The Sideshow*. The central figure in the large painting carefully measures out the wine,

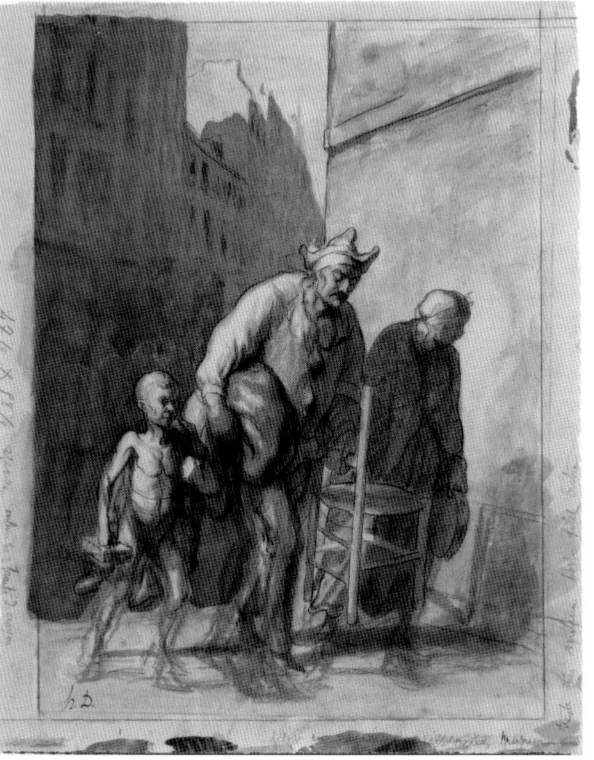

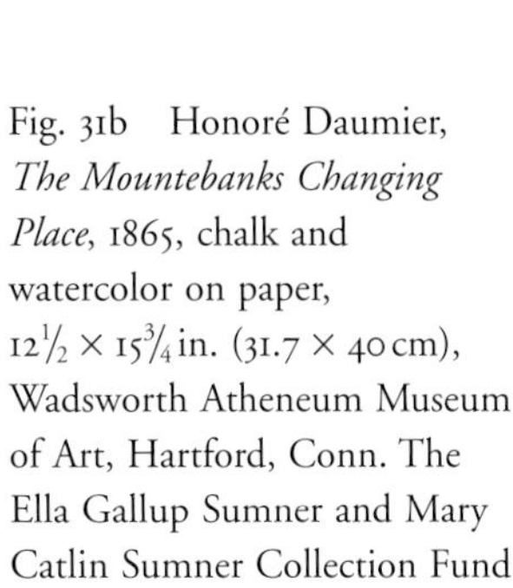

Fig. 31b Honoré Daumier, *The Mountebanks Changing Place*, 1865, chalk and watercolor on paper, $12\frac{1}{2} \times 15\frac{3}{4}$ in. (31.7×40 cm), Wadsworth Atheneum Museum of Art, Hartford, Conn. The Ella Gallup Sumner and Mary Catlin Sumner Collection Fund

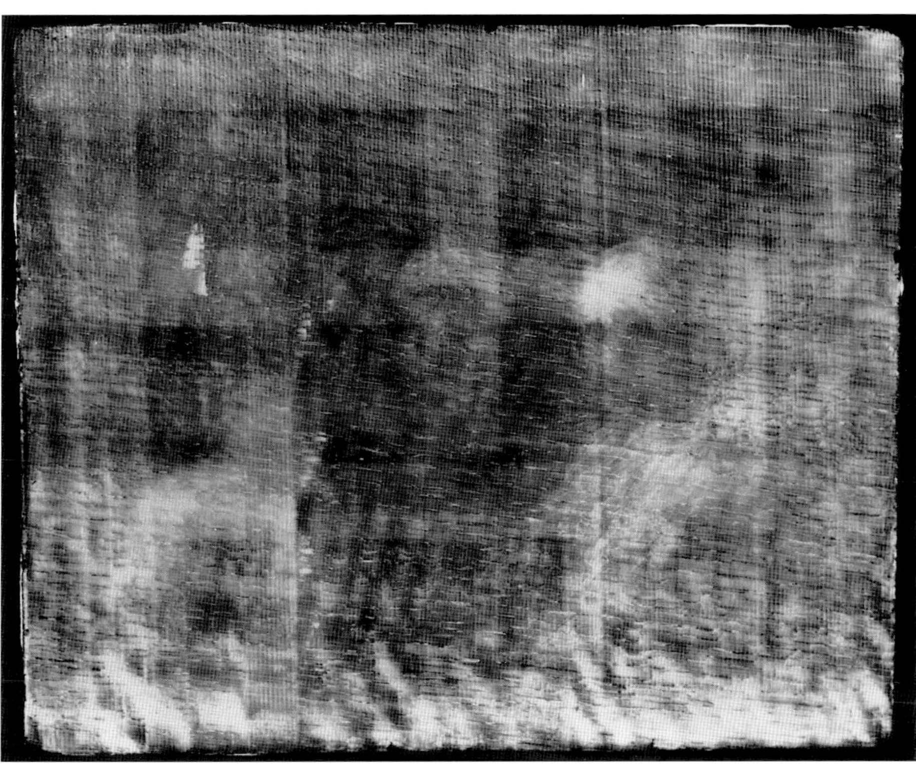

Fig. 31c X-ray photograph of cat. 30

while the older Pierrot at right and young acrobat at left quietly look on.

On the tavern wall at right above the head of Pierrot is a framed image of a striding figure with staff in hand. He is *le juif errant*, "the Wandering Jew," a type known from innumerable popular prints mostly published, since the eighteenth century, in the French town of Épinal and distributed across Europe by colporteurs. Many artists and writers at midcentury were fascinated by these woodcuts. In 1850 Gustave Courbet used an image of the Wandering Jew as the basis for his lithograph of the Fourierist evangelist Jean Journet (The Metropolitan Museum of Art, New York) and four years later for his painting *The Meeting* (Musée Fabre, Montpellier).[8] Daumier's friend Champfleury also employed an image of the Wandering Jew as the frontispiece of his 1869 *Histoire de l'imagerie populaire.* Equally significant was the enormous popularity of Eugène Sue's novel *The Wandering Jew*, issued in installments from 1843–1844, published in a single large volume a year later, and performed on the stage of the Théâtre de l'Ambigu in 1849. The novel describes the corruption of a powerful and avaricious Jesuit order and the poverty and vulnerability of a family named Rennepont whose descendants were scattered across Europe. For the radical Sue, the Jew was a powerful symbol of ancient crimes and modern oppression. He was at once the figure who, according to the Christian Apocrypha, refused to comfort Christ on his way to Crucifixion and a personification of the modern proletariat, who, denied home and succor, is compelled perpetually to wander the earth. In the "Interval"—the intermission or entr'acte—following chapter 16 of Sue's novel, the Jew says:

> For eighteen centuries, the powerful and the happy of this world have said to the toiling people what I said to the imploring and suffering savior. "Go on, go on!" And the people, sinking with fatigue, bearing their heavy cross, have answered in the bitterness of their grief: "Oh, for pity's sake! A few moments of repose; we are worn out with toil"—"Go on! Go on!" . . .

Sue's radicalism, like that of his contemporaries Courbet and the anarchist philosopher P.-J. Proudhon, was adorned with the ugly mask of anti-Semitism; his anti-Semitism, in turn, was made into a plea for charity, tolerance, and even emancipation. Daumier's *Saltimbanques*, presided over by a print of the Wandering Jew, belong to this unsettled and contradictory world. His protagonists have found "a few moments of repose" in the midst of their wearisome and unrewarding toil. They have halted their wanderings to have a drink in a tavern. In a little while, they will again pick up their tambourines, drums, and fiddles and position themselves on the barker's platform or behind the curtains of the sideshow.

1 Observations in the Technical Notes relied in part on a private conversation with Elizabeth Steele, Conservator, The Phillips Collection, Washington, D.C., and on Maison, 1961, pp. 17–20.
2 Venturi, 1939, vol. 2, p. 208.
3 Vollard, 1937, p. 93.
4 Baudelaire, 1975–1976, vol. 1, pp. 295–297.
5 Maison, 1968, no. II-43, pl. 196.
6 Clark, 1973b, pp. 121–122.
7 Victor Fournel, *Ce qu'on voit dans les rues de Paris*, Paris, 1858; *Les Spectacles populaires et les artistes des rues*, Paris, 1863, cited in Schapiro, 1978, p. 74.
8 Nochlin, 1967, pp. 209–222.

32

Constant Troyon
French, 1810–1865

Bull and Chickens
1850–1860

Oil on panel, 23¾ × 17¾ in. (60.5 × 45.1 cm)
Signed lower left: "C. Troyon"
M.1979.60

Provenance: (Constant Troyon sale, Paris, Hôtel Drouot, 22–23 January 1866, second day, lot 103, as *Boeuf et poules dans une prairie*, for Ff 1,720 to); Morel. [M. Knoedler & Co., Paris and New York, by 1906]. Dr. Jacob Arnold Carp (1871–1942), Helmond, Holland, 1919–1942; Hendricus Egbertus ten Cate (1868–1955), Almelo, Holland, by 1942 (sale, London, Sotheby's, 3 December 1958, lot 85, as *Bull in a Meadow*, to); H. A. D. Thomas, Amsterdam, still in 1963–1964; [E. J. van Wisselingh & Co., Amsterdam, by 1964, stock no. S9024, as *Le Taureau*, to]; Mrs. Julia A. M. McInnes, Winnipeg, in 1964, by descent to; Dr. D. C. McInnes, Winnipeg, still in 1973, to; [B. Laing, half share with E. J. van Wisselingh & Co., sold 1974 to]; Norton Simon, gift 1979 to; Norton Simon Art Foundation.

Exhibition: Amsterdam, 1963a, no. 25, ill., as *Le Taureau*.

References: Hustin, 1893, p. 60; Soullié, 1900, p. 107; Hannema, 1955, vol. 1, no. 111.

Technical Notes: The painting was executed on a vertically grained hardwood panel, which has been cradled, perhaps to repair a long vertical crack located 6 inches from the right side. The panel at the present time has no planar distortions or active cracks. The panel was not prepared with a ground layer. Microscopic examination of the surface reveals light-colored underpainting beneath the bull and the sky. The sky was begun with a quickly brushed layer of light gray, then a slightly darker blue-gray was applied wet into wet. Where gaps in the paint occur, the red-brown color of the unprimed panel provides a warm tonality. The bull was painted with several shades of brown applied over the light-colored underlayer; this handling, in the front half of the animal, lets the transparency of occasional thinner strokes of paint suggest the glistening coat. Where light hits the back of the bull, the paint is quite rich, both dragged and stippled as a final touch on the brown shape. Tiny shapes at the horizon at the right edge (black, brown, white) enliven the scene but are not identifiable. Two animals at the left side were an afterthought: they are painted on top of the sky and the grass, whose brushstrokes remain visible. Generally, the painting is well preserved. Some chemical abrasion has possibly occurred in the dark-shadowed areas of the foreground, and the letters of the signature appear to have been thinned. The painting was treated in 1989, at which time varnish was partially removed. Several spots of minor retouching compensate for small paint losses. The present varnish is moderately yellowed and unpleasantly thick. (RW)

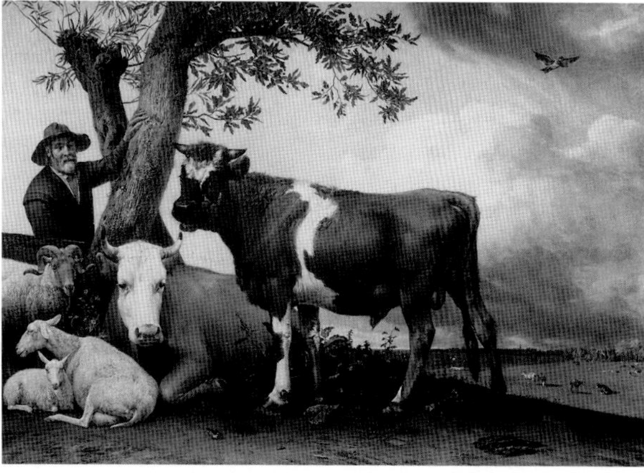

Fig. 32a Paulus Potter, *The Young Bull*, oil on canvas, 92¾ × 133⅜ in. (235.5 × 339 cm), Royal Cabinet of Paintings Mauritshuis, The Hague

Constant Troyon was born in 1810 and trained in Sèvres, the small town west of Paris associated with the manufacture of painted porcelain. His early training was with artists employed in the decoration of porcelain with picturesque rural scenes rather than in the studios of the École des Beaux-Arts in Paris. Thus, he was fully prepared to join the group of artists of the Generation of 1830 who rebelled against the Roman-centered classical landscape traditions of French art, replacing them with the patient study of the rural landscape of France itself under the aesthetic impetus of the only indigenous northern landscape tradition—that of seventeenth-century Holland. In fact, in 1847, when he was thirty-seven years old, Troyon made a crucial trip to Holland, where he studied works by Aelbert Cuyp and Paulus Potter and made a firm decision to become a painter of rural animals and their human keepers. From that point, he painted hundreds of works representing cattle, work horses, and barnyard animals, few of which he dated and some of which he exhibited with generic titles. This makes it particularly difficult to date works by Troyon or to decide which, among the large number of paintings surviving by him, he sent for public exhibition.

Bull and Chickens was made on a hardwood panel, which Troyon elected not to prime, preferring to make ample use of its orange-brown color as the unifying undertone of his composition. It was not sold in Troyon's lifetime and made its first appearance in his January 1866 studio sale, where it is listed as *Boeufs et poules dans une prairie* (*Bull and Chickens on the Plain*). It sold for a decent, but unspectacular, price to a collector who is known only by his last name, Morel. Its next owner was Dutch and much of its subsequent history took place in the very country that Troyon visited in 1847. There are

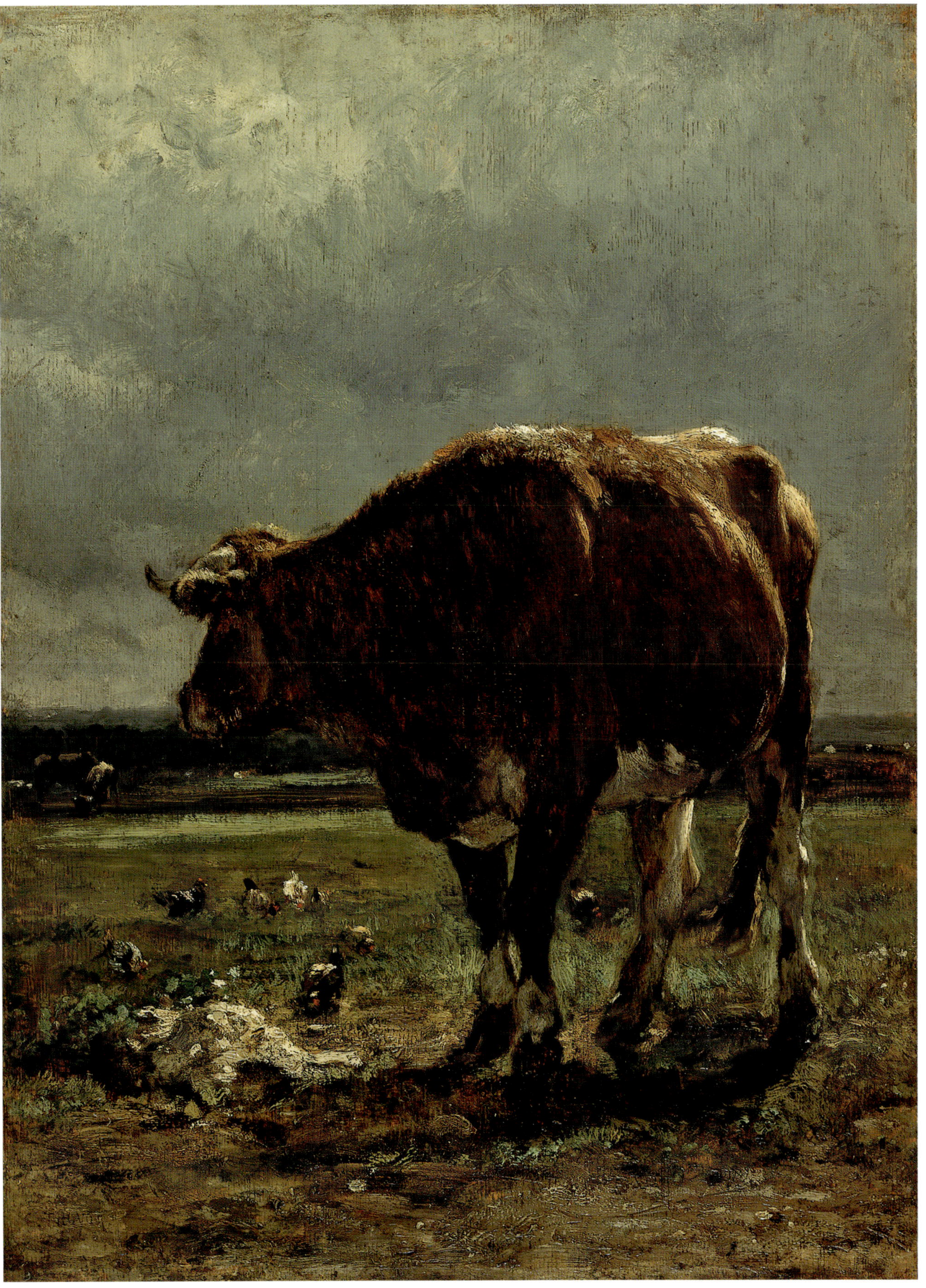

no recorded prints or early photographs of it in the literature.

Troyon adopted a startlingly simple composition, situating his bovine subject in the center of the compositional field and selecting a viewpoint so that its body and legs are roughly proportional to the panel on which they are painted. Unlike the famous painting by Paulus Potter in the Mauritshuis, *The Young Bull* (fig. 32a), Troyon's animal subject faces into the pictorial world, looking at two distant companions and grandly surveying the group of tiny chickens who seem occupied by bits of grain neglected by the giant beast above them. The sky is cloudy and troubled, and the bull turns toward his companions as if to gather them against the impending weather. There are numerous precedents for cows and bulls in this pose in the painting of Aelbert Cuyp, but none is exact enough to have acted as a precise prototype. Rather, Troyon seems to have studied seventeenth-century Dutch paintings in museums and accessible private collections in both France and Holland and to have internalized these lessons.

It is tempting to make connections between Troyon's rural animals and the peasant figures by his colleague Jean-François Millet who inhabit pictorial landscapes of remarkable similarity. Millet's figures were routinely compared to beasts (*les bêtes humaines*) in the critical literature of the 1850s and 1860s. And many critics of rural animal painting made links between the cattle or sheep in the paintings and human life. Thus, animals were allowed passions, worries, and doubts that they embodied just as clearly as their human counterparts in rural painting. Yet these connections are rarely more than generic, and none of Millet's works can be compared specifically to any particular painting such as the present canvas.

Although it has been commonly assigned dates in the early 1850s, it is just as likely that the present canvas dates from the late 1850s or even the early 1860s. It is both attractive enough and small enough that it would easily have found a buyer had it been painted as early as 1850. Instead, it made its recorded debut in Troyon's death sale, suggesting that it was a later work.

33

Constant Troyon
French, 1810–1865

Thatched Cottage by the Sea
c. 1855–1860

Oil on panel, $10\frac{1}{2} \times 13\frac{3}{4}$ in. (26.7 × 34.9 cm)
Signed lower left: "C. T."
N.1976.15

Provenance: Sedelmeyer (sale, Paris, Hôtel Drouot, 30 April 1877, lot 98, as *Paysage. Chaumière au bord d'une mare,* for Fr 2,150 to); Étienne de Roy. [Galerie Barbizon, Paris, sold 1976 to]; Norton Simon, bequest, 1993 to; Jennifer Jones Simon Art Trust.

Reference: Soullié, 1900, p. 19.

Technical Notes: The painting's support is a panel made from a single board; the edges are hand-beveled on the reverse. The wood is in very good condition, with no cracks and a very slight convex warp. The panel was not primed, and, occasionally, in areas where the paint is thin or absent, its warm color is influential. Rich paint was applied in complex, multiple layers. Troyon first painted a medium gray in the sky; after painting the white clouds, he brushed a more vibrant blue in the upper portion of the sky and over the edges of the clouds. Brush marking of the lower layers remains distinct. Paint thickness ranges from moderate impasto to thin glazes of semitransparent paint. Shadows in the cottage, such as the underside of the thatched roof, are thin glazes. The painting is very well preserved. Small losses at the edges are probably related to framing. The painting was superficially cleaned and varnished in 1981. An older discolored varnish is most noticeable in the sky. Retouching is minimal: the two poles standing in the water have been strengthened, and there are several small dots in the fisherman's jacket. (RW)

This small picture is both delightful and ingratiating. Indeed, it is almost like a miniature in its inclusion of a great deal of pictorial incident on a small surface. A ragged fisherman in the central foreground walks into the landscape, balanced at left by a thatched cottage or storage building and at right by two poles jutting up from the edge of the bay. Closer to the spectator in the foreground are three fishing baskets, one upside down and two lying on their sides, forming a kind of still life in the landscape. The middle ground is occupied by a stretch of blue-green water, with two small boats in it, and in the background is a coastal town, almost certainly in Normandy, where Claude Monet painted obsessively in the late 1860s. The distant shore arcs from the left middle ground to the right background. At the center left of the beach are a line of gray and white structures, painted with just two or three tiny brushstrokes, but which are sufficient to suggest either bathing cabins or, more likely, drying racks for the sails used by both fishermen and pleasure boaters. Farther to the right is a Norman church with spire and a number of other, less easily distinguishable buildings. But the entire effect of the beach, the hills, the spire, and the buildings is that of Sainte-Adresse, so familiar to us in somewhat later paintings by Eugène Boudin, Frédéric Bazille, and Monet. The direction of the view is virtually identical to that later employed by Monet in the *Beach at Sainte-Adresse* of 1867 (fig. 33a), and the younger artist actually painted his fisherman's cottages precisely like that in Troyon's painting in 1867 and 1868.[1]

The cottage is set into a mound, hillock, or dune. It is made of brick, wood boards weathered gray, and a tangle of brown-gray thatch. Two stone, brick, and cement walls, covered by a wooden roof, form another shed or stall, possibly for storing baskets, nets, and other fishing gear or for keeping an animal. The battered wood door of the cottage is swung open, and a blue cloth, smock, or chemise hangs from the hinge or a hook at the top. The pink and orange-red of the bricks forms an arresting contrast with the blue of the shirt. Otherwise the picture is dominated by blue (sea), yellow-ocher (grasses in the foreground), white (clouds), gray (opposite shore, foreground), and green (the patches of grass in the extreme right foreground, left foreground, and distant shore at left). The shape, direction, and texture of the brushstrokes suggest the character of the objects themselves—horizontal and architectonic for the bricks, horizontal but liquid and overlapping for the water, feathery for the thatch. The poles, probably used for hanging and drying the nets, are a lovely wavering line of brown with a thin edge of white and help establish an

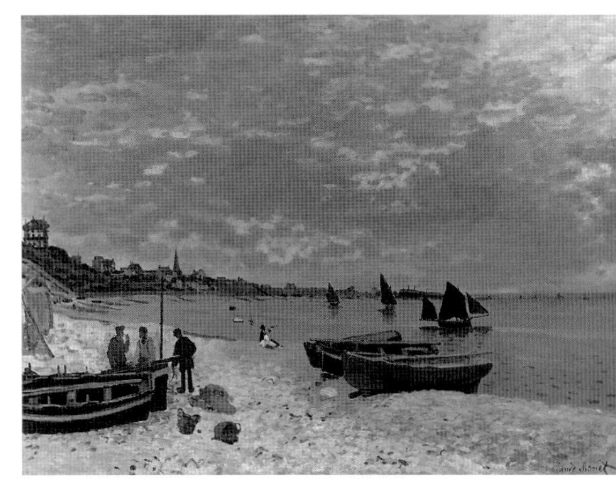

Fig. 33a Claude Monet, *Beach at Sainte-Adresse*, 1867, oil on canvas, $29\frac{7}{8} \times 40\frac{5}{8}$ in. (75.8 × 102.5 cm), The Art Institute of Chicago, Mr. and Mrs. Lewis Larned Coburn Memorial Collection

almost measurable scale and create a clear recession. The painting is painted directly on the panel, without white or other ground; thus, the warmth of the wood establishes the basic tonality of the painting, its grain, and the underlying texture.

Thatched Cottage by the Sea was initialed by its artist and sold in his lifetime. It does not appear in the death sale of 1866 and makes its first documented appearance in the 1877 sale of the Sedelmeyer collection. Perhaps because of its modest dimensions and slight aesthetic ambitions, it has remained a resolutely private painting, with no recorded exhibition history and vast gaps in a provenance between its second owner, Étienne de Roy, who bought it in 1877, and its acquisition by Norton Simon nearly a century later. An oddity in the oeuvre of Troyon, the painting might well be ascribed to another artist were it not for the initials in the lower left corner. The painter generally preferred to paint either inland or on the coastal plains, where he concentrated on animals.

Because it was relatively freely painted on an unprimed panel, the painting may well have been executed over two or three days in the landscape itself. The white sail of a pleasure boat suggests that Troyon, like many Frenchmen, was visiting Sainte-Adresse during the balmy summer months, and it is even possible that the small painting was a souvenir of the trip. The absence of the villas that were to dot the hill behind the beach suggests that the painting was made before 1860, when they began to appear, that is, well before Monet's aunt built her villa that was later to be immortalized by the painter. Monet himself painted a huge landscape of the same beach in 1865, accepted for the Salon of that year (see fig. 84a). The younger artist situates himself on the beach itself and makes a work intended to convey the full sweep of the landscape to an urban audience. Troyon's aims are more delicate and modest. Yet, in his cloud-filled scene with such carefully observed atmosphere, he predicted more of Monet's Impressionist achievement of the 1870s and 1880s than even Monet himself. The scumbled touches, carefully layered chromatic observations of the thatched cottage, and precise color distinction between beach and sky make it clear that, although this work is a small masterpiece, it was not painted by a small master.

1 D. Wildenstein, 1974, nos. 94 and 114.

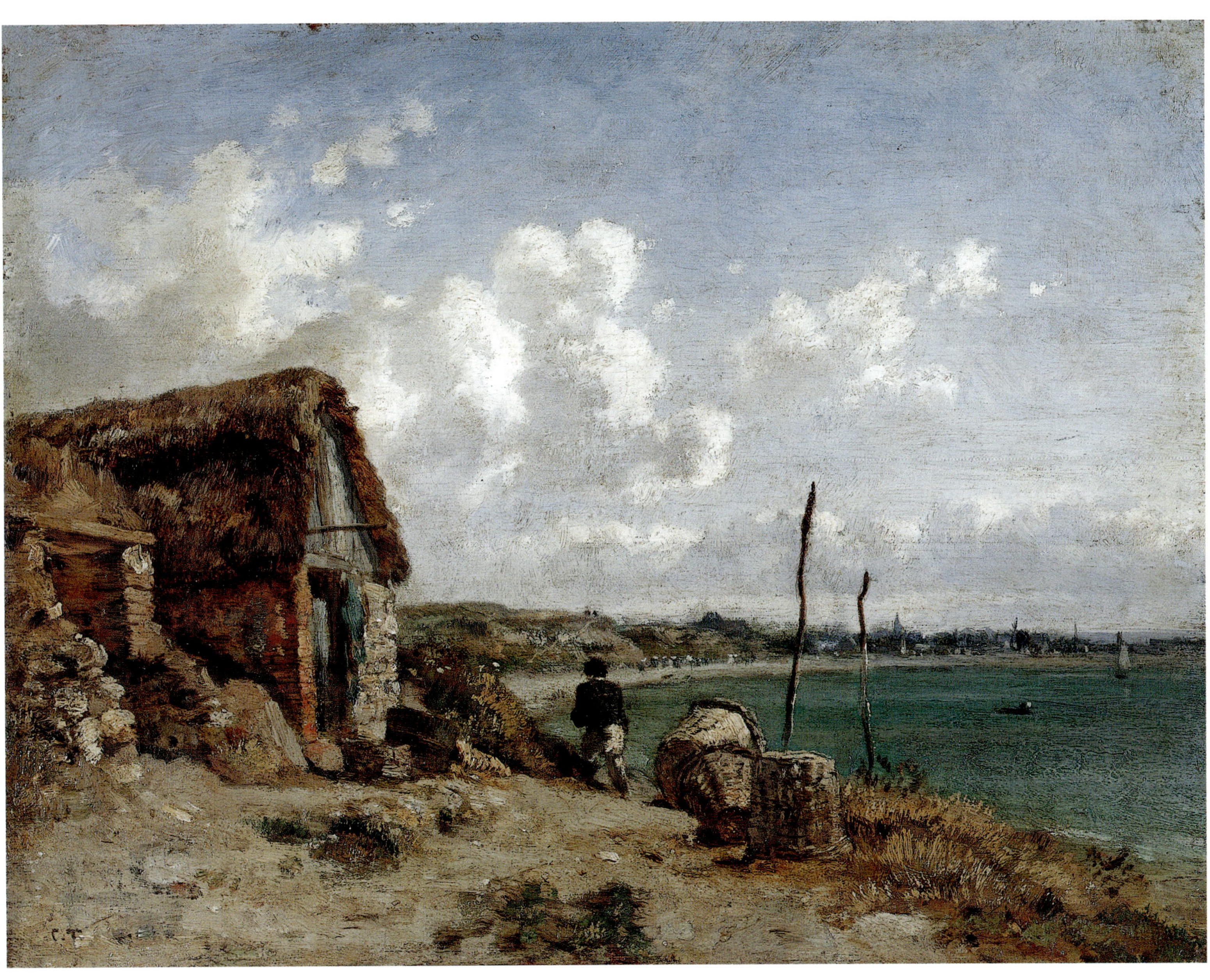

33

34

Jules Dupré
French, 1811–1889

Large Trees at Water's Edge
c. 1865

Oil on canvas, 38 × 30 in. (96.5 × 76.2 cm)
Signed lower left: "Jules Dupré"
F.1983.11

Provenance: Laurent-Richard, by 1871? (sale, Paris, Hôtel Drouot, 7 April 1873, no. 27, as *Grands Arbres au bord de l'eau*, for Ff 17,050). [M. Knoedler & Co., New York, sold 8 November 1889, for $10,000, to]; Corcoran Gallery of Art, Washington, D.C. (sale, New York, Sotheby Parke-Bernet, 3 May 1979, lot 40, to); Norton Simon, gift 1983 to; The Norton Simon Foundation.

Exhibition: Possibly London, 1871, no. 100, as *La Mare aux chênes*, as collection of Laurent-Richard.

References: Corcoran, 1915, no. 93; Corcoran, 1939, no. 113; Aubrun, 1974, no. 310, p. 164, ill.

Technical Notes: The original support is a plain-weave canvas with its tacking edges intact; it is glue-lined. In 1989 the upper right corner of the painting was separating from the lining canvas and it was reglued at the edges; however, this did not address completely the delamination, and there are two small air pockets at the upper right (1 inch from the right side, ¾ inch from the top) with lifting paint flakes. The stretcher is a replacement, constructed of heavy stock without a crossbar; the keys are ADS metal wedges. The smooth ground layer is pale gray. The opaque paint is directly applied in a free and vigorous handling, covering the ground entirely. It is quite thick, its points and ridges of impasto unaltered by the lining. There is a small loss of paint and ground at the lower left (4½ inches from the left side and 3 inches from the bottom, just above the signature). First noted in 1979, it was secured with adhesive but left unfilled and remains conspicuous because of its location. At this same time darkened varnish was selectively removed and replaced with multiple layers of acrylic resin. The thick, glossy varnish distorts significantly the values of texture and color. (RW)

Jules Dupré's painting exemplifies many of the pictorial and thematic concerns of the informal association of men who lived and worked in or near the French village of Barbizon. The Barbizon painters—Dupré, Théodore Rousseau, Narcisse Diaz, Constant Troyon, Jean-François Millet, and a few others—rejected the formality and historical associations visible in the works of a previous generation of classically inspired landscape artists, such as Pierre-Henri de Valenciennes and Achille-Etna Michallon, and embraced instead a more picturesque aesthetic derived from seventeenth-century Dutch art and the then-modern English School. These preferences were not the consequence of a desire for novelty or simply a wish to overthrow a reigning paradigm. They were instead part of a larger change in the culture of artist production, the economics of artistic exhibition and sale, and the understanding of nature. Dupré had a very independent mind-set, preferring the company of a few, similarly autonomous artists to the hierarchical society of the École des Beaux-Arts, and the humble fields and forests of rural France to the antique ruins and classical monuments of the Roman Campagna. In this manner, Dupré and the other Barbizon artists generally expressed their solidarity with a Romantic antiurban and anticapitalist sensibility also represented in the work of older contemporaries, such as the French artist Eugène Delacroix and the English painter John Constable.

Signs of the latter artist's influence are clearly apparent in *Large Trees at Water's Edge.* Constable's propensity for placing prominent, yet indefinitely modeled human figures in his landscape scenes—as in his impressive, vertical "six-footer" *The Lock* (fig. 34a)—is repeated in Dupré's painting. Dupré in fact met Constable in England in 1834 and thus had direct exposure both to the man and to his late landscape style, characterized by thick impasto and darkly toned greens and browns, highlighted by flecks of white, blue, red, and orange. *Large Trees at Water's Edge*, however, is less

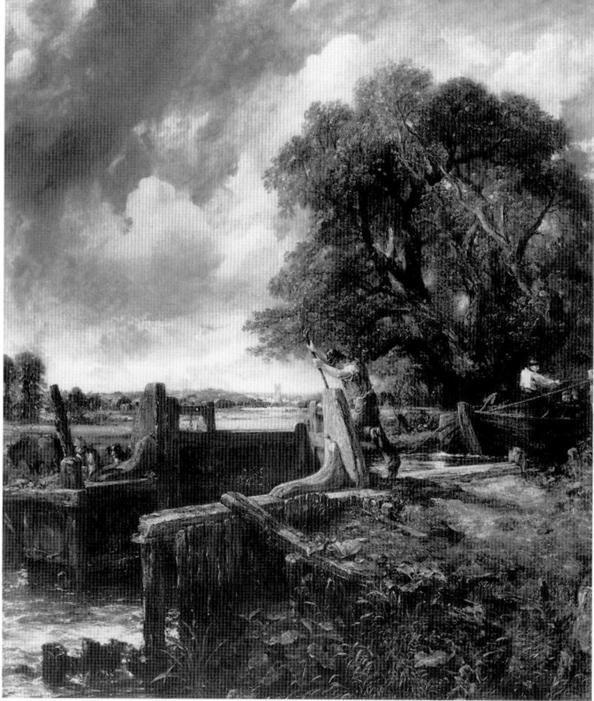

Fig. 34a John Constable, *The Lock*, 1824, oil on canvas, 56 × 47½ in. (142.2 × 120.7 cm), © Carmen Thyssen-Bornemisza Collection on loan at the Museo Thyssen-Bornemisza, Madrid

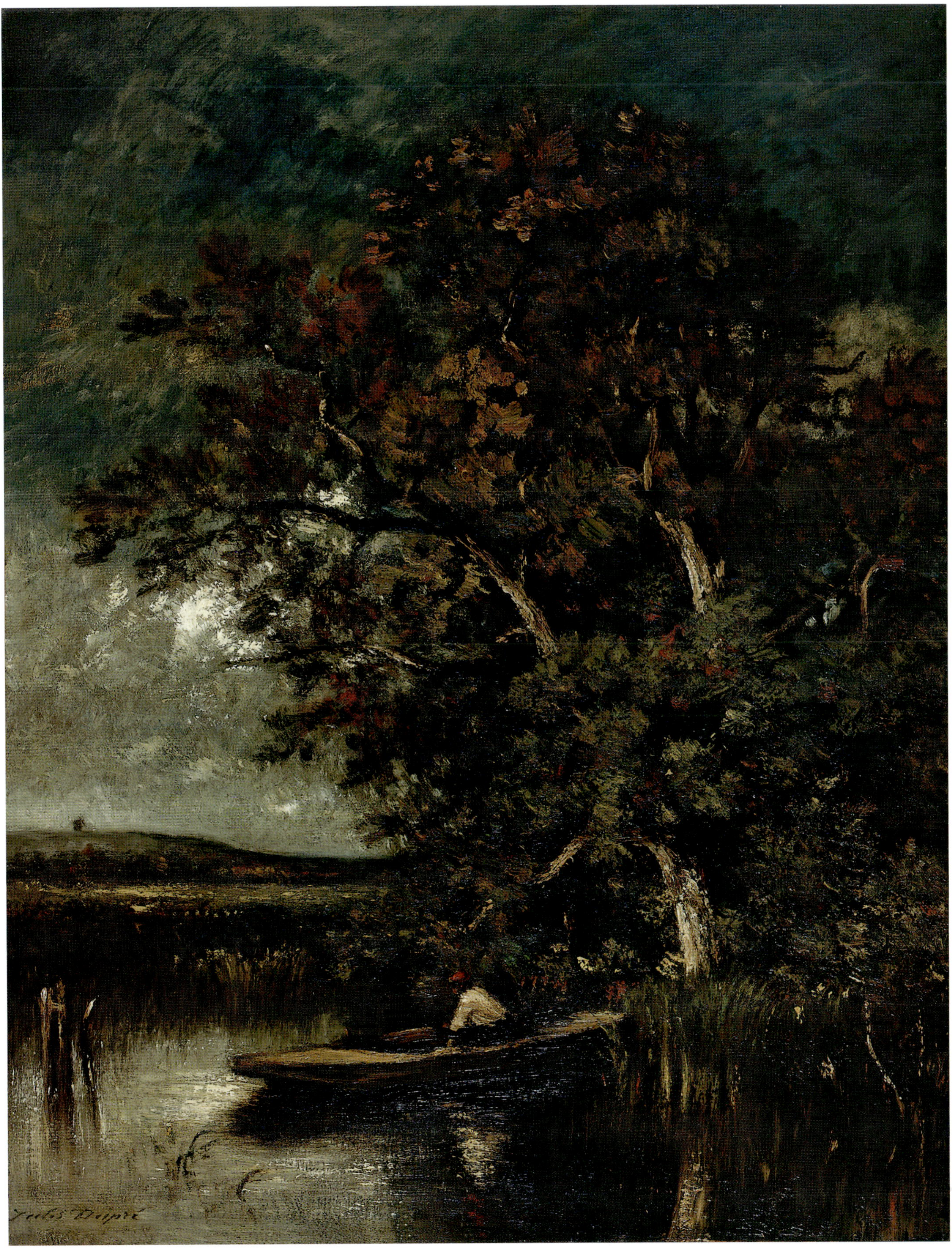

compositionally intricate than Constable's work, and less obviously dramatic. It shows a single figure in a small flatboat in the foreground, beneath a great, arcing oak tree. The main trunk of the tree is reflected at lower right in the shallow pond. Above, the trunk divides into two and then into many smaller branches laden with dark green leaves, blotting out most of the sky. The sky that remains is nevertheless a palpable presence, its blues, grays, and whites as tactile as the leaves it caresses. Dupré is said to have stated about one of his pictures, "The sky is behind the tree, in the tree, and in front of the tree."[1]

In the distant background at left is a long, low hill, on top of which is visible a distant windmill. In the water at lower left, on a line coincident with the man and the tree trunk, is a post for tying up the boat. The painting is thickly painted all over, with especially thick impasto—almost constituting shallow relief—in the white shirt of the fisherman. (The reflection in the water is almost equally thickly painted.) The consequence of Dupré's highly animated surface and yet stable composition is an almost vitalist conception of nature. That is, the suggestion that landscape elements—water, trees, sky, and light reflections—are nearly autonomous or self-determining. They are subject to no overarching mechanical forces and to no human discipline. The sentiment is one that will be found as well in Dupré's closest colleagues at Barbizon, Rousseau and Diaz, and one that conforms to the radical sensibilities of the so-called Generation of 1830.

Neither the date of the picture nor the location of its subject can be stated with precision. The painting, however, bearing the title *Grands Arbres au bord de l'eau,* was reproduced in etching by Émile Boilvin on the occasion of the April 1873 Hôtel Drouot auction of pictures belonging to M. Laurent-Richard, thus providing a terminus post quem. It was in fact one of twelve works by Dupré sold in that auction and achieved a price, 17,050 francs, midway between the highest, 38,000 (*La Mare aux chênes*), and lowest, 6,850 (*Rue de village, au coucher du soleil*). The description of the painting in the Drouot catalogue does not give any indication of the geographic setting of the picture, but the gentle hills in the background evoke either the region around Barbizon or the forests near L'Isle-Adam northwest of Paris, where the painter settled in 1849.

By the time of the Laurent-Richard sale, Dupré had regained much of the acclaim that greeted his first Salon appearance in 1835. He exhibited thirteen works at the fine arts section of the 1867 Exposition Universelle in Paris and was awarded medals that supplemented the Legion of Honor given in 1849 by the government of the Second Republic. By now, Dupré was being rediscovered by a younger generation of painters—the Impressionists—who themselves, like the Barbizon painters before them, would redefine the character of the French landscape.

1 Aubrun, 1974, p. 34.

35

Pierre-Étienne-Théodore Rousseau
French, 1812–1867

The Fisherman, Early Morning
c. 1865

Oil on canvas, $39^{1}/_{4} \times 53$ in. (99.6 × 134.6 cm)
Signed lower left: "TH. Rousseau"
F.1976.14

Provenance: Collot, Paris. Duc de Morny, Paris. Monsieur de Ferrol, Paris. Émile Gsell (1838–1879), Vienna, in 1872. Émile Gavet (1830–1904), Paris. By 1883 Mme Isaac Péreire, Paris, sold 1910 by heirs to; M. Knoedler & Company, New York, sold 1911 to; George F. Baker, New York, by inheritance to his heir; Mrs. William Goadby Loew, New York, by 1932, by inheritance to her daughter; Mrs. Robert E. Strawbridge Jr., by inheritance to; Robert E. Strawbridge III, New York. Private collection, New York. [Wildenstein, New York, sold 1976 to]; The Norton Simon Foundation.

Exhibitions: Paris, 1883b, no. 84, p. 54, ill., as *Le Pêcheur* (etching by Gustave-Marie Greux); New York, 1920b; New York, 1931c, no. 10; London, 1932, no. 398; New York, 1963, no. 61, ill.; New York, 1975, no. 58; on loan, Champaign, University of Illinois, Krannert Art Museum, 3 January–2 August 1977.

References: Sensier, 1872, p. 220; *American Art News*, 1912, p. 1; *Gazette des beaux-arts*, 1912; Blanche, 1932, p. 88, ill.; Schulman, 1999, p. 275, no. 512, ill.; G. Thomas, 2000, p. 27, fig. 12.

Technical Notes: The original support, a fine, plain-weave fabric, has a double lining. The adhesive appears to be aqueous and the fabrics are similar basket weaves. A later stretcher supports the painting. When tacking edges were removed some paint was cut as well. The cream ground leaves the crowns of the threads covered but texturally present, and the ground shows in areas of no or very thin paint. Painting began with a dark, medium-rich paint for the landscape that was at least partially wiped or even scraped, exposing the primed canvas crowns. Some of these areas were mistaken as abrasions and toned. Pasty and vehicular paints in dabs, dashes, and strokes with moderate impasto of pure and mixed earth, black, white, and green (possibly emerald) colors create an autumn appearance. The light-colored sky shows the use of wider brushes and paint in several layers applied wet in wet. The paint of the sky goes over the brown and other colors of the landscape and pierces the already painted trees, but one green of the trees thinly veils the sky at parts of the horizon. The condition of the painting seems fairly good. On the left the sky at the horizon has a square about 5 inches in both dimensions of later overpaint. The varnish is thin and fluoresces bluish in ultraviolet light. Two small cleaning tests exist at about the center in the landscape. (JF)

Along with Jean-François Millet and Camille Corot, Théodore Rousseau was a key figure in the establishment of the Barbizon School. This school was not an art academy or atelier; nor was it an artistic brotherhood or avant-garde. It was not even a unified artistic tendency: there are enormous differences among landscape paintings by the three artists mentioned above, not to mention between them and works by the half dozen or so other artists associated with Barbizon, including Charles-François Daubigny, Narcisse-Virgile Diaz de la Peña, Jules Dupré, Henri-Joseph Harpignies, Charles Jacque, and Constant Troyon. The term *Barbizon School* is itself a post hoc invention coined as late as 1903, according to the research of Nicholas Green, that is, some seventy years after the artists in question first began to paint in the forested region surrounding the small village of Barbizon, some thirty miles southeast of Paris.[1]

And yet the artists of the Barbizon School shared an essential conviction that lends coherence to their diverse endeavors. They proposed that the ideal relation between humans and nature was one of congruence not conflict, integration not opposition. The attitude was more original—and more radical—than it may at first appear. Though an idealized harmony between people and nature was the defining feature of Virgil's *Eclogues* (37 B.C.E.) and of the centuries of landscape art that drew upon it—from the frescoes of the Boscoreale Villa (c. 50 B.C.E., The Metropolitan Museum of Art, New York) to the paintings and theories of the French painter and theorist Pierre-Henri de Valenciennes in the late eighteenth century—the Barbizon artists for the first time erased the presumed hierarchy between the two. The ancient forests, rocky gorges, and grassy plains of the region were worthy of respect and preservation for their own sake; the men and women who inhabited these lands—and the artists who depicted them—were themselves the product of the natural forces of birth, growth, respiration, reproduction, decay, and death. The perspective is the precise inversion of the attitude of modernization and development that generally prevailed in this dawning age in France of industry and capitalist expansion.

Rousseau's large painting is a seductive scene of a summer morning in the French countryside. A pair of large trees and a barefoot man with a little black dog dominate the middle ground. The raggedly dressed fisherman walks toward the viewer, carrying a bag full of fish at his right side and some poles and fishing nets on his left shoulder. Behind him is a pond, whose shallow, placid waters reflect a pair of distant trees. To the right, some sheep graze in a forest clearing. At left is a dark, densely grown copse. Yet the most remarkable aspect of the painting is the sun, hidden behind the central trees and casting dramatically exaggerated shadows from that point across the foreground of the painting. Hence, the painting has the quality of a landscape silhouette, with forms starkly delineated against the brilliant light of the summer sun. Rousseau learned this device from studying the landscapes of the seventeenth-century French classical painter Claude Lorrain, who often made the light of the sun into the real subject of his otherwise historical and mythological landscapes.

Rousseau's painting has one main and two subsidiary areas of interest. The path on which the man is walking widens considerably in the foreground, so that the spectator enters the picture at a single place and is presented with three alternative types of landscape, one wild (left), one pastoral with grazing farm animals (right), and one cultural and recreational (center). It is a world that is expansive, both wide and deep. This, Rousseau seems to tell us, is what the countryside should mean: the freedom to fish in the morning and hunt in the afternoon. There is little here that elicits criticism or cogitation. Rather, Rousseau evokes a world at ease, in which human instinct and pleasure are encouraged in a landscape that is at once ordered and unbridled. A similar effect is achieved in the roughly contemporaneous *The Charcoal Burner's Hut* in the Dallas Museum of Art (fig. 35a).

Rousseau constructs space by paint texture, hue, and tone. The left foreground is painted thickly, with strongly defined texture, and greater attention is paid to surfaces here than in the rest of the painting. This area advances visually by virtue of its tactility. The trees above and to the right of the walking man are more thinly painted, lighter and paler in color, as if washed out from the light and atmosphere. In the distance, the sky and land meet and evaporate into a Claudian blue, atmospheric perspective. The landscape is actually Claudian in its intense spatial ordering, color, and light, but there is nothing classical or conventionally beautiful about Rousseau's pictorial world. It is left to the greens, browns, oranges, yellows, and blues—the blue blended with all the other colors—to create an overall pictorial balance.

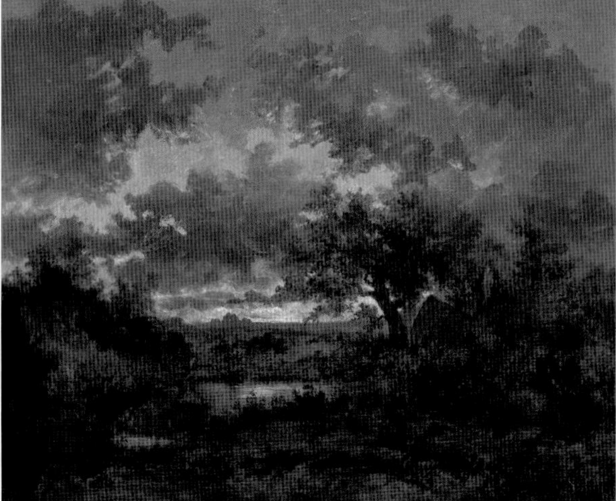

Fig. 35a Pierre-Étienne-Théodore Rousseau, *The Charcoal Burner's Hut*, c. 1850–1855, oil on canvas, $31\frac{1}{2} \times 39\frac{3}{8}$ in. (80 × 100 cm), Dallas Museum of Art, The Art Museum League Fund

Unfortunately, there is absolutely no record that this large and important landscape was exhibited in Rousseau's lifetime. It is likely, however, that such an imposing painting did appear either in a Salon exhibition, at an important exhibition in a commercial gallery, on the occasion of a world's fair, or even at a memorial exhibition. As is often the case with midcentury French landscape paintings, this one has had a number of recorded titles and could easily have been published with yet another. One of its early owners was the French collector Isaac Péreire, whose widow is listed as its owner at the time of its publication in a beautiful 1883 book entitled *Cent Chefs-d'oeuvre* (One Hundred Masterpieces) published by the commercial gallery of Georges Petit sixteen years after Rousseau's death in 1867. Here, it is described as a spring scene and placed, somewhat inexplicably, in L'Isle-Adam rather than in or around Barbizon or Chailly, where it appears to have been painted.

Since it was exhibited at the Royal Academy of Arts in London in 1932, the painting has been firmly and conclusively dated to 1853, but there is no evidence for this. The painting itself bears neither inscription nor date, and its first publication in 1883 has no date. In 1931, when it was published by Knoedler Galleries in New York, it was dated (with no more evidence, but with more justification on stylistic grounds) to 1865, and only in the catalogue for the great commemorative *Exhibition of French Art, 1200–1900* at the Royal Academy in London in 1932 did the date 1853 first appear. The painting was famous enough in 1912 to warrant a notice in the *American Art News* (listed as *Le Pecheur*) saying that it

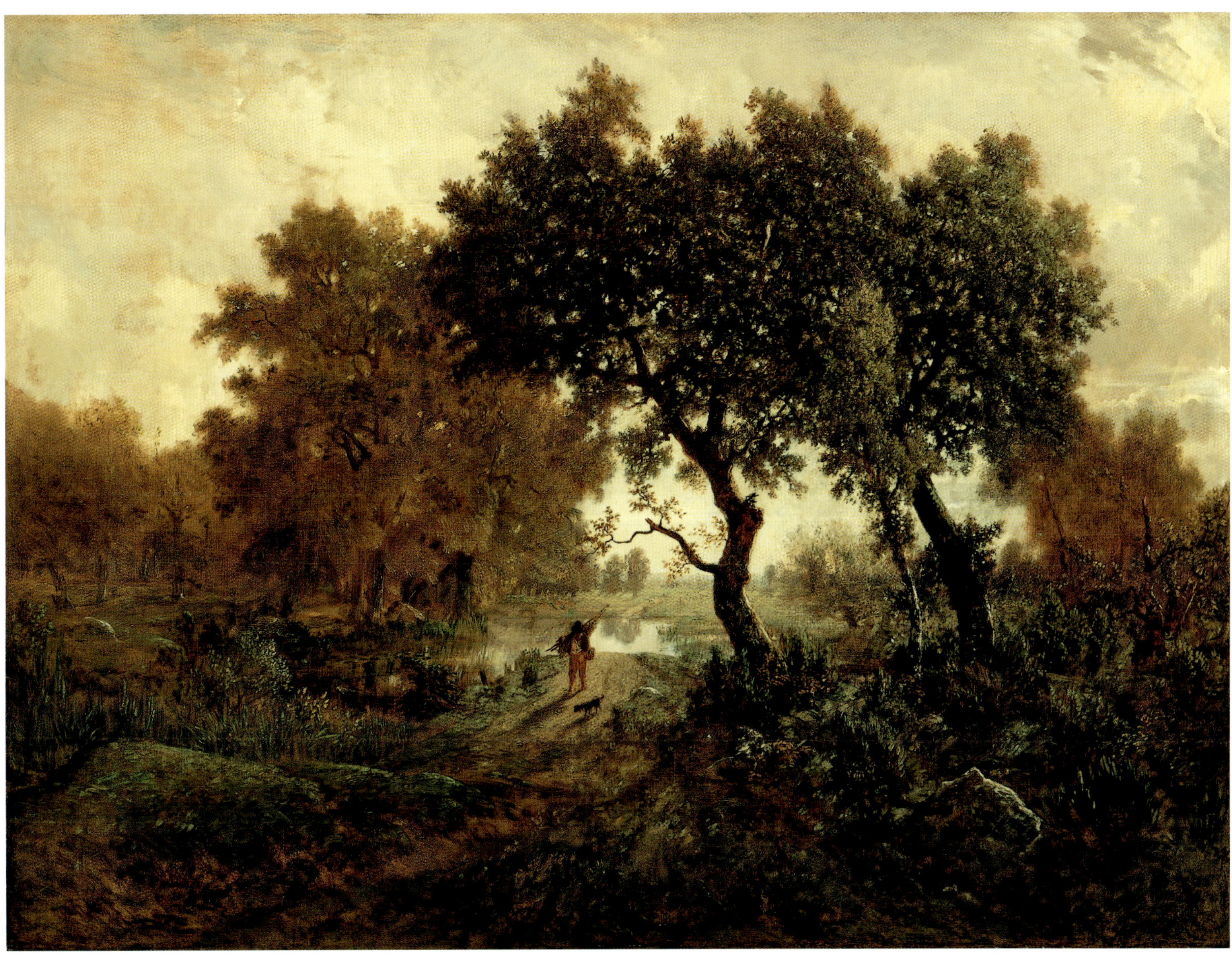

35

was sold to Mr. George F. Baker for $200,000, then the highest price ever paid for a Barbizon painting (according to this unreliable source). This extraordinary price (equivalent to nearly $4,000,000 today) makes it clear that, on the eve of World War I, Barbizon paintings were still at the top of the market in the United States. Curiously, Norton Simon paid only $75,000 for the painting when he acquired it in 1976, reflecting the subsequent decline in the reputation of that school.

The great American scholar of Barbizon painting John Minor Wisdom saw the painting for the first time just before it was acquired by The Norton Simon Foundation and assessed it as "one of the 12 most important Rousseaus [to] exist" and as "one of the top half dozen Rousseau paintings in America and the finest sold since World War II." When pressed, he listed the major paintings in the Cleveland Museum of Art, the Walters Art Gallery (now Museum), the Toledo Museum of Art, and at Middlebury College as the others in its league in the United States. Wisdom dated it to "the last years of Rousseau's life," effectively disputing the undocumented date of 1853 that the painting had borne silently since 1932.[2] On the basis of Wisdom's verdict, Simon bought the painting for the full asking price.

1 Green, 1990.

2 Correspondence, Norton Simon Museum curatorial files.

36

Charles-Émile Jacque
French, 1813–1894

Return to the Fold
c. 1878–1880

Oil on canvas, $32\frac{1}{4} \times 26\frac{1}{4}$ in. (81.8 × 66.6 cm)
Signed lower left: "C. Jacque"
N.1979.11.3

Provenance: Mrs. Francis Sydney Smithers, gift 1938 to; Corcoran Gallery of Art, Washington, D.C. (sale, New York, Sotheby Parke-Bernet, 3 May 1979, lot 43, to); Norton Simon, bequest 1993 to; Jennifer Jones Simon Art Trust.

Exhibitions: On loan, Washington, D.C., Smithsonian Institution, Renwick Gallery, July 1971–?; on loan, Princeton, University Art Gallery, 14 May–20 July 1979.

References: Corcoran, 1939, no. 191, ill. p. 58; Fanica, 1995, p. 114, ill.

Technical Notes: The original support is a fine, plain-weave fabric with the tacking edges removed. The painting is lined with wax resin and tacked with large tacks to a 5-part butt-join stretcher that may be original. The ground is light gray–cream and thick, but the canvas-weave texture is still present. The picture was probably first laid in with dark brown paint. The scene was then built up with pasty opaque paint, scumbles, and glazes of brown and black. Obvious brushwork in the opaque colors contrasts with smooth, dark areas. The figure appears underpainted with dark gray that may be part of this first lay-in or "underdrawing." With the exception of the blacks and browns, colors are mixed with a good deal of white. Light purple is used in the sheep at left (on the whites) and in the black dog. In the light paints at right what appears to be wrinkling is actually cracking with little losses that had been set down probably during the lining. Apparently the canvas shrunk somewhat since there is overlapping of paint. This can be seen throughout the white walls. The sheep in the shadow are much abraded in the lower left area. The signature is abraded and has some reinforcement. Additional abrasion occurs in the window at the upper right, in the darks inside the doorway, on the girl, and in the shadows of the pink drape. Ultraviolet light shows retouching around the edges and two horizontal areas of retouching at the upper right. The lining flattened the paint considerably. The varnish is shiny overall, saturating, and not too thick. In ultraviolet light it is streaky, fluoresces bluish green, and appears very dense over the signature. (JF)

The artistic device that gives this painting its animation and intimacy is the low vantage point: the spectator is afforded a sheep's-eye view. As the animals clamber over the threshold of the sheepfold, the viewer watches from behind while the sheepdog and the farm woman with staff ensure a safe passage and a secure night. This anecdotal element accounts for the sentimentality of the picture. The artist's empathy with his subjects has led some commentators, with a touch of condescension, to label Jacque "the Raphael of sheep."

But Jacque was more than an ingratiating animal painter. Unlike Rosa Bonheur, he emphasized the interaction of human and animal life, and interrogated the past and present of French rural society. Trained as an engraver and illustrator, he early on developed an ability to observe and understand the most telling details of physiognomy and deportment, and to record the salient characteristics of local landscapes, including Barbizon, where he lived from 1849 to 1854; Montrouge, just outside Paris, where he kept a studio; Pau; and other regions. This discernment is evident in his prints as well as paintings. His etchings, including *The Return* (fig. 36a), deeply influenced by Rembrandt, as well as such other seventeenth-century Dutch masters as Nicholaes Berchem, are precise and naturalistic, yet highly expressive. They are both intimate and nostalgic, invoking an earlier age, when the rural economy was governed by seasonal cycles, times of day, and the vagaries of weather, rather than the demands of a modern, national market and a cash economy. This is why Jacque, in his paintings and etchings, so often depicts the return of sheep to their fold at day's end, or else depicts morning, noon (such as *Noonday Rest*, Tweed Museum of Art, Duluth), spring (as in *Springtime*, The Metropolitan Museum of Art, New York), summer, and dramatic weather events.

Return to the Fold, like the works cited above, balances accurate details of animal, human, and architectural

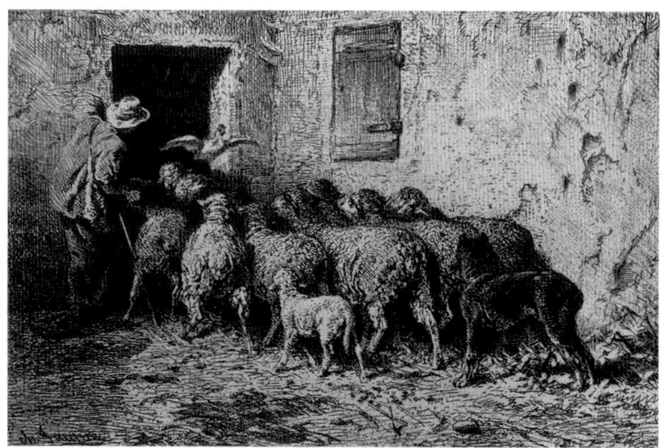

Fig. 36a Charles-Émile Jacque, *The Return*, 1878, etching and roulette, The University of Michigan Museum of Art, Ann Arbor, Gift of Carl Fredric Clarke

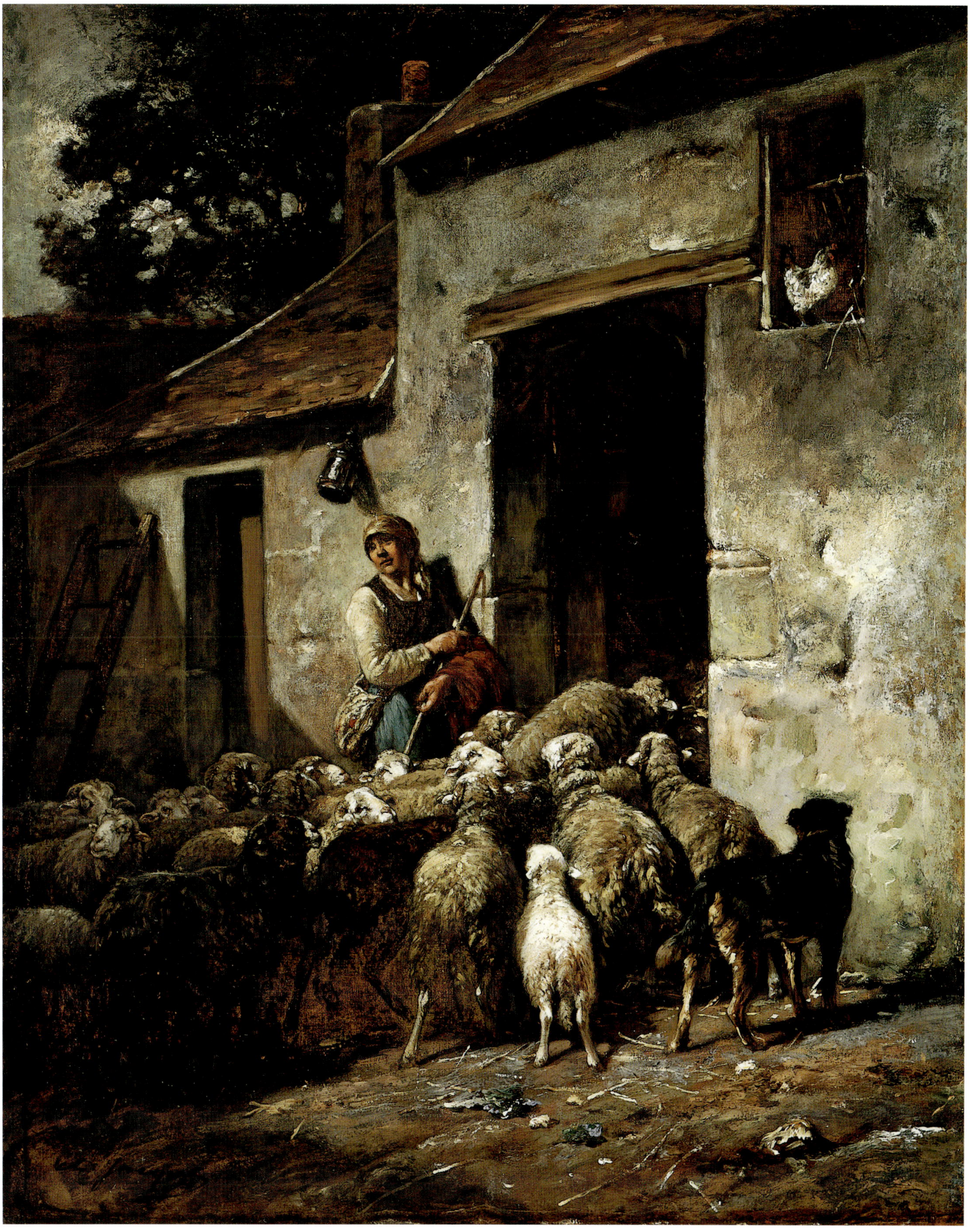

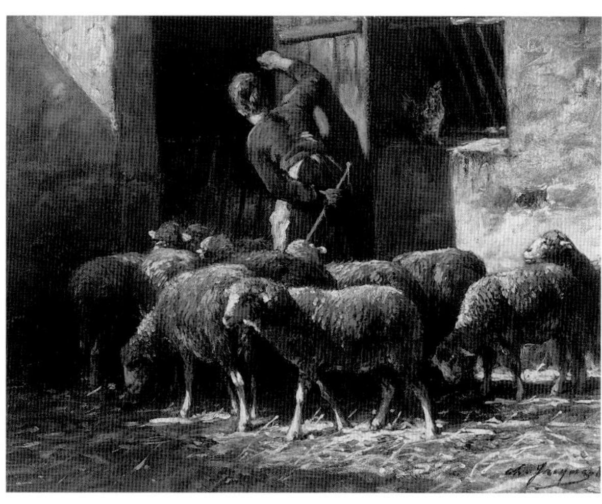

Fig. 36b Charles-Émile Jacque, *Return of the Flock*, 1889, oil on panel, 9½ × 13 in. (23.5 × 33 cm), Tweed Museum of Art, University of Minnesota, Duluth

physiognomy with sentimental content. The sheep, according to the art historian Pierre-Olivier Fanica, are *béarnaise* from the region of Pau, noted for their oily wool and relative heterogeneity of color.[1] The rooster, perching in the window at upper right and keeping a proprietary watch on the proceedings, is undoubtedly a well-known local variety; in his spare time Jacque raised and studied poultry and wrote a monograph called *Le Poulailler: Monographie des poules indigenes et exotiques*, published in 1858.

The wall and doorway in the present picture, as in many others by the artist, is as carefully studied as the sheep and poultry. It is thickly painted with irregular brushstrokes and palette knife smears, to ensure that the surface of the painting better approximates the mossy and lichen-encrusted stone and stucco walls of an old farmhouse. But it also thereby resembles an artist's palette; this is an instance of Jacque's Realism, the insistence, marked in the work of Gustave Courbet, that the fiction of representation be revealed even amid the artifice of storytelling. (Other genre, landscape, and animal painters of the time, such as Jules Bastien-Lepage and J.-F. Raffaëlli, associated with the term Naturalism, endeavored to have the artistic medium disappear before the authority of the subject.)

Jacque was a prolific artist whose total oeuvre may number more than three thousand paintings and several thousand more drawings, etchings, and engravings. By

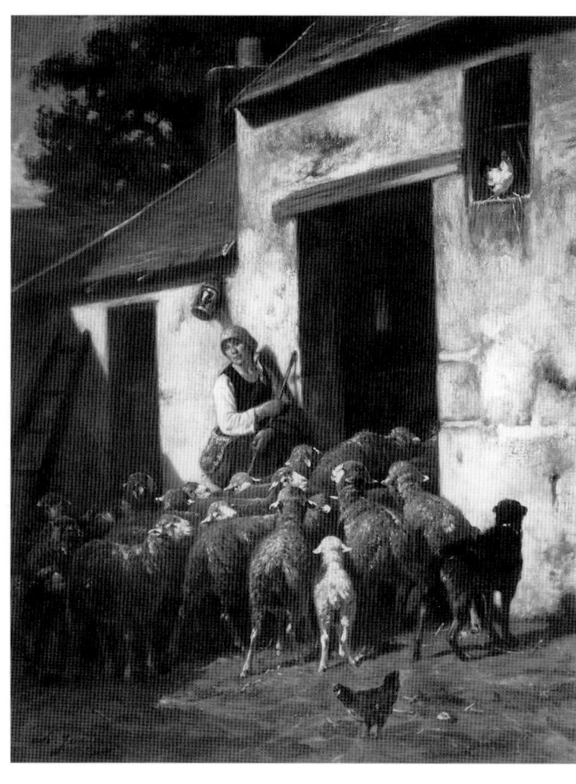

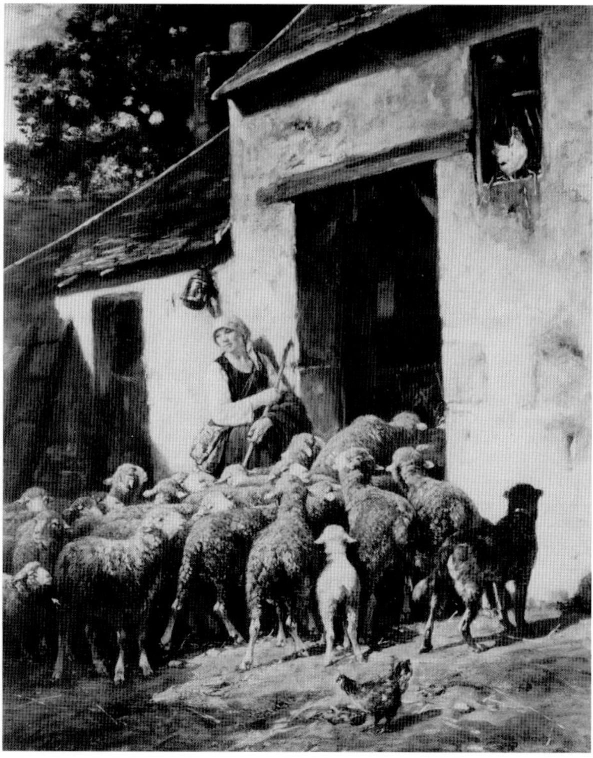

Fig. 36c (*right*) Charles-Émile Jacque, *Sheep*, oil on canvas, 37⅞ × 25³⁄₁₆ in. (96.2 × 64 cm), The Philbrook Museum of Art, Tulsa, Gift of Laura A. Clubb

Fig. 36d (*far right*) Charles-Émile Jacque, *Return to the Fold*, c. 1878–1880, oil on canvas, 32 × 26 in. (81.3 × 66 cm), Fisher Gallery, University of Southern California, Los Angeles

the 1880s he was quite successful, especially in England and the United States, and maintained an atelier in which his sons were employed; he also inspired many artistic imitators and forgers. The present painting, however, is undoubtedly autograph and may be compared with other works by Jacque from late in his career, including *Leaving the Stall: Morning* (1878, private collection) and *Return of the Flock* (fig. 36b). A replica or different version of the present painting, somewhat more generalized, but apparently in better condition, is in the Philbrook Museum of Art in Tulsa (fig. 36c). Another is in the Fisher Gallery, University of Southern California (fig. 36d).

The picture has been significantly overcleaned and abraded. The dark sheep in the left middle of the picture is almost completely lost, the animals immediately to the left and right almost equally so. There are also significant areas of thin, abraded paint in the bodice of the figure, her lower face beneath her chin, her eyes, and elsewhere.

1 Fanica, 1995, p. 114.

37

Thomas Couture
French, 1815–1879

Reverie
1840–1841

Oil on canvas, $21\frac{5}{8} \times 20\frac{1}{2}$ in. (54.9×52.1 cm)
Signed with initials center left: "T. C."
N.1979.11.5

Provenance: [Boussod, New York, sold 6 November 1890 to]; [M. Knoedler & Company, New York, stock no. 6646; sold 22 November 1890, to]; Corcoran Gallery of Art, Washington, D.C. (sale, New York, Sotheby Parke-Bernet, 3 May 1979, lot 58, to); Norton Simon, bequest 1993 to; Jennifer Jones Simon Art Trust.

Exhibitions: Paris, 1841, no. 429; on loan, Santa Fe, Museum of New Mexico, 1 July–13 August 1959; Lexington, 1973.

References: *Le Constitutionnel*, 1841; Pelletan, 1841, p. 2; *L'Artiste*, 1841, p. 332; Corcoran, 1915, no. 143, p. 58; Corcoran, 1939, no. 80; Boime, 1980, pp. 86, 91–92, 89, ill.; Didier Aaron, 1987, fig. 14a.

Technical Notes: The open, plain-weave canvas with tacking edges removed was strengthened with an aqueous lining to another canvas. The 5-part stretcher may be original. On top of a medium-thick light gray ground lies a textured gray paint that affects the appearance of the entire surface. The vigorous handling of this layer is visible in the X-ray. The flesh was painted with thick local color that retains the texture of the brush. Application was wet in wet with little blending. The background and the figure's hair consist primarily of dark browns that were thin enough to flow off the peaks of the textured underlayer, something that was perhaps aided by the artist's wiping. Strips on the right and bottom edges about ¼-inch wide are unpainted. Remnants of a yellow varnish are visible. The present varnish, possibly a natural resin, fluoresces greenish in ultraviolet light. The painting was cleaned in 1979 and varnished with Rembrandt picture varnish. (JF)

This modest painting of a female head is undoubtedly the work of Thomas Couture, who is known today chiefly as the painter of *Romans of the Decadence*, one of the most reproduced paintings of the nineteenth century. Today the vast canvas is shown prominently in the Musée d'Orsay, Paris, and there represents the pinnacle of French academic achievement at midcentury. We also know Couture as one of the principal teachers—perhaps pictorial advisors would be a better term—of Édouard Manet. This painting represents a dark-haired young woman who, though posing without a blouse, is discreetly covered with a diaphanous but unrevealing fabric wrap. Her head leans slightly forward and her dark eyes are downcast. Thus, she is neither an academic nude nor a portrait, but exists in an in-between state, part model, part muse, part allegory. The painting was purchased in 1890 for $1,350 from M. Knoedler & Company by the Corcoran Gallery of Art in Washington and is thus one of a number of paintings acquired by Norton Simon at a large sale of works from the Corcoran in 1979. The Couture was purchased by the Corcoran at the height of the artist's reputation, most likely from the family of the artist, who had relations with the dealer through their American friends, Mr. and Mrs. Childe Hassam. Couture's work was known in America because, in addition to Manet, he had been the teacher of the influential American artist William Morris Hunt (this fact is noted by hand on the 1890 accession card at the Corcoran), and his surviving daughter was then close to Childe Hassam. The Corcoran celebrated Couture's effect on American art by its acquisition of this painting.

As soon as Norton Simon acquired the painting, he sent it to the conservation studio of Bernard Rabin in Maplewood, New Jersey, where it was X-rayed and, within days of its acquisition, examined by Anne Coffin Hanson of Yale University and Fred Licht of the Institute of Fine Arts. Licht dismissed the picture as "a very bad painting, and even if it is a Couture, not a very good example of his work."[1] Hanson was more careful, refusing to attribute the painting securely in spite of its Corcoran provenance and the comparatively high price it fetched in 1890. However, when she returned to New Haven, she wrote a letter to the Norton Simon Museum about the painting, in which, after lengthy and concrete analysis, she concluded that it is most likely the work of Couture and that its signature is both old and genuine.[2] The extent of the scholarly attention paid to this unassuming painting does not get interesting, however, until it arrived in California and the American scholar of French academic art Albert Boime went to see it.[3]

Although immensely knowledgeable about academic painting technique, Boime immediately accepted the attribution of the painting to Couture on the basis of documents as much as style. He identified it as having been exhibited by Couture at the Salon of 1841, where the twenty-six-year-old artist was represented by five paintings, one of which was entitled *Reverie.* Boime also supplied the Museum with the relevant passages in the contemporary criticism (which were probably already known to art historian William Hauptman[4]) and which seem to strengthen his case.

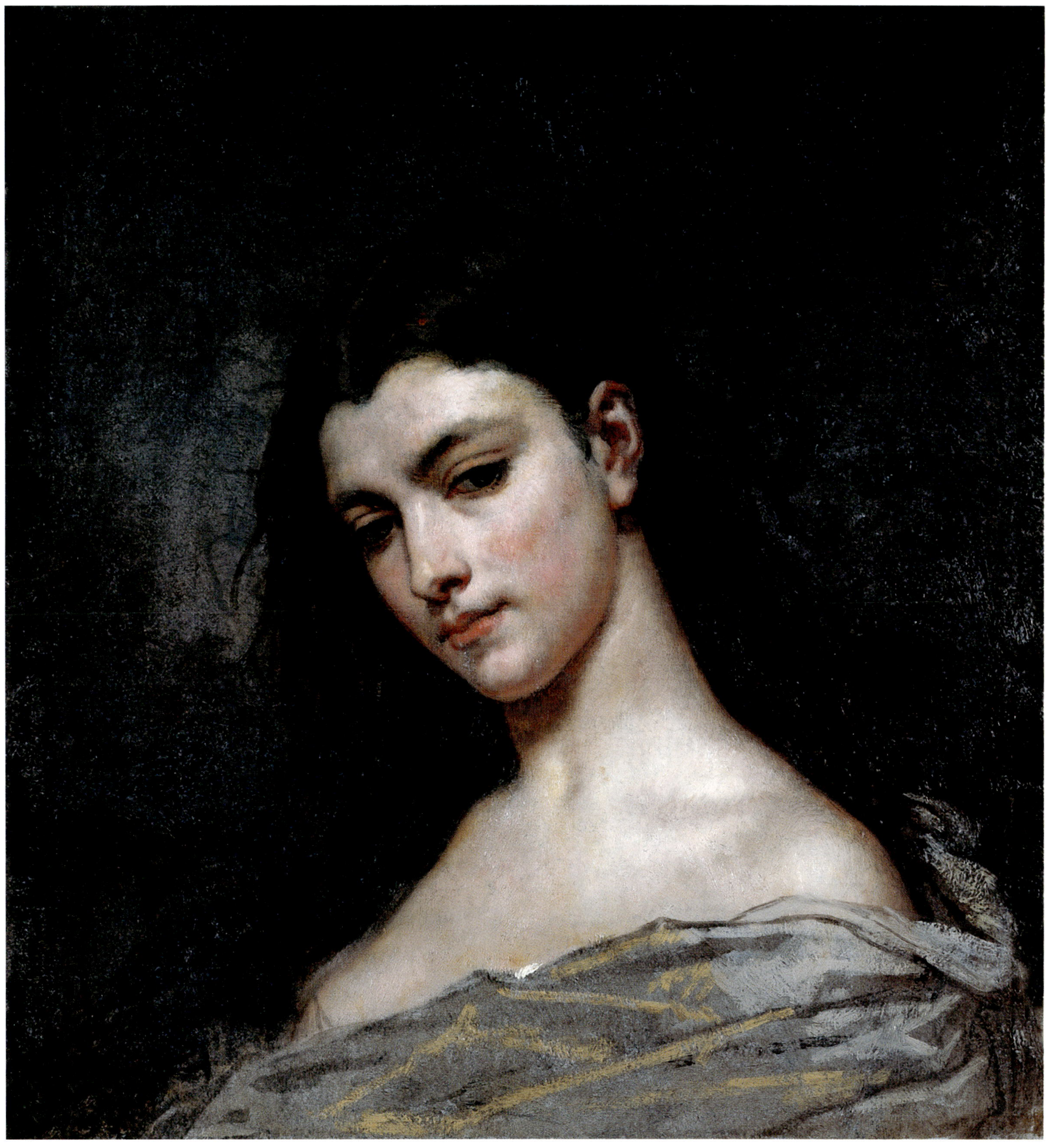

37

An anonymous reviewer in *L'Artiste* wrote about "*La Rêverie*, une jeune fille dont la chevelure flotte dans un désordre harmonieux, un air de mélancolie tout à fait ravissant, une suavité délicieuse dans les lignes de la bouche et du cou" (*Reverie*, a young girl, flowing hair in harmonious disorder, an air of melancholy entirely delightful, a delicious suavity in the lines of her mouth and throat). Reviewers in *Le Constitutionnel* and *La Presse*, though less rhapsodic, made specific comments about the painting, one of them referring to it as "sa charmante tête de jeune fille" (his [Couture's] charming head of a young woman), making it clear that *Reverie* was not an elaborate picture with a full-length figure. This and the careful modeling support the retitling of the painting to its original *Reverie*. It should be noted that this does not mean "dreaming" in the sense of sleeping, but the more generic associations of the English word *reverie*, which has a sense of thoughtful daydreaming, sometimes erotic. We sense, in looking at this young woman's head and upper body that her mind is elsewhere, that she is in a state of suspended consciousness fully acceptable as reverie. It is thus comparable to a series of early, moody pictures by the great Realist Gustave Courbet, including his self-portrait, *Man with a Pipe* (c. 1848–1849) and *Peasant Girl with a Scarf* (cat. 41). The young Courbet in fact had moved from Ornans to Paris late in 1839 and would certainly have seen Couture's contributions to the Salon in 1841. Boime has written powerfully about the tradition in academic painting that the young Couture was dutifully following, the *tête d'expression* (expressive head), which had been codified in French academic practice by Charles Le Brun in the seventeenth century. The aim of the exercise was to represent an emotion or a state of mind rather than an individual, using the head and neck alone as conveyors of this quality. Couture chose "reverie" in 1840, one of many newly represented states associated with Romanticism and bourgeois leisure.[5]

In 1979 Hanson seems to have been puzzled by the loose brushstrokes that Couture applied to the primed canvas under the final painting. These can easily be seen in the X-ray made by Bernard Rabin that same year, which look startlingly like a sketchy landscape whose bottom is the right edge of the present canvas. Hanson was correct to discount this idea, thinking it odd that a landscape sketch would be so freely brushed onto the canvas. She failed to mention, however, the distinct possibility, in line with the academic practice set forth in the scholarship of Boime, that Couture, like other academic painters at midcentury, covered the surface of the painting with a coat of dark brown paint called *ébauche*, which toned the surface, forming a midvalue background onto which the painter applied darker and lighter tones.

1 Memorandum, 7 June 1979, Norton Simon Museum curatorial files.
2 Letter, 9 June 1979, Norton Simon Museum curatorial files.
3 Memorandum, 27 June 1979, Norton Simon Museum curatorial files.
4 Letter, 29 August 1973, Norton Simon Museum curatorial files.
5 Boime, 1971, p. 41.

38

Émile-Gustave Couder
French, c. 1847–1903

Floral Still Life with a Cat
1872–1873

Oil on canvas, 46 × 58 in. (116.9 × 147.3 cm)
Signed lower right: "E. Gue Couder"
N.1979.16

Provenance: The artist (sold at the Paris Salon of 1873 to); William Corcoran; Corcoran Gallery of Art, Washington, D.C. (sale, New York, Sotheby Parke-Bernet, 3 May 1979, lot 56, to); Norton Simon, bequest, 1993 to; Jennifer Jones Simon Art Trust.

Exhibitions: Paris, 1873; on loan, Washington, D.C., Smithsonian Institution, Renwick Gallery, July 1971.

References: Corcoran, 1915, no. 78; Corcoran, 1939, no. 76.

Technical Notes: The ground is light in color and possibly commercially applied on a plain-weave, medium-fine canvas. It is lined with an aqueous adhesive to a fabric of basket weave with approximately three threads grouped in the warp and weft. The tacking edges of the painting and the lining were cut to the design, and a double strip lining was added to attach the painting to a 5-part wood stretcher that has metal expanders at the joins. The paint was flattened by the lining. There is a tear about 3½ inches long at the lower right. The shape and values of the design were laid in with dark colors. Then, local color was applied for the middle tones. The dark underpainting, where it is left practically uncovered, acts as shadow. The condition is good with only a few problems. Some of the dark colors have generalized abrasion and there are numerous small losses and restorations. The painting was cleaned in 1979 and varnished with dammar, B72 and Rembrandt Picture Varnish. (JF)

Émile-Gustave Couder is all but forgotten today; nothing is recorded of his birth date, but we know that he debuted in the Salon of 1869 and exhibited until the end of the century, before his death in 1903. During his lifetime Couder was a competent academic painter of still life. The closest painter to Couder familiar to the American audience is Henri Fantin-Latour, but the latter had such important ties to the vanguard of Édouard Manet and has sustained such intense examination in the twentieth century that close comparison with Couder is not advisable. It seems likely that Norton Simon bought this painting in 1979 as an affordable French academic flower painting to complement his large collection of floral still lifes from the late sixteenth through the nineteenth centuries. Indeed, it was painted less than a decade after the great floral still life by Gustave Courbet (cat. 42) and a decade or two before those of Pierre-Auguste Renoir, Paul Cézanne, and Fantin-Latour. Curiously, Simon bought no floral still lifes by other academic painters in spite of the fact that the genre was very strong in the nineteenth century, particularly among women artists, whom he otherwise admired.

The American collector William Corcoran bought this painting in 1873, when he visited Paris for the first time since the Franco-Prussian War and the Commune, which kept foreigners away. He is said to have purchased two flower paintings by Couder from the Salon for 2,500 francs in the spring of 1873. The purchase was approved by the board of Corcoran's museum in August of that year. In response to Couder's sinking reputation in the twentieth century, Simon paid only $2,200 for the painting when it was auctioned by the Corcoran to raise funds for other acquisitions in 1979. The Corcoran had already relieved itself of the painting in 1971, when it was lent for the inaugural reopening of the Smithsonian Institution's Renwick Gallery in Washington with its High Victorian central gallery, in which the painting indeed looked splendid. The Corcoran indicated that the Couder was sent to the Smithsonian as a long-term loan but in fact sold the painting later.

The most interesting aspect of the Couder is less its manner of painting than its attitude toward its subject. Most floral still-life paintings position a large vase in the center of the picture and allow the flowers to dominate the upper half of the composition. Here, as if to revitalize the tired genre, Couder created a plausible narrative in which a domestic cat, playing in the hushed confines of a paneled room in a private home, has just knocked over the vase of flowers, fortunately without breaking the blue-and-white painted porcelain vase. Whereas earlier painters of still life had stressed the impermanence of living things by emphasizing the transitoriness of the flowers themselves, Couder added a thoroughly modern dynamism to the scene. The cat, startled and retreating from its handiwork, is "in trouble."

Though we know very little about Couder, this painting indicates that he must have had grand ambitions. His painting was undoubtedly inspired by the most famous of all French still-life paintings—and a work that has been on continuous public display since 1728—Jean-Siméon Chardin's *The Ray* (fig. 38a). The pictures are identically sized and both feature cats on the left side of the composition. (Chardin included cats in at least four other slightly later and smaller works.) In addition, both sought to dazzle the spectator with action as well as stillness. The difference, of course, is that Chardin's

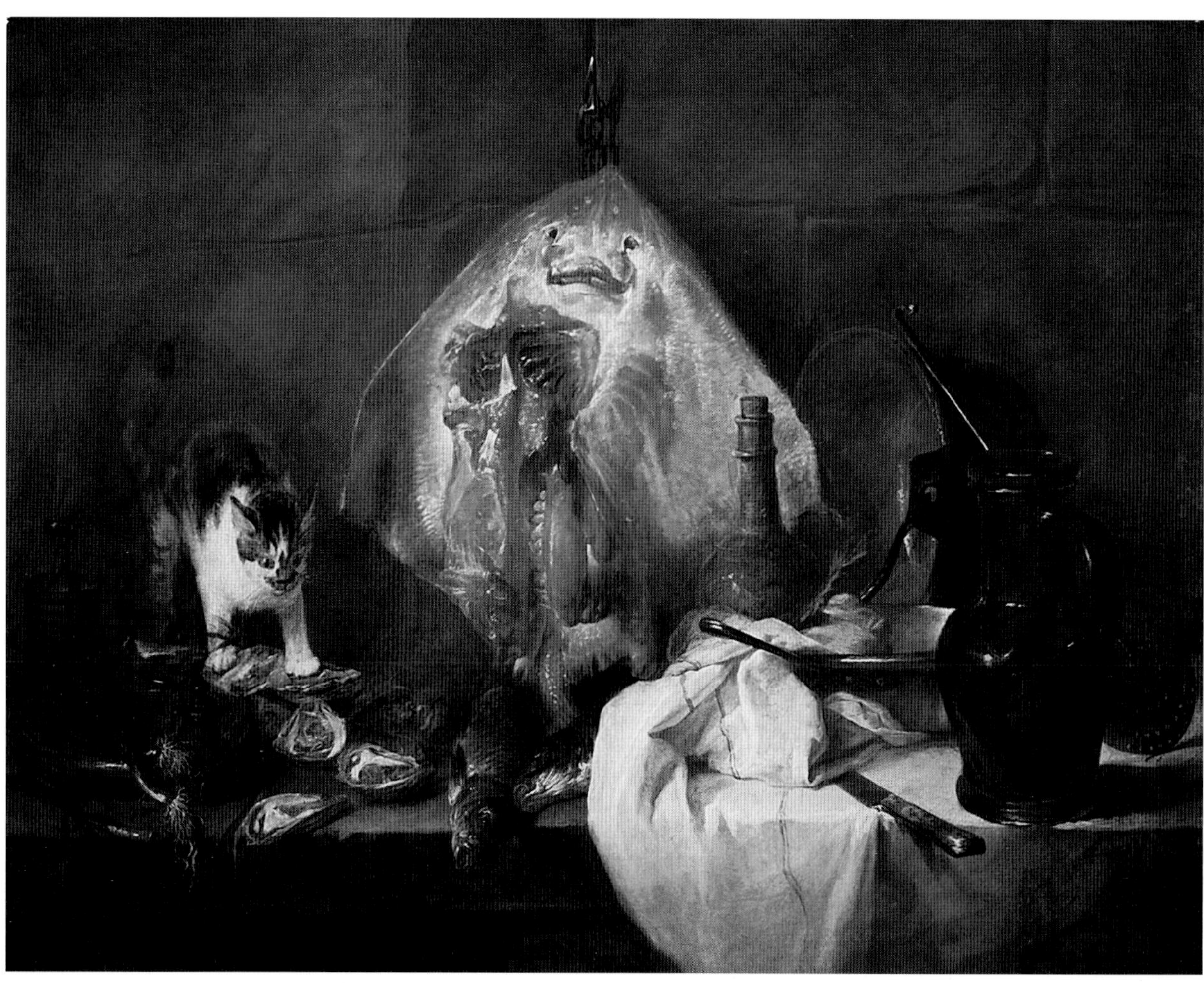

Fig. 38a Jean-Siméon Chardin, *The Ray*, oil on canvas, $45\frac{1}{8} \times 57\frac{1}{2}$ in. (114.5 × 146 cm), Musée du Louvre, Paris; photo: Erich Lessing / Art Resource, NY

picture (and the rest of his still-life oeuvre) features a formality and poignancy that are absent from Couder's essentially anecdotal, even vaudevillian, painting.

It is interesting to speculate on Couder's life. Was he a late son of Jean-Alexandre Rémy Couder, who was born in Paris in 1808 and died there in 1879? This latter artist, a student of Baron Gros, did paint still lifes, though he is listed as predominantly a painter of history and genre. This seems thoroughly likely, although the artists' biographer Emmanuel Bénézit is usually scrupulous about documenting such relationships. Perhaps he never found a birth date or birth certificate for Émile-Gustave Couder. If the latter made his debut at the Salon of 1869, he would have been born about 1847 or 1848, when Jean Couder was forty.

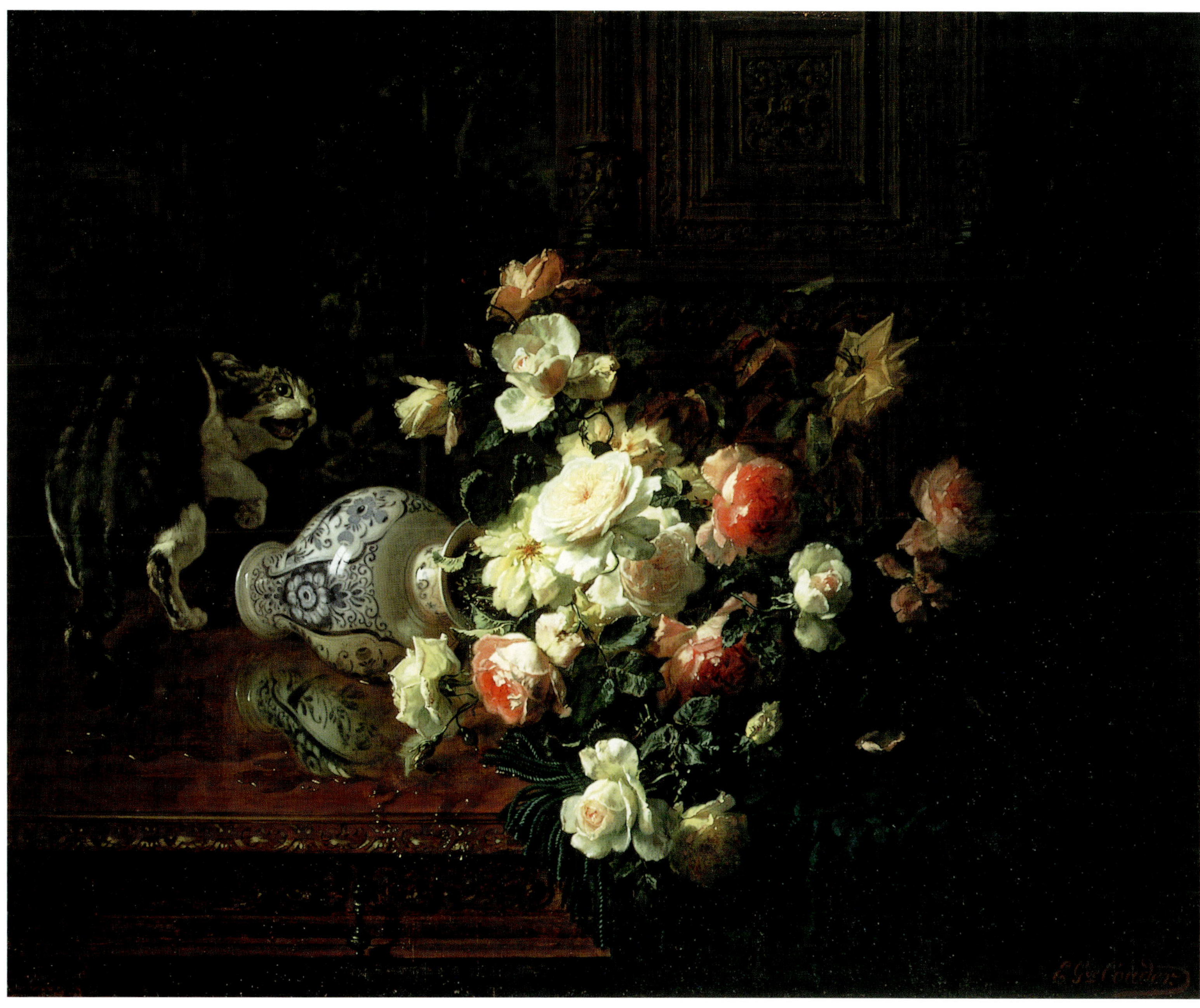

39

Charles-François Daubigny
French, 1817–1878

Village on the Seine near Vernon
1872

Oil on canvas, 33⅝ × 57⅝ in. (85.3 × 146.2 cm)
Signed and dated lower left: "Daubigny 1872"
M.1966.2.4

Provenance: [M. Knoedler & Company, New York, sold 1899 to]; Corcoran Gallery of Art, Washington, D.C.; [E. V. Thaw and Co., New York, sold 1966 to]; Norton Simon Art Foundation.

Exhibitions: On loan, Santa Fe, Museum of New Mexico, 1 July–13 August 1959; Irvine, 1967, pp. 8, color ill., 9; Princeton, 1972, no. 20, p. 75, ill.; San Francisco, 1974, no. 15.

References: Corcoran, 1903, no. 85, p. 42; Bryant, 1915, pp. 188–189, fig. 112; Steadman, 1973b, p. 9, ill.; Hellebranth, 1976, no. 87, p. 34, ill.

Technical Notes: The original fine, tight, plain-weave canvas was lined with an aqueous adhesive to medium-weight plain-weave fabric. The original tacking edges extend about ¼ inch on each side. The stretcher with metal expanders is later. The paint is thick with a creamy consistency. Brushes of various sizes made long strokes, some with wavy patterns, and also short dabs. In the sky it is evident that the artist used a knife in part for application. Paint was applied wet in wet but also wet over dry paint, and numerous layers were used to build up the landscape and sky. Most of the forms were painted over the landscape paint, and no initial brown lay-in is evident. Local colors—green, very light sky blue, and pink—are prominent, and there are dashes of what appear to be pure blue, red, orange, and white. Black is also used, for example, in one long stroke that skips over the set paint below. The painting has a synthetic varnish, but remnants of the earlier varnish show a greenish fluorescence in ultraviolet light. Paint layers are in good condition with a medium crackle pattern, stretcher marks just showing, and a few losses. The lining had limited effect on the paint surface. Layering of the rich paints produced very fine contraction crackle and wrinkling. (JF)

Charles-François Daubigny was an extremely successful landscape painter in the mid–nineteenth century whose works were highly valued by conservative Salon jurors and Impressionist artists alike. His luminous, atmospheric, and naturalistic views of the Forest of Fontainebleau and of the Oise, Seine, and Marne river valleys were exhibited at the Paris Salons beginning in 1840, and he received first-class medals in 1853, 1857, and 1867. He had a prominent place at the Exposition Universelle of 1855, was granted public commissions in 1860 to decorate a staircase and room of the new Louvre, and was awarded a Legion of Honor in 1874.[1] By the 1860s the novelty of his painterly touch—its rapidity, fluidity, and often-perfunctory character—was increasingly remarked by critics, sometimes with condescension. Théophile Gautier's comment in his Salon review of 1861—"it is really a pity that this landscape artist, having so true, so apt and so natural a feeling for his subject should content himself with an 'impression'" —has been taken as an anticipation of the critical reception of the Impressionist artists more than a decade later.[2]

In fact, though Daubigny supported the Impressionists from his position as a Salon juror in the late 1860s, his own paintings differ markedly from those by the younger artists. They are uniformly more sober than Impressionist works—distinguished by dark underpainting and a wide tonal range—and they lack the characteristic intuitive, abbreviated, and expressive touch. In this way, Daubigny's landscapes have much more to do with fellow Barbizon painters—he was a close friend of Camille Corot and painted with him, Théodore Rousseau, and Jules Dupré at Valmondois, L'Isle-Adam, and at locations near the Forest of Fontainebleau—than with the Impressionists who followed. Nevertheless, Daubigny's generous encouragement of Claude Monet, Pierre-Auguste Renoir, and even Paul Cézanne (the latter was viewed by most art critics in the late 1860s and early 1870s as an anarchist and a madman) helped ensure that his own reputation would be secure after his death in 1878.

Daubigny's *Village on the Seine near Vernon* is a panoramic view of a marshy landscape on the upper reaches of the Seine near Giverny, where Monet later lived and built his magnificent water gardens. The differences between the two artists' paintings of these proximate locations, however, could hardly be greater. Whereas Monet in the 1890s depicted in his water lily pictures a horizonless, phantasmagoric landscape of reflection, translucency, and watery immersion, Daubigny represents in 1872 an intensely palpable world, weighted with history, labor, and contingency. The low horizon and extensive view derive from Dutch landscape paintings of the seventeenth century, especially by Jacob van Ruisdael and Philips Koninck, and the idealized integration of village, church, and agricultural labor—and the wide range of hue—from the painting of the Englishman John Constable of the 1820s. Daubigny's picture is thus an exercise in topographic and naturalist art, mapping a specific location in the Île-de-France and documenting its life and labor.

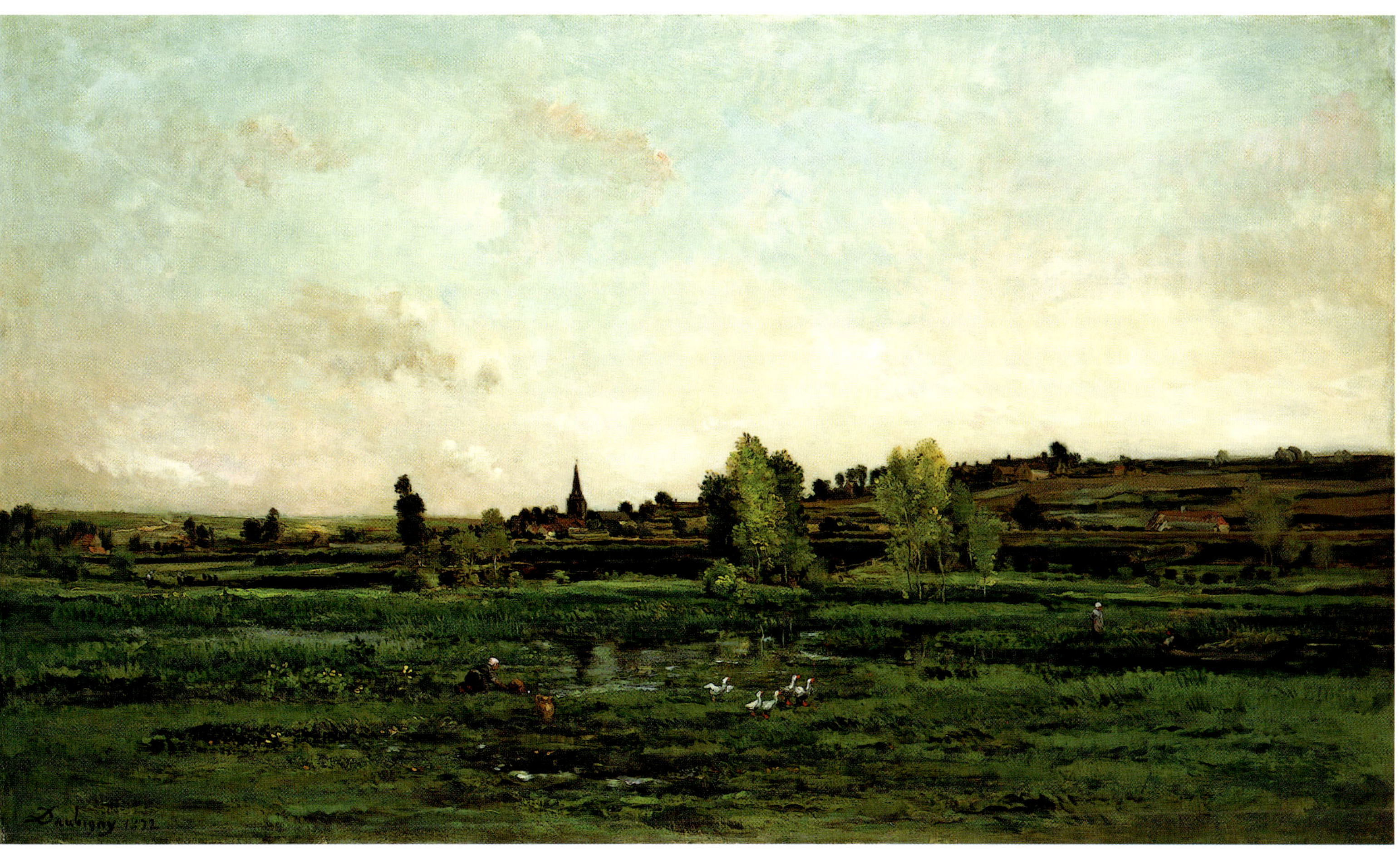

39

The composition consists of an extensive foreground comprising green marsh grasses and a shallow, meandering stream. Visible are a kneeling peasant woman at center left, five gray-white and orange squawking ducks in the center, a peasant woman standing to the right, and a man seated in a small boat or barge near her. The middle ground is marked by three clumps of slender trees painted with feathery touches, beneath which are four long, broad horizontal stripes of dark- and light-toned paint—purple-brown, blue-green, purple-brown again, and yellow-green—suggesting the visual compression of space. In the background can be seen a village and church steeple at middle left and a gentle hill with farmlands at right. The presence of the trees and church are an explicit (and conventional) sign of the artist's faith in the combined authority of nature and the Christian religion, but they serve more than a symbolic function: they divide the composition into discrete vertical sections, permitting the entire scene to be more easily grasped and measured. This is especially necessary since the foreground is rather vaguely rendered, and more than half the painting is composed of a variable and measureless sky, articulated only by irregular wisps of white, gray, pink, yellow, and blue.

Village on the Seine near Vernon was not exhibited at the Salon, and its history before it was purchased by the Corcoran Gallery of Art in 1889 is unknown. Because its sale is not recorded in any of the available auction records of the period, and because it is not listed among the works sold from the artist's atelier on his death in 1878, it is possible that the picture was sold directly from the artist's studio and did not pass through the hands of his dealer, Paul Durand-Ruel. In this circumstance, according to the art historian Lynne Ambrosini, the artist might have orally assigned the work a title on the spot, without otherwise recording it.[3] This circumstance may help account for the confusion in the literature concerning the subject of this work, and many others. Though the present picture has been known as *Hamlet on the Seine near Vernon* at least since 1903, when it was exhibited in Washington, D.C., under that title, two nearly identical compositions, in Tokyo (Motoyama Collection) and Rochester (fig. 39a)—albeit smaller and painted on panel—are titled *Near Andrésy.* There is, however, no

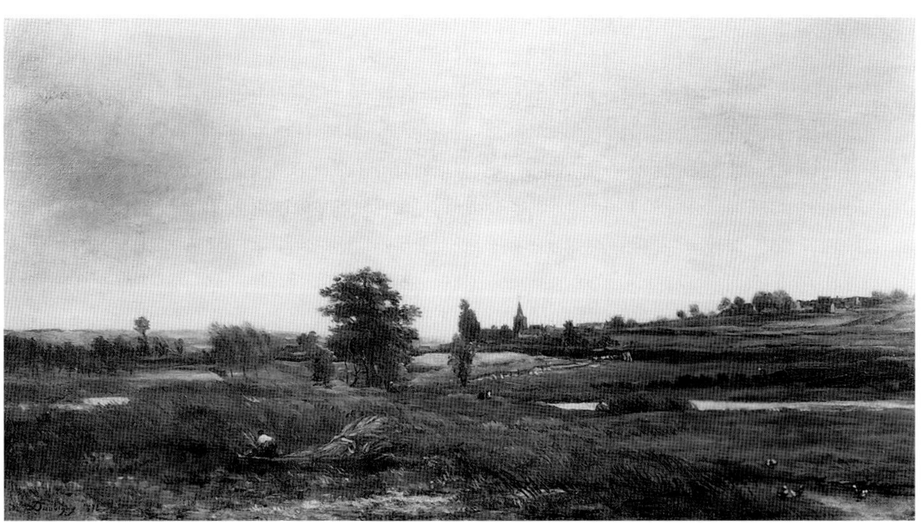

Fig. 39a Charles-François Daubigny, *Near Andresy*, 1872, oil on panel, 17 × 32½ in. (43.2 × 82.5 cm), Memorial Art Gallery of the University of Rochester: George Eastman Collection of the University of Rochester; photo: James Via

reason to give special credence to these Andrésy ascriptions, which were probably based on a supposed resemblance between the church in the Daubigny paintings in Tokyo and Rochester and the churches in two more securely titled pictures, *La Terrasse d'Andrésy*[4] and *Andrésy*.[5] In fact, a close examination of the church in the Tokyo, Rochester, and Pasadena paintings reveals that it is not the one in the Andrésy pictures, nor the actual, thirteenth-century St.-Germain d'Andrésy. Neither, however, does the church in the present work resemble in the slightest the Church of Notre-Dame de Vernon, later painted by Monet in 1883 and 1894. In all likelihood, therefore, the present picture depicts—as its title states—a village, as yet unidentified, near Vernon.

1 Hellebranth, 1976, pp. xi–xii.
2 Gautier, 1861, p. 121. See also the comments of Zacharie Astruc in 1859, "[Daubigny] is the painter par excellence of simple impressions." Astruc, 1859, p. 303. Cited in Tinterow and Loyrette, 1994, p. 366.
3 Oral communication with the authors.
4 Present location unknown, Hellebranth, 1976, no. 47.
5 Present location unknown, Hellebranth, 1976, no. 48.

40

Henri-Joseph Harpignies
French, 1819–1916

A Farmhouse
1875

Oil on canvas, 11 × $16\frac{1}{4}$ in. (28 × 41.2 cm)
Signed lower left: "H. Harpignies"
F.1969.38.8

Provenance: [Huinck & Scherjon, Amsterdam]. Hendricus Egbertus ten Cate (1868–1955), Almelo, Holland, in 1955 (sale, London, Sotheby's, 3 December 1958, lot 75, to); [Thos. Agnew & Sons, Ltd., London, stock no. 19232, 1958 to]; Robert Ellis Simon, bequest 1969 to; The Norton Simon Foundation.

Exhibitions: Los Angeles, 1965; San Francisco, 1974, no. 19, ill.

References: Hannema, 1955, vol. 1, no. 72, vol. 2, pl. 52.

Technical Notes: The support is a lightweight, fine-weave canvas; it has been lined with the original tacking edges retained and tacked to the original keyed stretcher. Weave transference from pressure in lining has slightly exaggerated the canvas texture. The lining is quite old, but adhesion between the two canvases appears to be strong. The thin ground of warm white was commercially applied; the tacking edges indicate that it has darkened. A light golden brown underpainting was painted down the left side, beneath the trees, the middle ground, and the foreground; across the center of the painting beneath the landscape elements at the horizon; and beneath the foliage at the right side, positioning these compositional elements on the white ground. The painting was primarily created with layers of thin paint for the darker tones, followed by dabs of green to depict foliage. The sky is extremely thin, with thick white clouds. The sunlit houses are brushed with thicker, opaque paint. Brush marking is seldom visible and may have been softened by lining. Abrasion is extensive. The dark brown shadows, vulnerable in cleaning, and the light brown underpainting have been significantly thinned throughout the painting. In some areas, the stronger paint remains on top of the abraded underpainting, with the ground partially exposed. Some greens, such as those at the right side, exhibit the artist's facile brushwork, and in the lighter colors of the buildings the paint appears to be unaltered. Varnish in the sky was reduced in an early undocumented treatment. The present varnish is discolored and brittle. (RW)

Harpignies sustained his long life and career—he died in 1916 at the age of ninety-seven—by living and painting with modesty and equanimity. He studied in 1846 with the minor landscape painter Jean-Alexis Achard (1807–1884) and traveled to Rome, Naples, and Capri three years later, gaining an understanding of the pastoral tradition, identified with Claude Lorrain and subsequent generations of French painters including Pierre-Henri de Valenciennes and Jean-Joseph Xavier Bidaud. Harpignies at this time also developed a strong appreciation for the works of Camille Corot, which combined Italian color and light with French topography and vernacular architecture. He returned to Italy in 1863, remaining there for nearly two years, but most of his mature art addressed the landscape of central France, especially the surroundings of the small town of Hérrison in the Aumance Valley in the Auvergne and the region of the river Loire and its tributaries, the Nievre and Allier, depicted in *The Bridge-Canal at Briare* (1883, The Philbrook Museum of Art, Tulsa, Okla.).

This small picture represents a large, late-Norman-style farmhouse bordered by a pond. The waters are perfectly still and extend from the lower right edge of the canvas to a narrow point beyond the irregular green banks at left. In the foreground, the bank of the pond is gray-brown and muddy, eroded by the tramping hooves of grazing animals. Small clumps of grass or algae interrupt the surface of the water. In the middle of the pond at right, a boat plies the water; its slender form—turned into a clothespin shape by its reflection—disrupts both the placidity of the waters and the calm, clear reflection of the manor house and farm buildings. The stone walls of the latter radiate the warm sun of midday, and its jumble of slate roofs, steep gables, and overhanging eaves disrupts the irregular or rounded contours of the trees and shrubs. The water in the right foreground is unperturbed; the gables of the house and farm buildings appear as brown, green, and beige upside-down triangles. Here the truths of pastoral and Impressionist painting appear to coincide.

A Farmhouse was probably painted *en plein air*, sometime in the mid-1870s, at a site near the towns of Hérisson and Chateloy. It is composed of muted greens, blues, grays, and browns, but the latter colors have been thinned during an improper cleaning. As a result, the areas of brown-toned ground—especially visible in the water in the right foreground—have greater pictorial salience than they may originally have had. The left side of the painting is comparatively more densely covered with color, and there the brushstrokes are larger and more expressive. The upper two-thirds of the canvas are

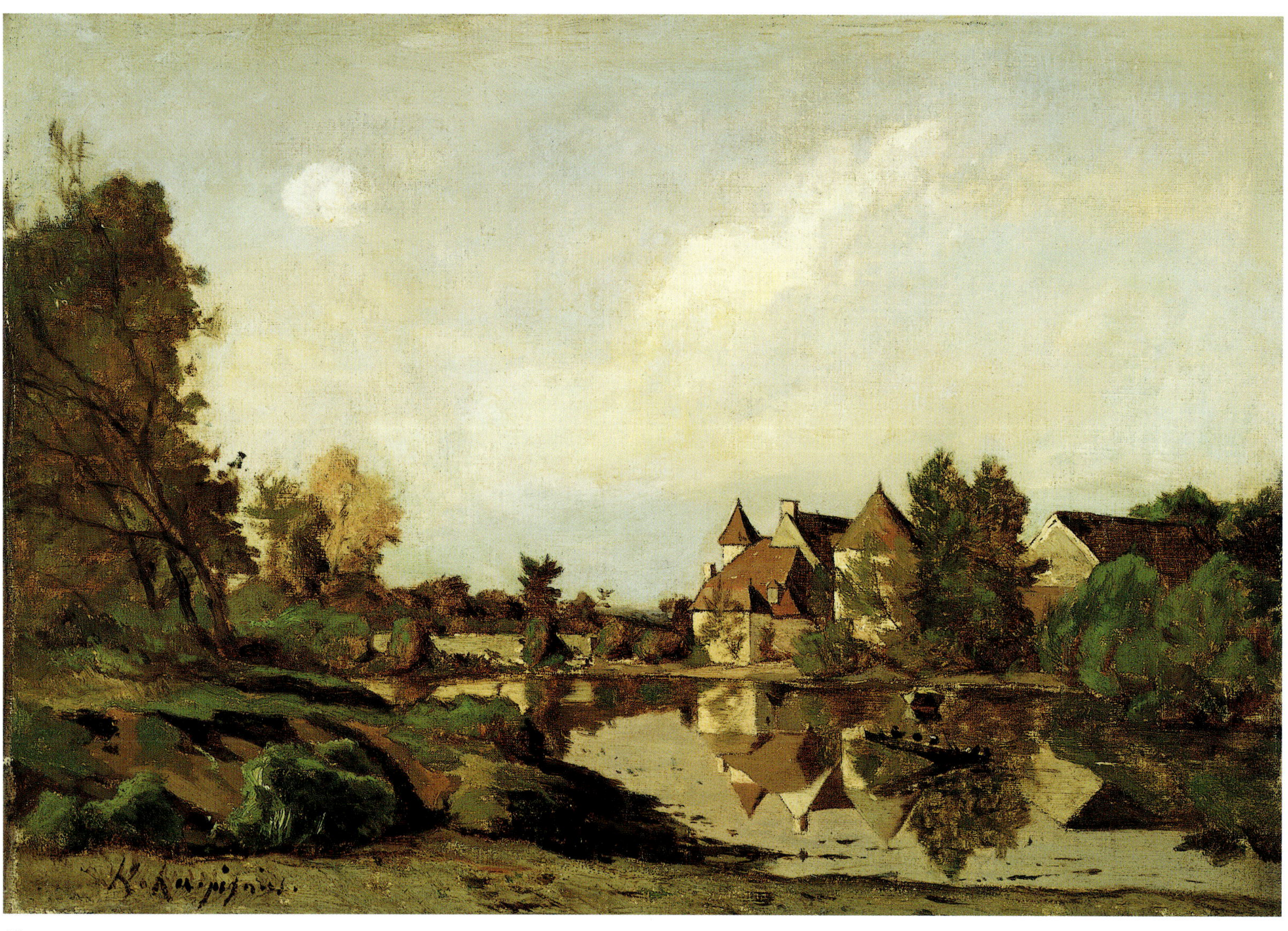

40

filled with a blue-gray sky with a diagonal trail of clouds pointing like an arrow to a spot on the horizon between the pyramidal roof of a tower at right and the yellow-brown of a tree at left. There is nothing significant about this spot, except that it marks the farthest point that the eye of the spectator may travel. The picture is thus organized and composed by means of a simple and conventional formula: the rocky foreground at left, watery middle ground at right, and architecture and foliage in the center and left background are treated as distinct, planar zones. In this way, the spectator is encouraged to imaginatively enter the scene, pass a few moments in the warmth of a summer day in rural interior France, and then pass on to other business. Landscape painting, even when practiced at a high level of sophistication, was not always—as it was for many Barbizon painters, the Realists, and the Impressionists—a matter of nationalism, science, experimentation, autonomy, and the avant-garde; it could simply aim to provide a pleasant and brief diversion from daily cares.

41

Gustave Courbet
French, 1819–1877

Peasant Girl with a Scarf
c. 1849

Oil on canvas, 23⅝ × 28¾ in. (60 × 73 cm)
Signed lower right: "G. Courbet"
M.1989.2

Provenance: The artist, to; M. Weill; D'Ol*** (sale, Paris, Hôtel Drouot, 9 December 1876, lot 20, as *Tête de femme*); [Galerie Durand-Ruel, Paris]; A. H. Stirlin, Zurich, by 1935, by inheritance to; H. R. Stirlin, Zurich and St.-Prex, Switzerland, still in 1955, sold to; [Drs. Fritz and Peter Nathan, Zurich]; [Acquavella Galleries, New York, sold 1966 to]; John T. Dorrance Jr., Gladwyne, Pa. (sale, New York, Sotheby's, 18 October 1989, lot 2, color ill., to); [Acquavella Galleries, New York, sold in 1989 to]; Norton Simon Art Foundation.

Exhibitions: Zurich, 1935, no. 49, pl. XX; Paris, 1938b, no. 32, pl. XII; La Tour de Peilz, 1950, no. 15; Besançon, 1952, no. 19; London, 1953, no. 12, pl. V; Venice, 1954, no. 16; Lyon, 1954, no. 20; Paris, 1955b, no. 38, pl. 31; Paris, 1959b, no. 30; Bern, 1962, no. 16; Paris, 1977, no. 17.

References: Léger, 1929, pl. 22; *Gazette des beaux-arts*, 1938, no. 32; *Les Amis de Gustave Courbet*, 1955, ill. p. 24; Fernier, 1977, vol. 1, no. 210, p. 40, color, p. 131, ill.

Technical Notes: This earliest of the paintings by Courbet that Norton Simon bought exhibits a smooth, blended handling of paint. Brushstrokes are visible, however. In the flesh, for example, short strokes going in all directions visibly give texture to the surface. On a light-colored ground the artist laid out his forms and shadows in thin, translucent dark brown and black paint. On this underpainting he modulated the forms with local color applied wet in wet. This underpainting acts as shadow at the top of the head scarf. Shadows in the scarf are also created with thin black paint glazed over the lighter colors. It appears that the outlines of the face and arm were drawn very summarily with graphite. The drawing is visible under magnification around the face, nostrils, mouth, and arms, and curved lines indicate volume in the arm. There is one significant pentimento that is visible under normal viewing conditions. The hand was originally higher on the girl's face. Adjustments along the arm are also noticeable. The picture has been extended about ¼ inch on each side by turning up the tacking edges of the original plain-weave canvas. This was presumably done when the picture was lined to a similar fabric with an aqueous adhesive. The remainder of the tacking edges was removed. The stretcher is of a later date than the picture. The condition of this picture is good. There are only a few losses and surface abrasions. The signature area is difficult to read in ultraviolet light because of toning, restorations, and thick varnish. The artist first signed the painting with a deep purple color, and on top of that the signature is picked out with a vermilion color. The former has contraction cracks and most of the latter is probably restoration paint. (JF)

When an earnest young painter showed his teacher, Gustave Courbet, the figure of an angel he had been painting, the master is said to have thundered: "Why do you make an angel? Have you ever seen one? No, I thought not! Put that aside and paint a portrait of your father whom you see every day."[1] Courbet's quip, reported by his friend the critic Jules Castagnary may be apocryphal, but it is a vivid summary of his aesthetic; he was a Realist and a materialist who preferred to paint a concrete and seen world rather than an ideal and vaporous one. Courbet rejected the classical tradition in European art and embraced popular and vernacular art. His portraits, nudes, genre scenes, landscapes, and still lifes are rendered with a directness and asperity that distinguish them from works by artists who trained at the official French École des Beaux-Arts and exhibited at the Salons. His over-lifesize genre scenes from early in his career—including *After Dinner at Ornans* (1848, Musée des Beaux-Arts, Lille), *The Burial at Ornans* (1849, Musée d'Orsay, Paris), *The Stonebreakers* (1849, Gemäldegalerie, Dresden, destroyed), and *The Peasants of Flagey* (1850, Musée des Beaux-Arts, Besançon)—were efforts to create a new, accessible, popular art with as much grandeur and monumentality as the old, elite, and pompous art of history painting. Courbet's efforts to reinvent the high art of easel painting were coincident with some of the most momentous political and economic upheavals of the nineteenth century—the 1848 Revolution and the Paris Commune of 1871. Ever since, critics and art historians have debated the actual function and significance of Courbet's art in those revolutions and their aftermath.

Courbet himself insisted on the public, political significance of his challenge to artistic orthodoxy. To be a materialist and a Realist, he claimed, was to embrace the cause of the working people of France in their struggle for economic equality and political enfranchisement. "I am not only a socialist," he wrote to a newspaper editor in 1851, "but also a democrat and [a partisan of the] republic, in short a supporter of all that the revolution stands for, and first and foremost I am a Realist."[2] A decade later he stated: "By reaching the conclusion that the ideal and all that it entails should be denied, I can completely bring about the emancipation of the individual, and finally achieve democracy. Realism is essentially democratic art."[3] He bluntly asserted that the art of painting must leave behind its former indebtedness to the ideal, and that if his materialist vision were accepted, "it would be impossible for painting to consist of any other things than the representation of objects which the artist can see and touch."[4] This emphasis on material specificity, particularity, and individuality, finally, is consonant with the views of his friend the anarchist Pierre-Joseph Proudhon, whose 1865 essay "Art and Its Social Role" was much admired by Courbet. In common with Proudhon, the artist stated in several letters that the strength of France—and the best hope for its future—lay, not in its central government, but in its separate and distinct regions, its independent communes, and its fully autonomous citizens.[5]

All the essential phases of Courbet's career are represented in the Norton Simon collections, but landscape and still life dominate. These paintings are quintessential examples of the artist's materialist method. Courbet's materialism, we must note at the outset, is not a function of naturalism, illusionism, trompe l'oeil, or other tried-and-true pictorial devices. Rather, it is manifest in the physical structure of the paintings—in their dense and sometimes clotted surfaces, their purposeful, spatial naiveté, and their assertion that paintings are intended to be seen, not seen through. All artworks, of course, are at some level materialist: all are composed of chemical and organic components, and all possess a physical structure. But some demand that we examine them first on this ground and not on some other, such as narrative, anecdote, or illusion. This is not to claim that Courbet's works are only optical, or only tactile, or that they denote, as one recent art historian has argued, the achievement of a union between painter-beholder and painting.[6] Rather, it is to state that Courbet's works at the Norton Simon Museum, like his best paintings elsewhere, are made in such a way as to forbid any examination or interpretation that overlooks pictorial surface, composition, and structure. They assert the worth of nature, human labor, and autonomy; they argue both that matter has a history and that history is composed out of matter; and, finally, they propose that it is the business of art to examine and understand the facts of the physical world as well as independent, lived experience.

Like a number of other paintings from Courbet's first decade of professional activity, *Peasant Girl with a Scarf* is concerned with the placement of a figure in the landscape. Though this may seem a simple matter—artists since Giotto have depicted humans in a natural setting—the relation was especially fraught during the 1840s and 1850s. The French countryside, like the English a century before it, was then undergoing a period of particularly rapid modernization and rationalization. The resulting disruption to long-standing patterns of rural life and to the structure of rural wages, prices, and labor had literally revolutionary implications. Courbet attempted to engage this modern history in his art; his great trilogy of paintings from 1849–1850 was precisely concerned with the transformation of peasants into impoverished proletarians (*The Stonebreakers*), with the role of the bourgeoisie in the countryside (*The Peasants of Flagey*), and with the survival of ancient, popular traditions in the face of progress (*The Burial at Ornans*).[7] Other artists, too, explored these subjects, including Honoré Daumier, Jean-François Millet, and Jules Breton, but Courbet's uniqueness lay in the fact that he explored the question of the relation of humans and nature from both an intensely physical and a rigorously historical perspective. For him, the drama of modernization had visible effects on actual living bodies and on nature. Hard work changed the physiology of men's and women's bodies; the collision of classes made the interaction of people and places awkward and unpredictable; doubts about the past and the future made expressions, gestures, and movements unreadable. Political struggles over wealth and resources and human efforts to dominate nature made the latter appear alternatively anodyne and sublime, pacific and violent, innocent and erotic.

Courbet explored this conflict of person and place in small as well as large pictures, in *tableau historique* (his description of the enormous *Burial at Ornans*) and in more modest genre scenes, landscapes, and portraits. *Peasant Girl with a Scarf*, like many of his early self-portraits, figure studies, and landscapes, is a drama of physical proximity and emotional distance. A young rural woman—possibly the artist's sister Juliette—gazes longingly to the right, as she rests her chin on her left hand. Her upper body inclines slightly toward the spectator while her left elbow is planted on a leafy mound or hillock. Her patchwork gray dress is gathered halfway between bosom and waist, truncating her torso, and her right arm is entirely missing. Orange and sepia

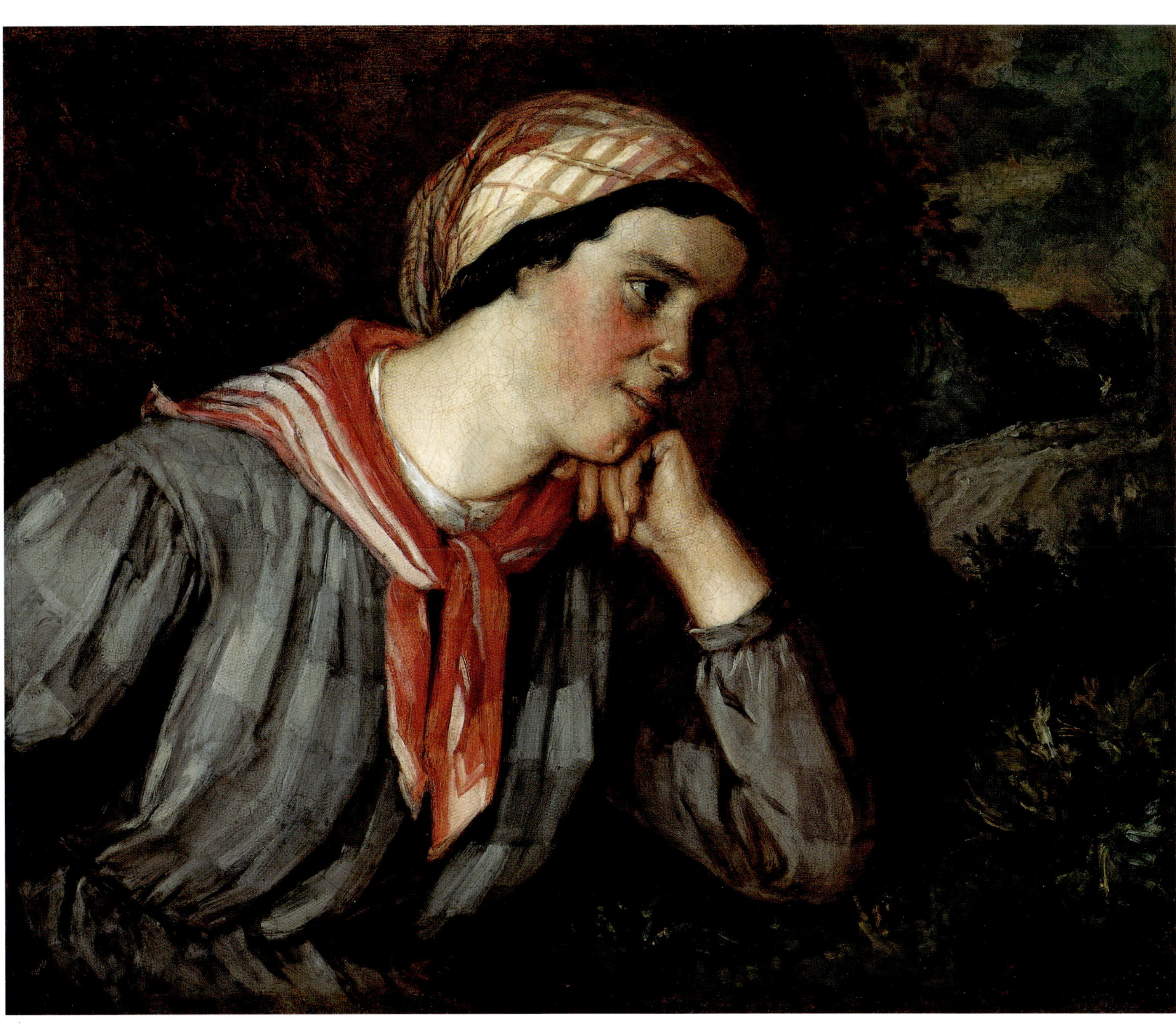

41

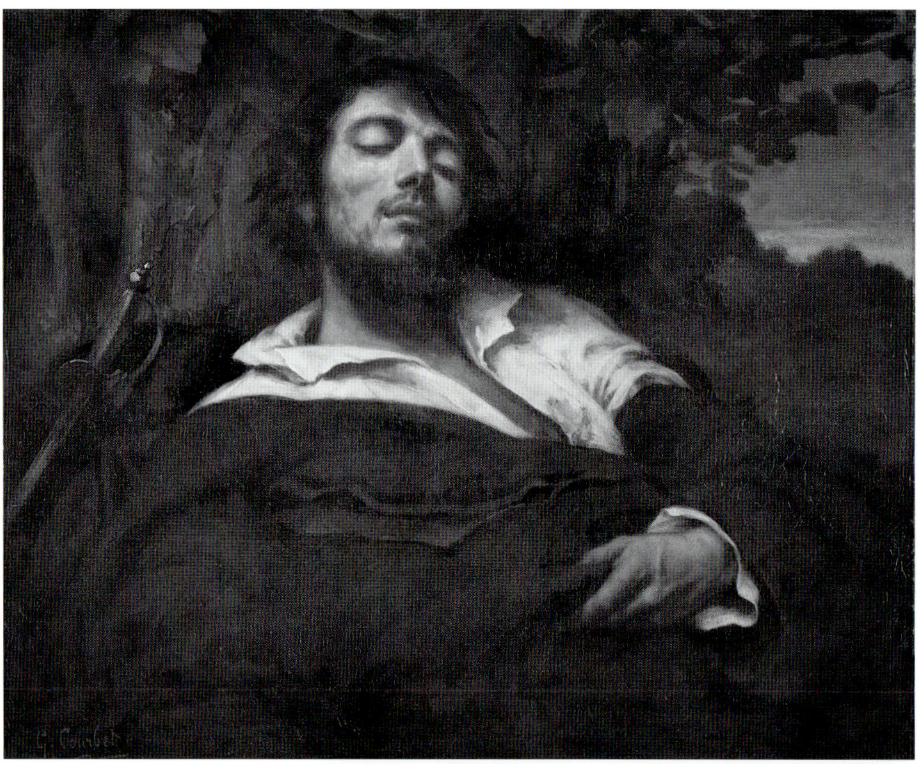

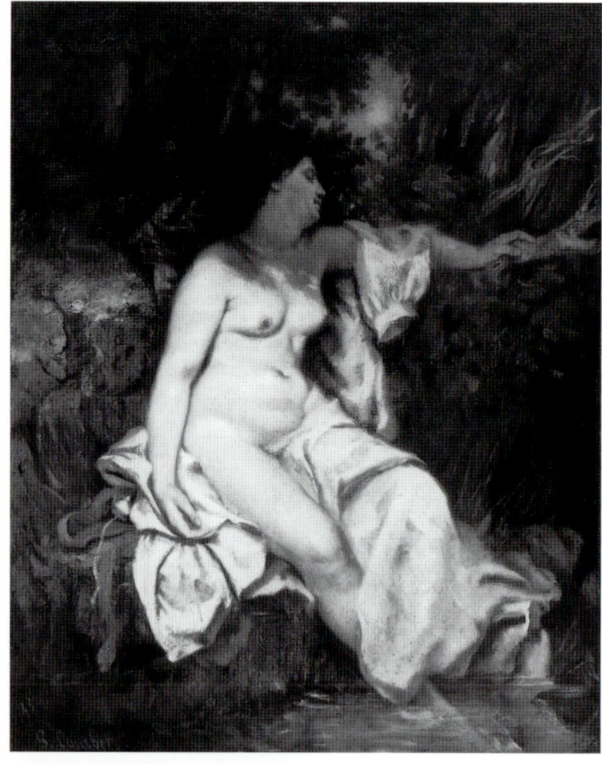

Fig. 41a (*above left*) Gustave Courbet, *Self-Portrait as the Wounded Man*, 1844–1854, oil on canvas, 31⅞ × 38³⁄₁₆ in. (81 × 97 cm), Musée d'Orsay, Paris; photo: Erich Lessing / Art Resource, NY

Fig. 41b (*above right*) Gustave Courbet, *Bather Sleeping by a Brook*, 1845, oil on canvas, 32 × 25½ in. (81.3 × 64.8 cm), The Detroit Institute of Arts, City of Detroit Purchase

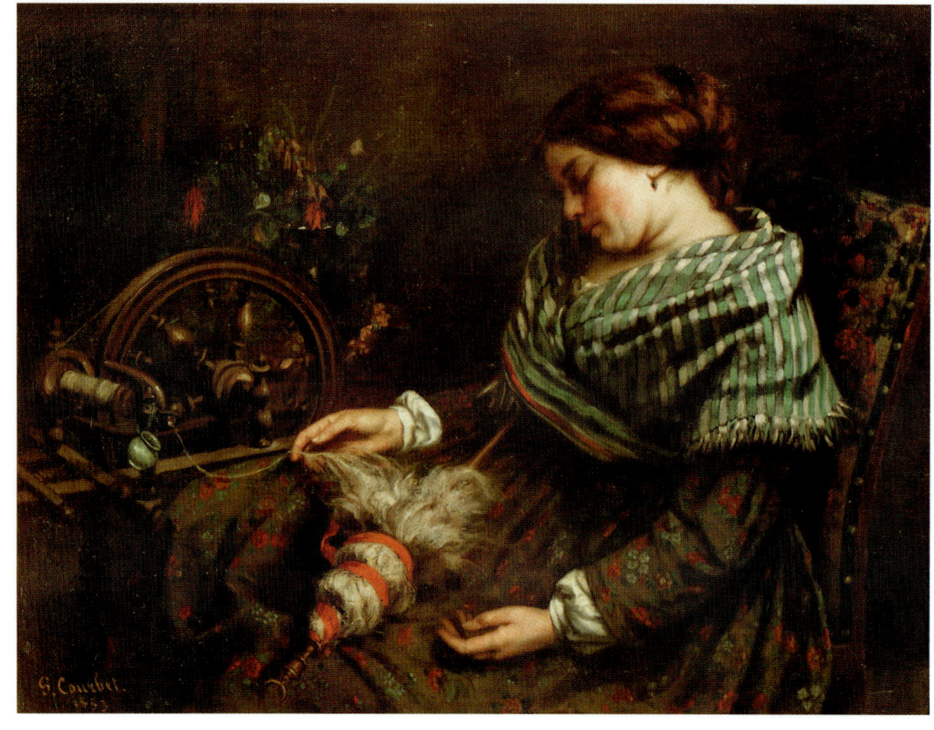

Fig. 41c Gustave Courbet, *The Sleeping Spinner*, 1853, oil on canvas, 35½ × 45⅝ in. (90 × 116 cm), Musée Fabre, Montpellier; photo: Erich Lessing / Art Resource, NY

brown paint frame her head, shoulders, hand, and wrist. At her forearm, the background becomes darker brown or black, perhaps even the result of bituminous paint; below that, a dark green is visible. Is the peasant girl standing on level ground or sitting on a slope? The latter seems more likely, but we cannot be sure; her pose simply does not fit the given facts of the landscape. The result of these ambiguities—like those seen in *Self-Portrait as the Wounded Man* (fig. 41a) and *Bather Sleeping by a Brook* (fig. 41b)—is an uncertainty or even opacity of genre, identity, and iconography. A portrait, viewers were led to believe, should have a vertical format and pose; a genre scene should have figures more vaguely rendered, and a literary subject should be more easily identifiable.

Like two later pictures of women in landscapes, *Woman with a Garland of Flowers* (c. 1856, private collection, Paris) and *Women on the Banks of the Seine* (1856, Musée d'Orsay, Paris), *Peasant Girl with a Scarf* imparts an artificial atmosphere. There is something slightly too forced about her flushed and ruddy cheeks and her red-and-pink kerchief pointing insistently downward. Like the women reclining on the grassy banks of the river Seine in Courbet's better-known painting, she may be thinking of her lover—the small, vaguely painted figure just visible at the far right of the canvas. Hélène Toussaint has suggested that the work may have been inspired by *Petite Fadette* (1849), an early Realist novel by George Sand that tells the story of twin brothers in love with the same peasant girl.[8] The failed suitor enlists in the army, leading to dreams of lost love. This novel, widely read in 1849, may also provide a date for the painting, which appears on stylistic grounds to be from the late 1840s. Courbet rarely based paintings on contemporary literary works; he was more often concerned with individual men and women, social types or classes, and mythic patterns.

The Sleeping Spinner (fig. 41c), like the *Peasant Girl with a Scarf*, portrays a young peasant woman insensible to the material world around her; it recalls depictions of Fate, the Nereids, and Penelope at her loom. The *Peasant Girl*, correspondingly, may have been intended to invoke the broad theme of innocence versus budding desire, or even to suggest the myth of Proserpine, the mortal who is abducted by Pluto while picking flowers in a meadow but returns to earth each spring. Courbet's peasant girl, like Proserpine, can be seen as a symbol of springtime, abundance, and eternal return. But the awkwardness of the painting's composition, the ambiguities of identity, costume, and location, and, most of all, the physical closeness of the figure to the viewer render its myth and allegory "Realist." The girl and the picture represent a uniquely modern conflict of emotional distance and material proximity, and of desire and its denial. *Peasant Girl with a Scarf*, like others of Courbet's Romantic early pictures, represents a dream and a very physical reality all at once.

1 Quoted in Castagnary, 1882, p. 23, in *Modern Art in Paris: Exhibitions of Realist Art*, selected by Theodore Reff, New York, 1981, no. 3.

2 Quoted in *Bulletin des Amis Gustave Courbet*, no. 52 (1974), p. 12.

3 Quoted in Riat, 1906.

4 Quoted in Castagnary, 1864, p. 183.

5 An excellent summary of Courbet's politics—and indeed his entire life and career—is the entry by Klaus Herding in Turner, 1996, vol. 8, pp. 50–61. Also see Herding, 1991.

6 Fried, 1990, passim.

7 See Clark, 1973a.

8 Toussaint, 1977, p. 93.

42

Gustave Courbet
French, 1819–1877

Vase of Lilacs, Roses, and Tulips
1863

Oil on canvas, $25\frac{5}{8} \times 21\frac{3}{8}$ in. (65 × 54.3 cm)
Signed and dated lower right: "Gustave Courbet 63"
M.1979.24

Provenance: [Jos Hessel, Paris, sold 27 April 1917 to]; [Bernheim-Jeune, Paris, stock no. 20.880, sold 16 March 1918 to]; Fasset-Arbouin, Paris. [Galerie Daber, Paris, sold to]; [Fritz Nathan, Zurich, sold 24 April 1957 to]; [Paul Rosenberg & Co., New York, stock no. 5696, sold 22 March 1962 to]; [Galerie Alfred Daber, Paris (for Michel Fert, Geneva?), sold ½ interest to]; [M. Knoedler & Company, New York, stock no. A8314, sold 12 February 1963 to]; Mrs. Arthur Lehman, New York. John Loeb Sr., New York,? consigned 1973 to; [M. Knoedler & Company, New York, stock no. A8314, sold 1973 to]; [Walter Feilchenfeldt, Zurich, jointly owned with]; [Reid & Lefevre, London, sold 11 December 1973 to]; [Paul Rosenberg & Co., New York, stock no. 6459–2749, sold 1979 to]; Norton Simon Art Foundation.

Exhibitions: Paris, 1917b, no. 8; Paris, 1919, no. 14; Philadelphia, 1959, no. 43, ill.; Paris, 1962a, no. 11, pl. IX; Bern, 1962, no. 26, ill.; London, 1973, no. 2; on loan, Princeton, University, Art Museum, 14 March–17 June 1979; on loan, Phoenix, Art Museum, 19 June–26 September 1979

References: Léger, 1929, pl. 31, p. 96; Hazama, 1933, ill. no. 20; Fernier, 1977, vol. 1, no. 364, pp. 206–207, ill.

Technical Notes: The support is a plain-weave canvas of fine to medium weight. The original edges have been cut off; however, cusped threads visible on the X-radiograph indicate that the dimensions are unchanged. At the upper left, a complex vertical tear had been repaired before the application of a glue lining. The smoothly applied ground is warm white or cream. Microscopic examination of the surface shows a thin red-brown layer above the white ground; thin portions of the dark background allow it to show through. Paint was applied fluidly in multiple layers over a thinly painted dark background. Courbet made several changes in the composition, portions of which remain visible through the paint of the final version, such as the red blossom behind the lilacs at the upper left. There is a complete tulip shape to the left and above the large yellow flower in the center; in the finished painting its yellow bloom is almost covered at top and bottom by dark green leaves. There was a third small white flower to the left of the two visible ones; it is now painted over with part of a lilac and a green leaf. Courbet modified contours and texture with additions of loosely brushed and sometimes stippled paint and occasionally thin glazes. The well-preserved paint film exhibits very small, thin contraction cracks, visible only with magnification. It is possible that cleaning has slightly thinned the dark paint in the background at the upper left. The natural resin varnish is slightly uneven but not discolored. (RW)

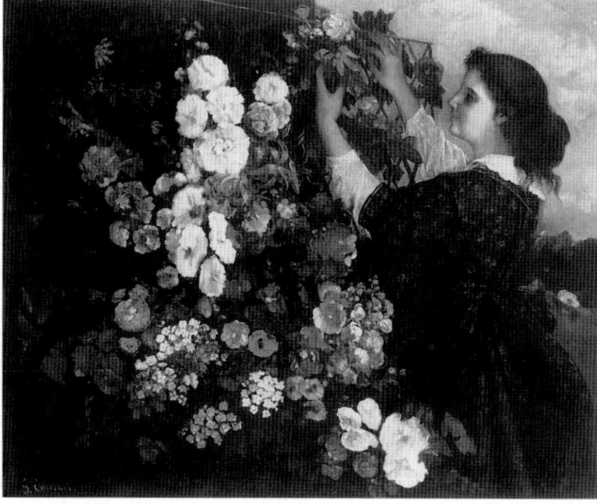

Fig. 42a Gustave Courbet, *The Trellis*, 1862, oil on canvas, $43\frac{1}{4} \times 53\frac{1}{4}$ in. (109.8 × 135.2 cm), Toledo Museum of Art, Purchased with funds from the Libbey Endowment, Gift of Edward Drummond Libbey

Courbet's still lifes are among the marvels of his production. The floral paintings, made as a contribution to a long-standing but minor tradition in French art, were created in a brief burst of activity in the mid-1850s (*Bunch of Flowers*, 1855, Hamburger Kunsthalle; replica in the Metropolitan Museum of Art, New York) and then again in 1862–1863. This example is dated 1863, at the end of the second and more sustained of those two periods. Although there is little evidence for the early provenance of the majority of these later flower paintings, they have a clearly commercial quality, indicating they were made first of all for the trade. Small arrangements of flowers, each of which presented different compositional and coloristic problems, were perfect aesthetic investments for the modest bourgeois collector.

The varied flowers in Courbet's still life—depicted with considerable accuracy—were grown in the gardens and hothouses at Rochement near Saintes in western France. The owner of this estate, Étienne Baudry, was a reform-minded progressive who was seriously interested in both art and gardening and was Courbet's host for about a year from May 1862 until May 1863. It was in this large establishment with its fine horticultural library that Courbet painted his second series of floral still lifes, the masterpiece of which is *The Trellis* of 1862 (fig. 42a). In all these paintings, Courbet mixed natural flowers with others grown in hothouses. This combination recalls Dutch still-life painting of the seventeenth century, which was in general also seasonally diverse. In addition to its

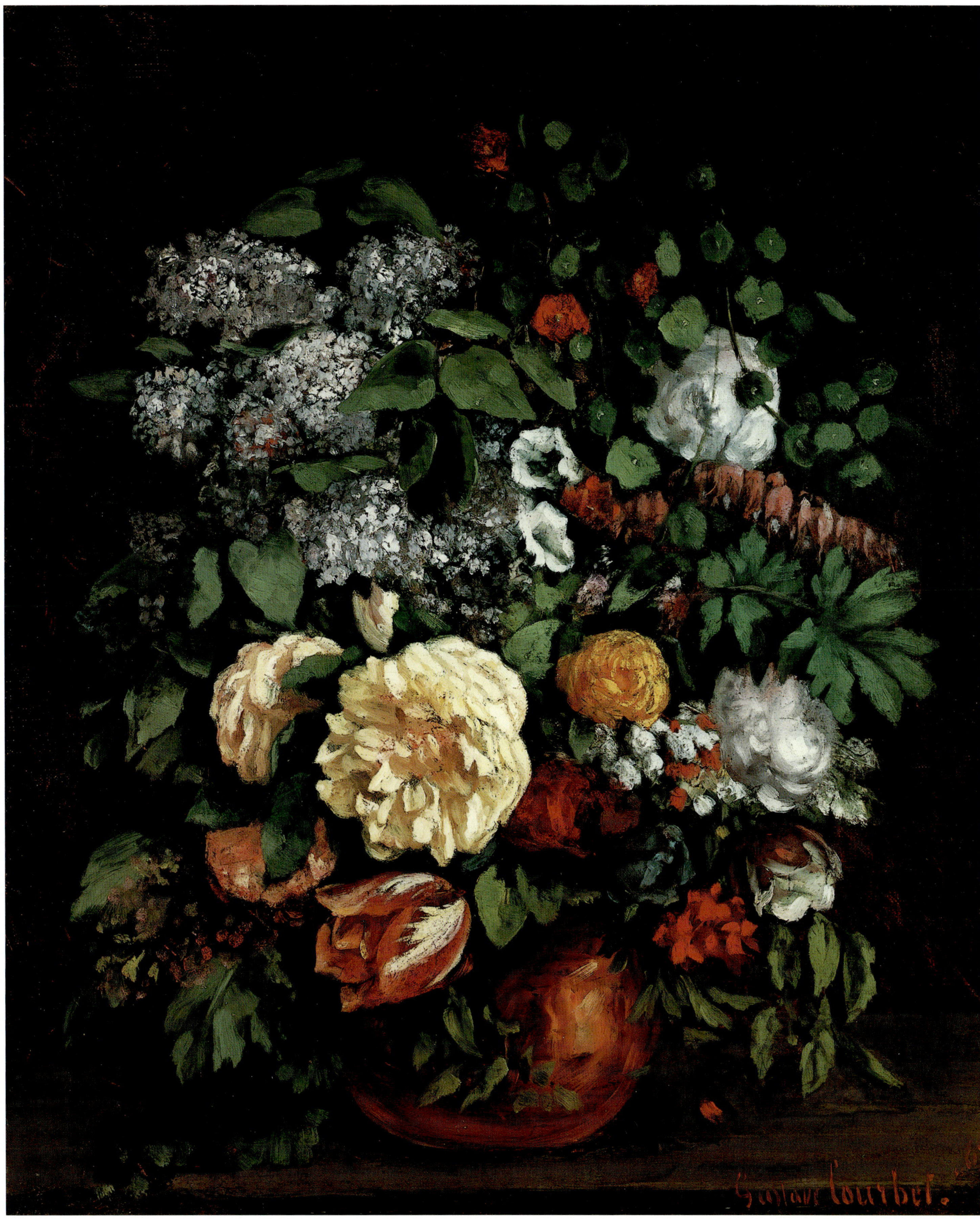
Gustave Courbet.

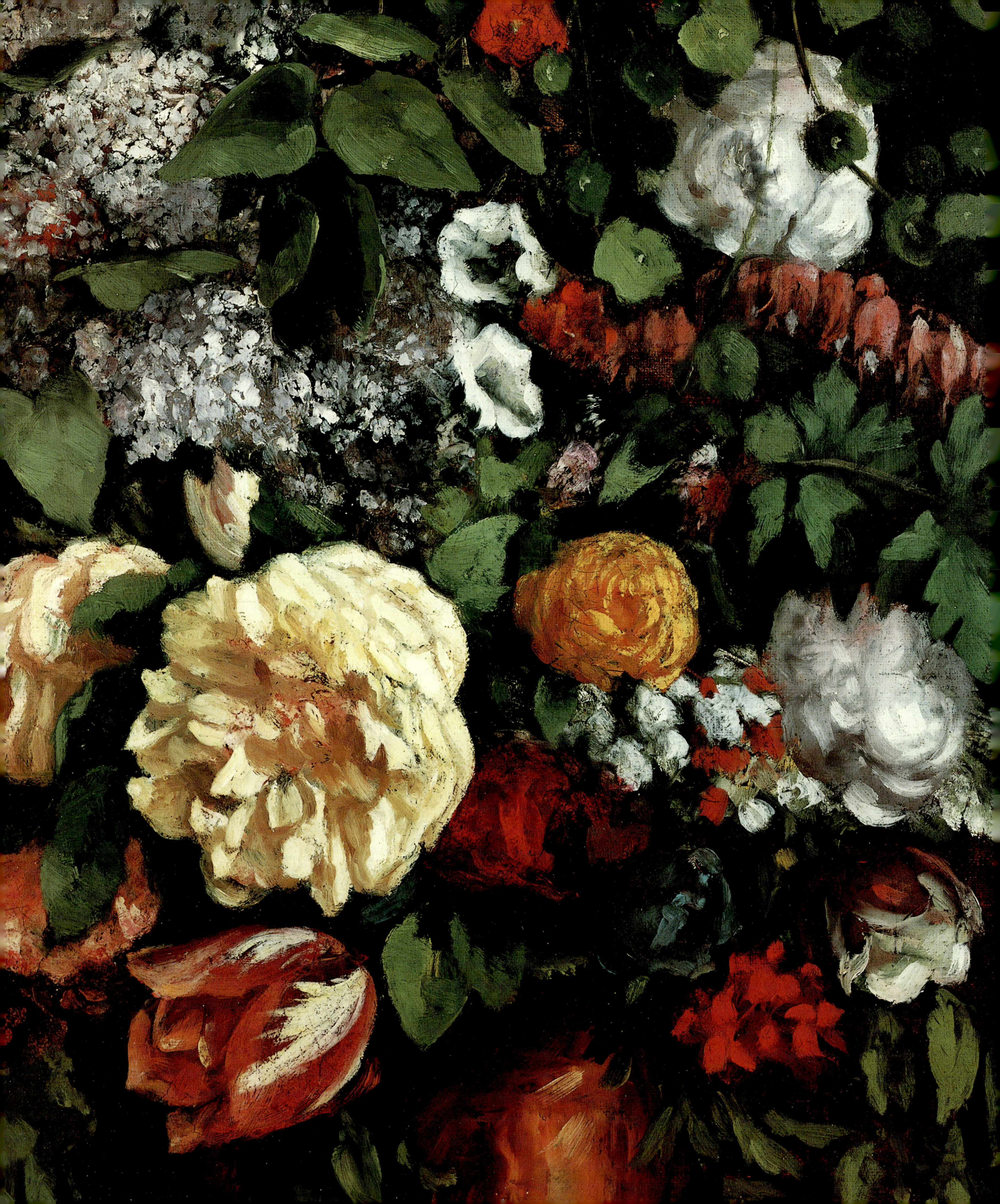

seasonal variety, Courbet's painting depicts flowers with blooms that varied greatly in longevity. The distinctive poppies or nasturtiums in the upper right are very short-lived when cut and placed in water; the heartier roses at the right have a very long period of bloom.

The colors of flowers and the art of flower arrangement have long been associated with the art of painting. Artists' skills in mimicking the color of flowers are testimony to their sympathy with nature itself. The creation of beautiful and visually compelling bouquets of flowers is akin to the composition of colors and shapes on canvas; both are artificial constructions of natural forms for domestic interiors. The Japanese art of ikebana, which began to receive sustained attention in France just at the time when Courbet took up still-life painting, is an excellent example of the blending of nature and artifice. Like the Shinto masters of Japanese flower arrangement, Courbet had a deep reverence for nature; unlike them, though, he displays in his work a greater concern for color than for line, for matter than for space, for abundance than for spirit.

Indeed, like most painters who preceded him in this genre, Courbet allowed the represented flower arrangement to fill virtually the entire surface of the canvas. Yet where many earlier artists created an illusionistic space in which their arrangement sits, Courbet allowed the flowers to emerge from an almost spaceless dark background. Only the position of what appears to be a copper or copper-colored ceramic container on a simple ledge encourages us to read the flower arrangement in any kind of pictorial space. In this respect, Courbet seems to have tipped his hat to the great Romantic painter Eugène Delacroix, whose two most ambitious floral paintings were exhibited in 1849, at the same Salon in which Courbet showed *After Dinner at Ornans* (Musée des Beaux-Arts, Lille), the brooding group portrait that is arguably his breakthrough painting. (The latter picture was actually acclaimed by Delacroix.) Delacroix's death in 1863 might in fact have provoked Courbet to push himself to paint a floral tribute to the great colorist.

Despite his renowned audacity and originality, Courbet painted this work in a manner that is consistent with the long tradition of flower painting. Using paintbrushes of varying sizes and widths, he applied his pure, viscous paint in a thoroughly academic manner, in overlapping strokes on a ground prepared with a dark brown *ébauche*. This accentuates the luminosity and chromatic intensity of the blossoms in contrast to the dark, dull background. Courbet was already known as the master of crude subjects painted equally crudely with a palette knife. This work shows no trace of that tool, almost as if Courbet were repudiating, at least in part, the consciously low aesthetic with which he was strongly associated. Indeed, except for the copper pot, the painting has thoroughly bourgeois aspirations—the hothouse flowers being as much a luxury as the painting itself. Not a hint of Courbet's rural origins or his fascination with small-town life is evident in this supremely confident exercise in urban flower painting. Only the density of composition and the plenitude of the color reveal this still life to be the creation of the arch materialist of paint.

43

Gustave Courbet
French, 1819–1877

Marine
c. 1865–1866

Oil on canvas, $19\frac{3}{4} \times 24$ in. (50.2×61 cm)
Signed lower left: "Gustave Courbet"
F.1970.12.P

Provenance: Jean-Baptiste Faure (1830–1914), Paris. [Durand-Ruel, Paris]. F. Lindet, by 1902 (sale, Paris, Hôtel Drouot, 6 May 1953, lot 8, ill.); [Galerie Jacques Dubourg, Paris, sold December 1953 to]; [Roland, Browse & Delbanco, London, sold 29 March 1954 to]; R. C. Pritchard (sale, Geneva, Christie's, 6 November 1969, lot 170, ill.). [E. V. Thaw and Co., New York, sold 1970 to]; The Norton Simon Foundation.

Exhibitions: Paris, 1867; Bristol, 1968, no. 20; on loan, Richmond, Va., Museum of Fine Arts, 19 June 1970–5 March 1973; San Francisco, 1973, no. 22, ill.; Los Angeles, 2006, no. 36, ill.

References: Fernier, 1977, vol. 1, no. 499, ill.; Faunce, 1993, pp. 110–111, pl. 32; Levine, 1994, p. 8, fig. 11; Eisenman, 2003, p. 140, ill.

Technical Notes: Courbet's *Marine* was painted on a medium-thick off-white ground on plain-weave canvas. Probably at the time of the lining, the tacking edges were removed right up to the paint, sometimes taking a bit of the design. X-radiographs show wide cusping along the perimeter. The stretcher is later. In the sky the first paint layer is deep blue. The foreground uses gray underpainting, while the green area below the horizon line has dark red beneath. Such underpainting acts much like a dark ground, setting off the lighter colors on top. On the surface Courbet judiciously applied touches of pure colors but he also toned back some areas with thin, translucent films that appear to contain particles of black pigment (note sky at upper left). Parallel lines probably from the application of paint with a palette knife are visible in a number of areas under normal viewing conditions and in X-radiographs, but brushstrokes are also visible on the surface. No changes in design are detectable. The condition is very good with few losses or restorations and almost no abrasion. In addition, the texture of the paint is well preserved. The surface coating, probably synthetic, does not appear discolored. (JF)

Courbet's Realism comprised two radical ideas: first, that the artist must attend to the material, observed world in all its social, scientific, and historical complexities and contradictions; and second, that a painting be treated as a concrete, physical surface and not as a mere window through which the painter and audience gaze with longing, admiration, or wonder. To reject either of these positions was to identify with an *ancien* political regime rooted in pretense, arbitrary power, and corruption, and an old artistic order wedded to trickery, elitism, and the denigration of honest, physical work. As Courbet matured and his practice advanced, and as opportunities for engagement with class and political struggles were increasingly foreclosed, the second of Courbet's two approaches to Realism came to predominate. His *Marine* of about 1865–1866 is not engaged with the social and historical complexities of its place and time, but it is nevertheless an extraordinary and innovative experiment in Realism: it offers an interrogation of the physical constituents of paint, the bases of illusionism, and the artifice of landscape art.

Courbet visited Trouville, on the northern coast of France, in the summer and fall of 1865 and painted, by his count, twenty-five seascapes with autumn skies, "each one more free and extraordinary than the last."[1] Twenty-five seascapes and ten *marines diverses* were exhibited in 1867 at the great Courbet retrospective held at the Rond-Point de l'Alma—the so-called Pavilion of Realism—adjacent to the grounds of the Exposition Universelle. This *Marine* may have been one of them. It most closely resembles a slightly larger picture of the same title in the Wallraf-Richartz Museum (fig. 43a) and another, probably painted at Deauville, also on the northern French coast, in 1866.[2]

The quality and originality of these three canvases would certainly have justified their inclusion in Courbet's exhibition. The Norton Simon *Marine* is one of his pictures from the 1860s about which it can truly be said that large details appear totally nonobjective. The artist's treatment of sand and water—considered separately—does not resemble those primal elements so much as broad, liquid, horizontal rivers of paint. Ironically, it is the sky, the most ethereal of substances, that is painted with the greatest degree of exactness, its blotches and puffs recalling the famous cloud studies of the English artist John Constable. This does not mean, however, that representation is altogether abandoned by Courbet. In place of a conventional verisimilitude derived from close attention to the surface texture of objects and their location in space, Courbet has devised a kind of substitute illusionism contrived from the matter and process of painting. By pulling paint across the surface of his canvas with a palette knife, Courbet revealed gray undertones and cool hues that suggest the pools of water that remain after a tide has receded. In this sense, Courbet has matched the unique quality of oil paint—its

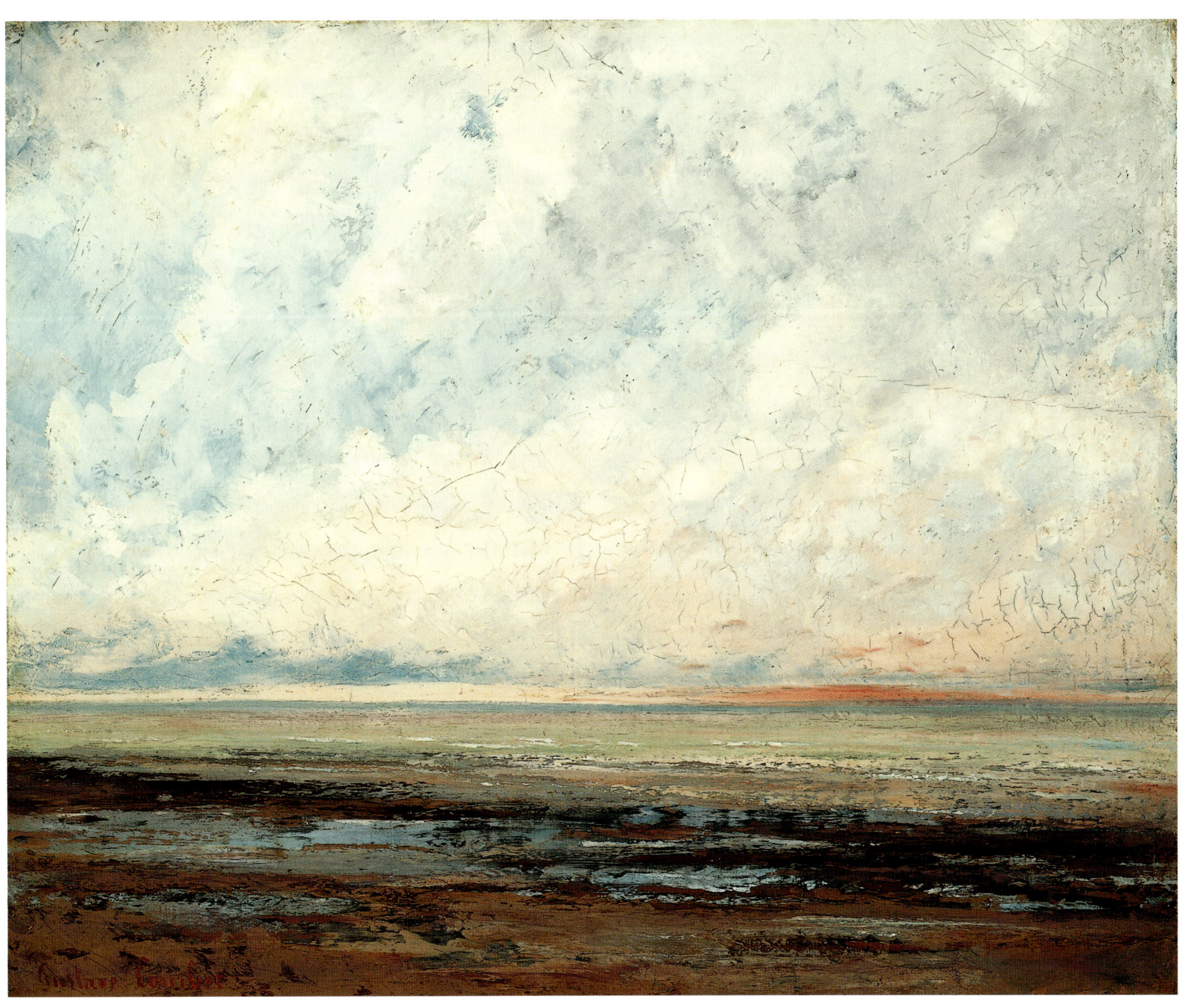

43

Fig. 43a Gustave Courbet, *Marine*, 1865, oil on canvas, $21\frac{1}{4} \times 25\frac{3}{16}$ in. (54 × 64 cm), Wallraf-Richartz Museum, Cologne

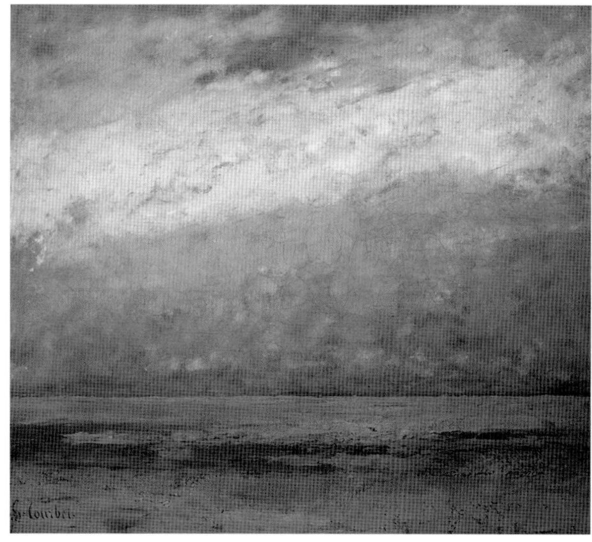

viscosity and plasticity—to the character of the place and matter he has chosen to represent.

Nevertheless, despite their mimetic effectiveness for modern audiences, these marine paintings were not easy for Courbet's contemporaries to understand or appreciate. The unusual range of hues—dominated by pink, melon, orange, gray-blue, and a dozen shades of brown—was far more intense and high-keyed than was usual in seascapes of this period, for example, those by Eugène Isabey, who was also active in Trouville at about this time. In addition, the complete elimination of history, anecdote, architecture, boats, or even figures must have been startling to audiences used to seeing such subjects as sea bathing (for example, in canvases by Eugène Boudin), the departure of a fishing fleet (Johan Barthold Jongkind), and the triumphal arrival of naval officers or other grandees (Isabey). Finally, the extreme flattening of planes or telescoping of depth—effected by the near uniformity of tone and denseness of texture—tends to deny the spectator imaginative entry into the world of the picture. The effect, as Klaus Herding has noted, is of a kind of solid wall of paint, which—far from suggesting Impressionist intangibility—connotes solidity, mass, and matter.[3] Courbet's paintings may thus fairly be judged the most Realist when they are the most abstract.

1 Courbet to his father, 17 November 1865, in Arts Council of Great Britain, 1978, p. 162.
2 Private collection, Washington, D.C.; Fernier, 1977, no. 591.
3 Herding, 1991, p. 93.

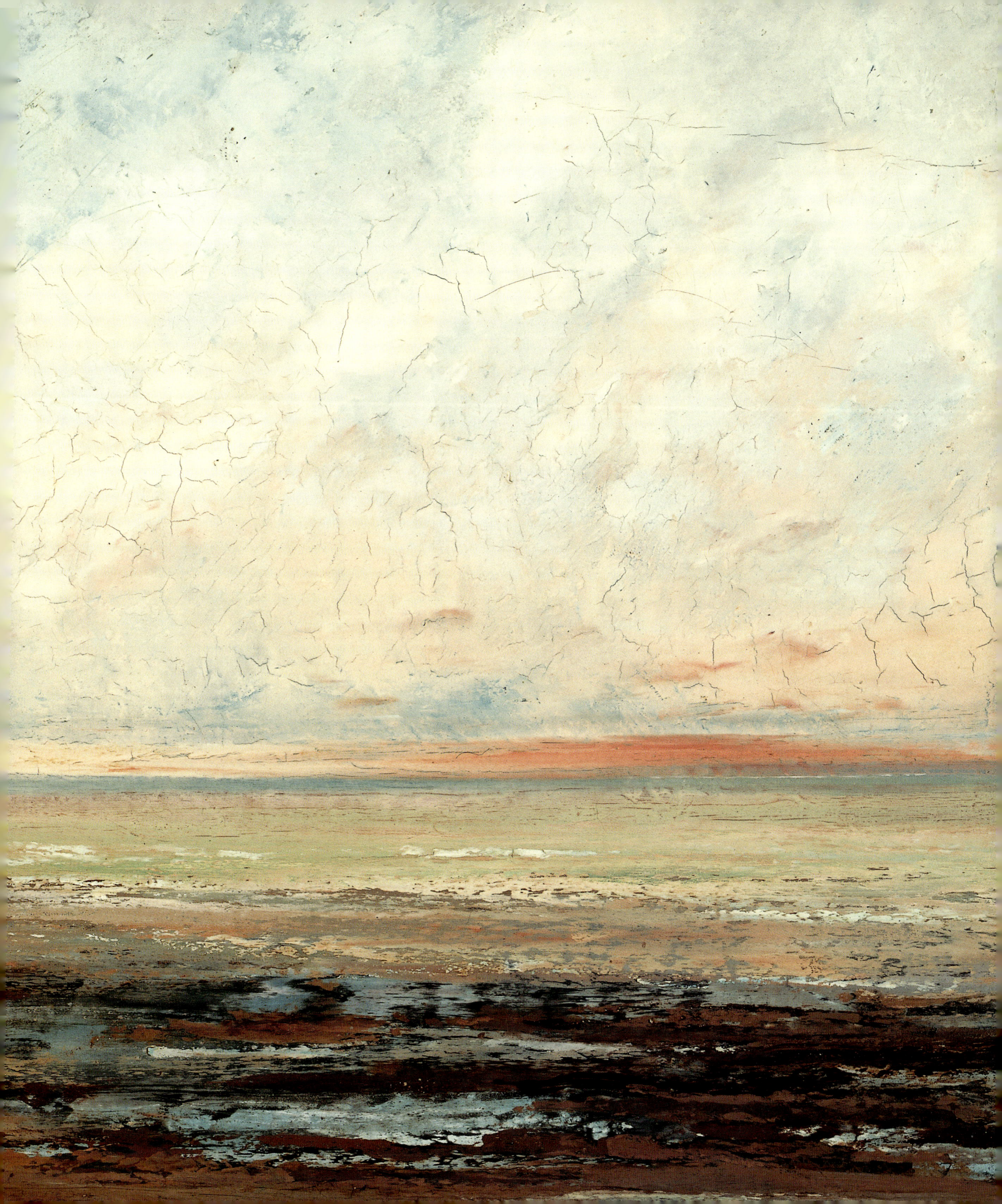

44

Gustave Courbet
French, 1819–1877

Stream of the Puits-Noir at Ornans
c. 1867–1868

Oil on canvas, 39⅜ × 59¼ in. (100 × 150.5 cm)
Signed and inscribed in orange-red lower left: "G. Courbet / Ruisseau du Puits-Noir a Ornans"
Somewhat overpainted date above signature and to the right: "68"
M.1976.13

Provenance: Alexandre Berthier, 4th prince of Wagram, Paris (1883–1918), until 1906. [Galerie Georges Petit, Paris, 1906]. [Galerie Heinemann, Munich; 1908]. Hugo Schmeil, Dresden, by 1914 (sale, Berlin, Galerie Paul Cassirer, 17 October 1916, lot 8, ill.). Mr. and Mrs. Thomas Mitchell, Beverly Hills, Calif., by 1950. [Paul Kantor Gallery, Beverly Hills, Calif., stock no. K1724, sold 1965 to]; Norton Simon, gift 1976 to; Norton Simon Art Foundation.

Exhibitions: Dresden, 1914, no. 18; Pomona, 1950, ill.; on loan, Boston, Museum of Fine Arts, 17 June–17 November 1965; on loan, Los Angeles, County Museum of Art, 5 January 1970–1 August 1971; San Francisco, 1973, no. 23, ill.; Los Angeles, 2006, no. 13, ill.

References: Meier-Graefe, 1912a, p. 161, ill.; Meier-Graefe, 1921, pl. 32; Hazama, 1933, ill. no. 11; Fernier, 1977, vol. 1, no. 196, ill.; Arts Council of Great Britain, 1978, p. 165; Chu, 1993, p. 42, fig. 2; Eitner, 2000, p. 109, 112 n. 22, fig. 2; G. Thomas, 2000, p. 75, fig. 44.

Technical Notes: The plain-weave, medium-weight canvas is lined with an aqueous adhesive to fabric that is tacked to an old, though probably not original, stretcher. Original tacking edges are removed up to the design, but some unprimed canvas beyond remains, and wide cusping shows on all sides. The rich, directly applied paint on the surface of this painting is immediately noticeable. What is not so apparent, however, is Courbet's use of complex paint layers on a dark ground. The almost black preparation, probably applied with a palette knife, is thick and rich. It is this dark layer setting off the opaque paints on top that creates the illusion of space and atmosphere. A warm, translucent paint layer similar to an imprimatura covers the cooler-colored ground. Over this Courbet blocked out his design with an underpainting of translucent warm tones. The artist laid in the larger light areas, such as the sky, gray background at center, and ocher foreground, leaving major forms such as the large tree trunks reserved. He built up the reserves with dabs of opaque and pasty or thin and translucent paints. Finally, surface paints such as the finer tree branches were applied. More than one layer of paint produce the smooth, light areas such as the sky. It consists of a thin, loosely applied turquoise blue over a solid, light purplish blue. The first layer must have been fairly dry before receiving the top layer. Courbet employed brush and knife, the former giving strokes, dashes, and jabs to the surface and the latter providing smooth passages and ridges. He flecked paint from a brush for some effects and scored the surface for fine tree branches. The X-ray shows minor, if any, pentimenti. The painting is in good condition, though there are about six areas of loss in the lower left quadrant. All are clearly visible in the X-ray. Restoration (visible in ultraviolet light) hides contraction cracks located in the triangle formed by the two largest trees at lower left. The lining secures a system of large cracks. The surface is well preserved with only limited abrasion so that fine, thin strokes of the tiniest tree branches remain mostly intact. Presumably, wrinkles developed in the smooth sky during the drying process. The varnish, probably synthetic, is only slightly discolored but nonsaturating. The signature and date use orange-red paint, but the more blocky letters of the lower inscription have a different red paint highlighted with light red. To the right of the lower inscription, remnants of another scraped and/or overpainted inscription extend for about 7½ inches. In ultraviolet light the letters *rbe* appear in the obliterated inscription, and the letter *C* is detectable to the left of the *rbe*, and in ultraviolet light a letter (e?) follows *noir*. (JF)

The Stream of the Puits-Noir at Ornans depicts a particular section of the Breme—a small tributary of the river Loue—as it courses through a wooded gorge known as the Puits-Noir. The secluded site, some 2½ miles from the artist's birthplace of Ornans in the Franche-Comté, was known to Courbet from childhood. He first painted it during the winter and spring of 1853–1854 and exhibited one version, *The Stream of the Puits-Noir, Valley of the Loue* (fig. 44a), beside ten other of his works at the Exposition Universelle in Paris in 1855. Courbet returned to the location about a decade later, but now generally preferred an adjacent site, where the limestone outcroppings are lower, a large boulder dominates the right foreground, and the water a bit less agitated. This latter spot became the basis for *The Covered Stream* (fig. 44b) and its numerous, subsequent variants. In all, there are twenty-nine known paintings that appear to represent the Puits-Noir; all but one are smaller than the Norton Simon picture.[1] The present painting is the only winter landscape in the group, which suggests that it was not a studio replica but made from studies on the spot. Since Courbet is known to have spent the winters 1853–1854 and 1854–1855 at Ornans, and since in January 1854 he wrote to his friend and patron Alfred Bruyas that he "has three landscapes in the works," it is possible that the present painting was at least begun at this time.[2] Nevertheless, the picture has definite stylistic traits that suggest a later date, probably about 1867–1868, and there is a partially overpainted date of "68" on the canvas.

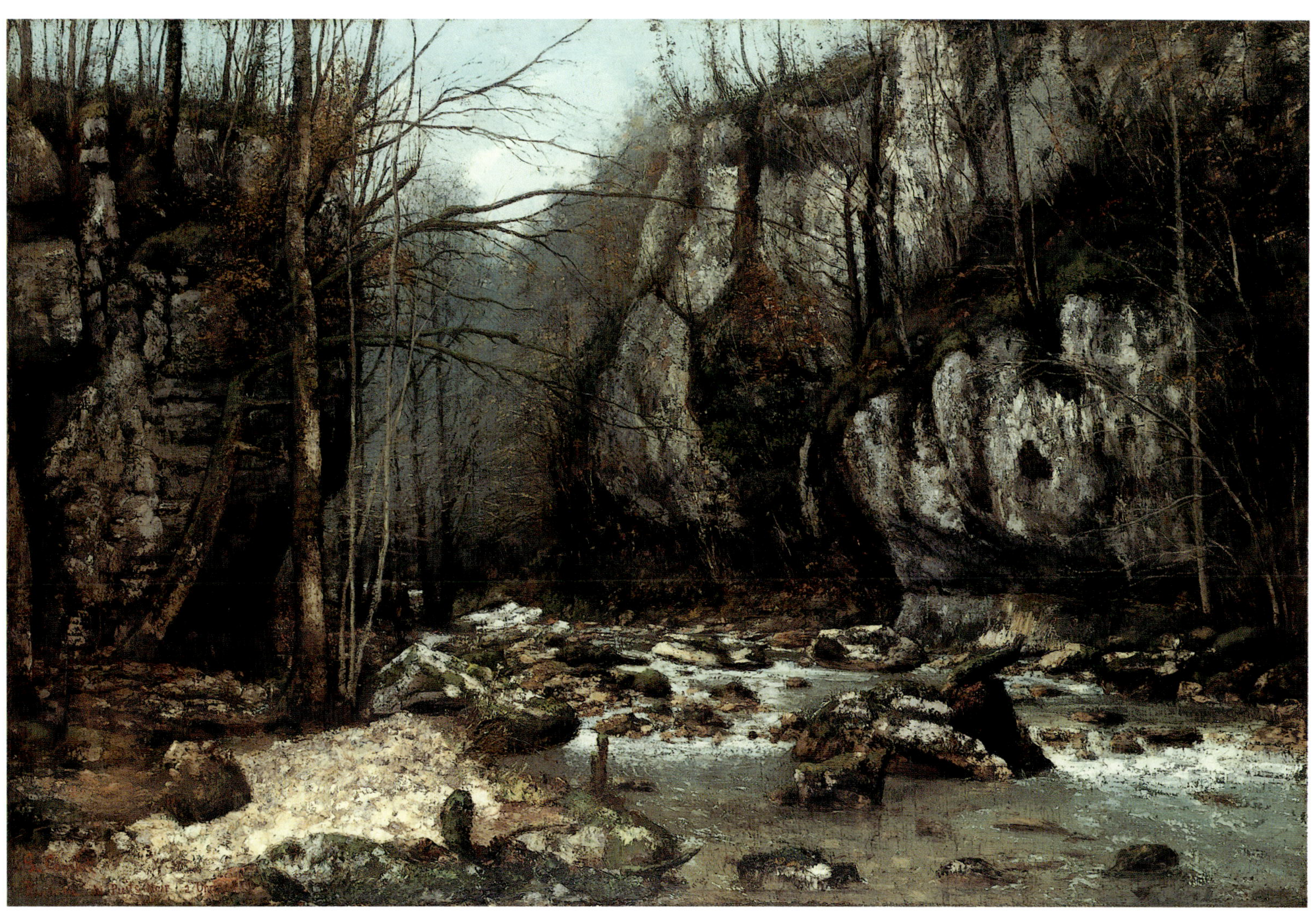

44

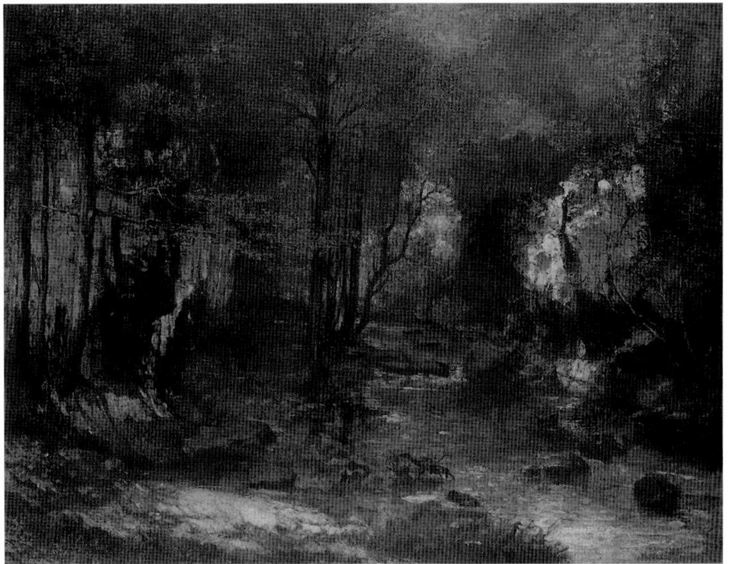

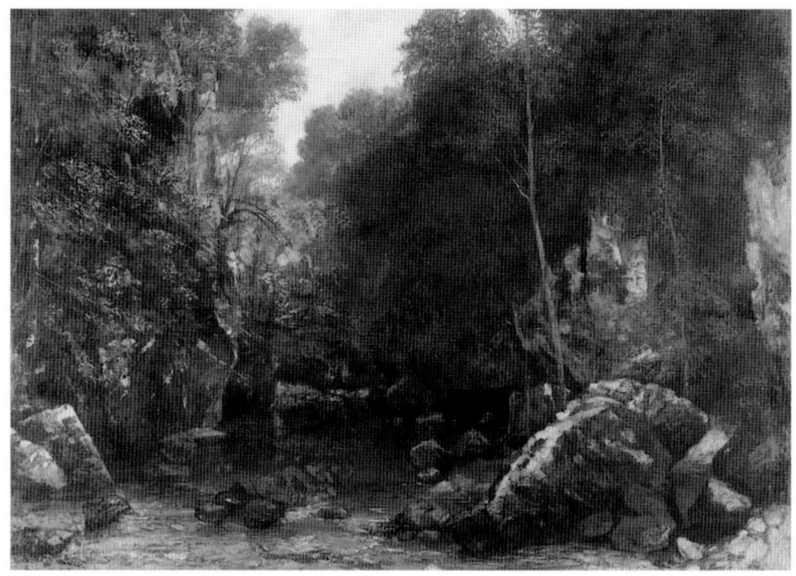

Fig. 44a (*above left*) Gustave Courbet, *The Stream of the Puits-Noir, Valley of the Loue*, 1855, oil on canvas, 41 × 54 in. (104 × 137 cm), National Gallery of Art, Washington, Gift of Mr. and Mrs. P. H. B. Frelinghuysen in memory of her father and mother, Mr. and Mrs. H. O. Havemeyer

Fig. 44b (*above right*) Gustave Courbet, *The Covered Stream*, 1865, oil on canvas, 37 × 53⅛ in. (94 × 135 cm), Musée d'Orsay, Paris; photo: Réunion des Musées Nationaux / Art Resource, NY

The gorge called Puits-Noir was formed by the seasonal expansion and contraction of stone, the penetration of plant roots and burrowing insects into small crevices, and especially the effect of water, which in contact with limestone forms a highly corrosive carbonic acid that can quickly break down rock and create deep channels. The formation of the streambed required many millennia, and the process is obviously ongoing. Courbet's *Stream* is a compelling interrogation of the varied materials and processes that compose this site. River waters, stirred into foam by collision with submerged and extruded rocks, are forced into shallow rapids in the lower middle of the painting; at the lower right, the water cascades off a low, rocky shelf before it is becalmed. Boulders, rocks, and pebbles of all sizes dominate the painting. The metamorphosed outcroppings at left and right are rounded, swelling forms, while the rocks in the streambed and along the banks are more broken and angular. Many of the rocks are covered with moss—especially those in the center of the stream—and some have gray-white lesions on them, suggesting the presence of lichen. At the lower left of the painting there is a bright, trapezoidal shaped patch of sand and gravel, washed onto the bank during a period of high water or flood. Broken and rotting tree trunks jostle for attention amid the boulders and rocks; some are cigar shaped and pitched at jaunty angles—like the one that overhangs the dark sienna boulder near the bottom right. Two stumps, one fat, one thin, stand erect near the bottom center of the picture. Leafless trees line the banks of the stream. Two of them in the left foreground have thick trunks and are composed of the same clotted paint—applied with a spatula or palette knife—as the rocks and boulders. The trees at the right and those that recede into the middle and background have a very different material character. They are generally more thinly painted with visible brushstrokes that trace the lengths of the trunks. At the top of the painting, there is visible a V-shaped patch of sky; it is painted with approximately the same density of oil and pigment as the smooth areas of water at the bottom.

Courbet's *Stream of the Puits-Noir at Ornans* in fact is fairly thickly painted all over. There are no precise contour lines, no carefully calibrated tonal modeling, and no effort to use color to construe spatial depth. Warm and cool hues are as likely to be seen in background areas as in foreground areas. Darks and lights are balanced across the surface of the picture and throughout its depths. Texture and scale alone are employed to organize space. But these latter instruments have an additional function: they inform the viewer about the material quality and variety of the water, rocks, trees, and sky on view, and their histories. The young trees are lightly painted and have an open surface structure. Older trees are more densely pigmented; they have nearly a mineral or fossil character. The large tree at the left indeed appears to grow out of the rock itself; just to its left, a section of the cliff face is treelike in shape, highlighting the drama of the meeting of organic and inorganic nature. The transition from plant to mineral is also marked on the boulder at the right with its blanket of soil and green grasses. Courbet's painting is thus a study of the physical character of an especially beloved place near the artist's home in Ornans. Nature is made temporal and contingent in Courbet's art, as surely as the human world in other paintings is understood to be the result of historical change, struggle, conflict, and cooperation.

The principal discovery that emerged from the most recent physical examination of the painting is the existence of an earlier signature and date in the lower left corner, most of which is actually beneath a second red-orange signature and inscription that dominate our view of the painting. Since Courbet actually was in Ornans during the autumn of 1868, when the painting was initially dated, it seems clear that he worked on this large painting from life. Yet the complete absence of any evidence of its ownership or exhibition within Courbet's lifetime makes it impossible to do anything other than speculate about Courbet's decision to rework the painting and to add another signature and inscription. It would seem that such a decision would have been made when the painting was sold to a prominent collector or sent for a major exhibition, most likely the latter, since it was standard for artists to sign paintings in orange-red for the Salon exhibitions so that their paintings could easily be identified. The painting's first recorded owner was the prince of Wagram, who, with fifteen paintings by Courbet, was among the greatest of the artist's collectors, but this collection was formed at the end of the nineteenth and early part of the twentieth centuries, well after Courbet's death in 1878. It is possible, given the stylistic oddities of the painting, that it was left by Courbet with his friend Édouard Ordinaire, with whom he stayed in the autumn of 1868, and that Ordinaire's son, Marcel, a follower of Courbet, reworked and inscribed the painting after Courbet's imprisonment and later exile in Switzerland.

1 Fernier, 1977, no. 466, location unknown.

2 Chu, 1992, no. 54-I, p. 121; cited in Eitner, 2000, p. 108.

45

Gustave Courbet
French, 1819–1877

Cliff at Étretat, the Porte d'Aval
1869

Oil on canvas, 25¾ × 32 in. (65.4 × 81.3 cm)
Signed and dated lower right: "G. Courbet '69"
F.1969.6.2

Provenance: Édouard-Napoléon-César-Edmond Mortier, 5th duc de Trévise, Paris (1883–1946). [Galerie Alfred Daber, Paris, sold 1949 to]; [Paul Rosenberg & Co., New York, stock no. 5371, sold October 1950 to]; Mr. and Mrs. R. Sturgis Ingersoll, Pennlyn, Pa., sold 1969, through Jane Wade, to; The Norton Simon Foundation.

Exhibitions: Paris, 1949, no. 16, ill.; New York, 1956a, no. 16, ill.; Philadelphia, 1959, no. 43, ill.; on loan, Phoenix, Art Museum, 18 August–15 December 1969; on loan, Los Angeles, County Museum of Art, 16 December 1969–26 March 1973; San Francisco, 1973, no. 24, ill.

References: Riat, 1906, p. 268; Bénédite, Laran, and Gaston-Dreyfus, 1911, pp. 97–98, pl. XLI; Bénédite, Laran, and Gaston-Dreyfus, 1912, pp. 81–82, pl. XLI; Lindon, 1958, pp. 356, fig. 4, 357; Fernier, 1977, vol. 2, no. 718, p. 97, ill.

Technical Notes: The support is a plain-weave canvas, wax-lined to canvas with the original tacking edges intact. It is tacked to a 6-member keyed stretcher that is probably original. Adhesion between the two canvases is uniformly strong. In the lower left quadrant, two damages to the original canvas, visible on the X-radiograph, have been well repaired. Microscopic examination shows that Courbet applied a warm white underpainting on top of the commercial priming, leaving only the dark green land at the upper left and center in reserve. Beneath the remainder of the painting, there is a red-brown, semitranslucent underpainting, occasionally visible in gaps of the paint. He then applied opaque but fairly liquid paint in multiple layers, often thickly and in broad strokes. Contrasting with the textured areas of beach, cliffs, and unquiet water, the sky is painted with perfectly smooth, delicately modulated colors, with no visible brushstrokes or ridges from a palette knife. The X-radiograph shows a changed position of some of the rocks in the right foreground, where originally they were smaller and more numerous. At the left side, it appears that Courbet first painted a strong spray against the larger dark rock and then replaced it with the dark pool of water and the light-colored sailboat at the left. The X-ray also shows more areas of dense pigment in the water at the center right, suggesting that the tonality may originally have been lighter but was later changed to darker blues. In normal vision, the small voids in the blue water near the horizon appear to be losses. However, the microscope reveals various colors of blue dribbled and dragged across them, but not quite in a continuous layer. Earlier restoration is undocumented. There is a minimal amount of scattered retouching in the sky at the upper right. (RW)

Étretat is a small town on the coast of Normandy, trapped in a valley between two great cliff formations. At the beginning of the Second Empire (1852–1870), the extension of the trunk railway line from Le Havre opened up this formerly secluded fishing village to tourism. Within a generation, it was a fashionable resort and second-home destination for wealthy Parisians. Country villas began to dot the hillsides and cliffs of Étretat, and hotels and inns replaced many of the humble homes and shops of the traditional fisherpeople who had inhabited the site for generations. The town was particularly cherished by writers, musicians, and artists, and its residents and guests included Alphonse Karr, Guy de Maupassant, Jacques Offenbach, Eugène Isabey, Eugène Boudin, Johan Barthold Jongkind, and Claude Monet. From 10 August to 17 September 1869 Courbet stayed in Étretat at the cottage-studio belonging to the marine painter Alfred Le Poittevin, uncle of de Maupassant. Accompanied by the Barbizon painter Narcisse Diaz, Courbet saw the sights and at once began to plan, sketch, and paint at least eight canvases representing the cliffs of Aval, also known as La Porte d'Aval. The largest and best of these, *The Cliff of Étretat after the Storm* (fig. 45a), was exhibited at the Salon of 1870. Courbet also painted another identically sized version and another, larger variant of the composition.[1] Gustav Arosa, the great collector and guardian of Paul Gauguin, owned the one of identical dimension, and this has occasionally been confused with the Norton Simon painting (fig. 45b). Courbet also started work on the approximately two dozen versions of *La Vague* (*The Wave*), his best-known, most audacious, and most notorious series of sea paintings.

The motif here is found at the south end of the half-mile-long, crescent-shaped beach and boardwalk that dominate the town. At the opposite, north, end of Étretat is the Porte d'Amont, also painted by Courbet in 1869 and, three years later, by Camille Corot (fig. 45c). As Corot's picture indicates, and as verified by guidebooks and postcards from the era, the south end of the beach was dominated by fishing and the north by bathing. In 1885 Claude Monet painted both ends of the beach of Étretat without any people, treating the cliffs as if they were examples of monumental architecture, like Rouen Cathedral. In the early twentieth century, the beach and cliffs were the subject of works by Georges Braque and

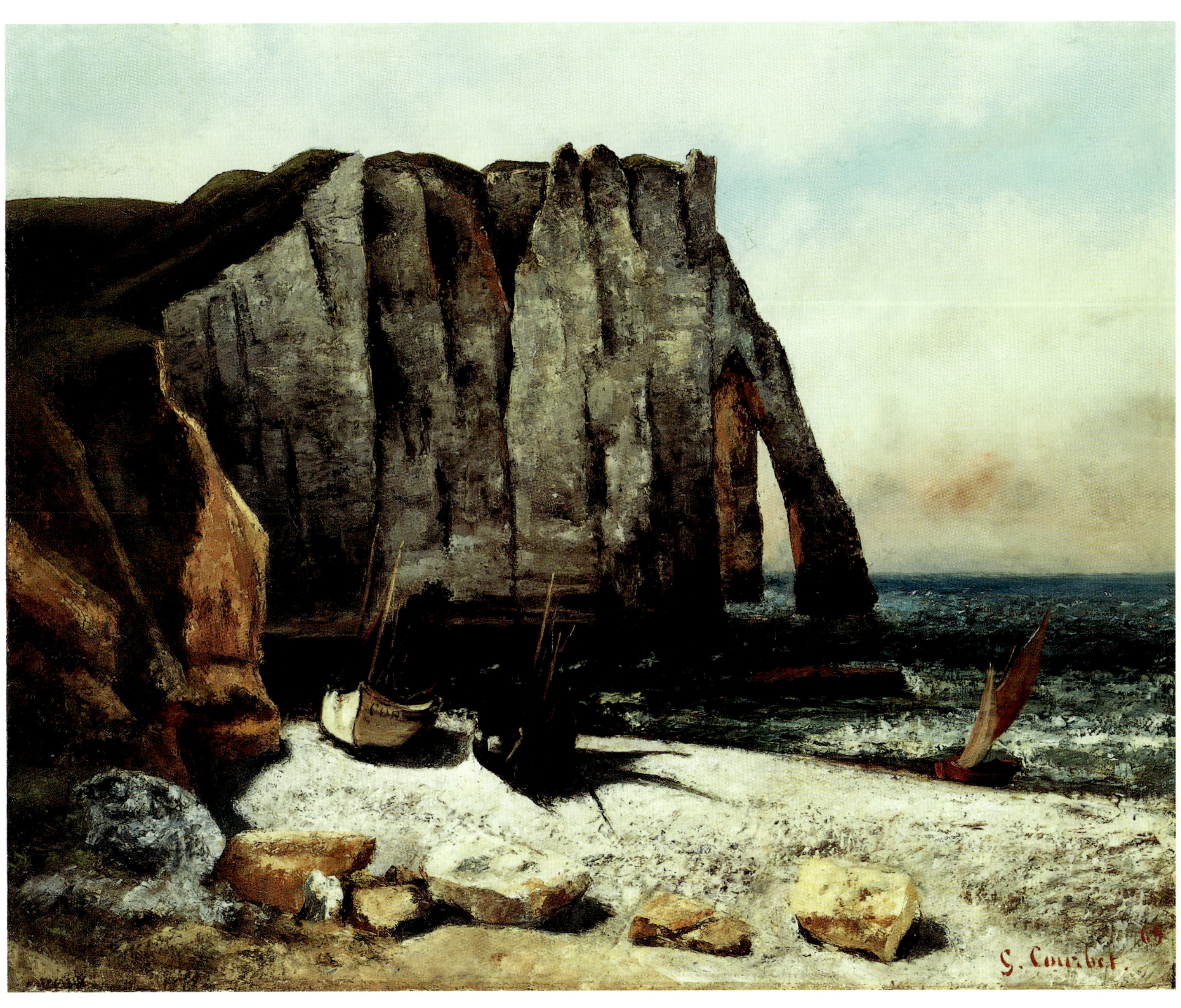

45

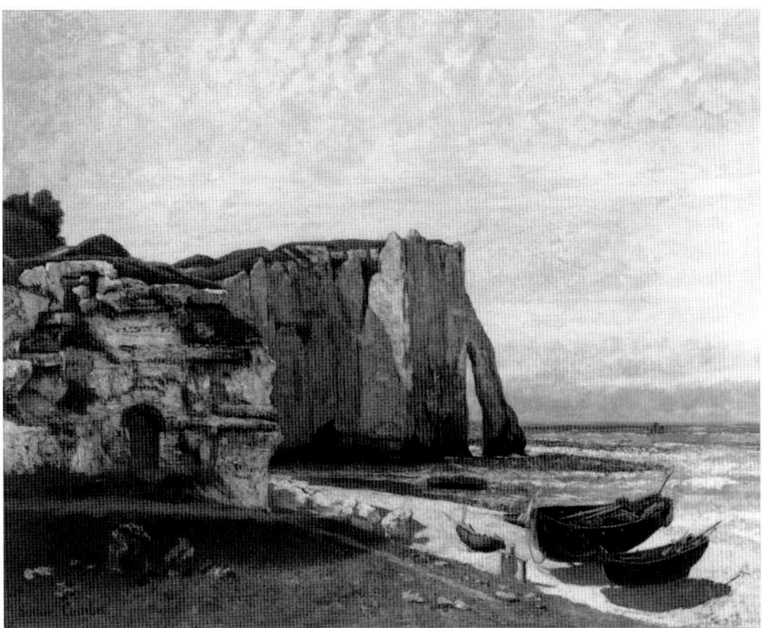

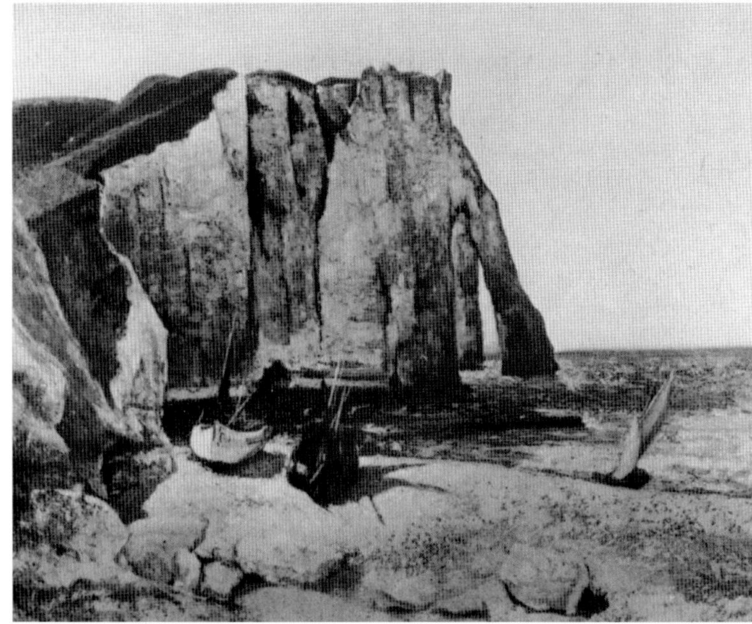

Fig. 45a (*above left*) Gustave Courbet, *The Cliff of Étretat after the Storm*, 1870, oil on canvas, $52\frac{3}{8} \times 63\frac{3}{4}$ in. (133 × 162 cm), Musée d'Orsay, Paris; photo: Réunion des Musées Nationaux / Art Resource, NY

Fig. 45b (*above right*) Gustave Courbet, *Étretat*, 1869, oil on canvas, $25\frac{3}{4} \times 32$ in. (65.4 × 81.3 cm), location unknown; photo: Fernier, 1977, no. 721

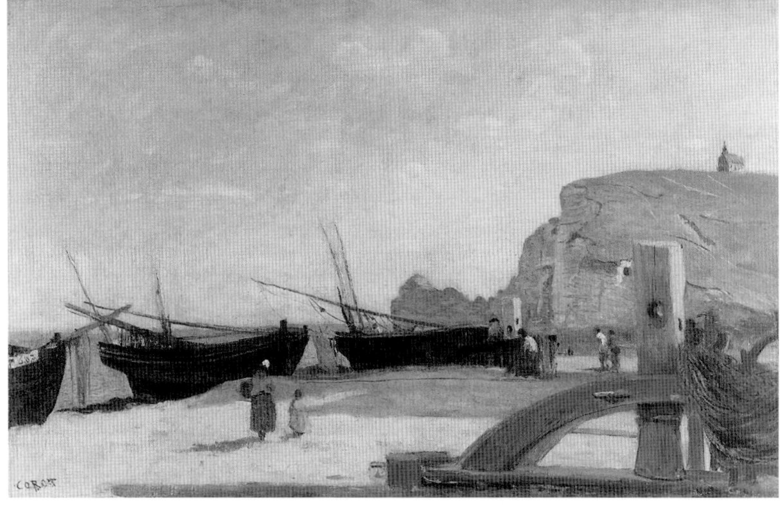

Fig. 45c (*right*) Jean-Baptiste-Camille Corot, *View of the Cliffs of Amont (The Beach, Étretat)*, 1872, oil on canvas, $14 \times 22\frac{1}{2}$ in. (35.5 × 57.1 cm), St. Louis Museum of Art

Henri Matisse. The latter's paintings of La Porte d'Aval—so different from Courbet's that they might be parodies—are especially striking. *Large Cliff with Fish* (fig. 45d), for example, is vertical in format, thinly and broadly painted, and focused on an array of dead fish in the foreground, not the eponymous cliffs beyond.

The present painting is a superb and solidly constructed seaside landscape, which concentrates all our attention on the strength and endurance of the massive limestone cliffs. In the foreground, a line of boulders functions as a still life, giving a detailed sense of the particularity of the local geology. Even the hardest of nature's materials, we are informed, are subject to fracture and fragmentation; the changing forces of wind and water ceaselessly sculpt the surface of the great cliffs, creating works of natural art. In the left middle ground is a pair of fishing boats, tossed on the beach like children's toys. At the right a third boat is depicted; it still sports its sails as if it has just arrived, or else has been readied for departure and awaits its human occupants. Apart from the boats, however, there is little in the picture that points to the anecdotal or the quotidian. Instead, an abstraction is created by flatness and spacelessness. This is partly attributable to the quality of light and partly to the odd density and opacity of the surface. The light possesses softness and limpidity, suggesting it had passed through a translucent filter of glass in the artist's studio. The rock face, composed of narrow, vertical panels of gray and black with traces of sienna, seems made out of clay molded by the human hand rather than hewn by geological processes; the effect is heightened by the very detail and tectonic specificity, as we have seen, of the

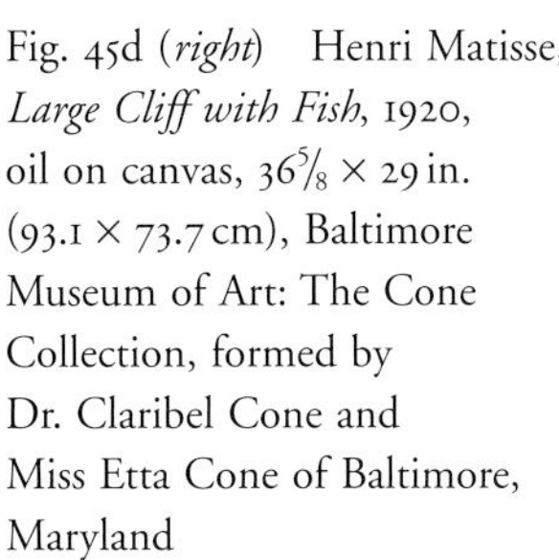

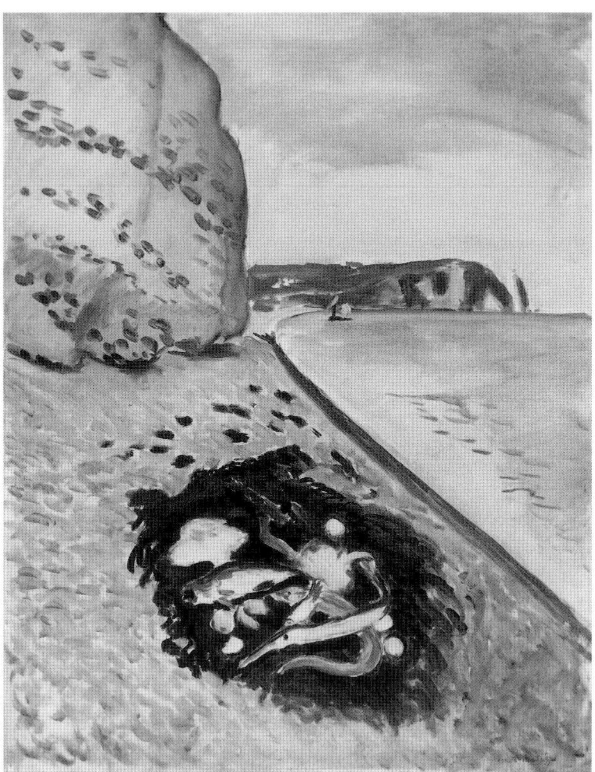

Fig. 45d (*right*) Henri Matisse, *Large Cliff with Fish*, 1920, oil on canvas, $36\frac{5}{8} \times 29$ in. (93.1 × 73.7 cm), Baltimore Museum of Art: The Cone Collection, formed by Dr. Claribel Cone and Miss Etta Cone of Baltimore, Maryland

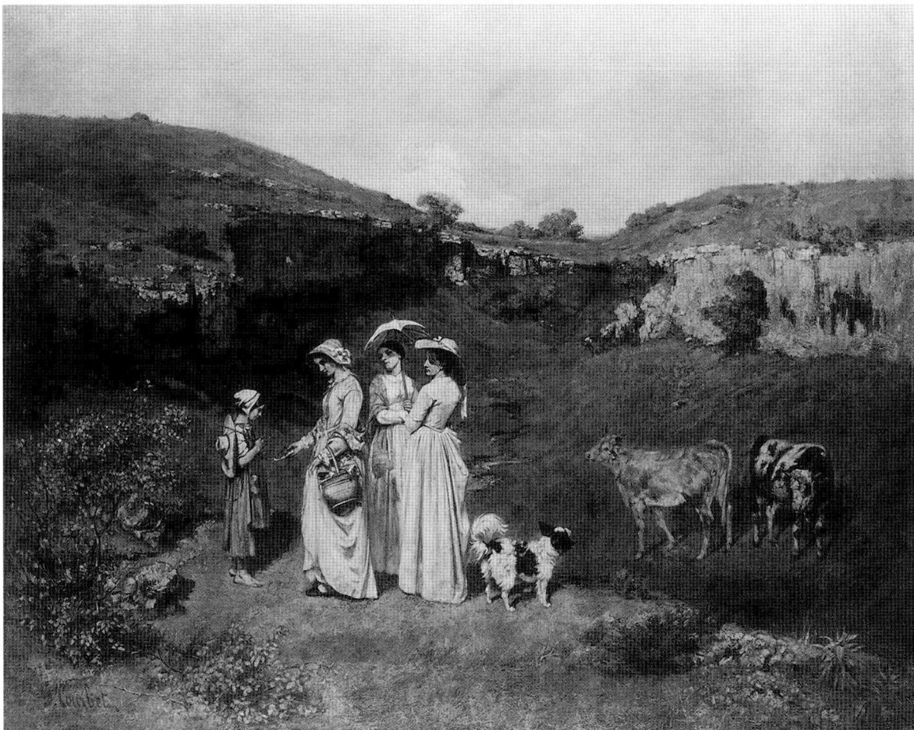

Fig. 45e (*below*) Gustave Courbet, *Young Women from the Village*, 1851, oil on canvas, $76\frac{3}{4} \times 102\frac{3}{4}$ in. (195 × 261 cm), The Metropolitan Museum of Art, New York, Gift of Harry Payne Bingham, 1940

foreground boulders. The gray-green carpeted hills above have a smooth, polished aspect, tending to obscure our perception of depth and scale. Indeed, a real ambiguity of surface and depth is apparent in the picture: the brown cliffs at lower left cast a shadow on the beach from which they appear to rise; at their top, however, the same cliffs are part of the ridge that joins the distant gray cliffs. Far and near are thus brought into awkward proximity. The effect is akin to that found in some of Courbet's paintings of the landscape near his native Ornans, such as *Young Women from the Village* (fig. 45e), one of his most important figural works of the 1850s.

The beach, water, and sky, too, have an artificial, constructed aspect. At the bottom of the picture, white, gray, and brown flecks of paint jostle for position above visible brown underpainting. The water is composed of alternating, horizontal bands of white-green, gray-green, blue-black, and green-blue. Small gaps in the paint surface in the upper right portion of the sea expose further brown underpainting. The water at left, which passes between the rocks and the beach, just above and to the left of the two boats, is opaque brown-black and creates a hole and a spatial depth where there otherwise would be none. Here, finally, is visible the conjunction of sand, cliffs, rocks, and water. The sky, however, is the most remarkable part of Courbet's painting. It is smooth, densely painted (the crackle indicates the thickness), and polished, like a sky by Yves Tanguy or Salvador Dalí. The line where it meets the cliffs is crisp and precise, making the rocks appear backlit and lending a preternatural glow to the whole image. That luminous sky, combined with the toylike quality of the boats and the ambiguous perspective, gives the whole picture a childlike and Surrealist air. In this, it recalls once again *The Young Women of the Village*, whose odd perspective and awkward modeling recalled to critics in 1852 sign paintings and children's art. This is an indication of the purposefully vernacular, popular character of Courbet's art, and of the artist's manner of insistently highlighting the artificial, material, and crafted character of things—even natural things, like the sand and waves, cliffs and sky of Étretat. *The Cliff at Étretat, Porte d'Aval,* though clearly touristic in feel and made for the market, nevertheless exposes Courbet's continuing commitment to an art freed from academic constraint and devoted instead to a directness or honesty of sight and a freedom of painterly touch.

1 Fernier, 1977, nos. 720 and 721.

46

Gustave Courbet
French, 1819–1877

Apples, Pears, and Primroses on a Table
1871–1872

Oil on canvas, $23\frac{1}{2} \times 28\frac{3}{4}$ in. (59.7×73 cm)
Signed, inscribed, and dated lower right: "Ste. Pélagie / G. Courbet 71"
M.1999.2.1

Provenance: [Durand-Ruel, 1872]. [W. Craibe Angus, Glasgow]. John Glas Sandeman, by 1878, still in 1886. Thomas Glenn Arthur, by 1888, to; James Arthur, by 1901. [Ian MacNicol, Glasgow]. ?Private collection, Scotland, by 1962. Mrs. Margaret (Leslie) Wilson by 1963, sold 30 July 1968, through Ian MacNicol Galleries, Glasgow, to; [Reid & Lefevre, Ltd., London, stock no. 141/68, as *Nature morte. Pommes, poires et primulas sur une table, Saint Pélagie*, sold 31 October 1968 to]; [Galerie Castiglione, sold 20 December 1968 to]; [Paul Rosenberg & Co., New York, stock no. 6336, as *Nature morte, pommes, poires et primulas sur une table*, sold 29 August 1969 to]; The Norton Simon Foundation, transferred 1999 to; Norton Simon Art Foundation.

Exhibitions: Glasgow, 1878, no. 135; Edinburgh, 1886, no. 1136; Glasgow, 1888, no. 746, as *Apples and Pears Piled on a White Cloth: in the Background a Pot with a White Pelargonium*; Glasgow, 1901, no. 1279; London, 1963, no. 7, ill.; Edinburgh, 1967, no. 18, p. 29; London, 1968, no. 10, color ill.; on loan, Washington, D.C., National Gallery of Art, 11 September–28 December 1969; on loan, Los Angeles, County Museum of Art, 29 December 1969–15 November 1971; on loan, Toledo, Museum of Art, 16 November 1971–6 March 1973; San Francisco, 1973, no. 25, ill.; on loan, Toronto, Art Gallery of Ontario, 10 February–28 August 1981.

References: MacColl, 1901, ill. opp. p. 146; Riat, 1906, p. 330; Reid, 1962, pp. 2–3, ill.; Crombie, 1968, pp. 379, 381, ill.; Rewald, 1973, p. 273; Toussaint, 1977, p. 189; Fernier, 1977, vol. 2, p. 131, no. 780, ill.; Faunce and Nochlin, 1988, p. 91; Fried, 1990, pp. 246–248, pl. 14; Faunce, 1993, pp. 126–127, pl. 40; Przyblyski, 1995, pp. 268–273, 278–281; Przyblyski, 1996, pp. 28–37, fig. 1.

Technical Notes: The support is a plain-weave, medium-weight canvas. It remains unlined and is tacked to its original stretcher. A small hole at the center of the top tacking edge may have been caused by previous framing hardware. A small tear in the large apple near the center has been well repaired. The thin white ground was commercially applied. A dark brown underpainting covers the ground, over which Courbet directly applied the remainder of the paint in vigorous brushwork. The white tablecloth was painted last, leaving small areas of dark brown exposed to serve as shadows and outlines. There is no impasto. The texture of brushwork is well preserved. It is not clear if chemical abrasion has occurred. The possibility of solvent-related thinning of the brown paint seems most likely at the upper left among the leaves of the primrose, where white particles have been exposed more than elsewhere in the dark brown areas. The painting was cleaned in 1979, but curatorial files contain no details of the treatment. Ultraviolet light reveals the fluorescence of natural resin varnish intermittently and unevenly over the surface, interspersed with areas where it has been completely removed. Small areas of retouching are in the background: beneath a primrose leaf at the left side, lightly scattered in the floor of the background, the small tear in the apple, and a small bit in the apple at farthest left. The varied and discontinuous surface coatings produce an unpleasant effect. The most recent varnish is a nonsaturating, rather thick material applied above the partial remains of an older varnish. (RW)

This is among the masterpieces of Courbet's oeuvre. If one were to make a list of the most perfectly realized five among his many surviving still-life paintings, this would rank near the top, and it has been admired continuously since the nineteenth century. Yet the painting is associated with one of the bleakest moments in the painter's life, when he was incarcerated in the Ste.-Pélagie prison for his role in the toppling of the Vendome Column during the Commune in 1871, the year the painting is dated. Indeed, Courbet boldly inscribed this painting—and more than a dozen others—with the name of the prison itself, trumpeting his own chastisement and exclaiming that his individuality, creativity, and talent could not be stifled by mere prison bars. In fact, this picture was probably painted, not in prison, but in the comfortable salon of the clinic run by a Dr. Duval at Neuilly, where the artist was sent at the end of 1871, when his health began to fail.

Courbet's sister Zoë described the present painting in a letter of 1872 to the artist's longtime friend Alfred Bruyas. She said it was

> a large painting, a dozen pears, apples, etc., heaped pleasingly on a table, then a fireplace in the back of the room, with [Courbet's] dressing gown on an armchair. The whole composition is delightful. Gustave is enchanted with it. He says that he has never achieved such gracious effects of color. He made it with love and is enchanted by his success. He would like to show it to you.[1]

Zoë Courbet's account is accurate, as far as it goes, and she may be forgiven for having overlooked in a letter to the artist's most important patron some disturbing elements in the painting.

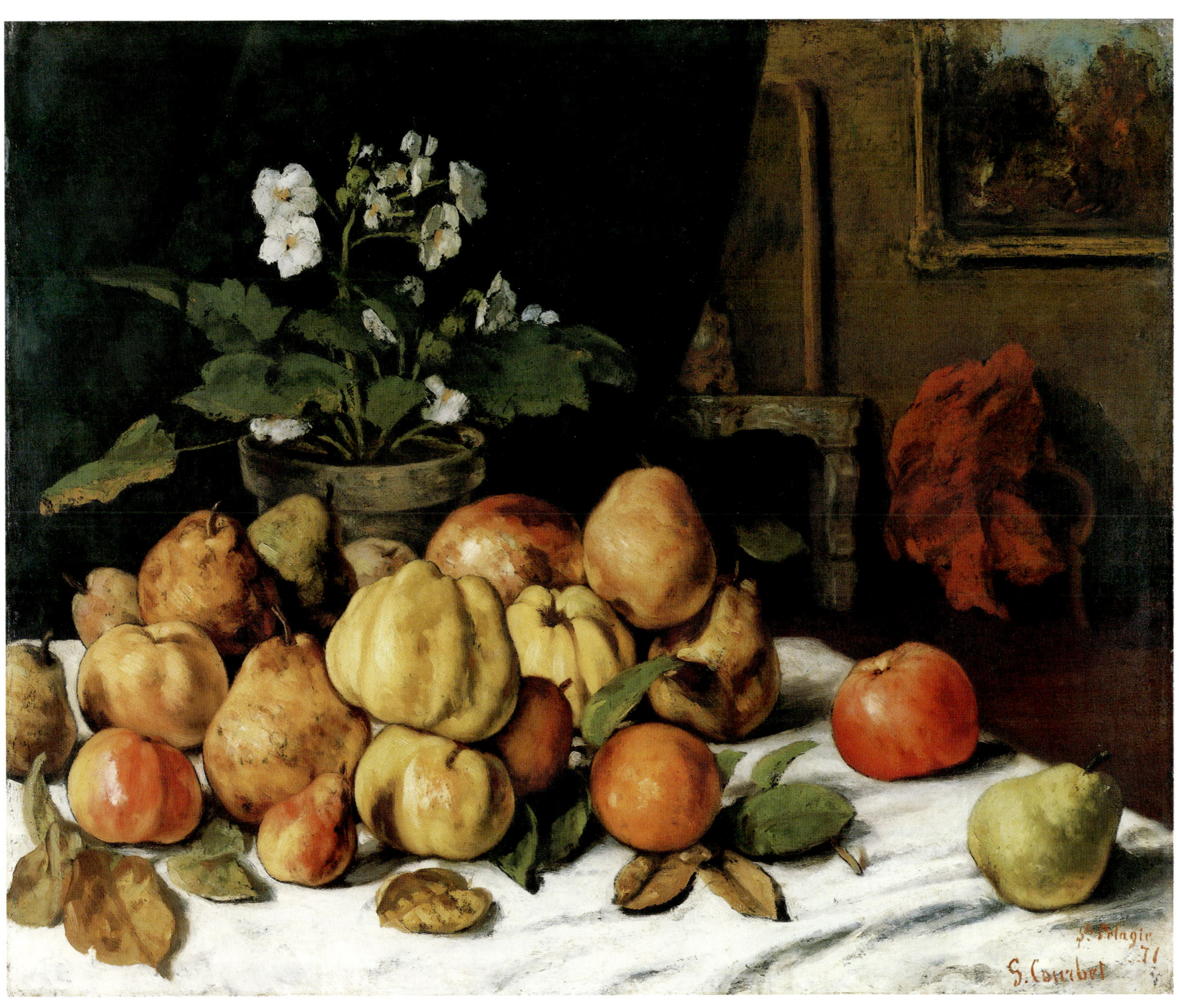
Ste Pélagie
71
G. Courbet

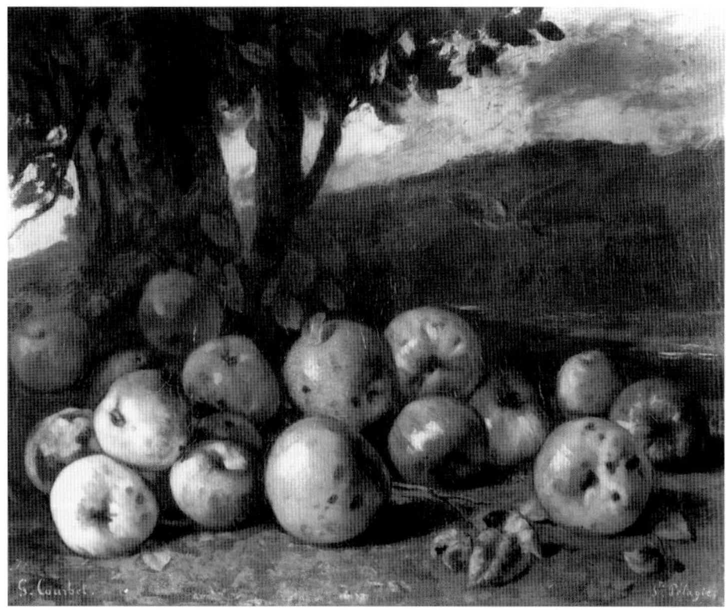

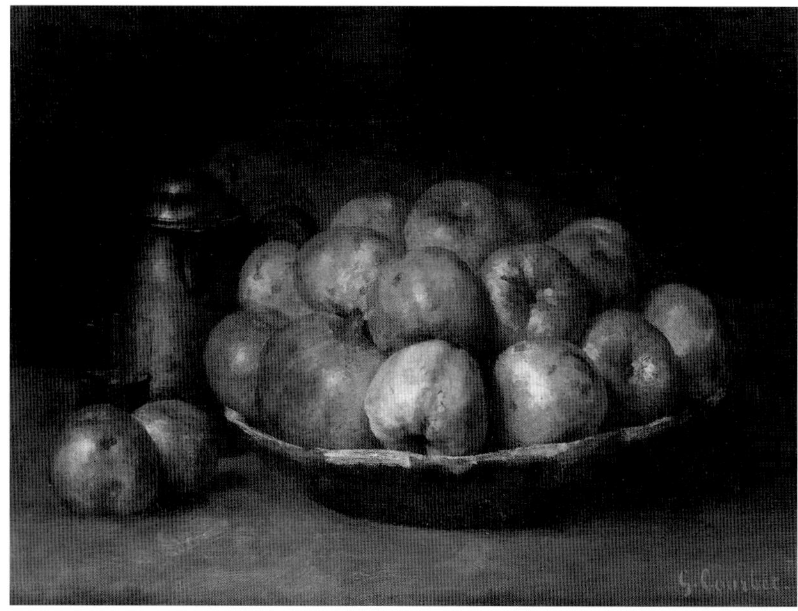

Fig. 46a (*above left*) Gustave Courbet, *Still Life with Apples*, 1872, oil on canvas, 23¼ × 28¾ in. (59 × 73 cm), Museum Mesdag, The Hague

Fig. 46b (*above right*) Gustave Courbet, *Still Life with Apples and a Pomegranate*, 1871–1872, oil on canvas, 17⁹⁄₁₆ × 24 in. (44.5 × 61 cm), National Gallery, London

Courbet's still-life motif consists of a pile of ten pears, eight apples (or possibly seven plus a large pomegranate), and one orange in front of a potted primrose on a casually draped white cloth placed atop a table. These constitute an accidental ensemble more than a formal arrangement; the folds in the cloth indicate that Courbet may even have gathered up all the fruit in a heap and put it on the table at once, allowing the red, yellow, and orange globes to fall and spread in a pattern determined more by chance than by conscious intention. The art historian Michael Fried, in one of the few sustained analyses of the painting in the considerable Courbet literature, treats the fruits as if they are an imbedded representation of the naked body of a woman.[2] His assumption that the casual and horizontally determined positioning of the fruit forces us to consider them collectively rather than individually, however, is not sustained by an actual examination of the painting. Instead, the almost inchoate nature of the arrangement forces us to look at each individual fruit—and Courbet contrasts them by their axes and by the groupings and separations. The effect is similar to that seen in *Still Life with Apples* (fig. 46a) and may be distinguished from the more classical, compact, and Chardinesque *Still Life with Apples and a Pomegranate* (fig. 46b).

The fruits themselves are fascinatingly diverse: there are two varieties of pears and two or three of apples. While most of these fruits are native to the temperate north of France (Normandy, Brittany, and the Île de France) with its rich, loamy soils and cold winters, the orange and pomegranate were cultivated in the warm, dry air of southern France, Spain, or northern Africa; these semitropical fruits were undoubtedly purchased from a luxury fruit seller in Paris. The orange leaves scattered among the fruits are both green and brown, indicating that while working on the painting, Courbet may have pulled some leaves off the oranges and eaten the fruit—the orphaned leaves then quickly turned brown. The blooming primroses are in an ordinary terracotta pot like those purchased from a commercial nursery. Courbet has not bothered to place the pot in another, more attractive container,[3] indicating both that he preferred the simple earthen color and unadorned form of the terracotta to other, more decorative, vessels and that he wished the spectator to recognize the hothouse origin of the plant. Thus the primrose, like the orange, pears, apples, and pomegranate, raises questions concerning the local or remote origins of the fruit and flowers, their planting, harvesting, transportation, sale, freshness, and decay. More than in the case of traditional still lifes possessing *vanitas* or other allegorical references, Courbet's work suggests history, contingency, vulnerability, and change. This significance is of course greatly increased by the circumstance of the painting's creation, and its inscription. There is something extremely poignant—and more than a little paradoxical—about a still life of flowers and fruit in a prison cell or asylum. It represents an infusion of color and vitality in places characterized by colorlessness and torpor; it suggests freedom and cultivation in a location where both are excluded as matters of law and discipline. The fruit and flowers in Courbet's chamber will wither and die no less certainly than its human inhabitant. Moreover, by placing his signature and Ste.-Pélagie inscription so prominently in the lower right, Courbet strongly associated himself—his politics and imprisonment—with the still-life elements.[4]

The foreground still life is juxtaposed to a background—partially hidden behind the folds of a very dark greenish blue curtain—that represents a bourgeois drawing room. The viewer sees a marble mantelpiece with a mirror and a gilded clock on top of it. Next to this is a carved wooden chair on which Courbet placed a large, animated, and casually folded piece of reddish drapery—his dressing gown, according to Zoë—which may be considered a kind of artist surrogate. Above this is a landscape painting in a gilded frame resembling one by Courbet himself. Although a precise identification of this small landscape is impossible, it looks like several pictures of the artist's beloved, native Jura, including *Passage of Deer at Twilight* (c. 1870, Musée d'Orsay, Paris), *The Covered Stream* (see fig. 44b), and *Solitude* (1866, Musée Fabre, Montpellier). Courbet's many landscapes of this region, as we have seen, including the *Stream of the Puits-Noir* (cat. 44), emphasize geographic specificity, independence, enclosure, and refuge. Thus the inclusion of a Jura landscape in *Apples, Pears, and Primroses on a Table*, like the depiction of a landscape painting-in-a-painting in his renowned *The Painter's Studio* (1855, Musée d'Orsay, Paris) makes an appeal to what the artist called "the rule of freedom," and this at the very moment when his own liberty was most clearly denied.

Of the fifteen still lifes inscribed with the words *Ste. Pélagie*, this is the largest and most important. Yet, it has not once been exhibited in France and has thus been alienated from Courbet's career as represented in the canonical collection of his paintings at the Musée d'Orsay in Paris. The historian of modern French art will inevitably see numerous rhymes between *Apples, Pears, and Primroses on a Table* and subsequent still lifes by Paul Cézanne, Paul Gauguin, Georges Braque, Henri Matisse, and other modern artists, but there is in fact little likelihood of any direct influence. Though it has been extensively published, the painting was not shown at any of the important Courbet exhibitions from the memorial event of 1882 to the present. The painting was first acquired in 1872 by the great Parisian dealer Paul Durand-Ruel after its exhibition in his galleries. Soon after that, the picture entered the collection of the prominent Scottish dealer of modern French and Netherlandish art, Craibe Angus in Glasgow; a dozen years later it was sold to T. G. Arthur and remained in Scotland for the next ninety years, until its appearance on the London art market in 1963. The painting's entire early provenance thus illustrates the ties between art dealers in France, Great Britain, and the Netherlands, and the commercial significance of modern art in Paris, Glasgow, Amsterdam, and London. This history of ownership also reveals some of the indirect ways that works by artists from one generation may be glimpsed by artists from the next. Craibe Angus's purchase of the still life was probably facilitated by his father-in-law, H. J. Jan van Wisselingh, a Dutch dealer in Amsterdam and an early friend and supporter of the artist.[5] Van Wisselingh's son, Elbert Jan, ran a branch of the firm in Paris, frequently transferring paintings by Hague School artists to Goupil and Co. (later the firm of Boussod and Valadon). The latter gallery, in turn, employed Vincent van Gogh in its London branch in 1873 and at its Paris salesroom the following year. By this time, Gustave Courbet had left France to live in exile in Switzerland, and *Apples, Pears, and Primroses on a Table* was transferred to Scotland. But other pictures by the great Realist remained behind and were an undoubted inspiration to van Gogh and Henri de Toulouse-Lautrec.

1 Pierre Borel, *Le Roman de Gustave Courbet*, Paris, 1922, pp. 128–129; cited in Przyblyski, 1996, pp. 28–37.

2 Fried, 1990, pp. 246–248.

3 See, for example, Fernier, 1977, vol. 1, nos. 300, 302, 362, and 364–369.

4 The link was apparently clear to Courbet's contemporaries: a caricature by Faustin in May 1872 in the Parisian weekly *La Chronique illustrée*, depicts the related *Still Life with Apples*—rejected from the Salon of 1872—with an over-large signature and inscription. See Przyblyski, 1996, p. 30.

5 See Courbet's *Portrait of H. J. van Wisselingh*, 1846, in Fernier, 1977, vol. 1, no. 68.

47

Gustave Courbet
French, 1819–1877

Henri Rochefort
1874

Oil on canvas, 25½ × 21¼ in. (64.8 × 54 cm)
Signed lower left: "G. Courbet"
F.1972.18.1

Provenance: Brenet, in 1893. Gates, in 1900. [Durand-Ruel, Paris, sold 20 January 1906 to]; Weigand. Otto Gerstenberg (1848–1935), Berlin, by 1929, by inheritance to his daughter; Margarete Scharf, by descent in; Gerstenberg family [according to Peter Nathan], sold by 1962 to; [Drs. Fritz and Peter Nathan, Zurich, sold 7 March 1964 to]; [Paul Rosenberg & Co., New York, stock no. 6092–2160, sold 31 May 1972 to]; The Norton Simon Foundation.

Exhibitions: Paris, 1893, no. 974; Bern, 1962, no. 82; on loan, Phoenix, Art Museum, 5 June 1972–9 February 1973; San Francisco, 1973, no. 26, ill.

References: Lemonnier, 1888, p. 67; Riat, 1906, p. 283; Meier-Graefe, 1912a, p. 119, ill.; Meier-Graefe, 1921, pl. 114; Léger, 1929, pp. 195, 202; Zurich, 1935, under no. 130; Léger, 1948, p. 165; Courthion, 1948, vol. 1, p. 303; Fernier, 1977, vol. 2, no. 1022, p. 225, ill.

Technical Notes: The support is a plain-weave canvas of medium weight with the original tacking edges remaining. The painting has been glue-lined. Some weave transference is discernible, although it is not pronounced. There are two small bulges at the bottom of the left edge, where the painting is delaminating from the lining. This condition was first noted in a condition summary in 1973. The tacking edges are weak at the turnover and have split intermittently, presumably during restretching. The canvases are tacked to what appears to be the original keyed stretcher. The smooth, thin ground is beige. There is a reddish brown imprimatura over the entire picture surface, seen most clearly at the juncture of the coat collar, small necktie, goatee, and the flesh tones of the neck. The white shirtfront was rapidly applied over the imprimatura, apparently with a palette knife. The quickly painted black coat leaves exposed a considerable amount of the imprimatura. The paint was applied with very little brush marking. The modeling of the face is extremely smooth; delicate and subtle transitions of color are finely handled. The black coat and the white shirt were directly and rapidly applied in a thin layer. Earlier restoration appears to have included cleaning of the face and the shirt. As revealed by ultraviolet examination, the thinly painted black coat may never have been cleaned; the same goes for the hair and the darkest areas of the face. It is not clear if the area of the black coat at the proper left neck/shoulder area was very thinly painted or has been slightly abraded. The present varnish is slightly discolored with an orange-peel texture over the entire surface. Ultraviolet light reveals an unusual color in discontinuous blotches, which might indicate an additive of some sort to one of the surface coatings. (RW)

Henri Rochefort (1831–1913) was a celebrated French journalist, editor, and political chameleon. In 1863 he became editor of *Le Figaro* and five years later founded the satirical and bitterly anti-Bonapartist *La Lanterne.* During these years, he was continually threatened and harassed by government agents, arrested, released, fined, forced into duels, and sent into exile. He returned to France in 1869, founded another journal, *La Marseillaise,* and was promptly elected to the national legislature, where he gloried in his skill, as one early biographer put it, "not as an orator but an interrupter."[1] Soon he was once again imprisoned for calumnies directed against Emperor Louis Napoleon, but his freedom and political reputation were restored during the Franco-Prussian War. In 1871, after France's defeat, Rochefort supported the Commune and put all his journalistic weight behind the fragile new regime. He survived the brutal reprisals that followed the defeat of the Commune but, like his friend Courbet, was condemned to imprisonment. In 1873 Rochefort was transported to the French penal colony at New Caledonia in the Pacific, but he had one more trick up his sleeve. During the night of 19 March 1874 he managed to escape in a small boat with five other convicts, making his way first to Australia, then to the United States, England, and Switzerland. In 1880, after the amnesty of Communards, he returned to Paris, resumed his career as a journalist—he founded *L'Intransigeant*—and regained his notoriety, first as the ardent supporter of the putschist General Boulanger and later as a vicious anti-Semite. Rochefort's passage from radical Republican to protofascist was far from unique in the late nineteenth century, but no one was more public, provocative, and, in the end, pestilential.

Rochefort's biographers universally describe him as charming, modest, and droll in person, but fierce in the public sphere. Speaking in the legislature or writing on the front pages of *L'Intransigeant,* he was, in the American vernacular, a colossal bigmouth, and he knew it. It is thus easy to imagine that Rochefort's greatest aphorism—and his one true gift to posterity—was partly directed at himself: "France has thirty-six million subjects, not counting subjects for complaint." The present portrait conveys something of this great ego and volubility. Though the picture is generally rather gloomy, there are bright highlights on Rochefort's large forehead,

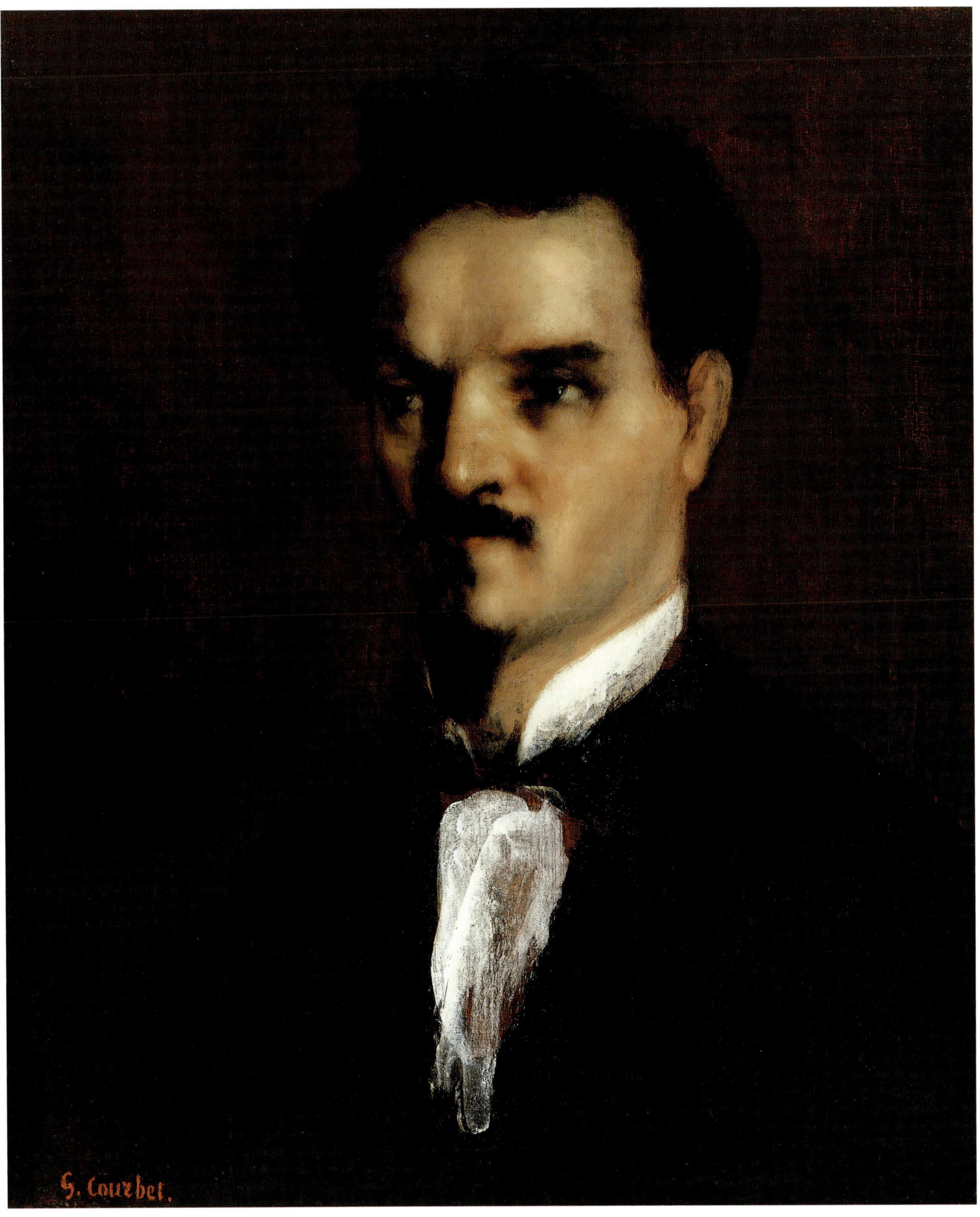

47

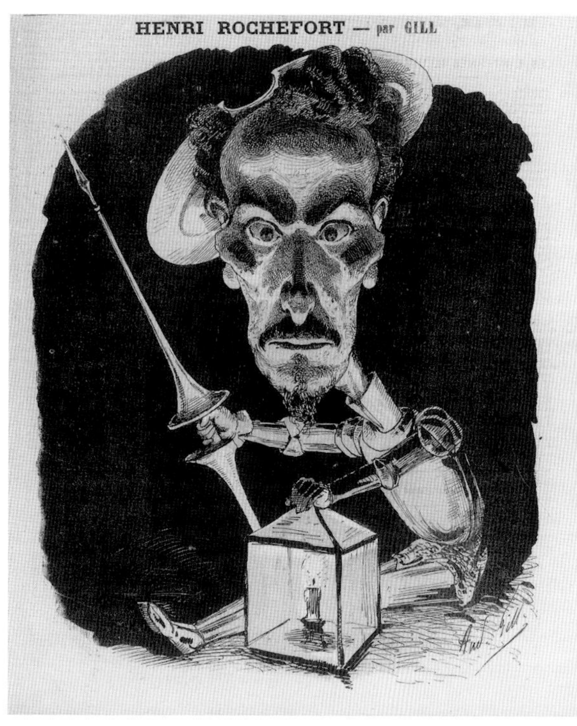

Fig. 47a André Gill, *Caricature of Rochefort*, in *L'Éclipse*, 7 June 1868

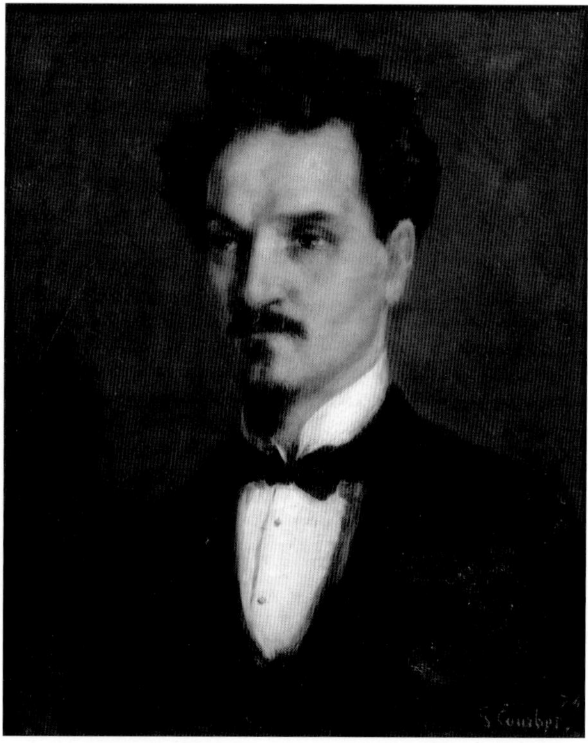

Fig. 47b Gustave Courbet, *Henri Rochefort*, oil on canvas, 25⅝ × 21¼ in. (65 × 54 cm), Châteaux de Versailles et de Trianon; photo: Arnaudet; H. Lewandowski. Réunion des Musées Nationaux / Art Resource, NY

tip of nose, cheeks, and chin. The entire head is shaped like a letter V, an effect reiterated by the identical shape of goatee and cravat. The result of this chiaroscuro and this repetition is a powerful sense of relief, and an emphasis on the swelled forehead and angular jaw. These were the very elements of Rochefort's physiognomy that contemporary caricaturists most often focused on, as is apparent in the charged portrait by André Gill in *L'Éclipse* (fig. 47a), depicting the journalist as a gaunt Don Quixote wielding his lance and *lanterne*. Courbet himself described Rochefort as "an animal who possesses only one beautiful thing: that's his jaws. He has the teeth of a horse!"[2] The present painting is not among Courbet's most beautiful or resolved portraits—it is lugubrious and without color—but by slightly exaggerating the triangularity of the head and face, it effectively conveys something of the egoistic character of the sitter.

Henri Rochefort was painted during a visit of the sitter to the artist at La Tour-de-Peilz in Switzerland in 1874. Courbet made a second nearly identical portrait of his fellow Communard, giving one to Rochefort and keeping the other for himself. Rochefort strongly disliked the portrait and gave it, two years later, to his friend Paul Pia. That work, perhaps brighter and a bit more angular than the Simon painting, was given by Pia's daughter in 1914 to the Musée national de Versailles (fig. 47b). The present painting likely remained with the artist until his death in 1877 and subsequently passed through the hands of a number of French dealers and collectors, including Durand-Ruel. In 1929 it was acquired by Otto Gerstenberg (1848–1935), a wealthy Berlin insurance executive who accumulated an extraordinary collection of old master and modern paintings and prints. In addition to amassing the most complete collection of graphic works by Henri de Toulouse-Lautrec ever assembled, he bought Degas's great painting *Place de la Concorde* (c. 1877, State Hermitage Museum, St. Petersburg). The latter painting, along with much of the Gerstenberg collection, was seized by the Nazis sometime just before or during World War II. Most of the artworks assembled by this great Jewish collector—including Courbet's portrait of the anti-Semite Rochefort—survived the war.

1 Lermina, 1884, p. 208.

2 Lemonnier, 1888, p. 67.

48

Johan Barthold Jongkind
Dutch, 1819–1891

View of Harfleur
1852

Oil on canvas, 17 × 23½ in. (43.2 × 59.5 cm)
Signed and dated lower right: "Jongkind 1852"
F.1969.8.2

Provenance: [Adolphe Beugniet & Bonjean, Paris]. [Boussod-Valadon, Paris]. [Georges Petit, Paris]. [Galerie Schmit, Paris, sold 1969 to]; The Norton Simon Foundation.

Exhibition: San Francisco, 1974, no. 17, ill.

References: Hefting, 1975, no. 90; A. Stein, 2003, p. 1852, fig. 97; Auffret, 2004, p. 314, ill.

Technical Notes: The plain-weave canvas has been lined with the original edges cut off; slightly cusped threads are visible at the top edge only. There is a small repaired hole to the left of the chimney in the upper right quadrant; no other damages to the support are evident. The stretcher, presumably the original, has a Parisian colorman's stamp on the crossbar. The cream-colored ground almost completely masks the canvas weave, providing a smooth painting surface, which was toned with beige paint. Microscopic examination revealed no preparatory drawing. Paint was applied wet into wet, and often wet over dry. Jongkind adjusted certain parts of the composition by painting over them, as seen in raking light, particularly in the lower right quadrant between the boat and the standing man. Lining has smoothed the brush marking slightly. The lower, dark portion of the painting has both deep mechanical cracks and contraction cracks, which reveal lighter colors below. It appears that there has been no chemical abrasion; rubbed areas are related to the artist's technique. Retouching is minimal, including the small hole at the upper right. The varnish is evenly glossy and clear. (RW)

Johan Barthold Jongkind's superb small townscape represents the Norman port city of Harfleur, east of Le Havre, at the mouth of the Lezarde River. It is among numerous French landscapes and townscapes painted in the first years of the 1850s by the great landscape painter. The Dutch artist had come to France in 1846 as a fully formed painter in his early thirties to study with the then famous French painter of Norman seascapes and landscapes Eugène Isabey. While there, he met Isidore Pils and Thomas Couture and began a lifelong career as a Franco-Dutch painter. Thus, it was Jongkind who brought to French landscape practice lessons learned from his own Dutch traditions, injecting a sense of history into a national landscape that had become bogged down in its Italianate and classical traditions.

View of Harfleur is one of the earliest French works by Jongkind in an American public collection. Jongkind studied the humble town port with both respect and determination. He represented a busy scene, even though there is not a great deal of human activity. Instead, the activity is all that of Jongkind himself, who marshaled the strongly conflicting horizontals, verticals, and diagonals and the jumble of architecture in the middle ground with the two boats in the foreground, sitting on the tidal banks of the river and waiting for high tide to be released from their muddy prison. A male figure in gray with a red-brown cap works on the larger of the two boats, overseen by a man at right, on the quay, with hands on his hips. At left, a woman and child stand, looking out toward the spectator.

The picture is composed with heavy masses in the right foreground, balanced by lower, slightly more distant forms at left, and a regular rhythm of chimneys, spire, and pediments. The extreme foreground seems to open up beneath our feet, especially at left, where the woman and child stand, recalling the harbor scenes of J. M. W. Turner. Jongkind animated the scene by representing it under the shifting light of a cloud-filled windy day. Although the figures appear in shirtsleeves, the smoke from the chimneys in the middle ground suggests briskness in the air. Jongkind employed a subdued palette of greens, grays, and browns, with highlights in white, light gray, and distinct points of color—the *tricouleur* red, blue, white as well as pink and sienna. There exists a watercolor of the subject (fig. 48a), published by François Auffret, the biographer of the artist and president of the Friends of Jongkind.[1]

Jongkind's desire to master humble Norman landscapes surely came both from his own familiarity with similar scenes in his native Holland and from the contemporary vogue for Norman views given impetus by the *Voyages pittoresques*, luxuriously illustrated travel guides with lithographic illustrations by artists such as Jongkind's teacher, Isabey. With the advent of the railroad in midcentury, French, Belgian, and Dutch city tourists were able to travel to the seacoast for summer holidays and weekend vacations. The bracing sea air and traditional life of the fishing villages of the north coast of France were considered healthful antidotes to the crowded conditions and pollution of modern urban life. For this reason, urban vacationers formed a ready market for such small scenes of Norman villages as this one. To create desire for these small pictures, Isabey, Jongkind, and their colleagues painted larger landscapes for

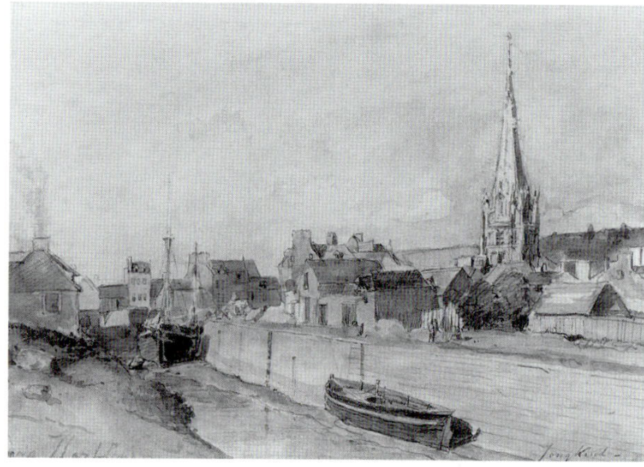

Fig. 48a Johan Barthold Jongkind, *View of the Lezarde*, 1850, watercolor on paper, $9 \times 12\frac{5}{8}$ in. (23×32 cm), private collection, Paris

exhibition at the annual Salon, and Jongkind sent to the Salon of 1851 a particularly imposing and successful view of Harfleur, now in the Musée de Picardie, Amiens (fig. 48b). Interestingly, it includes several smokestacks for the tanneries and fish-packing plants that were modern components of this fishing community. However, in his smaller paintings made for the private market, like the present painting and an identically sized painting of the same year representing the port of Harfleur at sunset, all such contemporary elements were eliminated, allowing the collectors from Paris, Lille, Amsterdam, or Brussels to imagine a world unspoiled by industrialization.

It is salutary to contrast the representations of Norman fishing villages by Jongkind with those of both his teacher, Isabey, and his followers among the Impressionists. Isabey represented the drama and difficulty of the life of the fishermen. His seas pound against the shore, his fishing boats lurch in treacherous waters, his wives and children stand in full gales blowing from the threatening sea. By contrast, Jongkind stressed the continuities of human life in this arduous industry, preferring a harmonious and picturesque world to the Romantic and dramatic one of his teacher. Likewise, his Norman views can be starkly contrasted with those painted by Eugène Boudin, Claude Monet, and Édouard Manet a decade or more later. For these latter artists, the Norman world was one of hotels, restaurants, country houses, and beach parties. The fishermen and their families who had survived there for centuries had finally been displaced.

1 Auffret, 2004, p. 315.

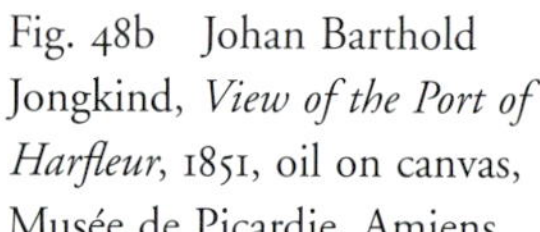

Fig. 48b Johan Barthold Jongkind, *View of the Port of Harfleur*, 1851, oil on canvas, Musée de Picardie, Amiens

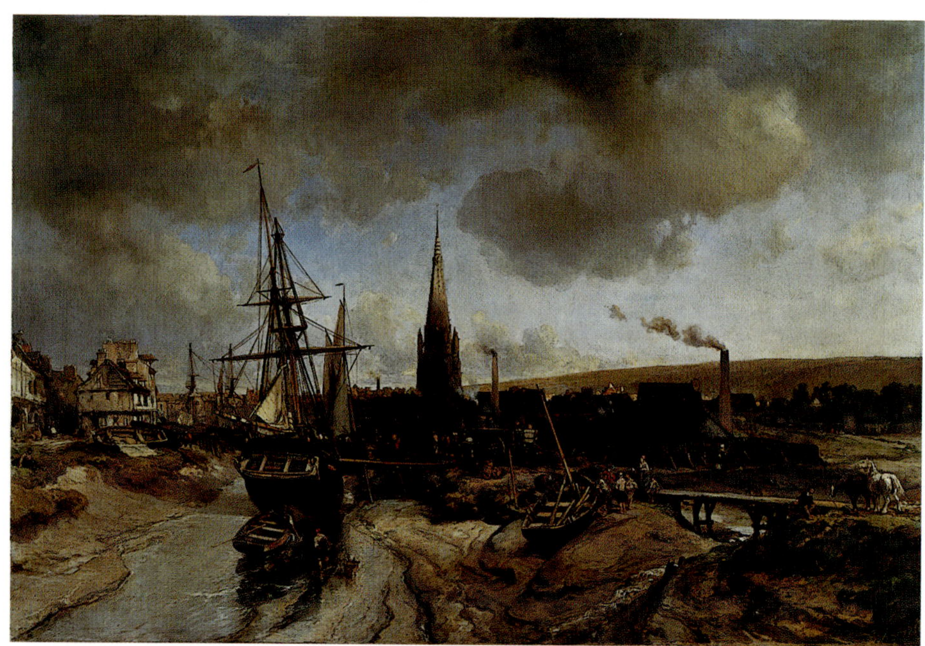

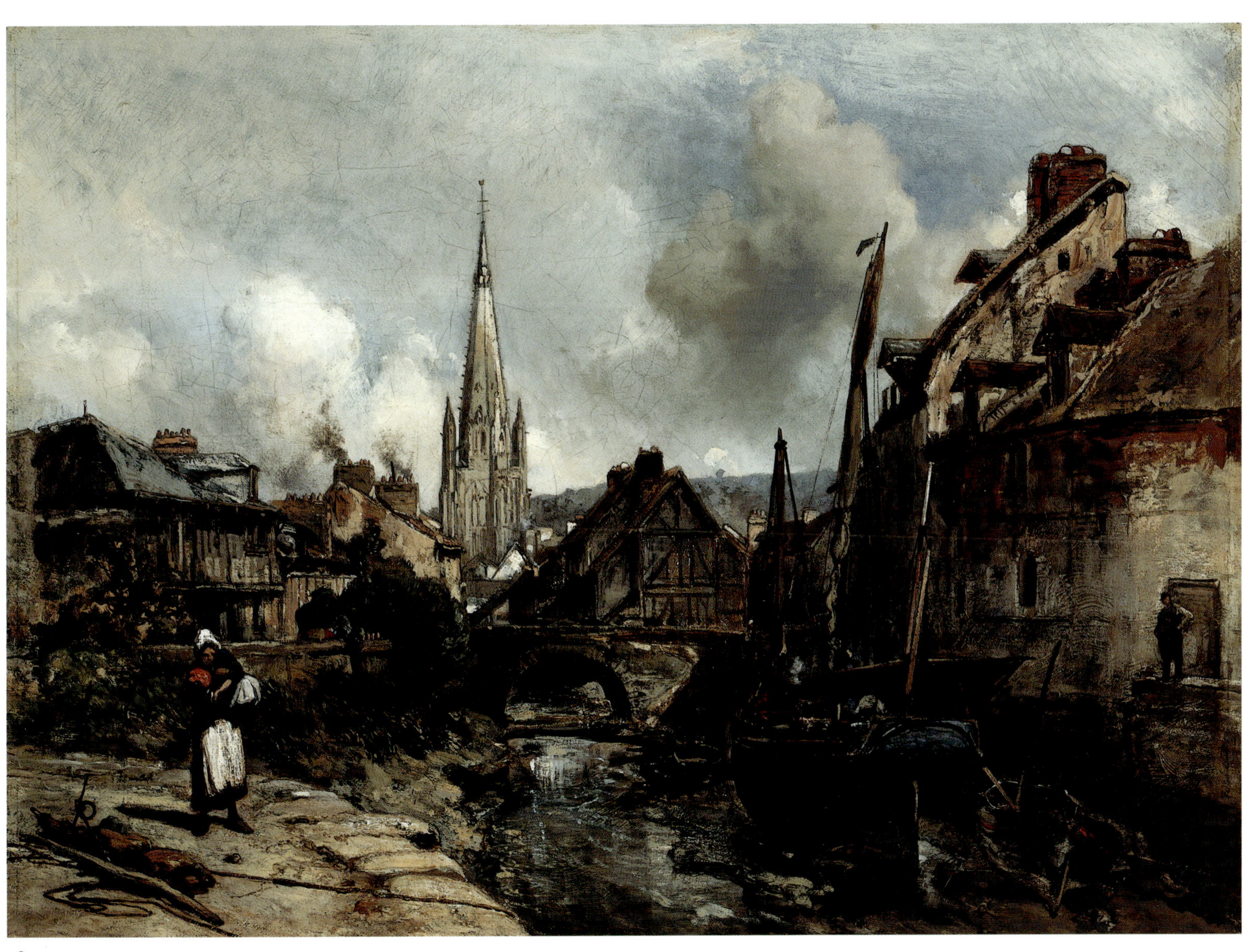

48

49

Johan Barthold Jongkind
Dutch, 1819–1891

The Church of St.-Médard and the Rue Mouffetard
1871

Oil on canvas, 17 × 22$\frac{1}{16}$ in. (43.2 × 56 cm)
Signed, dated, and inscribed lower right: "Jongkind 1871, Paris"
Inscribed verso on the stretcher upper right: "a Mons. Simon l'Eglise S. Medard au 1868 en Avril"; and lower left: "a droit rue des Patriarches au milieu Rue Daubenton"
M.1968.7

Provenance: Théophile Bascle, Paris (sale, Paris, Hôtel Drouot, 12–14 April 1883, no. 116, as *Vue de l'église de Saint-Médard, à Paris*). René Lucas by 1899, consigned, in partnership with Galerie Jacques Dubourg, Paris, to; [Arthur Tooth & Sons, London, sold March 1937 to]; R. A. Peto, London, and Bombridge, Isle of Wight, still in 1964. Private Collection [?Saint Albin or Sabin], Paris. [Arthur Tooth & Sons, London, by 1967]; [Drs. Fritz and Peter Nathan, Zurich, sold 1968 to]; Norton Simon Art Foundation.

Exhibitions: Paris, 1899b, no. 103, as *Paris; L'église Saint-Médard*; London, 1937a, no. 41; London, 1949, no. 16; London, 1967a, no. 4, ill.; Princeton, 1972, no. 34, ill.; San Francisco, 1974, no. 18, ill.

References: de Goncourt, 1885, in Hefting, p. 368; Hefting, 1975, no. 557, p. 229, color ill.; A. Stein, 2003, p. 1871, fig. 644.

Technical Notes: The painting is in its original state, apparently having never been removed from this stretcher. The reverse of the commercially primed canvas carries a Parisian colorman's stamp. The original edges remain. The canvas is desiccated and somewhat weak, and it is beginning to tear away from the tacks on the left side. A painted inscription in French and the artist's signature are on the back of the stretcher. The corners of the stretcher have opened slightly. The thin, cream-colored priming has probably darkened with age and is now light tan. The canvas texture remains visible throughout most of the painting. The scene was rather thinly painted, although the buildings were rendered with thicker, more opaque paint. The sky was blocked out with translucent washes of liquid paint, and then strengthened with scumbled white at the right. The center of the sky is made with thickly applied, opaque white paint. Painted after the sky, the town and figures were crisply rendered with a lively palette. Their edges were sometimes modified by additional brushstrokes of foreground paint. Paint was applied in dabs and short, quick brushwork. The light portrayed is that of a bright day with no shadows. Several minor damages to the paint layer have occurred: a small hole at the top right, a small hole at the bottom left corner, a small hole at the upper left, a short diagonal scrape at the top edge, and several small losses of paint and ground at the right end of the top edge. These have all been retouched. Additionally, retouching in the sky is in rather large areas at center left and two smaller areas near the top center. The brittle varnish saturates poorly; it is moderately yellowed. (RW)

By the 1860s Jongkind came to be closely involved with the development of a kind of painting we now call Impressionism. Rather than base his studio landscape paintings on watercolors and drawings done outside and create an annual immense canvas for the Salon, he took smaller canvases directly out of doors and rendered his sensations of a place in a single day. Indeed, many of his paintings of that decade bear on their surface a date that includes the day and month as well as the customary year. This gives Jongkind's canvases a sense of immediacy that is apparent both from their freely brushed surfaces and from the fact that they are so precisely dated. We are encouraged to think of the artist not as someone who works in the privacy and limited light of his urban studio but as a man who lives and paints outdoors in the same metropolitan world.

The second painting by Jongkind in the Norton Simon Museum, while not dated to the day, carries the year 1871 on its surface and the word *Paris* in addition to the artist's signature. The coincidence of this date and place makes it clear that Jongkind was referring to the most unsettled year in the recent history of the French capital—the year in which radical citizens of Paris took their city from a conservative government, just put into place after the Franco-Prussian War, and reasserted the principles of individual liberty and civil rights proclaimed and fought for during the French Revolution and subsequent revolutions in 1830 and 1848. The tumultuous events of 1871 as they related to scores of paintings have been amply studied by historians and art historians. Few artists played a more powerful role in these events than the Dutch painter Jongkind. A man of the left, Jongkind was famous for living a life of real simplicity, associating himself with workers and *petits commerçants* rather than with the *haute bourgeoisie* who were the most important purchasers of art. For that reason, he preferred to make small paintings, to sell them through modest dealers for reasonable prices, and to give many of them away to his friends, sometimes in exchange for favors such as lodging or food. Such gifts are not infrequently inscribed to particular men and women whose names we know but whose identities and professions are lost to us. This small painting is one such gift: to a M. Simon, whose name is recorded as the recipient of the painting on the back of

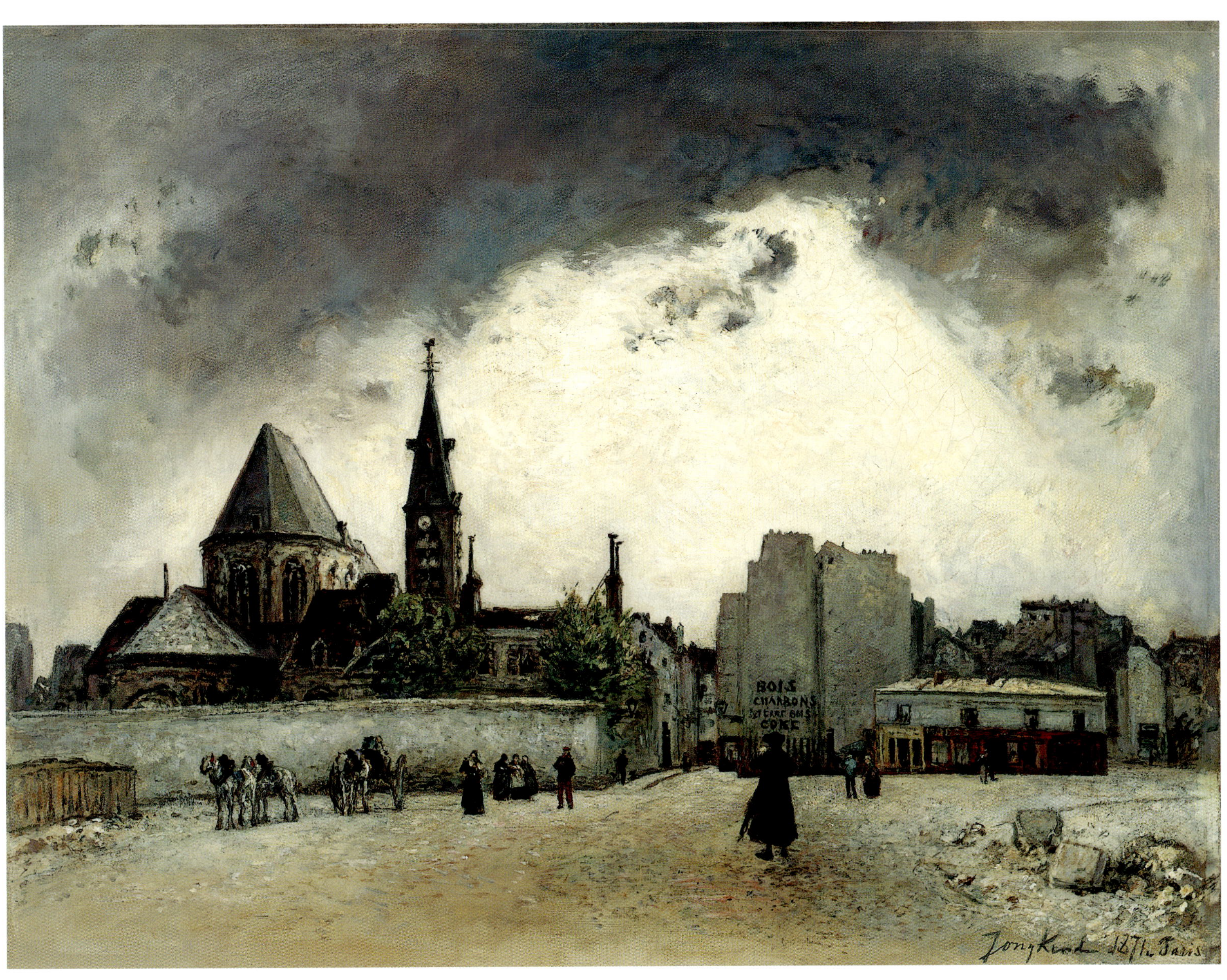

49

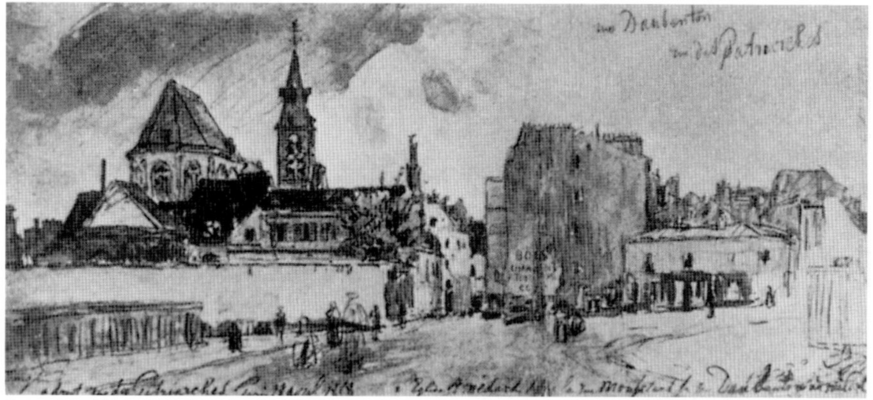

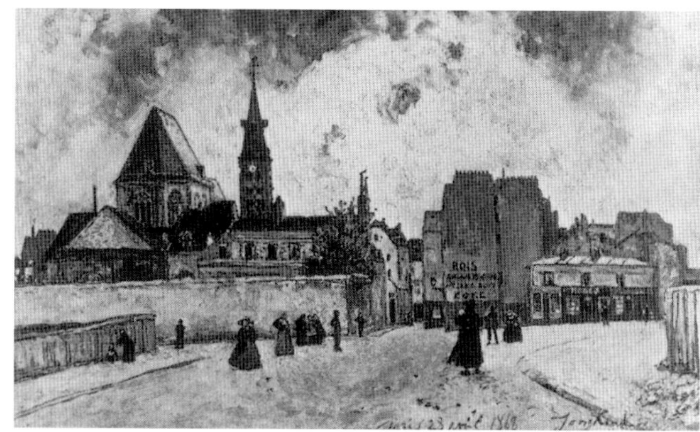

Fig. 49a (*above left*) Johan Barthold Jongkind, *The Church of St. Medard and the Rue Mouffetard*, 1868, watercolor on paper, location unknown; photo: Hefting, 1975, no. 473

Fig. 49b (*above right*) Johan Barthold Jongkind, *The Church of St.-Médard and the Rue Mouffetard*, 1868, oil on canvas, location unknown; photo: Hefting, 1975, no. 471

the canvas and who, due to the sheer commonness of his surname and the absence of a first initial or name, has no known existence outside that inscription.

The modest picture for M. Simon is a panoramic view of the small plaza outside the Parisian Church of St.-Médard in the working-class neighborhood bordering the rue Mouffetard. Jongkind includes debris, possibly from a destroyed barricade of the Paris Commune, in the lower right near his signature, date, and place. The foreground is otherwise empty, except for the figure of a Catholic cleric with his back to the spectator. This slightly comic figure faces a sign, painted on the wall of a building in the middle ground, which reads BOIS/CHARBONS/TERRE BOIS/COKE (Wood/coal/briquettes/coke). Another sign on a shopfront at right says MODES (fashion). There is an irony to this juxtaposition of signs since in a working-class district like this, heating in winter is important and fashion something that one aspires to rather than possesses. Light breaks through the clouds, suffusing this humble urban scene with color, particularly in the foreground with little touches of red, pink, and light blue-gray. A team of work horses without a wagon at foreground left and a horse hitched to a wagon behind them occupy a prominent place; there are no carriages, no large wagons, no elegant horses and riders such as those that would ride down one of the new *grands boulevards* of Paris. To the left stands a woman with long blue dress and white bib, and to her left three more women, equally sketchily painted, and then a soldier, slightly more forward in space—and thus clearly separated from the three ladies—and then, farther back in space, walking away from the viewer, up the rue Mouffetard, is a one-legged man, clearly a wounded man or *motile de la guerre* of the Franco-Prussian War or even the more recent Commune. To the right of the Catholic cleric, in the middle ground, are two more figures in working-class garb, and farther to the right, away from the spectator, are two more figures, one of whom has red pants and is probably a soldier. No fashionable women, no well-dressed men, no government officials in uniform, no doctors or professionals can be found in this cityscape of the people.

The painting is dated on the back 1868, with an inscription that reads (at the top of the stretcher), "a Mons. Simon l'Eglise S. Medard au 1868 en Avril," and at the bottom of the stretcher, "a droit rue des Patriarches au milieu Rue Daubenton." Thus, although we are placed in the city with the precision of a guidebook, the date on the back conflicts with that on the front. This raises a series of fascinating questions, none of which can be conclusively resolved. It may be that in 1871 Jongkind simply wanted to register on the back of the canvas the moment when he had had his first actual impression of the motif, and that the present canvas was copied from—or based on—an earlier one. He may also have wanted to indicate that the original impression was 1868, but that he has now, in 1871, returned to the motif and made an updated version of it. The date on the painting itself is clearly an homage to the events of that fateful year, bringing history into the mundane realities of working class life in Paris. A fence at right that had been included in watercolors dated to 1868 (figs. 49a and 49b)—each dated on the front, at bottom, to 28 April 1868—is here absent, replaced by debris, the product either of the demolition of a building on the site or, more tantalizingly, of a barricade. Jongkind painted the subject again in 1890, just a year before his death,[1] calling it then *Souvenir de l'église Saint Médard et la rue Mouffetard*, signifying that the late painting represented a freely painted "memory" of the place rather than an actual return to the working-class neighborhood where the painter had spent much time in the 1860s.

Throughout the 1860s Jongkind had a particular interest in street scenes in Paris that showed the effects of modernization—Haussmannization, as some of his contemporaries called it, placing the blame for this transformation on the policies of Napoleon III's *préfet de la Seine*, Baron Haussmann. In the same year that he first essayed this scene, 1868, Jongkind painted the *Demolition of the Rue des Francs-Bourgeois-St.-Marcel*, signing and dating the canvas to the very day of execution, 19 April 1868, just nine days before the first versions of the St.-Médard pictures. The construction fences in all the canvases are signs of modernization and change, of the rebuilding of Paris under the Second Empire.

If only we knew the identity of M. Simon. Was he wounded in the war, a member of the Commune, or simply a left-wing friend? What did he do for Jongkind so that he was given this particular painting? The detailed inscription of the place on the verso of the canvas suggests either that M. Simon was not strictly familiar with the place—that he needed to be told—or, more tantalizingly, that he was involved with an activity that occurred at that precise intersection of three small Parisian streets at a charged point in French history. The unremittingly snobbish French writers Edmond de Goncourt and Philippe Burty paid a visit to Jongkind years later, on 4 May 1882, and this encounter is recorded in Goncourt's journal. On that day, Jongkind showed them a series of paintings of the streets of Paris in the "Quartiers Mouffetard next to Saint-Médard," suggesting the importance of this series to the painter later in life. Goncourt seems to have adored the picturesque old painter, whom he described as "very great" and who seems to have pointed out to the wealthy duo that he spent no more than three thousand francs a year on his living expenses. There is little doubt that Burty and Goncourt spent more in a week than that, and, by stressing his frugality, Jongkind was making clear his sympathy with the working class in one of its most cherished Parisian districts. Goncourt tells us that the showing of works of art lasted "several hours" and that Jongkind "talked a good deal." One wonders what he said to these two wealthy gentlemen.

1 Hefting, 1975, no. 818.

50

Adolphe-Joseph-Thomas Monticelli
French, 1824–1886

Midsummer
1860–1870

Oil on panel, 15⅝ × 23½ in. (39.7 × 59.7 cm)
Signed lower right: "Monticelli"
F.1983.13

Provenance: [Knoedler & Co., New York, sold 18 August 1954 to]; [Paul Rosenberg & Co., New York, stock no. 5558, sold 23 February 1955 to]; The Phillips Collection, Washington, D.C., sold 10 April 1961 to; [Paul Rosenberg & Co., New York, stock no. 5969, sold 15 February 1980 to]; Norton Simon, gift 1983 to; The Norton Simon Foundation.

Exhibitions: Birmingham, 1973, no. 11; Pittsburgh, 1978, no. 19, colorpl. 5

Technical Notes: The painting appears stable. The support is a cradled hardwood panel with a horizontal grain. A rectangular wood insert at the top center may have repaired a defect in the panel; the edges of the insert have been inconspicuously retouched. Two cracks in the panel are closed and secure. Like the other two paintings by Monticelli in the collection, this one also has no ground layer. The artist left the wood exposed throughout the foreground and within the tree branches; especially in all the trees, the color of the wood is an important element in the painting's tonality. The opaque paint is applied in a very loose and spontaneous manner. The figures of the children, the goat, and the clouds are executed in relatively thick paint. However, the paint profile is curiously soft, and the varied dabs and blotches of color often lack crisp outlines. It is not clear if the surface texture has been altered by cleaning. Ultraviolet light suggests that the paint medium contained resin, which may have been a factor in the paint consistency. The sky was cleaned and revarnished in 1980. The four sides of the rectangular insert at top center were overpainted, and additional scattered retouching is located throughout the sky. A larger repair is located in the central part of the sky, which appears to cover a damaged area. (RW)

If American painting has its Albert Pinkham Ryder and Charles Blakelock to confuse and befuddle its most careful students, French art has Adolphe Monticelli. Each of these men was at once an eccentric outsider and a participant in the great vanguard drama of national painting. Each was fervently admired by artists now judged central in the history of modern art, and yet each rests in a kind of permanent artistic limbo. Blakelock and Ryder have their proponents today, but these scholarly advocates fight against long odds. So, too, the deck has been stacked against the American, French, and Dutch supporters of Monticelli.

The first problem is Monticelli's resolutely Italian name. Like that of Émile Zola, it has no obviously Gallic character, and since the history of art is organized according to national schools, Monticelli—a Frenchman with an Italian name—appears homeless. Indeed, were it not for the fervent admiration of another immigrant, Vincent van Gogh, we would know little today about Monticelli's career. For reasons that will become obvious when their paintings are compared, van Gogh was passionately interested in the paintings of Monticelli, in spite of the fact that the Provençal artist died in 1886, the year that van Gogh moved to Paris for his longest and last stay in the artistic capital of the world. The Norton Simon collections possess three works by the misunderstood Provençal painter. Surprisingly, they were acquired decades after other American museums purchased or were given their works by Monticelli.

Midsummer is probably the earliest of the three paintings, though there is no solid evidence to support the date (1871) previously ascribed to it. Like most of the paintings that constitute his oeuvre, *Midsummer* was not dated by Monticelli himself, and the most assiduous student of his work, Aaron Sheon, dated the painting to 1866–1868 in the most critically astute study of his work in print, an exhibition catalogue for a retrospective organized by the Carnegie Institute in Pittsburgh.[1] Even this date is difficult for an independent appraiser of the painter's style to accept, since there is little evidence on which to construct a solid chronology of Monticelli's art. In the two most important books on the artist—the lavish and fascinating study by André Alauzen and Pierre Ripert published in Paris in 1969 and Sheon's catalogue—the dating of works is largely unexplained, unconvincing, and, in many cases, visually illogical. The earnest student of Monticelli must enter the turbulent waters of dating and connoisseurship without an authoritative guide.

Midsummer has neither a nineteenth-century provenance nor exhibition history. It first appeared in the Phillips Collection in Washington, D.C. The Phillips sent the painting to Paul Rosenberg & Co. in exchange for another Monticelli, and Rosenberg sold the panel to Norton Simon in 1980, when the latter also purchased another Monticelli from Eugene Thaw. The painting has undeniable technical and iconographic affinities with the work of Monticelli's friend and mentor Narcisse-Virgile Diaz de la Peña. Monticelli seems to have met Diaz by 1856, probably through the intercession of their mutual friend, the Provençal painter Émile Loubon. Little is known of their precise interaction, but one can easily see the impact of Diaz's thickly painted forested landscapes with exotic figures on Monticelli's landscapes of the 1860s. Unfortunately, there are so many discrepancies of

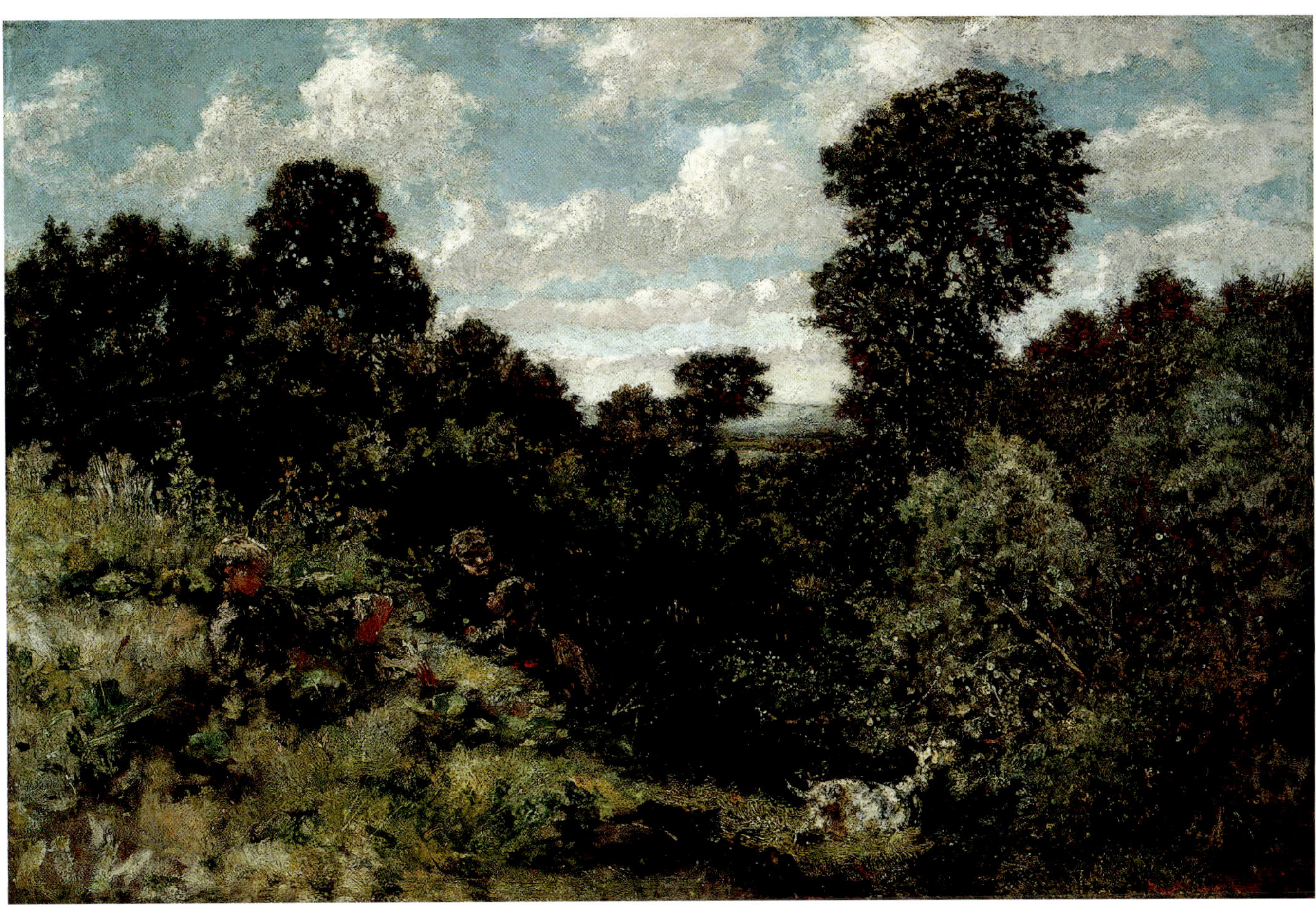

50

title in the Monticelli (and Diaz) literature that it is impossible to draw any conclusions about the precise links between the two painters. Rather, Diaz's imagery and to a certain extent technique, along with the palette-knife paintings of Gustave Courbet, led Monticelli to produce canvases with thick, wet-on-wet facture by the early or mid-1860s. This technical device in turn must have had as decisive an effect on the palette-knife paintings of the young Paul Cézanne as it was later to have on the young van Gogh.

Monticelli worked mostly on panels, largely because his paint was so thick that it would not have been supportable by stretched canvas. Also, Monticelli painted directly on the warm brown of the wood itself, without the application of a white or colored ground of paint. In this, he followed the practice of so-called *value painting* practiced by the academic artists chronicled by Albert Boime in his classic book *The Academy and French Painting in the Nineteenth Century* (1971). These men and women tended to paint a warm brown paint layer, working toward darks and lights from a middle tone similar to wood. This is clearly the case with *Midsummer*, which is among the most carefully painted works in Monticelli's entire oeuvre. (It was for this reason an odd choice for deaccession by the Phillips Collection.) In composing the painting, Monticelli responded to a landscape that is clearly northern France, perhaps near the Forest of Fontainebleau, where Diaz also painted. We are on the crest of a small hill, populated by a woman and two children playing in a sunny field that dominates the lower left. Behind and beneath them is a forest of oak trees that gives way to a luminous plain with a distant lake or pond very like those painted by Diaz and Théodore Rousseau many times in the 1850s and 1860s. A white goat nibbles at foliage in the lower right, and Monticelli signed the painting in red in the same quadrant. Because of the intensely painterly facture, nothing in the composition is remotely in focus, and the center of the composition is devoted to a deep, dark void of blackish brown into which the pleasant figures might sink. Thus, although similar in many ways to contemporary and earlier paintings by Diaz, *Midsummer* is a completely original work of art.

1 Pittsburgh, 1978, no. 19.

51

Adolphe-Joseph-Thomas Monticelli
French, 1824–1886

Flowers
1870–1880

Oil on panel, $24\frac{1}{4} \times 19$ in. (61.6×48.2 cm)
Signed lower right: "Monticelli"
M.1968.45

Provenance: ?Doctor Hippolyte Mireur (1841–1914), Marseille (sale, Hôtel Drouot, 28–30 March 1900, lot 74, as *Fleurs dans un vase* to); ?Lutz. [Derrick Morley, London, sold 11 May 1967, ½ share, to]; [Reid & Lefevre Gallery, London, stock no. 54/67, sold 1968 to]; Norton Simon Art Foundation.

Exhibitions: London, 1967b, no. 14; Philadelphia, 1969, no. 5; Princeton, 1972, no. 23; San Francisco, 1974, no. 23, ill.

References: Vincent, 1956, p. 200; Sheon, 1967, pp. 445, 448 n. 15, fig. 3; Steadman, 1972, p. 37; Steadman, 1973a, p. 11 ill.

Technical Notes: The support, a vertically grained hardwood panel, has been thinned to a thickness of ⅛ inch. A 1¾-inch wood strip is attached to the top edge, and another strip ½ inch wide, is attached to the bottom edge. The enlarged panel has been adhered to a wood backing, and the entire structure cradled. The X-radiographs indicate that the original composition was complete before the wood strips were added, and their purpose is unexplained. The join of the top addition is stable and tightly closed. The bottom strip is not held rigidly in place, and the join is opening at the left side. At the top edge, a vertical crack penetrates all layers, including the wood backing. A condition report from 1980 notes this same crack with a length of 2¼ inches at that time, but it has lengthened to 4 inches. X-radiographs reveal a large number of insect channels. They may exist throughout the entire painting; however, they are most clearly seen in the dark areas of the X-ray, along the left and the right sides. Almost all are below the surface except for a few at the right side, where the holes are visible from the front. There is no ground layer or any visible preparation on the original panel; the added strips were both prepared with a white ground. The paint has a loose handling of heavily textured paint mixed on the palette. Visible portions of the unprimed wood support provide a warm, dark tone. The thick impasto remains well preserved. The remains of aged natural resin, throughout most of the dark colors, and applications of newer varnish have not made a coherent surface. The varnishes vary tremendously in gloss, transparency, and saturation and generally are extremely unpleasant. (RW)

Precise dating of Monticelli's flower paintings is virtually impossible. Technically similar in startling ways, they seem to fall almost completely into the last decade of the painter's career before his death in 1886. Yet, in looking at earlier works in other genres, it is clear that Monticelli had the capacity to paint these densely impastoed canvases as early as 1860. *Flowers*, like the

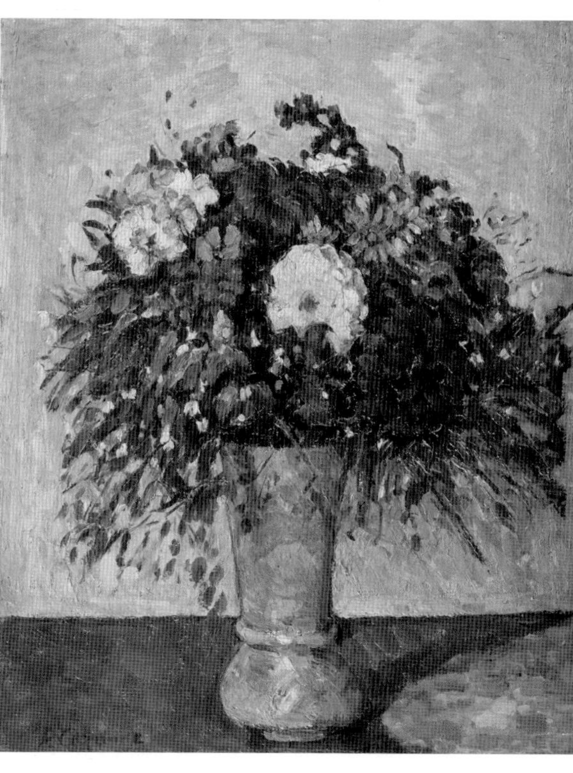

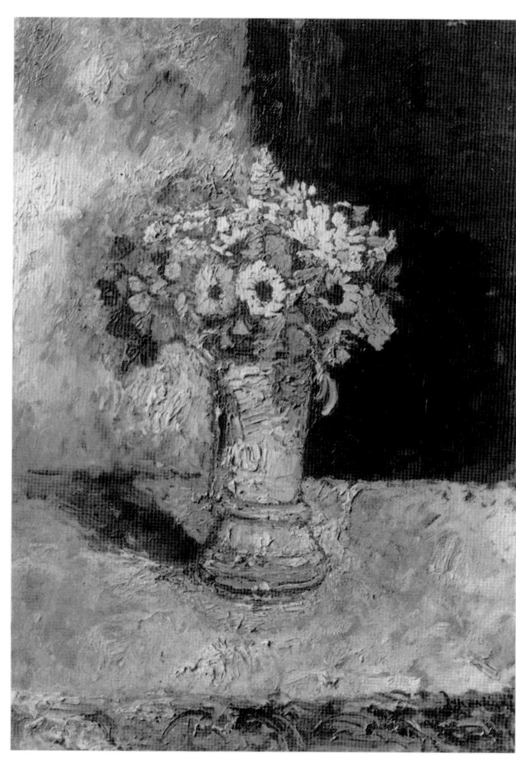

Fig. 51a (*right*) Paul Cézanne, *Flowers in a Blue Vase*, c. 1877, oil on canvas, $22 \times 18\frac{1}{8}$ in. (56×46 cm), State Hermitage Museum, St. Petersburg; photo: Scala / Art Resource, NY

Fig. 51b (*far right*) Adolphe-Joseph-Thomas Monticelli, *Vase of Flowers*, c. 1874, oil on panel, $24\frac{3}{4} \times 17\frac{3}{4}$ in. (63×45 cm), Musée des Beaux-Arts de Lyon; photo: © Studio Basset

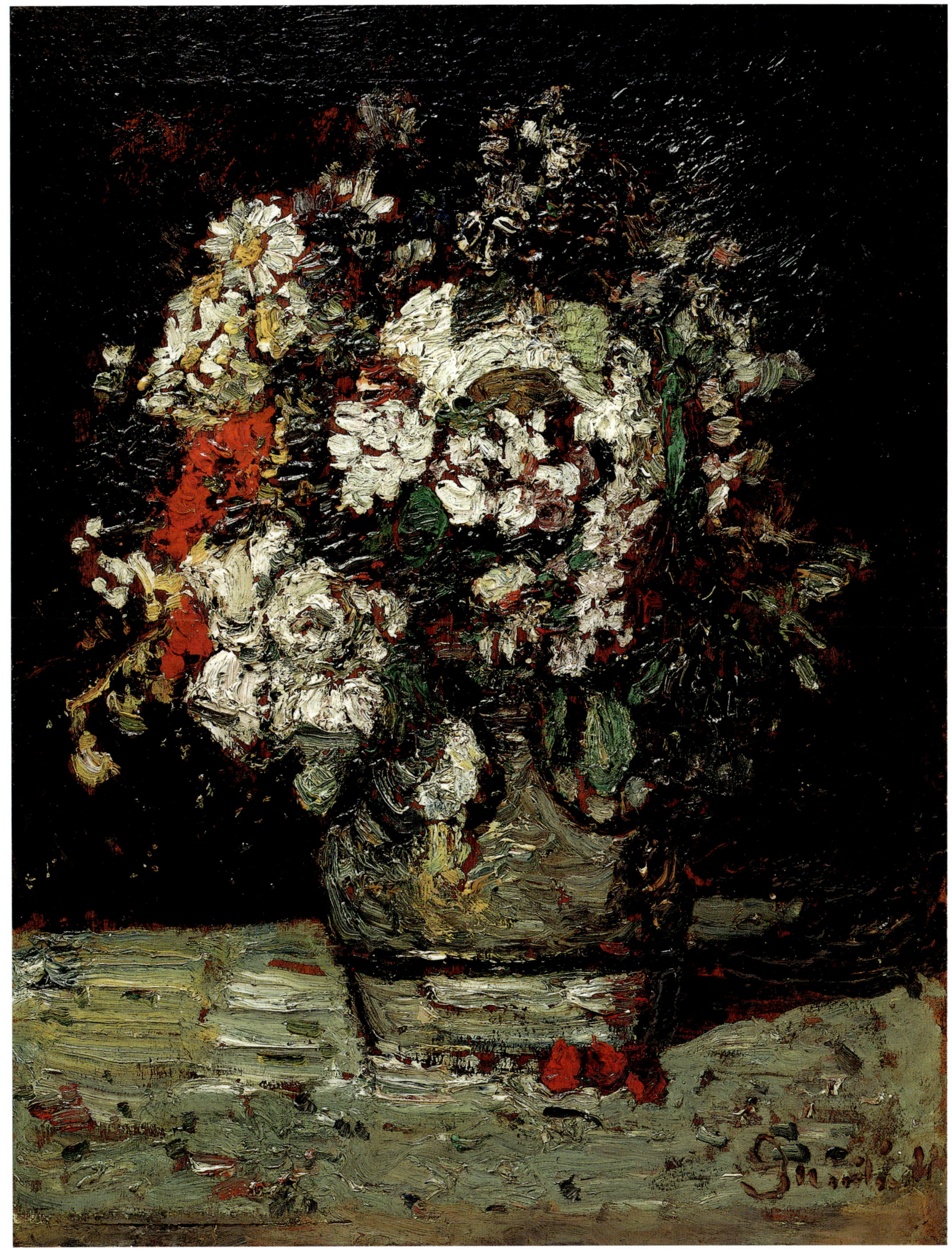

51

others, is signed but not dated and, also like most of Monticelli's paintings, made its earliest appearance after the painter's death. And, although there are startling relations to the flower paintings by Vincent van Gogh in the early 1880s, those to the floral still lifes of Paul Cézanne and Camille Pissarro in the 1870s are even closer. It is fascinating, for example, to compare Cézanne's *Flowers in a Blue Vase* (fig. 51a) with Monticelli's *Vase of Flowers* (fig. 51b). Although the arrangements of flowers in the vases are clearly different, the vase itself and the very idea of the painting are essentially identical, and both of these canvases have clear affinities with the present floral still life. Indeed, the relations between the thick painting of Monticelli and that of Pissarro and Cézanne has yet to be dealt with systematically in the art historical literature devoted to either of these vanguard artists. Yet, not only did Monticelli know Dr. Paul Gachet, in whose house Cézanne painted many of his still lifes in the 1870s, but the Provençal connection between the two men was strong. Indeed, the very idea of making crude, erotic, and emotionally resonant painting that Cézanne formed in the mid-1860s had already been explored by Monticelli at the beginning of the same decade. And, since Monticelli's works were exhibited in Paris (at his dealer Delarbeyrette) and in Provence (at the Société Artistique des Bouches-du-Rhône) throughout the 1860s, Cézanne could have been well acquainted with his production even without knowing the older artist personally.

Flowers is painted on a thin, planed mahogany panel with strips added at the top and bottom, probably before the panel was cradled. A careful examination suggests that it was relatively quickly and simply painted, and that it has been unevenly cleaned. Almost all the white or light-colored portions of the panel have been zealously cleaned, while the darker areas and the background look almost like a primordial soup of congealed varnish over paint. These latter areas have been left alone, possibly because they were painted with colored or tinted varnishes that would be disturbed by cleaning. The unevenness of the cleaning causes *Flowers* to disintegrate, as the whites advance and appear to separate from the darker areas. One wonders whether Monticelli himself may have coated even the light areas of the painting with tinted varnishes to hold the picture together visually. Microscopic examination of the large white area at the center of the bouquet that does not appear to be a flower shows that Monticelli toned one side of that area with a green-tinted varnish and the other with a brownish varnish. If this is true for the rest of the painting, it could have looked significantly different—and significantly better—than it does today. It is worth adding that Vincent van Gogh or his brother Theo owned a superb floral still life by Monticelli, which remains, with five other paintings by the artist, in the collection of the Van Gogh Museum in Amsterdam.

52

Adolphe-Joseph-Thomas Monticelli
French, 1824–1886

The Olive Oil Seller
c. 1880

Oil on panel, 20 × 15¾ in. (50.8 × 40 cm)
Signed lower left: "Monticelli"
M.1980.9

Provenance: Delas (sale, Paris, Hôtel Drouot, 19 June 1901, lot 13, as *La marchande de tou-caou*, passed). Claude Roger-Marx (sale, Paris, Galerie Manzi Joyant, 11–12 May 1914, lot 63, to); [Galerie Druet, Paris]. François Honnorat (1853–1921), by descent to; Heirs of F. Honnorat (sale, Marseilles, Hôtel des Ventes, 28–29 December 1928, lot 15, ill., passed; sale, Marseilles, Hôtel des Ventes, 29 December 1936, lot 15, ill., as *L'Italienne ou la Marchande d'olives*). (sale, Nice, Galerie Robiony, 9 June 1965, lot 107, ill., as *L'Italienne ou la Marchande d'olives*). (sale, London, Christie's, 12 December 1969, lot 17, ill., sold 2,800 gns. to); Williams. [E. V. Thaw & Co., Inc., New York, by 1978, sold 2 July 1980 to]; Norton Simon Art Foundation.

Exhibition: Pittsburgh, 1978, no. 72, colorpl. 30.

Reference: Alauzen, 1969, p. 360, fig. 464.

Technical Notes: The support is a vertically grained panel that has been cradled. A few insect channels and holes are visible both in the panel and in some cradle members, suggesting that the cradle was attached early. There is no ground layer, which allows the wood to contribute notably to the overall tonality of the painting. Thick, opaque paint was applied in very free brushwork, painted wet into wet and also wet over dry in numerous layers. Brushstrokes are unrelated to form. The buildup of thick, heavy paint prevents any determination of the artist's sequence of painting. The painting remains well preserved. Areas where wood is exposed are not paint losses but were created by the abrupt end of a brushstroke. In 1980 the painting was selectively cleaned. Examination with ultraviolet light reveals a thick natural resin varnish throughout the background, with reduced varnish in the light areas. Residues of brittle yellow varnish in the recesses of the impasto, combined with the thickness of the recent synthetic varnish, detract from the vitality of the surface. (RW)

Of the three works by Monticelli in the Norton Simon collections, the present painting is both the most exciting and the most enigmatic. Known throughout most of the twentieth century as either *La Marchande de l'huile* (*The Seller of Olive Oil*), *La Marchande d'olives*, or *L'Italienne*, its earliest recorded title is *La Marchand de tou-caou* (*The Vendor of "Very hot!"*). It represents a seated female wearing an elaborate costume that has been called both "Italian" and "Provençal" and relates to several of the Italianate peasant costumes used by Camille Corot for his late figural paintings.[1] Monticelli painted such figures rarely, preferring to use historical or exotic costumes that create the illusion of theatrical or operatic representations of history or literature. Although he worked with Narcisse-Virgile Diaz de la Peña in the countryside around Paris and professed to adore the landscape and peoples of his native Provence, he preferred pictorial realms that are fictive and mysterious.

Only one other painting in Monticelli's published oeuvre includes a female figure in the same or similar costume, and it is among the six works by Monticelli owned by Vincent van Gogh (fig. 52a). Called *The Italian Woman* already in the nineteenth century, it seems to clinch the identification of the figure in the Simon picture as Italian, rather than Provençal, though the costume is clearly a studio prop and likely bears only a general resemblance to actual clothes worn by Italian rural people. Similar costumes had been favored by European artists from the early nineteenth century, for example, by Achille-Etna Michallon in his *Peasant Outside of Rome* (fig. 52b).

The painting raises fascinating questions of pictorial legibility, beginning with confusion about just what it is the model appears to sell. We clearly see a seated female figure with brown hair, wearing a costume with a green skirt adorned with an added stripe at its hem. Over this, she wears a long patterned apron with either an embroidered or a heavily woven pattern. Her blouse and vest are also well described, and she appears to have a large, flat-bottomed ceramic bowl, like a paella dish, in her lap. But once we move beyond the figure itself and attempt to assign names to other parts of the picture, the mysteries multiply. Is she indoors or outdoors? Seated on a wall, cushioned bench, or a stone? What is the light-colored form at her feet? What is the large pale yellow, tan, and olive-colored form, or sequence of irregular forms, to the right of the figure? Is it light shining through an unseen window or through the opening of a tent? Is it a piece of thick cloth that might be raised to form a market stall? And, what exactly is she holding in

Fig. 52a (*right*) Adolphe-Joseph-Thomas Monticelli, *The Italian Woman*, 1879, oil on panel, Van Gogh Museum (Vincent van Gogh Foundation), Amsterdam

Fig. 52b (*far right*) Achille-Etna Michallon, *Peasant outside of Rome*, 1817–1821, oil on paper, mounted on canvas, $14\frac{3}{8} \times 9\frac{7}{16}$ in. (36.5 × 24 cm), Musée du Louvre, Paris; photo: Réunion des Musées Nationaux / Art Resource, NY

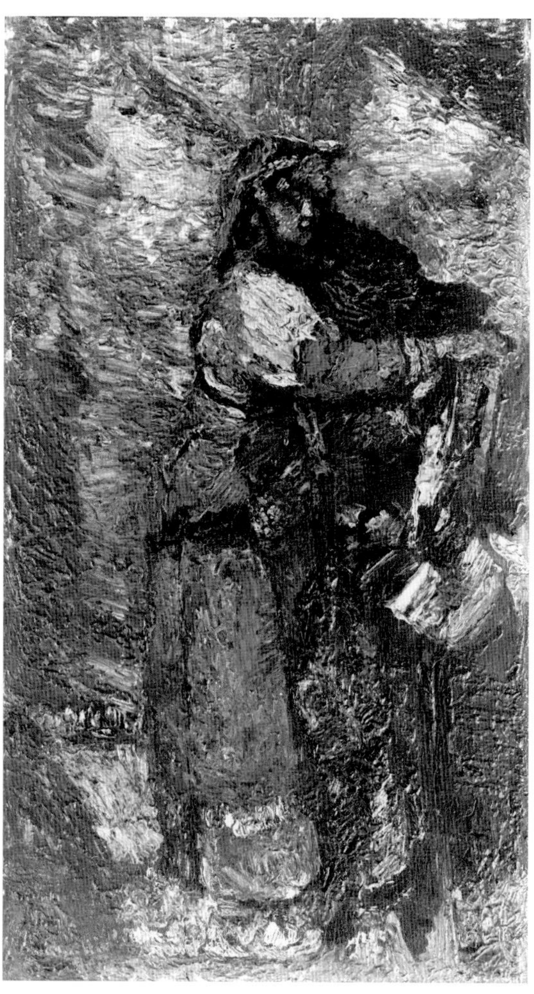

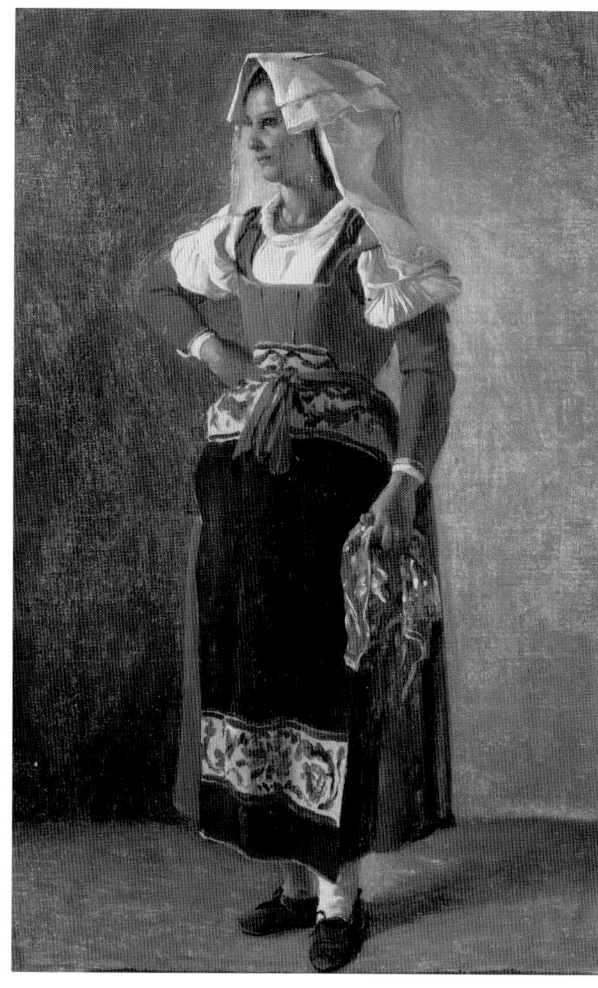

her hand? Most viewers of the area around her hands and the ceramic bowl conclude that she is holding a small bird, suggesting that other forms in the painting might also be birds that circle around her flat bowl of water, darting in and out of the sun. If she is a seller of exotic birds, she fits well with Monticelli's occasionally Romantic tendencies. It would have been comparatively easy for the artist to witness such a seller in the bird markets in his native Marseilles, where he lived between 1871 and his death in 1886. When he decided to paint a colorfully dressed woman selling songbirds that fly freely around her, all he had to do was hire a model, rent a costume, and buy two or three birds.

Yet, the Provençal words *tou caou* translate in French to "très chaud" or, in English, "very hot," which seems a very unlikely thing for either a bird merchant or an oil merchant to shout to attract customers. If, however, she is intended to represent a woman selling cool water on a hot Marseilles day, one could explain both the expression and the birds. But this too is unlikely, as the only vessel one would not use for cool water on a hot day is a flat dish. Indeed, it almost seems as if no one in either the nineteenth or the twentieth century has cracked the significance of the various titles, all of which, in spite of their precision, are likely to be wrong. Indeed, the picture might as easily be called *Gypsy with Tambourine* as *Bird Seller*, *Italian Woman*, *Olive Seller* or *Olive Oil Seller*.

It is fascinating to contrast the present painting with Monticelli's equally thick flower painting (cat. 51). Whereas the floral still life is comparatively simple in its

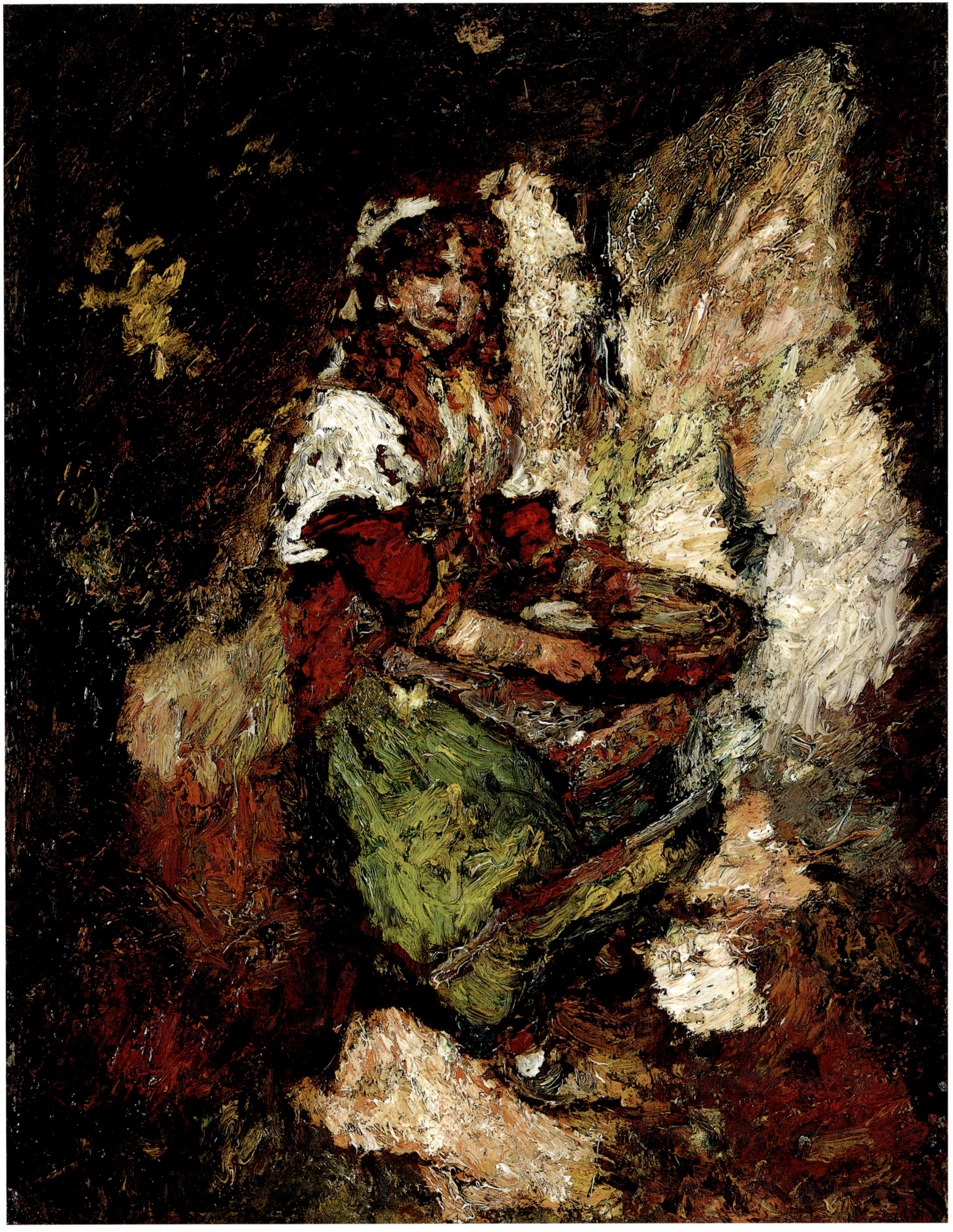

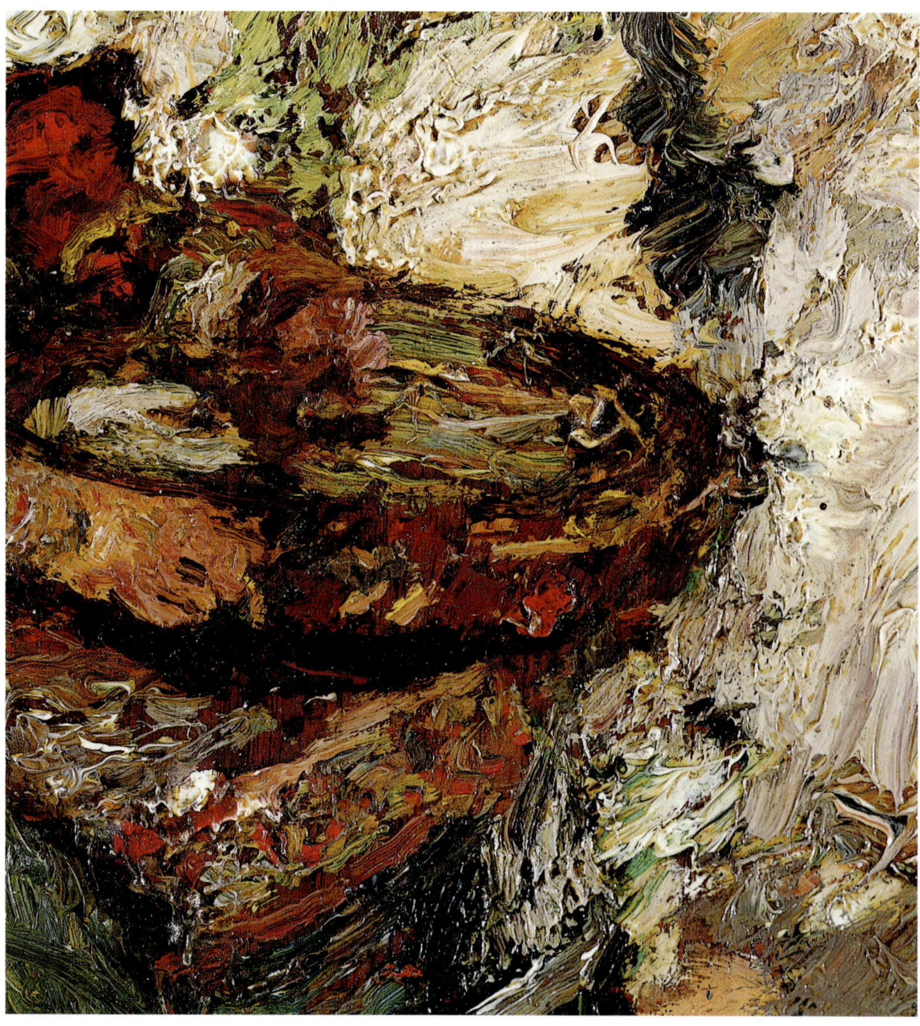

Fig. 52c Detail of cat. 52

chromatic structure, the present painting is very complex. The viewer can choose almost any area in the floral still life and find a passage of thickly applied oil paint with a single dominating color. Over these areas, Monticelli may have applied tinted varnishes to add richness. There are no chromatically simple passages in *The Olive Oil Seller.* Instead, Monticelli combined three to five different hues on a loaded brush and applied them to the panel to obtain passages of real complexity. It is even likely that he lightly brushed still other colors to the tops of the thick impasto after it had dried, thereby introducing scumbling into his arsenal (fig. 52c). The entire effect of the painting is of deliberation and control, in spite of the fact that the paint is thick and, for that reason, apparently spontaneously laid on. Instead, Monticelli analyzed his subject chromatically and then composed color mixtures to achieve results that are almost completely original in painting of Monticelli's generation. Claude Monet, Vincent van Gogh, and Paul Gauguin were to achieve similar chromatic complexity with paint, but none of them did it the same way, or quite so early.

1 See Robaut, 1905, nos. 1427, 1433, 1562, and 1996.

53

Louis-Eugène Boudin
French, 1824–1898

Beach at Trouville
1873

Oil on panel, $8\frac{1}{4} \times 16\frac{1}{4}$ in. (21×41.3 cm)
Signed lower left: "E. Boudin"
Inscribed and dated lower right: "Trouville 73"
F.1968.10

Provenance: [Adolphe Beugniet, Paris]. ?Private Collection, Paris. ?Georges Meyer-Heine, Marseilles, sold 5 June 1957 to; [Galerie Alfred Daber, Paris, sold 17 April 1968 to]; [M. Knoedler & Co., New York, stock no. A9243, as *Beach Scene*, sold 5 June 1968 to]; The Norton Simon Foundation.

Exhibitions On loan, Kansas City, Nelson Gallery of Art, 1968–1969; on loan, Los Angeles, County Museum of Art, 1969–1972; San Francisco, 1973, no. 34, ill.

Reference Schmit, 1973, no. 848, p. 301, ill., as *Scène de plage à Trouville.*

Technical Notes: The label on the reverse of the lightweight wood panel tells that "Beugniet 10 Rue Laffitte Paris" prepared it. The grain of the wood runs horizontally and the reverse has a rough, narrow bevel along the perimeter. A light blue-gray ground covers the front of the panel and thick brown paint coats the reverse. While paint appears to be mostly pasty and opaque with mixtures usually containing white and applied wet in wet, the artist made use of glazes as well. Brushstrokes ranging from about $\frac{1}{8}$ to $\frac{1}{4}$ inches wide remain visible, and in the sky in particular the impressions of the tips of the brush bristles were distinctively left. In general the sky and landscape were painted before the figures were placed. Numerous changes to the forms are obvious from the textures on the surface. The broadly painted landscape is in sharp contrast to some of the forms, for in a single small figure fine, individual strokes of what appear to be translucent turquoise, light ultramarine, pure ultramarine, medium ultramarine, white, and gray are visible under magnification. The surface coating, possibly a natural resin, fluoresces a greenish tone. In the valleys of the paint remnants of an older yellow varnish remain. The painting is in good condition with only some restoration along the edges. It must have been framed when the paint was still soft because a ridge exists along the perimeter. (JF)

54

Louis-Eugène Boudin
French, 1824–1898

Beach at Trouville
1880

Oil on panel, $5\frac{7}{8} \times 9\frac{7}{8}$ in. (14.9×25.1 cm)
Signed lower right: "E. Boudin"
Dated lower left: "7 bre 1880"
P.1980.2.1

Provenance: The artist, sold before 1891, for Ff 200, to; [Galeries Durand-Ruel, Paris, sold 14 December 1920 to]; Devilder, Roubaix, France. [André Schoeller (1879–1955), Paris, sold 4 May 1936 to]; [Arthur Tooth & Sons, London, stock no. 9735, as *La Plage*, sold 25 May 1936 to]; earl of Hardwicke. Cary Grant, Beverly Hills, Calif., gift 1980 to; Norton Simon Museum.

Reference: Schmit, 1973, vol. 2, no. 1305, p. 25, ill., as *Trouville. Scène de plage.*

Technical Notes: The grain of this small lightweight panel runs horizontally. A light gray-blue ground of medium thickness appears to have been carefully applied. The cradle has four stationary horizontal members and four movable vertical ones. No preparator's marks are visible. As in the other Norton Simon Boudin paintings, the landscape was laid out with pasty paint wet in wet first. This paint generally shows brush marks, and in the sky a distinctive brushwork shows the tips of the brush bristles. The figures were painted on top of the landscape, but landscape colors were used to adjust the outlines of the forms. The darks used in the forms are rather thin. Fine contraction cracks are visible with low magnification in a number of areas. The condition is very good, but the thick yellow varnish, which fluoresces yellow-green in ultraviolet light, obscures the colors. Around the red umbrella detachment of the varnish creates a blanched appearance. A few fine horizontal mechanical cracks are barely visible. The raw sienna dot at the upper left appears to be an original. (JF)

55

Louis-Eugène Boudin
French, 1824–1898

Beach at Trouville
1888

Oil on panel, 5⅝ × 9⅜ in. (14.3 × 23.8 cm)
Signed lower right: "E. Boudin"
Inscribed and dated lower left: "Trouville 88"
P.1980.2.2

Provenance: Charles Ricada, Paris (sale, Paris, Hôtel Drouot, 20 March 1893, lot 32, for Ff 400). Georges Feydeau, Paris (sale, Paris, Hôtel Drouot, 11 February 1901, lot 23, as *Sur la plage*, for Ff 1,400, to); [Durand-Ruel, Paris, sold 20 March 1920 to]; Devilder, Roubaix, France. [André Schoeller (1879–1955), Paris, sold 4 May 1936 to]; [Arthur Tooth & Sons, London, stock no. 9736, as *Sur la Plage, Trouville*, sold 25 May 1936 to]; earl of Hardwicke. Cary Grant, Beverly Hills, Calif., gift 1980 to; Norton Simon Museum.

Reference: Schmit, 1973, vol. 2, no. 2247, p. 357, ill., as *Trouville. Scène de plage.*

Technical Notes: The support is a thin, cradled wood panel. The cradling consists of 4 vertical stationary members and 4 horizontal sliding bars. The entire system is very light in weight. There is an extremely thin white ground and there may also be a light mauve paint layer over the ground. Paint is directly applied wet in wet with no blending, and colors are mixed with white, with the exception of a few small dashes of pure color. The tent and umbrella at right, the central dark figure, and surrounding dark forms were laid in first, followed by the sky and then the landscape. Remaining forms were applied over the landscape. The thick yellow varnish must be a natural resin and no earlier varnish is evident. The condition of the paint is very good with only a few scattered losses. The signature seems to have been reinforced by the artist. (JF)

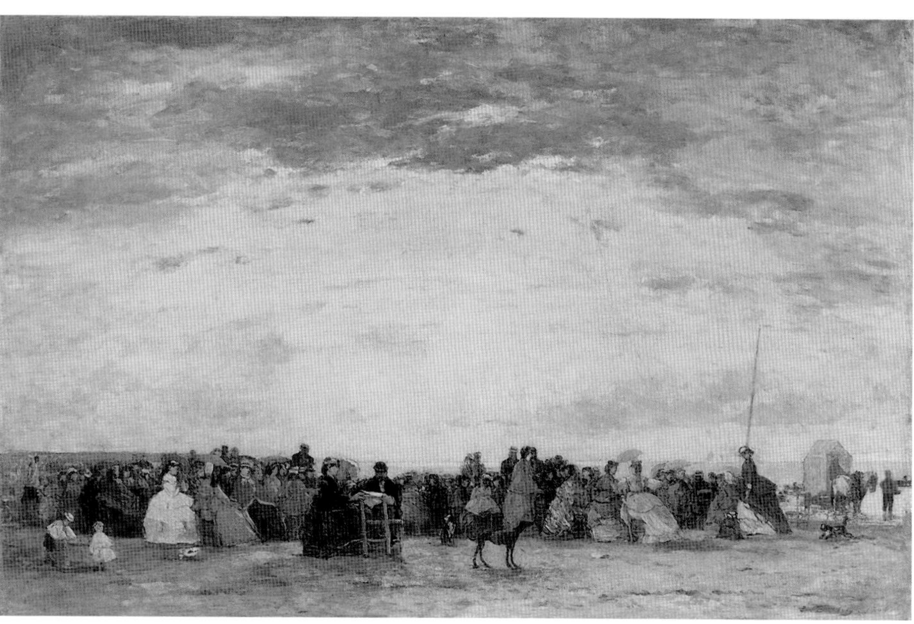

Fig. 53a Louis-Eugène Boudin, *Vacationers on the Beach at Trouville*, 1864, oil on canvas, 26½ × 41 in. (67.3 × 104.1 cm), The Minneapolis Institute of Arts

In 1973 the great Parisian art dealer Robert Schmit published a magisterial three-volume catalogue raisonné of the paintings of Eugène Boudin. Before the Schmit catalogue, scholars and collectors knew that the Impressionist painter's oeuvre was huge, but had no way to quantify it. Schmit, working with extensive archives, did for the famously prolific Boudin what Alfred Robaut had for the equally productive Camille Corot—arranged and published all the paintings known to him. The three volumes include entries for an astonishing 3,651 paintings made between 1850, when the artist was twenty-six, and 1898, when he died less than a month after his seventy-fourth birthday. (Vivien Hamilton, in a later study of Boudin, claims more than 4,000 paintings and 7,000 works on paper.[1]) Thus, we now know that the painter made at least seventy-five works per year, on average—more than one a week throughout a long working life. This kind of easy productivity is comparatively rare in the history of modern art. Certain artists, like Corot, Claude Monet, Pierre-Auguste Renoir, and, famously, Pablo Picasso equaled or surpassed Boudin's output, but most of the Norman painter's friends and colleagues worked more fitfully and in a manner that suggests struggle rather than ease. For Boudin, painting was as natural as eating or drinking, and works of art sprang from his nimble hands with short gestation periods and easy births.

The earliest of the four works by Boudin in the Norton Simon Museum (cat. 53) is a small painting on panel, signed and inscribed with the place in which it was made and the year—Trouville, 1873. It is the first of ninety works dated to that year in Schmit's listings and one of six small paintings on panel made on the beach at Trouville in the summer of 1873. The town itself had been painted literally hundreds of times by the artist, who turned forty-nine in the summer of 1873. He went there mostly to paint fashionable Parisians, who had flocked to Trouville and the neighboring town of Deauville in the summer months beginning in the 1850s. Boudin himself had made his first paintings of Parisians on the beach at Trouville in the early 1860s, and undertook a major pictorial campaign in the summer of 1863, when he painted no less a Parisian than the Empress Eugenie and her attendants strolling along the windswept beach.[2] In virtually every summer after that, Boudin returned to Trouville, never tiring of the movement of fashionably dressed men and women along

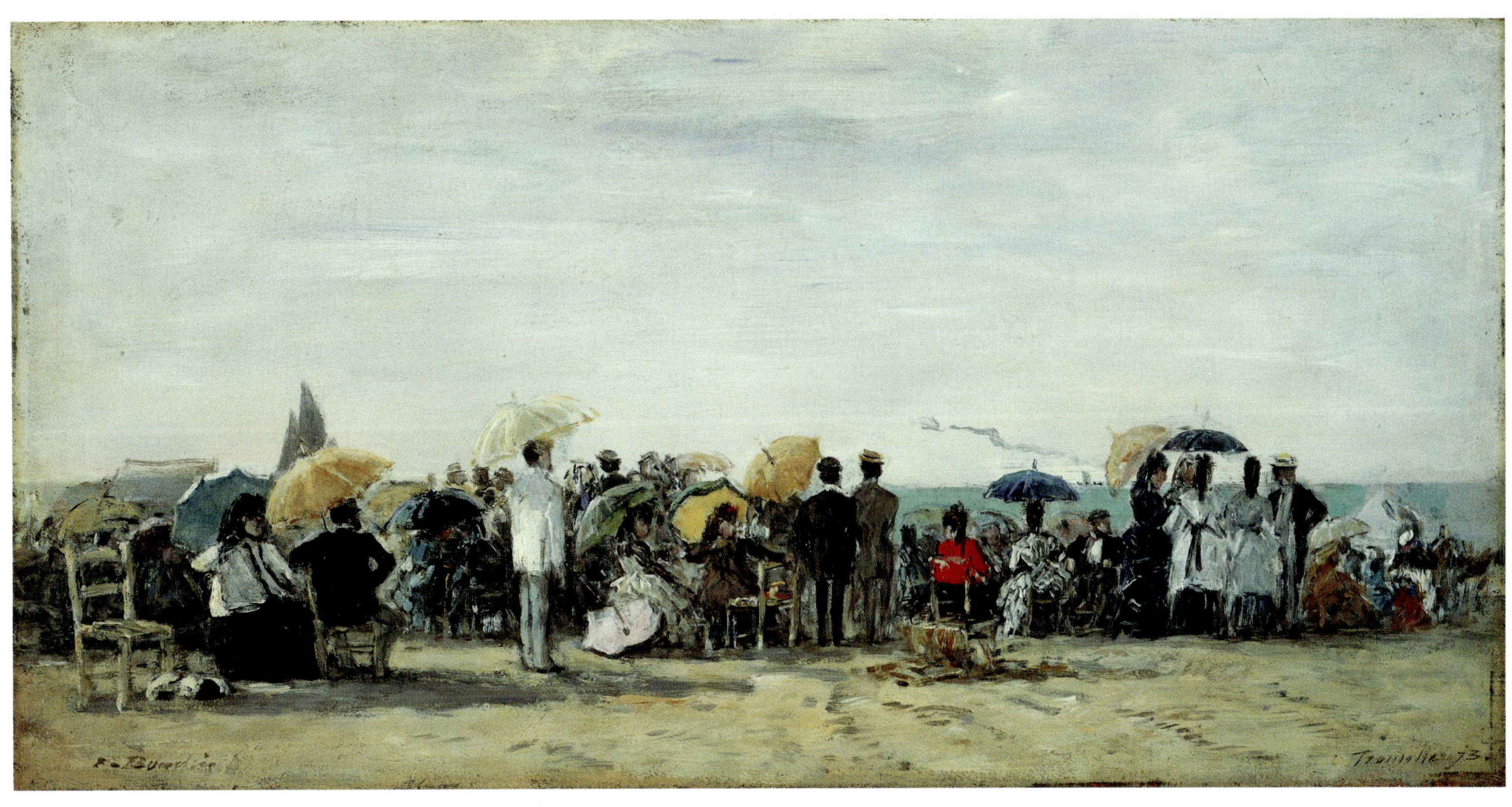

53

the beach (fig. 53a). Indeed, he was such a fixture at Trouville that the haut monde of Paris, who frequented the best hotels and private houses in the area, came to rely on his presence as part of the mystique of a summer at Trouville. If Boudin is painting us, they must have thought, surely what we are doing must have significance. And significance they had, because Boudin's submission of Trouville beach paintings to the Salons of 1864, 1865, and 1867 were accepted, making such modern subjects a familiar part of landscape practice years before the Impressionists began to exhibit similar paintings.

By 1873 this imagery must have soothed Parisian viewers, most of whom had had to forgo their summer trips of 1870 due to the Franco-Prussian War. This unenforced ban on luxury summer travel affected Boudin, too, and there are no beach studies inscribed as having been painted in Trouville until the summer of 1871, when he returned again. In 1872 the pattern of beach painting in July and August was firmly reestablished, continuing more or less uninterrupted throughout the remainder of the 1870s and 1880s.[3] The majority of these paintings were made on small panels, which were easier to carry and to pack than stretched canvases and much less likely to blow away in the wind. Owing both to the patronage of Norton Simon himself and to the generosity of Gary Grant, who gave two Trouville beach panels to the Norton Simon Museum in 1980, the Museum has three panels made on the beach at Trouville in the summers of 1873, 1880, and 1888. Thus, a small bouquet of plein-air beach scenes by the acknowledged master of that genre allows modern visitors to measure the painter's success within the limits of this iconography.

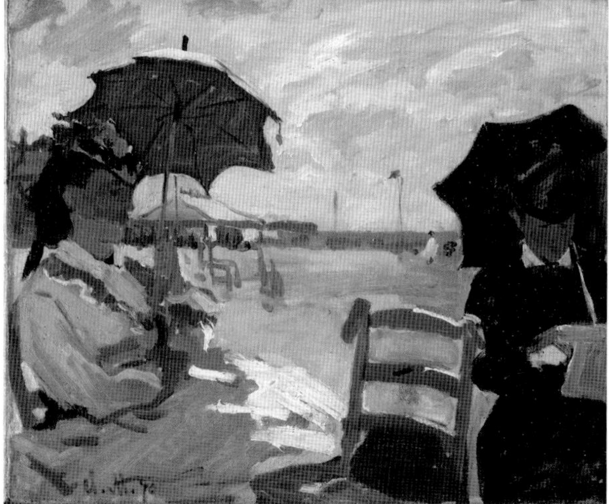

Fig. 53b Claude Monet, *The Beach at Trouville*, 1870, oil on canvas, 14¾ × 18 in. (37.5 × 45.7 cm), The National Gallery, London

The largest of the three (cat. 53) is the earliest. In it, one sees men, women, and a single dog arranged in and around groups of wooden beach chairs in the middle ground of the composition facing the sea. In a certain sense, the painting is modern because none of the figures acknowledges the viewer, and we see the majority of them from the back as if they are unaware of our analysis of their clothes, positions, and movements. The absence of children and nannies (though the small figure in red on the far right may be a child with her nanny) and the fact that all the figures are well-dressed indicate that Boudin observed this figural group either before a Sunday midday or on an early summer evening, as the people met on the beach to take the air before going into their hotels or country houses for dinner (the long shadows around the foreground figures suggest the latter). Their children were elsewhere, either playing after church or having an early supper and preparing for bed. The majority of the women wear evening black and white, enlivening their wardrobes with chromatically varied parasols in yellow, green, cream, and blue. The men wear white, gray, and black, and at least three of them wear jaunty straw hats. At least two of them seem concerned about damage from the sun to their pale, urban skins. A plume of smoke at right is the residue of the engine of a steamship plying the tranquil waters of La Manche. All seems well in this world, but, as in almost all works by Boudin painted on the beach at Trouville, his figures are treated as miniaturized social betters, whom the painter can observe from a distance without physical or conversational interaction. How different this view is from those painted on the same beach in the spring of 1870 by Monet, particularly the spectacular small painting in the National Gallery, London, representing Madame Monet and Madame Boudin (fig. 53b).

Careful examination of this panel shows that Boudin painted it on a cool blue-gray ground and that, after applying the beach and the sky, he worked to arrange his figures in plausible groups, fiddling with the silhouettes with particular care. The group of women in the middle distance to the right of center appears now with a blue parasol, but Boudin originally had given the third woman a parasol too, which must have been pictorially confusing, so he deftly removed it. And the pale yellow parasol of the male figure at center left was originally in a different position. Indeed, a close examination of that section of the painting suggests that Boudin may even have started the composition with a larger female figure, which he rethought, miniaturized, and regendered.

The second Boudin beach painting made in Trouville (cat. 54) is signed and dated July 1880. Although it lacks

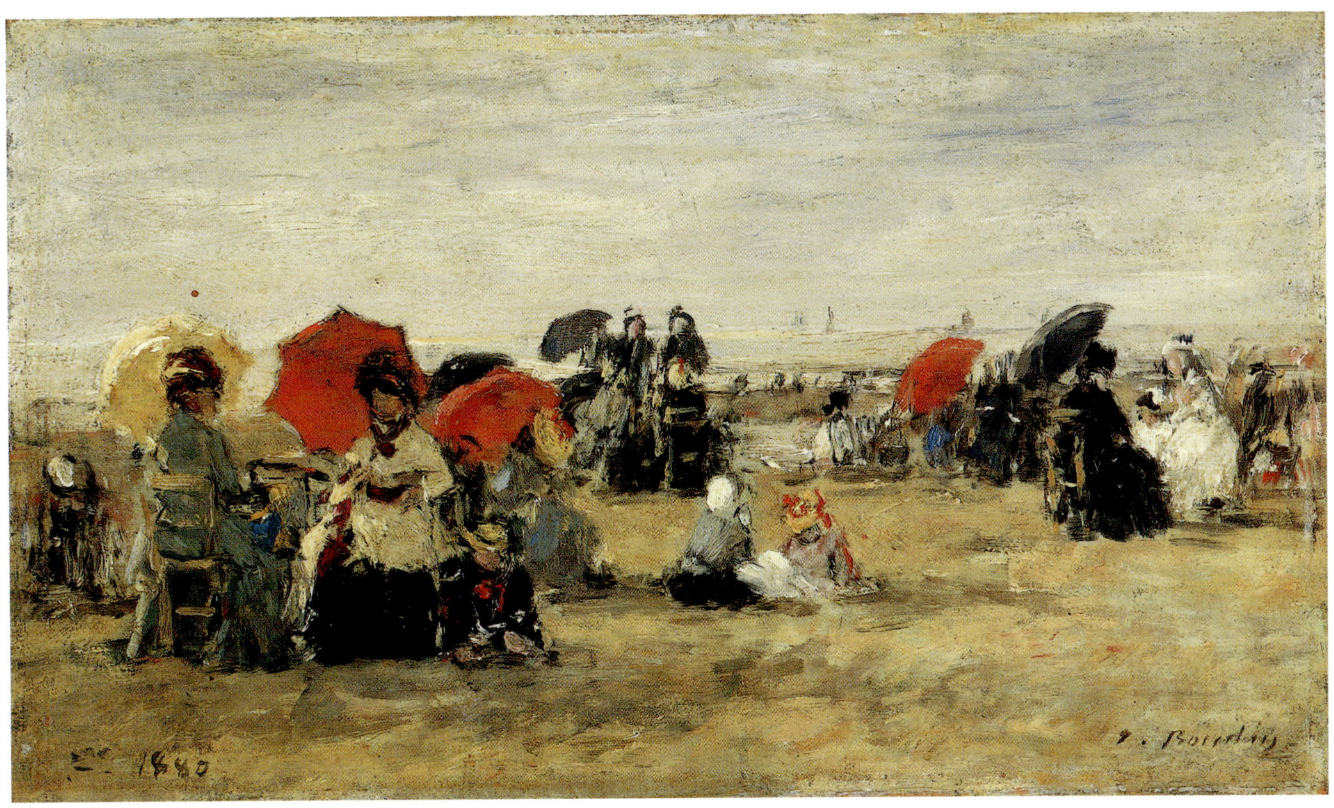

54

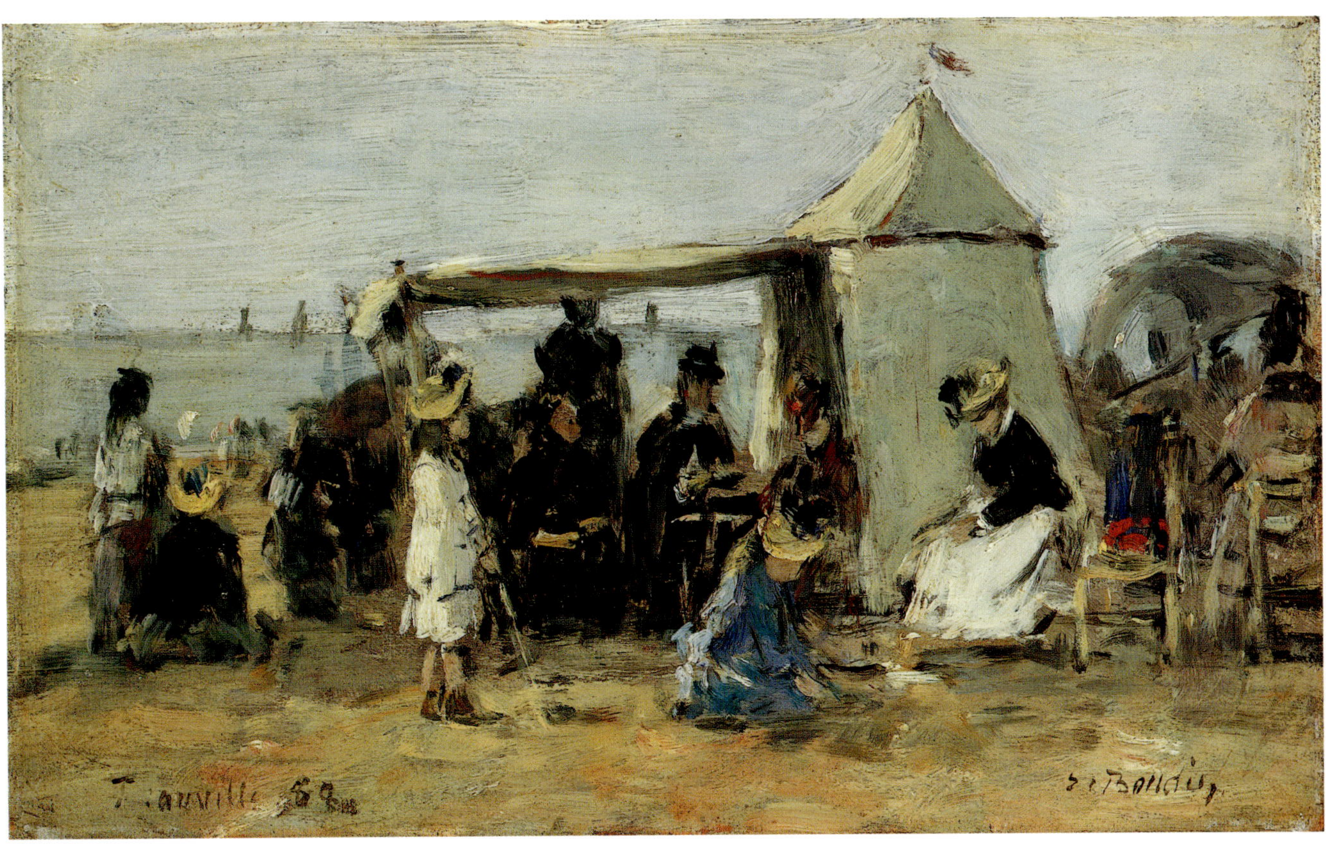

55

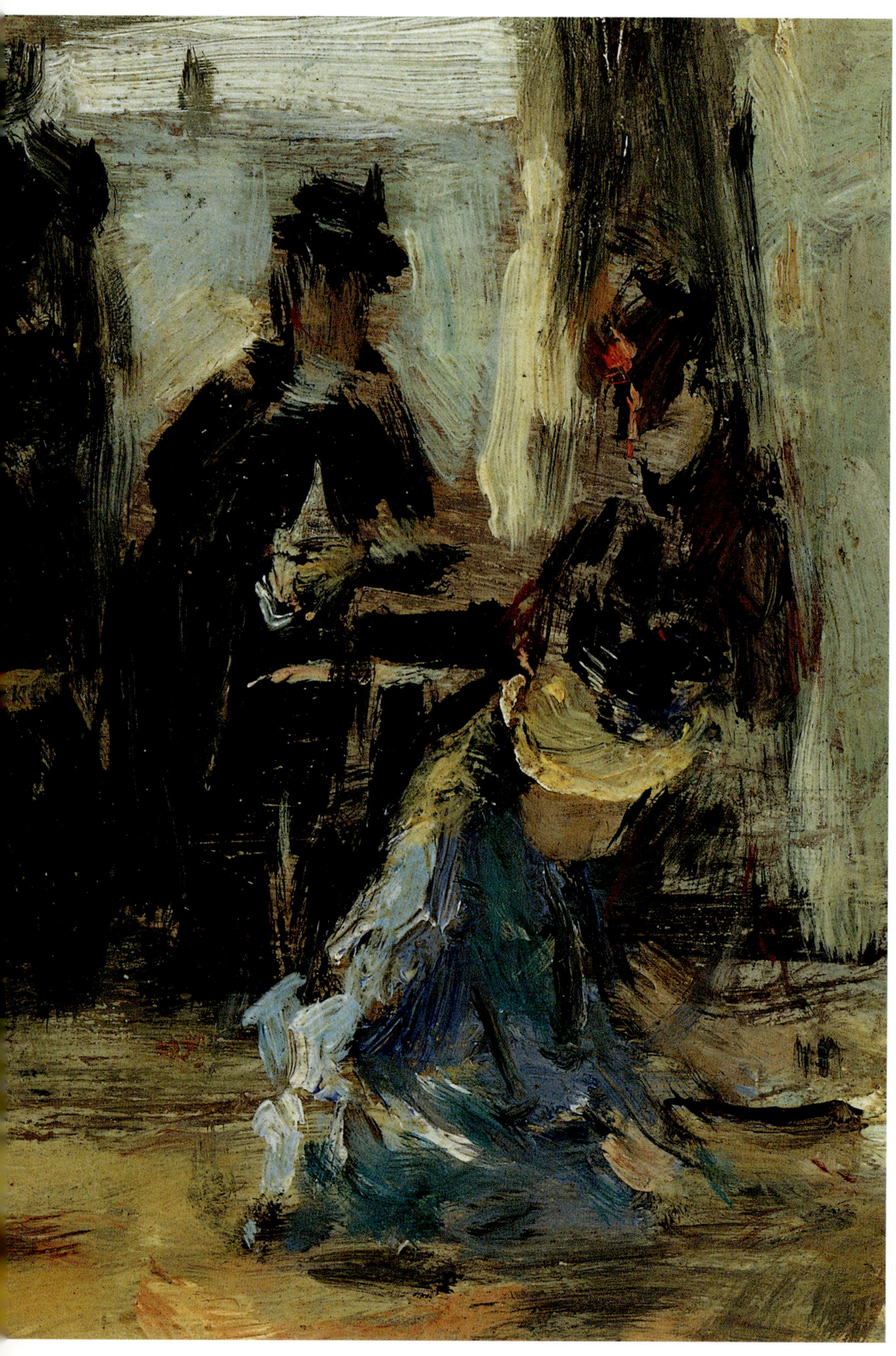

an inscription identifying the site as Trouville, it is so like other similar views from that summer that there is little doubt about the site. It is one of seventeen surviving panels and one small canvas dated to that summer by Boudin, a considerably larger production than the six for 1873. In this case, Boudin represents a scene with women, children, and servants, but no men, suggesting even by his July date on the panel that it was made before the men joined their wives for the annual extended vacations of August. Here, Boudin seems to have been prompted to paint the scene by the presence of three red parasols that give spice to the composition, playing wonderfully against the red-trimmed hat of the little girl who sits in the center with her nanny. The women hold the parasols in such a way that we know that the day is not windy, and, although we see distant sailboats, the women and children seem unaffected by the sea and actually ignore it in their conversations and little games. Hence, though it seems utterly similar as a type to the 1873 painting, the 1880 Boudin actually deals with different social and gender dynamics as they unfold on the beach. In this way, they are like the short evocative stories of Guy de Maupassant.

The final of the three beach paintings (cat. 55) was inscribed with the place, signed, and dated 1888 by Boudin. It is the only Trouville beach panel to survive from 1888, although there are three views on canvas of the harbor[4] and two views of the mouth of the river at Trouville at low tide.[5] It seems almost as if Boudin had finally wrung all the pictorial interest he could from bourgeois beach scenes and turned his attention increasingly to the life and landscape of the indigenous population, becoming in old age an invigorated version of the painter he had been as a youth. The 1888 panel represents women and children sitting and chatting around a rented canvas beach cabin, undoubtedly near the casino-club. The figure at the center of the composition, visually decapitated by the tent flap, seems to be the sole man in the painting, but he is so sketchily defined that one cannot be sure of his gender. The painting is unusual among the bourgeois beach scenes in being positioned so close to the figural subject. It is as if Boudin was so at home in the setting that he could approach his subjects on the beach, rather than lurking near the embankment, watching from a distance, as in most of the other panels. The first owner of the painting, Charles Ricada, must have been with Boudin that summer, because two other small panels of the sea at low tide were dedicated to him. One is inscribed to "Mr. Ricada" rather than the preferred French "M. Ricada," suggesting that the man was English or American. However, Schmit confidently proclaims Ricada's home as Paris, and his non-French name surely indicates that he was an expatriate. Perhaps he purchased the Simon painting—one of twenty-four Boudins he owned—from the artist, who, liking his new patron, made two additional panels for him. The latter paintings are of an identical vertical dimension and must have been conceived as a pair, creating a plausible trio of summer beach pictures for Mr. Ricada.

All three Trouville beach paintings by Boudin in the Simon collections fascinatingly situate these supremely urban vacationers in the midst of nature itself. Nothing impinges on them except water, sand, and wind, and, were it not for their elaborate clothing and the temporary canvas buildings and portable wooden chairs, they exist visually at the mercy of nature. In fact, all of these figures arranged themselves on a vast sand beach directly in front of a long row of hotels, restaurants, and houses in addition to the famous casino-club, to which many of them belonged. None of this is present in Boudin's beach scenes at the Norton Simon. Instead, his figures are displayed like insects in a petri dish or cells on a glass slide for examination by the artist. We suspect, of course, that they can leave when it rains or the season shifts with unpleasant results, but, in Boudin's world, they are there for our delectation and analysis, as they were for his. Charles Baudelaire was almost dead when Boudin stormed the Norman beaches looking for urbanites in the summer of 1863. How delighted the poet-critic would have been by the portability of urban modernity. We might call Boudin's bourgeois beaches the parks and boulevards of the sea.

1 Hamilton, 1992, p. 9.
2 Schmit, 1973, vol. 1, no. 280, Burrell Collection, Glasgow.
3 The most intelligent survey of this visual obsession is Hamilton, 1992.
4 Schmit, 1973, vol. 2, nos. 2249–2251.
5 Schmit, 1973, vol. 2, nos. 2244, 2245.

56

Louis-Eugène Boudin
French, 1824–1898

Low Tide, Berck
1886

Oil on canvas, $19\frac{3}{4} \times 24\frac{1}{8}$ in. (50.2 × 61.3 cm)
Signed and dated lower left: "E. Boudin 86"
M.1992.1

Provenance: Belvallette, Paris by 1899. Brosset Heckel, Lyon (sale, Paris, Hôtel Drouot, 18 November 1966, lot 14, to); [Stephen Hahn Gallery, New York, sold 1967 as *Figures on the Beach* to]; The Norton Simon Foundation, transferred 1992 to; Norton Simon Art Foundation.

Exhibitions: Paris, 1899a, no. 84; San Francisco, 1974, no. 22, ill., as *Figures on the Beach.*

Reference: Schmit, 1973, vol. 2, no. 2148, p. 319, ill.

Technical Notes: The fine- to medium-weight canvas does not appear to have any ground. While there is a possible layer of a light blue or green visible on the center right edge and at the lower right corner, this must be oil paint that is intermittently applied. The sky is underlaid with a darker gray paint that also appears discontinuous. Paint of local color is directly applied wet in wet in most cases without attempts to disguise the manner of application. Careful visual examination and the X-ray reveal changes and adjustments. The tight, plain-weave canvas gives only a slight texture to the paint surface. The canvas with tacking edges may never have been removed from the 5-part butt-join keyable stretcher. What appears to be a natural resin varnish covers the surface, but one wonders if the painting were originally varnished, especially since it is on an unprimed canvas that has now been darkened by saturation. (JF)

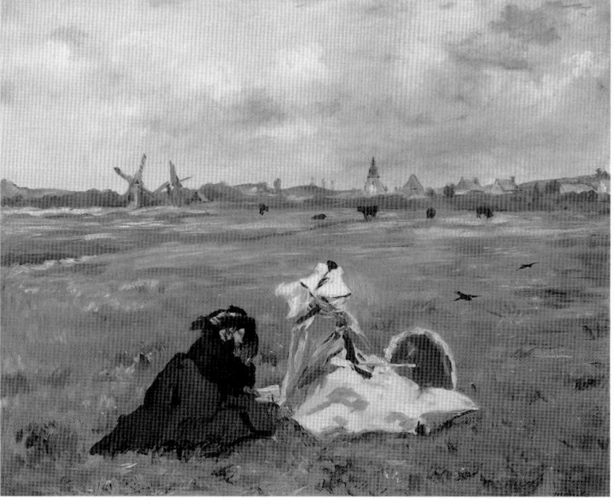

Fig. 56a Édouard Manet, *The Swallows*, 1873, oil on canvas, $25\frac{5}{8} \times 31\frac{7}{8}$ in. (65 × 81 cm), Foundation Collection, E. G. Bürhle, Zurich

Schmit lists only forty-two paintings by Boudin dated to 1886, the year in which this subtle study of seaside atmosphere was painted. These include the usual clutch of panels made in July and August on the beach at Trouville, studies of the harbors at Deauville and Le Havre, and a series of coastal landscapes painted in Berck-sur-Mer and nearby Étaples on the very northeast reaches of the French coast of the English Channel. Édouard Manet had visited the two towns with his wife and mother in the summer of 1873, and Parisians came to prefer the more rugged charms of these bleak coastal reaches to the manicured beaches, casinos, and resort hotels of Deauville and Trouville. Indeed, not only did Boudin visit these comparatively remote coastal sites in 1888, but he did so off-season, when the figures tend to be locals rather than the fashionable Parisians he painted in Trouville.

The painting has been known for many years as *Figures on the Beach*, but recent research has conclusively identified it as *Marée basse, Berck*, which was among the large group of canvases selected by Boudin's friends for inclusion in the memorial retrospective of the painter's work organized at the École des Beaux-Arts in 1899, the year following his death. How different it is from Manet's genre scene of 1873 (fig. 56a), painted outside the same town. Manet centered his composition on the figures of his wife and mother sitting listlessly in a field. Behind them, the windmills and church tower of the town itself remind us just how Dutch or Flemish this part of France really was. For Boudin, the figures who animate his landscape world are natives who scurry about at water's edge at low tide looking for oysters and clams. He gives us no hint of the town in which they live, allowing them the liberty of free range. They seem almost like chess figures as they move through the space that they themselves calibrate. The whole of their environment is shifting, and Boudin's famous command of grays, beiges, and various whites seems to be the true subject of this almost subjectless picture.

Boudin painted an even larger painting of a startlingly similar scene in the same year. This work, entitled *Marée basse à Étaples*, was given by the Rothschilds to the Musée des Beaux-Arts in Bordeaux (fig. 56b), and it, like the present painting, was included with its current title in the memorial exhibition of 1899. The two paintings are so startlingly similar that one almost wonders whether the Norton Simon picture was used partially as the basis for the larger canvas, which was surely painted as much in the studio as in the landscape itself. The two towns are close enough that the elderly painter or his friends might easily have forgotten whether Boudin was in one or the

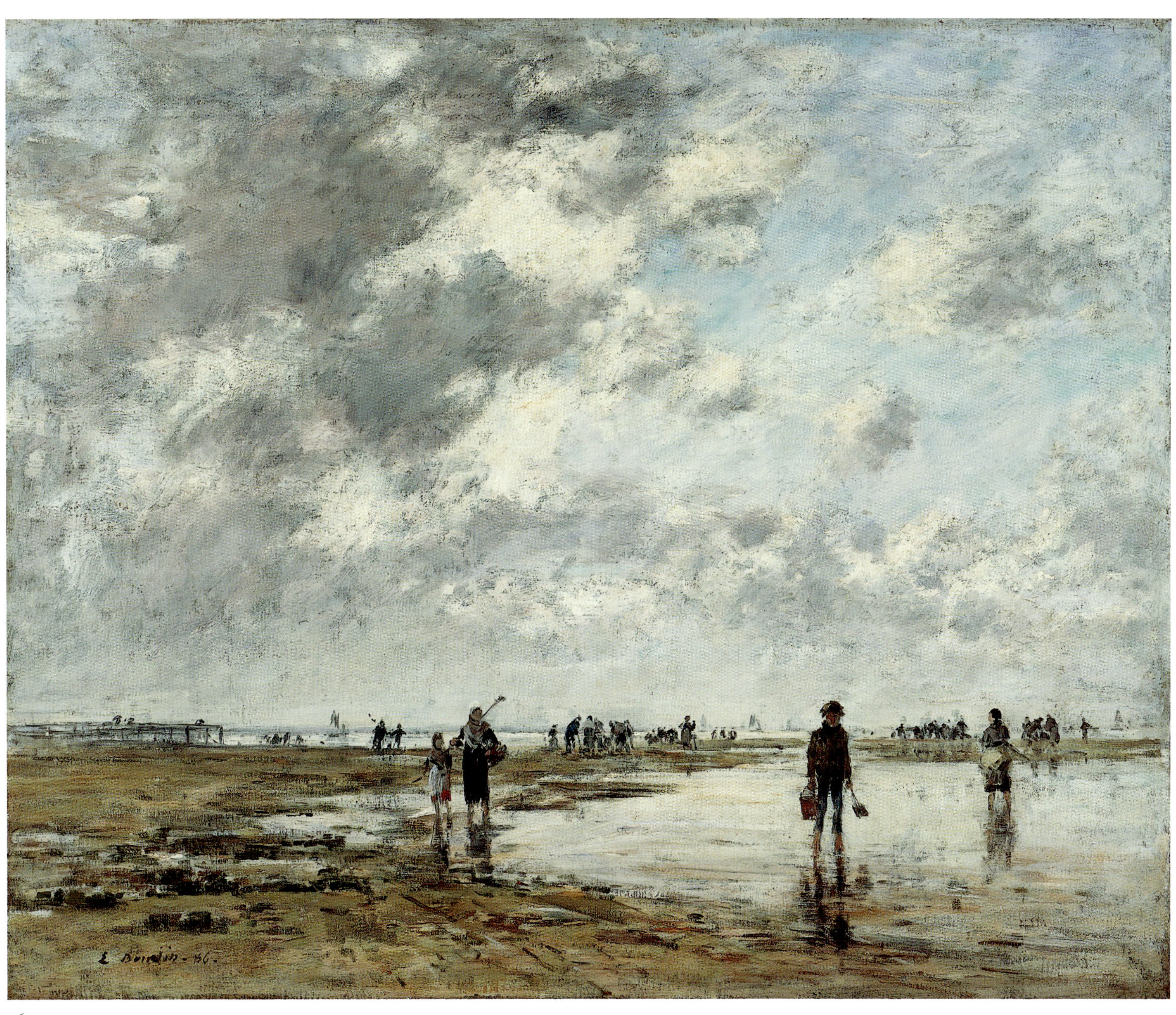

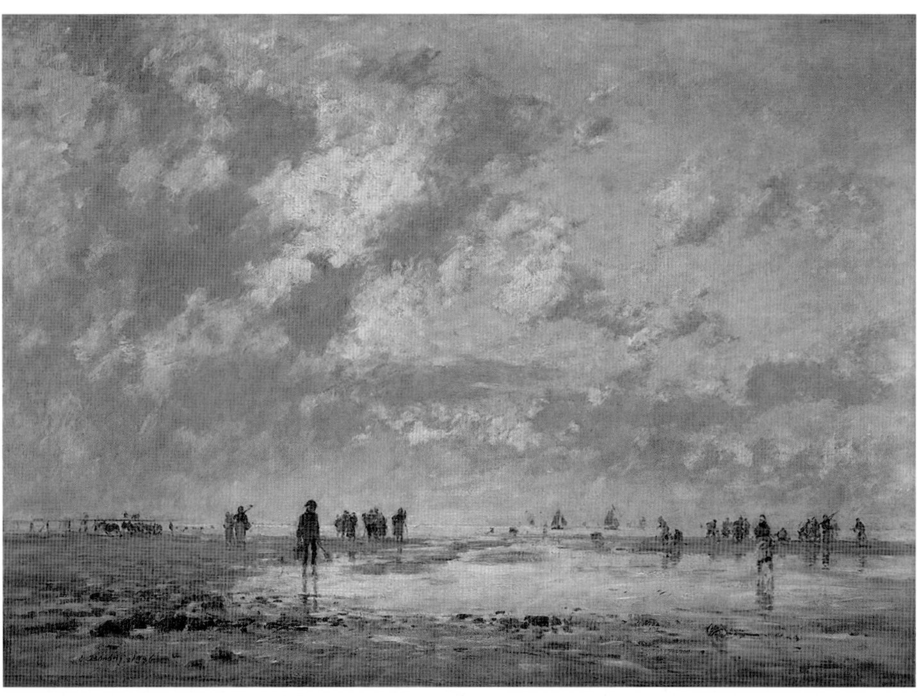

Fig. 56b Eugène Boudin, *Marée basse à Étaples*, 1873, oil on canvas, $31\frac{1}{8} \times 42\frac{7}{8}$ in. (79 × 109 cm), Bordeaux, Musée des Beaux Arts; © M.B.A. de Bordeaux/ photograph Lysiane Gauthier

other when the two paintings were made thirteen years before the memorial exhibition. In all likelihood the smaller painting discussed here was made largely *en plein air* and Boudin then used it to set a chromatic and compositional standard for the larger painting of the same year.

Remarkably, the present work has survived more than a century stretched on its original stretcher without being lined. This means that its delicately brushed pictorial surface is perfectly preserved, allowing us to marvel at Boudin's subtle, yet authoritative, touch. Recent examination has suggested that Boudin may have painted the work without applying a ground to the canvas. It is definitely not commercially primed, as so many of Boudin's canvases were. Instead, the artist chose a very tightly woven canvas and may have painted it directly with no ground. If that is the case, it is likely that he would not have varnished the painting, allowing the resulting dry surface to look almost like a pastel. Boudin was, by 1886, such a confident painter of the effects of light, water, and sand that he could render diverse effects almost instinctively. Yet, even with all his confidence, Boudin made small adjustments as he worked. A series of curved brushstrokes accessible even to the naked eye become, when viewing the X-ray, clear evidence that Boudin started the composition with a boat or two in the foreground, and that the figure of the boy digging clams in the foreground was actually painted over the earlier beached boat. We must be thankful that Boudin's second-tier reputation saved this work from overzealous restorers. Had it been by Monet or Manet, its fate would most likely have been different, and we would not be able to learn as much as we have from its subtle surface.

57

Pierre-Cécile Puvis de Chavannes
French, 1824–1898

The Legendary Saints of France
c. 1877–1878

Gouache on paper, mounted on canvas, three panels, Panel A: $86\frac{1}{4} \times 110\frac{1}{8}$ in. (219 × 279.7 cm); Panel B: 86 1/4 × 142 in. (219 × 360.7 cm); Panel C: $86\frac{1}{4} \times 110\frac{1}{2}$ in. (219 × 280.7 cm)
F.1978.38.1–3

Provenance: [Alfredo Sidès, New York, by 13 November 1935, in partnership with]; [René Gimpel (1881–1944/45), New York]. Hirschl & Adler, New York, consigned 3 March 1960 to; [Hirschl & Adler, New York, gift c. 18 December 1969 to]; Norton Simon, gift 1978 to; The Norton Simon Foundation.

Exhibition: Paris, 1904, no. 16.

References: Price, 1972, nos. 193–195; Wattenmaker, 1975, p. 173; d'Argencourt and Foucart, 1977, p. 136; Chennevières, 1979, fig. 3.

Technical Notes: *The Legendary Saints of France* consists of three oversize gouache-on-paper cartoons. It has suffered a great deal of damage through inappropriate previous treatments and remounting. Despite some cleavage in the paper support, many repairs, and unsympathetic overpainting, the work is relatively stable, but extremely fragile. The work is a virtual collage, as it contains inserts, overlays, and corrections made by the artist as design directions changed. Whole figures have been cut and adhered on top of previously rendered figures. Paper joins are irregular and do not correspond to available paper sheet sizes, but rather to design changes. There are 54-inch-wide paper expanses between joins, indicating access to oversize paper supplies. The paper was laid down on canvas and covered completely in gouache; the paper support is textured like the underlying canvas. However, there are $\frac{1}{4}$-inch borders around the perimeter of the three panels, where the paper is free of media and can be examined. These borders reveal a darkened, embrittled, thick paper wrapped around the strainers. The design layer is executed in relatively thin layers of gouache, with a characteristic matte appearance. The saints' halos in Panel A have an added gilding effect, as bronze or another powder was added to the medium. Panel B does not share this effect, and the halos are a distinct brown gouache. Brushwork is clearly evident, and the artist's style utilized outline and broad contour strokes, with matte, solid color infill to mimic fresco. The work was removed from its strainer, rolled, and restretched in a 1976 treatment, maintaining the original mounting canvas. The canvas support is darkened owing to age and adhesives. The condition of the frieze varies in the three panels: for panel A, the primary support extends within $\frac{1}{2}$ inch of the edges of the secondary support, and the border is wrapped by a narrow strip of Kraft paper. There are gaps in this wrapping paper around the perimeter. For panel B, the canvas mount reveals nail holes and ragged fabric across the top. This is due to a previous remounting, perhaps the 1976 treatment. For panel C, the primary support extends within $\frac{1}{2}$ inch of the edges of the secondary support, and the border is wrapped by a narrow strip of Kraft paper. (SSB)

The compositional and iconographic challenge faced by Puvis de Chavannes in painting his procession of the legendary saints of France above his narrative cycle at the Church of St.- Geneviève in Paris was the following: How is it possible to represent a line of twenty saints in such a way that each one is identifiable and yet the whole group constitutes an organized community? In addition, how is it possible to compose a painted frieze, figures occupying a single, shallow plane, that nevertheless conveys a semblance of the three-dimensionality of life? The problem is an ancient one in art and aesthetics—processional friezes are found in the Parthenon and on the Ara Pacis—and Puvis was not alone among nineteenth-century artists in attempting to devise a modern solution. In the 1830s and 1840s the sculptor David d'Angers placed shallow, crowded, narrative reliefs on the sides of the bases of many of his large-scale commemorative statues. These friezes were purposely simple and direct, at times even crude, in style to appeal to the broadest possible audience. In 1841 the painter Paul Delaroche completed his mural *Hemicycle,* also known as *Artists of All Ages,* for the École des Beaux-Arts, a vast panorama that depicted an assemblage—part procession and part colloquy—of more than seventy artists from antiquity to the eighteenth century. And a decade later, Jean-Léon Gérôme exhibited a frieze of extremely naturalistically painted figures titled *Nations Bringing Their Tribute to the World's Fair in London* (National Ceramic Museum, Sèvres).

Puvis's solution to the problem of the frieze at St.-Geneviève was to organize these patron saints of French provincial cities into three discrete groups, separated by the same intercolumniation that divided the narrative cycle below. The result is a parade of figures that is at once flat and robust, unified yet individual. The halos and gold-patterned background behind the saints emphasize the decorativeness and two-dimensionality of the frieze, but the figures' placement makes it appear as if they were actually marching behind the fluted half-columns. They walk, stand, bless, converse, gaze heavenward, and cast their glances earthward as individuals. In the left panel, a young man, accompanied by a child, is apparently cured of blindness by Saint Lucien, bishop of Beauvais. In the center panel, a dragon accompanies the slow perambulation of Saint Martha of

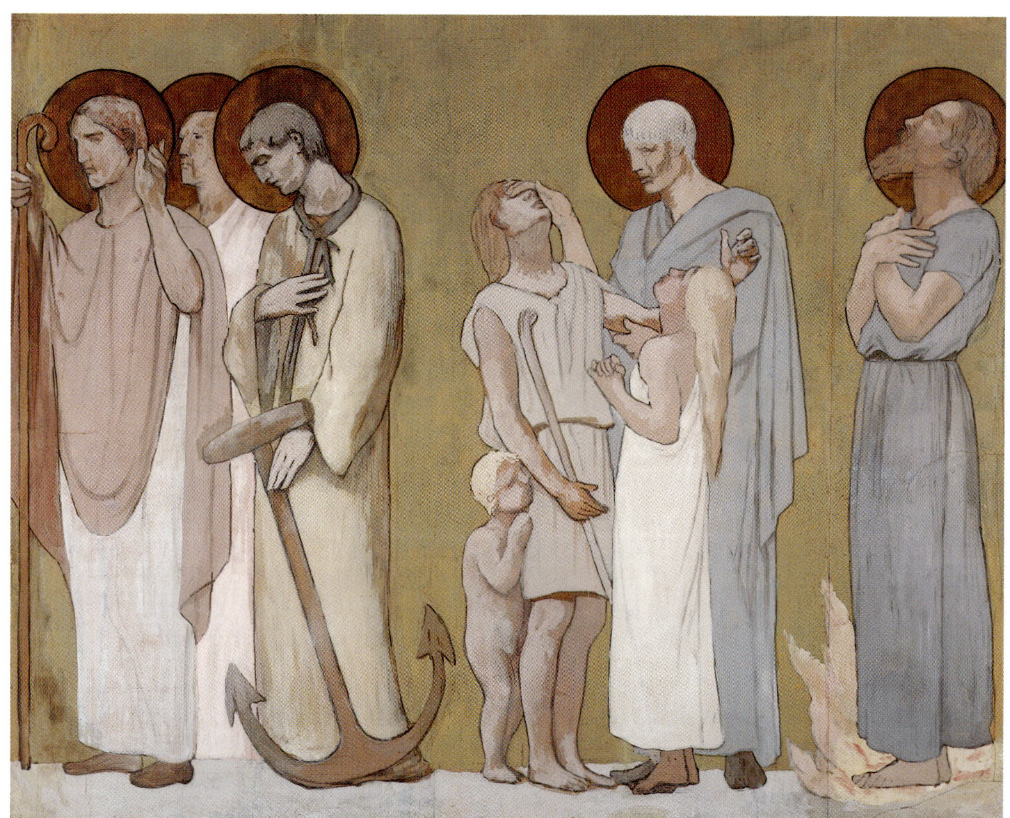

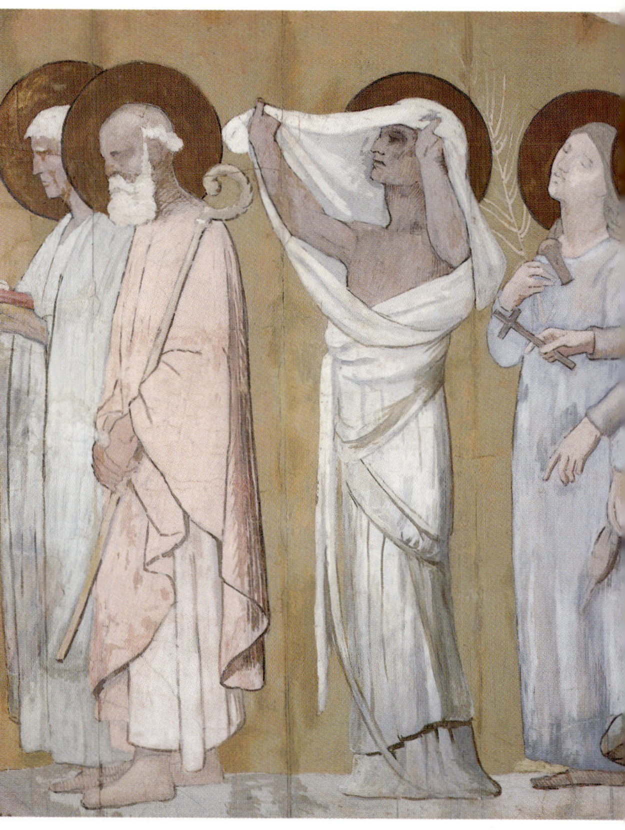

57

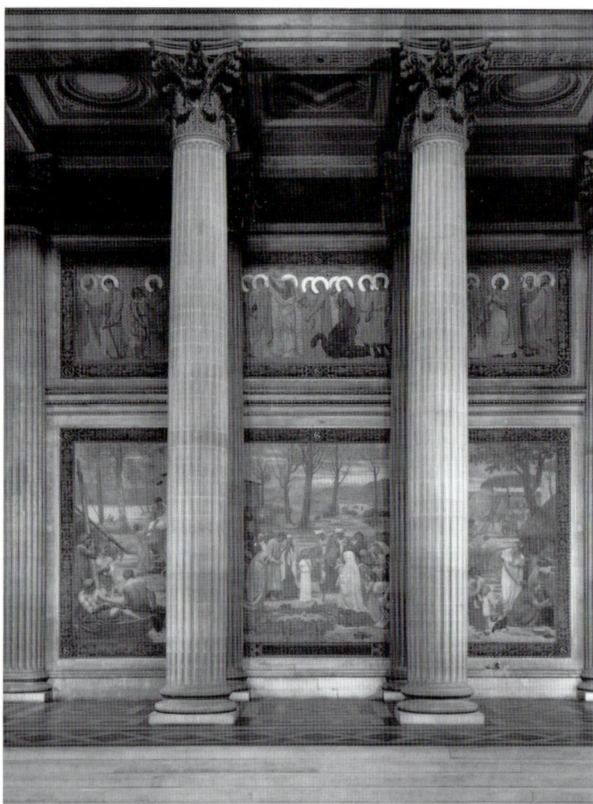

Fig. 57a Pierre-Cécile Puvis de Chavannes, *Legendary Saints of France* and *The Pastoral Life of St. Geneviève*, installed in 1877, Panthéon, Paris

Provence, Saint Columbia of Sens, and Saint Madeleine of Provence. In the right-hand panel, Saint Trophimus, bishop of Arles, and Saint Paul, bishop of Narbonne, stop to chat.

The present panels are full-scale gouache-on-paper studies for the mural paintings in the Panthéon (fig. 57a). According to the research of Aimée Brown Price, Puvis's working method often consisted of a progression from small studies—in charcoal, red or black chalk, pencil, sanguine, or watercolor—to larger oil sketches using thinned oil, gouache, and other media, to full-scale oil sketches or cartoons, and finally to finished work.[1] He also often painted reduced replicas of his large-scale murals, as in the case of the Norton Simon *Pastoral Life of Saint Geneviève* (cat. 58) and the *Legendary Saints of France* in the Philadelphia Museum of Art (fig. 57b). The oil sketches and cartoons of Puvis, such as the *Study for Saint Geneviève as a Child in Prayer* (Van Gogh Museum, Amsterdam), *The Sacred Wood* (Clemens-Sels Museum, Neuss), and *The Benefits of Peace* (National Gallery of Canada, Ottawa), are often his most experimental and formally audacious works.

The Legendary Saints of France achieves an unusual formal unity by virtue of its extreme simplification of forms and its muted tonal range of pinks, browns, blues, and greens all mixed with white. The bodies of the saints are elongated, recalling the stone saints surrounding the

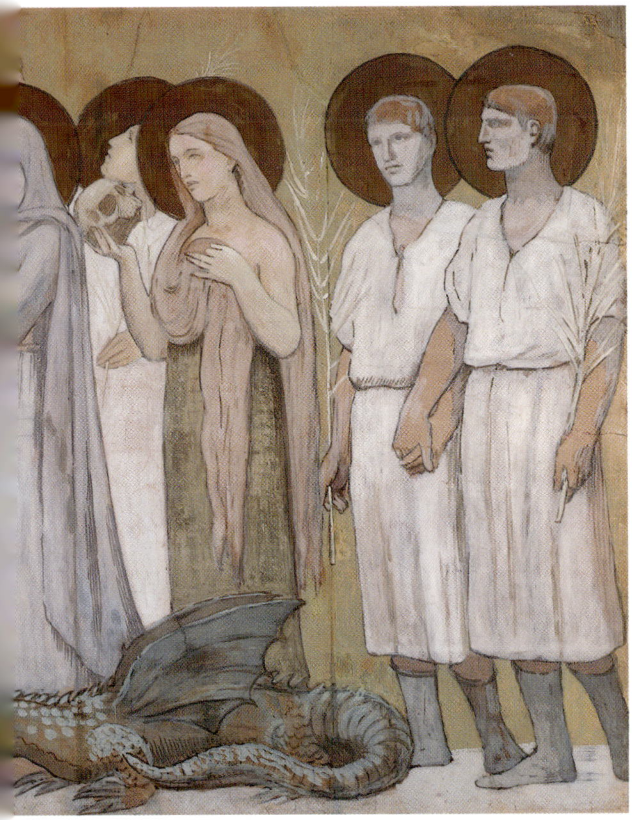

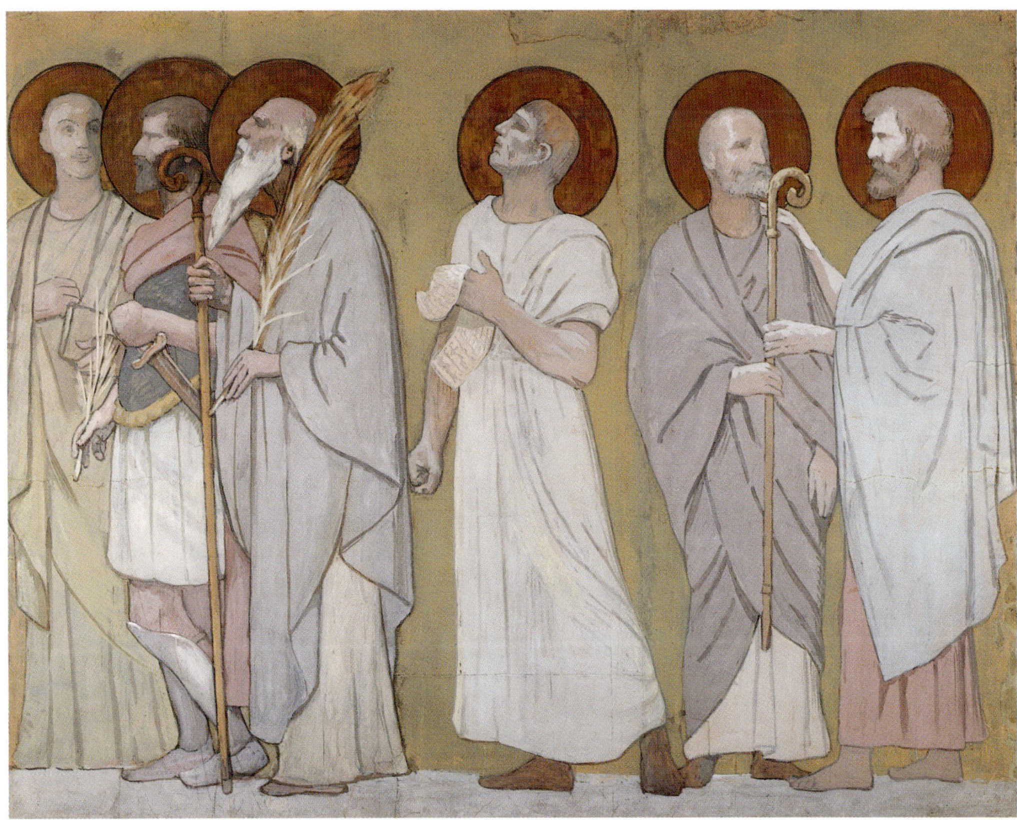

east portal of the south transept (c. 1220) at the Cathedral of Chartres. (The elongations of Puvis's figures appear even greater by virtue of the way in which they extend nearly the entire height of the support. They stand on a narrow white ground plane, like a ledge or catwalk.) The figures are broadly and thinly painted and in some cases consist of little more than sepia outline and gouache infill. Modeling is thus perfunctory: the neck of the boy in the left panel who is being cured of his blindness is painted with a dark pink-brown pigment and his lower neck in a much brighter hue of pink; there is no transition or half-tone to join the two parts. The effect of Puvis's unusually simple and direct form and color is at once monumentality and a saintly noncorporeality. The figures are stony, as if marble dust or plaster were mixed with their blood. And they march in a slow, even lugubrious procession, enacting for all eternity their miraculous acts of kindness and cure or displaying the means of their martyrdom.

1 Oral communication with the authors. Also see Aimée Brown Price, "Puvis de Chavannes' Critical Fortune," in Lemoine, 2002, pp. 61–69.

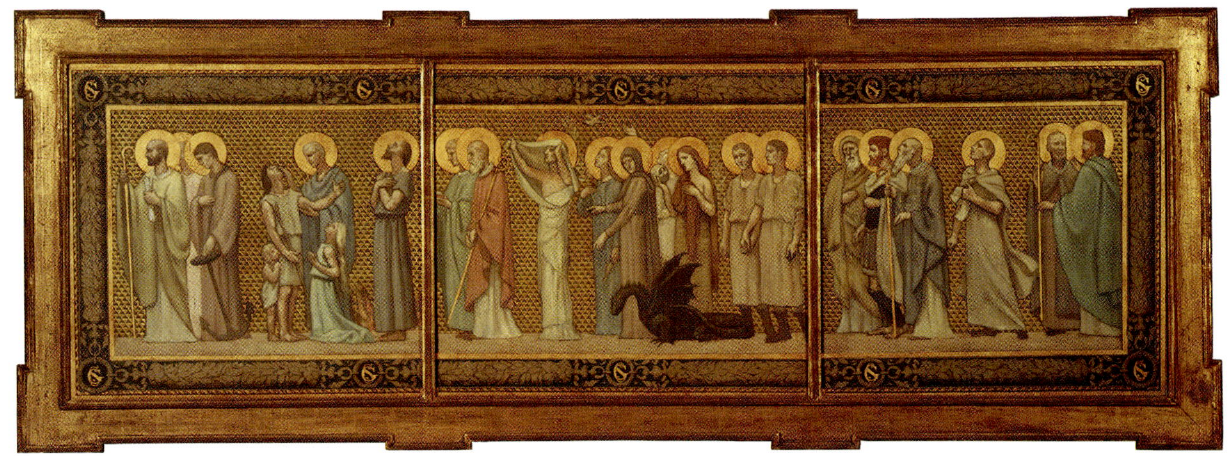

Fig. 57b Pierre-Cécile Puvis de Chavannes, *Legendary Saints of France* (reduced version), c. 1879, oil on canvas, three panels, panel A: $30\frac{1}{4} \times 32\frac{1}{2}$ in. (76.8 × 82.5 cm); panel B: $30\frac{1}{4} \times 35$ in. (76.8 × 88.9 cm); panel C: $30\frac{1}{4} \times 32$ in. (76.8 × 81.3 cm), The Philadelphia Museum of Art, given by Dr. and Mrs. Richard W. Levy; © The Philadelphia Museum of Art / Art Resource, NY

58

Pierre-Cécile Puvis de Chavannes
French, 1824–1898

The Pastoral Life of Saint Geneviève
1879

Oil on canvas, three panels, Panel A: 53 × 32¼ in. (134.5 × 81.9 cm); Panel B: 53 × 35⅛ in. (134.5 × 89.1 cm); Panel C: 52¾ × 32¼ in. (134 × 81.9 cm)
Signed and dated lower right: "P. Puvis de Chavannes '79"
M.1968.49

Provenance: Catholina Lambert (1834–1923), Patterson, N.J. (sale, New York, Plaza Hotel, 21–24 February 1916, lot 186, to); F. von Hellman [for?]; I. Johns [?], or John Quinn (1870–1924), New York.[1] Mr. and Mrs. James Byrne (or Byron),[2] consigned 18 June 1923 to; [Durand-Ruel, Paris, photograph no. A1310, sold before the end of 1923 to]; Art Institute of Chicago,[3] inv. no. 23.954, sold January 1955 to; [E. & A. Silberman Galleries, New York, sold 5 December 1963 to]; Huntington Hartford Collection, Gallery of Modern Art, New York, sold January 1968 to; [Hirschl & Adler Galleries, Inc., New York, sold July 1968 to]; Norton Simon Art Foundation.

Exhibitions: Paris, 1887, no. 1; Paris, 1889, no. 561(?); New York, 1894, no. 10(?); Brooklyn, 1956, no. 26, ill.; South Hadley, 1966, no. 31, ill.; Princeton, 1972, no. 25, ill.; San Francisco, 1974, no. 30, ill.; Amsterdam, 1994, no. 74, ill.

References: Michel and Laran, 1912, pp. 41–44; Metropolitan Museum of Art, 1916, p. 134; Art Institute of Chicago, 1923, p. 110, cover ill.; Art Institute of Chicago, 1924, pp. 117–120; *Art News*, 1924, p. 1; Art Institute of Chicago 1925, pp. 56, ill., 149, no. 627 (1932 ed., pp. 51–53); Minneapolis Institute of Arts, 1930, pp. 44–46; Venturi, 1939, vol. 2, p. 95; Price, 1972, nos. 201–203, pp. 461–464; d'Argencourt and Foucart, 1977, pp. 9, 136, 138–139, under nos. 114, 120; Boucher, 1979, pp. 64, 66, under nos. 74, 77; Trudzinski, 1987, p. 222; Price, 1994, no. 74, pp. 152–154, 155, ill.; Thomson, R., 1994, p. 477; Price, 1995, p. 129; Lemoine, 2002, p. 204 nn. 50 and 51.

Technical Notes: Three separate paintings, of uniform height but slightly differing widths, combine visually to make a single composition, which is surrounded by a faux-painted frame, ornamented with a typical French twisted border at the outside and the monogram of *SG* regularly spaced in the decorative border. The materials and construction are identical in each of the three panels. The heavy, plain-weave canvas retains the original tacking edges and is unlined. The fabric is becoming brittle, and in several places a tacking edge has split or the canvas is torn around the tack holes. There are no damages to the canvas within the painted portion. These are probably the original stretchers. The canvases were prepared with a double ground, which can be seen on the tacking edges and in several losses. The first (lower) layer is rosy beige; the second (upper) layer is medium gray. Both layers may be oil bound, judging by the thickness and the gloss. In spite of the thickness of the grounds, the canvas texture remains evident. It appears that the artist's preliminary drawing was done with graphite or charcoal, although this is difficult to determine because the painting has been varnished, changing the refractive index. Opaque paint in a rather thick and pastelike consistency was dragged over the textured canvas support with a brush. Occasionally there are multiple layers. For example, there was more than one application of blue in the sky, as the first layer, slightly less viscous, fills in the canvas weave recesses; then a thicker, heavier layer was brushed over this, not entirely covering it. Generally, the paint is very well preserved. There is very little cracking. In the left panel, there are several minor paint losses in the blue sky at the left beside the tree. Paint appears to have been brushed on more quickly, leaving more gaps and more exposed ground, as in the boat at the bottom. In the central panel there are two conspicuous paint losses in the standing figure at the center right. There is a diagonal feather crack through the lavender mountains at center left. Scattered abrasion and scuffs are at all edges, and there are several tiny flake losses in the sky. The right panel is slightly more worn than the other two, with minor damages at the edges. The canvas seems more fragile and the paint appears to be less supple, with mechanical cracking and small losses. The surface is heavily soiled along the left side. The paint is abraded in many areas, but it is unclear whether it was the artist's intention or the result of an intervention; for example, the tree trunk at the upper right appears multilayered as well as rubbed down. The faux frame consists of a decorative border at the tops and bottoms in addition to the outer sides of the left and right panels. The design, painted in gold with glazes to deepen shadows, was drawn freehand with thin gray lines. A small amount of shading and subtle highlights were employed to suggest three-dimensionality. No record of earlier restoration was found. Microscopic examination revealed no retouching or remains of darkened varnish left from cleaning. The surfaces have been varnished, however, and it is possible that the paintings have had no previous treatment other than the adjustment of canvas tension, as evidenced by the opened stretcher corners. (RW)

In 1874 the French painter Pierre Puvis de Chavannes was awarded a commission for a set of mural paintings for the Panthéon, then properly called the Church of St.-Geneviève, in Paris. According to the contract between the artist, Philippe de Chennevières, directeur des Beaux-Arts, and l'Abbé Bonnefoy, the latter's ecclesiastic assistant, the subject of the murals was to be "The national-religious history of France during the first four centuries, A.D."[4] The commission further stipulated that the mural ensemble occupy two tiers of wall: the lower section was to represent the "education of the young Saint Geneviève" and the "pastoral life of the same saint," and the upper register, "a procession of holy persons." Moreover, according to Chennevières and Bonnefoy, the murals had to be readable as single compositions, even though they were to be separated into thirds to accommodate the fluted Corinthian half-columns that divided the wall. Puvis began work on the commission at once, and the murals—they are actually oil paintings on canvas—were completed and fully installed by the late spring of 1878 (see fig. 57a).

As the art historian Aimée Brown Price has shown, the mural project at St.-Geneviève was extremely important both to government officials and to the career of Puvis. The massive, Neoclassical church, designed by Jacques-Germain Soufflot and built between 1755 and about 1790, was transformed in 1791 into a *Panthéon des Grands Hommes* in honor of founding and fallen figures of the Revolution. The public, patriotic significance of the building was reiterated in 1830, when the sculptor David d'Angers was commissioned by the new government of the July Monarchy to decorate a pediment relief with the subject "To Great Men the Fatherland is Grateful." Twenty-one years later, after another change of regime, Napoleon III had the edifice reconsecrated as part of an effort to deemphasize the revolutionary history of France and to strengthen the entente between church and state. The building remained a church until 1885, when it was once again turned into a pantheon of national heroes, the function it retains to this day.

In the year of Puvis's commission, the French nation was in a politically and economically perilous state. Napoleon III's capitulation to Prussian forces at Sedan in September 1870 and the subsequent surrender of the French army left the country demoralized and militarily vulnerable. The loss of territory along the German border and the imposition of crushing financial reparations further weakened the state. And finally, the rise and defeat of the Paris Commune of 1871—the first self-described "communist" insurrection in European history—revealed the depth of the social and class conflicts that divided France. In 1874 the ruins of the burned Tuileries Palace and Hôtel de Ville—just a short walk from the hill crowned by St.-Geneviève—could still be seen, and Paris remained under martial law.

The redecoration of the Church of St.-Geneviève, which engaged the talents of more than a dozen artists besides Puvis, was thus clearly an effort of the new "Government of Moral Order" to concentrate public attention on the sacred and heroic origins of Paris and the French nation and to reinvigorate a flagging patriotic spirit. The life and legend of Saint Geneviève in fact had been frequently invoked during the Franco-Prussian War—she was said to have protected fifth-century Paris from Attila the Hun—and her cult remained powerful in the war's aftermath. Puvis's mural project, his first in Paris, was thus an extraordinary chance for him to set his work before an eager public, influential patrons, and the best artists in the nation. By all accounts, he did not squander the opportunity. His full-scale cartoon for *The Pastoral Life of Saint Geneviève* (fig. 58a), exhibited at the Salon of 1876, was described by the critic Charles Yriarte as "a heroic achievement,"[5] and the final mural was claimed by Chennevières to have created an "immense sensation . . . like a festival of art."[6]

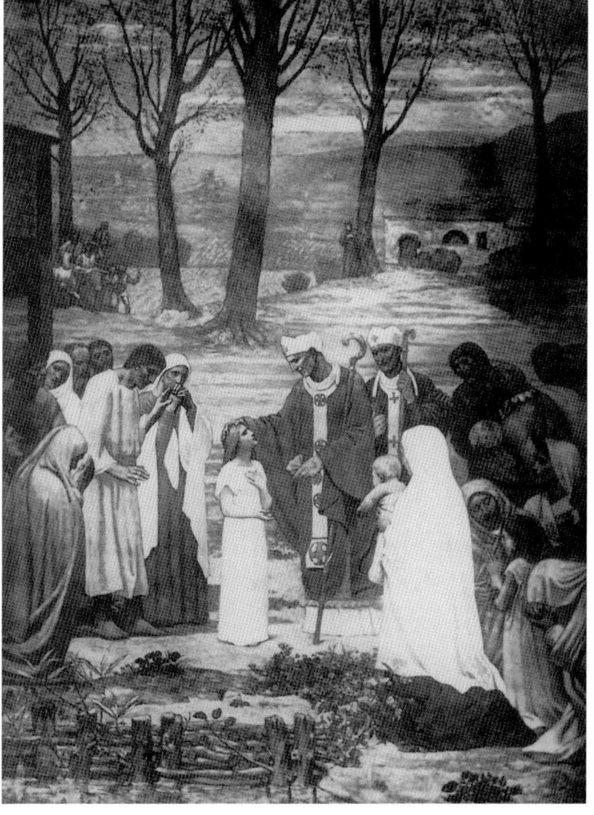

Fig. 58a Pierre-Cécile Puvis de Chavannes, *The Pastoral Life of Saint Geneviève*, oil on canvas, Musées Royaux d'Art et d'Histoire, Brussels

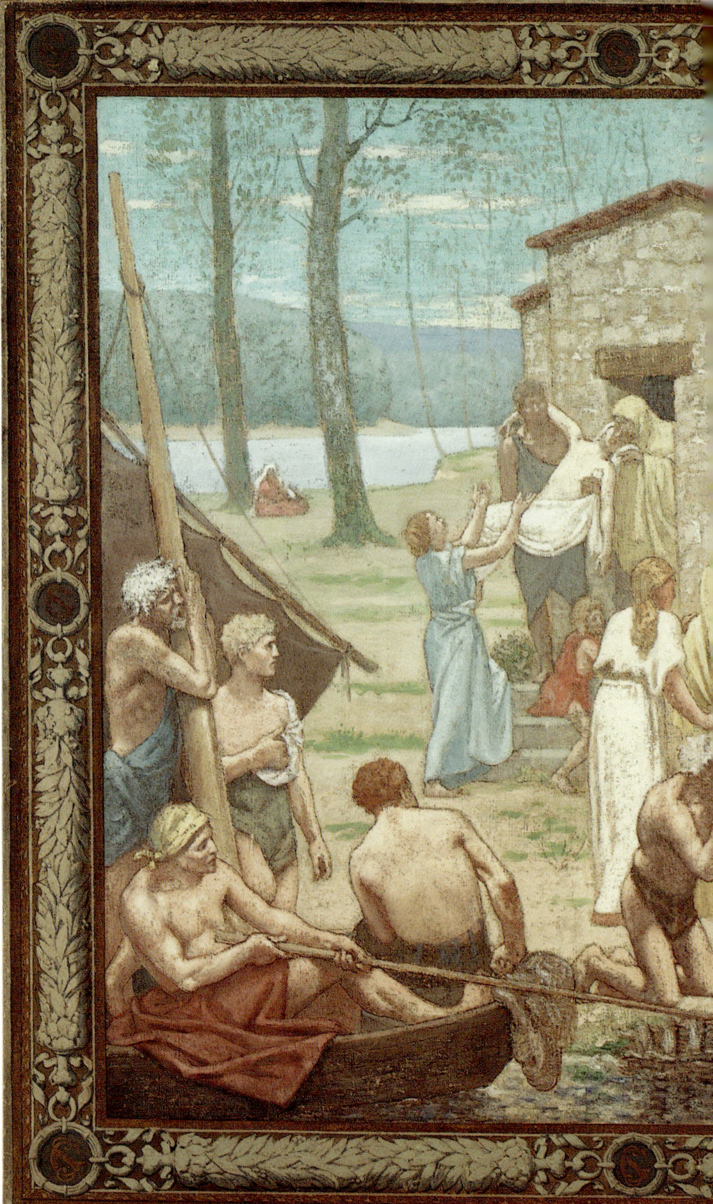
58

The Pastoral Life of Saint Geneviève in the Norton Simon collection is a reduced, later replica of the original mural in the Panthéon, but it exhibits all of the formal and iconographic elements that occasioned its great celebrity and acclaim. A still smaller version, formerly in the James J. Hill collection, was painted in 1874 (fig. 58b). The three canvases represent the moment when the young girl entered the stage of French history. The inscription below the central panel reads (in translation): "In the year 429, Saint Germain of Auxerre and Saint Loup de Troyes, on their way to England to fight the Pelagian heresy, arrive in the vicinity of Nanterre; in the crowd gathered to meet them, Saint Germain distinguishes a child marked for him with a divine seal. He foretells to her parents the high destiny to which she has been called. That child was Saint Geneviève, patron saint of Paris."[7] The composition of the central panel, which conveys the bulk of the narrative, is an ingenious one. The bishop-saints and townspeople form a block, linked by overlapping forms, common gestures, and shared expressions of piety. The crowd, however, has parted in the middle to make room for a young, blond girl dressed in white. She is the future Saint Geneviève, shown in a posture of supplication and humility. Saint Germain places his right, ungloved hand on the top of her head and voices the prophesy. At the left, the child's parents stand and listen with rapt attention; to the right, a kneeling woman presents her infant child for benediction. Above the figures to the right is a farmhouse, to the left a manger and a distant view of Nanterre. And beyond that, a line of blue-purple hills culminating in Mont Valérian, the hill that dominates the western approach to the city of Paris. A row of five trees in the middle ground reaches up into the cloud-streaked blue sky; the largest of them stands above the figure of the young girl. She will be the source of strength and succor for untold generations.

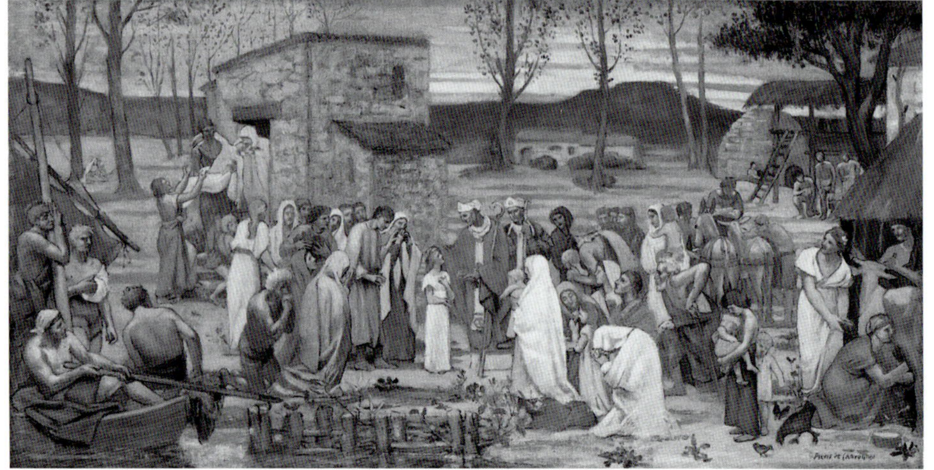
Fig. 58b Pierre-Cécile Puvis de Chavannes, *Sketch for "The Pastoral Life of Saint Geneviève"*, 1874, oil on canvas, 20½ × 40½ in. (52 × 103 cm), Private collection; photo: Christie's Images

The panels at left and right depict the early economic, social, and spiritual life of the community. On the left, according to Puvis's own account quoted by Chennevières, "some boaters [on the Seine] approach the bank and contemplate the scene, while from a hovel, a sick youth is carefully brought forward in order that he

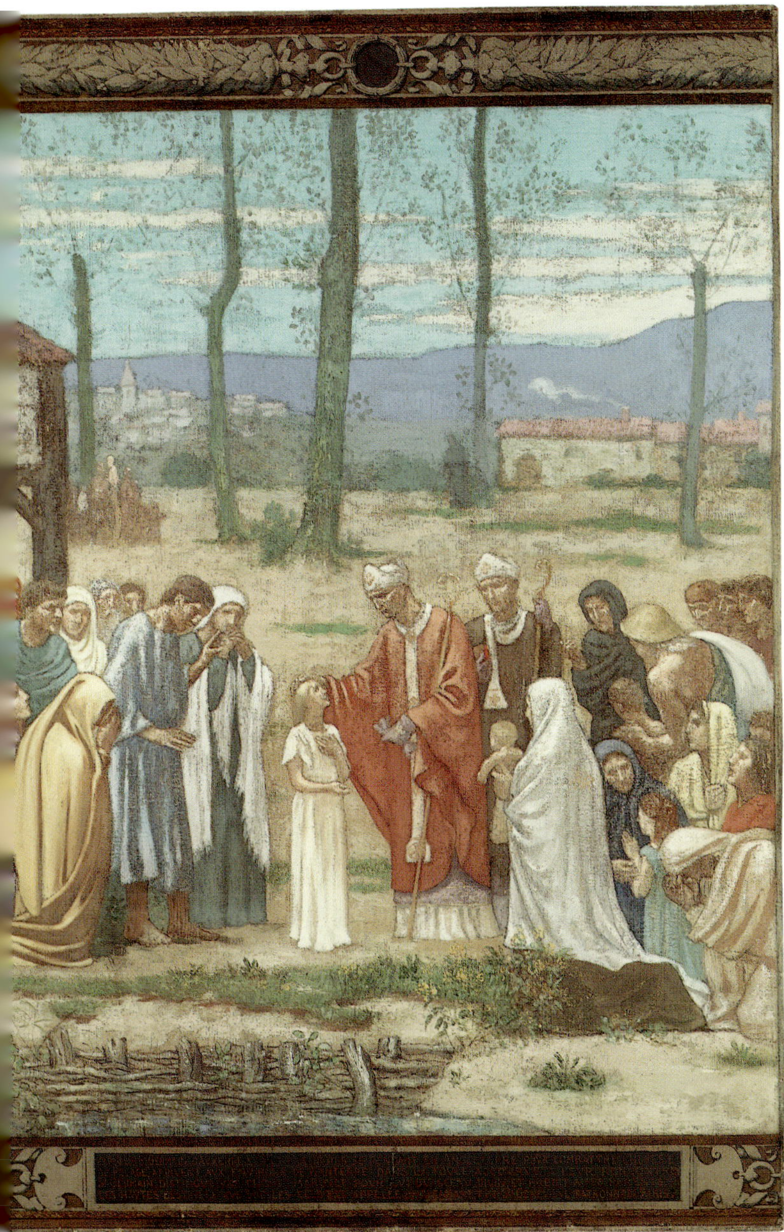
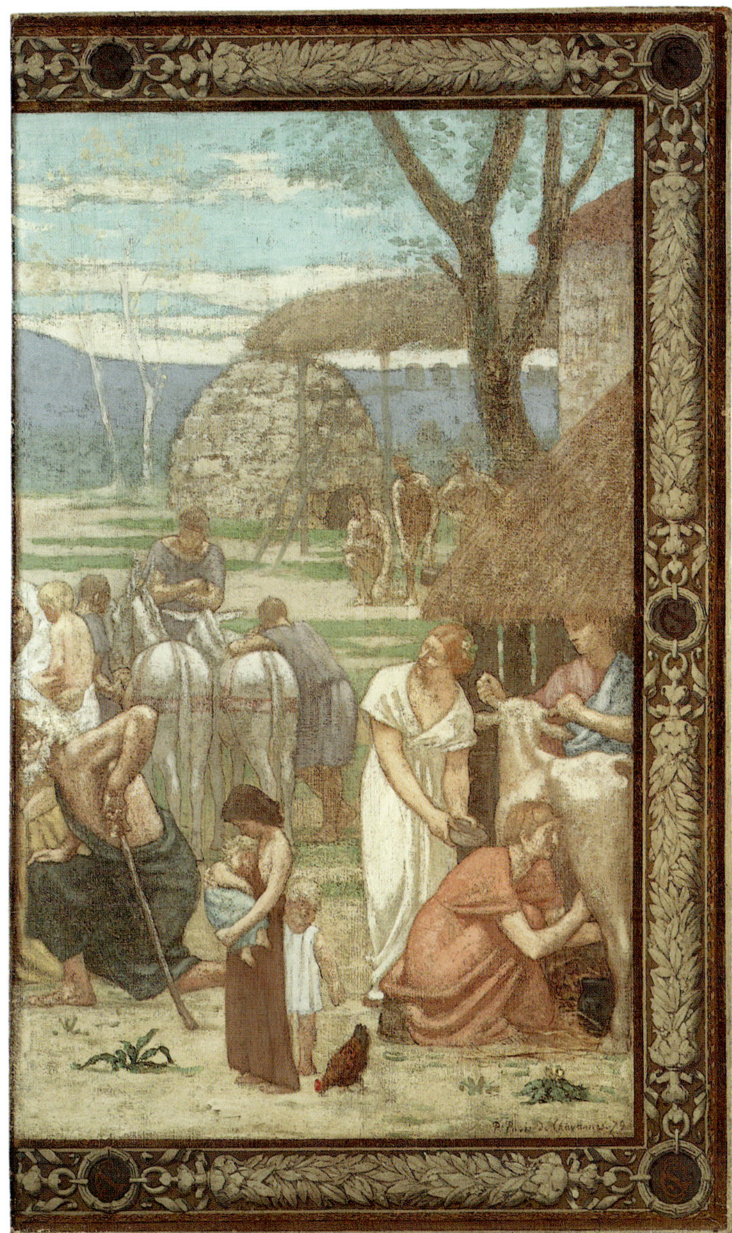

may be touched and cured by the bishop-saints." On the right are vignettes of farming, animal husbandry, and primitive craft: three girls work together to milk a cow, some potters in the background (Puvis called them "semi-savages") tend their wares and observe the scene, a hen pecks in the foreground. "The right panel," Puvis added, "is full of emotions . . . ; an old man crippled with age painfully attempts to kneel down; a young beggar keeps her distance, a little like a pariah, with the weight of a big child asleep in her arms . . . while the attendants of the bishops rest, indifferent to the impression they are creating all around them."[8]

Throughout his long career, Puvis de Chavannes was extremely skilled at succinctly conveying the basics of often complex narrative and allegorical programs. His large mural projects for the Amiens Museum, *Ave Picardia nutrix* (*Hail, Picardy the Nourisher*, 1865) and *Ludus pro patria* (*The Family*, 1882), are ingenious summaries of local legend, national myth, and contemporary anthropological thinking. Like the Norton Simon triptych, they appealed to lay and learned audiences alike and conveyed an extremely conservative social and political message, preaching nationalism, Catholic piety, and the acceptance of social and sexual stratification.

Yet Puvis's art was widely admired by some of the most politically and artistically radical artists of the nineteenth and twentieth centuries, including Édouard Manet,

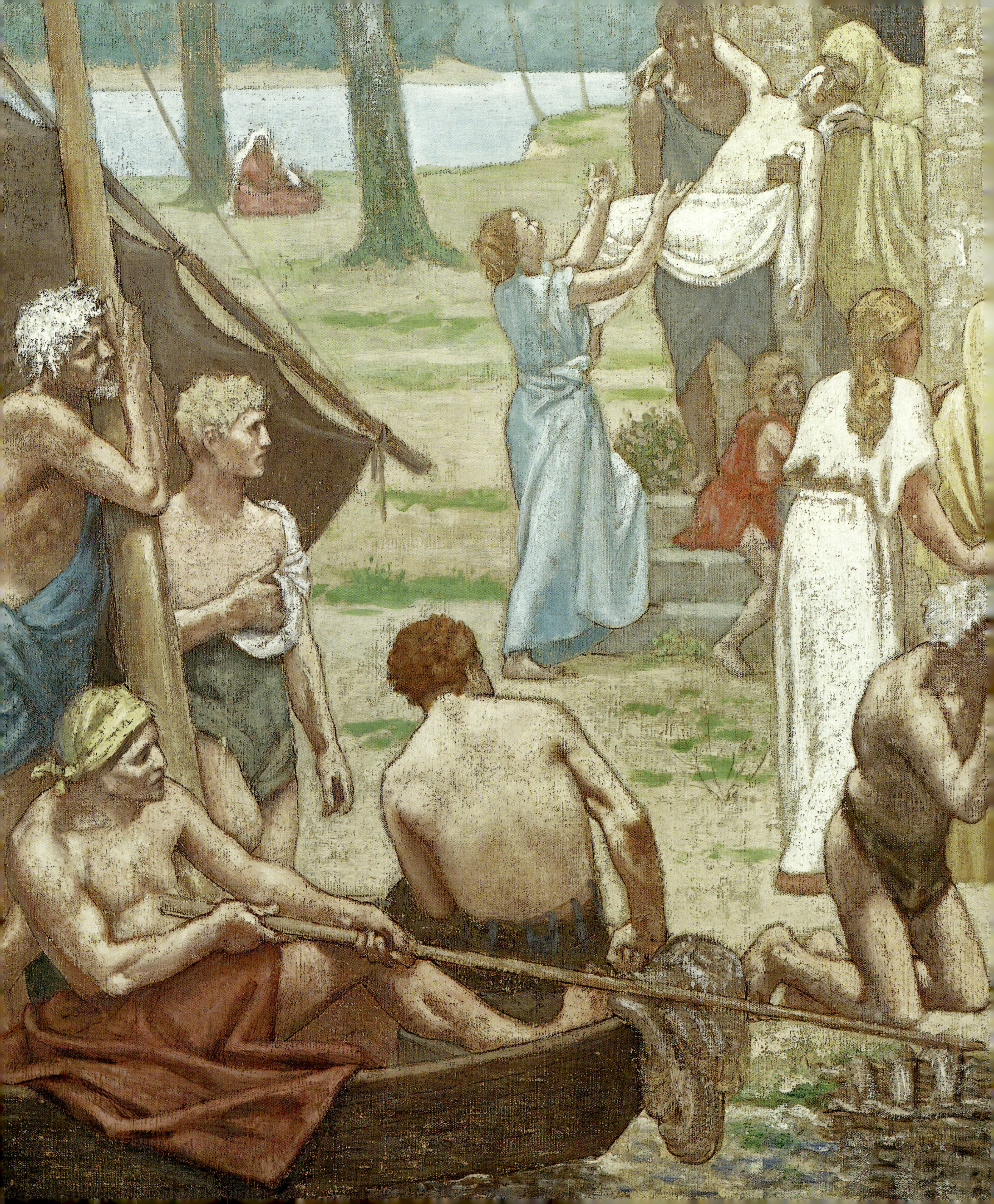

Vincent van Gogh, Paul Gauguin, Georges Seurat, and Pablo Picasso. The reason for his popularity among such diverse audiences must be his thematic and formal ingenuousness. The cool, flat colors in *The Pastoral Life of Saint Geneviève* (the canvases are in a superb state of preservation), combined with some passages of almost Impressionist handling, especially in the water at the bottom of the left and center panels, placed the artist among the young avant-garde of the mid-1870s as well as the Salon favorites Alexandre Cabanel, William-Adolphe Bouguereau, Paul Baudry, and Ernest Meissonier. The thin paint, Giottesque forms, and frank exposure of the texture of the canvas associated the work with both antique and late medieval art, and with a new generation of modernists who insisted on recognition of the fictive nature of representational art. This modern archaism was such an important aspect of Puvis's reputation that it alone explains why the great modernist collector John Quinn owned this triptych along with fifty other works by Puvis. It also makes clear just why the Art Institute of Chicago, whose collection of modern painting is the best of any American art museum, trumpeted its acquisition of the Norton Simon painting in the 5 April 1924 issue of *Art News* just two years before it acquired Seurat's *Sunday Afternoon on the Island of La Grande Jatte* (1884–1886), which is heavily indebted to Puvis. Fortunately for Norton Simon, the Art Institute pruned its Puvis holdings, trading this superb painting for other modernist works at the Silberman Galleries. From there, it was acquired by Huntington Hartford for his Gallery of Modern Art in New York. Not many major paintings have been owned by three museums in one century.

1 According to Price, 1972, p. 461, the buyer was "I. Johns"; Lemoine, 2002, p. 204 nn. 50 and 51, provides the only evidence that John Quinn owned the work; other references indicate von Hellman.

2 Caroline Durand-Ruel confirmed the name as Mr. and Mrs. James Byrne from company stock books; other sources suggest the name might be "Byron."

3 Price, 1972 and 1974, mentions Wert D. Walker in the provenance of the picture, however, the sale from Durand-Ruel was directly to the Art Institute of Chicago, purchased with funds from Mr. Walker.

4 Price, 1994.

5 Yriarte, 1876, pp. 694–695.

6 Chennevières, 1885, pp. 72–73.

7 "L'an 429, St. Germain d'Auxerre et St. Loup de Troyes se rendant en Angeeterre [*sic*] pour combattre l'hérésie de Pélage, arrivent aux environs de Nanterre; dans la foule accourue à leur rencontre, St. Germain distingue une enfant marquée pour lui du sceau divin, et prédit à ses parents les hautes destinées aus quelles [*sic*] elle est appelée, cette enfant fut Ste. Geneviève patronne de Paris." The inscription differs slightly from that in the Panthéon.

8 Chennevières, 1885, pp. 72–73.

59

William-Adolphe Bouguereau
French, 1825–1905

Monsieur M.
1850

Oil on canvas, $34\frac{1}{4} \times 27\frac{3}{4}$ in. (87 × 70.5 cm)
Signed and dated lower left: "W. Bouguerea(u) / 1850"
M.1977.13.1

Provenance: [Établissement Rustique, Vaduz, Liechtenstein, consigned to]; [Heim Gallery, Ltd., London, sold 1977 to]; Norton Simon Art Foundation.

Exhibition: Paris, 1850, no. 338.

Reference: Vachon, 1900, p. 145.

Technical Notes: The support, a plain-weave canvas, has the original tacking edges at the left side and the bottom. The canvas has been wax-lined, and additions approximately $2\frac{3}{8}$-inch wide were added to the original support at the top and right sides. This is supported by the X-radiograph, which shows cut edges of fringed canvas at both the top and the right, near where the strip lining would join the sides of the original canvas. Another painting, beneath the portrait and upside down, appears to be a seated or standing male nude: his head turned to the left, his torso, both arms, and proper left leg are fully developed, but his right leg is not as clearly seen (fig. 59c). The X-ray also reveals numerous damages to the original canvas. The off-white ground has a gritty, granular character (also distinctly visible on the X-radiograph), which imparts a prominent texture to the surface of the entire painting. The added portions at the top and right each have an uneven, bumpy surface; the characteristics of a ground layer, if any, are undetermined. The paint is smoothly brushed and blended wet into wet with subtle color modulations. Almost no brush marking is visible. In much of the dark areas, chemical abrasion has occurred. The above-mentioned damages have been retouched. The added widths at top and right sides have been thickly and broadly overpainted. Under ultraviolet light, the milky blue fluorescence suggests that the varnish is an aged synthetic resin. However, there is a variety of fluorescence including some older natural resin, which remains in much of the dark coat. The varnish above the additions at the top and right is dull and rather blotchy. (RW)

The life, career, and reputation of William-Adolphe Bouguereau exemplify the successes and failures of artistic instruction offered by the École des Beaux-Arts in Paris in the mid–nineteenth century. Enrolled there in 1846 and placed in the studio of François-Édouard Picot (himself a pupil of Jacques-Louis David), Bouguereau quickly achieved official and public success. Awarded a Premier Grand Prix de Rome in 1850, he studied at the Villa Medici for nearly four years and attained a real proficiency in the techniques and manners of the Baroque and Renaissance artists who had made Rome the European capital of art for more than two centuries, from about 1500 to 1750. Bouguereau's ambitious early canvases—primarily devoted to classical and religious subjects—reveal carefully staged and balanced multifigure compositions, warm, subdued colors, and high finish. The same deliberate approach to painting, requiring initial oil sketches, subsequent pencil, chalk, and charcoal drawings taken from life, and the final application of successive layers of paint to canvas, would characterize all his later practice.

By the late 1850s Bouguereau was receiving commissions from both church and state and regularly exhibiting at the annual Salons. His many Christian subjects—the deaths of martyrs, the life of Christ and the saints—are pious in spirit and sentimental in feeling. His paintings of classical subjects, such as *Apollo and the Muses* (Grand Théâtre de Bordeaux, Bordeaux) are frankly derived from Raphael, Poussin, and Ingres but display a greater concern with anecdote and theatricality. His contemporary history paintings, including *Napoleon III Visiting the Flood Victims of Tarascon in 1856* (1856, Hôtel de Ville, Tarascon), are fewer in number and both theatrical and nakedly propagandistic. Finally, Bouguereau's genre subjects, especially his many depictions of mothers and children such as *First Caresses* (fig. 59a), are ingratiating, often to the point of being saccharine.

Bouguereau's paintings were eagerly collected by wealthy patrons in both France and the United States and widely reproduced in engravings, photogravures, lithographs, and even postcards. By this means, his works became better known and admired than those of perhaps any other artist of his time. It was this very aspect of his art, its apparent meretriciousness combined with the artist's unalloyed devotion to academic rules, that prompted scorn from the Impressionist artists and their followers. Indeed, by the end of the nineteenth century, the increased regard for French modernism led to a precipitous decline in Bouguereau's reputation.[1] By the 1920s Bouguereau was almost a forgotten figure among

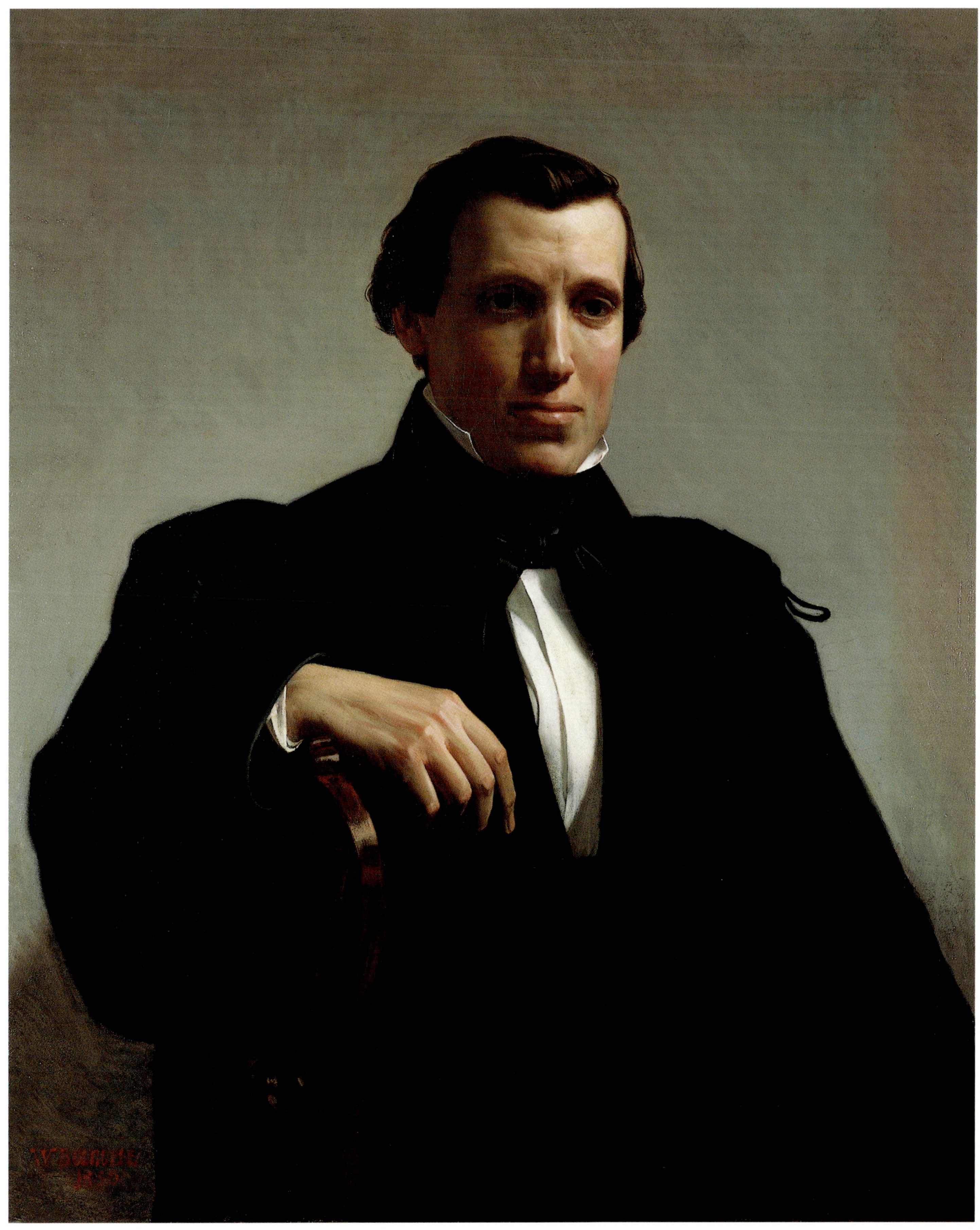

59

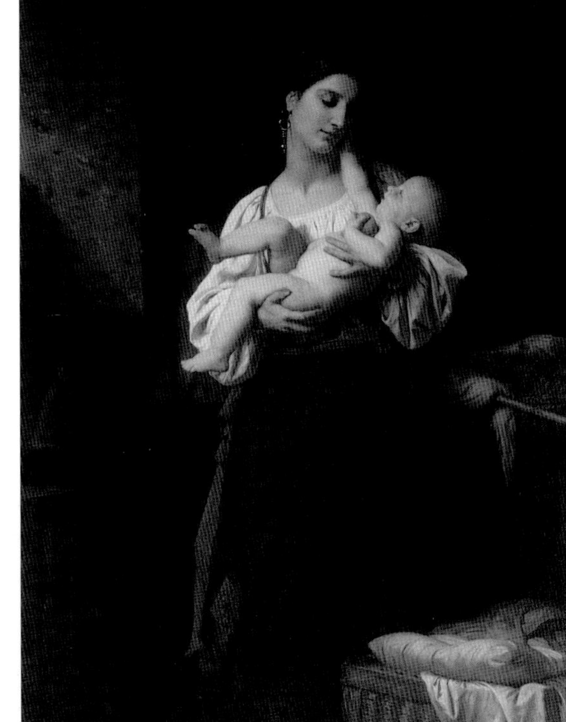

Fig. 59a William-Adolphe Bouguereau, *First Caresses*, oil on canvas, Lyndhurst, Tarrytown, NY

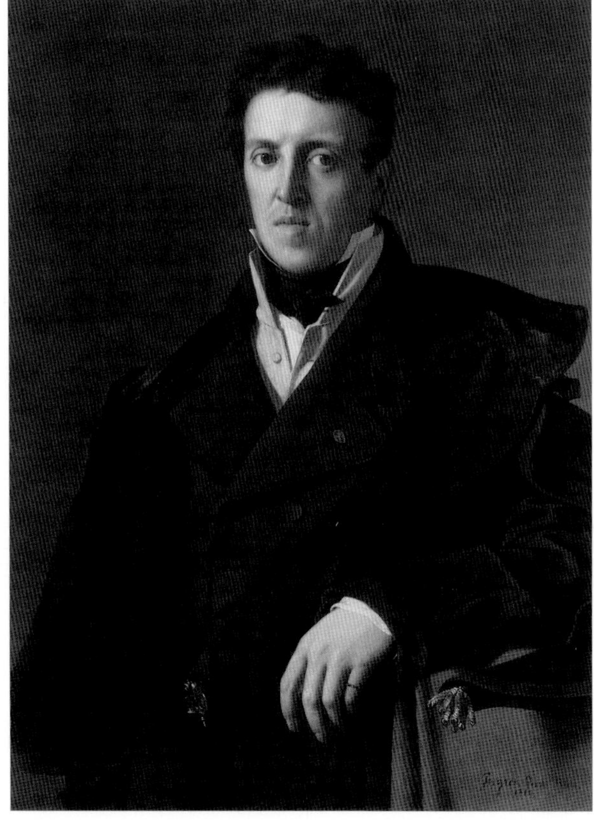

Fig. 59b Jean-Auguste-Dominique Ingres, *Marcotte d'Argenteuil*, 1810, oil on canvas, 36¾ × 27¼ in. (93.5 × 69.3 cm), National Gallery of Art, Washington

European and American artists, critics, and the general public. Norton Simon's acquisition of *Monsieur M.* in 1977 and *Allegory of the Arts* (cat. 60) in 1979 occurred at a moment when the presumed opposition of academic and modern art was undergoing an extensive reevaluation. The latter was recognized to have been enmeshed in a web of economic and political forces that belied claims of utter independence; the former was understood to have attained a genuine popularity that exceeded the control of state institutions. Bouguereau's works are today rightly recognized as important exemplars of both academic method and bourgeois taste; they are also highly valued by the art market.

In addition to his religious, historical, and genre paintings, Bouguereau produced many portraits in the course of his long career. *Monsieur M.* was exhibited at the Salon of 1850–1851. This was only the second time the young Bouguereau had shown at the Salon (his name was misspelled *Bouquereau* in the official catalogue), and the portrait received little notice. Indeed, Bouguereau's submission that year was dominated by his dark and cannibalistic *Dante and Virgil in Hell* (private collection). The recent conclusion of revolutionary hostilities (what Karl Marx called the "civil war in France"), the expressive freedom sanctioned during this brief, republican interlude between the July Monarchy and the Second Empire, and the temporary establishment of a jury-free submission policy may have stimulated Bouguereau's venture into the macabre. Never again would his art be as nightmarish and Romantic as it was in 1850. Never again would his portraits, such as *Monsieur M.*, be so simple, direct, and free of sentimental cant.

If *Dante and Virgil* represented Bouguereau's Mr. Hyde, *Monsieur M.* was his Dr. Jekyll. Given that the handsome sitter was identified only by initial, it is likely that he was a member of Bouguereau's family, circle of friends, or else a young bourgeois of some wealth and ambition. (It was customary at this time to leave unidentified the subject of portraits, unless the sitter was prominent in the government, the church, or the world of arts and letters.) The modern young man is shown seated and half-length, his right arm and limp hand resting on the back of an armless chair that we would today describe as typically Second Empire. He exhibits an undemonstrative if not vacant expression, and his eyes are

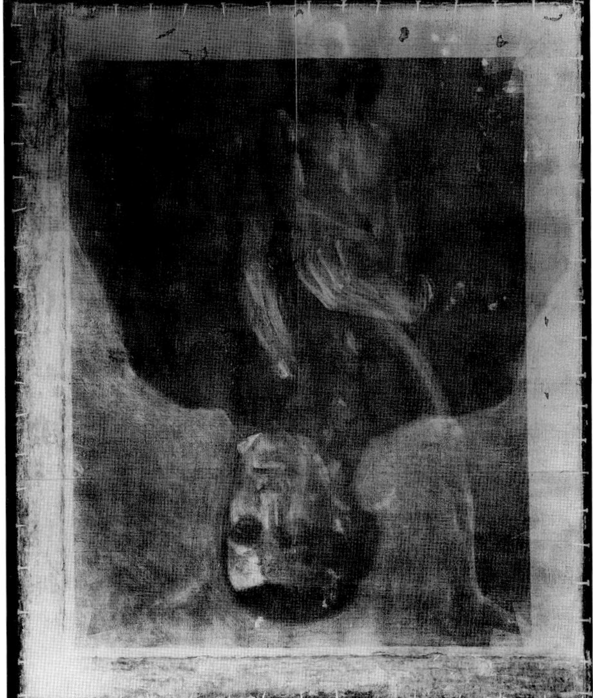

Fig. 59c X-ray photograph of cat. 59

dull. Judging by the epaulets on his shoulders, he is a professional of some kind, possibly a lawyer, though he is not wearing the typical hat, gown, and cravat worn in the courtroom by the *avocat*. The stability and sobriety of the pose and its polished finish recall the incisive but icy contemporary portraits of Hippolyte Flandrin and the later, nearly photographic portraits of Léon Bonnat. Bouguereau's own later portraits, including that of his sister Catherine Bouguereau (1854, private collection) and the three-quarter-length *Portrait of Aristide Boucicault* (Bon Marché collection, Paris), are considerably more animated and ingratiating.

Colin Bailey of the Frick Collection remarked on the almost startling similarity between Bouguereau's portrait and an early portrait by Ingres of 1810 representing Charles Marcotte (fig. 59b).[2] Given these similarities of physiognomy and pose, it is tempting to identify the sitter of Bouguereau's portrait as Joseph Marcotte, son of Charles Marcotte, who would have been seventy-seven years old in 1850. It would have been logical for the young Bouguereau to pay discreet homage to the great Ingres by creating a rhyming portrait of a son painted by an artistic "son" of Ingres.

The paper label pasted on the upper left of the canvas is the original Salon number. The X-ray photograph (fig. 59c) indicates that the portrait was painted over an *académie*, a study of a long-haired, bearded, and well-muscled male nude facing left. The figure may have functioned as a preliminary study for one of the figures in the artist's early history paintings, such as *Ulysses Recognized by His Wife after His Return from Troy* (1849, Musée des Beaux-Arts, La Rochelle) or *Zenobia Discovered by Shepherds on the Banks of the River Araxes* (1850, École Normale Supérieure des Beaux-Arts, Paris). The young Bouguereau, having received a commission from a Monsieur M., apparently turned his unneeded canvas upside down and painted his portrait. He subsequently added two strips of canvas at top and right to give the figure a bit more space to breathe. Examination of old photographs of the picture indicates that at some later point, the strips were folded over, perhaps to hide the disfiguring number, perhaps to fit a preexisting frame, or perhaps simply because an owner of the work found the compact format more satisfying.

1 When Pierre-Auguste Renoir was given his first pair of glasses in the 1910s, he reportedly threw them on the ground and proclaimed, "Merde! Je vois comme Bouguereau!" ("Shit! I see like Bouguereau!").

2 Communication in the Norton Simon Museum curatorial files.

60

William-Adolphe Bouguereau or Elizabeth Gardner Bouguereau
French, 1825–1905, or American, 1837–1922

Allegory of the Arts
c. 1890–1895

Black and white chalk on buff paper, mounted to linen, $20 \times 52\frac{5}{8}$ in. (50.8×133.7 cm)
Signed lower right (on pedestal base): "W. BOVCVEREAV"
M.1979.62

Provenance: Private collection (sale, New York, Sotheby's, 2 April 1976, lot 151, ill., to); Norton Simon, gift 1979 to; Norton Simon Art Foundation.

Technical Notes: The drawing is executed in black and white chalk on buff artist's paper, which has been adhered to a linen secondary support. This linen-lined support is attached to ragboard with hinges around the perimeter. Several layers of ragboard are glued to a wooden strainer inside the frame package. The paper support suffers from overall embrittlement owing to its linen backing and unknown adhesives and from structural damage around the perimeter. The drawing has severe water damage around the perimeter, as well as adhesive residues from a previous window mat. The residues are disfiguring, as is the water damage in the lower right corner and along the bottom edge. These damages are primarily outside the design area but extend into the design in two places: the lower right corner, in the figure's feet, and the seated figure, fifth from right. Both of these areas may have been retouched to compensate for the damage. The weakened support was treated in October 2003 to reinforce weak and missing corners, a large loss $15\frac{3}{4}$ inches from the left edge at the top, and a $\frac{3}{8}$-inch loss 11 inches from the right edge in the figure's chest area. (SSB)

This large, horizontal drawing was likely made in preparation for the painting of a canvas or panel intended to be set above a door or window, or as part of a decorative ensemble. The figures of children stand or sit on stone ledges, benches, or floors in a shallow niche. They are arranged in three groups with five children at left, five in the center, and four more at right. It is not known if the work was ultimately executed in oils or if the project remained uncompleted. The drawing is clearly an allegory of the arts, based on the example of François Boucher, among other eighteenth-century artists, who used putti or small children to represent the arts of painting, sculpture, architecture, poetry, and music. At the left, two children are tying decorative swags; beside them another child, a boy, makes music by blowing a pair of panpipes. The standing child with wings is the poetic muse, who accompanies a seated poet or writer. In the middle is a little girl-child with palm branches who stands over two children who draw, thus indicating that *dessin* is the foundation and crown of the visual arts. The standing, almost adolescent girl accompanies a seated boy with a hammer; the latter represents sculpture. Beside him, a boy leans over holding a small sapling, indicating the need to nurture the arts, as one does a delicate plant. Next to him, a seated boy decorates a clay pot, and beside him, a small child uses a hammer and small chisel to decorate or chase a metal bowl. At the far right, another child hangs up a banner or cartouche.

There is no date on the drawing. If the work is indeed by the academic master William-Adolphe Bouguereau, whose name is inscribed on the base of the stone seat on which slouches the pubescent girl at center right, it was likely made toward the end of his long career, when images of melancholy and piety became rare and pictures of happy children, such as *Childish Idyll* (1899, private collection), more numerous.[1] But Albert Boime, Gerald Ackerman, and Damien Bartoli have doubted the attribution of this drawing to Bouguereau: the first scholar primarily on iconographic grounds (the profusion of children is otherwise unknown in the painted and graphic oeuvre)[2], and the latter two on the basis of style (Ackerman believes the skill and strength of drawing are not at the same, high level as that of Bouguereau,[3] and Bartoli states that the conception of space differs from that of the academic master[4]).

The signature appears to be of the same vintage as the rest of the drawing. But notwithstanding the signature, the work cannot with surety be attributed to Bouguereau. Indeed, it is not even certain that the drawing is French. One attractive candidate for authorship is Elizabeth Gardner Bouguereau, an American painter from Exeter,

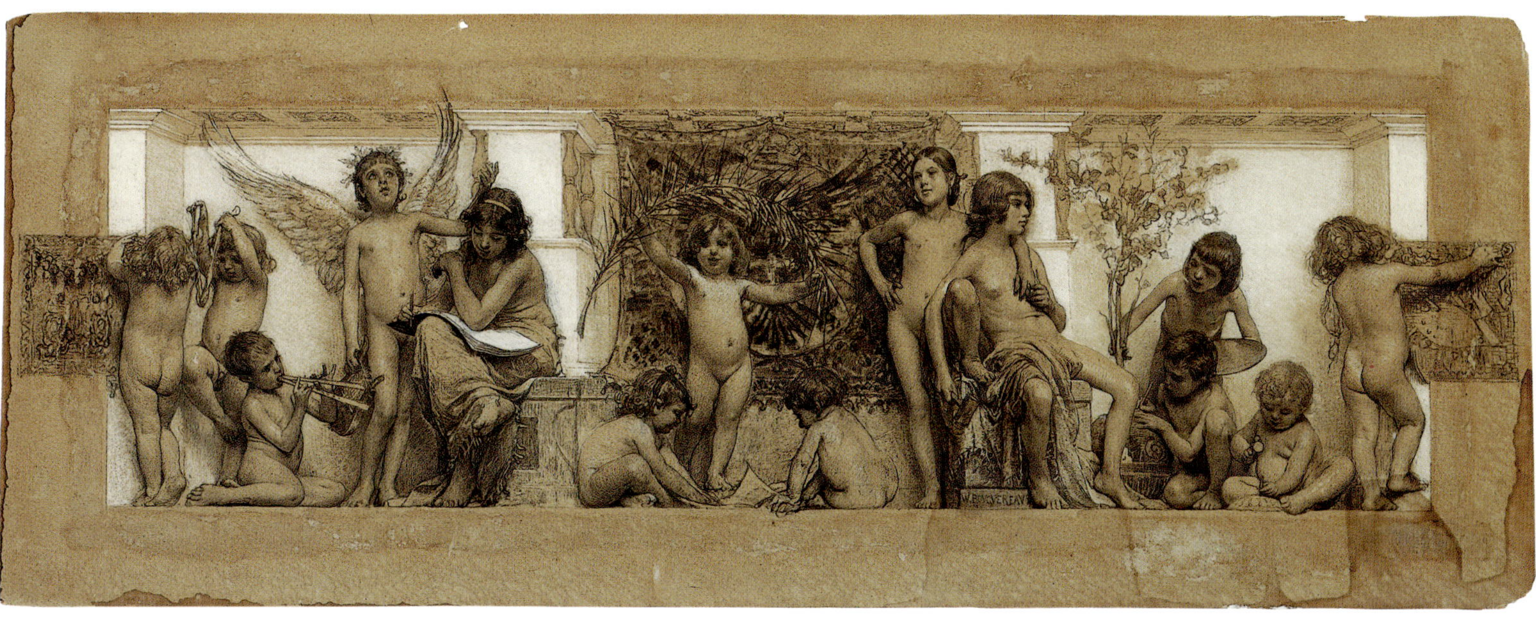

60

New Hampshire, who went to Paris in 1864 and soon thereafter (dressed as a man to evade the prohibition of women students) entered the art school at the Gobelins Tapestry factory.[5] She subsequently enrolled at the Académie Julian (in woman's clothes), where she met and studied with the older William-Adolphe. She later married the celebrated artist. Elizabeth Gardner enjoyed considerable success in the Paris Salons, exhibiting there no fewer than twenty-five times. Her work is strongly indebted to that of her mentor and partner, and her later pictures, including *In the Woods* (1889, private collection) and *Soap Bubbles* (1891, private collection), feature young and adolescent children. If the drawing is by Elizabeth Gardner Bouguereau, the presence of William-Adolphe's signature is more easily reconciled, though not justified.

1 Montreal, 1984, pp. 252–253.
2 Memorandum, 29 March 2005, Norton Simon Museum curatorial files.
3 Letter, 2 April 2005, Norton Simon Museum curatorial files.
4 Letter, 16 May 2005, Norton Simon Museum curatorial files.
5 Montreal, 1984, p. 52.

61

Anselm Feuerbach
German, 1829–1880

Old Woman Seated
1853

Oil on linen, 43 × 33⅝ in. (109.2 × 85.4 cm)
F.1975.01

Provenance: Private collection, Paris. [Galerie Fischer, Lucerne, in 1929]. William Dieterle, Hollywood and Germany; by inheritance to; Elizabeth (Mrs. William) Dieterle, Vogging, Germany, sold 1975 to; The Norton Simon Foundation.

References: Uhde-Bernays, 1929, no. 86; Ecker, 1991, no. 113.

Technical Notes: The canvas is plain-weave and medium-weight and was lined in 1975 with PVA Heat Seal to linen and stretched onto an expansion bolt stretcher. Original tacking edges are still present. The canvas has a medium-thick cream-colored ground that covers the top tacking edge but only a part of the others. The design is drawn on the ground with a brush and black paint. The flesh was laid in with dark red-brown paint and then worked up with local color. There are numerous losses of varying sizes to the paint layers and there appear to be two tears to the support. In ultraviolet light the background is generally dark, indicating that it may be thinly overpainted to hide the numerous little losses. (JF)

Few paintings by the German portraitist and history painter Anselm Feuerbach survive in American public collections, and this situation contributes to the general lack of knowledge of nineteenth-century German painting outside Germany. Although almost a household name among literate Germans at the end of the nineteenth century for his large-scale *Battle of the Amazons* (1872, Stadtmuseum Fembohaus, Nuremberg) and *Fall of the Titans* (1874–1880, Great Hall, Akademie, Vienna), his name is scarcely recognized outside Germany today except by art historians. Given the resolutely Francocentric nature of the Norton Simon nineteenth-century collections, it is unusual to find such a work there. Yet, an undocumented early Parisian provenance perhaps explains the aesthetic appeal of the work to Simon. And, its twentieth-century German provenance, in the collection of William Dieterle, the film director who worked with Jennifer Jones, the second Mrs. Norton Simon, makes clear why it is the lone nineteenth-century German painting in the Museum.

The painting has been dated to 1853 by the major scholars of Feuerbach's oeuvre, and there is no reason to doubt this. It is either a painted sketch or an unfinished painting, most likely the latter, given its large scale and the lack of clear relation to another composition. As the conservation report states, the work is not in good condition, but what does remain attests to Feuerbach's powerful sense of composition, particularly in the silhouette of the figure. There is little doubt that the work was a portrait that, for reasons that are undocumented, did not advance beyond this early stage. As such, the picture is a reminder that Feuerbach, whose finished paintings have smooth surfaces without strong brushwork, used his brush and paint with real spontaneity in the early stages of his paintings. The woman's mass and her strong personality are clearly felt. She confronts the viewer as she confronted Feuerbach himself in 1853. It shares many qualities with the contemporary oil sketches of Thomas Couture and with later ones by his most famous pupil, Édouard Manet. Given the fact that Feuerbach resided in Paris from 1851 to 1854, it is possible that the picture was made there and was a considered response to works by Couture, then at the height of his fame.

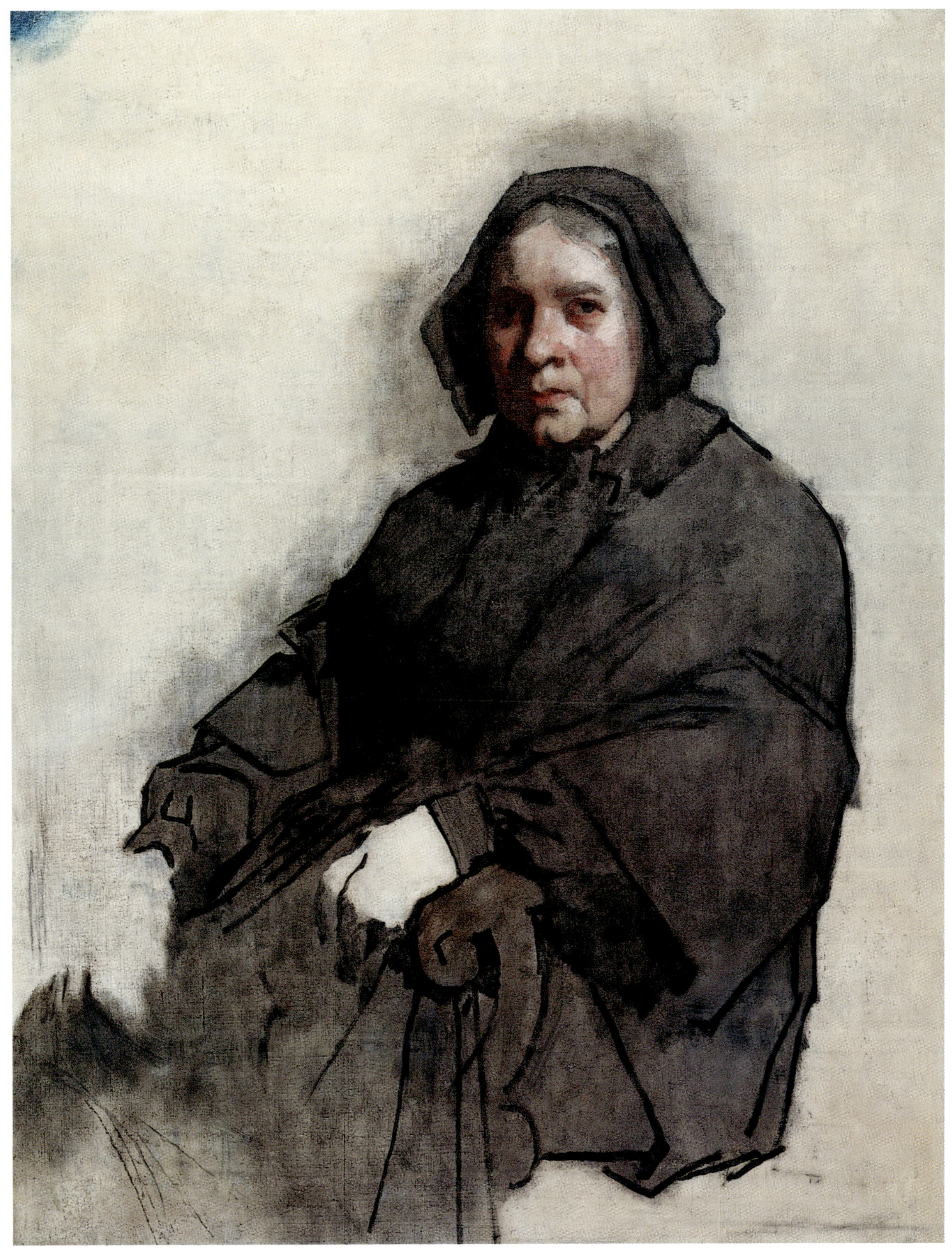

61

62

Paul-Désiré Trouillebert
French, 1829–1900

Still Life with Plums
1865–1880

Oil on panel, $6\frac{3}{8} \times 14\frac{1}{4}$ in. (16.2 × 36 cm)
Signed lower left: "Trouillebert"
M.1979.11

Provenance: [?Galerie Georges Petit, 1906]. Sale, Champetier de Ribes, Drouot Rive Gauche, Paris, 26 May 1977, lot 46. [Galerie Abels, Cologne, by 1978, sold 1979 to]; Norton Simon Art Foundation.

Exhibitions: Paris, 1906, no. 90; Cologne, 1978, no. 24, ill.

Technical Notes: The support is a horizontally grained wood panel approximately ½ inch thick. The sides have a machine-tooled bevel. A small, thin, horizontal crack is at the left side, 2½ inches from the top; it appears to be stable. A reddish brown ground layer is visible in the fissures of numerous contraction cracks. A rather pronounced surface texture is evident when the panel is viewed in raking light with magnification; it is especially noticeable in the more thinly painted dark background, where there are striations in various directions separate from the brush marking of the design layer. The fluid handling employs strong, quick brushwork. The background color is directly applied over the red-brown ground. Small, short strokes on the plums, which describe the volume, are applied over a thin underpainting of red-violet, which delicately modifies the blue. The leaves also are quickly brushed in a direct and assured application of rich paint. The foreground is slightly built up with several values of yellow-ocher, the uppermost and lightest being in the lower center. The painting is in very good condition with the exception of the cracks that may have resulted from the artist's application of thick paint before the underpainting had completely dried. The varnish is not noticeably discolored. Retouching is conspicuous only because of differences in surface gloss. (RW)

Were it not for its prominent signature at lower left, it would be difficult to assign this delightful small still life on panel to Paul-Désiré Trouillebert. Modern scholars and connoisseurs know this artist as a minor landscape painter who worked in the manner of his mentor, Camille Corot. Indeed, Trouillebert's capital moment as an artist came when the famous writer Alexandre Dumas fils acquired a landscape by Trouillebert thinking that he had purchased a major painting by Corot. The resulting publicity created such a stir that Trouillebert's career took off. Trouillebert was first accepted to the Salon of 1865, when he was already thirty-six years old, but he failed to make much of an impression until the Salon of 1882, when he exhibited a large composition with bathers that was much discussed in the critical press. Although he is known to have painted portraits and genre scenes, few of these are noted in the literature that records the movement of Trouillebert's works through the public sales. Indeed, neither Emmanuel Bénézit nor Hippolyte Mireur, each of whom recorded the sale of hundreds of works by the artist between 1883 and 1951, cites more than a handful of still-life and genre scenes by the artist. (He did paint a fair number of outdoor genre scenes, including an *Island of the Grande-Jatte* that was sold in 1885, a year before Georges Seurat painted his famous scene of the same site.)

This small painting is, thus, virtually impossible to date. Painted on a panel, which is covered with a reddish brown *ébauche* or ground, the work represents a branch cut from a plum tree and laid on the surface of a table or along a wall. Trouillebert did no elaborate arranging of the elements of his still life; his picture is an informal study of spherical fruits still attached to a leafed branch, rather than a fully developed composition. It is a confidently and relatively quickly painted analysis of natural forms. Any French painter who tackled a still life with plums had to contend with the ghost of the greatest French still-life painter of the eighteenth century, Jean-Siméon Chardin, whose representation of a simple bowl of plums challenged generations of French painters. By electing not to arrange the plums, but rather to study them on a branch, Trouillebert was deflecting our sense of his competition with Chardin. One of the plums has disengaged itself, while the others are obedient in their attachment to their branch. This independence notwithstanding, all of them will either die at an equal rate or be simultaneously baked into a *tarte aux prunes.*

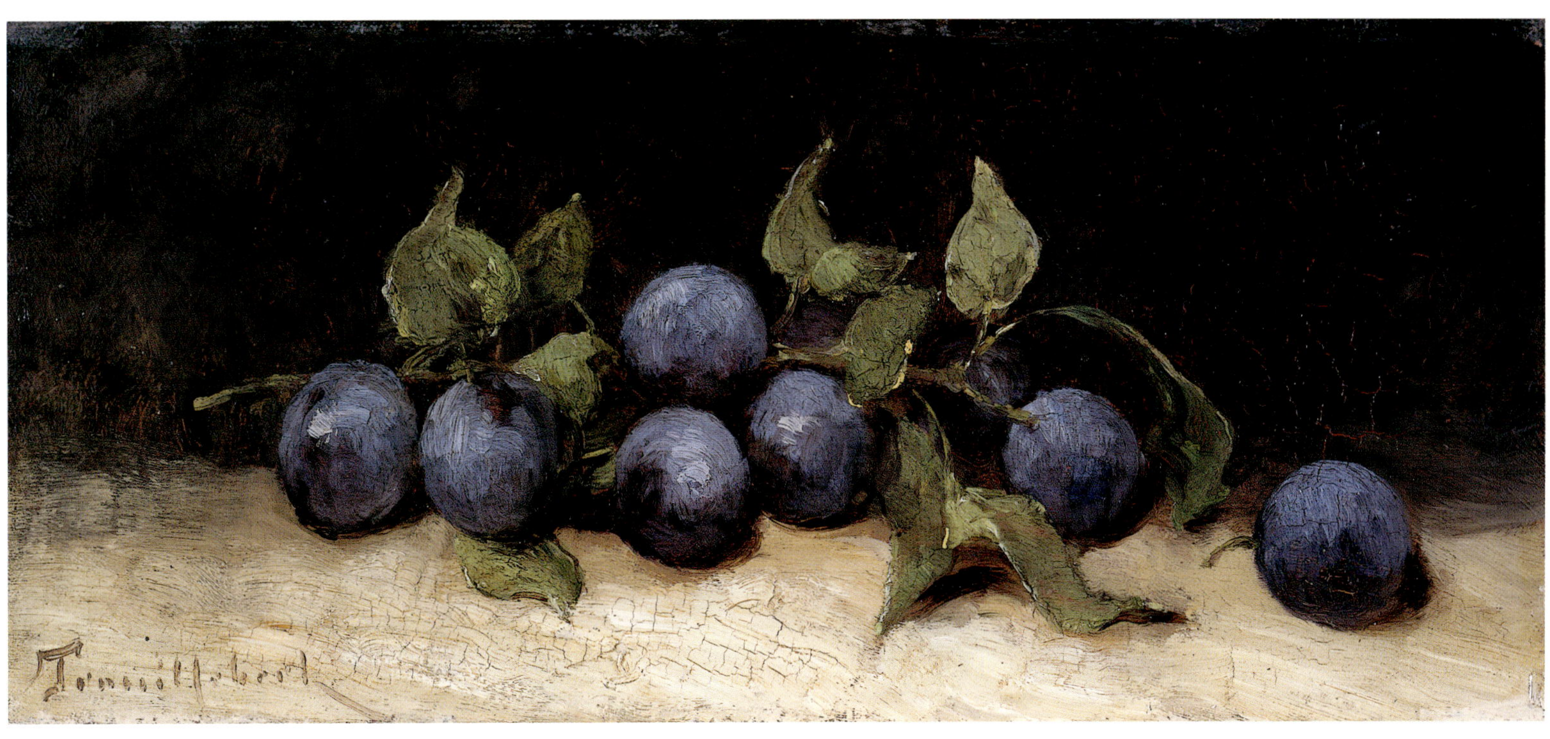

62

63

Camille Pissarro
French, 1830–1903

The Boulevard des Fossés, Pontoise
1872

Oil on canvas, 18¼ × 21⅞ in. (46.4 × 55.5 cm)
Signed and dated lower right: "C. Pissarro, 1872"
M.1975.20

Provenance: [Durand-Ruel, Paris, deposited by Durand-Ruel with Jules Féder, his banker at the Banque de l'Union Général, which went bankrupt in 1882. Durand-Ruel recovered painting on 22 June 1892 from Picq, who was overseeing the bankruptcy proceedings. Sold 3 October 1940 to]; [Sam Salz, New York, sold 22 November 1940 to]; [Paul Rosenberg, sold 8 May 1942 to]; [Durand-Ruel, New York, sold 1 February 1946 to]; Jakob Goldschmidt (d. 1955), Berlin (until 1933) and New York (1933–1955) (sale, London, Sotheby's, 28 November 1956, lot 126, sold for $23,800 jointly to); [Thos. Agnew & Sons, London, and A. Tooth & Sons, London, consigned November 1956 to]; [M. Knoedler & Co., New York, stock no. CA4952, sold, as stock no. A6533, 13 March 1957 to]; Norton Simon, gift 1975 to; Norton Simon Art Foundation.

Exhibitions: Baltimore, 1936, no. 1; San Francisco, 1938, no. 16; New York, 1946a, no. 5; New York, 1953b; Los Angeles 1965; on loan, Toronto, Art Gallery of Ontario, 10 February–26 August 1981.

References: Pissarro and Venturi, 1939, vol. 1, no. 171, vol. 2, pl. 35; Georges-Michel, 1945, ill. following p. 68; Cogniat, 1974, ill., n.p.; Pissarro and Snollaerts, 2005, no. 277.

Technical Notes: The painting is in very good condition. The support has been lined with the original tacking edges retained. Both canvases are aged and brittle, but there are no apparent damages to either, other than a very small hole at the center of the top edge. The keyed stretcher appears to be the original. As seen on the tacking edges, the ground layer is quite thin. It probably was off-white initially, but it has darkened to beige. There also is a rosy cream-colored underpainting that extends over the entire surface. The paint layer's original surface texture has been well preserved, as lining has not noticeably altered the profile. However, it is possible that Pissarro painted on a ground that was both thin and absorbent, and the saturated quality of the paint, now glossy with varnish, is changed from an original matte finish. The paint has been applied with a rather small brush in a multilayered, heavily worked technique of overlapping strokes and dabs of paint. Pissarro has painted both wet into wet as well as using a fairly dry brush over dried paint, working and reworking to build up the painting. The X-radiograph confirms that white and white mixtures (i.e., in the sky and light-colored areas of the buildings) were done after the trees, rooflines, and road had been established. This also can be seen with the microscope. The surface coating, an aged synthetic resin, has yellowed. In 1986 the painting was superficially cleaned to remove surface dirt. (RW)

In August 1872 Camille Pissarro arrived in the town of Pontoise after an absence of more than four years. In the meantime, he had worked in the region of Louveciennes, Bougival, and Marly with Claude Monet, Pierre-Auguste Renoir, and Alfred Sisley and had spent a pictorially eventful period in the London suburbs during the Franco-Prussian War and the Commune. There, he had not only seen paintings by John Constable and J. M. W. Turner and worked in conjunction with Monet and Charles-François Daubigny, but he had also married his common-law wife, Julie Valley, and legitimized their children. On his return to France, Pissarro discovered that German troops had lived in the family's house on the route de Versailles in Louveciennes, damaging many works of art. For that and other reasons, the Pissarro family decided to move back to the town of Pontoise late in the summer of 1872.

When Pissarro arrived, the family rented a small house with an even smaller front garden on the rue Ravet in the town of Pontoise itself. This modest dwelling proved too small, and, early the next year, the family moved to the hamlet of L'Hermitage, where they had lived in the late 1860s. It was, perhaps, in his restless search for a new place to live that Pissarro explored a good deal of the landscape of Pontoise and its suburbs in the autumn of 1872. He painted the banks of the Oise River; the streets that entered the city from the north, east, and west; a series of rural paths and fields east of the town; an urban and an open-air market; a major view of the most imposing plaza in the town; and an important series of large-scale paintings representing the four seasons, this latter project taking him into 1873. It was, in short, a singularly productive period in his career, culminating in the first cycle of decorative paintings in the history of Impressionism.

Of the twenty-seven paintings made in Pontoise during those months (nearly seven per month), twenty-five are landscapes, and none of them represents the same view. They are, in short, exploratory in nature. With the exception of four relatively large canvases that would have been difficult to achieve completely *en plein air*, the remaining landscapes, small in scale, were relatively easy to carry back and forth from the Pissarros' centrally located house near the Jardin de Ville to the motifs. Many of them depict landscapes with yellowing foliage seen under cloudy, unsettled skies. Thus, they are works

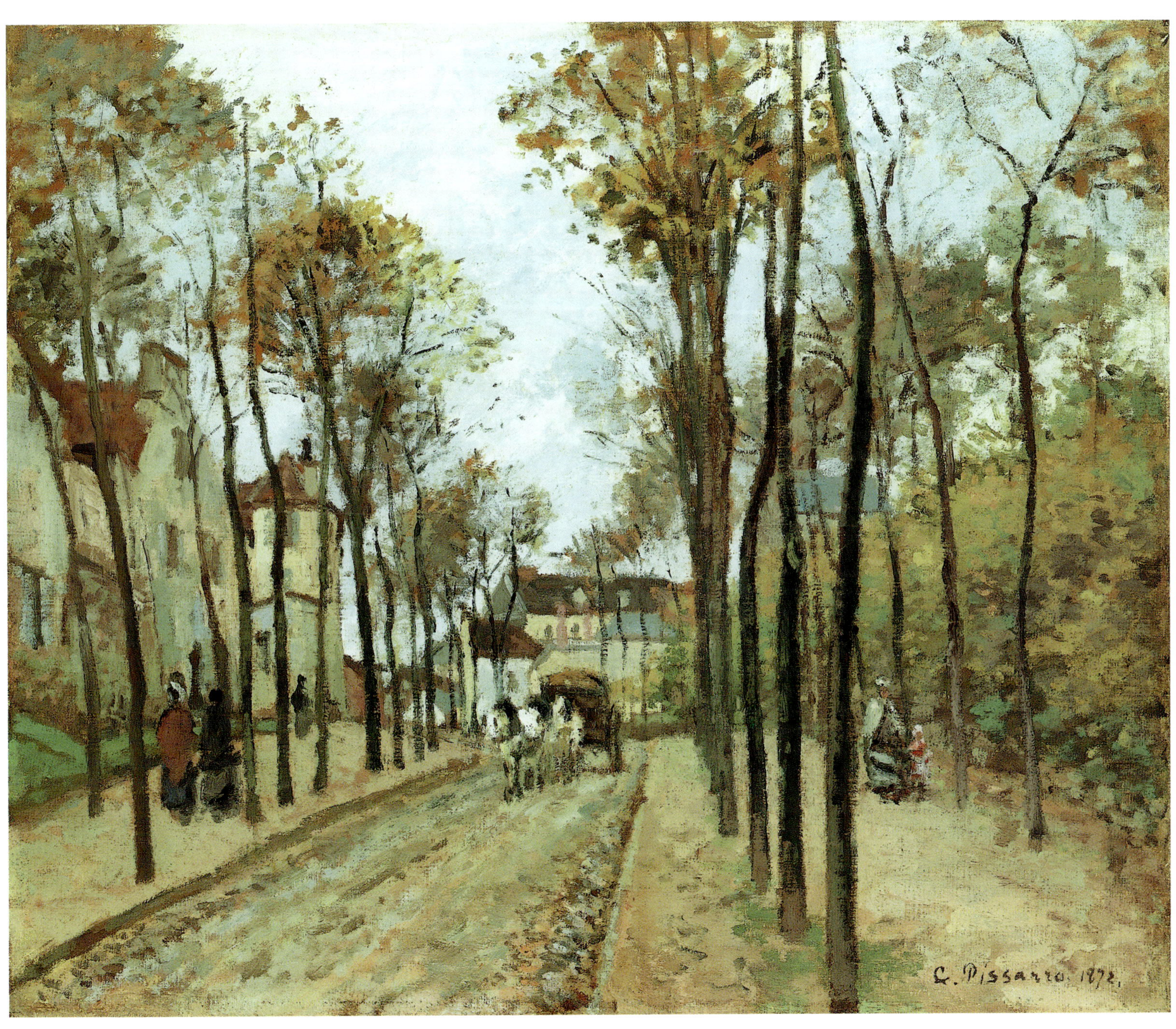

63

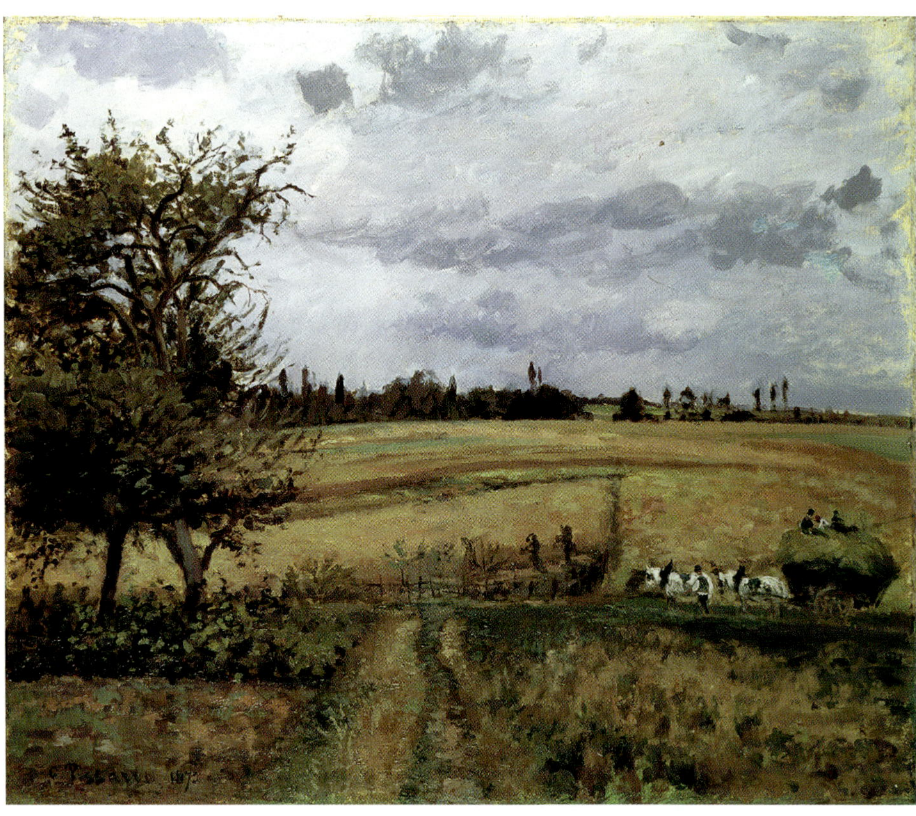

Fig. 63a Camille Pissarro, *Landscape in Pontoise*, 1872, oil on canvas, $18\frac{1}{8} \times 21\frac{5}{8}$ in. (46 × 55 cm), Ashmolean Museum, Oxford

that respond not only to the season in which they were made but also to the English landscape tradition in which Pissarro had immersed himself in 1870–1871.

The present landscape represents a street in the city then called the boulevard des Fossés (Boulevard of the Moats), now called the boulevard Jean Jaurès. Although it appears to be an old street in an old town on a blustery autumn day, the boulevard des Fossés had, in fact, been constructed outside the medieval walls of the city in the former moats during the early 1860s, shortly before Pissarro himself had first moved to the city in 1866. It was a Second Empire street just like the boulevards in Paris that were shortly to become the subject of paintings by Monet, Renoir, and Édouard Manet in the 1870s. The boulevard des Fossés joined the new railroad station, the rue Impériale, and a series of plazas and gardens constructed in the ruins of formerly ecclesiastical properties in Pontoise, most of which had been inaugurated as recently as 1864. The small trees that had been planted less than ten years earlier in the landfill of the moats had grown enough to be respectable in the autumn of 1872, when Pissarro painted this subtle urban view.

The canvas chosen by Pissarro was a standard size favored by landscape painters for more than a generation for medium-size studies. Pissarro had bought the canvas already stretched and mounted commercially with a group of others of various dimensions that he used during this period. The size of the canvas was the painter's preferred format for plein-air landscapes at this time, most probably because it was small enough to enable him to seize an impression of seasonal light and time and big enough to make a real effect in a domestic interior. In all, he painted eight landscapes on canvases of identical dimension that autumn. One of them was purchased by Edgar Degas and kept by that assiduous collector throughout his life (fig. 63a). The majority of these landscapes represent urban spaces or roads and forthrightly address issues of transience that Pissarro had become sensitized to, first through his work with Monet in Louveciennes and then through his exposure to the informal traditions of English landscape painting.

To paint the Norton Simon landscape, Pissarro walked along the rue Ravet until it intersected with the boulevard des Fossés near the place du Vieux Cimetière, where he was painting one of the larger canvases of that season. From this large and then unfinished plaza, he walked downhill toward the Oise River and, about halfway down the street, turned around and set up his easel on the side of the road looking toward the place du Vieux Cimetière. He chose a section of the boulevard near a vegetation-covered hill and across the street from the buildings. There he could work in relative tranquillity without being bothered by passersby. He also elected to depict an evenly lit, overcast light, which was common during the fall season and did not necessitate precise shadows and particular color temperatures for which he would have to wait to be able to paint at another session. Pissarro could work on the painting in the morning or the afternoon over a period of several days or more than a week without being unfaithful to the visual character of the motif observed in this diffuse light. The presence of three female figures and one child suggests that the painting was done during the week. The figures are all well dressed, and the part of town selected by Pissarro was near two areas of bourgeois houses. All three women wear shawls, and this fact, together with the yellowing of the foliage, forces us to feel a chill in the air. This is not an easy, summertime landscape with Parisian tourists, like those painted in Argenteuil or the beach resorts of France by Monet or Renoir. Instead, Pissarro shows us the rhythms of small-town daily life in off season.

Chromatically, the painting has a wide range of hues—many grays, browns, purples, and greens. The lines that define the trunks and branches of the trees are applied with a dry brush atop already dry pigment, and those in the upper right corner are particularly fanciful and free. What looks at first like a single carriage in the middle distance becomes, at closer inspection, a single, small, covered carriage following a small cart. Both horses are white and thus at first look like a pair. Pissarro manages the effect of a chilly wind by constructing virtually the entire painting with small, overlapping patches of paint that give color rather than contour to the forms they represent.

In spite of its subtlety and beauty, it is difficult to associate this painting with any of the numerous unidentified landscapes exhibited by Pissarro during his lifetime. How easy it would be for it to have become simply *Rue à Pontoise*, *Paysage avec une rue*, or even *Automne*. Its earliest recorded owner was the distinguished German collector Jakob Goldschmidt, who lived in Berlin until 1933 and then in New York until his death in 1955. In his townhouse at 34 East Sixty-fourth Street, the Pissarro (called there simply *Landscape*) hung in the living room with paintings by Honoré Daumier, Manet, Renoir, Degas, and Henri de Toulouse-Lautrec and in the company of a Chinese sculpture and an Italian Renaissance bronze.

64

Camille Pissarro
French, 1830–1903

The Poultry Market at Pontoise
1882

Oil on canvas, 31⅞ × 25⅝ in. (81 × 65 cm)
Signed and dated lower left: "C. Pissarro 82"
M.1984.2

Provenance: Collection of artist, sold 15 December 1887 to; [Boussod & Valadon (Theo van Gogh), Paris, sold same day 15 December 1887 to]; [Guyotin, Paris]. [Bernheim Jeune, Paris, c. October 1916, sold 14 March 1922 to]; [Durand-Ruel, Paris, sold 20 February 1923 to]; Albert Poullot, Paris, still in 1930. [Jacques Dubourg, Paris, by 1937, still in 1938]. [C. W. Kraushaar Art Galleries, New York, in 1939, still in 1942]. Mlle Janine Darrigol, Paris, by 1956 until at least 1962. [Galerie Schmit, Paris, sold 6 November 1967 to]; Norton Simon, sold 28 January 1981 to; [E. V. Thaw & Co., New York]. [Acquavella Galleries, Inc., New York, sold 3 December 1984, to]; Norton Simon Art Foundation.

Exhibitions: Paris, 1883a, no. 52; Basel, 1917, no. 83; Paris, 1928a, no. 36; Paris, 1930, no. 57; New York, 1932b, no. 6; London, 1937c, no. 33; New York, 1939b, no. 13, ill.; Los Angeles, 1940, no. 55; Paris, 1956, no. 51, ill.; Bern, 1957, no. 66, pl. VI; Paris, 1962b, no. 22, ill.; New York, 1981, no. 4, ill.; Tokyo, 1984, no. 37.

References: Tabarant, 1924, pl. 22; Charensol, 1928, p. 188, ill.; Édouard-Joseph, 1934, vol. 3, p. 144, ill.; Pissarro and Venturi, 1939, vol. 1, no. 576, vol. 2, pl. 120; Venturi, 1939, vol. 1, p. 62; Cogniat, 1974, p. 39, ill.; Lloyd, 1979, pp. 7, 15, fig. 28; Shikes and Harper, 1980, p. 157, ill.; Lloyd, 1981, p. 91, ill.; Schirrmeister, 1982, fig. 9; Brettell, 1990, pp. 25–28, ill. 27; J. Pissarro, 1993, no. 247, p. 208, ill.; Jirat-Wasiutyński and Newton, 2000, pp. 71, 73, no. 30, ill. (X-ray); Pissarro and Snollaerts, 2005, no. 873; Brettell and Fonsmark, 2005, p. 172, fig. 131.

Technical Notes: The fine, plain-weave canvas is a standard size that was available to artists prestretched. The stretcher is most probably the original. A colorman's stamp on the reverse of the linen is partially obscured by the vertical crossbar of the stretcher, but the first three letters are REY and the final three are ROD. The painting has been strip-lined with the original tacking edges retained. There is no mention of this treatment in the file, and it may have occurred in New York between 1981 and 1984, during the time the painting was not in the Simon collection. The smooth, off-white ground is extremely thin. The paint retains its original profile. Dragging a somewhat dry brush with colors mixed on the palette over already dry paint, Pissarro has employed small strokes of paint to establish larger, textured color blocks. The paint surface is built up and reworked over and over. The multiple layers of paint vary in thickness. In some areas, where he has reworked less, the canvas texture remains visible, as opposed to the most thickly layered areas, where the canvas texture is completely masked. Transmitted light reveals a dense network of very thin microcracks distributed throughout the entire painting. The cracking may have been caused or exacerbated by restretching. It would appear that there have been occasional problems with flaking in the past. There are numerous small losses of paint and ground starting from the bottom left corner and extending intermittently up the left side. In addition to small, unfilled flake losses, there are numerous larger losses, which have been filled and retouched. There is a minor area of abrasion and paint loss at the upper right, while at the bottom right corner there is a larger amount of lost paint and ground, which has been toned in and is inconspicuous. Retouching is located in the central portion of the bottom edge, the left end of the bottom edge, the upper end of the left edge, and across the top edge. The painting is varnished. (RW)

The Poultry Market at Pontoise has long been considered a masterpiece among the small group of major figure paintings produced by an artist more often associated with landscape. Its lengthy and distinguished bibliography nonetheless begins twenty-five years after the painter's death in 1903, and none of these sources makes any mention of its position in Pissarro's oeuvre during his lifetime. Indeed, its first documented appearance was, until very recently, thought to be an exhibition held in 1928 at the Durand-Ruel Gallery in Paris. It occupied pride of place in the beautifully selected memorial retrospective of Pissarro held at the Orangerie in 1930—perhaps the most important Pissarro exhibition of all time—but it did not enter a museum collection until its acquisition by the Norton Simon Art Foundation in 1984.

Recently, members of the research team compiling the second scholarly catalogue raisonné of Pissarro's oeuvre for the Wildenstein Institute have demonstrated that the painting was, in fact, included in the artist's first one-person exhibition held at the Durand-Ruel Gallery in Paris in 1883, a little-studied but important event.[1] Here, it appeared as *Marché à la volaille*, one of four representations of market scenes. Although the exhibition was a modest success for Pissarro, no critic singled out the present canvas for discussion, in spite of the fact that several critics mentioned the various representations of markets as an important component of the showing.

Careful examination of the surface of the painting makes it clear that Pissarro labored over its complex and chromatically sophisticated surface for a long time, and, given the fact that the artist failed to include it among the large number of figure paintings and gouaches submitted to the 1882 Impressionist exhibition, we must

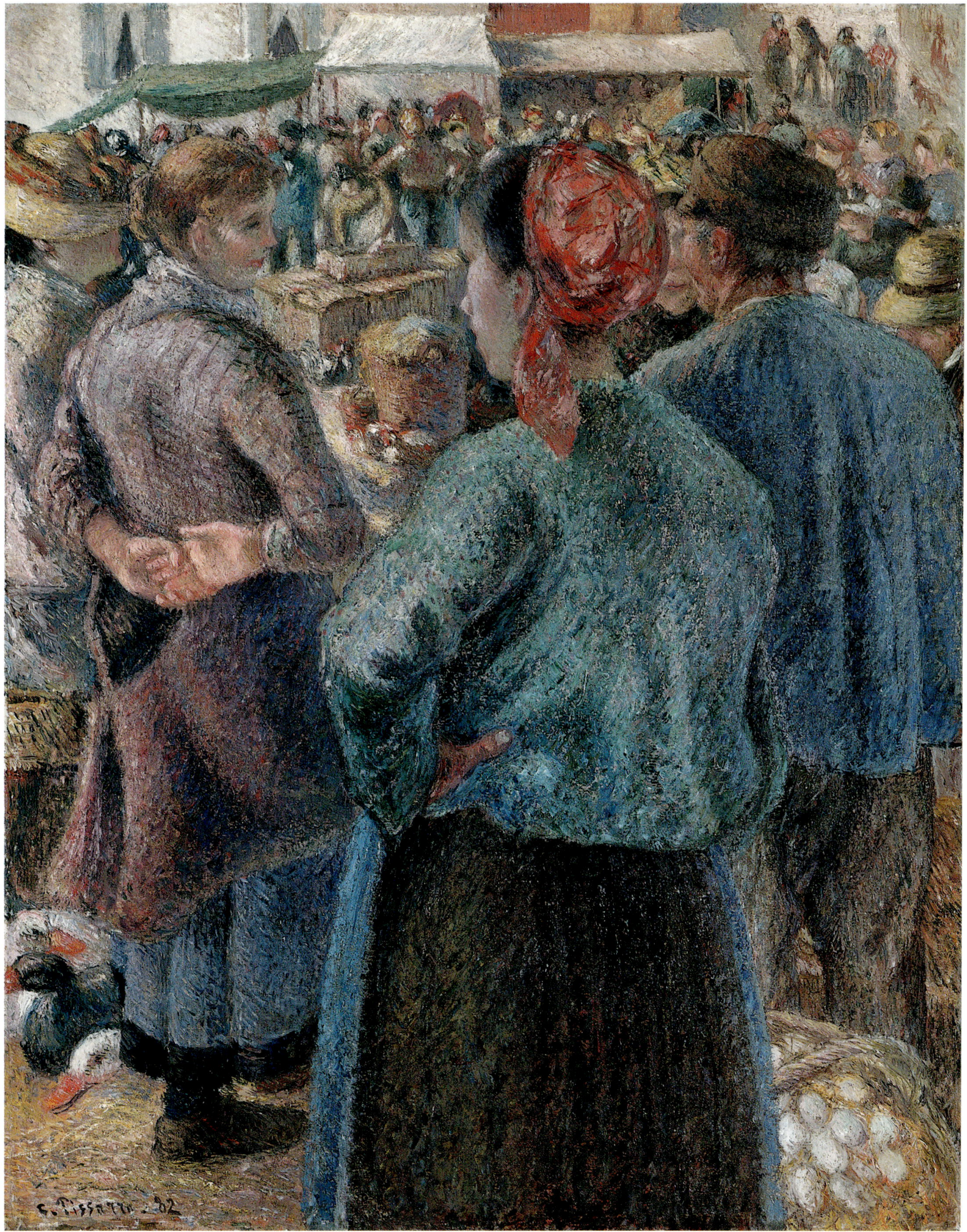
C. Pissarro . 82

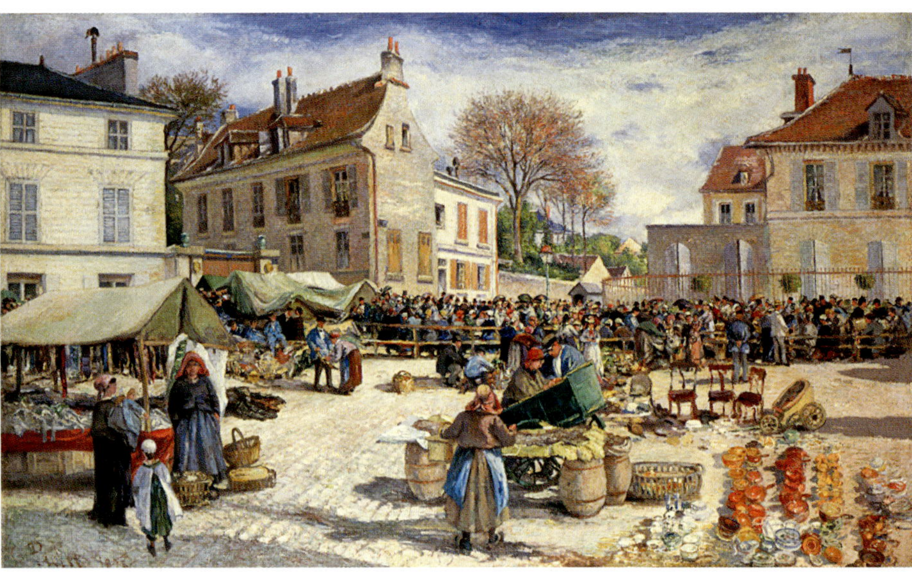

Fig. 64a Ludovic Piette, *The Marketplace in Front of the Town Hall at Pontoise*, 1876, oil on canvas, $43\frac{3}{4} \times 73\frac{1}{4}$ in. (111 × 186 cm), Musée de Pontoise

conclude that, in spite of its 1882 date, it was not completed until after March, when that exhibition was held. Had he completed it by that time, surely he would have included his first major oil painting of an urban market in the venue in which the artist made his "debut" as a figure painter. Indeed, with its group of ambitious, multifigure compositions by Pierre-Auguste Renoir and Gustave Caillebotte, as well as Pissarro, along with the landscapes of Claude Monet and Alfred Sisley, the exhibition in 1882 was powerful proof that the Impressionist movement, even without Edgar Degas, was as devoted to the human figure as to the suburban and rural landscape. This in itself was a major shift in Pissarro's career. He had submitted no figure composition to the 1881 Impressionist exhibit, whereas thirteen of the twenty-three oil paintings and all eleven gouaches in the 1882 showing represented figures who dominated their landscape or urban settings.

A good many writers about Pissarro have stressed his preference for rural rather than urban subjects and for the agricultural rather than the commercial aspects of modern life. In this, his work is routinely compared with that of his great predecessor Jean-François Millet. Pissarro himself is famous for having at once linked and separated his enterprise as a rural artist from that of Millet, stressing, in so doing, his Jewishness (Pissarro used the word *Hebrew*, while he called Millet *biblical*) and, thus by implication, his own connections to mercantile rather than agricultural practice. Yet, we know from his extensive reading in anarchist literature and particularly in his early enthusiasm for agricultural work as a part of the balanced life, that a good many of the meanings that Pissarro associated with rural labor were, in fact, modern and politically progressive. Unlike Millet's toiling peasants, whose activity seems at the service of fate, Pissarro's rural workers both work and rest, do a good deal of their work in groups (that is, collectively), and take the products of their labor to urban markets for direct sale to consumers. They are in their own way as fully modern as the urban figures represented by Degas, Renoir, and Berthe Morisot. The fact that they are emphatically not bourgeois figures and that they produce, sell, and consume allows them to serve as models for the kind of progressive anarchism that Pissarro and many of his friends sought.

Richard Thomson and Joachim Pissarro have noted the many links between Pissarro's representations of markets and the writings of anarchist philosophers and theorists from Pierre-Joseph Proudhon onward.[2] They have also pointed out the precedents for Pissarro's market scenes both in the painter's own representations of markets in the Virgin Islands and Venezuela in the early 1850s and in Salon painting of the 1870s and 1880s by many French artists. Yet, the majority of important academic paintings of rural markets were exhibited in Salons of the later 1880s and early 1890s, after the Norton Simon painting was completed, and Pissarro would have shied away from any such sources for both political and aesthetic reasons. The most important sources for the Impressionist market scenes of Pissarro are rarely noted in the Pissarro literature. These can be found in the work of the artist's anarchist friend, the minor painter Ludovic Piette, who exhibited nine paintings of markets, including four of Pontoise, in the Impressionist exhibition of 1877. These works were particularly noted in the extensive press garnered by the third and most important of the eight Impressionist exhibitions.

It is fascinating to compare Piette's large painting *The Marketplace in Front of the Town Hall at Pontoise* (fig. 64a) from the 1877 exhibition with the present painting of five years later. Shared by Pissarro are Piette's brilliant palette and a fascination with the shapes and textures of baskets, containers, and stalls. For Piette, however, the human figures in the market are dominated by their setting and are miniaturized to such an extent that one might even call these paintings urban landscapes in the manner of Canaletto. With Piette, we observe the teeming market from a safe aesthetic distance, almost as if we were upper-class tourists sitting in a private room of a restaurant on the second floor.

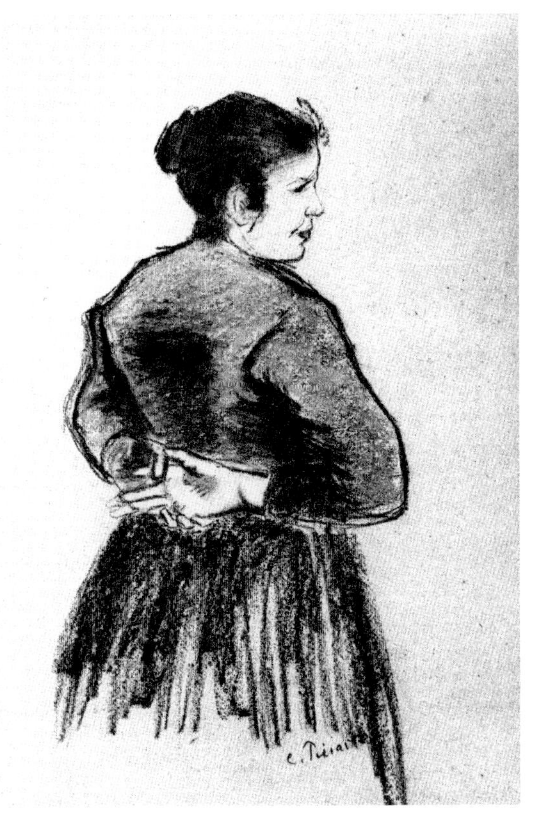

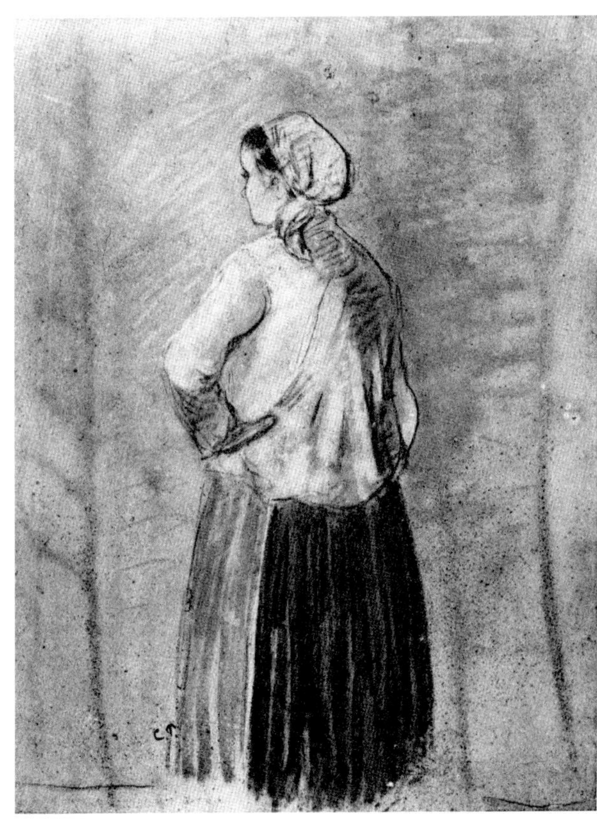

Fig. 64b (*right*) Camille Pissarro, *Young Woman, Hands Behind Her Back*, 1880–1881, pastel, $21^{1}/_{8} \times 14$ in. (51×35.5 cm), location unknown; photo: Pissarro and Venturi, 1939, no. 1575

Fig. 64c (*far right*) Camille Pissarro, *Peasant Woman from the Rear, Left Hand on Hip*, 1880–1881, pastel, $25^{3}/_{16} \times 18^{7}/_{8}$ in. (64×48 cm), location unknown; photo: Pissarro and Venturi, 1939, no. 1584

For Pissarro, the human figure utterly dominates the composition, acting as a dramatic *répoussoir* for the score of tiny figures who maneuver excitedly in the middle ground. Indeed, it is the weighty repose of these foreground figures, together with the verticality of the pictorial format, that gives the painting the sense of being a concentrated slice of the market scene pictured by Piette. Unlike Piette and his distant spectacle, Pissarro almost shoves his viewer into the market, allowing us a sense of the handwoven clothing of the figures, of the steadfast durability of their shoes, of the sheer weight of the fabric folds that define their columnar bodies. Because none of the three principal figures in the Pissarro faces the viewer nor acknowledges our presence, we are at once immersed in and detached from the market.

Perhaps the most interesting aspect of *The Poultry Market at Pontoise* in contrast with similar scenes by Piette is the limited nature of its setting. Whereas Piette was fascinated with the architecture of the seventeenth- and eighteenth-century buildings around the marketplace, Pissarro crops his setting so dramatically that we see more of the tents and awnings for the temporary sheds than of the solid buildings that shelter them. Thus, it is the figures that dominate the setting, suggesting that the market is a humanscape and not an urban view with staffage figures.

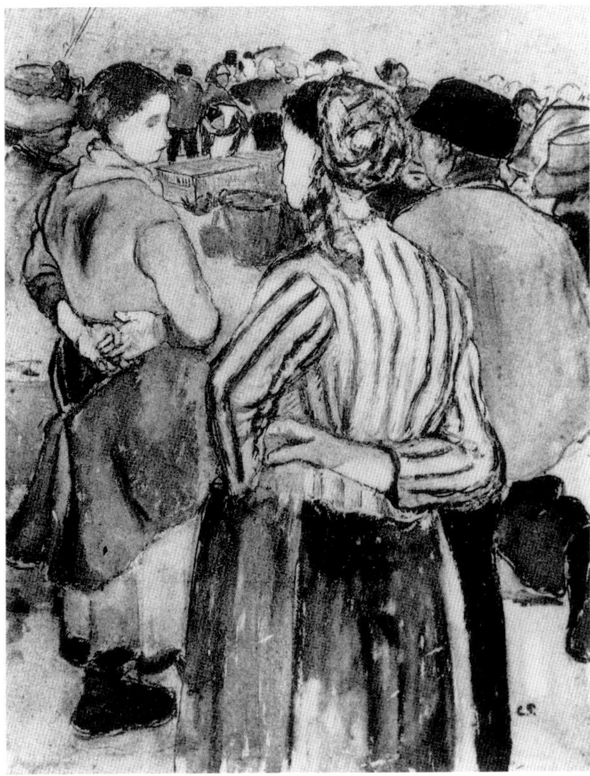

Fig. 64d Camille Pissarro, *The Market at Pontoise*, c. 1882, tempera or gouache, $31^{7}/_{8} \times 25^{5}/_{8}$ in. (81×65 cm), location unknown; photo: Pissarro and Venturi, 1939, no. 1364

It is clear when examining *The Poultry Market at Pontoise* in detail that Pissarro has based the three principal figures on drawings done from hired models

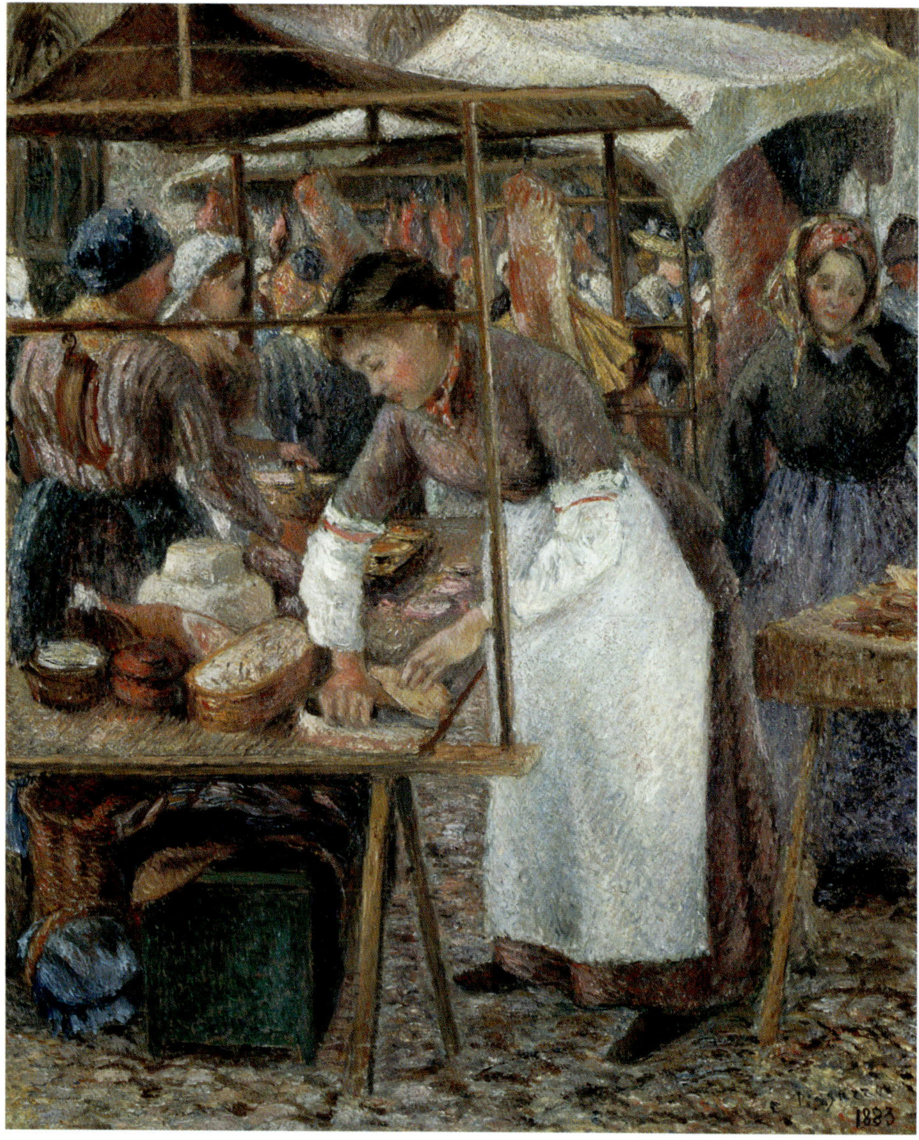

Fig. 64e Camille Pissarro, *The Pork Butcher*, 1883, oil on canvas, $25\frac{1}{4} \times 21\frac{3}{8}$ in. (64.1 × 54.3 cm), Tate Gallery, London; Art Resource, NY

posed simply in his yard or studio and transposed into a market setting. Although Pissarro's drawings remain largely unpublished, several sheets survive that may have served the artist when he conceived of the Norton Simon composition. Two of these, *Young Woman, Hands Behind Her Back* (fig. 64b)[3] and *Peasant Woman from the Rear, Left Hand on Hip* (fig. 64c),[4] are directly related to the composition and may be identical in figural scale to the figures in the painting. Nonetheless, nothing in their poses or gestures is particular to any aspect of marketing, and the figures are not unlike others used by Pissarro in harvest scenes or representations of rural rest. Examination of the X-ray of the Norton Simon market scene suggests that Pissarro may even have transferred black chalk or charcoal drawings of these figures onto the primed canvas from another source, in this case the two drawings just mentioned. In addition, an identically composed tempera or gouache painting published in the 1939 catalogue raisonné (fig. 64d)[5] is exactly the same size as the present painting, suggesting that transfer processes could well have been used. However, Pissarro did not simply transplant figures from one figural context to another, as did both Degas and Paul Gauguin at the same period. Instead, he chose a set of figures for a particular situation for which they had exclusive use.

It is difficult without a detailed physical examination of all the related works to decide just how Pissarro transferred his figures from one to another support or pictorial context. Perhaps because none of the figures is reversed in position from that in the final paintings, we cannot imagine a kind of printed transfer process like that used by Degas and Gauguin. (If Pissarro had elected to adopt such a process, the figure in the painting would have appeared in reverse). It is also possible that Pissarro thoroughly wetted a sheet of paper, printed it using the single-figure drawings as support, and then placed the still-wet transfer itself on the primed canvas of the new support. Had he done this, the figure would have appeared doubly reversed, or identical to the original orientation. Even though there are a handful of squared figure drawings from the early 1880s by Pissarro, none of the sheets related directly to the Norton Simon canvas is squared. That fact, together with their scalar similarity, suggests that Pissarro was beginning to use more experimental modes of transfer.

Pissarro's market scene is alive with closely observed detail. The particularity of the baskets and the hampers is almost ethnographic, and Pissarro was evidently fascinated with the color, pattern, and visual weight of the fabrics used for the clothing in the painting. The full-scale tempera or gouache study, for example, gives the female figure in the foreground a striped blouse rather than the turquoise blue solid fabric seen in the final painting, and the same figure has her right hand behind her back in the tempera painting, while the male figure on the right, who is standing on both feet in the Norton Simon painting, rests his right knee on a container or hamper. Physical examination of the painting proves that Pissarro made many small changes to the composition as he labored to complete it for the 1883 exhibition. The large female figure on the left with her hands twisted behind her back had dark hair in both the figure drawing and the tempera multifigure study. When working on this figure in the Norton Simon painting, Pissarro

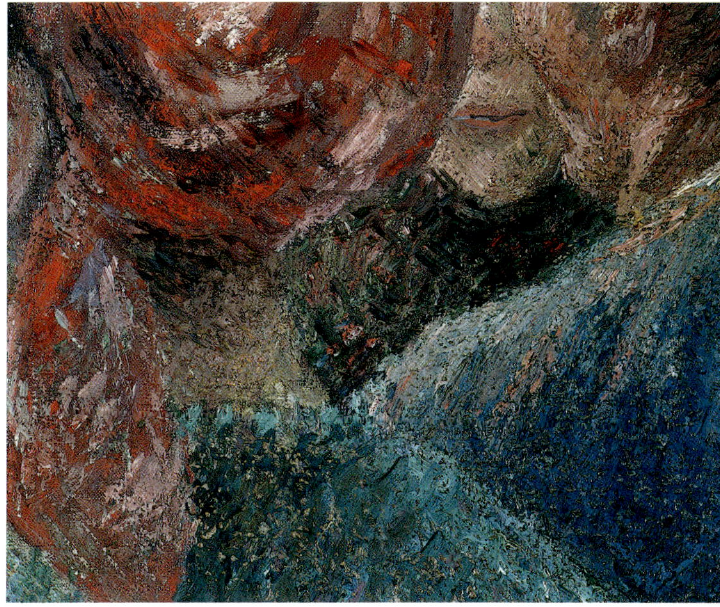

Fig. 64f Detail of cat. 64

worked with another model and attempted to show more of her face, before deciding on the strict silhouette of the final figure.

The Poultry Market at Pontoise is among the best-preserved figural paintings of Pissarro's career. Perhaps because it did not enter an American museum collection until 1984, it survived without being subjected to relining using either glue or wax. Thus, its intricate and physically complex surface retains its visual life. Unfortunately, however, the work has been varnished, and a skein of small, shiny highlights is visible when the varnish on the crests of the paint catches the light. It is known that Pissarro did not varnish his paintings of the 1880s, allowing this standard procedure to occur only if the dealer or collector insisted on it. He preferred the flat, dry honesty of an unvarnished surface, just as he tended to frame his paintings in plain, uncarved, unornamented wooden moldings that were either painted or simply stained.

Pissarro worked on another oil painting of a market in Pontoise in 1882–1883, completing it as well in time for the 1883 exhibition. This work, *The Pork Butcher* (fig. 64e), has compositional ambitions similar to those in the present picture but focuses on the actual work of a single female butcher, who appears to be slicing fat from a section of pork used for bacon. Pissarro seems to have used the same model, his niece Nini, for the butcher as for the blond girl on the left in the Norton Simon painting. *The Pork Butcher* became more famous than *The Poultry Market at Pontoise* because it was given by the artist's son Lucien to the British national collections in 1944, making it easily available for reproduction and critical comment. However, it is at once smaller and more compositionally simple than the Norton Simon painting, which remains the early masterpiece of figural genre by Pissarro.

The painting is alive with tiny, quivering touches of paints—commas, elongated dots, lines, small patches, and slightly gestural touches. None of these marks is large enough or curved enough to possess any eloquence as gesture. Instead, Pissarro seems to have been obsessed with small areas of color that read monochromatically from a distance but are actually covered with scores, even hundreds, of smaller touches of diverse colors (fig. 64f). This system is far from the "constructive stroke" developed about this time by Paul Cézanne in conjunction with Pissarro. Instead, it more closely resembles the highly wrought, gestureless color surfaces employed by Pissarro, Georges Seurat, and Paul Signac beginning in 1884–1885. Pissarro did not meet Seurat until October 1885, more than two years after he finished this painting. But, judging from its surface alone, the older painter had as much to teach the younger about color and facture as he had to learn. It is precisely this aspect of Pissarro's color theory and color technique in painting that has yet to be fully studied as a major source for the better-known and ostensibly more rigorous "dotted" technique of the Neo-Impressionists. In recognition of its chromatic brilliance, this painting appeared on the cover of the November–December 1971 issue of *Color Engineering: The Journal of Color Science and Technology*. Unfortunately, nothing even remotely interesting was written about the painting in that context. We await a full reappraisal of color painting in France in the early 1880s, a subject that will be based on close analysis of paintings like *The Poultry Market at Pontoise.*

1 Conversation between the author and Durand-Ruel et Cie.

2 J. Pissarro, 1993, pp. 152–182, and R. Thomson, 1990.

3 Pissarro and Venturi, 1939, vol. 1, no. 1575.

4 Pissarro and Venturi, 1939, vol. 1, no. 1584.

5 Pissarro and Venturi, 1939, vol. 1, no. 1364.

65

CAMILLE PISSARRO
French, 1830–1903

Landscape with Flock of Sheep
1889 and 1902

Oil on canvas, $23\frac{3}{4} \times 29$ in. (60.3×73.7 cm)
Signed and dated lower left: "C. Pissarro, 1902"
Signed and dated lower right (partially painted over): "Pissarro, 89"
P.1964.24

PROVENANCE: Collection of the artist, sold February 1902 to; [Bernheim Jeune, Paris, February 1902]. [Galerie Jerome Friedmann, Hamburg (sale, Berlin, Rudolph Lepke, 29 October 1912, lot 75)]. Baron Heinrich Thyssen-Bornemisza (1875–1947), Schloss Rohoncz, by 1930, presumably still in 1939. M. Stolliard, Cannes, sold 1956 to; [Wildenstein and Co., sold 1957 to]; Mrs. Reese Hale Taylor, Pasadena, Calif., life bequest 1964 to, and received 1997 by; Norton Simon Museum.

EXHIBITIONS: Munich, 1930, no. 405, as *Landschaft mit Schafherde*; Los Angeles, 1991, no. 61, ill.

REFERENCES: Pissarro and Venturi, 1939, vol. 1, no. 1259, vol. 2, pl. 246; Sérrulaz, 1955, fig. XI; Bailly-Herzberg, 1980–1991, vol. 5, no. 1882, p. 222; Ward, 1996, pp. 178, 326, n 5; Luckhardt and Schneede, 2001, pp. 223–224, ill.; Pissarro and Snollaerts, 2005, no. 873.

TECHNICAL NOTES: The support is a rather lightweight, fine, plain-weave canvas, evenly stretched and in sound condition. The unlined canvas retains the original tacking edges and appears to have never been removed from this stretcher. The corners have been opened slightly to tighten the canvas. The smooth, cream-colored ground is a thin layer. Two signatures are visible: what is doubtless the later one is at the bottom left along with a date of 1902. Another signature at the bottom right has been painted over, leaving the last five letters of *Pissarro* and the date 1889 only partially legible. The painting is very well preserved with no losses or abrasion. The two signatures and dates indicate that Pissarro reworked portions of the painting. Presumably the darker clouds in the sky (which are the upper layer and are made up of larger, more fluid brushstrokes) are later modifications. In the lower portion of the painting, the darker colors (e.g., an olive green that covers the earlier signature) are less delicate, and the artist may have changed the tonal values to a lower key. Paint was applied in juxtaposed and superimposed dabs and generally covers the ground entirely except in the sky at the top edge and the sides. There is a network of very fine cracks, widely spaced throughout the painting, and it is unvarnished. (RW)

LANDSCAPE WITH FLOCK OF SHEEP was painted in the village of Éragny-sur-Epte, a small agricultural community some sixty miles northwest of Paris to which Pissarro and his family moved in 1884. It is a picture whose apparent simplicity belies a stunning complexity. In the foreground of an extensive plain, a flock of sheep, so tightly packed that its outline resembles a cigar, is tended by a shepherd and a dog. In the middle distance, the pastureland is bounded at right by a line of trees, receding in space and descending in size, and at left by a long hedgerow, also receding toward the horizon, and diminishing in size. In the center, far beyond the sheep, are three small, dark masses that may be trees. Beyond the trees and hedges, and masking the distant horizon, is a line of low hills, made nearly immaterial by the intervening atmosphere and light. The sky fills the entire upper half of the canvas and is dominated by the heavy mass of threatening blue-gray clouds at the upper right. This much is easy to describe.

More difficult is to account for the variation in the size and direction of brushstroke as well as the color temperatures used to construct forms and constitute spatial planes. The fields of grass are composed of short or long diagonal strokes of paint, sometimes parallel, sometimes intersecting. The sheep are all made from short, parallel, diagonal daubs of color. The sky and clouds above are painted with a much broader brush, and the strokes are long, looped, and intersecting. (This part of the canvas was evidently painted more than a decade after the rest; the dark clouds are painted on top of an earlier paint layer and may be compared with those in the sky of *The Pont Neuf* [1902, Szépmüvészeti Múzeum, Budapest].) In the extreme foreground, crisscrossing strokes of red-brown and ocher, combined with smaller daubs and hatchings of red and violet, act as a foundation on which the rest of the composition is built. Beyond this is a succession of narrow bands, each parallel with the arc of the distant horizon, composed of variations of complementary green and red, orange and blue, or yellow and violet and adjacent hues of yellow, light green, olive green, light blue, and dark blue. (The actuality of color variation far exceeds the available vocabulary.)

The flock of sheep stands out from the surrounding landscape by virtue of its handling and color, predominantly red, blue, and white, brushed and daubed wet on wet to produce an almost solid mass of form. Only the two modestly nonconformist sheep in front have a definitive lamb shape; were it not for them, the viewer would not easily be able to discern the pink-blue mass as animals at all. They are instances of what

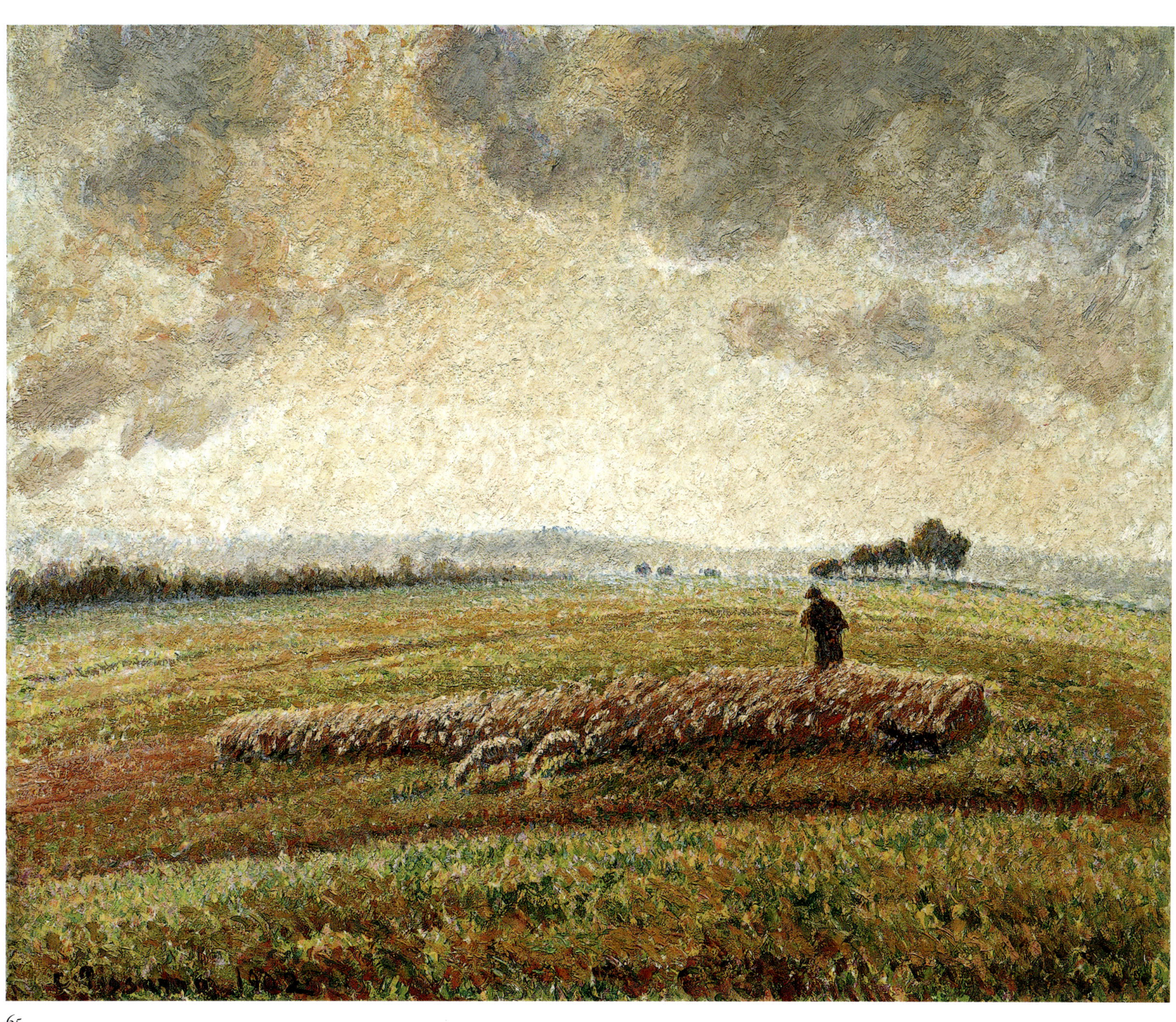

65

E. H. Gombrich called "the etcetera principle,"[1] the idea that a few, strategically placed naturalistic forms can persuade viewers that a great mass of freely applied paint actually represents familiar people and things. This principle is, of course, essential to Impressionism and underlies Pissarro's practice almost from the beginning. Even the dog at the right conforms to the solid shape of the flock; it stands out only by virtue of silhouette and color—dark brown, with a few small spots of blue, green, and yellow. Finally, it should be noted that the progression of colors and brushstrokes is not entirely in one direction: lines of warm color and dark tonality sometimes occur in the middle as well as the foreground; large daubs of paint occasionally interrupt the general diminution in size from foreground to background.

The dominant aesthetic and ideological effect of Pissarro's painting is to force a reckoning with a set of oppositions that in fact constitute a dialectic: openness and closure, liberty and constraint, freedom and conformity, autonomy and heteronomy. The tight phalanx of sheep, dog, and human slowly progresses across a large plain, upon a wide earth beneath a vast and changeable sky. Closeness is more palpable in an arena that is nearly boundless; personal freedom is more keenly felt in the context of work, cooperation, and responsibility; individuality only has meaning in the context of community and society. The arc of the horizon in Pissarro's painting is like the curvature of the earth itself, giving the painting a planetary scale. The confined spaces of Éragny constituted for Pissarro a whole world, and in the course of twenty years there, he created more than two hundred paintings, and many hundreds more watercolors and drawings.

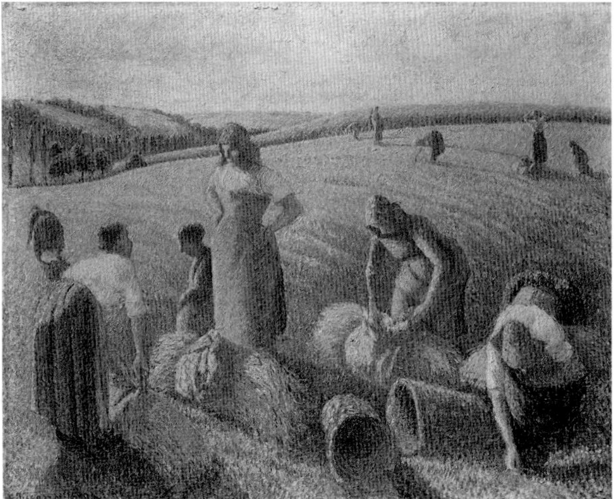

Fig. 65a Camille Pissarro, *The Gleaners*, 1889, oil on canvas, 25¾ × 31⅞ in. (65.5 × 81 cm), Kunstmuseum, Basel

In *Landscape with Flock of Sheep* Pissarro may have been reprising in paint the views of his friend the anarchist geographer Élisée Reclus, who had argued in a series of publications, beginning with *L'Homme et la terre*, that human and natural history cannot be separated and that sound stewardship of the earth is essential to the establishment of an ideal social order. He further argued that individuals must gain an understanding of the social, historical, and geographic totality to achieve a proper self-consciousness, the essential precondition for freedom. "Man is nature becoming self-conscious,"[2] Reclus wrote, summing up ideas of a "dialectics of nature" such as that represented by Pissarro in the present picture.

Landscape with Flock of Sheep is one of several canvases of a similar subject painted by Pissarro at Éragny in the late 1880s and early 1890s. It may be compared with the slightly earlier, more Neo-Impressionist *The Flock of Sheep*[3] and the exactly contemporaneous *Flock of Sheep in a Field after a Harvest*.[4] The latter painting, like *The Gleaners* (fig. 65a) and the great *Apple Picking at Éragny* (1888, Dallas Museum of Art), exhibits the same curved horizon as the present work and must be considered to represent a key moment in an audacious and highly experimental phase in the artist's career. The Norton Simon picture unfortunately suffered the same fate as most of Pissarro's works of the late 1880s—it was unsold—and was partly repainted and redated in 1902. Pissarro made little effort in 1902 to obscure the earlier date and signature, perhaps because he believed—as did his anarchist friend Reclus—that nature and history constitute an integrated whole that should not be denied by an artist. His painting is in a superb state of preservation; it has never been relined, restretched, or varnished, and the luminosity of its myriad colors is undimmed.

1 Gombrich, 1962, pp. 184–185.
2 Reclus, 1875–1894, vol. 1, p. 1.
3 Private collection, Pissarro and Venturi, 1939, vol. 1, no. 723.
4 Private collection, Pissarro and Venturi, 1939, vol. 1, no. 736.

66

Camille Pissarro
French, 1830–1903

View of Berneval
1900

Oil on canvas, $28\frac{3}{4} \times 36\frac{1}{4}$ in. (73×92.1 cm)
Signed and dated lower right: "C. Pissarro, 1900"
N.1967.4

Provenance: Paul-Émile Pissarro (1884–1972), youngest son of the artist, in 1930, still in 1939. [Sam Salz (1894–1981), New York, sold April 1957 to]; Florence Homolka. (sale, London, Sotheby's, 28 June 1967, lot 46, ill., to); Norton Simon, sold May 1981, ⅓ share, to; [William Beadleston, Inc., New York]; Norton Simon (sale, London, Christie's, 19 May 1982, lot 20, ill., bought in); [William Beadleston, Inc., New York, sold April 1984, ⅓ share, to]; Norton Simon, bequest 1993 to; Jennifer Jones Simon Art Trust.

Exhibition: Paris, 1930, no. 103; Paris, 1934e, no. 2

References: Kunstler, 1930, no. 24, ill.; Pillement, 1930, p. 260; Kahn, 1934, p. 2; Pissarro and Venturi, 1939, vol. 1, no. 1143, vol. 2, pl. 227; Cogniat, 1974, p. 74; Pissarro and Snollaerts, 2005, no. 1331.

Technical Notes: The original support, a fine, plain-weave fabric with tacking edges extending to the back edge of the stretcher, is lined with an aqueous adhesive to a slightly heavier plain-weave canvas. The painting is tacked onto a 5-part wood stretcher that may or may not be original. The canvas is preprimed with a medium-thin grayish ground that allows the canvas texture to show. A lead white oil layer may cover the design rectangle. The painting was directly painted and built up of thick layers of pasty paint. Application was wet in wet with brushes of various sizes. There are dabs, short and longer parallel strokes, and looser, more fluid strokes in the sky. Local colors mixed with white predominate, but there are also apparently pure colors such as dark green, a few earth colors, and limited spots of yellow and what is probably vermilion. Forms were adjusted over surrounding paint and the little gate was applied over the already set paint of the landscape. At the upper left in the sky, the artist applied white paint first and then shaped the clouds with the application of blue. Obviously cleaned in the past, the painting was revarnished with a synthetic resin that looks flat and plastic. In ultraviolet light it appears somewhat bluish. Traces of an earlier yellowed natural resin varnish can be seen in the crevices of the paint. The condition is very good, but the lining did flatten paint to some degree and the varnish is inappropriate. (JF)

By the early 1880s Pissarro's aesthetic was fully formed, comprising a tendency toward overall pictorial harmony reminiscent of that of Camille Corot and an ordered complexity of surface—sometimes obscuring the motif—suggestive of the works of his informal pupil Paul Cézanne. Pissarro's landscapes, peasant paintings, and market scenes, such as *The Poultry Market at Pontoise* (cat. 64), convey a sense of immediacy and animation but possess a weight and sobriety that suggest the artist's almost reverential attitude toward his subject. Always an avid reader and reflective thinker, Pissarro had by this time begun seriously to engage the new anarchist literature, especially the writings of the Frenchman Pierre-Joseph Proudhon, author of *Du principe de l'art et de sa destination social* (1865), and a little later, the Russian Pyotr Kropotkin, author of *Paroles d'un révolte* (1884). These authors and others, including Élisée Reclus and Jean Grave, confirmed Pissarro's sense of righteous grievance at his own and others' exclusion from the prosperity and therefore autonomy enjoyed by the class of urban proprietors and governmental elite. What he wished to emulate was not, however, the attitude and social position of this minority assembly of exploiters, but that of the peasants, the majority class of small, rural landholders and ordinary laborers. He believed they represented the true national patrimony and the basis of a future community that would triumph when the oppressive state had been toppled. For the remainder of Pissarro's career, his work would oscillate between the country and the city—the peasant and the urban dweller—and his particular Impressionism would represent an attempt to encompass the facts and sensual appearance, the reality and dreams, of this bifurcated epoch.

Approaching the end of his life, Pissarro concentrated with even greater fervor than before on this dual artistic allegiance. His dozens of depictions of Rouen and Paris are perhaps the greatest of all topographic records of those cities during the fin de siècle, and his renderings of peasant and rural subjects near his home at Éragny are no less exemplary. Pissarro's paintings of Berneval-sur-Mer, a small resort community near Dieppe in Normandy, are thus somewhat anomalous; they are neither urban nor truly rural, and the gratification they offer is above all scenic and picturesque.

Pissarro visited Berneval in July 1900 and made at least seven paintings there. The view in the present painting, like that in a slightly smaller composition (fig. 66a), is from an elevated position, probably the porch of the Grand Hôtel de Berneval, and includes a garden gate at left, about a dozen houses or chalets scattered across the

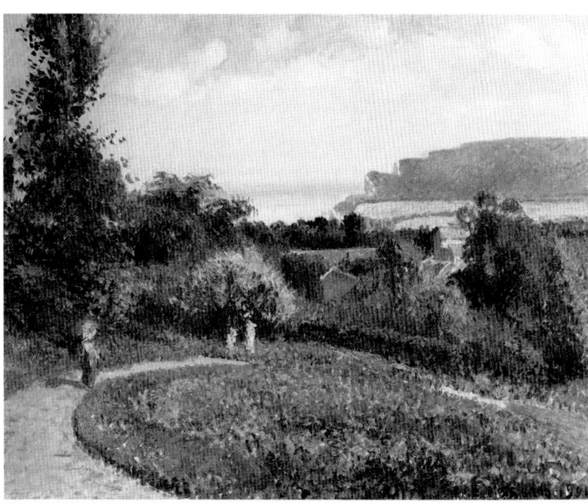

Fig. 66a Camille Pissarro, *The Hotel Garden at Berneval*, 1900, oil on canvas, 25⅝ × 31⅞ in. (65 × 81 cm), private collection

middle ground from left to right, and the dramatic zigzag of cliffs facing a limpid summer sea. The colors of the landscape—with shades of green, orange, pink, and violet in the fore- and middle ground, and green, light brown, blue, gray, and pink above—reprise the hues of paintings Pissarro made at Pontoise and Éragny in the late 1870s and 1880s. And Pissarro's habit of masking the geometric form of buildings by interposing freely painted trees and other foliage, first developed in a series of highly innovative canvases exhibited at the Impressionist exhibitions of 1874, 1876, and 1877, is similarly repeated in *View of Berneval*. Nevertheless, the elevated perspective, extensive view, and essentially picturesque quality of the landscape most of all recall the artist's contemporaneous paintings of the Louvre, Pont Neuf, and boulevard de l'Opéra in Paris rather than his earlier works. In each case, the composition is very carefully weighted, balanced, and clarified, and the spectator is given an easy path of access into an extensive and monumental pictorial space. In this manner, the distance between Berneval and the urban world that was Pissarro's chief occupation at this time is to an extent erased.

Pissarro was one of a legion of French artists who painted the cliffs and beaches of Berneval and nearby areas. By the end of the nineteenth century, the resort towns of Normandy were well known as favored destinations for wealthy men and women from across France, Europe, and the United States. The development of major rail lines from Paris to Rouen and Le Havre in 1847 opened up the region for tourist development, and by the 1860s a number of wealthy entrepreneurs had built seaside villas. The many new hotels and guesthouses on the Normandy coast, often provisioned with cabanas for changing into swimming clothes and bathhouses for hydrotherapy, also attracted middle-class tourists lured by the promise of cures for fatigue and a variety of ailments. Artists, too, flocked to Normandy, and the names of towns are now nearly inseparable from the artists who represented them: Sainte-Adresse: Claude Monet and Alfred Stevens; Trouville: Eugène Boudin and Gustave Courbet; Étretat: Courbet and Monet; Deauville: Boudin; Berck-sur-Mer: Édouard Manet; Honfleur: Johan Barthold Jongkind; Villers-sur-Mer: Constant Troyon; and Villerville: Charles-François Daubigny.

Berneval has two additional claims to fame, beyond the pictures by Pissarro. Pierre-Auguste Renoir visited the hamlet several times, painting *Mussel Collectors at Berneval* (The Barnes Foundation, Merion, Pa.), exhibited at the 1879 Salon, and *Landscape with People at Berneval* (1898, State Hermitage Museum, St. Petersburg). And Oscar Wilde found refuge in Berneval in 1897 after release from his two-year imprisonment following a criminal conviction for sodomy. There he stayed in a small hotel under the pseudonym Sebastian Melmoth, wrote *The Ballad of Reading Gaol*, and tried to maintain contact with his few remaining friends. His description of the town of Berneval in a letter to Carlos Blacker evokes the social world of Pissarro's landscape:

> Well, I am in a little chalet, with a garden, over the sea. It is a nice chalet with two great balconies, where I pass much of my day and many of my nights. Berneval is a tiny place consisting of a hotel and about twenty chalets: the people who come here are *des bon bourgeois* as far as I can see. The sea has a lovely beach, to which one descends through a small ravine, and the land is full of trees and flowers, quite like a bit of Surrey, so green and shady. Dieppe is ten miles off. Many friends, such as the artists Will Rothenstein and [Charles] Conder, have come to see me for a few days.[1]

Pissarro did not have many friends come to visit him at Berneval, and there were no peasants for him to paint, as there were at Éragny, only *des bon bourgeois*. Thus he focused his attention, as Wilde had three years before, on

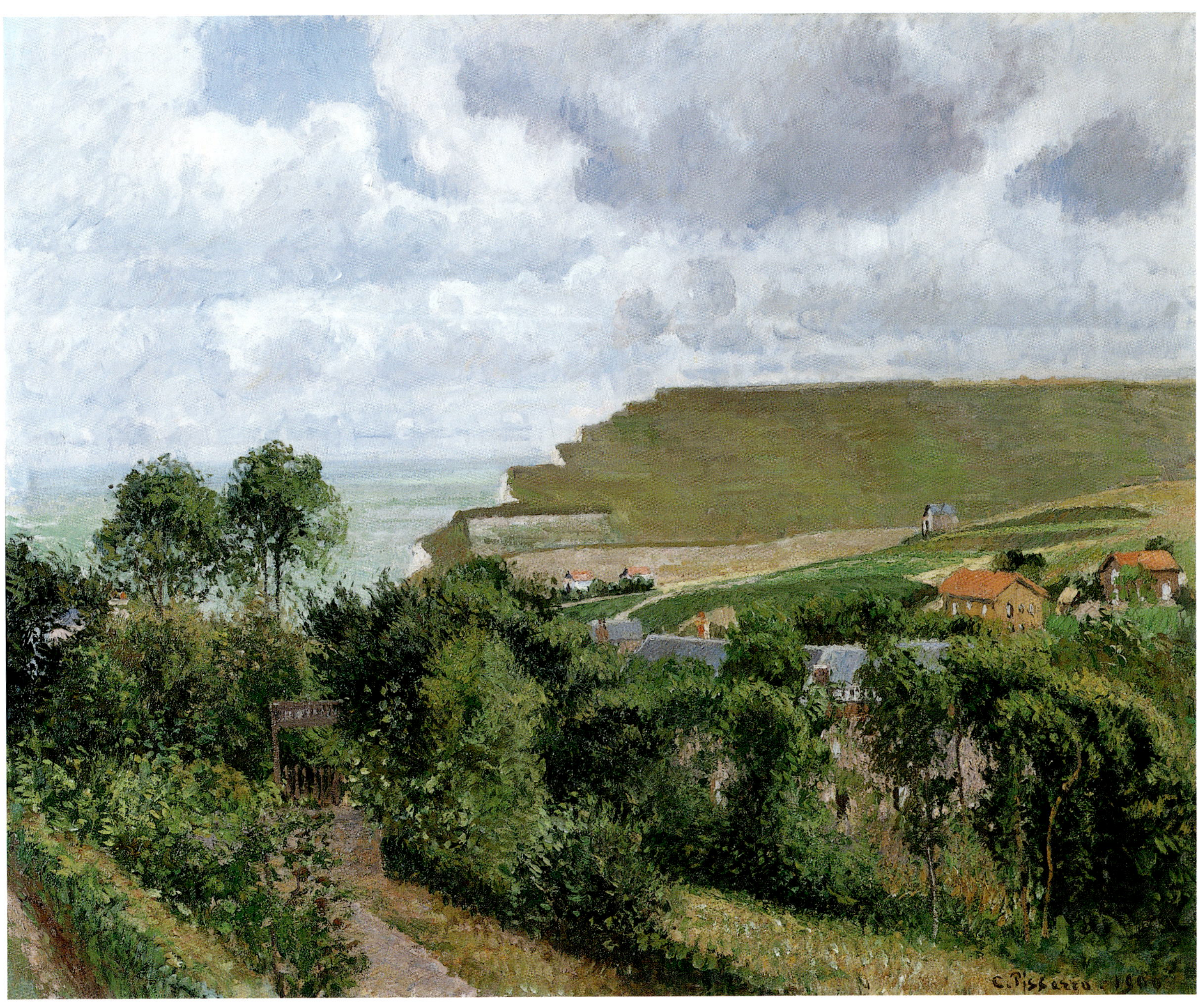

the chalets, trees and flowers, ravine, beach and cliffs. The latter in fact have an odd, almost autonomous character in Pissarro's painting, receding in an ordered progression of steps that appears quite artificial. The adjacent plains are similarly unnatural and awkward, seeming to be tilted up nearly to vertical, paralleling the plane of the picture. Perhaps it was his unfamiliarity with this motif, neither rural nor urban, neither wild nor domestic, neither traditional nor modern that created a jarring ambiguity in the middle of this picturesque scene. Pissarro could not easily project his anarchist dreams on this quiet resort populated by the discreet bourgeoisie. The rusticity and self-reliance of peasants were not on offer here, and the frantic energy and modernity of Rouen and Paris—the harbingers of an imagined proletarian revolution—were nowhere to be seen amid the quiet paths and scenic bluffs of Berneval. Pissarro may have come here precisely to escape from his own fervid dreams and ambitions, but that achieved distance may help explain why he found the place so difficult to represent.

1 *The Complete Letters of Oscar Wilde*, edited by Merlin Holland and Rupert Hart-Davis, New York, 2000, p. 911, 12 July 1897.

67

Édouard Manet
French, 1832–1883
Still Life with Fish and Shrimp
1864

Oil on canvas, 17⅝ × 28¾ in. (44.8 × 73 cm)
M.1978.25

Provenance: Jean Dollfus, by 1884. Mme Besnard, Paris. Marquis de Biron, Paris, by 1902–at least 1926. [Paul Rosenberg, Paris]. [Durand-Ruel, Paris]. Edith Dunn (Mrs. Alfred Chester) Beatty, London, by 1932, by inheritance to; Sir Alfred Chester Beatty (1875–1968), London and Dublin, sold 16 March 1955 to; [Paul Rosenberg, New York, stock no. 5166, offered 12 March 1959 and subsequently sold 29 January 1960 to]; Donald Ellis Simon, Los Angeles, gift 1971 to; The Norton Simon Foundation, Los Angeles (sale, New York, Sotheby Parke-Bernet, 3 May 1973, lot 28, ill.); [New York, Sotheby Parke-Bernet, sold privately 21 May 1978 to]; Norton Simon Art Foundation.

Exhibitions: Paris, 1865a; Paris, 1884, no. 55, as *Nature morte*; Paris, 1885, no. 321, as *Poissons et crevettes*; London, 1932, no. 467, no. 439 in cat., as *Poissons*; Liverpool, 1933, no. 579; Claremont, 1963, no. 46, p. 6, ill., as *Still Life*; Los Angeles, 1965; Philadelphia, 1966, no. 96, ill., as *Salmon and Pike [Poissons]*; on loan, Los Angeles, County Museum of Art, 4 August 1970–20 May 1971; on loan, Minneapolis, Institute of Arts, May 1971–August 1972; Milwaukee, 1977, pp. 150, 151, ill.; on loan, Princeton, University, Art Museum, 30 June 1978–16 April 1979.

References: Duret, 1902, no. 120, p. 222; Moreau-Nélaton, 1906, no. 61; Duret, 1926, no. 120, p. 251; Moreau-Nélaton, 1926, vol. 1, p. 62, fig. 64, vol. 2, no. 55, pp. 86, 128, fig. 338; Tabarant, 1931, no. 89, pp. 130–131, 578; Jamot and Wildenstein, 1932, vol. 1, no. 99, p. 128, vol. 2, fig. 411; *The Studio*, 1932, p. 78; Tabarant, 1947, pp. 96, 535, 604, fig. 88; Orienti and Venturi, 1967, no. 78, p. 94, ill.; Rouart and Wildenstein, 1975, vol. 1, no. 82; Hanson, 1979, p. 70, pl. 28; Kennedy, 1987, pp. 45, ill., 49 (App. 2), 50 (App. 3), 51 (App. 4); Darragon, 1991, fig. 116; Bajou-Charpentreau, 1993, pp. 91, 117, fig. 57; Rubin, 1994, pp. 178–179, fig. 69; Armstrong, 2002, p. 272, fig. 140.

Technical Notes: The medium-weight support is a slightly open-weave fabric in a basket weave, that is, double threads for both warp and weft. The unlined canvas is somewhat brittle, worn through at each corner; however, there are no areas of damage. It is tacked to what appears to be the original keyed stretcher. The smooth, thin ground leaves the canvas texture evident throughout most of the painting. It is cream or light tan-colored and remains visible on the reverse where it seeped through the open weave. A white underpainting, lighter than the ground, was painted beneath the fish and the cutting board. With the base color of white, Manet added rose-white strokes over it and then continued above with varied tones of gray, up to the previously placed dark contour. The underside of the salmon and the parsley indicate that Manet worked wet into wet as he went back and forth to establish the shapes; this is also evident in the needlefish. The dark contours of the two fish are different colors: the upper contour of the needlefish is a dark gray made with blue, and the lower contour of the salmon is a dark gray made with raw umber. The dark background is not entirely opaque, and the light-colored ground is occasionally visible through thinner parts of the brown paint. The paint is in excellent condition. A minimal amount of very fine cracking is located just to the left of the salmon's tail. There is a tiny loss above the salmon's head, a group of tiny losses at the upper right edge, and small losses at the bottom left and the bottom right corners. Ultraviolet light indicates that selective cleaning has removed the thick natural resin varnish from the fish, shrimp, and the cutting board. The remaining old varnish, a rather thick natural resin, is discolored and no longer saturates well, modifying the luminosity of the background. Retouching is located at the center of the right edge, intermittently along the left edge, several small dots in the drawer knob at lower center, and small dots in the upper left background. (RW)

Still Life with Fish and Shrimp was one of the pendants listed by Manet in a letter of January 1865 to his dealer Martinet; its partner is *Still Life: Fruit on a Table* (fig. 67a), and the two were exhibited together in February of that year.[1] The painting remained unsold until after the artist's death in 1883, when it was included in an inventory of the contents of Manet's studio, valued at one hundred francs and marked as "prisé," that is, appraised for sale. At that time, it was photographed by Lochard, who gave it the title *Salmon* and noted that it was painted in 1864 at Boulogne-sur-Mer. The picture was exhibited again, with its pendant, in the great posthumous exhibition of 1884 sponsored by the École Nationale des Beaux-Arts, where it was also photographed—this time by Godet—in an ensemble of smaller works flanking the great *Déjeuner sur l'herbe.* It was titled in the catalogue *Still Life*, stated as belonging to one M. Jean Dollfus, and assigned a date of 1869, perhaps because Lochard's title led to confusion with a larger, later painting called *Salmon*, also painted in Boulogne (fig. 67b). The Norton Simon picture subsequently entered the literature as *Fish and Shrimp* (sometimes as *Salmon, Pike, and Shrimps*) and has generally been recognized as a fine, early still life by the artist.

While the letter from Manet to Martinet does not preclude the possibility that the work was painted in Paris—Manet was installed at his new studio on the boulevard des Batignolles by mid-November 1864—the

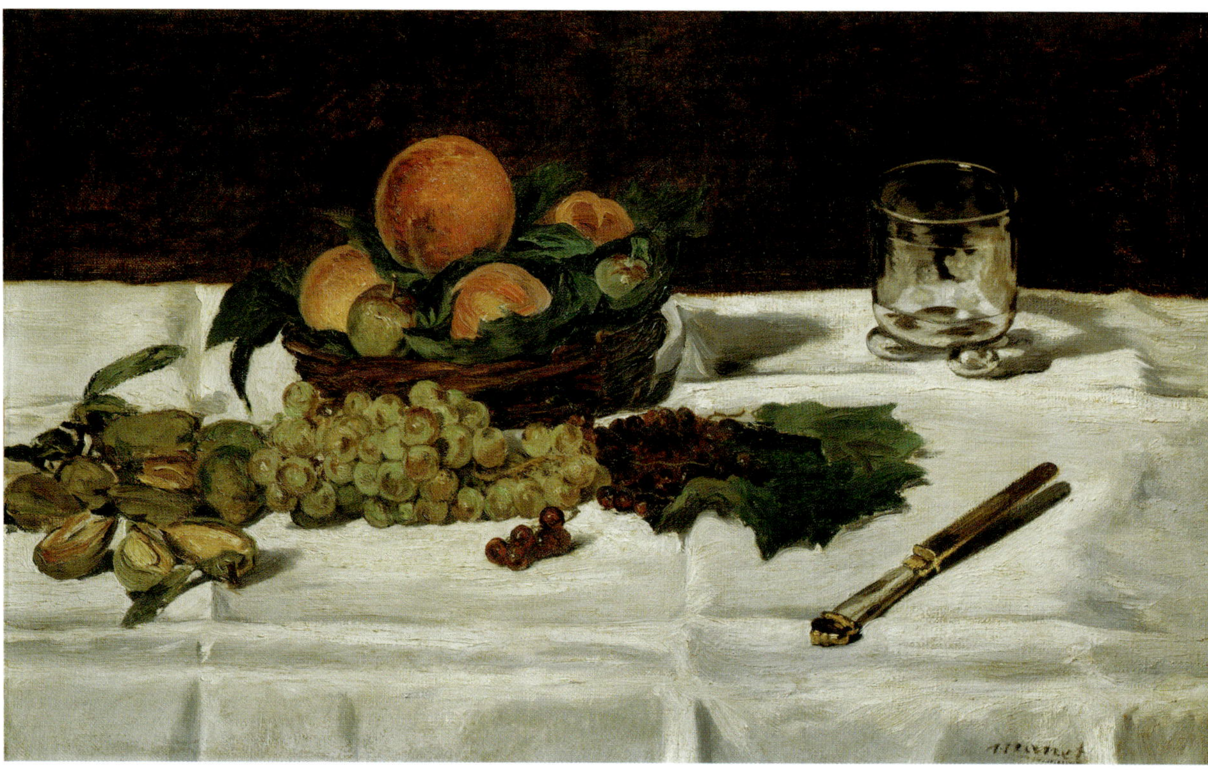

Fig. 67a Édouard Manet, *Still Life: Fruit on a Table*, 1864, oil on canvas, $17\frac{3}{4} \times 28\frac{3}{4}$ in. (45 × 73 cm), Musée d'Orsay, Paris; photo: Erich Lessing / Art Resource, NY

subject matter and quickness of execution strongly suggest it was made during the artist's summer holiday at the seaside resort on the English Channel. Boulogne remains today the leading fishing port in France, and Manet would have seen dozens of ready-made still lifes of fresh fish as he walked the streets of the small city. But it would be a mistake to suppose that Manet's painting was based solely on observation. The genre of still life—and especially of fish still life—was undoubtedly very familiar to him; examples by seventeenth-century Netherlanders such as Jan Davidsz. de Heem and Claesz could be seen in museums, private collections, and in the Paris salerooms. Interest in the still-life paintings of Chardin was revived in the 1840s by the critics Jules Champfleury and Théophile Thoré, and there appeared in the annual Salons at that time still lifes by a group of painters from Lyon—Antoine Vollon, François Bonvin, and François Vernay—that recalled the seeming rusticity of the earlier master. The Louvre began collecting Chardin in earnest in the 1850s, and Manet may also have seen still lifes by the artist in 1860 in exhibitions at 26, boulevard des Italiens and at the Galerie Martinet (where he himself would exhibit a year later). Martinet exhibited additional Chardins in 1863, and in that year Edmond and Jules de Goncourt published the first version of their classic study of the artist, which later appeared in their book *L'Art du XVIIIe siècle* (1880–1884).

Manet's *Still Life with Fish and Shrimp* is like its still-life antecedents in a number of respects. As one of a pair, it recalls the first efforts in this mode by Balthasar van der Ast in the early seventeenth century. But unlike works by that artist or by others in the so-called Bosschaert dynasty (named after the flower painter Ambrosius Bosschaert, who was brother-in-law of van der Ast), it lacks any clear symbolic or allegorical reference, as for instance to *vanitas*, the five senses, the four elements, or natural and artificial wonders. Manet's still life can be more closely associated with Claesz's *Still Life with a Herring* (fig. 67c), with which it shares a common subject, size, scale, tonality, and point of view. Each picture depicts a fish placed horizontally on a table occupying the lower quarter of the picture plane. In

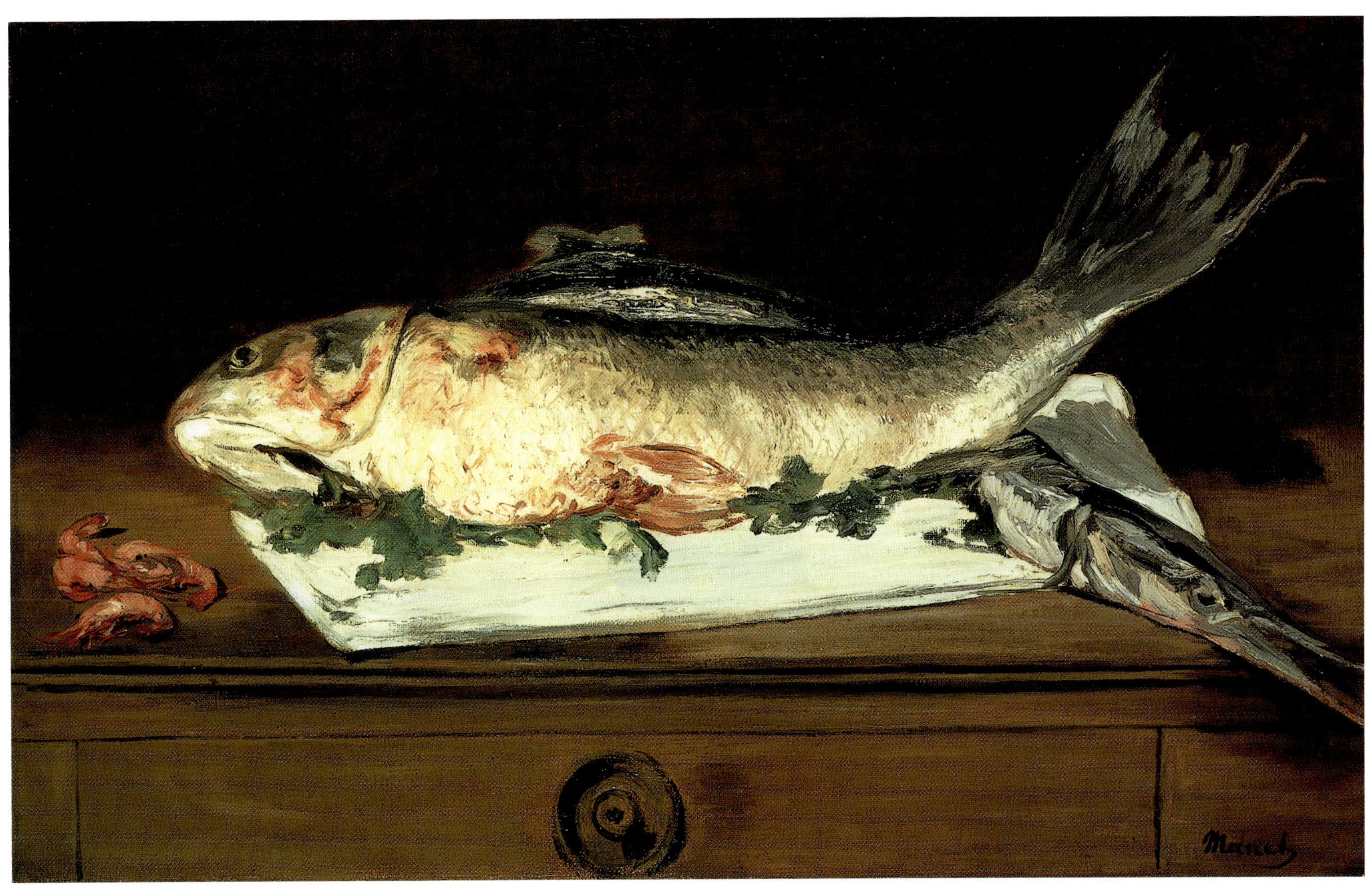

67

Fig. 67b Édouard Manet, *Salmon*, 1869, oil on canvas, 28$^{3}/_{8}$ × 36$^{1}/_{4}$ in. (72 × 92.1 cm), The Shelburne Museum, Shelburne, Vermont

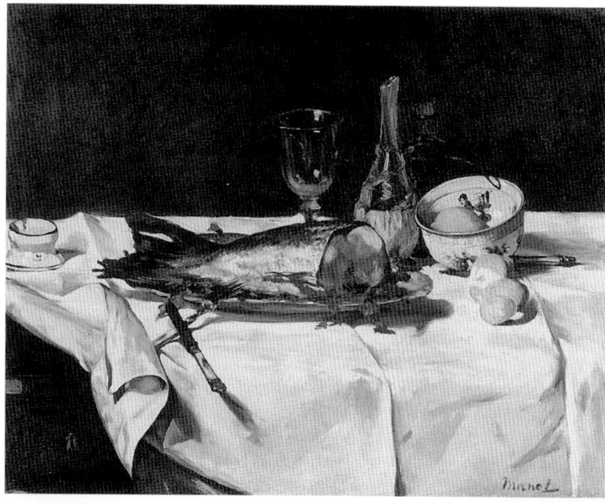

Fig. 67c Pieter Claesz, *Still Life with a Herring*, 1636, oil on panel, 14$^{3}/_{16}$ × 19$^{5}/_{16}$ in. (36 × 49 cm), Museum Boijmans van Beuningen, Rotterdam

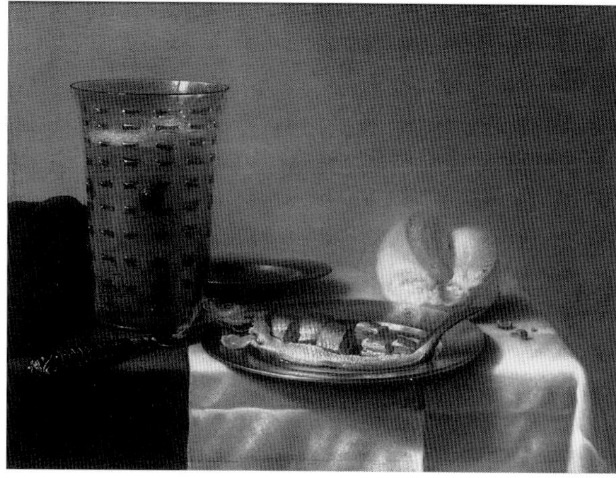

addition, each shows the head and raised tail of the fish, and each contains an element of trompe l'oeil: the salver on which Claesz's fish is set overhangs the table and threatens to topple over into the viewer's space; the elongated jaw of the second fish in Manet's painting (it appears to be a needlefish, family *Belonidae*) droops over the right corner of the cutting board and table on which it is laid. The differences between Claesz's work and Manet's, however, are significant and instructive. The former shows a cured fish as the centerpiece of a meal that also includes bread and beer; the fish has been cut into sections and partially eaten; and the fine glass, cutlery, and plate indicate the wealth of the consumer. It is thus a scene of consumption and bourgeois domesticity very much in step with the ideology and self-understanding of a rich and powerful maritime nation. Manet's picture, by contrast, lacks clear marks of either national chauvinism or the quotidian. The fish and shrimps are laid on what appears to be a slab or cutting board but are not accompanied by any kitchen implements; they are decorated with sprigs of green parsley, to be displayed before cooking. We are presented with what may be called the raw facts of fish and still-life painting: two fish and a handful of shrimps were purchased at the market, set down, adorned with parsley, and painted. The point of view here is that of the worldly gentleman, cosmopolitan, or flâneur. The components that constitute this still life are no more salient for the artist-observer than if they were flowers, shoes, or dead rabbits; they are observed with a connoisseur's combination of keenness and dispassion.

This matter-of-factness suggests Manet's greater indebtedness to Chardin than to the Dutch artists. Indeed, his first recorded still life, *Oysters* (fig. 67d), is a reprise of Chardin's *Le Plat de ouitres*, which the artist likely saw when it was auctioned at Hôtel Drouot in the late spring of 1861.[2] Manet's larger and slightly later *Fish (Still Life)* (fig. 67e) was clearly based, as Charles Moffett first proposed, on Chardin's *The Silver Tureen* (fig. 67f) exhibited at Martinet's in 1860.[3] *Still Life with Fish and Shrimp* does not appear to be modeled on any single painting by Chardin, but it has compositional features common to many still lifes by the earlier artist. The restricted space surrounding the fish mimics the circumscription in a number of Chardin's works, including *Still Life with a Hare* (fig. 67g), also shown at Martinet's. In addition, Manet's effort to open up the composition at right—the tail of the salmon and the head of the needlefish suggest an open scissors—is derived from a gesture seen in many still lifes by Chardin. What is different about Manet's painting is its immediacy. The liquidity of the paint and the comedy of composition—note the awkward change in scale from shrimp to salmon—forbid sober contemplation or intellectual immersion. Though the little picture is not nearly as ostentatious as *Olympia* on her divan or *Dead Christ with Angels*—each painted by the artist just a few months before—there is a common element of travesty, and a similar frankness about the truth of painting and the falseness of allegory and symbolism.

Fig. 67d Édouard Manet, *Oysters*, 1862, oil on canvas, $23\frac{5}{8} \times 26$ in. (60×66 cm), National Gallery of Art, Washington, Gift of the Adele R. Levy Fund, Inc.

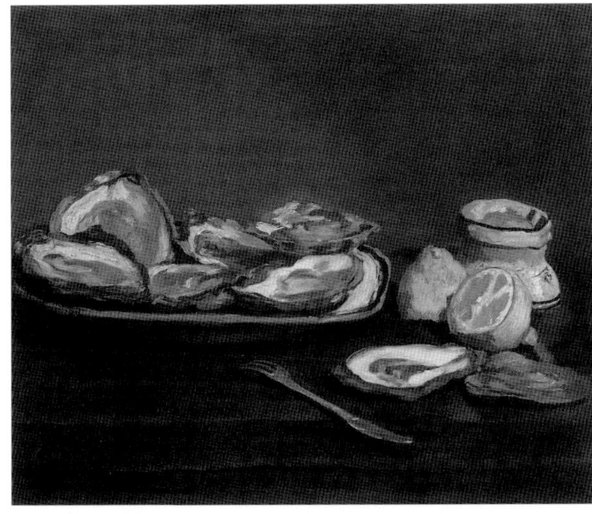

Fig. 67e Édouard Manet, *Fish (Still Life)*, 1864, oil on canvas, $28\frac{7}{8} \times 36\frac{1}{4}$ in. (73.4×92.1 cm), The Art Institute of Chicago, Mr. and Mrs. Lewis Larned Coburn Memorial Collection

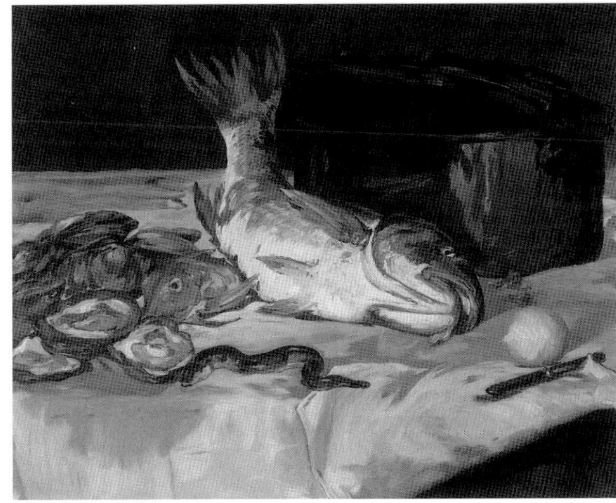

It is precisely this parody and this honesty that give the painting, like others by Manet of the same period, something of the character of a modern manifesto. The directness, comedy, and handmade character of *Still Life with Fish and Shrimp* suggest an impatience with the conventional, belabored approaches to the genre on offer at the official Salon exhibitions. (The nearly perfect preservation of the painting easily permits us to evaluate the facture.) Like Vollon or the Spanish-inspired Théodule Ribot, Manet looked back to the seventeenth and eighteenth centuries for inspiration, but unlike them, he rejected anything that may be called historicism, the deliberate revival of a past style or subject without regard to its salience in the present. In Manet, Claesz and Chardin have been reborn as modern, ironic positivists who know the difference between a nice, fresh fish bought at market and an allegory of wealth and vanity.

1 Moreau-Nélaton, 1926, vol. 1, p. 62.

2 The painting, titled *Une Table de cuisine*, was offered in the Montmarque sale (Mireur, 1901–1912, vol. 2, p. 151).

3 Cachin et al., 1983, p. 216.

Fig. 67f (*right*) Jean-Siméon Chardin, *The Silver Tureen*, oil on canvas, $30 \times 42\frac{1}{2}$ in. (76.2×107.9 cm), The Metropolitan Museum of Art, Fletcher Fund, 1959

Fig. 67g (*far right*) Jean-Siméon Chardin, *Still Life with a Hare*, c. 1730, oil on canvas, $25\frac{5}{8} \times 32$ in. (65.1×81.3 cm), Philadelphia Museum of Art, Gift of Henry P. McIlhenny; photo: Graydon Wood, 1993

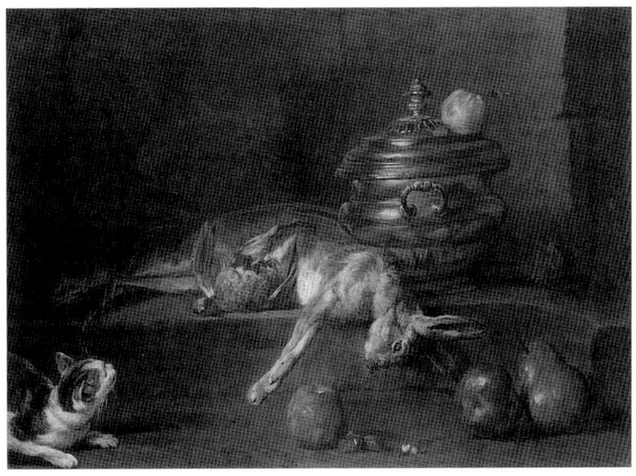

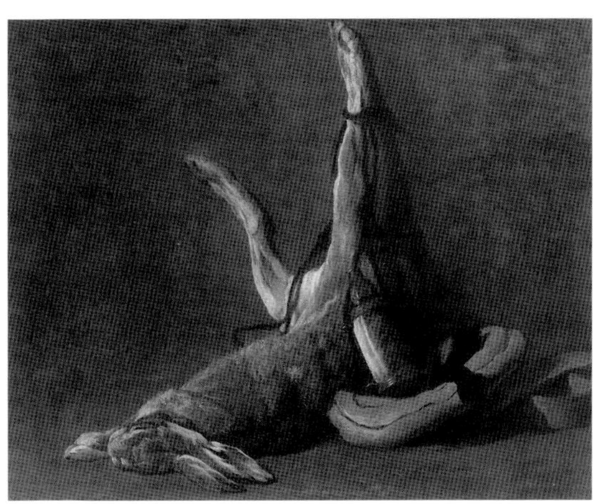

68

ÉDOUARD MANET
French, 1832–1883

The Ragpicker
c. 1865–1870

Oil on canvas, 76¾ × 51½ in. (194.9 × 130.8 cm)
Signed lower right: "Manet"
F.1968.9

PROVENANCE: The artist; sold 1871–1872 for Ff 1,000 to; [Durand-Ruel, Paris, for Ff 1500 to]; Ernest Hoschedé (1837–1890), Paris (sale, Paris, Hôtel Drouot, 5–6 June 1878, lot 45, as *Le Mendiant*, for Ff 800 to); Duquesne, Paris. Fernand Crouan, Nantes, by 1884. Rothermundt, Blasewitz (near Dresden), by 1906–1921. [Paul Cassirer, Berlin]. Josef Stransky (1872–1936), New York, by 1921. Adolph Lewisohn (d. 1938), New York, by 1926, to; [Wildenstein & Co., New York and Paris, by 1931]. [Wildenstein & Co., New York, reacquired c. 1950, later sold to]; H., Geneva (Mr. Schlepfer), by 1964–at least 1967; [Wildenstein & Co., New York; sold 1968 to]; The Norton Simon Foundation.

EXHIBITIONS: London, 1872a, no. 31, as *A Beggar*; Paris, 1884, no. 44, as *Le Mendiant*; Berlin, 1906, no. 189, ill.; Buffalo, 1930, no. 32, ill.; St. Louis, 1931, no. 17, as *The Beggar*; Paris, 1932, no. 37, ill., as *Le Mendiant*; Philadelphia, 1933, p. 19; San Francisco, 1934, no. 118; Boston, 1935, no. 25; New York, 1937a, no. 15, pl. XV; Toledo, 1937, no. 13, ill.; Amsterdam, 1938, no. 141; Detroit, 1954, no. 20, ill.; Lausanne, 1964, no. 350, ill.; Philadelphia, 1966, no. 76, ill.; Paris, 1967, no. 29, ill.; on loan, New York, Metropolitan Museum of Art, March 1968–January 1969; on loan, Los Angeles, County Museum of Art, January 1969–September 1972; San Francisco, 1973, no. 29, ill.; on loan, Princeton, University Art Museum, 11 December 1980–14 July 1981.

REFERENCES: Duret, 1902, no. 95; Moreau-Nélaton, 1906, no. 117; Rosenhagen, 1906, pp. 442, 434, ill.; Duret, 1910, no. 95, p. 224 (1912 ed., no. 95, p. 228); Meier-Graefe, 1912b, fig. 48; Waldmann, 1923, pp. 46, 35, ill.; Duret, 1926, no. 95, p. 248; Moreau-Nélaton, 1926, vol. 1, no. 44, p. 109, fig. 121, vol. 2, pp. 47, 128, fig. 339; Watson, 1926, pp. 31, 18, ill.; Bourgeois, 1928, p. 67, ill.; Venturi, 1929, p. 154; Tabarant, 1931, pp. 146–147, 578, no. 106; Wilenski, 1931, p. 245; Jamot and Wildenstein, 1932, vol. 1, no. 153, pp. 89, 137, vol. 2, pl. 22, fig. 45; Tabarant, 1932a, no. 37, p. 33; Tabarant, 1932b, p. 141; Lambert, 1933, p. 375, fig. 13; *Art News*, 1933, p. 11; McMahon, 1937, p. 8, ill.; *New York Times*, 1937, sec. 9, pt. 1, n.p., ill.; *Art Digest*, 1937, p. 9, ill.; Venturi, 1939, vol. 2, no. 95, p. 190; Florisoone, 1947, pp. 19, 21, 24; Tabarant, 1947, pp. 115–116, 323, 492, 536, 605, fig. 113; Orienti and Venturi, 1967, no. 97, p. 95, ill.; Daulte, 1967, p. 143; Mélikian and Wildenstein, 1967, p. 76 (English ed., p. 58, ill. [detail]); Bodelsen, 1968, no. 45, pp. 339–340; Hanson, 1968, pp. 74, 77, fig. 19; Caby, 1968, p. 5, ill.; Rouart and Wildenstein, 1975, vol. 1, no. 137, ill.; Alpers, 1976, pp. 36, 37, fig. 14; Steadman, 1976, p. 222, colorpl. A; Weisberg, 1978a, pp. 286, 287, fig. 12; Hanson, 1979, p. 65; Alpers, 1988, p. 79, fig. 3.48; Herbert, 1988, p. 63, fig. 64; Distel, 1990, p. 104; Darragon, 1991, fig. 121; Stevenson, 1992, pp. 105, 104, ill.; Perutz, 1993, p. 67; Brombert, 1996, pp. 106, 306.

TECHNICAL NOTES: The condition of the painting is good. The original support is a fairly tight, medium-weight, plain-weave fabric that has been lined to canvas with an aqueous adhesive. The tacking edges are partially extant and are covered with a thin off-white ground, indicating that this was a preprimed canvas; the stretcher is later. The thick and opaque paint is directly and vigorously applied with brushes ranging in width from about ¼ to ¾ inch. Manet did not use glazes or scumbles; instead, his shadows are opaque darks directly applied. The artist first laid out at least some of the design with dark brown paint that differs from a traditional design sketch in that it is rather thick and appears to contain a white pigment. While some paint may be applied over already set paint, much of the painting is wet in wet. There is little or no blending on the surface to achieve a chiaroscuro for the costume or flesh; rather, brushstrokes follow form to declare volume. Contrarily, the colors of the beard and background are painted into one another wet in wet for the fuzzy quality that suggests texture for the beard and atmosphere for the background. The beard in the X-ray shows numerous areas of scraping that were subsequently repainted. The repaint is consistent with the earlier paint and is no doubt Manet's, but it is distinguishable with magnification and does not entirely match surrounding paint. The X-ray and surface texture indicate that the artist fairly completely painted the white shirt before painting the sack over it. The artist made numerous slight changes including the placement of the stick and hand and the shadow cast by the man's right foot. A more significant change perhaps is in the still life at lower left; elements of it in the lower left corner were painted out. There is a tear about 7 inches long in the background to the right of the man's left knee. Unfortunately, the varnish is thick and nonsaturating, and small losses and the few larger ones in the background have been freely overpainted. (JF)

THE FIRST MENTION of *The Ragpicker* is in a list, prepared by Manet and dated December 1871, of paintings the artist recently sold to the art dealer Durand-Ruel: "Four Philosophers (which include *The Drinker* and *The Ragpicker*)."[1] Two of the four pictures (figs. 68a and 68b) are now in the Art Institute of Chicago. The third is undoubtedly *The Absinthe Drinker* in the Ny Carlsberg Glyptotek, Copenhagen (fig. 68d). The last is the present painting. *The Ragpicker*, unlike the other three, all of which appeared in Manet's privately financed exhibition at the Exposition Universelle in 1867, has no exhibition history before 1872 and therefore—given its size and evident ambition—is unlikely to have been completed before 1867. It is, however, closely

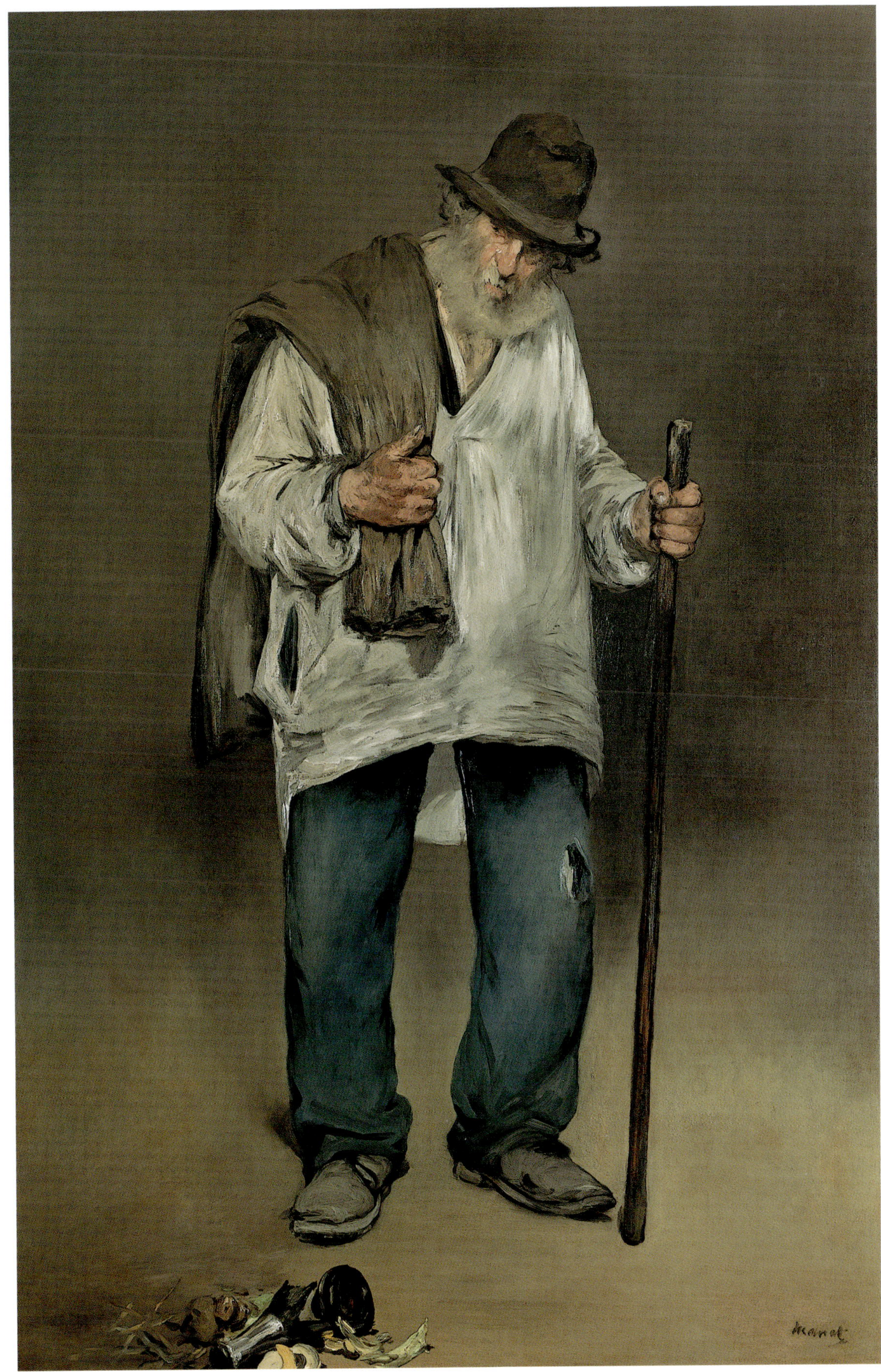

Fig. 68a (*right*) Édouard Manet, *Beggar with a Duffle Coat (Philosopher)*, 1865, oil on canvas, 73⅞ × 43¼ in. (187.7 × 109.9 cm), The Art Institute of Chicago, A. A. Munger Collection

Fig. 68b (*far right*) Édouard Manet, *Beggar with Oysters (Philosopher)*, 1865–1867, oil on canvas, 73¾ × 42½ in. (187.3 × 108 cm), The Art Institute of Chicago, Arthur Jerome Eddy Memorial Collection

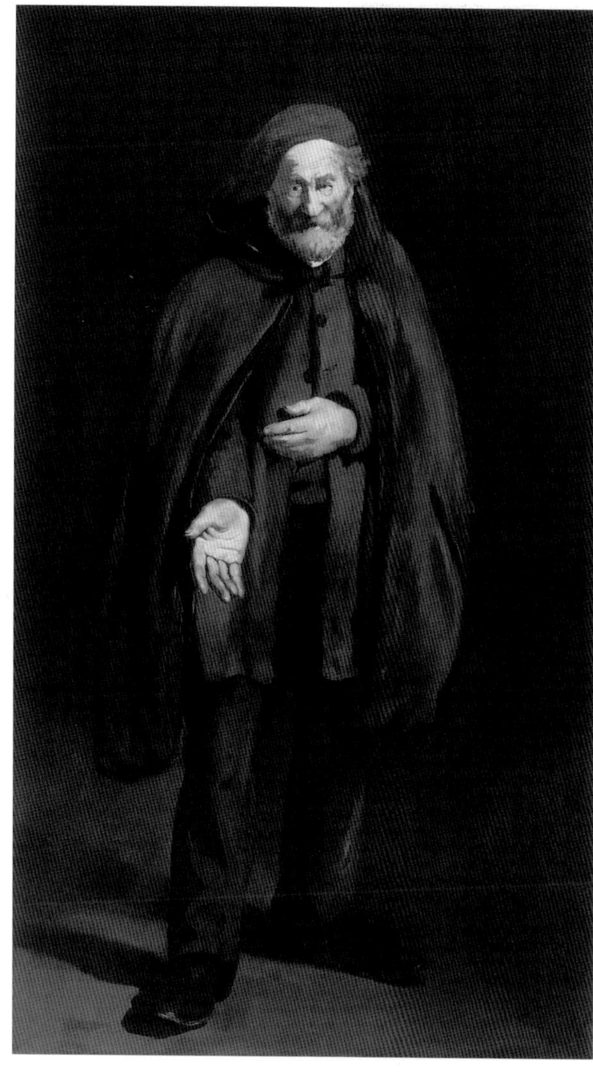

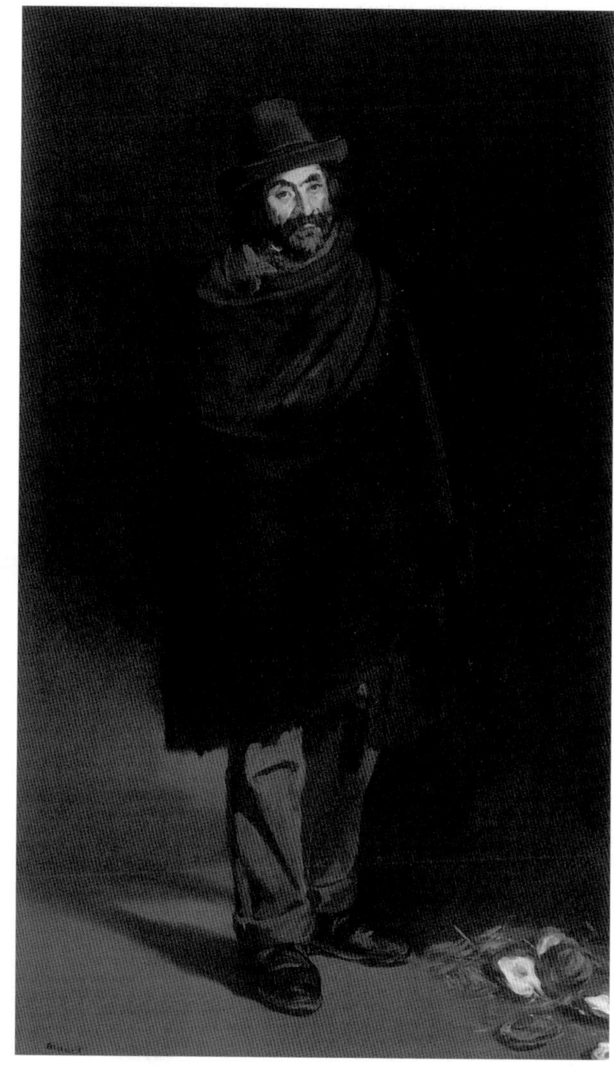

connected in style and subject—as Manet attested—to the earlier works, and it is entirely plausible that *The Ragpicker* was begun in the mid-1860s and finished later in the decade. Indeed, the four philosophers possess a strong family resemblance, although no two are precisely the same size, and the Norton Simon painting is significantly larger. Each is just under life-size and features a single, standing, male figure in a dark, amorphous setting. All the men are bearded and unkempt, and three of the works have strong still-life elements in the foreground. The exception is *Beggar with a Duffle Coat (Philosopher)* (fig. 68a), which is also unique by virtue of the more frontal address of the figure.

Though Manet titled the painting *The Ragpicker* (*Le Chiffonnier*) in his list for Durand-Ruel, it was first exhibited in London in 1872 with the title *A Beggar*, perhaps because the earlier name was thought to have less resonance for an English audience. In addition, the new title more clearly associated the work with another work by Manet called *The Philosopher*, also exhibited in London, although we are not certain which of the two Chicago pictures it was. The pictorial and iconographic origin of both canvases can be traced to the "beggar-philosophers" painted by prominent seventeenth-century Flemish, Dutch, and Spanish artists, including Peter Paul Rubens (fig. 68c), Jusepe de Ribera (fig. 68e), and Rembrandt van Rijn (fig. 68f). Manet's chief sources of inspiration, however, were Diego Velázquez's portrait of the actor Pablo de Valladolid (fig. 68g) and his paintings of Moenippus and Aesop in the Museo del Prado (figs. 68h and 68i).

"I am in a great hurry to see all those beautiful things and seek the counsel of maestro Velazquez," Manet wrote to his friend Zacharie Astruc on the eve of his trip to Spain in the late summer of 1865.[2] Manet was part of a small horde of French travelers to the peninsula in the decade and a half following the marriage in 1853 of Napoleon III to Eugenia de Montijo (the future Empress Eugénie), but his interests were unusually focused. He had made copies after paintings by Velázquez as early as

Fig. 68d (*right*) Édouard Manet, *The Absinthe Drinker*, 1858–1859, oil on canvas, 71¼ × 41¾ in. (181 × 106 cm), Ny Carlsberg Glyptotek, Copenhagen; photo: Ole Haupt

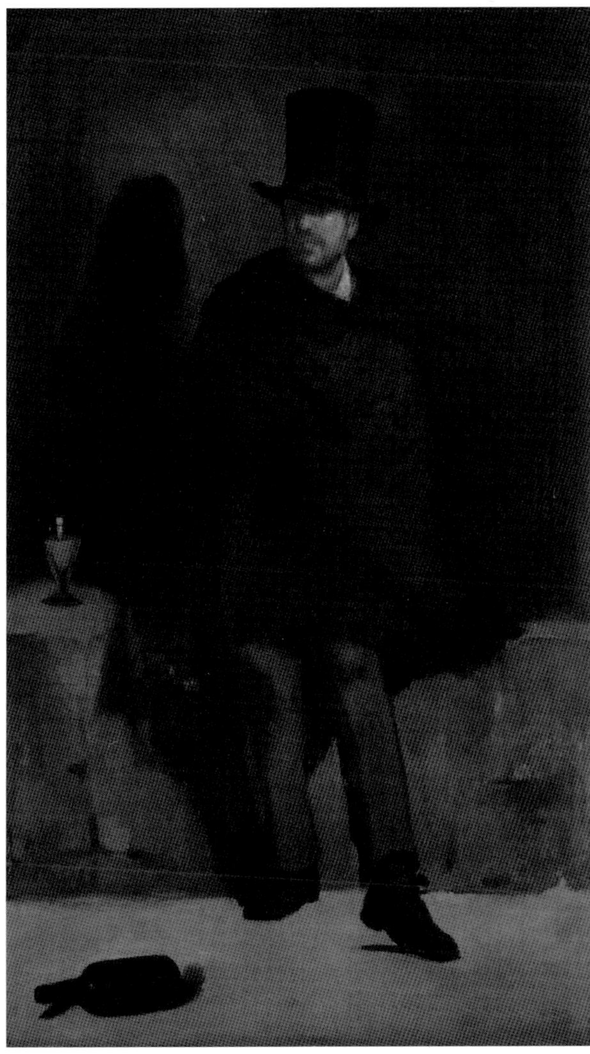

Fig. 68e (*below right*) Jusepe de Ribera, *Archimedes*, 1630, oil on canvas, 49¼ × 31⅞ in. (125 × 81 cm), Museo del Prado, Madrid

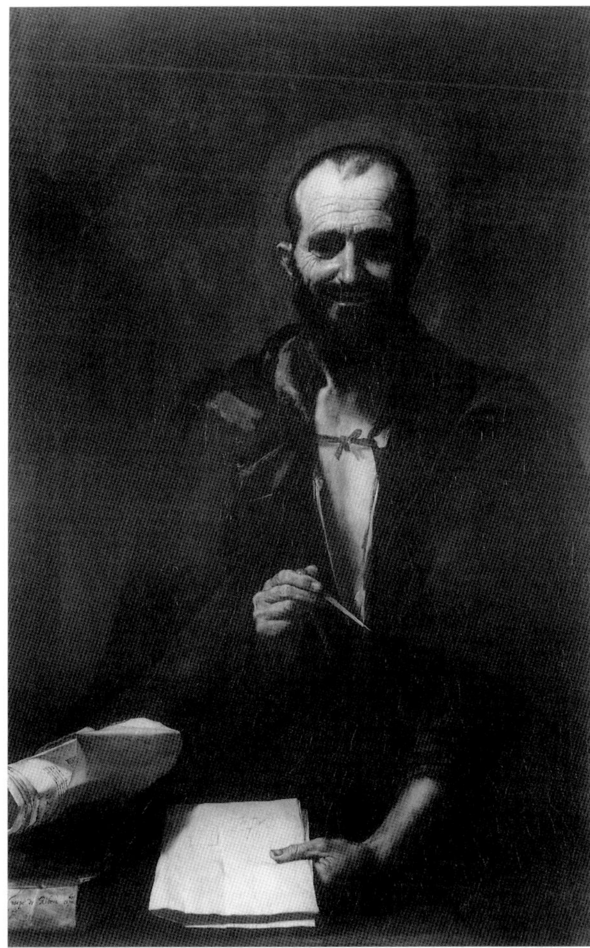

Fig. 68c (*below*) Peter Paul Rubens, *Democritus*, 1638, oil on canvas, 70½ × 26 in. (179 × 66 cm) Museo del Prado, Madrid

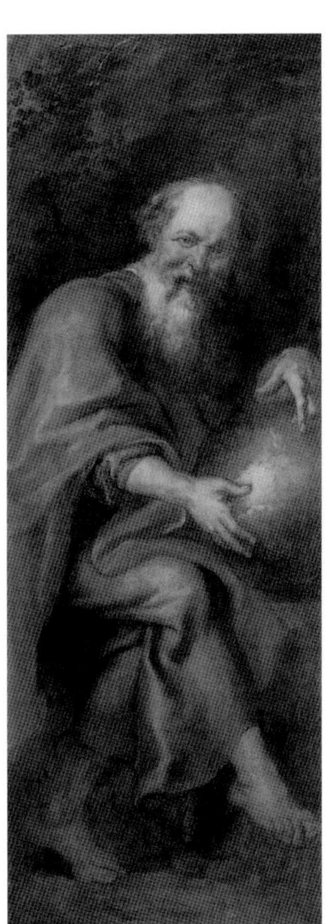

1859 and continued to paint Spanish subjects until the moment of his departure for Spain. He wrote from Madrid to his friend the painter Henri Fantin-Latour that "the philosophers [of Velázquez] were astounding pieces" and "alone worth the journey," and that the *Pablo de Valladolid* was "perhaps the most astounding piece of painting ever done."[3] After his return to Paris, Manet continued to enthuse: "The entire trip is worth making just for the work of Velázquez," he wrote Astruc in mid-September. "I saw in Madrid some thirty or forty [of Velázquez's] portraits or paintings, all of them masterpieces; he is greater than his reputation and he alone is worth the exhaustion and the unavoidable discomforts of a trip to Spain."[4]

The Ragpicker, however, painted after Manet's return to France, does not convey the energy and excitement attested in his letters. Where *Still Life with Fish and Shrimp* (cat. 67) appears spontaneous, *The Ragpicker* and the two paintings in Chicago were painted in several campaigns and are almost labored. This is particularly true of the larger Norton Simon painting, which may have occupied Manet intermittently between 1865 and 1870. Its contours were laid down once, adjusted, fixed again, redrawn, and readjusted. Although this may well be the result of the extended period of gestation, it also attests to a certain anxiety of influence. Velázquez's *Moenippus* and *Aesop* (figs. 68h and 68i) are painted with a freedom and expressiveness that Manet attempted to emulate but could not surpass. Pentimenti are clearly visible in several places in *The Ragpicker*: the left side of the head, the left edge of the sack flung over the old man's right shoulder, the right side of the left hand, and both sides of his staff. X-rays of the canvas reveal still greater uncertainties or changes of heart: a mysterious, clublike form extends from the upper left corner of the canvas to the man's right hand; another runs from the

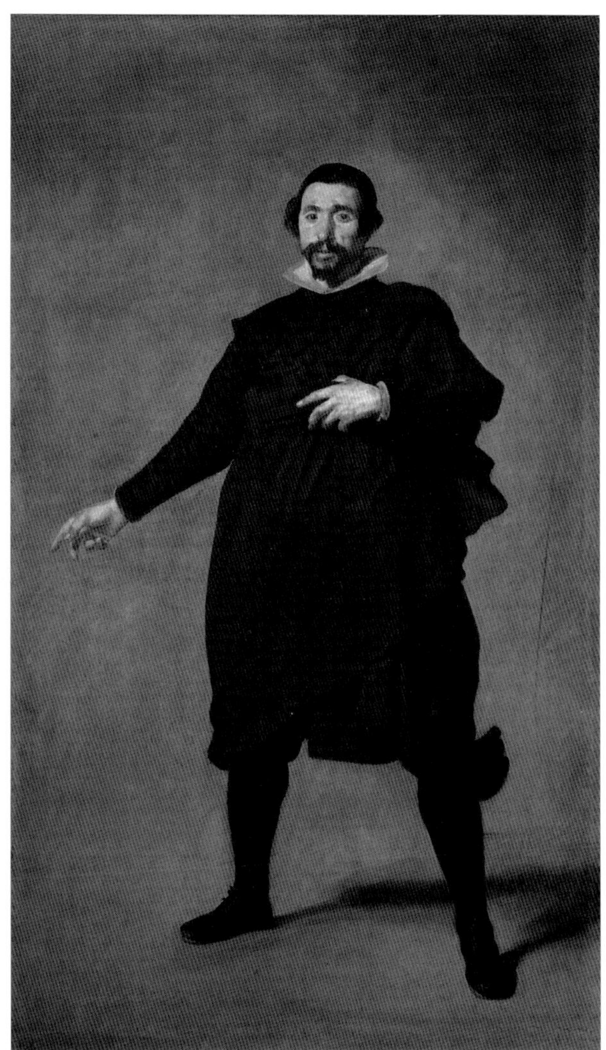

Fig. 68g Diego Velázquez, *Pablo de Valladolid*, 1632, oil on canvas, $82\frac{1}{4} \times 48\frac{3}{8}$ in. (209 × 123 cm), Museo del Prado, Madrid; photo: Scala / Art Resource, NY

middle, right edge of the canvas to the waist of the figure. Where the earlier still life uses color, texture, and composition to convey the blunt physicality of its subject, the later painting is veritably minimalist in means: a gray tonality dominates the limited range of hue (blue, brown, rose), the paint surface is inexpressive in the extreme (an effect unfortunately exacerbated by the relining and flattening of the canvas), and the composition is quite static. Finally, where the one picture is naturalist, the other is allegorical: it says one thing ("this is a beggar or ragpicker") but means another ("he is a philosopher or a criminal"). Indeed, *The Ragpicker* appears conservative when seen beside other paintings from the late 1860s, such as *The Reader* (1868–1869, Musée d'Orsay, Paris) and *Departure of the Folkstone Boat* (1869, Philadelphia Museum of Art).

Manet's model can be identified as the painter Joseph Gall, who either lived or had a studio near Manet on the rue Guyot, where *The Ragpicker* was painted. Gall appears in paintings dated as early as 1861, but more fully in 1865–1866. Born in 1807, Gall would have been in his late fifties when Manet asked him to pose. His strong nose and straggling beard made him an ideal choice for a world-weary, if determined, beggar-philosopher. Given the fact that all the other paintings representing the figure of Gall are securely dated to 1865–1866, it seems likely that Manet began this painting at that time as well.

The ragpicker or beggar was a well-known social type in Manet's France. Charles Baudelaire titled a poem "The Ragpicker's Wine" (Le Vin des chiffonniers), and guidebook authors frequently described the picturesque personage—a holdout from Paris before the age of Baron Haussmann's renovations of the city—traversing the streets collecting rags to sell to paper manufacturers. A tiny, early sketch for *The Ragpicker* conveys a greater sense of this movement than the finished painting.[5] There the figure strides forward as the ground plane passes beneath his bowed legs. The sketch also recalls a slightly different iconographic tradition, the Wandering Jew, a type described in countless popular songs, prints, and

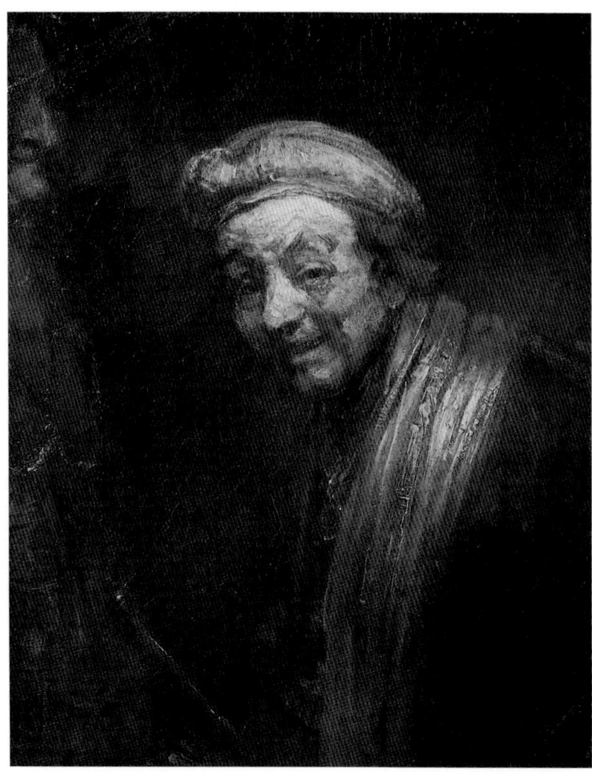

Fig. 68f Rembrandt van Rijn, *Self-Portrait as Zeuxis*, 1669, oil on canvas, $32\frac{1}{2} \times 25\frac{5}{8}$ in. (82.5 × 65 cm), Wallraf-Richartz Museum, Cologne

Fig. 68h (*right*) Diego Velázquez, *Moenippus*, c. 1639–1640, oil on canvas, 70½ × 37 in. (179 × 94 cm), Museo del Prado, Madrid; photo: Erich Lessing / Art Resource, NY

Fig. 68i (*far right*) Diego Velázquez, *Aesop*, c. 1639–1640, oil on canvas, 70½ × 37 in. (179 × 94 cm), Museo del Prado, Madrid; photo: Scala / Art Resource, NY

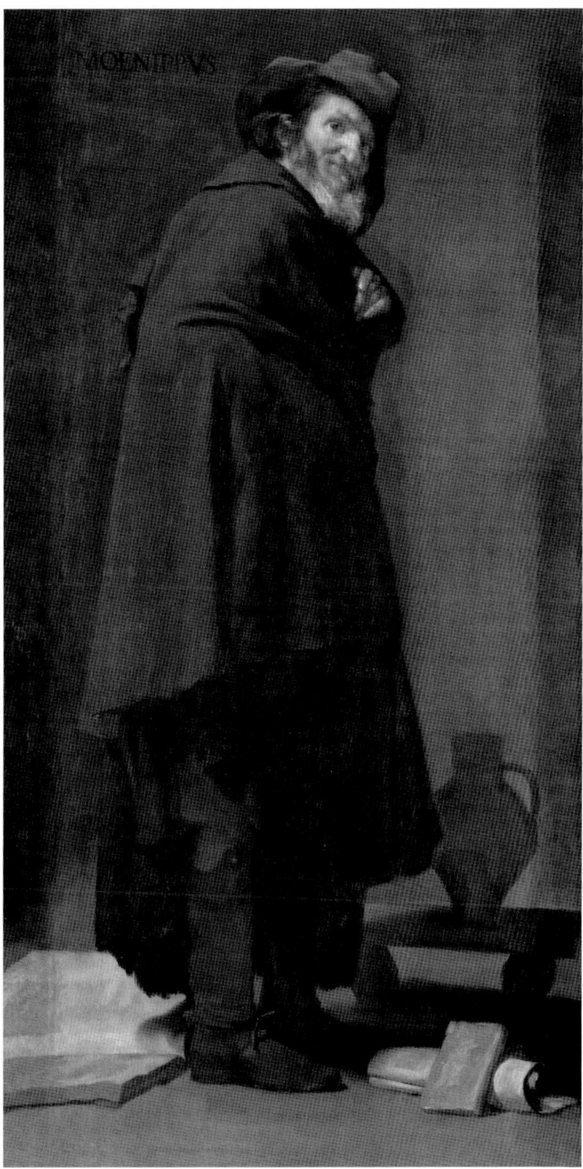

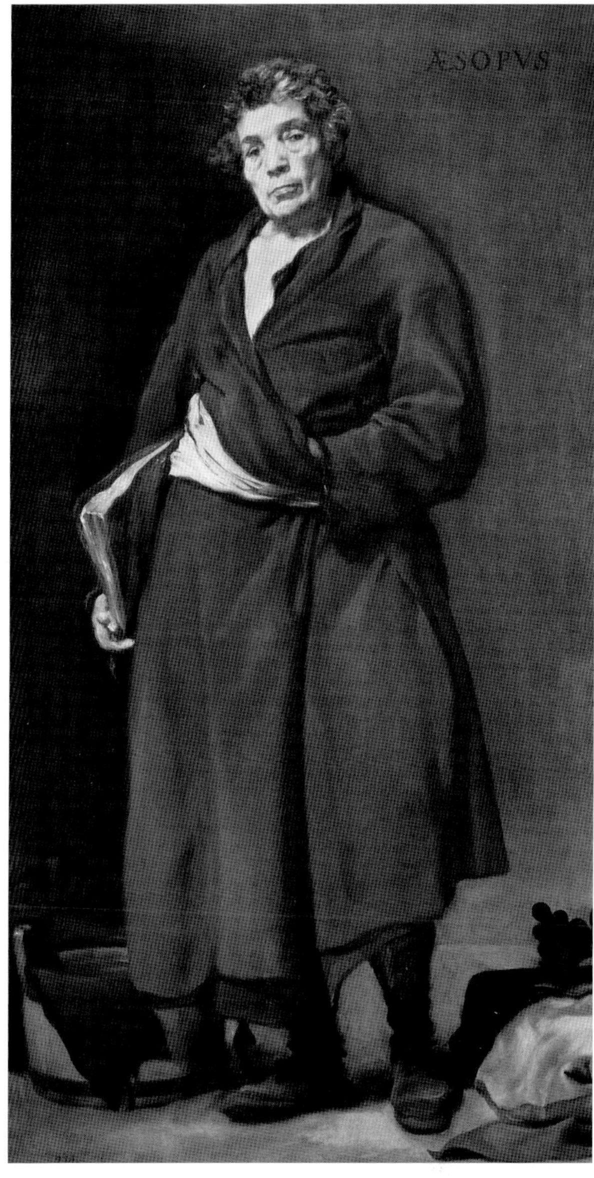

broadsides, and in the famous, eponymous novel of the Paris underworld by Eugène Sue (1845).

According to popular fiction, the ragpicker was a natural vagabond, a wanderer who possessed a greater liberty and happiness than the bourgeoisie in their offices. If he occasionally went hungry and homeless, died young, and suffered the ignominy of burial in a common grave, it was because he had chosen a life of freedom. Sometimes, however, a different image prevailed. During times of social upheaval, for example in the immediate wake of 1848 and the coup d'état of Louis Napoleon in late 1851, or in the period leading up to the rebellion of 1870–1871, street people—urchins, mountebanks, peddlers, beggars, ragpickers, and petty thieves—assumed a more sinister aspect. They were then seen as dangerously mobile in their political affections, as potential revolutionaries, and as likely to slit the throat as pick the pocket of a *bon bourgeois*. These men and women—members of what the French historian Louis Chevalier, using terminology borrowed from the French Second Empire, called the "classe dangereuse"—were the frequent target of police roundups and popular derision.[6] When in 1867 Manet exhibited his *Beggar with Oysters (Philosopher)* (fig. 68b) beside fifty other works in an old barracks on the avenue de l'Alma, he was subjected to widespread derision. One caricaturist represented his bearded philosopher with a dagger in his hand.[7] *The Ragpicker* does not appear quite so threatening. He is more picturesque than proletarian, and the element of social protest in the picture is confined to a single element: the poverty of the man is highlighted by comparison with the residue of a late-night *repas* at his feet. The broken champagne bottle, oyster shells, and lemon peel become in Manet's hand a brilliantly painted still life of the frivolity and corruption of the beau monde. Although it was considered by Manet as part of a group of beggar-philosophers, its larger scale, longer gestation period, and greater physical complexity suggest that Manet painted it as a summation as much as a part of a series. Curiously, the great collector Jean-Baptiste Faure, who bought the Copenhagen and the two Chicago paintings from Durand-Ruel, did not elect to purchase the Norton Simon picture, which entered the collection of the department store magnate Ernest Hoschedé and was sold in his bankruptcy sale in 1878 for the paltry sum of eight hundred francs.

1 Moreau-Nélaton, 1926, vol. 1, p. 130.

2 Moreau-Nélaton, 1926, vol. 1, p. 73.

3 Moreau-Nélaton, 1926, vol. 1, pp. 71–72. Manet made a small copy of the painting (Rouart and Wildenstein, 1975, vol. 1, no. 103) and used it as a basis for his *Tragic Actor—Philibert Rouvière as Hamlet* (National Gallery of Art, Washington, D.C.).

4 Brombert, 1996, p. 179.

5 Rouart and Wildenstein, 1975, vol. 2, no. 467 (Musée du Louvre, Cabinet des Dessins, Paris).

6 Chevalier, 1973.

7 Caricature by Randon in *Le Journal Amusant*, 29 June 1867.

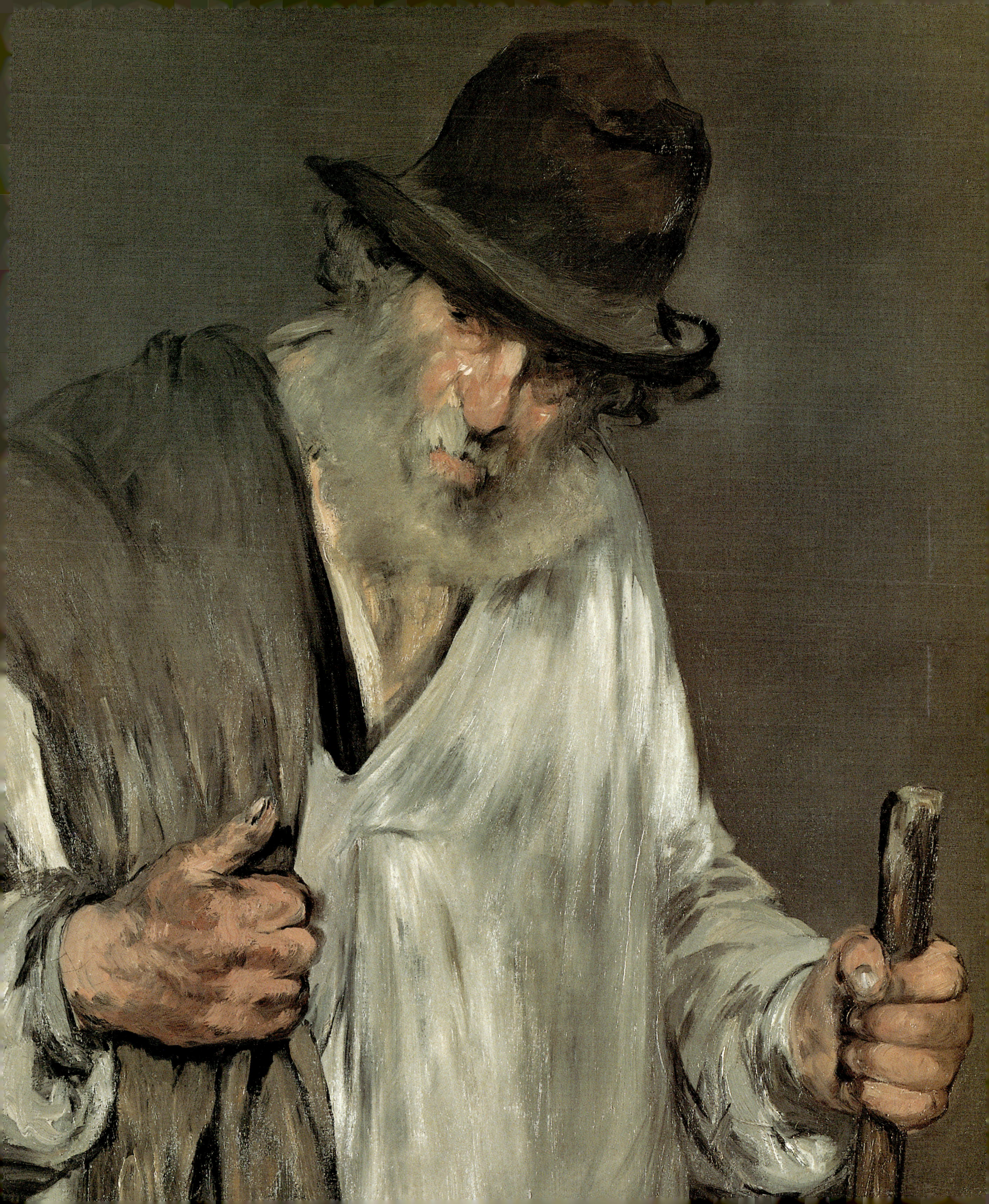

69

Édouard Manet
French, 1832–1883

Madame Manet
1874–1876

Oil on canvas, $23\frac{7}{8} \times 20$ in. (60.6×50.8 cm)
Signed lower right by Manet's widow: "Ed. Manet"
M.1973.4

Provenance: The artist; gift(?) to; George Moore, London, until at least 1932, by bequest to; Lady Cunard, London, by at least 1936, by bequest to; Sir Robert Abdy, consigned 30 September 1952 to [Arthur Tooth & Sons], but sold 17 November 1952 to; [Wildenstein & Co., New York, sold 18 July 1956 to]; Norton Simon, gift 1973 to; Norton Simon Art Foundation.

Exhibitions: Dublin, 1899, p. 5; London, 1936c, no. 35; London, 1943, no. 14; Detroit, 1954, no. 19; Los Angeles, 1965; Philadelphia, 1966, no. 103; San Francisco, 1973, no. 28, ill.; on loan, Norfolk, Chrysler Museum, 7 November 1980–21 July 1981.

References: *The Times*, 1899, p. 5; Duret, 1902, no. 105, p. 37, ill.; Moreau-Nélaton, 1906, no. 106; Meier-Graefe, 1912b, p. 222, fig. 125; Waldmann, 1913, pp. 52, ill. 43; Moreau-Nélaton, 1926, vol. 1, no. 14, pp. 86 n. 1, 95, fig. 114; Tabarant, 1931, no. 120, pp. 161, 578; Jamot and Wildenstein, 1932, vol. 1, no. 144, p. 135, vol. 2, fig. 163; Tabarant, 1947, pp. 80, 129–130, 134, 536, 606, fig. 123; Courthion, 1953, vol. 1, pp. 96, ill., 97, vol. 2, p. 53; Orienti and Venturi, 1967, no. 107, p. 96, ill.; Rouart and Wildenstein, 1975, vol. 1, no. 116, p. 113, ill.; D. Sutton, 1976, p. 171, fig. 7; Darragon, 1991, fig. 91; Armstrong, 2002, pp. 21, 24, fig. 12.

Technical Notes: The original fine, plain-weave support must have been commercially prepared with the thin cream-colored ground. It has been lined with an aqueous adhesive to fabric. The X-ray reveals that the original canvas with tacking edges removed does not quite go to the edges of the newer stretcher. The painting has a discontinuous fine crackle pattern. The condition is good, but there are some scattered small losses and abrasions, and later toning often covers original paint. This is especially true in the foreground, the lips, and the shadows in the face. This delicately painted portrait seems to have been done rapidly, but much of the painting is built up of washes, scumbles, and glazes. It appears that the artist first drew the form in brown paint and at the same time painted the shadows, and the sketch is visible around the eyes and between the neck and chin, where it acts as part of the shadow in the finished painting. The face was built up with thicker flesh tones and then with scumbling. Thin scumbles of different shades of gray create much of the coat. The background was first brushed in with a thin dark gray color that must have been wiped before the application of glazes and scumbles that seem to contain some blue, yellow, or green pigments, but the color is very faint. The head was shifted lower and the outline of the hair changed at some point. The pentimento can be seen to the top and left of the present head even though Manet tried to paint it out. His overpaint created a denser area of gray paint. The present varnish is synthetic. (JF)

Manet's wife, a Dutch pianist whose maiden name was Suzanne Leenhoff, was engaged by the Manet family as a music teacher for their children in 1850 or 1851, when the future painter was eighteen years old. By the spring of 1851, she was pregnant, presumably by one of the Manet men, and she gave birth to a son on 26 January 1852. The son was introduced in Parisian society as her younger brother and remained unlegitimized (his father was identified as a mysterious Koella on his Dutch birth certificate) even when Manet himself married Suzanne in 1863. A good deal of ink has been spilled on the identity of Léon Leenhoff's father, with scholars equally divided between Manet's father and Manet himself. In any case, the painter waited until a year after his father's death before marrying his former music teacher. By all accounts the marriage was a happy one, although the couple had no other children, and Mme Manet outlived her husband by twenty-three years.

Manet painted his wife rarely, and three of the six securely identified portraits of her are unfinished, including the present work. Oddly, the obviously posthumous signature has never before been identified as such, and, given what one knows of the history of the painting, its existence is all the odder. The history of this painting—both its exhibition history and its provenance—is unusually difficult to document. Its first owner, George Moore, made the painting available to Théodore Duret and Julius Meier-Graefe, who included photographs of it in the earliest complete monographs on Manet in 1902 and 1912. However, there is no record of it as a gift to Moore or a purchase by him, despite the fact that the English artist was introduced to Manet in 1879 and made frequent trips to Paris in subsequent years. It is not possible to link the painting directly to one of the portraits of Mme Manet listed in the inventory of Manet's possessions at the time of his death in 1883, but the signature, which resembles others put on paintings by his widow, suggests that it was acquired by Moore from the sitter after 1883.

The painting has most recently been dated to 1866, when Manet seems to have begun a small series of four paintings of his wife. There are two reasons for this dating. The first is the existence of a "Portrait de Mme.

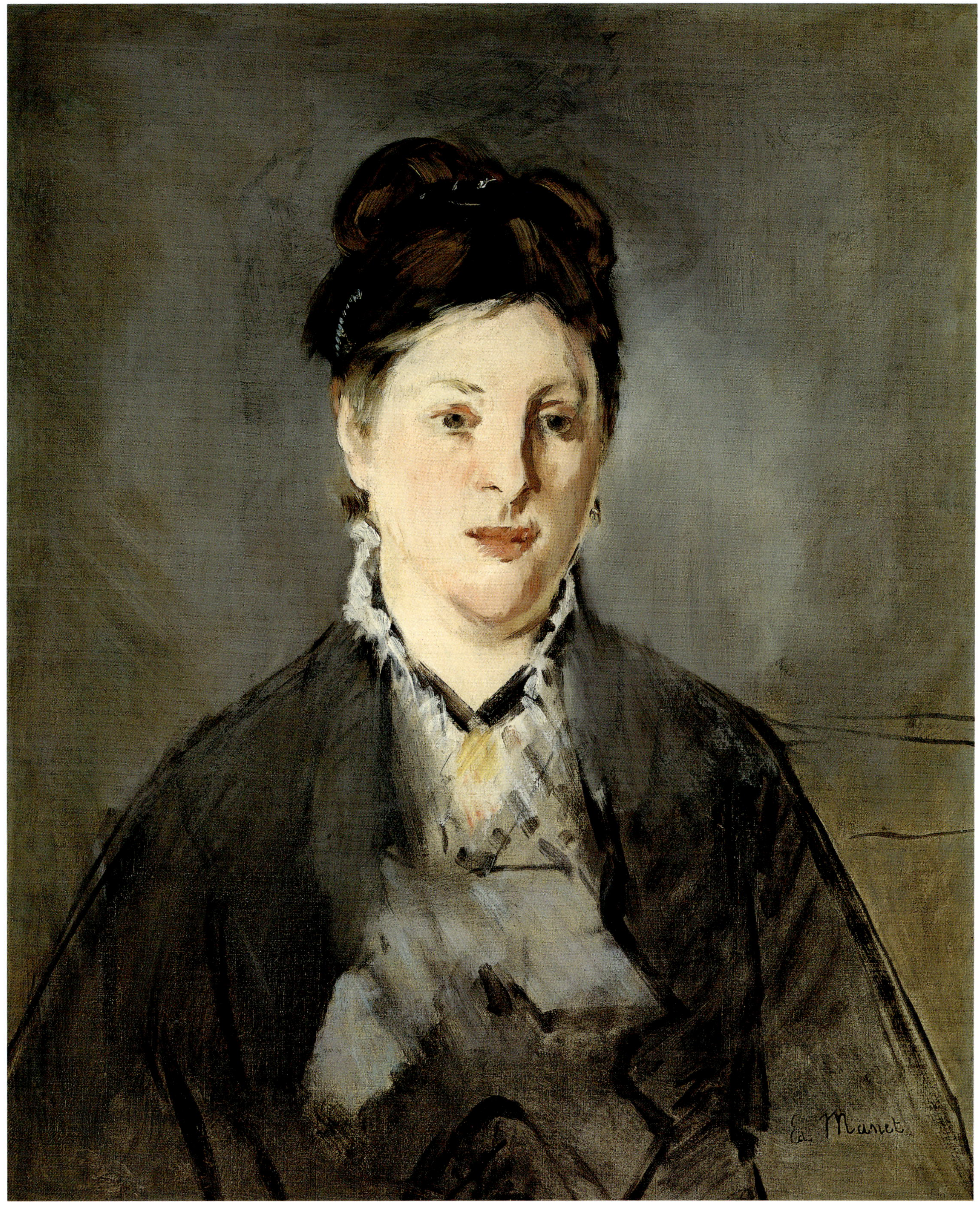

69

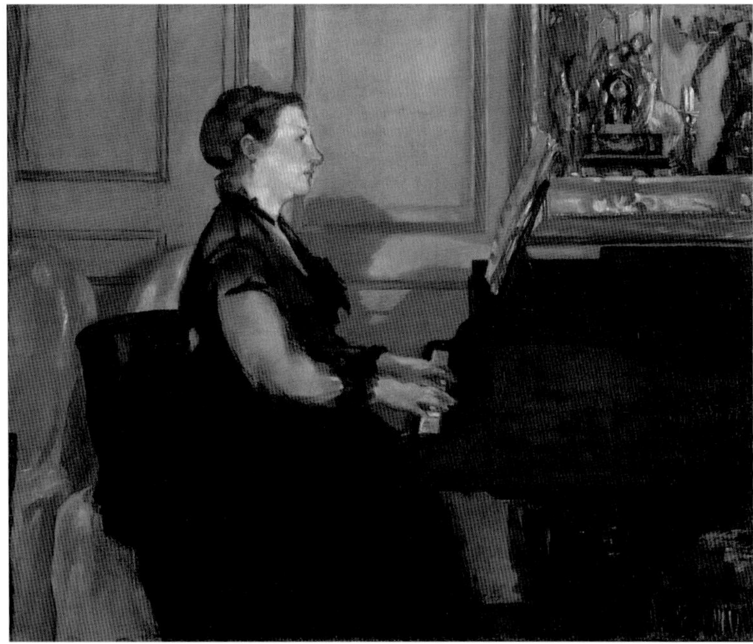

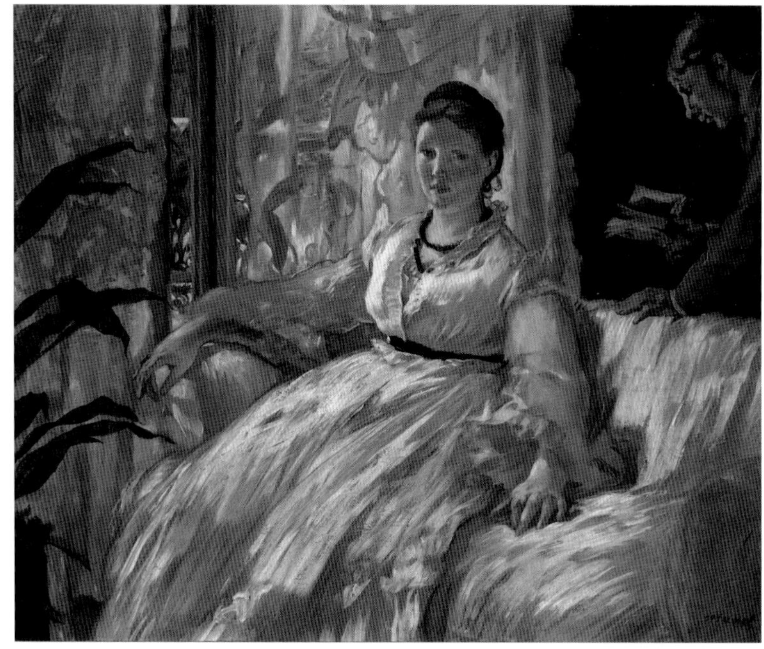

Fig. 69a (*above left*) Édouard Manet, *Mme Manet at the Piano*, 1867–1868, oil on canvas, 15 × 18⅛ in. (38 × 46 cm), Musée d'Orsay, Paris; photo: Erich Lessing / Art Resource, NY

Fig. 69b (*above right*) Édouard Manet, *Mme Édouard Manet and her son, Léon Koella-Leenhoff*, 1869, oil on canvas, 24 × 29⅛ in. (61 × 74 cm), Musée d'Orsay, Paris; photo: Erich Lessing / Art Resource, NY

Fig. 69c (*right*) Édouard Manet, *Madame Édouard Manet*, c. 1874–1876, oil on canvas, 39½ × 30⅞ in. (100.3 × 78.4 cm), The Metropolitan Museum of Art, New York, Bequest of Miss Adelaide Milton de Groot, 1967; photo: all rights reserved, The Metropolitan Museum of Art

M" as no. 14 in the catalogue of the 1867 exhibition of fifty major paintings by Manet in a privately constructed pavilion built in conjunction with the Exposition Universelle in Paris in that year. The second is a mention of a "Portrait d'une dame" as "barely dry" in an article published by Émile Zola in January 1867.[1] Yet neither document supports unequivocal identification of the Norton Simon portrait as either of these works. In the first case, it is highly unlikely that Manet would have included such a sketchily painted (and, on stylistic grounds, probably later) picture in such an important selection of his paintings. In fact, it is more likely that the "no. 14" portrait of Mme Manet was, instead, the 1863 portrait of Manet's mother now in the collection of the Isabella Stewart Gardner Museum in Boston. Another listing in the 1867 catalogue, for no. 8, is entitled *Portrait de M. et Mme M*, and this is clearly the 1860 double portrait (Musée d'Orsay, Paris) submitted by Manet to the Salon of 1861. It is likelier that the "Mme M" in both paintings was the artist's mother. The second mention of the painting derived from a studio visit by Zola to Manet's studio in 1866. It was actually misquoted by Adolphe Tabarant in his catalogue of 1931 to read "Portrait de Mme M."[2] In fact, Zola's essay clearly called the painting "Portrait d'une dame," further severing the traditional link between this painting and the year 1866.

The earliest commentators on the painting date it to 1868 without giving any clear reason. Both Duret and Meier-Graefe knew Mme Manet and might have decided on a date for the picture based either on discussions with her or on guesswork determined by her presumed age in the painting. This latter method is notoriously difficult for Mme Manet, who seems to be of quite different ages in two more easily datable portraits, one of 1867–1868 (fig. 69a) and the other of 1869 (fig. 69b). Unfortunately, the most closely related portrait of Mme Manet, the unfinished work in the collection of the Metropolitan

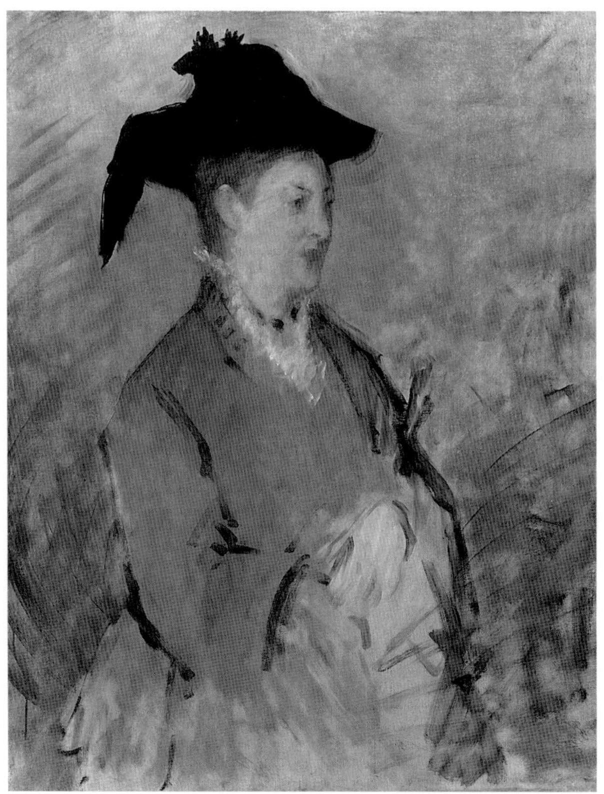

Museum of Art (fig. 69c), has no documentary association that might aid in establishing a date for both pictures. Stylistically, both the Norton Simon and the Metropolitan portraits have more in common with Manet's loosely painted works from the mid- and later 1870s than they do with his thick and tightly finished works from the 1860s, and the link between the painting and its first owner, George Moore, would argue for a later date. In fact, Manet's latest completed portrait of his wife, signed in 1879 (*Mme Manet in the Conservatory*, National Gallery, Oslo), represents her looking not a good deal older than she appears in the Norton Simon and Metropolitan portraits, giving us further confidence in dating both these paintings to the mid-1870s.

The most beautifully written and seemingly convincing essay about the present portrait remains unpublished. Produced in the early 1970s by John Russell for Simon, the essay repeats all the mistakes corrected above, but its discussions of the painting itself and of the relationship between Manet and his wife are beautifully apt. Russell calls the portrait "a private painting: direct, fresh, and unemphatic," refers to its "relaxed, unaggressive style," and calls it a "touching memorial to an alliance which, though it was made legal in October 1863, had run a clandestine course since Manet's 20th year." Russell also quoted the Italian painter Giuseppe de Nittis as saying that Mme Manet "had a serenity that nothing could disturb."[3]

Indeed, this painting, as skillful and easy as it is, succeeds in capturing the placid composure of Manet's wife. She sits with no hint of discomfort, her hair arranged with a cleverly painted decorative comb and band, and her clothes sketched with a brio completely lacking in the sitter herself. Her gaze is completely disengaged from that of the painter-viewer, as if she is lost in thought, and, unlike the two portraits of the late 1860s in the Musée d'Orsay, she is shown with no hint of a domestic context. Four awkwardly painted lines to the right of the figure allude either to moldings or to the chair in which she sits, but Manet seemed uninterested in physical context, preferring to concentrate on her face. Russell's use of the word "unemphatic" is crucial here, because Mme Manet seems not to have any distinctive qualities in this representation. She is simply present, accepting of her role as model, and little of the intense chemistry of gaze that animates Manet's portraits of Victorine Meurent or Berthe Morisot gives spark to the painting. Indeed, Manet's interest in the representation of boredom and lassitude has often been discussed, and even Meurent herself adopts this bland passivity in Manet's Salon painting of 1874, *The Railroad*, in the National Gallery of Art in Washington. Interestingly, Manet's period of pictorial investigation of boredom centers in the mid-1870s, when he painted in both Paris and Argenteuil. The Norton Simon portrait of Mme Manet surely dates from these years.

1 Zola, 1867, p. 59.

2 Tabarant, 1931, no. 120, p. 161.

3 Essay, c. 1971, Norton Simon Museum curatorial files.

70

Paul-Camille Guigou
French, 1834–1871

The Village of Saint-Paul on the Banks of the Durance
1865

Oil on canvas, $25\frac{1}{2} \times 59\frac{1}{4}$ in. (64.8 × 150.5 cm)
Signed and dated lower right: "Paul Guigou. 65"
F.1968.8

Provenance: Havard, France (sale, Paris, Palais Galliera, 3 December 1967, lot 30, ill., as *Le Village près de la rivière*); [Arthur Tooth & Sons, Ltd., London, sold 1968 to]; The Norton Simon Foundation.

Exhibitions: Paris, 1865b, no. 983, as *Vue de Saint-Paul-la-Durance (Bouches-du-Rhône)*; San Francisco, 1974, no. 25, ill.; Chicago, 1978, no. 65, ill.

References: Pigalle, 1865a, p. 28, ill.; Bonnici, 1989, no. 127, pp. 160, ill.; Lamort de Gail, 1989, vol. 1, no. 59, ill.

Technical Notes: The support is a plain-weave canvas; it has been wax-lined with the original edges retained. The commercially applied, cream-colored ground has darkened slightly to light brown. It is rather thin and leaves the canvas texture evident. Beneath the middle horizontal band (mountains, village, trees) the ground was toned with a thin light brown paint; it is visible most clearly in the trees at the right side, where the artist lightly dabbed on spots of paint for the foliage. In the sky, lean paint was brushed directly over the ground; the hills and village are depicted in thicker opaque colors, blended wet into wet. The river was quite thinly painted and appears to have been further thinned by cleaning. Glazes and shadows, such as in the trees, also were vulnerable to solvents; shadows and midtones in the central landscape have been affected. The surface is varnished with a synthetic resin. There are a small retouch in the sky at upper left, a small spot at the bottom left corner, and a larger area that covers losses at the upper right corner. (RW)

The Provençal landscape painter Paul Guigou was thirty-one years old when he submitted to the Salon of 1865 a large landscape entitled *Vue de Saint-Paul-la-Dourance (Bouches-du-Rhône)*. Its ambitious scale and forthrightly Provençal title make it clear that the young artist wanted to bring the glories of his home landscape directly to the capital city of Paris. In this, he was following the strategy of his teacher, the first great painter of Provence, Émile Loubon, and setting a precedent for his fellow Provençal Paul Cézanne. Cézanne too was in Paris in 1865, and there is little doubt that he saw this painting. His own attempts to succeed at the Salon failed consistently throughout the 1860s, and we have absolutely no idea what he thought of the work of his colleague. There is also no evidence whatsoever that they ever met. Yet, were it not for the twentieth-century fame of Cézanne, we would know little or nothing today of the oeuvre of Guigou, whose death at thirty-seven cut short a brilliant career.

Although Guigou was praised widely by writers in Provence in the years following his death, his career languished in obscurity in the first half of the twentieth century. Indeed, it was not until the French-Swiss historian of Impressionism, François Daulte, wrote a fervent article that this heretofore minor artist gained luster throughout the world.[1] Daulte called Guigou a "Pure Provençal," relishing the anti-Parisian and regional quality of both his style and his imagery. Although we do not know quite how he came to the artist, Norton Simon

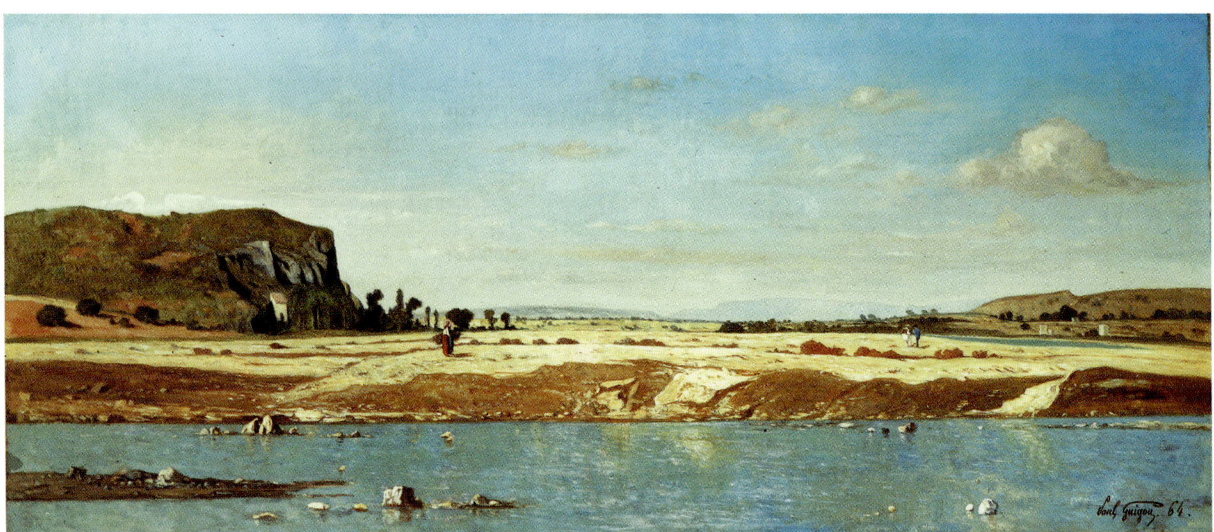

Fig. 70a Paul-Camille Guigou, *The Banks of the River Durance at Saint-Paul*, 1864, oil on canvas, $24\frac{3}{8} \times 58\frac{1}{4}$ in. (62 × 148 cm), The Art Institute of Chicago, Searle Family Trust

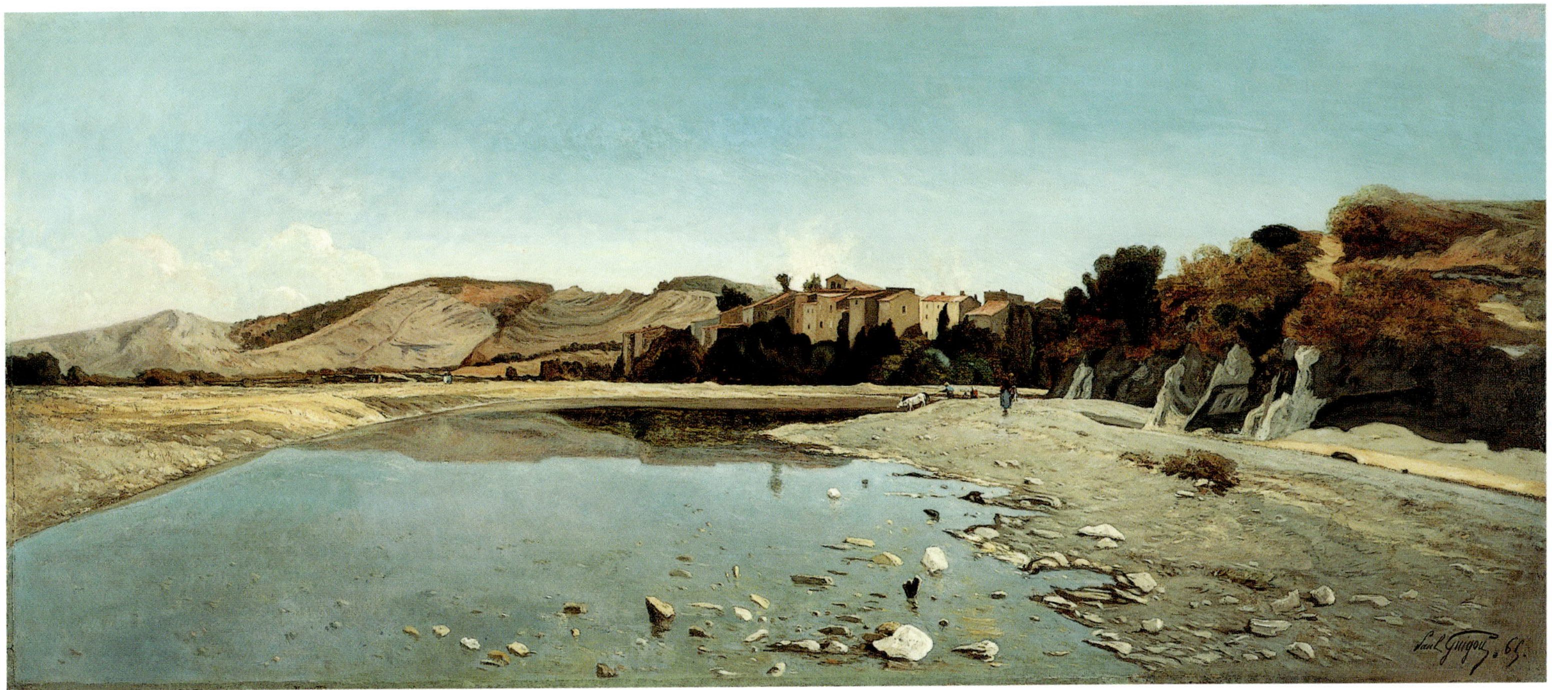

70

Fig. 70b (*right*) Paul-Camille Guigou, *The Village of Saint-Paul on the Banks of the Durance*, 1865, ink on paper, Pigalle, *L'Autographe au Salon de 1865*, 13 May 1865

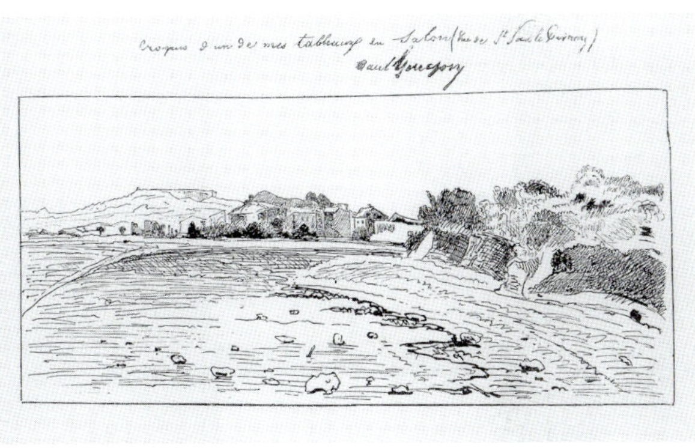

was the first international collector of real importance to recognize the prescient genius of Guigou. In addition to the three paintings that remain in the collection of the museum that bears his name, he also owned (and sold in a public sale) another of Guigou's Salon paintings—one of 1864, purchased in 1984 by the Art Institute of Chicago (fig. 70a). No international private collector seems to have believed so intently in Guigou as did Norton Simon. Of the thirteen works by Guigou in American museums listed by Claude-Jeanne Bonnici in 1989, the Norton Simon Museum is the only institution with more than a single work.

This, the earliest of the three paintings by Guigou that remain in the museum, is also the greatest. Its inclusion in the Salon of 1865 cannot be doubted, because a pen-and-ink drawing of the picture was published in a collection entitled *L'Autographe au Salon de 1865* by Pigalle on 13 May of that year (fig. 70b). This was also the first year in which a major landscape by the future Impressionist Camille Pissarro was also accepted at the Salon (fig. 70c), and it is instructive to compare the two works. Pissarro was four years older than Guigou and had worked extensively in the Île-de-France with Camille Corot, Antoine Chintreuil, and Gustave Courbet. Both Pissarro and Guigou chose a small town on the banks of a French river. The rivers of France had been proudly represented as part of the national natural patrimony for at least two centuries. The allegorical sculptures in the great pools at Versailles represented these rivers, which had been, in a prerailroad era, the symbols of French communication, trade, and power. Both artists elected to represent secondary rivers—the Marne leads into the

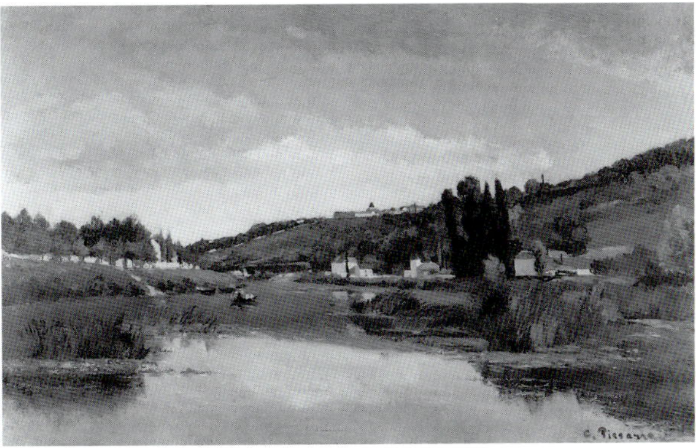

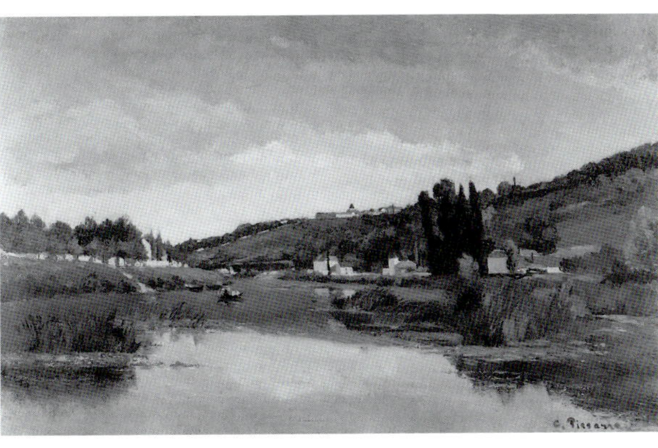

Fig. 70c Camille Pissarro, *The Marne at Chennevières*, c. 1865, oil on canvas, $37\frac{1}{4} \times 56\frac{5}{8}$ in. (94.5 × 144 cm), National Gallery of Scotland, Edinburgh

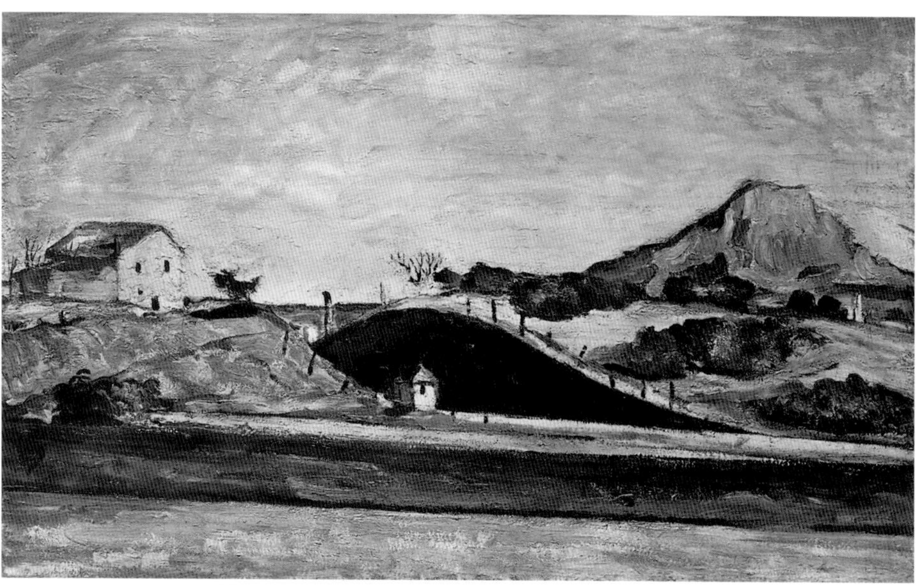

Fig. 70d Paul Cézanne, *The Railroad Cutting*, 1867, oil on canvas, 31½ × 50¾ in. (80 × 129 cm), Neue Pinakothek, Munich

Seine not far from the site of the former's painting, and the Durance flows into the Rhône near Saint-Paul-la-Durance, the site of Guigou's work.

The two paintings have an element of sleepy provinciality, of a history and a life removed from the bustle of the capital. In this way, they are like Balzac's "Scenes of Provincial Life," which had entertained and amused Parisians in literary form more than a generation earlier. Both paintings aggrandize the ordinary. Both are composed in large, simple rhythms and are free from historical or allegorical allusions. Both place the action safely in the middle ground, creating a powerful distance between the viewer and the scene viewed. Together, these works constituted part of the submission by French landscape painters at midcentury of the countryside of France for the benefit of its capital. In this, they are an important component of the great region-versus-nation debates that filled French political and cultural life during these decades. For Guigou, the radical aspect of Provence was its blinding, white light, its emptiness, and its lateral extent. Where Pissarro's largely horizontal composition seems to open up in the center, Guigou's scatters our attention to the peripheries of the vast, extended space.

The most extraordinary aspect of Guigou's painting is its severity and relative dryness of surface. In contrast to Pissarro, who composed his painting with thick strokes of paint manipulated à la Courbet with the palette knife, Guigou applied his paint relatively thinly, confining it to areas of the design conceived almost like pieces of a puzzle drawn onto the surface. There are few seductive painterly strokes that add verve and personality to the surface. That asperity is today exaggerated due to some abrasion of the picture surface from an earlier cleaning. Instead, the painter seemed content to represent his native Provence in an almost naïve or neoprimitive manner. We do not know today whether this approach is a result of Guigou's aesthetic intentions or of his relative lack of skill with the medium of oil paint at this early point in his career. His teacher, Loubon, was much less dry in both execution and composition, preferring rhythmic curves and relatively thick paint. And, to make matters more interesting, we know that Guigou spent the summer of 1864 in Saint-Paul-la-Durance, when he began this painting, with Adolphe Monticelli, whose equally Provençal aesthetic was translated into deep, generally dark colors and thick paint.

It is fascinating to compare this and Guigou's 1867 Salon painting *La Durance à Cadenet*[2] to Cézanne's first great landscape of Provence (fig. 70d), which shares so many aspects of form and even facture with Guigou's work. It is perhaps one of the injustices of history that Guigou was killed in the Franco-Prussian War, while Cézanne, with his father's money, evaded the draft and hid in his mother's isolated house in L'Estaque. Also, Patrice Marandel noted the many formal and chromatic links between this landscape by Guigou and those by another fellow southerner, Frédéric Bazille from Montpellier.[3] He made particular links to what he called the virtually brutal views of the medieval walls of Aigues-Morte, the latter of which were surely known to Cézanne.

1 Daulte, 1960.
2 Bonnici, 1989, no. 166.
3 In Chicago, 1978, p. 128.

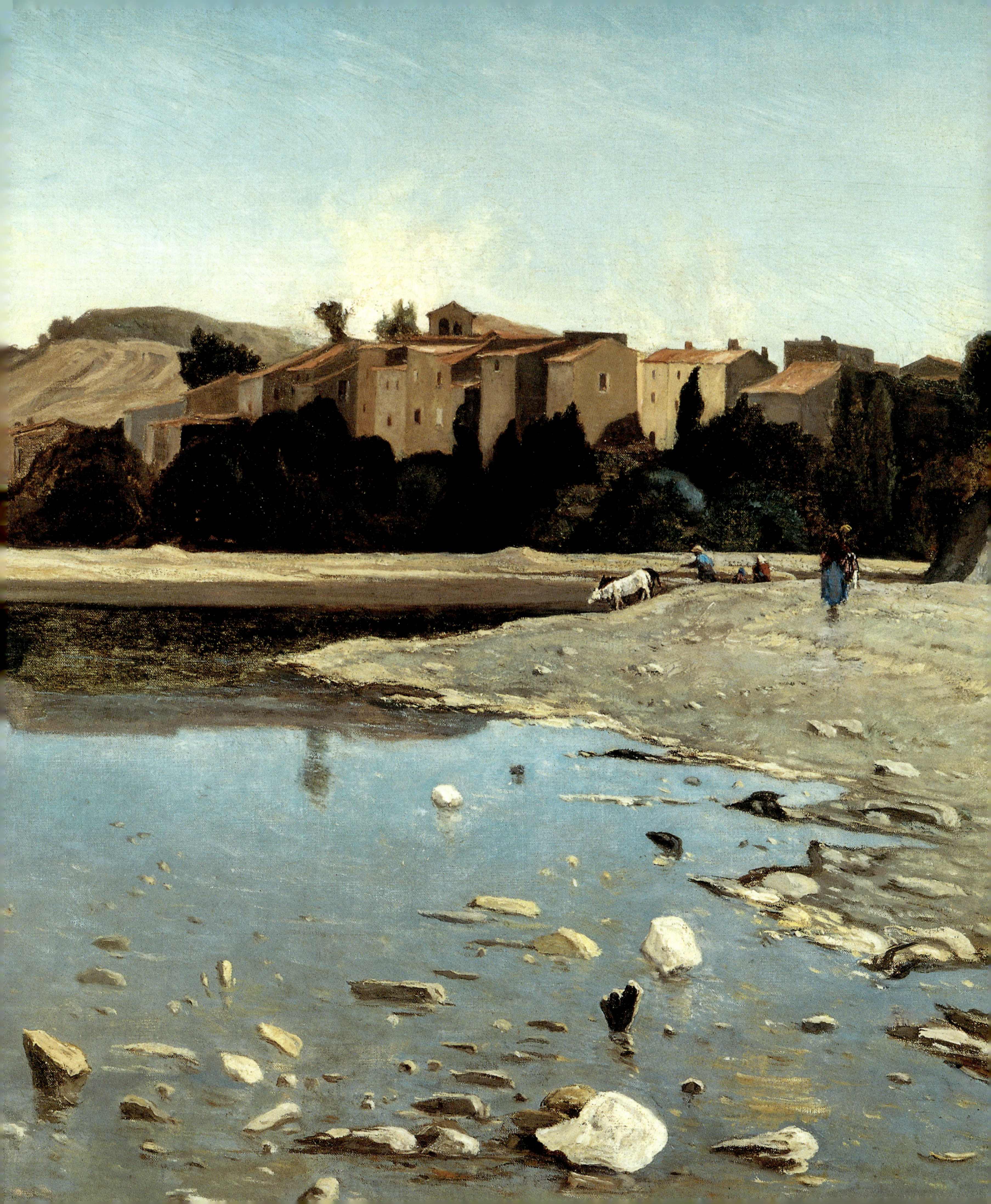

71

Paul-Camille Guigou
French, 1834–1871

Landscape in Martigues
1869

Oil on canvas, 11 × 18¼ in. (27.9 × 46.4 cm)
Signed and dated lower right: "Paul Guigou 69"
M.1973.3.1

Provenance: Trotti, Paris, 20 April 1911, to; [Hector Brame, Paris, in partnership with Tempelar, stock no. 2493 (2717), sold 2 May 1911 for Ff 800 to]; Strölin, Paris. Götz. [Galerie Daber, Paris, by 1939]. A. Askin, New York. [Arthur Tooth & Sons, Ltd., London, by 1972, sold 1973 to]; Norton Simon Art Foundation.

Exhibitions: Paris, 1939b, no. 9, as *Étang de Caronte, Martigues*; on loan, Phoenix, Art Museum, 21 June 1973–23 May 1974; San Francisco, 1974, no. 26, ill.

References: George, 1939, p. 5, ill.; Bonnici, 1989, no. 229, pp. 121, 184, ill.; Lamort de Gail, 1989, vol. 1, no. 143, p. 124, ill.

Technical Notes: The plain-weave canvas support has been lined with the original edges retained. It was restretched onto the original stretcher. A small hole near the center, above the mast of the sailboat, was repaired before lining. The commercially applied, smooth, off-white ground is moderately thick, partially filling the canvas weave. It has darkened slightly with age. The landscape was composed in a rather loose handling, working from the top down, background to foreground. The opaque paint retains a slight texture of brush marking. Above the signature there is a pentimento of an earlier signature and what appears to be *68*, now almost covered by the green paint of the foreground. Microscopic examination of the paint surface with raking light reveals an unusual amount of fine grit embedded in every color. Additionally, in certain details of the painting, there appears to be fine sand or mica on the paint surface. For example, in the foreground, the sand/mica is not present in the green grasses, but it is in the flower blossoms. Similarly, it is in the woman's skirt but not all of her costume, seeming to be an indication of an intentional embellishment of the paint. The painting is well preserved overall. It was cleaned and revarnished in 1982. Minor retouching is located at the upper left corner and the upper left edge, the top of the right edge, in the middle of the sky, and in the repaired hole above the sailboat. The synthetic varnish is slightly yellowed. (RW)

Martigues is one of the most picturesque towns in southern France, associated equally with wild horses on the famous grasslands called the Camargue and with the Mediterranean. It was also the hometown of the brilliant, if repetitive, landscape painter Félix Ziem and figured prominently in the Provençal literary revival of the second half of the nineteenth century. Indeed, the guidebook literature that shaped French perceptions of the landscape in the railroad era extolled the virtues of this isolated fishing community in Provence. Yet, first in 1868 and then finally in 1869, when Guigou painted this small panoramic study of the Mediterranean landscape, the mystique of Martigues was in its infancy. The painting is one of at least four works by Guigou to represent the small town, and was also among his last. Guigou lost his life less than two years later in the Franco-Prussian War, an early death that effectively removed him from the larger history of French modern art until the revival of his reputation in the 1960s.

This small painting was published in the newspaper *Beaux-Arts* in 1939, thirty years before that revival began. Then for sale at the Galerie Daber, it was a typically modest work from the painter's oeuvre. Composed in the panoramic format preferred by Guigou, it represents the coastal pathway near Martigues, looking east along the Golfe de Fos toward the distant city of Marseille in the right background. Carrying a basket on her head, a woman walks slowly toward the viewer on the path that fills the left half of the composition. Guigou patiently defines the spatial recession of the path by emphasizing the strong shadows of trees, many of which are not in the pictorial area, but inflect it with their shadows. The space of the path recedes dramatically into the middle distance and is contrasted by Guigou to the deeper, but laterally defined space of the intensely blue bay. Hence, Guigou contrasts depth with width, and the two almost collide in the center of the painting. Here he places two floating forms, the closer one a dark barge moored near the grassy path and the more distant one a sailboat, probably for leisure sailing rather than for fishing, that moves dramatically—its sails stretched into taut curves by the wind—on a line parallel to the picture plane. The slow movement forward of the staffage figure contrasts with the fast, lateral movement of the sailboat, and the almost cloudless blue sky is further enlivened by the movement of the birds, which swoop through space in the middle distance. The wind appears to have carried with it fine grains of sand from the beaches of the Mediterranean; they are embedded in the paint.

There is little doubt that this small painting was conceived as an independent and saleable work of art,

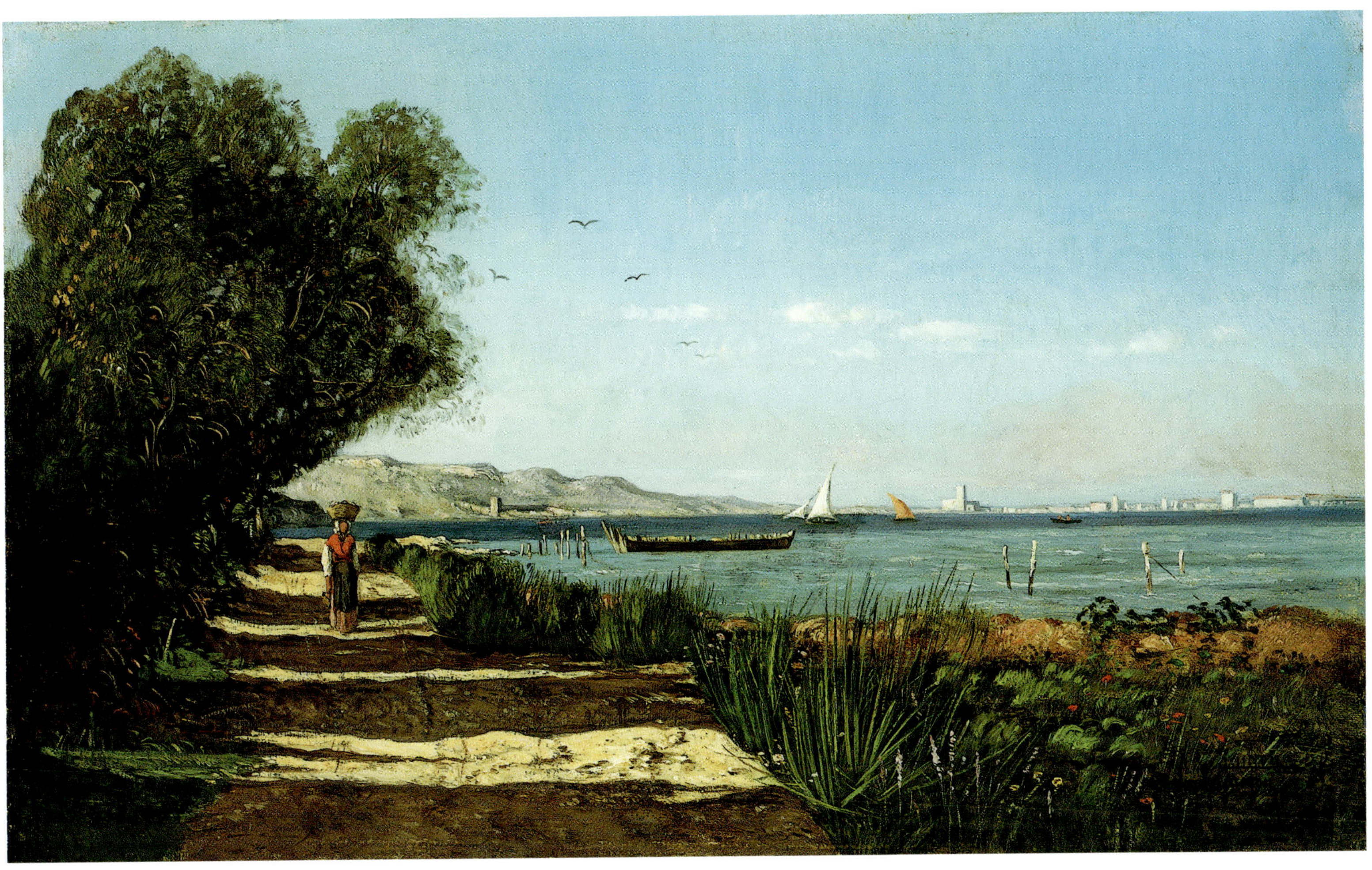

71

made for the amateur market. Its first recorded owner, a M. Trotti, lived in Paris and sold the painting to the respected dealer Hector Brame in 1911. Surely, the work had its ultimate origin in the collection of the painter's descendants, known to M. Brame, who played a crucial role in selling works by Guigou to Parisians before the mid-twentieth-century rise in his reputation. The fact that the painting is as deliberately composed—as formulaic, in a way—as it is, indicates that it was painted only partly in situ, constructed from drawings and perhaps oil sketches of an even smaller scale. The existence of an earlier signature and date of 1868 indicates that the work was made in two campaigns. It was probably at the time of its acquisition by Brame early in the twentieth century that it was glue-lined onto a new canvas and framed for sale.

72

Paul-Camille Guigou
French, 1834–1871

Landscape in Southern France
1870

Oil on panel, $7\frac{1}{8} \times 17\frac{7}{8}$ in. (18×45.5 cm)
Signed and dated lower right: "Paul Guigou 70"
N.1979.1.2

Provenance: (Sale, London, Sotheby's, 8 July 1971, lot 16, as *Paysage et chaîne de montagne*, to); Marubeni-Iida Co. (sale, London, Sotheby's, 5 July 1973, lot 4, ill., as *Paysage la Camargue*, to); H. Breny. Private collection, France. [Wildenstein & Co., Inc., New York, sold 5 January 1979 to]; Norton Simon (sale, New York, Christie's, 29 May 1981, lot 32, unsold), (sale, New York, Sotheby's, 27 May 1982, lot 27, ill., unsold), bequest 1993 to; Jennifer Jones Simon Art Trust.

Reference: Lamort de Gail, 1989, vol. 1, no. 178, ill.

Technical Notes: The landscape was painted on a small cardboard. It has been set into a thin hardwood panel that is cradled. The wood margins at each side of the painting measure ¼ inch. The thin white ground leaves the surface texture of the cardboard slightly visible in raking light. Rich paint was applied with fluent brushwork. A dark blue-black layer covers the ground of the entire painting; it modifies the upper colors and influences the tones in the sky. The distant trees at the horizon were painted with an extremely thin ocher-colored paint, over the blue, creating an atmospheric green. For the grasses in the foreground, light strokes of paint were applied last with a delicate touch, as they pushed only slightly into the wet paint beneath. An X-radiograph reveals Guigou's free and spontaneous brushwork, marked by his use of white throughout the painting. There are numerous microlosses in the middle section of the painting, which appear to be flake losses, exposing the blue underlayer; high magnification shows the difference between these losses and the blue that is exposed in the rubbed effect of the trees at the horizon. A brief treatment report from 1982 mentions "blisters" that required consolidation. At that time the painting was also cleaned and varnished. Retouching is located throughout the sky in small dots, a slightly larger area in the sky at top left center, and the top left corner. (RW)

Were it not for the signature and date of 1870 at lower right, it would be difficult to assign this superb small painting to Paul Guigou. Its comparative softness of surface and its complex, painterly touch has little in common with other, earlier works by this short-lived artist. Yet, its imagery and its format are completely consistent with Guigou's oeuvre. Hence, rather than reading it as an anomaly in his career, it might be wiser to consider the small painting as the indication of a new phase in the painter's work, a phase cut short by his death the following year.

Like many works by Guigou, the painting is composed in bands that run strictly parallel to the panoramic pictorial surface. Its subject is undivided grassland, giving credence to the second published title of the painting, *Paysage la Camargue* (*Camargue Landscape*). The Camargue is among the most distinctive landscapes of Provence. Immense grassland that runs for miles inland from the fishing town of Martigues, the Camargue has its own unique inhabitants, its own bands of wild horses, and its own lore. Although easy to enter, the Camargue is so dense with tall grasses that a naïve visitor can easily become disoriented and lost. It is perhaps because the grasses in Guigou's picture are comparatively short and because one can easily see a female figure in the middle ground that the cataloguers of Guigou's work rejected this 1973 title when they published their catalogue raisonné in 1989. Their caution is understandable in spite of the fact that one knows that Guigou painted in and around Martigues and that there are short grass areas as well as distant mountainous hills in the Camargue.

The composition of the painting is anchored, not by a prominent tree or a hill, but by the spindly construction to the left. This structure is like those that protect small trees in their early growth or provide support for the vertical growth of a vine. Yet, neither tree nor vine is visible, and close examination of the painting suggests that it is, rather, a ladder with a tripod support. It simply sits in the landscape, a human intrusion in what seems an utterly natural world. Nothing in the foreground helps explain its presence. The flowers, grasses, and small, scrubby shrubs grow where the winds left their seeds, and the woman in the middle ground was clearly placed there only for scale. She guards no animals, stoops to gather no plant, and carries the result of no harvest. In many ways, the small painting suggests the superb horizontal landscapes of 1872–1873 painted in the north of France by Camille Pissarro, the Impressionist master who never knew Guigou.

Technically, the painting is fascinating. It was painted on a support of thin, textured cardboard that has been

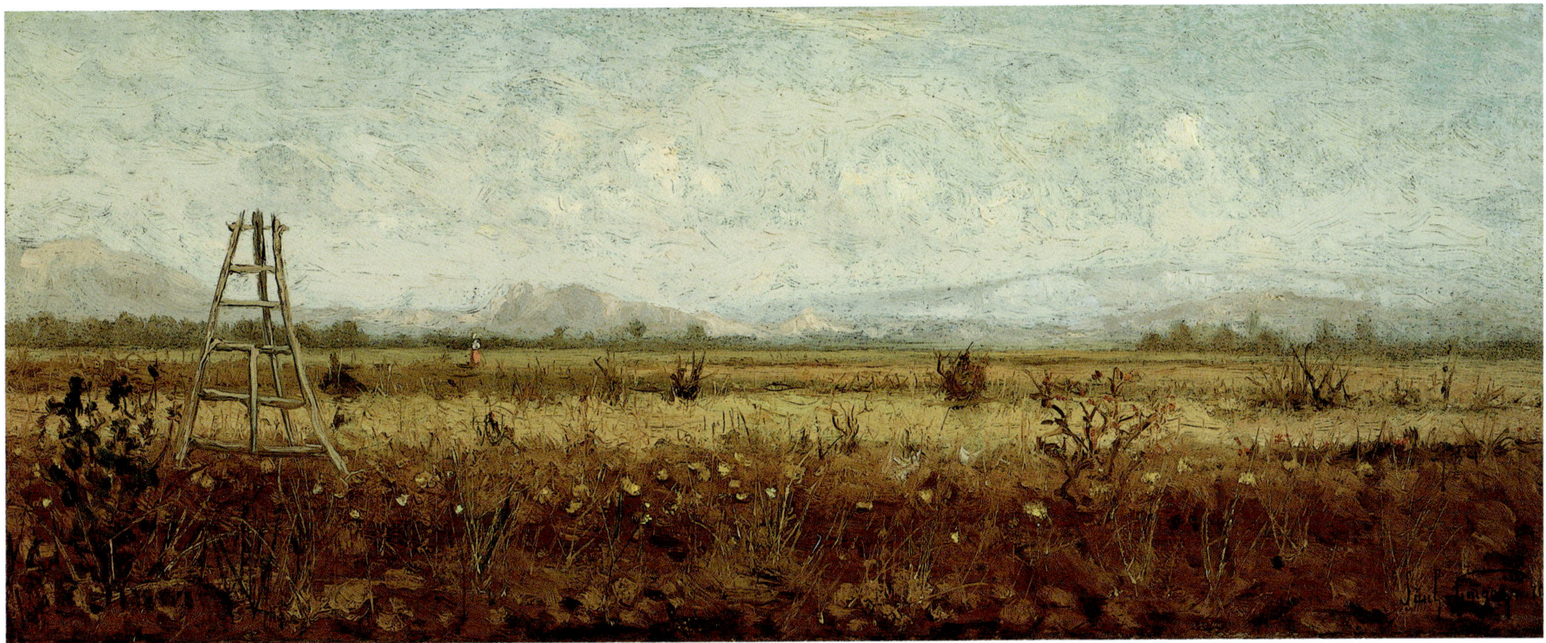

72

inset, probably after the artist's death, in a mahogany panel composed of two pieces that were carefully cradled. Hence, a small painting on cardboard—a fragile and ephemeral work of art—has become a panel painting, one of the oldest and most durable forms of pictorial expression in Western art.

The painting is included in one of the two separate catalogues raisonné compiled of Guigou's work and published in 1989, but not in the other. Claude-Jeanne Bonnici includes many similar works but omits any reference to the present painting, perhaps intending to create doubts about the attribution. However, the perfectly authentic signature and date and the completely typical style, subject, and medium of the painting—comparable to many other small painted studies on cardboard and wood made in the last year of Guigou's life—make its attribution to the artist secure. In fact, the proportions of the composition are precisely those favored by Guigou.

73

Stanislas-Victor-Édouard Lépine
French, 1835–1892

A Courtyard on the rue de la Fontenelle, formerly *Figures in a Courtyard of a Château*
1874–1878

Oil on canvas, $17\frac{1}{2} \times 12\frac{1}{2}$ in. (44.5 × 31.8 cm)
Signed lower left: "S. Lépine"
F.1967.1

Provenance: (Sale, Paris, Hôtel Drouot, 7 February 1879, lot 30). [Arthur Tooth & Sons, London]; Hervitt, London. Sir Alfred Chester Beatty (1875–1968), London and Dublin, by 13 March 1940 (sale, London, Sotheby's, 28 June 1967, lot 1, as *Personnages dans la cour d'un château*, to); The Norton Simon Foundation.

Exhibitions: Paris, 1895a, no. 84; on loan, Los Angeles, County Museum of Art, 16 July 1969–26 August 1974; San Francisco, 1974, no. 29.

References: Kennedy, 1987, p. 50 (App. 3), as *Intérieur de cour*; Schmit and Schmit, 1993, no. 220, ill., as *Montmartre, une cour rue de la Fontenelle (l'Atelier). Printemps.*

Technical Notes: The original support is a plain-weave canvas, probably medium weight. The top, left, and right tacking edges have been cut off; the bottom tacking edge has been opened out, adding ½ inch to the painting's height. The painting was lined to include the expanded bottom edge. A 4-inch vertical tear through the center of the painting was repaired before it was lined. A smooth, cream-colored ground remains visible on the original tacking edge at the bottom. It completely covers the canvas texture. Paint was applied in multiple layers. Much of the paint is rather heavily worked, both wet into wet and wet over dry. Edges are blurred. The paint is generally well preserved; however, lining has smoothed the paint profile, softening the brushwork. Although X-radiography does not show changes in composition, microscopic examination indicates several areas that were reworked by the artist, such as that surrounding the signature and the light-colored portion of the central foreground, the figure of the woman, and the borders of the courtyard path. Other changes are probably from a previous undocumented restoration. The upper layer of the standing male figure in the doorway and the woman in the courtyard show some abrasion, especially in black shadows, making the contours of the skirt and the black shirt poorly defined. Several letters of the signature also are slightly abraded. The painting was cleaned and revarnished in 1990. (RW)

Stanislas Lépine emerged from the legion of the students of Camille Corot to achieve his own modest success as a landscape and cityscape painter. Although nearly forty years younger than Corot, he impressed the older artist at his debut at the Salon of 1859 and worked in Corot's close circle until the older artist's death in 1875. Unfortunately, Lépine lived a comparatively short life, dying in 1892 at the age of fifty-seven. But, even more unfortunately for art historians, he continued the practice of his teacher by signing, but almost never dating, his paintings, leaving the modern student of his oeuvre a formidable task in putting them in order. In certain ways, this is less a problem than it would be for an artist who responded quickly to artistic fashion. Lépine seems not to have been swayed by the developments of Impressionism or the various offshoot vanguard movements, continuing to paint the urban and rural landscapes of Paris and his home landscape of Normandy as if Corot had never died. Like his colleague Léon Lhermitte, he practiced a kind of landscape perfected by French artists in the 1830s well into the second half of the century.

This wonderful vertical urban study is one of at least four closely related works painted by Lépine. We know that the artist lived and worked in Montmartre throughout his professional life, spending summers with his parents and family in his native Caen. Although he ranged widely throughout the city of Paris and its surrounding suburbs, he tended to avoid the newly constructed boulevards and other completely modern aspects of the Second Empire city. Instead, he preferred to paint enduring forms, devoting particular attention to the small streets and courtyards of old Montmartre. This small village on the top of a large butte was incorporated into the city of Paris only in the nineteenth century. Even Corot and Georges Michel, who had painted there early in the century, represent it as a completely separate hilltop village dominated by its famous windmills. These picturesque sites—with their dramatic views of the city and of the plains of Montmorency stretching north of Paris—were to become leisure gardens as the century progressed, and both the Moulin de la Galette and the Moulin Rouge trafficked on the memories of a rural village characterized by its windmills. Many painters favored this region of the city, and one could mount a wonderfully evocative exhibition of nineteenth- and early-twentieth-century paintings of Montmartre by artists including Paul Cézanne, Camille Pissarro, Pierre-Auguste Renoir, Vincent van Gogh, Pierre Bonnard, Henri de Toulouse-Lautrec, and Pablo Picasso. Lépine has little of the superstar reputations of these vanguard artists, but he was considerably more faithful than any of them in his devotion to Montmartre.

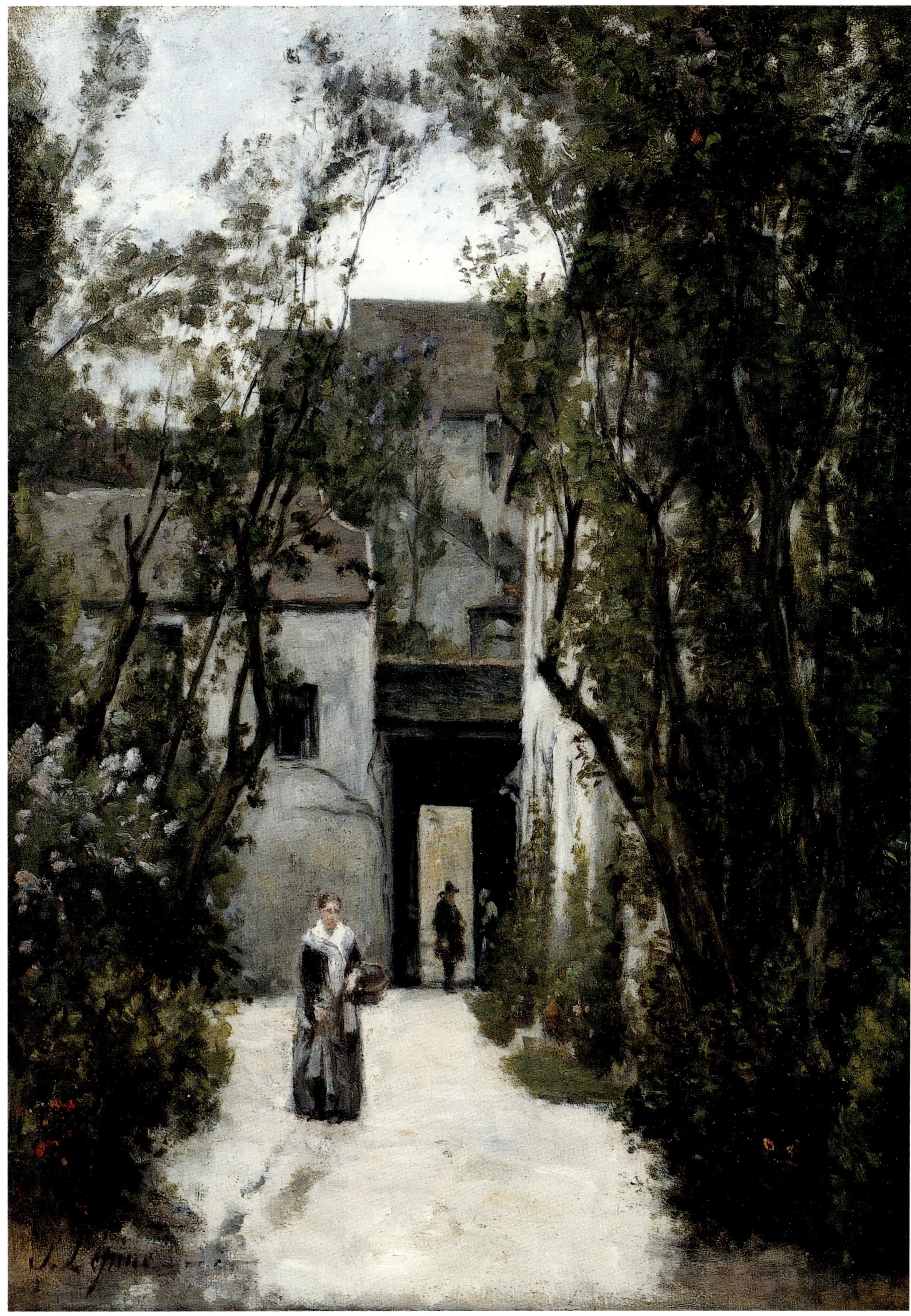

73

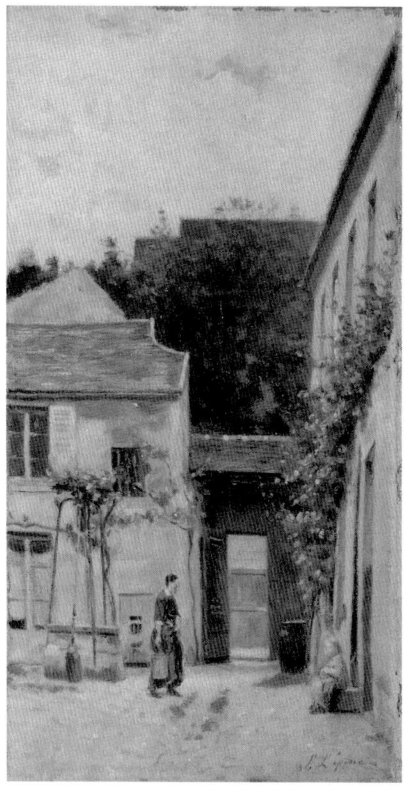

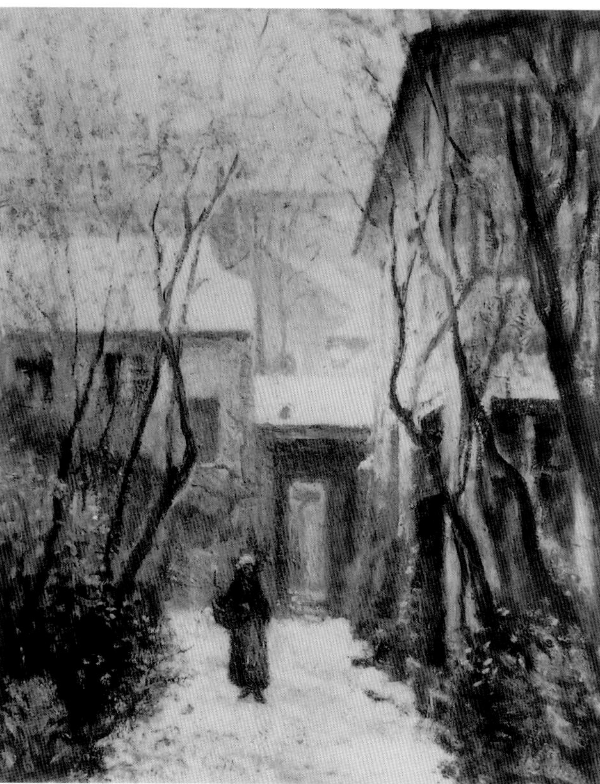

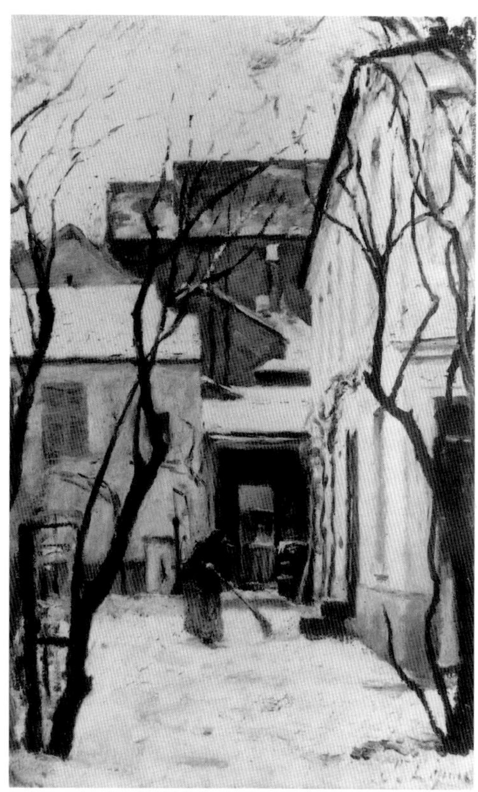

Fig. 73a (*above left*) Stanislas-Victor-Édouard Lépine, *The Courtyard*, c. 1880, oil on canvas, $13\frac{1}{4} \times 7\frac{3}{16}$ in. (33.7 × 18.3 cm), The Art Institute of Chicago, Mr. and Mrs. Martin A. Ryerson Collection

Fig. 73b (*above center*) Stanislas-Victor-Édouard Lépine, *Montmartre, Courtyard*, oil on canvas, Archives of Thos. Agnew & Sons, Ltd., Witt Library, Courtauld Institute, London

Fig. 73c (*above right*) Stanislas-Victor-Édouard Lépine, *Montmartre, Courtyard*, oil on canvas, Archives of Thos. Agnew & Sons, Ltd., Witt Library, Courtauld Institute, London

A Courtyard on the rue de la Fontenelle is one of several done in the small courtyard house on the rue de la Fontenelle where Lépine kept a studio for much of his life. Perhaps to vary his formats or simply to work from his own studio in inclement weather, Lépine preferred to arrange the architectural forms of the courtyard on variously scaled vertical canvases, mostly of a small dimension. This one is among the largest and finest of the group, and it entered the collection of Sir Alfred Chester Beatty, who owned as many as five works by Lépine. Another comparable view was given by the great collector Martin Reyerson to the Art Institute of Chicago in 1933 (fig. 73a), and the Witt Library in London has photographs from the Agnew Archives of two small paintings formerly in the collection of Alexander Young (figs. 73b and 73c), both painted in winter. Clearly, Lépine and his dealers found a ready market for these small, delicate, and inexpensive paintings that record a portion of Paris that played a large role in the image of the city taken home by foreign tourists.

The work was painted directly on a vertical canvas that is in good condition save for a small vertical tear at the center that forced someone early in its history to line the canvas. It is possible that this was done during Lépine's lifetime, because surface examination makes clear that the entire area of the foreground courtyard was painted at a later stage in the life of the composition, and some of the paint actually covers an inscription or even a date that originally followed Lépine's signature. The latter, too, is partially overpainted. The inclusion of lavender and white flowering bushes at the right suggests that the painting was made in the spring, when lavender bushes were in flower. Lépine seems to have fiddled extensively with the figure of the foreground woman with her wicker basket. (Is she the painter's wife coming for a noon visit?) Yet, these alterations are not present in the X-ray made of the painting shortly after its acquisition by Norton Simon. It is worth noting that the foliage is painted in almost precisely the same loosely brushed manner favored by Corot in the last decades of his life.

The entire rue de la Fontenelle, one of the oldest and most picturesque in Montmartre, was destroyed just after Lépine's death to make way for the great Basilica of Sacre Coeur, which dominates the northern skyline of Paris today. This small painting of a house on the rue de la Fontenelle, its smaller companion in the Art Institute of Chicago, and the other paintings made in the area of Lépine's studio are perhaps the best indicators we have of a modestly charming area of Paris that is forever lost.

74

Stanislas-Victor-Édouard Lépine
French, 1835–1892

The Pont Neuf, Paris
c. 1875–1879

Oil on canvas, 9 × 13 in. (23 × 33 cm)
Signed lower left: "S. Lépine"
F.1969.8.1

Provenance: (Sale, Paris, Hôtel Drouot, 7 February 1879, lot 37). Picq, Paris (sale, Paris, Hôtel Drouot, 7 May 1898, lot 38, as *Vue de Paris: Le Petit Bras de la Seine*). Louis Schoengrun, Paris (sale, Paris, Hôtel Drouot, 7 February 1901, lot 21, as *Le Petit Bras de la Seine, au Pont-Neuf*). Alexander Young, London (sale, London, Christie's, 1 July 1910, lot 213, to); Murray. [Leopold Megret] (sale, London, Christie's, 9 July 1928, lot 145, as *Bridges on the Seine*, bought in or to); [?]Lord Lamborne (Amelius Mark Richard Lockwood [1847–1928]), London. [Allard & Noël, Paris]. [Galerie Schmit, Paris, by 1968, sold 1969 to]; The Norton Simon Foundation.

Exhibitions: Paris, 1968, no. 59; San Francisco, 1973, no. 41.

Reference: Schmit and Schmit, 1993, no. 74, ill., as *Le Petit Bras de Seine au Pont Neuf.*

Technical Notes: The fine, plain-weave canvas is unlined. Although it is oxidized and brittle, it is undamaged and tautly stretched under even tension. The canvas is double primed with a pale gray ground, providing a smooth surface that covers the canvas texture. Lépine drew lines on the primed canvas with thin gray paint to establish the outer dimensions of the picture area. The paint is exceptionally well preserved and retains its original brush marking. Softly worked contours were applied with fairly small brushes with a wet-into-wet technique. Distance and shadowed areas are rendered by pale lavender. Although somewhat thin, the paint is not transparent or liquid. White is mixed into the majority of the colors. Lépine used many grays and no real blacks. The light areas of the painting have been cleaned in a previous restoration; there is an extremely thin layer of varnish at the left side, the lower right corner, and the bridge across the center. The surface was not revarnished after cleaning, leaving the central, light areas of the sky and water unsaturated and matte. (RW)

This small painting of the little branch of the Seine River south of the Île-de-la-Cité first appeared in a large sale of paintings by Lépine held at the Hôtel Drouot in February 1879. This gives us a terminus ante quem for its date and enables us to know that, perhaps at that point, it entered the collection of a M. Picq. This man is undoubtedly the same as a M. Picq-Véron, who also owned the Norton Simon Sisley (cat. 78). One of four works by Lépine in the Picq sale of 1898, this small painting is typical of the canvases painted along the Seine in abundance by Lépine in the 1870s and 1880s. In his site selection, Lépine prefigured the late urban views along the Seine painted by Camille Pissarro in the years after Lépine's death.

The Norton Simon canvas is small and painted in a delicious wet-on-wet manner. We are standing on the left bank of the Seine, and our elevated point of view and position over the river indicate that we are standing on the west side of the Pont St.-Michel (The St.-Michel Bridge), then as now the main connection between the Latin Quarter and the Île-de-la-Cité. The painting was made in late autumn or winter looking downriver toward the pavilions of the Palais du Louvre, which dominate the center of Lépine's composition. The buildings on the right are those that border the famous place Dauphine, the first public square built in Paris during the reign of Henri IV, who also ordered the construction of the Pont Neuf. Lépine omitted all but the very edge of the Conciergerie, the most monumental building in the vicinity. His is a humble Paris, observed by an habitué walking across the Seine, not a dazzling Paris of monuments made for the delectation of tourists. Indeed, had Lépine turned in the other direction, he would have been forced to include the facade of no less a monument than Notre-Dame de Paris. Here, we see four barges and a lone rowboat beached for scale on the opposite quay.

In the context of the Norton Simon collections, this Lépine joins Pierre-Auguste Renoir's sublime *Pont des Arts* (cat. 88), painted a decade earlier, and Lépine's own later view of the Île-St.-Louis (cat. 75) in giving contemporary pictorial life to the Parisian quays of the Second Empire and early Third Republic. Jean-Baptiste Armand Guillaumin's view of the Seine at Charenton (cat. 95), painted a year or so earlier, was made within a half-hour walk of the setting for this small painting. By contrast to the earlier works by Renoir and Guillaumin, the two paintings by Lépine are almost painfully modest, uninvolved, and comparatively monochromatic.

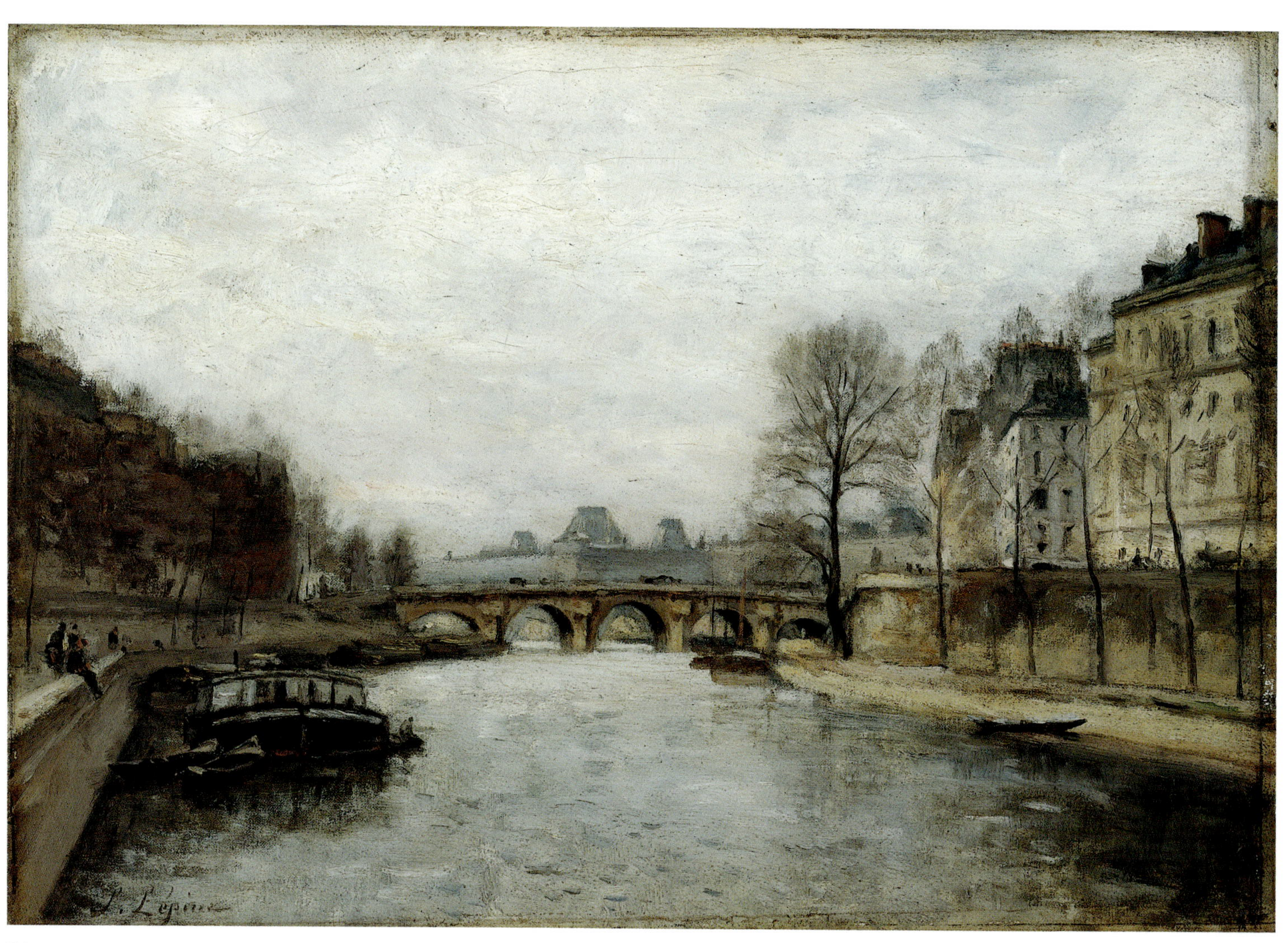

74

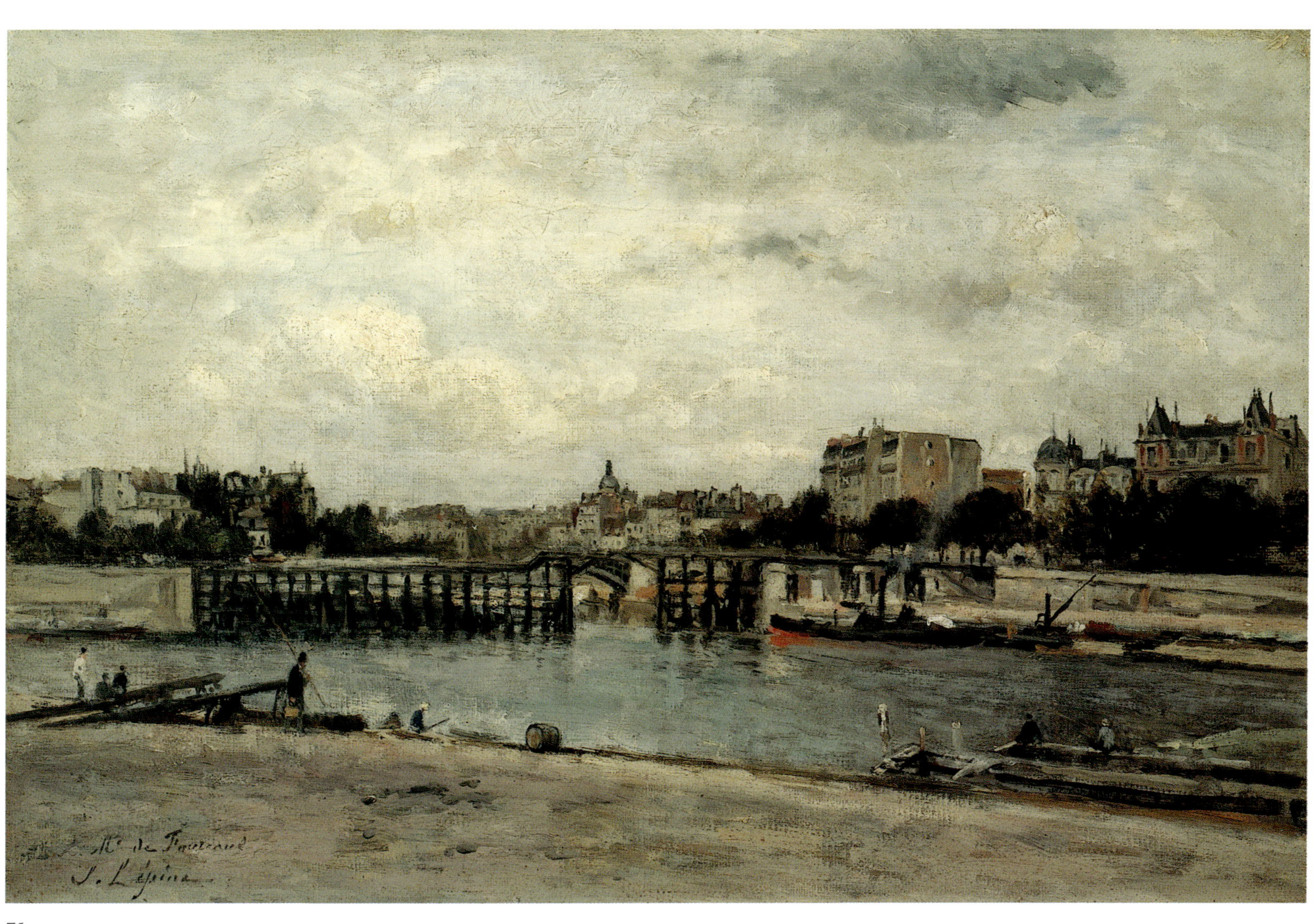

75

75

Stanislas-Victor-Édouard Lépine
French, 1835–1892

The Pont de l'Estacade, Paris
c. 1880–1884

Oil on canvas, $10^5/_8 \times 16^1/_8$ in. (27 × 41 cm)
Signed and dedicated lower left: "à M. de Fourcaud S. Lépine"
M.1969.19

Provenance: Louis de Fourcaud, Paris (sale, Paris, Hôtel Drouot, 29 March 1917, lot 43, ill., for Ff 4,200 to); [Boussod, Valadon, Paris, stock no. 31250, for Ff 9,000 to]; [J. Allard, 4 January 1918]. Mme L. Ferrey, Paris (sale, Paris, Galerie Georges Petit, 18 April 1921, lot 33, ill., to); Gerson. [Georges Petit, Paris]. François Estier, Paris (sale, Paris, Hôtel Drouot, 5 December 1940, lot 32, ill., for Ff 32,000). [Galerie Schmit, Paris, as *Vue de Paris*, sold 20 March 1969 to]; Norton Simon Art Foundation.

Exhibitions: Princeton, 1972, no. 29, ill.; San Francisco, 1974, no. 28, ill.

Reference: Schmit and Schmit, 1993, no. 36, ill., as *La Seine à l'Estacade pendant la construction du Pont Sully.*

Technical Notes: The support is canvas; a 2-inch diagonal tear in the sky at center left and a small hole at the lower left have been well repaired. The painting has been glue-lined with the original edges cut off. An off-white ground was probably commercially applied in a smooth layer. It may have been thick enough to mask the canvas weave, but the present surface with its pronounced weave is a result of lining pressure. Much of the sky was painted wet into wet, although there are occasionally superimposed brushstrokes above dried brushstrokes. The river appears to have been laid in with a mauve color, then modified by subsequent loose brushstrokes, which allude to the reflection of the bridge. Small brushstrokes describing the buildings at the horizon are superimposed over the larger brushstrokes of the pale sky, indicating that the sky was painted first. Many of the details of the figures on the riverbank were painted after the lower paint layer had dried. The paint texture has been partly smoothed by lining. There is minimal cracking, primarily in the sky and visible with magnification. Previous cleaning has been done with care. (RW)

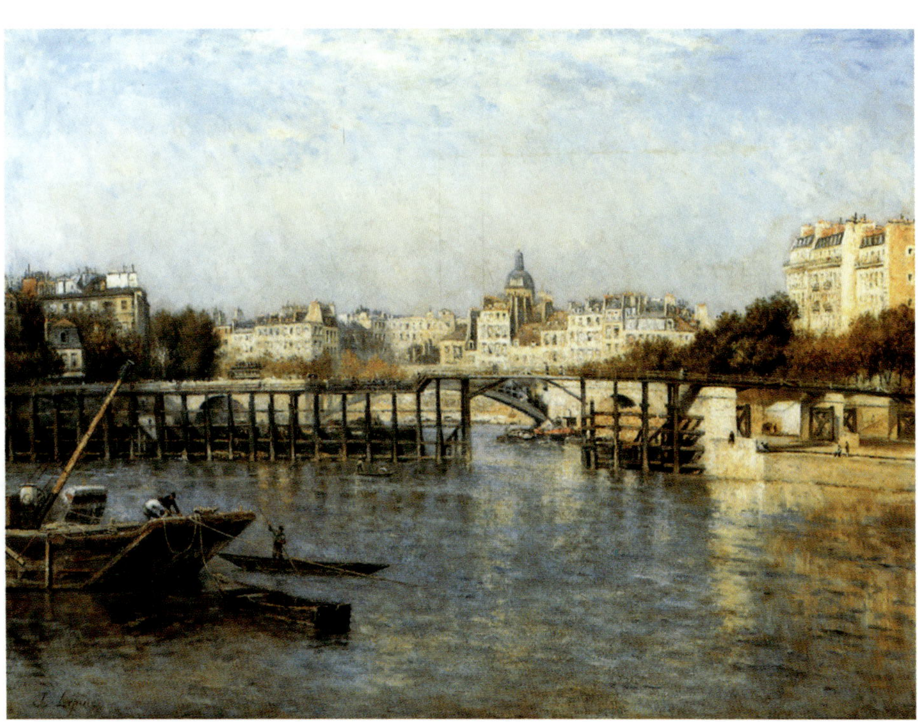

Fig. 75a Stanislas-Victor-Édouard Lépine, *The Seine at l'Estacade*, 1882, $49^1/_4 \times 67$ in. (125 × 170 cm), private collection

In the spring of 1885 Lépine submitted a large and fully finished view of the Parisian quays to the Salon (fig. 75a). Listed as number 1561, *The Seine at l'Estacade* (125 × 170 cm, nearly four by six feet), this painting remains to this day one of the masterpieces of Lépine's oeuvre and among the largest canvases ever executed by this modest painter. Like his Salon paintings of 1886 and 1888, which also represent stretches of the Parisian quays (in a somewhat smaller format), this painting seems to be his attempt to rival the great series of paintings of the ports of France painted by the late-eighteenth-century master Joseph Vernet. Unfortunately, unlike those of Vernet, Lépine's paintings have never been grouped in a museum exhibition, depriving today's audiences of an understanding of Lépine's pictorial ambitions.

In painting the smaller Norton Simon canvas, Lépine chose a site on the quai St.-Bernard (then the Port aux Vins), where Paul Cézanne had lived and worked early in the 1870s. Looking northwest from the quay, across the river to the quai Henri IV, Lépine surveyed a wider landscape panorama in this small painted sketch than he did in the larger Salon painting. Yet the main features of the composition and the point of view survive. Surely Lépine would not have carried the Salon canvas onto the quay itself, preferring, as had his master Camille Corot, to work outdoors on a small scale and to apply formal and chromatic lessons learned there to the preparation of the larger canvas. Though it is possible that he might have taken the large painting to the quay on one or two occasions to apply finishing touches and to sprinkle throughout figures and other particularizing forms, Lépine remained thoroughly academic in his working method. It is perhaps because of its academic character that the Norton Simon painting was dedicated to a M. de Fourcaud, its first owner. Louis de Fourcaud was no less than a professor at the Académie des Beaux-Arts, a

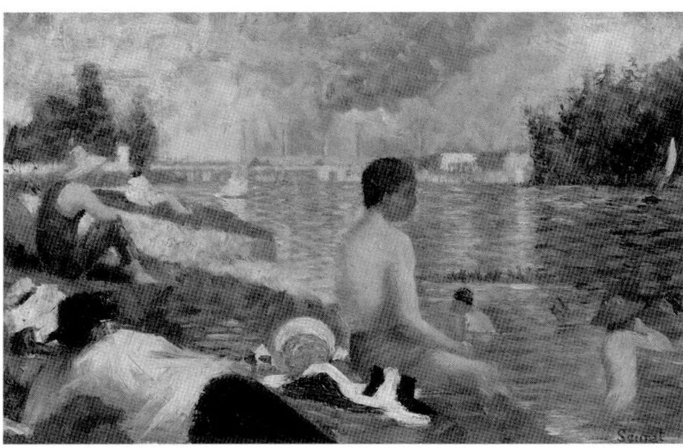

Fig. 75b Georges Seurat, *Final Study for the "Bathers at Asnières"*, 1883, oil on panel, $6\frac{1}{4} \times 9\frac{7}{8}$ in. (15.8 × 25.1 cm), The Art Institute of Chicago, Adele R. Levy Fund

man who worked against the Impressionists and may have had a hand in assuring that Lépine's large painting fared as well as it did in the Salon of 1885.

The dome at the center of the composition belongs to the Church of St.-Louis and St.-Paul on the rue St. Antoine (with its great painting by Eugène Delacroix and its sculpture by Germain Pilon). At the far left is an indication of the gardens and a small pavilion of a city house designed by Louis Le Vau and decorated by Charles Le Brun, which is one of the few buildings from the seventeenth-century development of the Île-St.-Louis to survive intact. It is opposed pictorially to large and new Third Republic apartment buildings on the right bank. Lépine was to paint another view from the same quay two years later and submit it to the Salon of 1886. The earlier view looks down the large branch of the Seine toward the Baroque church. The later one looks down the small branch of the Seine toward Notre-Dame de Paris. In both cases, the ecclesiastical form provides a central focus to the landscape.

It is fascinating to compare Lépine's horizontal painting in the Norton Simon collection with the exactly contemporary studies of the Seine painted by the young—and equally academically trained—Georges Seurat in the western suburbs of the city (fig. 75b). Both artists chose to conceive of their paintings on "Sunday," when the workers of Paris were free to loaf and fish in the waters of the Seine. Yet, whereas Seurat centered his composition on the smokestacks of the suburbs, Lépine allows the church to dominate his cityscape. Each man was fascinated by the fishermen along the Seine, and Seurat made individual studies of them for inclusion in larger paintings. Lépine shows us seven such figures working along the deserted docks. One lone steamboat, at the right center of the painting, gives off subtle pictorial evidence of steam, and a single barrel of wine reminds us that we are on the Port aux Vins.

The Pont de l'Estacade was a temporary structure built to control the flow of the Seine during the long period of construction for the Pont de Sully, the double bridge located on the east end of the Île-St.-Louis. The French word has Italian origins in the word *steccata*, or "post," and refers to a bridge-dam made from long posts planted in a river to close or divert it temporarily during construction. Hence, in painting this temporary structure, Lépine was celebrating the continuing modernization of the capital city during the Third Republic. He may have also been celebrating the resurrection of the city after the disaster of the Franco-Prussian War of 1870–1871 and the sharp economic downturn that followed the crash of 1873. The Pont de l'Estacade burned, collapsed, and was rebuilt repeatedly throughout the nineteenth century. It finally disappeared in 1938.

76

Ignace-Henri-Jean-Théodore Fantin-Latour
French, 1836–1904

White and Pink Mallows in a Vase
1895

Oil on canvas, 21 × 19½ in. (53.3 × 49.5 cm)
Signed lower right: "Fantin"
M.2003.1

Provenance: The artist, sold to; Mrs. Edwin Edwards, London, sold by 1911 to; John Postle Heseltine (1843–1929), London. [J. B. Bennett & Son, Glasgow]. William A. Cargill, Carruth, Bridge of Weir, Scotland (sale, London, Sotheby's, 11 June 1963, lot 25, ill.). [Hallsborough Gallery, London, by 1965, to]; [Acquavella Galleries, New York, sold by 31 October 1967 to]; The Norton Simon Foundation, transferred 2003 to; Norton Simon Art Foundation.

Exhibitions: London, 1965, no. 16, ill.; New York, 1966b, no. 18, ill.; San Francisco, 1973, no. 27, ill.

References: Fantin-Latour, 1911, no. 1595; Wykes-Joyce, 1966, p. 12, color ill.

Technical Notes: The support is a fine, plain-weave canvas that has been wax-lined. The present stretched dimensions now include approximately ¼ inch of the original tacking edges at each side. Adhesion between the two canvases is uniformly strong. The off-white ground is extremely thin and does not fill the canvas weave. The nearly monochromatic background paint is extraordinarily thin; it may have been rubbed or brushed with a very liquid paint. The flowers are painted with opaque, rich paint, then scored with the brush handle to create the striations in the blossoms. The bulbous portion of the glass vase is quite transparent, with a slight addition of transparent light green. The white flowers are thickly painted and opaque; the pink flowers appear to be alizarin crimson with additions of white to vary the shades of pink and are quasi-transparent, allowing the thread tops to show through in widely varying degrees of opacity/transparency. The left side of the glass vase has been outlined or drawn with graphite, charcoal, or very dry paint. The paint film shows no abrasion or alterations and is uncracked. There is a small repair at the lower left part of the table. No earlier condition reports were found. The synthetic varnish is fairly thick and creates a uniform gloss. (RW)

With wonderful floral still-life paintings by Gustave Courbet, Pierre-Auguste Renoir, and Paul Cézanne, how could the Norton Simon collections not have a floral still life by the nineteenth-century master most faithful to that genre, Henri Fantin-Latour? Although born in Grenoble to mixed French-Russian parents, Fantin-Latour was trained in Paris and, by suppressing his first name, Ignace, was able to pass completely as a Frenchman. His oeuvre is large and iconographically diverse, but he remains known to the public at large—and to most scholars—as a painter of floral still lifes. It is a cliché, by now, to begin an entry or short essay on French floral still-life painting by reminding the reader that it was near the bottom of the hierarchy of genres codified by the French Academy. Yet, although this is technically true, virtually every great French painter of the eighteenth and nineteenth centuries practiced the genre, and the number of minor artists who devoted their careers to floral painting is staggering. Fantin-Latour was neither a great French painter nor a minor practitioner of floral still life. Although he attempted to attain greatness through his allegorical and musical paintings, his still lifes earned him a steady living, and he plays a major role in any study of nineteenth-century floral painting. In this, he is different from any of the other great artists—from his friend Édouard Manet to Henri Matisse—in that floral still life dominated his oeuvre. In fact, he exhibited floral paintings at the Salons from the 1860s (fig. 76a) in addition to his more intellectually ambitious paintings of literary and allegorical subjects.

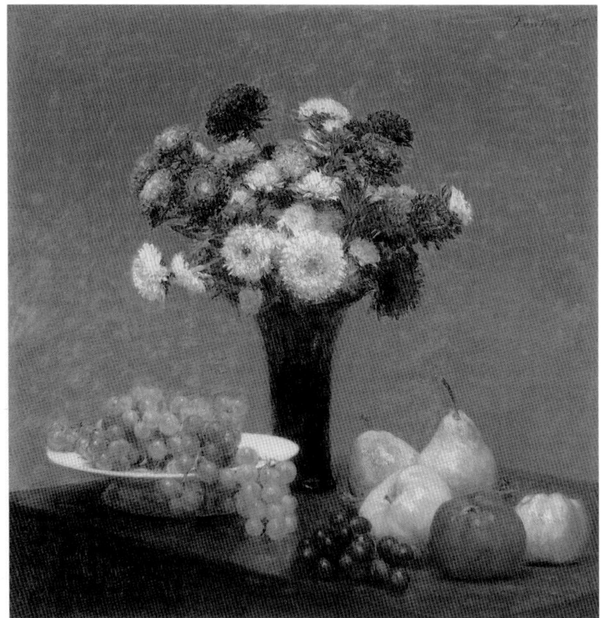

Fig. 76a Ignace-Henri-Jean-Théodore Fantin-Latour, *Asters and Fruit on a Table*, 1868, oil on canvas, 22⅜ × 21⅝ in. (56.8 × 54.9 cm), The Metropolitan Museum of Art, New York, The Walter H. and Leonore Annenberg Collection, Gift of Walter H. and Leonore Annenberg, 2001, Bequest of Walter H. Annenberg, 2002

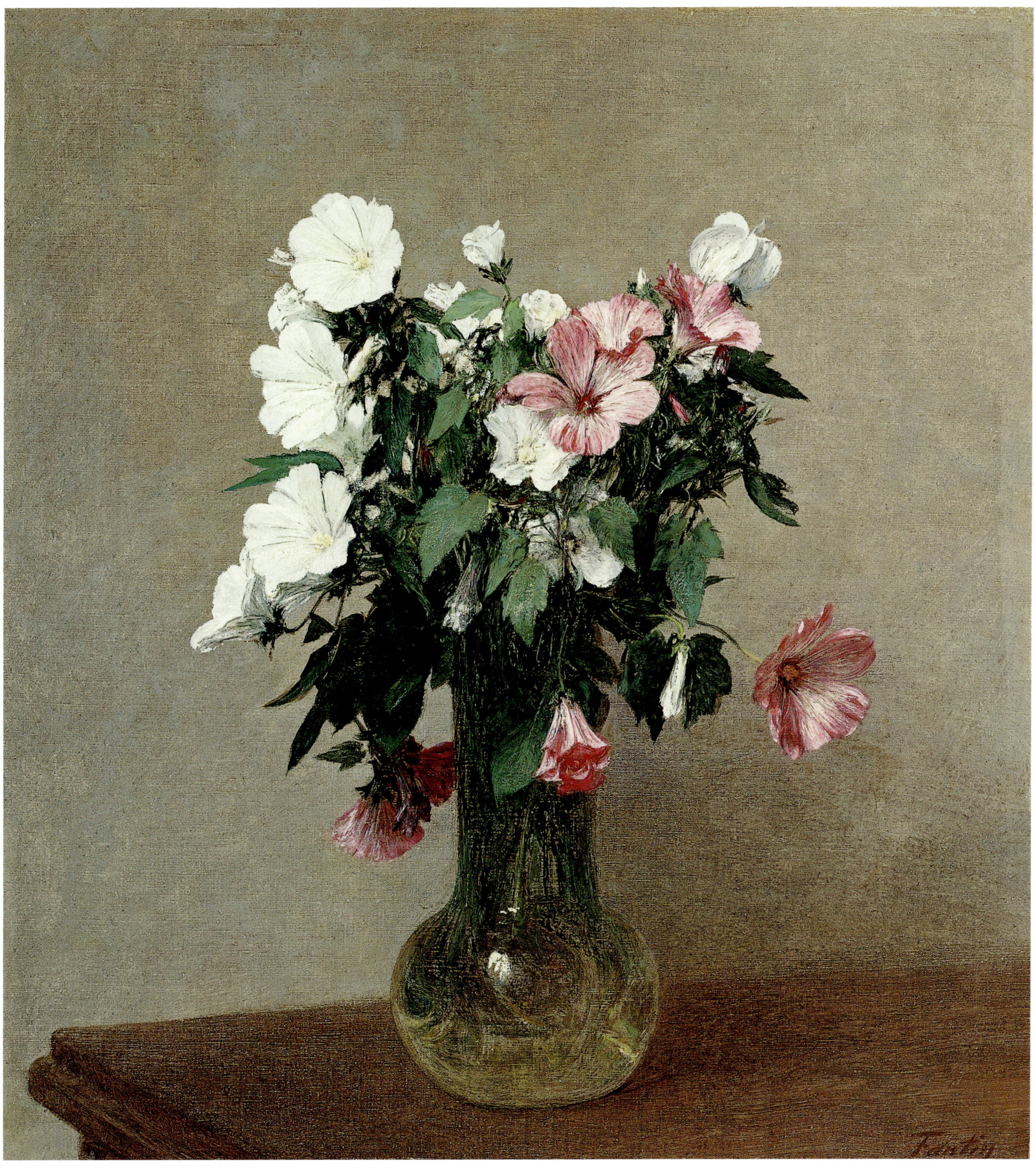

This small painting is neither the most ambitious nor the most important of Fantin-Latour's highly prized floral still-life paintings. Made in 1895, toward the end of the artist's long and productive career (he stopped painting in the genre the year before his death in 1904), it represents summer flowers gathered from the large garden of the house he shared with his wife, the floral still-life painter Victoria Dubourg, whom he had married in 1876. The effect of the painting is of almost startling simplicity. Unlike the floral paintings by Courbet and Renoir in the Norton Simon collections, Fantin's flowers are not arranged but simply cut from their stalks in the garden and placed without artifice into a simple clear-glass vase filled with water. All of this rests in the center of a composition at the edge of an off-center, unadorned wooden table in front of a gray-white plaster wall. There are no pictures on the wall, no decorative accessories, no painted patterns on the vase, and even the light is a soft, interior light, probably suffused through lace curtains from a distant window.

The effect of the painting is almost pearlescent. All the glory and subtlety of the painting can be found in the flowers themselves. The whitest whites are the petals of the white mallows, and the striation of the pink mallows is represented with matching striations of pink and white paint. The effect of the still life is of short-lived life and freshness, as mallows cannot long maintain their peak of bloom when cut from the plant. Indeed, Fantin takes care to show us that certain of them have not yet opened (and never will), while others have wilted already. There is, in this, as in most floral still lifes, a hint of melancholy at the transience of life. Indeed, Fantin almost forces us to remember that, before they were cut, the mallows were part of a large flower garden that was, in totality, almost a riot of blooming color. In the vase indoors, at the end of their life, their glory is lonely.

Rosamond Westmoreland's examination of the painting revealed an almost startling thinness of the ground and of the paint used to describe the table, the vase, and the wall. Against this ground, through which the canvas almost breathes, Fantin laid in the individual leaves and petals of the flowers in a manner he had been practicing for decades. In this, he proves once again that practice does make perfect. The painting is so remarkably unremarkable that until acquired by Norton Simon in 1967, it had never been in a famous collection or great exhibition. Rather, it provided at least four owners and hundreds of thousands of visitors to the Norton Simon Museum a moment of simple pleasure experienced by Henri Fantin-Latour in the summer of 1895.

77

Alexander Alexandrovich Kiselev
Russian, 1838–1911

The Mill
1890

Oil on canvas, 29½ × 49⅛ in. (75 cm × 125 cm)
Signed and dated lower left, in Cyrillic: "AKilselev 1890"
M.1987.1.4

Provenance: (Sale, London, Sotheby's, 1 May 1987, lot 44, ill., to); Norton Simon Art Foundation.

Technical Notes: The support, a plain-weave, medium-weight canvas, is unlined; it remains strong and supple. It has been commercially primed with a thin off-white ground that leaves the canvas texture evident. The paint layer is in excellent condition apart from frame abrasion at the perimeter. Applied directly over the light ground, the paint is thin but not liquid. Brush marking remains visible although the canvas texture is predominant. The blue of the sky was smoothly brushed down to the horizon; white clouds were worked wet into wet into the blue where contours merge. Reserves were left for the trees at the right and for part of the large tree at the left. Shadows are translucent brown. The foreground was painted with blended colors, often very smooth, with scattered accents of foliage and leaves. In the foreground, especially at the lower right, small areas of barely tinted ground layer were left to represent the sandy earth. The painting has been cleaned unevenly in an earlier treatment, and portions of the sky appear more yellowed than others. (RW)

This large and brilliantly painted landscape is one of the finest nineteenth-century Russian landscape paintings in any public institution in America. The painter, Alexander Alexandrovich Kiselev, like most important artists of the nineteenth century in Russia, was trained at the St. Petersburg Academy, founded in the eighteenth century and headquartered in a magnificent building on the Neva River. There, he learned to make art in a manner that had been invented in Italy in the sixteenth century and codified in France in the seventeenth and eighteenth centuries. In Russia, this mode of training produced a professional class of artists who were as well educated in the craft and the aspirations of art as those of any European country. And, after the opening of the Hermitage Museum in 1852, these artists were also able to study the works of major European painters, just as their counterparts in Paris, London, Vienna, Munich, or Berlin did. Two years older than the great French Impressionist painter Claude Monet, Kiselev was trained in an artistic system that valued long periods of study, hierarchical processes of preparation, and highly finished exhibition paintings. As a result, the Russian's landscapes have a much more elaborate and studied look than do contemporaneous paintings by Monet and his Impressionist colleagues.

It would be wrong, however, to deny the importance of avant-garde and modern tendencies in nineteenth-century Russian art. Indeed, the artists of Artel' Khudoznikov (Artists' Cooperative Society), a movement to take art from the academies that was founded in 1863, formed the nucleus of a group generally called the Wanderers or the Itinerants (Peredvizhniki), which dominated Russian aesthetics and art practice from 1870 (four years before the first Impressionist exhibition) until 1923. These men believed that both art and its imagery should extend throughout and encompass the entire nation of Russia, rather than being confined to the two cultural capitals, St. Petersburg and Moscow. One part of their enterprise was to mount self-juried exhibitions in regional cities; the other was to begin a collective pictorial representation of Russia in all her vastness and cultural variety. Although Kiselev was not one of the most important members of this large collective—that honor would go to Ivan Kramskoi, Vasily Perov, and Nikolai Ge—he was more than a little affected by its tenets, and the present painting is surely proof of that. Indeed, by 1890, when this painting was made, many otherwise academic artists as well as important plein-air painters such as Isaak Levitan who were not technically members of the group sent paintings to their exhibitions, and it is likely that this work, with its large scale and Cyrillic signature, was intended for exhibition—either at the academy itself or in one of the exhibitions of the Wanderers. If so, however, this information is not recorded.

We know nothing of the site selected by Kiselev—there is neither an inscription on the painting nor a historical title that can help us solve that mystery. Yet, part of the painting's charm—as well as its meaning—is in the sheer rural anonymity of its subject—a wood mill building next to a recently constructed wood dam in "Anywhere" Russia. The capital city is as far away culturally from this landscape world as it might have been physically, and Kiselev was trying to bring the delights of the Russian countryside directly into its capital city, St. Petersburg, where he lived, worked, and exhibited. Anyone familiar with Russian realist fiction of Kiselev's time will be able to imagine scores of passages of prose from authors like Anton Chekhov, Ivan Goncharov, and Ivan Turgenev that evoke the same or similar rural worlds.

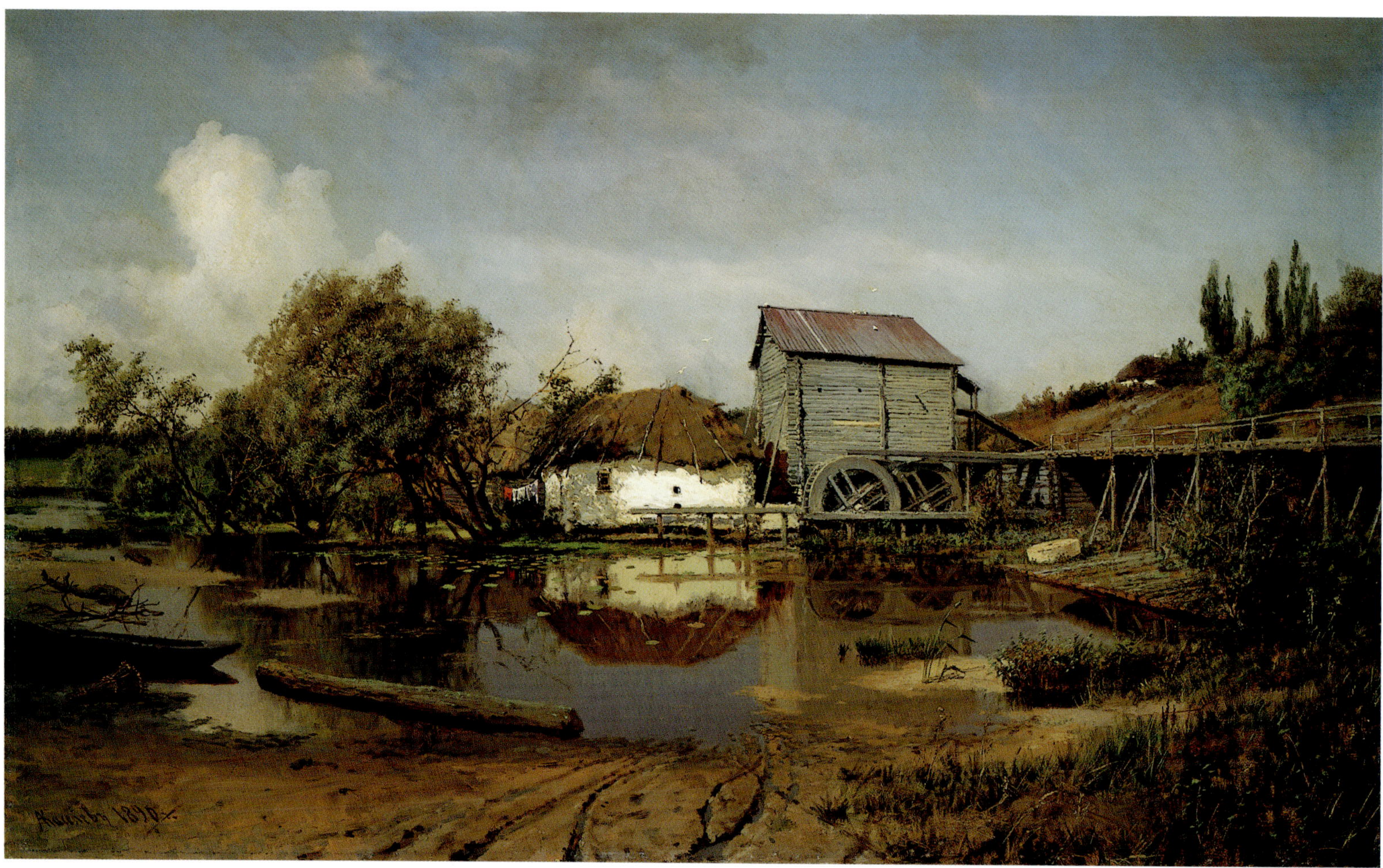

77

Kiselev was not, however, indebted to any Russian writer when he painted this work. Rather, he was thinking as much about the seventeenth-century Dutch landscapes by artists like Jan van Goyen and Jacob van Ruisdael, of which the Hermitage had particularly splendid examples. In painting this work he managed to create a pictorial world with its own authority and energy, in spite of its sources from two centuries earlier. Indeed, he focused on a relatively newly constructed mill building and dam—an improvement undoubtedly financed by a wealthy landowner to harness the power of the slow-moving river—which is placed next to a small thatched dwelling of considerably greater age. And even this is covered with a new coat of lime wash so that it commands the center of the picture in all its brilliance. And, to separate Kiselev's world even further from that of Chekhov and other writers, we quickly observe that, although this painting represents a fully humanized landscape, it is utterly devoid of actual human beings. The flat fishing boat is empty; the laundry, barely moving in the wind, was hung some time ago; the bridge over the dam has no foot traffic; no water flows over the ready paddles; a fishing trap sits empty in the far right corner. Perhaps, as is so often the case in Russian rural fiction, everyone is sleeping. Indeed, the only one awake in the utter stillness of this landscape world is Kiselev.

78

Alfred Sisley
English, 1839–1899

Louveciennes in the Snow
1872

Oil on canvas, 20 × 28¾ in. (50.8 × 73 cm)
Signed and dated lower left: "Sisley 72"
M.1996.3

Provenance: Picq-Véron, Ermont-Eaubonne, sold 25 June 1892 to; [Durand-Ruel, Paris, sold 17 July 1892 to]; Henri Vever, Paris (sale, Paris, Galerie Georges Petit, 1–2 February 1897, lot 112, as *Effet de neige*, for Ff 2,200 to); Mme Rambaud (probably Raimbaud). Mme Cancurte, Paris. [Hector Brame, Paris, sold 25 January 1951 to]; [Arthur Tooth & Sons, Ltd., London, stock no. 2533, sold 27 February 1951 to]; Audrey E. Pleydell-Bouverie, London, by bequest to; [David Gibbs, New York, sold 25 September 1968 to]; The Norton Simon Foundation, transferred 1996 to; Norton Simon Art Foundation.

Exhibitions: Paris, 1897, no. 142; Paris, 1917a, no. 30; London, 1951, no. 4, ill.; London, 1954a, no. 33, pl. 3; Philadelphia, 1969, no. 14; Berkeley, 1970, no. 299; San Francisco, 1973, no. 40, ill.; on loan, New York, Metropolitan Museum of Art, 18 December 1980–26 August 1981.

References: Daulte, 1959, no. 52, ill.; Stevens, 1992, p. 44.

Technical Notes: Apart from having been varnished, the painting is in pristine condition, having never been removed from its original stretcher. The delicate profile of the brushwork remains clear and unaltered. The plain-weave canvas is unlined; it is oxidized, quite dark, and rather brittle. It is tacked to a 5-member stretcher, constructed with mortise-and-tenon, keyed corners and a single crossbar. Tiny holes at the top center and bottom center of the canvas have an unpainted margin around the hole, probably from where the fabric was held with a tack to a board while painting outside. The smooth ground is pale gray, with a slight yellowing from the varnish layer. The surface texture seems to illustrate the Impressionists' desire to incorporate the subtleties of the canvas weave: Sisley's use of a partly dry brush leaves tiny gaps in the paint, which, in combination with the thin ground barely covering the canvas threads, imparts a faint texture. The directly applied paint is lean and delicately brushed. Red-brown grasses are quite thin, not completely covering the canvas texture, painted in fast strokes both horizontally and vertically. In the foreground and the trees, Sisley used a slightly dry brush with small, controlled strokes, not filling in the irregularities of canvas texture. The subtle coloring of the winter sky was achieved with a first layer of pale gray; the clouds were then painted in scribbles, with a slightly darker blue-gray. The relative dryness of the paint meant that superimposed brushstrokes in the sky remained crisp over the first layer. Occasional areas of the ground are left exposed, such as the pathway at the lower center; it functions as a tonal value in its own right. The painting overall is thinly painted with no impasto. It appears that the painting has never been cleaned, as indicated by the absence of any staining on the reverse of the canvas where solvents and varnish might seep through cracks. The varnish is an aged synthetic resin, and it is considerably yellowed, affecting the overall appearance of the snowy landscape. (RW)

The single work by Alfred Sisley in the Norton Simon collections epitomizes the style and quality of that Anglo-French artist. Painted in 1872, Sisley's most important year of production, it was acquired directly from Sisley by the great collector Picq-Véron, who lived in the resort town Ermont-Eaubonne. This gentleman amassed a collection that included at least sixteen paintings by Sisley, all of which were sold to Sisley's dealer, Durand-Ruel, in the summer of 1892, perhaps after M. Picq-Véron's death and seven years before Sisley's own death. Picq-Véron was, with the opera singer Jean-Baptiste Faure (who owned thirty Sisleys) and the Rouen businessman Depeaux (who owned more than fifty), one of a handful of faithful collectors who followed Sisley's career, buying judiciously to form collections that were, before their respective dispersals, mini-retrospectives of the painter. Two other men, Décap and Feder, about whom little is known, owned fifteen paintings each by Sisley, and these five collectors absolutely dominated what might be called the early Sisley market. No twentieth-century collector has followed them in their fidelity to this subtle and elusive artist.

Alfred Sisley, as his name suggests, was born to English parents in Paris. His mother and father both descended from wealthy families involved in manufacturing, and his father exported silk flowers from Paris to places throughout the world. After a period of education in England, Sisley returned to France and renounced his interests in the family business. By 1862 he had entered the Paris studio of the French painter Charles Gleyre, where he met his soon-to-be fellow Impressionists Claude Monet, Pierre-Auguste Renoir, and Frédéric Bazille. By 1863 the four young artists were painting together in the Forest of Fontainebleau, and by 1866 Sisley's submission to the official Salon was accepted, and another two works were accepted to the Salon of 1870. This brief biography is similar to that of his companions Monet, Renoir, Camille Pissarro, and Bazille. Yet, whereas the early careers of those artists are well documented, with scores of paintings, the catalogue raisonné of the paintings of Sisley contains only twelve works that survive from an entire decade of activity. The quality of five of these works is so high that one yearns for the discovery of a

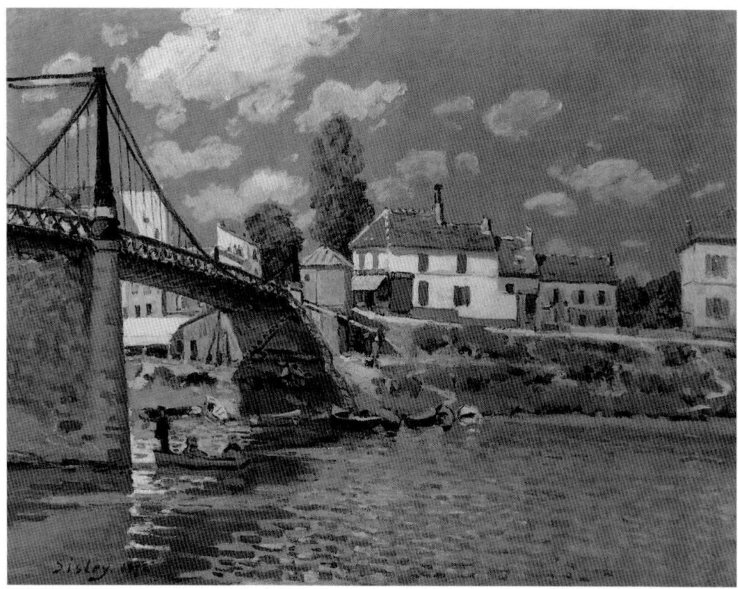

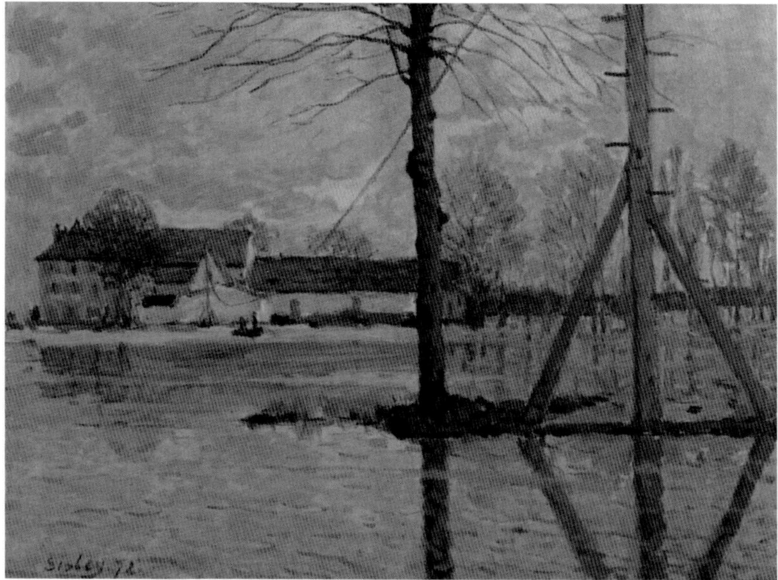

Fig. 78a (*above left*) Alfred Sisley, *Bridge at Villeneuve-la-Garenne*, 1872, oil on canvas, $19\frac{1}{2} \times 25\frac{3}{4}$ in. (49.5 × 65.4 cm), The Metropolitan Museum of Art, New York, Gift of Mr. and Mrs. Henry Ittleson Jr., 1964

Fig. 78b (*above right*) Alfred Sisley, *Le Bac de l'Île de loge, inundation*, 1872, oil on canvas, $17\frac{3}{4} \times 23\frac{5}{8}$ in. (45 × 60 cm), Ny Carlsberg Glyptotek, Copenhagen

cache of other early works by Sisley. The same lack of productivity (or perhaps Sisley's own destruction of early work) continued in 1870–1871; only four works by Sisley are dated 1870, and there are no surviving works dated to 1871. There are, however, nine signed but undated paintings that are conventionally assigned dates from 1870 to 1872 that might be the result of Sisley's work during the first three years of the 1870s.

The year 1872, by contrast, was stunningly productive for the reclusive Sisley, and thirty-one paintings survive that are signed and dated to that single year—nearly twice the output of the entire previous decade. The present painting is among the largest and best preserved of this group, and its virtually unbroken provenance begins with Picq-Véron, who bought two other 1872 paintings by Sisley. Both Depeaux and Faure bought two paintings of 1872 (figs. 78a and 78b), and the greatest living French painter, Édouard Manet, purchased a work from 1872 as well. Clearly the painter's fortunes had begun to rise. It is worth remembering that this sudden burst of activity came after a particularly difficult time for Sisley. Not only did he and his family have to endure the Franco-Prussian War and the ensuing Commune, but, throughout those same years, 1870–1871, Sisley's father had become seriously ill, made a series of disastrous business decisions, lost most of his money, and died, leaving his young painter son, who had married in 1866 and already had two children, virtually destitute. For the first time in his life, it became necessary for Sisley to live off his artistic production.

In 1871 Sisley rented a small house at 12, rue de la Princesse, in the hamlet of Voisin near the small suburban town of Louveciennes. Renoir's mother lived nearby, and that artist, although a soldier in the French army during the war, kept in close touch. Pissarro had also lived a short walk away for several years, and Monet worked in nearby Bougival just before the war. Hence, Sisley moved to what has often been called "the cradle of Impressionism" and used this already well-pictured landscape as his source of inspiration for what was his first year of professional artistic activity. During 1872 Sisley recorded the annual flooding of the Seine at nearby Port Marly, made a lengthy summer trip to nearby Argenteuil to work in the company of his friend Monet, hiked along the Seine to Bougival, followed the main road both east and west to Sèvres and St.-Germaine-en-Laye, and, finally, holed up in his small house during the winter, recording the snowy winter of 1872–1873 in a series of five paintings, of which the Norton Simon's is the largest. Durand-Ruel bought three of these paintings from Sisley in February 1873, and Picq-Véron may already have owned this painting because, being the largest of the group, it would surely have appealed to the profit-conscious dealer, had he been able to buy it. Indeed, Durand-Ruel bought fifteen of Sisley's 1872 paintings in that year and the first two months of 1873, giving the painter a steady, if small, income, which was undoubtedly enriched through private sales to Manet, Picq-Véron, Faure, and others.

Unlike the vast majority of Impressionist paintings in American museums, the Norton Simon Sisley remains on its original stretcher and has not been lined on a new canvas with glue or wax. Hence, it looks today almost as it did when Sisley painted it in either January or February 1872 (snowfall was measured in both months). In spite of its size and importance, it is recorded as

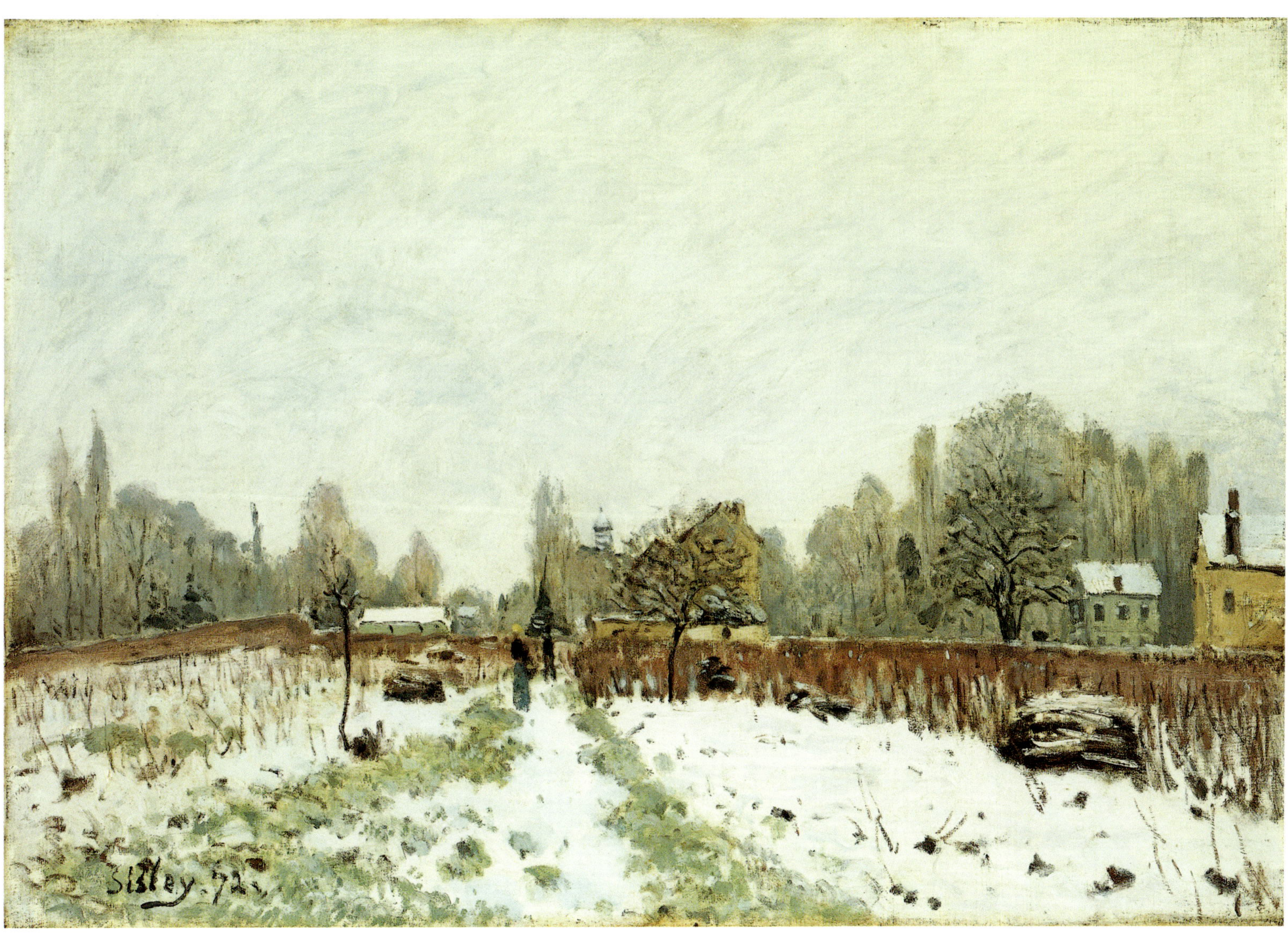

78

having been exhibited only once in Sisley's lifetime and that was a commercial retrospective held in 1897, just two years before the painter's death. The painting is deft, subtle, and modest in its ambitions. Its landscape motif, a pathway through a common field less than a five-minute walk from the center of Louveciennes, is arranged so that all the forms clump together in the middle distance, well away from the viewer. Precisely in the center, Sisley shows us the little bell tower of the unremarkable church in the center of Louveciennes.

The sky is relentlessly gray and heavy, and the entire picture is composed of closely related tones of celadon, warm grays, beiges, deep greens, browns, and various pale grays. Perhaps because it was painted out of doors in cold weather, it was made quickly, with the main areas brushed in with thinned paint applied in quick, rhythmic strokes with relatively large brushes on a commercially primed pale gray ground. When this undercoat was dry, Sisley took smaller brushes and drew in details—the barren trees, the pile of wood, the clumps of grass, the two figures who move resolutely through the landscape. The sense of actually being there as Sisley himself transcribed the scene is quite strong, and the painting, like many of Sisley's from 1872, has an effect of immediacy that extends from the visual to the tactile. We feel the cold, humid air as it gathers itself for another bout of snow.

79

Paul Cézanne
French, 1839–1906

Uncle Dominique
c. 1865–1867

Oil on canvas, $18\frac{1}{8} \times 15$ inches (46.1×38.2 cm)
M.1968.31

Provenance: [Ambroise Vollard, Paris]. Auguste Pellerin (d. 1929), by 1923, Paris, by inheritance to; Jean-Victor Pellerin, Paris (sale, Paris, Galerie Charpentier, 8 June 1956 to); [Davey (Knoedler, stock no. 6380)]. Frances Vogel (Mrs. A. L.) Spitzer, New York, by 1959, still in 1967; [Jane Wade, Ltd., New York, sold 17 September 1968 to]; Norton Simon Art Foundation.

Exhibitions: Paris, 1936c, no. 1; London, 1939, no. 3; New York, 1959, no. 4, ill.; Philadelphia, 1967; Philadelphia, 1969, no. 2; Princeton, 1972, no. 32; San Francisco, 1974, no. 44, ill.

References: Rivière, 1923, pp. 196, 155, ill.; George, 1931, p. 80, pl. 90; Raynal, 1936, p. 146, pl. LVIII; Rivière, 1933, p. 13, ill.; Venturi, 1936, vol. 1, no. 79, pl. 21; Novotny, 1937, pl. 2; Barnes and de Mazia, 1939, pp. 11 n. 13, 74 n. 50, 311 n. 14, 402, no. 5; Cézanne, 1937, pl. 2; Schildt, 1946, fig. 21; Dorival, 1948, pp. 25, 128, 137, pl. 7; W. Hess, 1957, p. 335, ill.; Orienti and Picon, 1970, no. 60, p. 61, ill.; Steadman, 1972, p. 38; Steadman, 1973a, p. 12, ill.; Schapiro, 1973, p. 56; Therond, 1987, p. 4; Gowing, 1988, pp. 104, 109; Rewald, 1996, vol. 1, no. 102, vol. 2, p. 34, ill.; J. Pissarro, 2005, pp. 75, 84, pl. 8.

Technical Notes: Very thick opaque paints, applied with palette knife and brush, are seen in the face and light background. The blacks and blues, though more medium rich, are very thickly applied as well. The jacket was first laid in with blues and then worked up with black and probably a pure blue. The support is a heavier plain-weave canvas that is lined with an aqueous adhesive to fabric. Tacking edges and perhaps a bit of paint were removed from the edges. The condition seems good, but there is some question about the waxy surface and possible restoration in the lower part of the picture. The yellowing fluorescing varnish is no doubt later and rather thick. The X-ray shows some adjustments and possible but indecipherable changes. The light paints have large cracks. (JF)

Much has been written about the series of nine portraits painted by Paul Cézanne in the late summer and autumn of 1866 using, as his model, his maternal uncle Dominique Aubert.[1] Aubert was Cézanne's mother's younger brother and served as a bailiff in the law courts of Aix. He was married and the father of two daughters about the same age as Cézanne himself, and these young women may also have served as models for the painter. Aubert must have had time on his hands in the latter part of 1866, for he modeled for his nephew, then an unknown amateur painter in the first decade of his career, more often than did any other sitter. Only Cézanne himself, his wife, and son modeled for more paintings than Dominique Aubert. Thus, we can think of Cézanne's project as a portrait painter as a family enterprise.

Cézanne spent this period in Aix in the company of various friends, who, fortunately, wrote letters to others that give shape to the period. Cézanne's childhood friend Antony Valabrègue wrote an often-quoted letter to the novelist Émile Zola in November 1866. "Fortunately, I only posed one day. The uncle is more often the model. Every afternoon, there appears a portrait of him while Guillemet belabors it with terrible jokes."[2] This passage tells us that Cézanne conceived of his portraits as part of a larger project and that he painted them quickly, in fact, in a very few hours. Knowing this from a reliable witness—who was himself the victim of a Cézanne portrait—allows us to interpret them as pictorial exercises made by a young artist who was beginning to form a system of painting.

Many writers—from early commentators like Antoine Guillemet and Georges Rivière to the British formalists Edward Fry or Lawrence Gowing—consider these works to be exercises in paint modeling in which Cézanne took up the challenges set by the two prevailing vanguard French painters of the period of Cézanne's youth, Gustave Courbet and Édouard Manet. From Courbet, Cézanne borrowed the tool of the painter, the palette knife, and a sense that the material qualities of paint itself are essential to the meaning of a painting. From Manet, he borrowed the pictorial inclination to reduce to their minimum the number of gestures required to evoke a form, thereby creating a pictorial image of unmatched concentration and power. Other writers, particularly the brilliant and prolix amateur art historian Albert Barnes, link Cézanne's enterprise to an even longer pictorial tradition, making particular mention in his analyses of these 1866 portraits to the paintings of Titian, Tintoretto, Rembrandt, and Hals. All of these notions have resonance with the paintings themselves, but few of the writers take up the challenge of speed that is at the center of Valabrègue's passage.

What Cézanne attempted to do was to achieve pictorial results that have a power and an immediacy communicated by the painting as a material object. The painting becomes, thus, a performance of a short duration that risks all. This is true of all nine surviving "afternoon pictures" representing Dominique Aubert.

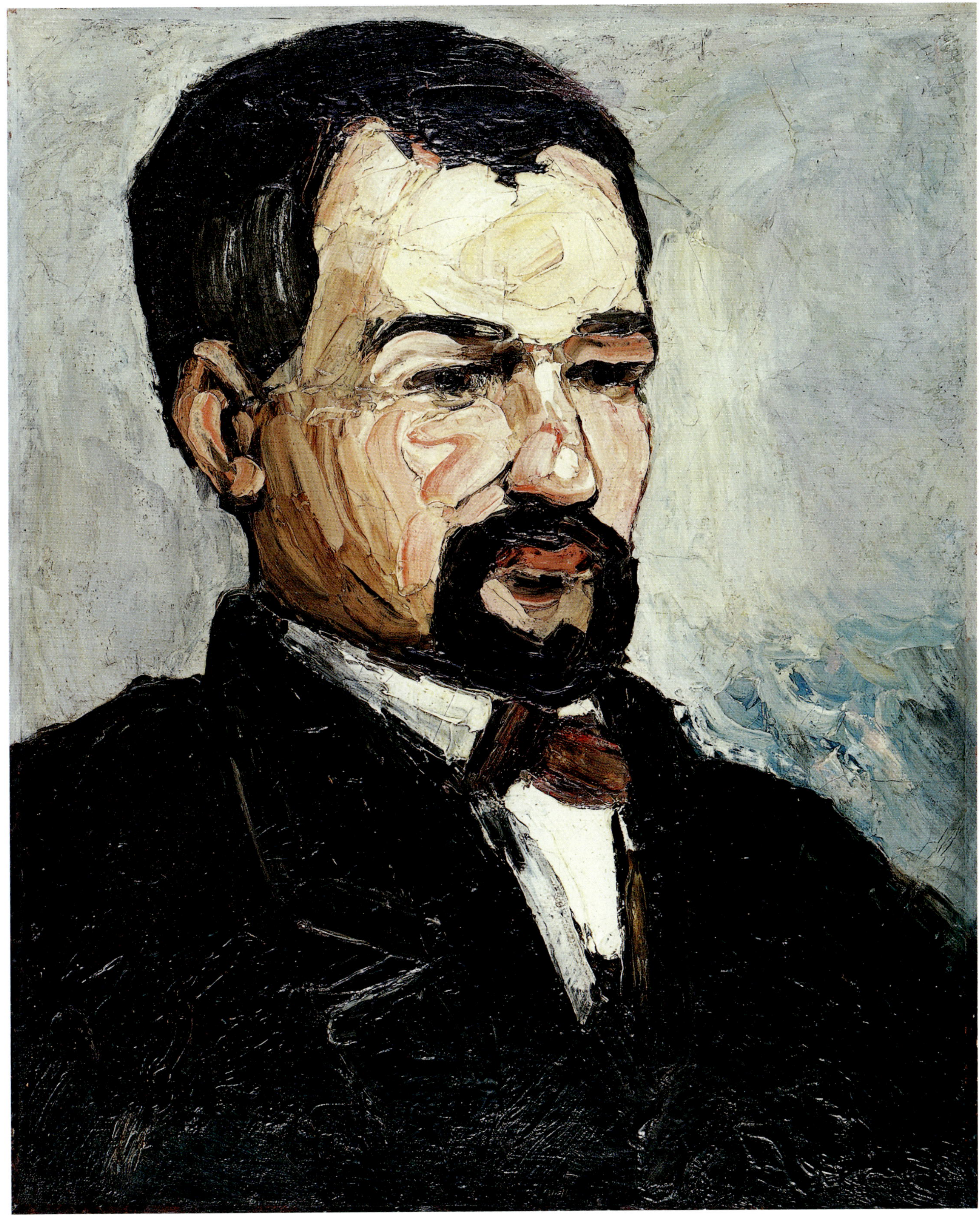

79

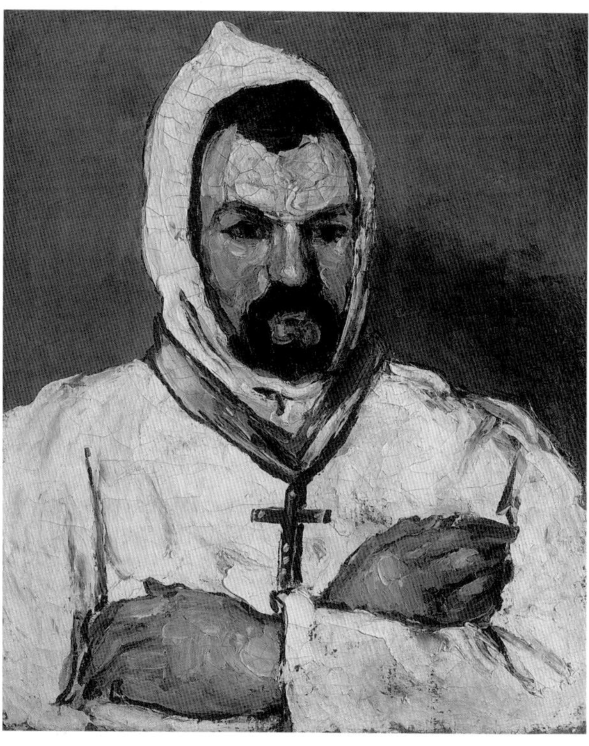

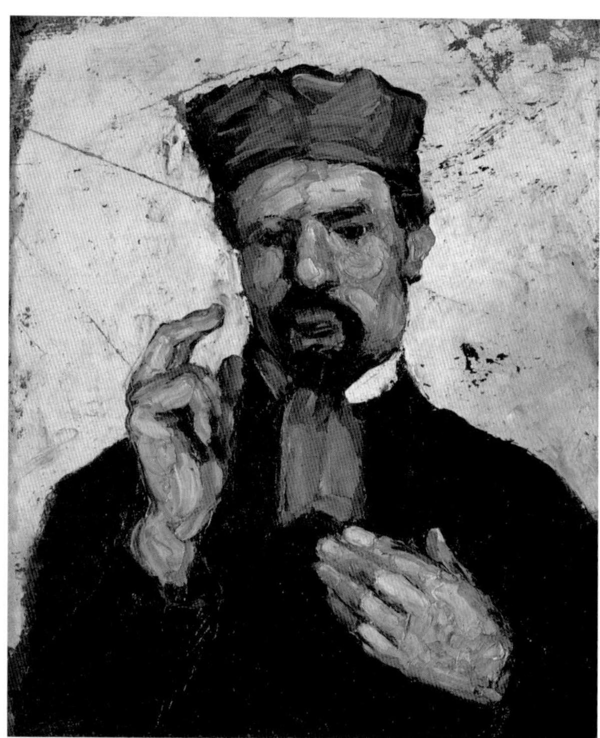

Fig. 79a (*right*) Paul Cézanne, *Dominique Aubert, the Artist's Uncle, as a Monk*, c. 1866, oil on canvas, 31⅜ × 25¼ in. (79.7 × 64.1 cm), The Metropolitan Museum of Art, New York, The Walter H. and Leonore Annenberg Collection, Gift of Walter H. and Leonore Annenberg, 1993, Bequest of Walter H. Annenberg, 2002

Fig. 79b (*far right*) Paul Cézanne, *Uncle Dominique as a Lawyer*, c. 1866, oil on canvas, 24⅞ × 20½ in. (62 × 52 cm), Musée d'Orsay, Paris; photo: Erich Lessing / Art Resource, NY

Cézanne used so much paint and applied it in such large gestures that he risked turning the entire painting into a mess with the application of any given stroke. As he mixed several hues on the palette to create the chromatic semblance of a passage in the sitter's face or clothing, he had to be careful not to allow them to mix too much, because he clearly wanted to retain a sense in the stroke of the material nature of color. This accomplished, he then laid the colors onto the canvas with a single stroke that had to fit into a visual schema of other strokes that, if they overlapped in the course of painting, would produce unintelligible results. Through the use of unprecedented quantities of paint in each stroke, Cézanne makes the viewer aware of paint as a literal medium for the gestures of the painter. Thus, painting becomes mediated action in a completely new way. No precedents—either from Cézanne's own time or from the earlier history of European painting—prepare us for this. One wonders, in addition, how many failures were scraped off the canvas to allow nine acceptable performances to remain.

Another idea that emerges from Valabrègue's short passage is that Cézanne's uncle was a model rather than himself the subject of a portrait. Though this may seem a philosophically hazy distinction, it is a crucial one. Earlier commentators on Cézanne's early portraits are divided on their significance as *portraits*. One extreme is exemplified by Barnes, who wrote that "Cézanne's early portraits are definite delineations of particular individuals, with emphasis upon the particularities of the sitter, his cast of countenance, posture, or psychological disposition."[3] The other extreme is found in Bernard Dorival's excoriatingly powerful passage in his monograph on Cézanne published in English in 1948. "In fact so great is his indifference to his models that they all have a family look: we end by wondering when looking at a portrait by him, whether it is one of the many portraits of Uncle Dominique or one of his not less numerous self-portraits. For he never tried to detail the features or the expressions of those he painted: he had no desire to apprehend and recreate an individual life. A model was nothing but a pretext."[4]

Yet, in a slightly later passage on the same page, Dorival subtly admits the truth of Barnes's assertion.

> His inspiration could only be excited by a brutal shock such as that a human face can provide, a human face mysteriously fashioned, etched, brightened, and tarnished by life. If he was built in this way, his need for expressive models becomes understandable—models wasted by grief like the woman whose features he painted in 1864 [Rewald 75?], or full of character like Uncle Dominique whose face with its high forehead, sunken eyes, bushy eyebrows, large nose, thick lips, heavy chin, beard, mustache, and frowning vulgar ugliness had a violent expression well suited to excite his emotions.[5]

Clearly, the painter can have it both ways in making a

Fig. 79c Paul Cézanne, *Uncle Dominique in Profile*, 1866, oil on canvas, 15½ × 12 in. (39.5 × 30.5 cm), Fitzwilliam Museum, University of Cambridge

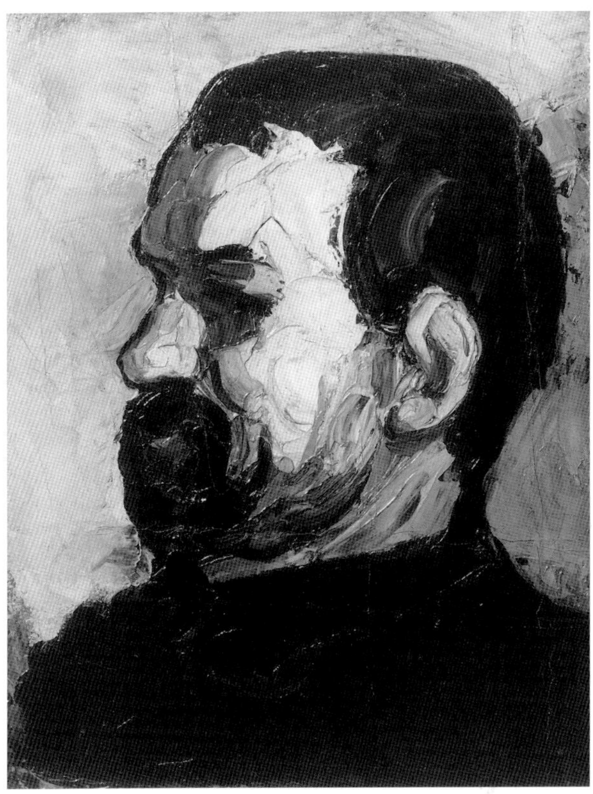

portrait—he can paint another in such a way that we understand both.

The principal reason that we accept Valabrègue's notion that Aubert was a model rather than a subject is that Cézanne posed and dressed him in various ways. First of all, he was allowed to play roles, both as a monk (fig. 79a) and as a lawyer (fig. 79b) (what every bailiff either wanted to be or wanted to mock?). But, more often, Cézanne simply made shifts in costume elements, size of canvas, and point of view. These are best summarized by Henri Loyrette's list: "in full face, profile, and three quarters views, in bust and half-length, behatted, beturbaned, and becapped."[6] Of these combinations, the Norton Simon canvas is a three-quarter bust portrait with no apparent costume elements added to the mix. It is, thus, a straightforward portrait of Aubert himself, and it can be grouped with three others (Rewald 104, 109, and fig. 79c) that represent Aubert without hands or hats. These concentrated analyses of a human head resting on its clothed shoulders are as devoid of pictorial gimmicks as possible. They represent actual encounters between two men, one of whom literally remakes or forms the second.

Of the four straight portraits, three represent Aubert looking off, outside the pictured area. Thus, we are permitted to look at the sitter without the uncomfortable sensation of being looked at by him. In this, Cézanne departs from the portraits and figural groups of Manet, for whom the idea of the picture as itself capable of the gaze is paramount. Cézanne eschews this, more often than not, preferring to empower the viewer, allowing us both time and psychological space to confront the sitter. This is, in itself, a relief, because the paintings themselves are so physically confrontational. They seem to leap out of their frames, pushing from the confines of the canvas with the power of polychrome relief sculpture. The backgrounds are, by and large, reduced to the absolute minimum—the heads touch or are occasionally cut off by the top of the canvas in seven of the nine Aubert portraits. This physical urgency of being literally in the face of the sitter creates a sense of impolite proximity or aggressiveness. We are simply too close to the sitter for comfort. This confrontational quality to the Aubert portraits brings us to two other passages about them that are important to understanding the paintings. One of these is another passage from a letter written by Valabrègue to Zola, but one routinely neglected in the considerable bibliography devoted to the early portraits. This passage, quoted in Dorival's monograph of 1948, is as essential to understanding these portraits as is that dealing with speed and modeling: "Paul is a terrible painter for the attitudes he makes his sitters take in the midst of a debauch of color. Every time he paints one of his friends, he seems to be taking revenge on him for some hidden insult."[7] This notion of the paintings as both physically and psychically aggressive is somewhat more difficult for us to understand after the onslaught of similarly violent portraits that litter the history of twentieth-century art (perhaps the most recent examples of portraits by Francis Bacon, Leon Kossoff, and Lucian Freud serve as the best comparisons). Yet, in the mid-1860s, such pictorial behavior was aberrant and even dangerous, and the fact that Cézanne performed these pictorial transgressions on his friends and family, as Valabrègue points out, makes their lack of social decorum even more extreme.

The second passage can be found in a letter from Cézanne's painter-friend Antoine Guillemet to the Puerto Rican painter Francisco Oller, who was, himself, a good friend of Camille Pissarro and, by association, Cézanne. In the letter from 1866, Guillemet places Cézanne in a vanguard lineage similar to that discussed above, but more powerfully expressed: "Courbet becomes a classic [in the face of the new Cézannes]. He's done some superb things, next to Manet he is traditional, and Manet will one day seem so in turn next to Cézanne. . . . Today's gods will not be tomorrow's. To arms! Let our febrile hands seize hold of the knife of insurrection, let's tear down and rebuild. . . . Paint with heavy impasto and dance on the belly of the terrified bourgeois."[8] This passage, written the year after the anarchist philosopher Pierre-Joseph Proudhon's powerful book, *De l'art et de sa destination sociale* was published, makes us realize that the way Cézanne chose to paint his uncle was socially transgressive and, more important, antibourgeois. As Valabrègue himself said, Cézanne's pictorial practice was itself aggressive, and its victims were the painter's own friends and family members.

The Dominique Aubert who emerges from the Norton Simon portrait is a man who, though respectably dressed and posed for representation, possesses a troubling physicality and proximity. He is decidedly not a Parisian, as he lacks refinement and presents an air of darkness and crudity popularly associated with Provence. He is also utterly alone, with no props or setting to mitigate the sheer strength of his presence. In this, he is representationally the opposite of the photographic portraits of the period with their curtains, plants, views, and details of costume. One wonders why this evidently good-natured man posed so often and so willingly for his nephew and what he thought of Guillemet's interpretations of the paintings still wet on the canvas? One might say, on the basis of negative evidence, that he avoided any chance of representation later in his life, bowing out, like Cézanne's father, of the painter's cadre of models shortly after making his appearance on the scene. There are no later portraits of Dominique Aubert, and, hence, no chance for us to measure changes in his appearance and in his relationship with his nephew. Perhaps he too became discouraged by the fact that Cézanne's career sputtered even before it started, as he was rejected time and again from the Salon, even with his portraits (the somewhat earlier portrait of Valabrègue was rejected from the Salon of 1866 over the protests of Charles-François Daubigny).

It is fascinating, too, that only one of the nine Aubert portraits was kept by the sitter, and this is the strangely unportraitlike caprice in which Cézanne represented his uncle "Dominique" as a "Dominican" monk (fig. 79a). All the others remained with the painter and were purchased late in his lifetime by his dealer, Ambroise Vollard. Of these, seven entered the single greatest collection of works by Cézanne in history, that of Auguste Pellerin, whose heirs sold them over time. Five of the nine can be found today in public institutions: the Metropolitan Museum of Art has two and there is one each in the Musée d'Orsay, the Fitzwilliam, and the Norton Simon. The portrait in the Reinhardt Foundation, formerly owned by Monet, is not acceptable as a part of the group (see n. 1).

The Norton Simon version is remarkably well preserved. Although it was lined, probably early in the twentieth century, this was surely done to provide a more secure backing for the heavy paint resting on its surface. It may even be that the diagonal cracks in the lower left and upper right corners were from diagonal braces in a homemade stretcher used by Cézanne when he painted. It is, in light of this, fascinating to speculate on the manner in which these works were painted. Certain artists who look at the canvas today refuse to believe that it was painted vertically (that is, on the easel). These observers maintain that the sheer weight and viscosity of Cézanne's pigments would have forced the strokes to "sink" on an easel, suggesting that these canvases may have been among the first in the history of art to have been painted on a table or other horizontal surface. This seemingly trivial detail of a painting's construction is, in the end, more important than it at first seems. A painting when constructed on a table is no longer the window onto the world that it had been for centuries in Western pictorial theory.

1 Rewald, 1966, vol. 1, nos. 102–109 and 111. A putative tenth, Rewald 110, in the Oscar Reinhardt Foundation in Winterthur, does appear to represent Dominique Aubert, but it is decidedly different in both style and attitude and may have been painted later.
2 Rewald, 1996, vol. 1, p. 100.
3 Barnes, 1939, p. 74.
4 Dorival, 1948, p. 25.
5 Dorival, 1948, p. 25.
6 In Cachin et al., 1996, p. 88.
7 Valabrègue to Zola, 1866, in Dorival, 1948, p. 138.
8 Guillemet to Oller, 12 September 1866, in Ponce Art Museum, 1983, p. 227.

80

Paul Cézanne
French 1839–1906

Vase of Flowers
1880–1881

Oil on canvas, $18\frac{1}{2} \times 21\frac{3}{4}$ in. (47×55.2 cm)
F.1968.1

Provenance: The artist; sold c. 1896 to; [Ambroise Vollard, Paris, sold c. 1910 to]; Andries Bonger (1861–1934), Amsterdam, by inheritance to; Mrs. Andries Bonger, Almen, the Netherlands, sold 1966 to; [Walter Feilchenfeldt, Zurich, sold 16 March 1967 to]; [Paul Rosenberg & Co., New York, stock no. 6264, sold 14 December 1967 to]; The Norton Simon Foundation (sale, New York, Christie's, 19 May 1982, lot 23, unsold).

Exhibitions: Cologne, 1912, no. 134; Berkeley, 1970, no. 273; San Francisco, 1973, no. 43, ill.

References: Venturi, 1936, vol. 1, no. 358, vol. 2, pl. 98, no. 358; Rewald, 1956, pp. 96–97 n. 36; Gowing, 1956, p. 188; Orienti and Picon, 1970, no. 487, ill. p. 109; Rishel, 1983, p. 17, fig. 8a; Benjamin, 1989, pp. 191–193, fig. 54; Homburg, 1992, pp. 135–137; Homburg, 1996, pp. 122, 149 n. 385, fig. 75; Rewald, 1996, vol. 1, no. 478, vol. 2, p. 153, ill.; Cachin et al., 1996, p. 573.

Technical Notes: The primary support is a loose-weave canvas in a standard size 10 (55 × 46 cm), available from artists' suppliers. It was prepared with a thin white ground that does not mask the rather grainy canvas texture, a type of support Cézanne often chose.[1] It has been glue-lined with the original tacking edges cut off; the stretcher probably dates from this lining. X-radiography reveals a small, thin tear in the canvas at the upper left. Additional small, very minor damages are a small gouge at the bottom left and two small tears at the center left. Painted directly on the white ground, the painting is composed of greens, mauve, pink, lavender, purple, and blue, with a touch of complementary orange at the top center flower and the bottom in the vase. The ground was left exposed around the flowers and at the bottom on either side of the vase; it is partially visible through the sketchy brushwork of the background, providing a slightly luminous effect. The background was painted last, as observed at the outer contours of the flowers. Thickly painted shadows within the bouquet are deep blue. Paint was applied wet into wet, with colors often mixed on the palette. The paint exhibits tiny hairline cracks throughout. It is generally well preserved, with no evidence of previous interventions other than the lining, which has smoothed the paint profile. A few tiny losses of paint and ground are associated with the above-mentioned damages. A small tear at the upper left has been retouched. It is possible that the painting was left unvarnished by Cézanne and not varnished until it was lined; the present varnish has no discoloration. (RW)

Cézanne painted a small group of floral still-life paintings in 1876–1877, two of which he included among the sixteen pictures he submitted to the second exhibition of his work in the third group exhibition of the Impressionists, held in rented rooms in Paris in the spring of 1877. Though modest in number, this pair of paintings was part of a small series of floral still lifes that ended only a few years before Cézanne's death, when he wrote several letters to his dealer Ambroise Vollard about a painting of flowers that he had been working on for months and finally dropped after more than a year in January 1903.[2] To this, one might add the wonderfully naïve flowers in his earliest decorative painting, made in 1860 and 1861 for the Jas de Bouffan. And there are also several potted flowering plants that make their appearance in still lifes with fruits and flowers that owe their aesthetic impetus to the St.-Pélagie still lifes of Courbet (see cat. 46). But, in thinking about these paintings as somehow essential to Cézanne, we must remember that they number only 34 in a surviving oeuvre of 954 paintings.

It is, however, no accident that, of the four paintings by Cézanne in the Norton Simon collections, two are floral still lifes. Mr. Simon's interest in this type of painting extended throughout the history of the European easel picture, making it possible while touring the Norton Simon Museum to find a flower painting or two in virtually every gallery. There are several reasons for this. First is the obvious sensuality of flower paintings, which, minor as they are in terms of the ambitions of the great artist, address fundamental issues of color harmony and balance. Even theorists of the art museum in eighteenth-century France compared the arrangement of paintings on a gallery wall to the positioning of flowers in a garden bed, and similar connections between paintings and flowers could extend for pages.[3]

This floral still life by Cézanne is part of a small group of paintings—still lifes, urban views, and portraits—made in the artist's apartment at 32, rue de l'Ouest in the Montparnasse section of Paris. Cézanne had already made a large number of still-life paintings from 1877 to 1879 on that street at number 67, but the wallpaper in the room in which he painted there is clearly different from that in the Norton Simon and other paintings from 1880 until he moved again in 1882. The strongest representations of this wallpaper can be found in *Fruits, Napkin, and Milk Jar* (fig. 80a) and *Self-Portrait* (fig. 80b).

How fascinating it is, therefore, to compare Cézanne's treatment of that wallpaper in those two paintings with the same paper in the present floral still life. The other still life seems most obsessed with getting it right, because Cézanne represents all aspects of the paper—its strong

Fig. 80a (*right*) Paul Cézanne, *Fruits, Napkin, and Milk Jar*, 1880–1881, oil on canvas, $23\frac{5}{8} \times 28\frac{3}{4}$ in. (60 × 73 cm), Musée de l'Orangerie, Paris; photo: Erich Lessing / Art Resource, NY

Fig. 80b (*far right*) Paul Cézanne, *Self-Portrait*, 1880–1881, oil on canvas, $13\frac{1}{4} \times 10\frac{1}{4}$ in. (33.6 × 26 cm), The National Gallery, London

Fig. 80c (*below*) Paul Cézanne, *Flowers in a Red Vase*, 1880–1881, oil on canvas, $18\frac{1}{4} \times 21\frac{7}{8}$ in. (46.3 × 55.5 cm), private collection; photo: Christie's Images

diagonal diamonds, its floating central star, and its corner diamonds. In the *Self-Portrait*, he pulls the diamonds apart, pushing them across the surface at will, and completely omits the central stars. The Norton Simon still life takes the opposite tack, reducing the diamonds to two lines in the upper left of the composition and completely omitting the corner diamonds that are such an important feature of the London self-portrait. Only the central stars remain, and these are placed irregularly across the surface so that they play roles determined more by the colors and characters of the flowers and the vase than by the dictates of their own regularity. So much for truth to appearances.

The multicolored, multispecie nature of this arrangement of flowers links this painting of them to other works made by the artist in 1876–1877 and to an undated floral still life Camille Pissarro painted about 1877–1878. The decision to paint the same bouquet more than once enabled Cézanne to use a range of colors and to study the relationship between discrete touches of

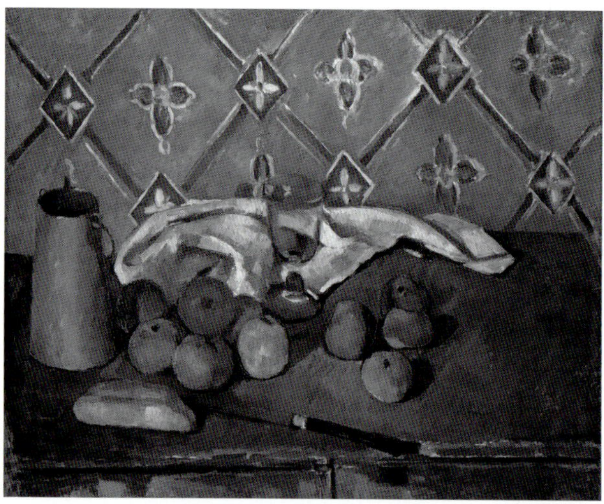

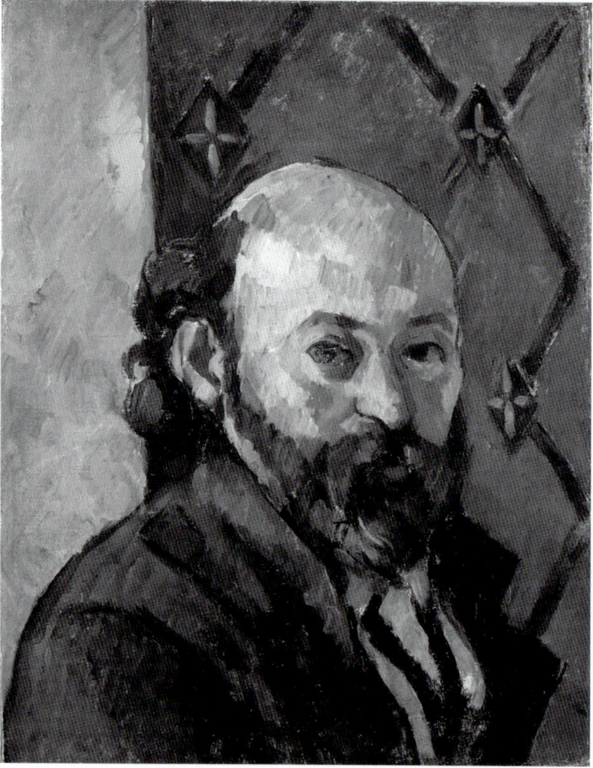

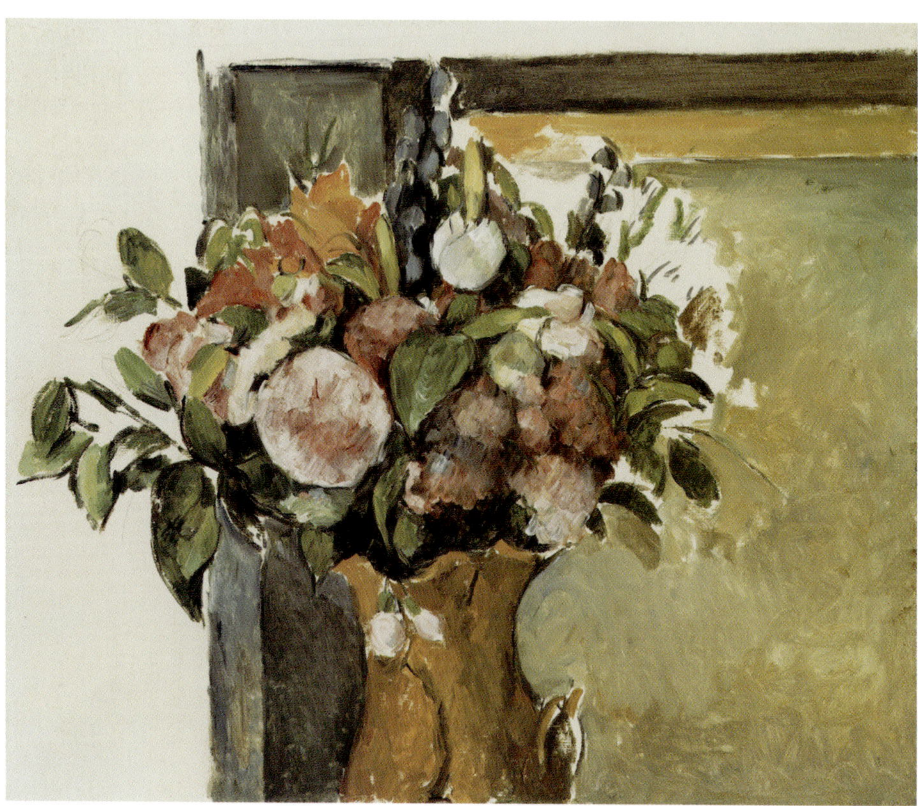

paint and the petals or leaves of the observed bouquet. In painting the Norton Simon flowers, he selected a vase that has been inexplicably called Rococo,[4] but which is a relatively simple pitcher rather than a vase. In fact, he painted the arrangement twice—once, in the Norton Simon painting, while the flowers sat on a table or chest, and a second time (fig. 80c), where they appear to be on the floor seen against a piece of furniture or a fireplace. These works were painted on canvases of identical dimensions, clearly as a way for the painter to study the effects of varying light and background on a single subject. It is even possible that, as he painted throughout

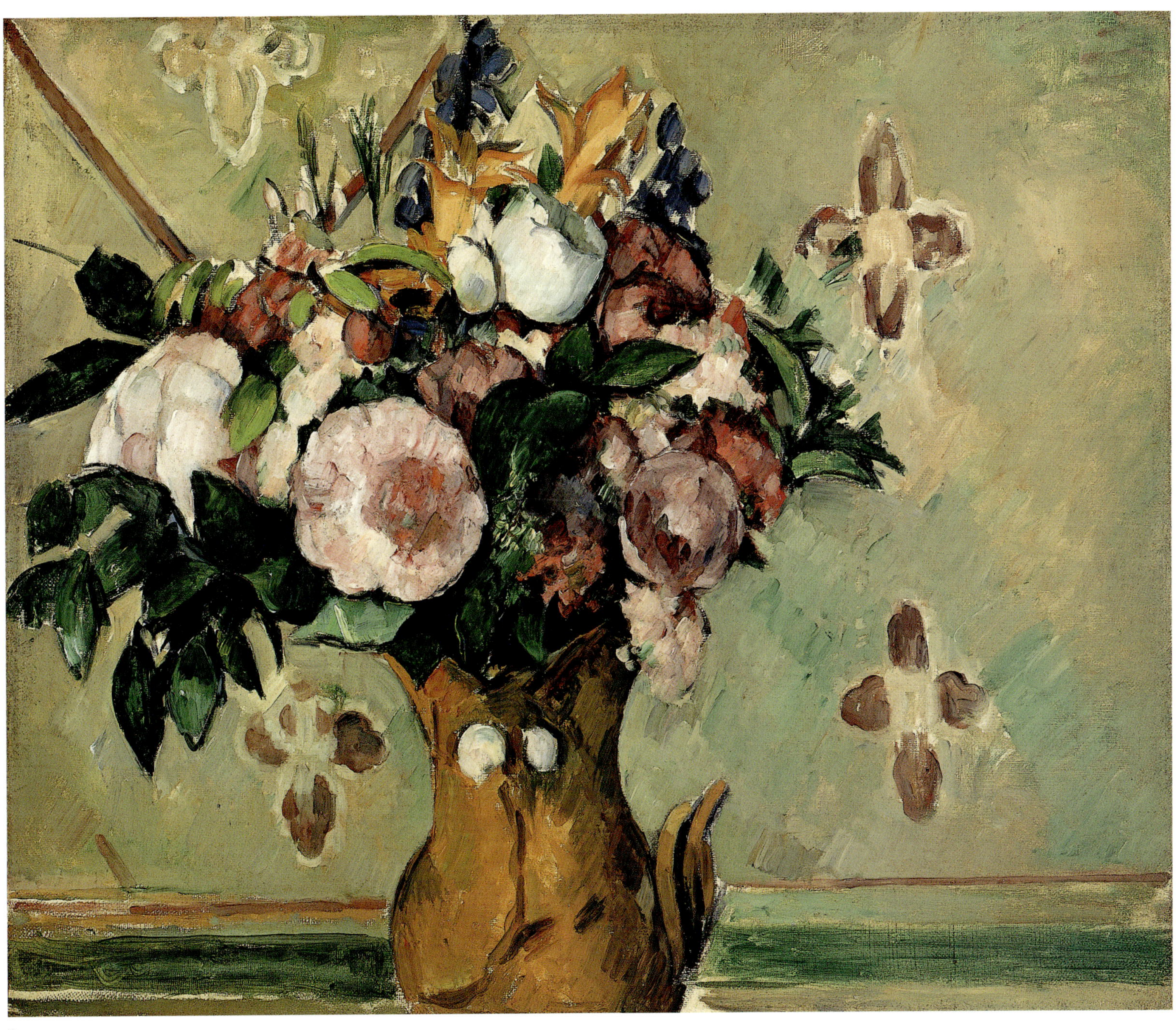

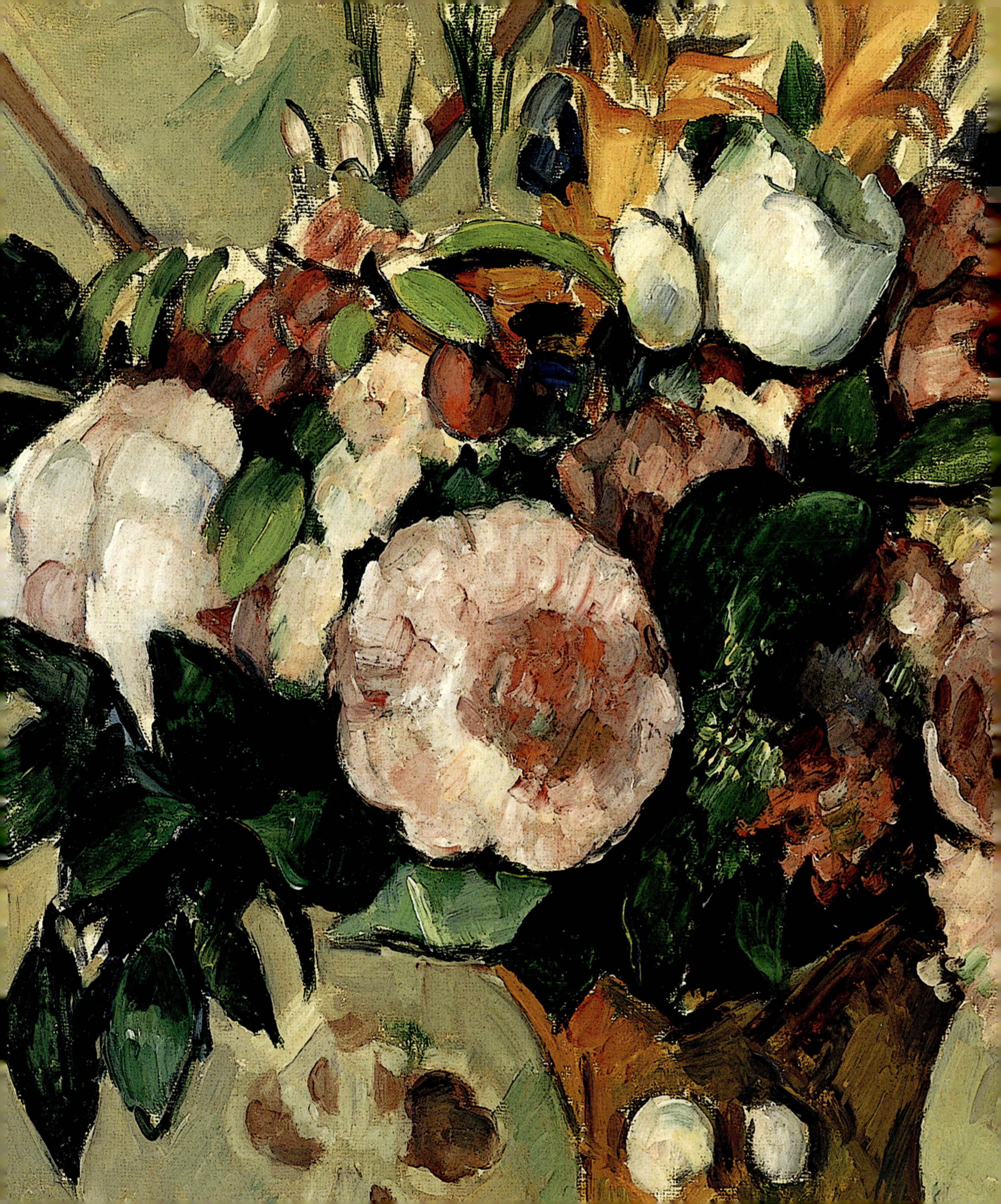

the day, Cézanne shifted the position of the vase of flowers so as to catch light as it moved through the room that he used as a temporary Parisian studio. This explanation is perhaps the answer to the quandary about the status of the two paintings evoked by Joseph Rishel in an eloquent catalogue entry on *Flowers in a Red Vase* (fig. 80c).[5] Rishel noted the comparative rarity of such compositional pairings in Cézanne's oeuvre and flirted briefly with the idea that the less finished still life might have served as a study for the Norton Simon work. In all probability, the two works were made simultaneously rather than sequentially, with Cézanne choosing to work more concertedly on the Norton Simon canvas.

The most unusual—even remarkable—aspect of the present still life and its pair is that each represents a vertical subject on a horizontal canvas. Indeed, when looking quickly at the Norton Simon painting, certain observers have even felt that it must be a fragment of a once-larger canvas. There are several reasons why this is not so. First, it is painted on a canvas of a standard size. Second, its pair is virtually identically composed with similar cropping. Third, although the canvas has been lined, X-rays reveal convincing evidence of cusping on all four edges, making it completely clear that the canvas retains its original dimensions.

Although Cézanne most often used traditional formats for his paintings, retaining vertical formats for portraits, certain figure studies, and floral still lifes and horizontal ones for landscapes, genre scenes, and tabletop still lifes, he is known to have broken those conventions on occasion. Two wonderful portraits of his wife and son respectively painted in the late 1870s[6] present the sitters' heads and shoulders on horizontal canvases and study the relationships between the heads and the contours of a large red armchair. And Cézanne had already painted a vertical floral still life on a horizontal canvas in 1876–1877.[7]

Yet none of these precedents really prepares us for the compositional originality of the present still life. Because the wall behind the vase of flowers is strictly parallel to the picture plane and because the table or chest on which the vase is placed is completely horizontal, Cézanne sets up the painting almost as a visual chess game of moves of color, shape, and texture along a pictorial surface that is, in almost all senses, rendered as flat. The pictorial tensions prompted by this decision are enhanced by Cézanne's decision to crop the vase in an almost photographic manner at the base and by its asymmetrical positioning left of center. The massing of the arrangement, too, veers left, forcing Cézanne to balance the composition through the placement of the two disembodied wallpaper stars on the right. He also establishes a secondary diagonal grid with the wallpaper diamond in the upper left. This is subtly balanced through the application of the paint in diagonal bands related to the diamonds on the right side of the composition. Cézanne chose to use strong colors boldly, deliberately placing them to enhance chromatic difference through contrasts of hue and value. He also painted the flowers in such a way that it is difficult to determine their specie. Is the central flower a rose, a peony, or a large chrysanthemum? Are the spiky yellow-orange flowers at the top too small to be the daylilies they resemble? The questions could go on.

In its studied contrast between orthogonal and diagonal, between thick and thin paint, between hard and soft, warm and cool, flat and volumetric, this small painting is an eloquent formal study using a vase and some flowers as a pretext for painting. Its assurance is so total that it immediately appealed to Cézanne's most important and faithful dealer, Ambroise Vollard, who purchased it from the artist in 1896, only to sell it fourteen years later to the Dutch collector of modern French art Andries Bonger. Through Bonger, the shy Symbolist from Bordeaux, Odilon Redon, learned of the existence of the painting and copied it. Fortunately, this copy (cat. 83) entered the Norton Simon collection as a gift of Mr. Simon's friend Mr. Neison Harris of Chicago.

1 Callen, 2000, pp. 33–34, 36–37, states that Cézanne used the cheaper weight *étude* canvas, until his father died in 1880, whereupon he was able to buy better quality canvases. Still, he continued to use the *étude* and was nearly the only painter who seems to have regularly chosen it.

2 Rewald, 1986a, p. 251.

3 Michel Faré, *La Nature morte en France*, Geneva, 1962.

4 Rishel, 1983, p. 17.

5 Rishel, 1983, p. 17.

6 Rewald, 1996, vol. 1, nos. 387 and 465.

7 Rewald, 1996, vol. 1, no. 314.

81

Paul Cézanne
French, 1839–1906

Farmhouse and Chestnut Trees at Jas de Bouffan
1884–1885

Oil on canvas, $36\frac{1}{8} \times 28\frac{11}{16}$ in. (91.8 × 72.9 cm)
M.1995.1

Provenance: The artist; gift to; Fannie Toure (a servant at Jas de Bouffan), until 1943 to; private collection, Hyères (woman who cared for Mme Toure in her old age); ?private collection, Paris; Chadourne, Paris, sold 1 April 1950 to; [Paul Rosenberg & Co., New York, stock no. 5382-901, sold 1 October 1957 to]; Robert Ellis Simon, bequest 1969 to; The Norton Simon Foundation, transferred 1995 to; Norton Simon Art Foundation.

Exhibitions: Los Angeles, 1965; San Francisco, 1973, no. 44, ill.

References: Rewald, 1939, pl. 60; Rewald, 1948a, pl. 60; Rewald, 1948b, no. 45, p. x, ill.; Rewald, 1950, no. 45, p. x, ill.; Auzas, 1950, pl. XII; Venturi, 1951, p. 47, pl. XIV, fig. 51; Sargeant, 1952, p. 83, color ill.; Rewald, 1968, fig. 57; Orienti and Picon, 1975, p. 124; Steadman, 1976, p. 223; Rewald, 1986a, p. 14; Rewald, 1996, vol. 1, no. 595, vol. 2, p. 198, ill.; Cachin et al., 1996, p. 579; Feilchenfeldt, 2006, pp. 198, ill., 199; Conisbee and Coutagne, 2006, p. 88, fig. 13.

Technical Notes: Cézanne used inexpensive ecru canvas for this picture. A thick and light-toned ground, possibly applied by the artist, covers a thin, commercially applied, off-white ground. Though tacking edges no longer exist, cusping remains visible along all edges of the painting in the X-ray so that one can with some confidence say that the design dimensions remain intact. The painting was lined to canvas with an aqueous adhesive and restretched on a later stretcher. Initially Cézanne seems to have roughly blocked in some of the design with fluid blue paint, but some of these lines such as the parallel and vertical ones at about the center of the picture do not seem to have much to do with the composition. The artist made only minor changes. Colors, though limited to green, ocher, and blue (including gray-blue), achieve a greater range by virtue of density, consistency, and application (wet in wet or wet over dry) and type of stroke. As is typical with the ecru canvas, the ground here developed a fine crackle pattern following the open canvas weave. These cracks have now darkened and transferred to the thinner paints on the surface. The X-radiograph shows three losses of canvas (repaired with inserts) along the upper part of the work, and tears that measure anywhere from about 1 to 3 inches in length. Only limited surface abrasion exists. A sprayed synthetic varnish inappropriate for the painting and now gray and dirty covers the surface. (JF)

This large and imposing landscape is one of many painted by Cézanne on the estate owned by his father outside Aix-en-Provence. Called the Jas de Bouffan (House of the Winds), the property surrounded a large eighteenth-century house at the end of a long allée of mature chestnut trees. Adjacent to the main formal house was a group of lower farm buildings and sheds that also served as subsidiary spaces for the house itself. Cézanne was attracted to vernacular rural architecture in both Provence and the north of France. These buildings, with their irregular contours, sagging roofs, and mismatched openings, seem to elude any precise sense of historical time, giving an air of timelessness to the landscapes in which they are set, making them the opposite of the utterly contemporary or modern landscapes painted by Cézanne's fellow Impressionists in the suburbs and watering holes outside Paris. *La France profonde* is the subject of Cézanne's deeply classical pictorial world, whether in the north or in the south.

Cézanne's attitude toward the Jas de Bouffan was conflicted throughout his life, largely because it was the property of a father from whom he was forced, at first, to conceal his long-term relationship with Hortense Fiquet and the existence of their son, Paul, born in Paris in 1872. Cézanne's father discovered the alliance early in 1878 by opening a letter addressed to his son, a letter that mentioned "Mme Cézanne and little Paul." He completely refused to endorse the alliance and essentially forbad the normalizing of relations, threatening to cut off Cézanne's allowance and even to disinherit his son. Although Cézanne himself could visit his parents at the Jas de Bouffan between 1878 and some months before his father's death in 1886, he could not bring Hortense or young Paul, who stayed in Paris or were forced, when in Provence, to live in Marseille or in a small house owned by Cézanne's mother (who knew about the liaison and the child) in distant L'Estaque on the coast. The psychic tensions that this continuation of childhood had for Cézanne when he stayed at the house of his father cannot be exaggerated, and they clearly affected his paintings of his father's prized property.

Why, we must ask, did Cézanne paint this property scores of times in the 1880s, before himself assuming control of it at his father's death in October 1886? When there, he was forced to play the role of dutiful son, never mentioning his common-law wife and son in his father's presence. Was it simply a matter of ease and convenience for Cézanne to take his easel and paint supplies outside the house into the gardens and fields surrounding it? Or could one say that his numerous representations of the outbuildings and trees around the house constitute an

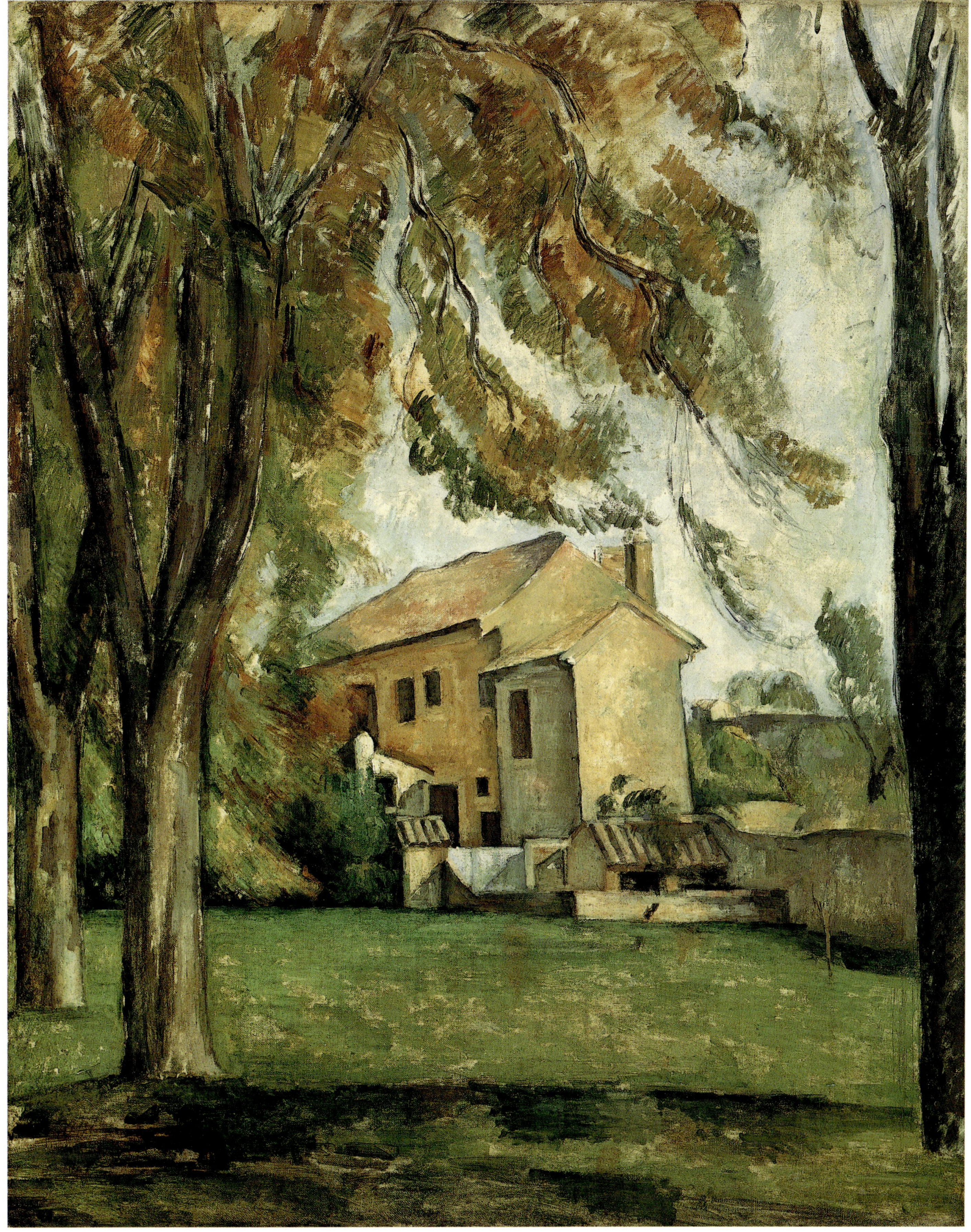

81

avoidance of the Jas itself, which is, in most cases, notable for its absence? Even in the present picture, the large house would have fallen within the visual field of the painting, but was deliberately screened by the chestnut trees whose gesticulating branches fill the left side of the composition and the sky.

John Rewald, the most patient and persistent scholar of Cézanne in the last century, learned of the existence of this painting only in the late 1940s, when it emerged from total obscurity in a private Provençal collection. Completely unknown to Lionello Venturi, the first cataloguer (1936) of Cézanne's paintings, it is both autograph and important, and Rewald proved that the work had been given by Cézanne to Fannie Toure, known as a servant at the Jas de Bouffan. Mlle Toure kept the painting until her death in 1943, leaving it to a caregiver. Rewald had published a photograph of it in 1948, and it emerged on the larger market in 1950. Fannie Toure's identity and history were published only in 1996 in an entry prepared by Rewald.[1] In this entry, Rewald recounts a tale obviously told to him either by Mlle Toure herself or the caregiver (no source is cited) that links the gift of the painting to the cholera epidemic in Marseille in the summer of 1884 (June through October, according to Rewald). Apparently, Mlle Toure's family insisted that she return home to escape contagion, and Cézanne gave the picture to her at that time. This enabled Rewald to date the painting to the early part of 1884.

While fascinating and at least partially believable, this story raises more questions than it answers. First of all, it is the clear record of a gift, very rare in Cézanne's practice and the only one recorded to a family servant in his life. Cézanne is known to have given works to friends like Camille Pissarro and Joachim Gasquet, but these gifts are so rare that this one must be considered exceptional. Why, we must ask, did Cézanne make this unusual gift and, as a corollary question, why this particular painting? Cézanne included the farm buildings that feature as the central motif of the Norton Simon canvas in six paintings that are datable to the mid-1880s (figs. 81a and 81b) and four others,[2] and two of these[3] are as large and finished as the one he gave to Mlle Toure. Yet none of these paintings treats the farm buildings as the central element of the composition as they clearly are in the present canvas. In all other cases, they are shown on one side or the other of a composition in which they are balanced by trees or by the towering facade of the main house. Also, as Rewald pointed out, the present painting is the only representation of the farm buildings on a

Fig. 81a (*below left*) Paul Cézanne, *Chestnut Trees at Jas de Bouffan in Winter*, c. 1885–1886, oil on canvas, $28\frac{7}{8} \times 36\frac{3}{8}$ in. (73.3 × 92.5 cm), The Minneapolis Institute of Arts, The William Hood Dunwoody Fund

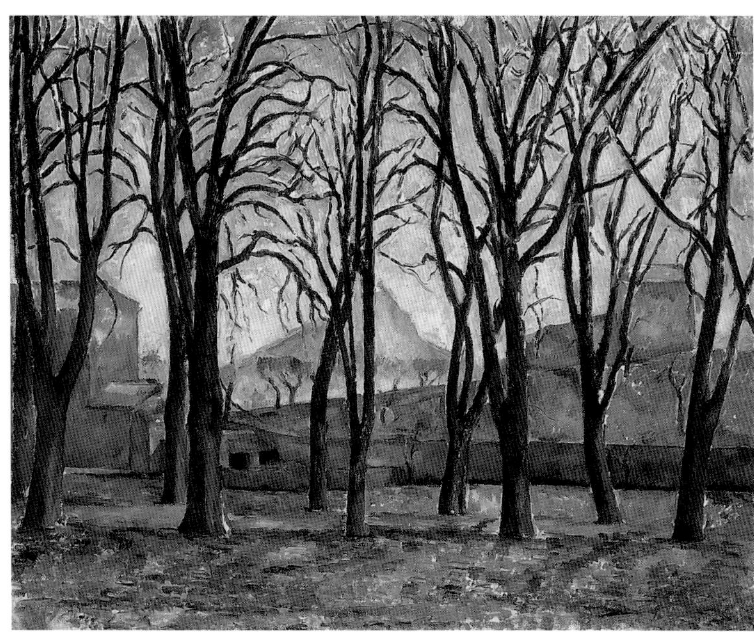

Fig. 81b (*below right*) Paul Cézanne, *Farm of Jas de Bouffan*, 1887, oil on canvas, $23 \times 28\frac{3}{8}$ in. (58.5 × 72 cm), The Barnes Foundation, Merion, Pa., BF 188; © Reproduced with the Permission of The Barnes Foundation™ All Rights Reserved

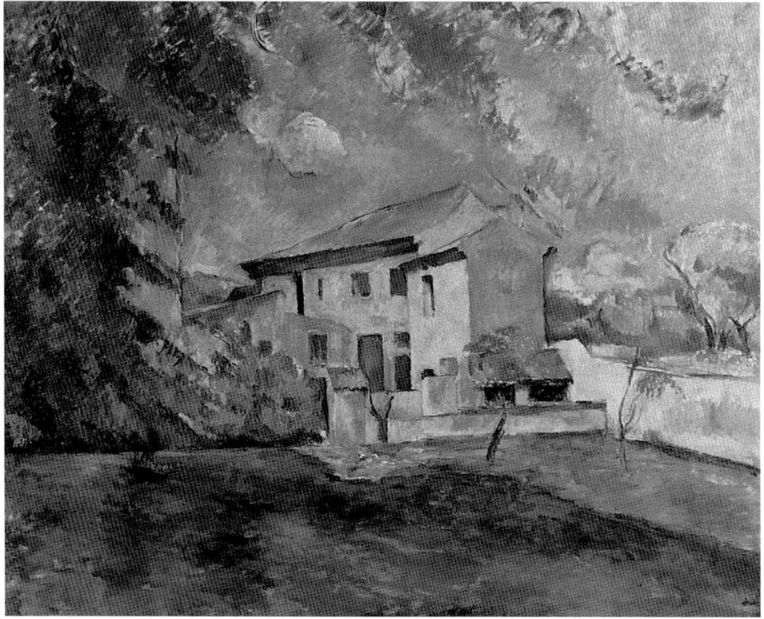

Fig. 81c Paul Cézanne, *Mont Sainte-Victoire with the Large Pine*, c. 1887, oil on canvas, 26 × $35\frac{1}{2}$ in. (66 × 90 cm), The Samuel Courtauld Trust, Courtauld Institute of Art Gallery, London

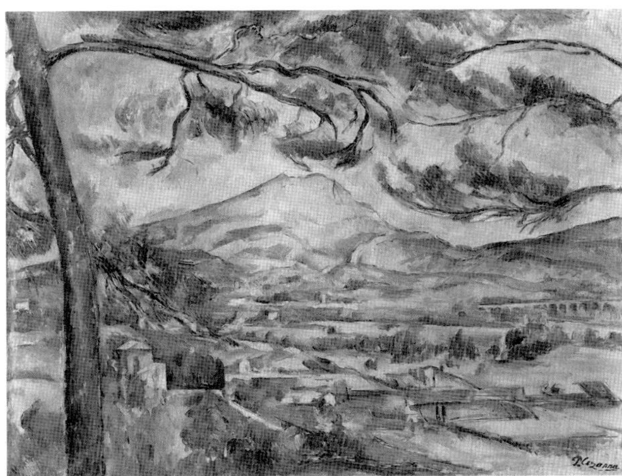

vertically oriented (or "portrait") canvas, making it still more unusual and linking it to a small group of paintings made in Gardanne in 1885–1886 and in L'Estaque and Aix in the mid-1880s.

When we look at these seven paintings in the context of Cézanne's other works from the 1880s, it is difficult to place the Norton Simon canvas as early in the sequence as its presumed date of early 1884 would indicate. If it could be conclusively proven that the gift of this painting was made in 1884, it would provide an anchor for a systematic redating of many other canvases. In fact, Rewald himself dated the painting to 1885 when he first published it in 1948, and, when he worked at the maddening task of putting Cézanne's undated paintings in a reliable sequence for the 1996 catalogue raisonné (a task at which he, like all others, failed), he noted through placement the relation between the distinctly gestural foliage in the sky of this work and that in two famous paintings of the Mont St.-Victoire at the Courtauld Institute (fig. 81c) and the Phillips Collection, Washington, D.C., respectively. These have always been dated to the later 1880s, generally to 1886–1887, and share remarkable similarities in facture with the Norton Simon painting. All are decidedly different from two earlier representations of the same motif,[4] datable to the early part of the decade. When, therefore, was the Norton Simon painting made?

There is plausible circumstantial evidence to link the painting to Cézanne's life even more closely than Rewald has yet done. Biographers of Cézanne, following the lead of Rewald himself, have long known of an emotionally tumultuous love affair that Cézanne had in 1885, the existence of which can be gleaned from veiled references in several letters that Cézanne wrote to Émile Zola in the spring and summer of that year. None of the letters gives any hint of the identity of Cézanne's lover, and the painter himself was forced to spend a good deal of time with Hortense Fiquet and his son in the midst of his romantic suffering for another woman during the summer of 1885. One letter actually asks Zola to act as a go-between for Cézanne, suggesting that the writer send letters (now lost, unfortunately) to the woman, who, thus, must not have been in Aix. Was Fannie Toure Cézanne's lover? Was she forced to leave Aix for reasons perhaps completely unconnected to the cholera epidemic? Did Cézanne make this unique gift of a painting as a record of their emotional union?

The answer is mostly likely yes to all these questions. Cézanne's life in the spring of 1885 was turned completely upside down both physically and emotionally. In March he contracted a painful—and probably psychosomatic—case of neuralgia, forcing him virtually to stop work. The letters to Zola make it clear that the woman who incited his passion was not in Aix-en-Provence, at least not in the spring of 1885. Had Fannie Toure been forced to leave by her family, as Rewald tells us? Did Cézanne give her the painting and then find himself so lost and emotionally wrought that he was forced to think about his commitment to his common-law wife in the face of his passion for another, younger, woman? Clearly we cannot answer these questions without access to Cézanne's letters to the woman, probably destroyed or lost. Yet the sheer fact of this unusual gift as well as its timing in Cézanne's life make it likely that the recipient of the shy painter's obsessive love was none other than Fannie Toure.

If this is the case, then surely the Norton Simon painting represents the place of their meetings or trysts, the ramshackle farm buildings adjacent to the main house. There, perhaps, they could meet privately, away from the prying eyes and ears of the painter's family. Surely, Cézanne's decision to make those buildings the central motif of this painting was both deliberate and related to the desires of the painting's recipient. His farm buildings are framed by the gesturing branches of the chestnut trees, which seem almost to reach out from the sky to touch them. This fascination with painting as touch is as strong here as in any painting from the 1880s, and surely it was not an accident. And, just as surely, the comparative haste of execution, with a relatively straightforward and even lackluster application of greens in the lawns and the extreme simplification of the palette, suggests that Cézanne completed the painting with some speed, choosing the largest size canvas in his arsenal at that point. The foliage and branches of the trees are painted with evident haste, and close examination reveals that Cézanne drew the branches and foliage with brush and blue-gray paint both before and during the process of painting.

Comparing the various versions of these simple buildings in Cézanne's oeuvre of the period reveals that, while he accepted the relative placement and scale of the buildings with some fidelity in all versions, he made subtle, but deliberate, alterations of the size, placement, and location of the windows and doors in the larger of them. In only one of the seven can one find an entrance door accessible to the viewer.[5] And in several others, Cézanne virtually eliminates the openings altogether, stressing the plastic geometries of the building's forms. The Norton Simon and the closely related Barnes (fig. 81b) versions both treat the buildings in real detail, with deeply shaded recesses for the windows and doors and a sense of the buildings' interiors, hence as a place the viewer is encouraged to enter in the mind.

One also wonders, given the emotional importance of this affair to Cézanne in 1884–1885, whether the two versions of *Leda and the Swan*[6] and the mysterious small erotic paintings[7] he painted at about this time could all be expressions of Cézanne's thwarted love affair. How odd it is that the Norton Simon painting, which is so classical and seemingly devoid of such emotions, could open this small chapter in a great painter's emotional life.

1 Rewald, 1996, vol. 1, no. 595, p. 397.
2 Rewald, 1996, nos. 538, 567, 600, and 611.
3 Fig. 81a and Rewald 567.
4 Rewald, 1996, nos. 511 and 512.
5 Rewald, 1996, no. 538.
6 Rewald, 1996, nos. 447 and 590.
7 Rewald, 1996, nos. 591–594.

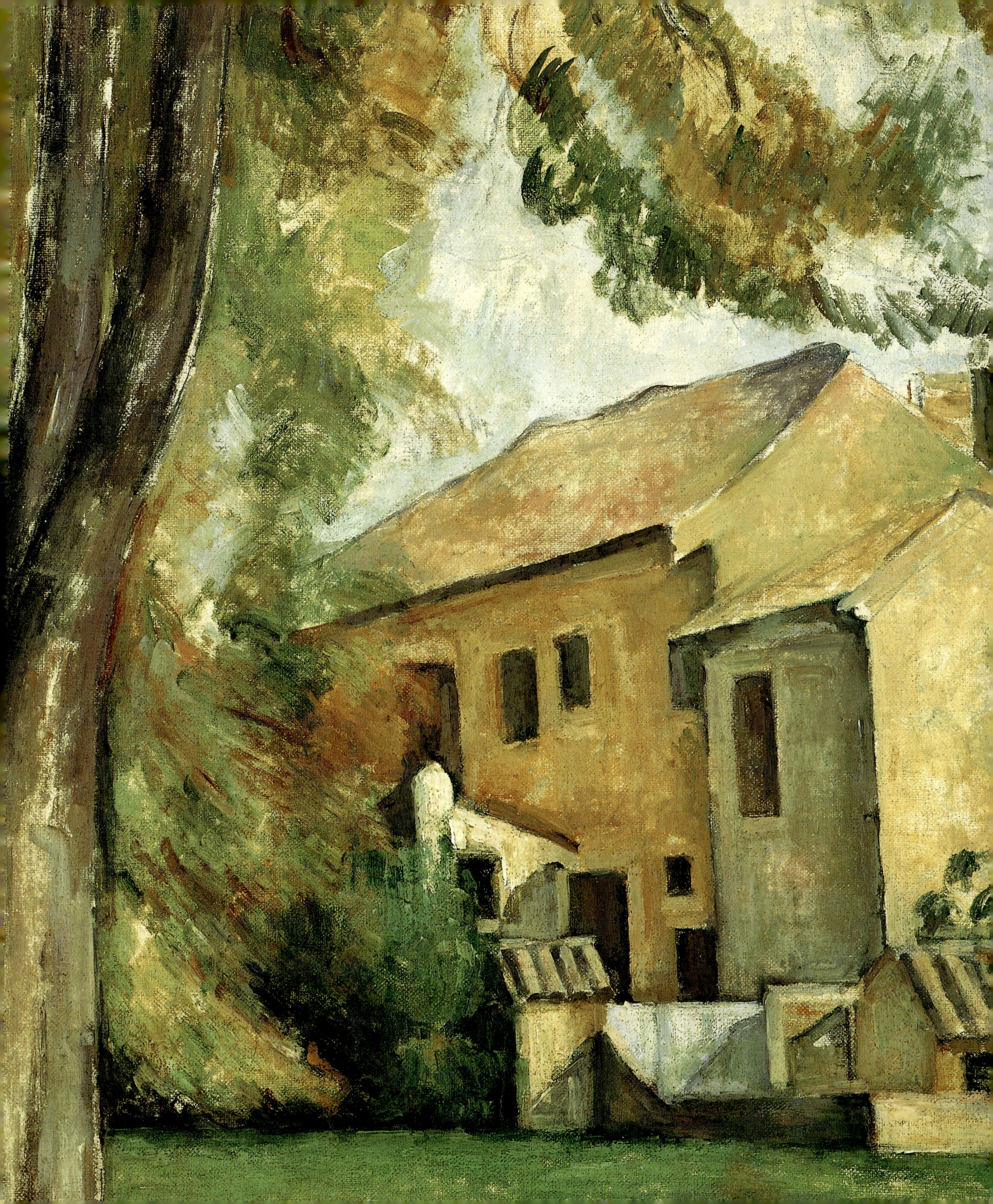

82

Paul Cézanne
French 1839–1906

Tulips in a Vase
1888–1890

Oil on paper, mounted on board, $28\frac{1}{2} \times 16\frac{1}{2}$ in.
(72.4×41.9 cm)
M.1976.12

Provenance: The artist, sold c. 1896 to; [Ambroise Vollard, Paris, stock no. 4040, as *Fleur de lis rouge dans un pot vert quelque fruits à côté*]. Egisto Fabbri, Florence, sold for Ff 3,000 to; [Ambroise Vollard, Paris, stock no. 3365, as *Nature morte, bouquet de tulipes*, by 1904]. [Paul Cassirer, Berlin, in March 1905, to]; Julius Stern, Berlin, by April 1905 (sale, Berlin, Cassirer und Helbing, 22 May 1916, lot 8, ill., as *Rote Tulpen in einem grünen Topf*, to); Sally Falk, Mannheim, sold 11 April 1918 to; [Paul Cassirer, Berlin, sold 20 April 1918 to]; Meta (Mrs. Franz) Schütte, Bremen, still in 1927, by descent to; Mme Irene von Le Suier (née Schütte), Bremen. [Paul Rosenberg, Paris]. Edith Dunn (Mrs. Alfred Chester) Beatty, London, by 1936, by inheritance in 1952 to; Sir Alfred Chester Beatty (1875–1968), London and Dublin, consigned December 1961 to; [Arthur Tooth & Sons, London, sold 15 January 1962 to]; Norton Simon, Los Angeles (sale, New York, Sotheby's, 2 May 1973, lot 8, color ill., to); [Wildenstein & Co., Inc., New York, on behalf of]; Norton Simon, gift 22 December 1976 to; Norton Simon Art Foundation.

Exhibitions: Paris, 1904, no. 30 or 3; Berlin, 1909, no. 28; Cologne, 1912, no. 131; Berlin, 1914b, no. 37, ill.; Paris, 1939a, no. 29, ill.; London, 1939, no. 35, ill.; London, 1946, no. 5; on loan, Dublin, National Gallery of Ireland, September 1954–?; Los Angeles, 1965.

References: E. Bernard, 1908, p. 479, ill.; Meier-Graefe, 1910, p. 75, ill. (1913, p. 73, ill., 1923, p. 77, ill., 1927, p. 356, pl. XLVII); Cézanne, 1912, no. 5, ill.; Vollard, 1914, pl. 45; Meier-Graefe, 1918, p. 142, ill. (3rd ed., 1922, p. 174); Westheim, 1918, p. 234; *Kunst und Künstler*, 1919, p. 203, ill.; Deri, 1919, vol. 1, pp. 197–198, vol. 2, pl. 41 (Berlin, 1920, vol. 1, pp. 197–198, vol. 2, pl. 41; Berlin, 1923, vol. 1, pp. 191–192, vol. 2, pl. 43); Zeisho, 1921, fig. 13; Friedländer, 1922, pp. 229, 40, ill.; Rivière, 1923, p. 73, ill.; Pfister, 1927, fig. 82; Waldmann, 1927, p. 498, ill.; Bertram, 1929, pl. XIX; Fry, 1929, p. 136, ill.; Rivière, 1933, p. 77, ill.; Venturi, 1936, vol. 1, no. 618, vol. 2, pl. 618; Cogniat, 1939, pl. 56; Duret, 1939, p. 167, ill.; Dorival, 1948, pp. 55–56; Orienti and Picon, 1970, no. 825, ill. p. 124; Rewald, 1986a, p. 179, ill.; Kennedy, 1987, p. 51, App. 4; Dorn, Hille, and Kronjäger, 1994, no. 57, pp. 122, 152, 122, ill.; Rewald, 1996, vol. 1, no. 721, vol. 2, p. 249, ill.; Cachin et al., 1996, p. 565 (installation photograph of 1904 Salon d'Automne); Feilchenfeldt, 2006, p. 150, ill.

Technical Notes: The painting was executed on a heavy paper prepared with a white ground, estimated to be a glue/chalk type. Damages to the paper were extensive: a very uneven surface with tears, cracks, ridges, and unexplained depressions, and a horizontal tear at the approximate center from side to side. An early restoration included attachment with glue to a finely woven fabric, then two layers of multiple-ply cardboard, which were mounted on plywood. The unpleasant surface was worsened by a brittle, very yellowed varnish. The date of this restoration is unrecorded, but in 1973 a comprehensive treatment was undertaken. Areas of lifting paint were consolidated, the varnish and old retouches were removed, and old fillings were minimized. The varied supplementary materials from the reverse were removed; the paper was deacidified and adhered to 8-ply rag board, then mounted on a solid panel composed of balsa wood blocks sandwiched between birchwood veneers. In the final phase of restoration, small missing areas of the original paper support were replaced with inlays of paper. After varnishing, the losses were retouched. An earlier condition of flaking left numerous pinpoint losses, many of which are still visible although not conspicuous because of Cézanne's loose paint handling. Overall the treatment was quite successful and normal viewing is not compromised. (RW)

This beautiful floral still life was among thirty-one paintings by Cézanne selected for exhibition at the Salon d'Automne in 1904. This was one of the largest public exhibitions of paintings by Cézanne held during his lifetime, surpassed only by the 1895 and two 1898 exhibitions held at the private Paris gallery of his dealer, Ambroise Vollard. In all these exhibitions, including even the considerably earlier Impressionist exhibition of 1877, Cézanne was represented by a large number of floral still-life paintings. In fact, these constitute a greater proportion of the work he exhibited during his lifetime than they do of his total surviving oeuvre. The reason for this is obvious—marketability. It is easier to imagine a wealthy client purchasing a stylistically radical painting of flowers than a similarly vanguard representation of a human figure or figural group or even a landscape or kitchen still life.

Cézanne had begun painting floral still lifes under the impetus of Camille Pissarro in the 1870s, and the two men worked together, using the same vases and even arrangements during that decade. In the 1880s and early 1890s Cézanne continued practicing this minor genre, usually either in Paris while visiting his wife or on days with inclement weather.[1] Of the fifteen floral still lifes Cézanne painted, *Tulips in a Vase* is dated by most scholars to the latter part of the period and is considered, together with *The Blue Vase* (fig. 82a), his masterpiece of

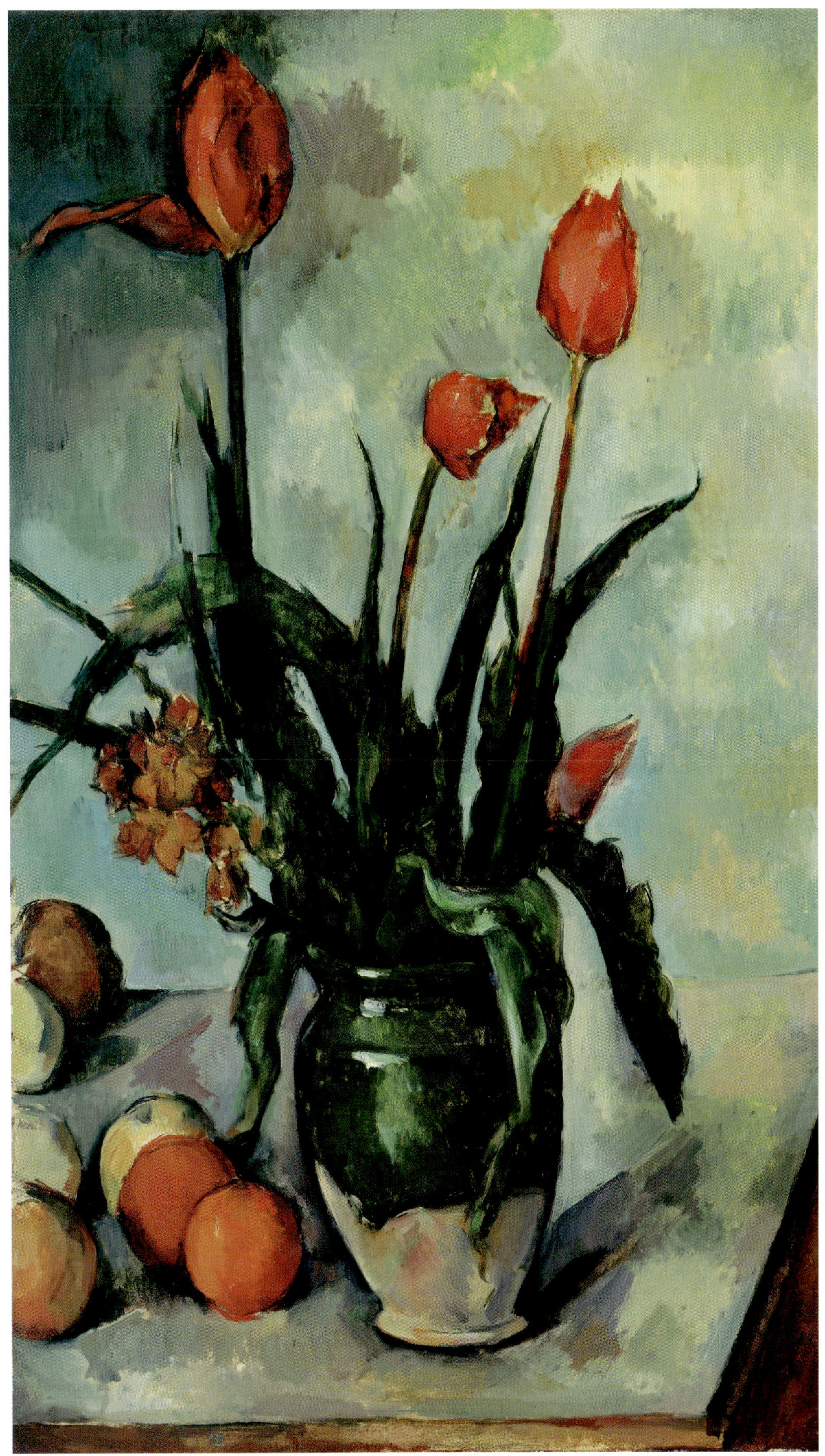

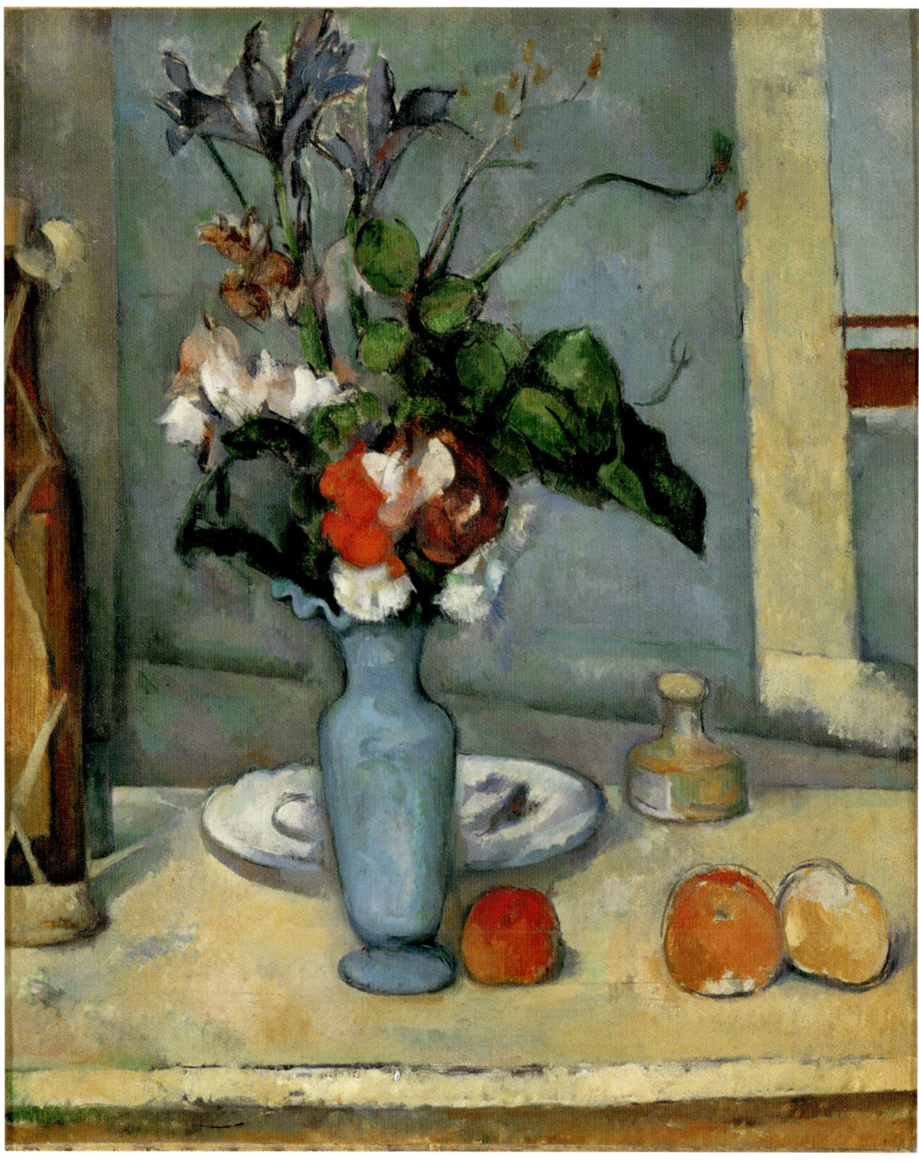

Fig. 82a (*above*) Paul Cézanne, *The Blue Vase*, c. 1889–1890, oil on canvas, $24\frac{3}{8} \times 20\frac{1}{8}$ in. (62 × 51 cm), Musée d'Orsay, Paris; photo: Erich Lessing / Art Resource, NY

floral still life. It is perhaps no accident that these two paintings were both shown in the 1904 Salon d'Automne, an exhibition seen by many future Fauve painters. Both paintings held considerable sway over the pictorial imagination of Henri Matisse, who was simultaneously investigating the color painting of Paul Gauguin, but who painted homages to these two still lifes by Cézanne throughout much of the remainder of his long working life.

Together with another painting of the same arrangement now in the Art Institute of Chicago (fig. 82b), this is Cézanne's only rendition of tulips, the flower associated with both the Netherlands and early spring. Much ink has been spilled on Cézanne's possible use of artificial flowers so that his arrangements could be sustained during the long periods during which he worked on the paintings. Other writers have even interpreted Cézanne's choice of tulips for the Norton Simon and Chicago pictures as an indication of his preference for the almost geometric clarity of their forms and for the fact that they can last in water for a long enough period to be painted. Yet it is clear that, whether he painted flowers from the garden in Provence or from flower shops in Paris, he could easily have obtained fresh blooms and replaced the old ones. And even a superficial examination of the tulips in the Norton Simon work makes clear that, when certain of the blooms were painted, they were considerably past their prime. In fact, the flower that gestures in the upper left corner of the present composition is about to lose one of its petals, suggesting that Cézanne, like many earlier painters of floral still lifes, was interested as much in the theme of death and decay as he was in chromatic beauty.

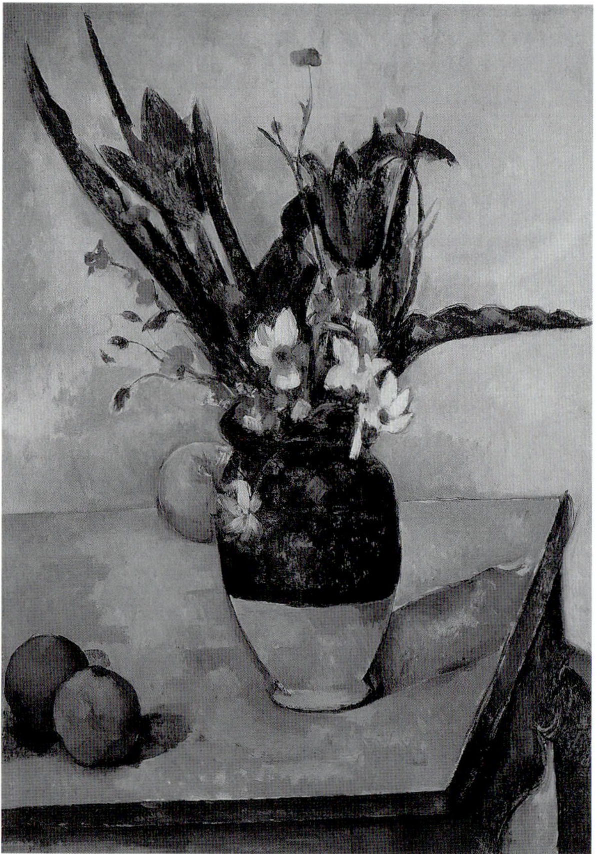

Fig. 82b (*right*) Paul Cézanne, *The Vase of Tulips*, 1890–1892, Oil on canvas, $23\frac{1}{2} \times 16\frac{5}{8}$ in. (59.6 × 42.3 cm), The Art Institute of Chicago, Mr. and Mrs. Lewis Larned Coburn Memorial Collection

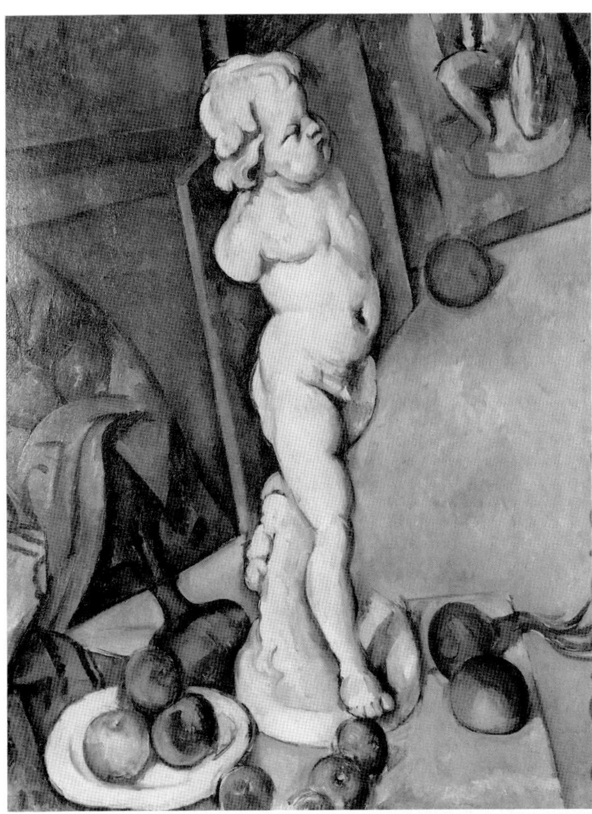

Fig. 82c Paul Cézanne, *Still Life with Plaster Cast*, c. 1894, oil on paper, mounted on board, $27\frac{1}{2} \times 22\frac{1}{2}$ in. (70×57 cm), The Samuel Courtauld Trust, Courtauld Institute of Art Gallery, London

In the last twenty years, scholars working on Cézanne have begun to speculate about his Parisian oeuvre, and certain writers have suggested that many of the floral still lifes, including the famous *Blue Vase*, were painted in Paris, where Cézanne spent considerable periods of time in the 1880s and 1890s. John Rewald even pointed out in his lengthy entry for the Norton Simon still life in the 1996 catalogue raisonné that the evidently Provençal origin of the ceramic olive jar that serves as a vase does not, in itself, mean that the painting was made in Provence. Indeed, we can find this or similar green-glazed olive jars in paintings by Cézanne known to have been painted in Paris or the north of France.

Another clue that might aid us in our speculation about the geographic origins of this still life is the table. Although it is treated generically, the exactly comparable still life in Chicago represents the table in greater detail. It is a rather complex and, for Cézanne, refined pale wood table with a curved skirt and protruding corner legs with pronounced curves. As such, it is decidedly different from the simply made pine and deal tables that are common in Cézanne still lifes and might well have been in Cézanne's wife's rather nice apartment along the quai d'Anjou on the Île-St.-Louis, which the couple rented in 1888 and remained in for many years. The same table appears in four paintings by Cézanne, all of which have been associated with Paris, and all of which were painted in periods when Cézanne worked for long periods of the year in the capital.[2] If this still life was painted in Paris, that fact alone makes it possible to speculate more precisely about its date. Cézanne was in Paris for most of 1888 and the first several months of both 1889 and 1890, when this work was most likely made.

Two remarkable aspects of *Tulips in a Vase* make it unique among his floral still lifes. The first is its extremely long and narrow proportions, which are completely unlike those of any of the many standard sizes of stretched canvases used by Cézanne throughout his life. The second—and related—aspect is that, although it appears to be an oil painting on canvas, it is in fact an oil painting on paper made at a time in Cézanne's life during which he worked extensively in watercolor. To our knowledge, only one other painting on paper by Cézanne is recorded in the literature, the famous *Still Life with Plaster Cast* (fig. 82c). This latter painting is one of the anomalies of the artist's career, and, because of its oddities of composition and meaning, it has one of the longest bibliographies of any Cézanne still life. Because of its relatively straightforward composition and subject matter and its complete absence from exhibitions since 1965, *Tulips in a Vase* has never been treated with comparable depth. Nor has it been technically linked to the Courtauld painting on paper.

As a direct result of their paper supports, these paintings have a surface quality that relates them to Cézanne's watercolors. And, perhaps also because they are on paper, each is an unusual size. In both cases, Cézanne tackled a vertical subject observed in an interior with complex relationships to its background. For the Norton Simon still life, this demanded a format that more closely resembles a Chinese hanging scroll than a Western easel painting. It is highly likely that, rather than ordering a specially made canvas sized to the task at hand, Cézanne opted to cut a large sheet of paper to the exact dimensions that suited him. The ease and convenience of this, together with the fact that he had become accustomed to painting on paper with watercolor, made paper an ideal solution to the formal problems posed by each of these unusual subjects. It is fascinating that, unlike Édouard Manet and Edgar Degas who routinely cut down or added to compositions using a variety of

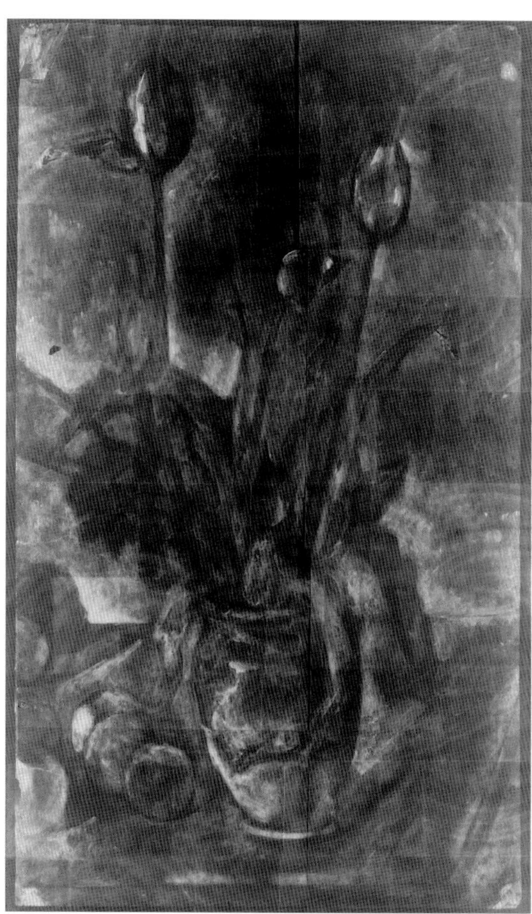

Fig. 82d X-ray photograph of cat. 82

techniques, Cézanne followed the by-then standard Impressionist practice of working on prestretched, presized, and preprimed canvases of standard sizes. This must have been done both because of availability of supplies and for convenience when framing, exhibiting, or selling works.

The Norton Simon still life exhibits several fascinating qualities apart from its size and medium. Chief among these is its chromatic structure. Cézanne rarely painted compositions in which reds and oranges of such vivid directness were placed in a single picture. When Mme Cézanne wears a red dress, she is not seated in an orange chair or placed next to a still life with orange fruits. Indeed, the brilliant interplay between the oranges in the lower left and the green glaze of the olive jar gives the bottom of the picture such an intensity that Cézanne was forced to represent what was surely the pale yellow-brown wood of the tabletop in the same icy blues and pale greens that he used for the wall behind the flowers. Hence, local color is less interesting to him than chromatic contrasts and harmonies.

The X-ray (fig. 82d) reveals another intriguing aspect of the painting. It is perfectly clear that Cézanne painted the olive jar in its entirety before filling it with the thick, almost waxy tulip leaves that erupt from it. He then crammed the stems and leaves of four tulips in the green jar and devoted almost as much pictorial attention to the complex folds and curves of these pulpy green leaves as he did to the blossoms. This dark and tumultuous center of the still life is balanced by the arena of whitened pastels that palpitate around it. Cézanne reveled in the freedoms of the painter by making the tabletop visually disappear to the right of the vase and flowers. He allows us to believe in its existence by the visual insertion of a brown triangle in the lower right corner. This flat geometric form plays in a game of two and three dimensions with the spheres of the fruits (probably both oranges and apples) and the freer forms of the tulips and their dramatic leaves.

Rewald has pointed out that Cézanne used at least two Provençal olive jars in his still lifes—one with a straight edge between the green glaze and the gray-beige of the ceramic itself and the other—this one—with a curvilinear line that makes the green glaze appear to have erupted from the mouth of the jar.[3] Yet, if this is the case, Cézanne used both jars in painting the Chicago and the Norton Simon arrangements. It is likelier that Cézanne was as free with his decisions about the precise visual character of the vase as he was with the proportions of tables or patterns of wallpaper.

The Norton Simon still life was purchased from Vollard by the great German dealer Paul Cassirer and was in various German collections until 1936. It thus played a role in the German understanding both of French painting in general and of Cézanne in particular. Known to Hugo von Tschudi and Julius Meier-Graefe, the two most important figures in the German acceptance of French modern art, the Norton Simon still life was evidently thought important enough that it was owned by the great connoisseur Edith Dunn (Mrs. Alfred Chester) Beatty, most of whose collection is currently in the National Gallery of Ireland in Dublin.

1 These are Rewald, 1996, vol. 1, nos. 469–478, 660, 675, and 719–721, all dated by Rewald to the early 1890s.

2 Rewald nos. 680, 719, 803, and 825. A cruder and simpler table with a similar skirt and straight legs appears in two very late still lifes—Rewald 934 and 936—made in Provence as well as in modern photographs of Cézanne's studio in Les Lauvres (see Rewald, 1986a, p. 250).

3 Rewald, 1996, no. 721.

83

Odilon Redon
French, 1840–1916

Vase of Flowers, after Cézanne
1896

Oil on canvas, $18\frac{1}{4} \times 21\frac{3}{4}$ in. (46.4 × 55.2 cm)
M.1973.7

Provenance: Probably from artist or Mme Redon to; Ary Leblond (aka Aimé Merlo [1880–1958]), Paris, by 1934, by inheritance to; Henriette Merlot Ary-Leblond, Paris, by 1934–at least 1964. M. Renevey, Paris(?) L. Lefebvre-Foinet, Paris, by 14 February 1968, ½ share with; Sunion Fine Arts, Vaduz, Liechtenstein; ½ share sold back 7 November 1968. [E. J. van Wisselingh & Co., Amsterdam, stock no. S8702, in 1967, sold 1970 to]; Neison Harris, Northbrook, Ill., gift 1973 to; Norton Simon Art Foundation (sale, New York, Christie's, 19 May 1982, lot 23, ill., unsold and returned to); Norton Simon Art Foundation.

Exhibitions: Paris, 1910a, no. 8; Paris, 1934b, no. 32; Paris, 1951, no. 166; The Hague, 1957, no. 178; Pont-Aven, 1961, no. 146; San Francisco, 1974, no. 50, ill.

References: Bacou, 1956, vol. 1, p. 176; Rewald, 1956, pp. 96–97; Redon, 1960, pp. 306–307; K. Berger, 1964, no. 260; Moueix, 1969, vol. 2, letter XII, pp. 89–90; Rewald, 1986b, pp. 229, 242–243 n. 37; Benjamin, 1989, pp. 191–192, ill. opp. 192; Homburg, 1992, pp. 135, 136 n. 52, fig. 7; A. Wildenstein, 1992, vol. 4, no. 2042, p. 45, ill.; Homburg, 1996, pp. 122, 149 n. 385, fig. 76; Rewald, 1996, vol. 1, p. 319.

Technical Notes: The medium-weight, plain-weave canvas has dimensions that were a standard size for commercially available canvases. It has been wax-lined with the original tacking edges retained, probably to repair a small hole at the top center. The cream-colored ground is very thin, leaving the canvas with a slight surface texture. It possibly has darkened slightly from impregnation with wax. Paint was applied quickly in the thinly painted sketch. Redon positioned the vase and bouquet and wall design directly onto the ground, then brushed in the thin background paint. The flowers were brushed over the background in opaque paint. The paint is well preserved and brush marking remains distinct. No residues of discolored material are evident in the recesses of the canvas texture, and it is likely that the painting has never been cleaned. The present varnish is probably the first. (RW)

By the late 1870s, at a time when Naturalism of one kind or another dominated both the Salons and the independent exhibition venues organized by artists and dealers, Redon had developed a highly mysterious and evocative graphic style—evident in charcoal drawings and lithographs alike—that he called his *noirs*. The term effectively described at once the predominant formal and expressive aspect of his works; they are often dark, densely worked compositions whose subject may derive from mythology, folklore, literature, and the secret world of dreams and nightmares. These brooding and enigmatic works of art, such as *Devil Carrying off a Head* (c. 1875, Musée d'Orsay, Paris), articulate an antimodern pessimism and nostalgia that are dialectically opposed to the hopefulness and promise of the Impressionist landscape.

During the 1870s and 1880s, when Redon was developing his *noirs*, he paid little attention to painting and drawing with color. Nevertheless, there are a handful of compelling oils, pastels, and gouaches from this period, including *Figure Holding a Winged Head* (c. 1876, private collection). Not until the late 1880s and 1890s, however, did Redon begin to explore the expressive potential of color. Now he became associated with the French Symbolists and Nabis, meeting or corresponding with the painters Paul Gauguin, Maurice Denis, and Paul Sérusier and the poets Stéphane Mallarmé and Émile Verhaeren. A participant in the prevalent generational withdrawal from modernity and the quotidian, Redon embraced religious and mystical themes in his art and sought to understand the capacity of color as a vehicle for aesthetic and spiritual transport. After 1900 still-life drawing and painting were the chief arenas for this intense exploration of color. However, Redon's confrontation with the art of Paul Cézanne in the mid-1890s must be counted a signal event in his progress toward becoming one of the two greatest masters of still life in the first decade of the twentieth century. (The other was Henri Matisse.)

A handwritten by note by Arï Redon in the Norton Simon Museum files recounts the origin of this oil painting by his father:

> One day in 1896, Mr. André Bonger (brother-in-law of Theo van Gogh and great admirer of Odilon Redon, whose collection still exists in Holland), was in Paris and bought a canvas by Cézanne. Since he had to go to London, he left the canvas at Redon's house. During his absence, my father amused himself by copying the picture, and when Bonger returned to Paris, probably earlier than he intended, he found the copy on the easel. Not thinking it possible that the canvas could be

other than the one he owned, he exclaimed: "You are really too nice, Monsieur Redon, to have cleaned the picture, which was very dirty; one can now see all the colors, which were very dull." My father laughed heartily, and showed Bonger the original, which was at the side. The original Cézanne is still in the collection of Mrs. Bonger. It is number 358 in Venturi's catalogue, and dated about 1880.

The anecdote seems fanciful. It recalls various legends in the history of art, from the ancient account of the Greek artist Zeuxis painting a still life of fruit so naturalistically that birds rushed to peck at it, to the story that the young Picasso's talent was so prodigious that his artist-father was compelled to lay down his brushes for good. But Arï's tale may be true: after all, the pictures by Cézanne (cat. 80) and Redon actually exist in the Norton Simon Museum. The only doubtful part of the account is that so astute a collector and connoisseur as Bonger did not immediately detect in the freshly painted still life the hand of Redon. His picture reveals an approach to color, contour, structure, relief, and pictorial meaning that is very different from Cézanne's.

Redon's *Vase of Flowers* is generally softer and warmer than Cézanne's original (cat. 80). It is also less architectural and more atmospheric. The contours of the pitcher, leaves, flowers, tabletop, and wallpaper in Redon's canvas are less clearly marked than in Cézanne's and consequently stand out in less relief. Cézanne's vase has some visibly bare patches, creating a highlight that helps lend the pitcher volume. Redon's, by contrast, is essentially monochrome, composed of yellow-brown and touches of brownish green.

Cézanne's brushstrokes are more expressive than Redon's; the paint is pulled around the contours of the flowers and leaves to help stamp out their form. Similarly, the large pink chrysanthemum in the middle of Cézanne's still life (there are actually daubs of blue-green and brown-green in the center of the flower) is constructed from more than a hundred short, overlapping brushstrokes; this may be called Cézanne's improvised illusionism, whereby the physical juxtaposition and overlapping of daubs of paint construct forms in space. Redon's pink flower, for its part, is constructed along completely different principles; he used a small brush and employed a flurry of mostly short, feathery brushstrokes to create a single, soft, and unnaturally colored dream flower.

The comparison of Redon's with Cézanne's *Vase of Flowers* inevitably leads to the conclusion that even when the former was most trying to paint like Cézanne, he could not help being himself. What, then, was Redon's purpose in making the copy, other than to have some fun at his friend Bonger's expense? After all, he did not copy the architectonic, analytic approach to surface and form of the master from Aix. Nor did he pay much attention to the hard contours of the objects in Cézanne's still life, nor concern himself with its specific color modulations. Instead, Redon was engaged in a creative reinterpretation of Cézanne's work, a translation of one artist's style though the hands, mind—and especially imagination—of another. For that is what mostly excited Redon. He admired Delacroix even more than he did Cézanne and cherished Charles Baudelaire's remark that, for the Romantic painter, imagination was "queen of the faculties." Redon thus used his own imaginative powers to dematerialize a still life by Cézanne and make it his own. His *Vase of Flowers* may be seen as a significant step toward his extraordinary floral still-life oeuvre of the following decade. Most of these later works are pastels and positively psychedelic in their vividness. That brilliant body of work is only hinted at here, but the route from the earlier to the later still life is nevertheless clearly traced in Redon's copy after Cézanne.

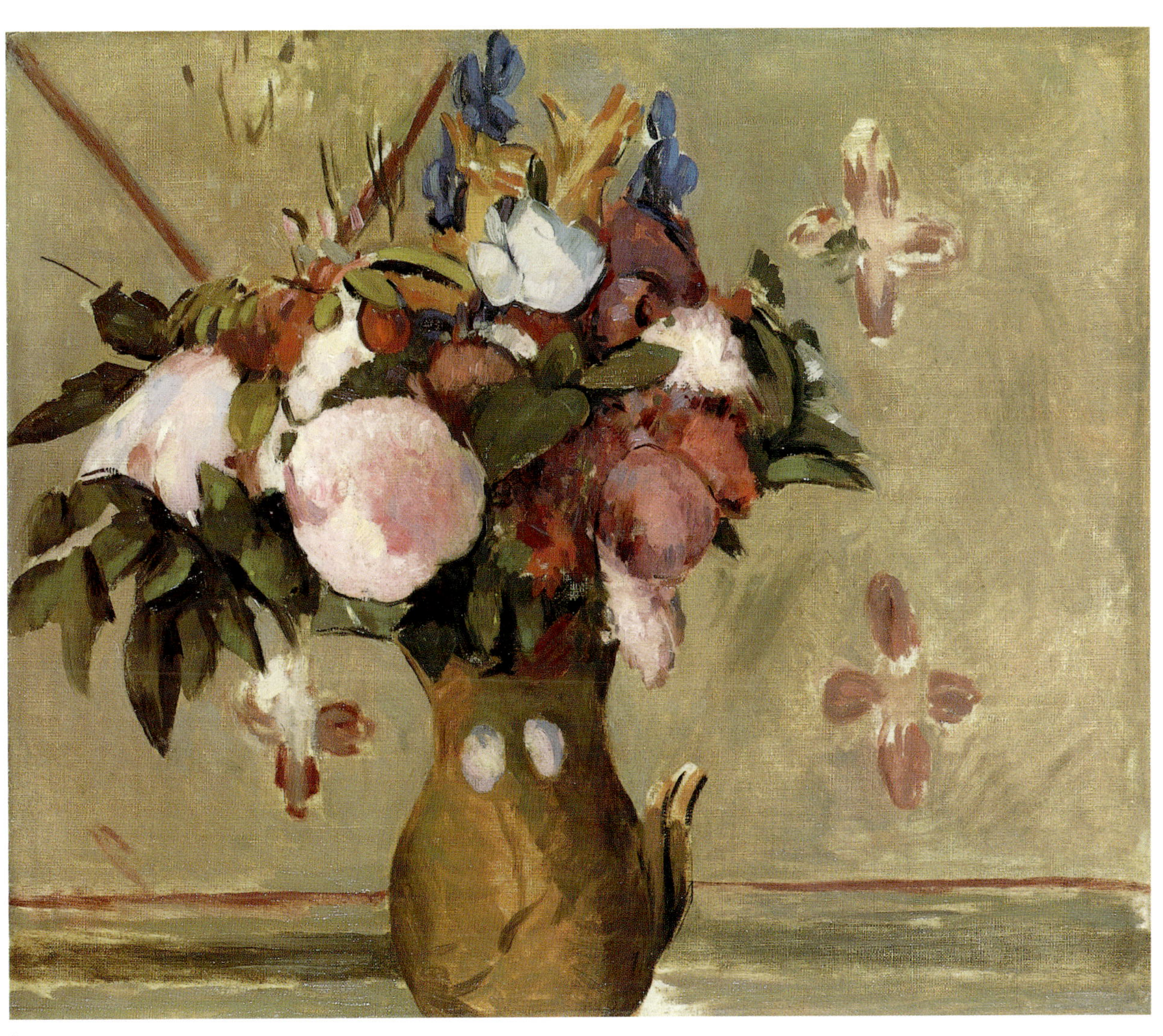

83

84

Claude Monet
French, 1840–1926

Mouth of the Seine, Honfleur
1865

Oil on canvas, $35\frac{1}{4} \times 59\frac{1}{4}$ in. (89.5 × 150.5 cm)
Signed and dated lower right: "Claude Monet 1865"
F.1973.33.2

Provenance: The artist, sold 1865 for Ff 300 to; Alfred Cadart, Paris. Rousselle, sold 24 July 1922 to; [Bernheim-Jeune, Paris, stock no. 23.095, sold 28 September 1922 to]; Georges Bernheim, Paris, still in 1924, possibly 1926. Y. de Saint-Albin, Paris. Jacques de Saint-Albin, Paris, by 1959. Remond, Geneva. [Wildenstein & Co., Inc., New York, by 1968, sold 1973 to]; The Norton Simon Foundation.

Exhibitions: Paris, 1865b, no. 1524; London, 1936a, no. 19, as *Embouchure de la Seine, environs de Honfleur*; Paris, 1959c, no. 1, ill.; on loan, Toledo Museum of Art, 10 January–26 August 1974; San Francisco, 1974, no. 38, ill.; on loan, Atlanta, High Museum of Art, 19 November 1980–4 August 1981.

References: Privat, 1865, p. 190; Pigalle, 1865b, p. 76 (with pen drawing by "B. T."); Mantz, 1865, p. 26; Mantz, 1877, p. 3; Le Roux, 1889, p. 2; Bricon, 1900, pp. 297–298; Cahen, 1900, pp. 106–107; Thiébault-Sisson, 1900, p. 3; Duret, 1902, p. 61; Dewhurst, 1904, p. 39; Lanöe-Villène, 1905, p. 280; Duret, 1906, pp. 95, 101 (3rd ed., 1922, pp. 66, 71; 4th ed., 1939, pp. 70, 76); Grappe, 1909, p. 17; Dubosc, 1910, p. 4; Alexandre, 1921, pp. 34, 36, ill. opp. 36; Geffroy, 1922, pp. 27–28; Duret, 1923, p. 19 (ill. of pen sketch by "B. T." 1st pub. in Pigalle, 1865); Mauclair, 1924, p. 6; F. Fels, 1925, p. 2; Chavance, 1926, p. 147; Gimpel, 1927, p. 173; Régamey, 1927, p. 76; M. Fels, 1929, p. 73; Léger, 1930, p. 6; Lathom, 1931, p. 47; Grappe, 1941, p. 13; Tabarant, 1942, p. 425; Graber, 1943, pp. 166–167; Malingue, 1943, p. 15; Bazin, 1947, p. 10 (2nd ed., 1953, p. 26); Reuterswärd, 1948, pp. 28, 30, 31, fig. 1 (pen drawing by "B. T." in Pigalle, 1865; here erroneously titled *Pointe de la Hève*); Robiquet, 1948, p. 62; Cassou, 1953, p. 17; Mathey, 1956, p. 37; Stoll, 1957a, pp. 33–34; Stoll, 1957b, p. 40; Monet, 1957, p. 198; Rich, 1957, p. 28; Degand and Rouart, 1958, p. 32; Lethève, 1959, pp. 29–30; Seitz, 1960, pp. 10, 16, 46, fig. 5; Mathey, 1961, pp. 63, 66; Rewald, 1961, p. 122, ill.; Gimpel, 1963, pp. 253–254; Mount, 1966, pp. 76–77, 86, 87, 90–91, 95–97, 403; Taillandier, 1967, p. 93; D. Wildenstein, 1967a, vol. 4, pp. 466, 470; D. Wildenstein, 1967b, pp. 14, 16; Bortolatto, 1972, no. 8, p. 88, ill.; Isaacson, 1972, pp. 20, 98 n. 8, 102 n. 29; Kimbell Art Museum, 1972, pp. 200, 202; D. Wildenstein, 1974–1991, vol. 1, no. 51, ill., vol. 4, p. 408; Hefting, 1975, no. 28, p. 355; Steadman, 1976, pp. 220–222, fig. 1; Isaacson, 1978, pp. 14, 193, fig. 2; Petrie, 1979, p. 16, fig. 8; House, 1981, p. 6, fig. 2; Gordon and Forge, 1983, pp. 15–17, ill.; Stuckey, 1985, p. 32, ill.; B. Bernard, 1986a, p. 254, ill.; B. Bernard, 1986b, p. 17, ill.; Moffett, 1986, p. 95, fig. 3; National Gallery of Scotland, 1986, p. 18, fig. 4; Skeggs, 1987, pp. 24, 25, ill.; Mathey, 1992, p. 72, ill.; Levine, 1994, p. 4, fig. 5; Kostenevich, 1995, pp. 132, 134, fig. 2; Seiberling, 1994, p. 41, fig. 3; Tucker, 1995, pp. 19–20, pl. 20; D. Wildenstein, 1999, p. 29, color ill.; Brenneman, 2001, p. 31, color fig. 14; Shimada and Sakagami, 2001, p. 32, fig. 12; Hodge, 2002, p. 11, color ill.; Eisenman, 2003, pp. 139, ill., 140–141; Czymmek, 2004, p. 62, ill.

Technical Notes: With pasty local color the artist seemingly painted this picture directly mostly wet in wet with no blending, leaving artifacts of his brushes. It is surprising to find, then, that he painted the sky with pure, transparent washes of blue and black (sometimes one over the other) on the dense light color applied to the upper half of the picture to indicate the sky while giving form to the clouds. Monet began with a plain, almost tight-weave fabric. The painting has been lined with an aqueous-based adhesive to a slightly heavier fabric. Original tacking edges, which run to the back edge of the stretcher, extend the painting by almost $\frac{1}{4}$ inch on each side on the front. The lining and stretcher could date from about the mid–twentieth century. A cream-colored ground, commercially applied, allows the texture of the crowns of the canvas weave to show. Extensive ground losses exist on the tacking edges. The artist made no significant changes that are visible in raking light or in the X-radiograph. The one exception may be at the right side, where a boat or sail may have been painted out. Otherwise, one sees only minor adjustments around forms. Colors are mainly mixed with white, and the extensive use of earths give a sense of serious veracity. However, there are some bright pure colors, such as the blue glazes in the sky and in the lower central part of the ocean and the small dabs of red, green, and blue in the landscape and ships. The painting is in very good condition, with only minor abrasions in the upper left and lower right quadrants and losses along edges and corners. The surface coating appears to be synthetic with a plastic appearance and in ultraviolet light fluoresces an even, dense, bluish color. (JF)

Claude Monet's ambitious *Mouth of the Seine, Honfleur* was exhibited at the Salon of 1865, along with *Pointe de la Hève at Low Tide* (fig. 84a), and both were sold to the art dealer and print publisher Alfred Cadart for three hundred francs each.[1] Monet was obviously pleased by his Salon debut and his first sales; before the works were shipped off to their purchaser, he had them reproduced by a commercial photographer. After the Salon, the artist immediately traveled to Chailly near Barbizon to begin work on his next canvas, the monumental *Luncheon on the Grass* (Musée d'Orsay, Paris). Having mastered and transformed the genre of marine painting, the confident twenty-five-year-old artist would now conquer life-size figure painting.

Mouth of the Seine, Honfleur is in fact a kind of manifesto. It announces the end of classical marine

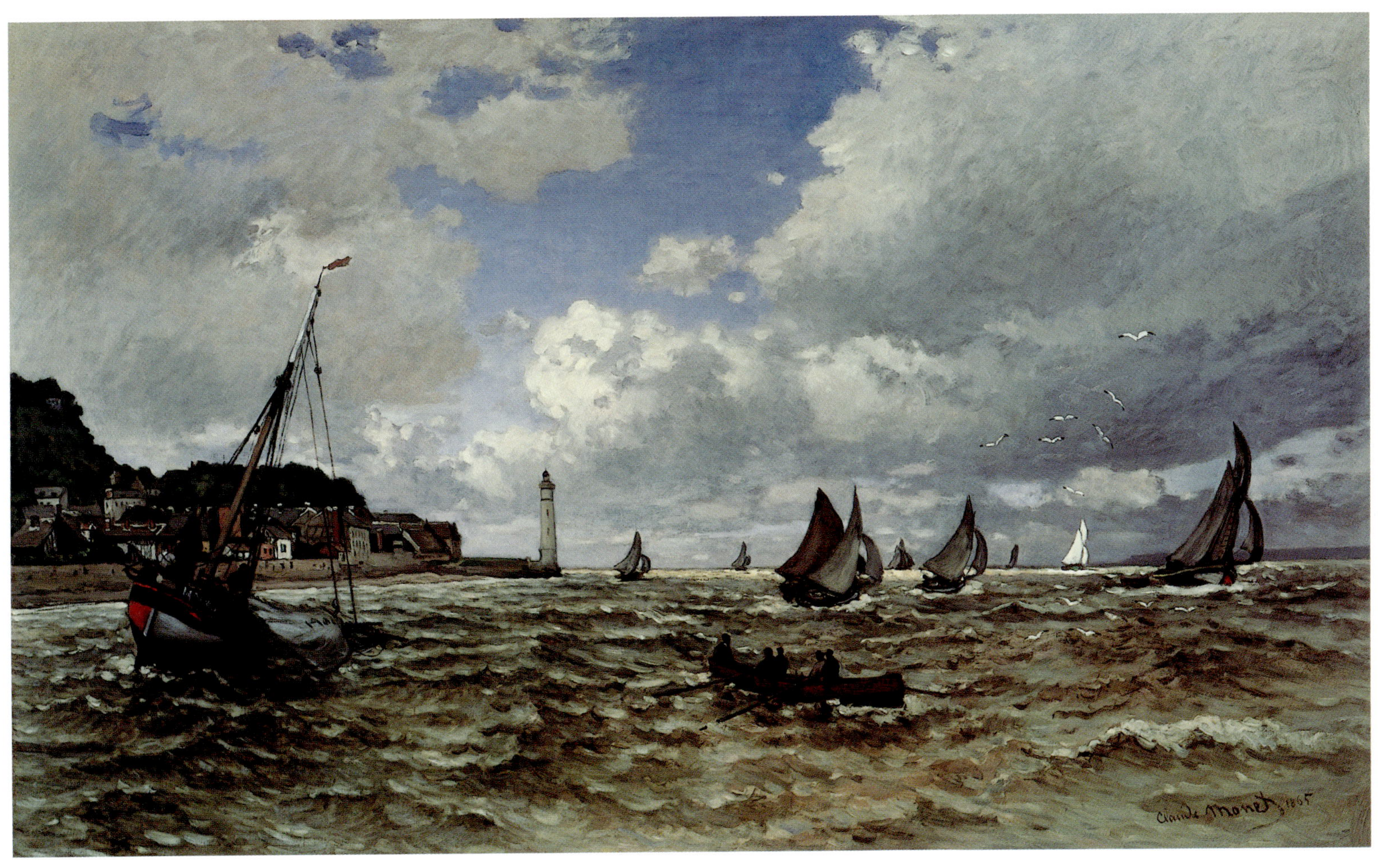

84

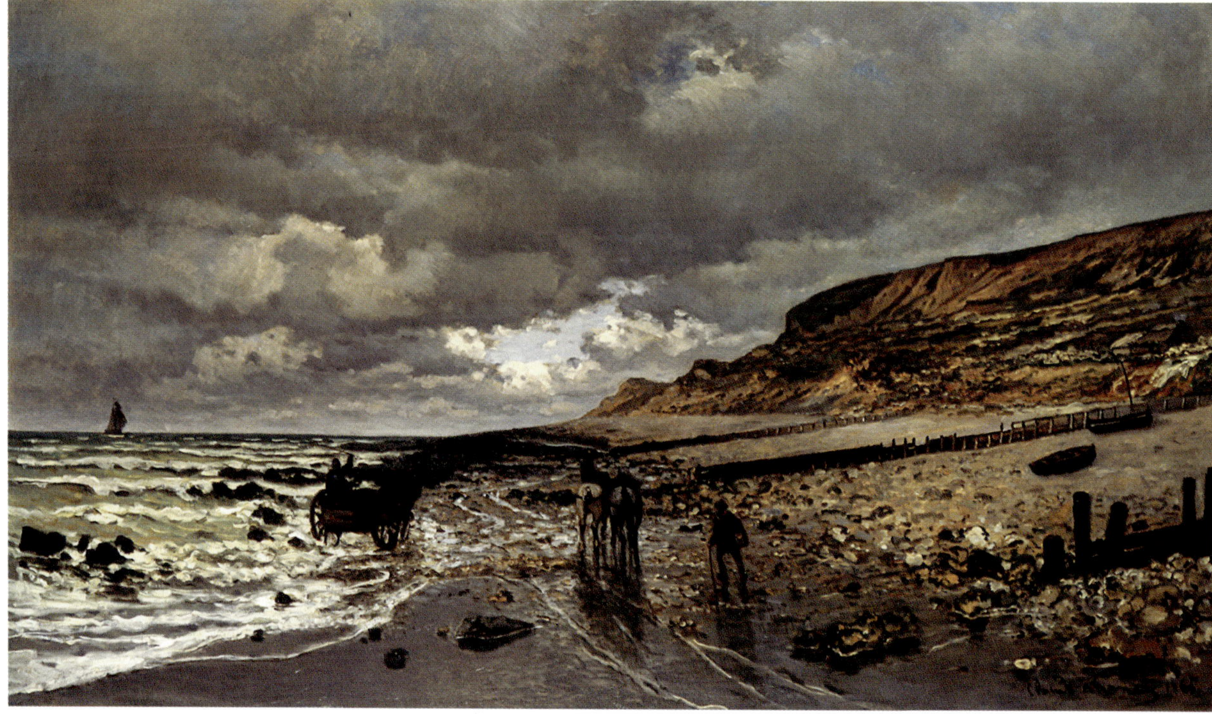

Fig. 84a Claude Monet, *Pointe de la Hève at Low Tide*, 1865, oil on canvas, 5½ × 59¼ in. (90.2 × 150.5 cm), Kimbell Art Museum, Fort Worth

Fig. 84b James McNeill Whistler, *Harmony in Blue and Silver—Trouville*, 1865, oil on canvas, 19½ × 29¾ in. (49.5 × 75.5 cm), Isabella Stewart Gardner Museum, Boston

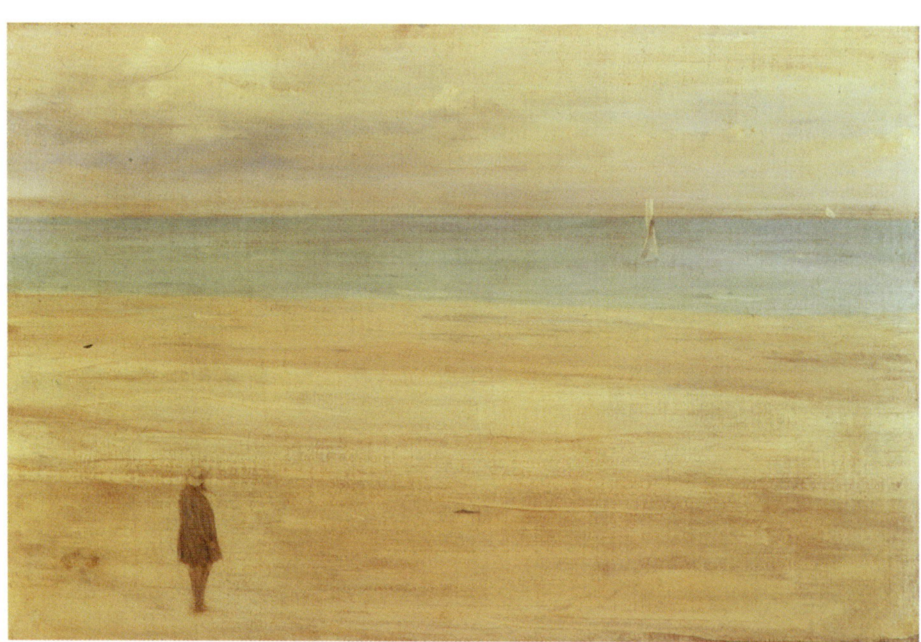

painting in France and the emergence of a new, modern genre. The transformation would be completed a decade later by Monet and the other Impressionists, but the hallmarks of the new art are plainly visible here. They are apparent in the form and color of the marine, its consequent disengagement with narrative and history, and its assertion of the independent validity of painting apart from literary and visual precedent.

Monet's early paintings, such as *Mouth of the Seine, Honfleur* and *The Entrance to the Port of Le Havre* (cat. 85), provide clear instances of the artist's recognition of the cultural and even political weight borne by landscape in art. They indicate the residual thrall of the classical tradition in French art, the great influence of the radical painter Gustave Courbet, and, most of all, the effort to jettison the oppressive burden of the past. *Mouth of the Seine, Honfleur* marked the artist's Salon debut and competed for press attention in 1865 with *Olympia*, Édouard Manet's scandalous depiction of a poor and nearly naked, but clearly self-possessed, prostitute (Musée d'Orsay, Paris). The latter work was the more audacious, but Monet's work was itself quite experimental in character and must be seen alongside other modern seascapes of the period. In 1864 Manet painted three marines recognized at the time as influenced by Japanese ukiyo-e prints, including *The Kearsarge at Boulogne* (private collection), and in 1865 Courbet created almost three dozen Normandy marines that are unprecedented in their reduction of pictorial incident to the basic superposing of sand, sea, and sky, including *Marine* (cat. 43). James McNeill Whistler painted side by side with Courbet at Trouville, but rather than engaging the materiality of air, water, and land, he explored the abstract interaction of tone and color, as in *Harmony in Blue and Silver: Trouville* (fig. 84b). Beside these highly experimental marines, Monet's *Mouth of the Seine, Honfleur*—painted about six months earlier than the works by Courbet and Whistler—appears at first glance

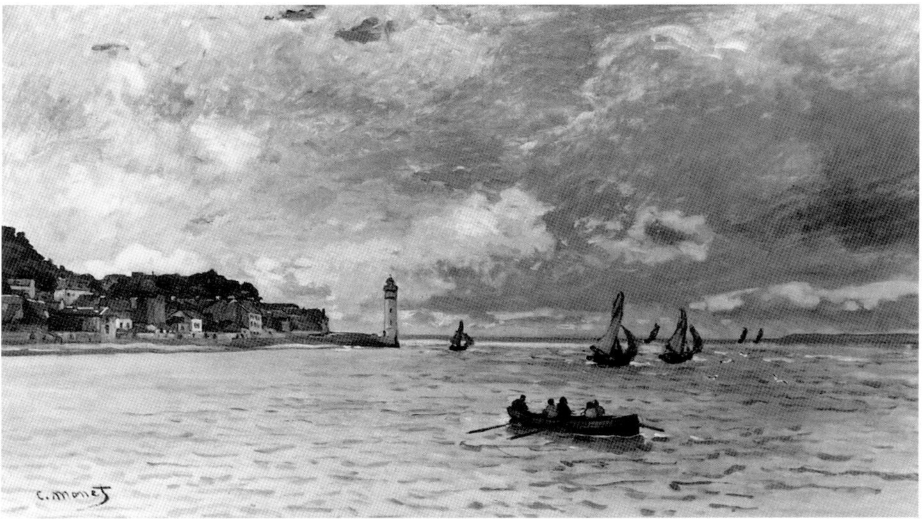

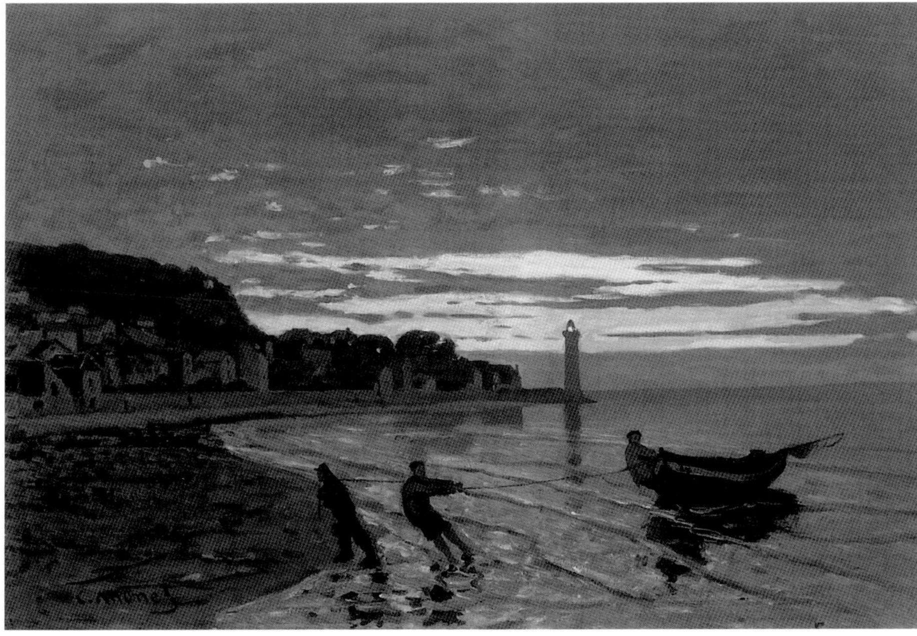

Fig. 84c (*top*) Claude Monet, *The Lighthouse at Honfleur*, 1864, oil on canvas, $21\frac{1}{4} \times 31\frac{7}{8}$ in. (54×81 cm), Kunsthaus, Zurich

Fig. 84d (*above*) Claude Monet, *Towing a Boat, Honfleur*, 1864, oil on canvas, $21\frac{3}{4} \times 32\frac{3}{8}$ in. (55.2×82.1 cm), Memorial Art Gallery of the University of Rochester, Gift of Marie C. and Joseph C. Wilson

more conservative and anecdotal; it includes a plethora of objects and figures, as well as meteorological and architectural details.

Monet's large marine was painted, not *en plein air*, but in the studio in Paris; it was based on a number of more freely brushed *études* made on site, the most important of which were *The Lighthouse at Honfleur* (fig. 84c) and *Towing a Boat, Honfleur* (fig. 84d). While at work on these studies, Monet stood before his easel on the long jetty that dominates the harbor at Honfleur, with his back to the boat basin, facing open waters, a lighthouse, and a hill known as Le Mont Joli. The large finished painting of Honfleur depicts an array of fishing boats crossing the choppy waters of the Seine estuary. At left a large boat with lowered anchor lists hard to the right, weighted down by its nets, tackle, and extended otter board (the wooden beam used to balance a boat while it is lowering a trawl). Other nautical dramas, too, are carefully staged: a rowboat with five men aboard pulls hard against the strong current; additional fishing boats—some may be smaller shrimpers—run and heel before the stiff wind.

A single boat near the horizon at right is picked out by the sun, its glimmering white sail making it seem like an apparition beside the dull gray of the others. A flock of gulls, approximated by the conventional V-shaped schema taught to children, is illuminated by the same sunbeams. At the left of the picture are Le Mont Joli and at its base a jumble of gray stucco and half-timber facades, brick chimneys, and steeply pitched roofs leading to the Hospice and old lighthouse, its little black cupola like the dot of an upside-down exclamation point. Georges Seurat painted the same lighthouse in 1886 (National Gallery of Art, Washington, D.C.), placing it in his middle ground as he looked beyond it to the very jetty on which Monet had stood twenty years before. The young Neo-Impressionist painter may in fact have intended homage to Monet—*Mouth of the Seine, Honfleur* was already well known—but the pairing is more significant because of the light it sheds on the development of marines in particular and modern landscape in general. The two pictures mark the start and finish of a twenty-year process of pictorial clarification, refinement, reduction, abstraction, and democratization. The end, however, was foretold in some ways at the beginning.

Monet's big picture was a success with Salon critics, and at one level it is indeed pitch-perfect. It is clearly an ambitious and even patriotic *tableau* that records a well-known port of France, thereby recalling the great series of the ports of France painted by Joseph Vernet between 1755 and 1765, and before them the harbor scenes of Claude Lorrain. Vernet's pictures were lavishly praised in 1767 for their ideal—and not merely literal—truth by the great critic Denis Diderot, and Monet may have hoped to find his own Diderot at the Salon of 1865. But though his two marines were singled out for general praise, and even said to be highlights of the Salon, they were judged to be neither fully *idéales* nor clearly *réeles*. In fact, they were treated with just a bit of uncertainty and some condescension: "youthful and naïve," wrote one critic;

"dull in tonality, like the paintings of Courbet . . . but with great simplicity of aspect," commented another.[2] Indeed, Monet's marines were neither fish nor fowl, and critics would have been hard-pressed to find a stylistic or aesthetic category in which the painting could be placed. Like his companions at Honfleur in 1864—Frédéric Bazille, Eugène Boudin, and Johan Barthold Jongkind—he had begun the process of disassembling the conventions of marine painting, only he worked on a larger scale than they did. "There is a first rank seascape painter in him," Émile Zola wrote in 1868, "but he interprets the genre in his own way, and I see this as further proof of his intense love for the reality of the present."[3]

One mark of Monet's originality is his unusual treatment of light. Sea and sky are dominated by a single tonal register and temperature—gray-green below, gray-blue above—preventing us from seeing a plausible deep space. The deep blue opening in the clouds—it recalls the sky in Eugène Delacroix's *Scenes of a Massacre at Chios* (Musée du Louvre, Paris)—is a diagonal, jagged gash, but its location well above the horizon means that it does little to actually extend the pictorial space. The sea consists of a thousand open arcs in multiple shades of green, gray, and blue, like so many painted mustaches or seagulls. An area of calligraphic painting, hinting at eddies and backflows, is visible above the artist's signature at lower right. Warm color is limited mostly to a few highlights, for example, the red on the hull of the ship at left and the red of the matched ship at the far right pointed in the opposite direction. This to-and-fro of warm color maintains spatial balance and keeps pictorial focus on the middle plane of the picture.

The horizon in the center of the painting is where deep space should be found, but this is precisely where it is ostentatiously denied. The bright yellow-white line that extends, with wavering intensity, from the base of the lighthouse to just beyond the boat at far right is a thin band sandwiched between a narrow gray stripe above and a heavier, blurred, and slightly wavering gray-green band below. The result is a flat space on the horizon, a dense, painterly zone, which functions like a mirror, reflecting the spectator's gaze back to the pictorial surface rather than permitting it to pass into the distance. That reflection is one of Monet's key innovations in this picture. It is an effect clearly visible in his subsequent, fully Impressionist landscapes and marines, from those made at Argenteuil in the 1870s, such as *Riverside Walk at Argenteuil* (1873, National Gallery of Art, Washington, D.C.) to those painted while on holiday in Venice in 1908, such as *S. Giorgio Maggiore* (Art Institute of Chicago).

1 Monet to Arsène Alexandre, 6 December 1920, in D. Wildenstein, 1974–1991, vol. 4, p. 408.

2 Quoted in Geffroy, 1922, p. 28.

3 Émile Zola, "Mon Salon: Les Actualistes," in *Écrits sur l'art*, ed. Jean-Pierre Leduc-Adine, Paris, 1991, p. 208.

85

Claude Monet
French, 1840–1926

The Entrance to the Port of Le Havre (formerly *The Entrance to the Port of Honfleur*)
c. 1867–1868

Oil on canvas, $19\frac{3}{4} \times 24\frac{1}{8}$ in. (50.2×61.2 cm)
Signed, dated, and inscribed lower left: "A son ami Lafont, 1870, Claude Monet"
M.1999.2.2

Provenance: The artist; gift 1870 to; Antoine Lafont, Paris. [Durand-Ruel, Paris, c. 1900]. (sale, Paris, Hôtel Drouot, 28 June 1943, lot 18, ill., as *Dieppe: Bateaux de pêche sortant du port* to); Mettey. Private collection, Paris. [Anstalt für Kunst und Kultur (Wildenstein),[1] by 1952(?)–consigned 29 January 1969 to]; [Reid & Lefevre, London, stock no. 8089, returned 1969 to]; [Anstalt für Kunst und Kultur (Wildenstein)]; [Galerie Castiglione, Schaan, Liechtenstein; offered May 1969 and subsequently sold 19 December 1969, through Reid & Lefevre, London, to]; The Norton Simon Foundation, transferred 23 November 1999 to; Norton Simon Art Foundation.

Exhibitions: Paris, 1952a, no. 16; London, 1969, no. 6, ill.; on loan, Phoenix, Art Museum, 20 February–20 June 1970; on loan, Los Angeles, County Museum of Art, 22 June 1970–May 1971; on loan, Minneapolis, Institute of Arts, May 1971–October 1972; San Francisco, 1973, no. 35, ill.

References: D. Wildenstein, 1971, no. 3, p. 19, color ill.; D. Wildenstein, 1974–1991, vol. 1, no. 87, p. 161, ill.; Martini, 1978a, no. XI, p. 12, ill.; Monneret, 1978–1981, vol. 1, s.v. "Lafont"; Kostenevich, 1995, p. 134, fig. 2.

Technical Notes: The near-fine, plain-weave canvas support is lined to a similar fabric with an aqueous adhesive. Tacks hold the painting onto an old wood stretcher, and original tacking edges extend to the back edge of the stretcher. The canvas was commercially prepared with a light cream or gray ground that is medium thick and nearly fills the canvas weave. It appears that very light pink paint covers the ground (design area only), and its warm tonality must have some optical effect on the other colors, especially the greens. While dashes of color and wet-in-wet painting show speedy application, underlayers that retained crisp texture of the brush must have been well set before paint was applied over them. Colors appear local, fresh, and pure—composed only of simple mixtures mainly with white pigment—but glazes and scumbles figure prominently. For example, the rowboat at the right has a thin glaze of ultramarine over the gray of the hull, and the steamer has a thick red layer under a thin pink. The sky's gray underpaint affects the tonality of the thinly applied pinks and blues on top. During the first application of the paint for the sky and sea, reserves were left at least for the pier, lighthouse, and the rowboat in the foreground, but some of the ship's sails and the other rowboat, for example, were applied over the paint of the sea. (JF)

We know from a letter that Monet was in Honfleur in February 1867, to prepare new works for exhibition at the Salon.[2] After a period of work in Paris, he returned to the Normandy coast late in the year—this time to Le Havre—to work on some more pictures of boats and shipping. *The Entrance to the Port of Le Havre* appears to have been painted in late 1867 or early 1868. The small painting is an extremely fresh and freely painted study for a now lost or destroyed work called *Ship Passing the Jetty of Le Havre*, known to us only through Salon reviews and caricatures published in June 1868 (fig. 85a), and from two other studies, *The Jetty of Le Havre in Bad Weather* (private collection) and *A Seascape, Shipping by Moonlight* (fig. 85b). Indeed, the latter picture, though slightly larger, may have been conceived as a kind of pendant to the Norton Simon picture since it represents the exact same location and point of view, but at night. Still another picture, the identically sized *Seascape: Storm* (fig. 85c), represents the same boat depicted in *The Entrance to the Port of Le Havre* but without any other boats or architecture. Though the present work, like the pictures in Edinburgh and Williamstown, has generally been said to represent the jetty and lighthouse at Honfleur, there is no early exhibition history to confirm the title, and comparison with period photographs suggests that the scene actually depicts Le Havre (fig. 85d). This identification is further buttressed by an inscription on the back of the Edinburgh picture (not in Monet's hand) that reads "Marine, temps . . . Port du Havre" and by the previously mentioned association of these three works with the large, lost marine—indubitably representing the port of Le Havre—shown at the Salon of 1868. Both *The Entrance to the Port of Le Havre* and *The Jetty of Le Havre in Bad Weather* were given to Monet's friend the

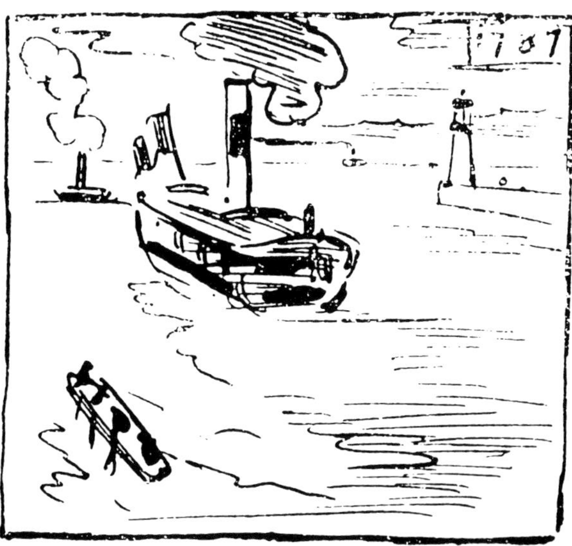

Fig. 85a Chassagnol-Neveu, caricature of Monet's *Ship Passing the Jetty of Le Havre*, in *Tintamarre-Salon*, 1868

Fig. 85b (*right*) Claude Monet, *A Seascape, Shipping by Moonlight*, 1866, oil on canvas, $23\frac{3}{8} \times 28\frac{9}{16}$ in. (59.5×72.5 cm), National Gallery of Scotland, Edinburgh

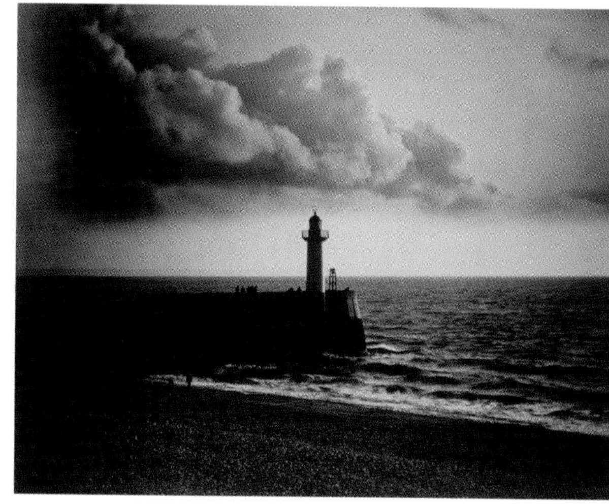

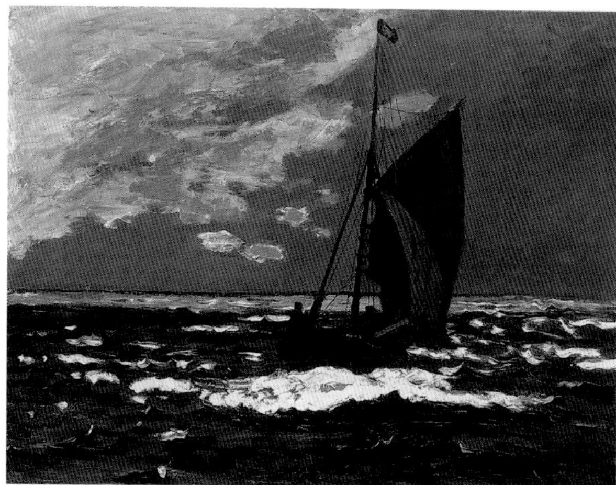

Fig. 85c (*right*) Claude Monet, *Seascape: Storm*, 1866, oil on canvas, $19\frac{3}{16} \times 25\frac{1}{2}$ in. (48.7×64.7 cm), Sterling and Francine Clark Art Institute, Williamstown

Fig. 85d (*above, far right*) Gustave Le Gray, *Lighthouse and Jetty, Le Havre*, 1856–1857, albumen print from collodion-on-glass negative, $12\frac{1}{16} \times 16$ in. (30.6×40.6 cm), Victoria and Albert Museum, London; © Victoria and Albert Museum, London / Art Resource, NY

journalist and left-wing politician Antoine Lafont in 1870; the simple dedication "A son ami Lafont" in Monet's hand is visible at the bottom of the two pictures.

The two early Monets in the Norton Simon collections should be understood as important monuments in the origin and development of an independent or autonomous modern art. Though viewers of Monet's landscapes—including *The Mouth of the Seine at Honfleur* and *The Entrance to the Port of Le Havre*—are provided a spectacle of nature and human design, they are given little opportunity to move and breathe inside the world of the picture; nearly all essential information in each work is given in two dimensions. The rowboats, skiffs, and steamers are painted with the same broad strokes of paint regardless of their putative locations in space, and the whitecaps and wakes are little more than horizontal or curling strokes of paint. A more honest or matter-of-fact work of art could hardly be conceived. And without some kinetic or psychological identification with the people or things in the artwork, a key element in landscapes before the modern period, viewers are kept at an emotional and ideological remove from the imagined world of the painting. Narrative, anecdote, history, and idealization—all attributes of older, classically influenced landscape art—are severely circumscribed. In place of all that is a pleasure derived from contemplating the artwork's most basic decorative and representational capacities, what the poet Stéphane Mallarmé called in 1876 "the clear and durable mirror of painting."[3] This was the beginning, we may justly say, of the project of democratic painting in which all parts are equally finished and all equally worthy of attention. It is democratic, too, in its implied appeal: audiences are not required to have any special classical training or other elite schooling in order to understand the painting. Impressionist works—from those by Monet to those by Georges Seurat—are thus the first European efforts at what may be called autonomous art, that is, painting emancipated from the conventions of genre, from the requirement to tell a story, or from the necessity to convey a specific understanding of the social and historical or even geographic relationship between the worlds within and without the picture.

1 According to Lefevre Gallery's "for sale" book (sale no. 8089), the painting was "on sale from Anstalt für Kunst und Kultur (Wildenstein)" on 29 January 1969 and was returned to Anstalt für Kunst und Kultur at an unknown date. Information provided by Lefevre Gallery, London, March 2001. No further documentation has been found for the "Anstalt" provenance, nor is its location mentioned in the Lefevre books.

2 D. Wildenstein, 1974–1991, vol. 1, no. 13, p. 444.

3 Stéphane Mallarmé, "The Impressionists and Édouard Manet," in Moffett, 1986, p. 35.

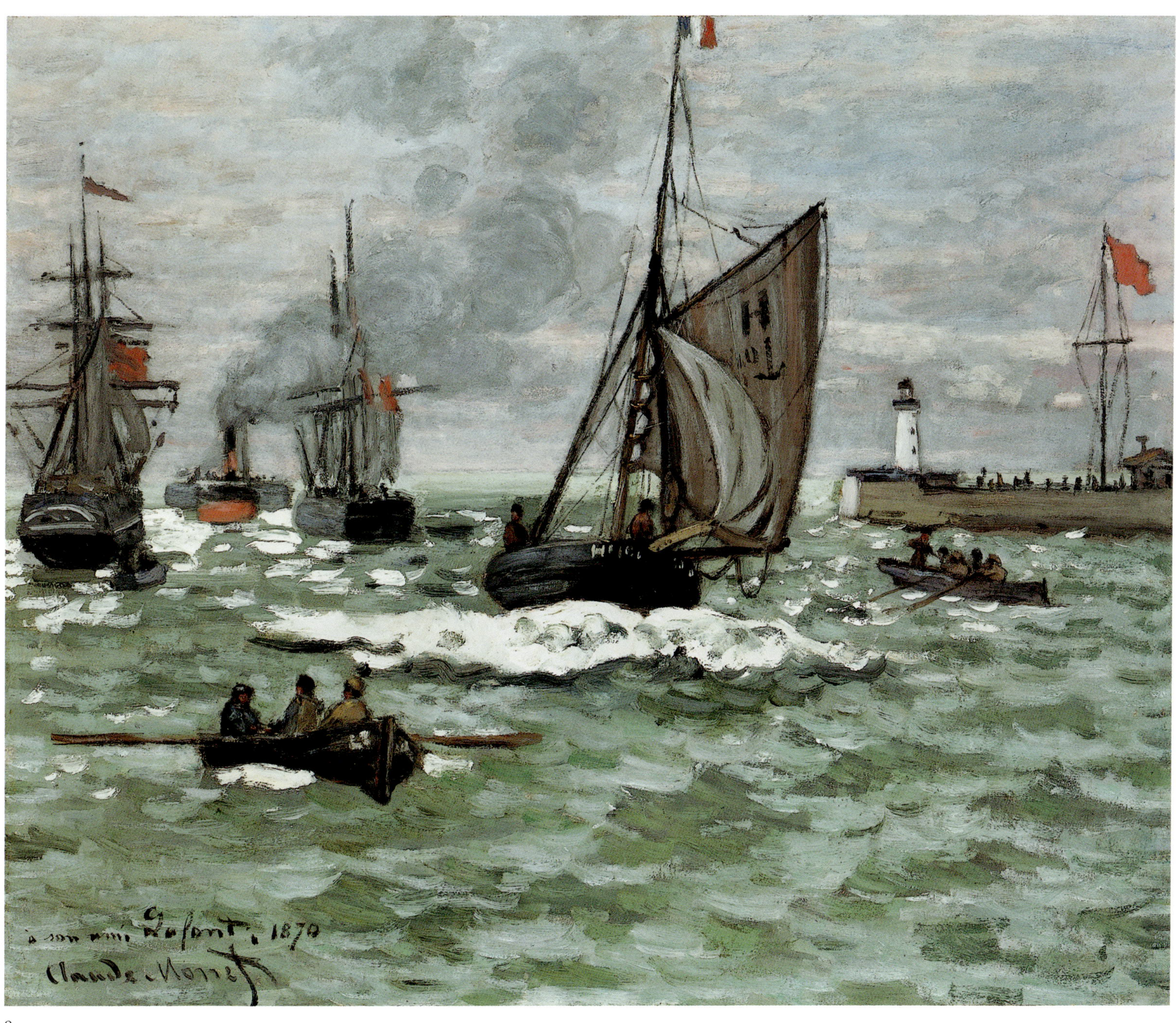

85

86

Claude Monet
French, 1840–1926

The Artist's Garden at Vétheuil
1881

Oil on canvas, $39\frac{1}{2} \times 32$ inches (100.3×81.2 cm)
Signed and dated lower right: "Claude Monet 81"
F.1975.9

Provenance: The artist; sold 9 February 1882 to; [Durand-Ruel, Paris]. d'Alayer, Paris. [Durand-Ruel, Paris, in 1931, still in 1935]. ?[Arthur Tooth & Sons, London, by 1936]. [Durand-Ruel, New York, by 1940]. [Sam Salz, New York]. [E. V. Thaw, New York, sold by at least 1959 to]; Mr. and Mrs. William Goetz, Los Angeles. Mr. and Mrs. Benjamin E. Bensinger, Chicago, by at least 1969, owned jointly with the Art Institute of Chicago (sale, London, Christie's, 15 April 1975, lot 31, color ill., to); [Wildenstein & Co., New York, sold 1975 to]; The Norton Simon Foundation.

Exhibitions: Possibly Paris, 1882, no. 70, as *Coin de jardin à Vétheuil*; possibly New York, 1886, no. 250; London, 1905; Boston, 1915; New York, 1920a, no. 27; New York, 1924; New York, 1931b, no. 34; Chicago, 1933, no. 7; Paris, 1935b, no. 36; London, 1936a, no. 5; New York, 1940a, no. 5; New York, 1945a, no. 40, ill.; San Francisco, 1959, no. 42, ill.; Los Angeles, 1967, no. 33, ill.; Chicago, 1969; New York, 1969, no. 16, color ill.; on loan, Phoenix, Art Museum, 25 July–1 December 1975; on loan, San Francisco, California Palace of the Legion of Honor, 5 January–15 June 1976.

References: Venturi, 1939, vol. 1, p. 226; Rewald, 1973, p. 470, ill.; D. Wildenstein, 1974–1991, vol. 1, no. 683, p. 406, ill.; Wise, 1975, no. 51, pp. 104–105, ill.; Dyrness, 2001, between pp. 96 and 97, pl. 3.

Technical Notes: The condition of this painting is very good. Although it has been lined, cleaned, and varnished, the impasto and colors seem very well preserved with very few losses. Tacking edges of the fine, plain-weave fabric of medium weight have been trimmed at the back of the stretcher, cutting some of the unused tack holes away. The secondary tack holes correspond to some holes in the stretcher, supporting the theory that this butt-joined 6-part stretcher is original. The commercially applied ground is light gray, thick, and smooth. The artist himself may have applied a second, thinner, ground layer that varies in color from cream to darker and sometimes bluish gray. Paint is pasty. It was directly applied, sometimes with several colors on a brush wet in wet and wet over set paint, leaving brushstrokes and impasto. Most colors are mixed with white but otherwise are bright and pure. Using no underdrawing, the artist built up the image making numerous changes along the way. The most interesting include the apparent change in the line of the house and in the staircase as seen in the X-ray. The application of the blue sky and present buildings over previously applied green paint is visible with magnification. The former is visible in the X-ray and the latter by examination with magnification. Obvious to the eye and in the X-ray is the slight change of placement of the jardinières. Remnants of an earlier yellowed varnish that was removed can be detected in some paint crevices. The painting was revarnished with a material that does not fluoresce in ultraviolet light. (JF)

In October 1878 Monet and his friend and former patron, Ernest Hoschedé, rented a house on the Chantemesle–La Roche-Guyon road on the western edge of the village of Vétheuil. Their landlords were "les dames Elliott," who lived in a large Neo-Renaissance house just up the hill and who may have been Americans. The small house they selected for their families, like others in the village, stood immediately on the main road between the center of Vétheuil and the next town of La Roche-Guyon. For the annual sum of six hundred francs, the Monets and the Hoschedés had access to the house, a small side garden, and an orchard across the street, with an outdoor staircase leading down to the Seine River, where Monet docked his *botin*, or painting boat. Life in this house was not easy. In addition to the Monet family with their two children, the Hoschedés had six children, and, although Ernest Hoschedé was often away in Paris trying to raise funds after his bankruptcy in June of that year, the house was crammed with children and probably two or three servants, creating a total population of fourteen or fifteen people.

If this was not enough, Monet's market collapsed, largely as the result of the bankruptcy art sale of Ernest Hoschedé in 1878. The former department store magnate owned sixteen paintings by Monet, all of which sold at very low prices, effectively devaluing the painter's entire production. And, to heap disaster on disaster, Camille Monet, the artist's wife, was very ill after the death of their second child in March of that year, and her condition deteriorated continuously until her death on 5 September 1879. From that point, the lives of the two families went from bad to worse. The servants quit in February 1880, possibly prompted by a scandalous article about the Monet and Hoschedé households in the Parisian rag *Le Gaulois* in January 1880.

It is precisely this house, with all its terrible associations, that we see on the right in *The Artist's Garden at Vétheuil*, a painting of such sunny optimism that it is difficult to imagine the darkness and difficulty associated with the house. If ever a painting embodied the truth of the saying "Time heals all wounds," it is this one. In fact, Monet's life had become increasingly stable later in 1880, and on 24 May 1881 he wrote to the

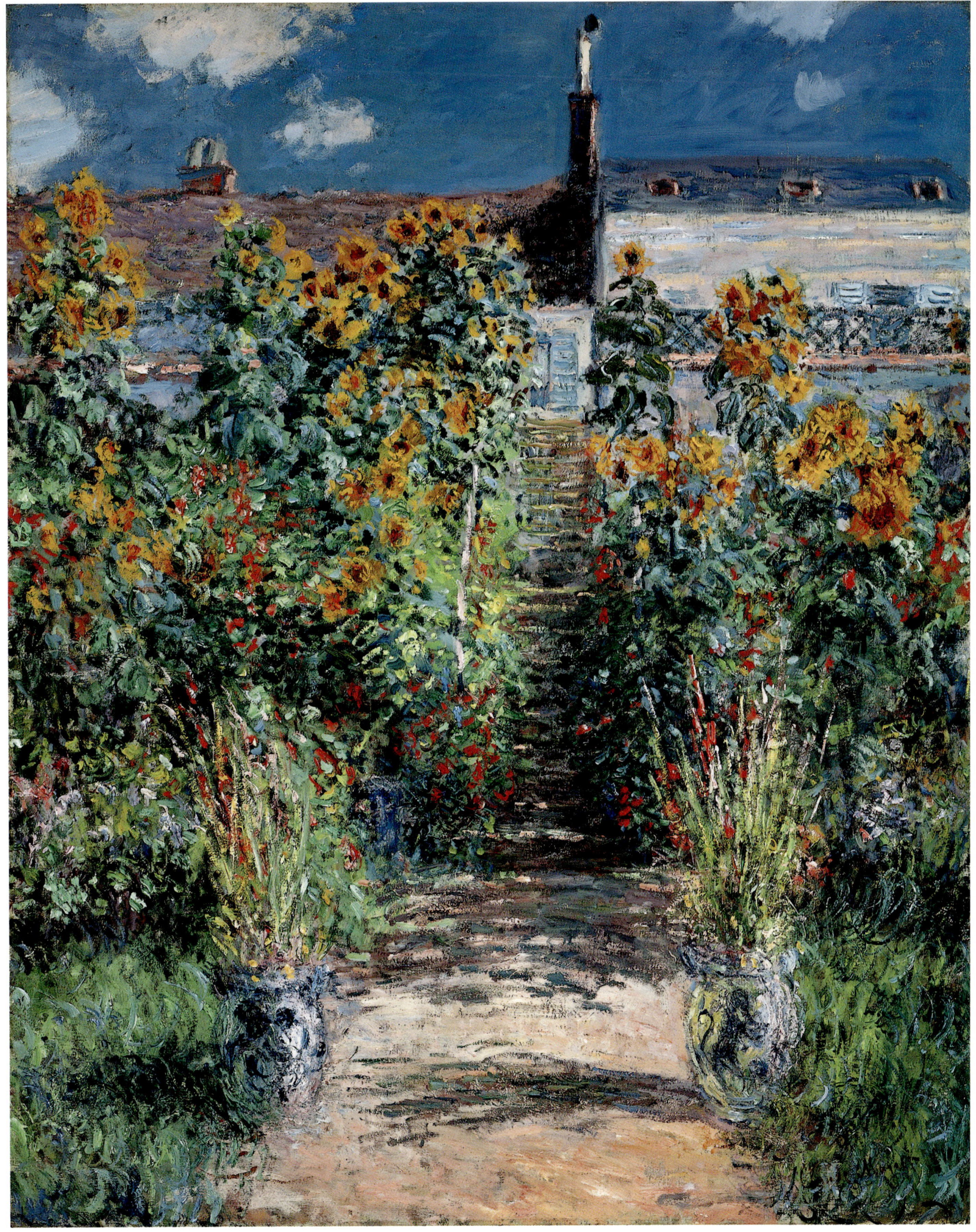

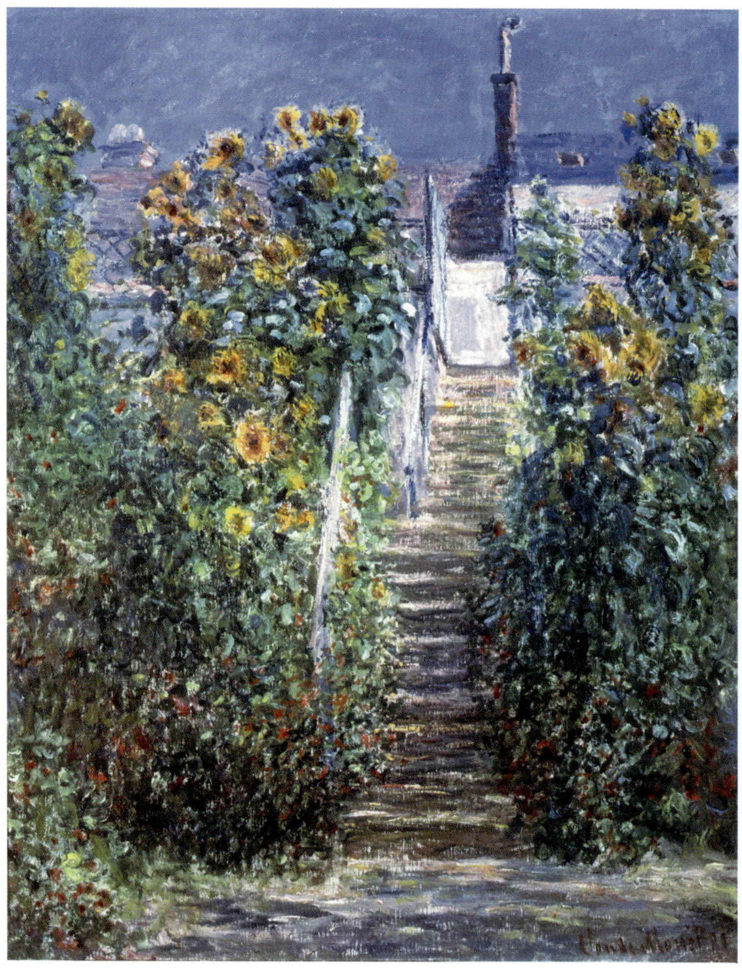

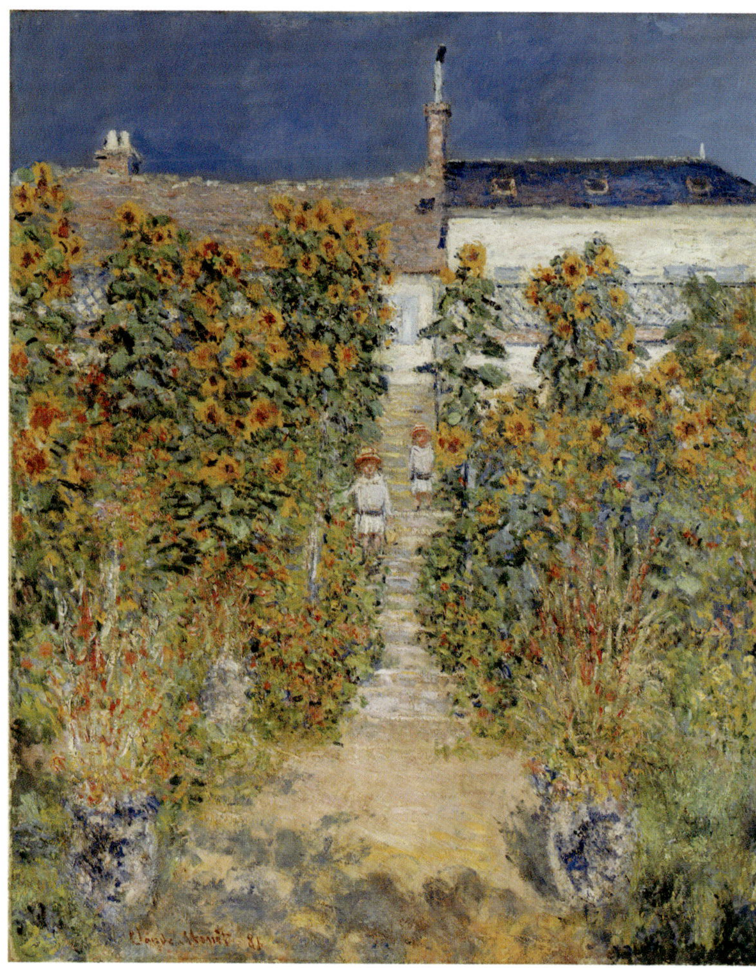

Fig. 86a (*above left*) Claude Monet, *The Artist's Garden at Vétheuil*, 1881, oil on canvas, 31½ × 25⅝ in. (80 × 65 cm), private collection, New York

Fig. 86b (*above right*) Claude Monet, *The Artist's Garden at Vétheuil*, 1881, oil on canvas, 39⅜ × 31½ in. (100 × 80 cm), private collection; photo: Christie's Images

novelist Émile Zola, living in nearby Medan, to inquire about "pretty areas on the banks of the Seine" with "good schools for my son Jean."[1] The blended family of Hoschedé and Monet children was working better, and Monet was selling paintings at better prices. He even submitted a major painting, *Lavacourt*, to the Salon of 1880, where, although poorly hung, it received enthusiastic press comments and was even illustrated in a lengthy review of the exhibition in the prestigious journal *La Gazette des Beaux-Arts*. And, in March 1881 he had taken a trip to the Norman fishing town of Fécamp to paint seascapes to counter the suburban landscape imagery that had dominated his art for a decade. Monet was emerging from poverty and depression and demonstrating real professional resilience in the summer of 1881 when he painted this gardenscape. Indeed, he made more money from sales of his art in 1881 than he had in any year since 1873, when his career had its first peak, and he had begun a long and gradual professional climb that was to result in real wealth within a decade.

This painting, in fact, is one of four closely related canvases representing the same garden scene. Because the paintings are not the same size, they cannot be considered in any way as a series meant to be shown together in a manner that Monet would perfect a decade later with his so-called haystack paintings. Of the four, all but the largest were begun in the summer of 1881. The four canvases can be divided into two subgroups—the "dark" paintings (figs. 86a and 86b, shown together in the Chicago Monet exhibition of 1995) and the "sunny" paintings (the Norton Simon version, fig. 86c, and the one in the National Gallery of Art, fig. 86d, which have never been shown together). In each group, one painting is smaller than the other, almost suggesting that the smaller work was a "study" for the larger. This is probably not the case with the "dark" paintings, since Monet preferred to work simultaneously on various versions of a particular composition rather than in a hierarchical manner. In addition, there are numerous differences of palette, composition, and handling in the two "dark" paintings. However, it is interesting to speculate about whether Monet considered the Norton Simon painting and the painting in a private collection (fig. 86b) to be a pair. They were sold to Monet's most faithful dealer,

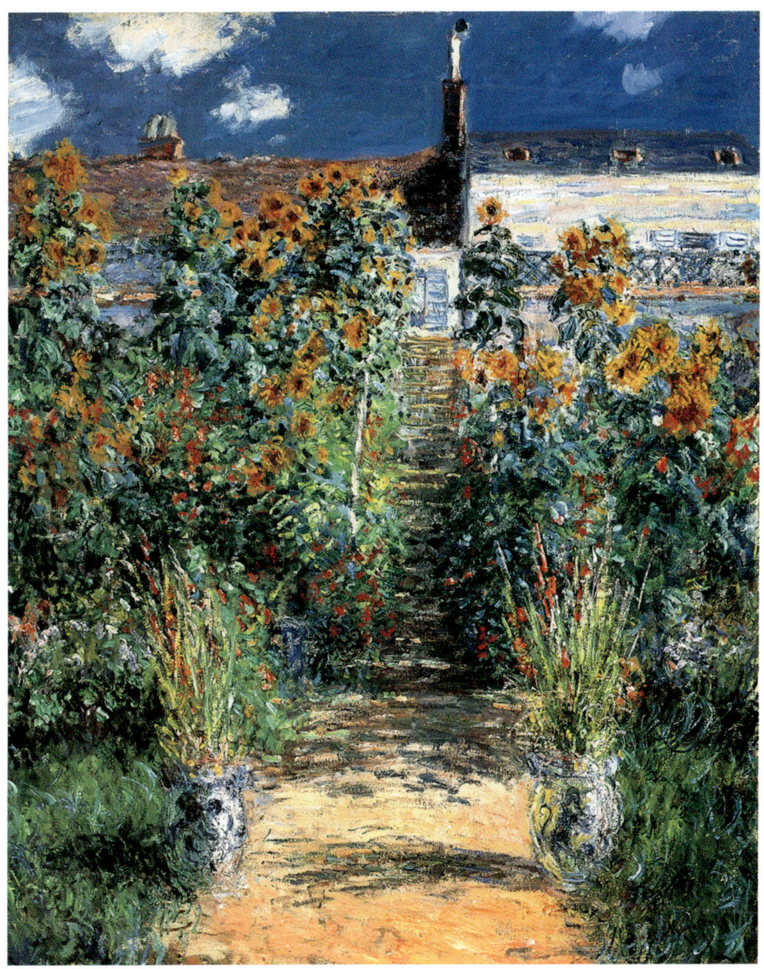

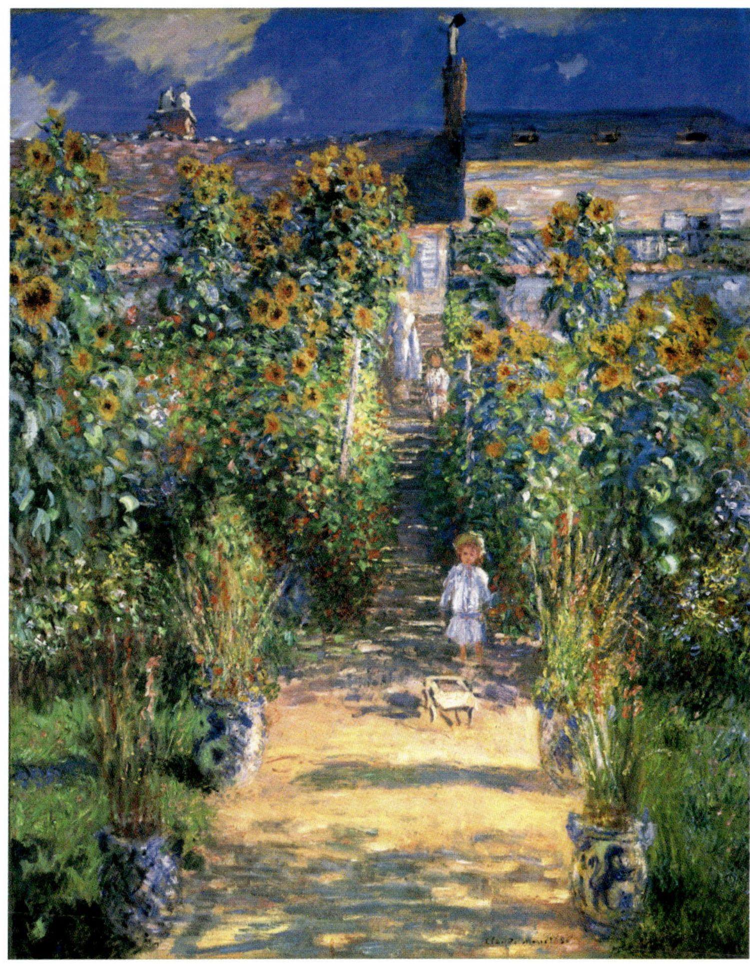

Fig. 86c (*above left*) Cat. 86

Fig. 86d (*above right*) Claude Monet, *The Artist's Garden at Vétheuil*, 1881, oil on canvas, 59⅝ × 47⅝ in. (151.4 × 121 cm), National Gallery of Art, Washington, Ailsa Mellon Bruce Collection

Durand-Ruel, on the same day in February 1882 and are of identical dimension and composition, as were two other garden pictures of the same summer, likewise bought from Monet by Durand-Ruel on a single day in December 1881.[2] Unfortunately, there is no positive proof of this idea of an original pairing, since the paintings were neither exhibited nor sold in such a manner.

It is clear, however, that the Norton Simon painting served as a study for the final work of the group, the large painting at the National Gallery of Art in Washington (fig. 86d). On 1 October 1881 Monet wrote to Durand-Ruel that he had begun a large painting and that he wanted to do a lot of work before leaving Vétheuil.[3] The National Gallery painting is the largest work from that year to survive and shares with the Norton Simon painting identically placed clouds and a startlingly similar chromatic structure. Indeed, the flower garden represented would not have been at its full height in October (sunflowers go to seed, after all), suggesting that Monet based the larger painting as much on the smaller one as on the garden itself. Essentially, Monet adapted the composition to the larger format simply by adding a nearly identical row of flowerpots to the bottom of the bigger painting. He was evidently so pleased with the effect of the Norton Simon painting that he wanted to monumentalize it.

Whatever his intentions, Monet seems not to have finished the large painting in 1881, although it must have been far enough along for him to sell the Norton Simon "study" on 9 February 1882. Signed and dated 1880, the large painting remained in Monet's possession for many years, before it was sold to the dealer Georges Bernheim, whose first recorded purchase of a painting by Monet was in 1913. This is why Monet misdated the work to 1880, since he had sold all three earlier paintings and could not remember when he had originally worked on it at the time he signed and dated it decades later. An X-ray examination of the Norton Simon painting reveals that Monet had considered inserting one and possibly two figures on the staircase, both of whom he painted over with foliage and stairs as the work progressed, and both of whom appear with a standing female figure in the large version. The figures have been identified as little Michel Monet on the steps with a woman (either Mme

Hoschedé or a servant) and Jean-Pierre Hoschedé at the base of the staircase. All of the figures face the painter as if in greeting.

Perhaps the most fascinating aspect of the paintings is the ways in which they effectively disguise the fact that the main public road west of Vétheuil passed directly in front of the house and between it and the trellised fence at the top of the double staircase, effectively dividing house and garden. Monet was to perform similar feats at Giverny, where his garden was divided by a railroad track that ran between the orchard garden and the water garden. Just as we have no idea of the existence of the public road in the Vétheuil garden paintings from 1881, so too we never see the railroad tracks in Monet's numerous landscapes of the gardens at Giverny. It is clear that when he made the four paintings of 1881 Monet was aware that this would be his family's final summer in Vétheuil. Although his lease ended in October, the family stayed on until December, when they moved to the larger town of Poissy, which Monet had actually mentioned in the May letter to Zola. The summer garden paintings of 1881 were conceived as a form of pictorial farewell to the town of Vétheuil, and they put a very good face on it.

The Norton Simon painting is a marvel of color painting. Monet worked on it with broad brushes, laying in the major areas of the composition with textured paint and then covering almost the entire surface with deft touches that glisten on the surface. It is fascinating to compare it with the dotted surface of Georges Seurat's *Sunday Afternoon on the Island of La Grande Jatte* of 1884–1886 (Art Institute of Chicago), a painting that attempts to record the effect of brilliant summer sunshine using scientific analyses of color and perception. Even accounting for the instability of the younger artist's experimental pigments, the picture by Monet wins hands down in its capturing of brilliant sunshine. Indeed, Monet had such extensive experience painting motifs like this one that he had little need of theories. A detailed examination of the painting by Joseph Fronek suggests that Monet may have started it with a much lower horizon line and considerably more sky. If this is the case, it may well have been the first of the three works surviving from the summer of 1881. The patterns of the shadows tell us that Monet worked on it in the mornings, perhaps dividing his day into garden mornings and *botin* or river afternoons, when it would have been more pleasant to be on the cooler Seine. Fascinatingly, the presumed pair with the Norton Simon painting (fig. 86b) has minimal shadows from the chimney and the flowerpots, suggesting that it was painted nearer midday, and figure 86a has a less-pronounced shadow from the chimney, suggesting that Monet worked on it in the late morning. Hence, we can surmise that Monet breakfasted and started his summer painting day by working in the garden on the three paintings successively.

When the present painting and its pair were purchased from Monet in 1882, they were described in the stock book of Durand-Ruel by the title *Coin du jardin, Vétheuil* (*Corner of the Garden, Vétheuil*). A painting of that title appeared in the only surviving handwritten catalogue of the seventh Impressionist exhibition of 1882. Unfortunately, the painting is not singled out with sufficient clarity in the critical press devoted to the exhibition for us to know which of the two works with that title was selected for display. Either would have looked superb in 1882, when Monet defied the odds and started the second, and most successful, phase of his long career. Although the garden he represented in Vétheuil lacks the horticultural variety of the painter's earlier garden in Argenteuil or his later one in Giverny, it has considerable verve. With lots of sunflowers, four blue-and-white ceramic pots he had purchased for the Argenteuil garden, and some other flowers grown from seed, a dreary slope of a hillside in Vétheuil becomes a paradise-on-a-budget.

1 D. Wildenstein, 1974–1991, vol. 1, letter 218, p. 442.
2 D. Wildenstein, 1974–1991, vol. 1, nos. 680 and 681, p. 404.
3 D. Wildenstein, 1974–1991, vol. 1, letter 223, p. 443.

87

JEAN-FRÉDÉRIC BAZILLE
French, 1841–1870

Woman in a Moorish Costume
1869

Oil on canvas, 39¼ × 23¼ in. (99.7 × 59 cm)
Signed lower right: "F. Bazille"
M.1997.2

PROVENANCE: Marc Bazille (the artist's brother [1845–1923]), by inheritance to; Mme Meynier de Salinelles, Montpellier, by 1941, by inheritance to; Mme Penchinat [or Pinchinat] de Salinelles, Nîmes, by 1959 (sale, Paris, Palais Galliera, 14 June 1967, unnumbered lot). [E. V. Thaw & Co., Inc., New York, sold 23 December 1969 to]; The Norton Simon Foundation, transferred 1997 to; Norton Simon Art Foundation.

EXHIBITIONS: Paris, 1910c, no. 18, as *Femme mauresque*; Montpellier, 1927, no. 30; Paris, 1935a, no. 4, ill.; Montpellier, 1941, no. 30; Paris, 1950b, no. 49; Montpellier, 1959, no. 33; on loan, Phoenix, Art Museum, 20 February–18 June 1970; on loan, Los Angeles, County Museum of Art, 19 June 1970–15 November 1971; on loan, Toledo, Museum of Art, 16 November 1971–6 March 1973; San Francisco, 1973, no. 38, p. 121, ill.; Chicago, 1978, no. 47, ill. pp. 10 color, 99; on loan, Atlanta, High Museum of Art, 20 November 1980–5 August 1981.

REFERENCES: Hamel, 1910, p. 13; Poulain, 1932, no. 34, pp. 135–136, 217; Laprade, 1935, pp. 1, 8; Guérif, 1943, p. 24; Sarraute, 1948, pp. 81–82, no. 34; Daulte, 1950, pp. 1, ill., 8; Daulte, 1952, no. 45, pp. 69, 143, 150, 184–185, ill.; Bezombes, 1953, no. 302, pp. 185, 103, ill.; Daulte, 1970, no. 226, p. 88, color ill.; Dolan, 1990, pp. 99, 100, fig. 1; F.-B. Michel, 1992, pp. 247–248; Marandel, 1992, pp. 66–67, 75, 163, fig. 30, color ills. pp. 66, 67 (detail); Daulte, 1992, no. 50, pp. 69, 122, 125, 134, 137, 143, 175–176, 68, color ill.; Bajou-Charpentreau, 1993, pp. 172–173, fig. 89, p. 163 (X-ray); Bonafoux, 1994, pp. 48, 49, color ill.; Schulman, 1995, no. 49, pp. 189–190, ill., p. 190 (X-ray); Pitman, 1998, pp. 169–170, 178–179, 261 n. 4, fig. 111; DelPlato, 2002, pp. 233, 235, fig. 7.3.

TECHNICAL NOTES: The X-ray shows another painting beneath the standing woman (fig. 87b). Viewing the left side of the present picture as the top of the first composition, the X-ray exposed a partially draped female nude lying on a bed. The white and light green paint at the upper right of the present picture corresponds to drapery in the first picture. With minimum painting out and no detectable scraping—the original design is partially visible in raking light—Bazille painted *Woman in a Moorish Costume* over the reclining nude. He used opaque, pasty paint alla prima in detectable brushstrokes wet in wet (see the breast, for example) and wet over dry. The rough, dark green paint following the upper form of the standing figure either adjusts her outline or, less likely, hides paint from the first picture. The fine, plain-weave canvas has a thick white-gray ground. It was lined to a heavier fabric after the tacking edges were removed. The stretcher, most likely original, has the vertical bar asymmetrically placed to the left of center, signifying that the stretcher has been reduced in width. Old stretcher marks that are visible in the X-ray lead to the speculation that the first composition was cut on the bottom. The painting has a synthetic varnish, and ultraviolet light shows only a few small restorations. (JF)

FRÉDÉRIC BAZILLE IS the sole painter associated with the young Impressionists who never lived to see the group coalesce. Killed in the Franco-Prussian War in 1870 at the age of twenty-nine, he had no effect on the public phase of Impressionism. Indeed, his canvases remained for the most part in the collection of his wealthy Protestant family in Montpellier, France, inaccessible to the critics and scholars who defined the Impressionist movement in the late nineteenth and early twentieth centuries. Nonetheless, Bazille was central to the formative decade of Impressionism, playing roles in the movement that straddled those of patron and colleague. Wealthier than Claude Monet, Pierre-Auguste Renoir, or Alfred Sisley, he often intervened financially in their respective crises. When his works of the second half of the 1860s are placed in the same context as theirs, it becomes clear that his pictorial contributions to the movement's beginnings more than matched those of his longer-lived, and hence more famous, friends.

The single work by Bazille in the Norton Simon collections is one of his greatest. Painted in the penultimate year of the artist's life, it is among the handful of what we might call "late-early" works that explain just why Édouard Manet, Monet, and Renoir admired the tall, young artist from Montpellier. The painting represents a dark-haired model engaged in tying the sash of her North African costume. She is shown in an undifferentiated space—most likely the painter's Paris studio—with three "props," a striped man's shawl, a sheathed dagger, and a brass tray, all arranged around her. Bazille signed the painting with a flourish in the lower right corner and left us many pictorial clues in the area around the central figure that he reworked the canvas repeatedly. Thus, the painting projects an image of both artistic control and careful pictorial deliberation. Each of the carefully selected items that surround the figure is perfectly placed, and no area of the composition is left unresolved.

Unfortunately for its contemporary interpreter, the painting seems never to have been exhibited in the artist's lifetime. Mentioned once in an undated letter written to his parents sometime in 1868–1869, the painting was made while Bazille also worked on his portrait of

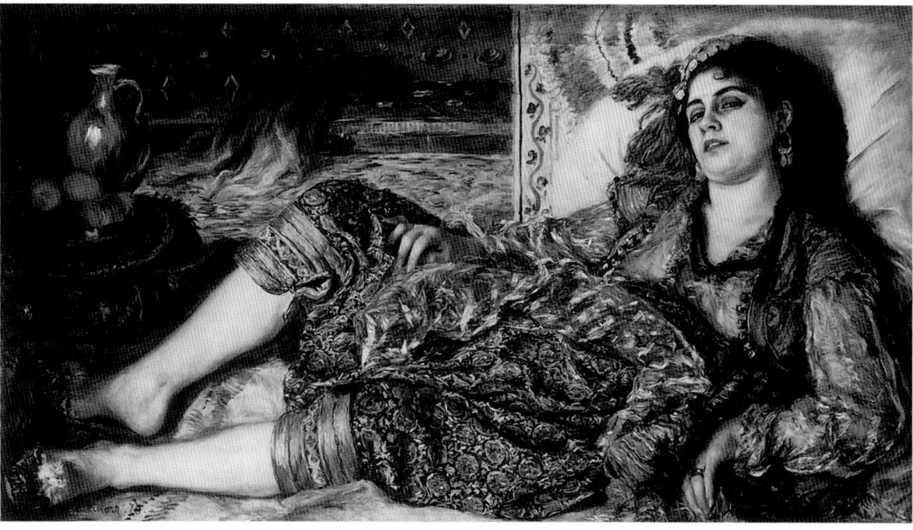

Fig. 87a Pierre-Auguste Renoir, *Odalisque*, 1871, oil on canvas, 27¼ × 48¼ in. (69.2 × 122.6 cm), National Gallery of Art, Washington, Chester Dale Collection

Edmund Maître, dated 1869, and based on what the painter called "a Moorish model."[1] What, we must ask, did he mean by "Moorish"? The word had no national connotations in the 1860s, evoking instead images of medieval, pre-Christian Spain rather than any contemporary country in the north of Africa. Yet, the word *model* does help, because it makes clear that the painting was made in the artist's studio from a hired model rather than on a trip to North Africa. Thus, it takes its place in the long and productive history of urban Orientalist exoticism, about which much has been written in the past generation. Several writers, particularly Patrice Marandel, who, with Dianne W. Pitman, is the most important twentieth-century scholar of Bazille's work, have stressed this fact, comparing and contrasting Bazille's painting with those by Jean-Léon Gérôme, Henri Regnault, and Renoir.

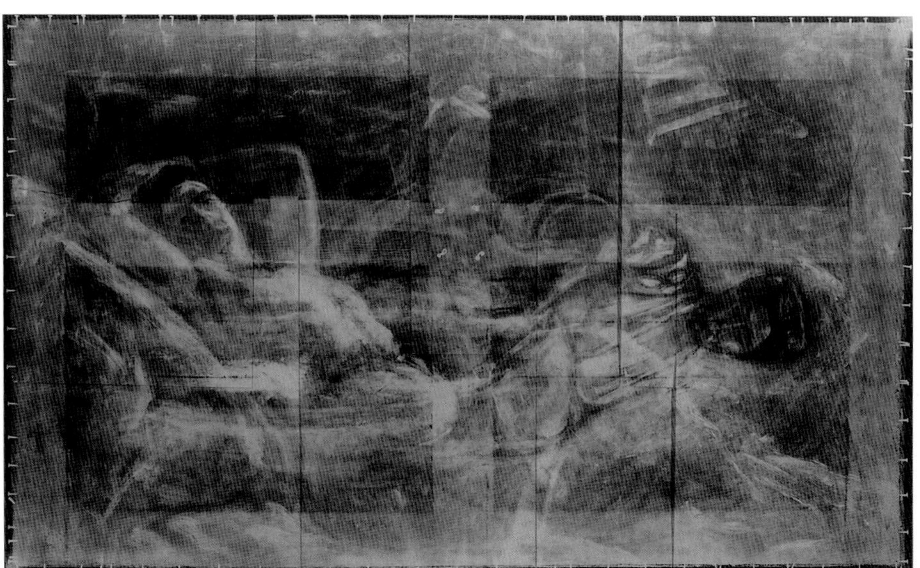

Fig. 87b X-ray photograph of cat. 87

Many writers who have addressed the painting have indicated that Bazille's model in 1868–1869 was the same woman used by his close friend Renoir one year later in his *Odalisque* (fig. 87a). Although her name is mentioned only once in the literature devoted to Bazille,[2] the woman is well known in the Renoir literature as his French mistress, Lise Tréhot, who was associated with Renoir throughout the second half of the 1860s, was painted by him at least from 1867 until her marriage to an architect in 1872, and who is known to have had two children by Renoir. The physical resemblance between Tréhot as painted by Renoir and the "Moorish model" in the present painting is unmistakable. She may also have appeared in several other paintings by Bazille, including *Nu couché* and *Femme nue de dos* in the Musée Fabre, Montpellier, and *Jeune Femme aux yeux baissés* in the Mitsubishi Collection, Tokyo. Although none of the paintings is dated, the group indicates the closeness of Renoir and Bazille in the second half of the 1860s and corroborates the fact that they often painted together.

Lise Tréhot had black hair, dark eyes, a full figure, and a sultry look, which, to a northern Frenchman, would have seemed more foreign than French. Fortunately for Bazille, she was accustomed to posing in the nude and was, in addition, exotic enough in her looks that he could pass her to his parents as "a Moorish model" without raising fears on their part of an illicit romance. Bazille painted her reclining on a divan in a fully realized painting underneath the present composition, and this fact is revealed by an X-ray that has already been published and discussed in the extensive literature devoted to Bazille (fig. 87b). This painting is utterly conventional in composition. However, it is interestingly prudish, in that the model, although erotically charged in her pose, is decorously covered with a negligée. She does, however, look forthrightly at the painter-viewer in such a way as to make us complicit in a sexual drama. There is no such drama in the finished painting, which is characterized by a cool detachment and modesty, with the exception of the barely visible nipple of the model's breast.

Indeed, the model is absorbed in her task, her eyes lowered to inspect her sash. It almost seems as if she is readying herself to pose and thus has not assumed a fixed pose for the artist. This fact gives the painting a decorous

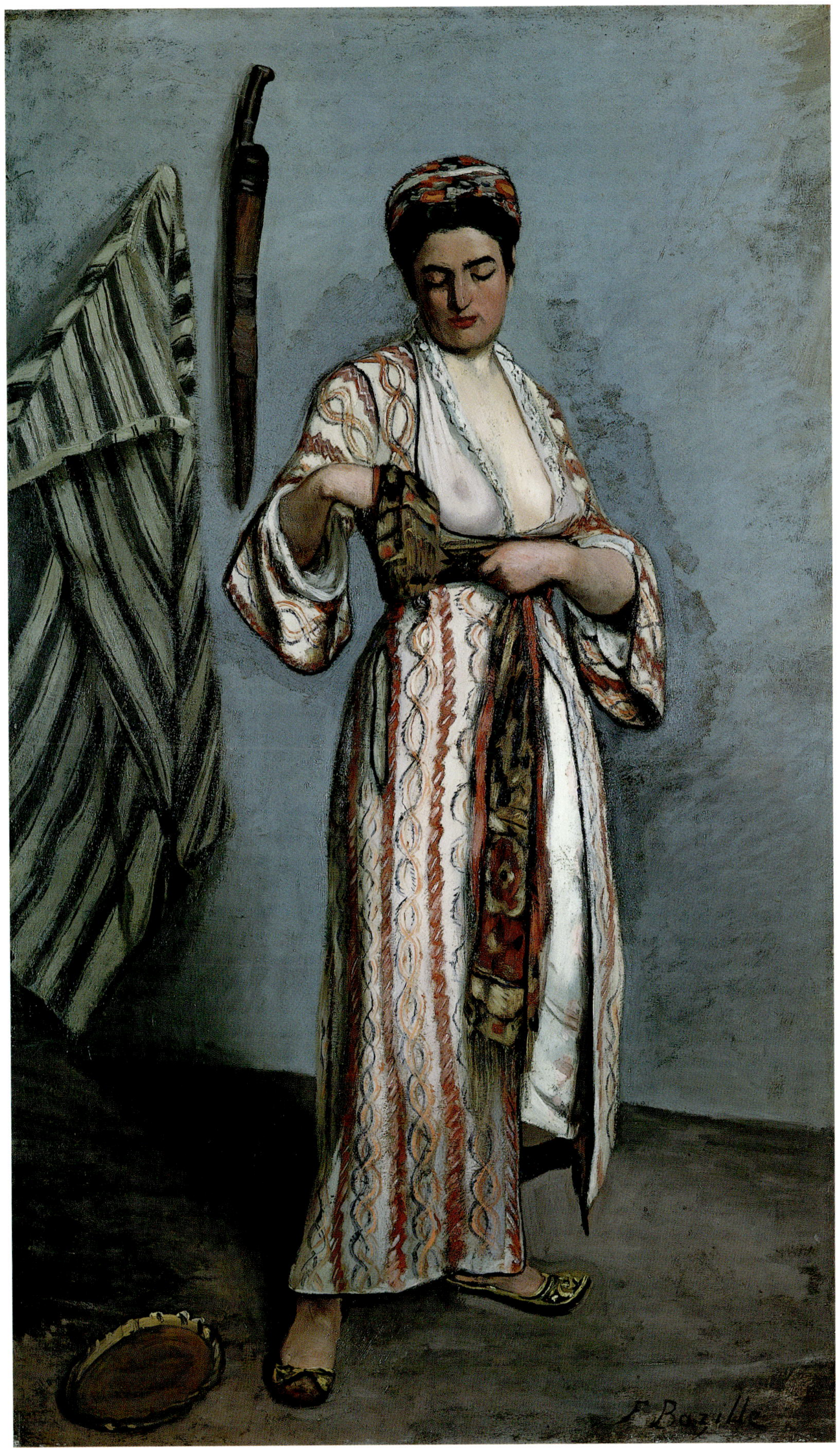

87

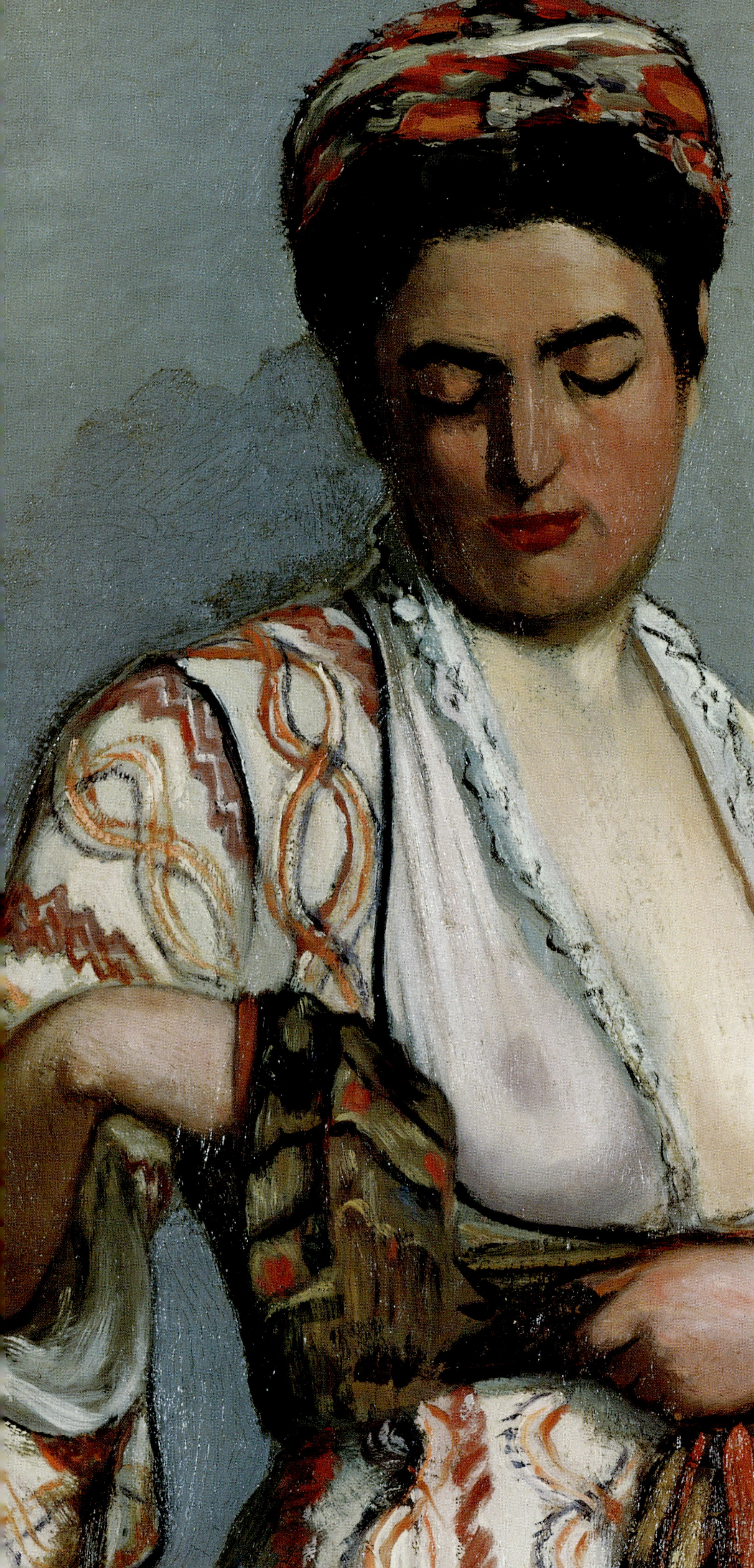

quality, which is in strict contrast with the rejected painting beneath it. Bazille's emphasis on studio practice and on the artificiality of Orientalism is fascinating, especially when we recognize the connections between Bazille's work and the 1867 novel by the Goncourt brothers, *Manette Salomon.* A brilliant article by Thérèse Dolan makes it clear that several of Bazille's paintings of 1868–1869 relate closely to passages from the Goncourts' novel about the life of a Jewish artist's model in 1850s Paris. Dolan points to a lengthy passage rather late in the novel in which Manette discovers Oriental costumes in the painter Coriolis's armoire, tries them on, and is transformed into "la vraie femme d'Ionie—la femme de séduction."[3] All of this suggests the superb Orientalist scenes painted by Eugène Delacroix after he visited a Muslim house in Morocco in 1832. It also reminds us of the fact that only Jewish women could pose freely for Western men in North Africa, a social and religious condition that affected both Delacroix in 1832 and Renoir in the early 1880s. Manette, too, was Jewish and in the Goncourts' novel was understood by anti-Semitic French readers as a negative influence on the Catholic painter Coriolis. (By contrast, the Bazilles were Protestant.)

Although this seems to go a bit far afield, there is as direct a link between Delacroix's Orientalist paintings and this work by Bazille as there is between the Goncourts' novel and the painter from the Midi. Indeed, Alfred Bruyas, the great collector of contemporary art from Bazille's native city, Montpellier, had just given a large part of his private collection of contemporary art to the Musée Fabre in Montpellier in 1868. Among this large gift arranged in a special gallery was Delacroix's 1847 masterpiece, *Algerian Women in Their Apartment* (fig. 87c). Delacroix had died in 1863, four years before Bruyas's gift and also before Bazille's reintroduction to the Romantic painter's canvas at the opening of the Bruyas Gallery. What is therefore clear is that there are three major sources for Bazille's Orientalist masterpiece, a Realist novel, the death of Delacroix, and the gift of a major collection of contemporary French painting to his hometown museum in Montpellier. Bazille used each of these sources as an impetus to creation rather than as a model to follow closely. His finished work has a vigor of composition, an originality of touch, and a psychological detachment found nowhere in the works by the Goncourts or Delacroix.

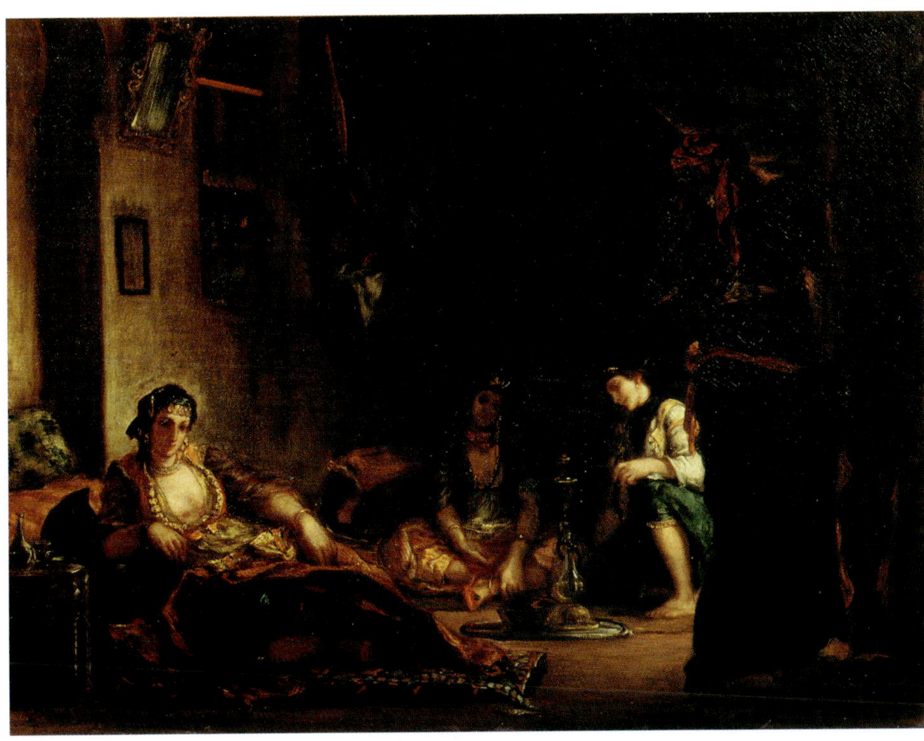

Fig. 87c Eugène Delacroix, *Algerian Women in Their Apartment*, 1849, oil on canvas, $33\frac{1}{8} \times 43\frac{3}{4}$ in. (84 × 111 cm), Musée Fabre, Montpellier; photo: Réunion des Musées Nationaux / Art Resource, NY

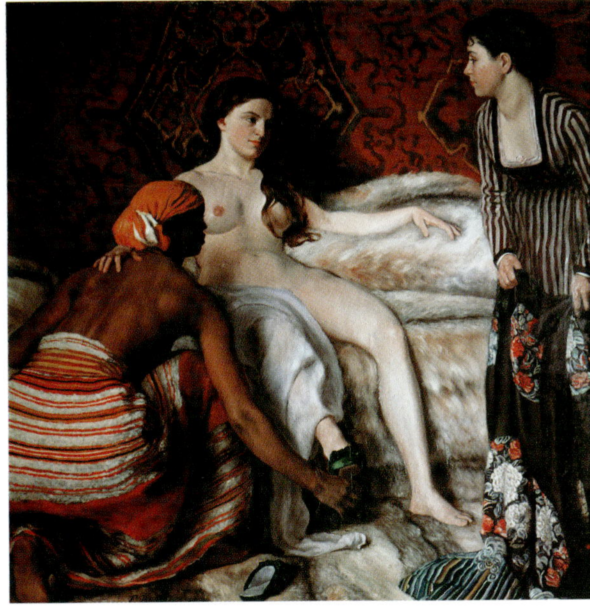

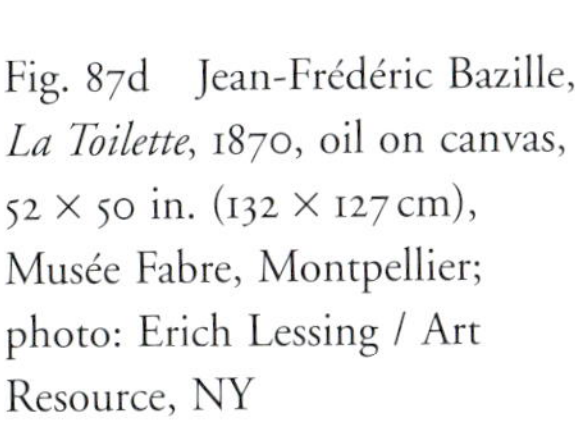

Fig. 87d Jean-Frédéric Bazille, *La Toilette*, 1870, oil on canvas, 52 × 50 in. (132 × 127 cm), Musée Fabre, Montpellier; photo: Erich Lessing / Art Resource, NY

How, then, are we to interpret this studio picture? Surely Manet can be counted a source for its dry paint surface and its modernist composition. One thinks of Manet's Spanish canvases of the first half of the 1860s as models for the exoticism of Bazille's work. Bazille worked on two major Salon paintings in 1869, one of male bathers out of doors and the other of a female nude and two attendants in an exotic Oriental interior. He submitted both to the Salon of 1870, but *La Toilette* (fig. 87d) was rejected, presumably because of its sexually charged exoticism and the awkwardness of the principal nude figure. Bazille used Lise Tréhot again as the model for a Caucasian servant to the red-haired nude who is being washed and dressed. This large and ambitious painting courts failure with a real determination. The earlier and simpler painting in the Norton Simon Museum succeeds by attempting less and accomplishing more. Indeed, when Renoir completed *Odalisque* in 1870, just before the death of his friend Bazille later in the year, he embraced convention. By posing Lise in exotic costume and having her recline enticingly while she looks longingly into the viewer's eyes, Renoir attempted to use the art of painting to seduce his viewer. Bazille was at once more modern and more ambiguous in his aims, and we can never know whether his standing Lise in Oriental costume is dressing or undressing for her viewer.

1 Sarraute, 1948, p. 82.
2 Bajou-Charpentreau, 1993, p. 172.
3 Dolan, 1990, pp. 102–103.

88

Pierre-Auguste Renoir
French, 1841–1919

The Pont des Arts, Paris
1867–1868

Oil on canvas, 24 × 39½ in. (60.9 × 100.3 cm)
Signed lower right: "A. Renoir"
F.1968.13

Provenance: The artist; sold 31 March 1872 for Ff 200 to; [Durand-Ruel, Paris, stock nos. 1131 and 178, until at least 1875/1877]. comtesse de Rasty, Paris. [Galerie Matthiesen, Berlin, 1929]. (Max Silberberg and Hugo Simon sale, Paris, Galerie Georges Petit, 9 June 1932, lot 25, ill., bought in); Dr. van Kricken to; Mme Perls/Frank Perls, Paris, sold December 1936 for $12,900 to; [M. Knoedler & Co., Inc., New York; jointly owned with Carstairs Gallery, New York, stock no. A1802, sold 3 June 1941 for $19,500 to]; Richard N. Ryan, New York, by inheritance to; Mrs. Richard N. Ryan, New York, subsequently married to W. Clifford Klenk, Wainscott, N.Y. (sale, New York, Parke-Bernet Galleries, 9 October 1968, lot 8, ill., to); The Norton Simon Foundation.

Exhibitions: London, 1872b, no. 37; New York, 1939a, no. 34, ill.; New York, 1940c, no. 18; New York, 1950, no. 2, ill.; Dayton, 1951, no. 46, ill.; Detroit, 1954, no. 59, ill.; Los Angeles, 1955, no. 4, ill.; New York, 1958, no. 1, ill.; Washington, 1959, no. 39, ill.; Dallas, 1961, no. 56, ill.; New York, 1965, no. 3, ill.; New York, 1966a, no. 28, ill.; Philadelphia, 1969, no. 10, ill.; on loan, Los Angeles, County Museum of Art, 28 August 1969–16 February 1971; on loan, New York, Metropolitan Museum of Art, 17 February 1971–23 January 1973; Chicago, 1973, no. 6, colorpl. III; San Francisco, 1973, no. 36, ill.; on loan, South Bend, University of Notre Dame, Snite Museum of Art, 8 October 1980–3 September 1981.

References: Meier-Graefe, 1929a, pp. 28–29, fig. 14; Rewald, 1937, p. 19, ill.; Lord, 1939, p. 40, pl. B; Brian, 1940, pp. 6, ill., 7; Rewald, 1946, p. 147, ill. (1961 and 1973 eds., pp. 272, 354, ill. 167); Goldwater, 1958, p. 60, ill.; Nochlin, 1971, pp. 20, 22, 240, fig. 6; Champa, 1973, pp. 14–15, 46, fig. 21; Willis, 1973, p. 52, ill.; Schulze, 1973, p. 42; Patterson, 1973, pp. 43–45, ill.; Mullins, 1974, pp. 36–37, ill.; Rewald, 1974, fig. 7 (detail); Wheldon, 1975, pp. 37–38, ill.; Steadman, 1976, pp. 222, ill., 228; Callen, 1978, pp. 9, 30–31, pls. 8, 9; Martini, 1978b, p. 12, pl. VIII; Bell, 1978, pl. 9; Duret-Robert, 1978, p. 100, fig. 14; Monneret, 1978–1981, vol. 2, pp. 165–166; Oakley, 1980, p. 7, pl. 3; D. Thomas, 1980, p. 7, ill.; R. Thomson, 1982, p. 330, pl. 45; Gaunt, 1982, p. 4, fig. 11; White, 1984, pp. 26, 40, 285; C. Schneider, 1985, pp. 49, 50, fig. 2; Distel, 1985, pp. 19, 27 n. 4, 181, fig. j; Herbert, 1988, pp. 7–9, pls. 9, 10; Monneret, 1989, p. 34, fig. 1; Clarke, 1991, pp. 111–112, fig. 108; Stevenson, 1991, pp. 13, 42, 52, 84, color ill., 42–43; Bade, 1992, p. 20, ill.; House, 1994, p. 15, fig. 1; Brettell, 1996, pp. 118–119, fig. 63; Bailey, 1997, pp. 249–250, 337 n. 23; Callen, 2000, pp. 120, 184, color fig. 173; Goldin, 2001, p. 127; Néret, 2001, p. 22, ill.; Rubin, 2003, pp. 78–82, color ill., fig. 63 (detail), Forgione, 2005, pp. 665–666, ill.

Technical Notes: Because of the numerous layers of opaque paint (3 or more in most places, with impasto and brushstrokes), the surface of this picture gives little indication of its plain-weave, medium-weight fabric support. At the lower left edge, for example, there are three fairly thick layers of paint: a gray color on the off-white ground and then two layers of blue paint above that. The local colors are all mixed with white except for a few accents of bright red. Brush sizes vary from about ½ inch wide in the sky to a narrower size and shorter strokes in the cityscape. Paint was applied wet in wet but usually over paint that had set below. It seems that the artist first laid in at least part of the basic design in a light, opaque gray. Most buildings, for example, have a gray underpainting. A light pinkish or gray underpainting exists in various points of the sky; the warmer pink color projects the blue color on top while the gray gives depth. Though the application seems entirely direct, there are very thinly applied opaque paints, particularly in the sky, that allow the color below to show through to create a sense of atmosphere. Figures were painted onto the ocher layer that is also the quay on which they walk, but the gray of the walls behind is painted around them. In these numerous layers of paint the artist reworked some forms. The top of the barge located at lower left was once peaked and the roofs in the background show numerous adjustments in the X-ray. The ground, thick enough almost to fill the canvas weave, may be commercially applied. The painting, lined with an aqueous adhesive to a similar type canvas, no longer has its original tacking edges. However, in a few areas slivers of original canvas edge covered with ground remain. The 5-part butt-join stretcher may or may not be original. The cracks in a pattern of medium-wide intervals show dark, probably because they expose gray underpainting. A few minor losses exist and show in ultraviolet light as being restored. The signature remains in good condition beneath a discolored varnish layer. The painting was cleaned in 1990 and varnished with Soluvar. Remnants of an earlier discolored natural varnish exist. Several questions remain: a strip about 1-inch wide along the top is different in texture and color from the rest of the painting. In the X-radiograph and under ultraviolet light the strip appears different as well. Age characteristics and lack of any other evidence to the contrary suggest that the strip is original. The paint around the dome appears smeared. This paint appears turquoise under normal viewing conditions and shows dark in ultraviolet light. However, here, too, age characteristics suggest that it is original. (JF)

We know from Claude Monet's letter to his friend Frédéric Bazille, provisionally dated 20 May 1867,[1] that Monet and Renoir were working on a series of views of Paris in the spring of 1867; Renoir's *Pont des Arts* is surely one of them. Monet had already applied to the minister of the fine arts, the comte de

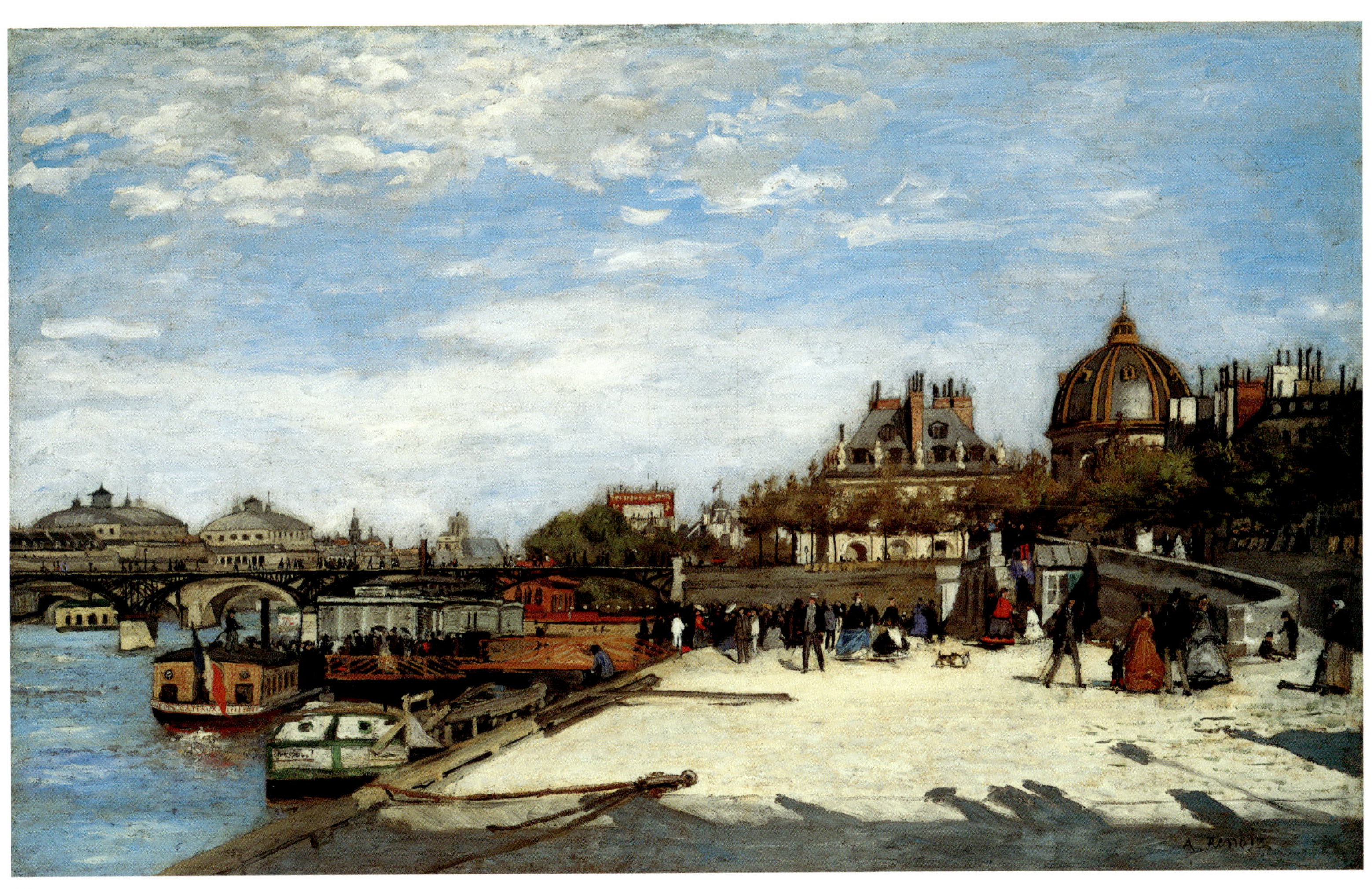

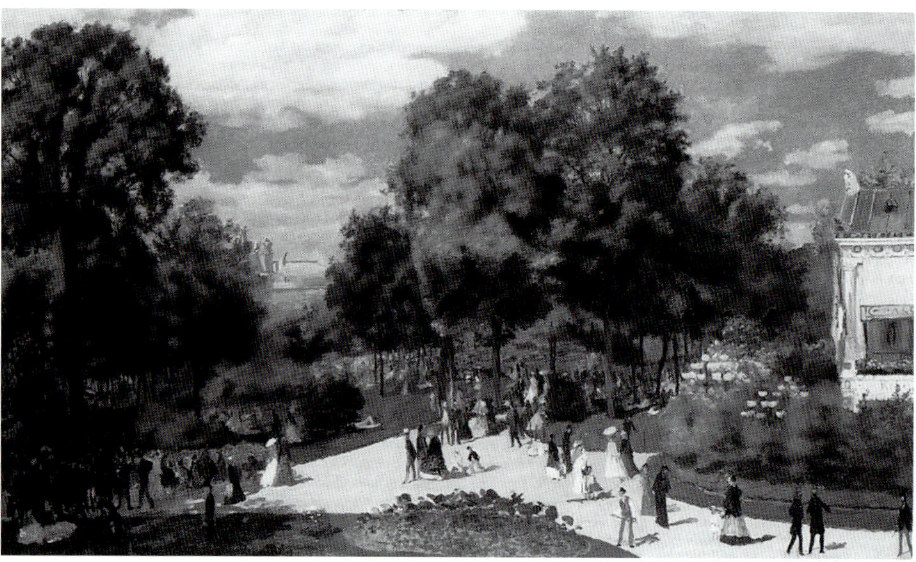

Fig. 88a Pierre-Auguste Renoir, *The Champs-Elysées during the 1867 Exposition Universelle*, 1867, oil on canvas, 30⅛ × 52 in. (76.5 × 132.1 cm), private collection

Fig. 88b Édouard Manet, *Exposition Universelle*, 1867, oil on canvas, 42⅛ × 77½ in. (107 × 197 cm), National Gallery of Norway, Oslo

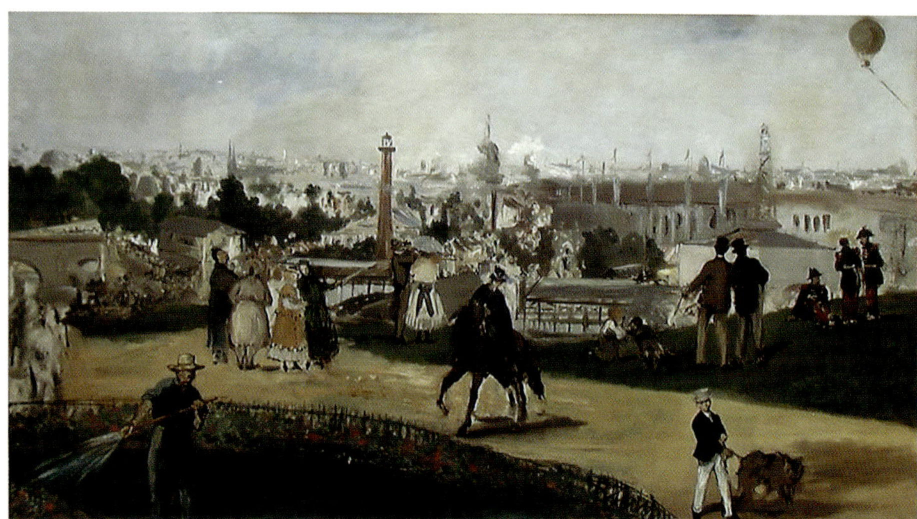

Nieuwerkerke, on 27 April of that year, for permission to paint from Claude Perrault's colonnades at the Louvre.[2] And it is obvious that the two young artists (Monet was twenty-seven and Renoir twenty-nine) were fired up to make a series of Paris views in connection with the Exposition Universelle being held in Paris in May.

In many ways, 1867 was the apogee of the Second Empire. Most of the major urban projects instigated by Napoleon III and his minister Baron Georges Haussmann were either completed or well under way, and the great capital city awaited the hordes of provincial and foreign tourists who would flock to Paris for the exposition. Seemingly, everyone got on board. Émile Zola began to serialize his first Parisian novel, soon to be called *Thérèse Raquin*. Jacques Offenbach premiered his operetta *La Vie parisienne*. Gustave Flaubert was hard at work on his novel of urban realism, *L'Éducation sentimentale*, which appeared in 1868. And Édouard Manet—the painter of modern urban life par excellence—decided to rent a building and mount a private retrospective of his career just outside the precincts of the exposition. We also know a good deal about the appearance of Paris that summer because a record number of guidebooks and photographs prepared for visitors to the exposition were published. The most spectacular was La Bédolière's guidebook of Paris and its environs, which acts even today as the most detailed record of tourist Paris during the Second Empire. And, there is little doubt that Flaubert's friend Maxime du Camp was hard at work assembling material for his magisterial multivolume portrait of Paris, *Paris, ses organes et ses fonctions*, which was published in 1869. Nearly every serious artist, musician, and writer in Paris was making a representation of his or her city, which had by then supplanted Rome as the capital of European art.

Although there is still no reliable catalogue raisonné of Renoir's paintings, we know of two major works begun or completed in 1867 that can be linked to this collective artistic project. The Norton Simon painting is the smaller but better known of the two. Its companion, *The Champs-Élysées during the 1867 Exposition Universelle* (fig. 88a), which remains in a private collection to this day, has rarely been reproduced in color and has not been exhibited in more than a generation. Together, these two pictures, when combined with the three major works of 1866–1867 painted from the Louvre by Monet, are the most important urban view paintings of the Second Empire, surely the greatest single period of modern urban development of the nineteenth century. Both of Renoir's paintings are larger than any of Monet's three modestly scaled canvases (figs. 88c, 88d, and 88e). To this group of five paintings by the two future Impressionists we can add Manet's own *Exposition Universelle* from 1867 (fig. 88b). Manet's painting, like that by Renoir of the Champs-Élysées, seems to have been intended to represent the city during the exposition. Unfortunately, these works have never been assembled for exhibition, even in Theodore Reff's tantalizing *Manet and Modern Paris* at the National Gallery of Art, Washington, in 1982. Hence, the greatest urban paintings since Canaletto's Venice, Bellotto's Vienna, or Turner's London are known only from scattered reproductions and one lengthy

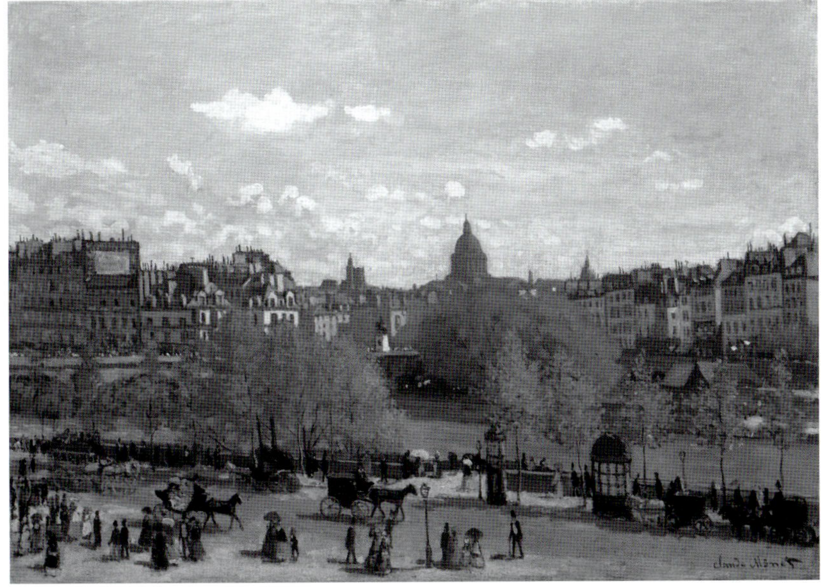

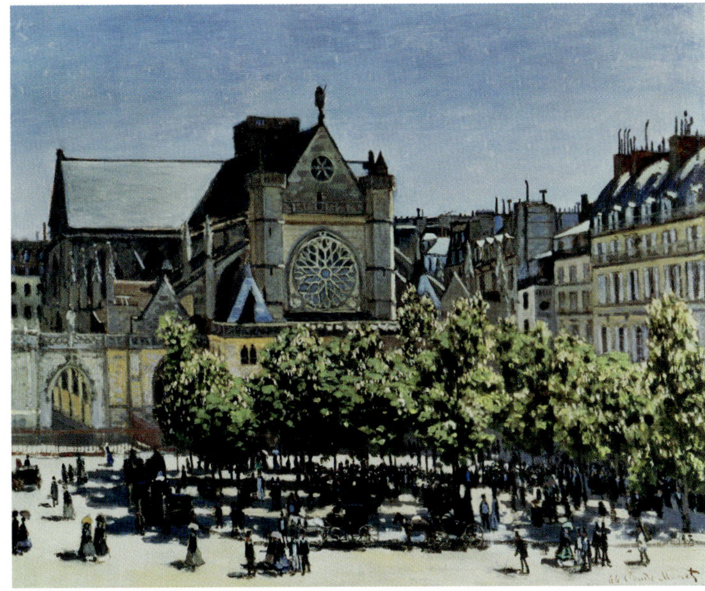

Fig. 88c (*above left*) Claude Monet, *The Quai du Louvre*, 1867, oil on canvas, 25⅝ × 36¼ in. (65 × 92 cm), Gemeentemuseum, The Hague

Fig. 88d (*above right*) Claude Monet, *Saint-Germain-L'Auxerrois, Paris*, 1867, oil on canvas, 31⅛ × 38⅝ in. (79 × 98 cm), Nationalgalerie, Staatliche Museen zu Berlin; photo: Bildarchiv Preussischer Kulturbesitz / Art Resource, NY

discussion in Robert L. Herbert's important book on Impressionism (1988).

Even before its acquisition by the Norton Simon Foundation in 1968, Renoir's *Pont des Arts* had entered the world of scholarly discourse about Second Empire painting. Although it was included neither in the pathbreaking exhibition devoted to that era of French culture organized by the Philadelphia Museum of Art in 1978 nor in the Metropolitan Museum of Art's *Origins of Impressionism* of 1994, it has been published many times, often in color, and written about extensively by art historians from Julius Meier-Graefe through John Rewald to Kermit Champa and Robert L. Herbert. (It has not, however, played a major role in the poststructuralist and other theory-based writing of young art historians from the last generation.) Thus, it has joined Monet's *Garden of the Princess* (fig. 88e) as one of a handful of Second Empire representations of Paris that epitomize the politics and aesthetics of that great capital during the years of its modern redefinition.

Where in Paris does Renoir take us? We are standing with him on the Port du St.-Pères below the Quai Malaquais, accessible to us via the ramp on the right. Immediately behind us is the Pont du Carrousel, an almost new bridge completed in 1834 that linked the left bank with a vast new archway through the Louvre, one of the most glorious of the Second Empire building projects. In fact, Hector Lefuel's famous Louvre "guichets," as they were called, were actually under construction in 1867 when Renoir made his painting. The shadows of *promeneurs* on the Pont du Carrousel decorate the foreground of Renoir's composition. From this shady and protected vantage point, we look almost due east, up the Seine, and see a span of urban monuments starting at the left with the Second Empire pair of theaters at Châtelet, crossing the Seine along the crowded 1801–1803 cast iron Pont des Arts, passing by the leafy square du Vert Gallant at the point of the Île-de-la-Cité, and ending, on the right, with Louis Le Vau's side facade and dome of 1662 for the Institut de France.

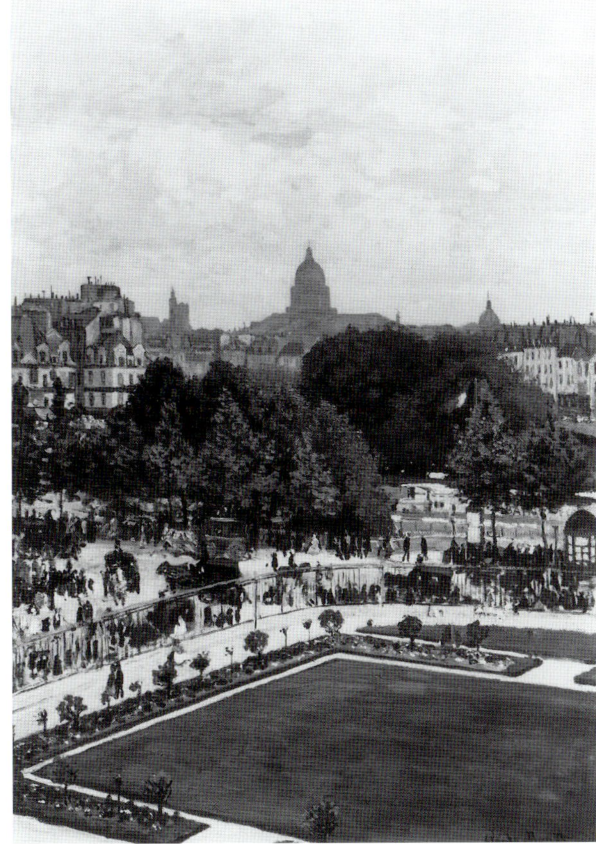

Fig. 88e Claude Monet, *Garden of the Princess*, 1867, oil on canvas, 36⅛ × 24⅜ in. (91.8 × 61.9 cm), Allen Memorial Art Museum, Oberlin

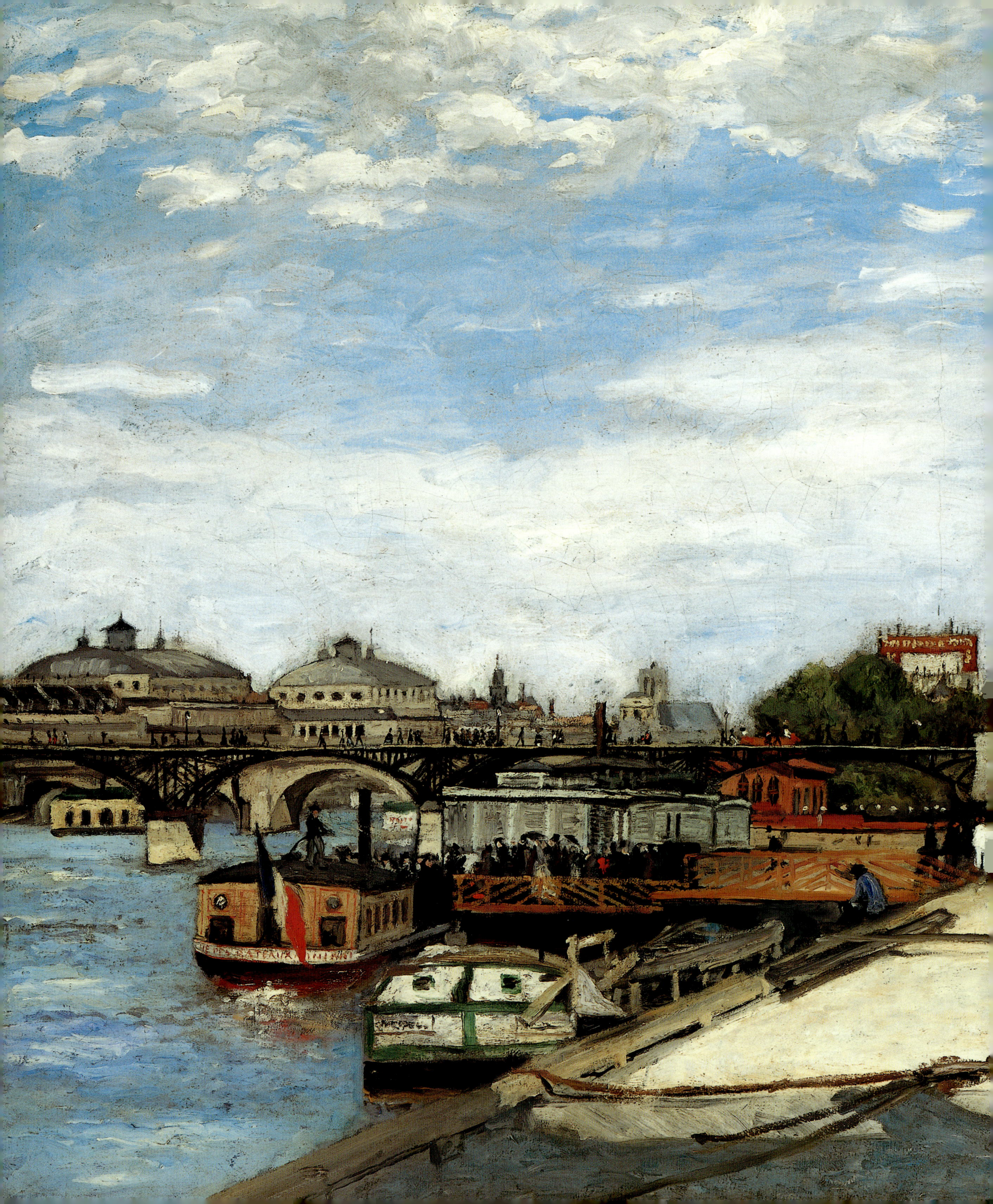

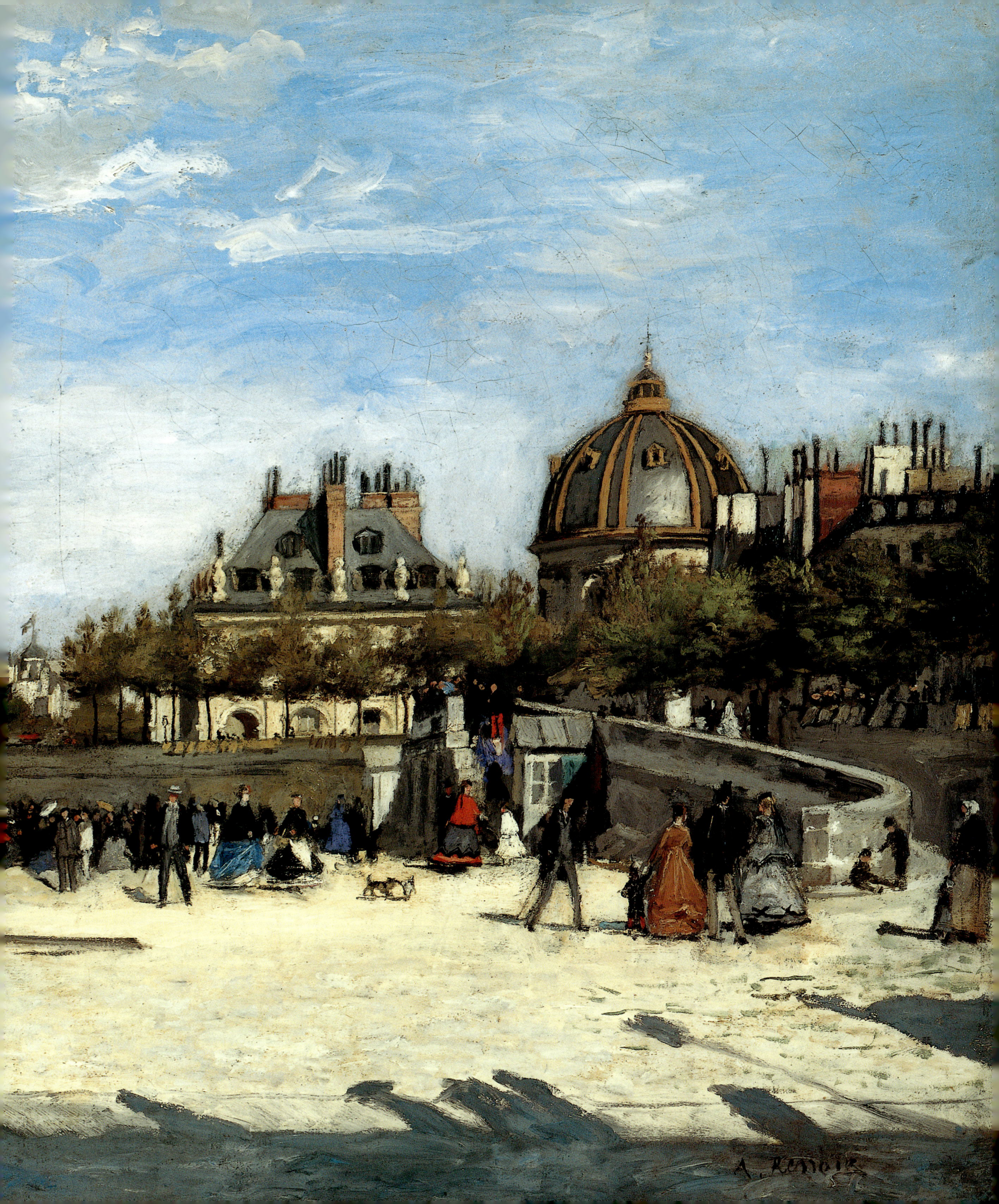

Any Parisian would put the time as afternoon and the season as summer. In all probability, the painter intended us to think of the city as observed during the Exposition Universelle, which opened in May of that year. However, the painting, though signed, is undated, forcing us to dissociate it from a particular year, and there are few clues in it that would allow us to date it with precision to any particular year in the 1860s. The vast crinoline dresses worn by the women in the middle ground are similar to those worn throughout the late 1850s and 1860s in popular imagery and in the paintings of Eugène Boudin, Monet, Franz Xaver Winterhalter, and many others.

Renoir's choice of vantage point is fascinating, because it is painted in a part of Paris particularly associated with art. Immediately to the left, but outside Renoir's framed view, is the long side facade of the Musée du Louvre, the windows of whose recently renovated Grande Galerie could be seen simply by turning one's head. Immediately to the right, but also off-view, is Félix Dubon's handsome river facade for the École des Beaux-Arts, which had given the famous school a quayside presence only since 1862. Yet, just as Monet elected to paint Paris from the Louvre, almost so as to be forced not to include the building itself, Renoir selected a wide expanse that could easily have included both the Louvre and the École des Beaux-Arts. He chose to leave them out, concentrating instead on the teeming life along the quays, ports, bridges, and, of course, the river Seine itself.

The Port du St.-Pères was one of the most active places in Paris from which to catch ferryboats or to go for a bracing swim in the waters of the Seine. We see crowds of people waiting to get on a yellowish ferryboat with a triumphant tricolor flag, and just beyond it are the walls of two river bathing establishments—frequented by the working class and petty bourgeoisie—that Honoré Daumier and other popular illustrators of the Second Empire lampooned. The quay immediately in front of us is full of people, but they are safely away from the painter-viewer, permitting us to look at them directly but at the same time allowing us the luxury of social distance and a slightly condescending gaze. The viewer is thus at once spatially involved and psychologically or socially detached from Renoir's urban panorama, and this distance, in an odd way, is reinforced by the foreground shadows of the figures who come and go on the bridge above and behind us.

As Richard Thomson has pointed out in his article on dogs in nineteenth-century French painting, two pet dogs (he calls them "errant, autonomous dogs") cavort in the middle ground, giving us the fun of attempting to identify their human owners.[3] Men, women, and children mix with genial ease, suggesting a holiday or a Sunday in the city rather than workaday reality. A worker or perhaps a sailor, in his blue *blouson*, sits with his black dog on the side of the river. The background is crowded with scores of other tiny figures, who climb the stairs to the quay itself, shop in the stalls along the quay, or cross the Pont des Arts. The connoisseur of Paris will recognize the top of the tower at the Bastille, a church tower, and numerous chimneys that punctuate the sky. Renoir's treatment of the sky is also pleasant and eventless in its banality, refusing to allow our attention to leave the city and its inhabitants on this glorious, balmy day.

The painting is so unproblematic, so empty of discord or dissension, so optimistic that we yearn simply to be there. Joining Renoir on the quay on a gorgeous day in the center of the greatest cultural capital in nineteenth-century Europe was made as easy as possible. Indeed, one wants to link the painting to those of Canaletto or Michele Marieschi, who painted Venice during feast days or at the arrivals of important people. The same ease of access, the same generality of view, the same sense of pleasurable detachment can be found in Renoir's two views of 1867 Paris. Yet several writers, most notably Robert L. Herbert and John House, have worked a little too hard to find purposeful artistic statements concerning working-class life and social conflict in them. For each author, the figures of the worker/sailor and the working-class woman with two children on the right side of the middle ground speak to the social complexities of Parisian urban culture in the Second Empire. The inclusion of these types, they argue, was not a morally or socially neutral act by Renoir. For House, Renoir was "quietly indicating here that social and economic divisions remained, even in the sunlit modern world."[4]

There is good reason to believe—based on both the physical evidence of the canvas and a later account of Renoir's habit of painting in cities—that the working-class figures were observed by Renoir while he worked, and that any statement his paintings may make is therefore inadvertent or neutral. Indeed, like the staffage figures that litter middle grounds throughout the history of urban view painting, they were selected for their variety of pose, costume, gender, age, color, size, and position so as to make the scene appear to have been actually observed. Several writers of the *Pont des Arts* have observed that Renoir painted the architecture, vegetation, and water first, before adding the majority of the figures, as if populating an urban set.[5] William Gaunt and others tell us that when Renoir was painting the Pont Neuf in 1872, he painted the cityscape's architectural element and then worked from a café, while his brother stopped passersby with small queries so that they would stand still long enough for Renoir to paint them.[6] One wonders whether Monet did that in 1867. If the painting intends any statement, it is that the modern city is composed of a melange of social types—highborn and vulgar, sophisticated and ignorant, the in-set and the plebeians.

Many writers have discussed the easy spaciousness of Renoir's cityscape. Unlike the three works by Monet and Renoir's own painting of the Champs-Élysées, all of which were painted from above, Renoir here places the viewer firmly on the ground. Rather than a detached and expensive balcony view of the urban spectacle—such as the painter Gustave Caillebotte later offered—Renoir allows us to imagine that we and he could simply stroll into the painting. We are in the cool shadows of the bridge and are not, therefore, easily viewable by the sunstruck figures. The shadows of the figures strolling on the bridge above us are angled because of the direction of the light in such a way that their diagonal shadows double as perspective-exaggeration devices that almost force us into the painting. If ever a painting uses diminution of human scale to make architectural space legible, it is this one. From the proximate midsize figures on the port to the tiny, but countable, figure-ants that move to and fro across the Pont des Arts of the painting's title, Renoir's urban world is filled with figures that open up the vast city to the painter-viewer.

Linda Nochlin, in her short but brilliant discussion of the painting, compares it to Jan Vermeer's *View of Delft*, arguably the most famous urban view painting in the history of art.[7] We must remember, however, that for all its reliance on formulas of urban painting perfected by the Dutch in the seventeenth century and the Italians in the eighteenth, Renoir himself had seen remarkably few works of this type. He had never been to Holland and, unlike his other Impressionist friends, would never go. Nor had he visited either London or Venice by 1867 and consequently knew only the paltry Venetian view paintings in the Louvre. Indeed, *Pont des Arts* has much more to do with the recent paintings of Monet and his teacher Boudin than it does with the great tradition of European urban view painting to which it makes such a brilliant contribution. For some, its relative tightness and coldness of facture are off-putting. The French art historian Sophie Monneret actually went so far as to call it "cold and realist and announcing nothing of his future manner of fantasy and the Impressionist touch."[8] One must remember that what one might call Renoir's schizophrenia of touch was to be a recurrent feature of his work. It is not far from this cold representation of a warm day in Paris to the hard, almost enameled surfaces that dominated his production in the mid-1880s.

The "series of Paris views" to which Monet referred in his letter of May 1867 actually were painted by the two artists. But they seem to have had little immediate effect on audiences or peers. None was exhibited in the 1860s, although most of them sold to collectors in the early 1870s. Several writers have pointed out the relatively devalued status of the Norton Simon painting when it was first sold to Durand-Ruel in 1872. Reputedly, the dealer paid only two hundred francs for this masterpiece of urban view painting and four hundred francs for an 1860s floral still life.[9] This same ambivalence dogged this great painting until its "rediscovery" by Julius Meier-Graefe in 1929. Since that time, it has suffered no reversals of fortune.

There is, however, a persistent and puzzling question concerning its date. Certain scholars have conclusively published it as having been painted in 1867, while others with equal conviction say 1868. None seem to have evidence to substantiate their views. Indeed, only the Monet letter places this "series" in time, but it provides us with no terminus ante quem. As Joseph Fronek has learned, and relayed in conversation in front of the painting, scholars like William Gaunt and Anthea Callen are correct in pointing out the relative technical complexity of the painting, with its patiently observed architecture over which Renoir overlaid his figures and clouds. Since the larger painting by Renoir of the Champs-Élysées (fig. 88a) is the only one of the five paintings by Monet and Renoir to be dated 1867 on the canvas, it is probably prudent to assume that it was the only one completed in that year. The largest of the three canvases by Monet (fig. 88d) is actually dated 1866 by the artist—a date logically disputed by many, including Daniel Wildenstein in the catalogue raisonné.[10] It seems wise to assume that both artists worked hard on their canvases in 1867, but that they completed them somewhat later. The seasonal variety in the three paintings by Monet cannot be denied, and, by 1868, Renoir's so-called cold manner of Paris painting had softened when he painted the glorious view of skaters in the Bois de Boulogne (William I. Koch Collection). So, 1867–1868 it is.

1 D. Wildenstein, 1974–1991, vol. 1, letter 32.
2 D. Wildenstein, 1974–1991, vol. 1, letter 84.
3 R. Thomson, 1982, p. 330.
4 Herbert, 1988, pp. 7-9; and House, 1994, p. 15.
5 Callen, 1978, p. 30; and Gaunt, 1982, pl. 4.
6 Gaunt, 1982, pl. 4.
7 Nochlin, 1971.
8 Monneret, 1989, p. 34.
9 Stevenson, 1991, p. 13. Stevenson says that the floral still life sold for 300 francs, while the more reliable Barbara Ehrlich White records 400 francs in White, 1984, p. 40.
10 D. Wildenstein, 1974–1991, vol. 1, no. 84, places it in the spring of 1867, stating that Monet subsequently dated the painting 1866.

89

Pierre-Auguste Renoir
French, 1841–1919

Seated Nude
c. 1872

Oil on canvas, 14¾ × 10 in. (37.5 × 25.4 cm)
Stamped lower left: "Renoir"
F.1982.1

Provenance: [Galerie Jacques Dubourg, Paris]. Mrs. Othon Friesz, sold 24 April 1957 to; [Paul Rosenberg & Co., New York, stock no. 5695, offered 12 March 1959 and subsequently sold 15 March 1962 to]; Norton Simon, gift 1982 to; The Norton Simon Foundation.

Exhibition: Los Angeles, 1965.

References: Daulte, 1971, vol. 1, no. 81, ill.; Fouchet, 1974, n.p., ill.

Technical Notes: There have been several alterations to the painting's original condition. The fine, plain-weave canvas has been glue-lined to a slightly heavier canvas, and the height has been extended by approximately ⅜ inch at the top edge. It appears that no additional canvas was attached; the increased area created by the lining was filled, textured, and retouched. A strip has been nailed across the top edge of the stretched painting, revealed by the X-ray, which shows a second set of longer tacks across the top. The original stretcher was retained. The thin ground layer barely covers the thread tops. The pale gray color may be a mixture of raw umber and white. The paint surface has been slightly altered by lining, with the canvas weave exaggerated, along with tiny pits and bumps, which may have been caused by debris that remained on the reverse of the original canvas before lining. The extremely thin, liquid paint was applied in washes or veils of muted color. It is in fair condition. There is extensive pinpoint flaking in the right leg, the left thigh and knee, the abdomen and chest. Microscopic examination shows distinct edges of the losses, which seem unlike those of chemical abrasion; however, they occur in light-colored areas, which suggests a possible link with cleaning solvents. There are several very small additional losses at the bottom edge and at the upper right edge, which are unrelated. The deteriorated varnish is yellowed and quite brittle. Ultraviolet light indicates it is a thick natural resin. (RW)

Renoir's oeuvre contains many images of the nude—mostly, but not exclusively, female, and this subject is so completely identified with him that the general public in Europe and the United States think of him primarily as a painter of naked women. He started with this subject in the 1860s, painting a hefty model—his mistress Lise Tréhot—as a Diana and used the same model for other large-scale exhibition pictures of the female nude in the late 1860s and very early 1870s. In the mid- and later 1870s, the period of high Impressionism, the representation of the nude waned in his oeuvre as he worked harder to investigate modern-life subjects and left to his colleague Edgar Degas the task of painting Realist nudes.

There are, however, exceptions to this rule, and several of Renoir's most ingratiating small-scale paintings of the 1870s represent the female nude. This superb small painting of a seated nude has been confidently dated 1872 by François Daulte in his incomplete catalogue raisonné of Renoir's oeuvre. However, the painting has no nineteenth-century provenance, bibliography, or exhibition history to support this claim. The translucent, abraded signature at lower left, "Renoir," appears to be a studio stamp, indicating that it was sold after the artist's death.

This small painting is nevertheless a tour de force of painterly performance. Its scale and wonderfully loose brushwork indicate that Renoir painted it in one sitting, while his model posed for him. By representing her without a clear setting—we see no chair, sofa, or bed on which she sits, nor do we know quite what supports her arm and head as she rests—we are encouraged to think less of her social status or identity than of her participation in the tradition of the painted nude in European allegorical painting. And, rather than represent her undergarments and clothing, as Gustave Courbet and Édouard Manet generally had done, Renoir covers her with a few wisps of abstracted drapery, veiling but not hiding the dark triangle of her pubic region. Hence, this woman is at once an allegory of beauty, sleep, or sensuality, and an actual woman to be desired.

Yet, we suspect from her hair color, body type, and what we know of Renoir's life in the late 1860s and early 1870s that she is Lise Tréhot, who had posed for Renoir for nearly five years when, in 1872, she suddenly left the painter and married a young architect. This small picture was made for the kind of guiltless male delectation that has been much discussed—and equally much derided—by feminist historians of art. The male artist-voyeur has arranged and painted her—with soft, boneless curves and pubic zone in the dead center of the picture—simply for the imaginative consumption of the spectator. The message of this picture is thus anything but complex.

If we accept the identity of the woman as Lise and the style of the painting as a fluid one that preceded the tiny strokes and broken surfaces of Renoir's paintings of the mid-1870s, the 1872 date for this painting is entirely plausible. One imagines it was retained by the artist for his own stimulation, or else meant for the collection of a well-born gentleman, who would have commissioned a superbly rich small frame to surround its corporeal luxury. It could easily have fit into the collections of Renoir's earliest clients, like Victor Chocquet or Eugène Murer, and hung on the same wall with others by Eugène Delacroix. It is, indeed, to the sensuous liquidity of Delacroix's touch that Renoir pays homage in this painting. Few, if any, painters of his own generation had the skill to paint it.

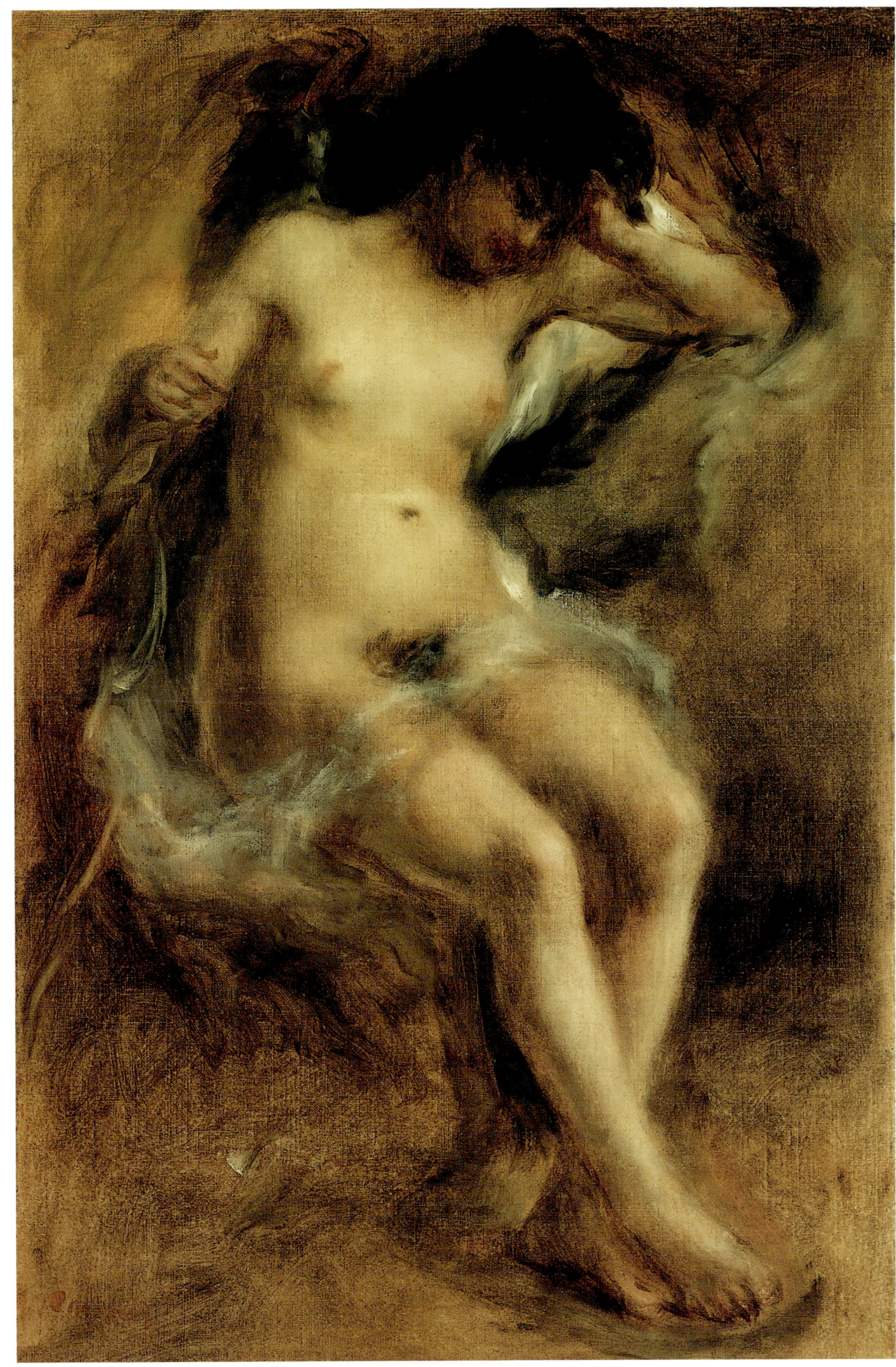

89

90

Pierre-Auguste Renoir
French, 1841–1919

Bouquet of Lilacs
1875–1880

Oil on canvas, 21¼ × 25¾ in. (54 × 65.5 cm)
Signed lower right: "Renoir"
N.1979.4.2

Provenance: The artist, sold 13 June 1881 to; [Durand-Ruel, Paris, stock no. 1072 (also Durand-Ruel stock no. 1138 in 1891), sold 26 May 1897 to]; [Durand-Ruel, New York, stock no. 1720, resold 22 September 1936 to]; [Durand-Ruel, Paris, stock no. 13766, sold 22 September 1936 (same day) to]; Mme de la Chapelle, Paris; sold September 1936, through [illegible in Knoedler stock book], to; [M. Knoedler & Co., New York, owned jointly with L. Carré, Paris, Knoedler stock no. A1740, sold 4 February 1937 to]; Dorothy Willard, New York, sold 19 December 1950 to; [M. Knoedler & Co., New York, stock no. A4473, sold 13 February 1957 to]; Mrs. Ralph J. Hines, Southampton, N.Y. Mrs. Joan F. Thayer, Cambridge, Mass., by 1961. [E. V. Thaw & Co., Inc., New York, sold 10 January 1979 to]; Norton Simon, bequest 1993 to; Jennifer Jones Simon Art Trust.

Exhibitions: New York, 1914, no. 4; on loan, Cambridge, Mass., Fogg Museum, Harvard University, 20 December 1961–1966; on loan, Seattle, University of Washington, Henry Gallery, 21 February–28 August 1979.

References: Perruchot, 1958, p. 611, ill.; Whelan, 1998, pp. 84–85, ill.

Technical Notes: The paint is very well preserved; the paint profile retains the points and ridges of its original state. The support is a fine, plain-weave canvas of light to medium weight with the original tacking edges intact. The canvas has been glue-lined, with the edges of the lining canvas trimmed to the dimensions of the original. A 1983 report referred to it as unlined, but this is incorrect. The lining is well adhered and the painting is taut. There are faint stretcher creases at the left and right sides. The keyed stretcher appears to be the original. The ground as seen on the tacking edges is extremely thin and probably porous. The X-radiograph shows that a second, slightly thicker ground (or underpainting) was applied with broad strokes of a palette knife over the picture surface, not extending completely to the edges. Renoir applied rather wide brushstrokes of fairly thin paint in the background. The bouquet is built up of flowers painted with vivid colors dabbed quickly over the white ground; paint was mixed on the palette and sometimes blended slightly on the canvas. The rich jewel-like colors—-blues, greens, alizarin, violet—-are superimposed in layered, light, tiny strokes. The flowers appear to have been painted before the background paint had dried. The quick dabbing of paint permits the white underpainting to show through occasionally. The textured brush marking retains its original clarity and immediacy, though it is diminished somewhat by the yellowed varnish. Much of the paint has a dense pattern of fine contraction cracks, most clearly evident in the dark background. There appears to be no chemical abrasion or other damage. Ultraviolet light reveals an area of delicate retouching at the lower left edge and in thin cracks at the bottom center. The aged natural resin varnish is brittle and yellowed. It has pooled in the recesses of the paint surface and detracts from the vibrant coloring. (RW)

Few painters in the history of French art painted flowers more convincingly and subtly than Renoir. Yet, until relatively recently, this part of his career has been little known and still less thoroughly documented. Even this superb painting of lilacs and other flowers presents many mysteries. Although signed, it was not dated by Renoir, and there is absolutely no supporting evidence for the traditional ascription of 1875. We know that Renoir sold it to the great dealer Durand-Ruel on 13 June 1881, but neither Durand-Ruel nor its next dealer, Knoedler, records a date for the execution of the work. Renoir exhibited only three still lifes—all with flowers—in the three Impressionist exhibitions in which he participated in the 1870s: an imposing floral still life from the late 1860s shown in the first exhibition of 1874 and two unidentified paintings in the third of 1877, titled *Bouquet of Wildflowers* and *The Dahlias*. Unfortunately, this information does not help us with the Norton Simon painting, which does not seem to represent wildflowers and is definitely not a painting of dahlias. The work is recorded as having been exhibited only once in Renoir's lifetime, and then in New York in an exhibition without a catalogue produced just three years before the painter's death. It is therefore difficult to discuss the date of the painting with any degree of precision.[1]

Renoir seems to have painted flowers throughout his life. One of the principal received ideas of Renoir studies is that, because he began his career as an apprentice painter of flowers and pleasant scenes on porcelain, he retained a lifelong proclivity for these easy subjects. Occasionally his floral works are very large and formal, painted as a contribution to decorative flower painting of the sort begun in France by Jean-Baptiste Monnoyer in the seventeenth century. More often, however, Renoir's floral still lifes are small and seem to have been made for ready sale. The fact that they figure among the paintings he sent to the Impressionist exhibitions suggests that Renoir painted such pictures as a sort of advertisement for the rest of his production. In this, they are like certain of his anonymous portraits, the public exhibition

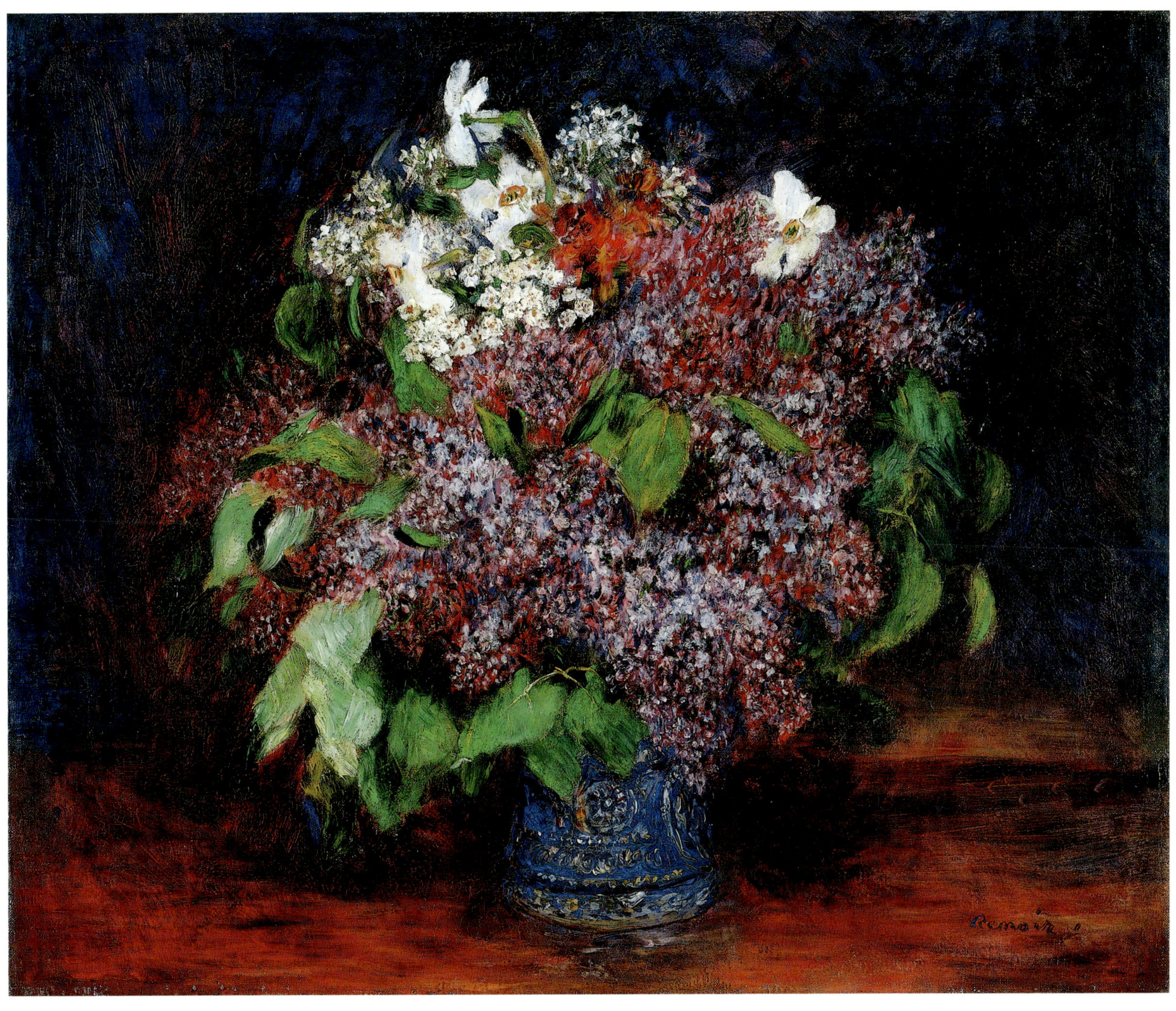
Renoir

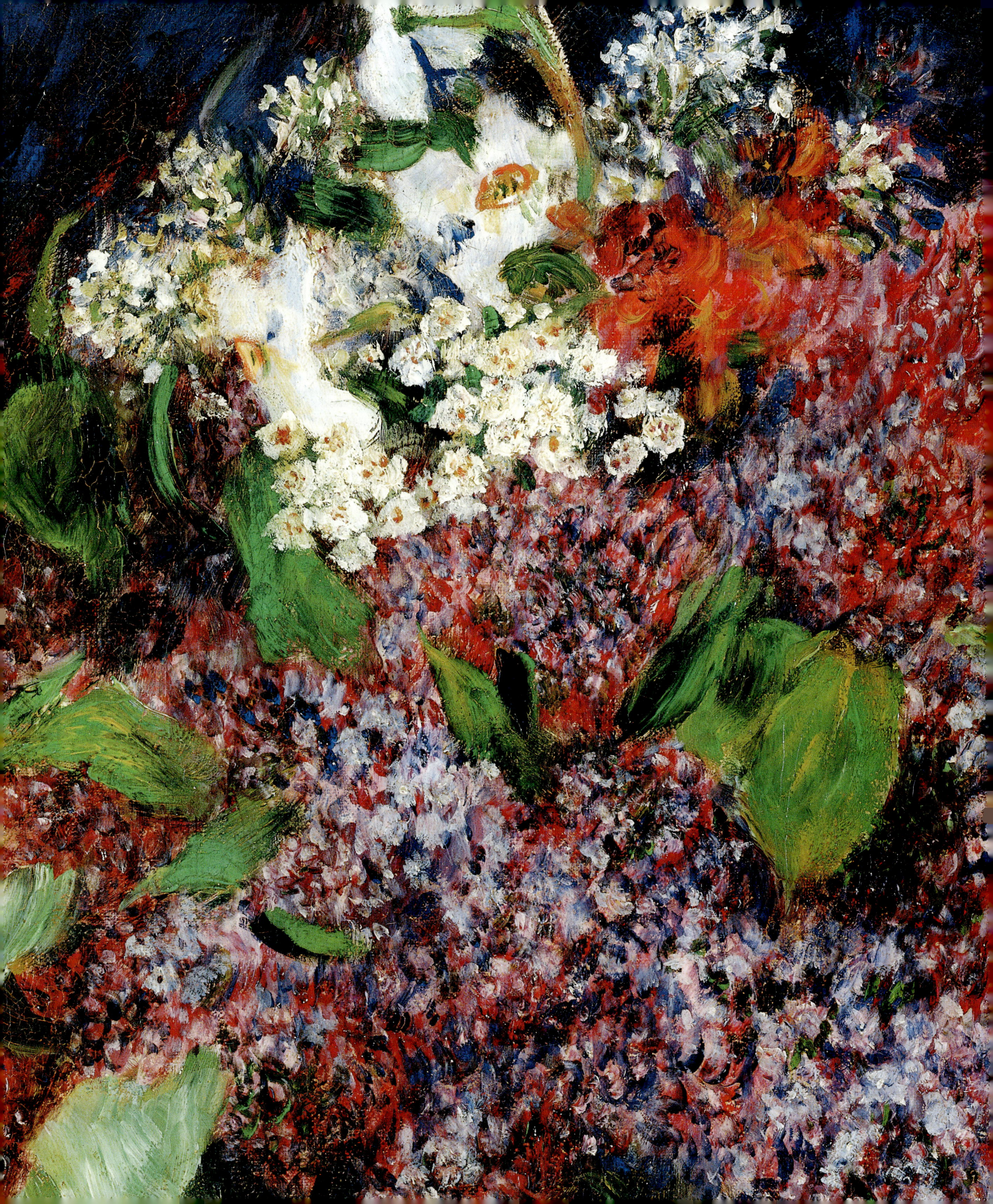

of which produced later private commissions. Unfortunately, Renoir's contribution to the genre of flower painting and its markets has not been separately studied, even in a persuasive article.

In painting this group of early spring flowers, Renoir elected to use the very dark background that had become de rigueur for French flower painting of the seventeenth and eighteenth centuries but that had become a little unfashionable in the 1870s. Here the rich colors—plums, saturated reddish purples, reds, whites, yellows, and pale blues—seem to glow against the deep blues, greens, and orange-browns of Renoir's background. The brilliant green leaves of the lilac seem almost to dance across the palpitating surface of blossoms. Yet, where traditional French floral still lifes treated petals and leaves with painstaking clarity and focus, Renoir seems to suggest their forms with jabs and small touches of paint and with large shapes that read as brushstrokes. Although dominated by the lilacs of the painting's title, the still life is crowned by an assortment of jonquils and other flowers that contrast with the deeply recessive colors of Renoir's background and lend drama to the composition.

Like his colleagues Camille Pissarro, Claude Monet, and Paul Cézanne, Renoir liked to use exotic vases in which to arrange his flowers. This one is difficult to identify. Its deep Ming blue color and complex pattern make one think that it might be Chinese cloisonné, but there is not enough evidence to clinch an identification, and it is not close enough to vases in other paintings for us to pinpoint the source of its exoticism. Whatever the significance of *Bouquet of Lilacs* for Renoir's career, it makes its principal contribution to the Norton Simon collections as Renoir's entry in the tradition of modern floral painting inaugurated by Gustave Courbet with such paintings as *Vase of Lilacs, Roses, and Tulips* (cat. 42).

1 *Bouquet of Lilacs* has been published only in the context of flower painting (see References, above). Unfortunately, neither author provides a discussion of the painting.

91

Pierre-Auguste Renoir
French, 1841–1919

Young Woman in Black
c. 1875–1877

Oil on canvas, $13\frac{1}{8} \times 10$ in. (33.2×25.5 cm)
Signed upper right: "Renoir"
N.1963.5

Provenance: Eugène Murer, Paris and Auvers-sur-Oise, by 1887. Georges Viau, Paris (sale, Paris, Galeries Durand-Ruel, 4 March 1907, lot 66, ill., as *Jeune femme* for Ff 4,100 to); [Bernheim-Jeune, Paris, to]; Paul Harth, Paris, for Ff 300,000 to; [Bernheim-Jeune, Paris, stock no. 26,935, sold 31 December 1938 for Ff 400,000 to]; [Reid & Lefevre, London]. [Galerie Étienne Bignou, Paris]. William A. Cargill, Carruth, Scotland (sale, London, Sotheby's, 11 June 1963, lot 36, color ill., to); [Arthur Tooth & Sons, Ltd., London, for]; Norton Simon, bequest 1993 to; Jennifer Jones Simon Art Trust.

Exhibitions: Paris, 1904, no. 5; Paris, 1938c, no. 17; Los Angeles, 1965; San Francisco, 1973, no. 37, ill.

References: Alexis, 1887, no. 39; Gachet, 1956, p. 171; Daulte, 1971, vol. 1, no. 165, ill.

Technical Notes: The support is a fine, plain-weave canvas; it has been glue-lined to canvas with the original tacking edges removed. The X-radiograph reveals very slightly cusped threads only at the left side. Adhesion between the two canvases appears to be uniformly strong. The painting is tacked to a 5-member stretcher with mortise-and-tenon, keyed corners. All keys are present. The smooth ground is white or cream-colored. The paint is applied wet into wet over the light ground with fluid brushwork. To model the face Renoir used thin, cool hues for shadowed areas, while highlights are created with lighter, opaque paint. His technique employs multiple layers of thin paint, as well as dabs and strokes of a fully loaded brush. A small amount of impasto accentuates the black hat and the white flower. The surface texture may have been slightly altered by the pressure of lining, transferring a faint pattern of canvas weave to the front surface. Except for minimal losses of paint and ground around the edges, the paint is very well preserved. Small white dots, which are particularly noticeable at the left and right neckline-collar and at the center of the collar, are revealed to be gaps in the paint, caused by Renoir's rapid brushstrokes with dryish paint, which was not liquid enough to create a continuous stroke. The painting was treated in 1990 and varnished with synthetic resin. There is a slight amount of retouching in the losses around the edge, as well as a few dots at bottom center. (RW)

Throughout the mid-1870s Renoir worked concertedly to prepare his masterpiece, *Ball at the Moulin de la Galette*, exhibited in the 1877 Impressionist exhibition and now in the Musée d'Orsay. We know from witness accounts—and mostly from those of his enthusiastic friend the writer Georges Rivière—that Renoir worked either at home on the rue St.-Georges or in a street-level studio facing a small garden on the rue Cortot. The artist's friends came and went throughout the day, allowing him many occasions to paint them—alone and in small groups. These paintings, most of them small, were sold cheaply or presented as gifts to members of the painter's circle, one of whom, Eugène Murer, the first owner of *Young Woman in Black*, is known today as a close friend of Camille Pissarro. He owned a pastry shop in Paris on the boulevard Voltaire and kept a house in Auvers-sur-Oise near that of the more famous Dr. Gachet. He was actively collecting Impressionist art in the 1870s and owned work by Pissarro, Renoir, Claude Monet, Paul Cézanne, Alfred Sisley, Armand Guillaumin, and others. His collection was published in 1887 in the left-wing journal *Le Cri du Peuple*, when this painting made its first appearance. As one of the earliest collectors of Impressionism, Murer has been discussed in the admirable documentary work of Anne Distel, curator of painting at the Musée d'Orsay, and makes frequent appearances in the various biographies devoted to the life of his friend Pissarro.[1]

The fact that Murer owned this painting and that this ownership is not recorded in the painting's next publication, as part of the equally famous collection of Georges Viau, sold in 1907 in Paris, suggests that it might well have been disposed of in an early undocumented sale or perhaps given as a gift. The work is one of many similar head studies of young female models painted by Renoir in the mid-1870s in his Montmartre studio. All of these works share small formats and seem to have been made as part of a larger project of representing young Parisians in Renoir's circle. They are, in a way, painterly notes or artistic exercises of the hand and wrist, the making of which enabled Renoir to paint such figures convincingly when he included them in large, multifigure compositions such as the *Ball at the Moulin de la Galette*. In the 1887 publication of Murer's collection, the Norton Simon head is listed under number 39 as "modiste à la marguerite, adorable petite tête" (dressmaker with a daisy, adorable little head).

The model has not been identified by name in any published source and is, thus, one of many of Renoir's sitters who can be considered as representations of a Parisian type rather than as portraits of an individual. Most of these figures share common features, to which

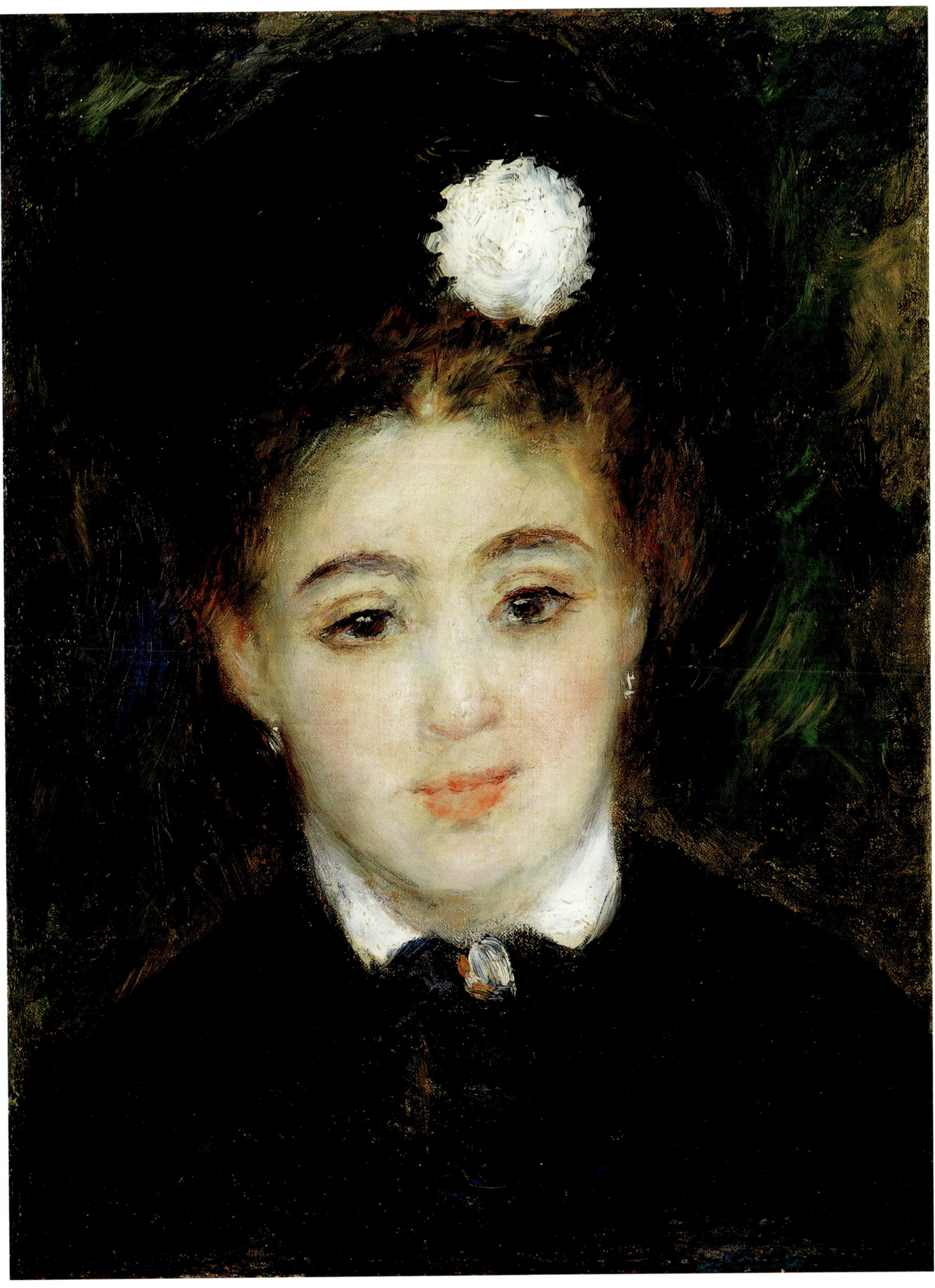

91

the painter was evidently attracted—dark eyes, strong eyebrows, tiny noses, and small, neatly positioned mouths. She appears to be in her twenties and is presented in formal clothes for the street with what is surely a silk flower in her black hat. Her brooch, high color, small earrings, and black hat make her seem utterly respectable and bourgeois.

Yet the fact that her earliest recorded title calls her a *modiste* (dressmaker) suggests that she is from the working class. From the evidence of the painting alone, there is no reason to classify this young woman as anything other than bourgeois. Her proper street attire and her discrete jewelry indicate comfortable prosperity and modesty, and no attribute of a dressmaker is present. Even her flower, identified in the title for the painting recorded in 1887 as a white daisy, hardly seems to be as evocative as the white or red camellias that adorned the great courtesan in Alexandre Dumas's *La Dame aux camélias.* Given that there are many errors of fact in other matters in the article of 1887, the title might simply be entirely an invention either of the writer or of Murer himself. Yet we must not take it lightly, in spite of the fact that it may be technically incorrect. What it first suggests is that, for this left-wing journal, the identification of the woman as a worker may have carried positive connotations, rather than the faintly salacious overtones to the term *dressmaker* in bourgeois fiction and as well as in the scholarly writing of art historians who work on Edgar Degas, Édouard Manet, and other urban figure paintings.

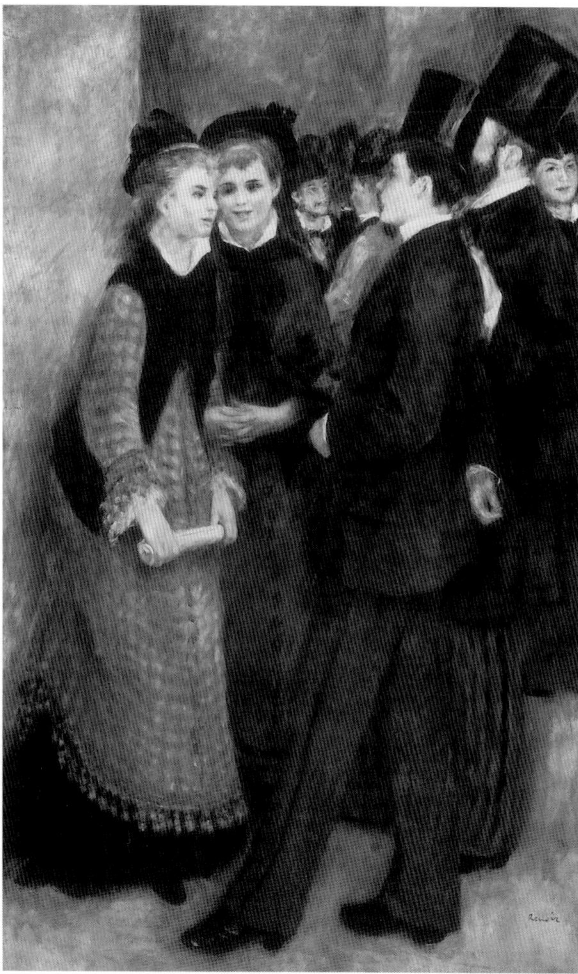

Fig. 91a Pierre-Auguste Renoir, *After the Concert*, c. 1877, oil on canvas, $73\frac{3}{4} \times 46\frac{1}{4}$ in. (187.4×117.4 cm), The Barnes Foundation, Merion, Pa., BF 862; © Reproduced with the Permission of The Barnes Foundation™ All Rights Reserved

This positive connotation, however, was surely intended neither by the collector nor his cataloguers. Indeed, Murer's collection is recorded as including a large number of paintings with decidedly sexually suggestive titles, including the first-name-only identification of models in a manner common for prostitutes and sexually available artist's models. We are treated to "the inseparables" (whose names were Eva and Laurenzie), *The Polish Girl, Blondinelle the Ingénue,* and *Margot, Souvenir of Youth.* And one painting, number 40, is called *Interior of a Harem in Montmartre, Nude Women.* Surely our pretty little unnamed *modiste* would fit well into that world.

Georges Rivière discussed Renoir's models of the mid-1870s in a much later essay of 1921, published after Renoir's death. His precise discussions of Nini, Margot, and several others do not allow us to identify the particular model in *Young Woman in Black,* although she looks startlingly like the woman posed frontally in Renoir's major painting of 1877, *After the Concert* (fig. 91a). She also bears a striking resemblance to Henriette Henriot, whom Renoir painted throughout the mid-1870s and who served as the model for his monumental *La Parisienne* of 1874 (National Museum and Gallery, Cardiff). Henriot, a moderately successful actress, whose career has been extensively discussed by Colin Bailey in his superb study of Renoir's portraits,[2] possesses the kind of wide-eyed innocence that Renoir found irresistible, and he painted her several times, even in a role *en travesti,* dressed as a man.

Renoir evidently thought enough of small paintings like this to have included several in the Impressionist exhibitions of 1876 and 1877. There are listings for a *Head of a Woman* in the catalogue of the 1876 exhibition and two for a *Head of a Young Girl* and *Two Heads* in the 1877 exhibition. None of these works has been positively identified, and, given the inadequate state of Renoir's catalogue raisonné, it is not currently possible even to speculate whether the present work is one of them. It does, however, seem clear that Renoir, like many other artists working as part of what Edmond Duranty called "the new painting," strove to portray contemporary individuals anonymously. They serve simply as moderns, whose particular stories, like their names, are lost to us. They are figures in a collective portrait of Third Republic Paris. Their anonymity, though frustrating to the historian, is essential to their very modernity. And, as women, they are what Renoir's friend Rivière called *fillettes* (like the English "fillies") who are "essentialement parisienne."[3]

1 Anne Distel, *Impressionism: The First Collectors*, New York, 1989, pp. 207–215.

2 Bailey, 1997, cats. 19 and 20.

3 Berson, 1996, vol. 1, p. 179.

92

Pierre-Auguste Renoir
French, 1841–1919

At Renoir's Home, rue St.-Georges (formerly *The Artist's Studio, rue St.-Georges*)
1876

Oil on canvas, $18\frac{1}{8} \times 15$ in. (46×38.1 cm)
Signed lower right: "Renoir"
M.1978.13.2

Provenance: Eugène Murer, Paris, sold in 1896 to; Georges Viau, Paris (sale, Paris, Galeries Durand-Ruel, 4 March 1907, lot 64, as *L'Atelier de l'artiste (rue Saint Georges, année 1876)*, for Ff 4,900). [Durand-Ruel, Paris]. M. Hocquard, Paris. Antonio Santamarina, Buenos Aires, by 1933 (sale, London, Sotheby's, 2 April 1974, lot 15, as *L'Atelier du peintre, rue Saint-Georges*); [P. & D. Colnaghi, London, sold 1978 to]; Norton Simon Art Foundation.

Exhibitions: Rouen, 1896; Paris, 1904, no. 9?; Paris, 1912, no. 28; Paris, 1920, no. 14; Buenos Aires, 1933, no. 96, as *L'Atelier de la rue St. Georges*; Buenos Aires, 1947, no. 3?; Buenos Aires, 1962, no. 59, ill.; on loan, Princeton, University Art Museum, 31 May–18 December 1978.

References: Alexis, 1887, no. 44, as *Chez Renoir (cinq portraits de MM. Alphonse Daudet, Cabaner, Pissarro, Rivière, et Cordey)*; Vollard, 1919, p. 82, ill.; Rivière, 1921, pp. 61–62, 80, 111, 116, ill. opp. 62; Meier-Graefe, 1929a, no. 80, p. 128, ill.; Santamarina, 1942, p. 55, ill.; Drucker, 1944, no. 40, p. 199, ill. (1955 ed., no. 35, p. 150, ill.); Rewald, 1946, p. 307, ill. (1961 and 1973 eds., p. 382, ill.); Jedlicka, 1947, no. 27, ill.; Chamson, 1949, no. 17, ill.; Berr de Turique, n.d., fig. 16; Gaunt, 1952, fig. 16; Gachet, 1956, pp. 156–157, 164, 170, 172, 176–177, fig. 17; Daulte, 1971, vol. 1, no. 188, ill.; Delage, 1982, p. 58, fig. 28; Lloyd, 1981, pp. 38, 39, ill.; Gaunt, 1982, no. 21, ill.; White, 1984, pp. 74, color ill., 81; Shimada, 1986, p. 15, ill.; Bonafoux, 1986, pp. 124, ill., 190; Wadley, 1987, pp. 172, 361, colorpl. 58; Monneret, 1989, p. 66, ill.; Bailey, 1997, pp. 15, 16, 51 n. 249, 149, fig. 18; Néret, 2001, color ill. p. 189; Gaussen, 2002, pp. 97–101, color ill.; Feilchenfeldt, 2006, p. 22 (installation photograph of Durand-Ruel gallery).

Technical Notes: The fine, plain-weave canvas, which is lined probably with an aqueous adhesive to a similar type fabric, still has some of its original tacking margins, but brown tape on the edges prevents a complete appraisal. The X-radiograph reveals that the design was extended very slightly, $\frac{1}{8}$ inch at most on all sides except the top, when it was attached to the later stretcher. One is very aware of the surface and brushwork in this small painting. This is not the fault of the lining. Instead, the ground is thin and does not fill the canvas weave, leaving the canvas texture very obvious. Also, the open application of paint, much of which is in fine parallel strokes of color, covers the texture in only some areas of thickest paint. Colors are mostly pure or mixed with white; black seems to be present as do a few brown earth colors. The darkest shadows and the signature appear to be in Prussian blue. Very fine cracks may be seen with magnification, and larger cracks exist in the whites. The condition of the painting is very good with virtually no significant restoration. Whether or not the painting was meant to be varnished is not known, but given the technique, the role of the ground, and the overall canvas texture, this writer feels that it was not meant to be varnished. The painting was cleaned of a discolored varnish in 1990 and then revarnished. (JF)

Much has been written about the studios of nineteenth-century Parisian painters. Whether vast skylit lofts, cramped attic spaces, or comfortably furnished workrooms filled with cluttered cupboards, these spaces were considered alchemical because in them base materials—paint, charcoal, canvas, wood—were brought to life. Yet, we have long been taught to think that Impressionist painting was made entirely outside the studio—drawn and painted directly from life as it was manifested in the streets, rivers, fields, cafés, dance halls, and squares of Paris and its environs. This view has now been decidedly debunked. Historians of Impressionist art have reconstructed the artistic practice of Renoir, Claude Monet, Berthe Morisot, and the others and revealed it to be as complex and as layered as that of any academic artist.

Since the early twentieth century, this small painting by Renoir—one of the masterpieces of the Norton Simon collections—has been persistently identified as a representation of the painter's studio on the rue St.-Georges. This studio has been known not only as a place of work—for the solitary magic of art making—but also as a gathering place for Renoir's friends and admirers, that is, as a place of chatter, music, and easy sociability where Renoir also happened to work. Here he painted many small-scale figure studies from hired models and friends, many posed in natural positions. The life of the studio was most vividly and lovingly evoked by Georges Rivière, first in his lengthy reviews of the Impressionist exhibition of 1877 and, later, in his delightful monograph, *Renoir et ses amis*, published in Paris in 1921, just two years after the painter's death. Indeed, Rivière devoted an entire chapter to the studio, describing it with an almost obsessive interest in detail and culminating with the present painting, which Rivière published with a note identifying each of the five figures.

Rivière's focus on the painting is not surprising since he himself is its central figure. According to his lively account, he arrived daily at Renoir's studio with his

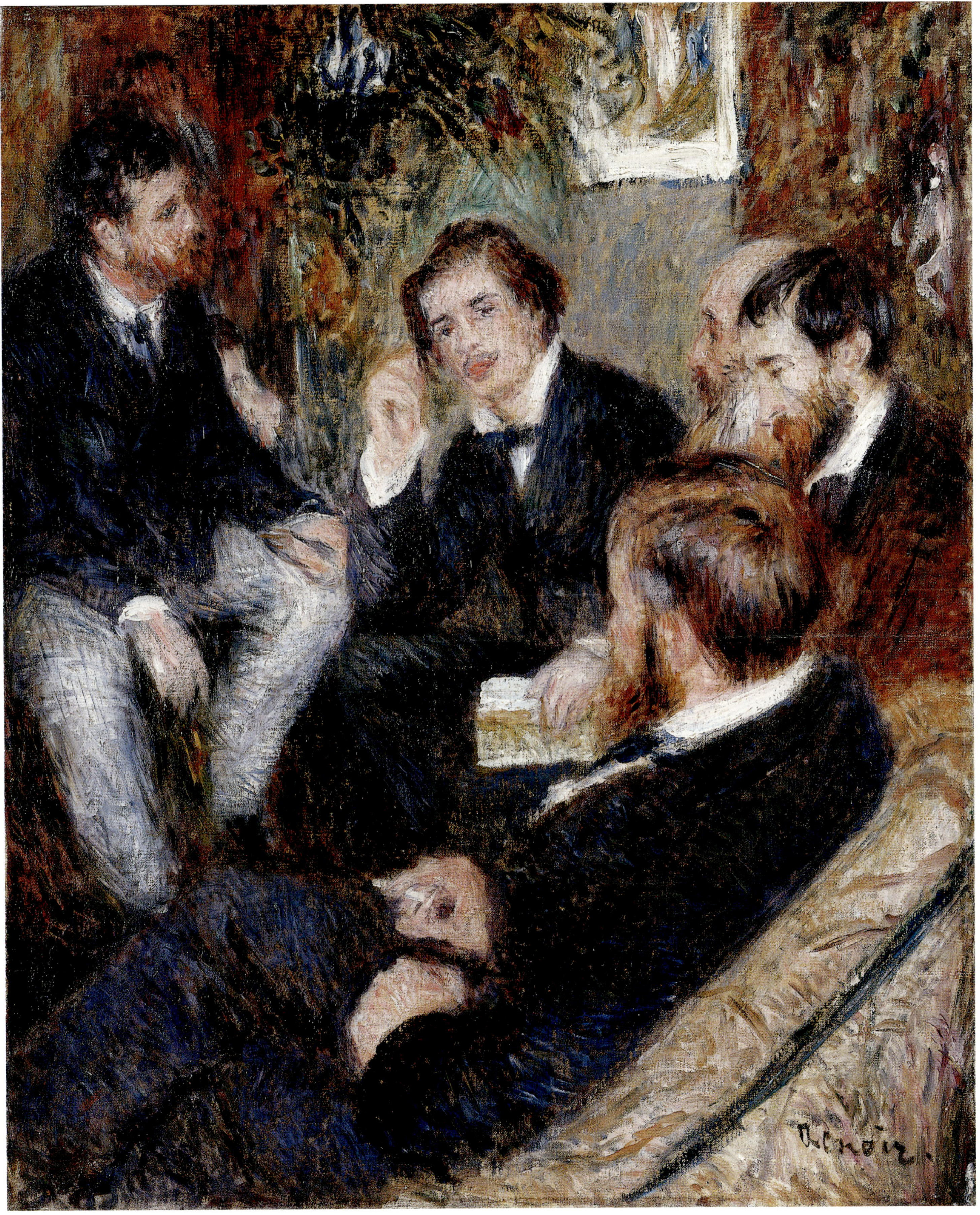
Renoir.

friends the minor painters Franc Lamy and Frédéric Cordey at about five in the afternoon. A little later, Eugène-Pierre Lestringuez, an amateur philosopher who worked in the Department of the Interior, would saunter in. All but one of these men figure in Rivière's identifications in Renoir's painting. The figure at the far left, seated alone with his hand on his knee, is identified as Lestringuez, whom Rivière discussed at length as a man fascinated by the occult and the relationships between modern sciences and earlier occult-based knowledge systems. Lestringuez, whom Rivière also identifies as a model in the *Ball at the Moulin de la Galette* (1876, Musée d'Orsay, Paris), appears to be listening to what Rivière is reading aloud. The young author holds a yellow paperback novel in his left hand—probably a Realist work by Émile Zola or the brothers Goncourt—seemingly having paused in his task. The others—Camille Pissarro, Cordey, and the composer Ernest-Jean Cabaner—form an open circle around Rivière, from which the painter-viewer is excluded.

The painting has been called *In the Studio* since 1907 in spite of the fact that there is absolutely no visual evidence that an artist could work in the room. There are no easels, palettes, unfinished paintings, portfolios of drawings, plaster casts, or *écorché* figures like those that abound in nineteenth-century French studios in photographs and paintings. Here, the studio—if that word may still fairly be used—seems more like a literary salon, where the refinements of art and culture are engaged and discussed. In addition to the protagonists, the picture shows a painting on a distant wall, a potted plant on a stand (probably a fern), and a well-upholstered sofa. Indeed, the setting, summarily suggested as it is, seems a good deal more comfortable and high-toned than the room Rivière described from memory more than forty years later. It is worth quoting at length the author's description because it has so little to do with the painting.

> The rectangular room had windows all along the long side that faced west. In summer the room was filled with sunlight despite the thick cloth curtains that were meant to filter it. The walls were papered in light gray and several unframed canvases hung there. Against the walls there lay piles of canvases, both used and unused, of which only the backs were visible. There was no other furniture except two easels, a few cane chairs of the most common design, two squat armchairs covered in very faded floral rep, a worn-out divan covered in material of indeterminate color and a whitewood table on which lay jumbled up tubes of colors, brushes, bottles of oil or spirit, and paint-stained rags.[1]

Instead of the canvases, windows, and general bohemian disarray mentioned by Rivière, the Norton Simon painting shows us five well-dressed bourgeois men sitting in chairs—one in respectable upholstery—in a rather dark room decorated with a single painting. The depicted picture does seem to be framed or bordered in white in the manner that became de rigueur in the late 1870s for advanced artists. Even this nod to avant-garde modernity does little to undercut the evident bourgeois respectability of the setting. The principal quality of the painting is an intimate sociability of a type that was becoming associated with urban culture. It is thus a painting about discourse as culture, about the interchange of ideas among disciplines, and about the conviviality of professional men. There are, one will note, no women present, which seems odd when one thinks of the easy sexuality of *la vie bohème.* There is little *bohème* in Renoir's painted room, forcing us once more to ask whether this painting actually represents Renoir's studio.

Perhaps the solution to this problem can be found in the first publication of the painting in the 1887 article in *Le Cri du Peuple* devoted to the collection of Eugène Murer. Here it was given a slightly, but crucially, different title. It is called *Chez Renoir (cinq portraits de MM. Alphonse Daudet, Cabaner, Pissarro, Rivière, et Cordey)* (*At Renoir's* [*five portraits of Misters Alphonse Daudet, Cabaner, Pissarro, Rivière, and Cordey*]). This presents us with two fascinating problems. First, the title itself, which, in the usual sense of the word *chez* would mean at Renoir's home, not his studio. And, in fact, Renoir had worked in his home on the rue St.-Georges until sometime in 1875 or 1876, when he rented a studio at 18, rue Cortot while maintaining his apartment on the rue St.-Georges as his residence.[2] There are two sources for this information, both published after Renoir's death. The first, Renoir's dealer Ambroise Vollard, states that Renoir rented space on the rue Cortot early in 1875, with money from a portrait commission. The second, Rivière, dates the move to May 1876. Neither author provides any evidence.

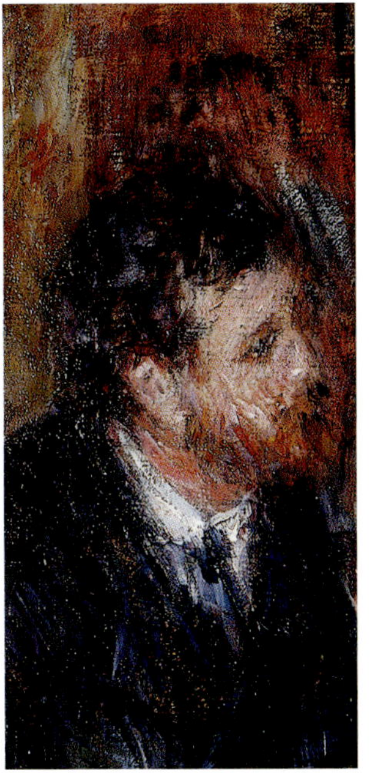

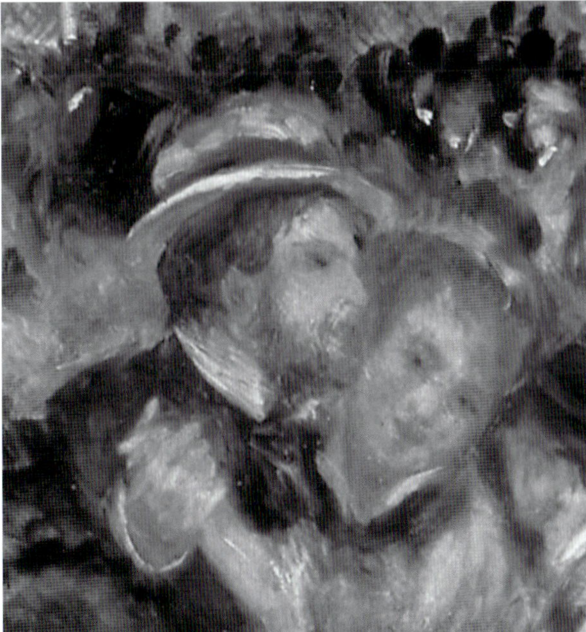

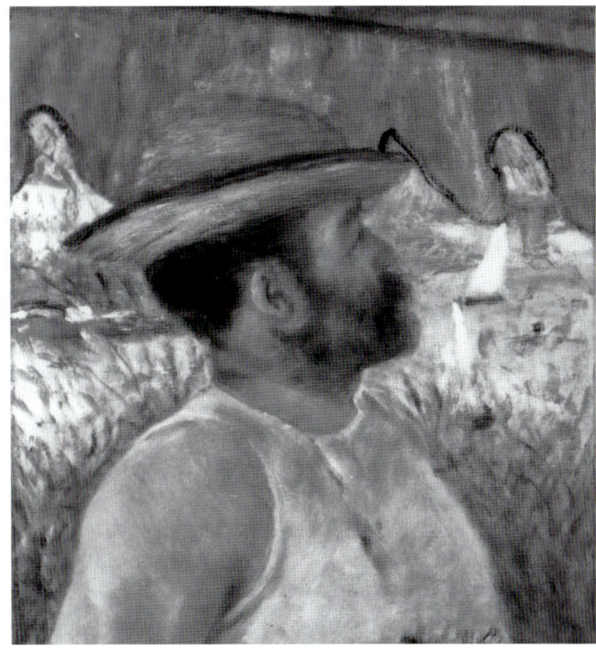

Fig. 92a (*above left*) Detail of cat. 92)

Fig. 92b (*above center*) Pierre-Auguste Renoir, *Ball at the Moulin de la Galette* (detail), 1876, oil on canvas, $51\frac{5}{8} \times 68\frac{7}{8}$ in. (131 × 175 cm), Musée d'Orsay, Paris; photo: Scala / Art Resource, NY

Fig. 92c (*above right*) Pierre-Auguste Renoir, *Luncheon of the Boating Party* (detail), 1880–1881, oil on canvas, $51\frac{1}{4} \times 69\frac{1}{8}$ in. (130.2 × 175.5 cm), The Phillips Collection, Washington, D.C.

Yet, when one combines this sketchy evidence with that of the first publication of the painting as *Chez Renoir* it seems likely that the painting's first owner, Eugène Murer—or his anonymous cataloguer—was correct. The painting most likely represents Renoir's living room on the rue St.-Georges and not his studio on the rue Cortot, with its famous garden and large windows. Yet, we must not give up totally on Rivière, who was, after all, in the painting. Why not assume that, although Renoir had rented a larger independent studio where he could work away from home as a professional painter and where he could paint in the garden, he also painted at home on the rue St.-Georges. Most accounts of Renoir stress his easy manner and his relative lack of interest in intellectual discussions and ideas. Although he evidently relished his role as witness to such performances and provided the occasion for them, he was actually happier representing them than participating directly. Indeed, this painting is rare in Renoir's representations of Parisian conviviality by virtue of its exclusion of women. Renoir strove here to represent a serious (read "men only") literary gathering, not a lighthearted exercise in relaxed social intercourse. And the presence of Pissarro, who was so evidently the patriarch of the Impressionist movement, gives the painting's gathering added intellectual and moral weight. Pissarro had not yet rented his Parisian apartment on the nearby rue des Trois Frères in 1876, when this picture was painted. Therefore, he had had to make the trip from Pontoise to Paris to attend Renoir's gathering.

In summary, the painting depicts a gathering of men at Renoir's home on the rue St.-Georges. They are seen reading and chatting, while the working artist, looking over the shoulder of Cabaner, paints their picture. The underlying seriousness of the picture—that is, its rejection of Bohemia—was very much in keeping with the larger efforts of Renoir and Rivière in 1876 and 1877 to banish from the public mind any of the associations of artistic and political insurrection that lingered from the first Impressionist exhibition of 1874. The new journal launched by Rivière in 1877, called *L'Impressioniste*, lampooned the widely held view that these artists were "intransigents" and "revolutionaries who like to sow discord in the camp of the artists." They were instead sincere artists whose artworks were simply "the result of sensations they have experienced."[3]

The main puzzle of *Chez Renoir* is now solved, but one small mystery remains: the identification of the figure at the left. Rivière is insistent that it is Eugène-Pierre Lestringuez(fig. 92a),[4] whose career and opinions he discusses at some length.[5] Murer, however, who was equally close to Renoir in the 1870s, maintains that it represents the then famous writer Alphonse Daudet. Either identification is perfectly plausible, and arguments could be made for each being the figure. Renoir did include likenesses of Lestringuez in both the *Ball at the Moulin de la Galette* and in his 1880–1881 masterpiece, *Luncheon of the Boating Party* (figs. 92b and 92c). In both cases, the figure is represented at almost the same angle as the figure in the present painting and is decidedly similar.

We also know that Renoir had met Daudet in the fall of 1876 through the publisher Georges Charpentier and had visited the writer at his country home in Chambrosay and even painted a portrait of his wife (Musée d'Orsay) in the same year. As a figure in Renoir's literary and artistic circle of 1876, Daudet would have been considerably more appropriate—and high-toned—than the civil servant Lestringuez. But, in this case, it is probably wisest to accept Rivière's own memory of Lestringuez. After all, why should he have omitted the celebrated Daudet when discussing his friend's career and a painting in which he himself was a sitter? And the resemblance to the two other documented portrayals of Lestringuez by Renoir in the period is too great to ignore.

At Renoir's Home, rue St.-Georges is an intimate painting of a human gathering—and of sociability, discourse, conviviality, and artistic sobriety—in which the artist specialized in the mid- and late 1870s. Though small in size, it stands prominently among a large number of other representations of cafés, millinery shops, gardens, restaurants, dance halls, and living rooms by Renoir, Edgar Degas, Claude Monet, and their Impressionist contemporaries.

1 Wadley, 1987, p. 75.
2 Distel, 1985, p. 298.
3 Eisenman, 1986, p. 57.
4 Bailey, 1997, p. 47 n. 111; and Distel, 1985, p. 211.
5 Rivière, 1921, p. 62.

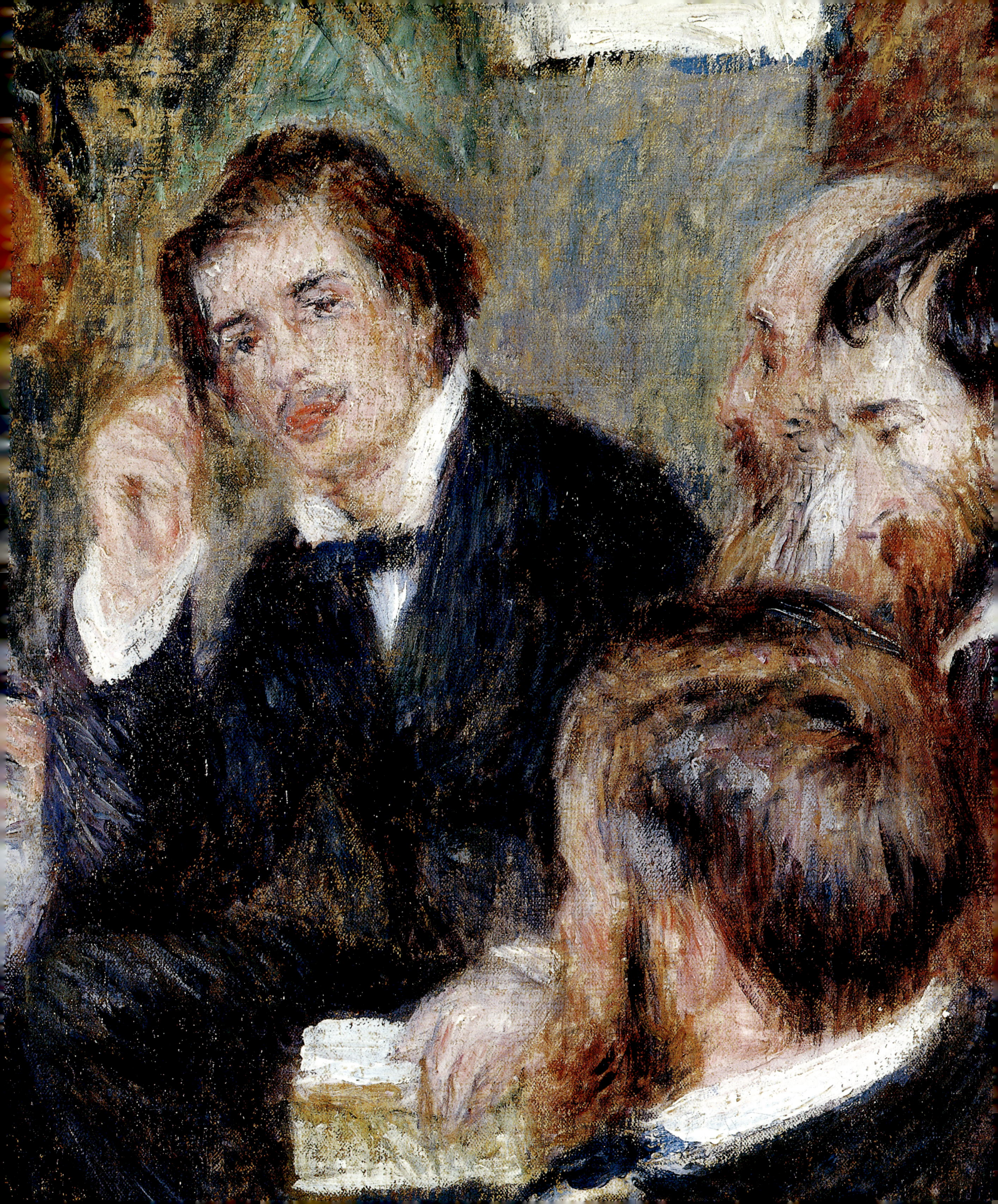

93

Pierre-Auguste Renoir
French, 1841–1919

Reclining Nude
c. 1892

Oil on canvas, 13 × 16⅜ in. (33 × 41.5 cm)
Signed lower right: "Renoir"
M.1969.02

Provenance: The artist, sold to; [Bernheim-Jeune, Paris]. Mme Olivier Sainsère, Paris, by 1927. Farjon, Paris. [Stephen Hahn, New York, sold 1969 to]; Norton Simon Art Foundation.

Exhibitions: Paris, 1927, no. 13, as *Femme nue*; Paris, 1953, no. 170, ill.; Paris, 1954a, no. 32; Montreal, 1967, no. 11, ill.; Philadelphia, 1969, no. 12; Princeton, 1972, no. 37, ill.; San Francisco, 1974, no. 41, ill.

References: Goulinat, 1925, p. 23, ill.; Daulte, 1971, vol. 1, no. 623, ill.; B. Schneider, 1984, p. 62, ill.

Technical Notes: Examination reveals the painting to be in very good condition. It is executed on a fine, plain-weave canvas with its original tacking edges intact and is lined. There is a small loss in the original canvas at the top right corner. The lining is uniformly well adhered. The smooth, thin ground is pale gray, possibly white with raw umber added. If it was an absorbent material, it may well have darkened with the infusion of wax adhesive. Magnification reveals an opaque, bright white underpainting over the ground layer, which Renoir applied out to each edge. The X-radiograph reveals strong, firm brushstrokes, which are unrelated to the final uppermost image and presumably are from the application of the white underpainting. The paint is well preserved, with the crisp edges of brushwork seemingly in their original state. As seen with magnification, Renoir covered the background, sky, and foreground with thin washes of color in a very liquid state, and then apparently rubbed it even thinner, leaving the color only in the recesses of the canvas weave; in this way he created a pastel, insubstantial backdrop for the more solidly conceived figure, which is painted with opaque, thicker paint. With the microscope it is evident that the dark brown fringe of the cloth near her left foot was painted on top of the thin, rubbed paint of the foreground. At first glance (a previous report from 1986 stated that the painting had been overcleaned) the white thread tops would suggest that some solvent abrasion had occurred, but careful study indicates that there is no abrasion other than that which was intended by the artist. There is a small loss of brown paint at the center right, which is old, and several tiny losses of ground and underpainting in a small vertical line at the top end of the right edge. The painting was cleaned in 1969, and the varnish is clear and evenly glossy. (RW)

Renoir turned to the female nude with real enthusiasm in the early 1880s, particularly after his trip to Italy in 1881. While in Naples, Rome, and Venice, Renoir had gloried in the painted bodies of Titian, Veronese, and later Baroque painters and, on his return to Paris, began to conceive of major paintings that represented, not modern leisure, the subject of his greatest works in the 1870s and very early 1880s, but groups of female nudes. His earliest works in the new manner were painted in a rather dry style, which, after his completion of the famous *Bathers* (1887, Philadelphia Museum of Art), he gradually softened to create his fluidly curvilinear late style. This persisted virtually unchanged from the late 1880s until he recomplicated his facture about the time of World War I.

This small nude, one of hundreds painted by Renoir in the last thirty years of his life, is surely quite early in the sequence. Its completely assured smoothness of surface relates it to the larger nudes dated by exhibition and sales to the late 1880s and early 1890s. Many of these nude women are set into landscapes and seascapes so that the dialogue between the body and its natural setting, so important in pastoral poetry from antiquity forward, is fully explored. This removal of the female nude from the Realist context of the city means that male viewers can fantasize about her without guilt or direct self-association. It also naturalizes the woman in a way that stresses her fecundity and her participation in the endless cycles of nature. Here, Renoir places the figure between land and sea, as if allowing the aquatic realm access to this mythic woman. The waves that push into the land, the gentle undulations of the land itself—all of the setting finds its analogue in the female figure. She is, of course, reclining. How could she stand in such a setting? How could she confront the viewer? She turns from us, allowing us guiltlessly to caress her with our eyes.

It is tempting, in the case of this small nude, to relate her not just to Renoir's own numerous exercises in this motif but also to the wonderfully evocative landscape monotypes by Edgar Degas. Although Degas and Renoir had drifted somewhat apart in the 1890s, each artist followed the other's career, and Degas's fabulous and evocative landscapes were featured in one of only two solo exhibitions he had in his long lifetime, at Durand-Ruel's gallery in September 1892. Arsène Alexandre wrote a beautiful review, and many connoisseurs were able to become acquainted with an aspect of the artist little known before. Degas also explored the relationship between the landscape and body, actually imbedding bodies in his imagined terrain so that landscape and body are one. Renoir must have seen this exhibition, and one

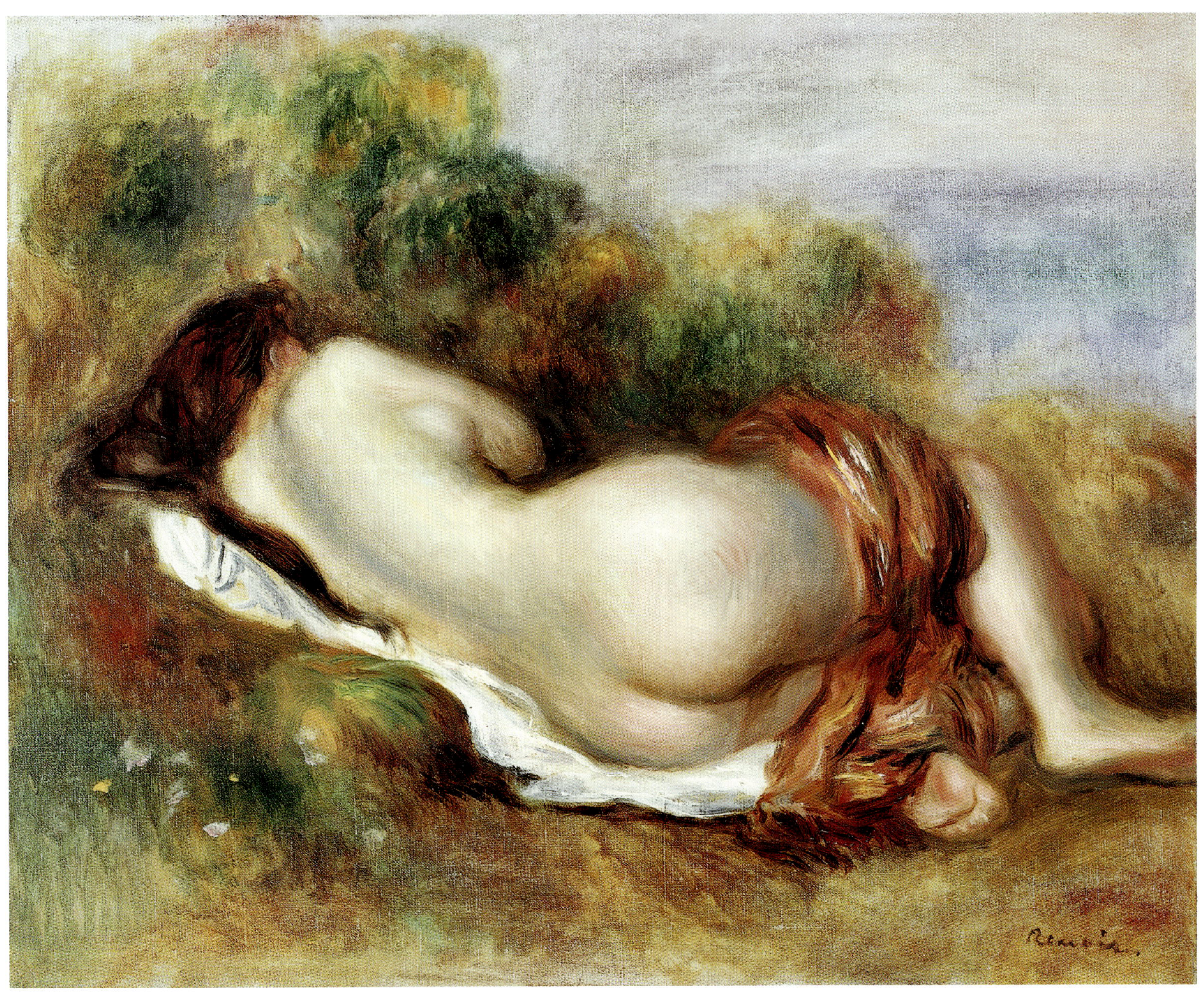

93

is tempted to date this small nude in a landscape—and probably others like it—to his experience of Degas's landscape worlds. For Degas, the landscape was virtual, an image that emerged through the artist's hand from the recesses of the mind rather than from an actual landscape. One feels very much the same sense of artifice and vitality when viewing Renoir's landscape with its perfectly proportioned, rounded nude. No such nude ever posed in such a landscape for a painter, not even for Renoir.

94

BERTHE MORISOT
French, 1841–1895

In a Villa at the Seaside
1874

Oil on canvas, 19¾ × 24 in. (50.2 × 61 cm)
Signed lower right: "Berthe Morisot"
M.1979.21

PROVENANCE: Probably sold by artist at (sale, Paris, Hôtel Drouot, 24 March 1875, lot 21, as *Châlet au bord de la mer*, for Ff 230 to Henri Rouart); [Ernest?] Hoschedé (1837–1890), Paris]. Edgar Degas, Paris, by 1896 (estate sale, Paris, Galerie Georges Petit, 26–27 March 1918, lot 83, as *Femme et enfant sur une terrasse au bord de l'eau* to); [Paul Rosenberg, Paris, buying for]; Mme Fernand Halphen, Paris, by inheritance to; Georges Halphen, Paris, sold May 1979 to; [Hirschl & Adler Galleries, Inc., New York, stock no. 6037, sold ½ share to Galerie du Cirque, Paris; sold 12 June 1979 to]; Norton Simon Art Foundation.

EXHIBITIONS: Paris, 1896, no. 124; Paris, 1961, no. 11; Paris, 1972, no. 49, p. 67, ill.

REFERENCES: Angoulvent, 1933?, no. 43; Bataille and Wildenstein, 1961, no. 38, pl. 6; Bodelsen, 1968, no. 783, pp. 334–335; J. Rey, 1982, pp. 24, 25, color ill.; Adler and Garb, 1987, pp. 92, 120, color fig. 35; Manet, 1987, p. 90, ill.; Herbert, 1988, p. 280, fig. 286; Thomson and Howard, 1988, pp. 126, ill., 127; Schirrmeister, 1990, pp. 107–110, 115 n. 13, fig. 7-4; Higonnet, 1992, pp. 36, 112; Dumas, 1997, pp. 43, 71 n. 211, 124, color fig. 158; Ives, Stein, and Steiner, 1997, no. 897; Clairet, Montalant, and Rouart, 1997, no. 38, p. 132, ill.; Patin, 2002, p. 47, color fig. 5.

TECHNICAL NOTES: The basic landscape—the sea, sky, and some of the terrace—was first laid in directly wet in wet with a reserve left for at least the upper part of the woman. The rest of the composition was painted over the first lay-in. For example, the curtain was painted over the sky and sea. In the center and left foreground there are numerous adjustments and changes; however, these cannot be interpreted even with the X-ray. There are a few visible drawn and inscribed lines that correspond to the design, but it is not clear how extensive this drawing is. The cream-colored ground of medium thickness must have been commercially applied. A similarly colored layer, but more medium-rich and probably oil, lies on the ground, but it does not extend over the tacking edges. The two layers together fill the canvas weave and give a fairly smooth surface. The support, a medium-fine, plain-weave fabric, has been lined with an aqueous adhesive to a similar material. It is attached to a 5-part butt-join stretcher that may be original, but the painting has been restretched. Remnants of a natural resin varnish can be detected, but the present coating is probably a synthetic. (JF)

BERTHE MORISOT PAINTED this deft study of the modern seaside vacation in the summer of 1874, a monumentally important year in her life. Just months before, she had dared the conventions of her gender and class by submitting work to an independent exhibition of artists, whose modified union or corporation she joined and whom we know today as the Impressionists. This was to prove a decisive moment in her life, and she exhibited in seven of the eight exhibitions organized by the group between 1874 and 1886; only Camille Pissarro was more faithful. Yet not even she could convince her mentor and friend, the great painter Édouard Manet, to join his younger colleagues in this endeavor. He watched in fascination from the sidelines as Morisot gained both notoriety and recognition as a member of this rebel group. Manet's abstention did not prevent the Manet family and the Morisot family from vacationing together in the summer of 1874 in the Norman seaside town of Fécamp. The two families went en masse to this small fishing village with its recently completed villas and seaside resort hotels, reveling in its bracing, breezy air while escaping the heat and claustrophobia of Paris. In Fécamp, Morisot's parents, sisters, brother-in-law, nephews, and nieces joined their counterparts in the Manet family, and, during that summer, Morisot received and accepted a proposal of marriage from Manet's brother, Eugène. Édouard Manet, however, declined to visit that summer, preferring to spend it working with his young male colleagues, Claude Monet and Pierre-Auguste Renoir, in the river town of Argenteuil.

In Fécamp, Morisot made a series of studies of women and children on holiday that are among the strongest and most subtle of her career. Of this summer series, there is no doubt that the Norton Simon painting is the masterpiece. Morisot completed it (probably later in her Paris studio), signed it, and submitted it in 1875 to one of the earliest Impressionist auctions, organized mostly by the dealer Paul Durand-Ruel. The auction featured paintings and works on paper by Monet, Renoir, Alfred Sisley, and, of course, Morisot. The auction has always been interpreted as a major setback in the history of Impressionist commercial ventures, with particularly low prices being paid for paintings by Monet and Sisley. Morisot, by contrast, fared rather well, and a painting by her called *Interior* (1872, Hiyashi Collection) set a record price in a sale filled with works that are now considered masterpieces of Western art.

The present painting was the first work in the catalogue listing of those submitted by Morisot, appearing under the title *Châlet au bord de la mer*, and it sold for a respectable 230 francs to Henri Rouart, the

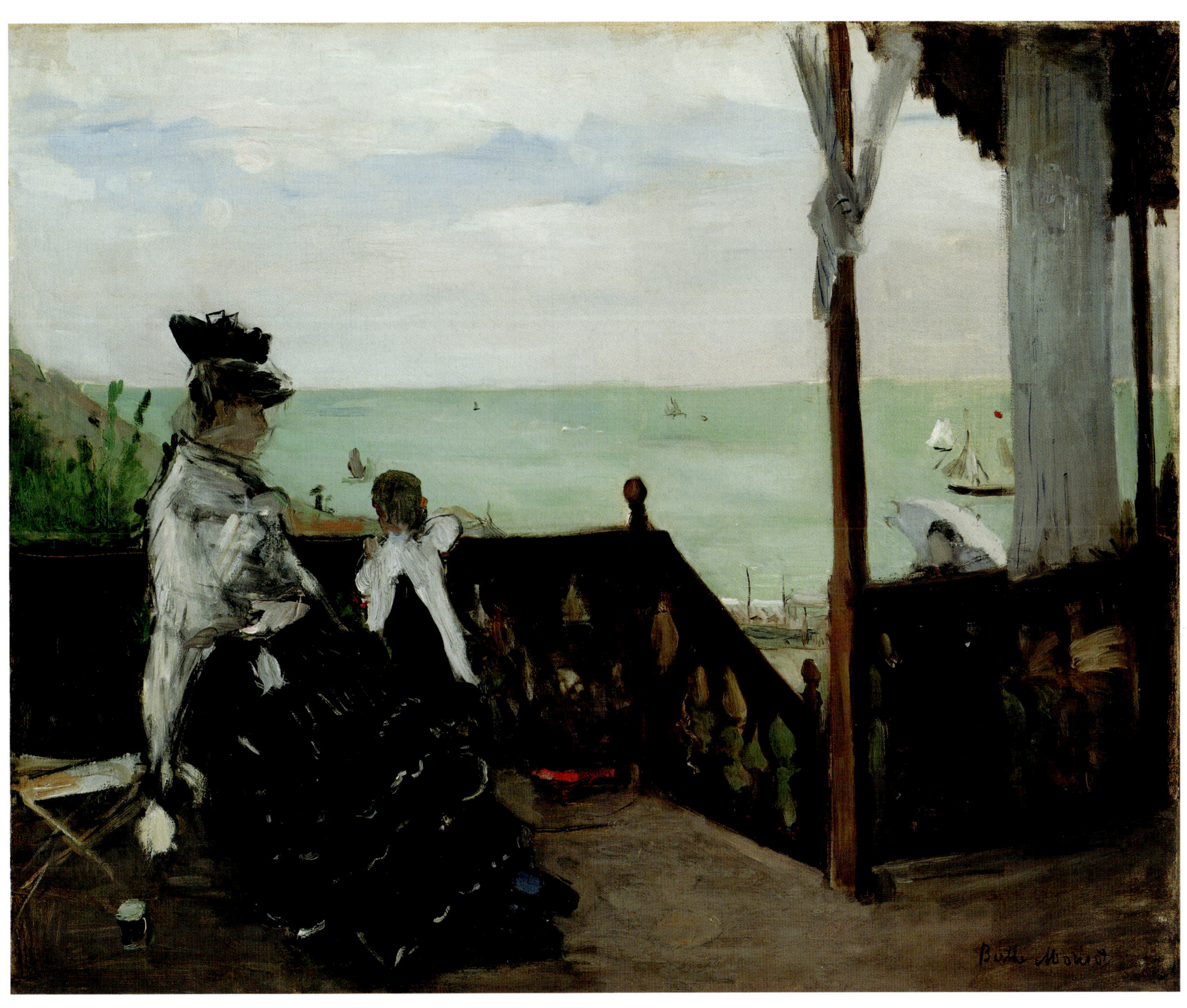

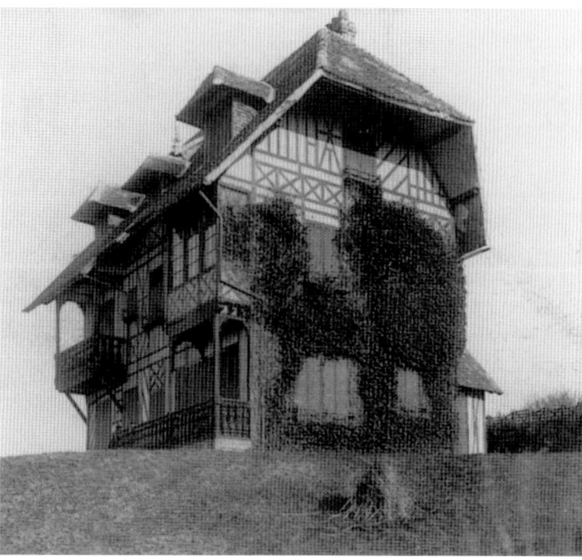
Fig. 94a Anonymous photographer, picture postcard of a villa on the cliff at Fécamp, c. 1900

industrialist and amateur artist. He, too, had exhibited with the Impressionists and was to become one of the greatest collectors of Impressionist painting. He was also a close friend of Morisot's Impressionist colleague Edgar Degas. Rouart, as the provenance demonstrates, seems to have owned the work for a short period, and he either sold or traded it to the department store magnate Ernest Hoschedé (who had purchased *Interior* at the 1875 auction), who in turn sold it (perhaps after his bankruptcy in 1879) to Degas (see cat. 86). All three men would be on any short list of major early collectors of Impressionism, Degas being perhaps its leading figure. Possibly because of its early sale (the painting was less than a year old when Rouart bought it), it seems never to have been exhibited in Morisot's lifetime, making its first recorded appearance in the great memorial exhibition held in 1896 with its catalogue preface by her friend the poet Stéphane Mallarmé.

Because of its important provenance and its easy availability to contemporary scholars, the Norton Simon painting has been discussed by virtually every writer associated with Impressionism and, particularly, with the oeuvre of Morisot. Its site has long been identified as Fécamp, a small fishing and resort town with a harbor and long pebble beach, squeezed between cliffs, about ten miles northeast of Étretat, famed for its massive rocks and cliffs, painted by Gustave Courbet, Monet, and others. But scholars are not at all clear whether the painting represents a private villa or the veranda of a small hotel. Unfortunately, no records help to identify just what residence the Morisot or Manet families rented that summer. There is, however, a wonderful photograph from a turn-of-the-century postcard of a similar villa perched, as was Morisot's, on the edge of a steep hill (fig. 94a). Whatever the precise site, the veranda is situated safely above the beach, seen below in Morisot's painting, creating an arena of privacy for the upper-class women and children of Morisot's circle. Morisot's figures are not men and women enjoying the seaside, such as in the scenes painted by the middle-class Monet earlier in the decade, or even by Morisot's upper-class male colleagues Manet and Degas. Indeed, Morisot never seems to have taken her easel onto the beach itself, perhaps out of fear of remarks from others, perhaps simply to maintain her sense of privacy. This pictorial reserve or discretion has been much discussed by feminist historians of the artist's career, some of whom interpret the painter's reliance on balconies, staircases, hillside perches, and other distancing devices as expressions of the imprisonment felt by Morisot and most other women of her class. Other writers stress the subjectivity of Morisot's vision and the honesty of her pictorial location. In either instance, her freely brushed pictures disclose many more aspects of women's lives and sociability than the jewel-like beach scenes of Eugène Boudin or the atmospheric and expansive views of Monet.

One historian of Morisot's oeuvre has concerned herself with the painter's interest in, and use of, couture fashion. Anne Schirrmeister has published an article dealing with this topic, which includes a discussion of the Norton Simon painting.[1] Like Morisot herself, Schirrmeister relishes the expensive and beautifully executed white piping on each of the four layers of ruffles on the female figure's day dress as well as her jaunty blue stockings. And although she ignores the wonderfully layered hat with its oddly square protuberances, Schirrmeister remarks on the woman's careful protection of her arms and shoulders from wind and sun, as she wraps herself in a pale shawl and protects her hands with gloves. The fact that the shawl does not quite match the dress is evidence of Morisot's lack of concern for high fashion and her concomitant reliance on the discreet—

and comparatively informal—dressing habits of real women of the upper classes in the privacy of their homes and other controlled spaces. Schirrmeister published two nearly contemporary fashion plates of similarly dressed mothers and daughters out of doors, making it clear how informal Morisot's mother and child are when compared with the starched and posed ideal women in the fashion plates. In the latter, the girls wear miniature versions of their mothers' elaborate dresses and stand with perfect posture. By contrast, the little girl in Morisot's painting is leaning against the balcony, protected from the dirt by a simple white smock over what seems to be an equally simple dress.

Everyone who has written about this charming painting remarks on the second woman who walks up the staircase, parasol on her shoulder. By this entrance, Morisot suggests that the foreground female is perhaps as elaborately dressed as she is and positioned as she is at the top of the stairs because she is expecting to receive a caller from another house or hotel. There is conveyed absolutely no sense of anxiety or surprise. Rather, Morisot's principal figure (some say that it is her sister Edna, already married with two children) sits placidly, giving no indication that she is about to rise, while her daughter looks unconcernedly over the rail, and sailboats move about in the water, appearing and disappearing as if to divert the women. On the floor at left is a glass of some unidentifiable refreshment, and on the floor at right, near the standing child, a dish or plate, perhaps containing some fruit.

When Morisot's friends, led by the executor of her estate, Pierre-Auguste Renoir, organized a memorial exhibition of her work in 1896, the year after her early death, the painting was already owned by Degas, who lent it. This immense exhibition did little, one suspects, to strengthen Morisot's reputation because it had so many works arranged in the rooms of a commercial gallery that viewers were as likely to be confused as enlightened, engulfed as they were by scores of small, subtle canvases. Oddly, the exhibition was entitled with both of Morisot's names—first her professional (and maiden) name, Berthe Morisot, followed, in parentheses, by her married name (Madame Eugène Manet). Also on the title page was the mention of a portrait of Berthe Morisot (photoengraved) by Édouard Manet and, finally, a preface by Stéphane Mallarmé. Three men seemed to be needed to pay homage to a single woman. Perhaps she would have been consoled by this, not so much because she needed approval but because she deserved it. Morisot was among the first great women artists who persistently signed her full name, Berthe Morisot, rather than hiding behind a genderless initial as B. Morisot.

1 Schirrmeister, 1990, pp. 107–110.

95

Jean-Baptiste Armand Guillaumin
French, 1841–1927

The Seine at Charenton (formerly *Daybreak*)
1874

Oil on canvas, $21\frac{1}{4} \times 25\frac{3}{8}$ in. (54×64.5 cm)
Signed and dated lower left: "A. Guillaumin 5.74"
M.1968.16.2

Provenance: Edmond Décap, Paris, sold 17 March 1900 to; [Bernheim-Jeune, Paris, stock no. 10.435, sold 17 March 1908 to]; Georges Hoentschel de Malherbe (1855–1915), Paris, by inheritance to; Mme Hoentschel de Malherbe, Paris (sale, London, Sotheby's, 24 April 1968, lot 94, to); Norton Simon Art Foundation.

Exhibitions: Princeton, 1972, no. 28, ill.; San Francisco, 1974, no. 27, ill.

References: Serret and Fabiani, 1971, no. 33, ill.; Guillin, 1990, p. 8, pl. 27.

Technical Notes: The support is a plain-weave canvas, lined to canvas, with the original tacking edges cut off. The lining is old; however, adhesion between the two canvases remains strong. A small hole at lower center has been repaired. Paper tape that covers the edges has been unevenly covered with a dark brown unidentified substance, which has spattered over the edges onto the painting. The paint strata are not distinct. Although there is a small paint loss at the bottom edge that would normally provide information under a microscope, a clearly differentiated ground layer was not found. It has been noted that Guillaumin sometimes painted on unprimed canvas.[1] The image retains its original character, but the paint has been significantly altered by the heat and pressure of lining. Not only have individual brushstrokes lost definition and three-dimensionality, but the canvas texture is probably more evident in some places because of weave transference. Various changes in the composition are glimpsed with raking light, which reveals underlying brushstrokes. At the lower right, the black railing down to the water originally may have extended farther out. Many aspects of earlier treatment indicate a careless approach. Repair of the hole at bottom center consisted only of filling and a faint toning to a pale gray. Residues of dark yellow-brown material in the recesses of brushstrokes suggest that cleaning was not thorough. The brown substance over the paper tape is unexplained, and the present varnish is on top of it. The painting was varnished in 1969; at the time of acquisition a conservation report noted the painting was unvarnished. (RW)

Of the artists associated closely with the early Impressionist movement, the least understood is Armand Guillaumin. There are many reasons for this, and, in the face of this superb Impressionist landscape, they need to be rehearsed. The first is the painter's poverty and backbreaking work early in his life. One knows from early letters and witness accounts that Guillaumin's life in his late twenties and early thirties was one of almost relentless penury. Unlike his close friends Camille Pissarro and Paul Cézanne, who could rely, when pressed, on the largesse of their comfortably middle-class families, Guillaumin had no such support. He often could not afford even minimal rent, staying with friends instead, and worked long hours at his menial job digging and hauling wet waste for the Department of Roads and Bridges of the City of Paris to make ends meet. Thus, his early production, which is considered by most critics and historians to be his finest, is almost painfully small. The second reason for Guillaumin's comparative neglect involves his impassioned left-wing politics, which, although he shared these views with Pissarro and the young Cézanne, seem to have made it difficult for Guillaumin to socialize with the haute-bourgeois members of the Impressionist circle like Edgar Degas, Berthe Morisot, and even Claude Monet. These views also made it difficult for Guillaumin to relate well to the other working-class member of the group, Pierre-Auguste Renoir, who, although he had a background similar to that of Guillaumin, was so intent on social assimilation that he had little room for unfashionably radical politics. The third reason for Guillaumin's failure as an Impressionist involves his long life and the fact that he won the lottery in 1891, which produced a sufficient private income that he could work in isolation, painting scores of mediocre canvases every year until his death in 1927. Hence, his late career numerically overwhelms his superb beginnings, forcing a careful historian to question even the quality of the early masterpieces.

Although it was painted when the artist was thirty-two years old, the Norton Simon canvas is number 33 in the most reliable catalogue raisonné of Guillaumin's oeuvre. This means that fewer than three dozen canvases survive from a full decade of artistic production. By contrast, Monet, Cézanne, and Pissarro each made well over two hundred paintings for the comparable decade in their respective careers. Yet, when confronted with almost any of the pictures that do survive from Guillaumin's first decade of work, we are in the presence of real originality, boldness, and mastery. This is certainly true of the present painting. This forthrightly industrial view represents a completely contemporary attitude toward the

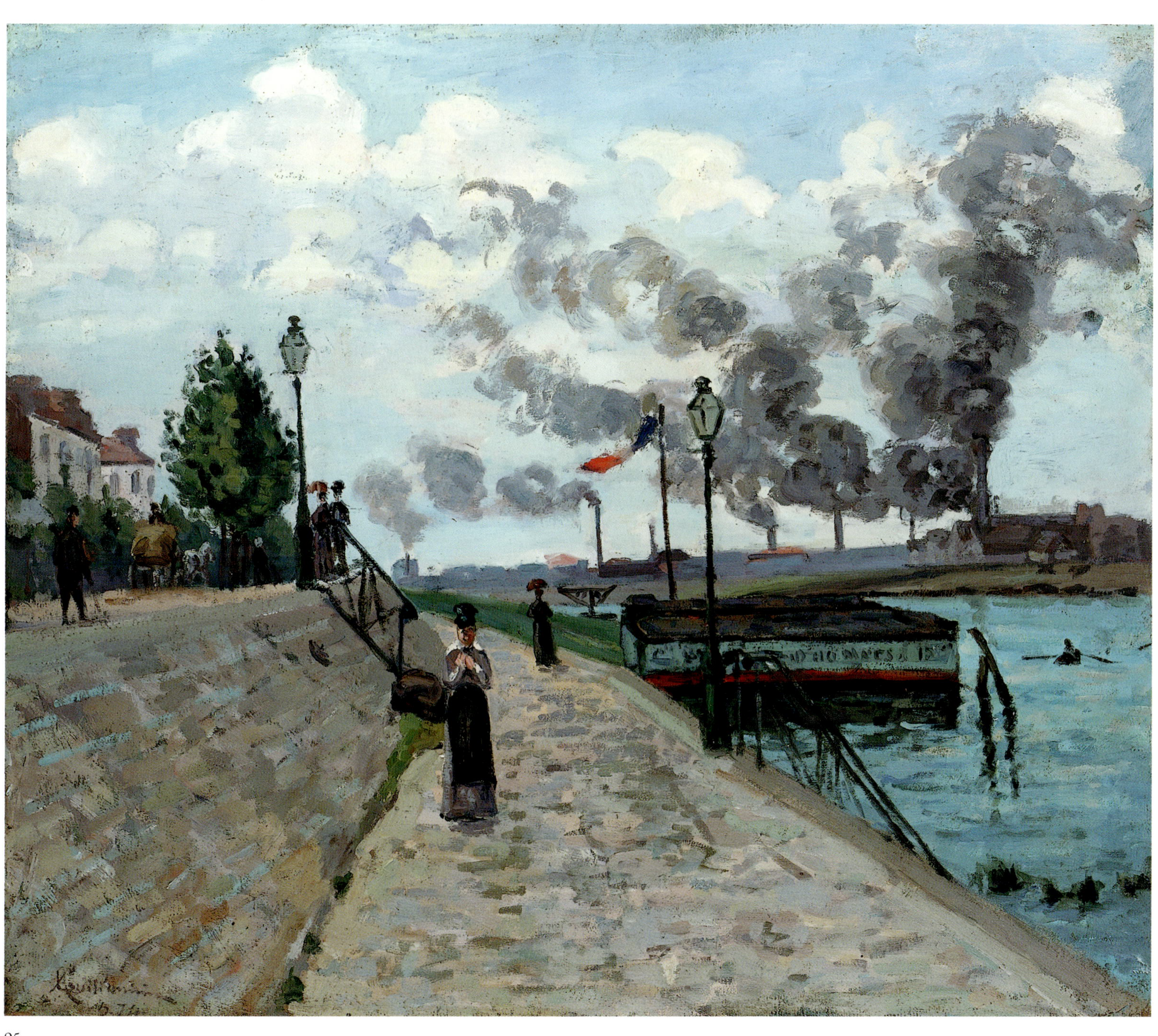

95

traditional art of landscape painting, glorying in the interplay between the clouds of industry and nature's clouds. Indeed, Guillaumin juxtaposed a scene of middle-class domesticity with one of full-scale industrialization in such a way as to suggest that the one is necessary for the other and that the modern landscape can aestheticize factory chimneys and smoke just as it can fashionable clothes and leisure boating. Of other Impressionists, only Pissarro had the courage to include industrial forms and industrial smoke in the landscape as integral to the experience of modern reality, and Guillaumin surely knew the older artist's views of the sugar refining factory in Pontoise, painted in 1873 (fig. 95a), the year before this view along the Seine during a period in which Guillaumin was often in Pontoise and Auvers.

The major difference between these two masterpieces of modern landscape involves paint handling and working method. Whereas Pissarro blocked in the major forms in his landscape with large brushes and correspondingly large areas of color, he blended these into a subtle landscape world with smaller brushes and hundreds of variously applied touches of paint. By contrast, the Guillaumin landscape almost seems like an underpainting, which the artist has worked up with minimal smaller touches. Thus, its effect is bolder and more immediate than the Pissarro, which aestheticizes industrial forms by treating them as elements in a carefully constructed and worked landscape composition. Guillaumin thrusts the subject, with its belching dark gray smoke, into our faces, and we can easily imagine him pushing the viscous paint into the sky area with big, crude brushes, applying it while the underpainting of the sky was still wet. Indeed, the painting itself remains wet-looking, as if it were still on the artist's easel, awaiting further touches. This sense of immediacy is made stronger by Guillaumin's decision to sign the painting with his name and to include not only the year, 1874, but also the month (he represents the month of May by using its number, 5), when the painting was made. This decision is comparatively infrequent in Impressionist practice, and Guillaumin himself practiced it rarely.

Thus, we know that this painting was made in the month following the first momentous event in Guillaumin's life as an Impressionist—the first organized exhibition of independent artists, soon nicknamed "Impressionist," held in April 1874 in the former studio of the photographer Nadar on the boulevard des Capucines. Guillaumin was an enthusiastic original member of this group, submitting three works, like his friend Cézanne, to the first exhibition. He sent pictures to the later exhibitions of this artistic coalition in 1877 (8 paintings), 1880 (18 paintings and 4 pastels), 1881 (10 paintings, 4 pastels, 1 watercolor), 1882 (13 paintings), and 1886 (17 paintings and 4 pastels), making him among the most faithful of the artists to the group's collective endeavors. It is very difficult to say whether the present painting was among these exhibited works because of the ambiguity of titles for Impressionist landscape paintings. Since its first appearance on the American art market in the 1960s, the painting has had the title *Point du jour* (*Daybreak*), and this is the title selected by Georges Serret and Dominique Fabiani in their catalogue raisonné of 1971. This title is obviously wrong, because the scene is full of sunlight and cannot in any way be construed as daybreak. The earliest recorded title for the work can be found in the records of Bernheim-Jeune Gallery in Paris,

Fig. 95a Camille Pissarro, *The River Oise near Pontoise*, 1873, oil on canvas, $17\frac{13}{16} \times 21\frac{5}{8}$ in. (45.3 × 55 cm), Sterling and Francine Clark Art Institute, Williamstown, Mass.

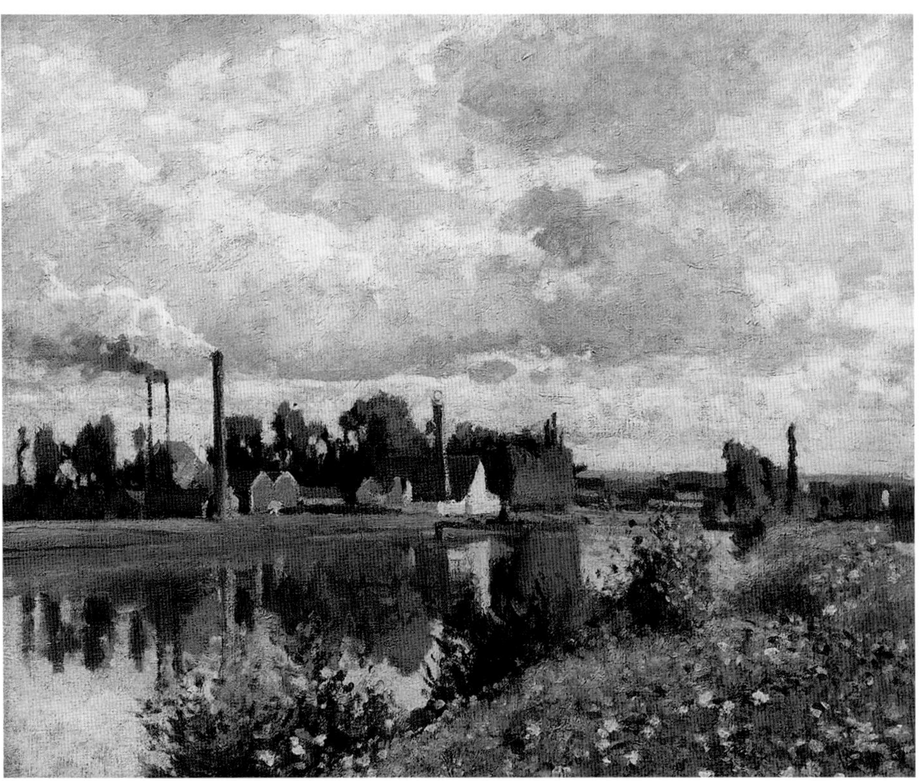

which calls the painting *La Seine à Charenton* (*The Seine at Charenton*). Charenton is an industrial suburb east of Paris, which Guillaumin visited frequently in the 1870s and 1880s, and this is surely a more apt title than its invented twentieth-century one. The painting is also associated with the major early Impressionist collector Edmond Décap, who purchased landscape paintings from other artists associated with the group, particularly Alfred Sisley (cat. 78), and who visited the Impressionist exhibitions.

The present work could not have been among the three paintings submitted by Guillaumin to the 1874 exhibition, because it had not yet been painted. Guillaumin skipped the 1876 exhibition, which would have been the logical next place for it to be shown. In 1877, the greatest of the eight exhibitions organized by the coalition, none of the titles listed in the catalogue could be a match, and in examining the later exhibitions, there are no works listed with "Charenton" in their titles, nor are there unidentified works that fit. Thus, in all likelihood, Décap purchased the work early from the artist himself, and it never appeared in public in the painter's lifetime. Perhaps a future historian of Impressionism will do what Serret and Fabiani failed to do: match early owners, titles, and works to those listed in the catalogues of the six Impressionist exhibitions that were Guillaumin's primary vehicle for public success in the first twenty years of his working life. In the absence of that close archival work, all else about his early career is speculation.

1 Callen, 2000, p. 67.

96

Giovanni Boldini
Italian, 1842–1931

Portrait of a Dandy (formerly *Portrait of Toulouse-Lautrec*)
1880–1890

Pastel on paper, 25 × 16¼ in. (62.9 × 41 cm) (irreg.)
Signed lower right: "Boldini"
M.1974.3

Provenance: [H. M. Calmann Gallery, London, to]; [E. V. Thaw & Co., Inc., New York, sold 18 March 1974 to]; Norton Simon Art Foundation.

Technical Notes: The primary support is blue laid paper, which is visible along the lower right and left edges of the sheet at the edge of the dark pastel medium. Laid lines and chain lines are clearly visible in these areas, and under the pastel. The paper is laid down on a thicker wood pulp paper. Eighteen nail holes around the perimeter of the artwork have rusted and perforate the support and medium. The support remains stable and planar, with the exceptions of buckling at the lower right corner near the signature and perforation from the rusty nail holes. While the blue laid paper is wrapped around the strainer at the top, left, and right edges, it is clearly lying on top of the backing sheet along the bottom edge. This orientation and the lower right corner creases indicate that the primary support was mounted after the portrait was executed, a complicated operation. The work is drawn in pastel, extending to the edges of the sheet in varying levels of thickness and application, and appears fixed in the dark area of the figure's jacket and unfixed in the head, hands, and background. The medium is in excellent condition, with the exceptions of a minor abrasion at the figure's collar and cracks in the hand and tie area, perhaps having separated in the mounting process. The work is stretched around a wooden strainer with a horizontal crossbar. The strainer-artwork assembly was previously separated from the glazing by wooden strips nailed through the artwork. These strips were removed in a 1989 treatment. (SSB)

Were it not for its perfectly readable and perfectly authentic signature at the lower right, it would be difficult to assign this superb pastel firmly to Giovanni Boldini. The Italian-born and -trained Boldini arrived in Paris in 1871, renting a studio first on the rue Frochot and then, nearby, on the much livelier place Pigalle. He used the city as a base for a thoroughly cosmopolitan career, which took him to almost every European capital. Like his later friends John Singer Sargent (they met by 1883), Paul Helleu, Joaquin Sorolla, and Anders Zorn, Boldini specialized in painting beautiful, rich people of the sort who, by the second half of the twentieth century, would be known as jet-setters. His sitters were English, French, Italian, Spanish, American, Chilean, Argentinean, and many other nationalities, but his talents lay firmly in the representation of women and their children. Men play a relatively minor role in his oeuvre. Yet he painted portraits of Sargent, James McNeill Whistler, and Edgar Degas, among other artists, and perhaps his most famous portrait represents the archetypal Parisian dandy (fig. 96a). Boldini used pastel and oil paint with equal flair, although his pastels usually employ a brilliant linear structure, absent from the Norton Simon work.

The present pastel was purchased by Norton Simon in March 1974 from the distinguished New York dealer Eugene Thaw as a portrait of Henri de Toulouse-Lautrec by Giovanni Boldini. Although an excellent photograph of the work is included in the Norton Simon website, it has never, to our knowledge, been published. Thus, it is not included in the 1970 catalogue of Boldini's work assembled by Ettore Camesasca and Carlo Ragghianti,[1] nor does it make a single appearance in the extensive literature devoted to Toulouse-Lautrec.

That its genuine signature confirms that Boldini was, in fact, its artist encourages us to try to establish firmly

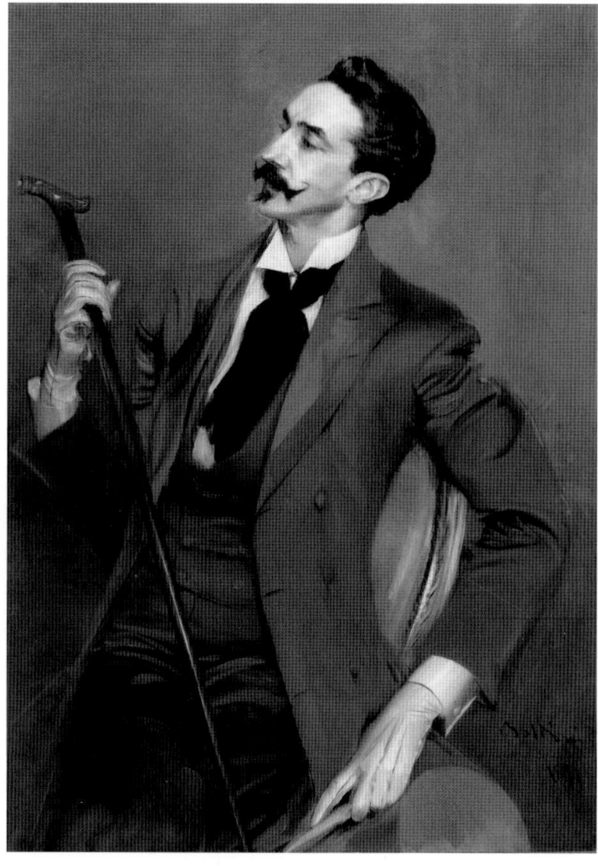

Fig. 96a Giovanni Boldini, *Count Robert de Montesquiou*, 1897, oil on canvas, 63 × 32½ in. (160 × 82.5 cm), Musée d'Orsay, Paris; photo: Réunion des Musées Nationaux / Art Resource, NY

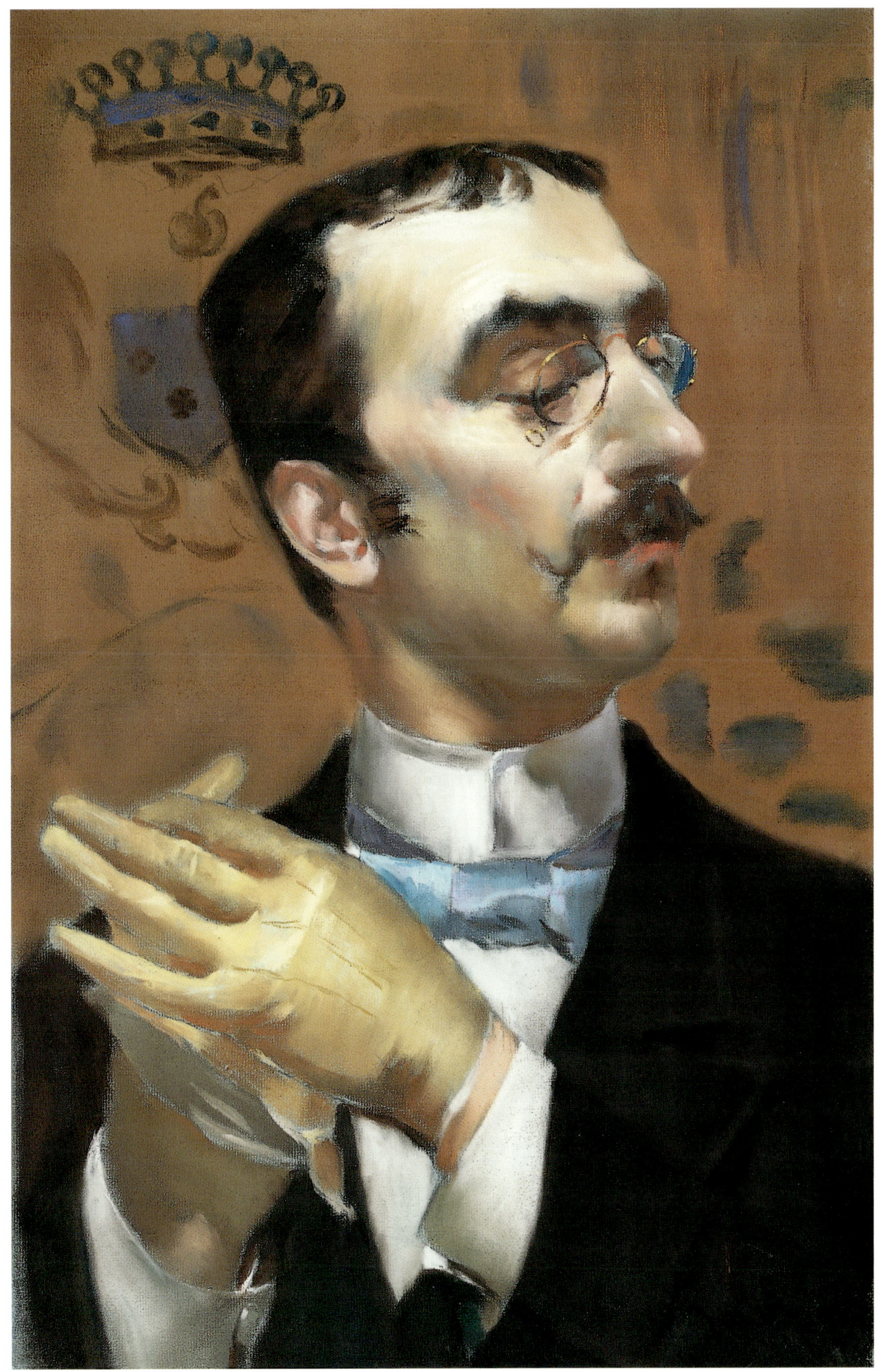

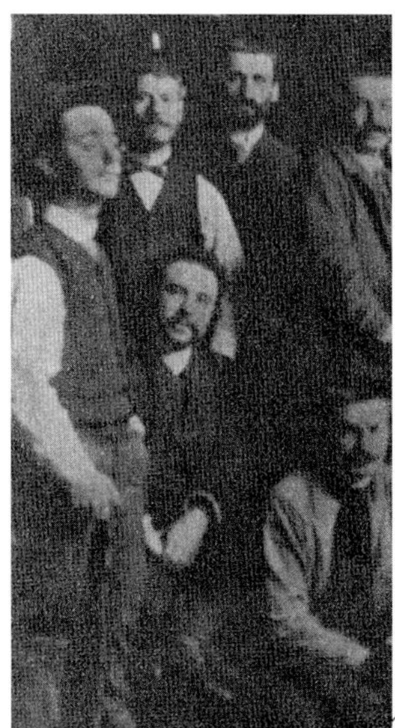

Fig. 96b Toulouse-Lautrec at Cormon's studio, c. 1883; photo: Dortu, 1971, fig. Ic. 135

whether it actually represents Toulouse-Lautrec. There are many published photographs and scores of self-portraits as well as drawn and painted portraits of Toulouse-Lautrec by others. The vast majority of portraits that represent the famous painter as an adult show him with a beard and most often wearing a hat. These two attributes have become, in a sense, signals that a short figure with these characteristics in any of a number of paintings and prints of the period is Toulouse-Lautrec. In the absence of both these cues, viewers of the Norton Simon pastel tend to doubt that it represents the famous artist. Yet there are so many other similarities of physiognomy—the prominent nose; the thick, dark eyebrows; the closely cropped hair; the fine, large hands—virtually identical to the same features recorded in the Toulouse-Lautrec iconography, that one wants to figure out a way that this could be the painter.

A well-known photograph of Toulouse-Lautrec made about 1883 and taken at the Atelier Cormon, where he was a student, shows him with a hat, without a beard, and wearing virtually identical pince-nez (fig. 96b). Even the angle at which the head is held is similar to that in the Boldini, though the nose is not quite as prominent as it is in the pastel. Another clue for the identity sleuth is the state of Toulouse-Lautrec's hair. In the Boldini, the figure is clearly beginning to bald and has combed his hair so as to discourage us from realizing this fact. If, one reasons, this was the case, it would explain both why he grew a beard (in compensation) and why he often wore a hat. Yet, there are several later photographs of Toulouse-Lautrec without a hat that show clearly that he had plenty of hair, even as late as 1896, either in the photograph showing him asleep[2] or that representing him in Maxime Dethomas's studio.[3] These and other later bareheaded photographs also show us a man with a much fuller face and with a brow with not quite such a Neanderthal ridge behind the eyebrows. Thus, after detailed examination, it is impossible to prove that this is Toulouse-Lautrec and easy to find reasons to assert that it is not.

The Toulouse-Lautrec problem also extends to the prominent coat of arms in the upper left corner of the pastel. If this actually represented the well-known family coat of arms of Toulouse-Lautrec (with the golden cross of Toulouse and three golden lions' mouths for Lautrec), we would be inclined to stretch a little to see the features of the famous painter in those of Boldini's sitter. Yet the arms, with their prominent crown above a single apple, which, in turn, is above a shield-shaped blue crest with three black crosses, can almost be read as a pastiche or joke, in line with the fawning silliness of the sitter. With so little to go on, it is futile to speculate on the identity of this dandy. Rather, it might be more profitable to conclude that the work was not intended to be a portrait in any strict sense, in spite of the clear individuality of the sitter. Boldini could just as easily have intended to represent a typical Parisian dandy, with all his false claims to an aristocratic pedigree and his absurd gestures. Indeed, our rather ruddy young man half shuts his eyes as he turns his head from the viewer and begins to remove his yellow kid gloves. These are as elegant as his blue silk tie and his gold pince-nez. Boldini shows us neither studs nor cufflinks, although he makes it clear that the sitter's collar and cuffs are well starched and pressed. The man seems disdainfully to turn from us, his viewers, and we are left to wonder why. If Boldini was making a character study of a pretender or a dandy, he certainly succeeded.

Fortunately, the condition of the pastel is beautiful. It was directly executed by Boldini on blue laid paper. After it was mounted on another sheet of paper and again on a secondary support (see Technical Notes), Boldini seems to have applied several small touches of gouache or pastel powdered into water or ether in the areas of the glasses and the shirt collar. These touches are so small and slight that they seem almost gratuitous, yet, when one mentally removes them, the pastel loses a certain amount of flair. Without an exhibition history or knowledge of the identity of the sitter, it is difficult to date this work with precision, but it seems to have been made in the 1880s, before Boldini arrived at his consistent and mature linear style.

1 Ettore Camesasca, and Carlo L. Ragghianti, *L'opera completa di Boldini*, Milan, 1970.
2 Dortu, 1971, vol. 1, fig. Ic. 183.
3 Dortu, 1971, vol. 1, fig. Ic. 182.

97

Gustave Caillebotte
French, 1848–1894

Canoe on the Yerres River
1878

Oil on canvas, $25\frac{7}{8} \times 31\frac{7}{8}$ in. (65.7×81 cm)
Inscribed with artist's signature by Renoir lower left: "G. Caillebotte"
N.1984.1.1

Provenance: Martial Caillebotte, Paris, c. 1894. Private collection, Paris; Pauline K. Cave (sale, New York, Sotheby's, 16 November 1984, lot 13, ill., to); Norton Simon, bequest 1993 to; Jennifer Jones Simon Art Trust.

References: Berhaut, 1978, no. 94, p. 114, ill.; Wittmer, 1991, no. 35, pp. 19, 51, 70, 76, 164, ill., 277; Berhaut, 1994, no. 88, p. 106, ill.

Technical Notes: The support is a plain-weave, medium-weight canvas; it has been glue-lined with the original tacking edges removed. No damages to the canvas are apparent, and the reason for lining was not determined. Adhesion between the two canvases appears to be uniformly strong. The thin ground, a warm pale gray, leaves the canvas texture visible, with a slightly grainy surface, including slubs in the canvas and occasional prominent threads. Microscopic examination did not reveal evidence of any preparatory drawing. Paint was applied with various sizes of brushes. The central foreground of light-colored paint was applied in crisp, horizontal strokes directly over the ground. Semidry brushstrokes of colors mixed on the palette often do not cover the ground; they drag over the canvas threads or sometimes over an underlying color, giving a shimmering quality to the reflection in the water. Caillebotte employed a wetter paint and small brushstrokes in the blue-green water. In the background (foliage on the riverbank) paint was applied in shorter strokes and dabs with softened contours. In the area of the rower's hat, the artist originally painted the shape of the hat as more rounded, as if the head were tipped down. Brush marking above each shoulder indicates that these areas also were reworked. Yellow paint beneath the blue-green water has produced a pentimento. No documentation was found regarding earlier treatment. Both the lining and varnishing have altered the probable original appearance of the painting. Heat and pressure have softened the profile of brush marking, and the effect of a loaded brush dragged over a textured canvas was diminished. The varnish is judged to be fairly recent, very likely applied at the same time as the lining. (RW)

Gustave Caillebotte is not as well known to the general public as Claude Monet, but his role in the development of Impressionism, and especially in the public dissemination of the style, was every bit as great. Though he did not show in the first Impressionist exhibition in 1874, he purchased there several important works, providing financial support to Monet, for example, when he needed it most. Two years later, Caillebotte exhibited eight paintings with the Impressionists, the following year six more, and no fewer than twenty-eight in 1879. At the same time, he continued to collect Impressionist works and to lend or give money to the most needy artists in the group. He did one more thing in 1876 that proved pivotal in the eventual establishment of Impressionism as the most well-known, admired, and avidly collected modern art: the twenty-eight-year-old artist drew up a will that made provision for an 1878 exhibition of Impressionist art and for a bequest to the French state of his prized collection of works by "the painters known as Intransigents or Impressionists," including Edgar Degas, Monet, Camille Pissarro, Pierre-Auguste Renoir, Paul Cézanne, Alfred Sisley, and Berthe Morisot.

In the event, Caillebotte lived for another eighteen years, and the 1878 exhibition was postponed until the following year. (Internal dissension and a bad economy made an exhibition in 1878 unpropitious.) But Caillebotte's bequest—accepted at first with reluctance—formed the core of the Impressionist collection at the Luxembourg Museum and later the Musée d'Orsay. His collection included Degas's *Women in Front of a Café, Evening* (1877), Cézanne's *Estaque* (c. 1878–1880), Monet's *The Luncheon* (c. 1873) and *Regatta at Argenteuil* (c. 1872), Pissarro's *St.-Denis Hill* or *The Red Roofs* (1877), and Renoir's *Ball at the Moulin de la Galette* (1876). The modern understanding and appreciation of Impressionism is thus unimaginable without the support and generosity of Gustave Caillebotte.

As already indicated, Caillebotte was more than just an impresario of Impressionism; he was a highly original and skilled practitioner of what Edmond Duranty in 1876 called "the new painting." Between about 1876 and 1882 Caillebotte's contribution to the movement was probably as great in number as that of any other artist, and his best paintings, including *Floor Scrapers* (1875, Musée d'Orsay), *The Pont de l'Europe* (1876, Musée du Petit Palais, Geneva), and *Paris Street: Rainy Day* (1877, The Art Institute of Chicago), rival the finest achievements of Degas, Monet, or Renoir. Indeed, they are unique pictorial interrogations of proletarian labor, the social geography of urban life, gender identity, and bourgeois leisure. His depictions of male swimmers, rowers, canoers, and sailors, including *Oarsmen* (1877, private collection) and *Bathers* (1878, private collection), constitute a serious examination of what would prove to be the most intense and long-standing preoccupation of twentieth-century European and American men of all social classes (besides war): sports.

Canoe on the Yerres River may be grouped among a large number of paintings of swimmers, fishermen, rowers, and canoers made by Caillebotte at Yerres in 1877 and 1878. The painter's family owned a château and thousand-acre estate on the edge of the small town, named for the adjacent, cool river waters, some fifteen miles southeast of Paris. Caillebotte spent summers there until the property was sold in 1879. The artist was himself a rower and yachtsman, and he bestowed on his paintings of male recreation on the river and its banks the intensity that is born of direct participation. His principal depictions of canoers on the Yerres are *Canoers Rowing on the Yerres* (1877, private collection), *Canoer in a Top Hat* (1878, private collection), and *Skiffs* (fig. 97a). The three were among the twenty-eight paintings exhibited by Caillebotte in the fourth Impressionist exhibition of 1879 and were intended to extend the range of his imagery to include the Parisian suburbs from the distinctly urban scenes that had dominated his submissions to the 1876 and 1877 exhibitions. In this, he was paying obeisance to his friends and mentors, Édouard Manet and Monet, each of whom had studied the leisure culture associated with the river in 1873–1874. *Canoe on the Yerres River* may be considered a study, or preliminary version, of figure 97a. It may alternatively be understood as simply unfinished.

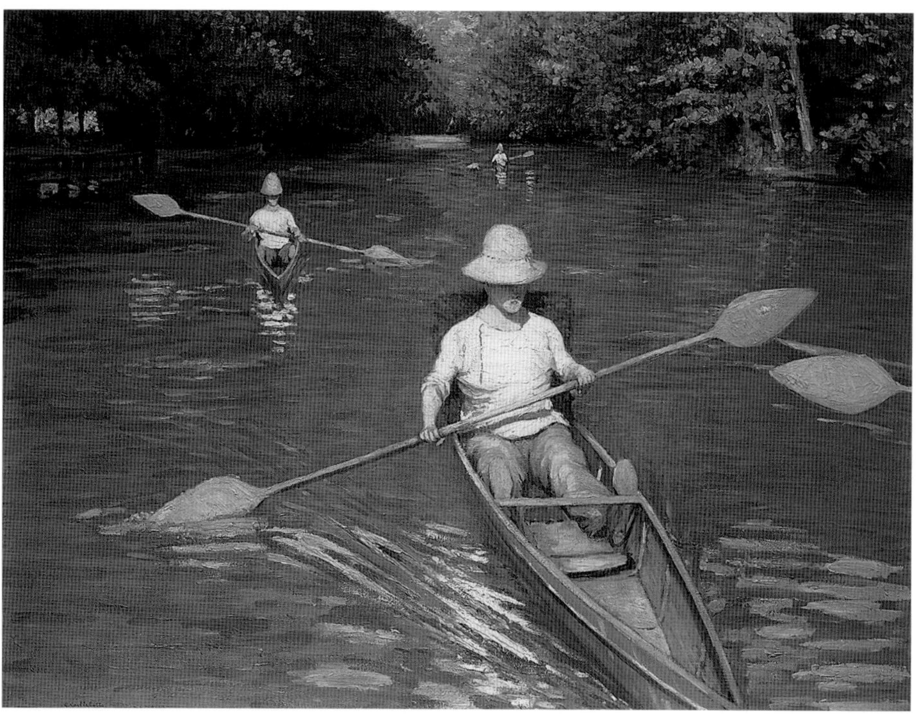

Fig. 97a Gustave Caillebotte, *Skiffs*, 1877, oil on canvas, 35 × 45¾ in. (88.9 × 116.2 cm), National Gallery of Art, Washington, Collection of Mr. and Mrs. Paul Mellon

In attempting the suburban and rural genres, Caillebotte was entering territory to which his talents were not obviously suited. He excelled in the representation of architecture, hard surfaces, and spaces made legible by the employment of linear perspective. Although this realm did extend to suburban gardens, with their rational ordering principles, his sensibility, like Manet's, was not suited to landscape. Hence, in painting water, vegetation, and atmosphere, he had to rely on the precedent of Monet, many of whose suburban paintings he already owned, as we have seen, and studied by the time he applied himself to similar subjects in 1878.

In painting the Norton Simon canvas, Caillebotte conceived a simple composition with the river and a male rower occupying the dead center of the pictorial format. Thus, the work is conceived more in terms of compositional strategies than point of view, and the spectator is unable to determine a perspective. Clearly above the rower, the viewer might at first imagine herself standing on the banks of the river looking down as the rower passes. Yet water occupies the entire foreground of the painting, making this position impossible. The spectator's vantage point is too high to be a fellow rower and too low to be an observer on a bridge that looks down on the river. Therefore, like the author of a traditional novel—an omniscient observer—the spectator must compose the scene in the mind rather than from visual evidence. In this, Caillebotte shows how little he understood crucial aspects of the naturalist aesthetic of his friends the Impressionists.

The second problem that Caillebotte encountered in making this painting was the transcription of water with oil paint. The artist's mentor, Monet, had worked on this pictorial problem—fundamental to the landscape

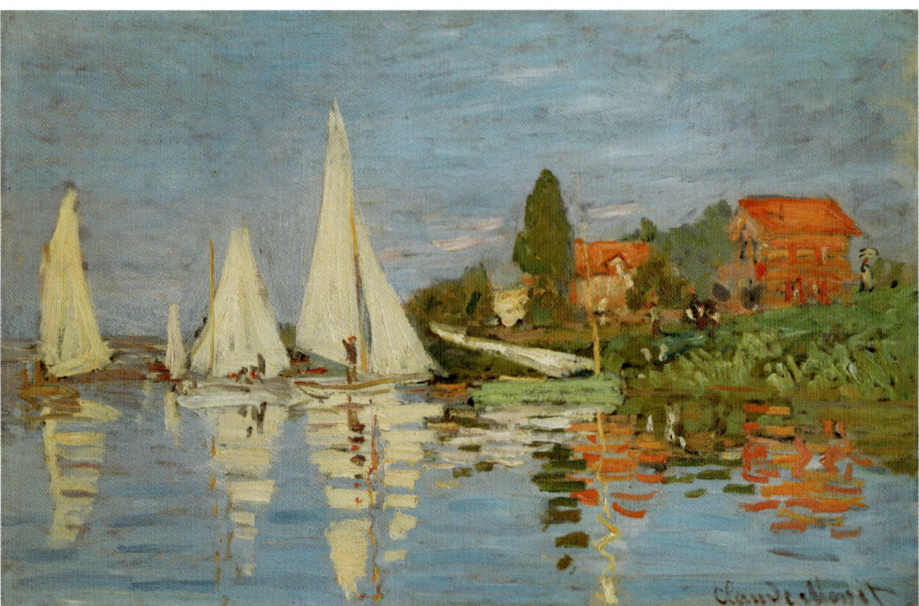

Fig. 97b Claude Monet, *Regatta at Argenteuil*, c. 1872, oil on canvas, 18⅞ × 29½ in. (48 × 75 cm), Musée d'Orsay, Paris; photo: Erich Lessing / Art Resource, NY

painter—from his teenage years and, by the early 1870s, could transform the thick and viscous medium of oil paint into a completely plausible representation of clear water. When looking at the water even in the paintings by Monet owned by Caillebotte when he began this canvas (fig. 97b), one senses both water and paint in equal measure, as if the variously liquid qualities of medium and subject were subsumed by the painter. For Caillebotte in 1878, this was not so easy. We read the strokes of paint that gather around the rower and his boat as thick lines of paint without ever actually accepting them as effects of light reflected in the water. And to represent the motion of the rower in the water, Caillebotte took on Degas, who, of all the Impressionists, was most adept at trapping the human body as it moved. By contrast, Caillebotte's rower is toylike and static as he maneuvers his double-headed paddle.

Indeed, the rower is clearly unresolved. He is large enough that his face would be easily recognized if his broad-brimmed hat or boater were not covering half his face, and yet the spectator is denied any significant clues to his identity. The relatively large size of the figure also renders perplexing its extremely approximate anatomy. Both arms and hands are shown in extreme foreshortening, but the consequence is that they appear small and stunted. The torso thus appears broad, even massive, by comparison. The legs are also severely foreshortened and equally stunted. The hat covers the upper half of the face, but there is no differentiation between the rest of the face and neck—they are a rudimentary column that rises from the crewneck of the bluish white shirt. The awkwardness of this head may be partly accounted for by the changed placement of the hat. A clear pentimento—a light arc or halo surmounting the top of the hat—indicates that it was originally perched on the figure's head at a steeper angle, covering slightly more of the face. The change exposed more of the face, but Caillebotte's insistence on the anonymity of his rower creates an anomaly: this is a face without eyes, nose, mouth, or chin. The viewer is led to wonder if this was initially intended to be a self-portrait. Something of the overall awkwardness and discomfort of the picture is explainable if we think this is the artist, who never unambiguously depicted himself in his paintings. For readers interested in details of geography and in the sartorial particulars of upper-class rowing, there is a long description of all the elements of the site and of the rower's straw hat in Pierre Wittmer's extraordinarily detailed book.[1]

Caillebotte elected never to finish this painting and did not include it in the 1878—or any other lifetime—exhibition. The painting nonetheless had sufficient charm and verve that it appealed to the eye of Caillebotte's executor—no less a painter of water than Renoir. When Renoir systematically surveyed Caillebotte's oeuvre after the painter's death in 1894, he identified a small group that were, in his view, sufficiently successful that they were candidates for signatures applied to the paintings under Renoir's own supervision in an attempt to make them more saleable. The Norton Simon painting bears one of these signatures.

Both paintings by Caillebotte in the Norton Simon Museum come from the collection of Pauline K. Cave, one of the first American collectors of Impressionist painting who recognized the importance of Caillebotte and, thus, participated with American museums in what has become a successful post–World War II revival of interest in the great collector's paintings. This began in earnest in 1964 when the Art Institute of Chicago purchased Caillebotte's masterpiece, *Paris Street: Rainy Day* and which resulted in 1995 in the French canonization of Caillebotte the painter with his first twentieth-century official retrospective in the Grand Palais.

1 Wittmer, 1991, p. 164.

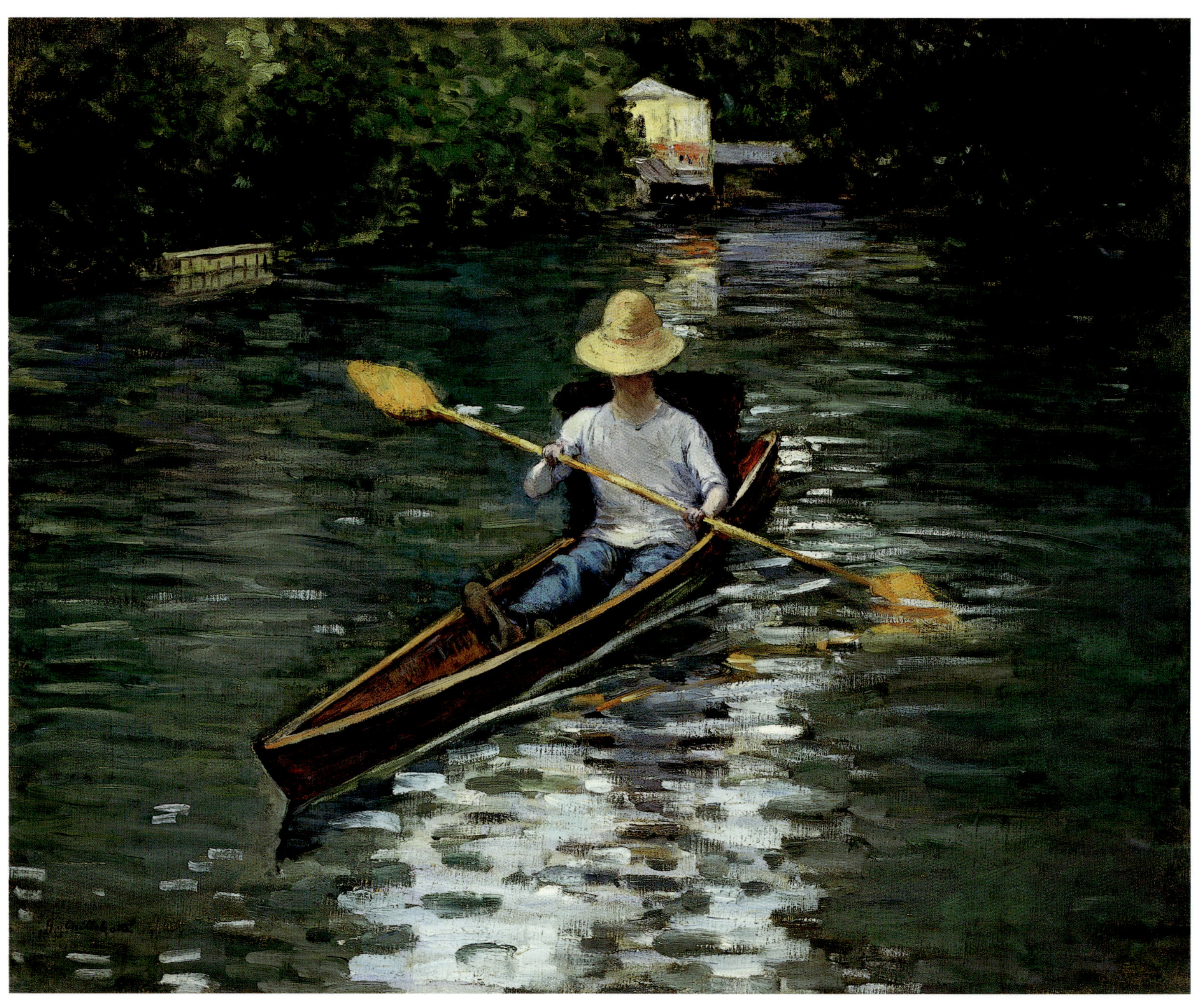

97

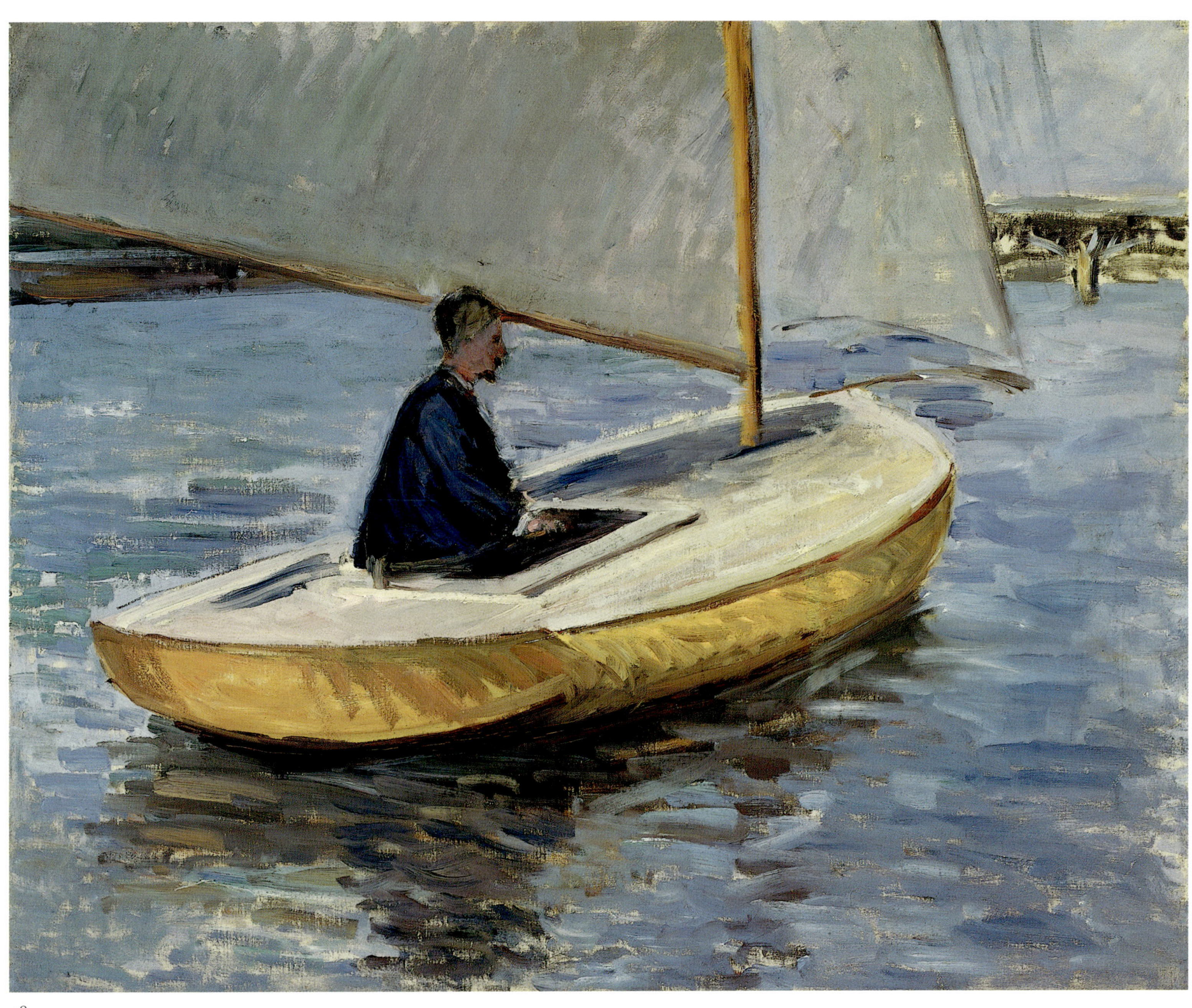

98

Gustave Caillebotte
French, 1848–1894

The Yellow Boat
1891

Oil on canvas, $28\frac{3}{4} \times 36\frac{3}{8}$ in. (73 × 92.5 cm)
F.1985.2.1

Provenance: Family of the artist; Mme Albert Chardeau, Paris, née Suzanne Caillebotte, in 1968. Pauline K. Cave (sale, New York, Sotheby's, 16 November 1984, lot 14, ill., to); The Norton Simon Foundation.

Exhibition: New York, 1968b, no. 48.

References: Berhaut, 1978, no. 395, p. 214, ill.; Berhaut, 1994, no. 467, p. 244, ill.

Technical Notes: The support is a medium-weight, plain-weave canvas; it has been lined with the original tacking edges cut off. Damages to the original support consist of a vertical tear approximately 4 inches long, at the right center, and two holes at the upper left and upper right, in the sails. The lining appears to be relatively recent; adhesion between the canvases is uniformly strong. The pine stretcher is constructed with mortise-and-tenon, keyed corners and may be the original. Paint was very quickly and directly applied over a cool white ground. The loose, sketchy brushstrokes leave much of the ground exposed, and there is no underdrawing or underpainting. As indicated by the brush marking from the first lay-in, the artist reworked the position of the boat and the mast. In the earlier version, the boat extended approximately 5 inches to the right of the final image. A pentimento of the previously painted mast can be seen, several inches to the right of the later mast. The multiple layers of paint in this area are thicker, completely covering the ground. The repair of the large vertical tear was not well done and remains rather obvious due to uneven filling; the amount of actual paint loss is not known. There are several small losses in the sails, and the retouching is visible with magnification. There is no evidence of abrasion, and it is possible that the painting has never been cleaned. The painting has been varnished, perhaps at the same time that it was lined. It is a synthetic resin, slightly yellowed. (RW)

By the mid-1880s Caillebotte had moved further and further away from his career as a painter-collector associated with the Impressionist movement. His large private income was sufficient for an independent life and his commitment to the production and exhibition of paintings waned when compared to his amateur pursuits of gardening and boating. Indeed, Caillebotte was such a passionate sailor in the decade before his death in 1894 that it might truly be called his vocation. His fascination with boat design, boat building, and boat racing has been well studied by David Travis, whose lecture on the subject is contained in the Museum curatorial files.[1]

The Norton Simon painting of 1891 probably represents the painter's friend Eugène Lamy, whose portrait he had painted two years earlier. Lamy is sailing a boat of the painter's design on the Seine. The bridge in the background is easily identifiable as the pedestrian and land bridge at Argenteuil near the painter's home at Petit Gennevilliers. Thus, the painting may be linked directly with works by Édouard Manet and Claude Monet done in the same stretch of the river more than fifteen years earlier, in 1874. One thinks particularly of the famous painting by Manet called *Boating* now in the collection of the Metropolitan Museum of Art (fig. 98a). By contrast to the Manet, which is an elaborate allegory of sex roles and politics disguised as a boating picture, Caillebotte seems to have had more directly descriptive aims. Yet, for whatever reason, he tired of the picture and left it in a state of incompleteness, never returning to it before his death three years later. In its arrested state, detailed interpretation is at once ungrounded and unwise.

Had the painting not made such a late entrance into the public world (it was still owned by the painter's brother and his descendants until 1968), the modern historian would be tempted to link it to the series of paintings by Pierre Bonnard of the great Swiss collector Ernest Hahnloser at sea in a boat. Unfortunately, it is likely that no great twentieth-century French painter—and here Henri Matisse and Albert Marquet come to mind—could have seen Caillebotte's uncompleted study of a new yellow boat slicing through blue waters. M. Lamy appears to have no control of the boat (we see neither ropes nor rudder) as it sails forever up the Seine.

1 Travis, 1995.

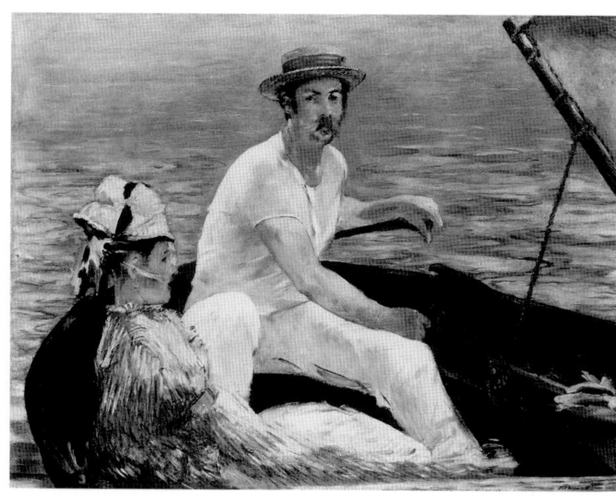

Fig. 98a Édouard Manet, *Boating*, 1874, oil on canvas; $38\frac{1}{4} \times 51\frac{1}{4}$ in. (97.2 × 130.2 cm), The Metropolitan Museum of Art, H. O. Havemeyer Collection, Bequest of Mrs. H. O. Havemeyer, 1929

99

Paul Gauguin
French, 1848–1903

Tahitian Woman and Boy
1899

Oil on canvas, $37\frac{1}{4} \times 24\frac{3}{8}$ in. (94.6 × 61.9 cm)
Signed and dated lower right: "99 / Paul Gauguin"
M.1976.8

Provenance: [Ambroise Vollard, Paris]. Moll, Vienna. Mrs. Austin Mardon, Ardross Castle, Scotland, 1923 (sale, London, Sotheby's, 24–25 November 1964, lot 32). [Hammer Galleries, New York, sold 5 January 1965 to]; Norton Simon, gift 1976 to; Norton Simon Art Foundation.

Exhibitions: Manchester, 1923, no. 18; Los Angeles, 1965; New York, 1968a, p. 31, ill.; San Francisco, 1973, no. 47, ill.

References: Meier-Graefe, 1904, vol. 3, p. 141; de Rotonchamp, 1925, no. 7, p. 221; G. Wildenstein, 1964, no. 578; Steadman, 1976, pp. 223, 225, fig. C; Sugana, 1972, no. 400, pp. 110, 112; Prather and Stuckey, 1987, p. 343; Eisenman, 1997, pp. 74, 76, ill., 77, 228.

Technical Notes: There has been much interest in the materials and techniques used by Paul Gauguin, and consequently, a number of his paintings have been subjected to a thorough scientific analysis.[1] The present work has not, but it is comparable to many of his other well-studied Tahitian paintings. The very coarse, open-weave fabric has approximately 4 or 5 threads per centimeter. At about this time Gauguin generally applied his own white ground, and this seems to be the case here. The tacking edges, still intact, are unprimed, and the ground ends irregularly along the edges of the picture area; the X-ray shows an uneven application of the ground. Gauguin generally sketched a composition with brush and thin dark blue paint and then applied paint in layers of simple strokes to build up forms, as he did for this painting. Pigments are as expected with little or no black. The X-radiograph may show a few changes but nothing concrete. Contraction cracks developed in both of the faces as well as in a few other places where paint seems to be denser. Most of the contraction cracks show the white of the ground, but those in the woman's face expose a dark layer of paint beneath the surface that could indicate reworking. According to Museum records the painting was infused with wax in 1966 and wax-lined to fabric and "revarnished" in 1968. The present surface coating appears to be a synthetic, and there is no evidence of an earlier varnish. Aside from the treatment of wax lining and varnishing the painting survives virtually intact except for drip marks in the lower right corner that were restored in 1968. (JF)

When Paul Gauguin departed for Tahiti in 1891, he was forty-three years old and the leader of a new direction in art. His paintings of Breton subjects—landscapes, portraits, children playing, women talking, and religious festivals—were recognized by a small group of young artists and critics as startling revisions of recent artistic practice. Works such as *The Yellow Christ* (1889, Albright-Knox Art Gallery, Buffalo) and *Two Children* (fig. 99a) feature broad zones of flat, almost uninflected color, shadowless forms distinguished from their backgrounds by dark blue lines and awkward anatomies. Gauguin's bodies have flat faces, almond eyes, pasteboard torsos, claw hands, and giant feet. His paintings were consequently nonnaturalistic; they exhibited neither the representational order and clarity of Salon art nor the dynamic and quotidian character of Impressionism. Such a bold assertion of artistic autonomy could not but attract a cultlike following. When the artists who constituted the School of Pont-Aven gathered at the Pension Gloanec or at Marie Henry's inn at Le Pouldu in Brittany, Gauguin was the sun, and his friends—Émile Bernard, Paul Sérusier, Jacob Meyer de Haan, and a dozen others—were the planets.

Gauguin had also, by 1891, attained a certain celebrity among avant-garde poets and critics in Paris. He was considered, alongside the poets Paul Verlaine and Arthur Rimbaud, "un maudit," a decadent who expressed in his painting, as Octave Mirbeau wrote at the time, "the irony of sadness, the threshold of mystery" and "the bitter and violent smell of the poisons of the flesh."[2] The young critic Albert Aurier, writing in the widely circulated avant-garde journal *Mercure de France*, passed a more sober verdict: Gauguin was the leader of a new school of "Symbolists" or "Synthetists." He added: "we are witnessing the agony of naturalism in literature and,

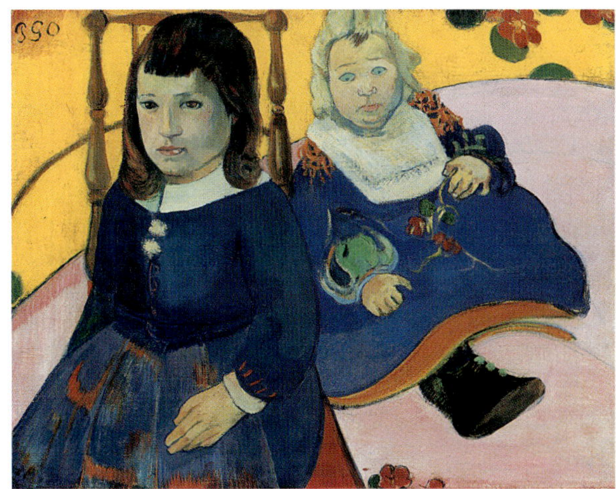

Fig. 99a Paul Gauguin, *Two Children*, 1889, oil on canvas, $18\frac{1}{8} \times 23\frac{5}{8}$ in. (46 × 60 cm), Ny Carlsberg Glyptotek, Copenhagen; photo: Ole Haupt

Fig. 99b Paul Gauguin, *Faaturuma (Melancholic)*, 1891, oil on canvas 37 × 26⅞ in. (94 × 68.3 cm), The Nelson-Atkins Museum of Art, Kansas City (Purchase: Nelson Trust)

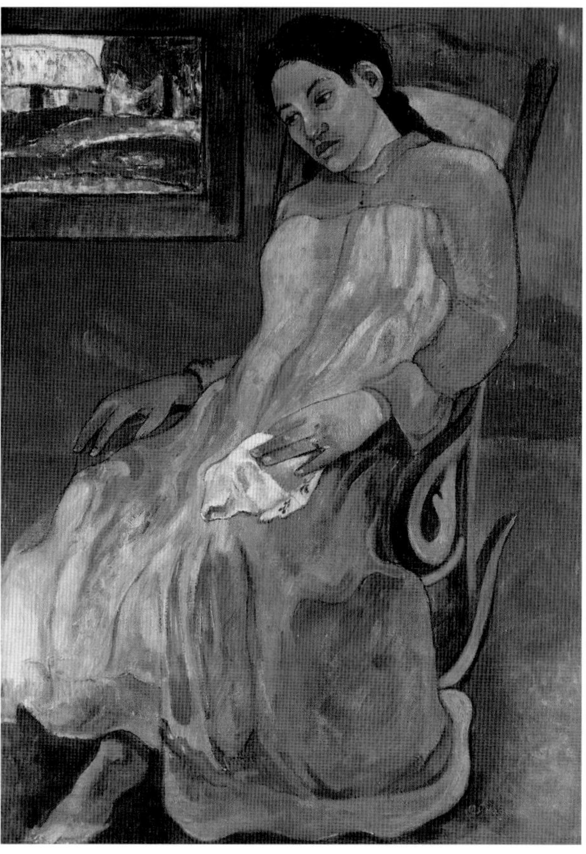

simultaneously, the preparation of an idealist, even mystical reaction, [and] we should wonder whether the plastic arts are revealing a similar evolution."[3] According to Aurier, the petit-bourgeois materialism (*proudhommesque*) that had generally characterized the former age was now passing from the scene, and a new, more spiritual, ideal, and symbolic outlook had arrived. The concomitant art—whose outlines he believed had been established by Gauguin—would reject quotidian, patriotic, and stereotypically exotic subjects and, equally, dispense with Impressionist or naturalist treatments. Instead, it would be suggestive, dreamlike, and decorative, the last term meaning that the art in question must consist of simple signs that transmit emotion and expression. Perhaps most of all, the new Synthetism must reject all previous artistic pieties; it must not be an allegory, a moral lesson, or an instrument of propaganda. Gauguin himself summarized the Symbolist aesthetic when he wrote: "The essence of a work, insubstantial and out of reach, consists precisely of 'that which is not expressed; it flows by implication from the lines without color or words; it is not a material structure.'" Gauguin's words here include a citation from Mallarmé, leader of the Symbolist poets.[4]

Notwithstanding his growing fame among the decadent subcultures of fin de siècle Paris, Gauguin decided to leave metropolitan France soon after the publication of Aurier's essay. His intention was to establish what he called a "Studio of the Tropics . . . where material life can be lived without money . . . and where living means singing and loving." There he would be unaffected, he thought, by the ongoing economic depression and the dispiriting struggles among artists to wrest a living from sales to the small contingent of independent-minded art dealers and collectors. He would occupy a hut, he said, in a state of "primitiveness and savagery," and if circumstances permitted, he would invite friends and family to join him in his exotic commune.[5] In the event, Gauguin remained isolated in Tahiti. Though he accepted (or purchased) the company of a few native lovers and friends, he was rebuffed by most colonials and Tahitians alike, and true comradeship eluded him. He worked alone, devoting himself primarily to representing the faces and bodies (they are not really portraits) of unknown indigenous women and conveying the vivid colors of local flora and his imagination. Two outstanding examples of Gauguin's first Tahitian manner are *Faaturuma (Melancholic)* (fig. 99b) and *Vahine no te tiare* (*Woman with a Flower*) (Ny Carlsberg Glyptotek, Copenhagen). In each picture, a native woman is shown in an attitude of contemplation and repose.

Almost a decade later, Gauguin returned to the subject of the seated woman with *Tahitian Woman and Boy*. He had in the meanwhile returned to France for nearly three years (May 1892–July 1895) and exhibited forty-six of his Tahitian works at the galleries of Durand-Ruel. Though sales were poor, the exhibition received tremendous publicity, probably because of the exotic subject matter and Gauguin's assertion of his own primitiveness. After his return to Tahiti he also painted his masterpiece, *Where Do We Come From? What Are We? Where Are We Going?* (1897–1898, Museum of Fine Arts, Boston), and soon thereafter attempted suicide by arsenic. Now, in 1899, he was living with a young woman named Pau'ura

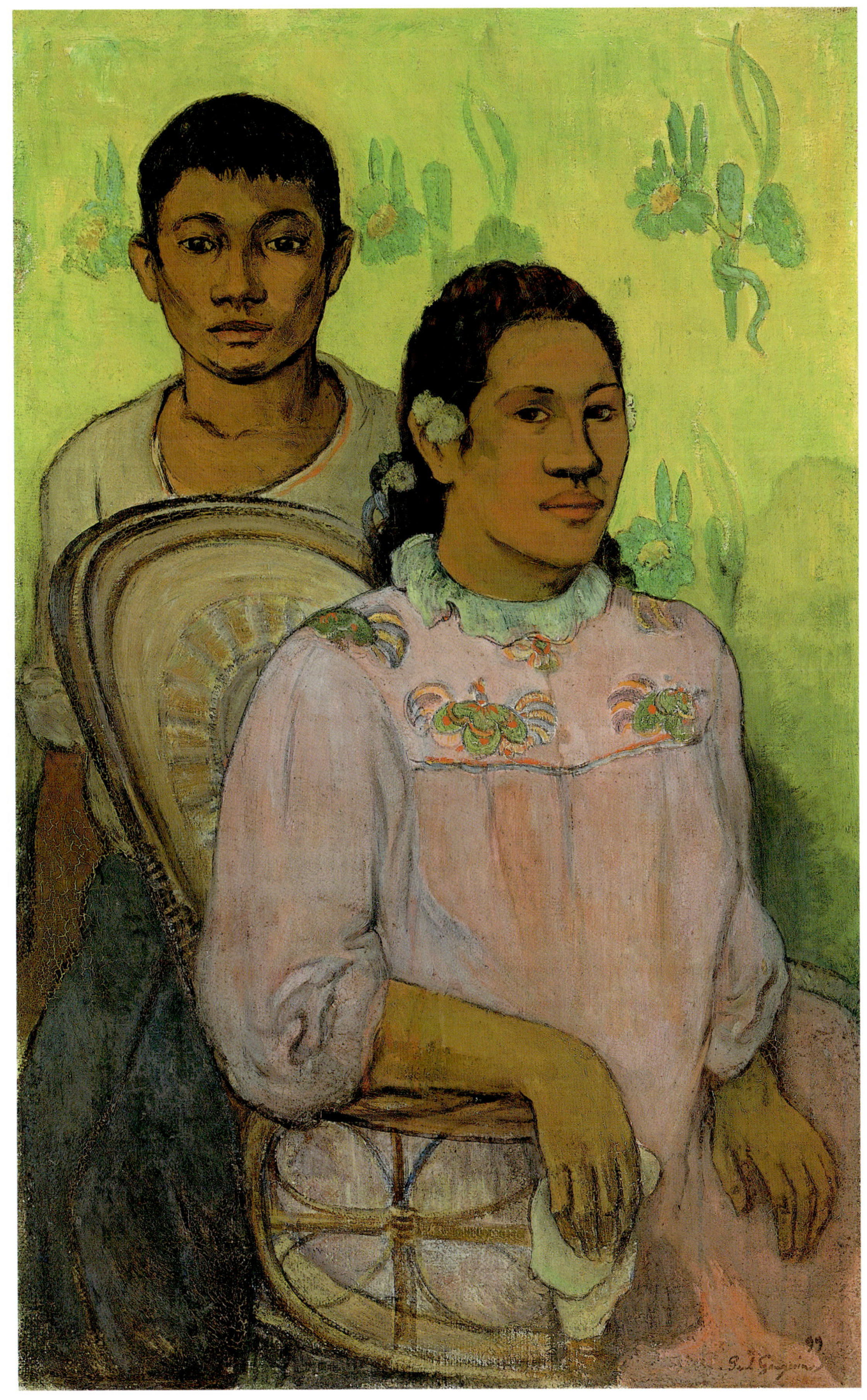

99

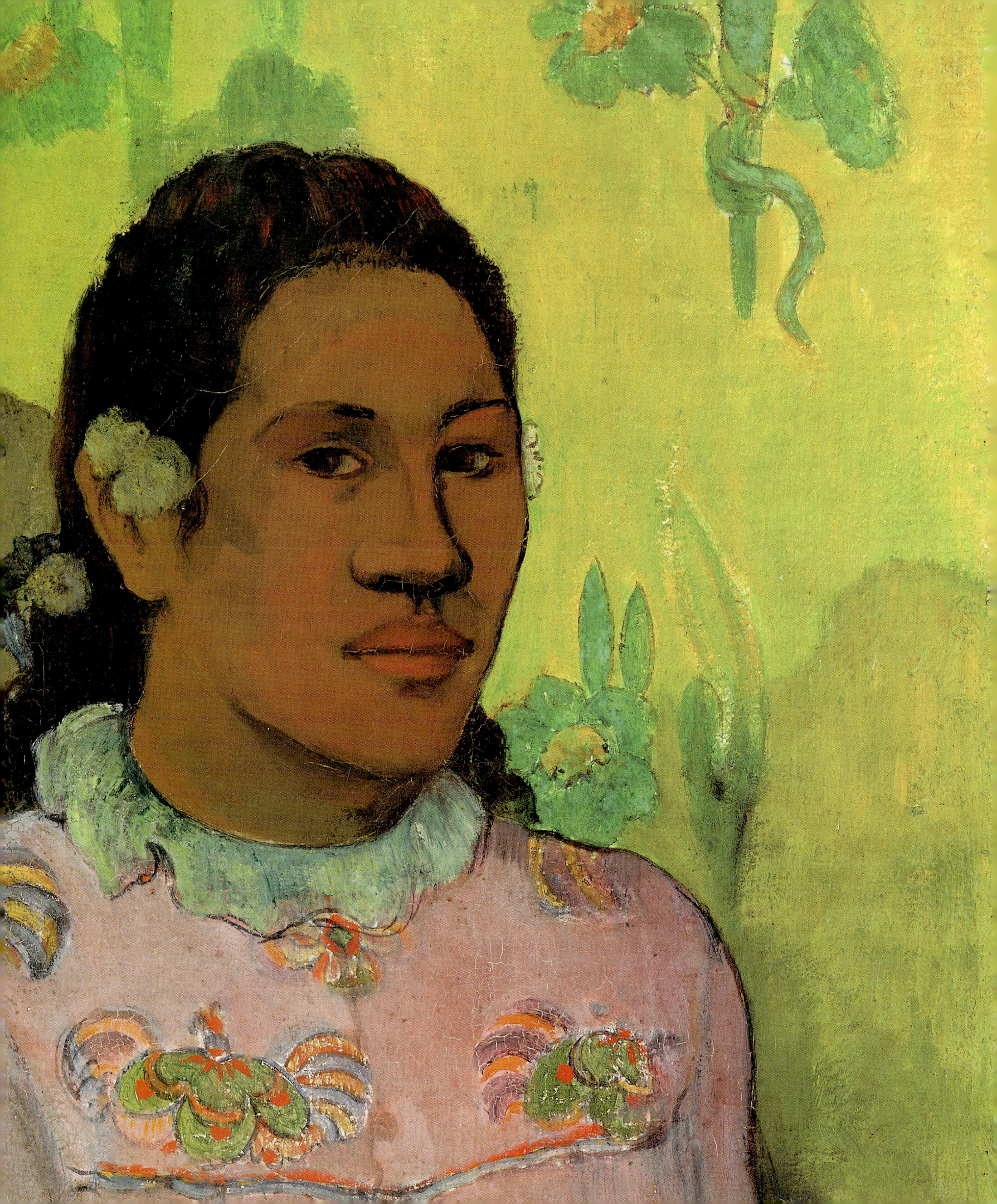

in a small thatched house at Punaauia, about fifteen miles from the capital of Tahiti, Papeete. He was broke, depressed, and often sick from the syphilis that would finally kill him. And yet the present picture possesses an unsurpassed coloristic exuberance.

Tahitian Woman and Boy is painted on a coarse, open-weave fabric—often called jute—of a size (the image size is approximately 36 by 23 inches) and proportion (a ratio of 3 : 2) that is more or less standard in his career from 1888 until his death in 1903. The two figures fill most of the vertical and the entire horizontal axis of the picture: the right arm and leg of the boy at left and the knees of the seated woman at right are cut off by the canvas edge. Though the woman is placed in front of the standing boy and though the rattan chair is clearly foreshortened, the space in the painting is extremely shallow. The arc of the chair back is blurred at right to diminish its recession, and the dark green shadow to the right of the seated figure is softly brushed—a memory of academic modeling—to bring the figure and the wall into closer proximity. The colors of the wall itself, with its superimposed flower pattern, lends a dreamlike insubstantiality to the space. They comprise several shades of Granny Smith apple green balanced by the pink-violet missionary dress adorning the poised young woman. Dashes of heat—the salmon orange circling the neck of the young man and the embroidered top of the dress—create flat, ornamented patterns on the surface of the rough jute.

The painting may be a portrait of Gauguin's lover, Pau'ura, and one of her relations, but this identification cannot be made conclusively. The young woman's face reprises that found in a number of Gauguin's paintings and drawings from 1891 to 1893, including *Vahine no te tiare, Eu haere ia oe?* (*Woman Holding a Fruit; Where Are You Going?*) (1893, The State Hermitage Museum, St. Petersburg), and the black chalk drawings made in 1891 from Tahitian models. In addition, the placement of the female figure—on a chair with an arc behind her—is like that seen in many earlier paintings, such as *Loulou* (1890, The Barnes Foundation, Merion, Pa.) and the great *Portrait of a Seated Woman* (1890, Art Institute of Chicago). The standing boy facing front in *Tahitian Woman and Boy* is unusual in Gauguin's oeuvre, though there are suggestions of his form, subject, and posture in a few earlier works. The two seated boys in *The Meal* (1891, Musée d'Orsay, Paris), their faces turned to the great carved bowl in the center of a table, are the only other such carefully rendered, young male physiognomies in Gauguin's career. The frontal posture in Gauguin's art is rare and generally reserved for carved figures, ghosts, and *tupapa'us*, or representations of the artist himself, as with *Parau na te Varua ino* (*Words of the Devil*) (1892, National Gallery of Art, Washington, D.C.) and the two versions of *Bonjour, Monsieur Gauguin* (Narodni Gallery, Prague). The perspective, however, is used in *Aita Parari te Tamari Vahine Judith* (*Annah the Javanese*) (1893–1894, private collection) and *Portrait of a Young Woman, Vaïte (Jeanne) Goupil* (fig. 99c).

Tahitian Woman and Boy may be an instance of Gauguin's nostalgia for a past time—the months before and after his first voyage to the South Seas, when he dreamed of an emancipated future. In 1899 Gauguin's lover gave birth to a child he named Émile, after the first, now deceased child he had in 1874 with his wife, Mette. The infant may also have recalled the child he might have had with Teha'amana in 1891, had she not miscarried or aborted. In addition, his thoughts now turned

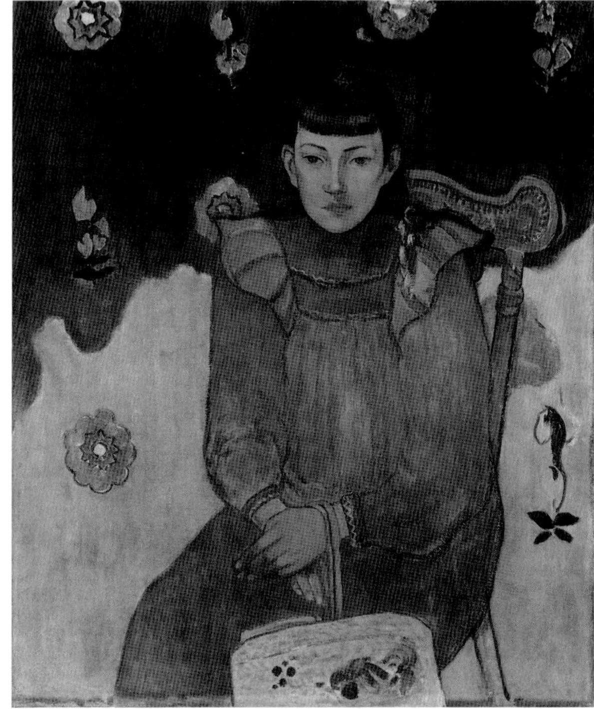

Fig. 99c Paul Gauguin, *Portrait of a Young Woman, Vaïte (Jeanne) Goupil*, 1896, oil on canvas, $29\frac{1}{2} \times 25\frac{5}{8}$ in. (75 × 65 cm), Ordrupgaard, Copenhagen, photo: Pernille Klemp

increasingly to his friend Vincent van Gogh, whom he had last seen ten years before and with whom he planned the Studio of the Tropics. Critics in Paris were now comparing works by the two men, and Gauguin needed to assert the superiority of his own originality compared with that of van Gogh. And in 1899 he even felt compelled to ask his friend Georges-Daniel de Monfreid to send him a packet of seeds—including sunflower seeds (veritable talismans of van Gogh)—so that he could plant a garden that would remind him of France. The vivid colors of *Tahitian Woman and Boy*, which recalls the background green-turquoise of van Gogh's *Self-Portrait Dedicated to Paul Gauguin* (see fig. 111b) is perhaps the strongest reminder of van Gogh and the vanished hopes of 1889. Gauguin's painting is a richly colored, coarsely textured surface and a decorative ensemble that, as the painter stated, "is unsubstantial and cannot be grasped."[6]

1 Christensen, 1993.

2 The Mirbeau quote is from *Le Figaro*, 18 February 1891, cited by Gauguin in Maurice Malingue, ed., *Paul Gauguin: Letters to His Wife and Friends*, trans. Henry J. Stenning, Cleveland, 1949, p. 162.

3 Albert Aurier, "Le Symbolisme en peinture: Paul Gauguin," *Mercure de France*, March 1891, pp. 155–164; republished and translated in Dorra, 1994, pp. 195–203.

4 Gauguin to André Fontainas, March 1899, cited Dorra, 1994, p. 209.

5 "Une Lettre inédite de Paul Gauguin," *Les Marges*, vol. 14, May 1918, p. 169.

6 Gauguin to Andre Fontainas, March 1899, cited in Dorra, 1994, p. 209.

100

Claude-Émile Schuffenecker
French, 1851–1934

Fernand Quignon
c. 1885–1890

Oil on canvas, $31\frac{7}{8} \times 25\frac{5}{8}$ in. (81 × 65 cm)
Stamped with artist's monogram lower right
M.1980.2

Provenance: Fernand Quignon, by descent in 1941 to his daughter; Marthe Quignon and Gaston Potiez (the sitter's son-in-law), to their son; Roger Potiez and his uncle, Jean-Roland Quignon, Paris (son of Fernand Quignon), to; Galerie André Watteau, Paris, to; (sale, London, Sotheby's, 30 April 1969, lot 46, ill., as *Portrait du peintre Fernand Quignou* [*sic*], to); [Spencer A. Samuels & Co., Ltd., New York]. [Barbara Mathes Gallery, Inc., New York, sold January 1980 to]; Norton Simon Art Foundation.

References: Porro, 1992, no. 193, p. 191; Grossvogel, 2000, no. 444.

Technical Notes: The original support is a medium-weight, plain-weave canvas, available commercially as a standard size. It has been wax-lined to canvas with the original tacking edges preserved. A right-angled tear in the background at the right center has been repaired, as has a small hole at the left side of the bottom edge. The lining is uniformly well attached, and the painting is tautly stretched on a new keyed stretcher. The cream-colored ground is moderately thick, leaving the canvas texture only slightly evident. The paint is opaque and has sufficient body to retain brush marking. It was applied in very loose, sketchy brushstrokes, often in a single layer applied directly over the light ground; small areas of the ground were left exposed throughout the background and around both hands. The figure was brushed in quick, straight strokes, in colors directly from the palette. Some additional colors are superimposed in the jacket and flesh tones, but without defining volume. The only suggestion of modeling is in the lighter paint on the proper left check and the front edge of the nose. The paint is well preserved; retouching is located only in the previously mentioned damages, carefully done. The surface is varnished. (RW)

Claude-Émile Schuffenecker is better known as a friend of Paul Gauguin than as a painter in his own right. He met Gauguin in 1872 when the two worked for the brokerage firm of Paul Bertin in Paris. They shared interests in art, music, and exotic cultures and together haunted the galleries and museums of the French capital. Schuffenecker passed on to Gauguin the lessons he learned at the ateliers of the Salon artists Paul Baudry and Carolus-Duran and advised the older man on drawing and the proper methods for mixing oil and pigment. Gauguin left Bertin's in 1877, and Schuffenecker departed four years later, but their friendship continued to grow, fertilized in part by the latter's frequent gifts of money. In the meanwhile, Gauguin's art developed from a kind of taut Impressionism toward something approaching Synthetism. In 1889 he painted *The Schuffenecker Family* (Musée d'Orsay, Paris) in this new manner, emphasizing the almost regal authority of Madame Schuffenecker and the deference of her husband, Émile. By 1890 Gauguin was deemed by the critic Albert Aurier to be the chief master of a new school of Symbolists, dedicated to an art that was built on abstract ideas, decorative surfaces, and the synthesis of vision and memory.[1] In a year, he would travel to Tahiti without help from Schuffenecker, who repeatedly refused to support his old friend's Pacific adventure.

Unlike Gauguin, Schuffenecker attained neither notoriety for his exotic travels nor great acclaim for his art. His painting retained many of the fundamentals of academic design, even when he essayed Impressionist or Symbolist subjects. His *Rocky Coast in Brittany* (1886, Musée des Beaux-Arts de Quimper), perhaps inspired by Claude Monet's paintings the year before of the same subject, combine Neo-Impressionist and Synthetist sensibilities while still displaying an underlying academic order. His *Self-Portrait* (c. 1890–1892, private collection), in which the conservatively dressed artist with a closely cropped beard is shown between Buddha and Christ, contains a balance of pictorial elements, careful foreshortening, and a clear arrangement of spatial planes. (The pairing of the two divinities is a likely reference to Édouard Schuré's mystical treatise *The Great Initiates*, 1889.) Despite his frequent stylistic reserve, Schuffenecker nevertheless exhibited his works at some of the most important avant-garde venues of the fin de siècle. He was a founding member of the Salon des Indépendants in 1884 and organized with Gauguin the now famous Volpini exhibition of Synthetist art on the grounds of the Paris Exposition Universelle of 1889. There, he exhibited twenty-three paintings, the majority of which were landscapes made in Brittany the previous year. By 1891 he had largely split with Gauguin—who anyway was now in Tahiti—and begun to associate with the mystical artists called the Nabis who later exhibited at the Salon de la Rose + Croix. After an artistic hiatus about 1903, Schuffenecker resumed his career as a painter and teacher. He continued to work in a loosely Impressionist manner and to teach at the Lycée Michelet in Vanves until his death in 1934.

Fig. 100a Maurice Meyer Studio, *Fernand Quignon*, photograph courtesy of the Comité Quignon, Fontenay-Tresigny, France

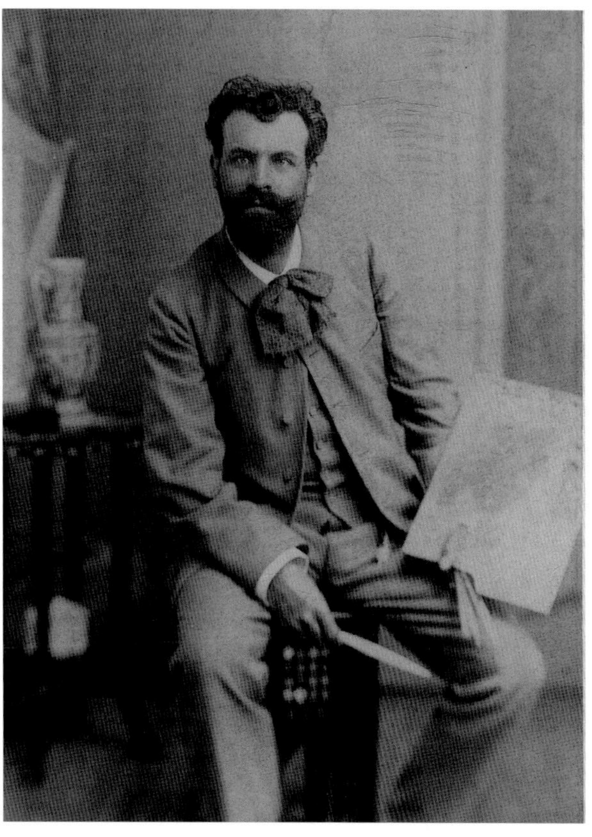

Schuffenecker's half-length portrait of his friend Fernand Just Quignon (1854–1941) depicts the now little-known landscape painter seated in a garden in front of a flowering trellis. He wears a brown and mauve jacket buttoned only at the top—exactly as shown in the contemporary studio photograph of the artist (fig. 100a) made by the studio of Maurice Meyer—a purple cravat, and a black vest. His right thumb is hooked into his vest pocket, while his left hand grips a pipe. He has a thick head of dark brown hair and a full red-brown beard and gazes impassively through forest green eyes. Despite the employment of divided color throughout the canvas and the particularly vivid use of red, orange, green, and turquoise for the face, the image is of a serious and self-important young man anxious to maintain a stolid aspect. Quignon was a fairly successful painter, winning awards at the Salon des Artistes Français in 1888, 1889, 1891, and 1900. He had, however, a peculiar knack for being in the right place at the wrong time. He spent three summers in Brittany at the Pension Gloanec from 1880 to 1882, a half decade before Gauguin stayed there, and he moved to Auvers-sur-Oise in 1883, seven years before Vincent van Gogh made the town his home. One might almost say he was an artist ahead of his time, but his landscapes from the 1880s onward are surprisingly conservative, composed of predigested motifs (farms, horse-drawn carts, churches, and fruit trees) organized on a single, middle-ground plane. Indeed, the highly conventional format of Schuffenecker's portrait and Quignon's stiff posture itself derive from the world of Salon painting to which the latter but not the former unambiguously belonged.

1 Albert Aurier, "Le Symbolisme en peinture: Paul Gauguin," *Mercure de France*, March 1891, pp. 155–164; republished and translated in Dorra, 1994, pp. 195–203.

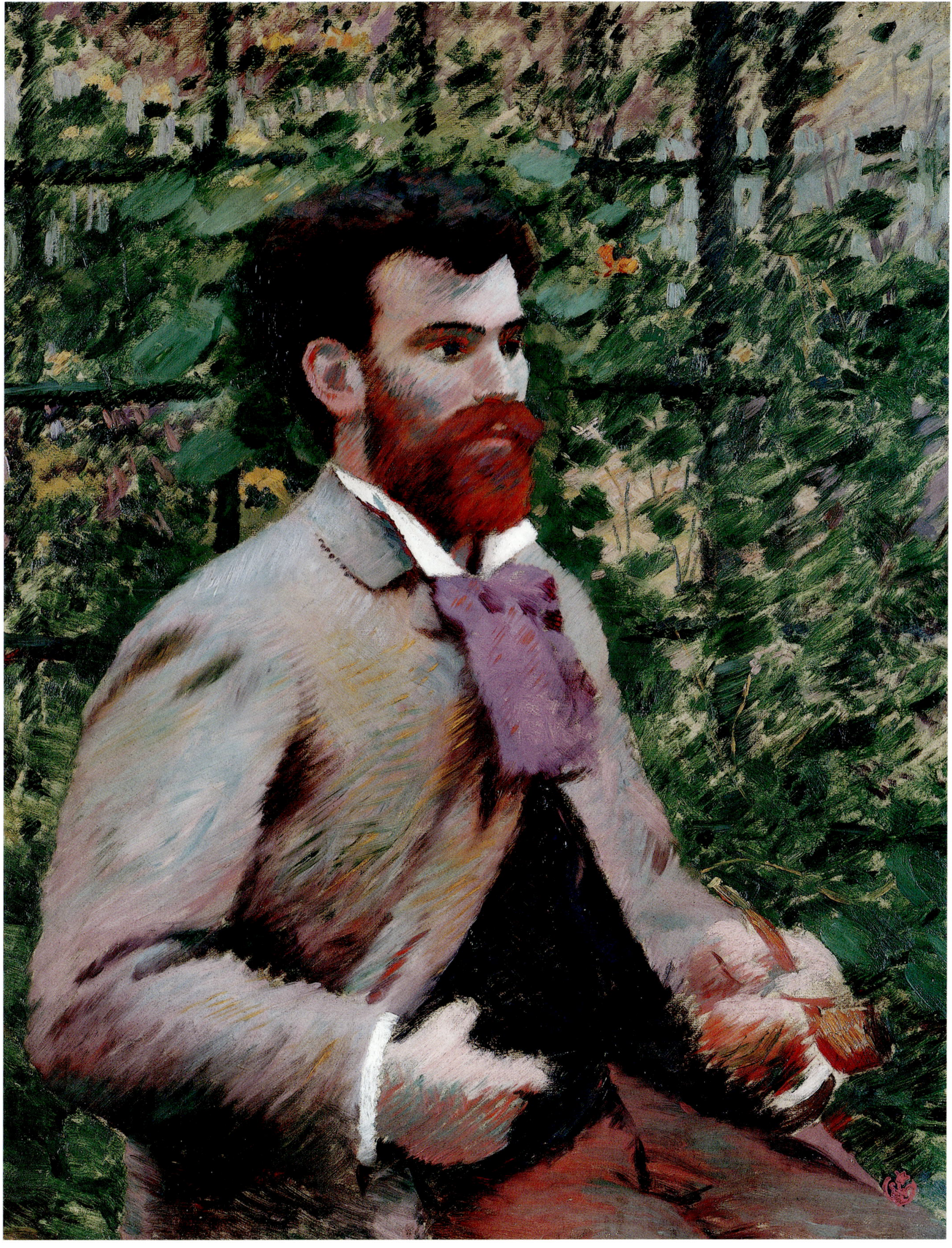

101

JEAN-LOUIS FORAIN
French, 1852–1931

Head of a Woman with Veil
c. 1878–1880

Oil on canvas, 13⅞ × 10⅞ in. (35.2 × 27.7 cm)
Signed upper right: "L. Forain"
M.1997.1.3

PROVENANCE: Alfred Beurdeley, Paris (sale, Paris, Galerie Georges Petit, 6–7 May 1920, lot 63, as *Tête de femme*, to); Couriot; [Jacques Dubourg, Paris]; G. R. A. van Stolk, Bergen. [E. J. van Wisselingh & Co., Amsterdam, stock no. S8849, by 1971, sold 19 September 1972 to]; Norton Simon (sale, New York, Sotheby Parke-Bernet, 2 May 1973, lot 5, color ill., bought in), (sale, London, Sotheby Parke-Bernet, 4 December 1980, lot 527, ill., bought in); Norton Simon, bequest 1993 to; Jennifer Jones Simon Art Trust, gift 1997 to; Norton Simon Art Foundation.

EXHIBITIONS: Amsterdam, 1971, no. 14, ill.; on loan, Phoenix, Art Museum, 13 October 1972–8 February 1973.

TECHNICAL NOTES: The support is a fine, plain-weave fabric that has been lined with an aqueous adhesive to a heavier plain-weave fabric. Some of the original tacking edges survive. It is tacked to a wood stretcher that is not original. The X-ray reveals a line of cracks and losses along the perimeter, about ¼ inch in from the present stretcher's edge, as if the painting had once been attached to a smaller stretcher. Along the perimeter there is a white band (about ¼ inch wide) painted over the original colors. The white paint appears old, since the line of cracking along the perimeter and the age cracks and losses exist in the white as well. It appears, then, that the painting was cut down, presumably by the artist, who may also have painted the white band to size his new dimensions, and then it was stretched onto a smaller stretcher, probably also by the artist. Later it was lined and stretched on the present slightly larger stretcher, and the white band was at least partially painted out to somewhat match the paint of the adjacent composition. The original paints are directly applied wet in wet with controlled brushwork and minimal blending. The artist used thin, possibly pure, colors (Prussian blue, black, and sienna, estimated) as well as pasty (those mixed with white). The dark blues of the hat and blue-green dress are scumbled with dark gray, but the yellow background is a thin application over the light-colored ground. The ground, which covers tacking edges and is probably commercially applied, allows some canvas texture to show. The varnish may be a natural resin and is later. The condition of the painting is good. Fine to medium crackle patterns exist, and there are scattered small losses in addition to those already noted. The varnish was removed and the painting revarnished in 1981. (JF)

THIS PORTRAIT OF an anonymous veiled woman is among the small masterpieces of Jean-Louis Forain's youth. Painted when the artist was in his mid-twenties and as the Impressionist movement was entering its full maturity, it represents a portly bourgeoise against a light-struck background that makes a playful mountain of her feathered blue-and-black hat. She is in strict profile, as if in emulation of a classical or Renaissance medal or quattrocento painted portrait, and her dark eye looks ahead without trepidation. As viewers, we are almost painfully close to her, but she seems unaware of our presence, and we are therefore free to gaze at her without social constraint.

Forain composed the work with thick paint and made compositional and iconographic allusions to the aesthetic of Édouard Manet and his followers Pierre-Auguste Renoir, Edgar Degas, and the urban Realists of the late 1870s such as Giuseppe de Nittis and Jean Béraud. It is, thus, easily datable by style alone to the last years of the 1870s, and, from the evidence of the signature, this dating is clinched. Florence Valdez-Forain, the artist's great-granddaughter and his most patient scholar, tells us that Forain changed his signature and professional name in 1880 from Louis Forain to Jean-Louis Forain, and the lone *L.* in front of Forain's surname in the upper right corner forces a date before mid-1880.[1]

The work relates to a small series of paintings of veiled women made by advanced French artists in the 1870s. Perhaps the finest of these is by Renoir (fig. 101a), but

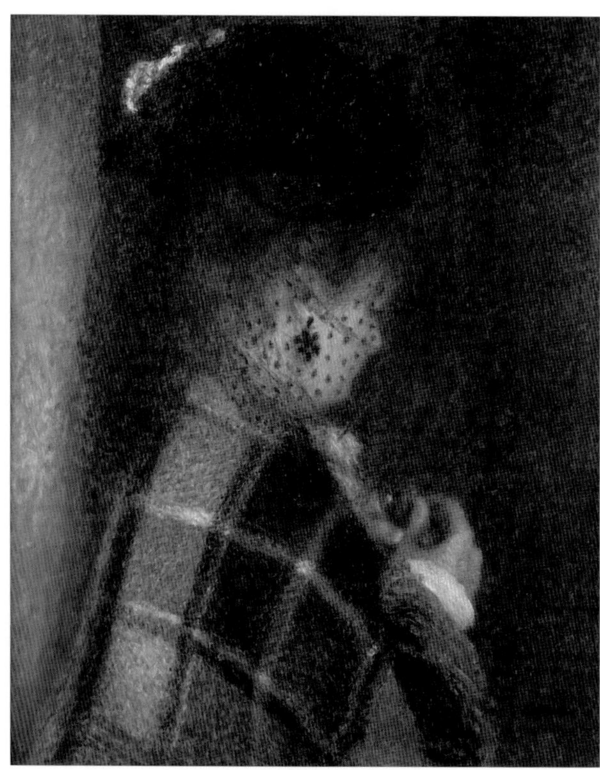

Fig. 101a Pierre-Auguste Renoir, *Young Woman Wearing a Veil*, c. 1875, oil on canvas, 24 × 20 in. (61 × 51 cm), Musée d'Orsay, Paris; photo: Réunion des Musées Nationaux / Art Resource, NY

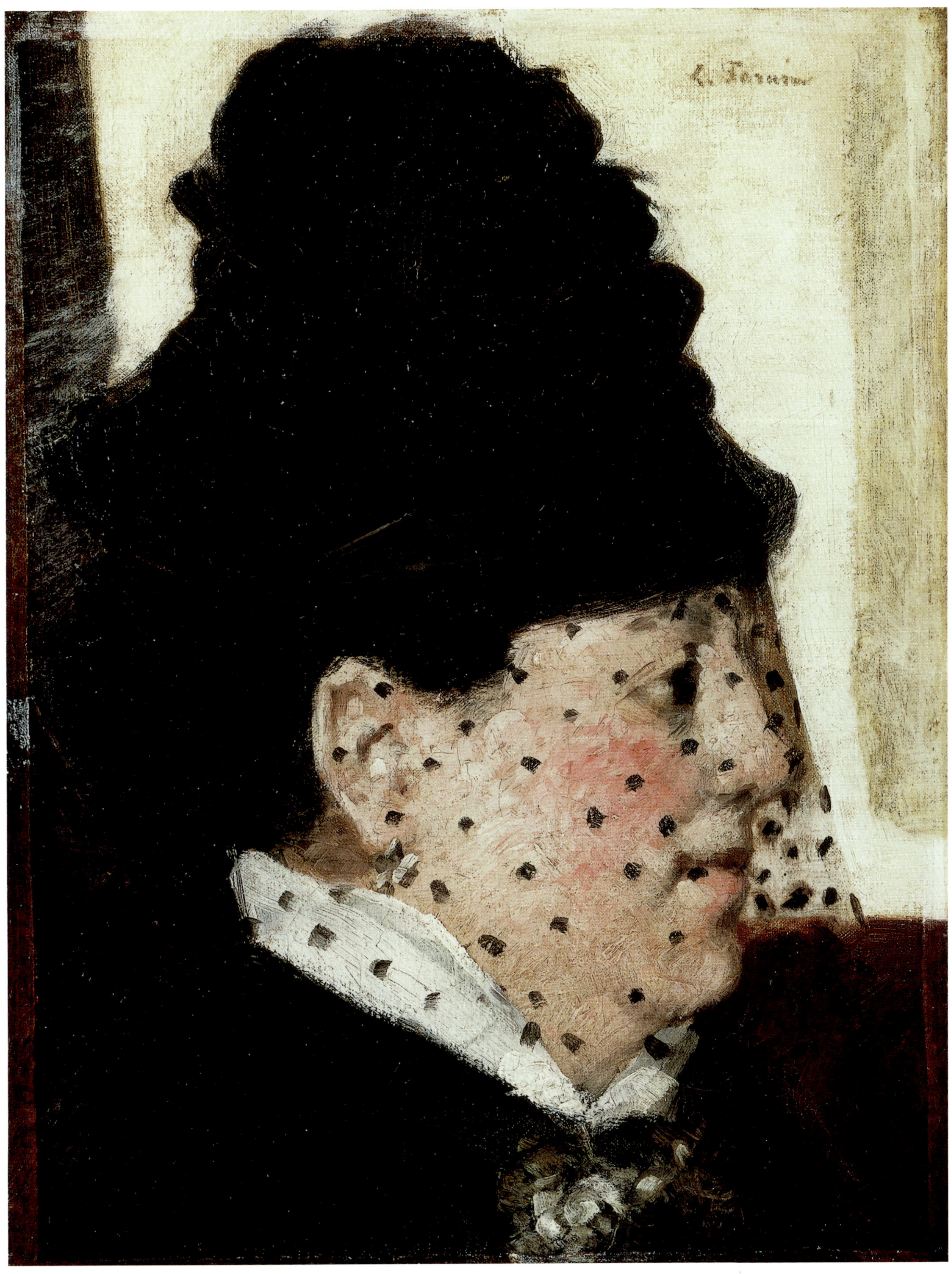

101

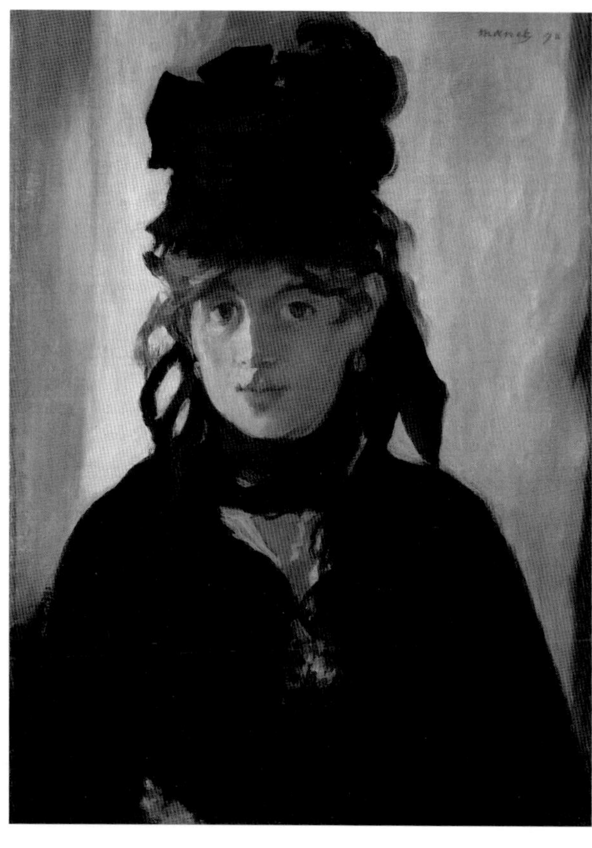

Fig. 101b Édouard Manet, *Berthe Morisot with a Bouquet of Violets*, 1872, oil on canvas $21\frac{5}{8} \times 15$ in. (55×38 cm), Musée d'Orsay, Paris; photo: Erich Lessing / Art Resource, NY

there are numerous other examples by Manet, Berthe Morisot, Degas, and Gustave Caillebotte. In the small painting's almost extreme reliance on a black-and-white silhouette, Forain suggests that he had seen Manet's famous portrait of Berthe Morisot (fig. 101b), then in the collection of its sitter, who, like Forain, exhibited with the Impressionist group. Morisot had been a faithful adherent of the artist cooperative from its inception in 1874. The younger Forain made his first appearance in 1877 and was included in three of the five other exhibitions that were organized by the group until 1886. It is even possible that the Norton Simon painting is one of the several now unidentified portraits of women—possibly the *Femme en noir*—exhibited at the eighth and last Impressionist exhibition in 1886.

In making this modest but powerful painting, Forain was throwing his hat into the ring of urban modernism. Following the lead of Naturalist writers like Émile Zola and Guy de Maupassant and Naturalist and Baudelairian painters who followed the example of Manet, Forain looked to commonplace sites in public Paris, thereby celebrating the newly cosmopolitan culture of that city, which had rebuilt itself into a vast urban theater in the Second Empire. Forain, like his compatriots, strolled the boulevards and streets of Paris, searching for figures whose clothing, pose, or features projected an emotional resonance they found of pictorial interest. Who knows what Forain himself saw in the pleasantly plump features of this woman? Did she remind him of his mother or aunt, or of a series of faces depicted by his dear friend Degas, including *Mademoiselle Marie Dihau* (fig. 101c) and *Portrait of a Woman*?[2] It is also possible that Forain had a less benign vision, seeing in his veiled, bourgeois woman the unappealing features of the women and men, shown in profile, at the left of Degas's celebrated *Women in Front of a Café, Evening* (1877, Musée d'Orsay, Paris) and *Portraits at the Stock Exchange* (1878–1879, Musée d'Orsay, Paris), exhibited at the third and fourth Impressionist exhibitions. Forain was a notable and outspoken misogynist (as well as an anti-Semite), and his depictions of women often contain a touch of venom mixed with naturalism.

Much has been written in recent years about the iconology of veiling in French Realist and Impressionist painting.[3] In certain cases, the veiling functioned in an almost erotic manner, faintly hiding beautiful women as they moved in the public sphere. Forain is clearly uninterested in that aspect of veiling, as his subject is stolidly middle-class and thus unappealing to male

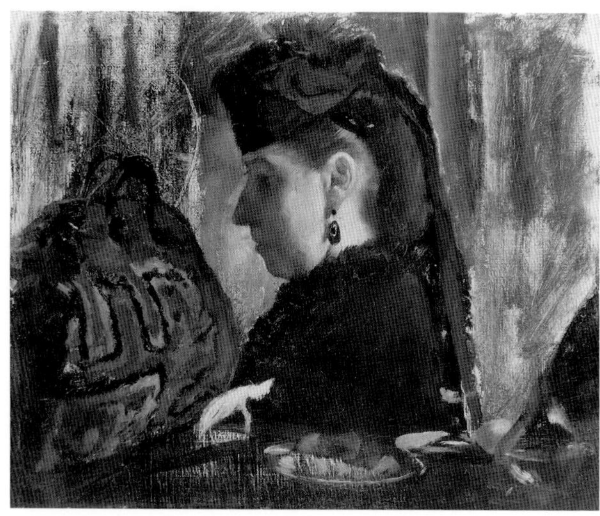

Fig. 101c Edgar Degas, *Mademoiselle Marie Dihau*, 1867–1868, oil on canvas, $8\frac{3}{4} \times 10\frac{3}{4}$ in. (22.2×27.3 cm), The Metropolitan Museum of Art, H. O. Havemeyer Collection, Bequest of Mrs. H. O. Havemeyer, 1929

voyeurs. Instead, Forain eternalizes her grief in miniature, giving us a portrait of a virtuous modern woman, unafraid of her public presence, because she had nothing to hide.

This minor masterpiece was first recorded in the large and important collection of the amateur collector Alfred Beurdeley, in whose posthumous sale it first appeared in May 1920 as *Head of a Woman.* Beurdeley's large collection consisted of a broad array of European old master paintings, with works by Spanish, French, Dutch, Italian, German, Flemish, and English artists including Murillo, Ribera, de Champaigne, Tintoretto, Canaletto, Reynolds, Raeburn, Boucher, and Fragonard. His taste for what was called "modern painting" in the 1920 catalogue was earnestly centered in the mid–nineteenth century, with Corot, Courbet, Chassériau, Ingres, Delacroix, Millet, and Rousseau. Of artists associated with the Impressionist movement, only Sisley and Forain appear. One can imagine this modest exercise in painted observation fitting admirably into this fundamentally conservative collection. Yet oddly, it is among the most modern works of Forain's oeuvre.

The painting has been lined and varnished in the twentieth century. Curiously, there is a small band of primed canvas that was included within the design area. At first, this looks like an incorporated tacking margin, but there is no evidence of former nail perforations, indicating that Forain intended this band to be part of the image. If this is so, it gives the work an additional air of experimental modernity.

1 Memorandum, 3 September 1998, Norton Simon Museum curatorial files.
2 Lemoisne, 1946–1949, no. 415, private collection.
3 Kinney, 1994, pp. 270–313.

102

Jean-Louis Forain
French, 1852–1931

At the Evening Party: Woman in White with a Fan
1883–1884

Pastel on paper, $21\frac{3}{4} \times 18$ in. (55.2×45.7 cm)
Signed and dedicated lower right: "à de Chaumont, son ami, JL. Forain"
N.1979.08

Provenance: de Chaumont. [?Galerie Brame, Paris, acquired 11 April 1900, sold 11 April 1900 to]; Gérard. Alfred Beurdeley (sale, Paris, Galerie Georges Petit, 2–4 June 1920, lot 139, ill., as *En soirée; femme blonde à l'éventail*, to); [Galerie Brame, Paris]. Beurdeley (sale, Paris, Palais d'Orsay, 16 May 1979, lot 120, color ill., to); [Galerie Cailleux, Paris, on behalf of]; Norton Simon, bequest 1993 to; Jennifer Jones Simon Art Trust.

Exhibitions: Paris, 1946, no. 608, as *L'Entrée au bal*; Paris, 1952b, no. 160, as *En soirée*; Paris, 1958, no. 78; Paris, 1978b, no. 13, as *En soirée (femme en blanc à l'éventail).*

Technical Notes: *At the Evening Party* is in good overall condition, despite a fair amount of previous treatment and remounting. The medium is pastel, which is unfixed, and may have faded from exposure to light. The pastel medium is layered and vigorously worked into the sheet in the background area behind the central woman's head and torso and applied lightly in other areas to allow the color of the sheet to come through as a ground tone. The pastel is drawn on one sheet of brown wove paper, which is fibrous and has embrittled edges. An X-ray reveals that the primary support was previously mounted on top of an oil painting of a horse and wrapped around the canvas and strainer. The pastel was separated from the painting in a 1979 treatment, and embrittled edges of the sheet were removed. The pastel was then strip-lined with Permalife bond paper and a glue, then a thick layer of mulberry paper, and wrapped around a 4-ply rag board adhered to birch plywood. The primary paper support is planar and secure. The edges of the remaining sheet are discolored and irregular and have tack holes. The entire right edge of the sheet is darkened due to previous contact with adhesives and tapes, and there are two stains (water or oil) in the central figure's skirt. There are numerous $\frac{3}{4}$–2-inch breaks in the sheet along the left and top edge. Despite these minor cracks and fissures, the sheet remains stable. (SSB)

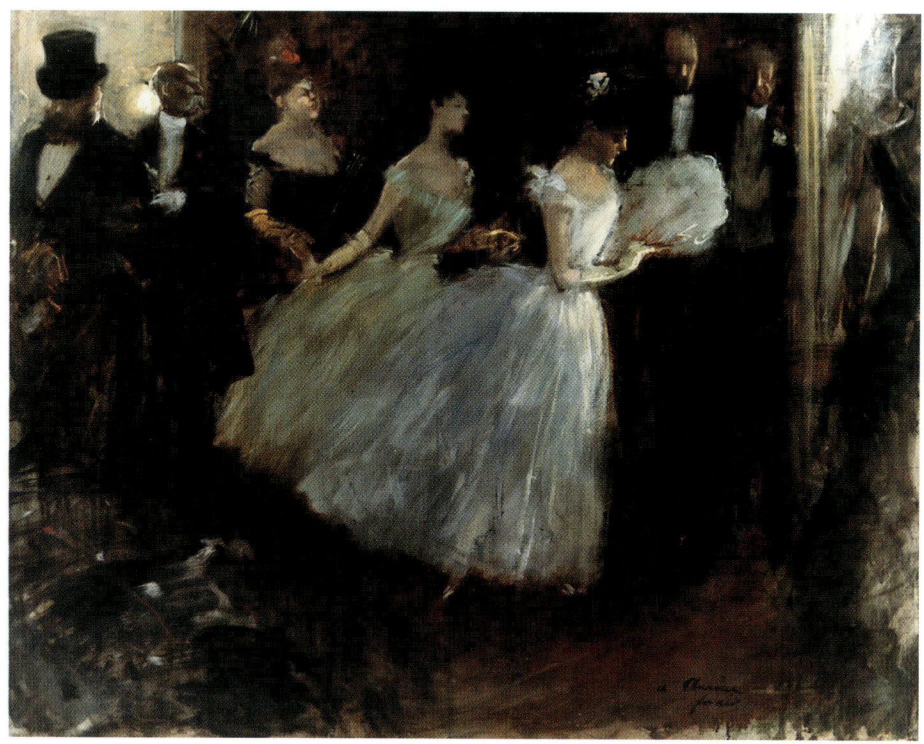

Fig. 102a Jean-Louis Forain, *A Soirée at the Opéra*, oil on canvas, $36\frac{3}{8} \times 28\frac{1}{2}$ in. (92.3×72.2 cm), private collection, Holland

This splendid pastel by Forain was inscribed in a fervent hand by its maker and dedicated to "M. Chaumont, my friend." Although undated, it has been placed about 1884 because of its iconographic associations with Forain's major Salon painting of that year, *The Buffet* (fig. 102b). This tightly executed painting was Forain's attempt to follow Pierre-Auguste Renoir in appealing to the official audience of the juried Salon exhibition as well as the modern urban audience of the independent artist cooperatives that competed with the Salon. *At the Evening Party: Woman in White with a Fan* is also related to another painting, *A Soirée at the Opera* (fig. 102a), a multifigure composition that includes a young woman with a fan posed in almost identical fashion. Although the Norton Simon pastel is related to both larger works, it was probably not made in preparation for either. Rather, all three seem to be part of a larger representational examination of urban bourgeois entertainment. In this way, they relate to similar paintings by the most important official artist of Parisian entertainments, Jean Béraud, such as *A Soirée* (fig. 102c). Béraud, in turn, followed the lead of official painters of the Second Empire, such as his teacher, the portraitist Léon Bonnat, and Ernest-Louis Meissonier. Forain's pastel was also obviously inspired by certain forthrightly modern works, such as Édouard Manet's *Masked Ball at the Opera* of 1873 (National Gallery of Art, Washington, D.C.) and Mary Cassatt's pastel *At the Theater* (The Nelson-Atkins Museum of Art, Kansas City), shown at the fifth Impressionist exhibition of 1880.

The Norton Simon pastel probably represents the young woman just before entering the major room of an elegant Parisian ball. At left are a woman who seems to have just removed her cloak and a maid standing stolidly,

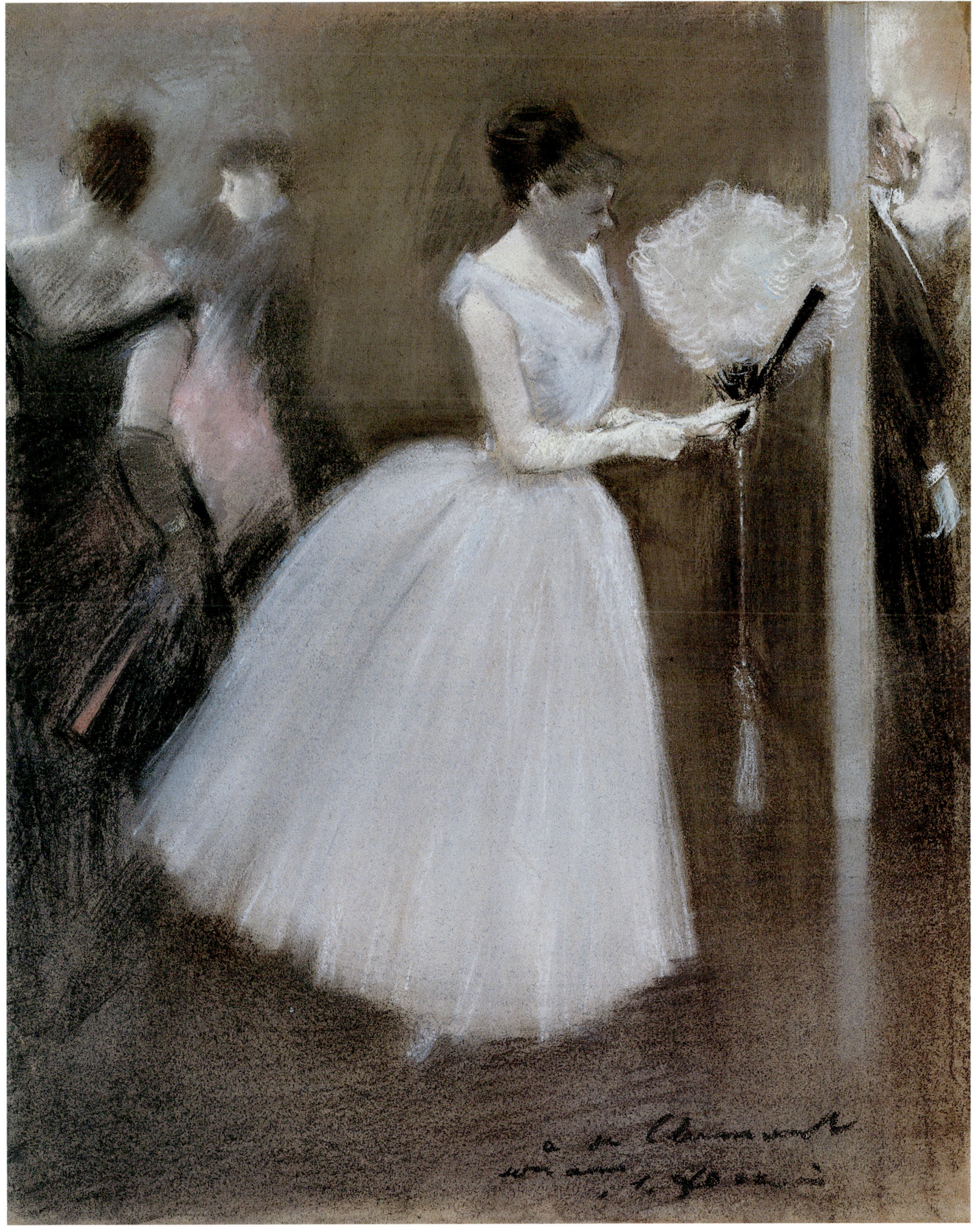

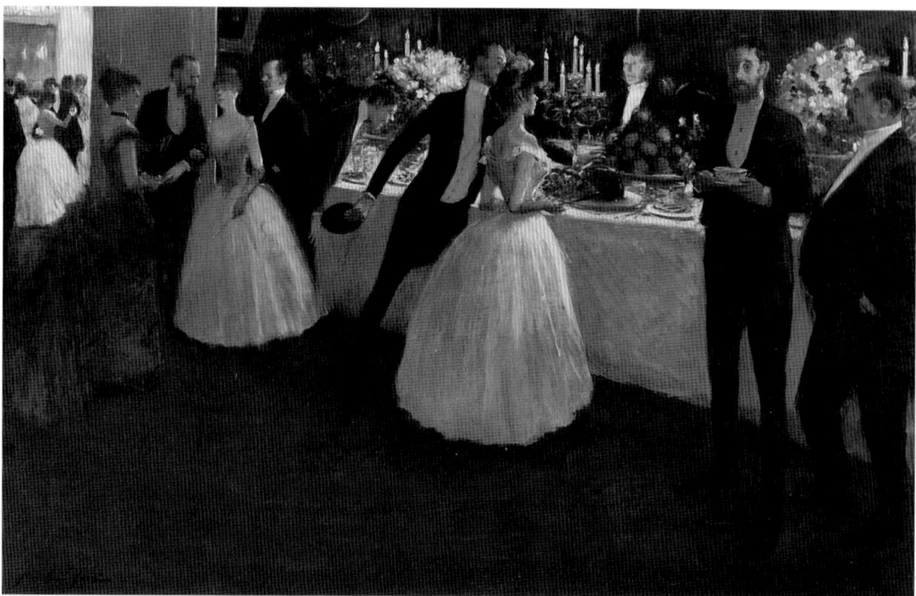

Fig. 102b Jean-Louis Forain, *The Buffet*, 1884, oil on canvas, $36\frac{3}{4} \times 58\frac{1}{4}$ in. (93.5 × 148 cm), Coll. Federation Mutualiste Parisienne, Paris; photo: Giraudon / Art Resource, NY

Fig. 102c Jean Béraud, *A Soirée*, oil on canvas, $25\frac{3}{4} \times 45\frac{5}{8}$ in. (65.5 × 116 cm), Musée d'Orsay, Paris; photo: Erich Lessing / Art Resource, NY

eyes down, to her right, the latter holding a light-colored cloak that may belong to the principal figure. This central figure seems to glide without weight toward the opening in front of her. She prepares herself for the act of entry by buttoning her evening glove and checking the position of her feathered fan. Thus, the two women in evening dress are both a study in contrasting value—one light, the other dark—and embodiments of successive moments in a process of entrance. A gentleman is shown leaning against the wall, perhaps in conversation with the amply endowed female figure in the room. He is unaware of the presence of the central figure.

Who are these women? Are they respectable women in a waiting room set aside for their gender, preparing to meet their husbands for a joint entrance? If so, the male artist and viewer are granted a glimpse of a private female space usually forbidden to sight. But the relation between the sexes in modern-life painting and drawing is rarely so straightforward, especially in works by Forain. The proximity of the male figure, the complete lack of architectural ornamentation, and the proximity of the entry room to that of the party itself suggest that this soirée may actually be taking place backstage in a theater or opera, such as that depicted in Forain's *Un Coin à l'Opéra* (location unknown), an ink drawing exhibited at the 1886 Impressionist exhibition.[1] If this indeed is a theater scene, the women are actually attractive escorts—not respectable women—for the wealthy, middle-aged gentleman at right. The ambiguity of class and meaning may be intentional: one of the marks of Manet's, Degas's and Forain's art is its refusal to abide by established social and Salon categories designating reputable from disreputable subjects and honest from immoral women. Indeed, if one interprets this pastel as one of a number of studies of an opera or ballet ball that culminate in *The Buffet*, this interpretation seems especially likely.

The title of the Norton Simon pastel has changed many times in its history. First published as *En soirée; femme blonde à l'éventail* (*At the Evening Party: Blond Woman with a Fan*) in the fifth and final of the Beurdeley sales in 1920, it has also appeared as *L'Entrée au bal* (*Entrance to the Ball*) in 1946, *En soirée* (*At the Evening Party*) in 1952, and, most accurately, *En soirée (femme en blanc à l'éventail)* (*At the Evening Party [Woman in White with a Fan]*) in 1978. The latter appearance in 1978 was the second time that the Norton Simon pastel was paired with *The Buffet* in an exhibition. Of the various titles, the last is perhaps the most acceptable, as the woman is decidedly not blond.

Forain had exhibited pastels at least since 1880, when a superb study of a woman with a large black fan appeared in the fifth Impressionist exhibition. (The work is now part of the nearly definitive American public collection of works by Forain at the Dixon Gallery and Gardens in Memphis, Tennessee.) The first pastels mark Forain's attempt to work in a medium almost completely associated with his revered master, Degas. Yet it must be remembered that whereas Degas was a restless experimenter with the technique of pastel, Forain stayed within the limits of the medium defined by artists of the eighteenth century, when pastels first became fashionable

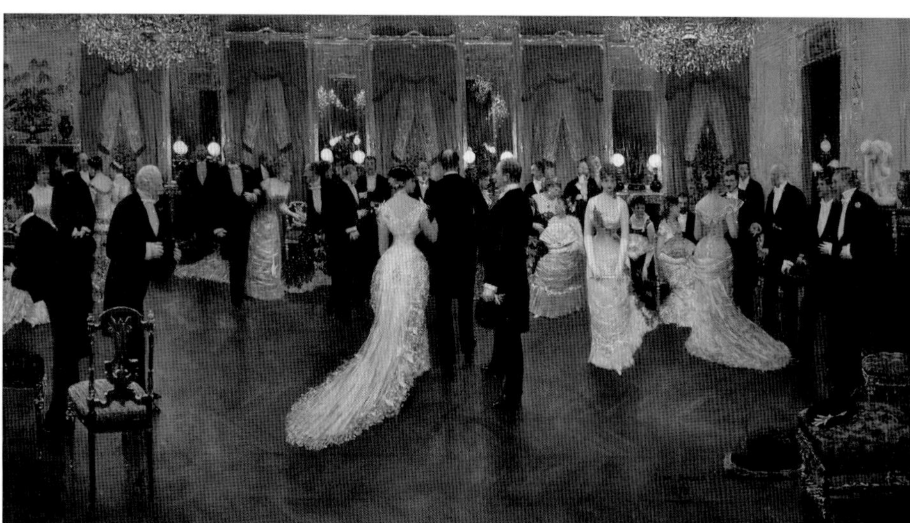

in France. In both the Dixon and the Norton Simon pastels, Forain worked with varying values of pastel crayons on light brown paper, using both the blunt tip and the sides of the crayon to represent the tonal masses of his composition. Once these were in place, he turned to the tip of the lighter-colored pastels and, with linear strokes, represented light glittering across the surfaces of fabric, feathers, and flesh. In this way, his pastels are in no way different from those of the eighteenth-century French artists, whose mastery of the medium had been extolled by the Goncourt brothers in their brilliant essays on eighteenth-century French art written in the 1860s. Fortunately, this pastel has never been varnished or fixed, and its surface, though slightly faded and abraded, retains the delightful, vellumlike dryness that the artist intended.

Like many ambitiously scaled pastels of the eighteenth and nineteenth centuries, this one was mounted onto canvas, probably after its completion. In this case, the canvas had already been used for the representation of a horse. This suggests that Forain himself might have done the mounting in order to save money, because had he sent it to his framer for mounting (as Degas and other artists did), he would have been billed for a new stretcher and canvas.

1 Berson, 1996, vol. 2, no. VIII-40, p. 242.

103

Jean-Louis Forain
French, 1852–1931

Hidden Truth
c. 1900–1905

Oil on canvas, $19^{11}/_{16} \times 24$ in. (50×61 cm)
Inscribed lower right with the artist's monogram
M.1979.48

Provenance: [Galerie Barbizon, Paris, sold 1975 to]; Norton Simon, gift 1979 to; Norton Simon Art Foundation.

Technical Notes: This sketch on a fine, plain-weave canvas has been lined with an aqueous adhesive to fabric. It is tacked to the back of a 5-part butt-join stretcher that could be original. The present rollover edges show no cracks, and since some of the sketch runs onto the tacking edges, the present dimensions deserve investigation. Although the canvas was preprimed with a medium- thick cream-yellow ground, the canvas texture nevertheless shows. A thin brownish imprimatura appears to cover the ground. The artist sketched out the scene with dark brown vehicular paint that was thin enough to run off the crowns of the weave. Washes of gray-blue were then applied along with a bit of green-blue to indicate sky color. A vehicular reddish, probably earth, color helps to describe the robes of the two figures in the left foreground. There are also a few highlights of light gray that, while opaque, are still fairly thin. The condition of the paint is very good with only light abrasions here and there. The synthetic varnish appears fresh and glittery. In ultraviolet light it fluoresces slightly bluish. (JF)

For those of us who live in the early twenty-first century, the most difficult aspect of Forain's career is his virulent anti-Semitism. Like his older friend Edgar Degas—and like thousands of other Frenchmen of his generation—Forain accepted as true the notion that France was a historically Christian nation into which Jewish outsiders had been improperly introduced, and that the effect of this unnatural attachment was at once poisonous and incendiary. The age of French toleration toward its Jewish population, which began with the 1789 revolution and peaked in 1870 on the eve of the Franco-Prussian War, was now past and would not return until after World War II, after the wholesale deportation and destruction of French Jewry. For most anti-Semitic Frenchmen of Forain's day, whose knowing association with Jews was minimal, these vicious beliefs were easily suppressed in daily life. But, when the so-called Dreyfus Affair erupted in France in 1898, Forain joined his anti-Semitic countrymen in an outpouring of invective and hatred against fellow citizens of Jewish descent, as well as their French sympathizers. This aspect of Forain's thinking and behavior is often mentioned in writing about him but relegated mostly to a sidebar in his small bibliography, which generally focuses instead on his attempts to unite in one artistic career the heritage of two great French artists, Honoré Daumier and Edgar Degas.

But anti-Semitism shaped and molded Forain's entire career, especially the three decades after 1898. His decision that year to join with fellow caricaturist Caran d'Ache and establish the satirical weekly *Psst!* was entirely based on his need to find a more pliant vehicle for his anti-Dreyfus and anti-Jewish crusade. The eighty-five issues of *Psst!* are indeed a compelling visual record of anti-Semitism in fin de siècle France. Forain's subsequent extreme nationalism and ultraconservative Catholicism, too—and the art that drew on these themes—were also outgrowths of his anti-Semitism.

Hidden Truth must play an important role in an investigation of Forain's anti-Semitism, but its presence in a museum founded by one of the greatest Jewish collectors in the history of art is surprising, to say the least (although Norton Simon may have been unaware of the iconography). Unlike the vast majority of works by Forain, which represent scenes from Parisian life, this small oil sketch seems to be a preparatory canvas for a visual allegory of the sort favored by French academic artists. At the left, we see two robed judges, one of whom wears a headdress easily related to others represented in the vast Dreyfus-oriented iconography recently studied by Norman Kleeblatt in the catalogue of an exhibition created for the Jewish Museum.[1] These figures—one fat and leering, the other fat and grotesque—are shown seated at the base of a huge outdoor sculpture similar to those representing the provinces of France at the periphery of the place de la Concorde in Paris. To the right of the composition are two male figures, hatless and wearing overcoats, who are masking and restraining a scantily clad and evidently classical female figure, who seems to represent both Truth and Justice. Behind this trio another man prepares to join the action, his coat blowing in an unseen wind. Behind all these foreground figures, an army gathers in the middle distance under threatening skies.

Previous efforts to argue that the work cannot be read unequivocally as anti-Semitic or anti-Dreyfusard—that it is an expression of Forain's general belief that the moral fiber of the French state was threatened by foreign and domestic enemies—is unsupported by the visual evidence. Indeed, the large-nosed tormenters of Truth (particularly the seated man at left, the central, standing figure, and the man on the far right) are clearly intended to be Jewish as is, perhaps, the seated judge on the right

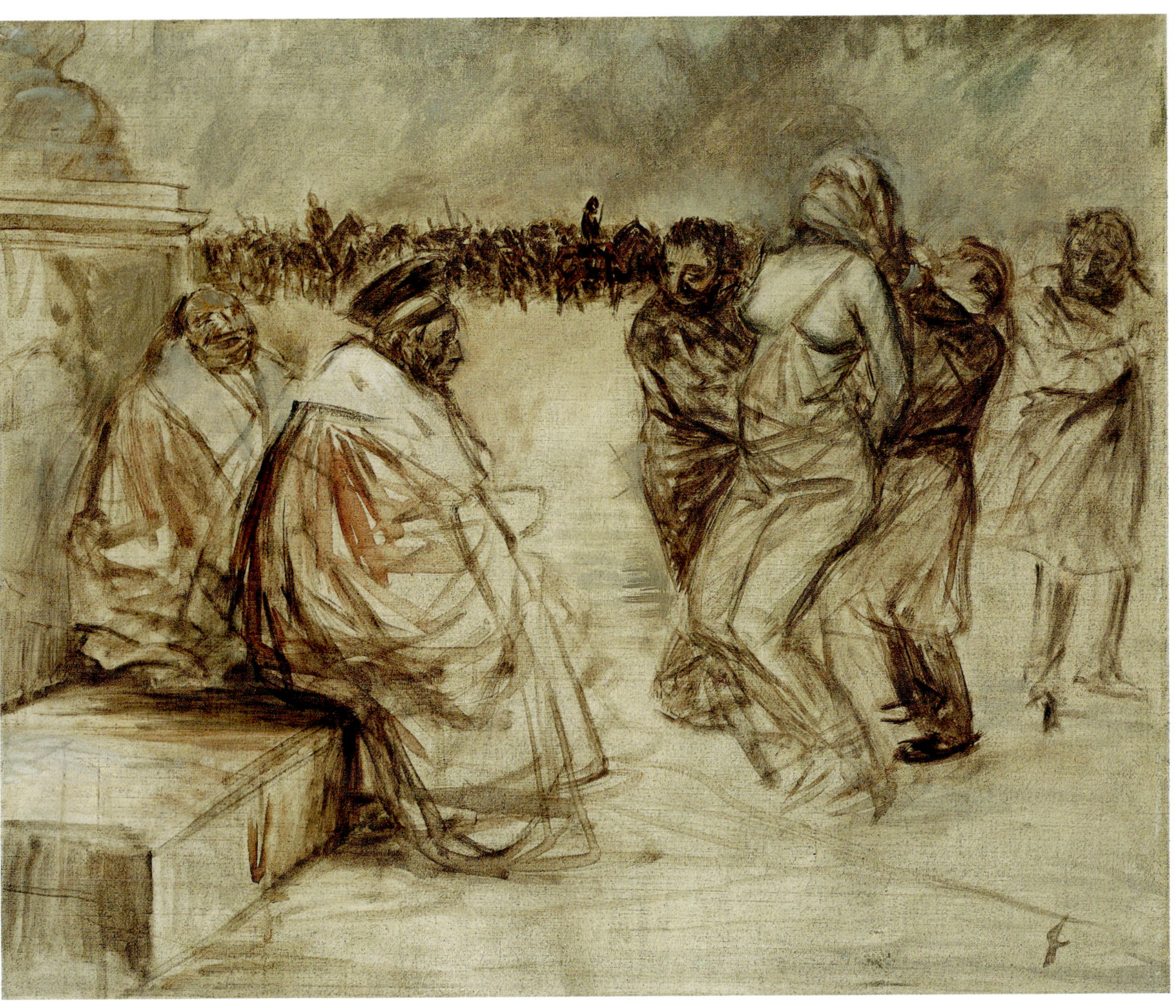

103

who is witnessing the struggle of "Truth-Justice." The unmasking of Justice and the restraining of Truth by Jews and their sympathizers was so evidently a part of Forain's intellectual, political, and moral makeup that it would be folly to attempt to generalize it away. Fortunately for posterity, he seems never to have sold this study, on which he placed a monogram, nor to have it taken it further by creating a larger allegorical painting for exhibition or public sale. The only mystery that remains in studying this work is why Norton Simon bought it in 1975.

1 Norman L. Kleeblatt, ed., *The Dreyfus Affair: Art, Truth, and Justice*, Berkeley, 1987.

104

Jean-Louis Forain
French, 1852–1931

The Widow and the Orphans
c. 1910

Oil on canvas, $41\frac{1}{8} \times 32\frac{7}{8}$ in. (104.5 × 83.5 cm)
Inscribed lower left with the artist's monogram
M.1979.41.1

Provenance: [Galerie Philippe Reichenbach, Paris, by 1964]; [Galerie La Cave, Paris, by 1978, sold 1979 to]; Norton Simon Art Foundation.

Exhibitions: Paris, 1964, no. 17, ill. as *Orphelins au tribunal*; Paris, 1978b, no. 35, p. 31, ill.

Reference: Faxon, 1982, p. 106.

Technical Notes: This sketch is very thinly painted with a subdued palette. The flat areas of the walls and floor are painted in thin veils of green, then gray, and then black or black over brown. These thin layers create the atmospheric colors for the space. Over this the forms are sketched in with a thin reddish brown as well as some touches of thicker paints. The original canvas, a tight, plain-weave, medium-weight fabric, remains unlined and tacked to a 6-part stretcher that must be original. Tacking edges wrap around to the back of the stretcher. The off-white ground that does not quite fill the weave was commercially applied. The artist set up grid lines (visible on the tacking edges) on the ground that must have helped transfer the image. Lines can also be seen under the design paint, marking off the floor and table legs. The lines and marks on the tacking edges, which are very precise, seem to be made with black paint or ink. The painting has what appears to be a sprayed synthetic varnish that is inappropriate. Except for the varnish, the painting is in very good condition. (JF)

This large painting first appeared in 1964 at a sales exhibition in Paris of material drawn largely from the painter's descendants. There it was given the title *Orphelins aux tribunal* (*Orphans at the Tribunal*), which was changed, with no cited evidence, to *La Veuve et les orphelins* (*The Widow and the Orphans*) when the painting made its second recorded appearance in the important Forain retrospective held at the Musée Marmottan in 1978. In the catalogue of that exhibition, the work was properly related to an etching by Forain entitled *Coming out of the Hearing* (fig. 104a), dated to 1909 by Alicia Craig Faxon in the definitive catalogue raisonné of Forain's prints.

In the Marmottan catalogue, the present painting was dated about 1910, that is, after the related prints. Although this seems an unusual assumption (in most of the history of art, prints postdate paintings), it remains plausible, particularly because there are numerous differences between print and painting. Like his mentor Edgar Degas, Forain often made prints independently of paintings, and it is not uncommon in the oeuvres of both these artists that pastels and paintings postdate prints. Because the print to which Forain's painting relates exists in eight recorded states with many impressions, Forain may have been working out the tonal, compositional, and iconological issues involved in the image in the small format of a copperplate and with the inexpensive media of paper and ink before tackling the painting. Joseph Fronek has discovered a grid and visible ink markings at the edge of the painting, indicating that Forain intended to transfer the composition. However, the print is not similar enough to have been involved in such a transfer.

What, precisely, do this painting and its related prints represent? It is clear that the two children at the front of the painting and its related print are vital to a particular court case, most likely because they are orphans. They are shown between two lawyers at the bar and under the protection of a woman dressed in black, who actually seems to shield them from the lawyers. All three main figures are in front of the bar, hence in the part of the courtroom where the judge presides. Thus, the viewer is placed in the position of judge rather than the courtroom audience, who occupies the middle ground at left, guarded by a policeman. In all probability, the only one of the three titles that might have been created in the

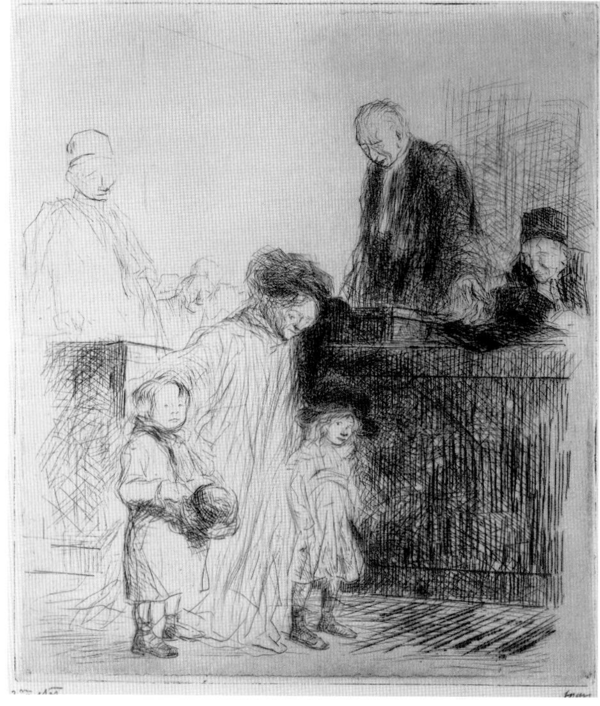

Fig. 104a Jean-Louis Forain, *Coming out of the Hearing*, 1909, etching, plate, $13\frac{3}{8} \times 11\frac{1}{2}$ in (33.9 × 29.2 cm); sheet, $24\frac{1}{2} \times 18\frac{11}{16}$ in. (62.2 × 47.5 cm), National Gallery of Art, Washington

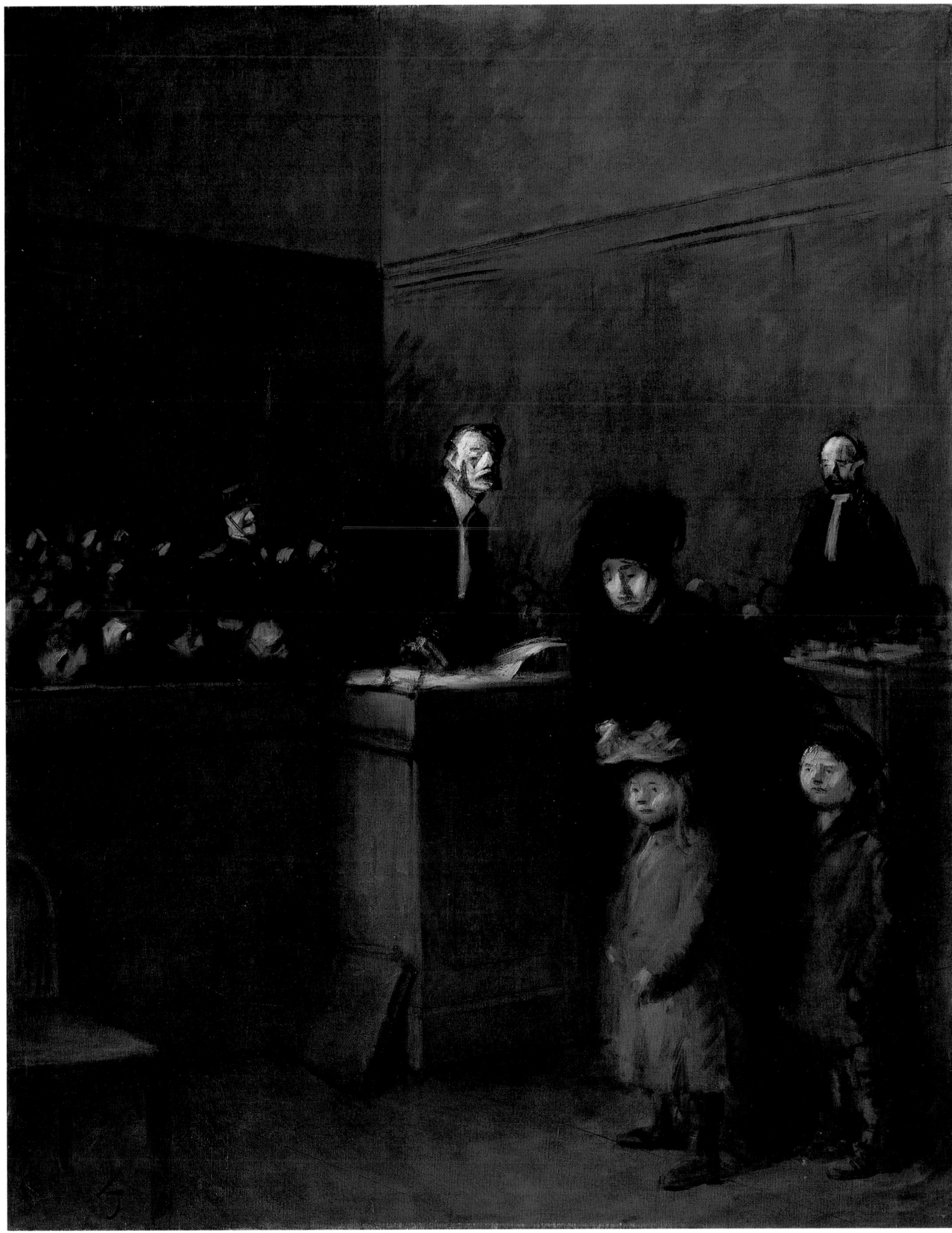

lifetime of the artist is that of the print (*Coming out of the Hearing*). Yet, it is not actually satisfying as a title when one confronts it with the work of art itself. It seems just as likely that the children are going in as coming out, particularly because they seem headed to an empty chair placed on the left of the composition in the painting, but absent in the print.

Throughout the composition, Forain struggled to be generic rather than particular in his description of features. We are not encouraged to think of the children or their protector as having names and being actual people. Rather, they are types, forcing us to accept them as part of the human condition of early-twentieth-century France. Forain visually placed their fate in the hands of the judicial system, which he, like his absent mentor Honoré Daumier, treats with a combination of contempt and understanding. Indeed, it seems as if all the figures in this painting are actors in a drama of justice or injustice that goes on every day in every city in every year. Forain seems intent on telling us that the outcome does not matter to anyone in the room, and that the children will one day be adults who will occupy the place of the adults in the background. Perhaps the most important aspect of the painting is that Forain placed the viewer in the role of judge without giving us enough information to decide the fate of the children. Thus, we too are in collusion.

105

Jacob (Isaac) Meyer de Haan
Dutch, 1852–1895

Still Life with Ham
c. 1889

Oil on canvas, 13 × 18¼ in. (33 × 46 cm)
F.1983.12

Provenance: Bellier. Private collection, Paris. [Galerie La Cave, Paris, sold 1978 to]; Norton Simon, gift 1983 to; The Norton Simon Foundation.

Exhibition: Paris, 1978a.

References: Weisblat, 1999, p. 110, fig. 19; Welsh-Ovcharov, 2001, p. 39, fig. 58.

Technical Notes: The support is a plain-weave canvas that has been lined and restretched on its original stretcher with the tacking edges retained. There is another painting beneath the visible one, as revealed on the top and the right tacking edges, but X-radiography does not provide useful information about this first design. The left and bottom tacking edges are unprimed. Because of the lining, it was not possible to determine if there is a ground layer beneath the first painting; there is a white ground layer above it, on the front surface only. Opaque, thickly applied paint depicts the objects on the table, with strong, descriptive brushwork. The palette is vibrant and varied. Light-colored highlights are quite thick. No consistent color was used for contours. The rose-mauve background paint is much thinner, especially as it approaches the right edge, where the white beneath it is occasionally visible. The foreground (tabletop) is more complex, executed in thinner, brushed-out layers frequently revealing the white ground, where colors are blended as the paint was applied wet into wet. The foreground paint is of uneven thickness, but this may be a change resulting from an earlier treatment. The possibility of wax in the medium has been raised but not investigated. There are occasional small flake losses throughout, and fractured paint at the edges has caused numerous losses. Lining has caused some flattening and smoothing of the paint. The present varnish is not discolored, but residues of older varnish in the recesses of brushwork are quite yellowed. In 1978 the painting was cleaned, lined, and varnished. (RW)

In the late summer of 1888, Jacob Meyer de Haan left his family home in Amsterdam to travel to Paris. He was the thirty-six-years-old son of a matzoh manufacturer and an artist of modest accomplishment. For the past decade, he had specialized in painting portraits and interior scenes with Jewish narrative subjects. His style combined academic and Naturalist approaches, recalling the work of his first teacher, J. F. Greive, the Hague School artist Jozef Israels, and the Berlin-born Max Liebermann. Meyer de Haan's *Is the Chicken Kosher?* (1880, location unknown),[1] however, is more anecdotal and humorous than works by any of these older artists. It offers at once an ingratiating glimpse at three elders of the Orthodox Ashkenazi community of Amsterdam and their Gentile servant, and a satire of a celebrated touchstone of Christian art, Caravaggio's *Supper at Emmaus.* His large painting of the trial of the seventeenth-century Jewish freethinker Uriel Acosta (1878–1888, location unknown)[2] is a more sober and ambitious exercise in the *genre historique,* but when it was exhibited in 1888, it was not well received by the conservative audience for which it was intended. Indeed, it may have been the poor reception of his chef d'oeuvre that drove Meyer de Haan to Paris, and soon after that, into the arms (or clutches) of Paul Gauguin.

After residing for several months in Paris with fellow Dutchman Theo van Gogh, Meyer de Haan was dispatched in April 1889 to Pont-Aven to study with, and provide financial support for, the chronically impecunious Gauguin. They were extremely close for about a year and a half, from the spring of 1889 to the late autumn of 1890, sharing quarters at the inn of Marie Henry in Le Pouldu, Brittany. It is difficult, at the outset, to imagine a more unlikely artistic marriage than that between the Jewish Naturalist Meyer de Haan and the Catholic Symbolist Gauguin, but in fact the two men were religious, political, and sexual nonconformists and had similarly advanced literary and artistic tastes. They shared an interest in comparative religion, Eastern and Hebrew mysticism, German idealist philosophy—chiefly Schopenhauer distilled through Thomas Carlyle—Japanese prints, and Breton folk art. They collaborated in the decoration of the inn at Le Pouldu, shared sexual intimacy with its eponymous owner (who bore a child to Meyer de Haan), and lived together in Paris in late 1890.

Indeed, though Gauguin undoubtedly made liberal use of his pupil's monthly stipends from home—he was what Meyer de Haan might have called a *schnorrer*—there is no real evidence of the sexual or other rivalry that has often been said to characterize the attitude of the master to the disciple. The great paintings and sculpture by Gauguin that include the face of Meyer de Haan—*Portrait of Meyer de Haan by Lamplight* (1889, private collection), *Nirvana: Portrait of Meyer de Haan* (1889–1890, Wadsworth Atheneum, Hartford), *Portrait of Meyer de Haan* (1889–1890, National Gallery of Canada, Ottawa), and *Contes barbares* (1902, Museum Folkwang, Essen)—are highly contrived Symbolist works, and there is little reason to assume that their physiognomic distortions are assaults on the character or religion of his friend and student. They are, in fact, some of the most compelling portraits of the age and suggest that Meyer de Haan possessed intellectual depths sufficient to inspire Gauguin to some of his finest achievements. Letters between the men reveal uninterrupted amity, and the two would most likely have continued their association in Tahiti after 1891 had not tuberculosis intervened. Meyer de Haan died of the disease in 1895. His own art was largely forgotten until the auction at the Hôtel Drouot in 1959 of the collection of Marie-Ida Cochennec, daughter of the painter and Marie Henry. That sale contained twenty-three paintings by Meyer de Haan but apparently did not include the Norton Simon still life.[3]

Meyer de Haan was not one of the inventors of Synthetism or Cloissonism; that distinction belongs to Gauguin, Émile Bernard, Louis Anquetin, and the other exhibitors at the Café Volpini exhibition in June 1889. But under the tutelage of Gauguin Meyer de Haan quickly learned the rudiments of the new style. Between April 1889 and October 1890 he produced more than thirty works of a pronounced modern character; they are generally vividly colored and emphatically two-dimensional. The best of these, including his fresco *Breton Women Scutching Flax (Labor)* (1889, private collection), painted for the west wall of the dining room of the inn, and *Maternity* (1889, private collection), are as fully realized as those of any of the other painters (excluding his teacher) active at Pont-Aven and Le Pouldu and often considerably more ingratiating. His still lifes are especially appealing: they are small and simply composed and contain objects of a decidedly plebeian cast—onions, apples, common flowers, Breton ceramic jugs, and glass tumblers. A modest picture titled *Still Life with Pitcher and Onions* (fig. 105a), made to decorate a door panel at the inn of Marie Henry, carried an inscription that conveys the mood of his entire still-life oeuvre: "I love onions fried in oil."

Still Life with Ham is one of the fourteen surviving still lifes painted during the months of Meyer de Haan and Gauguin's closest collaboration in the winter of 1889–1890. It is a picture of studied, formal, and culinary simplicity. A cured ham, perhaps a *jambon de Bayonne*, occupies the center of the canvas; behind it is a dark, rose-colored wall, and below it a still darker brown tabletop. To the right are seven vividly painted shallots (or small onions) and half a tumbler of red wine. The ham has a brown outer skin and a center with dark red areas of meat and greenish white and pink areas of fat. The meat sits on a blue plate, only a crescent of which is visible at left. The shallots appear almost sprightly. They are composed of warm yellows, oranges, and reds, outlined in several cases by complementary blues, violets, and greens. Each has a culminating, warm highlight. The glass of wine at right adds an architectural stability to the composition. It is like a broad, fluted column with straight edges and a perfect oval at the top.

The still life implies an immediate human presence: the dark purple wine is half drunk and the ham is half eaten. The shallots are there for art's sake—few people eat raw, unsliced onions—and as a kind of artistic signature. Had Meyer de Haan's name vanished from art history, he might have been known though his works as the "Master of the Raw Onions." But the ham is anomalous in Meyer de Haan's still-life oeuvre, and indeed there are no other *treife* (nonkosher products such as sausage, crustaceans, shellfish, etc.) of any kind. The choice of motif may be explained by the fact that Gauguin painted an almost identical composition entitled *The Ham* (fig. 105b) at exactly the same time. We do not know if the artists sat side by side before the ham, wine, and shallots, if they

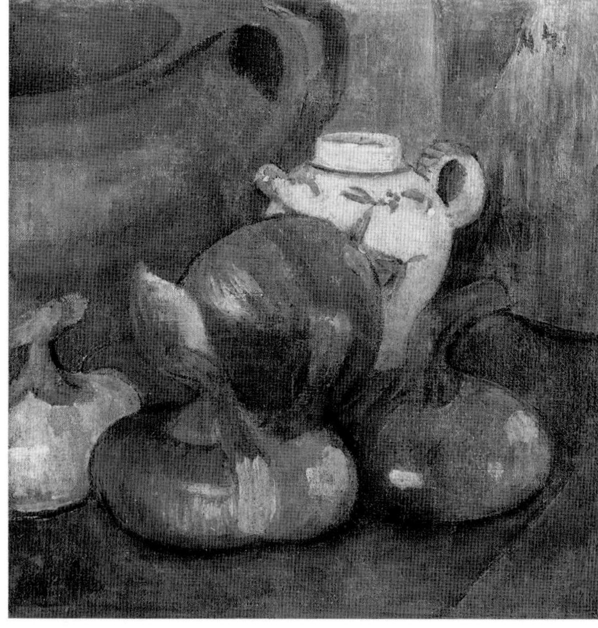

Fig. 105a Jacob Meyer de Haan, *Still Life with Pitcher and Onions*, c. 1889–1890, oil on canvas, 11¾ × 11¾ in. (30 × 30 cm), Musée des Beaux-Arts, Quimper

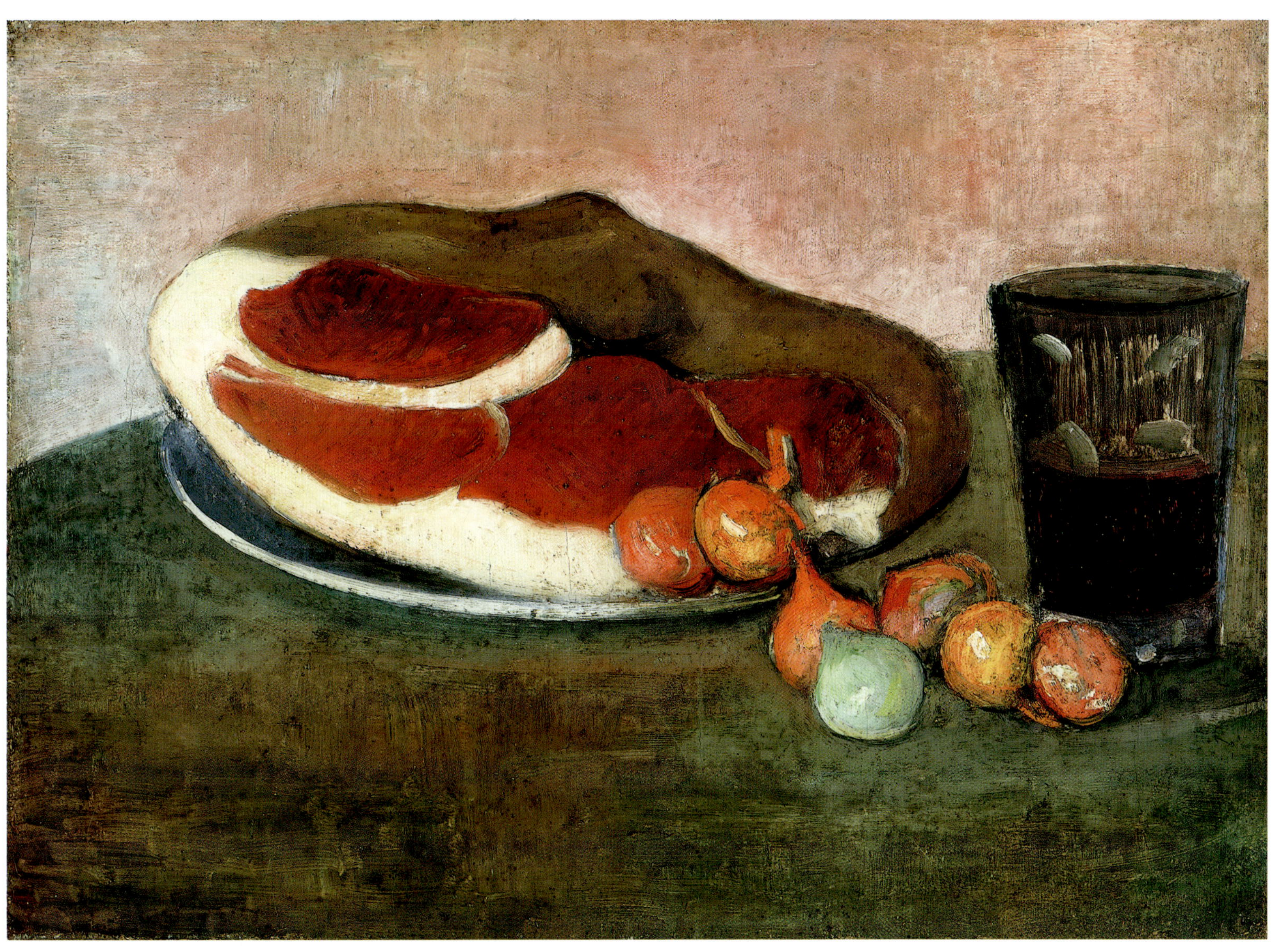

105

Fig. 105b Paul Gauguin, *The Ham*, 1889, oil on canvas, $19\frac{3}{4} \times 22\frac{3}{4}$ in. (50.1 × 57.7 cm), The Phillips Collection, Washington, D.C.

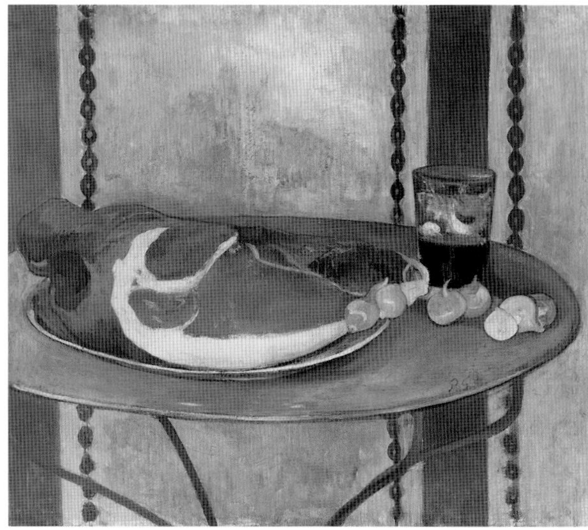

did so sequentially, or if Meyer de Haan copied Gauguin's composition, but it was almost certainly the non-Jewish artist who selected the subject. In so doing, Gauguin may have been teasing Meyer de Haan and not so subtly alluding to his picture of a decade before, *Is the Chicken Kosher?* The two men must then have shared an irreverent laugh together; they knew that in the present instance the answer was an unambiguous "No!"

1 Welsh-Ovcharov, 2001, p. 27, fig. 29.
2 Welsh-Ovcharov, 2001, p. 26, fig. 27.
3 The reference to the Hôtel Drouot 1959 sale was provided by the Galerie La Cave at the time of purchase. Two sales of Marie Henry's estate took place at Drouot Paris in 1959 (16 March and 24 June), but the picture is not listed in either sale, nor has it been located to date in any other Drouot auction in 1959.

106

Vincent van Gogh
Dutch, 1853–1890

The Back Garden of Sien's Mother's House, The Hague
May 1882

Sepia ink, gouache, and graphite on paper, laid on Bristol board, 18¼ × 23⅞ in. (46.3 × 60.7 cm)
Signed lower left: "Vincent"
M.1980.5

Provenance: [C. M. van Gogh, Amsterdam]; C. Mouwen Jr., Breda. Roell, Utrecht; [W. C. A. Huinck, Utrecht]; Henricus Petrus Bremmer (1871–1956), The Hague, 1928–1950. [Jon N. Streep, New York, sold 1955 to]; David Daniels, New York; (sale, New York, Sotheby Parke-Bernet, 14 May 1980, lot 212); [R. M. Light & Co., Inc., Santa Barbara, sold 4 February 1980 to]; Norton Simon Art Foundation.

Exhibitions: Amsterdam, 1932, no. 8; The Hague, 1950, no. 41; Minneapolis, 1960, no. 60, ill.; Newark, 1961, no. 54; Minneapolis, 1962, no. 118, pl. 29; Minneapolis, 1968, no. 61.

References: Faille, 1928, vol. 3, no. 942; van Gogh, 1936, p. 37; Vanbeselaere, 1937, pp. 130–131; van Gogh, 1958, vol. 1, nos. 184, 200, 202, 205, 210, vol. 3, nos. R8, R9; Faille, 1970, no. F942, pp. 647, 351, ill.; Hulsker, 1977, no. 147, p. 41, ill.

Technical Notes: The thin brown laid paper is mounted overall to Bristol board, with an additional laminate on the verso, creating a 0.5-mm thick composite. The drawing's mount to the Bristol is discussed by van Gogh: "The big one of the two . . . has become quite flat, because I used Bristol board, and the lines have greatly gained in quickness."[1] The drawing is executed in sepia-toned ink, white gouache, and graphite. The ink was applied first, highlighted in white gouache, and the graphite was applied last in a vigorous fashion, leaving impressions in the sheet. The sheet is in generally good condition; it has many creases and folds all along the right side of the work, especially in the lower right quadrant. The artist probably formed these creases in the lamination process. There is an embossed stamp showing through in the upper right corner, which reads "Bristol Board" in relief, where a portion of the primary sheet has been lost. (SSB)

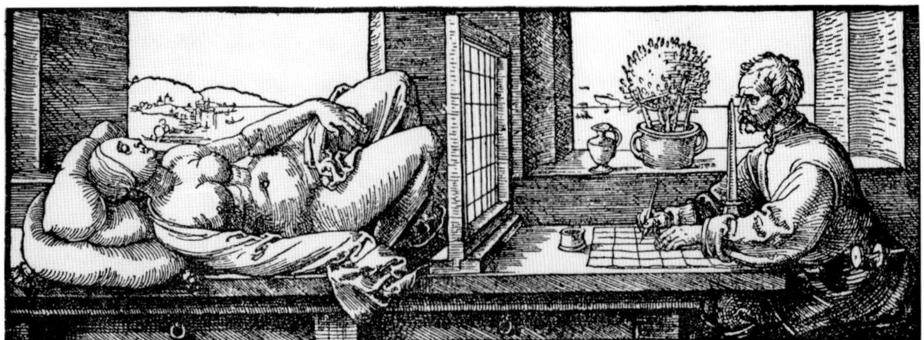

Fig. 106a Albrecht Dürer, *Draftsman Drawing a Nude*, woodcut from *Treatise on Perspective*, Nuremberg, 1527; photo: Foto Marburg / Art Resource, NY

Vincent van Gogh's drawing of the backyard and garden of the house belonging to the mother of Clasina (Sien) Hoornick is one of the most important of his early career. It was sent to his uncle C. M. van Gogh in late May 1882 along with six other drawings, in fulfillment of a commission for picturesque views of The Hague. There is, however, little that is charming or quaint about the drawing's subject: the garden is not yet in full blossom, the house was modern and nondescript, and it belonged to the mother of the artist's girlfriend, a former prostitute. It is therefore not surprising that it was received without enthusiasm. Van Gogh recorded his patron's cool reception: "Did I really think," [he asked,] "that such drawings could possess the slightest commercial value?"[2]

The drawing is nevertheless a tour de force of perspective rendering, exhibiting both a marked intelligence and a certain poignancy. In a letter to his brother Theo, dated 27 May, van Gogh expressed pride in the complex perspective employed in the large composition "of the court or yard where Sien's mother lives."[3] For some weeks he had been experimenting with a perspective frame modeled after a device rendered by Albrecht Dürer in an engraving called *Draftsman Drawing a Nude* (fig. 106a). Van Gogh specifically discussed Dürer's frame in a letter to Theo from early June and depicted his own, updated version of it in a sketch sent to his brother some weeks later (fig. 106b).[4] "It makes it possible," van Gogh wrote, "to compare the proportion of objects nearby with those on a more distant plane."[5]

The Norton Simon drawing is in fact composed of a succession of overlapping and superimposed gridded planes parallel to the picture surface, some perpendicular lines establishing spatial recession, and a number of homely objects and shapes framed by the governing geometry. The foremost plane consists of a fence made from two vertical posts and two horizontal beams; it very closely resembles the actual perspective frame used by van Gogh. At least four additional planes can be identified: a fence in the middle ground extending from the left margin to near the center of the drawing, an identical construction a few yards beyond that, and a lattice beneath a shelf or ledge on which rests an empty flowerpot, the bottom of a drainpipe, two potted plants, and a large birdcage. The house itself constitutes the last, farthest plane; it is made of brick, perforated by a doorway at center and at left by a large arched window composed of a grid of sixteen panes. Two additional windows are visible on the garden facade of the house overlooking the adjacent yard. A pair of small birdcages—possibly for pigeons—are visible above and to the left of the twin-paned transom windows.

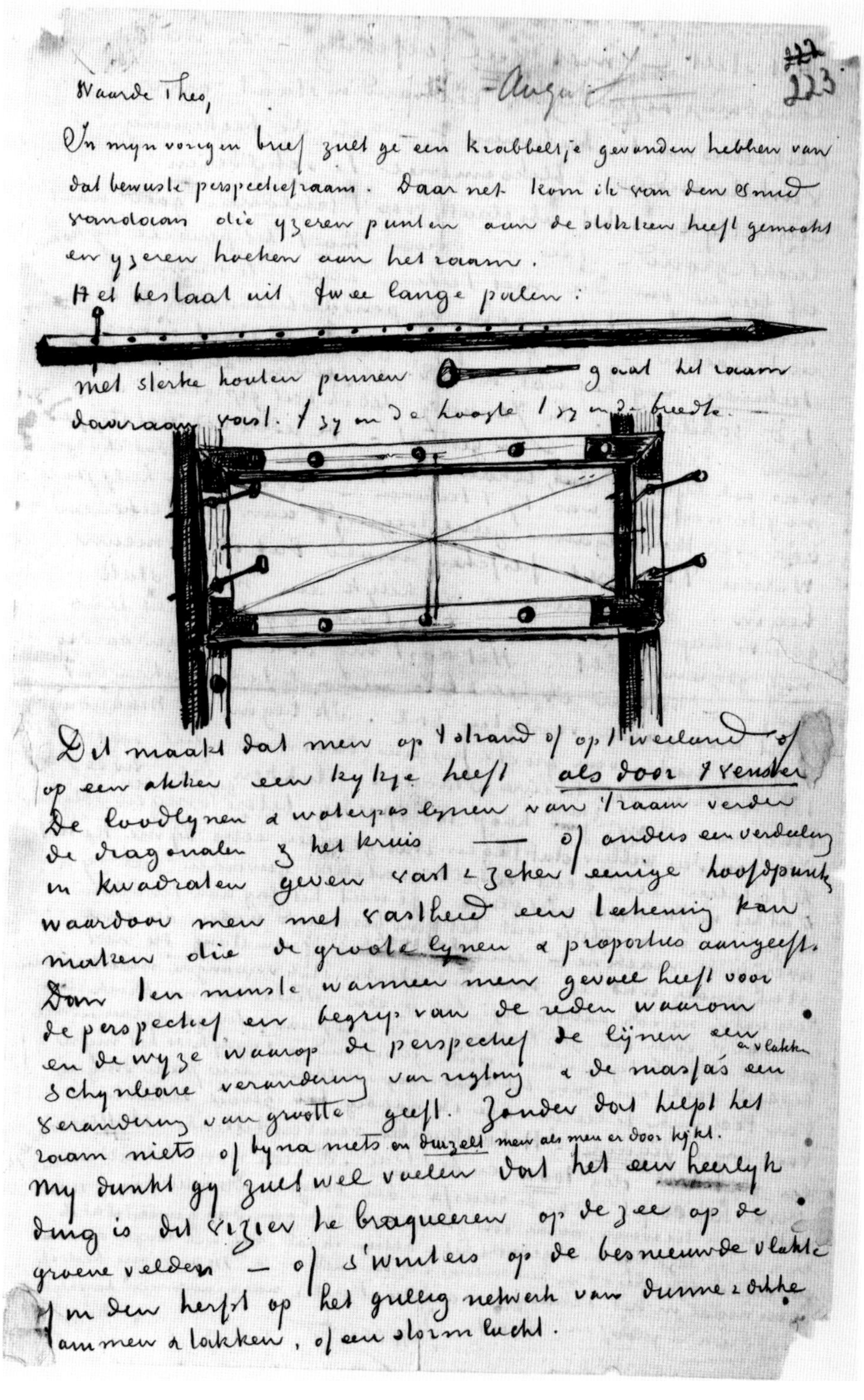

The railing, footpath, and plank fence at right all parallel the viewer's line of sight and function as orthogonal lines. The vanishing point of the drawing is approximately the bottom of the large birdcage. The presence of this cage, and at least two others—in addition to the spring season—must recall the parable devised by van Gogh in a letter to Theo from July 1880. Seeking to excuse his impracticality and what seemed to others his idleness, van Gogh compared himself to "a caged bird in spring . . . [who] is well aware that there is something for him to do, but he cannot do it." He continued:

> What is it? He does not quite remember. Then some vague ideas occur to him, and he says to himself, "The others build their nests and lay their eggs and bring up their little ones"; and he knocks his head against the bars of the cage. But the cage remains, and the bird is maddened by anguish.[6]

Van Gogh claimed to be that caged bird, misunderstood by others as idle and "living at ease," but in fact striving for liberty, action, and achievement. This large drawing is a perspective grid or cage that encloses the budding, espaliered trees at the right, the large fruit tree at upper right, and many other smaller flowers and plants. It is thus at once allegorical and mathematical, a picture about restraint and emancipation.

1 Van Gogh, 1958, vol. 3, no. R8.
2 Van Gogh, 1958, vol. 3, no. R9.
3 Van Gogh, 1958, vol. 1, no. 202.
4 Van Gogh, 1958, vol. 1, no. 223.
5 Van Gogh, 1958, vol. 1, no. 205.
6 Van Gogh, 1958, vol. 1, no. 133.

Fig. 106b Vincent van Gogh, *Sketch of a Perspective Frame*, in a letter from van Gogh to his brother, Theo (223), Van Gogh Museum (Vincent van Gogh Foundation), Amsterdam

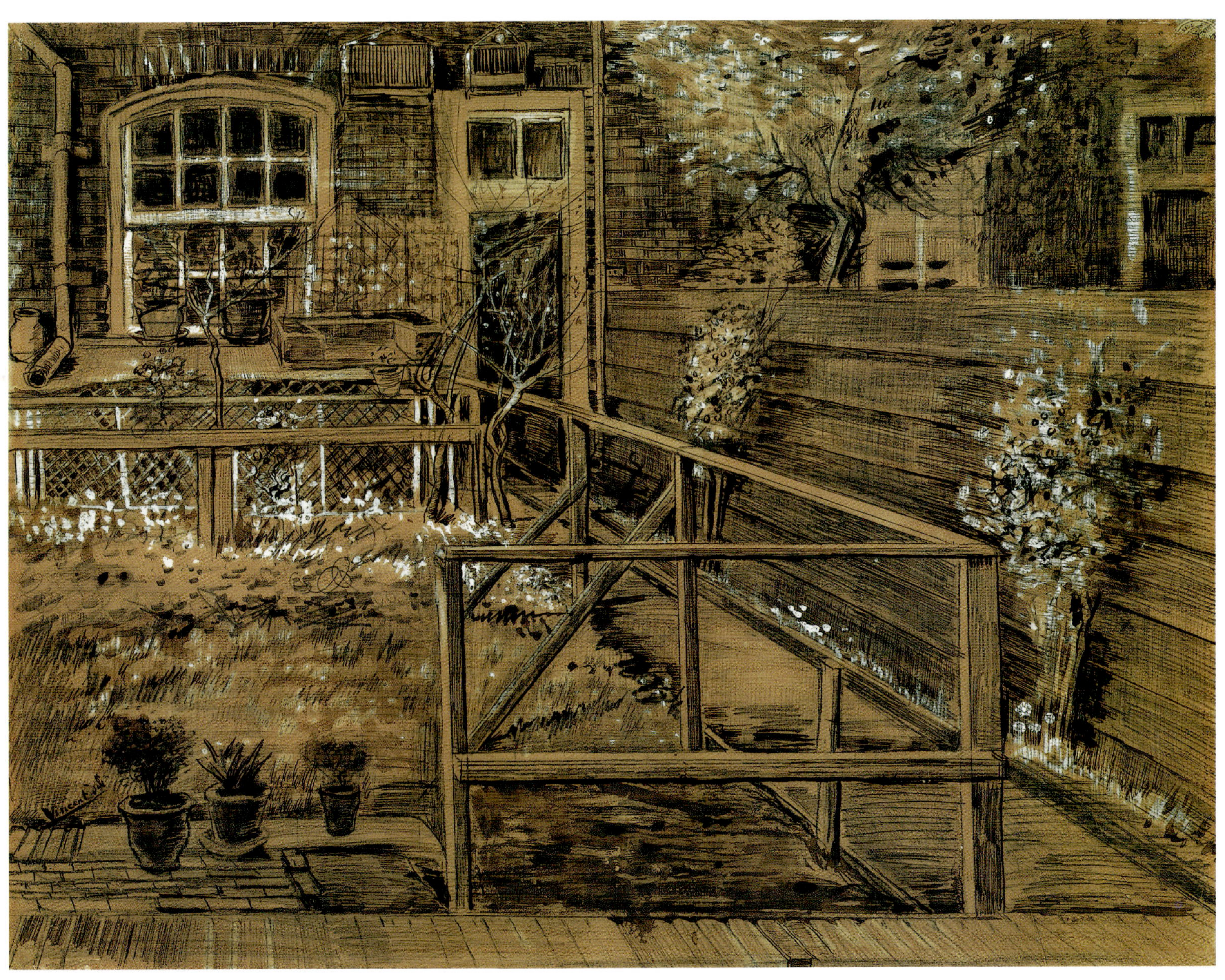

107

Vincent van Gogh
Dutch, 1853–1890

Still Life
November 1884

Oil on canvas, 15¾ × 22¼ in. (40 × 56.5 cm)
F.1972.44

Provenance: J. J. Biesing, The Hague; Henricus Petrus Bremmer (1871–1956), The Hague, c. 1910–1956. [E. J. van Wisselingh & Co., Amsterdam]. [Laing Galleries, Toronto]. Arnold Hofland, London, by 1963. [E. J. van Wisselingh & Co., Amsterdam, stock no. S3993, sold 1972 to]; The Norton Simon Foundation.

Exhibitions: Amsterdam, 1956, no. 18; Milwaukee, 1957, no. 77, ill.; Amsterdam, 1971, no. 17, ill.; San Francisco, 1974, no. 45, ill.

References: Faille, 1928, vol. 1, no. 57, vol. 2, no. 57, pl. XVI; Vanbeselaere, 1937, no. 57, pp. 284–285, 330, 346, 414; Faille, 1939, no. 62, p. 72, ill.; van Gogh, 1958, vol. 2, no. 387; Faille, 1970, no. F57, pp. 62–63, 614; Steadman, 1976, p. 223; Lecaldano, 1977, vol. 1, no. 66, p. 97, ill.; Hulsker, 1977, no. 539, p. 125, ill.; van Lindert and van Uitert, 1990a, p. 83; Tokyo, 1996, under no. 6, fig. 6a.

Technical Notes: The original plain-weave canvas has been glue-lined to a canvas of coarser weave, with the original tacking edges retained. The canvas is not well stretched, and there are conspicuous draws at the upper left and lower right corners. The lining canvas left no additional fabric at the edges, and all edges are covered with paper tape. The ground appears to be a thin, off-white layer, probably commercially applied. There may be a warmer white underpainting, or second ground. Past treatment has not been particularly beneficial; the lining has probably flattened the paint, and the brushstrokes now lack crispness. There are several small holes that have been poorly repaired, and cleaning has left darkened residues in the recesses of brushwork. An X-radiograph reveals a different composition beneath the still life, and comparison of the painting in raking light with the X-ray shows a correspondence of the surface topography with the original composition. The visible layer of rich paint was applied in a loose and quickly brushed handling. The background was more hastily covered with slightly thinner paint and covers less thoroughly. Some indications of light-colored lower layers are seen around the contours of the dark bottle in the center, as well as in the upper left and right background. The surface is heavily textured. Although the paint film has cracked throughout the surface, the fissures are not wide enough to permit identification of underlying colors. The varnish is thick, brittle, discolored, and nonsaturating. (RW)

In the winter of 1883–1884 Vincent van Gogh moved to Neunen in the Netherlands to live with his parents at the town parsonage. During the previous decade, he had lived in Etten, The Hague, Paris, London, Dordrecht, Amsterdam, Brussels, the Borinage (a coal mining district in Belgium), The Hague (again), and Drenthe. He had unsuccessfully pursued several careers, including preacher, language instructor, and art dealer, and recently concluded his affair with Sien Hoornick, a poor, single mother of two. Van Gogh's peripatetic way of life, unsuitable choice of partner (he was of the comfortable middle class and was expected to marry the same), and unconventional political views alienated him from family and friends. In 1883 he had no job and no income, and therefore little alternative but to live with his parents, who, van Gogh said, "feel the same dread of taking me into the house as they would about taking in a big rough dog."[1]

Many of van Gogh's paintings from this time have the provisional character of exercises—whether concerning proportion, composition, tone or color, anatomy or

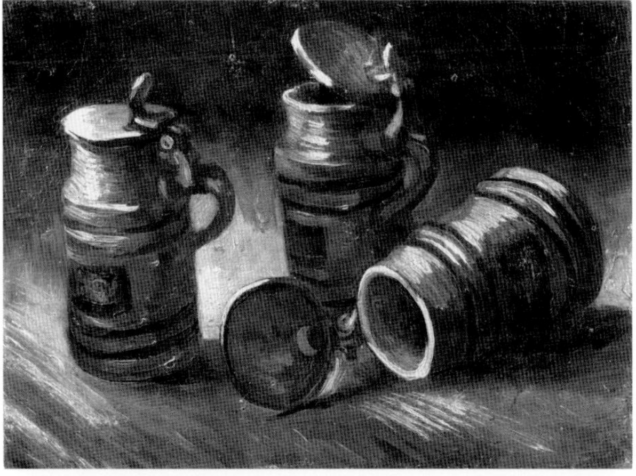

Fig. 107a Vincent van Gogh, *Three Beer Mugs*, 1884, oil on canvas, 12½ × 17 in. (32 × 43 cm), Van Gogh Museum (Vincent van Gogh Foundation), Amsterdam

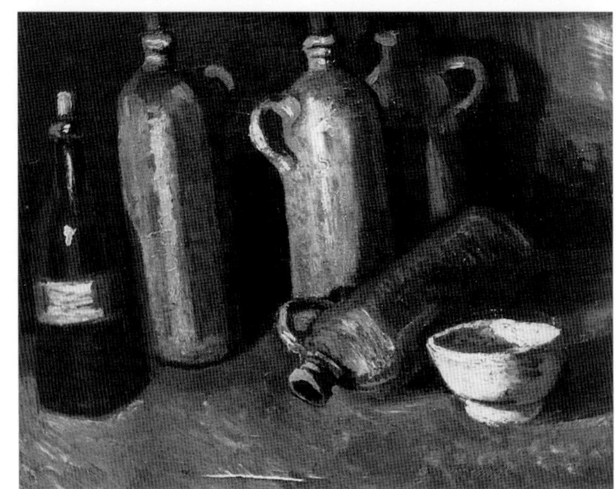

Fig. 107b Vincent van Gogh, *Still Life with Four Stone Bottles*, 1884, oil on panel, 13 × 16⅜ in. (33 × 41.7 cm), Collection Kröller-Müller Museum, Otterlo

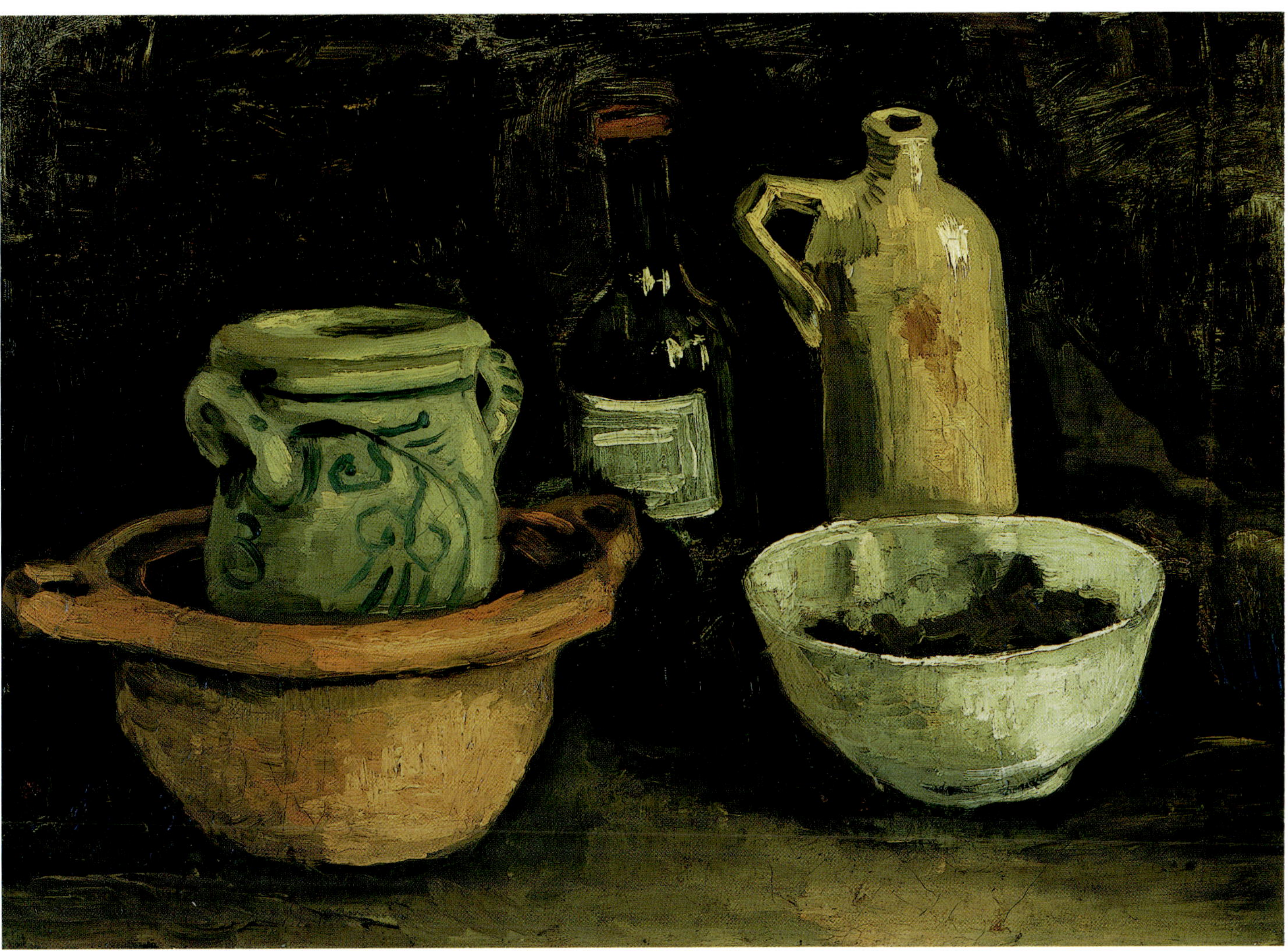

107

physiognomy. His *Still Life* is primarily a study of compositional balance, tone, mass, and volume, or what he called "the ABC of drawing and painting,"[2] though it is also quite full of feeling. It is one of fifteen still lifes painted in November 1884, a period in which he was actually giving painting lessons to several men and women, some wealthy and some from the working class. He often worked side by side with his students—correcting their works while composing his own—and considered his finished still lifes expressions of friendship and solidarity with his pupils.

These early still lifes were painted on canvases of two standard sizes, roughly 12 by 16 or 16 by 22 inches. The present painting is one the latter group and depicts five objects carefully arranged to create balance and near symmetry. The painting was almost certainly painted in Eindhoven, at the home of a former goldsmith named Hermans whom van Gogh described as a wealthy collector of "beautiful things, old jars and other antiques."[3] Van Gogh's painting contains three objects that must have been from Hermans's collection: at right, a plain white porcelain bowl, possibly Chinese; behind it a tall Selters container (c. 1800) of Westerwald type from the North Rhineland; and at left another Westerwald pot, possibly from the late eighteenth century. The latter pot in turn is set inside a crude earthen bowl used for mixing paint. (Additional collections of Westerwald pots, bottles, and tankards are depicted in other canvases, for example, *Three Beer Mugs* [fig. 107a] and *Still Life with Four Stone Bottles* [fig. 107b].) The Norton Simon still life, like the others, is thus at once an academic study of shape and balance and a reflection on the connection between collecting works of art and making them. Van Gogh had already begun to collect Japanese prints and English wood engravings and would soon begin to make considerable use of them in drawn and painted figures.

1 Van Gogh, 1958, vol. 2, no. 346.
2 Van Gogh, 1958, vol. 2, no. 386.
3 Van Gogh, 1958, vol. 2, no. 387.

108

Vincent van Gogh
Dutch, 1853–1890

Winter (The Vicarage Garden under Snow)
Probably January 1885, Nuenen

Oil on canvas, mounted on panel, 23 × 31⅛ in.
(58.4 × 79.1 cm)
F.1969.39.2

Provenance: C. Mouwen Jr., Breda (sale, Amsterdam, Frederik Muller & Cie, Amsterdam, 3 May 1904, lot 6, as *L'Hiver*, unsold). [Oldenzeel Art Gallery, Rotterdam]. Henricus Petrus Bremmer (1871–1956), The Hague, 1905; by descent to; his heirs. ?[E. V. Thaw & Co., New York, stock no. R8106]; ?[Reid & Lefevre, London]; [E. J. van Wisselingh and Co., Amsterdam, stock no. S2589, sold 22 October 1969 to]; The Norton Simon Foundation.

Exhibitions: Rotterdam, 1904, no. 37; Amsterdam, 1905, no. 27; Liège, 1946, no. 21, ill.; Paris, 1947, no. 21; Geneva, 1947, no. 21; Antwerp, 1952, no. 37; Munich, 1956, no. 82, ill.; Paris, 1960, no. 241; Amsterdam, 1963b, no. 12, ill.; London, 1966b, no. 15, ill.; San Francisco, 1973, no. 45, ill.

References: Faille, 1928, vol. 1, no. 194, p. 59, vol. 2, pl. L; van Gogh, n.d., no. 17; Vanbeselaere, 1937, no. 194, pp. 294, 252–253, 416; Faille, 1939, no. 209, p. 169; van Gogh, 1958, vol. 2, no. 394; W. Wilson, 1970, p. 44; Hulsker, 1970, p. 69; Faille, 1970, no. F194, pp. 104–105, 145, 618–619; Steadman, 1976, p. 223; Lecaldano, 1977, vol. 1, no. 96, pp. 98–99; Hulsker, 1977, no. 603, pp. 134, 136, 144–146, pl. 137; R. Berger, 1986, pp. 15, 22, 27; van der Wolk, 1986, no. 339, p. 290; van Heugten, 1995, pp. 68–69, fig. 4a; Tokyo, 1996, under no. 4, fig. 4a.

Technical Notes: *Winter* is painted over a painting of a woman sitting in a chair spinning thread (fig. 108b). In the X-radiograph the first image practically obscures the second. Obviously the artist did little to obliterate the earlier painting because the texture and some colors are visible through the surface of *Winter*. Instead, van Gogh incorporated some of the paints from *The Spinner* into his landscape. For example, white and gray around the spinning wheel became a sort of underpaint for the snow in the lower part of *Winter*. In both pictures paints are thick and opaque and are applied in a brushy, direct manner with impasto. Much of the application is wet in wet. The painting is on a plain-weave, medium-weight fabric with an off-white, medium-thick ground. It is adhered to a panel (estimated to be oak) of three planks with grain running horizontally that is beveled on the reverse. The perimeter of the painting was obviously cut, and the canvas support goes only to the edges of the panel. The condition of the present painting is good with only some scattered losses. Two tears at the bottom center of the canvas that are restored raise the questions when and why the canvas was adhered to panel. The painting was treated in 1973. The present varnish is dirty, and remnants of an earlier yellowed varnish can be seen in the paint crevices. (JF)

Winter (The Vicarage Garden under Snow) was probably painted in January 1885, a few months before *Head of a Peasant Woman in a White Bonnet* (cat. 109). A sketchbook now in the Van Gogh Museum, Amsterdam, includes a sketch for—or possibly after—the rather dark painting, as well as a reference to an issue of the popular French journal *L'Illustration* dated October 1884 (fig. 108a). In addition, van Gogh's letters from January 1885 refer to newly fallen snow and "two more studies of our garden when the snow was on the ground."[1] So *Winter* may be dated between October 1884 and January 1885, with the probability that it was made close to the later time. The dating is significant, because it informs us that van Gogh's conceptions of landscape and portraiture at this time were in lockstep. *Winter* is the landscape correlative of peasant paintings like *Head of a Peasant Woman in a White Bonnet.* A letter from the period indicates van Gogh's belief that certain places are as marked by poverty and hard labor as the faces of laborers and peasants.

> I've hardly ever begun a year [1885] with a gloomier aspect, in a gloomier mood, nor do I expect any future of success, but a future of strife.
>
> It is dreary outside, the fields a mass of lumps of black earth and some snow, with mostly days of mist and mire in between, the red sun in the evening and in the morning, crows, withered grass, and faded, rotting green, black shrubs, and the branches of the poplars and willows rigid, like wire, against the dismal sky. This is what I see in passing, and it is quite in harmony with the interiors, very gloomy, these dark winter days.
>
> It is also in harmony with the physiognomy of the peasants and weavers. I don't hear the latter complain, but they have a hard time of it.[2]

Van Gogh's landscape is more than just figuratively associated with contemporary paintings of peasants, weavers, and other laborers. An X-ray reveals that the

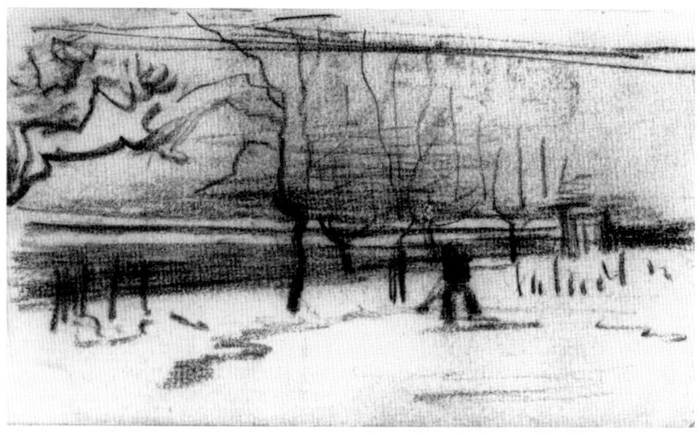

Fig. 108a Vincent van Gogh, sketch for *Winter* in Neunen Sketchbook, chalk and pencil on paper, Van Gogh Museum (Vincent van Gogh Foundation), Amsterdam

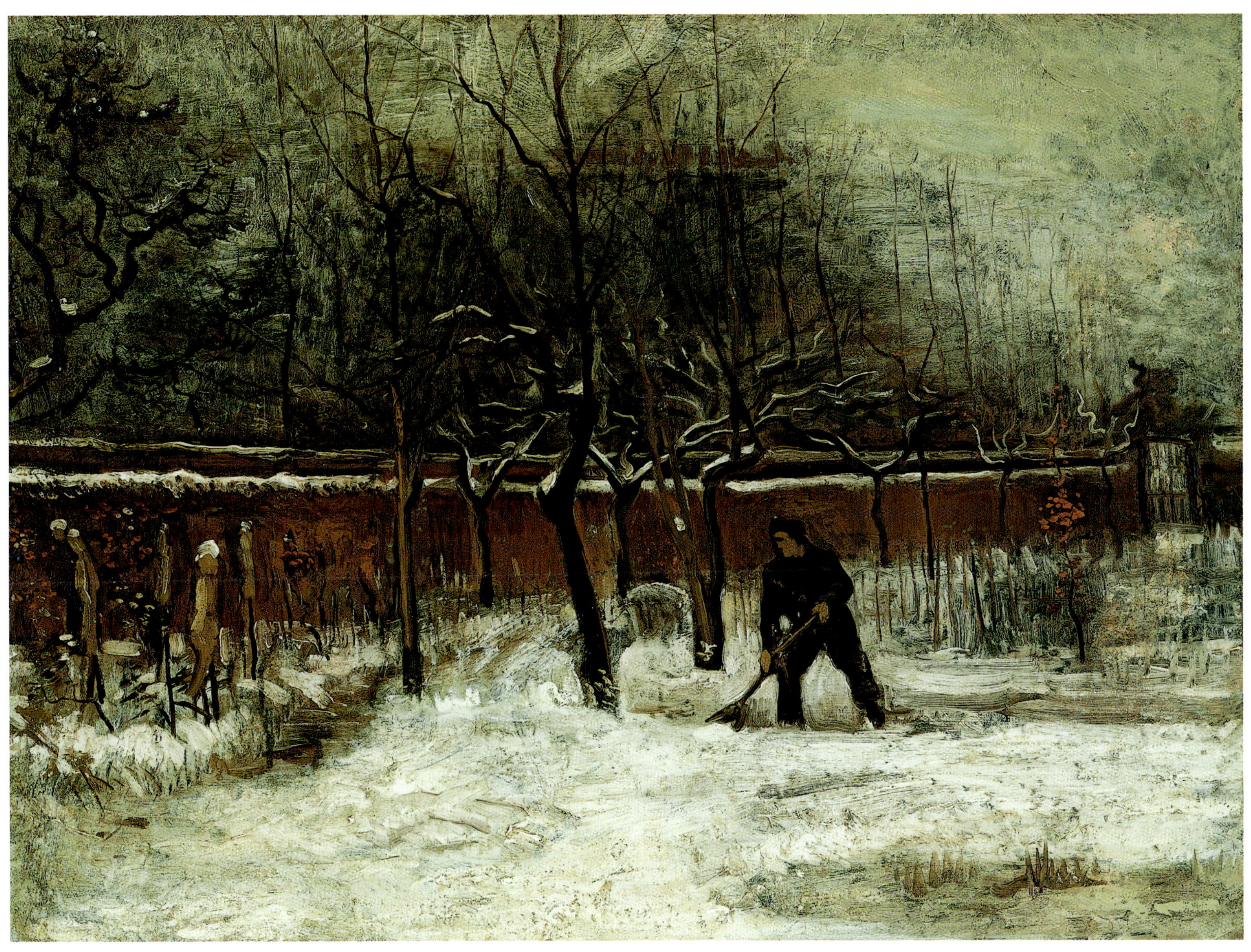

108

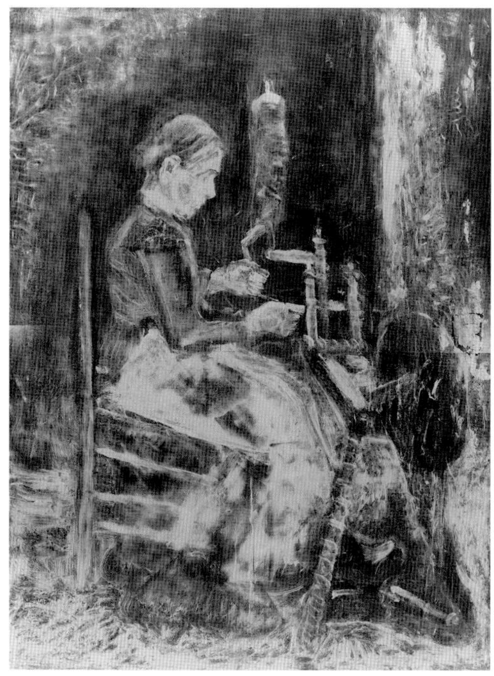

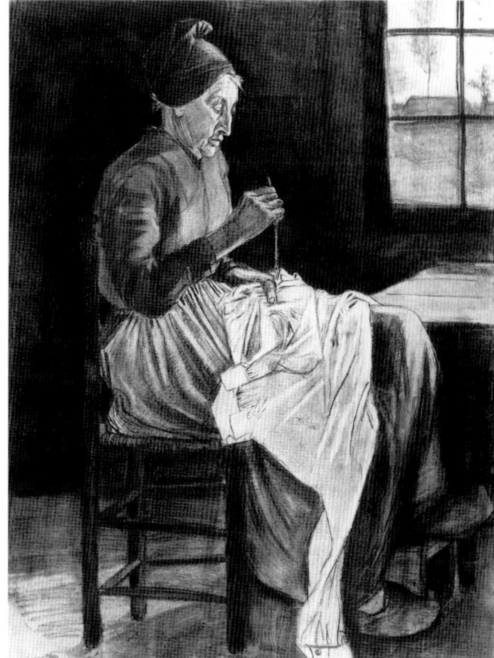

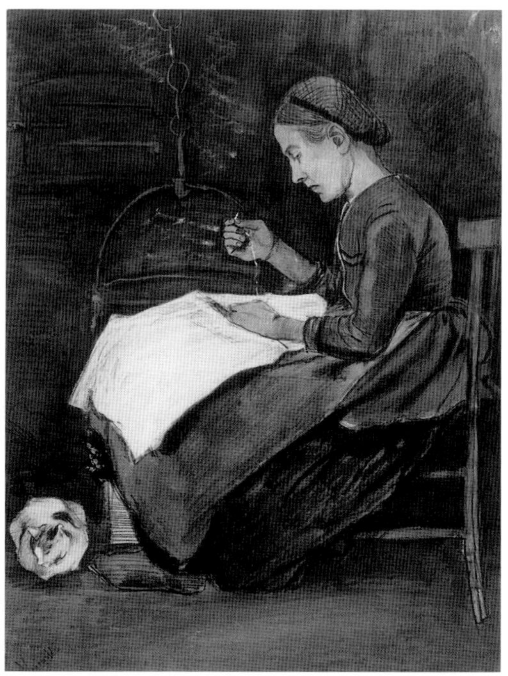

Fig. 108b (*above left*) X-ray photograph of cat. 108

Fig. 108c (*above center*) Vincent van Gogh, *A Woman Sewing*, 1881, black chalk, charcoal, and watercolor on paper, 24⅜ × 18¾ in. (62 × 47.5 cm), Collection Kröller-Müller Museum, Otterlo

Fig. 108d (*above right*) Vincent van Gogh, *Woman by the Fire with White Cat*, 1881, black chalk and watercolor on paper, 23⅝ × 18 in. (60 × 45.5 cm), Collection Kröller-Müller Museum, Otterlo

landscape is actually painted over an earlier painting of a woman in profile seated at a spinning wheel (fig. 108b). That painting, probably the "small one of that woman spinning" mentioned in a letter to Theo from late spring 1884,[3] is a reduced rendering of a now lost or destroyed painting of a woman "dressed in blue with a mouse-colored shawl." The drawing in the Kröller-Müller Museum, Otterlo (fig. 108e) may be related to this group of works.

Why van Gogh decided, six or seven months later, to rotate the canvas clockwise 90 degrees and paint a landscape over the "little woman spinning"[4] is unclear. It may have been that the earlier picture appeared to him a step backward in what he insisted to Theo was his steady artistic progress: the painting closely resembles in subject and composition a few of his large and ambitious figure studies made in Etten in the autumn of 1881 such as *A Woman Sewing* and *Woman by the Fire with White Cat* (figs. 108c and 108d). Alternatively, he may have been unsatisfied with the awkward perspective and foreshortening of the chair and spinning wheel. Of course, van Gogh was also especially short of money in January 1885, and he may have decided to reuse his small painting of a woman spinning simply in order "to go on working."[5] Whatever the reason for the overpainting, van Gogh drew some inspiration from the earlier work, as one can deduce from a study of the X-ray and the surface of the painting: one set of chair legs became the long top of the garden wall; the diagonal right leg of the spinning wheel became the path in the snow at lower left; and the geometry of bobbin and spindle at the center of the machine became the crouching, angular figure holding a shovel in the middle of this brooding landscape. The man with the shovel—painted with broad, short strokes reminiscent of the work of Honoré Daumier—appears to be clearing a path, but van Gogh, ever alert to the tragic dimension of his subjects, allows us to wonder whether he might instead be digging a grave.

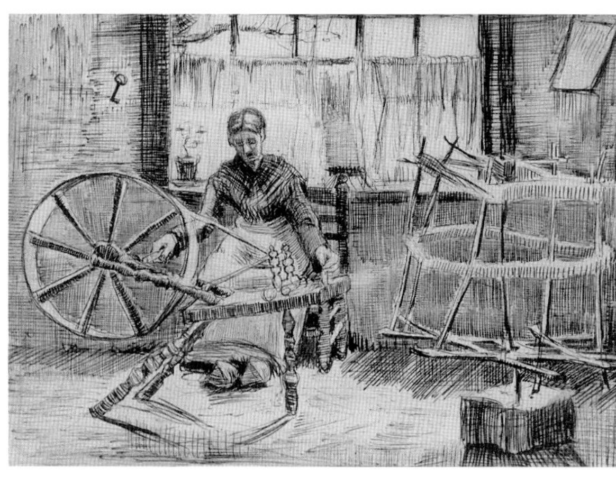

Fig. 108e Vincent van Gogh, *Woman Spinning*, 1883–1885, ink on paper, 5⅞ × 8¼ in. (15 × 21 cm), Collection Kröller-Müller Museum, Otterlo

1 Van Gogh, 1958, vol. 2, no. 394.
2 Van Gogh, 1958, vol. 2, no. 392.
3 Van Gogh, 1958, vol. 2, no. 370.
4 Van Gogh, 1958, vol. 2, no. 372.
5 Van Gogh, 1958, vol. 2, no. 387.

109

Vincent van Gogh
Dutch, 1853–1890

Head of a Peasant Woman in a White Bonnet
1885

Oil on canvas, 18½ × 13¾ in. (47 × 35 cm)
F.1985.1

Provenance: [Galerie d'Art Ed. Oldenzeel, Rotterdam, ca. 1902/1903, to]; Dr. H. J. Nieboer, The Hague, c. 1903/1904, by 1905; by inheritance to his daughter, Mrs. S. de Voogd-Nieboer, Rijswijk (sale, New York, Parke-Bernet, 14 March 1956, lot 89, ill., as *Head of a Peasant Woman*). [Hammer Galleries, New York]. (sale, London, Sotheby's, 6 December 1961, lot 61, ill., as *Tête d'une paysanne*, to); [R. M. Light, Boston, 1963]; Mr. and Mrs. David Bakalar, Boston (sale, New York, Sotheby's, 14 November 1984, lot 2, ill., as *Tête de paysanne au bonnet blanc*, to); The Norton Simon Foundation.

Exhibition Boston, 1962.

References: Faille, 1970, no. F85a, pp. 615, 72, ill., as *Head of a Peasant Woman with White Cap: Full Face*; Lecaldano, 1977, no. 149, p. 103; Hulsker, 1977, no. 694, p. 153.

Technical Notes: The dimensions in this portrait were extended about ¾ inch in the vertical direction and about ¼ inch in the horizontal by unfolding the tacking edges. What was not used of the tacking edges to extend the design was removed, presumably when the painting was wax-lined to canvas. The original plain-weave, medium-weight canvas was as recently as 1984 attached to a wood panel (compare *Winter*, cat. 108, that is also canvas on panel) with the dimensions of 18½ by 13½ inches. Presently stretched on a fairly old wood stretcher, it was first noted as on canvas only in 1984, but there is no documented explanation for the change in support or in dimensions. The medium-rich paint is thickly and directly applied with a good deal of impasto. Though applied wet in wet, the tones are not blended. In general, the artist initially laid in middle tones, then highlights and darker defining paints. The X-radiograph shows no design changes. Van Gogh may have applied a dark brown translucent paint to the ground as an underpainting or imprimatura layer. With magnification relatively large translucent particles show up in the paint surface. Some have dislodged, leaving cavities that extend down to the ground. As for the ground, it is only possible to say that it is light in color and possibly white. The condition of the painting is good though there are a few damages including some flattening of impasto. Five large vertical, mechanical cracks in the central area of the picture may be the result of rolling the canvas. The restoration of these cracks and a few small scattered restorations show clearly in ultraviolet light. A fine crackle pattern runs through the paint layers, and an even finer pattern of shallow contraction cracks that seems to have to do with the medium-rich technique affects only the surface paints. The painting was partially cleaned in 1984 and revarnished with B-67 that no longer saturates the darks. (JF)

In spite of doubts about his abilities and external obstacles, van Gogh's resolution to continue to live as an artist was unshakeable by 1884, as was his conviction that his work would be the realization of his radical moral and political beliefs. "There is an old civilization," Vincent van Gogh wrote to Theo in October 1884, "that in my opinion is declining through its own fault—there is a new civilization that has been born, and is growing, and will grow more. In short, there are revolutionary and anti-revolutionary principles."[1] Theo's withering reply to his brother, "it is more likely that [you] shall achieve something by making good pictures than by discussing revolutionary questions,"[2] prompted the artist to redouble his efforts to conclude an ambitious project of portraiture that he had begun two years earlier: a series of fifty head and bust-length portraits of proletarians and peasants—"Heads of the People" (he used the English phrase)[3]—that would function as a record of the life and character of his times. Van Gogh had seen a series of wood engravings with the same title in an English illustrated magazine called *The Graphic*[4] and was determined to try something similar in paint, "making figures *from the people for the people*."[5] At the same time, however, he would ennoble his painted heads and faces by emulating to some degree the manner of the great northern European masters with whom he was familiar. In 1881 he had drawn the daughter of Jacob Meyer (Kröller-Müller Museum, Otterlo) in direct imitation of a work by Hans Holbein. Two years later, his drawings of Clasina Hoornick and her mother, such as *Clasina (Sien) with a White Cap* (Van Gogh Museum, Amsterdam), exposed the influence of Albrecht Dürer's famous *Portrait of Barbara Dürer, the Artist's Mother* (1514, Kupferstich-kabinett, Staatliche Museen zu Berlin). Soon he would follow the example of Rembrandt, expressing in a letter his admiration for *The Syndics* and *The Jewish Bride*[6] and using *The Supper at Emmaus* as a compositional basis for his own *Potato Eaters*. Like the great Dutch master, he would even begin to sign his paintings with his given name, Vincent, instead of the patronymic, van Gogh.

In early February 1885 van Gogh reported his progress to Theo. He stated, "those fifty heads will be finished this winter."[7] *Head of a Peasant Woman in a White Bonnet*, probably one of the rapidly painted "new studies of the heads" announced by van Gogh in a letter to Theo from near the end of April,[8] was made in partial fulfillment of that pledge. It is part of a group of about ten surviving representations of Sien de Groot, the painter's mistress, and served as a preparation for the figure seated second from left in van Gogh's first large canvas, *The Potato Eaters* (fig. 109a). Though *Head of a Peasant Woman in a White Bonnet* functioned as a study, there is no reason to consider the painting anything but a finished work of art

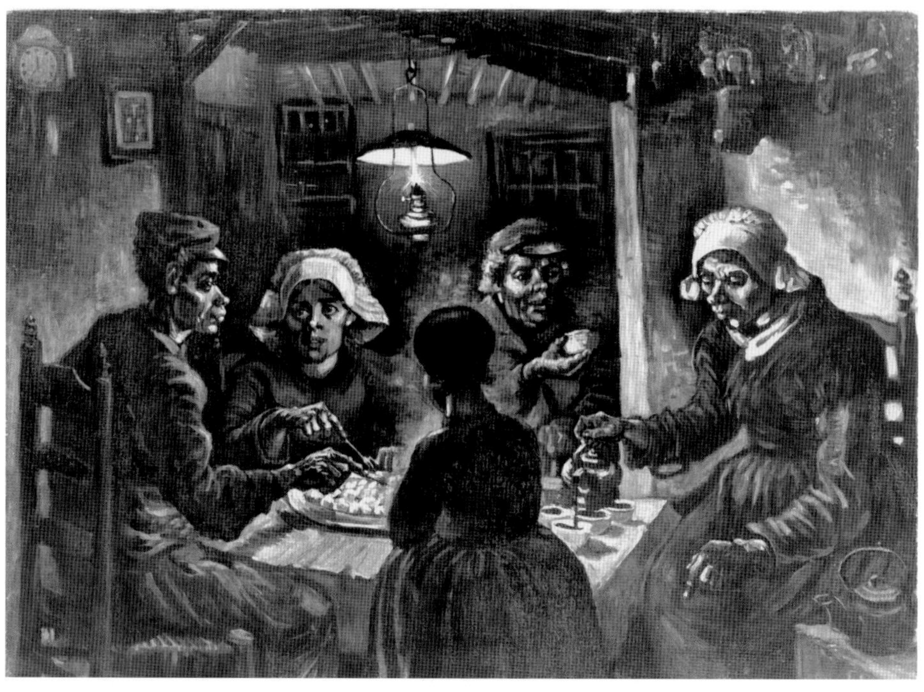

Fig. 109a Vincent van Gogh, *The Potato Eaters*, April 1885, oil on canvas, $32\frac{1}{8} \times 45\frac{1}{8}$ in. (81.5 × 114.5 cm), Van Gogh Museum (Vincent van Gogh Foundation), Amsterdam

in its own right. He spoke at this time of the difficulty of determining "where the study ends and the picture begins,"[9] and of his admiration for pictures that "were painted quickly . . . dashed off" from first to last "without any retouching whatever."[10] Impressionist artists had for more than a decade painted and exhibited works of startling spontaneity, and though van Gogh as yet knew hardly anything about the so-called new painting, he already admired its decisiveness. Impressionism would increasingly be for him, like the Romantic art of Eugène Delacroix and the experimental still lifes of the Marseille painter Adolphe Monticelli, the expression of a robust and masculine temperament. "At the point I am now," he wrote Theo in an important letter containing a sketch of *The Potato Eaters*, "I see a chance of giving a true impression of what I see." Paraphrasing the critic and novelist Émile Zola, he added that his own drawings and paintings were "not always literally exact, or rather never exact, for one sees nature through one's own temperament."[11]

Head of a Peasant Woman in a White Bonnet is inexact in its construction of volume and mass, but nevertheless quite carefully painted. The paint surface is dense and opaque, contours are carefully observed, and brushstrokes simulate the form and texture of the objects they represent. Indeed, the head and shoulders are neither smaller nor less fully rendered than those of the corresponding figure in *The Potato Eaters*. The sitter's face, neck, and head are framed by a kerchief and a starched and crumpled white-and-gray bonnet. A light highlight on the bonnet, forehead, bridge and tip of nose, upper lip, and chin creates an implied line that cleaves the face in two. The symmetrical division continues between her breasts, though here the line is informed by shadow, not by light.

Sien's head is thus shown fully frontal, a point of view that is unusual in the tradition of northern European portraiture—extending from Dürer to Jozef Israels—with which van Gogh was most familiar. Because both human faces and oil paintings are essentially flat, a frontal view tends to identify the former with the artifice of the latter, undercutting the animation generally deemed essential for the achievement of a good likeness. A frontal perspective is more common, however, in two unique representational circumstances: self-portraits and forensic portraits. In the former instance, the picture is intended—by means of its format—to clearly announce its distinctness from the rest of the artist's portrait oeuvre. The self-portrait may be considered in fact a separate genre in art history, and the artificial nature of the frontal view—that is, its relative flatness—is peculiarly suited to the representation of the painter. The painter, after all, is the one who, according to Renaissance art theory, magically wrests three-dimensional similitude from the two dimensions of the panel or canvas, and the frontal self-portrait renders the transformation visible. Indeed, the first and most famous self-portrait employing full frontality, Dürer's *Self-Portrait as Christ* (fig. 109b), emphasizes the nearly divine nature of the artist's inventive powers. The painter here resembles no one so much as Jesus Christ, and his picture is thus more iconic than it is naturalistic or narrative.

The second salient context for frontal portraits—modern forensic science—has an origin that returns us once again to Dürer, an artist for whom van Gogh, as we have already seen, had almost boundless enthusiasm. Dürer completed in 1523 his *Vier Bücher von menschlicher Proportion*, which, among other things, set out a systematic procedure for measuring and representing the

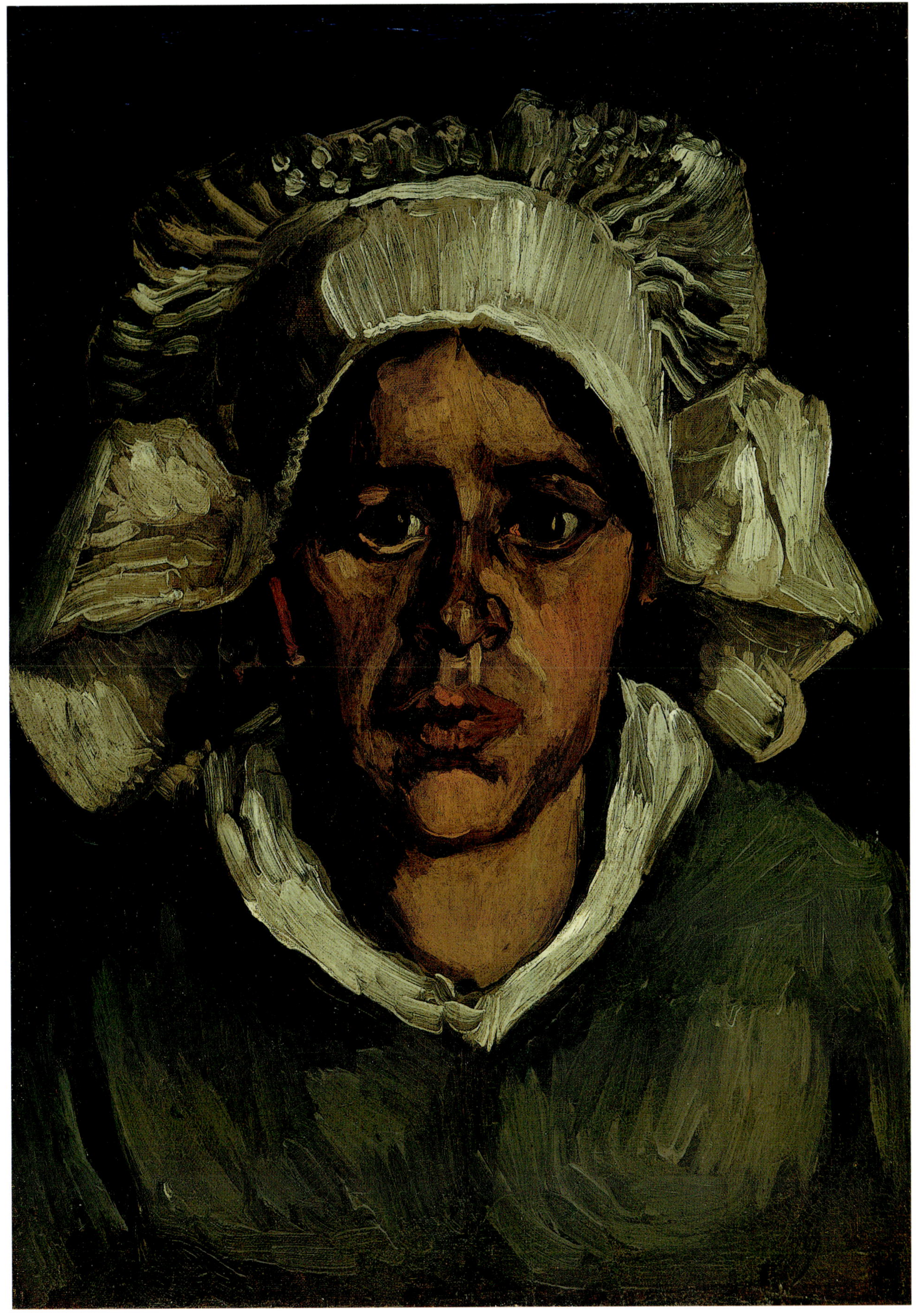

109

Fig. 109b Albrecht Dürer, *Self-Portrait as Christ*, 1500, oil on panel, 26⅜ × 19⅜ in. (67 × 49 cm), Bayerisches Staatsgemäldesammlungen, Alte Pinakothek, Munich

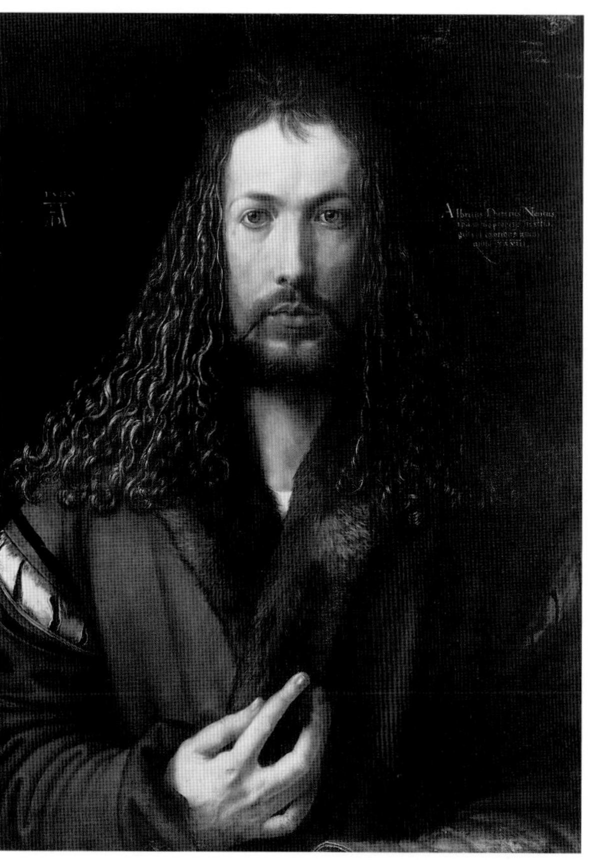

human body. His studies of actual bodies and heads, his efforts to discover precise, integral relations between the different body parts, and his diagrams of typical bodies seen from the front and sides announced the birth of anthropometry, a pseudoscience that would flourish in the nineteenth and early twentieth centuries. The latter practice of anthropometry was not, as it had been for Dürer, an effort (at once humanistic and theological) to reveal the consonance and unity of the human body by means of an investigation of the correspondence of its parts.[12] In the nineteenth century, this technique was widely used by criminologists to identify the salient physical features of the criminal class.

Van Gogh's portraits must be understood in this wider intellectual and pseudoscientific context. Though there is no specific evidence that van Gogh read the work of nineteenth-century criminologists, it is clear that he was concerned with depicting individuals as representatives of types or even races. In 1880 van Gogh stated that he had "read with great pleasure" an extract from the work of Johann Kaspar Lavater and Franz Joseph Gall, *Physiognomy and Phrenology*.[13] He collected hundreds of English wood engravings that explicitly portrayed physiognomic and social types, and especially admired Honoré Daumier for his creation of "types or heads of people."[14] In 1885, while at work on his fifty heads, he wrote Theo that he had received from his friend Anthon Rappard some drawings by Paul Renouard: "types of lawyers, criminals, etc."[15] And he stated numerous times in letters that the peasants represented in *The Potato Eaters* were a race apart whose lives were utterly different from "us civilized people," and that "one cannot help being the way one is."[16]

The frontality and physiognomic coarseness of the model in *Head of a Peasant Woman in a White Bonnet* informs us that she is intended to be seen as a representative of a type, the peasant, as much as a particular individual known to the painter. Her round eyes and raised brows, combined with the awkward angularity of her other features, convey childlike insouciance, sufferance, and quietism. The artist's promiscuous use of chiaroscuro suggests the closeness, dirt, smoke, and dim light of a peasant interior.

> . . . withered grass, and faded, rotting green, black shrubs. . . . This is what I see in passing, and it is quite in harmony with the interiors, very gloomy, these dark winter days.
>
> It is also in harmony with the physiognomy of the peasants and weavers. . . . The people are quiet, and literally *nowhere* have I heard anything resembling rebellious speeches.[17]

This latter disappointment—that despite their poverty and suffering the peasants he knows do not display a revolutionary temper—indicates clearly enough that van Gogh's interest in type or race differs from that of the criminologists. Though van Gogh, like most educated European men and women of his day, accepted the mistaken view that humankind was divided into distinct races with fixed physiological, social, and moral attributes, he did not uphold the racial superiority of white bourgeois over rough peasant or laborer. On the contrary, he viewed peasant and working-class life to be spiritually and physically superior to bourgeois ways of being and wished to become "a peasant painter." By that, he meant an artist who lived among the people he portrayed and came to know their lives, minds, and bodies, as it were, from the inside. Though his actual life among peasants was circumscribed by his class position, dependence on parents and brother, and personal reserve, he gained sufficient insight into their lives that he eventually abandoned many of the typological and racial preconceptions that guided early efforts such as the present painting.

Indeed, the fifty heads painted during the months before, during, and after work on *The Potato Eaters* are perhaps the last of van Gogh's efforts at specifically physiognomic or forensic portraiture. And in *The Potato Eaters* itself, this rationalist approach to composition is subsumed and mitigated within the narrative of the collective meal, with all its biblical and literary associations. Here van Gogh's major inspiration is not Dürer but Rembrandt—an artist who rejected all rules—specifically *The Supper at Emmaus* (1642, Musée du Louvre, Paris). Van Gogh remarked on the distinction between the studies and larger work when he wrote that "in the picture [*The Potato Eaters*], I give free scope to my own head in the sense of thought or imagination, which is not so much the case in studies, where no creative process is allowed, but where one finds food for one's imagination in reality, in order to make it exact."[18]

1 Van Gogh, 1958, vol. 2, no. 381.
2 Van Gogh, 1958, vol. 2, no. 384.
3 Van Gogh, 1958, vol. 1, no. 257.
4 Soth, 2000, p. 67.
5 Van Gogh, 1958, vol. 1, no. 251.
6 Van Gogh, 1958, vol. 2, no. 427.
7 Van Gogh, 1958, vol. 2, no. 389.
8 Van Gogh, 1958, vol. 2, no. 403.
9 Van Gogh, 1958, vol. 2, no. 396.
10 Van Gogh, 1958, vol. 2, no. 427.
11 Van Gogh, 1958, vol. 2, no. 399.
12 Erwin Panofsky, *The Life and Art of Albrecht Dürer*, Princeton, 1955, pp. 264–265.
13 Van Gogh, 1958, vol. 1, no. 138.
14 Van Gogh, 1958, vol. 1, no. 239.
15 Van Gogh, 1958, vol. 2, no. 389.
16 Van Gogh, 1958, vol. 2, no. 404.
17 Van Gogh, 1958, vol. 2, no. 392.
18 Van Gogh, 1958, vol. 2, no. 403.

110

Vincent van Gogh
Dutch, 1853–1890

Portrait of a Peasant (Patience Escalier)
August 1888

Oil on canvas, 25¼ × 21½ in. (64.2 × 54.6 cm)
Signed upper left: "Vincent"
M.1975.6

Provenance: Mrs. Johanna van Gogh-Bonger, Amsterdam, sold December 1899 to; Henricus Petrus Bremmer (1871–1956), The Hague, still in 1935, to; Mr. and Mrs. Edouard L. Jonas, Paris and New York, by inheritance to; Mrs. H. Harris Jonas, New York, by 1943, to; [Wildenstein and Co., New York, sold 1975, to]; Norton Simon Art Foundation.

Exhibitions: The Hague, 1898, no. 36; Rotterdam, 1904, no. 66; Amsterdam, 1905, no. 153; Cologne, 1912, no. 62, pl. 8; Copenhagen, 1922, no. 176; on loan, The Hague, Gemeentemuseum, 1924–1935; Springfield, 1935, no. 53; Cleveland, 1936, no. 320; New York, 1938, no. 46; New York, 1940b, no. 361, pp. 245, 247; New York, 1943b, no. 29, pp. 28, 70; New York, 1953a, no. 15; New York, 1955, no. 30; New York, 1972, no. 35; on loan, San Francisco, California Palace of the Legion of Honor, 6 January–14 June 1976.

References: Havelaar, 1915, p. 16; Faille, 1928, vol. 1, no. 443, vol. 2, no. 443, pl. CXVIII; Scherjon and de Gruyter, 1937, no. 62, pp. 90–91, 94; Faille, 1939, no. 478, p. 342; van Gogh, 1958, vol. 3, nos. 519, 520, 522, 528, 529, 534; Faille, 1970, no. F443, pp. 204, 628; Steadman, 1976, p. 223, pl. B; Lecaldano, 1977, vol. 2, no. 543, pp. 210–211; Hulsker, 1977, no. 1548, p. 355; van der Wolk, 1986, pp. 276–277; Feilchenfeldt, 1988, no. F443, p. 95; Dorn, 1990, no. F433, pp. 352–356; Palmer, 1990, pp. 72–74, ill. 75; van Uitert, van Tilborgh, and van Heugten, 1990, vol. 2, pp. 142, 146, fig. 55a; Sund, 1992, pp. 5–6, 11, 181–185, pl. 4; Arnold, 1995, pp. 144–145, 864, fig. 66; Dorn, 2000, pp. 8, 130, 152, 212, 218, 230, fig. 193; Shackelford, 2000, pp. 43, 45, fig. 37, 47 (detail); Jirat-Wasiuty_ski, 2001, pp. 177–191, fig. 11.2; Eisenman, 2002, pp. 17, fig. 0.5, 334; Sund, 2002, pp. 210–211, fig. 135.

Technical Notes: The support is a fine, plain-weave canvas with its original edges intact. It has been lined, first with glue, and then later infused with wax, presumably to arrest a problem of cleavage. The light-colored ground is exceptionally thin. The present color is golden beige, which undoubtedly is darker than it was originally; this could be due to the discoloration of a component in the ground, as well as having been impregnated with wax. The portrait is built up in multiple layers. A smooth pale green layer is beneath the hat and possibly under the face. The blue background was initially laid in with a smooth layer. The thick paint was strongly brushed with a ½-inch brush in the background; perhaps a smaller brush was used in the face and hat. The state of preservation is fairly good, though past restoration has not been beneficial. The impasto has probably been smoothed to some extent by the lining. There are countless tiny losses in the background. This condition, added to the uncommon number of cracks throughout the painting, may be something that occurred when the painting was off the stretcher. It is very likely that the color of the sitter's shirt has faded from a more vibrant coral color. On the bottom tacking edge, there is a small portion of what may be the unfaded color of the pink shirt. This tiny area was not completely cleaned and also was protected by the frame. (RW)

After a brief period of academic study in Antwerp from November 1885 to February 1886, van Gogh began an intense, nearly two-year residence in Paris. There he enrolled in the studio school of the Salon painter Fernand Cormon, but the training made little impression except to confirm him in his antipathy to conventional or academic approaches to portraiture, landscape, genre, and history painting. Nevertheless, the three or four months with Cormon were significant because it was during this time—the spring and summer of 1886—that van Gogh met Henri de Toulouse-Lautrec and Émile Bernard at Cormon's studio and gained firsthand knowledge of the work of the Impressionists Monet, Renoir, Degas, Sisley, Pissarro, and Seurat. He visited the eighth and last Impressionist group exhibition in May 1886 and learned the fundamentals of painting in "*intense* color and not a *gray* harmony."[1] His love of Dürer, Rembrandt, Honoré Daumier, and English wood engraving was now supplemented by admiration for Japanese prints, as well as the paintings of Eugène Delacroix and Adolphe Monticelli. In Paris, van Gogh even acquired the rudiments of an urban sophistication that at times eclipsed his rural, bookish reserve.

In November 1887 van Gogh joined forces with a small group of artists who called themselves "painters of the *petit boulevard*." Instead of representing the beauties of the countryside or portraying bourgeois men and women at play, these young artists—Bernard, Toulouse-Lautrec, Louis Anquetin, A. H. Koning, and Armand Guillaumin—depicted urban life and proletarian leisure. And instead of showing their artworks in the better galleries, they exhibited at unfashionable, indeed déclassé venues. (Their biggest exhibition was held at the cavernous, petit-bourgeois Grand Bouillon-Restaurant du Chalet in Montmartre.) Their subversive goal was to create a new, popular art, that is, to make paintings of the people and for the people. They even wished—at least, to the extent compatible with their artistic careers—to turn themselves into proletarians.

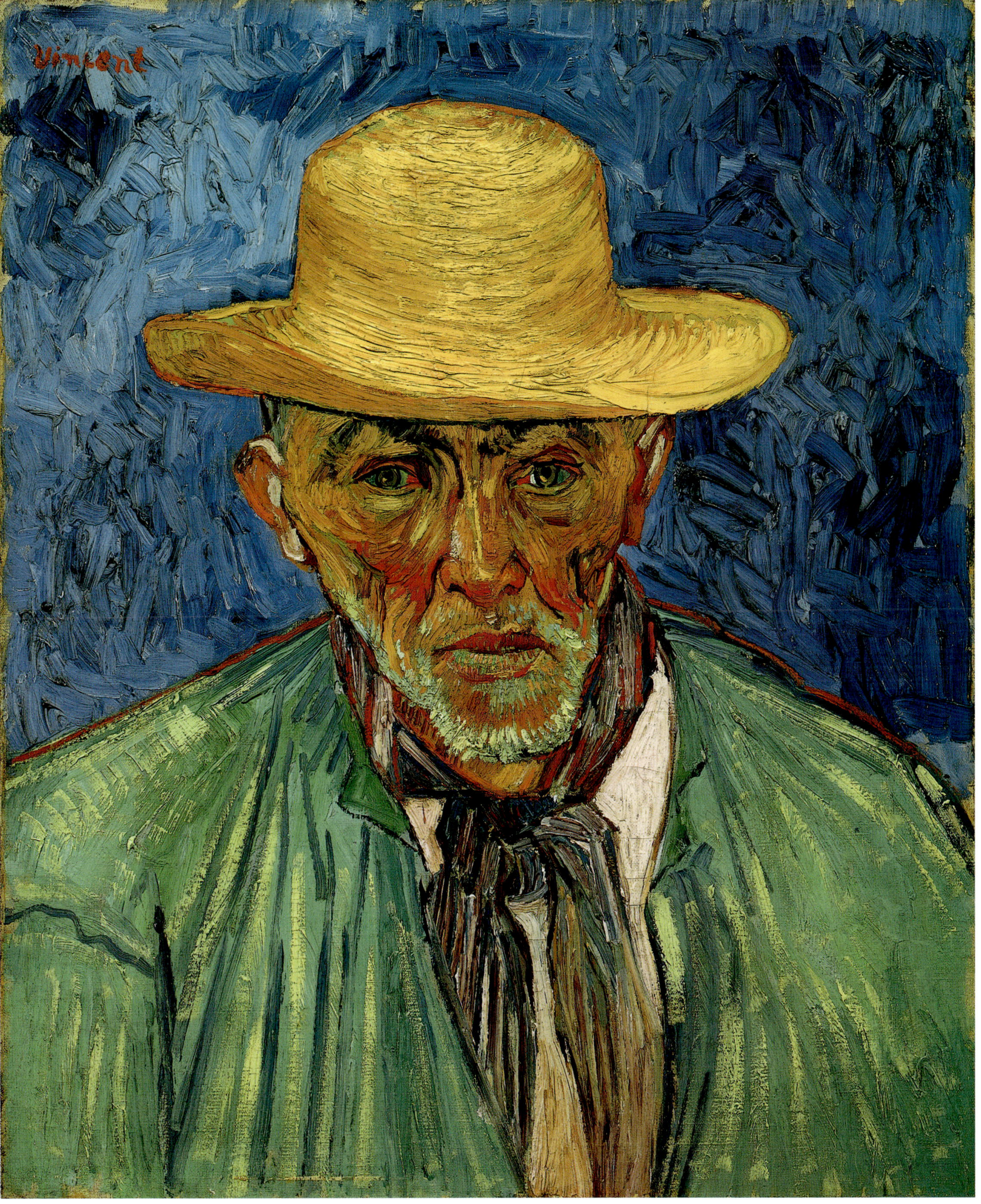
Vincent

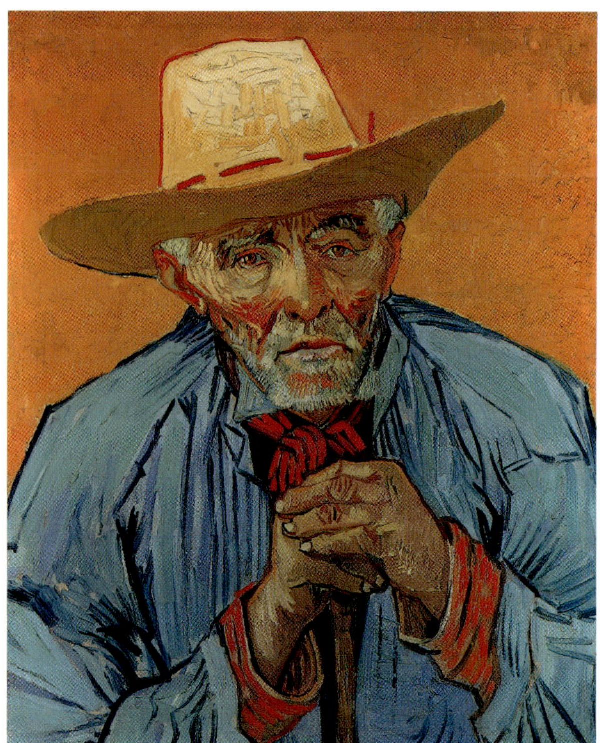

Fig. 110a Vincent van Gogh, *Patience Escalier*, August 1888, oil on canvas, private collection

But the cooperation and fellowship of the new painters of the *petit boulevard* was limited and short-lived. Personal and professional jealousies and animosities drove the artists apart. By the following February, van Gogh had determined to leave the French capital and establish in the south of France a commune for like-minded comrades. There he and his fellow artists would live cheaply, paint freely, and find sanctuary from what he saw as the corruption, selfishness, and competitiveness of the artistic life in Paris. In late February 1888 van Gogh moved to the city of Arles, in the heart of Provence, celebrated for its Roman amphitheater, medieval troubadour poetry, and the nineteenth-century nationalist poet Frédéric Mistral. At first, van Gogh lived in a hotel near one of the city gates in the northern precinct. Soon, however, he rented and began to decorate a small house, the Yellow House, on the place Lamartine just outside the gates. The task of decorating this house, the intended locus of a nameless "new religion," motivated van Gogh to accelerate his artistic experiments in advance of the arrival of his first and, in the event, only tenant, Paul Gauguin.

Van Gogh's paintings from Arles, made between February 1888 and May 1890, greatly extended the new artistic language that he and others had developed in Paris. Prismatic color was applied to the canvas more freely and boldly than before, and compositions were made more asymmetric and dynamic. The academic rules of perspective and modeling were freely manipulated, violated, or ignored. Line, color, and composition were understood—perhaps for the first time in the history of art—to be instruments of expression, not just tools of mimesis; they were intended to be used to depict the unseen worlds of thought and feeling as much as the visible realms of matter and identity. Physicality and the concrete were still important for van Gogh, as his works in the Norton Simon collections reveal, but they were seen as pathways to spirit. In this context, it is significant that van Gogh shifted his art historical attention from European to Asian precedents: Japan replaced Germany and the Netherlands as his cultural lodestone. Eastern faiths (especially Buddhism and the Shinto religion), with their perceived spiritual and animistic basis, trumped the Dutch Reform church with its greater emphasis on good works and salvation.

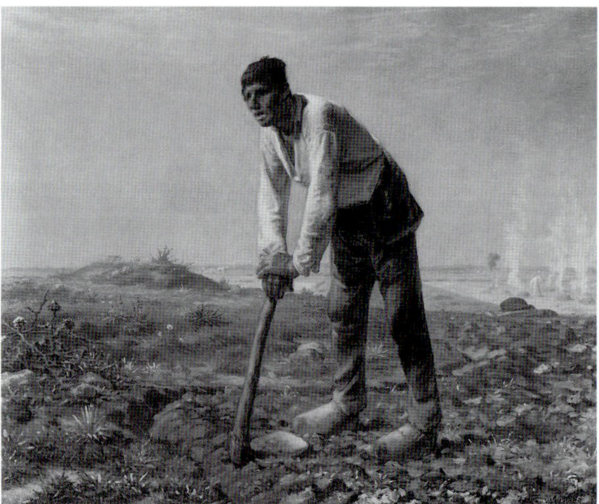

Fig. 110b Jean-François Millet, *Man with a Hoe*, 1860–1862, oil on canvas, $31\frac{1}{2} \times 39$ in. (80×99.1 cm), The J. Paul Getty Museum, Los Angeles

Portrait of a Peasant (Patience Escalier) was painted in early August 1888, and a second version, showing the peasant resting his hands on a stick (fig. 110a), was made a few weeks later. The Norton Simon portrait is a highly important example of van Gogh's reinvention of an artistic tradition. It is first of all a portrait, and as such remains firmly entrenched in a genre type that van Gogh specially embraced since his days at Neunen. Like his earlier portraits, such as *Head of a Peasant Woman in a White Bonnet* (cat. 109), it depicts a peasant, not someone high born, but unlike those, it is large and therefore grand and ambitious, colorful, and fully independent of a

Fig. 110c (*right*) Henri-Marie Raymond de Toulouse-Lautrec, *Young Woman at a Table ("Poudre de Riz")*, 1887, oil on canvas, $25\frac{5}{8} \times 22\frac{7}{8}$ in. (65×58 cm), Van Gogh Museum (Vincent van Gogh Foundation), Amsterdam

Fig. 110d (*far right*) Vincent van Gogh, *Portrait of a Peasant (Patience Escalier)* (cat. 110)

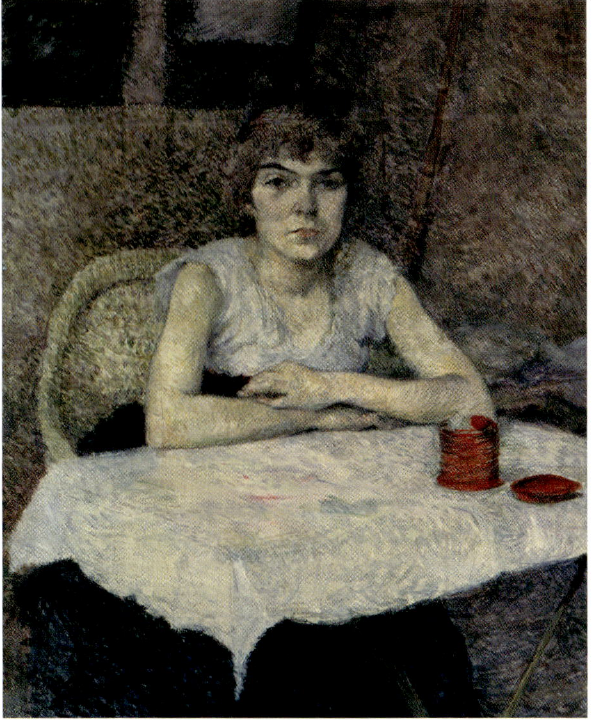

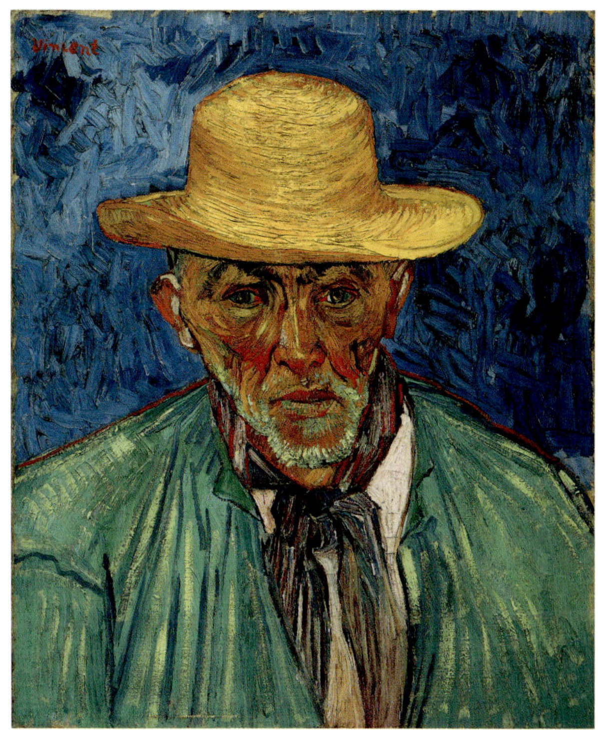

series. The figure is represented in a somewhat complicated pose: head and neck are craned slightly forward, suggesting a bit of a stoop, the right shoulder—outlined in red and blue—is pressed against the picture plane, while the face is turned slightly to the left. In addition, the peasant's hat is tipped just downward to the left, while the brim is turned up on the right, creating a hidden pocket of space. The eyes, ears, and nose are similarly asymmetrical, as are the smock, shirt, and cravat. Despite all this irregularity, the figure possesses considerable gravity and breadth, appearing over-life-size. (In fact, the head and shoulders are almost exactly life-size, but because we are used to looking at ourselves in diminished reflection on the planes of mirrors, they seem to us unnaturally large.)

In early August 1888 van Gogh wrote to Theo:

> You are shortly to make the acquaintance of Master Patience Escalier, a sort of "man with a hoe," formerly cowherd of the Camargue, now gardener at a house in the Crau. The coloring of this peasant portrait is not so black as in the "Potato Eaters" of Neunen. . . . I do not think that my peasant would do any harm to the de Lautrec in your possession if they were hung side by side, and I am even bold enough to hope the de Lautrec would appear even more distinguished by the mutual contrast, and that on the other hand my picture would gain by the odd juxtaposition, because that sun-steeped, sunburned quality, tanned and air-swept, would show up still more effectively beside all that face powder and elegance.[2]

The "man with the hoe" to which van Gogh refers is the eponymous painting by Jean-François Millet (fig. 110b). That work, which depicts an unnamed peasant leaning wearily on his hoe, was notorious in its day for its lack of idealization, *laideur* (ugliness), and supposed social criticism. Van Gogh thought his own peasant would be perceived equally crude and confrontational.

The Toulouse-Lautrec painting cited by van Gogh is *Poudre de riz* (fig. 110c), and it is interesting to place it next to *Portrait of a Peasant* (fig. 110d). The comparison reveals the experimental character of each artist's work. Van Gogh and Toulouse-Lautrec painted portraits of working people and invented new ways of conveying expression and social class. *Poudre de riz* is composed of small and discrete daubs, strokes, and hatches of color, dominated by closely valued white, gray, brown, and lilac. The tone and surface suggest face powder and the low, artificial glow of gas lamps. *Portrait of a Peasant*, in contrast, is painted with long, broad strokes of high-keyed orange, yellow, red, green, and turquoise. Complementary color subsumes adjacent color, and tonal difference is smothered by intense light and heat. In the letter cited above, van Gogh added:

> Again, in the portrait of the peasant I worked [as an] . . . arbitrary colorist. . . . I imagine the man I have to

> paint, terrible in the furnace of the height of harvest time, as surrounded by the whole Midi. Hence the orange colors flashing like lightning, vivid as red-hot iron, and hence the luminous tones of old gold in the shadows. Oh, my dear boy . . . and the nice people will only see the exaggeration as a caricature.[3]

The warm colors, van Gogh asserts, convey the atmosphere of August in Provence; the tanned skin tells of long years and hard toil beneath a southern sun. Of course, van Gogh knew that Monsieur Escalier was not now a peasant—he was formerly a goatherd from the Camarge, now turned gardener, or *journalier.* But he wished to invoke the peasant, a social type of great significance in French and European culture and politics. Two years later, van Gogh wrote to his sister Wilhelmina:

> I *should like* to paint portraits which would appear after a century to the people living then as apparitions. By which I mean that I do not endeavor to achieve this by a photographic resemblance, but by means of our impassioned expressions—that is to say, using our knowledge of color as a means of arriving at the expression and the intensification of character.[4]

Portrait of a Peasant (Patience Escalier) thus served two functions for van Gogh: it was at once a Realist representation of a peasant and an abstraction, that is, an interrogation of character by means of abstract form and color. Until his early death, van Gogh continued to believe he could reconcile these seemingly opposed definitions of modern art.

1 Van Gogh, 1958, vol. 3, no. 572.
2 Van Gogh, 1958, vol. 3, no. 520.
3 Van Gogh, 1958, vol. 3, no. 520.
4 Van Gogh, 1958, vol. 3, no. W22.

111

Vincent van Gogh
Dutch, 1853–1890

Portrait of the Artist's Mother
October 1888

Oil on canvas, 16 × 12¾ in. (40.7 × 32.3 cm)
M.1968.32

Provenance: [Ambroise Vollard, Paris]. Ann Rosenberg, Paris. E. Druet, Paris, sold October 1904 to; [Paul Cassirer, Berlin, sold May 1905 to]; Carl Moll (1861–1945), Vienna, by 1906–at least 1914. [Paul Rosenberg, Paris, by 1928]. Reverend Theodore Pitcairn, Bryn Athyn, Pa., by 1938 (sale, London, Christie's, 28 June 1968, lot 112, to); Norton Simon Art Foundation.

Exhibitions: Paris, 1901a, no. 20; Possibly Vienna, 1906, no. 34, as *Frau*; Vienna, 1909, no. 7, as *Frauenkopf*; Berlin, 1914a, no. 73; Vienna, 1925, no. 74; Dresden, 1926, no. 212; Paris, 1937, no. 87, pp. 29–30, ill.; New York, 1943b, no. 33, pp. 28, 74, ill.; Philadelphia, 1960; on loan, Portland, Oreg. Art Museum, 25 September 1968–21 April 1969; Berkeley, 1970, no. 302; Princeton, 1972, no. 33, p. 104, color ill.; San Francisco, 1974, no. 46, p. 106, ill.

References: Coquiot, 1923, p. 313; Faille, 1928, vol. 1, no. F477, p. 136, vol. 2, no. 477, pl. CXXX; Scherjon and de Gruyter, 1937, no. 104, p. 133; Huyghe, 1937, pp. 29–30, ill.; Faille, 1939, no. H502, p. 357, ill.; Wildenstein & Co., 1947, no. 33; Munich, 1956, p. 35, ill.; Elgar, 1958, no. 146; van Gogh, 1958, vol. 3, nos. 546, 548; Tralbaut, 1959, p. 13; Wallace, 1969, p. 8; Faille, 1970, no. F477, pp. 216–217; Steadman, 1972, p. 38, fig. 12; Steadman, 1973a, p. 12, ill.; Glynn, 1973, p. 89; Cornini, 1974, pp. 38, 200, fig. 45; Treble, 1975, p. 85, pl. 66; Steadman, 1976, p. 223; Lecaldano, 1977, vol. 2, no. 584, pp. 213–214; Fagles, 1978, pp. 54–55; Hulsker, 1977, no. 1600, pp. 368, 369; P. Wilson, 1981, p. 20; B. Bernard, 1985, p. 189; P. Sutton, 1986, p. 220, fig. 320; Crosman, 1988, p. 21; Feilchenfeldt, 1988, no. F477, pp. 19, 98; Gedo, 1989, pp. 136, ill., 137; Palmer, 1990, pp. 72–74, ill. 72; van Lindert and van Uitert, 1990b, p. 83, fig. 67; Arnold, 1995, pp. 152–154, 865, fig. 70; K. Sachs, 2000, pp. 130, 131, fig. 118; Druick and Zegers, 2001, pp. 200–203, fig. 62, color ill.; Goldin, 2002, p. 382, ill.; Feilchenfeldt, 2006, pp. 57–58, ill., 295–296, ill., 304, no. 13.

Technical Notes: The original support is a plain-weave, medium-weight canvas that has been lined with an aqueous adhesive to another fabric. Original tacking edges have been removed, but some scalloping is visible along the perimeter. The ground is creamy in color and fairly thin so that the crowns of the weave are bare. Van Gogh underpainted with thin applications of dark green for the background and red-gray for the dress, and it appears the flesh was laid in first with a reddish brown paint. The thick surface paint shows varied applications. Several sizes of brushes were used and strokes range from short to long. Brushstrokes follow form, and in the background brushstrokes created a grid pattern. At the figure's jaw the brush was quickly picked up from the thick paint to leave a ridge of thin impasto that scallops back over the initial stroke. Van Gogh applied a darker green at the brows and other features and then modeled up the flesh with light green paint. Under magnification crimson particles are visible on or in the flesh paint; perhaps this is a lake that has faded. Along the edge of the face there is a light grayish red line of thick paint applied over the green background. The crimson colors of the lips and the bonnet are set on a base of white paint. The thinly applied rich paint of the dress applied wet in wet so that the strokes follow form probably contains mostly a crimson lake and Prussian blue. The condition of the painting is good though impasto is slightly flattened. A fairly large crackle pattern exists in the paint and ground. The painting was cleaned in 1980 and revarnished with Acryloid B67 and B72. (JF)

The origin and progress of van Gogh's *Portrait of the Artist's Mother* may be gleaned from letters sent to his siblings Wilhelmina and Theo van Gogh. On about 8 September 1888 he wrote his sister: "I shall be very happy to have the picture of mother you speak of, so don't forget to send it."[1] A few days later, he wrote to Theo that he had received the picture (fig. 111a) and it "gave me great pleasure, because you can see that she is well, and because she still has such a lively expression." Van Gogh then compared it to his own most recent self-portrait (fig. 111b):

> But I do not care for it at all as a real likeness; I have just painted my own portrait, in my own ashen color, and unless we are painted in color, the result is nowhere near a speaking likeness. Just because I have taken a terrific amount of trouble to get the combination of ashen and gray-pink tones, I could not like the portrait in black and white. Would Germinie Lacerteux [the title of the Realist novel of 1864 by Jules and Edmond de Goncourt] really be Germinie Lacerteaux without her color? Obviously not. How I would like to have painted portraits of our own family.[2]

A month later, he informed Theo: "I am doing a portrait of Mother for myself. I cannot stand the colorless photograph, and I am trying to do one in a harmony of color, as I see her in my memory."[3] A few days later he again reported:

> I am working on a portrait of Mother, because the black-and-white photograph annoys me so. Ah, what portraits could be made from nature with photography and painting! I always hope that we are still to have a great revolution in portraiture. . . . the picture of

Mother, a size 8 canvas, will be ashen gray against a green background, the dress *carmine.* I do not know if it will be like her, but anyhow I want to give the impression of a blonde coloring. You will see it one day, and if you like, I will make one for you too. It will again be in a very thick impasto.[4]

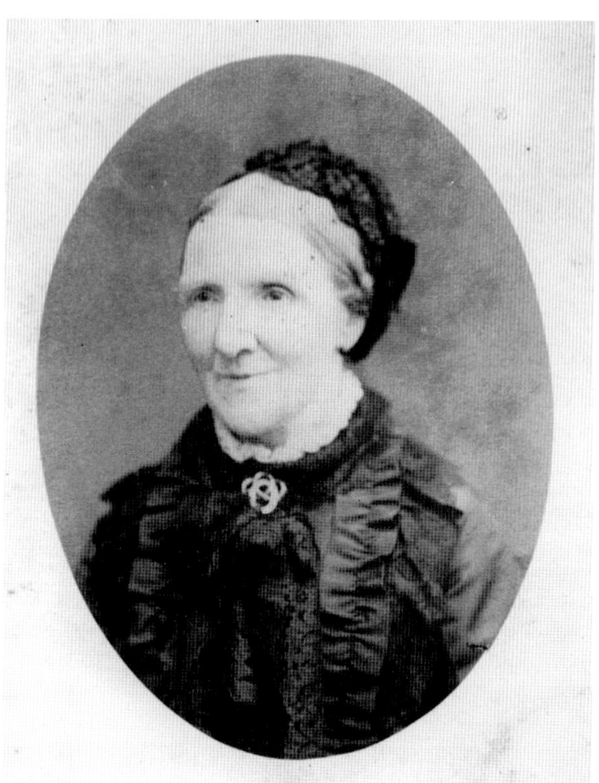

Fig. 111a Vincent van Gogh, *Anna Cornelia van Gogh-Carbentus, Vincent van Gogh's Mother,* 1888, photograph taken by Lavieter & Co., The Hague, Van Gogh Museum (Vincent van Gogh Foundation), Amsterdam

Finally, in mid-November, he confessed to Wilhelmina that "I don't like Mother's picture enormously."[5]

The sequence of letters indicates the shared origins of the great *Self-Portrait Dedicated to Paul Gauguin* (fig. 111b) and *Portrait of the Artist's Mother.* Each required a certain amount of melancholy self-examination and self-revelation, each shared a basic format, and each was part of a projected ensemble of family portraits. But whereas the first painting—judging from the artist's own comments and the verdict of posterity—was a great success, the second is something of a failure. *Portrait of the Artist's Mother* is not "a speaking likeness" but instead invariably reminds us of the black-and-white photograph from which it was derived. The photograph of the artist's mother generally associated with the painting is, in fact, reversed from it and there are numerous slight differences between the hats or headdresses between photograph and painting. It is actually possible that van Gogh had another photograph of his mother made at the same sitting. In the painting, van Gogh's mother's eyes are fixed in a lifeless gaze and her mouth is sealed shut. The gray-green skin color is nearly cadaverous, though some of this is the consequence of the fading of a fugitive red pigment on the surface layer of the paint. (The character of the change is visible on the bottom $\frac{3}{4}$-inch of the canvas, originally covered by the frame and now more vivid than the brown-carmine above.) Nevertheless, it is clear that van Gogh was inhibited in the painting of his mother. Fearing to manipulate or disturb the face and expression of his beloved (and sometimes feared) mother, van Gogh paid excessive deference to a photograph. The mother he "remembered" became an upright effigy of bourgeois propriety.

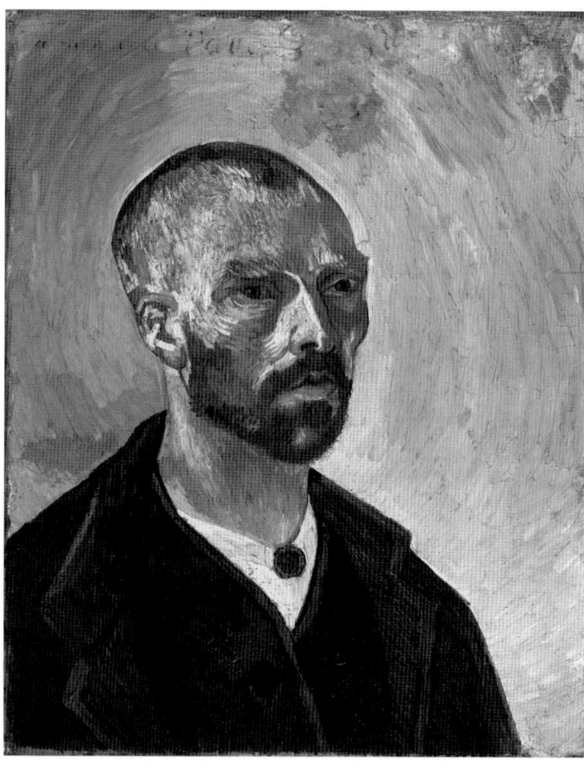

Fig. 111b Vincent van Gogh, *Self-Portrait Dedicated to Paul Gauguin,* 1888, oil on canvas, 24 × 19⅝ in. (61 × 50 cm), Fogg Art Museum, Harvard University Art Museums, Bequest from the Collection of Maurice Wertheim, Class of 1906

1 Van Gogh, 1958, vol. 3, no. W7.
2 Van Gogh, 1958, vol. 3, no. 540.
3 Van Gogh, 1958, vol. 3, no. 546.
4 Van Gogh, 1958, vol. 3, no. 548.
5 Van Gogh, 1958, vol. 3, no. W9.

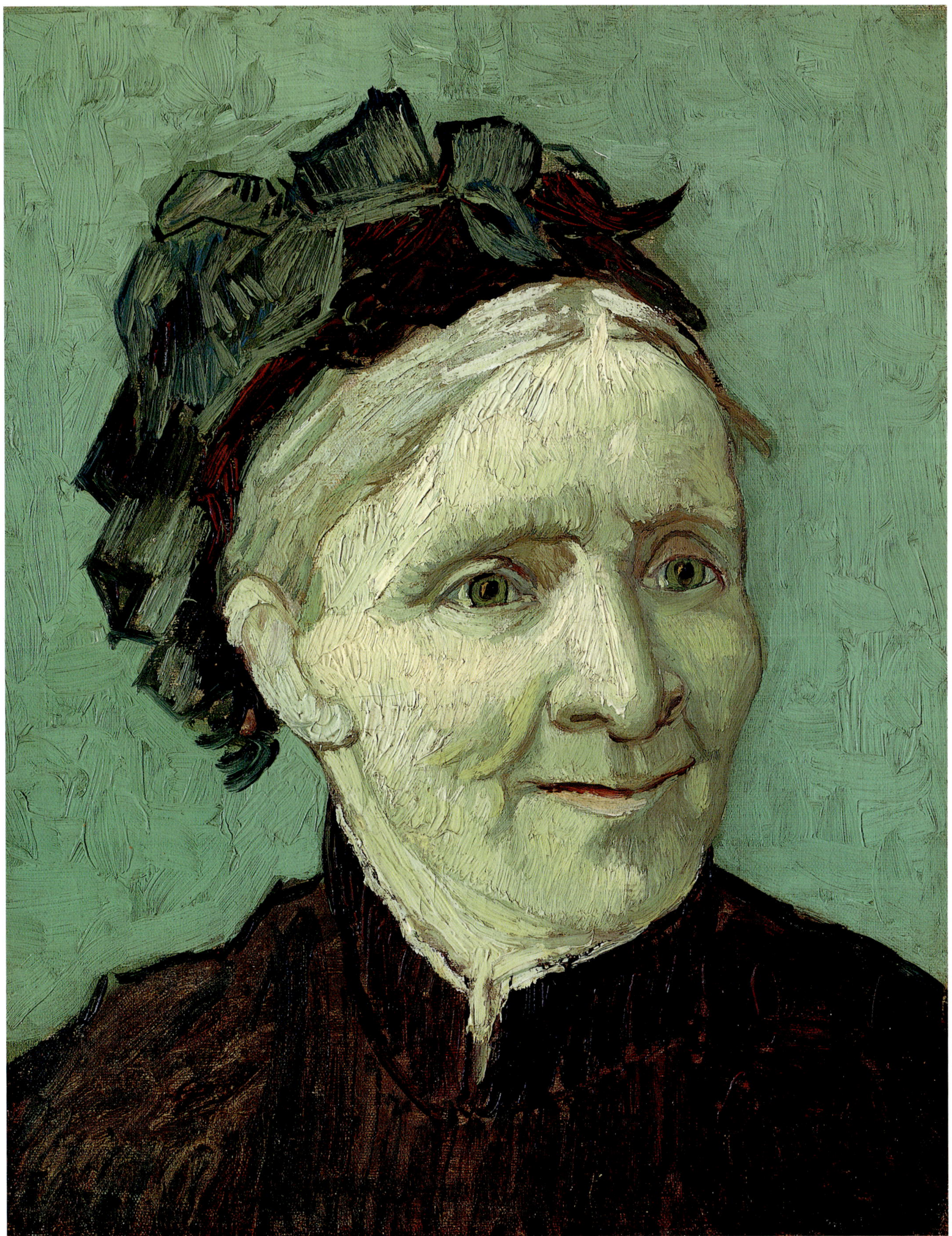

III

112

Vincent van Gogh
Dutch, 1853–1890

The Mulberry Tree
October 1889

Oil on canvas, $21\frac{1}{4} \times 25\frac{1}{2}$ in. (54×65 cm)
M.1976.9

Provenance: Camille Pissarro, Paris, by 1890, by inheritance to; Mme C. Pissarro, Paris; [Ambroise Vollard, Paris]. Alphonse Kann (1870–1948), Saint-Germain-en-Laye, by 1928, still in 1934, presumably inherited by; Michael Stewart, London.[1] [David Gibbs, London, sold 19 October 1961 to]; [Marlborough Fine Art, Ltd., London, sold 12 November 1961 to]; Norton Simon, gift 1976 to; Norton Simon Art Foundation.

Exhibitions: Paris, 1901a, no. 46; Paris, 1927; Paris, 1934a, no. 147, as *Olivier près Arles*; Los Angeles, 1965; San Francisco, 1973, no. 46, ill.; on loan, South Bend, Ind., University of Notre Dame, Snite Museum of Art, October 1980–August 1981.

References: Coquiot, 1923, p. 317; Faille, 1927, pp. 130, 107, ill.; Faille, 1928, vol. 1, no. 637, vol. 2, no. 637, pl. CLXXX; Scherjon and de Gruyter, 1937, no. 53, p. 247, ill.; Faille, 1939, no. 640/F637, p. 441, ill.; Faille, 1970, no. F637, pp. 636, 255, ill.; Lecaldano, 1977, vol. 2, no. 713, p. 223, ill.; van Gogh, 1958, vol. 3, nos. 609, 618, W16; Hulsker, 1977, no. 1796, p. 414, ill.; Johnson, 1979, pp. 98–99, fig. 2; Bailly-Herzberg, 1980, p. 65; B. Bernard, 1985, pp. 207, color ill. 282–283; Pickvance, 1986, p. 317, ill.; S. Stein, 1986, pp. 233, 260, 305, pl. 98; P. Sutton, 1986, p. 220; W. Wilson, 1987, pp. 90–91; Palmer, 1990, pp. 72–74, ill. 73; Arnold, 1995, pp. 700, 866, fig. 370.

Technical Notes: This luminous painting appears to be in or close to its original state, unlined and possibly never cleaned. The support is composed of two layers of fine, plain-weave canvas, tacked together and glued to the sides and back of the stretcher. X-radiographs reveal a second set of tacks below the tacking edge of the upper canvas. The absence of extra tack holes, the age and condition of the present tacks, and the absence of any disturbance at the edges of the thin gesso ground layer seem to indicate that the present double-canvas support is the original structure. The smooth ground layer is pale beige and extraordinarily thin. A cream-colored second ground or underpainting, painted in an opaque medium, provides greater luminosity and may have been intended to counter an absorbent ground. The painting, composed of energetic strokes of rich paint, employs quick, straight strokes in the sky and vigorous, descriptive brushwork in the tree. The paint is often layered with one color on top of another. The swirls of color are unblended, with several colors in a single brushstroke. In a few areas, a bit of the underlayer remains exposed. The profile of the impasto varies from delicate threadlike points to areas that appear to have been smoothed or flattened slightly, probably when the painting was stacked against another before it was dry. Restoration has been minimal, addressing only a small amount of flaking on three different occasions. There is no record of the painting having been cleaned, and in fact the present surface coating has the characteristics of aged egg white. Ultraviolet light produces no fluorescence. (RW)

On 24 August 1890, some four weeks after his brother's death by suicide in the town of Auvers, Theo van Gogh wrote to console his mother and sister: "Proofs of friendship and admiration of [Vincent's] talent and character are still coming in. [Camille] Pissarro . . . immediately wanted to exchange against a painting that pleased him . . . a mulberry tree golden yellow in the autumn against a blue sky."[2] Pissarro did acquire the painting, and it is easy to understand why. *The Mulberry Tree* is one of the most successful paintings van Gogh made at Arles and belongs to a pictorial and iconographic tradition that includes works by Pissarro himself. In acquiring the picture, the elderly artist was at once testifying to his affinity to Vincent van Gogh and providing an art historical evaluation of his work.

Drawings and paintings of single trees have long been staples of artistic education and practice. Leonardo da Vinci was sufficiently concerned with the challenge of representing trees to devise a theory, largely validated by recent research, that "all the branches of a tree at every stage of its height when put together are equal in thickness to the trunk."[3] Other artists were less empirical in their approach to nature and more concerned with the unique, expressive physiognomy of trees. Rembrandt, Jacob van Ruisdael, Meindert Hobbema, and other seventeenth-century Dutch artists made single trees or small groups of trees important foci of their expansive landscape compositions. In the late eighteenth century, the English artist Alexander Cozens, taking a lesson from Leonardo, invented a method for composing "beautiful" (serene) and "sublime" (awe-inspiring) forested landscapes by using two sheets of paper, India ink, and blots. But it was during the mid–nineteenth century, and especially in France, that depictions of single trees took on significance as symbols of national character, personal autonomy, and even radical republicanism.

At a time in France when political speech was often proscribed by law, the depiction of nature served as a vehicle for public debate about the relation of city and country, national versus local authority, and individual versus communal responsibility. And because of the inevitable comparison to heroic human figures, isolated

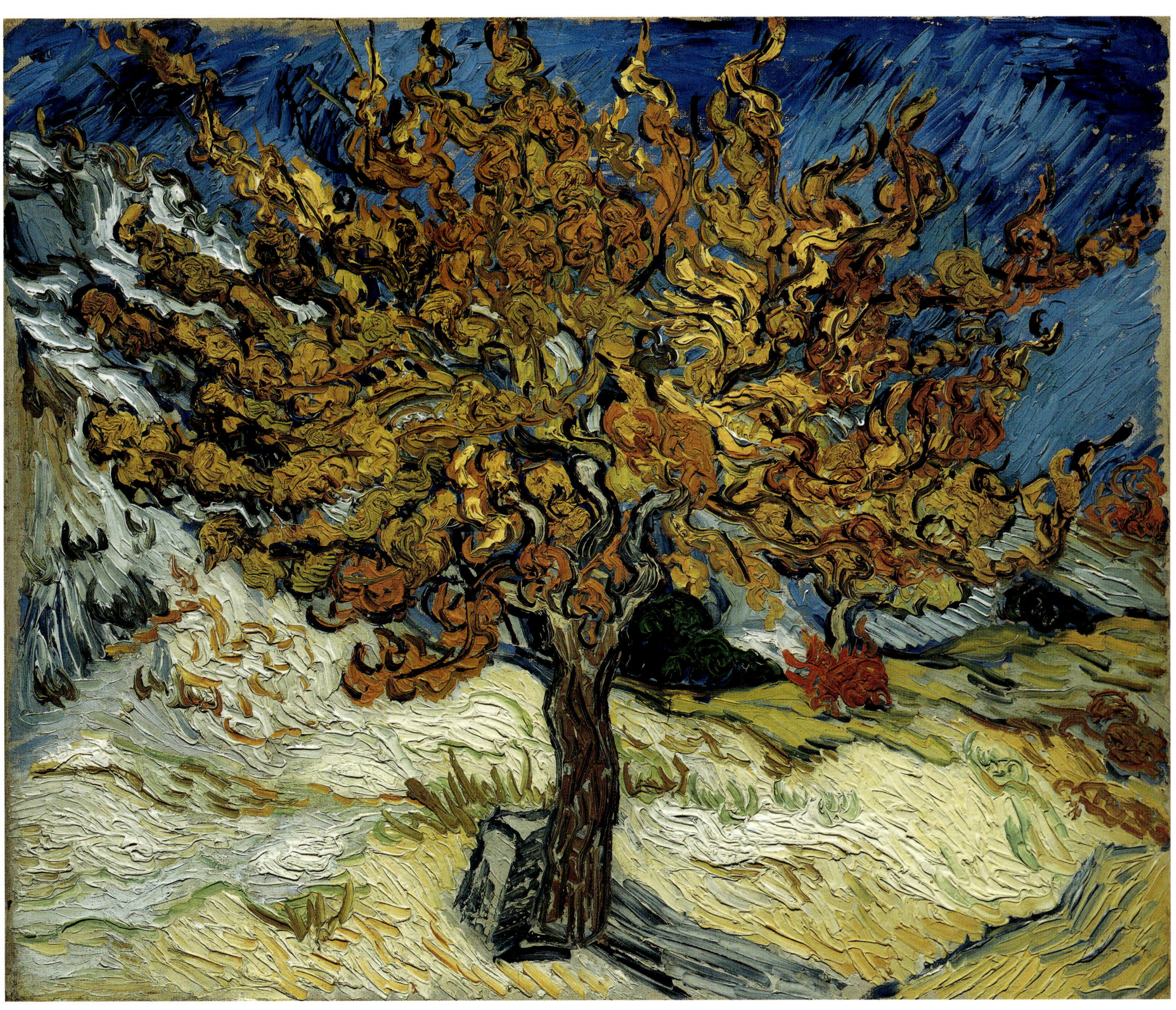

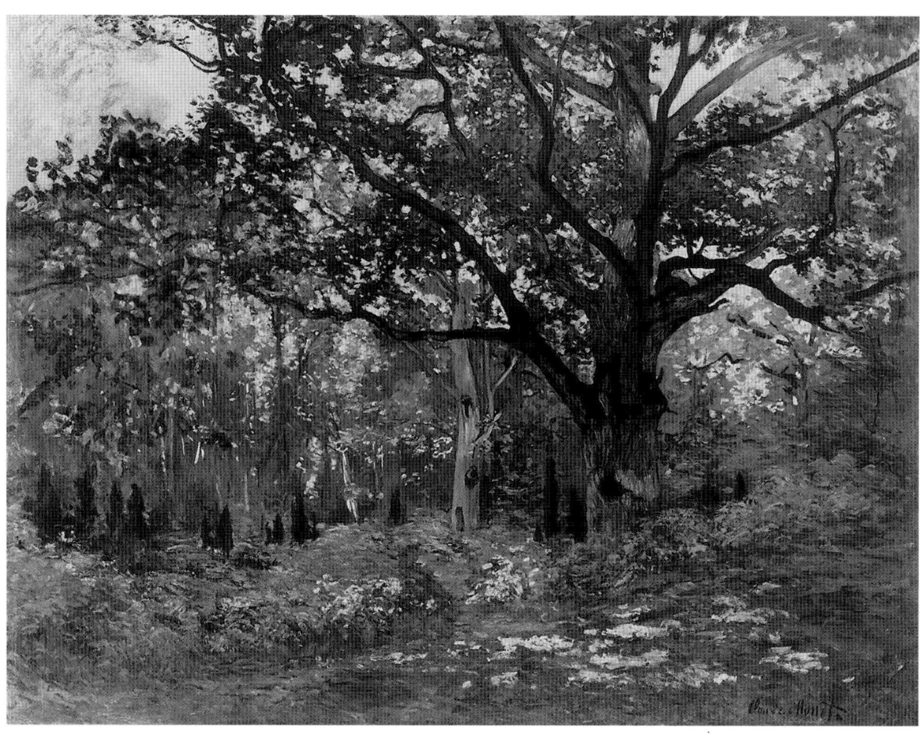

Fig. 112a Claude Monet, *The Bodmer Oak, Fontainebleau Forest*, 1865, oil on canvas, $37\frac{7}{8} \times 50\frac{7}{8}$ in. (96.2 × 129.2 cm), The Metropolitan Museum of Art, Gift of Sam Salz and Bequest of Julia W. Emmons, by exchange, 1964

trees were especially embraced as subjects by artists who wished to trumpet their independence from state cultural and artistic authorities. Théodore Rousseau's *An Old Oak near Fontainebleau* (c. 1852, Mesdag Museum, The Hague), Gustave Courbet's *The Oak at Flagey* (1864, Murauchi Museum of Art, Tokyo), and Claude Monet's *The Bodmer Oak, Fontainebleau Forest* (fig. 112a) all roused democratic sentiments and were likely have been known to both Pissarro and van Gogh. Therefore, when Pissarro saw van Gogh's *Mulberry Tree*—electric, palpable, dynamic—he knew that a great pictorial tradition was being revived.

The mulberry tree nearly fills its small canvas. The yellows, greens, and tan of the tree canopy are made with thick loops and swirls of paint creating peaks and valleys, like those seen on a pie or cake topped with meringue or frosting. The gray-brown tree trunk is flatter and the paint strokes more vertical than those that describe the leaves and branches. The land and sky are more thinly painted than the tree—underpainting is visible between some of the brushstrokes—giving it great physical presence, like a tapestry with gold and silver threads or a sculpted bas-relief. By virtue of this tactility and dynamism, *The Mulberry Tree* seems to possess a physiognomy and to project expression, chiefly ecstasy and independence. Indeed, the picture was interpreted by at least one attentive viewer as an image of the miracle of the burning bush from the book of Genesis.[4] In a letter written by Pissarro's grandson Paulémile to the great historian of Impressionism, John Rewald, he recalled some works owned by his parents: "We had several van Gogh's at Eragny: I often think of a small canvas representing a tree in Autumn which had the feeling of flames. I have never seen it reproduced . . . I wonder in what collection it can now be found?"[5] The accompanying crayon drawing showed *The Mulberry Tree* with orange and yellow flames in place of leaves and branches and flames engulfing the base of the trunk. Almost seven decades separated the painting from the letter, but the ecstatic impression the painting made was still vivid; *The Mulberry Tree* remains one of the artist's most compelling and visionary images.

1 Dr. Madeleine Korn has uncovered numerous Kann paintings inherited by Michael Stewart ("Alphonse Kann and Michael Stewart," International Provenance Research Colloquium, sponsored by the American Association of Museums, Washington, D.C., 15–16 November 2004).
2 S. Stein, 1986, p. 233.
3 J. P. Richter, *The Literary Works of Leonardo da Vinci*, London, 1939, vol. 1, fig. 1.
4 Johnson, 1979, pp. 98–99.
5 Letter, 18 November 1961, Norton Simon Museum curatorial files.

113

Georges-Pierre Seurat
French, 1859–1891

Angelica at the Rock (after Ingres)
1878

Oil on canvas, $32\frac{5}{8} \times 26\frac{1}{8}$ in. (83 × 66.2 cm)
M.1997.1.4

Provenance: Léon Appert (1837–1925, brother-in-law of artist), Paris, by descent to; Léopold Appert, Paris. ?Charles Hall Thorndyke (1875–1935). [Étienne Bignou, Paris]. Alphonse Bellier, Paris. [Jos Hessel, Paris, sold March 1930 to]; [Alex. Reid & Lefevre, London, stock no. 469/29, sold 20 February 1933 to]; [Étienne Bignou, Paris]. Private collection, England, by 1961–still in 1972. [Wildenstein & Co., Inc., New York, by 1976, sold 9 April 1982 to]; Norton Simon, bequest 1993 to; Jennifer Jones Simon Art Trust, gift 1997 to; Norton Simon Art Foundation.

Exhibitions: Glasgow, 1930, no. 21; London, 1930, no. 19, ill., as *Andromède*; Paris, 1936a, no. 1 bis, as *Andromède au rocher*; Norton, 1976, no. 54.

References: *Artwork*, 1930, p. 180, ill.; Rewald, 1943, pp. 2, 4, fig. 5 (French ed., 1948, p. 22, fig. 3); Cooper, 1946, p. 10; T. Hess, 1953, p. 172, ill.; Bonnet, 1957, p. 8; Rewald and Dorra, 1959, no. 1, fig. 1; de Hauke, 1961, vol. 1, no. 1, pp. 2–3, 262, ill.; Galeries nationales du Petit Palais, 1967, under no. 108; Courthion, 1968, pp. 13–14; Foucart, 1968, under no. 79; Chastel and Minervino, 1972, no. 1, p. 91, ill.; Galeries nationales de Grand Palais, 1974, under no. 107; R. Thomson, 1985, pp. 18, 227 n. 31; Rewald, 1990, pp. 18, 16, ill.; Grenier, 1990, no. 1, p. 16, ill.; Distel, 1991, pp. 6, 32, fig. 2; Herbert, 1991, under no. 8; M. Zimmermann, 1991, pp. 27–28, fig. 39; Düchting, 2000, pp. 10–11.

Technical Notes: The support is a medium- to lightweight, plain-weave canvas that has been lined. The edges may have been extended slightly on all four sides. Information about the original tacking edges is inaccessible. Using information from the X-radiograph, several damages to the canvas can be located as follows: three small losses at the upper right corner, a hole in the figure's lower abdomen, a hole or tear at the lower left, a vertical tear at the lower left in the rock, and a small hole at center left. A horizontal crack at the right center has raised edges, and a small vertical crack at the upper left also has raised edges. In other respects, the lining appears to be uniformly well attached. The painting is tacked to a keyed stretcher with a double crossbar; it may well be the original stretcher. The smooth, ivory ground is fairly thin, leaving the canvas texture evident. Seurat apparently drew his copy directly on the ground layer. Some traces of the preparatory drawing of the figure remain visible around the proper right foot, the left ankle and foot, the hands, and the facial features. The background was painted quickly and loosely in liquid, translucent paint, with sketchy contours. Angelica's hair is a secondary feature with almost no detail or descriptive brushwork. The figure is more controlled, brushed in thicker, more opaque paint. Some slight brush marking is in the arms, fingers, and forward leg. The sketchlike execution of the painting leaves the ground partially exposed in some areas such as the rock. Apart from the above-mentioned damages, which have been liberally retouched, the paint is generally in good condition, with little or no abrasion. The natural resin varnish is moderately yellowed. Ultraviolet light indicates that the varnish was removed from the figure in a previous treatment. (RW)

Georges Seurat was one of the most original and audacious artists of the nineteenth century, but his career began quite conventionally. Born in Paris, in 1875 he entered a municipal art school run by the Neoclassical sculptor Justin Lequien. There he copied from prints, drawings, and plaster casts of ancient Greek and Roman sculpture. According to the later testimony of his lifelong friend, the painter Aman-Jean (Amand-Edmond Jean), Seurat also admired and copied works by Jean-Auguste-Dominique Ingres. His Ingresque drawing *Young Woman*[1] and his drawing after *La Source* by Ingres[2] date from this time. The drawings are dominated by their strong contours, but in each case there is also the suggestion that the forms are extensions of the space that surrounds them. This attention to ambience and atmosphere—a kind of pictorial relativity—would become a distinguishing feature of the style of the mature draftsman and painter.

Three years later, in 1878, Seurat gained admittance to the prestigious École des Beaux-Arts and entered the atelier of Henri Lehmann, an accomplished, if conservative, painter and academic taskmaster who had studied with Ingres and taught Pissarro. During Seurat's eighteen months at the École, he toiled in the approved manner, though generally without enthusiasm and with a growing desire for alternative artistic models and methods. As he had at the atelier of Lequien, Seurat made drawings after plaster casts, copied prints, drawings, and paintings from approved Renaissance and Baroque masters including Raphael, Michelangelo, and Pontormo, and drew male and female nude models. He also carefully read Charles Blanc's long treatise on composition, color, expression, and harmony, the *Grammaire des arts du dessin*, then in its third edition (1876). And once again, the example of Ingres loomed before him. Now, however, his attraction must have been tainted by a measure of antagonism. Paintings by the archclassicist possessed a clarity and harmony that the young man likely saw as the

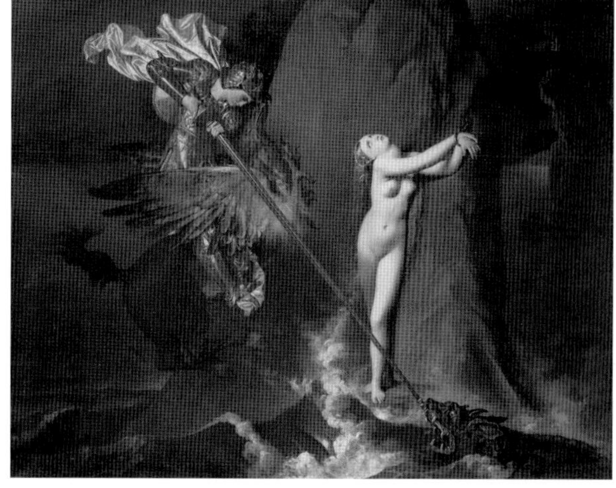

Fig. 113a Jean-Auguste-Dominique Ingres, *Roger Delivering Angelica*, 1819, oil on canvas, 57⅞ × 74¾ in. (147 × 190 cm), Musée du Louvre, Paris; photo: Erich Lessing / Art Resource, NY

very goal of art, but they also represented École pedagogy and an academic discipline that shackled his vision and imagination. Seurat would thus use the example of Ingres to develop an artistic style that depicted people and things both in their concrete isolation and in continuity with their surroundings.

Seurat's surviving works from this period at the École consist mostly of drawings. Of these, at least thirteen are copies after Ingres. His only oil painting from these years, *Angelica at the Rock*, was also copied from Ingres. It was most likely made in 1878 when the artist was about eighteen years old, and it bears no hints of the Neo-Impressionist style that would become Seurat's hallmark. Indeed, it is an apparently routine product of École instruction, copied from a single figure in a celebrated painting of 1819 by Ingres, *Roger Delivering Angelica* (fig. 113a), which was transferred from the Musée Luxembourg to the Louvre in 1878, the year Seurat made his copy.[3] Although Ingres also painted at least two single-figure studies of Angelica, one now in the Louvre, neither of these was accessible to the young Seurat in 1878 because each was in private collections. This is also true of the two later autograph variants of the subject, the earlier of which, now in the National Gallery, London, was later to be one of the gems of the private collection of Edgar Degas, who bought it in 1894.[4] In making his copy, Seurat omitted the gallant Roger, his hippogryph and lance, the fearsome dragon, the jagged rocks and breaking waves, and any other dramatic detail from this well-known episode in Ariosto's *Orlando furioso*. (Though little read today, *Orlando* was widely popular in the nineteenth century. In 1879, a year after Seurat painted his *Angelica*, a new French edition of the epic was published, containing more than six hundred illustrations by Gustave Doré. In 1892, a year after the artist's death, Émile Bernard began a massive project to illustrate *Orlando*.)

Seurat's *Angelica* lacks both the vividness of hue and the linear precision of Ingres's original. It is painted almost entirely in shades of brown and gray—essentially an exercise in grisaille—and resembles a sculpture in relief more than a finished painting. The dark tone constituting the figure's contour carves a shallow, indefinite niche in the featureless rock; Angelica thus seems to create her own space from a single plane, thereby conveying a unity of volume and mass. This clarity and compositional authority mark a significant early achievement for Seurat, but it does not make the painting itself a notable success. Anatomical and narrative credibility is strained to the breaking point in the work. Angelica's body is compressed between the top and bottom framing edges of the canvas, creating an awkwardness that exceeds even that in Ingres's own strange versions of the subject. It is almost as if Seurat

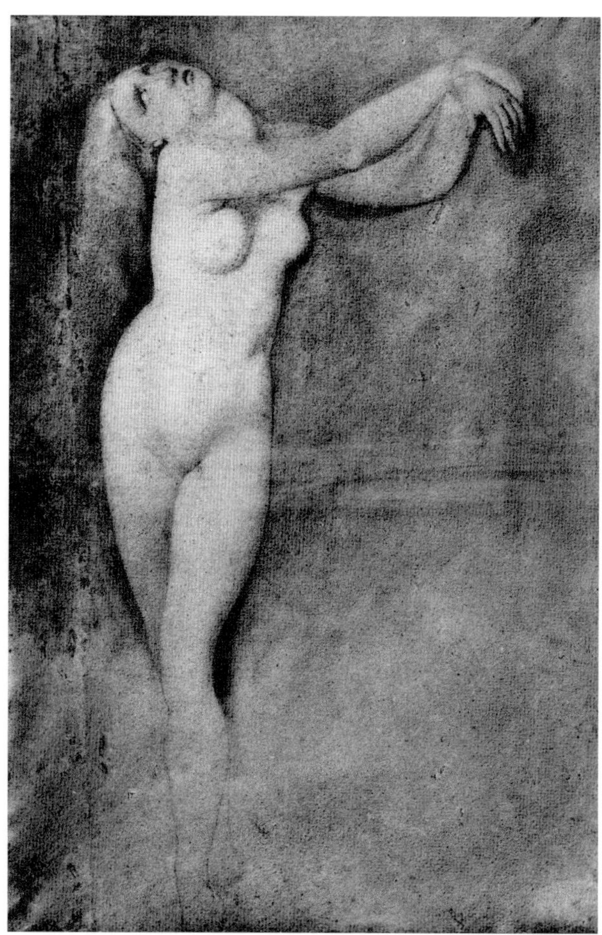

Fig. 113b Georges-Pierre Seurat, *Angelica at the Rock (after Ingres)*, 1878, black lead on paper, 16$^{15}/_{16}$ × 11 in. (43 × 28 cm), location unknown; photo: de Hauke, 1961, no. 315

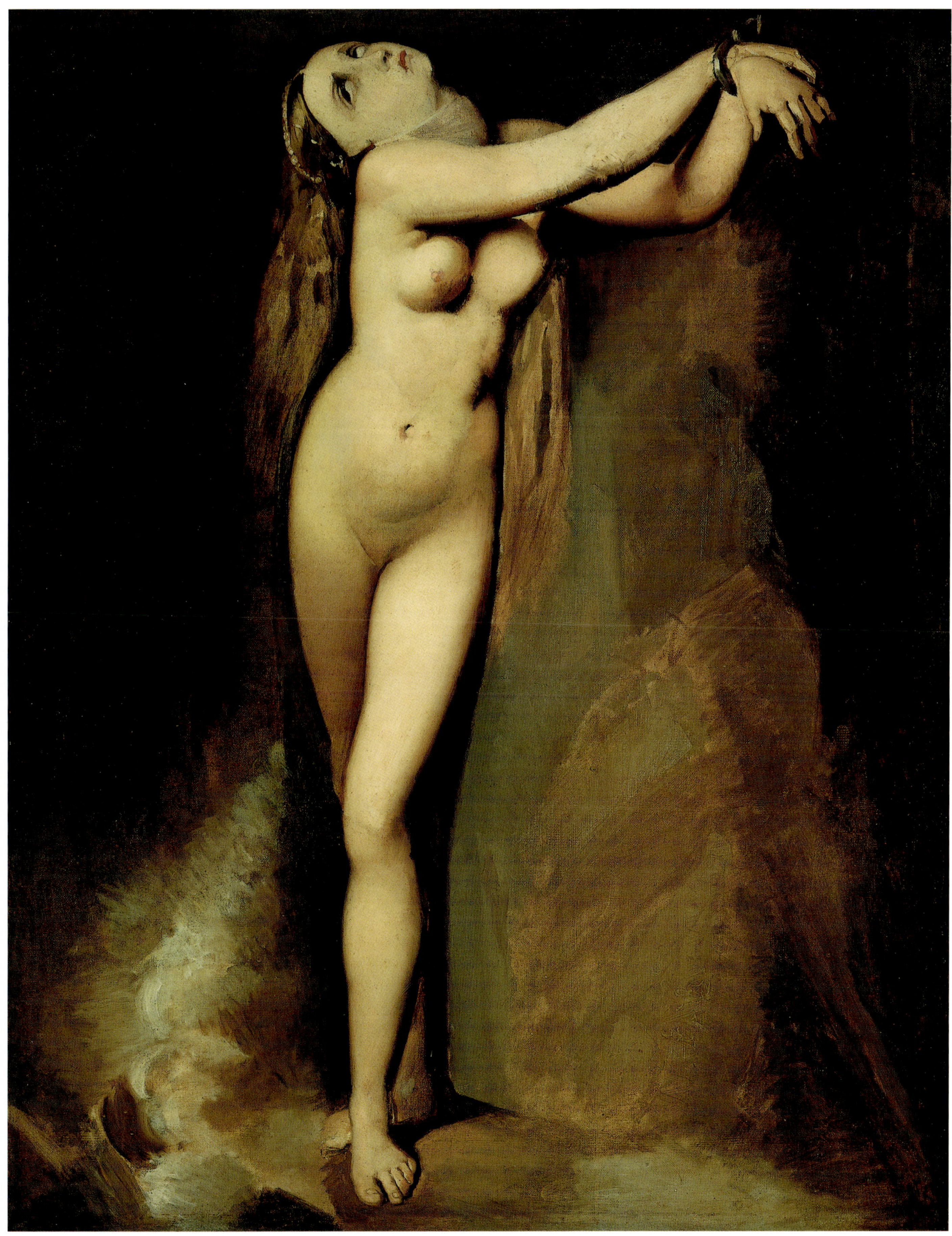

113

had begun his painting at the bottom and, reaching the top, found he had too little room left for the shoulders, neck, and head. Thus Ingres's anatomical distortions—justified by his desire to represent Angelica's intense feelings of pain and anguish—appear simply arbitrary and perverse in Seurat's painting. Seurat's smaller, preparatory drawing of Angelica (fig. 113b) affords the figure a bit more space and is consequently less awkward.

If *Angelica at the Rock* is not an entirely successful copy of a celebrated Neoclassical masterpiece, it marks a step in Seurat's deepening understanding of tone, modeling, volume, and composition. This knowledge would culminate a few years later in the invention of completely new styles of both drawing and painting. In his drawings for *Bathers at Asnières* (1884, National Gallery, London), such as *Seated Boy, Nude* (National Gallery of Scotland, Edinburgh), Seurat essentially eliminated line in favor of an overall tonalism and a continuity of figure and ground that render the one merely an aspect of the other. In the finished painting, the uniformity of touch, evenness of light, and balance of colors make the deep pictorial space consistent with the two-dimensionality of the canvas surface. The light umbra that surrounds the seated boy in the center of the canvas persuades us that he creates his own space, rather than occupies a preexisting one. This is precisely the effect first suggested in the Norton Simon *Angelica at the Rock.* It would appear again—now fully developed—in his mature divisionist canvases, including *Sunday Afternoon on the Island of La Grande Jatte* (The Art Institute of Chicago) and *La Parade* (The Metropolitan Museum of Art, New York).

1 De Hauke, 1961, no. 236.
2 De Hauke, 1961, no. 313.
3 G. Wildenstein, 1956, no. 124, p. 186.
4 G. Wildenstein, 1956, nos. 124, 125, 126, 127, 127 bis, 227, and 233, pp. 186–189, 210, 212.

114

Georges-Pierre Seurat
French, 1859–1891

The Stone Breakers, Le Raincy
c. 1882

Oil on canvas, 14¾ × 17⅞ in. (37.5 × 45.5 cm)
M.1968.28

Provenance: Léon Appert (1837–1925, brother-in-law of artist), Paris, by descent to; Léopold Appert, Paris, by descent to; Mme Vve Léopold Appert, Paris. ?Jacques and Pierre Puybonnieux, Paris, in 1934–still in 1952?. Private collection, Paris, in 1958. [Stephen Hahn Gallery, New York, 4 September 1968 to]; Norton Simon Art Foundation.

Exhibitions: Paris, 1908b, no. 34; Paris, 1957, no. 21; Philadelphia, 1969, no. 13; Princeton, 1972, no. 31, ill.; San Francisco, 1974, no. 47, ill.

References: Laprade, 1945, ill. p. 3; Laprade, 1952?, pp. 10, 94; Rich and Herbert, 1958, pp. 12, 27; Rewald and Dorra, 1959, no. 21; Herbert, 1959, p. 24 n. 4; de Hauke, 1961, vol. 1, no. 38, pp. 22–23, ill.; Courthion, 1968, p. 21; Chastel and Minervino, 1972, no. 39, pp. 93–94; Steadman, 1972, p. 37, fig. 10; Steadman, 1973b, no. 57; Alexandrian, 1980, p. 13, ill.; Rewald, 1990, p. 34, ill.; Grenier, 1990, p. 37, ill. no. 40; Distel, 1991, no. 8, p. 150, ill.; Herbert, 1991, under cat. 20, p. 38, ill.; M. Zimmermann, 1991, pp. 14, fig. 135 (detail), 92.

Technical Notes: The original support is a plain-weave canvas of fairly open weave. Remnants of the tacking edges indicate the fabric was weak and fragile; the corners, for example, had worn through and edges were frayed. There was a small hole at the upper right, at the right end of the hat worn by the figure at the right side. The painting was lined in 1968 and tacked to a new stretcher. The lining is well attached, and the painting is tautly stretched. The introduction of wax adhesive into the painting's structure removed or significantly altered some aspects of information about Seurat's method and technique. The remaining bits of the original tacking edges are unprimed. It appears that the front surface of the canvas was prepared with a white ground, intermittently visible with the microscope in a few places. It is also possible that the white layer was not a glue or chalk (gesso) ground but a white underpainting in an oil medium. It is unlikely, although possible, that the canvas had no ground. If there were none, the absorbent support would have produced a paint surface that was matte and chalky. Wax infusion may have altered the character of this layer, though not that of the oil paint in the design layer. Paint was applied to cover the canvas completely with repeated layers of hatching-type, crisscrossed brushstrokes, done wet over dry, leaving the brush marking of the lower layers visible. In the middle portion of the painting, the rectangular brushstrokes seem to represent the actual stone blocks. The paint has been slightly flattened by lining. The small hole was filled and retouched and the surface was varnished in 1968. (RW)

The Stone Breakers, Le Raincy is one of a group of seventeen small, freely sketched, Impressionist paintings by Seurat of laborers in a field. Eight depict stone breakers,[1] and the remainder peasants or agricultural laborers.[2] Most of these are single-figure compositions; the present painting is thus among the most significant of the group. When seen among Seurat's early drawings of workers, such as *The Axe*,[3] *Laborer at Work*,[4] and *Laborers in a Field*,[5] *The Stone Breakers* reveals the beginning of an ambitious project to represent working-class life and French class conflict in all its variety and complexity. Seurat's mature paintings, beginning with *Bathers at Asnières* (1884, National Gallery, London), which depicted, among other subjects, working-class and petit bourgeois bathers, harbor scenes in Normandy, and cabaret and circus entertainers and their audiences, were monumentalized interrogations of the same general theme.

Stone breaking is the very image of back-straining and monotonous work. In the nineteenth century, jailed French prisoners, inmates in English workhouses, and convicts transported to Australia and Tasmania all broke rocks as part of their punishment, restitution, or rehabilitation. In the United States, until the middle of the twentieth century (and in a few cases after), shackled prisoners in chain gangs could be seen breaking rocks in quarries or along rural Southern roads. But the work of breaking large stones into smaller ones was done by peasants and laborers as well as by prisoners. Boulders, large stones, and rocks are an obvious impediment to planting and plowing, so farmers, peasants, and agricultural laborers spent a considerable amount of time and energy breaking and hauling rocks. Gravel for roads and rubble for walls and concrete were largely supplied in the nineteenth century by day laborers breaking stones with sledges and long-handled hammers. Gustave Courbet claimed that his monumental *The Stone Breakers* (1849, formerly Dresden Picture Gallery, now likely destroyed), a scene of two battered proletarians breaking stones by the side of a country road, was inspired by an actual scene he had witnessed near his hometown of Ornans in the Franche-Comté. Seurat saw Courbet's celebrated and notorious picture in May 1882 at his memorial exhibition at the École des Beaux-Arts in Paris, and surely the sight of it profoundly affected the young artist.

Certainly Seurat's pictures of stone breakers were something of an homage to the Communard Courbet. Seurat himself had been taunted with the epithet "communard" while a student at Lehmann's, and he remained for the rest of his life a man of the left. To dedicate oneself to the depiction of laborers was to assert

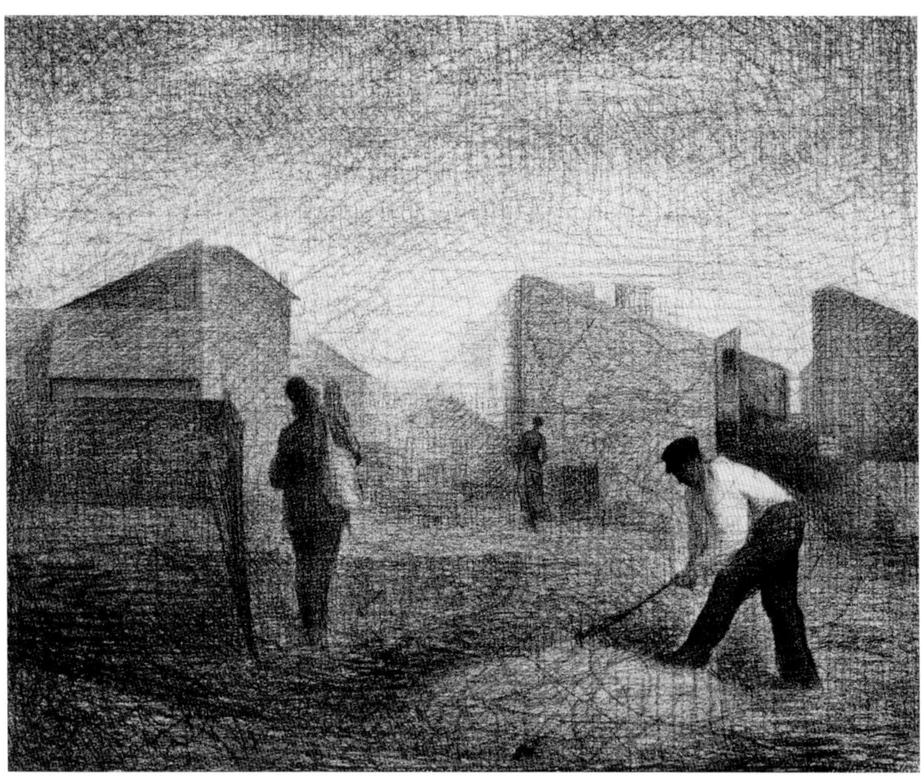

Fig. 114a Georges-Pierre Seurat, *Stone Breakers, Le Raincy*, c. 1881, Conté crayon on paper, $12\frac{1}{8} \times 14\frac{3}{4}$ in. (30.7×37.5 cm), The Museum of Modern Art, New York / Licensed by SCALA / Art Resource, NY

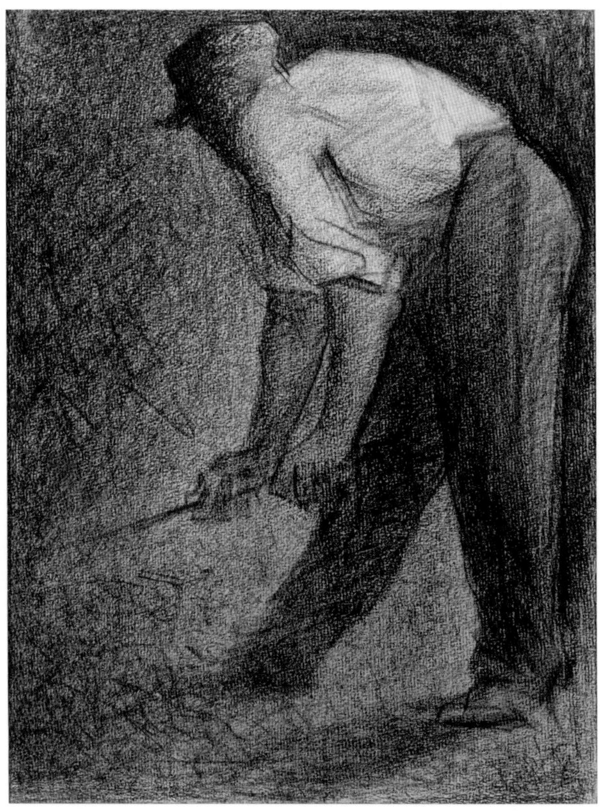

Fig. 114b Georges-Pierre Seurat, *The Stone Breaker*, c. 1881, Conté crayon on paper, $12\frac{3}{4} \times 9\frac{1}{16}$ in. (32.2×23 cm), Musée d'Orsay, Paris; photo: Réunion des Musées Nationaux / Art Resource, NY

sympathy for the working class and solidarity with their growing demands for economic and political equality. Seurat's first major drawing of stone breakers is the great composition at the Museum of Modern Art, *Stone Breakers, Le Raincy* (fig. 114a), which shows an industrial courtyard and figures engaged in alienated and poorly paid labor. None of the four figures in this Conté crayon drawing has any relation with the other, and each is essentially faceless. There are in addition three drawings of single stone breakers contemporaneous with the Norton Simon picture.[6] The first of these (fig. 114b) depicts a man in a posture nearly identical to the woman at right of the Norton Simon picture, except his hammer seems to be on the ground rather than in the air. It is not certain that the former was a study for the latter; each has a finished, autonomous character that suggests they were simply made as independent artistic works.

Seurat's painting is composed as a contrasting study of three figures; the hammer-wielding figures are presented in rough symmetry, with the woman in the center shown frontally, and the man at left and woman with hat at right shown in profile. Their long-handled hammers are suspended in midflight: at left it is seen at the top of its arc, and at right, halfway down. The three figures stand amid piles of rock and stone, and it is not clear which piles will grow smaller and which larger as they work, lending poignancy to what is already an image of a Sisyphean task. Nevertheless, it is possible to make a few small observations concerning the work that is performed and the character of the place. The stone blocks in the middle of the picture—just behind and to the sides of the cramped figure in dark blue at the center—are composed of large, rectangular (approximately $\frac{3}{4}$ inch long and $\frac{1}{2}$ inch wide) strokes of paint. These are mostly orange-pink in hue, with added tones of white mixed in. There are in addition about a dozen loosely handled blocks painted various shades of blue. In the foreground of the picture there is visible a smaller pile of blocky stones, each about half as large as those in the middle ground. These may be the product of labor expended on

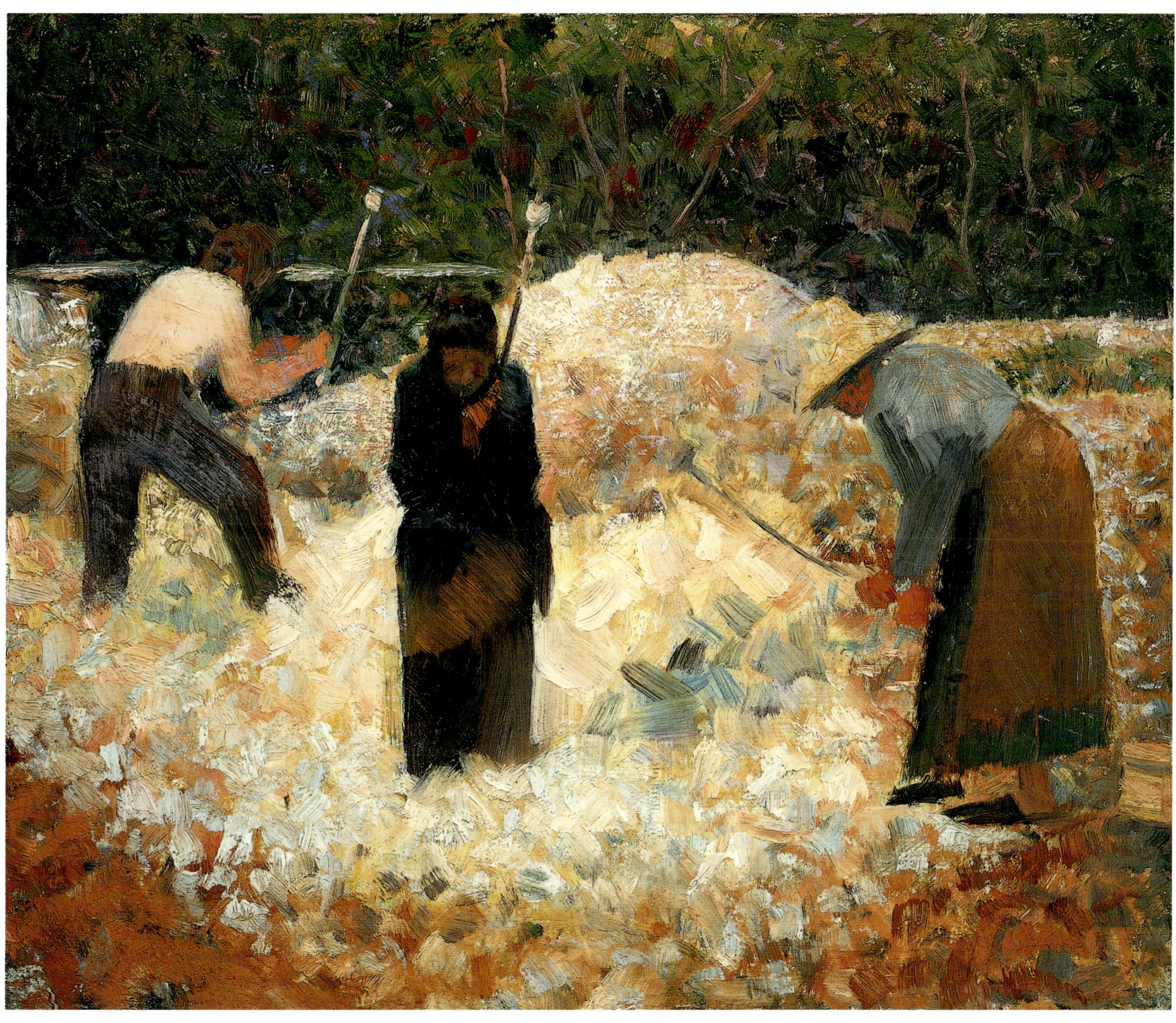

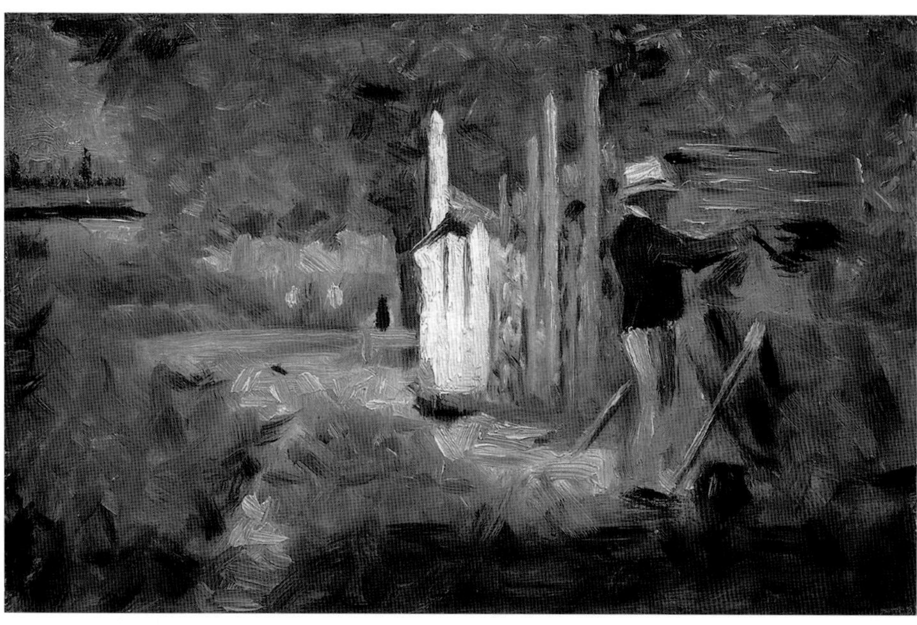

Fig. 114c Georges-Pierre Seurat, *Man Painting a Boat,* c. 1883, oil on panel, $6\frac{3}{8} \times 9\frac{1}{2}$ in. (16 × 24 cm), The Samuel Courtauld Trust, Courtauld Institute of Art Gallery, London

the larger blocks. But behind both piles is a third, still smaller collection of rocks composed of many colors, but especially gray and the complementary hues of orange and blue. The viewer is uncertain if the workers are breaking stones into three discrete sizes, or slowly and systematically crushing all rocks into uniform rubble. Thus, the passage of time, like the goal of labor in *The Stone Breakers,* is largely indiscernible.

The character of the place represented in *The Stone Breakers* is not simply a work yard in the middle of an industrial *banlieu,* as seen in figure 114a. Behind the figures is a wall of dense green foliage, highlighted with abbreviated, broad strokes of purple, indigo, dark red, and bright blue. A few tree trunks or shrubs are suggested with a pink-brown hue. We appear to be seeing a wall of vegetation bordering the far bank of a river; the line of white at the upper left, interrupted by the head and neck of the stone breaker on the left, indicates the line of the opposite shore. Thus the foliage below that line is actually the reflection of the distant foliage in the water. Perhaps then the fields at the right are agricultural. If so, this is a landscape in transition, caught between an agrarian past and the industrial future, frozen in time like the gestures and postures of the proletarian Three Graces.

Along with the other painted sketches of men and women at work from 1882–1883, such as *Fisherman* (Yale University Art Gallery, New Haven) and *Man Painting a Boat* (fig. 114c), *The Stone Breakers* marks a significant stage in Seurat's development as a colorist. The crisscrossed strokes visible across the lower two-thirds of the painting identify color and brushstroke as the same things. This was the nucleus of the discovery Seurat made three years later with the invention of Divisionism, that is, the technique whereby pure colors are allowed to meld in the eye of the observer rather than be mixed on the palette of the artist. The large strokes of color in *The Stone Breakers,* however (which are inevitably seen up close, because of the canvas's small size), cannot easily blend in the eye. The effect is therefore generally one of agitation, nervousness, and incompleteness, rather than the harmony he read about in the writings of Charles Blanc and which became his ultimate goal.

1 De Hauke, 1961, nos. 30, 31, 33, 36, 100, 101, 102, and 103.
2 De Hauke, 1961, nos. 32, 34, 35, 37, 39, 58, 60, 61, and 62.
3 De Hauke, 1961, no. 465.
4 De Hauke, 1961, no. 468.
5 De Hauke, 1961, no. 525, Musée d'Orsay, Paris.
6 De Hauke, 1961, nos. 555–557.

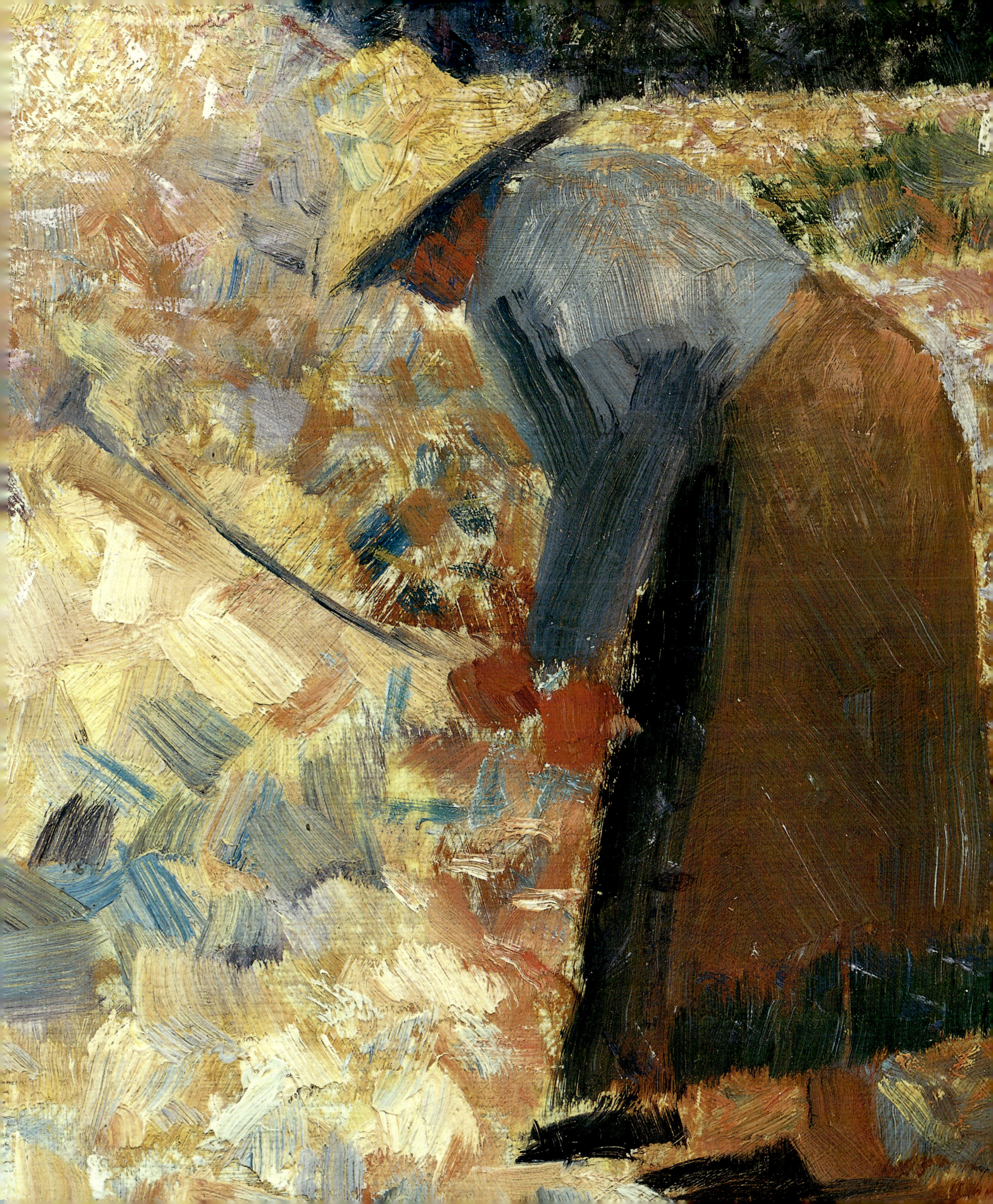

115

RODERIC O'CONOR
Irish, 1860–1940

Landscape with Cows
1890–1895

Oil on canvas, $25\frac{3}{4} \times 32$ in. (65.3×81.2 cm)
N.1979.10

PROVENANCE: [Galerie La Cave, Paris, sold 22 June 1979 to]; Norton Simon, bequest 1993 to; Jennifer Jones Simon Art Trust.

TECHNICAL NOTES: The support is a medium-weight, plain-weave fabric that has been lined with an aqueous adhesive. Original tacking edges are missing. The ground, probably applied by the artist, is thin and off-white. Marked by expressive brushwork and directly applied pure color, the composition nevertheless seems to have been well planned. The X-ray shows that the forms and the division of sky and landscape rarely deviated from their original placement. It is also apparent that there is an underlayer of paint in the sky that shows as horizontal brushstrokes in the X-ray. While most paints are pasty and opaque, some more translucent colors were enhanced by applying them over an underlayer of white paint. These include the orange at lower left and the dark green elsewhere in the landscape. Paint layers have only a few losses, and there are several areas of water damage, two long vertical lines at right center and a smaller region in the left half that was restored. An old discolored varnish was removed in 1979 and dammar and B-72 resin varnish was applied. (JF)

LANDSCAPE WITH COWS is a vividly colored landscape composed of three horizontal zones of complementary hue. The top zone is the largest of the three and depicts an unsettled sky painted with about two hundred mostly vertical strokes of paint measuring between 1 and 2 inches in length and $\frac{1}{4}$ and $\frac{1}{2}$ inches in width. At the left and right, a few horizontal green brushstrokes strengthen the contrast between the sky and the gentle red hills below. The palette and paint handling here are reminiscent of landscapes that Vincent van Gogh made in Arles and Auvers between 1888 and 1890. The central band of the canvas is the narrowest of the three. It is pinched slightly at the middle and composed of a varied ensemble of loops, lozenges, and short, diagonal stabs of red, yellow, orange, and green paint. It is itself horizontally divided into thirds, with reds and oranges dominant at the top, yellows and ocher in the middle, and greens below. The middle yellow section is more thinly painted than the rest, and in several areas—most notably in the center and near the left edge—the canvas weave and thinly primed canvas are clearly visible. The bottom zone of the painting, comprising cows and pasture, is crescent-shaped and dominated by warm reds and oranges. The bull strides jauntily from left to right and is painted a brilliant dark red, the color of coagulated blood. The cow in the center is yellow with red patches; its head is made up of just four vertical thumbprints of red and green. The grazing cow at the upper right is mustard yellow with nine dark green strokes of paint separating her from the flatly painted orange-brown grass. There are no cast shadows anywhere in the painting, although the contrast of complementary colors creates relief and spatial recession. The dominant cool blues of the sky recede from the viewer, while the warm oranges and reds at bottom advance. Thus *Landscape with Cows*, for all its painterly freedom and abstraction, narrates a basic, pastoral drama of grazing animals, fertile fields, and threatening sky.

The attribution to Roderic O'Conor, an Irish painter active in Brittany and befriended by Paul Gauguin, is entirely based on style. The painting is unsigned, has no known exhibition history, and no provenance before 1979. And though it does not closely resemble any specific works by O'Conor, there are many family resemblances between it and the painter's landscapes of the 1890s. *Landscape with Cows* is an ambitious, modern work. It clearly belongs among the class of paintings associated with the informal School of Pont-Aven, presided over by Gauguin, with members from Poland, Spain, the United States, Great Britain, and Ireland in addition to France.

O'Conor was educated at the Metropolitan Art School in Dublin beginning in 1879 and continued his training at the Académie Royale des Beaux-Arts in Antwerp before moving to Paris. He exhibited at the Salon in 1888 and at the Salon des Indépendants in 1892 and regularly thereafter. Throughout the 1890s he lived for long stretches of time in Brittany, especially the towns of Pont-Aven and Le Pouldu, though he also kept a studio and apartment in Paris. (O'Conor was independently wealthy.) After 1903 his attachment to Brittany and the surviving artists of the School of Pont-Aven began to fade, and he established new friendships among English artists and writers. His studio in the Latin Quarter was frequently visited by the women and men of the Bloomsbury Group, including Virginia Woolf, Vanessa Bell, and Roger Fry. In the decades after World War I and until his death in 1940, O'Conor appears to have grown increasingly reclusive. Well known to students of the Pont-Aven School, O'Conor's works are found in public and private collections in the United States in addition to his native Ireland.

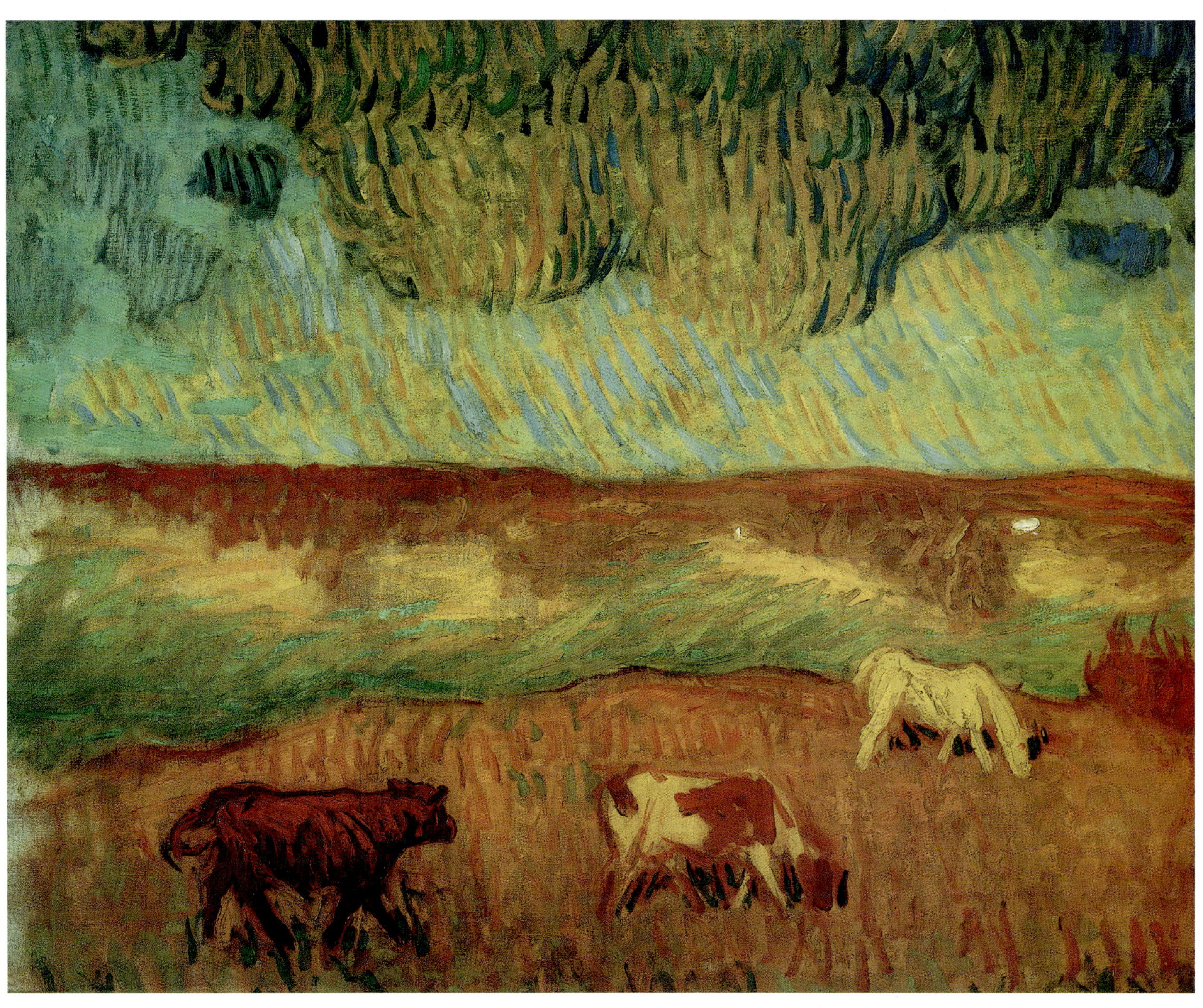

115

116

Louis Anquetin
French, 1861–1932

Portrait of a Man
1889

Pastel on paper, 24½ × 20 in. (62.2 × 50.8 cm)
Signed and dated lower left: "Anquetin / 89"
M.1977.03.01

Provenance: (Sale, Paris, Hôtel Drouot, 25 October 1945, lot 1). [M. Fouquet, Galerie des Deux Îles, Paris]. [Galerie La Cave, Paris, by 1976, sold 15 February 1977 to]; Norton Simon Art Foundation.

Exhibition: San Bernardino, 1980, no. 3, ill.

Reference: Brame and Lorenceau, 1991, p. 98, ill.

Technical Notes: The pastel is in very good condition, drawn on a wove paper primary support, covered entirely in medium. The medium was heavily applied in the black of the figure's coat and in lighter layers in the figure's head, allowing the brightness of the sheet color to illuminate the skin tone. The draftsmanship varies as well, as the head and torso are tightly rendered and the hands are drawn in a looser, more sketchlike manner. The primary support is mounted around the perimeter on sulfite board. The exact form of adhesion is not known, as wooden strips are nailed around the face of the work, and these strips may in fact be the means of attachment. However, in the lower left corner, there is a slight gap in the facing strip, and the edge of the primary support appears adhered to the board. Slight play in the secondary support indicates that the support is not laid down but is attached only at the perimeter. The wooden facing strips have caused some discoloration visible at the upper corners, especially a 7-mm area in the upper left, and a small 7-by-5-mm loss at the bottom left corner. There are stray marks in the white area surrounding the figure, probably made by the artist, and areas of possible abrasion. The area to the right of the figure's coat has shadows of previous lines, now covered in white pastel, indicating a correction by the artist. The upper right quadrant is flecked with brown spots on the surface of the sheet and medium. (SSB)

Louis Anquetin was a French painter whose renown is based on the invention by him and Émile Bernard of a method of painting called Cloisonnism. His best-known works in this style, two nearly identical pastel drawings and an oil painting (fig. 116a), were shown in 1888 at the exhibition of Les XX in Brussels and at the Salon des Indépendants in Paris. The pictures feature broad areas of warm and cool complementary colors bounded by thick black contours and a sinuous play with tapering lines, suggesting Art Nouveau or the Style Métro. The dark outlines of figures, architecture, and trees reminded the critic Édouard Dujardin of the strips of metal that bordered the colored compartments in medieval enamel work, hence the name Cloisonnism.[1]

Anquetin and Bernard undoubtedly liked the appellation lent by their friend Dujardin. They admired medieval and Asian enamels, leaded-glass windows, and, especially, Japanese woodblock prints and were striving to create a comparably simple, direct, and popular art. Indeed, Anquetin's exposure to Japanese prints at an exhibition, organized by Vincent van Gogh at the cabaret Le Tambourin in March 1887, was probably the precipitating event that led him from a lingering academic conception of form—learned at the studio of Fernand Cormon—toward a fully modern one. His contributions that year to the exhibition of the "painters of the *petit boulevard*" at the Grand Bouillon-Restaurant du Chalet—also organized by Van Gogh—included two works called *abstractions japonaises*, one of which may have been a version of the *Avenue de Clichy*. (The restaurant was very near the location depicted in the painting.)

Portrait of a Man, signed by Anquetin and dated 1889, is drawn in a style that is at once academic and Cloisonnist. A single uninterrupted contour may be traced from the back of the elderly gentleman's jacket at

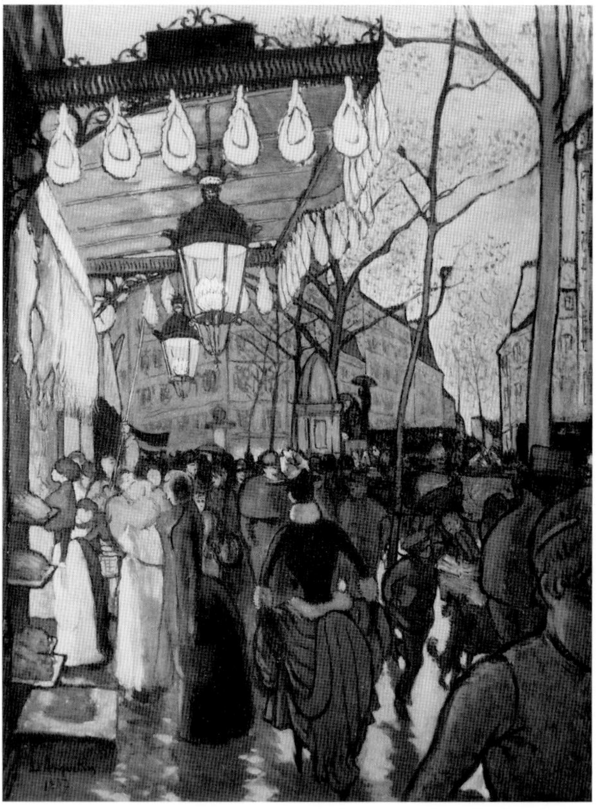

Fig. 116a Louis Anquetin, *Avenue de Clichy*, 1887, oil on paper, mounted on canvas, 27¼ × 21 in. (69.2 × 53.3 cm), Wadsworth Atheneum Museum of Art, Hartford, The Ella Gallup Sumner and Mary Catlin Sumner Collection Fund

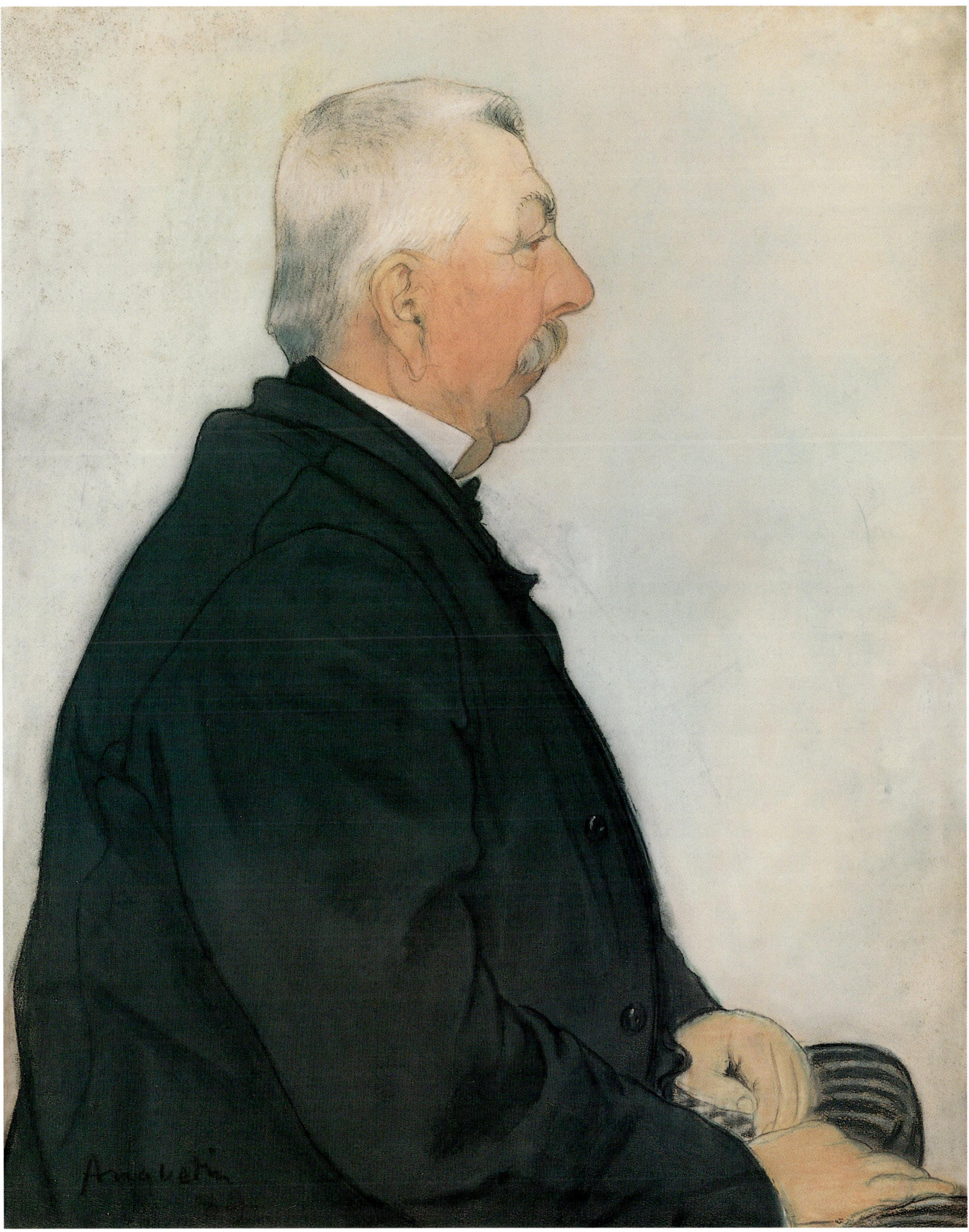

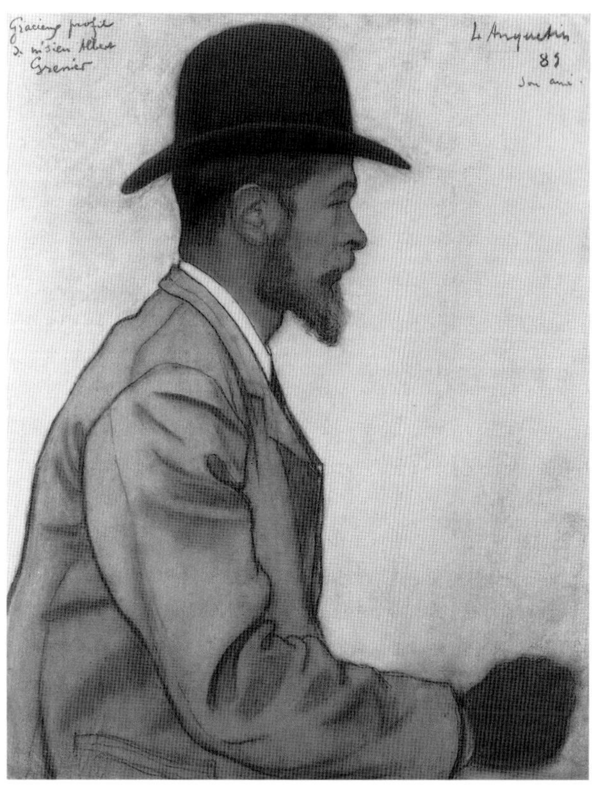

Fig. 116b Louis Anquetin, *Gracieux Profil de M. Albert Grenier*, 1889, pastel on paper, 25¼ × 19¾ in. (64 × 50 cm), private collection

lower left to the top of his head, down his nose, mustache, and chins, all the way to his pudgy hands resting on striped trousers. (Pentimenti indicate that the artist had originally placed the entire figure about two inches farther to the right.) At the same time, however, Anquetin's modeling of facial features is very careful, almost precise, and the mass and volume of the figure are strongly marked. The half-length profile format of the pastel is repeated in another work, also signed and dated 1889 (fig. 116b), but this time dedicated to the sitter, Albert Grenier. The Norton Simon pastel lacks a dedication, and the identity of the gentleman is unknown. Nor was the picture exhibited, so far as we know, in the artist's lifetime; the first record of its existence came in October 1945, thirteen years after the artist's death, when it was part of a large sale at the Hôtel Drouot in Paris. All we can say for certain about the sitter is that he is a man of advanced years, with thinning gray hair and many chins. He dressed for his portrait in a starched collar and black cravat, a sober, charcoal gray jacket, and striped pants. Like many men who sit for their portraits, he does not quite know what to do with his hands; they rest limply on his thighs. His eyes and mouth are impassive, the result in part of the broad mustache that covers the man's upper lip and the opening of his mouth. Given this restraint, we may surmise he was a person the artist respected or feared, perhaps a wealthy collector, art dealer, or family member.

1 Édouard Dujardin, "Aux XX et au Indépendants—Le cloisonisme," *La Revue Indépendante* 6 (March 1888), p. 488.

117

LOUIS ANQUETIN
French, 1861–1932

Portrait of a Woman (Marguerite Dufay?)
1891

Pastel on paper, $24\frac{3}{4} \times 20$ in. (63×51 cm)
Signed and dated upper right: "Anquetin 91"
M.1979.42

PROVENANCE: M. Huc, by 1928. [Galerie Nicolas Poussin, Paris, sold to]; ?Nusuvitch or Mescovitch. (sale, Lille, 29 May 1972, lot 50). [Galerie La Cave, Paris, sold 27 April 1976 to]; Norton Simon, gift 1979 to; Norton Simon Art Foundation.

EXHIBITIONS: Paris 1891, presumably no. 22; Paris 1928b, no. 1, as *Étude de femme.*

REFERENCES: Antoine, 1891, p. 157; Lecomte, 1891, p. 225; Welsh-Ovcharov, 1981, p. 254, fig. 96; Destremau, 1989, pp. 167, 171–172, 176 n. 13, fig. 28; R. Thomson, 1991, under no. 149, fig. 149c; Brame and Lorenceau, 1991, p. 115; Delannoy, 1996, p. 32.

TECHNICAL NOTES: *Portrait of a Woman* is a pastel on paper in good condition. The primary support is wove paper with a smooth texture, and the pastel is applied in heavy layers, with especially thick application in the figure's skin. The technique is varied, revealing stroke marks in the chest and arms, and appearing very smooth, moistened, and worked in the facial area. The paper support has a small 3-mm loss in the support at the upper left corner, the upper right corner has a small loss, and two tack holes are surrounded by tide lines. The upper right quadrant has abrasions that may have been repaired after glazing in a frame shattered during shipping. There are tiny spots in regular patterns, visible in the figure's face and throughout the work. These tiny spots do not disfigure the work, are noticeable under magnification, and may be due to previous mold or mildew damage. The support remains mounted to a sulfite board, similar to that of *Portrait of a Man*, with wooden strips nailed around the face of the work. A shiny adhesive is visible at the damaged area in the upper left corner, probably hide glue. Slight play in the secondary support indicates that the support is not laid down but is attached only at the perimeter. Labels fully documenting provenance on the verso of the backing board are recorded in object's file. (SSB)

BY 1891–1892 Anquetin had begun to leave Cloisonnism behind. He explored the work of Gustave Courbet, Honoré Daumier, Pierre-Auguste Renoir, and Paul Cézanne, and traveled back still farther in the history of art, admiring and partly emulating paintings by Peter Paul Rubens, Jacob Jordaens, and Frans Hals. He also became interested in caricatures and posters and in the expressive possibilities of exaggeration and caricature. *Portrait of a Woman* is an example of this later direction in Anquetin's career. His figure is Rubensian in amplitude, recalling *Helen Fourment as Aphrodite* (Kunsthistorisches Museum, Vienna), as well the female figures in many of Jordaens's mythological paintings. The insinuating smile and barely concealed bosom may also derive from the famous *Gypsy Woman* in the Louvre by Hals (fig. 117a), which Anquetin surely knew well. The caricature elements in the pastel, however, also recall some of Daumier's early lithographs and Courbet's pictures of women, including his tavern keeper, *Mme Gregoire* (c. 1858, The Art Institute of Chicago), and seminude figure, entitled *Intimité.*[1] Anquetin's corpulent woman displays with evident pride her particular charms—an extremely ample bosom—and indeed seems to offer her breasts to the spectator. They are supported (very improbably) on a white, gauzy shelf formed by her lowered bodice and seem veritably to break the plane of the picture and enter the viewer's space. Anquetin's caprice is reinforced by the swell of his sitter's cheeks, her arching mouth and eyebrows, double chin, round shoulders, and swollen forearms. Even the curly bangs on her forehead accentuate the basic erotic invitation. Below her bosom is an exaggeratedly pinched waist, drawn with black, gray and green; the bottom of her bodice is V shaped and points with alacrity to further pleasures available down below.

Anquetin's *Portrait of a Woman* reveals his stylistic mobility, if not restlessness. He adjusted contours, surfaces, shades, color, and touch according to the sex,

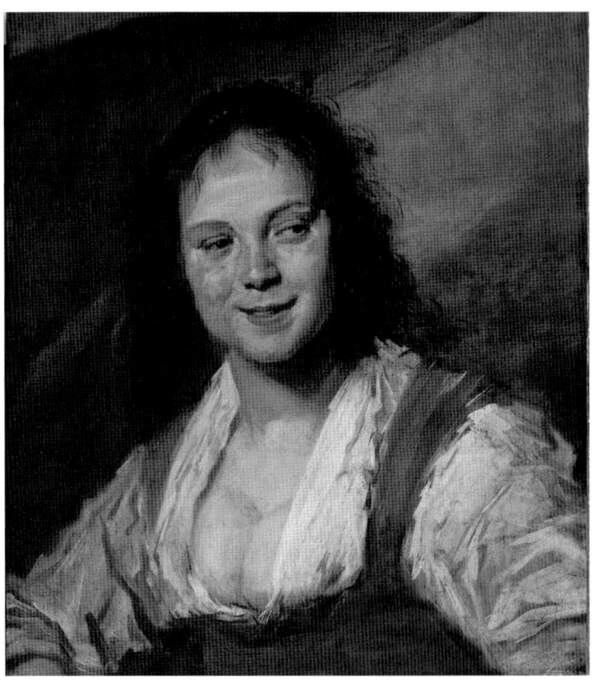

Fig. 117a Frans Hals, *The Gypsy Woman*, c. 1626, oil on panel, $22\frac{7}{8} \times 20\frac{1}{2}$ in. (58×52 cm), Musée du Louvre, Paris; photo: Erich Lessing / Art Resource, NY

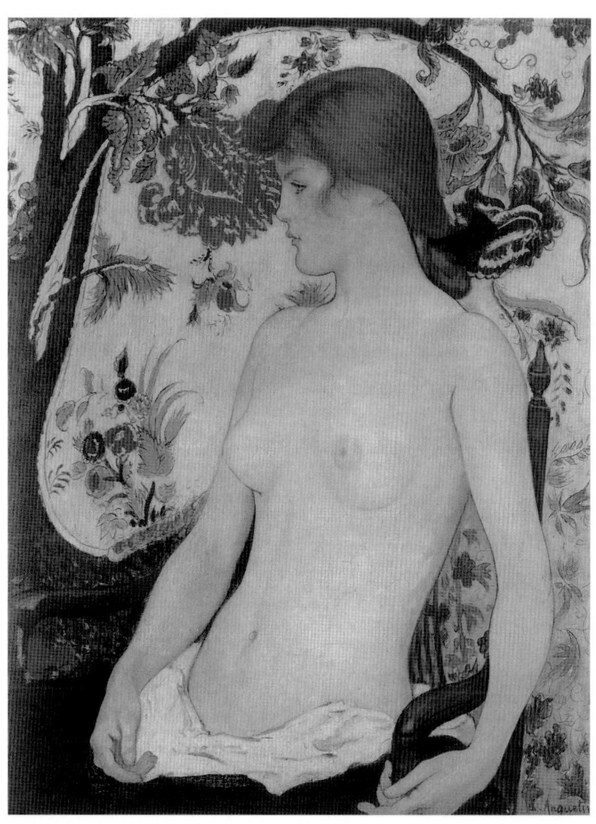

Fig. 117b Louis Anquetin, *Torso of a Young Woman*, 1890, oil on canvas, $29\frac{3}{4} \times 23\frac{3}{4}$ in. (75.5×60.3 cm), private collection

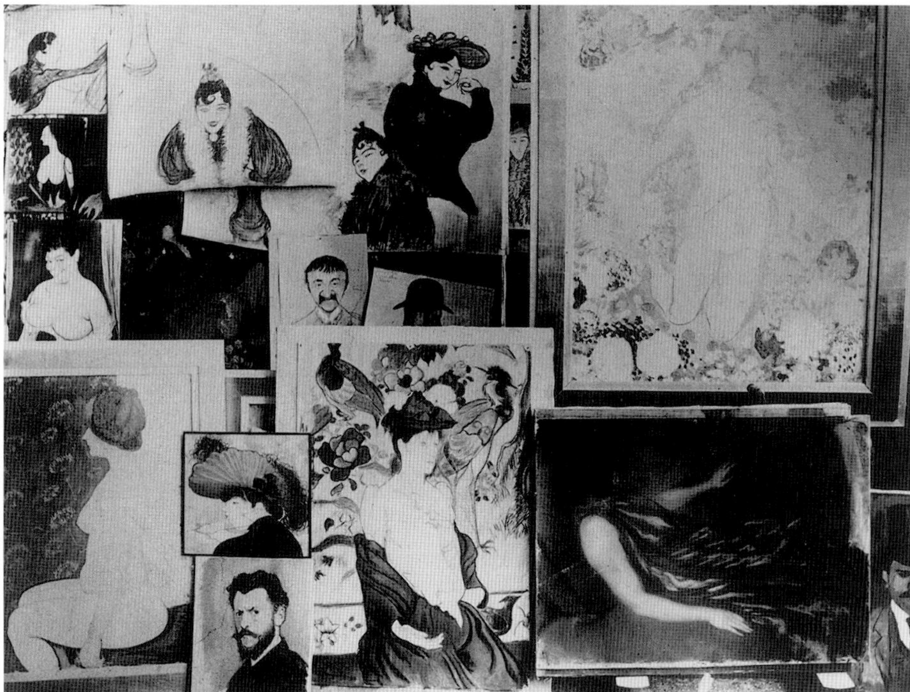

Fig. 117c The interior of Anquetin's studio, c. 1891–1892

character, and class of his sitters, and he did not shrink from exaggeration. In the same exhibition of the Salon des Indépendants in 1891 at which he displayed *Portrait of a Woman*, he also exhibited *Torso of a Young Woman* (fig. 117b) about which the critic Georges Lecomte wrote: "Her supple lines and languid chastity are of an exquisite purity; her pearly flesh confirms the candor seen in her Persian eyes and bright face."[2] The woman in the present picture is her precise opposite. She is gross and slatternly and her rictus grin is anything but chaste. Lecomte noted the opposition in his review and described her face as that of a "laughing simpleton who believes she is most attractive when she displays her nudity."

The identity of the sitter for *Portrait of a Woman* is uncertain, but it may be Marguerite Dufay, who, according to Charles Hiatt, was a "comique excentrique" notable for her girth and for singing and playing the trombone at several Paris cabarets.[3] Dufay was depicted by Anquetin in a lithographed poster from 1894, and the resemblance is clear. Anquetin and his chums from the Cormon Atelier, Henri de Toulouse-Lautrec and Albert Grenier, were regular customers at the many dance halls and cabarets of Montmartre near Clichy, including the Chat Noir, Mirliton, Reine Blanche, and Moulin de la Galette. Anquetin's other paintings and pastels of women with exaggerated anatomical features, including *Woman with a Blue Hat* (1890, private collection) and the others seen in an atelier photograph taken about 1891–1892 (fig. 117c), may thus also be of cabaret performers.

1 Fernier, 1977, no. 272, c. 1860, location unknown.
2 Lecomte, 1891, p. 225.
3 Hiatt, 1896, pp. 108, 113–114.

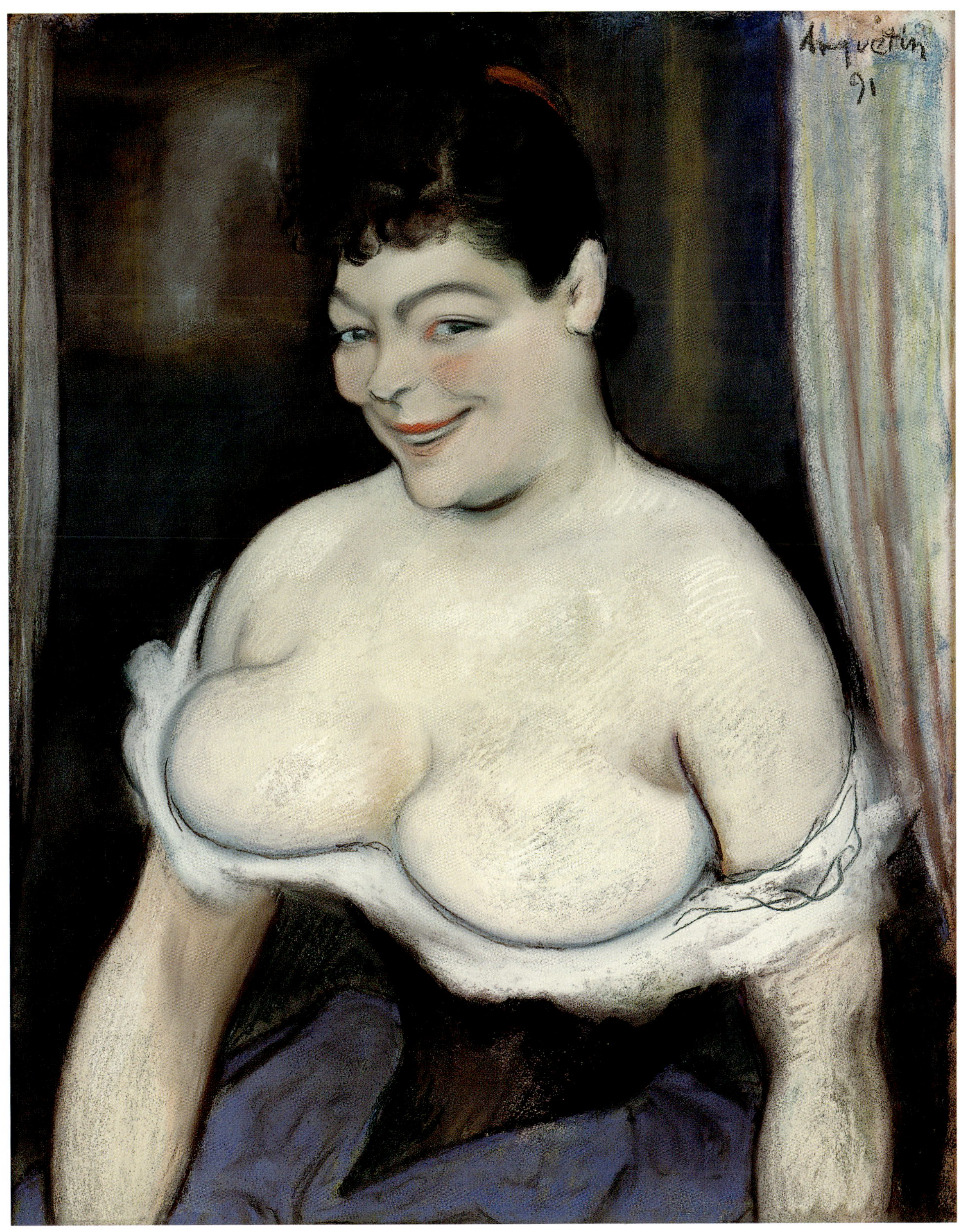

117

118

Louis-Georges-Eléonor Roy
French, 1862–1907

Figure in the Moonlight
1887

Gouache on paper, 9¼ × 11½ in. (23 × 29.2 cm)
N.1978.08.2

Provenance: Private collection, Paris; [Galerie La Cave, Paris, sold 1978 to]; Norton Simon, bequest 1993 to; Jennifer Jones Simon Art Trust.

Exhibition: Paris, 1978a.

Technical Notes: The thick, rigid sheet of wove paper is mounted to rag board with eight Japanese paper hinges. The rag board is mounted to two sheets of cross-laminated acid-free corrugated board. The mount board is only ⅜ inch larger than the sheet. The support is difficult to examine due to the present hinging system but may be a one-ply or Bristol board. The medium, gouache, is thickly applied in overlapping circles of color. Under magnification, the buildup of medium is clearly observed, with base matte colors under subsequent layers with varying binder and pigment content working up to shinier dots of color. The design extends to the edge of the sheet, without any border or unpainted area. The medium is stable and has characteristic craquelure where it is thickly applied. Generally, the greatest craquelure is above the artist's signature and diagonally up and to the right of the central figure's head. In addition, there are scattered thick blobs of paint and imbedded hairs in the work. (SSB)

Louis Roy was a painter, printmaker, and art critic who belonged to the circle of artists active in Pont-Aven and Paris around 1890. At Paul Gauguin's invitation, he exhibited some landscapes and still lifes in the Exposition des Synthetists—the so-called Volpini Exhibition on the grounds of the Paris Exposition Universelle of 1889—but failed to earn much attention or praise for his participation. Émile Bernard, one of the inventors of the flat, linear, and decorative style showcased at the exhibition, considered Roy's painting a "retarded" form of Impressionism. Roy nevertheless persevered, subsequently exhibiting at the Salon des Indépendants and the Exposition Impressionistes et Symbolistes at the Galerie Le Barc de Boutteville. Gauguin evidently thought enough of Roy to represent him in a portrait (fig. 118a).

Roy's greatest achievement was as a printer and publisher of prints. In 1894 he printed thirty proofs for each of the ten woodblocks by Gauguin for a deluxe edition of *Noa Noa*. The woodcuts were initially printed in black, with color added afterward by means of additional blocks or stencils. These prints were instrumental in the revival of the woodcut as a major artistic medium and are undoubtedly some of the greatest in the history of art. Roy also participated in the founding of the illustrated almanac *L'Ymagier*, edited by Alfred Jarry and Rémy de Gourmont. This splendid-looking publication was devoted to printing both new and old works of graphic art, including copies and restrikes of plates by Albrecht Dürer and other old masters, new prints by Armand Séguin and Henri Rousseau, and numerous *images d'Épinal*. (The latter are inexpensive woodblock prints devoted to popular themes, made at the town of Épinal in the eighteenth and nineteenth centuries.) Roy published his *À l'église* in issue five of *L'Ymagier* (July 1895, Spencer Museum of Art, Lawrence, Kan.).

Figure in the Moonlight is a dreamlike gouache representing an old man or woman with a cape, wooden clogs, and a cane walking down a path toward a sun that is setting on a distant horizon. The winding path is flanked its entire length by closely planted trees or high shrubs, and the sun sets beneath a large body of water or else a wide green-blue plain. Large trees frame the composition at left and right. The subject is clearly allegorical: it represents old age, the path of life, the passage to death, or the route to heaven. Similar subjects

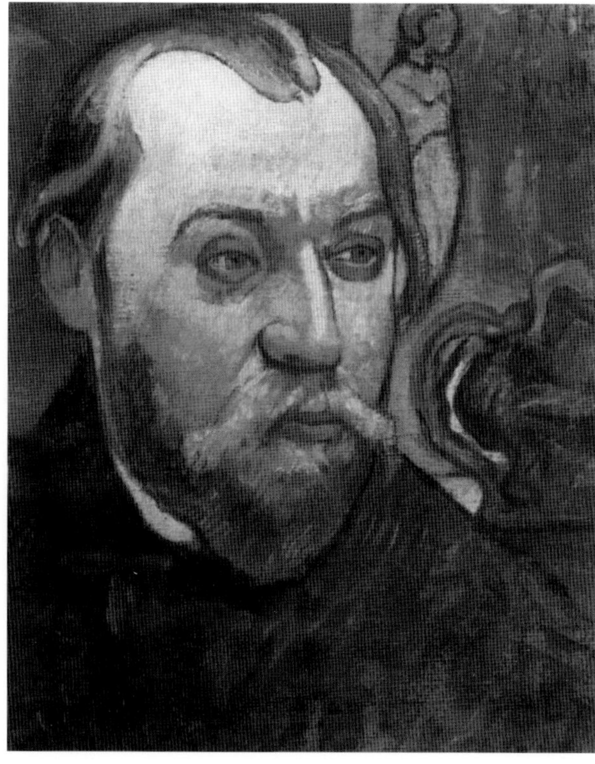

Fig. 118a Paul Gauguin, *The Painter Roy*, 1889, oil on canvas, 12⅞ × 15⅞ in. (32.7 × 40.3 cm), private collection

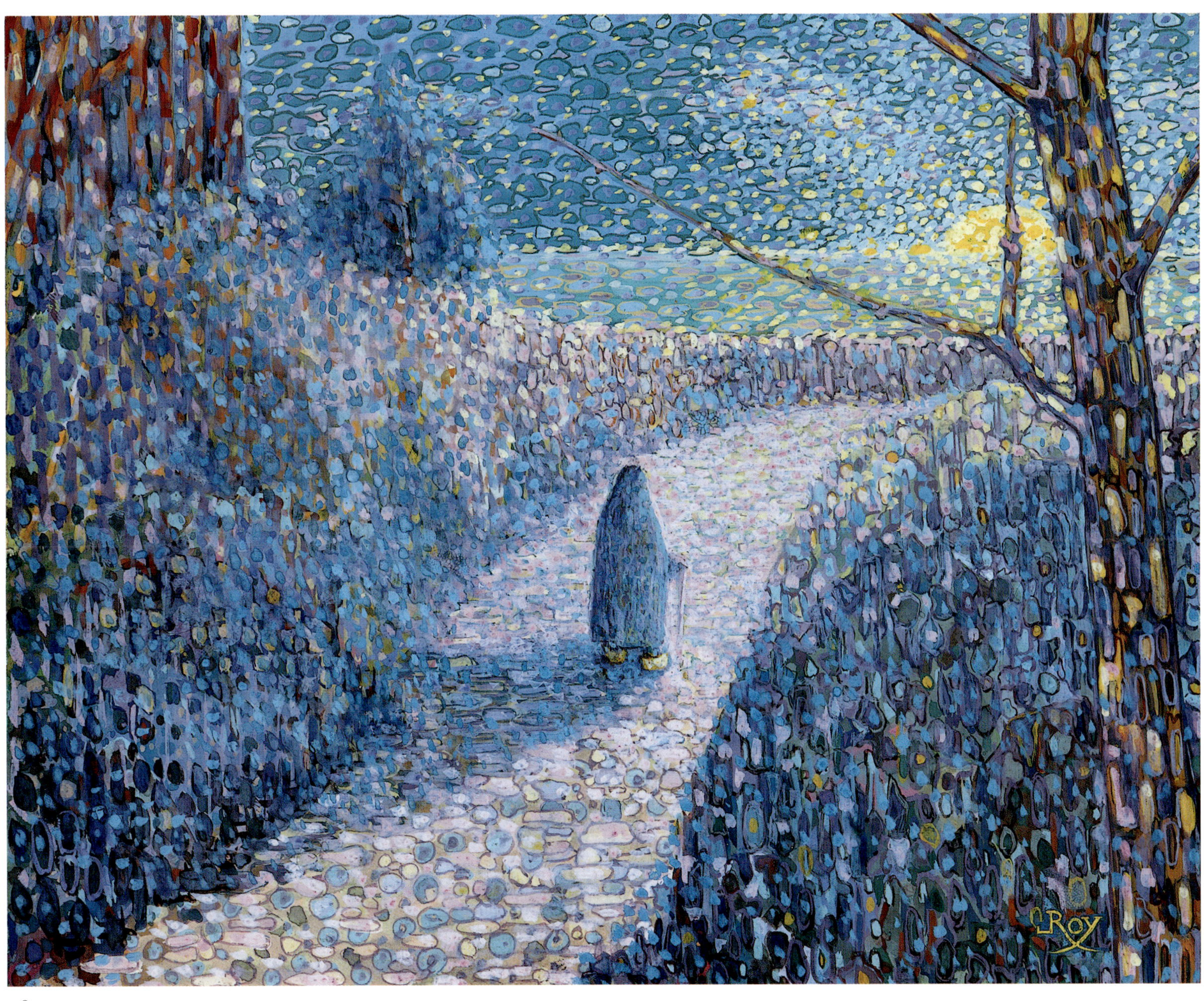

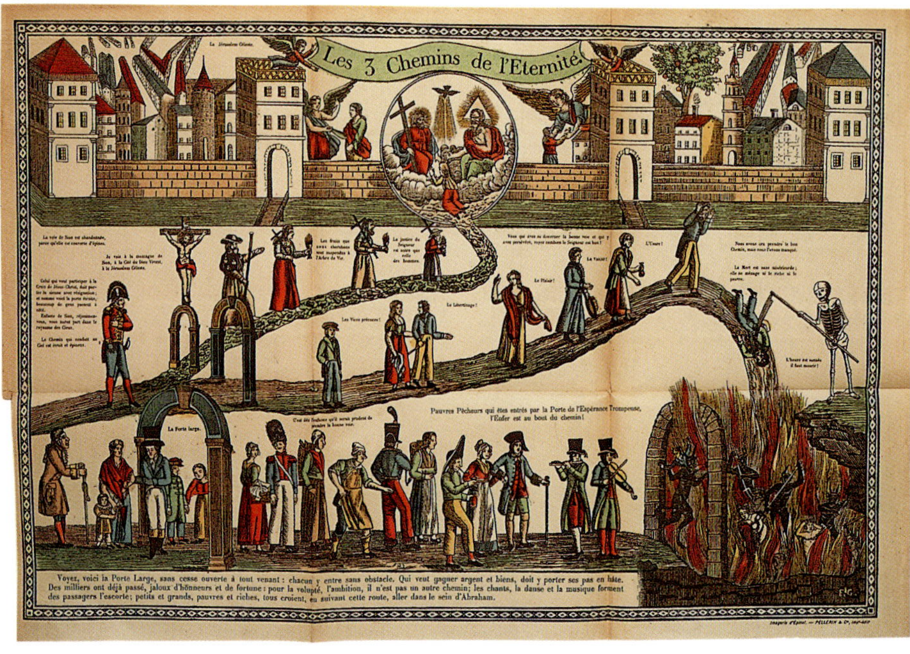

Fig. 118b Rémy de Gourment, *The Three Paths to Eternity*, appearing in *L'Ymagier* 6 (January 1896), engraving and woodcut, Spencer Museum of Art, University of Kansas, Lawrence

may be found in contemporary works by the Symbolist artists Paul Sérusier, Maurice Denis, and Odilon Redon, such as the latter's lithograph and drawing *Old Age*. The theme may also be derived from one of the many popular Épinal prints that passed before the eyes of the editors and printers of *L'Ymagier*. Issue six for example, from January 1896, included an Épinal print entitled *The Three Paths to Eternity* (fig. 118b), which depicts alternative routes to damnation and salvation. Only the uppermost trajectory, taken by penitent pilgrims carrying the cross and along a path covered with round leaves, leads to salvation. Roy's gouache painting, which probably dates from about this time, does not have this conventional Christian iconography, but it must have a roughly similar theme: the road to eternity or salvation.

What is most remarkable about the present painting is Roy's extraordinary technique. Every square inch of this small gouache is composed of myriad small dots, daubs, ovals, and dashes of blue, green, yellow, and especially pink, none more than about $\frac{1}{2}$ by $\frac{1}{4}$ inches. Many of the daubs, particularly those in the foreground, are separately outlined in adjacent and contrasting color and accented with small colored dots in the middle. The technique is basically Divisionist or Neo-Impressionist, but whereas Georges Seurat, Paul Signac, and their contemporaries employed it to create optical mixture and thereby simulate vivid half-tones, Roy does not primarily juxtapose complements. His optical mixture is incomplete, and each separate stroke remains separate and visible. The expressive effect of this handling is a dematerialization of the surface, a denial of space and volume, and the suggestion of a preternatural glow or energy. The Symbolist effect of the work, that is, its emphasis on an abstract idea or feeling more than a material place or thing, thus derives more from its peculiar form than its somewhat conventional subject.

119

PAUL SIGNAC
French, 1863–1935

The Seine at Les Andelys
1886

Oil on canvas, 18 × $25\frac{1}{2}$ in. (46 × 65 cm)
Signed, dated, and dedicated lower right: "À mon ami Albert P. Signac '86"
M.1968.27

PROVENANCE: Gift from artist to; Adolphe Albert (1855–1938). [Gallery Lorenceau, Paris, 1962, to]; (sale, London, Sotheby's, 23 October 1963, lot 54, ill., as *Vue des Andelys*, to); J. Horner. Private collection. [Stephen Hahn Gallery, New York; sold 20 August 1968 to]; Norton Simon Art Foundation.

EXHIBITIONS: Portland, 1968, no. 19; Princeton, 1972, no. 35, ill.; San Francisco, 1974, no. 48, ill.

REFERENCES: Groom, 1995, pp. 59, 60, fig. 2; Cachin, 2000, no. 126, p. 176.

TECHNICAL NOTES: The pristine condition of this unlined, unvarnished painting is rare. The support is a fine, plain-weave, unprimed canvas. It is not a standard size and was very likely cut from a larger piece of linen. The selvedge is at the bottom, and the tacking margins at the top edge and the right edge are extremely narrow. The reverse is lightly stained from absorbed oil in a pattern that relates to the areas of green paint on the front, as well as a few scattered spots of light salmon color. Paint was directly applied in a single layer, using juxtaposed small dots of colors, as well as longer strokes in the green on the hillside and the reflection in the river. In the quick brushing and dabbing of paint, raw canvas was frequently left exposed. Green foliage at right center and at the left upper center was done in small dabs. The white sky was painted across to the upper right, where a reserve was left for the green tree. Quick strokes of light blue were loosely hatched across the top of the sky and occasionally superimposed over green leaves. This sequence was duplicated at the lower left, in the white patch of reflected sky in the river. Brush marking is minimal, and the opaque paint leaves the canvas texture partially evident throughout. In the salmon pink riverbank, where the small areas of exposed canvas are rather evenly distributed between daubs of paint, and more clearly around the bend of the shore, the bare linen occupies a space of its own. Several spaces on the terraced hillside are also deliberate omissions of green paint. The subtle contrast in texture between the soft luster of the oil paint and the dry, matte linen remains distinct. Originally, the canvas would have been a lighter color, but it has darkened with age, probably shifting the overall tonality slightly, or lessening the contrast in the central area and the top right corner, where it interacts with the greens. The painting has remained unvarnished. (RW)

PAUL SIGNAC WAS one of the chief inventors of Neo-Impressionism—also called Divisionism and, more colloquially, Pointillism—a style of painting that employed small daubs, touches, or even dots of pigment to create a mosaic-like surface of color and light. Signac learned the method from Georges Seurat in 1885, through consultation with his friend Camille Pissarro, and from his own studies of the techniques of earlier nineteenth-century masters, especially Eugène Delacroix. Signac was also affected by a number of art theorists and scientists of his day, including Charles Blanc, author of the compendious *Grammaire des arts et du dessin*, as well as David Sutter, Ogden Rood, and especially Charles Henry's discussion of "optical mixture" in *Introduction à une esthétique scientifique* (1885).

Signac's initial efforts at Neo-Impressionist painting came in February 1886, when he retouched two works from the previous year, *Les Modistes* (Bührle Collection, Zurich) and *Snow, Boulevard de Clichy* (Minneapolis Institute of Arts). These and sixteen other canvases by Signac were part of a veritable Neo-Impressionist pavilion of the eighth and final Impressionist exhibition held in May and June that year in galleries on the rue Lafitte in Paris. The other works in the same style were by Pissarro and Seurat. The latter's *Sunday Afternoon on the Island of La Grande Jatte* (The Art Institute of Chicago) was the sensation of the exhibition and the touchstone for all future efforts in the Neo-Impressionist style. (The critic Félix Fénéon gave the movement its name in a laudatory review of the same year.) Soon after the close of the exhibition and after the hum of critical excitement had subsided, Signac traveled to the quiet town of Les Andelys in Normandy for rest and further artistic experimentation. *The Seine at Les Andelys* is one of ten surviving paintings of the town, the river, its surrounding hills and farms, and its inhabitants from that summer.

Signac's picture represents a bend in the river Seine at Les Andelys. The town is pressed close to the grassy embankment and sandy shore of the river, and a handful of abbreviated figures moves back and forth between each. One figure uses a wheelbarrow to unload a barge; another stands with a fishing pole. Like the people, the town seems divided between its devotion to labor and leisure. An orange-roofed and gray-green factory or incinerator with a smokestack is just visible at left, and a patchwork of planted fields can be seen on a hillside above (parallel brushstrokes are differently oriented in each patch). But the overall mood of the painting is relaxed and even a bit sleepy. The effect is increased by the lazy reflection of the town in the slowly moving river waters.

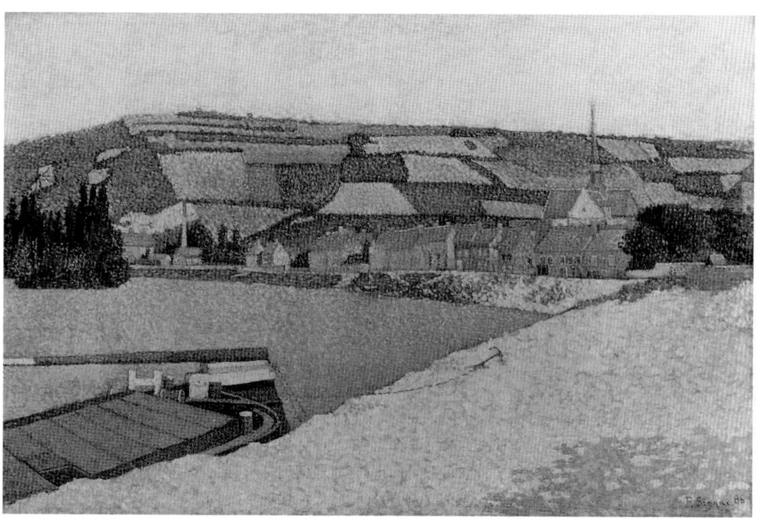

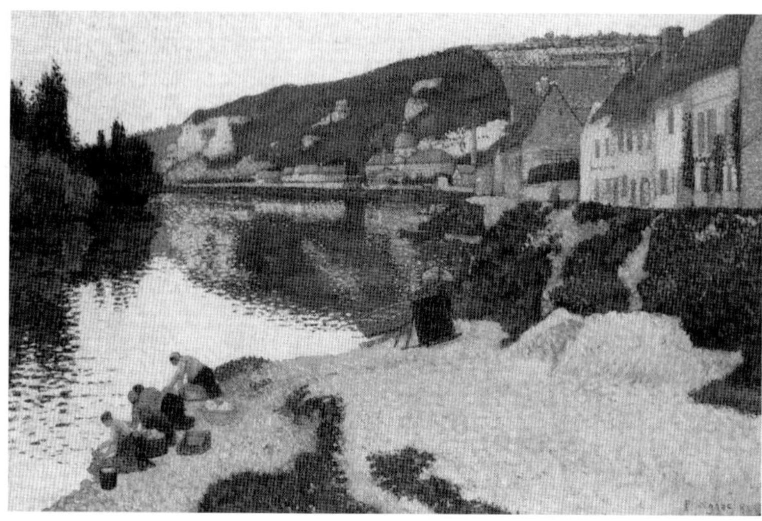

Fig. 119a (*above left*) Paul Signac, *Les Andelys, Cote d'Aval*, 1886, oil on canvas, $23\frac{5}{8} \times 36\frac{1}{4}$ in. (60 × 92 cm), The Art Institute of Chicago, through prior gift of William Wood Prince

Fig. 119b (*above right*) Paul Signac, *Les Andelys, Les Laveuses*, 1886, oil on canvas, $23\frac{5}{8} \times 36\frac{1}{4}$ in. (60 × 92 cm), private collection

The Seine at Les Andelys is not a fully developed Neo-Impressionist picture. It reveals typical Impressionist handling, long commas and shallow arcs of paint, as well as some short daubs. But there is also a crisscrossing of brushstrokes—seen for example on the tower, roof, and pediment of the church and on the roofs of the houses at right—that recalls Seurat's early paintings, such as *The Stone Breakers* (cat. 114). There is also present an anticipation of the Divisionism that will be fully manifest in the later, more fully developed treatment of the same subject now in the Art Institute of Chicago (fig. 119a). Here, optical mixture (which the artist also called "chromo-luminarism") is visible only in the blue-orange treatment of the roofs and windows of the two houses at right and in the light and dark green dots that constitute the foliage to the right of the houses. In the Art Institute picture, the entire canvas is painted in doctrinaire Neo-Impressionist style. This same high Divisionist finish is apparent in *Les Andelys, les laveuses* (fig. 119b), which more clearly represents the factories and smokestacks suggested at the left of the Norton Simon picture and adds a group of hardworking laundresses to the left foreground.

It was not uncommon at this time for Signac to make smaller, Impressionist studies for larger, Neo-Impressionist paintings. The strategy is repeated with *La Salle à manger* (1886–1887, Kröller-Müller Museum, Otterlo) and *Étude, salle à manger* (private collection) and with *Collioure, le clocher* (Kröller-Müller Museum, Otterlo) and *Collioure, le petit port* (private collection). The Impressionists themselves, Claude Monet, Pierre-Auguste Renoir, Alfred Sisley, and the rest, also made smaller sketches and studies for larger and more fully realized works, but rarely with so much formality and deliberation as Signac, Seurat, or Pissarro during his Neo-Impressionist phase. Indeed, these latter artists made no pretense at speed, spontaneity, or immediacy of execution, only intensity of effect. The present painting, in fact, exhibits greater animation than the larger, fully developed version. The brown of the unprimed linen canvas creates a warm base tone for the higher-keyed colors across the picture. The orange-pink hues—derived from Seurat's early palette—move forward off the canvas, while the various shades of green either sit flat on the surface, advance visually, or recede. The painting is thus both carefully and even scientifically rendered and yet marked by great animation, a combination that lay at the heart of the Divisionist project, but which is often absent from even its greatest examples. That this picture is in such a superb state of conservation—it has never been varnished, cleaned, or relined—allows us to judge accurately its important position at the dawn of Neo-Impressionism.

Signac dedicated and gave this painting to his friend the artist Adolphe Albert. Albert routinely exhibited at the Salon des Indépendants from 1886, when this painting was made, until 1938.

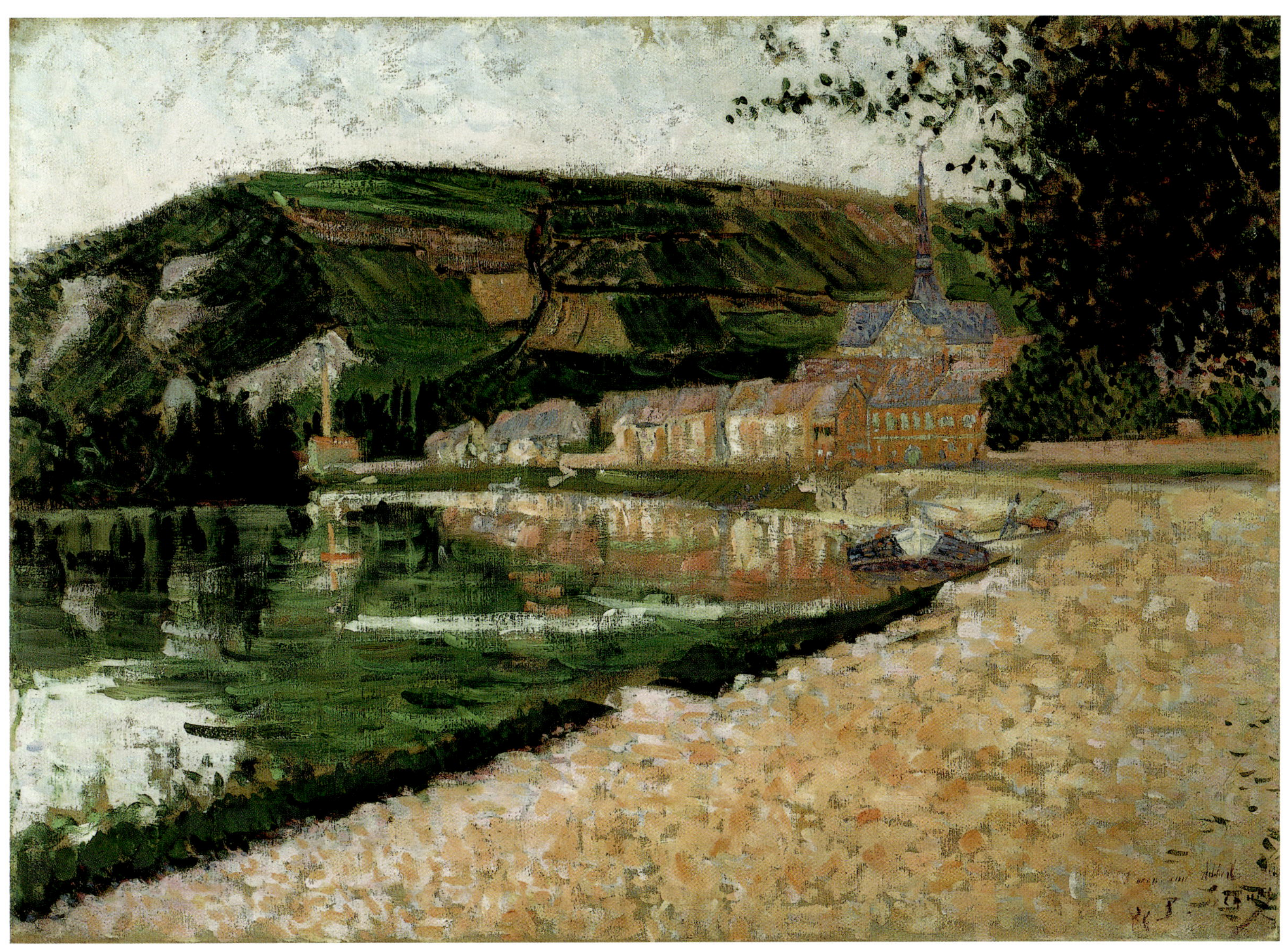

119

120

Paul Sérusier
French, 1863–1927

Still Life with Apples and Violets
1890–1891

Oil on canvas, 15 × 18⅛ in. (38.1 × 46 cm)
F.1983.14

Provenance: Estate of the artist, presumably by inheritance to; Mme Paul (Marguerite) Sérusier (d. 1950), presumably gift to; Mme Henriette Boutaric (d. 1984), Paris, still in 1964. George G. Frelinghuysen, Los Angeles (sale, Los Angeles, Sotheby Parke-Bernet, 4 February 1975, lot 303, ill., as *Nature morte aux voilettes*, to); [Paul Kantor Gallery, Beverly Hills, Calif., sold 21 March 1975 to]; Norton Simon, gift 1983 to; The Norton Simon Foundation.

Exhibitions: Paris, 1955a, no. 147; Copenhagen, 1956, no. 127; Mannheim, 1964, no. 251.

Reference: Guicheteau, 1976, no. 43, p. 205, ill.

Technical Notes: Bright primary and secondary colors and parallel brushstrokes characterize this picture. Earth colors and black are little used, and most colors are mixed with white. Since much of the paint is thick and applied in several layers, the texture of the twill canvas is just barely apparent in some areas. The medium-weight fabric cut just shy of the stretcher dimensions is lined with an aqueous adhesive to fabric and tacked to what may be the original stretcher (5-part butt-join). The lining was harsh and flattened the painting. Although the painting is fairly directly painted, the artist found it useful first to lay in most forms with certain flat colors. The yellow table and the book are underpainted with a pure translucent turquoise color, for example, and the purple shadow to the right of the table is underpainted with pure transparent green. The torso is underpainted with acid green that is fairly transparent and built up with flesh color and blue definitions and shadows. The oranges, by contrast, were developed with the local color only. The painting has various crackle patterns from medium interval to fine crazing, and tiny bits of paint have flaked from the edges of the cracks. There are additional scattered losses and restorations, but the paint is mostly intact. When the painting was cleaned in 1975, it was reported to have a yellowed varnish and a glue lining but remained in good condition. The present varnish must be synthetic; it appears thick, waxy, and inappropriate for the painting that the artist surely intended to remain unvarnished and matte. Ultraviolet light gives a bluish cast to the varnish and shows only some of the restorations. (JF)

Paul Sérusier was the most intellectual of the artists who worked in the circle of Paul Gauguin. As a young man, he acquired a rigorous education at the Lycée Condorcet in Paris and continued his course of improvement while an art student at the Académie Julian in Paris between 1885 and 1890. By the conclusion of his period of formal training, however, he had rejected nearly everything he learned from the academic masters in favor of an independent approach to form and spirit derived in equal measure from Plotinus, Richard Wagner, and especially Édouard Schuré, one of the founders of modern Theosophy. The latter's *The Great Initiates* (1889), which was widely read by artists, traced the origins of the human soul to a "divine archetype" or "cosmic essence" and the terrestrial body to the "womb of the earth," which gave birth to four races: red (America), black (Africa), yellow (Asia), and white (Europe).

Sérusier combined these ancient and modern mystical theories with the new Synthetist approach to painting of Émile Bernard and Paul Gauguin to construct a blueprint for a new, collective artistic practice. This newly invented tradition was meant to provide a rationale for the abstraction toward which a generation of artists had been groping. For them, pure colors and forms, independent of materiality and the vulgar world of things, offered a means to communicate the highest aspirations of humanity. In late 1888 Sérusier organized a brotherhood called the Nabis (Hebrew for "prophet") drawn from a group of disaffected young students at the Académie Julian, including Maurice Denis, Pierre Bonnard, Paul Ranson, and Henri-Gabriel Ibels. "I dream for the future of a purified fraternity," he wrote in 1889 to Denis, "made up only of committed artists, lovers of beauty and truth, who combine in their works and their lives that indefinable quality I translate by Nabis."[1] He introduced the group to some of the most advanced results of Cloisonnism and Synthetism, and shared with them his own painting *Bois d'amour* (a sketchy landscape painted on a cigar-box lid) made earlier that year at Pont-Aven, under the direct tutelage of Gauguin. According to Sérusier, the older artist took his charge out to some local woods and asked him: "How do you see those trees?" "Yellow," Sérusier answered. "Well then, make them your most beautiful yellow. How do you see the earth?" "Red," the disciple replied, "Then use your best red. . . ."[2] Sérusier's little painting was so admired and emulated by the group of Nabis that it soon became known as *The Talisman* (Musée d'Orsay, Paris).

The Nabis regularly exhibited together at several non-Salon venues between 1891 and 1896, and less often until 1900. Their group meetings, however, became infrequent

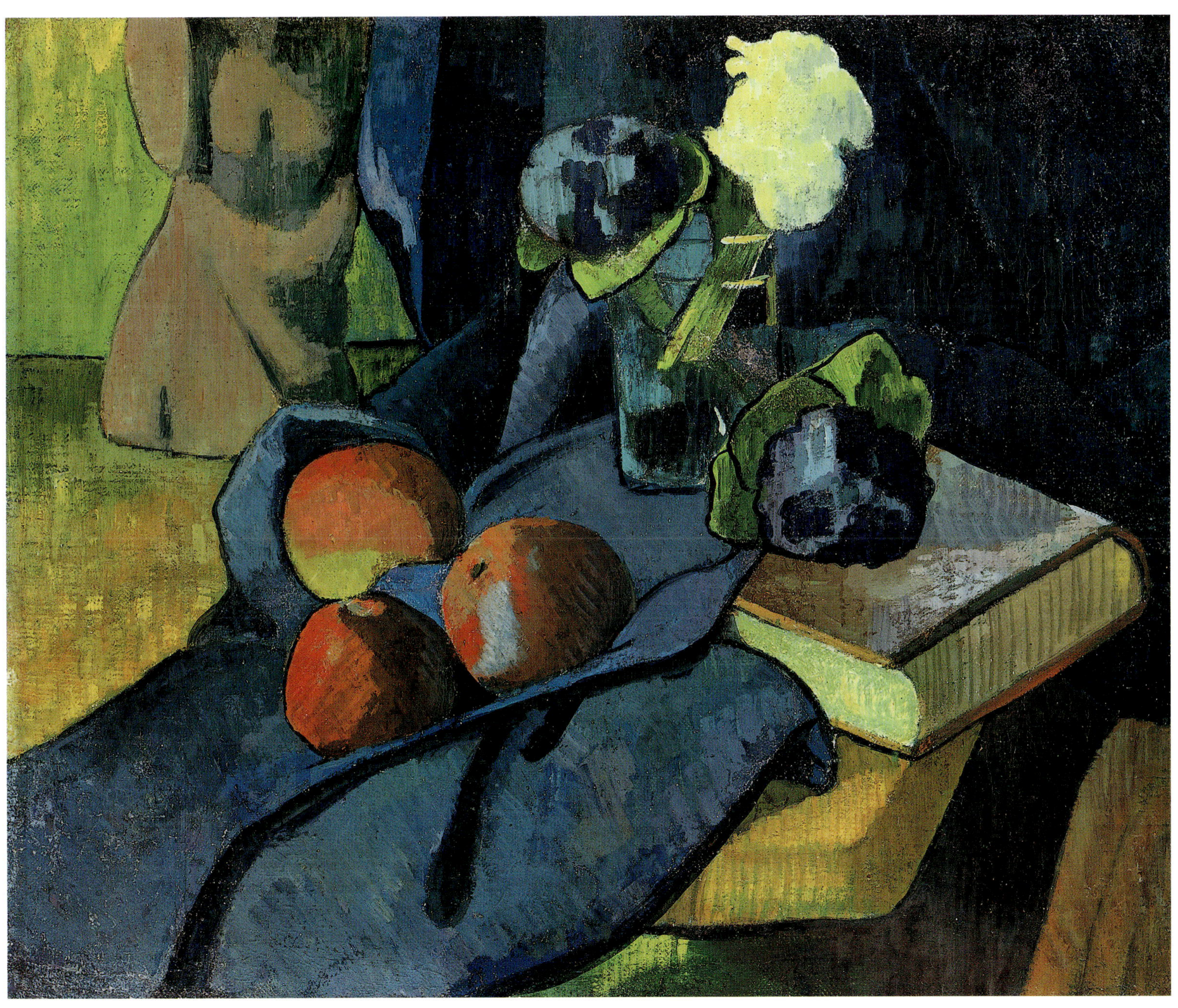

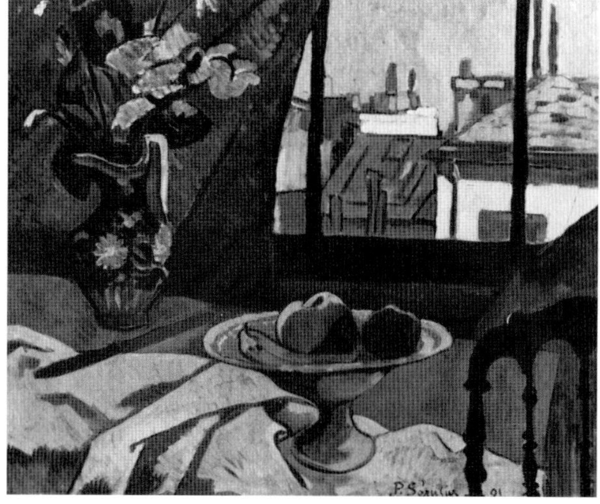

Fig. 120a Paul Sérusier, *Still Life with Apples and Flowers*, c. 1891, oil on canvas, 15 × 18⅛ in. (38.1 × 46 cm), location unknown; photo: Guicheteau, 1976, no. 44

after 1892, and they never achieved the unity of purpose envisioned by their founder. Sérusier nevertheless remained true to his initial spiritualism. His later lectures and publications, including his well-known *ABC de la peinture* (1921), argue forcibly that the artist's highest calling is to record the "correspondences" between the world of nature and the "mental images" that exist in the minds of all people.

Sérusier's oeuvre may generally be divided into three types: figure paintings, landscapes, and still lifes. Nearly all of the first two have Breton themes or settings, while his still lifes—though largely painted in Brittany—are composed of the usual arrangement of tables, fruit, flowers, ceramics, books and the occasional chair, window or lamp. *Still Life with Apples and Violets* is one of the two or three best works by the artist in this genre and among the best of a larger number of ambitious Nabi still lifes of that approximate date. It may be compared with Bernard's *Still Life with Flowers* (cat. 127) and *Still Life: The Blue Coffeepot* (1888, Kunsthalle Bremen) and Sérusier's own *Still Life with Apples and Flowers* (fig. 120a), signed and dated 1891.

Still Life with Apples and Violets is an extremely densely packed painting. It contains broad, flat, thickly painted areas outlined in thicker, dark blue and tightly interlocking shapes that recall leaded windows or cloisonné enamel. The colors of fruit, flowers, book, glass, tablecloth, tabletop, sculpted torso, and rear wall are fully saturated and possess little tonal modeling. Indeed, there is little light or air anywhere in the picture since the only glimpse beyond the jumble of things in the foreground is to a densely painted green wall in the left background and a dark indigo cloth at upper right.

Although Sérusier's brilliant colors owe nothing to the work of Paul Cézanne, his use of strictly regimented parallel strokes of paint clearly recalls the Provençal artist's "constructive stroke," so named by Theodore Reff.[3] Gauguin owned several paintings by Cézanne, one of which he used himself in 1890, in *Portrait of a Woman in Front of a Still Life by Cézanne* (fig. 120b). Sérusier's "constructive" still life surely dates from the same moment.

Unlike Cézanne, the greatest of all nineteenth-century still-life painters, Sérusier did not use color as a substitute for tonal modeling; the patchwork of colors jostle and abut one another but do not create rounded forms and palpable space. Rather, they remain flat, constituting an overall, fully pictorial correspondence with the visible, material world. Though Sérusier had little interest in Cubism when it was devised in Paris by Georges Braque and Pablo Picasso in 1907–1908, his *Still Life with Apples and Violets* contains the angularity and restlessness of that later art. The similarity is not coincidental, since Sérusier's theories and writings were well known to the next generation.

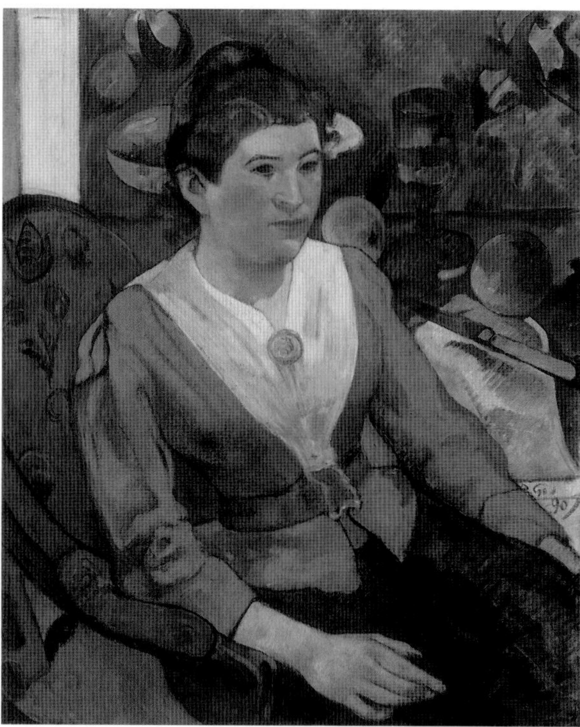

Fig. 120b Paul Gauguin, *Portrait of a Woman in front of Still Life by Cézanne*, 1890, oil on canvas, 25 11/16 × 21⅝ in. (65.3 × 54.9 cm), The Art Institute of Chicago, The Joseph Winterbotham Collection

1 Sérusier, *ABC de la peinture*, Paris, 1950; in Boyle-Turner, 1988, p. 19 n. 13.

2 Guicheteau, 1976, p. 19.

3 Theodore Reff, "Cézanne's Constructive Stroke," *Art Quarterly* 25, no. 3 (Autumn 1962), pp. 214–227.

121

Paul Sérusier
French, 1863–1927

Synchromy in Yellow
1900–1913, or 1915

Oil on canvas, 32 × 21½ in. (81.3 × 54.6 cm)
Signed lower right: "P Sérusier"
N.1976.20.2

Provenance: Estate of the artist, by descent to; Mme Paul (Marguerite) Sérusier (d. 1950), still in 1932. Marcel Guérin (d. 1948), by 1942. (sale, London, Sotheby Parke-Bernet, 8 April 1976, lot 214, ill., to); Norton Simon, bequest 1993 to; Jennifer Jones Simon Art Trust.

Exhibitions: Possibly Paris, 1913, no. 33; Tokyo, 1927; Quimper, 1932, no. 7.

References: Sérusier, 1942, p. 49; Guicheteau, 1976, no. 360, pp. 274–275, ill.

Technical Notes: The support is a medium-weight, loosely woven fabric with coarse, irregular threads and slubs. The original tacking edges remain; they are frayed and quite narrow. The canvas was not commercially primed, as the white ground was applied to the front surface only and it seeped through the interstices to the reverse. Microscopic examination reveals it to be very porous and chalky. It has chipped away in numerous places at the edges. Paint was applied with a fairly small brush in short, quick dabs of paint directly over the ground in a single layer. In the sky and foliage, colors were juxtaposed; in the foreground greens, the paint was brushed out. In numerous places the dry brush skipped and left gaps in the paint. The painting's condition is fair. The paint has an overall pattern of contraction cracking and a general appearance of being under bound, a possible result of the porous, absorbent ground. There are numerous small paint losses throughout, without retouching. The painting was cleaned and varnished in 1978. (RW)

Sérusier's best-known painting, *The Talisman* (1888, Musée d'Orsay, Paris), is a landscape, and landscape painting remained a touchstone for the artist from the beginning to the end of his career. As it was for Paul Gauguin, landscape for Sérusier was a means to establish a firm connection to a place and cultural heritage at a time when the artistic avant-garde seemed estranged from any determined audience, tradition, or location. For Gauguin, Brittany was simply one stop in an ongoing artistic and personal peregrination that ended with the artist's death in 1903 in the Marquesas Islands, among the most remote inhabited places on earth. For Sérusier, however, Brittany was the beginning, middle, and end of the journey. He explored Breton and ancient Celtic legend and folklore, convinced (as Gauguin was not) that he could discover the deep structure of the Breton land and soul and use it as the basis for a new painting that revealed the mystical connection between God, land, race, and individual. Thus, Sérusier made painting after painting depicting Breton figures engaged in ritualized actions—harvesting fruit, dancing, smelling flowers, and at prayer—as well as mythical figures such as elves, goblins, sorcerers, prophets, and angels. Sérusier also made landscapes without any figures at all, expressing by means of color harmonies the unique character of a place he understood as the land of the Celts.

In 1905 Sérusier began building for himself a house on the chemin de Duchen Glaz (now rue Paul Sérusier) in Châteauneuf-du-Faou, a small, picturesque town on the banks of the Aulne River in the Finistère department of Brittany. He first visited the town in 1891 in the course of his travels to Pont-Aven, Le Huelgoat, and other towns in central Brittany and made a more extended visit two years later. A painting from about 1896, *The Pilgrimage to Notre-Dame-des-Portes* (Musée des Beaux-Arts de Quimper), depicts the Romanesque church at the center of Châteauneuf, the town gates, the valley of the Aulne, and the surrounding hillsides planted with wheat and other grains. Sérusier's house had a fine view of these hills, and, beginning in 1906, he took advantage of this location to produce a number of gentle and undemonstrative landscapes, including *Synchromy in Yellow*.

The landscape is pastoral and autumnal, composed of green meadows in the foreground divided by a hedgerow and some trees; in the middle ground there rises an orange hill culminating in a wedge of blue-gray sky. A dark green field, shaped like a chevron, penetrates the orange trapezoid. At the bottom, three schematic cows graze or stare. The surface is painted loosely, even coarsely, with little concern to hide irregularly sized and shaped brushstrokes or to cover myriad small glimpses of the primed canvas beneath the paint. This open structure is especially apparent in the meadow and sky. To be sure, the picture is not entirely relaxed in handling and composition: there are areas of purposeful virtuosity, tension, and humor. The spiky shrubs and flat cows in the foreground are placed in such a way that their size may help us understand spatial recession, but they nevertheless seem to float on a light green sea. The hedgerow and trees mark a change in ground plane, but the second green meadow has no more modeling than the first, and thus it too is of uncertain dimension. The

Fig. 121a Paul Sérusier, *Landscape with Yellow Trees*, 1917, oil on canvas, 28 × 19¾ in. (71 × 50 cm), location unknown; photo: Guicheteau, 1976, no. 371

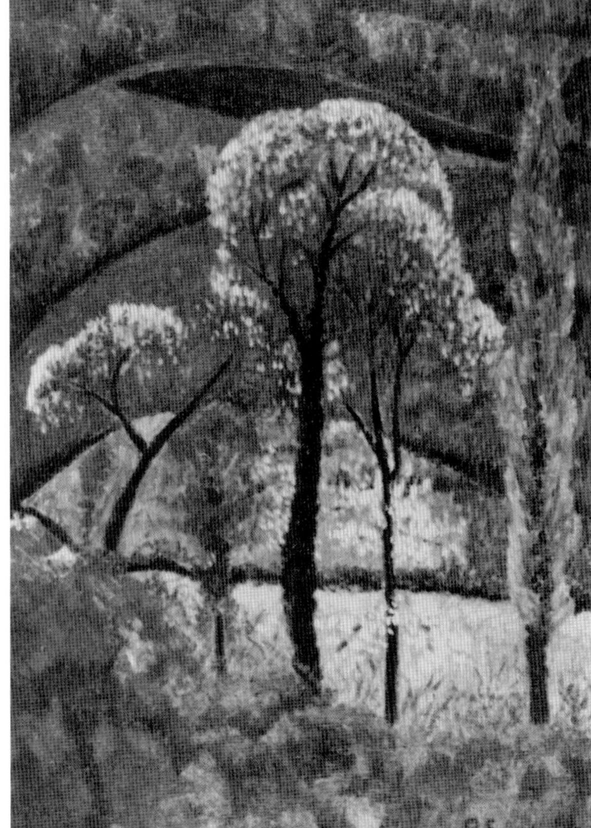

trees present their own mysteries: the one at left resembles a smokestack; the one at the center has three branching trunks and a lollipop canopy; the right-hand tree resembles a cypress, but the top of it appears to have a canopy of its own. Finally, the line of trees silhouetted against the sky at upper right are mere irregularly shaped extensions of the orange-green hill below.

Sérusier's painting is a decorative canvas in all the modern senses of the word. It is an ambience, an environment, and a mood far more than it is a representation of a place or thing. It is a tapestry of mostly warm colors and an organization of shapes and directions more than a precise reconstruction of nature or re-creation of specific plants and animals. And, finally, it is intended to be dreamlike and nonmaterial rather than quotidian and concrete.

The date of this picture, like that of many others by Sérusier, is uncertain since his oeuvre does not have a clear and one-directional stylistic development. A label on the verso indicates it was lent by Madame Sérusier to an "Exposition Artistique in Quimper" in 193[2] under the title *Synchromie en jaune* (no. 7). (The title *Vallée jaune*, also written nearby on the stretcher, was scratched out.) A painting with the title *Synchromie en jaune* was exhibited in Paris in 1913 at the Galerie Druet (no. 33). Assuming these are the same, the picture must date between 1906, when Sérusier moved into his well-situated house at Châteauneuf, and 1913. But the matter is more complicated. In the 1942 edition of Sérusier's *ABC de la peinture*, the painting was illustrated, titled simply *Paysage*, and assigned a date of 1915 in conformity with the date visible in the photograph. That date can no longer be seen on the canvas. The likelihood, therefore, is that the date was added by the artist, or someone close to the artist, long enough after 1913 that its exhibition year was forgotten. The numerals may subsequently have been removed by accident during a cleaning or on purpose to enhance the value of the work. Pictures made by Sérusier during his period of association with Gauguin are more desirable than those made long after, and when the picture was auctioned at Sotheby's in 1976 it was dated "circa 1892." There also remains the possibility that the picture is not the one exhibited in 1913 but was in fact painted in 1915 and accurately dated by the artist. Judging by style, the landscape most closely resembles four other vertical landscapes: *Landscape with Poplars*,[1] *Three Poplars in a Valley*,[2] *Autumn Landscape with Three Poplars*,[3] and *Landscape with Yellow Trees* (fig. 121a). The latter painting hung alongside the Norton Simon painting in the collection of the critic Marcel Guérin who sketched it, along with five other landscapes, in a letter from 1943 to Madame Sérusier.

1 Guicheteau, 1976, no. 221, signed and dated by the artist "07."

2 Guicheteau, 1976, no. 264, undated.

3 Guicheteau, 1976, no. 303, signed and dated "12."

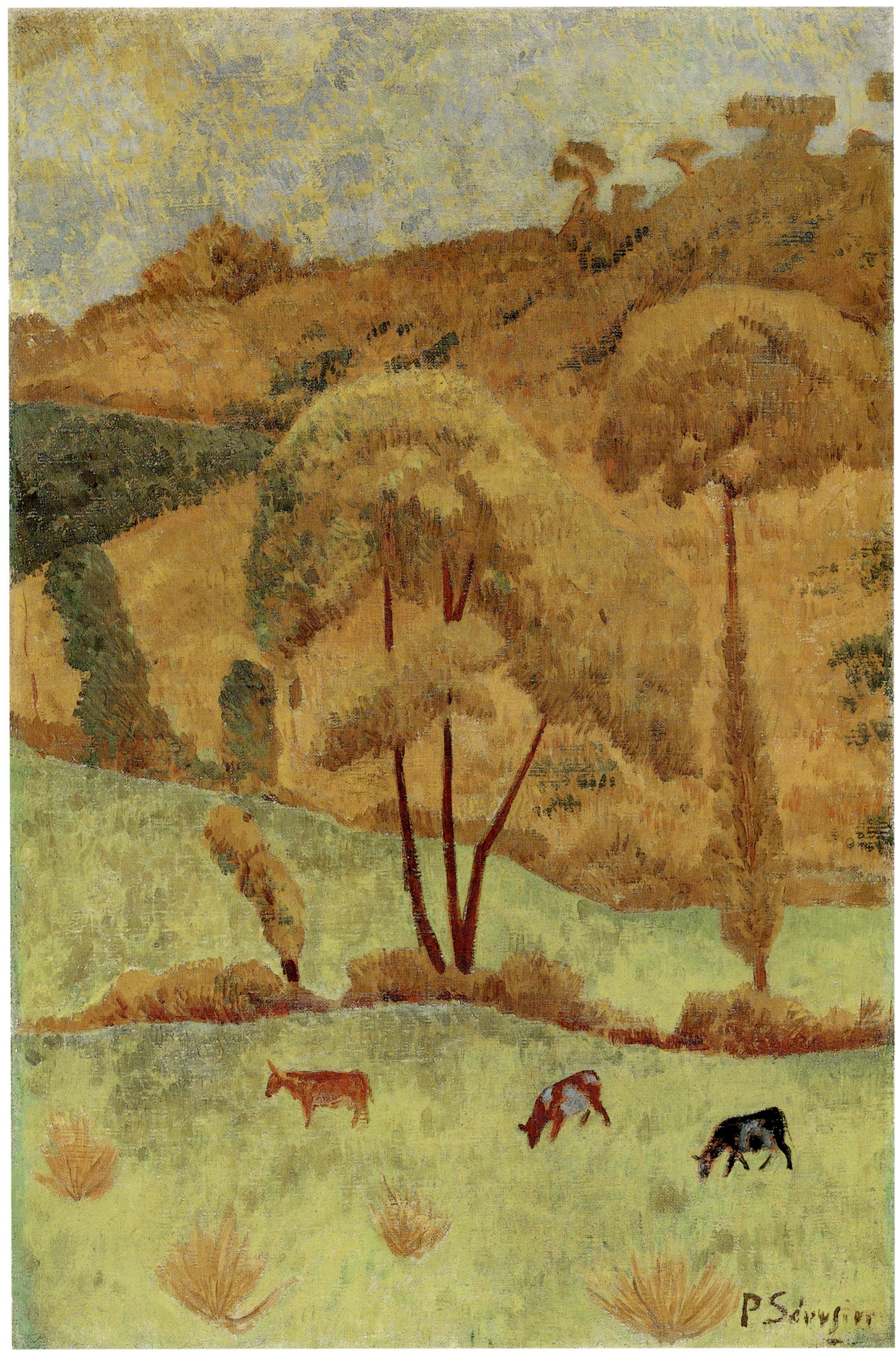

121

122

Henri-Marie-Raymond de Toulouse-Lautrec
French, 1864–1901

At the Cirque Fernando, Rider on a White Horse
1887–1888

Pastel and drained oil on board, $23\frac{5}{8} \times 31\frac{1}{4}$ in.
(60 × 79.5 cm)
Signed and inscribed upper right: "a mon ami Brua T-Lautrec"
M.1978.13.2

Provenance: [Galerie Georges Petit, Paris]. Antonio Santamarina, Buenos Aires, by 1933 (sale, London, Sotheby's, 2 April 1974, lot 23, to); [P. & D. Colnaghi, G.M.B.H., Zurich, sold 18 May 1978 to]; Norton Simon Art Foundation.

Exhibitions: Possibly Brussels, 1888, no. 10; Buenos Aires, 1933, no. 114; Buenos Aires, 1949, no. 168; Buenos Aires, 1950, no. 1; Buenos Aires, 1964, no. 4.

References: Joyant, 1926, vol. 1, p. 265; Dortu, 1971, vol. 2, no. P315, ill.; Stuckey, 1979, p. 126, fig. 6; Murray, 1991, pp. 131, 146, 148, 190–191, 246, fig. 89; R. Thomson, 1991, p. 234, fig. b; Brettell, 2002, pp. 277–281, fig. 145.3, 278.

Technical Notes: *At the Cirque Fernando* is in excellent overall condition. The work is painted on sulfite board or bookbinder's cardboard, a gray-brown pulpy, porous board with ragged and delaminating edges. The board is a visually midrange color tone and includes inclusions, shives, and unbeaten fiber bundles. The support is stable and in good condition; however, the edges of the millboard are ragged and worn. The support contains pinholes near the bottom edge at $7\frac{1}{2}$, $12\frac{1}{2}$, and $17\frac{1}{2}$ inches from the left edge, as well as staple holes approximately 6 inches from the top edge. Adhesive accretions are visible along the upper left and right edges. The design layer is pastel and drained oil, *peinture à l'essence*, on cardboard. Rapidly applied pastel is the predominant design material for the horse, the seated figure in the stands, and background imagery. The circus rider is painted largely in drained oil, directly on the millboard, without a ground layer. The media are generally stable, and minute areas of loss, due to previous insect damage, are visible under magnification. The work rests in a Plexiglas box, as do the other Toulouse-Lautrec works on cardboard. (SSB)

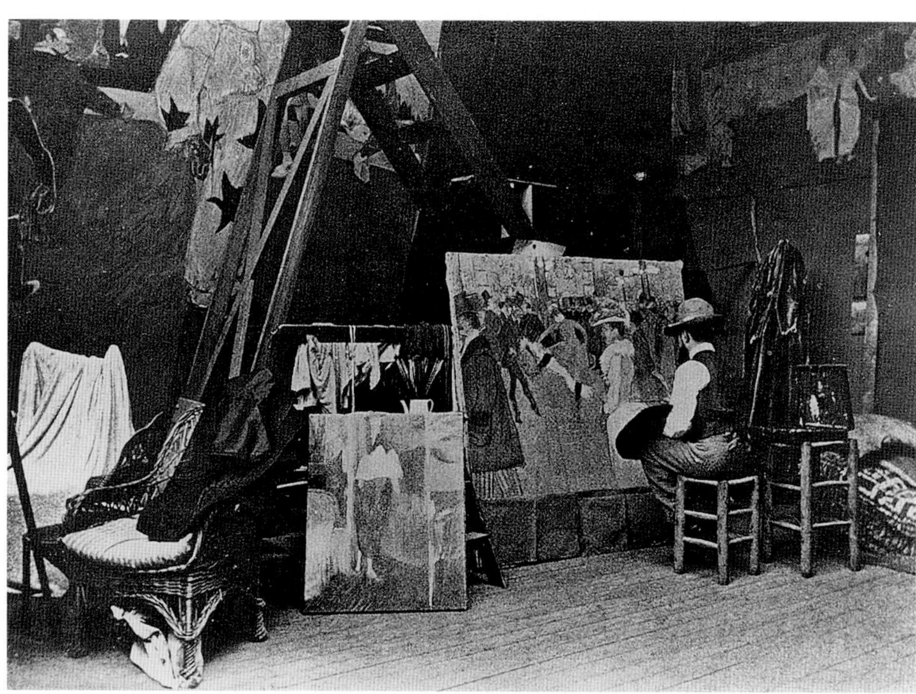

Fig. 122a Toulouse-Lautrec in his studio; the *Missing Ecuyère* visible on the left; photo: Dortu, 1971, fig. Ic. 158

Though Henri de Toulouse-Lautrec had an independent income, he chose to reside most of his adult life in Montmartre, among those who worked for a living. He moved there in 1886, stayed for twelve years, and became known as the preeminent painter of Montmartre, that section of Paris whose name still today invokes images of crowds, illicit sex, vulgar entertainment, and modern art and literature. The dissident character of the area has now largely evaporated, but in the 1880s and 1890s Montmartre was indeed populated by working people, anarchists, the poor, transients, prostitutes, entertainers, artists, and various other bohemians. It was also the location of a large number of popular clubs, cabarets, dance halls, and circuses whose names remain famous: Le Chat Noir, Le Mirliton, Moulin de la Galette, Moulin Rouge, and the Cirque Fernando. These locations provided Toulouse-Lautrec many of his subjects, including the present work.

In mid-June 1887 Toulouse-Lautrec wrote from Paris to his mother in Albi: "I'm busy doing a large panel for the circus. Unfortunately I'm afraid I shan't be able to finish until this winter at the reopening [of the Cirque Fernando]."[1] The "large panel" in question is almost certainly the so-called *Missing Ecuyère* (fig. 122a), known from a later photograph (where it is on the wall at left behind a studio ladder) and scattered remarks by the artist's friends.[2] Whether this over-life-size painting on canvas was ever exhibited at the circus or completed to the artist's satisfaction is unknown. A picture with the title *Ecuyère* was shown at the 1888 exhibition of Les Vingt in Brussels, though whether it was the *Missing Ecuyère*, *Equestrienne* (*At the Cirque Fernando*) (fig. 122b), or the smaller pastel and oil in the Norton Simon Museum remains unknown.

At the Cirque Fernando, Rider on a White Horse is a remarkable work. It has a somewhat antic aspect, but the

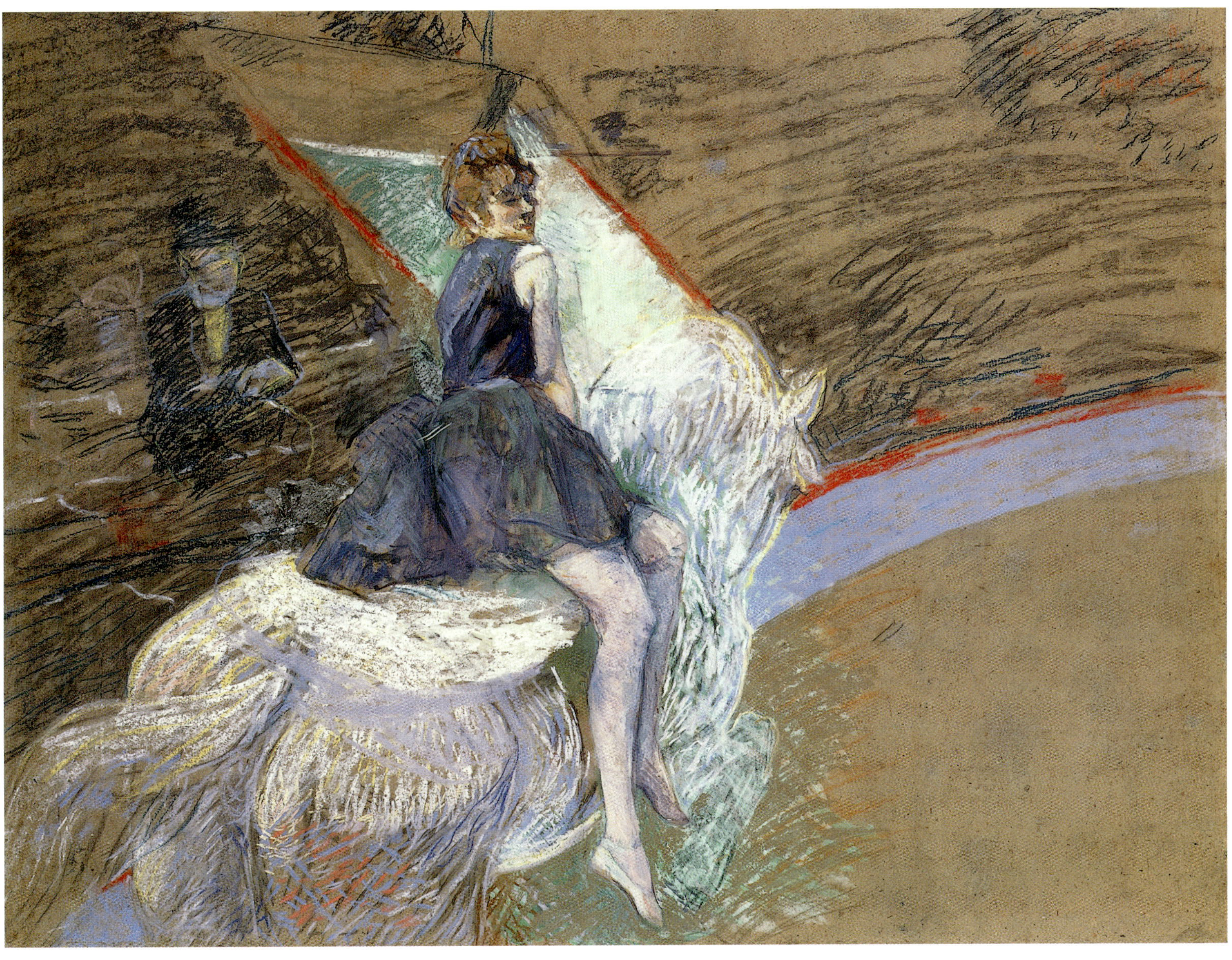

122

rider's face and body display a great expressive complexity. Despite its insistent sketchiness, the horse and equestrienne possess both volume and mass. This combination of comedy and sobriety, speed and gravity suggests that Toulouse-Lautrec's picture is a kind of modern, decadent Death on a Pale Horse, recalling images of the Four Horsemen of the Apocalypse. Indeed, the white horse is a phantom, composed of loose, shadowy pastel hatchings of orange, lilac, and brown on its croup, white for its back, and a jumble of blue, black, green, yellow, lilac, and white for its head, neck, and forelegs. The rider—modeled by the artist Suzanne Valadon—sits sidesaddle on her mount (except there is no saddle) and reaches down, presumably to grasp the horse's mane. She rests her chin on her right shoulder, revealing a face that is carefully rendered by means of small, dense, comma-shaped strokes of drained oil paint. Her eyes are shut or downcast, and her mouth is tightly closed. Suzanne's expression may be understood to connote either aloofness or erotic ecstasy.

More than the picture in Chicago or, judging from a single photograph, the *Missing Ecuyère*, the Norton Simon pastel and oil conveys movement and speed. The viewer focuses on the highly finished rider, while the background glides past in a blur. At left, a man, possibly the ringmaster, sits in a bleacher; his body is composed of horizontal black scribbles and zigzags. Above and to the right is the entrance to the ring, a trapezoidal space outlined in red and black and colored with turquoise. To the right of the horse are broad, flat stripes of lilac and

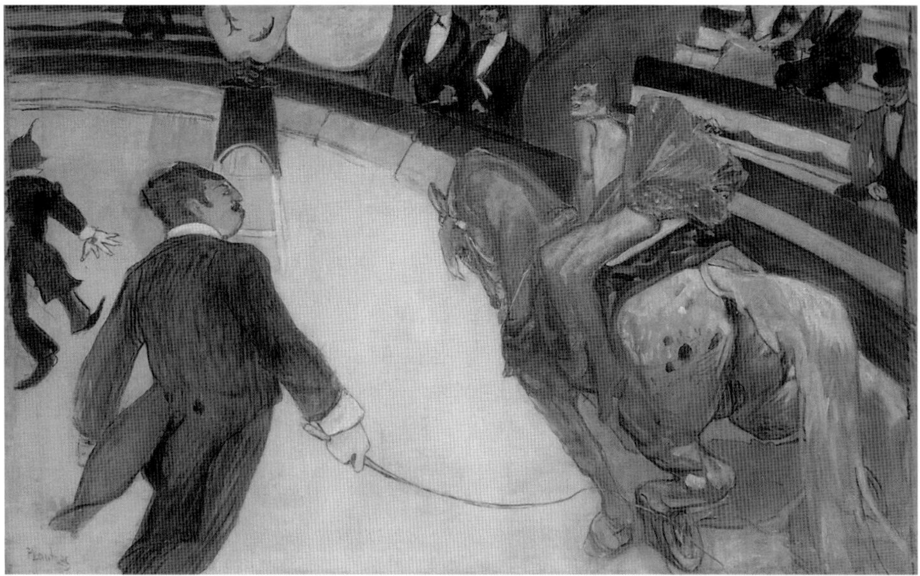

Fig. 122b Henri-Marie-Raymond de Toulouse-Lautrec, *Equestrienne (At the Circus Fernando)*, 1887–1888, oil on canvas, $39\frac{1}{2} \times 63\frac{1}{2}$ in. (100.3×161.3 cm), The Art Institute of Chicago, Joseph Winterbotham Collection

blue pastel like the lines of force in a Futurist picture; they help convey the sense of speed.

The subject of the drawing was at once quotidian and metaphoric. Circuses were a popular form of mass entertainment in fin de siècle Paris, and they came in several forms: large, permanent establishments located in the fashionable *quartiers*, such as the Hippodrome and Cirque d'Été; smaller institutions found in less stylish locations such as the Cirque d'Hiver and Cirque Fernando; and itinerant affairs pitched at primarily working-class audiences, like the Cirque Corvi. (The latter was painted by Georges Seurat in *Circus Sideshow* [1887–1888, The Metropolitan Museum of Art, New York]).

The Cirque Fernando was in its heyday when Toulouse-Lautrec painted it in 1887. It had already been depicted by Edgar Degas in his *Miss Lala at the Cirque Fernando* (1879, National Gallery, London) and would be again by Seurat in 1890–1891 (*Le Cirque*, Musée d'Orsay, Paris). The special attraction of the Cirque Fernando was its equestrian stunts, one of which involved a woman riding bareback around a ring and somersaulting through a hoop. This particular trick is the subject of the two larger *Ecuyère* pictures by Toulouse-Lautrec: each includes horse and rider, ringmaster, and a clown holding a hoop. It is also the subject, in part, of a well-known short story by Catulle Mendès, "L'Amant de sa femme," from *Monstres parisiens* (1882). In that story, a man is irresistibly compelled to return to his wife whom he had thrown out of his house years before for her adulteries. Now she is a circus performer, "starring at the Hippodrome, under a pseudonym, in the pageant of Riquet a la Houpe. . . . Looking older, she had rouge on her cheeks, shadow under her eyes . . . [and] stank deliciously of the heavy, cheap makeup and greasy face powder."[3] The Norton Simon painting and pastel lacks the narrative focus of Mendès's tale or the artist's own larger versions of the subject, but it does bring the bareback rider to life. The woman's face is heavily rouged, with deep shadows under her eyes. She is a metaphorical figure of decline and degeneracy, perhaps even, as in Mendès's story, of a near-fatal decline of national and masculine authority. Yet she is drawn and painted with extreme subtlety and is thus revealed as a very human victim of commercial exploitation. This understanding is Toulouse-Lautrec's own, perhaps unique, contribution to the representation of working women in late-nineteenth-century art. It is the insight—present from the beginning to the end of his career—that unites all three of his works in the Norton Simon Museum.

1 Herbert D. Schimmel, ed., *The Letters of Henri de Toulouse-Lautrec*, Oxford, 1991, no. 142, p. 113.

2 R. Thompson, 1991, pp. 231–233.

3 Catulle Mendès, "The Lover of His Wife," in *The Decadent Reader*, ed. Asti Hustveldt, New York, 1998, p. 836.

123

Henri-Marie-Raymond de Toulouse-Lautrec
French, 1864–1901

Red-Headed Woman in the Garden of M. Foret
Summer 1887

Oil on cardboard, 28⅛ × 22⅞ in. (71.4 × 58.1 cm)
Signed upper right: "T-Lautrec"
F.1973.37

Provenance: Nardus Collection. Pierre Decourcelle, Paris, by 1914 (sale, Paris, Hôtel Drouot, 16 June 1926, lot 74, ill., as *Femme en mauve dans le jardin du père Forest*, to); [Paul Rosenberg, Paris, sold 1926 to]; Albright Art Gallery, Buffalo, sold (by exchange) 1943 to; [Wildenstein & Co., New York, sold 7 July 1943 to]; Mr. and Mrs. Byron C. Foy, New York (Thelma Chrysler Foy sale, New York, Parke-Bernet, 13 May 1959, lot 12, color ill., as *Femme rousse dans un jardin*, to); Gordon Guiberson, Bel Air, Calif., consigned January 1965 to; [Wildenstein & Co., New York, sold April 1965 to]; Mr. and Mrs. Paul Mellon, Upperville, Va., returned February 1973 to; [Wildenstein & Co., New York, sold 31 December 1973 to]; The Norton Simon Foundation.

Exhibitions: Possibly Brussels, 1888, no. 1 or 2; Paris, 1914c, no. 27; on loan, Toronto, Art Gallery of Ontario, 1927; Chicago, 1930, no. 10; New York, 1931a, no. 10, ill.; Buffalo, 1932, no. 60; New York, 1946b, no. 5, ill.; New York, 1964a, no. 19; Washington, 1966, no. 151; San Francisco, 1974, no. 49, ill.

References: Joyant, 1926, pp. 267, 75, ill., as *Femme rousse assise de profil à gauche, en mauve*; Schaub-Koch, 1935, p. 178; Lassaigne, 1939, p. 165, pl. 52; Jourdain, 1948, pl. 6; Adhémar, 1962, p. 225; Sugana and Caproni, 1969, no. 233, p. 102, ill.; Dortu, 1971, vol. 2, no. P342, ill. p. 169; Steadman, 1976, p. 223, fig. 4; Stuckey, 1979, under no. 39, p. 149, fig. 1.

Technical Notes: The work is painted on sulfite board or bookbinder's cardboard, a gray-brown pulpy, porous board with ragged and delaminating edges. The board is a visually midrange color tone and includes inclusions, shives, and unbeaten fiber bundles. The support is in generally good condition; however, all the edges are slightly fragile and ragged. The medium is in very good condition. Visual examination reveals that it has a dry, aqueous quality, with only a few brushstrokes that appear to be oil, or perhaps *essence*. Similar works by Toulouse-Lautrec in public collections have been extensively studied to determine their media and binders, and the medium is indeed oil, despite its visual resemblance to gouache. (SSB)

Red-Headed Woman in the Garden of M. Foret depicts a young woman in a gray dress in a leafy garden. Her face is shown in lost profile, and her torso is cut off just below the waist by the picture frame. She has an ample bosom, a narrow waist, and abundant red hair tied in a bun. Her shoulder is at the eye level of the viewer and her eyes and head are inclined downward and to the left, toward a small, bare patch of ground. She is not looking at anything in particular, however; instead, she appears lost in thought.

The head and body of the model—in all likelihood she is Carmen Gaudin, who posed frequently for the artist in the mid- and late 1880s—is composed of a pair of diamond forms placed one on top of the other. The head is orange, pink, and green; the trunk is gray, blue, and white; and the brown of the cardboard support shows through in many areas. The outline of the torso is emphasized by the repetition of parallel lines within the body, lending it an architectonic character. This regularity is in marked contrast to the garden foliage, which is represented by means of varied, energetic, and multidirectional brushstrokes.

The light, color, and general vitality of the painting suggest it was begun, if not completed, out of doors. "The sky is unsettled," Toulouse-Lautrec wrote in an irreverent mood to his mother in July 1887, "and is sprinkling us with an unconcern that shows how little feeling the Eternal Father has with regard to outdoor painting."[1] *Red-Headed Woman* is likely one of the pictures painted that July, and one of the two pictures exhibited in 1888 at the Exposition des Vingt under the title *Rousse* (*plein-air*) (*Red-Headed Woman* [*Out-of-Doors*]).[2] The other painting is probably *Red-Headed Woman in the Garden of M. Foret* (fig. 123a). Two additional pictures of red-headed, working-class women in Foret's garden are *Woman in the Garden of Monsieur Foret* (fig. 123b) and *À Batignolle*.[3]

In 1889 or 1890 someone took a photograph of Toulouse-Lautrec painting *Portrait of Berthe la Sourde* (fig. 123c) in the same garden of Père Foret in Montmartre, located on the corner of the boulevard de Clichy and rue Caulaincourt. His position in the photograph—seated, feet flat on the ground, leaning forward and neck craning—is likely the same he assumed while painting *Red-Headed Woman*. The artist's eyes are on a line with the shoulders of the figure on the canvas and his seated model. When, in a few minutes, the artist and model stand up, the perspective of the diminutive artist will change; his eyes will still face her shoulder, and he will look up at her face. Taken together, the paintings and photograph reiterate the clear deference that

Fig. 123a (*right*) Henri-Marie-Raymond de Toulouse-Lautrec, *Red-Headed Woman in the Garden of M. Foret*, 1887, oil on cardboard, 25½ × 20⅞ in. (64.6 × 53 cm), private collection

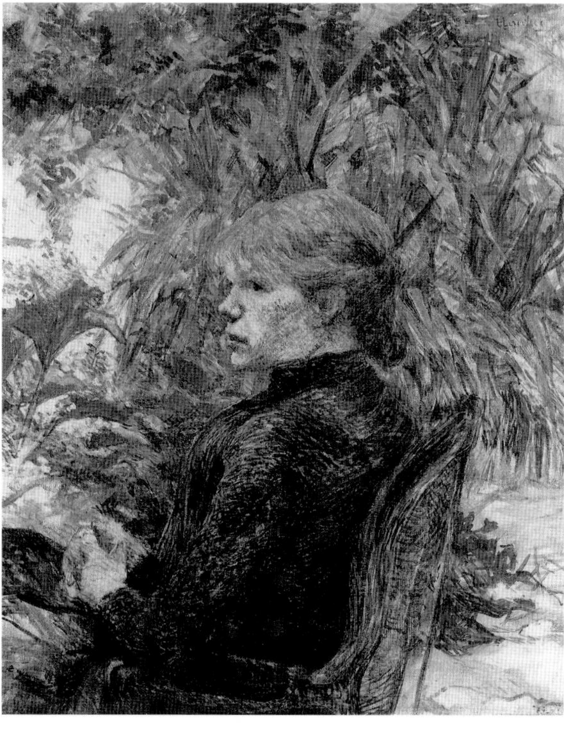

Fig. 123b (*far right*) Henri-Marie-Raymond de Toulouse-Lautrec, *Woman in the Garden of Monsieur Foret*, 1889–1891, oil on sized linen, 21⅞ × 18¼ in. (55.6 × 46.4 cm), The Metropolitan Museum of Art, Bequest of Joan Whitney Payson, 1975

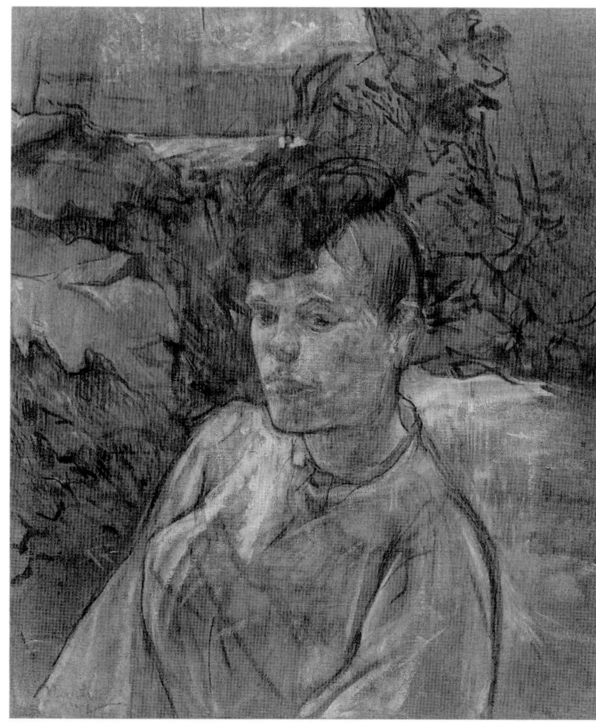

Toulouse-Lautrec generally showed his sitters, remarkable given his own elite class status. (He was the child of a long aristocratic lineage.)

Toulouse-Lautrec was not alone in depicting the appearance and lives of working-class women but was almost unique in his perseverance, the intensity of his gaze, and his lack of condescension. In this regard he surpassed Edgar Degas, whom he much admired, and can be compared only to his friend Vincent van Gogh. In 1886 the two studied at Fernand Cormon's atelier and the following year exhibited together at the Grand Bouillon-Restaurant du Chalet on the avenue de Clichy. The exhibition, organized by van Gogh, also included works by Émile Bernard, Louis Anquetin, A. Koning, and Armand Guillaumin. The venture was conceived in an effort to display modern painting with Naturalist themes on the *petit boulevard*, in mild opposition to the exhibitions of Impressionist pictures at elite galleries on the *grand boulevard*. That same year, Toulouse-Lautrec drew van Gogh's portrait in pastel (*Portrait of Vincent van Gogh*, Van Gogh Museum, Amsterdam) and publicly spoke out in defense of the older man when his work was derided on one occasion by a rival.[4] Van Gogh's most important effort at this time to depict a woman of the working class was *Woman at a Table in the Café du Tambourin* (Van Gogh Museum, Amsterdam), a somewhat exotic-looking portrait of his friend Agostina Segatori. It would not be until the great portraits of Madame Roulin in late 1888 that he would achieve the sober, interrogative qualities found in Toulouse-Lautrec's slightly earlier portraits, such as the *Poudre de riz* (fig. 110c) and *Red-Headed Woman*.

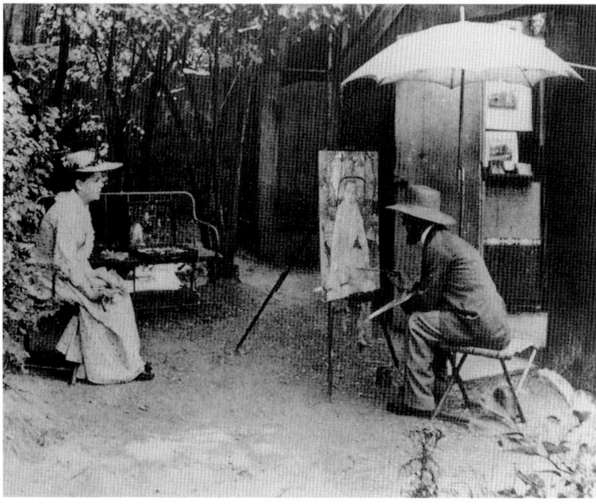

Fig. 123c Toulouse-Lautrec painting *Portrait of Berthe la Sourde* in the garden of M. Foret, Montmartre; photo: Dortu, 1971, fig. Ic. 161

1 Herbert D. Schimmel, ed., *The Letters of Henri de Toulouse-Lautrec*, Oxford, 1991, no. 146, p. 115.
2 Octave Maus, *Catalogue de la Ve Exposition des XX*, Brussels, 1888, n. p., in Dortu, 1971, vol. 1, p. 56.
3 Present location unknown, Dortu, 1971, p. 306.
4 Thadée Natanson, "Lautrec and Vincent van Gogh," in *Toulouse-Lautrec: A Retrospective*, ed. Gale B. Murray, New York, 1992, p. 108.

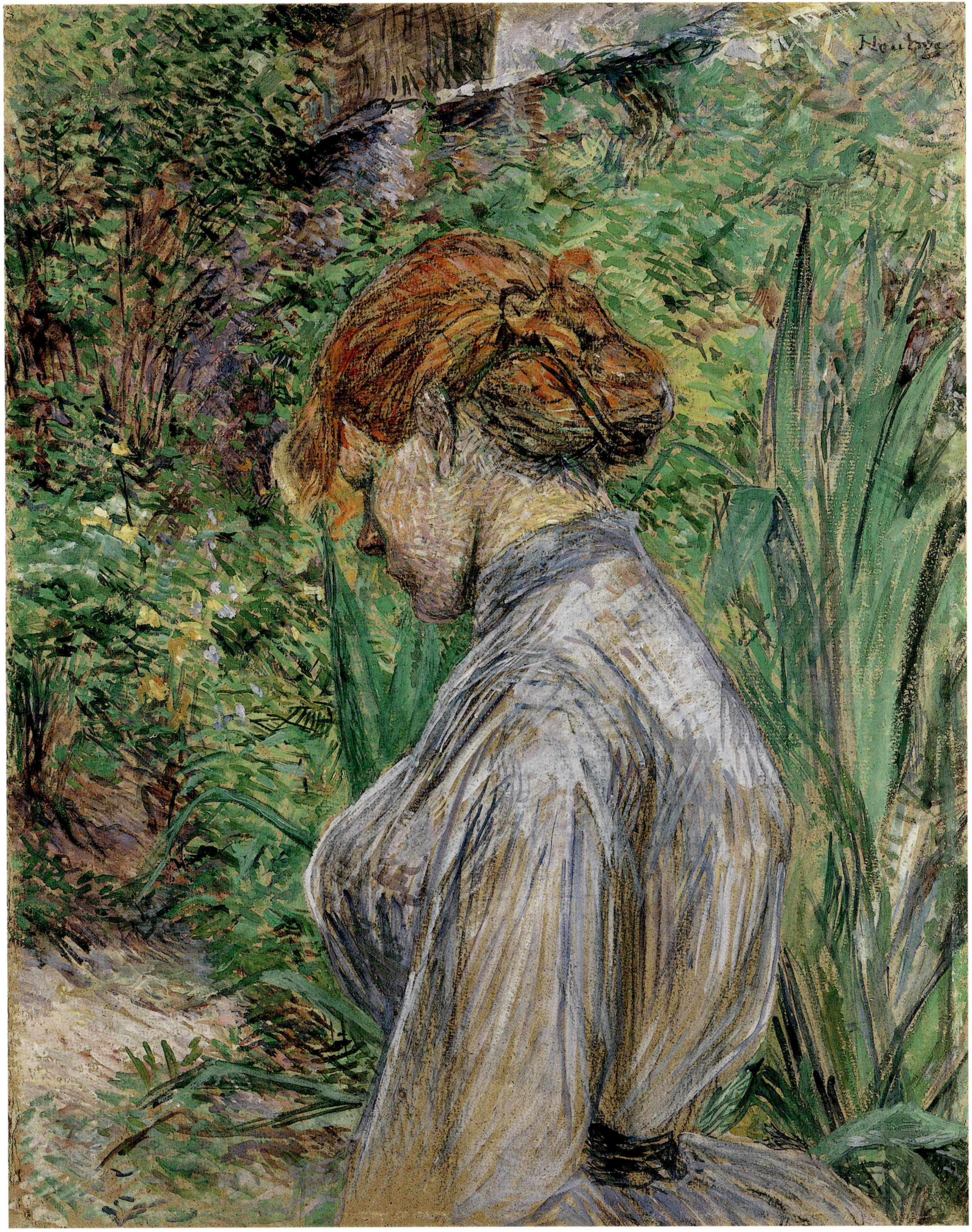

123

124

Henri-Marie-Raymond de Toulouse-Lautrec
French, 1864–1901

The Streetwalker (formerly *Portrait of a Prostitute*)
1892–1894

Oil on cardboard, 24¾ × 19⅛ in. (62.8 × 48.4 cm)
Signed lower right: "H T Lautrec"
M.2000.1.3

Provenance: [Jos Hessel, Paris]. [?Léon] Orosdi, by 1914. S. Sévadjian (sale, Paris, Hôtel Drouot, 22 March 1920, lot 21, ill., to); Heibel. [Paul Rosenberg, Paris, by 1926]. Mlle Jane Renouardt [?Renouard], Paris, sold 1938 to; [Paul Rosenberg, Paris and New York, after 1940, Paris stock no. 338, as *Pensionnaire de maison close*, New York stock no. 5095, as *Profil*; sold 20 February 1957 to]; Robert Ellis Simon, Los Angeles, bequest 1969 to; The Norton Simon Foundation, transferred 2000 to; Norton Simon Art Foundation.

Exhibitions: Paris, 1914a, no. 24 as *La Pierreuse*; Paris, 1914c, no. 77, as *Portrait de femme*; Paris, 1931, no. 106 as *Femme de maison ou pierreuse*; New York, 1945b, no. 9; New York, 1947, no. 13; Detroit, 1954, no. 128; Philadelphia, 1955, no. 52, ill.; New York, 1956b, no. 24; Los Angeles, 1965; San Francisco, 1973, no. 48.

References: Joyant, 1926, vol. 1, pp. 284, 199, ill.; Lassaigne, 1939, p. 127; Sugana and Caproni, 1969, no. 350, pp. 108–109; Dortu, 1971, vol. 2, no. P509, p. 313; B. Thomson, 1988, p. 131, pl. 57 (by Vuillard);[1] R. Thomson, 1991, p. 458, fig. d.

Technical Notes: The work is painted on sulfite board or bookbinder's cardboard, a gray-brown pulpy, porous board with ragged and delaminating edges. The board is a visually midrange color tone and includes inclusions, shives, and unbeaten fiber bundles. The support is in generally good condition; however, all the edges are fragile, chipped, and ragged. Primary damages in the support include two vertical gouges at the center top, a horizontal gouge left of center 5 inches from the bottom, a split in the upper left corner, and a horizontal split at the bottom center. The work is in very good condition. Visual examination reveals that the medium has a dry, aqueous quality in areas like the figure's hair and perhaps in underdrawing strokes, in contrast to areas like the figure's clothing and stole, which have the characteristics of oil. Similar works by Toulouse-Lautrec in public collections have been subjected to extensive study of their media and binders, and the medium is indeed oil, despite its visual resemblance to gouache. The verso of the millboard is painted blue and has several previous collectors' labels. (SSB)

A second portrait by Toulouse-Lautrec in the Norton Simon collections painted some six years after *Red-Headed Woman in the Garden of M. Foret* (cat. 123) marks a change in the artist's painterly style and thematic concerns. It depicts a heavy-set woman with puffy face and pasty skin seated and facing left. She is shown bust length, and her head is almost, but not quite, in profile—we can see just a bit of her right cheek, eye, and forehead. Her eyes, which appear crossed, are slightly downcast. Curls of hair fall on her forehead and drape the high collar of her rose-and-green-colored blouse. Her lips are parted, though she is not shown speaking. The wall behind her is orange with vertical streaks of red, yellow, and green, punctuated with the rough outlines of three pictures of identical size. To the left is an unidentifiable jumble of white and turquoise with smaller patches of blue and gray; it may represent an unmade bed or linens thrown over a chair, or may depict nothing specific at all. In many places, the tan of the cardboard support shows through the washes of thinned oil paint. The same figure—the same size, with the same slightly dissipated, slightly blank expression and seen from almost the same point of view—is represented in an important multifigure composition from this time, *A Corner of the Moulin de la Galette* (fig. 124a).

The Streetwalker is more broadly painted than *Red-Headed Woman* and dates from 1892–1894. It does not bear much relation to the work of Vincent van Gogh and is more closely related to contemporary paintings and pastels by Louis Anquetin, Jean-Louis Forain, Edgar

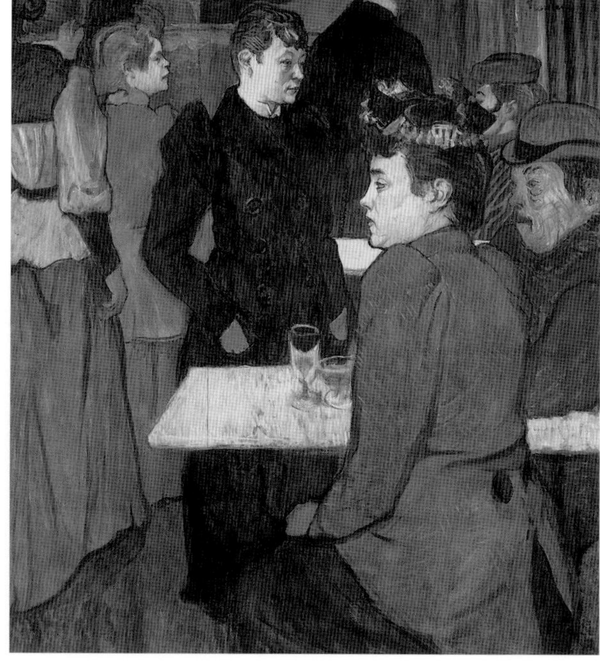

Fig. 124a Henri-Marie-Raymond de Toulouse-Lautrec, *A Corner of the Moulin de la Galette*, 1892, oil on cardboard, 39⅜ × 35⅛ in. (100 × 89.2 cm), National Gallery of Art, Washington, Chester Dale Collection

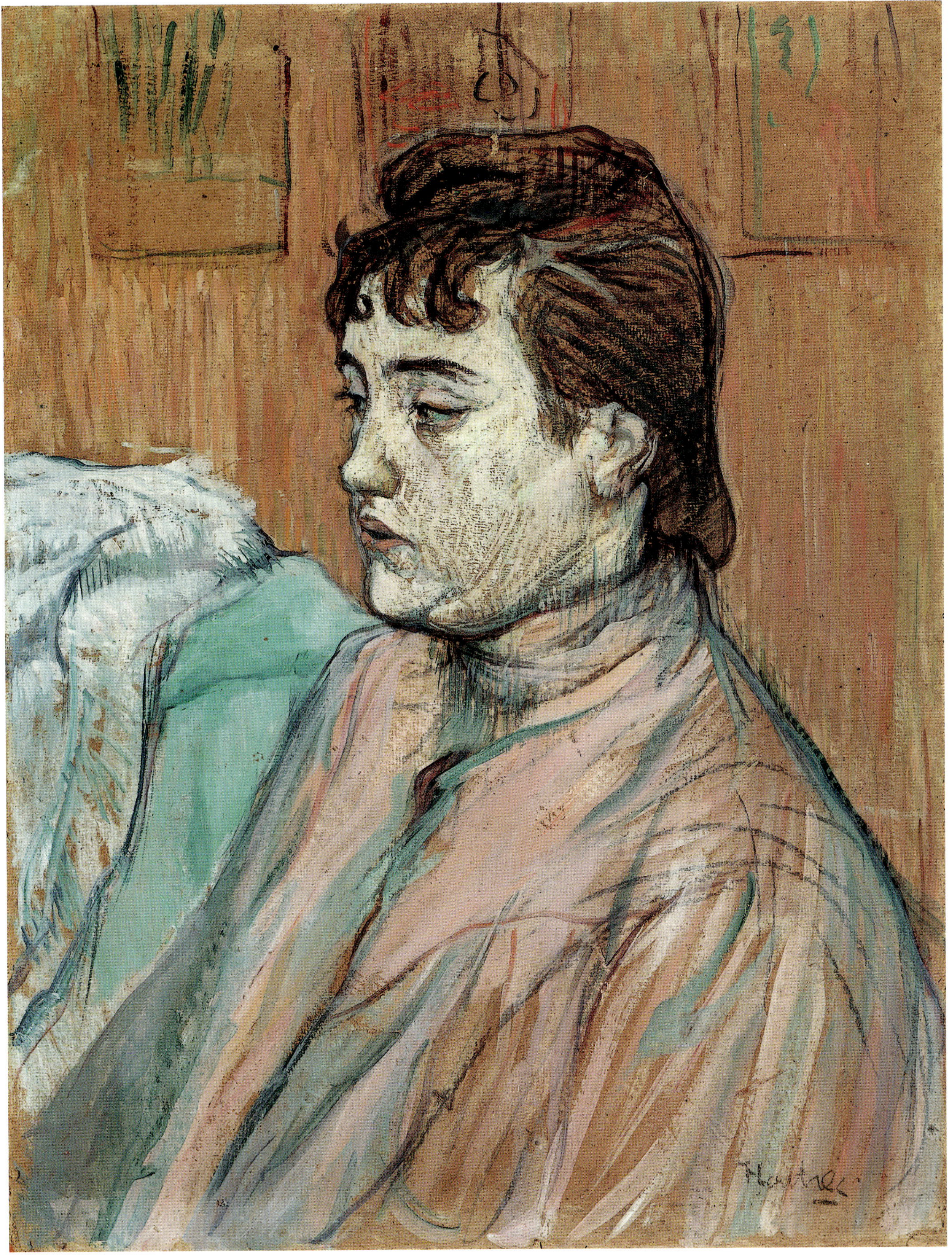

Degas, and perhaps Paul Gauguin. The subject and format of Toulouse-Lautrec's portrait generally recall works by the first two artists (see the discussion of Anquetin's *Portrait of a Woman*, cat. 117). The vertical streaks of orange, yellow, and pink in the background are reminiscent of some of the bath and brothel pictures of Degas from the late 1880s and early 1890s, such as *Study of a Nude* (David-Weill Collection, Paris) shown at the 1886 Impressionist exhibition. The mood of introspection and loss is reminiscent of Gauguin's *Faaturuma* (*Melancholic*) (fig. 99b), exhibited in Paris in 1893.

The earlier *Red-Headed Woman in the Garden of M. Foret* (cat. 123) was made out of doors, in a garden, whereas the later *Streetwalker* was painted indoors, perhaps even in a brothel. The one is dominated by the colors of nature, bright greens and yellows, and the other by unnatural colors associated with the hothouse decadence of fin de siècle interiors, orange, pink, and mauve. The one is inflected with myriad flecks and strokes of paint applied with apparent energy, the other composed of long lines and loops of paint put down with both deliberation and panache. Together, the two portraits describe the changes in a painter's career and the passage from one moment in the development of French modern art to the next. In *Red-Headed Woman*, Toulouse-Lautrec was an Impressionist who embraced Naturalist subjects, one of which was young, urban women of the working class. In the present painting, he was a confirmed Naturalist who explored Symbolist themes of decadence, degeneracy, and sexual license. In the 1890s Toulouse-Lautrec preferred to examine the closed interior of brothels and to chart on the human face and body the emotional and physical effects of this means of economic and social production and exchange. At the same time that he was depicting this extremely circumscribed interior life and space, however, he was also representing the world of Parisian public entertainments.

The present title, *The Streetwalker* (*La Pierreuse*) is the earliest that has been associated with the picture.[2] Toulouse-Lautrec would have heard the term regularly and read it in the novels of Stendhal, Alphonse Daudet, the Goncourt brothers, and Octave Mirbeau.[3] The term derives from the habit of certain lower-class prostitutes to frequent building sites—cluttered with cut stones, *pierres*—of Paris during the Napoleonic Empire. The term remained in common usage for most of the century, always to indicate a prostitute who was dirty, gross, and cheap. The artist himself used it in 1893 for his lithograph *Pauvre Pierreuse*, advertising a "Chanson réaliste."[4]

1 The painting is seen in Édouard Vuillard's *Lucy Hessel in the Small Salon, rue de Rivoli* (1903, private collection).

2 Paris 1914a, no. 24.

3 See, for example, Octave Mirbeau: "On s'imagine pas combine il y a de femmes, qui, chez elles, sont grossières de langage, ordurières de gestes, et degoutantes à force de vulgarité . . . de varies pierreuses!" cited in *La Grand Robert de la langue française*, Paris, 2001, vol. 5, p. 662.

4 Loys Delteil, *Le peintre-graveur illustré* (*XIXe et XXe siècles*), Paris, 1906–1930, vol. 10, no. 26.

125

Ker-Xavier Roussel
French, 1867–1944

Meeting of Women
c. 1893

Oil on canvas, $17\frac{7}{8} \times 29\frac{1}{2}$ in. (45.4 × 75 cm)
Signed lower right: "K × R . . ."
M.1977.3.2

Provenance: Collection of the artist, 1894–1944; Jacques Salomon (son-in-law of artist), Paris, presumably by inheritance 1944, but certainly by 1955. Antoine Salomon, Paris, by 1968. [Galerie La Cave, Paris, sold 15 February 1977 to]; Norton Simon Art Foundation.

Exhibitions: Paris 1944, no. 151 or 152; London 1954b, no. 43, ill.; Vevey 1954, no. 68; Paris 1955a, no. 133; Tokyo 1961, no. 242; London 1964, no. 4, fig. 6; Bremen 1965, no. 17, ill. p. 36; Munich, 1968, no. 212, p. 279, ill. (in Paris, no. 211, p. 333, ill.).

References: Alexandre, 1893, p. 3; Salomon, 1967, p. 39; Boyer, 1978, under nos. 107 and 108, p. 170; Musée du Petit Palais, 1986, p. 237; Frèches-Thory and Terrasse, 1991, p. 107, ill.; Huguette Berès, 1990, under no. 79; Frèches-Thory and Perucchi-Petri, 1993, under no. 97, pp. 226–227, 237; Groom, 2001, under no. 28, p. 113, fig. 1; Barruel, 2005, p. 32, fig. 11.

Technical Notes: The plain, open-weave canvas is tacked to a 5-part wood stretcher that shows signs of age. The design continues onto the tacking edges, which are unevenly cut at the back edge of the stretcher. A light gray ground almost fills the canvas weave. Thinly painted dark lines mark the rectangular areas, but the scene above is drawn with what appears to be charcoal. The ground is covered with a layer of pink paint that is probably oil. The design was then painted in short strokes with a small brush, leaving some of the pink to act as part of the design. For example, dabs of yellow and red delineate features of faces, leaving this pink base to show. Some forms consist of several layers. An example is the pink dress at right that has a bright red layer of underpaint covered with a gray-pink layer. Finally, the dark spots were added on top. White paint applied in a brushy manner covers the ground of the rectangles. The white is richer and denser on the right half of the picture. A dark ocher-gray paint was applied in a open, brushy manner over the white. The white underlayer has cracks that are visible with magnification, but the top layer seems to go over these cracks. Perhaps when this scene was cut out or edited to be presented as an easel painting, the dead space of the rectangles was enlivened with the brushy paint. A thin varnish covers the scene, but the rectangles are matte to semiglossy and thus apparently unvarnished, and so are the tacking edges. The condition of the painting is good with only a few small losses. There are also a limited number of noticeable cracks in the scene. (JF)

The peculiar format of this small oil painting is explained by the fact that it was a study for a decorative mural painting for the *mairie*, or city hall, of Bagnolet, a suburb southeast of Paris. The gray rectangles at left and right represent the spaces for doors or windows, and the gray area at bottom for a horizontal section of wall or wainscoting. Ker-Xavier Roussel was not in the end awarded the 1893 municipal commission, and his *Meeting of Women*, along with two smaller studies, *Conversation on a Terrace* (fig. 125a) and *Terrace of the Tuileries* (1893, Musée d'Orsay, Paris), was at some later date revised and sold as an independent easel painting. The paint surface clearly extends beyond its left and right tacking edges, indicating that the artist, or possibly a subsequent owner, decided to hide the narrow strips of architecture at left and white ground at right by folding them under the stretcher bars and cutting off the excess canvas. The result was a more cogent picture than the original maquette, closer in effect to the small, intimate, rectangular canvases that Roussel and his Nabi friends—Édouard Vuillard, Pierre Bonnard, and Maurice Denis—generally painted.

The painting depicts ten women standing or sitting in a beaux-arts-designed park composed of manicured and sculpted lawns, gravel walks, and stone benches and balustrades. Above the women are patches of blue sky and the branches and orange foliage of five large trees. Their regular spacing divides the canvas into five vertical segments, accentuating the regularity and calm of the scene. Gloria Groom has identified the location as the Terrasse des Tuileries looking south toward the Seine near the Pavilion de Flore, the westernmost wing of the Louvre.[1] There are six discrete groupings of figures in this elegant setting: the two large standing figures at right; the woman with her standard poodle near the patch of grass at left; the single reader seated on the base of the sculpture pedestal; the two figures in intimate conversation behind the solitary woman (one is seated on the stone bench, while the other kneels behind, resting her head on her hands); two standing figures to the left of the sculpture in front of the balustrade; and finally two more figures in the background at left, one seated and one standing. These distant figures are somewhat indistinct, but since Roussel intended them for a much larger composition, we must suppose their postures and attitudes would have been clarified at full scale. The women wear long, kimono-like dresses, several of which have fanciful, allover patterns of polka dots or parallel arcs, which tend to flatten their wearers' shapes. The women thus function pictorially as decorative extensions of the flat, Japanese-style trees and landscape, rather than

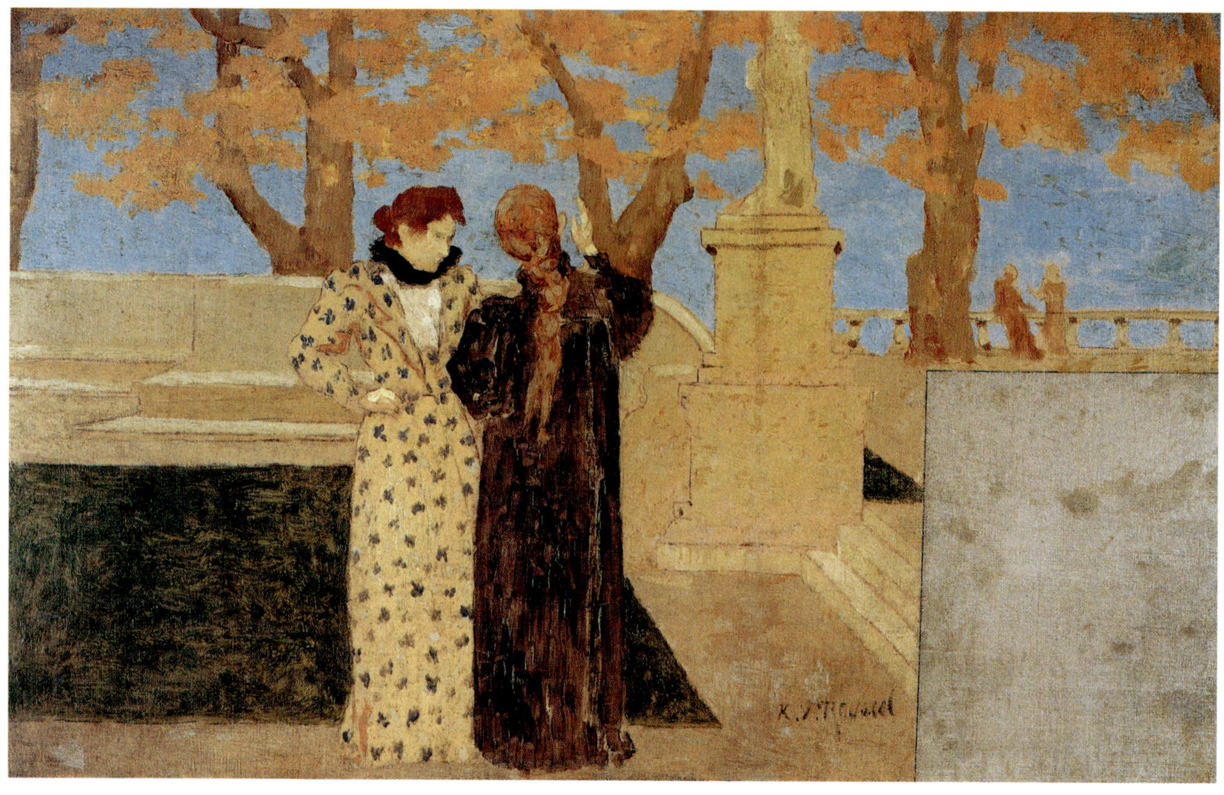

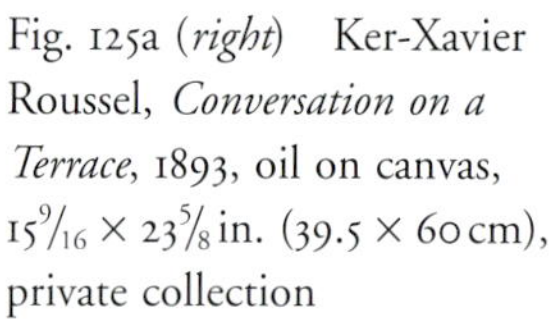

Fig. 125a (*right*) Ker-Xavier Roussel, *Conversation on a Terrace*, 1893, oil on canvas, $15\frac{9}{16} \times 23\frac{5}{8}$ in. (39.5 × 60 cm), private collection

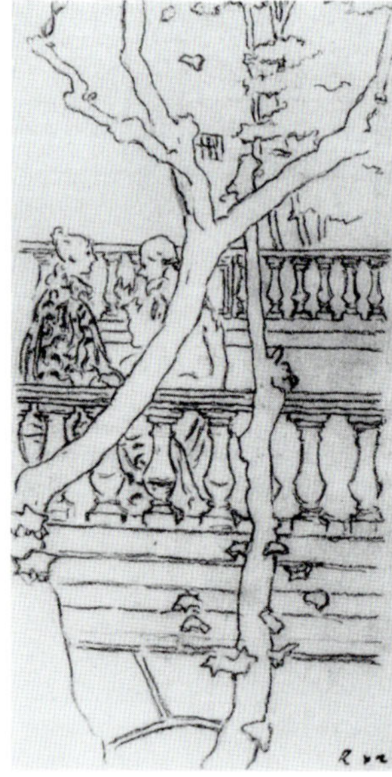

Fig. 125b (*above*) Ker-Xavier Roussel, *Two Women Conversing: The Terrace*, 1893, lithograph after an original drawing, reproduced in *Revue Blanche* 15 September 1893

being three-dimensional intrusions on the ornamental space. This Japonism is even more strongly accentuated in a contemporary lithograph by Roussel published in the Symbolist journal *La Revue blanche,* titled *Two Women Conversing: The Terrace* (fig. 125b). There, the women are fully subsumed by the decorative ensemble made up of the intersection of vertical and diagonal trees in the foreground and the parallel balustrades in the fore- and background.

The modernity of the figures in *Meeting of Women* is marked by their comportment as well as by their fashionable dress and abstracted form. The two in the foreground are broad, tall, and poised. The one at left presents a formidable back, like one of Henri Matisse's great series of relief sculptures called *The Back,* the first of

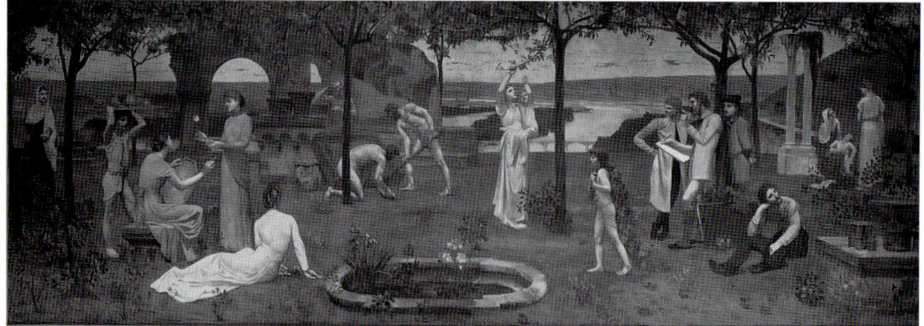

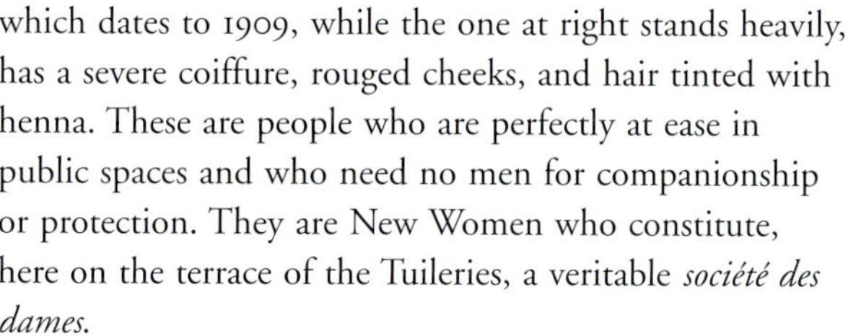

which dates to 1909, while the one at right stands heavily, has a severe coiffure, rouged cheeks, and hair tinted with henna. These are people who are perfectly at ease in public spaces and who need no men for companionship or protection. They are New Women who constitute, here on the terrace of the Tuileries, a veritable *société des dames.*

Yet for all its protofeminist contemporaneity, the painting is not without suggestion of classical allegory or symbolism. The very femininity of the subject suggests the tradition of allegorical painting in which women may stand for Peace, the Arts, Inspiration, the Seasons, Abundance, Justice, Liberty, or France. (Men are rarely allegories in French painting; they are heroes who act, not symbols who signify.) The most celebrated muralist of Roussel's day, and the artist who maintained—almost single-handedly—the tradition of large-scale allegorical representation until near the end of the nineteenth century, was undoubtedly Pierre Puvis de Chavannes. His *Inter Artes et Naturam* (*The Benefits of Peace*) (fig. 125c) was exhibited in 1890 at the Salon de la Nationale (also known as the Salon du Champ de Mars) and would have been well known to the younger artist. Its mélange of classically robed young men and women, children, laborers, artists, and poets constituted a utopian vision of a well-ordered, classless society in a future closely modeled on an idealized past. Roussel's mural idea, even

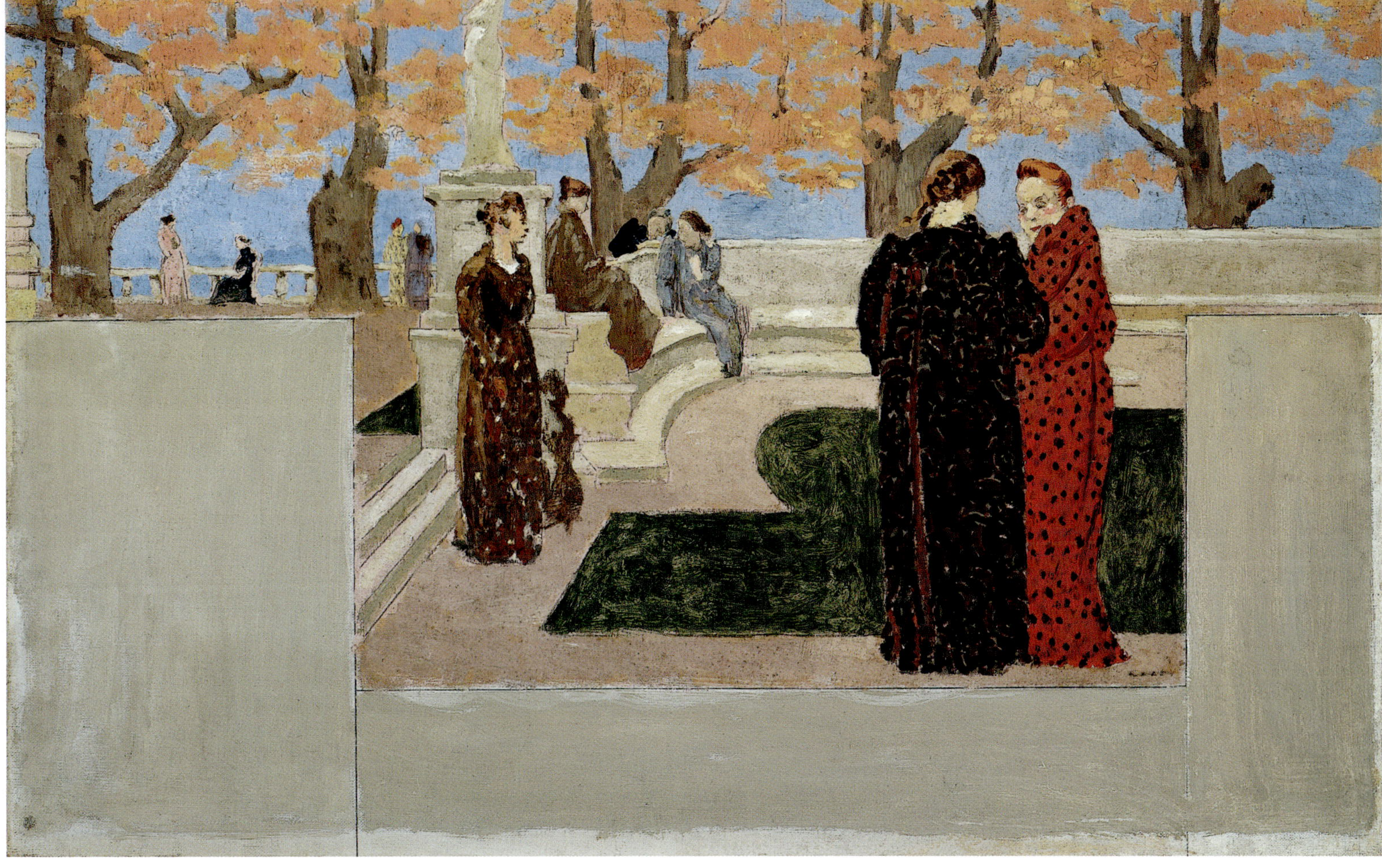

125

if accepted by the worthy citizens of Bagnolet, was not so ambitious. Its allusion to the arts and letters was limited to a single reading woman in the middle ground, seated beneath a sculpture that may depict the goddess Athena. Nor was it so dreamlike as Denis's *July* (1892, Gustave Rau Foundation, Zurich), exhibited at the Salon des Indépendants in 1892, which shows eight women in long gowns sitting and strolling on lawns in an imaginary garden or park. Nor was it as animated and modern as Vuillard's 1894 nine-panel ensemble for Alexandre Natanson, *The Public Gardens*,[2] which portrays the quotidian bustle of a contemporary space of bourgeois and petit bourgeois recreation. The very reticence of Roussel's *Meeting of Women*, in common with much of the rest of his work, made it oddly inappropriate for the public space of a bustling city hall, but at the same time marks the painting's quiet eloquence.

1 Groom, 2001, p. 113.

2 Salomon and Cogival, 2003, vol. 1, nos. V-39.1–V-39.5 (Musée d'Orsay, Paris), no. V-39.6 (The Museum of Fine Arts, Houston), no. V-39.7 (private collection, United States), V-39.8 (Musée d'Art Moderne, Musées Royaux des Beaux-Arts de Belgique, Brussels), V-39.9 (The Cleveland Museum of Art).

Fig. 125c (*facing page bottom*) Pierre-Cécile Puvis de Chavannes, *Inter Artes et Naturam (The Benefits of Peace)*, 1890, oil on canvas, $116\frac{1}{4} \times 326\frac{3}{4}$ in. (295 × 830 cm), Musée des Beaux-Arts, Rouen; photo: © Bridgeman-Giraudon / Art Resource, NY

126

Pierre Bonnard
French, 1867–1947

The Place Clichy, Paris
1900

Oil on cardboard (triptych); left panel, 13¾ × 9½ in. (34.9 × 24.1 cm); center panel, 13¼ × 20½ in. (33.7 × 52.2 cm); right panel, 13½ × 8¾ in. (34.3 × 22.2 cm)
Left panel signed lower left: "Bonnard"; center panel signed and dated lower left: "1900 Bonnard"; right panel signed lower right: "Bonnard"
F.1969.9.P

Provenance: [Jos Hessel, Paris]. Private collection, France. Daniel Varenne, sold 1968 to; [Hirschl & Adler Galleries, Inc., New York, consigned August 1968 to]; Norton Simon, returned September 1968 to; [Hirschl & Adler Galleries, Inc., New York, stock no. 5342, sold 7 May 1969 to]; The Norton Simon Foundation.

Exhibitions: On loan, Phoenix, Art Museum, 18 August–19 November 1969; Oakland, 1969, no. 11, ill.; on loan, Los Angeles, County Museum of Art, January 1970–September 1972; San Francisco, 1973, no. 50, ill.

Reference: Dauberville and Dauberville, 1965, vol. 1, no. 237, p. 241, ill.

Technical Notes: The support of all three panels is green cardboard with a firm surface. There is no ground layer, and the green support frequently remains slightly exposed. Bonnard may have prepared the surface to make it less absorbent before painting, but microscopic examination does not clarify this point. Paint was directly applied over the ground in feathery strokes. Superimposed strokes were applied over dry paint so that brushstrokes remained clear and distinct. Bonnard used dabbing and stippling as well as short, sketchy brushstrokes, deemphasizing color boundaries. As indicated by the X-ray, Bonnard painted without major changes; he reduced slightly the size of the horse pulling the cart in the center: its head originally extended farther to the right. When the three panels are unframed, it becomes apparent that their heights differ by a small amount and the design is not continuous from the center panel to the right panel. In the left and center panels Bonnard employed softer colors, greens and grays in multiple hues and values, using the brush with a light touch. In the right panel, brushstrokes are longer and firmer, and color areas are larger. The vantage point is different: the viewer is closer in the right panel. The paintings are well preserved and may never have been cleaned. Minor losses are found at the edges, where handling has caused small damages. There is a brittle and slightly opaque surface coating on each panel; the material has not been identified, but it is not typical of varnish. (RW)

A triptych is a picture composed of three parts with imagery generally derived from the Christian religion. The earliest triptychs are Byzantine icons, ivories, and reliquaries, and the most famous are by northern European painters. The form is ideally suited to mystery, revelation, and pageantry: a large central panel with a scene of the Annunciation, the Incarnation, or the Crucifixion is hidden from view by smaller side panels decorated with pictures of donors or saints that fold over the central scene. On a given, sacred day, the wings of the triptych are thrown open and one of the glories of the faith is revealed, to the astonishment of all. But can there be a triptych of modern life? Surely the form is an anachronism in an age of disenchantment.

Yet in the 1890s, the decade of the Nabis, Pierre Bonnard was master of this visual conundrum. His delightful gray-green painting *The Place Clichy, Paris* is one of three triptychs formerly owned by Bonnard's great friend, the art dealer Jos Hessel. The other two, *The Moulin Rouge* (fig. 126a), now split up, and *The Ages of Life* (fig. 126b), now with the Hessel descendants, are both larger and earlier. The first was signed and dated in 1896, the year of Bonnard's first important one-person exhibition at the Durand-Ruel gallery, and the second, though undated, was assigned the same year by Bonnard's cataloguers, Jean and Henry Dauberville. Bonnard made four additional triptychs in the 1890s for other patrons, before reprising the format in 1900 in the Norton Simon painting. They are the *Village Ensemble* (fig. 126c), composed of three tall, slender pastoral panels in oil; *The Course at Longchamp* (fig. 126d), depicting in successive panels the horses and jockeys, crowds and carriages, and standing spectators at the famous racecourse; *Jardin publique*,[1] three small tempera and pastel panels depicting an idealized urban park; and *Étude pour un décor de théâtre*,[2] three street scenes. These last two were painted in a loose, sketchy manner and are known only from photographs taken in 1916. No other painter of the Nabi circle was so ambitious in his effort to synthesize modern life—street scenes, rural retreats, and popular entertainments—with the sacredness and devotional content that still adhered to the triptych format. And no other patron than Hessel gave the artist such encouragement. The fact that Hessel owned three of the seven surviving triptychs suggests that they were considered more or less an ensemble of ensembles. The physical examination of the Norton Simon painting proves that the three panels are completely separate and of somewhat different dimensions. This suggests that they may not have been begun together and that their present triptych form may have been arrived at as the artist

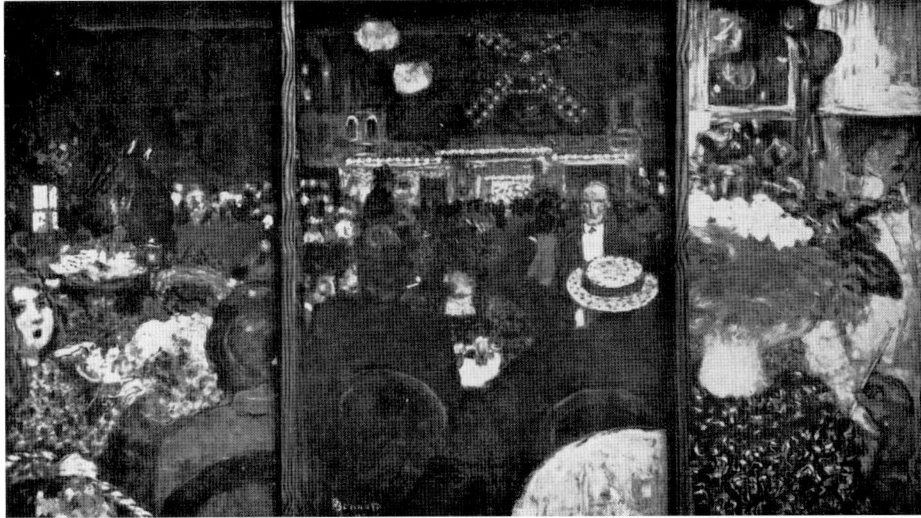

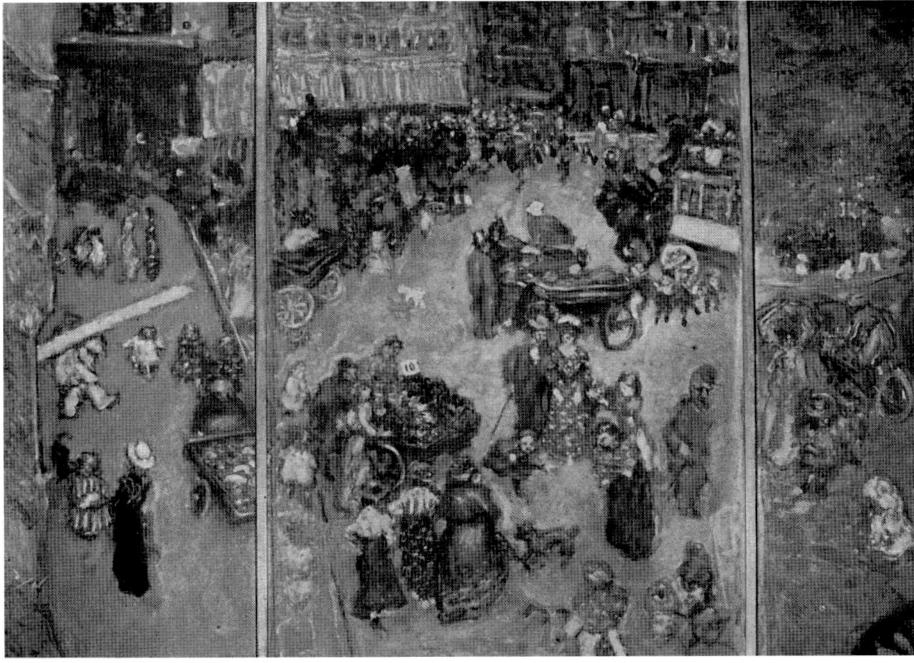

Fig. 126a (*top*) Pierre Bonnard, *The Moulin Rouge*, 1896, oil on panel, 24 × $39\frac{3}{8}$ in. (61 × 100 cm), location unknown; photo: Dauberville and Dauberville, 1965, no. 131

Fig. 126b (*above*) Pierre Bonnard, *The Ages of Life*, c. 1896, oil on canvas, $28\frac{3}{4}$ × $43\frac{1}{4}$ in. (73 × 110 cm), location unknown; photo: Dauberville and Dauberville, 1965, no. 136

worked on various urban scenes. Only detailed physical examination of the other triptychs will enable us to do more than speculate about their production.

In each of the Hessel triptychs, Bonnard's subject is the portion of northern Paris in the immediate neighborhood of the painter's studio at 65, rue de Douai, a small street one block south of the boulevard Clichy and very near the place Clichy (now called the place Blanche). This lively neighborhood, often called Les Batignolles, had been associated with the art world since Édouard Manet's time in the 1860s and had become an international artistic neighborhood by the mid-1880s. It was also an active center for Parisian nightlife, as the presence of the Moulin Rouge makes clear. The same region of the city, just south of Montmartre, had been painted by Edgar Degas, Pierre-Auguste Renoir, Camille Pissarro, Jean-François Raffaëlli, Henri de Toulouse-Lautrec, Vincent van Gogh, and others and was also the subject of many paintings by Édouard Vuillard as well as early works by Pablo Picasso. It is thus—in addition to its associations with entertainment and modern, urban life—an utterly artistic subject.

Bonnard himself made the city of Paris and principally the streets and boulevards near the place Clichy and place Pigalle into the chief subject of his out-of-door painting in the 1890s. In fact, Bonnard can be considered the major topographical painter of the region at the fin de siècle. A large number of these urban works were included in the 1896 exhibition of his work at the Durand-Ruel gallery, about which Pissarro—himself a major painter of urban subjects—wrote disparagingly to his son Lucien.[3] Indeed, Bonnard and his friend Vuillard were fast becoming the major young artists who acted as visual interpreters of fin de siècle Paris, all but supplanting the Impressionists in that role. With Bonnard as our visual guide, we peruse the rue Tholoze, the place Pigalle, the boulevard Clichy, the place Clichy, the avenues leading to the Barrières, and countless other streets and corners of this avant-garde neighborhood.

Although Bonnard painted many small works on panel, cardboard, and canvas as well as numerous prints and drawings that assay diverse aspects of his Parisian neighborhood, the three Hessel triptychs and the fourth depicting the racecourse (it was owned by Bernheim, Hessel's boss) are a synthesis of the artist's diverse experiments. Larger in scale, relentlessly formal, and symmetrical, the four urban triptychs suggest that the painter had major ambitions for them. Yet none was exhibited at all until the 1930s, and two of the three Hessel triptychs remained in his collection well into the twentieth century. The reason these works were long secluded may be that artist and patron viewed them as both intimate and experimental. Their format, derived, as indicated, from religious and devotional pictures, was conducive to extended contemplation and imaginative immersion. They were works intended for interiors, best enjoyed over a long period of time. Simultaneously, Bonnard's triptychs were extensions of a radical, avant-garde tradition that extended back to the German Nazarene painters and to the Pre-Raphaelites, earlier in

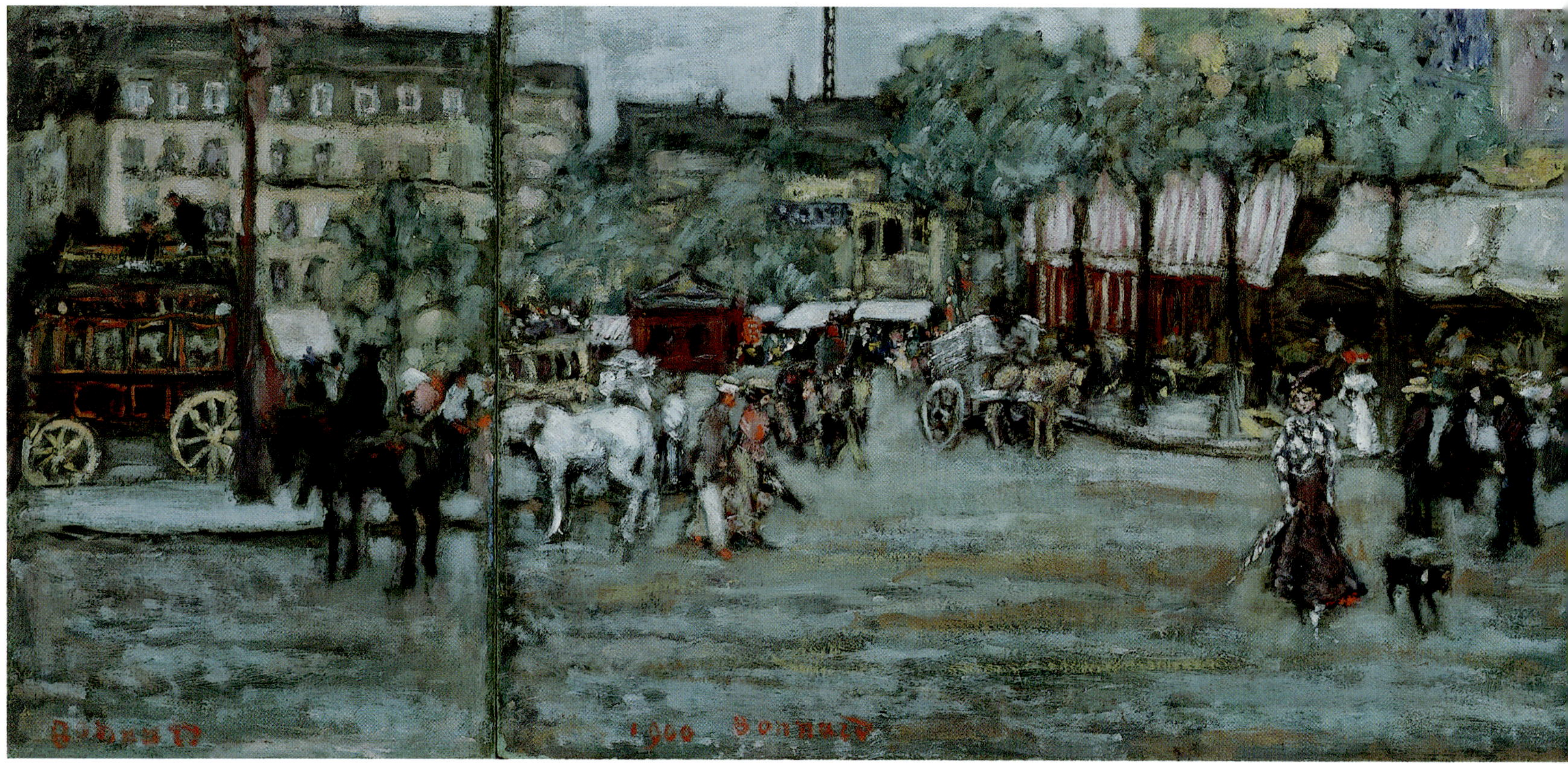

126

the century. Van Gogh, too, conceived of modern, secular triptychs when he described in a letter to his brother Theo his plan to flank his painting *La Berceuse* with two pictures of sunflowers. The result, he thought, would be a form of visual music that would project a sense of peace and rest, like a lullaby.[4] Bonnard's *The Place Clichy, Paris* projects more jazzy sonorities than contemplated by van Gogh—one can almost hear noise from the nearby, raucous Moulin Rouge—but he too tried to extend the reach of painting to the aural sense. This was an effort to discover the special, defining character of urban life and leisure, and it was an experiment later taken up by Fauvists, Cubists, and other inhabitants of Bonnard's artistic and popular neighborhood.

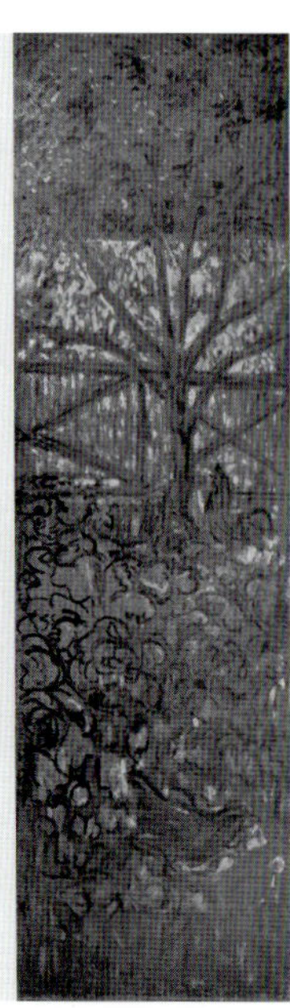

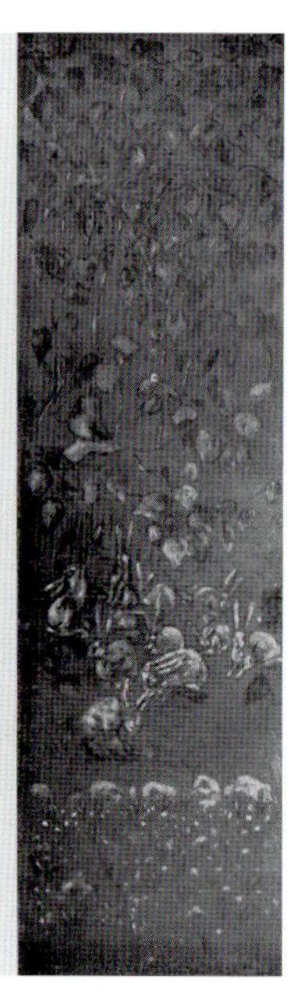

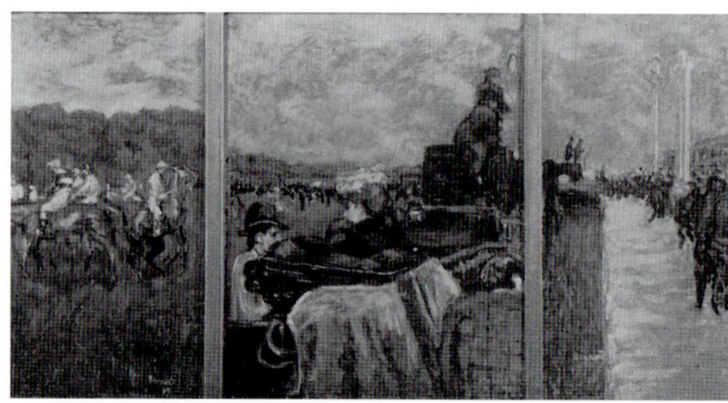

Fig. 126c (*right*) Pierre Bonnard, *Village Ensemble*, c. 1894, oil on brown fabric, triptych, each panel 67 × 19¾ in. (170 × 50 cm), location unknown; photo: Dauberville and Dauberville, 1965, no. 128

Fig. 126d (*far right*) Pierre Bonnard, *The Course at Longchamp*, 1897, oil on cardboard, 21¼ × 38⅝ in. (54 × 98 cm), location unknown; photo: Dauberville and Dauberville, 1965, no. 150

1 Dauberville and Dauberville, 1965, vol. 1, no. 148.
2 Dauberville and Dauberville, 1965, vol. 1, no. 149.
3 "Hideuse l'exposition qu'il a faite chez Durand . . . se symboliste se nomme Bonnard!" in *Correspondance de Camille Pissarro*, Paris, 1989, vol. 4, p. 159.
4 Van Gogh, 1958, vol. 3, no. 592.

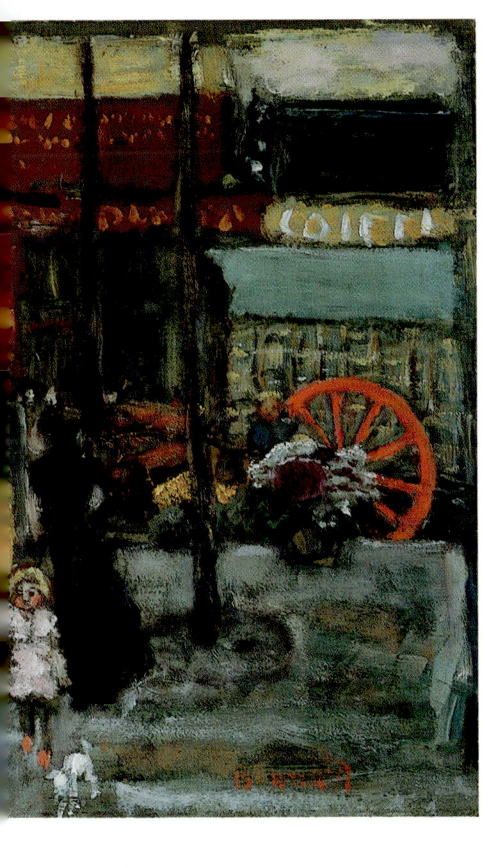

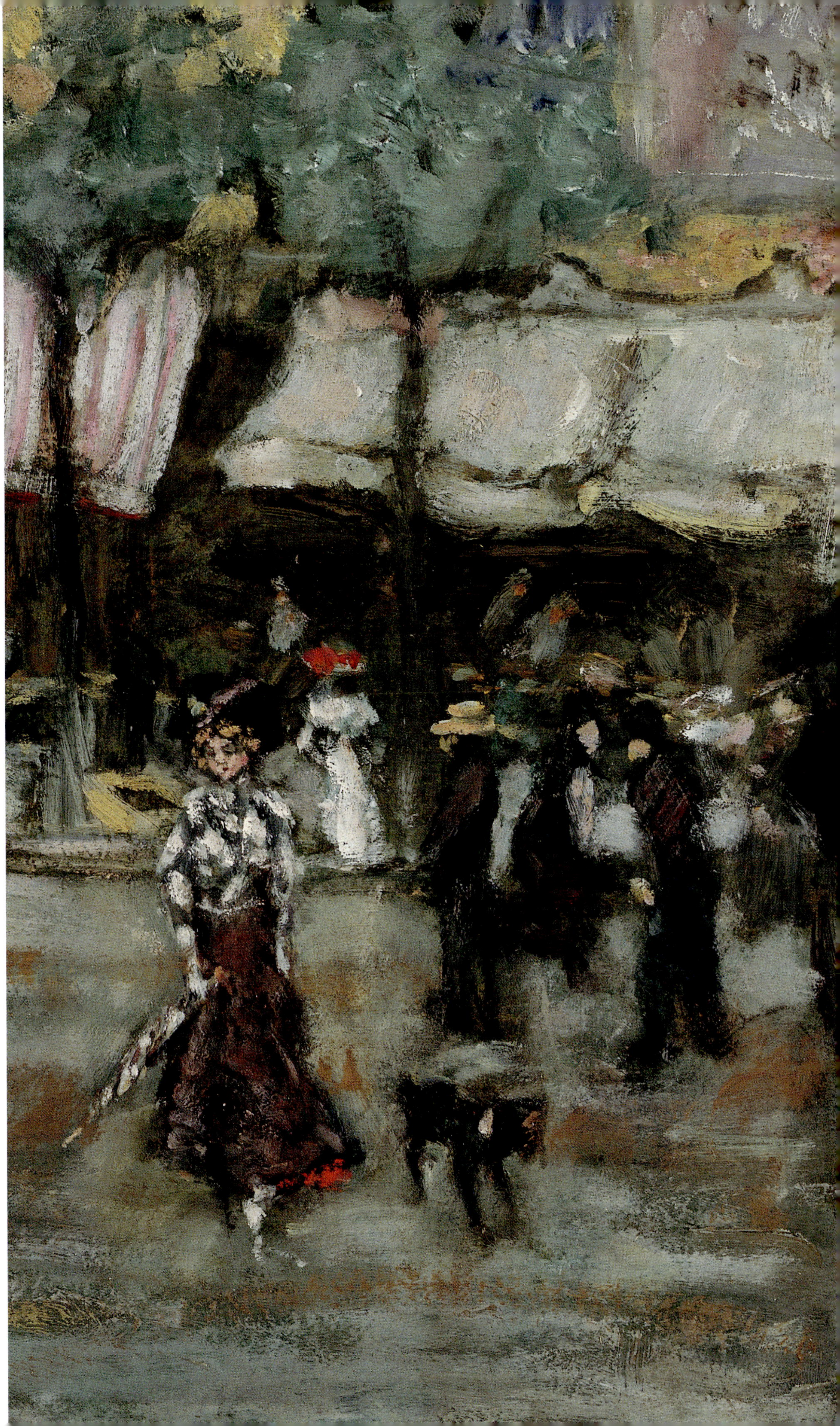

127

Émile Bernard
French, 1868–1941

Still Life with Flowers
1887

Oil on canvas, $19\frac{3}{4} \times 24$ in. (50.2 × 61 cm)
Signed and dated lower right: "Emile Bernard 87"
M.1997.1.2

Provenance: Émile Schuffenecker (1851–1934), Paris. Mme Clément Altarriba, Paris, by 1966. [Galerie Drouet, Paris, sold 9 June 1971 to]; [Hirschl & Adler Galleries, Inc., New York, by 1971, sold 6 February 1976 to]; Norton Simon, bequest 1993 to; Jennifer Jones Simon Art Trust, gift 1997 to; Norton Simon Art Foundation.

Exhibitions: Tokyo, 1936, no. 38, ill.; Paris, 1959a, no. 6; London, 1966a, no. 77a (Zurich, no. 92); Munich, 1966, no. 6, ill.; Bremen, 1967, no. 12, p. 77, ill.; Lille, 1967, no. 11, ill.; Pont-Aven, 1968, no. 2; Goteborg, 1968, no. 3.

References: Jourdain, 1958, p. 33, ill.; Luthi, 1982, no. 88, p. 19, ill.; Rapetti, 2005, p. 117, fig. 69.

Technical Notes: The original support, a plain-weave canvas, has been glue-lined. Three damages in the original canvas—a vertical tear at the lower right, a short vertical tear at the lower left, and a short horizontal tear at the lower right side of the begonia—may have been the reason for lining. The painting is tacked to a 5-member stretcher, which appears to be the original. Surface irregularities that look like bulges are from Bernard's heavily built-up paint. The white ground is a thin layer. The canvas texture remains evident only in the lower part of the painting, where the paint was thinly applied. Strong brushwork using thick, opaque paint depicts the flat spaces of the background and the table. The crimson strip across the bottom, which corresponds to the front edge of the table, was directly applied in a single thin layer. The dark painted boundary between these two distinct paint structures (thick and thin) contains multiple pigments from a full brush. The flowers and leaves are outlined on the yellow background with dark blue. Certain areas have been scraped back almost to the ground; an example is adjacent to the tulip leaf at the right. Flowers and leaves are strongly brushed with opaque paint worked wet into wet. The heavily worked paint in the rose-mauve tabletop was painted with longer brushstrokes, stopping at each contour (saucers, pots, shadows); it is most pronounced at the edge of the table where the paint thickness is three-dimensional. In conservation treatment in 2006, insecure areas of paint cleavage were stabilized and a discolored, heavy varnish was removed. Previous small repairs with discolored retouching were adjusted. The painting was left unvarnished. (RW)

Émile Bernard was only nineteen when he painted this masterful *Still Life with Flowers* in 1887. He had already been expelled from two art schools, become friends with Vincent van Gogh, Henri de Toulouse-Lautrec, and Paul Signac, and begun to collect Japanese prints. He recently concluded a six-month walking trip across Brittany, stopping long enough in Concarneau and Pont-Aven to make the acquaintance of Émile Schuffenecker, Charles Laval, and Paul Gauguin. Now he was back in Paris, preparing to exhibit some of his new works at a cavernous restaurant in Clichy, called the Grand Bouillon-Restaurant du Chalet. He was a member of an informal association of artists—comprising Louis Anquetin, Toulouse-Lautrec, and van Gogh—dubbed by the latter "the painters of the *petit boulevard*," who sought to create works of a decidedly popular character and to find equally democratic exhibition venues.

The paintings that Bernard made and exhibited in 1887 were experimental and, given the standards of the time, non-naturalistic. Though he claimed they were works in which ideas dominate the form,[1] the present painting in some ways suggests quite the opposite. The forms are so concretely asserted, the materials so insistently palpable, that intellectual concerns seem shunted aside. The picture appears to be crafted with chisel and wood rather than conjured from paint and brushes. It is in fact an early essay in the Cloisonnist style that soon became the hallmark of the so-called School of Pont-Aven. That style was first defined in March 1888 by the critic and dandy Édouard Dujardin. He said of Anquetin: "The painter traces his design with enclosing lines, within which he places his various tones juxtaposed in order to reproduce the desired sensation of general coloration. Drawing predicates color and color predicates drawing. And the work of the painter will be something like painting by *compartments*, analagous to cloisonné, and his technique consists of a sort of *cloisonnism*."[2] By 1889 the art had acquired a new name, Synthetist. In that year, Bernard exhibited twenty-five paintings, alongside seventeen others by Gauguin at the Impressionist and Synthetist Exhibition in a café on the grounds of the Paris Exposition Universelle. Now the innovations of the two artists had a wider audience than ever before.

Still Life with Flowers is a heavily worked, ambitious, and challenging painting. It represents two flowering, potted plants, tulips and begonias, on a wooden table. But the significance of the painting lies everywhere else but the flowers: the blue porcelain dishes that seem to hover above the table; the daggerlike towel at the upper left; the vertical stripes on the rear wall at left and right

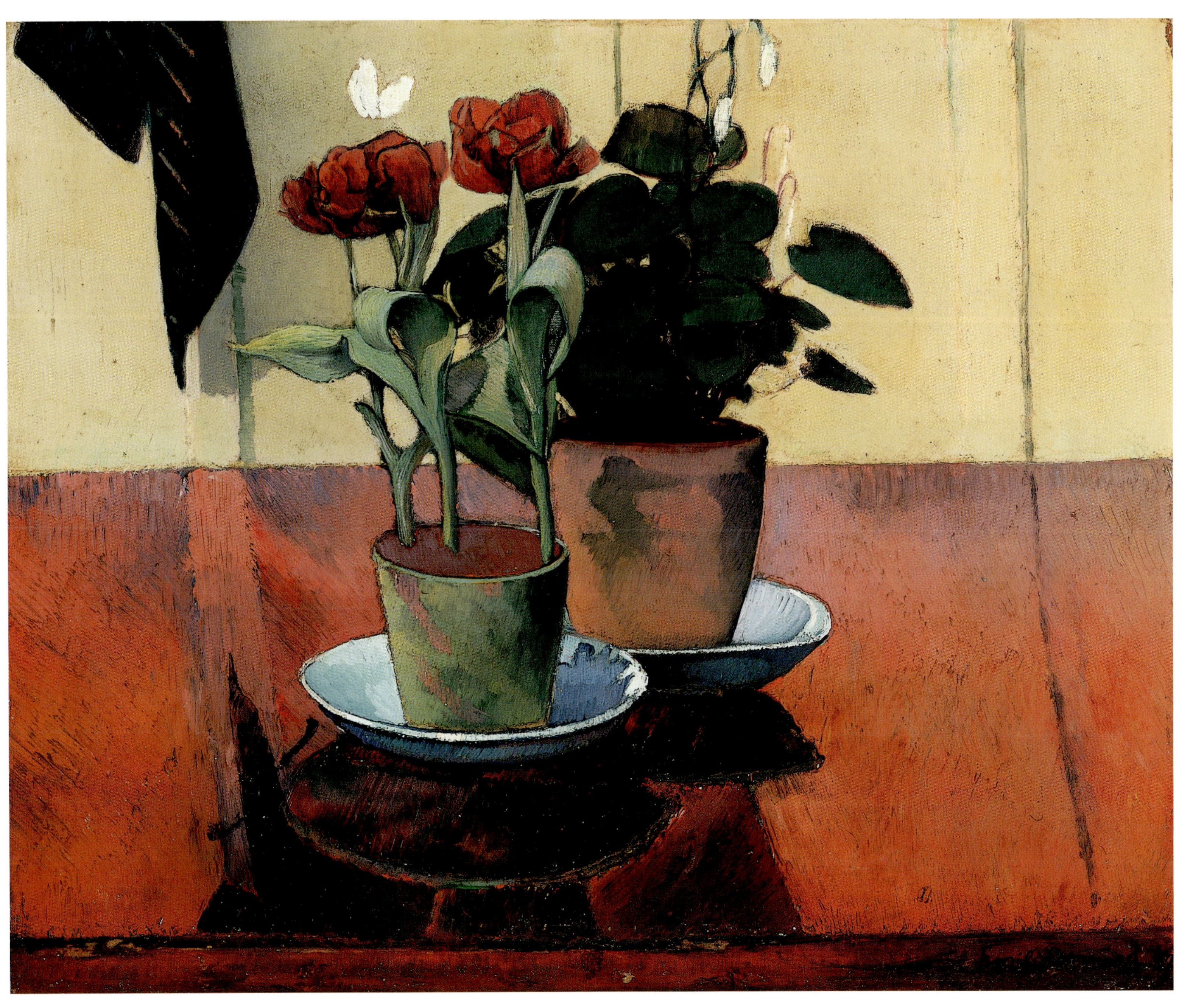

127

Fig. 127a (*right*) Émile Bernard, *Stoneware Pot and Apples*, 1897, oil on canvas, $18\frac{1}{8} \times 21\frac{1}{2}$ in. (46×54.5 cm), Musée national d'Art Moderne, Centre Georges Pompidou, Paris; photo: © Réunion des Musées Nationaux / Art Resource, NY

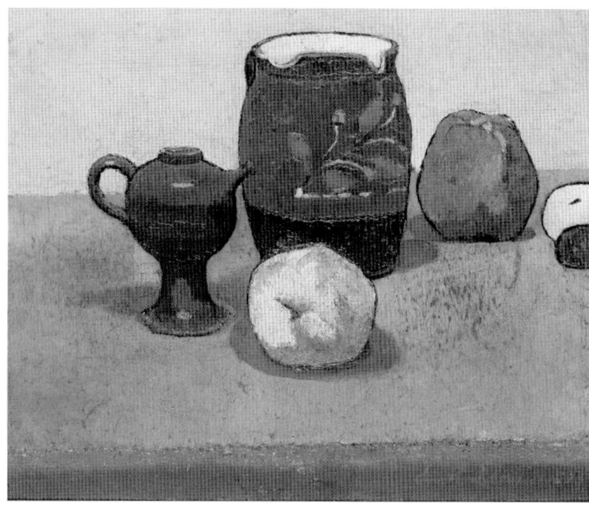

Fig. 127b (*far right*) Émile Bernard, *Portrait of Père Tanguy*, 1887, oil on canvas, $14\frac{1}{4} \times 12\frac{1}{4}$ in. (36×31 cm), Kunstmuseum, Basel

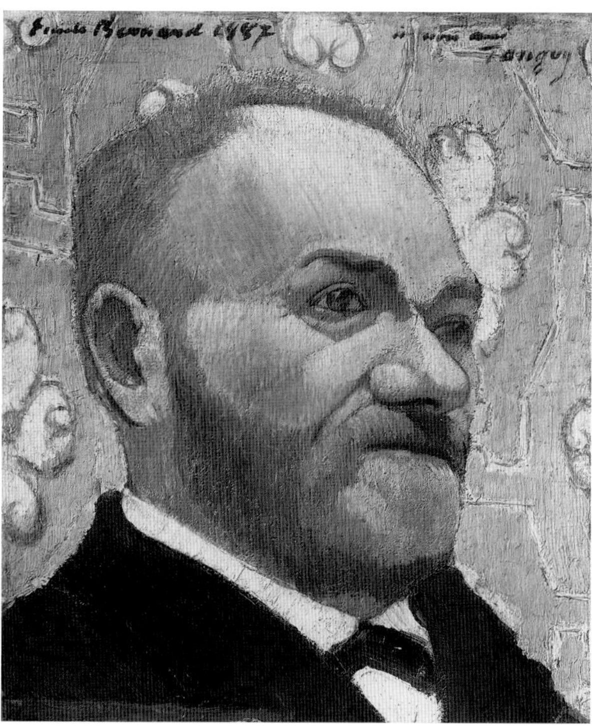

(inexplicably continued on the table only at right); the white butterfly frozen in place above the tulips; the inconsistent light sources and points of view; and, especially, the dark, illogical umbra of pots, dishes, and towel. The shadows are Bernard's special concern, for they seem carved or molded from wood or plaster. They possess considerable relief and have boundaries that bear little relation to objects to which they are ostensibly attached. For example, the lower edge of the shadow of the rear dish has a thick edge that passes through the shadow of the front one, and the bottom of the latter dish has an even thicker edge that creates a crescent-shaped channel through the broad rectangular shadow cast by the top edges of the flowerpots.

Bernard's picture revels in pictorial ambiguities and coincidences. The dirt around the left plant seems to rise above the lip of the pot, and the right edge of the right tulip coincides with the left edge of the right pot. It is as if the artist were looking at objects and things for the first time, with an innocent eye, that is, without any prior knowledge of perspective, modeling, or shading. The approach—a kind of pictorial populism—was shared by others in Bernard's circle, especially van Gogh. Both artists had an interest in crudely made objects of daily use, earthenware, rush seats, homemade wooden furniture, and simple patterns, and both made pictures that employ shallow relief and a visibly crafted surface. But one of the differences between Bernard and van Gogh is that the former's contrivances show, resulting in the labored and almost academic quality of *Still Life with Flowers*, its resemblance to an exercise in modern art. In this sense, the painting is made, as Bernard said, out of ideas more than forms.

Bernard's beautifully crafted still life with its pair of potted plants raises questions about the growth of art itself and of the various modes of its flowering. Among a small group of works by Bernard actually dated to 1887, it makes manifest the sheer precocity of the young painter. Yet, like the plants he represented, Bernard's was a hothouse career, fast in flowering and followed by a long, relentless decline into bitterness and utter pictorial confusion. This work, one of no more than thirty outright masterpieces of his career, all made between 1887 and 1890, was first owned by the shy Alsatian painter Émile Schuffenecker, who exhibited with Bernard, Gauguin, and others in the 1889 Impressionist and Synthetist Exhibition held at the Café Volpini at the Exposition Universelle of that year. This was the high point of Bernard's career, and, given the fact that Schuffenecker owned it, one is not stretching credibility to say that the painting was included in that landmark exhibition under the generic title *Nature morte* (*Still Life*) and that Bernard and Schuffenecker traded paintings after the exhibition. The Norton Simon collections contain works by six of the nine artists in that exhibition, and this one is among the finest. It compares favorably with two other paintings by Bernard from 1887, *Stoneware Pot and Apples* (fig. 127a) and *Portrait of Père Tanguy* (fig. 127b).

1 Luthi, 1974, p. 16 n. 6.

2 Dujardin, 1888, p. 490.

128

Émile Bernard
French, 1868–1941

Cupboard
1891–1893

Carved and painted wood, 95 × 59 × 20 in.
(241.3 × 149.9 × 50.8 cm)
N.1978.4

Provenance: M.-A. Bernard-Fort, Paris. [Sylvia Blatas, Paris]; Norton Simon, bequest 1993 to; Jennifer Jones Simon Art Trust.

References: Mornand, 1957, ill. opp. p. 32; Carrà, 1967, p. 237, ill.; Goteborg, 1968, ill. n.p.; Jaworska, 1972, p. 26; Luthi, 1974, pp. 15, 22, ill.; Luthi, 1976, pp. 7, ill., 12; Stevens, 1990, pp. 339, 340, 352–353, 61, ill.; Cariou, 1995, p. 91.

Technical Notes: The primary wood of the cupboard is chestnut, with additional use of oak and basswood or linden. Divided into upper and lower sections, the cupboard has two locking doors in the upper section held in place with iron hinges. The lower section has a drop lid, also attached with iron hinges. Carved and painted decoration is found on the left and right upper doors, the drop lid, the bottom front rail, the crest rail at the top of the cupboard, and the left and right stiles. In the doors and the drop lid, Bernard selected the boards so that their grain would repeat or emphasize his carved design in certain places. For example, in the standing woman on the proper right upper door, Bernard accentuated the folds in her skirt by gouging them out on the grain line. In the kneeling woman, the swirl of her skirt follows the wood grain. In both of the upper doors the design is an outdoor scene with four women. The proper right door was constructed from two chestnut boards, glued together with tongue-and-groove joints to make a rectangular panel. The proper left door was constructed from five chestnut boards. The panels were carved out to create an integral frame, and the figures in the settings are in relief. Several sizes of chisels and gouges were used. The wood has no priming or preparatory layer. The natural color of the chestnut wood was left unaltered in various parts, while other details or forms have been colored with paint or stained. Painted areas are extremely thin and intermittently placed within each scene. The carving on the drop lid, a single horizontally grained board, consists of scenes in two equal semicircles, which are divided by a stylized plant. Here also Bernard has integrated the wood grain with his design. The bottom front rail, below the drop lid, continues the design of the central woman whose chin is resting on her proper left hand. Carving is also found on the crest rail at the top and on the left and right stiles. The overall finish is wax, but it is not known if this was the artist's choice. The cupboard remained in use until 1990. (RW and John Childs)

The artists associated with Cloisonnism, Synthetism, and the School of Pont-Aven—including Paul Gauguin, Bernard, Paul Sérusier, and Jacob Meyer de Haan—were as interested in innovation in the decorative arts as in the fine arts of painting and sculpture. Indeed, they would not have accepted the idea of a hierarchical distinction between the two modes, believing each was the expression of individual imagination and lofty sentiment. Like the critics, artists, and designers of the English Arts and Crafts Movement who preceded them, they rejected on principle the alienated labor of industrial manufactures and what they saw as the soulless marketplace for art commodities. They thus practiced handcraft of all kinds (and tried to make painting once more into a craft) and endeavored as far as possible to insulate themselves from the judgment of anonymous Salon jurors and the rapaciousness of the art trade. This independent stance led them to look backward in admiration at art and design from the late medieval ages when, it was presumed, craft guilds fostered a collective approach to design and manufacture and artists knew for whom they were working and derived satisfaction from the relationship.

In France in the years around 1890 this anachronistic posture could be perceived by observers in either of two ways: on the one hand it seemed intensely democratic, with its embrace of precapitalist values of community and reciprocity, but on the other, it looked deeply conservative, with its implicit assertion of the transcendent value of medieval order, hierarchy, obedience, and faith. In fact, artists who emulated the art of "the Primitives" (the term then used for Italian and Flemish artists of the fourteenth and fifteenth centuries) were as conflicted about the political and social significance of their position as their audiences. They often shifted their religious and political allegiances from pagan to Christian and from left to right and back again. They were consistent only in their distrust of capitalist modernization.

Bernard was perhaps more pronounced a medievalist than any of the other Synthetists or artists of the School of Pont-Aven, and his strange career bears all the characteristic signs of this thinking. After leaving his home and school in Lille at an early age, he lived in Paris, enrolling in 1884—along with Henri de Toulouse-Lautrec, Louis Anquetin, and Vincent van Gogh—at the art school of Fernand Cormon. Following his expulsion in the spring of 1886, he traveled across Brittany (cat. 129), meeting Gauguin and independently developing the rudiments of Cloisonnism or pictorial Symbolism. After exhibiting with van Gogh and the other "painters of the *petit boulevard*" at the Grand Bouillon-Restaurant du Chalet, he returned to Brittany in August 1888, and for two months worked closely with Gauguin to forge the new Synthetist art. In 1889 he was one of the exhibitors at the *Exposition de peintres du groupe impressioniste et synthétist* organized by Gauguin and Émile Schuffenecker and held at the Café Volpini on the grounds of the Exposition Universelle in Paris. Two years later, the critic Albert Aurier published his article "Gauguin: Le Symbolisme en peinture," in which the young critic asserted that Gauguin was the leader of a new school of subjective, "idea-ist," synthetic (*synthétiste*), and decorative painters. Bernard was angered and appalled at what he felt was the slighting of his own achievement, and he resolved to break forever with Gauguin. His own artwork and life now began to careen in many directions. He became a critic and publisher, writing important texts in 1891 devoted to the art and aesthetic theories of Paul Cézanne and van Gogh. He now embraced a fervent Catholicism and exhibited in 1892 with the mystical Salon de la Rose + Croix. The following year he traveled to Italy before settling in Egypt, where he would remain until 1904. The remainder of his long career, Bernard died in 1941, was consumed with rejecting the formal innovations he himself had once championed, in the name of a Catholic fundamentalism that was inconsistent with the artistic independence he revered.

It is not known precisely when Bernard designed and built the armoire in the Norton Simon collections, nor for whom it was made. But there are sufficient clues to assign it a date between 1891 and 1893 and to believe it was made at the behest of immediate family or friends. The attribution to Bernard is securely based on style and the fact that it remained in the Bernard family until the 1920s. It is also mentioned in a number of letters from the artist's sister Madeleine (d. 1895) to Émile and their parents. "Émile has already used his tools for carving a bas-relief," Madeleine wrote her mother about 1891, "so we have not asked for the chest in vain."[1] Earlier suggestions that Gauguin carved the large, lower panel probably cannot be sustained.[2] Though the breadth and fluidity of the carving differ from the more cramped and angular approach to form in the upper two sections, the relief does not closely resemble any of Gauguin's sculpted work from the period of the two artists' collaboration from mid-August to late October 1888. Moreover, as MaryAnne Stevens has argued, it is hard to imagine the two finding sufficient time to work on this complicated project while they were busy inventing Cloisonnism or Synthetism in such paintings as *Breton Women in a Meadow* by Bernard and *Vision after the Sermon* by Gauguin.[3] By the spring of 1891, when Madeleine mentioned the carved chest in letters to her parents, Gauguin and Bernard had ended their association, and the former was preparing to leave France for Tahiti. In all likelihood, then, the cupboard was the result of a commission in early 1891, probably from the artist's parents, or else from his new patron, the comte de la Rochefoucauld who purchased several works of decorative art by Bernard, including a smaller cupboard (fig. 128a).

The chest is a two-tiered wooden cupboard whose basic form dates back to French, German, and Flemish prototypes from the sixteenth century. It is composed of two symmetrical, carved upper panels surrounding a planar central axis. Below these is a single, carved, horizontal panel separated from the upper zone by a horizontal axis. The cupboard is topped by elaborately carved finials and a broken arch and finished below by a carved apron and plain, rectangular legs. Decorative brass hardware has been attached to the vertical and horizontal axes and to the long posts at right and left. The composition of the cupboard was undoubtedly derived from earlier nineteenth-century Breton prototypes and was intended to be popular, primitive, or folkloric in aspect. The light application of color to the carved portions of the chest, in addition to the boldness and plasticity of the carving and the simplicity of its basic form, accentuated its folk character. This purposeful primitiveness may also have been inspired by furniture and designs created by the artists who worked for the design firm of William Morris and Co. during the 1860s and 1870s in England. These men and women, who included Morris, Ford Maddox Brown, Dante Gabriel Rossetti, and Edward Burne-Jones, sought to create simple, useful, and beautiful designs based on medieval prototypes. Their painted chests and cabinets are some of the finest examples of the international Arts and Crafts Movement, which flourished from the 1860s until World War I. Morris's writings were not widely known in France until several of his essays were translated in 1896, but the

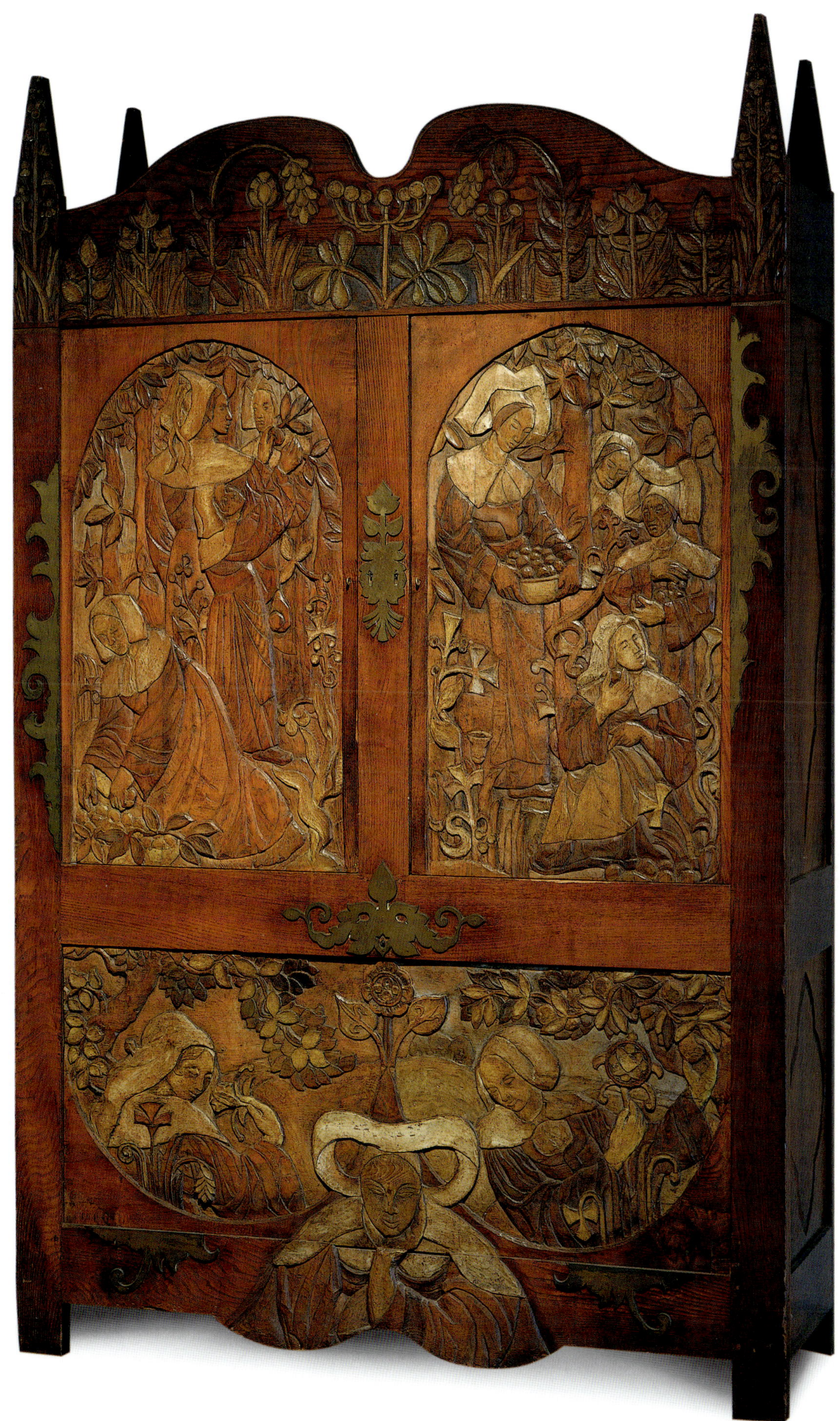

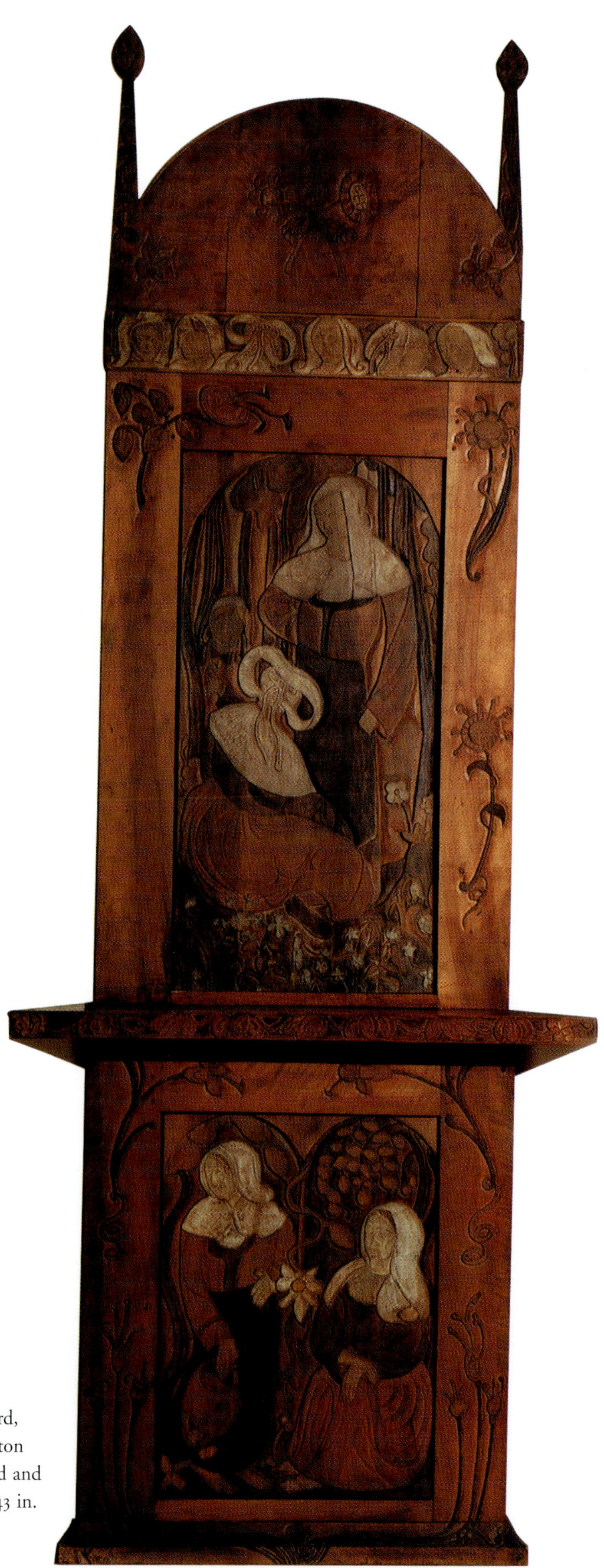

Fig. 128a Émile Bernard, corner cabinet with Breton scenes, 1891–1892, carved and painted wood, $108\frac{5}{8} \times 43$ in. (276×109 cm), private collection

designs and principles of his firm must have been known to Bernard's dear friend van Gogh—who briefly lived in London and was fluent in English—and, more significantly, to Gauguin, who alludes to them indirectly in essays written in 1889 for Aurier's journal *Moderniste illustré*.

Though the cupboard is largely conventional in its basic configuration of parts, its pictorial character suggests an affinity with another type of furniture: late Gothic, two-part altarpieces or diptychs. The carved upper doors are arched at the top, like the wings of many fifteenth-century altarpieces, and the horizontal panel below recalls a predella panel. Bernard may also have had in mind fifteenth-century *Schnitzaltars* (carved German altarpieces) when he began to carve his figures and landscapes.

The subject of Bernard's carved cupboard is not, however, conventionally religious, despite its derivation from Gothic and early Renaissance altarpieces and despite the artist's own fervent Catholicism. The eleven female figures depicted in the three main carved panels are dressed in the traditional Breton costume then generally worn only on festive occasions such as saint's days or during the religious and civic processions called *pardons*. They are all engaged in picking fruit and eating it. Brittany was known then (as now) for the quality of its apples and pears and their by-products, cider and Calvados. There is a visible narrative in the arrangement of scenes. In the upper left panel, three figures (one is a child) are picking fruit from the trees, while a kneeling woman in the foreground carefully piles them into a basket or bowl. In the upper right panel, three standing women are carrying the fruit in bowls from the orchard, while a fourth sits and gazes vacantly up and to her left, having just bitten into a piece of fruit.

The bottom panel shows three more women, arranged in a much more artificial and hieratic manner than in the compositions above. The setting is more magical than real, with a flowering apple tree at upper left that recalls the Hiroshige-inspired tree that divides the red field in Gauguin's *Vision after the Sermon* from 1888. A figure at left with her back to the viewer turns her head over her right shoulder and smells a fragrant blossom. At right, a woman turned forward casts her gaze downward across her right shoulder while pulling an apple from a tree with her left hand. In her right hand, she appears to hold an elaborate mirror, or else a scepter. At the bottom of the carved panel, extending to the lower front rail, we see a large, bust-length female figure facing forward, head cupped in her right hand, eyes closed and lost in reverie. She may represent Moraine le Fee (in English, Morgan le Fay; in Italian, Fata Morgana), the fairy goddess of Arthurian lore who ruled over "the Fortunate Isle" or "the island of Apples" and who was the nemesis of Queen Guinevere and Sir Lancelot. At the time that Bernard was at work on the cupboard, he was, according to his later memoir, *L'Aventure de ma vie*, also engaged in the study of Breton folklore, and he made a number of paintings and prints with medieval, troubadour, and Arthurian themes, including *The Knight's Combat* (c. 1890–1892, private collection) and *Les Fleurs du mal* (1892, private collection.) He specifically explored the tale of the enchantress Morgana—the Lady of the Lake—in 1892, when he undertook to illustrate Ariosto's *Orlando furioso*. The project was never realized, but the thirty-two surviving drawings attest to his interest in chivalric subjects and the theme of women smitten by love and desire. In Bernard's cupboard, the common Breton experience of picking, carrying, and consuming apples is the precondition for transport to a fairy isle of dream, temptation, and forbidden pleasure.

1 Undated letter from Madeleine Bernard to her mother, Émile Bernard Papers, J. Paul Getty Research Library, Los Angeles.

2 Jaworska. 1972, p. 26; and Luthi, 1974, p. 15.

3 Stevens, 1990, p. 340.

129

Émile Bernard
French, 1868–1941

Brittany Landscape
c. 1888–1889

Oil on canvas, 28⅞ × 39½ in. (73.3 × 100.3 cm)
N.1975.1

Provenance: Roderic O'Conor (1860–1940); presumably by inheritance to René Honta (d. 1955). Presumably in (sale, Paris, Hôtel Drouot, 7 February 1956). [Roland, Browse & Delbanco, London, and Hirschl & Adler Galleries, Inc., New York, sold 2 July 1957 to]; Walter P. Chrysler Jr., New York. [Knoedler Galleries, New York, and Hirschl & Adler Galleries, Inc., New York, stock no. 1906, sold 14 January 1975 to]; Norton Simon, bequest 1993 to; Jennifer jones Simon Art Trust.

Exhibitions: New York, 1957, no. 12, ill.; Dayton, 1960, no. 68, p. 76, ill.; New York, 1974b, no. 47, ill.

Reference: Roland, 1991, pp. 85–86.

Technical Notes: Two types or styles of painting exist in this picture. What is here called the original paint is mostly applied in parallel, moderately narrow strokes with medium-rich, predominantly pasty paints. In the lower right and in parts of the sky there is easily identified paint that differs in texture, application, and consistency. Even the crackle pattern differs from the "original." The support is a medium-fine, plain-weave canvas that is lined to fabric possibly with a wax resin. Original tacking edges have been removed so that the support is about ⅛ inch shy of the stretcher dimensions. The painting is tacked to a 6-part wood stretcher with butt corners and mortise and tenon at the crossbars. It could be original. The fairly thick off-white ground does not seem to go past the design region (see upper right corner). It has developed cracks following the weave of the canvas. The painting has been flattened somewhat from lining and there is some weave interference. There are small scattered losses and some general abrasion of surface paints. Cracking has caused some flaking. The surface has a thick, hazy, dirty synthetic varnish that is inappropriate for the picture. (JF)

Bernard had an unusual career. He was an extremely precocious artist, learning the rudiments of modernist art while still in his late teens and developing his own, original approach to painting by the age of twenty. From 1888 to 1892 he was among the most advanced and experimental painters in Europe. Just as the contemporary French composers Claude Debussy and Maurice Ravel employed chromaticism—notes outside the diatonic (seven-note) major and minor scales—to disrupt harmony and consonance, so Bernard employed color accidentals—unmodulated and dissonant hues—to undermine both mimesis and narrative, the twin foundations on which the edifice of European painting was built. Even Impressionism and Neo-Impressionism, which greatly reduced the significance of tonal value in painting, remained wedded to harmony and representation, reaching back to rules of color complementarity and pictorial expression implicit in the art of Eugène Delacroix and explicit in the writings of the theorists Charles Blanc and Eugène Chevreul. With Bernard's *Buckwheat Harvest* (1888, Josefowitz Collection, Lausanne) and *Breton Women with Parasols* (1892, Musée d'Orsay, Paris), and his friend Paul Gauguin's *Vision after the Sermon* (1888, National Gallery of Scotland, Edinburgh), the idea in art triumphed over the seen world, and one more institution of European culture was under fierce assault.

Brittany Landscape depicts an intensely domesticated landscape, with houses, trees, shrubs, fields, fences, walls, and hedgerows, but no people or animals. The terrain is organized in layers, with nine or ten distinct fore- and middle-ground planes, surmounted by four or five houses and a high horizon. Taken together, the planes form an irregular basin, consisting of sloping hills that meet in almost the exact center of the painting, a place marked by a clump of dark trees that appear to burst from the ground. The foreground below is a rocky, irregular slope, with several areas of exposed, orange-brown soil and red-brown rocky outcroppings, perhaps lichen-covered. Above, near the top of the basin, is an arc of trees, their six crowns rendered as green lollipops. The houses above them are simple affairs, plain, stuccoed boxes with peaked roofs colored blue or brown. To the left of the houses is the dark green crown of one or more great pine trees.

Unnatural, arbitrary, or accidental colors are used throughout the painting. At the middle right and extending as a tapering wedge are some manicured pale blue shrubs with pink and white highlights, articulated with vertical brushstrokes like those found in landscapes by Cézanne. A discordantly colored red and blue wall, bordered with four tall trees, emerges from behind these shrubs, only to disappear behind a clump of trees. Despite the arbitrariness of the color accents, the picture as a whole maintains its coherence, first because of the dominant green, and second because the configuration of planes creates a zigzag effect that leads the eye from foreground right to background left. Both surface plane and pictorial depth are given their due in Bernard's landscape.

Brittany Landscape is unsigned and undated but was most likely painted in late 1888 or 1889, during visits first to Pont-Aven and then Saint-Briac, though a few parts of

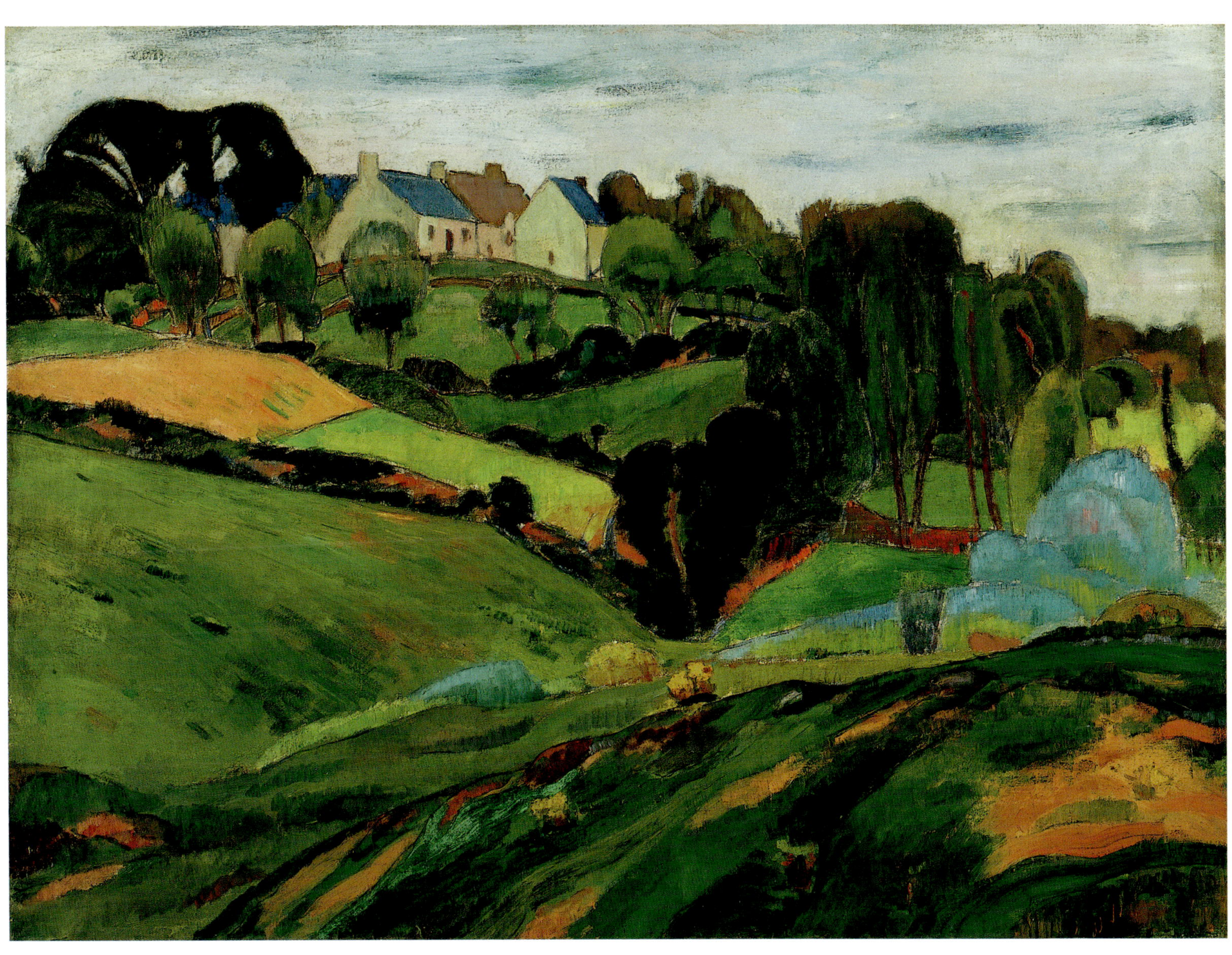

129

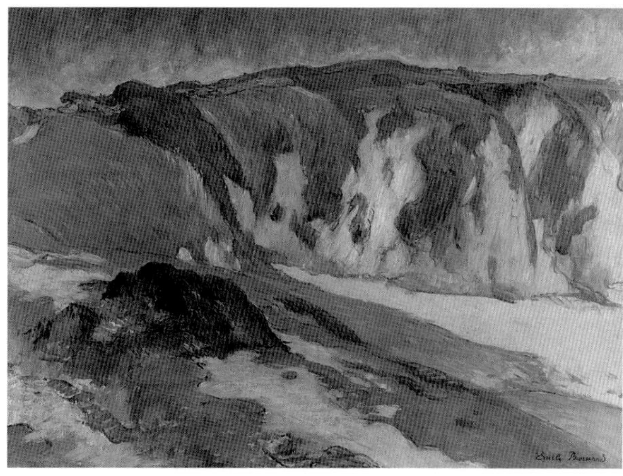

Fig. 129a Émile Bernard, *The Cliffs at Pouldu*, 1887, oil on board adhered to panel, $22\frac{1}{2} \times 30\frac{1}{2}$ in. (57 × 77.5 cm); photo: © Carmen Thyssen-Bornemisza Collection on loan at the Museo Thyssen-Bornemisza, Madrid

it—especially in the lower right—appear to have been painted later, perhaps by another hand. The picture should be placed midway in a sequence of Brittany landscapes with Synthetist touch and high horizon, beginning with *Harvest* (1887, private collection)[1] and *The Cliffs at Pouldu* (fig. 129a), and culminating with *Harvest on the Banks of the Sea* (1891, private collection).[2] The earliest of the three is constructed from a series of horizontal blocks of color, animated by a snaking path and the chunky shape of houses and stacks of grain. The last is a grand, abstract, and idealizing canvas with irregular geometric shapes and arcing contours that create an intricate, lock-and-key construction. The figures here are as abstract as the houses and grainstacks and anticipate the Cubist peasant pictures of the Russian Kasimir Malevich, such as the great *Harvesters* (1912, Stedelijk Museum, Amsterdam). Like Malevich, Bernard in his canvas of 1891 conceived of peasants or simple farm laborers as machines—anonymous, animate tools whose bodies and dispositions are shaped by the work they perform. The picture by Bernard that most closely resembles the Norton Simon landscape is probably *The Château of Rustephan Seen from the Heights of Pont-Aven* (1889, private collection),[3] which depicts the lands and architectural remains of a feudal estate that was later the subject of a novel by Bernard, *La Tour—un roman breton.* Each reveals a constructive, or synthetic, approach to the assembly of picture and landscape, and a common use of Cloisonnist outlining, especially visible around the houses and trees in the Norton Simon picture.

The absence of a signature on *Brittany Landscape* presents something of a puzzle. The most obvious answer is that the artist considered the work unfinished, but that is belied by the appearance of the work, which, apart from some purposely thinly painted areas such as the arc of trees and the zone where the houses meet the sky, is quite densely covered with paint. In fact, the bottom right of the picture and a few sections of sky exhibit broad, fluid brushstrokes so different from the constructed, Cézannesque *passage* work elsewhere that it is necessary to conclude that a later hand, perhaps not Bernard's, completed the painting, either to make the work more satisfying to the owner or to prepare it for sale. If the former, the hand may have been that of Roderick O'Conor, himself a Pont-Aven artist of some significance, whose widow was likely the last owner of the painting before it entered the art trade in 1956.

1 Luthi, 1982, no. 60.
2 Luthi, 1982, no. 289.
3 Luthi, 1982, no. 193.

130

Georges Lacombe
French, 1868–1916

Autumn: The Chestnut Gatherers
1894

Oil on canvas, 60⅛ × 93⅛ in. (152.7 × 236.3 cm)
M.1979.35

Provenance: Gabrielle Questroy Wenger (Lacombe's future mother-in-law), Versailles, 1894. Lucien Besnard (d. 1955), Alençon, by inheritance to; Mme Sanlaville (née Besnard); Mmes Sylvie Mora and Maldan-Lacombe by 1966; [Oscar Ghez/Modern Art Foundation, Geneva, by 1966], (sale, London, Sotheby's, 4 July 1979, lot 231, ill., to); Norton Simon Art Foundation.

Exhibitions: Paris, 1966a, no. 41; Paris, 1966b, no. 37; Geneva, 1968, no. 141, color ill.; Geneva, 1977, no. 23, color ill.

References: Joly, 1966, p. 13; Maillard, 1967, vol. 2, p. 343, ill.; Huyghe, 1969, vol. 1, no. 402, p. 133, ill.; Frèches-Thory and Terrasse, 1991, p. 151, ill.; Frèches-Thory and Perruchi-Petri, 1993, no. 43, p. 46, ill.; Hutton, 1994, p. 167, fig. 29; Ansieau, 1998, no. 29, pp. 11, 69–71, ill., 71, 140; Lambinet, 2003, p. 115.

Technical Notes: The heavy, plain-weave fabric still with its tacking edges is impregnated with wax; it was strip-lined with wax-resin in 1979. It is stapled to a newer stretcher over a loose lining. Although there is no ground as such, a brownish red oil layer coats the entire canvas. The artist used paints that were vehicular to medium-paste consistency. Colors are mostly mixed with white, but there are also transparent colors such as crimson and black. Unfortunately, the paint has an overall uniform dark appearance because it was impregnated with wax. In some areas paint was applied in several layers. For example, the yellow leaves often have bright yellow and orange paint on top of an orange layer. The flesh has an underpainting of light orange with the darker flesh color on top. The skirt of the second woman from the right was painted first with bright orange and then with dark mauve. The two central women in the foreground have black skirts with gray-green or black details or dark gray with black and crimson details. Outlines of forms were drawn both before and after the thicker paint was applied. There is a good deal of loss and general overall abrasion. The upper, thicker layers of paint show extensive crackle with loss from flaking, most significantly in the faces of the two women on the left and the dark skirts of the three foreground figures. There is a synthetic varnish and no evidence of an earlier coating. The painting was probably never meant to be varnished. The painting was surface-cleaned in 1979 in London, and old oil retouches and fills were removed. The losses were toned but not filled. (JF)

Georges Lacombe's *Autumn: The Chestnut Gatherers* is a large, colorful, but sober canvas. Five female figures (painted from the artist's fiancée, Marthe Wenger, who served as the model) stand, kneel, or process across an autumnal, forested stage. In the center foreground, a woman stands erect, in profile, with long blond hair, wearing a dark brown bodice and long skirt. She carries a large salver with shelled chestnuts, their ogival tips pointing upward. To the left, a woman with red hair and red bodice, seen in three-quarter view, kneels on the ground. With her big right hand, she wields a black rock, approximately the size of a softball, and is about to bring it down on a chestnut, still encased in its prickly, green husk. Chestnuts and chestnut husks, some opened like flower petals, others broken into pieces, lie on the ground in front of her. In the right foreground a third woman walks toward the first two. Her eyes are closed, her head is covered, and she is bent slightly forward, holding with her hands the bottom of her apron, carrying a load of chestnuts to be shelled. Her posture is almost that of someone giving obeisance, recalling the figure just to the left of the Tahitian Virgin Mary in Paul Gauguin's *Ia Orana Maria* (The Metropolitan Museum of Art, New York) and a figure from a sculpted relief from the Buddhist temple at Borobudur, Java, that was Gauguin's source. (Lacombe first saw Gauguin's work at Durand-Ruel's gallery in November 1893 and met and befriended the artist a few months later.) In the right middle ground of *Autumn: The Chestnut Gatherers* two more figures with headdresses are visible; one kneels on the ground, her right hand raised to shell chestnuts. (Some husks are visible on the ground behind her.) The figure to her right is slightly stooped and holds a large, coarse bag, presumably to collect the shelled nuts.

The ambient landscape is very much like a stage. The massive trees form an allée, leading the eye back to a flat yellow-green backdrop. Between the foreground and the background, four successive zones of space are visible: 1) that of the foreground figures, 2) that between the second and third row of trees, including the women in the middle ground at right, 3) that between the third and fourth row of trees, and 4) the last one, marked by the spaceless, airless, green, twilight sky. The repetition of colors creates an overall unity of mood: green for the crepuscular sky and chestnut hulls, the apron of the large, central figure, and the head scarf of the figure in the right foreground; orange-red for the ground and the leaves that hang from the trees; yellow for the large, footprint-size chestnut leaves that lie on the ground; and brown for the tree trunks, the bags that hold the chestnuts, and the

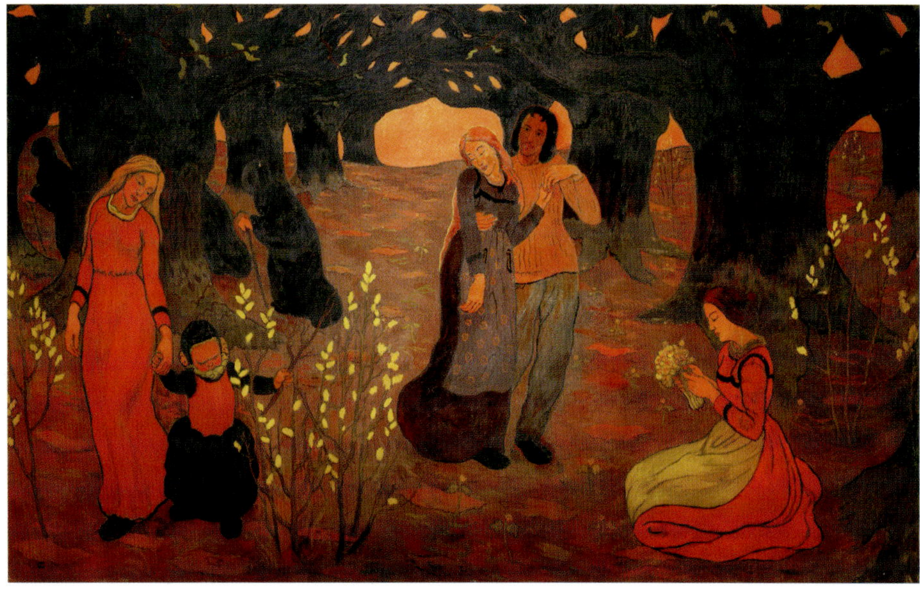

Fig. 130a Georges Lacombe, *Spring (The Ages of Life)*, c. 1892–1894, oil on canvas, $59\frac{1}{2} \times 94\frac{1}{2}$ in. (151 × 240 cm), Petit Palais, Musée d'Art Moderne, Geneva; photo: Erich Lessing / Art Resource, NY

Fig. 130b (*below left*) Georges Lacombe, Sketch for *Summer*, 1893–1894, pencil on paper, $10\frac{1}{8} \times 13\frac{3}{4}$ in. (25.5 × 35 cm), private collection

Fig. 130c (*below right*) Georges Lacombe, sketch for *Winter*, 1893–1894, pencil on paper, $10\frac{1}{8} \times 13\frac{3}{4}$ in. (25.5 × 35 cm), Musée Lambinet, Versailles

bodices of the women in the center foreground and the kneeling woman in the right middle ground. The unity of color and design and the stylized character of the mise-en-scène—along with the friezelike arrangement of the foliage along the top border of the canvas—recall verdure and other tapestry traditions. As with the other Nabi artists, including Édouard Vuillard, Maurice Denis, Ker-Xavier Roussel, Odilon Redon, Paul Ranson, and Paul Sérusier, Lacombe in this mural-size landscape sought to represent the world of dreams and the ideal, not the lived space of nature and quotidian life. Its inspiration was not the actuality of peasant labor but the imagined, timeless world of Breton songs and legends, such as those collected by Hersart de la Villemarqué in his celebrated *Barzaz-Breiz—Chants populaires de la Bretagne* (1839, republished 1893).

Lacombe began work on *Autumn: The Chestnut Gatherers* sometime after January 1894. (A label on the back of the picture indicates that the canvas was delivered to the artist on 2 January 1894.) It was just one of a projected four-painting series depicting the seasons of the year—and possibly also, by extension, the four ages of life—planned for the Versailles *hôtel particulier* (now destroyed) of the artist's future mother-in-law, Gabrielle Wenger. A second mural in the Musée d'Art Moderne in Geneva, the same size as the Norton Simon picture, depicts spring (fig. 130a). The whereabouts of the other two paintings is unknown; they may have been destroyed or never even painted. (Lacombe was independently wealthy and did not like to accept money for his paintings or sculptures. The pangs of necessity thus did not drive him to finish artworks.) The projected subject and composition of the missing seasons are known from two drawings.[1] *Summer* (fig. 130b) depicts bathers in a river; *Winter* (fig. 130c) shows skaters on a pond, with figures in the foreground warming themselves by an open fire. The finished *Spring* (fig. 130a) represents the same wooded landscape as the Norton Simon picture, with a male and female in the center, his right arm around her waist, his left hand holding her left hand as if they were dancing. A young woman in profile at lower right kneels on the ground, holding a bouquet of flowers. A mother and child walk holding hands in the foreground at left. In the middle ground behind them, an old woman, seen in profile, walks with a cane toward the left. Because of the movement of the two largest, central figures toward the right, the picture has an overall orientation the exact opposite of that in the Norton Simon picture. In addition, whereas it is twilight in the latter work, it appears to be daybreak in the Geneva canvas. The two pictures must have hung on opposite walls in Madame Wenger's parlor.

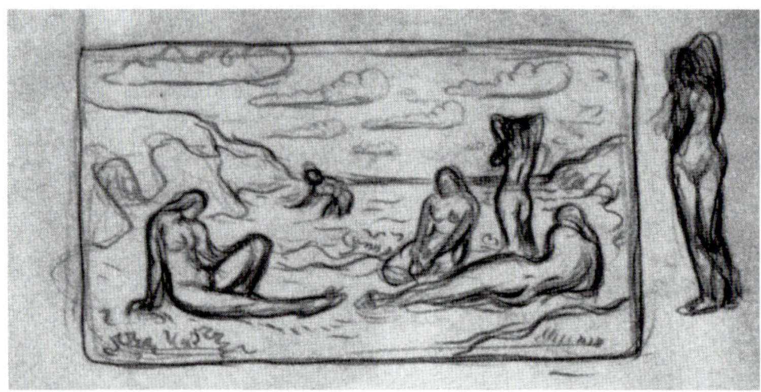

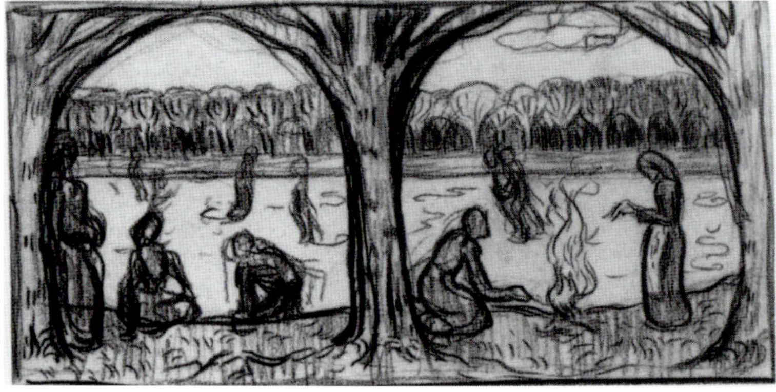

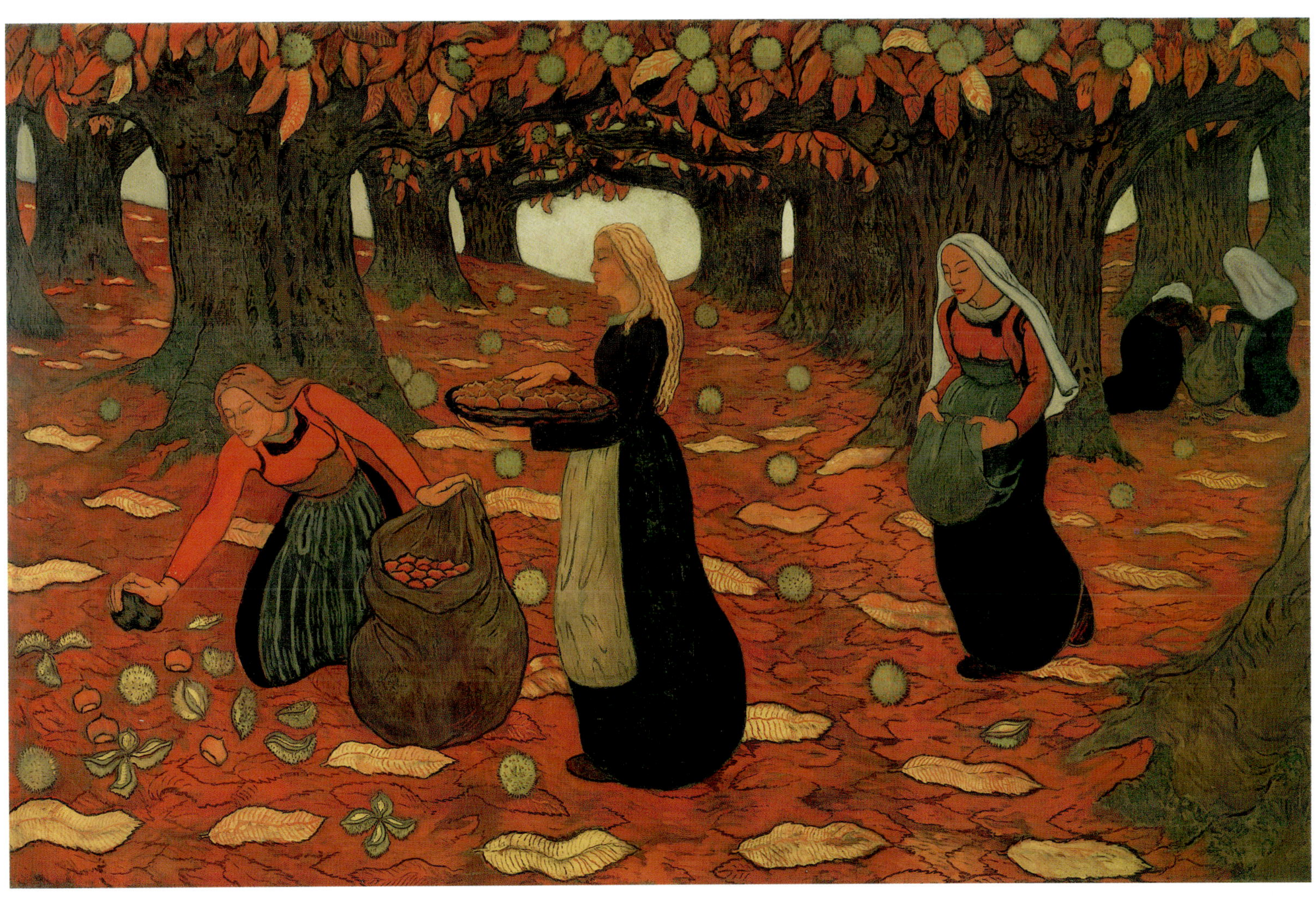

130

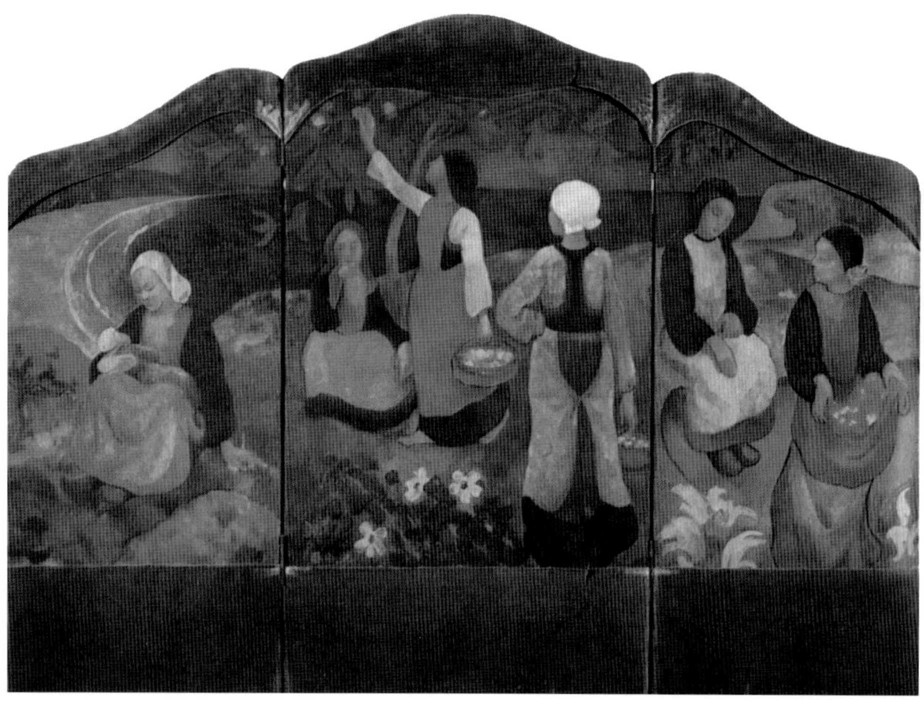

Fig. 130d Paul Sérusier, folding screen, 1891, oil on wood, 28¾ × 52⅜ in. (73 × 133 cm), location unknown

Paintings of the Four Seasons, the Labors of the Months, and the Seasons of Life are of course common in the history of art. The best known are those of Pieter Breugel the Elder and Nicolas Poussin, the latter of which Lacombe would have seen in the Musée du Louvre. In 1892 Pierre Puvis de Chavannes completed work on a pair of mural-size canvases, *Summer* and *Winter*, for the foyer of the newly restored Hôtel de Ville in Paris. The subject was also treated frequently by fellow Nabis Maurice Denis, Pierre Bonnard, Roussel, and Sérusier (fig. 130d). Sérusier in fact painted a decorative series devoted to the seasons (destroyed) for the atelier of Lacombe himself, the Ergastère at Versailles.[2] Lacombe's projected series, with its depictions of happy couples, children, old people—and in *Autumn: The Chestnut Gatherers*, robust, contented laborers—also stands in the tradition of utopian images. This iconographic lineage, which dates back to the age of Thomas More and Bruegel—the latter's *Land of Cockaigne* (1566, Alte Pinakothek, Munich) is the emblematic work—was revived in the nineteenth century by Dominique Papety. His *Dream of Happiness* (1843, Musée Vivenel, Compiègne) depicts about two dozen men, women, and children lounging or cavorting in a highly theatrical, woodland setting as they live out the utopian schemes of Charles Fourier, whose treatise *Unité universelle* is actually depicted at the lower right. Lacombe's *Autumn* is not nearly so programmatic as this, but its vision of pleasurable labor and carefree leisure is comparable to Paul Signac's anarchist and utopian *The Time of Harmony* (1894, private collection, Paris) and Henri Matisse's *Luxe, calme et volupté* (1904–1905, Musée National d'Art Moderne, Centre Pompidou, Paris).

Autumn: The Chestnut Gatherers is one of the two or three most important paintings by an artist better known as "the Nabis sculptor." It is in very good condition but has been darkened by the impregnation of wax from a relining. In addition, its surface has been made light-reflective rather than absorbent on account of a coat of varnish, undermining the sculptural quality of the figures. It may nevertheless be seen as an ambitious work of Nabi, Synthetist decorative art, comparable in scale and ambition—if not quite in painterly achievement—to Édouard Vuillard's *First Fruits*, also in the Norton Simon Museum (cat. 132).

1 Two studies for *Autumn: The Chestnut Gatherers* may be found at the Baltimore Museum of Art, and a third at the Petit Palais, Geneva.

2 Lambinet, 2003, p. 114.

131

Édouard Vuillard
French, 1868–1940

Dressmakers under the Lamp
c. 1891–1892

Oil on cardboard, 9⅝ × 10½ in. (24.5 × 26.7 cm)
Stamped lower left: "E Vuillard"
M.1979.41.2

Provenance: The artist's studio, to; private collection, Paris (probably Ker-Xavier Roussel[1]), by 1943, to; Jacques Salomon (son-in-law of Roussel), by 1955. [Galerie La Cave, Paris, sold 1 October 1979 to]; Norton Simon Art Foundation.

Exhibitions: Paris, 1943, no. 76; Basel, 1949, no. 11; Paris, 1955a, no. 188; Milan, 1959, no. 11; Albi, 1960, no. 10.

References: Chastel, 1954, p. 48, ill.; Easton, 1989, p. 44, fig. 23; Cogeval, 1993, color ill.; Salomon and Cogeval 2003, vol. 1, no. IV-77, p. 269, ill.

Technical Notes: The support is a thin cardboard, cut unevenly by hand at the top edge; magnification reveals drops of paint on and over this edge, demonstrating that the piece was cut before paint was applied. The wood content of the cardboard has caused it to darken considerably. The bottom right corner has broken and is almost separated from the painting; the top right corner is also broken and there are losses of both paint and support. There is no ground layer, although Vuillard may have prepared the cardboard with size to inhibit the absorption of oil. The tooth of the cardboard panel remains prominent in most areas of the painting. The medium appears to be oil, as indicated by the brush marking and the thickness of paint. The paint was directly applied onto the cardboard in a single layer, rather quickly brushed, often leaving gaps in brushwork, which expose the cardboard support. The paint film is well preserved with no evidence of chemical abrasion. There is a small repaired hole at top center. The painting has been varnished, significantly altering its appearance. By comparison, the unvarnished reverse of the support is a lighter, cooler beige tone than the varnished front surface. The varnish is yellow, nonsaturating, and brittle. A brief note in the file from 1979 states that dirt and varnish were selectively removed, but it is not clear if more varnish was added at this time. (RW)

The first evidence for the existence of this small early picture of Édouard Vuillard's mother and her dressmaking assistant is a brief, numbered entry in a 1943 exhibition catalogue of a Pont-Aven and Nabi exhibition in Paris. After that, it appeared in a variety of exhibitions, none particularly distinguished, before it entered the collection of the Norton Simon Art Foundation in 1979. The painting, made in one or perhaps two brief working sessions, displays brutal contrasts of tone and color and an absence of small transitional touches of paint. Thus it resembles an oil sketch, or *ébauche*. Nevertheless, it must be considered finished, and there exist a number of other works from the period 1889–1893 that reveal a nearly comparable directness, intensity, and immediacy. These include *Breakfast at the Window* (1892, private collection),[2] *Mme Vuillard's Dressmaking Studio* (1892, private collection),[3] and *Interior with Chiffonier* (1893, Kunstmuseum Winterthur).[4] *Dressmakers under the Lamp* is unusually raw, but it is not different in kind from other paintings completed by Vuillard in the early 1890s. Indeed, seen in context, it offers viewers an unusually clear perspective on the practices and motives of this little-understood artist.

Vuillard's painting places us in the apartment he shared with his mother, grandmother, and sister. (While it is tempting to identify the second figure in *Dressmakers under the Lamp* as the artist's sister, she was too young in the early 1890s to have served as the model for this woman, who is probably a paid assistant.) This small place was at once home, studio, and dressmaking establishment—its ambience changed not only with the light and the season but also with the uses to which its limited spaces were put. The largest of the rooms functioned as a dining room, receiving room, workroom, art studio, dressmaking studio, and probably guest bedroom—all by moving a modest assortment of furniture, lamps, and fabric coverings. Thus, the Vuillard flat was virtually a theater set—lighted by daylight, candle, and kerosene, and changing according to need—through which Vuillard's characters walked, acted, and spoke their lines in perfect ease. It was also an anachronistic space; by the end of the nineteenth century, most clothing production in France occurred in workshops and factories, not in homes. The segregation of home and workplace (of domesticity and labor) was one of the overwhelming facts of modernization in the nineteenth century, and yet it is largely denied in Vuillard's early paintings. Indeed, the sense of communality in this and his other early paintings—of the intimate relation between craft labor, eating, talking, and the artist's work of representation—is essential to Vuillard's achievement. When in 1892 the critic Albert Aurier spoke of the artist as "intimiste,"[5] the term struck a chord; it would be repeated in nearly all the subsequent literature on Vuillard. He was an intimist because he depicted quiet, domestic dramas that convey what André Gide called "a low tone, suitable to confidences."[6]

As already noted, Vuillard's painting cannot easily be understood on its own; it was part of a coherent, larger

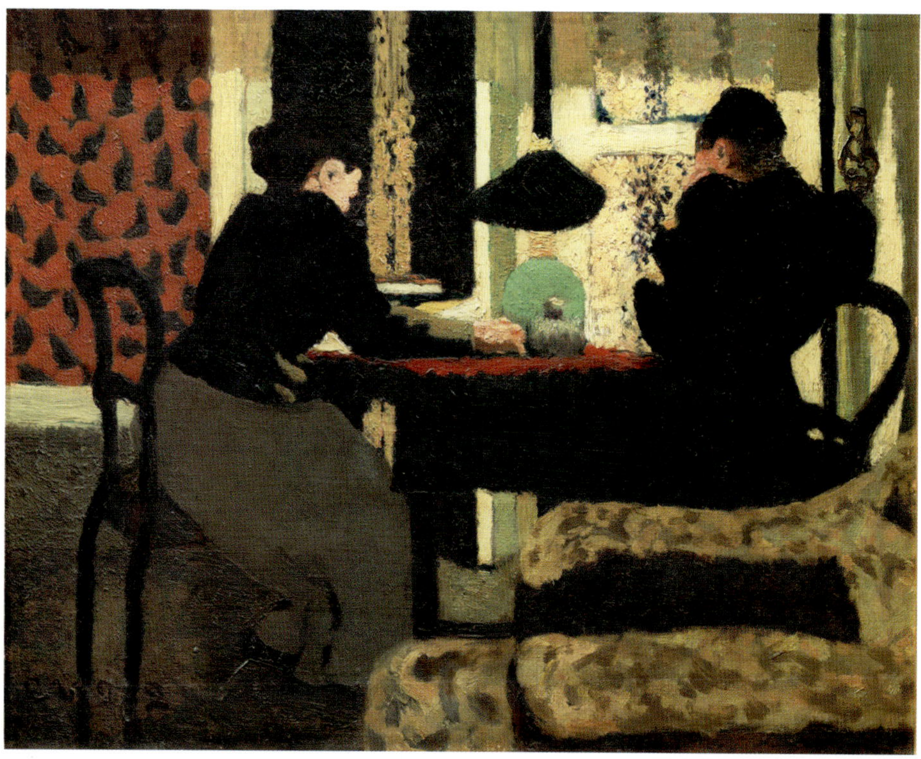

Fig. 131a Édouard Vuillard, *Two Women under a Lamp*, 1892, oil on canvas, $12\frac{1}{2} \times 15\frac{3}{4}$ in. (31.7 × 40 cm), L'Annonciade, Musée de Saint-Tropez

project of representation effectively studied by the art historian Elizabeth Easton. Many basic uncertainties remain, however. Easton's documentary research suggests that Vuillard's mother-muse was not the dressmaker she was long thought to have been—and as she is represented here—but was registered as a *corsetière* (corset maker), whose business began in the 1870s even before the death of her husband, Vuillard's father, in 1884. Nevertheless, the present painting and others like it are far too knowing in their engagement with the métier of sewing, textiles, patterns, and forms to have been fabrications. The bolts of printed and strongly colored cloth with which Vuillard's mother and assistant are generally shown working are not the stuff of underwear but of fashionable, middle-class couture. Indeed, *Dressmakers under the Lamp* and similar works make an elision between the painter's and dressmaker's occupation: each works with color and pattern and each composes finished designs from a few basic raw materials. This indeed is Vuillard's ambition, to assert the essential connection between several different types of decorative manufacture and to affirm the flat, ornamental character of painting. In his paintings, all depicted objects and surfaces—fabric, skin, limbs, torso, and light itself—are treated as one malleable, expressive substance. Like the other self-styled Nabi artists, who included Pierre Bonnard, Maurice Denis, Paul Sérusier, and Ker-Xavier Roussel, Vuillard asserted the expressive validity of form, color, and pictorial surface, independent of subject matter or content.

That this painting is first of all a decorative ensemble of color, shape, texture, and light does not mean, however, that it is without anecdote, narrative, or drama. Vuillard carefully manipulated artificial light to suggest that the picture was made either at night or on a dark winter afternoon as Vuillard's mother and her assistant worked with needle and thread under the strong, directed light of a kerosene lamp. Although the picture's current title (it cannot be attributed to the artist himself) identifies the figures as its subject, the painting actually seems to be as much about light as about women sewing. The small lamp that provides the illumination was painted on several other occasions by Vuillard, principally in his fine *Two Women under a Lamp* of 1892 (fig. 131a) as well as a marvelous panel of the following year, *The Green Lamp* (fig. 131b). The principal complexities of the painting concern light. We see two figures who are illuminated in contrasting ways. Vuillard's mother's face and body are strongly lit by the lamp, while her assistant sits between the painter-viewer and the source of light; she is thus shown in silhouette. Vuillard used this device,

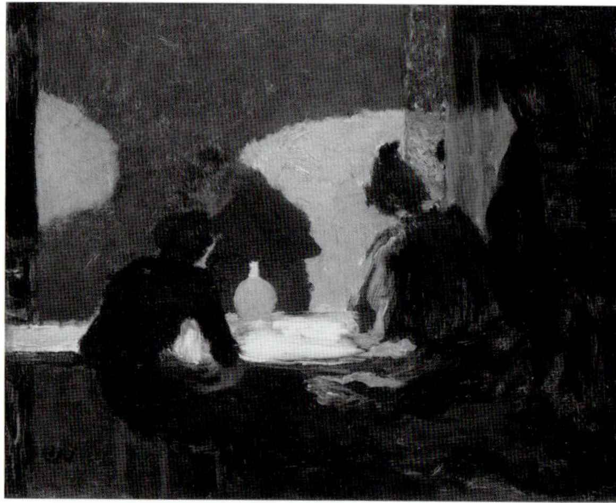

Fig. 131b Édouard Vuillard, *The Green Lamp*, 1893, oil on panel, 9 × 11 in. (22.8 × 28 cm), The Museum of Modern Art, New York

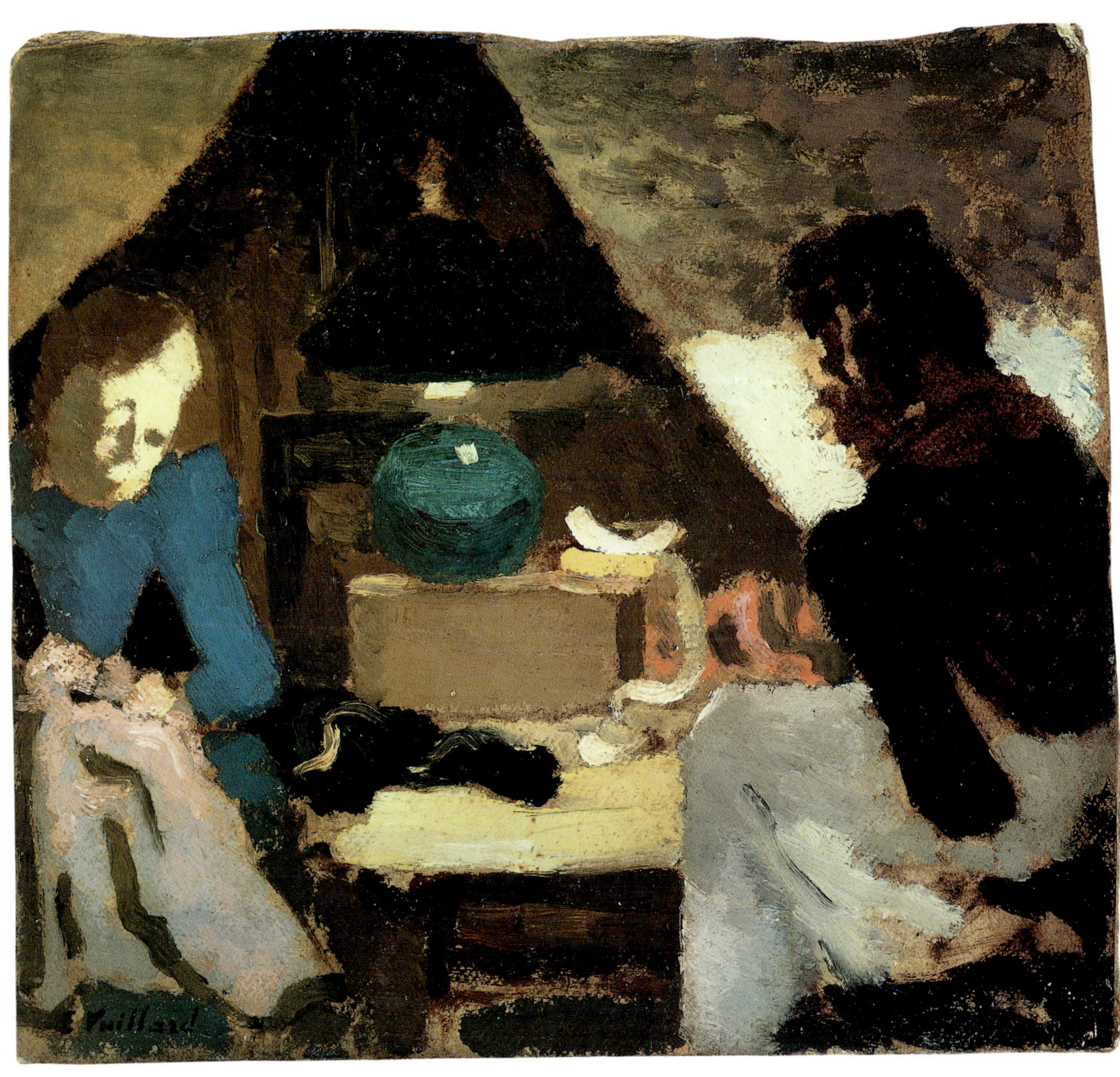

131

a classic representational problem on which all student artists work, in several other paintings of 1891 and 1892, differentiating them by using varying viewpoints. The Norton Simon painting is the only one in which the lamp is placed on a box so as to illuminate more than the top of the table. (Such an arrangement was likely made by Madame Vuillard to create a circle of light large enough to include the laps of the two women.)

The main difficulty in decoding this small painting is to make representational sense of the light in the room itself. The shade of the lamp is mirrored by what we first take to be a huge shadow of that shade that plays across the wall behind the figures. Yet the lamp seems also to cast light on that very "shadow," indicating that the two women are most likely seated in the small curtained alcove of a larger room. There is, in addition, some indication of a distant fireplace behind the lamp, further encouraging us to interpret the great diagonals to the left and right of the composition as curtains pulled back to reveal the room beyond.

The most disturbing aspect of the painting is the sheer ugliness of the female figure to the right. The small daubs of flesh color to the left of her head suggest an almost ghoulish countenance. This, when considered with the passageway through the curtains to a realm of darkness, lends a sinister quality to the representation, not unlike that seen in one of Vuillard's earliest family portraits, *The Family of the Artist* (1889, The Museum of Modern Art, New York).[7] These small pictures represent the isolation of a young and restless bachelor in an age-graded society of women, workshop assistant, sister, mother, grandmother (the latter of whom died in 1894). They also remind us of themes, some misogynist, some feminist, and some decadent, in the avant-garde theater of Vuillard's day, especially the plays of Henrik Ibsen and August Strindberg. The artist was intimate with this cosmopolitan and artificial world, which was also the world of Nabi art, no less than with the affective spaces of domesticity and craft. Throughout the 1890s he designed sets, playbills, and posters, first for the Théâtre Libre of André Antoine, and then after 1893 for the Théâtre de l'Oeuvre of Aurélian-Marie Lugné-Poë. It is even likely that his mother helped with the costumes. Thus Vuillard's art was stretched between two distinct social and artistic realms. It was his intense engagement with craft, pattern, and decorative surfaces that secured the liaison between them.

1 A large donation of pictures by Vuillard was made by his sister and her husband, Ker-Xavier Roussel, to the Musée National d'Art Moderne in Paris in 1944. These pictures were only part of the works that remained in Vuillard's studio at his death in 1940, and it is presumed that this painting remained in the Roussel collection, passed to his daughter and her husband, Jacques Salomon, and thence to their son, Antoine Salomon, who sold some pictures through Galerie La Cave.

2 Salomon and Cogeval, 2003, vol. 1, no. IV-75.

3 Salomon and Cogeval, 2003, vol. 1, no. IV-26.

4 Salomon and Cogeval, 2003, vol. 1, no. IV-90.

5 Aurier, 1892, p. 485.

6 André Gide, "Promenade au Salon d'Automne," *Gazette des Beaux-Arts*, 1 December 1905, trans. in Russell, 1971, p. 96.

7 Salomon and Cogeval, 2003, vol. 1, no. IV-2.

132

Édouard Vuillard
French, 1868–1940

First Fruits
1899

Oil on canvas, 96 × 170 in. (243.8 × 431.8 cm)
Signed and dated lower right: "E. Vuillard 1899"
F.1973.33.1

Provenance: Commissioned in 1899 by Adam Natanson (d. 1906), for 85, rue Jouffroy, Paris, by descent to his son; Thadée Natanson, Paris (sale, Paris, Hôtel Drouot, 13 June 1908, lot 63, to); Alexandre Natanson, Paris; lent to Léon Blum, Paris, 1910–1929; Alexandre Natanson, Paris (sale, Paris, Hôtel Drouot, 16 May 1929, lot 126, ill., to); Mme Bloch, purchasing for Léon Blum (d. 1950), Paris; Robert Blum, Paris; Walter P. Chrysler Jr., New York; [Wildenstein, New York]; private collection, Switzerland; [Wildenstein, New York, sold 5 November 1973 to]; The Norton Simon Foundation.

Exhibitions: Paris, 1904, no. 1287 or 1288, as *Verdure*; Munich, 1908; Paris, 1938a, no. 69, as *Dekoratives Panneau*; Basel, 1949, no. 239; Portland, 1956, no. 87, ill.; New York, 1964b, no. 22, ill.; San Francisco, 1974, no. 51, pp. 116, 117, color ill.

References: Ostini, 1908, p. 349; Segard, 1914, vol. 2, pp. 253, 262–266, 321; Chastel, 1946, pp. 53, 115; Roger-Marx, 1946, pp. 137–138; Bacou, 1964, p. 196 n. 33; Dugdale, 1965, p. 99; Brettell, 1981, p. 7; Bareau, 1986, p. 46; B. Thomson, 1988, pp. 49–50, 115, fig. 38 (detail); Warnod, 1989, pp. 54–55, ill.; Frèches-Thory and Terrasse, 1991, pp. 146–147, ill. 150; Dumas and Cogeval, 1990, pp. 31–33, ill.; Groom, 1990, pp. 147–165, 180–182; Benjamin, 1993, pp. 298–300, fig. 3; Cogeval, 1993, color ill.; Groom, 1993, pp. 65, 123, 124, 126, 127, 132, 145, pls. 195 (detail), 196, 199 (detail), 204 (study), 213 (1906 installation); Groom, 2001, under no. 41, fig. 1, color ill., p. 136; Cogeval, 2003, p. 204, ill.; Salomon and Cogeval, 2003, vol. 2, no. VII-63, pp. 573–575, ill.

Technical Notes: The fabric texture of the unprimed canvas shows in numerous areas, functioning to outline forms, and helps to create the impression of a tapestry. A dark stainlike paint applied to the canvas seems to map out the design. This creates a contrast to the light paint on top and imparts a darker, more somber overall appearance that may also be associated with old tapestries. Pasty paint is applied in brushstrokes, daubing and stippling with initial layers often applied wet in wet. Subsequent layers of paint were usually applied only after the preceding layer was set. Examples of layering include green brushed over blue and yellow over green. In the latter example the yellow was sometimes scraped before another layer of a different color was applied, as appears to be the case with the orange-red highlights in the lower center of the canvas. The colors are now darkened to some degree by the synthetic varnish that also discolors the fabric support. Originally, the surface was surely more matte but with greater variation of hue. Otherwise the painting is in very good condition with only minor losses and tears. Some of the original tacking edges survive on all sides, and the support has been lined with an aqueous adhesive to fabric and stretched on a later stretcher. (JF)

This enormous landscape—the largest of Vuillard's career—was painted in 1899 on commission from Adam Natanson, the wealthy father of the famous writer and editor Thadée Natanson, founder of *La Revue blanche*. Together with a slightly smaller landscape, *Window Overlooking the Woods*, in the Art Institute of Chicago (fig. 132a), it was installed in Natanson's *hôtel particulière* on the rue Jouffroy in Paris. Natanson, a retired banker, had conventional, even conservative, tastes, preferring gilt furniture, bibelots, and works of art in ornate frames to the modernist art and decor championed by his sons Thadée and Alfred. Vuillard seems to have responded to this conservative setting by electing to paint decorative panels that resemble large, so-called verdure tapestries from the sixteenth and seventeenth centuries. In *First Fruits*, Vuillard temporarily abandoned his preferred medium of distemper, or glue-based paint, for the more conventional oil paint on canvas. This decision, uncharacteristic at that period for Vuillard, was surely made by his client, who may have found the matte surfaces of distemper unpleasant and, perhaps, untested by time. Adam Natanson surely wanted something permanent, even if it was the work of a still young, experimental painter.

Never before had Vuillard, or any other modern painter, so closely approached the art of tapestry. Although his wonderful panels for Dr. Vaquez painted in 1896 (*Figures and Interiors*, Petit Palais, Paris)[1] have been compared to the famous late-fifteenth-century red-ground Unicorn tapestries at the Cluny Museum in Paris, the differences between the source and the result are so great that only the most general of connections can be made. With the Natanson landscapes, however, Vuillard seems to have taken the somewhat later verdure tapestry tradition as a strong prototype, borrowing the gray tonalities and the vegetal borders so common to the genre. In fact, when the painting was first exhibited at the Salon d'Automne in 1904, it was entitled simply *Verdure*. The term may be translated as "greenery," but it also refers to the typical tapestries of the Creuse River region, chiefly from the towns of Aubusson and Felletin, that were restricted in theme to rustic landscape and hunting scenes. Verdure tapestries, however, were also made in numerous towns in Flanders during the same

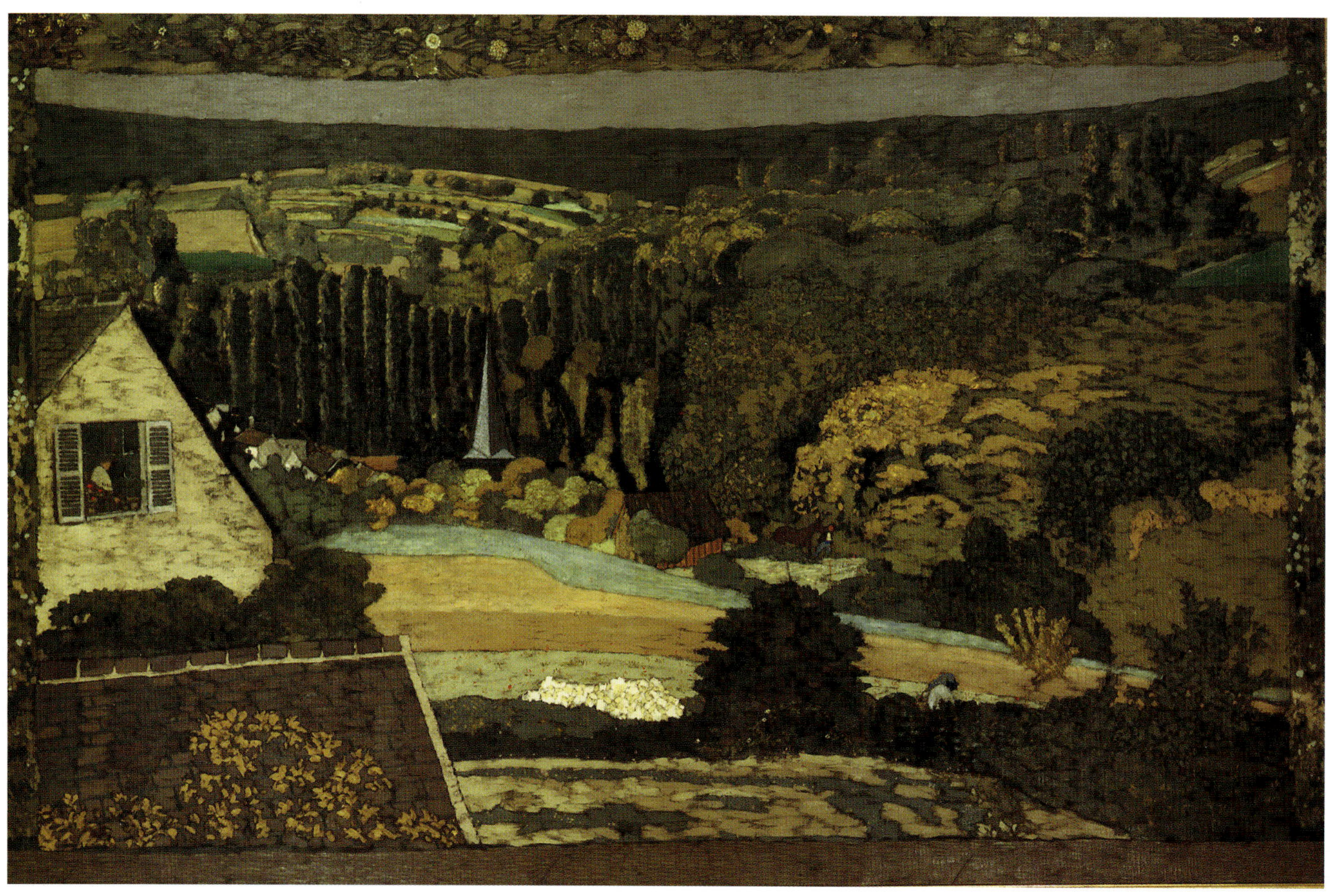

Fig. 132a Édouard Vuillard, *Window Overlooking the Woods*, 1899, oil on canvas, $96\frac{1}{8} \times 149$ in. (244.2×378.5 cm), The Art Institute of Chicago, L. L. and A. S. Coburn Fund, Martha E. Leverone Fund, Charles Norton Owen Fund, and anonymous restricted gift

period. Indeed, Vuillard's particular source was likely a set of twelve tapestries in the Musée du Louvre designed by Bernard van Orley from the Flemish workshop of Jan Gieteels. Now titled *Maximilian's Hunt*, the series depicts the hunts characteristic of each month of the year. The September tapestry (fig. 132b) is closest in general theme to Vuillard's painting and has a similar border, scale, colorways, and deep perspective.

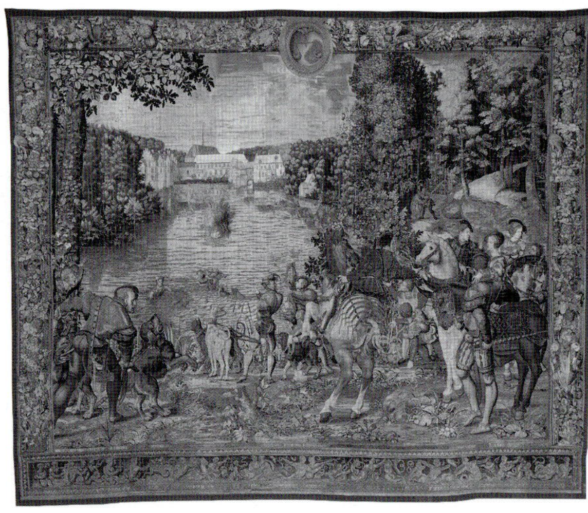

Fig. 132b After Bernard van Orley, *The Month of September*, from *Maximilian's Hunt*, 1531–1533, wool, silk, gold and silver threads, 14 ft. 5 in. × 18 ft. 6 in. (4.40×5.63 m), Musée du Louvre, Paris; photo: D. Arnaudet; © Réunion des Musées Nationaux / Art Resource, NY

Vuillard's principal compositional challenge in *First Fruits*, like that faced by French and Flemish tapestry designers, was to animate and differentiate a large surface with more or less uniform color. The landscape that unfolds beneath the spaceless gray sky is composed almost entirely of greens closely related in both value and hue. Whereas fine tapestries possess variety by virtue of their unique warp and weft, an oil painting must generally display variety by other means. Vuillard thus did not so much copy revered verdure prototypes as adapt modern landscape subjects to their planar structure. He divided his composition into discrete zones like those woven individually by tapestry makers before being assembled to form the larger panel. Vuillard also used subtly contrasting patterns, textures, and shapes to create modulations in this immense field dominated by four or five greens enlivened with browns, grays, off-whites, yellows, oranges, and blue-grays. Daisies of several types are dotted across varying green fields almost like printed flowers on wallpaper, and clusters of grapes are picked out in little dots of gray-blue that interact with the white-dotted red scarf of the woman working in the vineyard. The result is a mural that functions both as an independent work of art and as a grand "decoration"—a

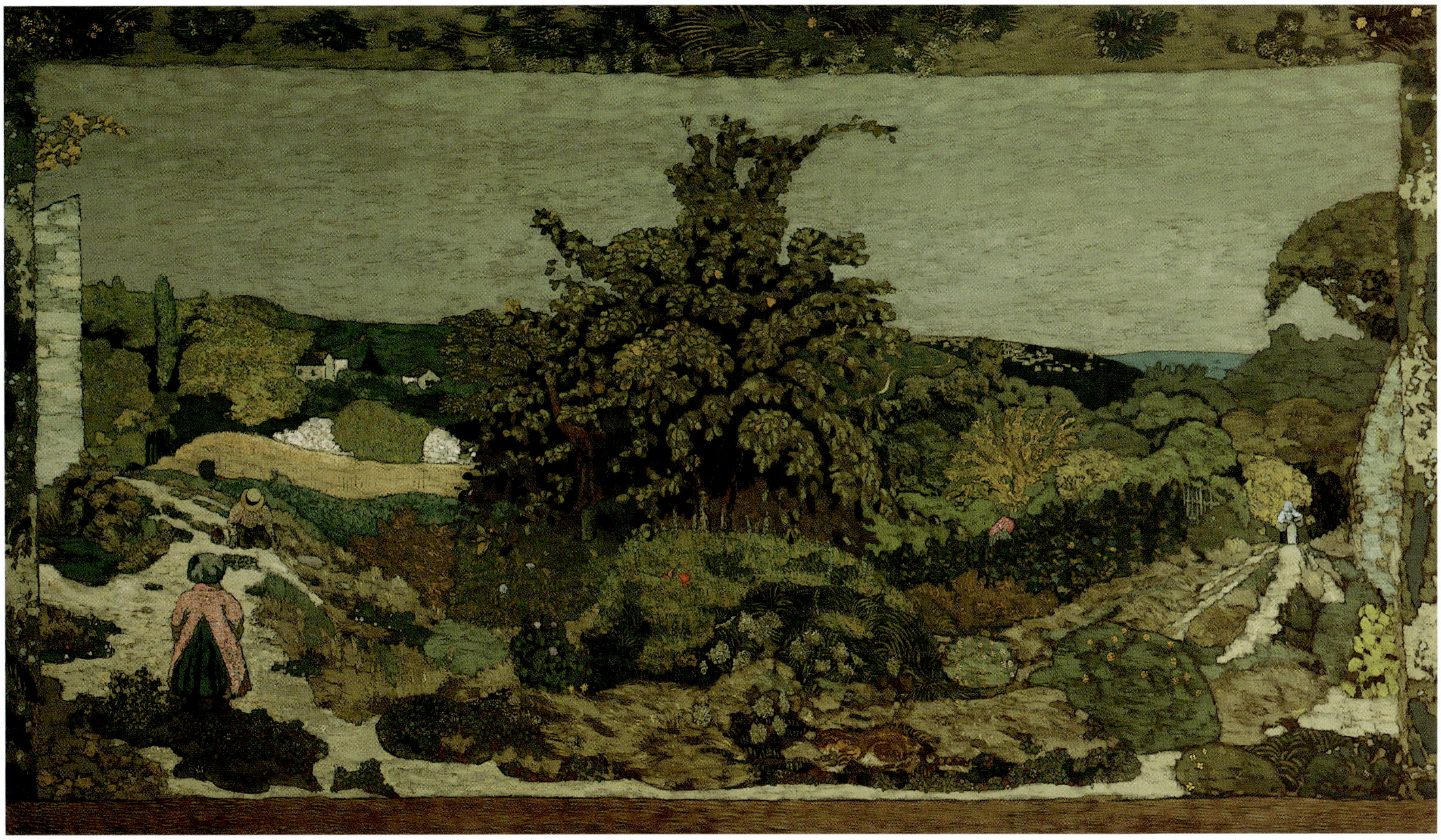

132

word favored by the Nabis and other Symbolist artists—that is inseparable from the room in which it is hung. The landscape motifs of the two Natanson landscapes have been identified by the art historian Gloria Groom as the countryside around the village of L'Étang-la-Ville, in the Île-de-France, where Vuillard's sister and brother-in-law, Marie and Ker-Xavier Roussel, rented a house called La Coulette shortly after the birth of their daughter Annette in November 1898.[2] The proud and childless Uncle Édouard doted on his young niece and recorded her alone or with her relatives in various environments throughout her childhood. She was too young to be the little toddler who stands alone in her pink smock and blue beret at the left of *First Fruits*, taking her "first steps"—the action mimics the title—in a rural landscape translated by her uncle from the verdant countryside in the hills just west of Paris. A photograph of the painting after it was reinstalled in 1906 in the dining room of Alfred Natanson at 92, boulevard Malesherbes, shows the grandchild of Adam (recently deceased), also called Annette, seated in a Chinese-style dining chair with a large table set for breakfast in front of her, and the vast *First Fruits* filling the wall behind her (fig. 132c). The painting was thus evidently a bond linking successive generations of Natansons, Roussels, and Vuillards. There is accordingly a genuine familial ease to the painting, and we are encouraged to linger in its paths, valleys, vineyards, and fields. Four figures, the child and three working figures, animate and give scale to various parts of this puzzlelike landscape. They are together a modern, pastoral, bourgeois retort to the Renaissance figures in van Orley's verdure tapestry, which had once belonged to Jules Mazarin and Louis XIV.

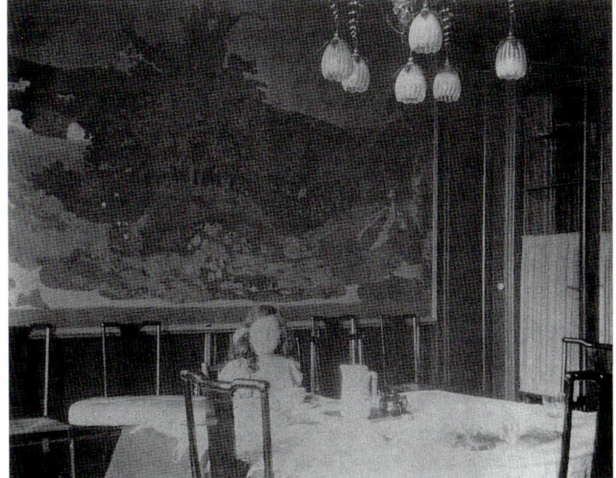

Fig. 132c Alfred Athis Natanson, *First Fruits* installed in the Natanson dining room, c. 1906, Archives Vuillard, Paris

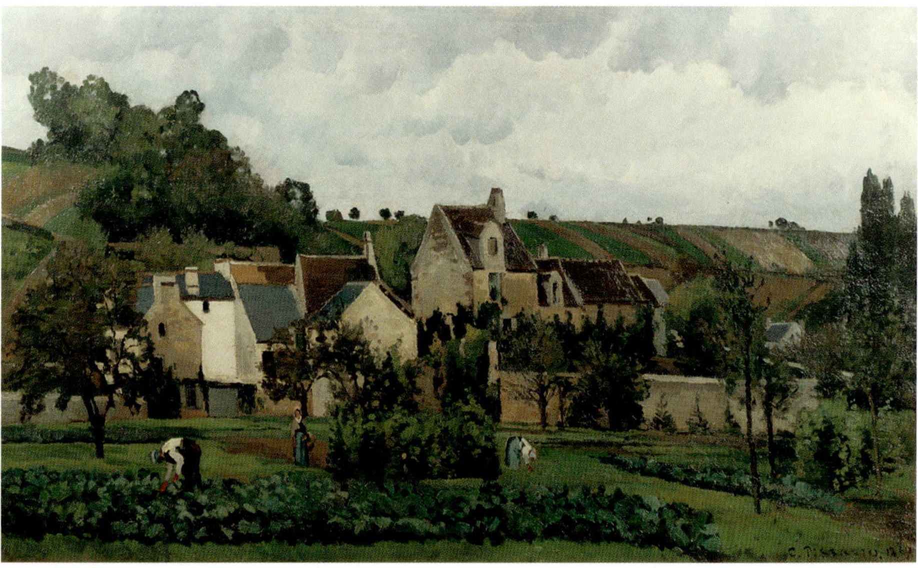

Fig. 132d Camille Pissarro, *The Hermitage at Pontoise,* 1867, oil on canvas, $35^{7}/_{8} \times 58^{1}/_{2}$ in. (91 × 150.5 cm), Wallraf-Richartz Museum, Cologne; photo: Erich Lessing / Art Resource, NY

First Fruits and *Window Overlooking the Woods* belong within the tradition of French and Italian painting known as pastoral, an association made in 1914 by Achille Segard in his fascinating study of "decorative" painting in France, *Peintres d'aujourd'hui: Les Décorateurs.* In a passage that is among the most beautiful and subtle ever written about landscape art, Segard deals with both canvases produced for Adam Natanson:

> This decorative painting is essentially peaceful, restful, noble in style, of great delicacy in the matching of tones, but a delicacy that is muted, as it were. It strikes a distinctly modern note. One cannot see with what one might compare it, either in the art of recent years or in the art of the past. It does have, however, affinities with the tapestries known as "verdures" of the century of Louis XIV. It is the perfect decoration for a study, a refuge for meditation. At the same time, this painting has a meaning. It gives instruction, for it invites contemplation. It describes for us—as the Georgics do—the touching beauty of an undulating landscape, the occult labors of germination, the delights of living in this harsh solitude. Monsieur Vuillard brings home to us what a contrast there is between all this tranquillity and the futile furor of big cities. He shows us where his preferences lie and invites us to share them. We divine, however, that this landscape has been seen by a city dweller accustomed to analyzing himself and to giving an account of the whys and wherefores of his emotions. We sense that it has been painted in a big city, and for an apartment in a big city. . . . In the elaboration of his works, the intellect remains predominant, even though it places itself at the service of [the artist's] visual sensibility.[3]

This passage reminds us of the existence of two traditions of landscape art in nineteenth-century France, the one realist, and the other idealist or pastoral. The first, identified with Gustave Courbet, Théodore Rousseau, Jean-François Millet, and later the Dutch-born Vincent van Gogh, emphasizes precisely what one might call the rustic odor of the earth. It is intensely materialist and historical, employing paint in such a way as to underscore the physicality and palpability of both the artwork and the motif. Realist landscape art also tends to depict peasants and rural laborers without idealization, and thereby to suggest that they are victims of a social and economic order that privileges urban dwellers, that is, bourgeois participants in a national and international money economy. The contrary tradition of idealist, classical, or pastoral landscape, by contast, derives from certain late antique poetic and artistic forms, interpreted in the seventeenth century by the artists Nicolas Poussin, Claude Lorrain, and Gaspar Dughet.

According to the rhetorics of pastoral poetry and art—extensively studied by William Empson and Raymond Williams[4]—the rural world outside a great capital city is remembered or evoked from a distance (either temporal or physical) by the poet or painter, as a place of refined order and subtly rendered ease. This form of pastoral is almost never erotic and can be experienced without Judeo-Christian guilt or shame. Some chief nineteenth-century French exponents of pastoral landscape are Pierre-Henri de Valenciennes, Camille Corot, Camille Pissarro, and, perhaps, Paul Cézanne. (The latter is somewhat of a special case, since he draws equally from the two traditions.) When the Realist critic Émile Zola in 1867 called the landscapes of Pissarro "grave and reasoned,"[5] he was evoking precisely the sense of classical or pastoral order that might be equally perceived in a Doric temple, a Roman bath, the Eclogues of Virgil, or the landscapes of Claude. Indeed, Pissarro's great green pastoral landscapes to which Zola referred bear a startling similarity to Vuillard's 1899 decorations (fig. 132d).

The artist who assumed effective control of the pastoral at the end of the nineteenth century was the great academic painter Pierre Puvis de Chavannes. The art historian Belinda Thomson is surely correct in pointing out that Puvis's death in 1898 focused renewed attention on the austere work of a man who had been

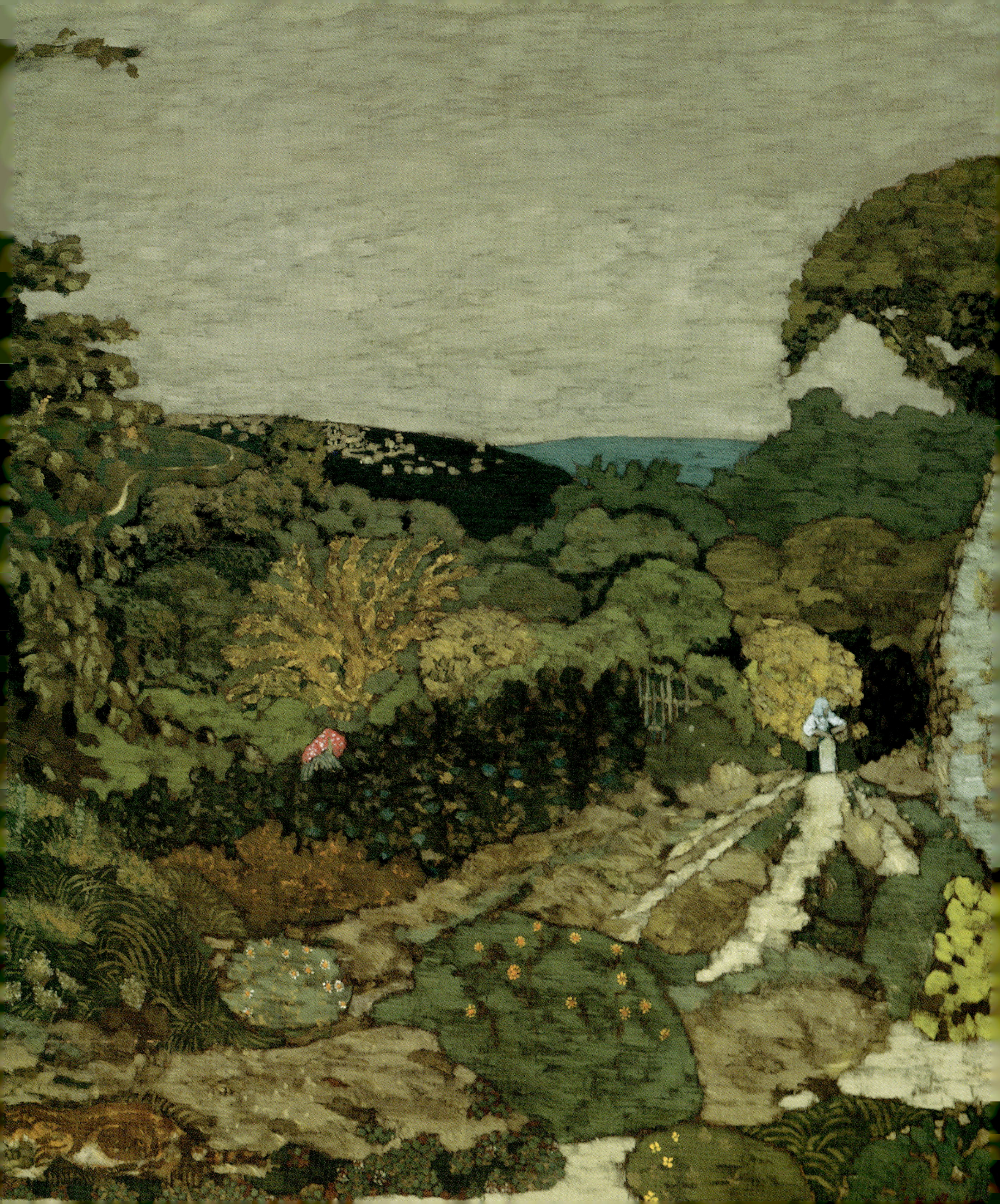

admired by two generations of avant-garde artists.[6] Puvis's famous paintings *The Sacred Grove* (1884–1886, Musée des Beaux-Arts, Lyon) and *Summer* (1873, Musée d'Orsay, Paris) are indeed possible sources for Vuillard's Natanson landscapes, but the relative emptiness and severe compositional rigor of Puvis seem at odds with the informal, interlocking masses of Vuillard. In the end, the verdure tapestries, with their material richness and textural complexity, are more compelling sources. Vuillard effectively engaged the broad tradition of the pastoral even as he invokes the local and urban pleasures of family and friends and the sanctuary of the *hôtel particulière.*

It is perhaps worth noting in conclusion the single animal in the vast Norton Simon painting, a mottled cat with a wonderfully furry body just to the right of center in the foreground of the vast composition. The cat seems to prowl silently through the landscape, its white belly peeking out and its long tale flaccid and flat in back of it. It seems to sniff the ground and to move slowly in the direction of the little girl at the far left. We assume, of course, that it is mousing and will soon pounce on its prey. It becomes our visual prey as we search the landscape. Guy Cogeval ends the beautifully written entry on the Natanson decorations in his catalogue raisonné with a suggestion that Vuillard himself considered them to be his finest works.[7]

1 Salomon and Cogeval, 2003, vol. 1, nos. V-97.1–V-97.4.

2 Groom, 1990, p. 124.

3 Segard, 1914, pp. 258–260, quoted in Salomon and Cogeval, 2003, vol. 2, p. 575.

4 William Empson, *Some Versions of Pastorale,* Norfolk, Conn., 1950; and Raymond Williams, *The Country and the City,* New York, 1973.

5 Zola, 1974, p. 74.

6 B. Thomson, 1988, pp. 49–50.

7 Salomon and Cogeval, 2003, p. 575; they also publish two small oil studies for the Norton Simon painting, nos. VII-59 and VII-60.

133

ÉDOUARD VUILLARD
French, 1868–1940

Lucie Hessel
c. 1905

Oil on cardboard, 16 × 18 in. (40.6 × 45.7 cm)
Signed upper right: "E. Vuillard"
Inscribed above signature: "à mon ami Lucie Hessel"
M.1977.1

PROVENANCE: Jos (d. 1942) and Lucie Hessel, Paris, c. 1900–still in 1930. Louis Carré, Paris. Vivian Prins, London. [Lefevre Gallery, London, sold 1977 to]; Norton Simon Art Foundation.

EXHIBITION: Paris, 1948, no. 47.

REFERENCES: T. Bernard, 1930, p. 22, ill.; Chastel, 1946, pp. 60, ill., 70–71; Wichmann, 1962, pp. 356, ill., 357; Salomon and Cogeval, 2003, vol. 2, no. VII-345, p. 712, ill.

TECHNICAL NOTES: It was not uncommon for Vuillard to use a support of unprepared cardboard as he did here. This particular board has a fabric texture that is visible through the surface of the paint, but it does not seem to be prepared in any other way. The ocher color of the board is important to the design where it was left unpainted. The bottom edge of the support was cut after the painting was complete, but the other edges seem mostly intact. The oil paint is pasty but fairly rich and worked wet in wet. Brushstrokes are evident and impasto is low. Although paint is directly applied, colors are nonetheless layered. For example, Madame Hessel's skirt consists of a yellowish layer with gray paint on top. The latter was applied after the first layer was set. Since the cardboard does not appear to have any original coating or preparation, it seems likely that the painting should have been left unvarnished, in which case the unpainted cardboard would have a lighter and more matte appearance. At present there is a thick, glossy varnish. (JF)

AFTER VUILLARD'S MOTHER and sister, Lucie Hessel was the most important woman in his life. The wife of the wealthy art critic and collector-dealer Jos Hessel, Lucie was a lifelong friend of the shy painter—at once muse, confidant, and, later, lover. The two are reported to have met in 1895, when Vuillard attended a dinner "chez Hessel au rue d'Argenteuil," but their relationship blossomed in the summer of 1900 at La Romanel, the summerhouse near Lausanne belonging to the Swiss Nabi painter Félix Vallotton, who had just married a cousin of the Hessels. From that moment on, they were virtually inseparable, and the painter was not only a frequent guest at the Hessels' country residence but served as the godfather of their adopted daughter. (He played this role largely because he was one of the close Catholic friends of the Jewish Hessels, who baptized their daughter and raised her as a Catholic.)

This small and informal portrait bears an inscription indicating that it was a gift from Vuillard to Lucie; the inclusion of her full name suggests that he did not want the gift to be interpreted by others in terms of too great an intimacy with a married woman. Lucie kept it throughout her life, and Vuillard himself kept a closely related painting (fig. 133a) until his death in 1940. Gloria Groom, among the most thoughtful and compassionate readers of the Vuillard journals kept by the Institut de France, has found no concrete evidence in them of an affair between the two but suggests it was nevertheless likely, discreetly referring to an analogous sexual relationship between Lucie's husband, Jos Hessel, and Vuillard's friend the painter Pierre Bonnard.[1] Indeed, the pressures felt by the participants in their *liaisons dangereuses* frequently erupted into small squabbles, threats, and scenes, some of which Vuillard patiently recorded in his journal.

Judging from Lucie Hessel's unflattering nickname "Le Dragon," we may assume that she was in every way formidable. Many friends and acquaintances described her as strong, opinionated, and especially domineering, even of Vuillard, and there is an indication that the Hessels referred to Vuillard as their "house painter." The present panel was in fact painted in the Hessels' rather grand apartment on the rue de Rivoli, directly across from the Tuileries Garden. Vuillard painted Lucie in the same room, *Lucie Hessel Posing*, in about 1904 (fig. 133b), a year or two before this more simplified Nabi panel. In

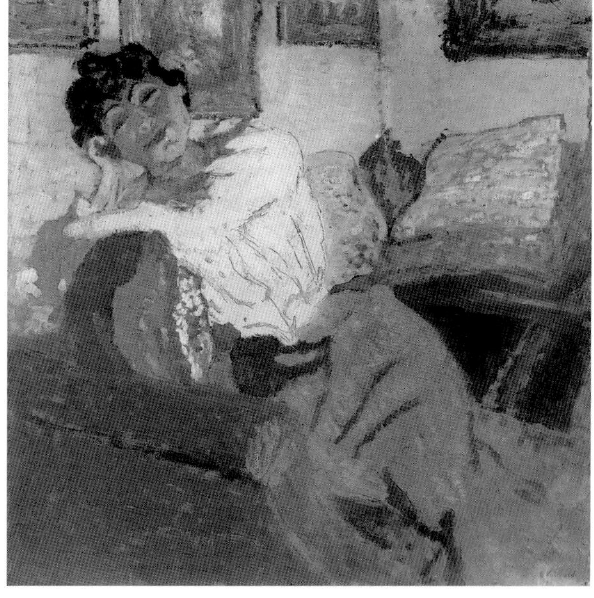

Fig. 133a Édouard Vuillard, *Madame Hessel on a Sofa*, c. 1905, oil on board, $21\frac{1}{2} \times 21\frac{1}{2}$ in. (54.6 × 54.6 cm), National Museums and Galleries on Merseyside, Walker Art Gallery, Liverpool

Fig. 133b Édouard Vuillard, *Lucie Hessel Posing*, c. 1904, oil on canvas, 31¼ × 28¼ in. (79.3 × 71.8 cm), private collection

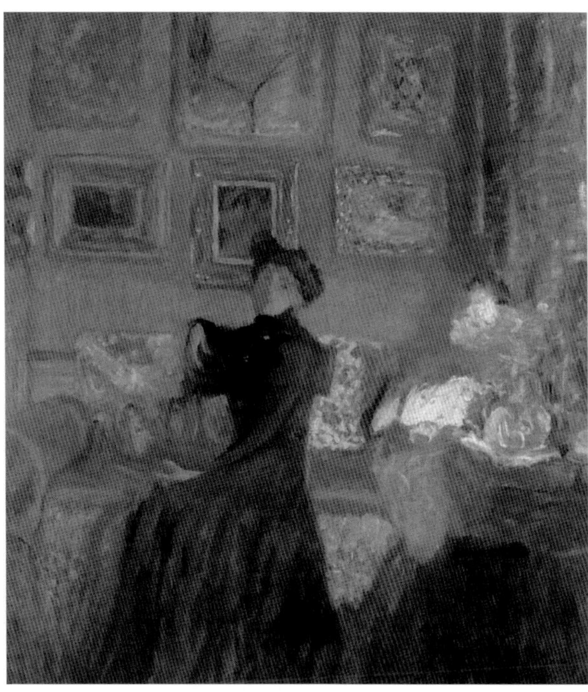

the earlier work, she leans against an arrangement of plump pillows on a pink sofa, looking into the painter-viewer's eyes, as if posing. She is thus confronting the viewer directly, refusing to sanction the distance generally maintained in Vuillard's Intimist interiors of the 1890s.

Yet in the Norton Simon painting it does not appear that Lucie Hessel is either conventionally sitting for a portrait or serving as a model, as she did for Vuillard on later occasions. Rather, it seems more likely that we are witnessing a languid conversation in the daytime, in which Lucie Hessel is either resting or listening to the painter, her lips pursed and her eyes almost shut. Only her vivaciously curled dark brown hair animates her repose. The simple gray skirt and the white, high-collared blouse she wears suggest that she is not dressed to receive but rather to welcome the painter into her home for an impromptu visit. There is, however, absolutely no sexual tension in the painting. Indeed, the opposite is true. We have no fear that Vuillard will disturb her languor; he paints her as placidly as she rests. Given the prominent dedication and provenance of this painting, it is possible that it was among the first depictions by Vuillard of the woman who was to dominate his life for the next four decades. By 1908 they saw each other daily, and despite the problems and setbacks in their relationship, it continued without interruption until Vuillard's death.

1 Groom, 1993, p. 2.

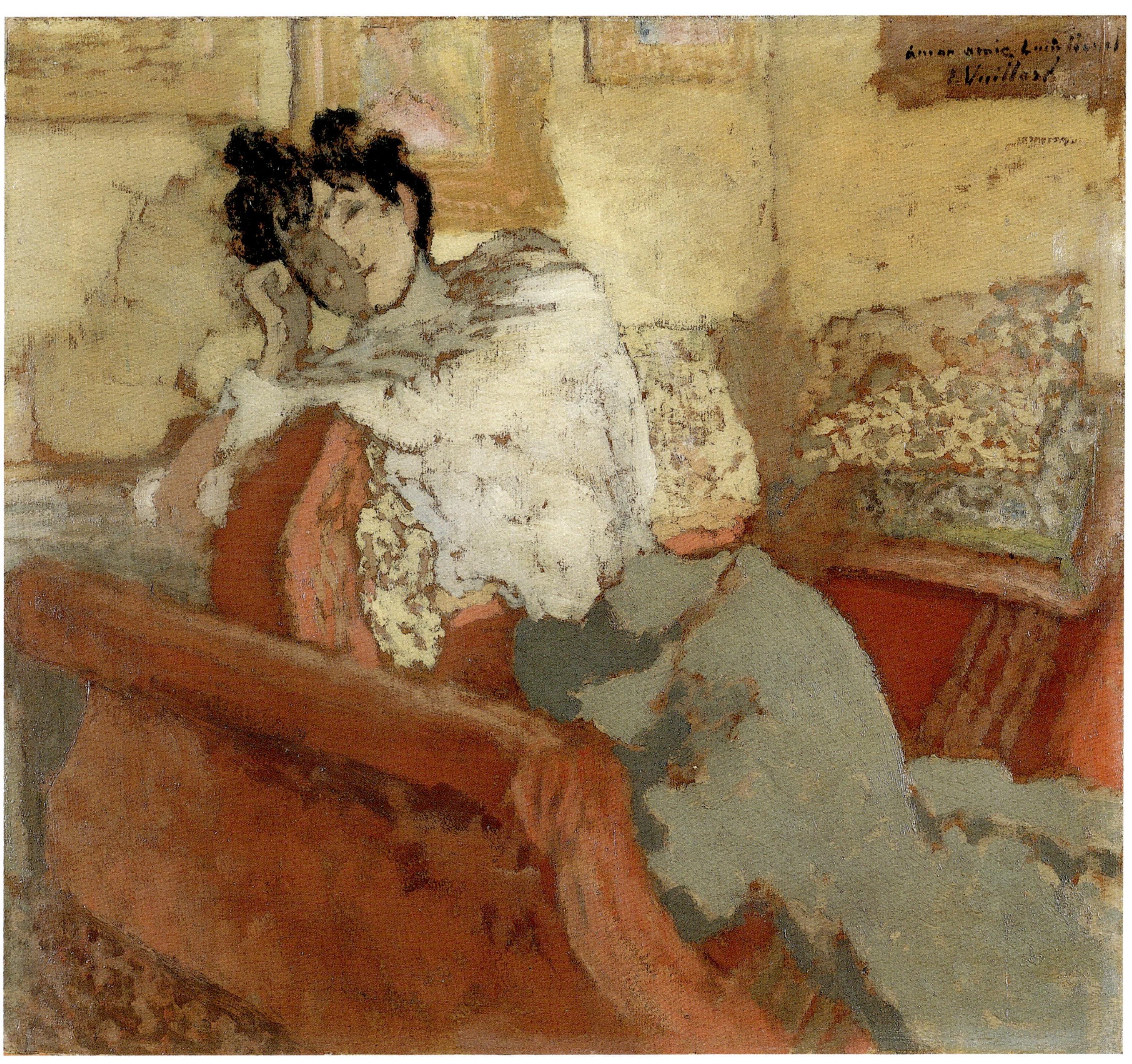

133

134

Édouard Vuillard
French, 1868–1940

The Pitch Pine Room (formerly *Denise Natanson and Marcelle Aron in the Summerhouse at Villerville, Normandy*)
Summer 1910

Oil on canvas, $18\frac{1}{4} \times 25\frac{3}{8}$ in. (46.4 × 64.4 cm)
Signed lower right: "E Vuillard"
F.1983.1

Provenance: The artist; sold 27 October 1910 to; [Bernheim-Jeune, Paris, stock no. 18352, as *La Chambre de pitchpin*, sold 13 January 1911 to]; [Léonce Rosenberg, Paris, to]; [Galerie Alfred Daber, Paris, to]; [Sam Salz, Inc., New York, to]; Edward G. Robinson (1893–1973), Los Angeles, by 1956, by inheritance to; Jane Bodenheimer Adler (Mrs. Edward G.) Robinson, Los Angeles (sale, London, Christie's, 17 May 1983, lot 32, ill., to); The Norton Simon Foundation.

Exhibitions: Paris, 1911, no. 4; Los Angeles, 1956, no. 72, ill.

References: Robinson, 1975, pp. 46, 47, color ill.; Salomon and Cogeval, 2003, vol. 2, no. VIII-372, p. 996, ill.

Technical Notes: The support is a commercially prepared, fine, plain-weave canvas. The gray ground is relatively thick, filling much of the canvas weave and covering the tacking edges. The canvas has been strip-lined and restretched on what appears to be the original 5-part butt-join keyable stretcher. Paint was applied with a brush in strokes and squiggles so that the gray ground shows in the design. The thick paint of the red coat appears to be several layers of paint applied wet in wet. The fuzzy signature was applied with a broad brush. The painting has been varnished and remnants of an older yellowed varnish can be detected in the impasto. The painting was probably not meant to be varnished, and the present varnish darkens the color of the ground in the design; this is particularly evident in comparison with the unvarnished tacking edges. (JF)

Vuillard, resolutely a Parisian, was also one of the great visual interpreters of country life as experienced by city dwellers with sufficient leisure and resources to own properties or rent them for months at a time away from the pressures of the French capital. Although he never himself owned country property, he was truly a connoisseur of such places, using his bachelor status and shy charm to secure invitations to the various country houses of the Natansons, Roussels, Hessels, Vallottons, and many other even grander friends. Although certain of these properties were in the Île-de-France, others dotted the rugged shores of Brittany and Normandy, just far enough from the capital that visits lasted for weeks or months rather than days or the weekend.

Here in these places of upper-middle-class rural privilege, Vuillard had sufficient time to observe urban sophisticates in various combinations practicing the well-tried habits of leisured country life. Certain of the houses—like those of the Natansons or Stéphane Mallarmé at Valvin—were relatively modest. Others were grand, newly constructed houses for a nouveau riche bourgeoisie, and surely this pine-paneled room at a Norman country house in Cricqueboeuf, rented by the Hessels in the summer of 1910, was among the latter. From its vast Art Nouveau chandelier to the beautifully carved staircase, the house was large, light-filled, and self-important. Only the wicker chair and the enormous informally flowered tablecloth allow us to think of this place as in any sense casual. But casual it was intended to be, as we can tell from the carefully identified human inhabitants of the room and the relaxed manner in which the work is painted. There exists a small *croquis* (pencil sketch) for the painting in a private collection (fig. 134a).

The little girl in her red smock reaching up for something on the table was Denise Natanson, the second daughter of Alfred Natanson and his wife, Marthe Melot. Her female companion was neither a servant nor a relative but, rather, Marcelle Aron, a cousin of the hostess, Lucie Hessel, and the future wife of the writer Tristan Bernard. Both Marcelle and Denise's mother, Marthe, were very involved in the theatrical circle around the Hessels, and the group, including Vuillard, was completely accustomed to one another. The unmarried and childless Vuillard was fascinated by relationships between children and unrelated adults and seems to have been thoroughly at ease in the company of children. He

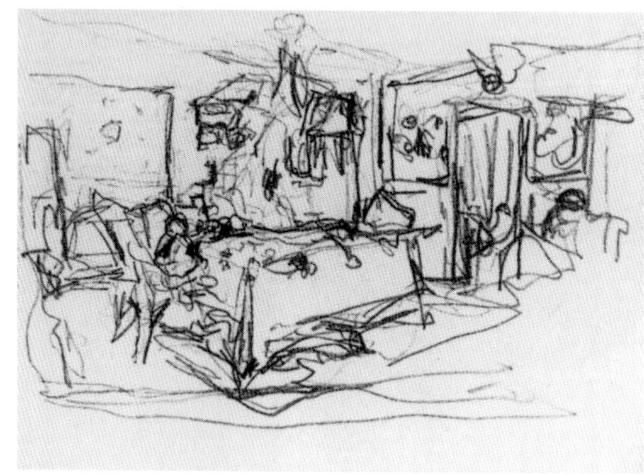

Fig. 134a Édouard Vuillard, preparatory drawing for *The Pitch Pine Room*, 1910, graphite on paper, $3\frac{7}{8} \times 5\frac{1}{16}$ in. (9.9 × 12.9 cm), private collection

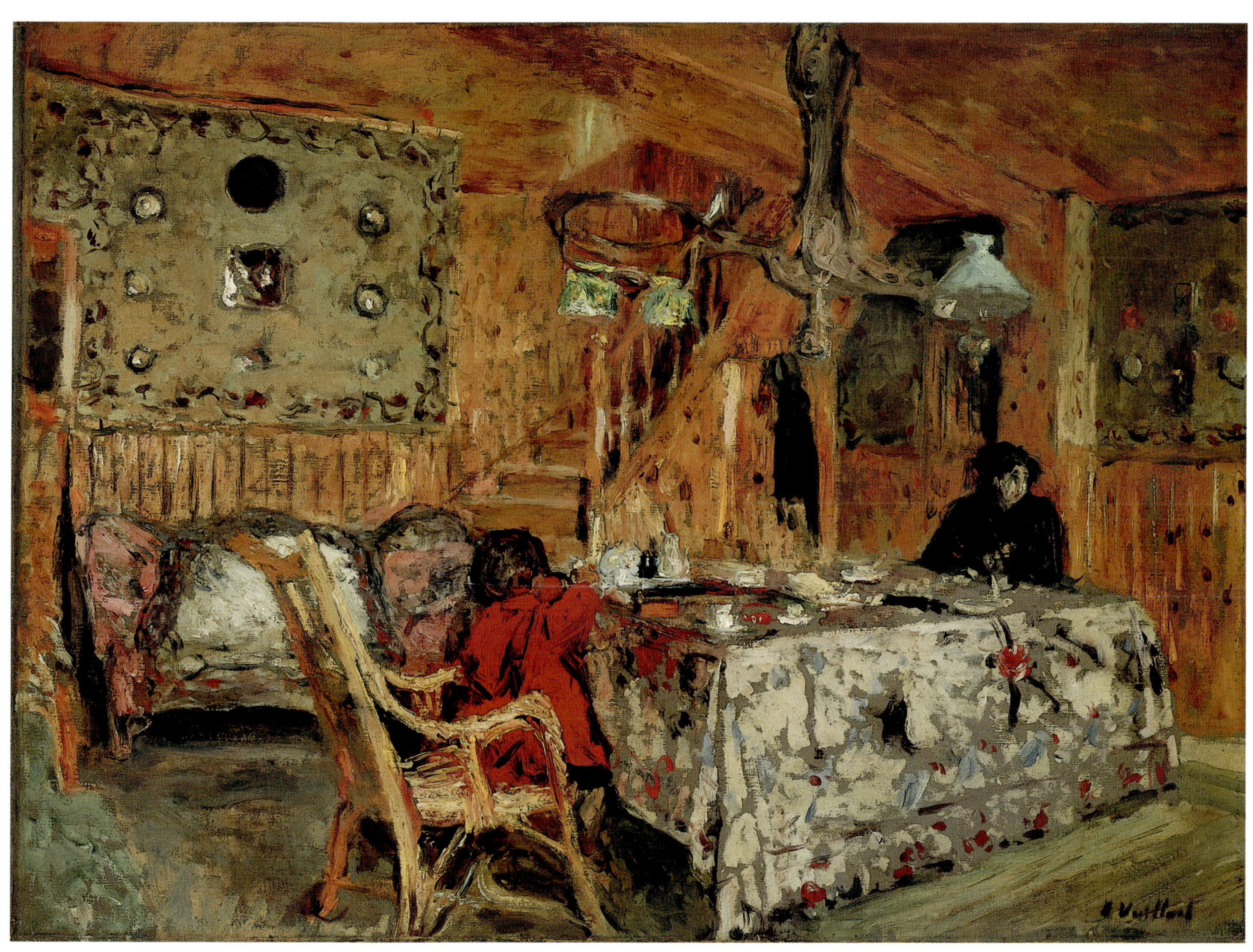

was like his friend Pierre Bonnard, who painted his own nieces and nephews throughout their childhoods, and their contemporaries, the French composers Claude Debussy and Erik Satie, each of whom wrote music specifically for and about children. The sense of being part of what might be called the extended family of friends and their children was a leitmotif of Vuillard from the time his niece was born in 1898 until World War I. In this ambience, Vuillard's desire for familiarity and closeness—apparent in early pictures of his home, mother, sister, and atelier—was gratified. The unblushing honesty of small children may break down adult reserve and permit an artist access to otherwise hidden recesses of heart and home.

The great German art historian Julius Meier-Graefe summarized Vuillard's aesthetic in 1908: "No artist has ever so suggested the soul of an interior—the sense of habitation. . . . We enjoy the same sort of intimacy with him as in conversation with certain agreeable people, when the talk results in a mutual perception of subtle things, when thoughts no longer require words for their interchange, and we are silent lest we should disturb them."[1]

1 Julius Meier-Graefe, *The Development of Modern Art*, London, 1908; cited in John Russell, *Édouard Vuillard, 1868–1940*, London, 1971, p. 98.

135

Maurice Denis
French, 1870–1943

The Entombment
1893

Tempera on paper, mounted on canvas, 43½ × 52 in. (110.5 × 132.1 cm)
Signed lower left, vertically: "M / A / V / D"
M.1977.3.3

Provenance: M. (?Christian) de Galéa, Paris, by 1970, probably by 1963. [Galerie La Cave, Paris, by 1976, sold 14 February 1977 to]; Norton Simon Art Foundation.

Exhibitions: Bern, 1951, no. 100, as *La Mise en tombeau*; Albi, 1963, no. 30, as *L'Enterrement dans mon quartier*; Paris, 1970, no. 58; San Bernardino, 1980, no. 15, p. 30, ill.

Technical Notes: The primary support is a thick machine-made paper with inclusions, possibly wood pulp, which are visible on the edges. The paper is very smooth and without texture. An edge strip on the upper left has detached from the painting and can be lifted to reveal the fact that the strip is painted underneath with matching medium from the primary painting. This indicates that the painting may have extended beyond the present edge and was effectively cropped by the present mount method. The painting is tempera on paper, which was later varnished. A clear strip of unvarnished, original medium can be observed along all four edges of the work, where the varnish ends. This unvarnished section reveals the matte, textured nature of the tempera and the lighter palette employed by the painter. The varnish has saturated the work overall, darkening the medium and creating a high-gloss sheen not originally intended. The work is in a poor state of preservation. While the artist may have mounted the painting to canvas, a subsequent owner had it varnished, which is inappropriate for tempera. There is also a great deal of pigment loss and improper retouching, especially in the figures' black cloaks. The paper support was mounted to canvas with an unknown adhesive, which has caused staining and darkening overall. The paper support is damaged and torn at the corners and back areas where it wraps around the strainer. In the primary design area, the work has numerous creases and fissures, probably due to the mount process, as paper, adhesives, and canvas expand at separate rates. (SSB)

Maurice Denis was a major painter and the leading theorist among the artists of the Nabis. (The word is Hebrew for "prophets.") This group, founded in late 1888 by a handful of dissident art students from the Académie Julian in Paris, was dedicated to the creation of an artificial and symbolic art that depicted the myths and mysteries that underlay various world religions. The effort paralleled the studies of comparative religion then being undertaken by such anthropologists as James G. Frazer, Arnold van Gennep, and Emile Durkheim, but without their scholarly rigor. Indeed, in place of intellectual discipline, the artists substituted esoteric enthusiasm, mystification, and a good measure of humor. By behaving as initiates in their own rites of passage and as adepts in their own mystical precincts (they ironically dubbed the apartment of the painter Paul Ranson at 25, boulevard du Montparnasse "the Temple"), the Nabis created both a sanctuary from a quotidian world they mocked and the basis for an avant-garde movement dedicated to the synthesis of dream, vision, spirit, and physical nature.

The formal inspiration for the Nabis was found in the Synthetist art and aesthetics of Paul Gauguin. The Nabi Paul Sérusier had worked with Gauguin at Pont-Aven in early 1888 and taken to heart the older artist's instruction that only the most vivid colors on his palette could effectively transmit his feelings before nature and the motif. Sérusier then painted a small and highly abstract painting of the Bois d'Amour in Pont-Aven and carried it, in late 1888, to Paris, where it was called *The Talisman* as a token of its perfect exemplification of Synthetist principles and its exalted status among the newly formed Nabis. A little over a year later, Denis set down in words his understanding of the aesthetic implications of Synthetist and Nabi art. He began his famous definition of "Neo-Traditionism" by stating: "a picture—before being a war-horse, a female nude or some little anecdote—is essentially a flat surface covered with colors arranged in a certain order."[1] What Denis meant by this was that all great works of art, including antique, primitive, and Christian art, share a common aesthetic integrity and spiritual worth. Moreover, art must take its lessons from the work of the old masters as well as the moderns, and from folk artists as well as Salon favorites if it is to achieve this spiritual depth and universality. The generality of the theory of Neo-Traditionism—and Denis would refine it for decades—encouraged an art among the Nabis that was quite varied; it ranged from small, bourgeois interiors depicted by Édouard Vuillard to large Catholic mysteries painted by Denis. In all cases, however, Nabi art emphasized pictorial simplification, flatness, and homogeneity of tone.

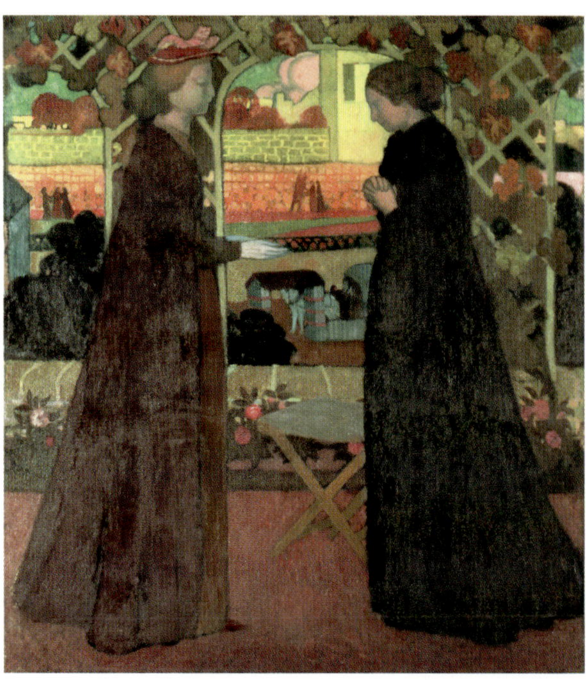

Fig. 135a Maurice Denis, *The Visitation*, 1894, oil on canvas, $40^{1}/_{2} \times 36^{5}/_{8}$ in. (103 × 93 cm), The State Hermitage Museum, St. Petersburg

From his early youth, Denis was a pious Catholic. And throughout his artistic career, he believed, as he wrote in his journal in 1886, that painting was essentially a religious art.[2] Such a position is unusual in the development of modern art, but certainly not unprecedented. The German Nazarenes at the beginning of the nineteenth century and some of the English Pre-Raphaelites at midcentury sought to renew and modernize Christianity by means of an art that rejected academic convention. Eugène Delacroix painted many religious paintings, one of which, *Jacob Wrestling with the Angel* (1861) in the Church of St.-Sulpice in Paris, was a veritable pilgrimage site for such modern artists as Gauguin, Vincent van Gogh, and Georges Seurat interested in the division of color and the visual impact of the contrast of complements. Denis painted his own *Jacob Wrestling with the Angel* (c. 1893, private collection) based on Delacroix's mural and Gauguin's famous painting of the same subject (*Vision after the Sermon*, National Gallery of Scotland, Edinburgh). Pierre Puvis de Chavannes was also renowned for religious works and Christian allegories, and his embrace of decorative works—whose pale tonalities highlighted the flatness of the pictorial surface and deemphasized volume and mass—were especially admired by the Nabis and Symbolists. Denis's three small panels for a girl's room, *September* (1891, Musée des Arts Décoratifs, Paris), *April* (1892, Kröller-Müller Museum, Otterlo), and *July* (1892, Gustave Rau Foundation, Zurich), all find their immediate precedent in works by Puvis.

Though Denis did not undertake any formal study of theology, he did attend in the early 1890s—in the company of Sérusier and other Nabis—several lectures on scholastic philosophy by Dominicans of the Paris Faubourg St.-Honoré. He also read widely in the field of history of religion and theology, even contributing to the conservative and hierarchical Thomist revival of the early twentieth century. Denis's art grew more religious and conservative as he matured. It contained fewer typical Symbolist themes, such as peasants, femme fatales, figures in contemplation of nature, and music, and a greater number of Catholic and Trinitarian subjects, such as *Visitation* (fig. 135a), *The Legend of Saint Hubert* (1897, private collection, Paris), and *The Virgin's Kiss* (1902, Folkwangmuseum, Essen). Denis embraced the idea that secularized religious paintings, visible outside the precincts of the church, were a valuable stimulus to piety and spiritual contemplation. Such religious works, including *The Entombment*, effected, he believed, a reconciliation of sacred and secular spaces and, like the Incarnation itself, the realms of materiality and the spirit. The Norton Simon picture is thus both a conventional modern burial and an Entombment of Christ, a Symbolist dream and an illustration of a Christian theme.

The elements of Denis's composition are organized in shallow relief, as if carved into the sides of a sarcophagus. A group of eleven figures in black conveys to the grave the body of a white-shrouded figure with a halo. The figures are mostly seen as silhouettes, lacking depth or substance. It is late winter or spring, perhaps Eastertime, since the forest of tall trees is bare and forsythias at right are in bloom. A few other flowers or discarded nosegays lie at the feet of the burial party.

1 Maurice Denis, "Définition du néo-traditionnisme," in *Théories (1890–1910): Du symbolisme et de Gauguin vers un nouvel ordre classique*, ed. L. Rouart and J. Watelin, Paris, 1912, p. 1.

2 Terrasse, 1970, p. 14.

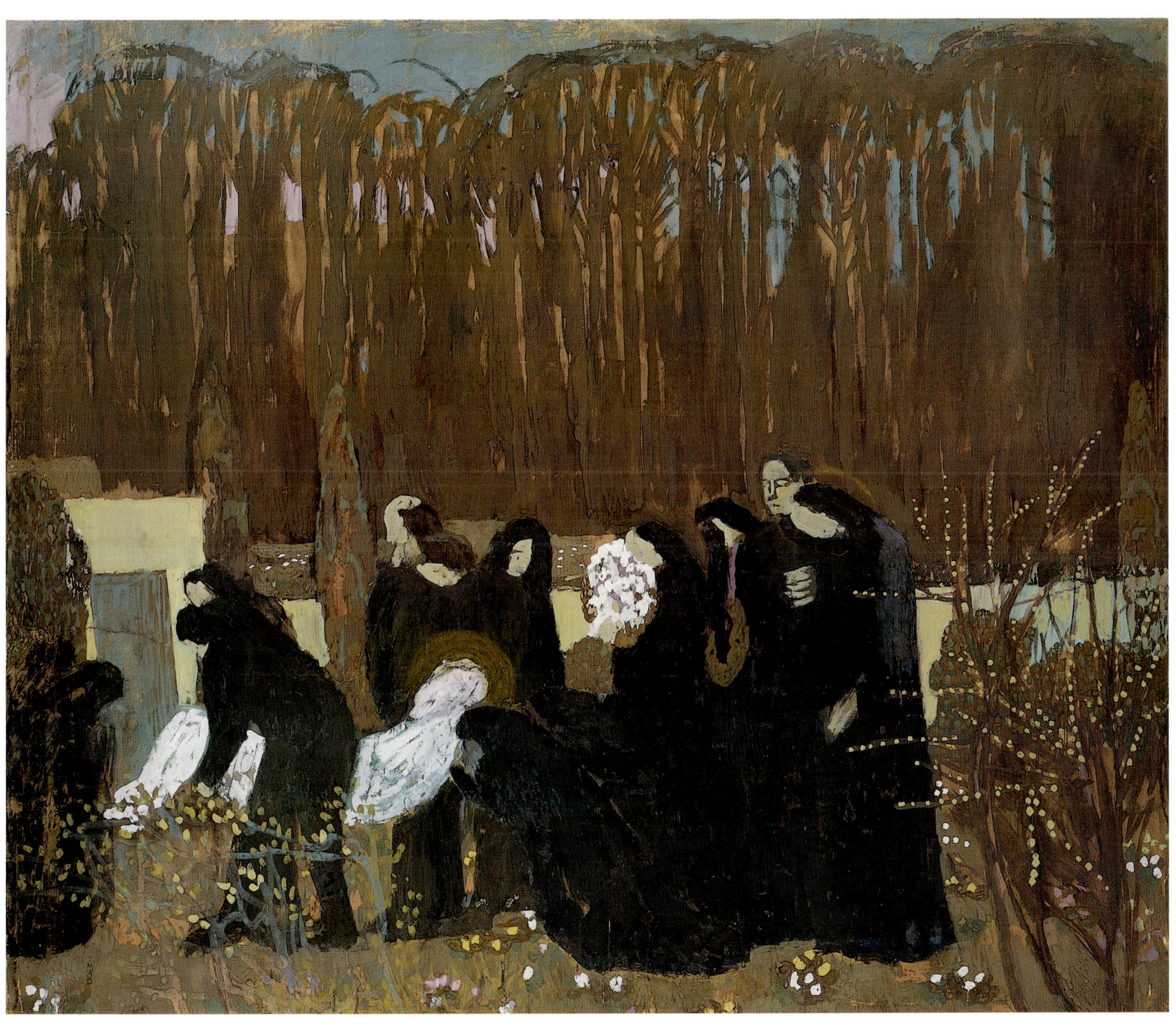

135

136

Piet Mondrian
Dutch, 1872–1944

View near the Weesperzijde, Tower of Blooker Chocolate Factory in the Distance

1899

Pastel on paper, 18 × 25¾ in. (45.5 × 65.5 cm)
Signed and dated lower left: "Piet Mondriaan '99"
F.1978.37

Provenance: (sale, Amsterdam, Paul Brandt, 15 April 1970, lot 303, ill., as *View of a Village on the Dutch Coast*); [E. J. van Wisselingh & Co., Amsterdam, stock no. T4125*/T9125, as *Landschap*, sold 23 December 1974 to]; Norton Simon, gift 1978 to; The Norton Simon Foundation.

Reference: Welsh and Joosten, 1998, vol. 1, A206, ill.

Technical Notes: *Landscape* is drawn on a cream-colored sheet of wove paper, which was removed from a rigid backing board in a 1975 treatment. There is graphite ruling around the edge of the sheet, indicating a trim line, especially noticeable along the bottom. The sheet has an embossed collector's stamp at the lower right with a man in profile and "S.V.H. Israels." The support remains stable and planar, despite a great deal of treatment. The upper left corner is missing, and there is a loss 9 inches from the upper left corner, measuring approximately ⅛ inch. The left, right, and bottom edges are trimmed square, but the upper edge is trimmed irregularly. The upper right corner is buckling due to the hinge or excessive adhesive. There are in the lower left corner a tack hole and a round indentation. The pastel is applied lightly, which allows the cream color of the sheet to provide highlights and a bright, warm tone in the areas without pastel. The medium is in good condition overall; however, there is water damage or a tide line in the center left of the pastel, 10½ inches from the left and 5 inches from the top. There are horizontal, squared-off losses or erasures of pastel in the lower half of the sky area, beginning 6 inches from the left and extending across the sheet. These pastel erasures are a part of the design motif, introducing a geometric element. The primary support is float-hinged to acid-free mat board across the top with three Japanese paper hinges. The work is matted in a stepped-window mat, to allow proper space between the face of the pastel and the glazing. (SSB)

Piet Mondrian was twenty-seven years old in 1899 when he made this intensely matter-of-fact pastel drawing. Its roots in Dutch art are deep—from the landscape drawings and etchings of Rembrandt to the charcoal landscapes produced by Vincent van Gogh in the early 1880s (cat. 106). Yet, while Rembrandt relished the rugged aspects of rural poverty and van Gogh stressed the harsh realities of Dutch rural life, Mondrian presents us with a relentlessly middle-class world with neatly drawn dwellings of wood and stucco arranged around a large, open field at the center of the composition. In the left foreground is the steep gable of a house with a small curtained window, a slender, smoking chimney, and a red-shingled roof. The diagonal line of a fence leads from the house to the vacant field, drawing attention to a lone grazing goat. To the left of the fence is the polder dike, studded with slanting posts, on which runs an avenue that slices diagonally from the foreground house to the middle of the drawing. There, the thoroughfare nearly disappears amid the confusion of small, suburban houses and businesses, but reappears to culminate at the T-shaped telegraph pole on the horizon. Four small, slender figures stand or amble along the street. To the right of the scene are some apple trees and beyond them a white-stuccoed house and an adjacent charcoal gray house with attached workshop.

Thanks to the patient work of Tom Brockmeier of the Amsterdam Municipal Archives, we now know that Mondrian represented the scene from the raised embankment of the Amsterdam–Utrecht railway, and that the drawing represents the Blooker Chocolate Factory built in 1883 along the Weesper Trekvaart canal.[1] The factory's tall smokestack, which must have dispersed everywhere the sweet, acrid smell of cacao, was omitted from the drawing. Brockmeier concluded that Mondrian left out the prominent smokestack for pictorial reasons, though the excision may with equal justice be called ideological: the smokestack would have given the subject a decidedly industrial character and thereby undermined its balanced rural-urban quality.

The pastel is large enough that we know it was not made in the out of doors but from a smaller study made on the spot. As such, it is a very carefully composed, almost abstract composition, built up from horizontal, vertical, and diagonal lines and a few basic colors: two greens, white, orange, blue, and red. It thus marks an early stage in Mondrian's quest to remove strong associative meanings from works of art and to achieve compositional clarity. Apparently, Mr. Simon was fond of saying that all of the future qualities of Mondrian could be found already in this pastel, and there is some

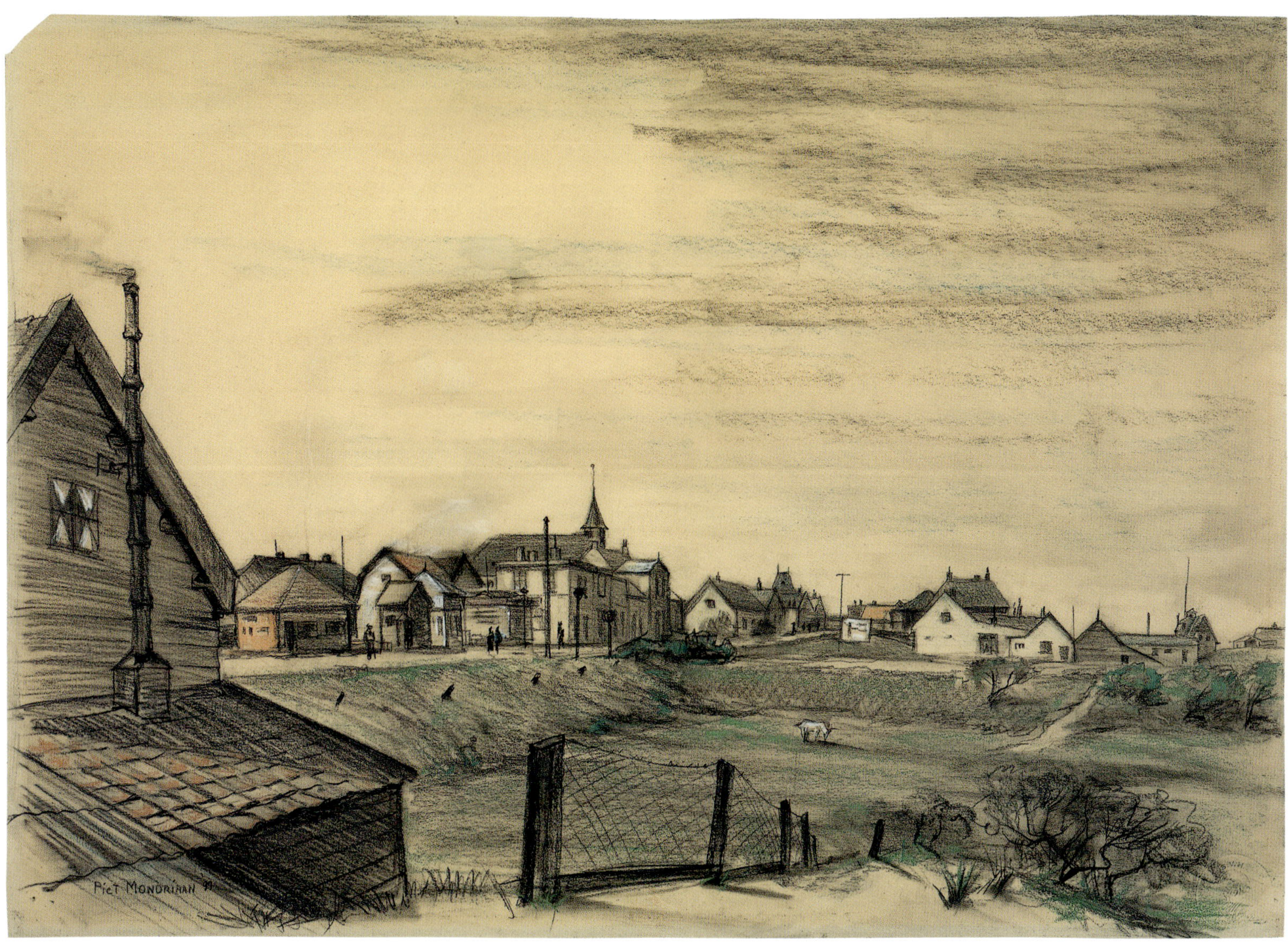

136

justification for his view. The black, linear, and geometric quality of the architectural composition; the disciplined lines of the clouds; the carefully filled-in areas of red, blue, green, and white; the use of a rectangular gum eraser to remove sections of black chalk in the sky and around the buildings, these are all features in an otherwise unremarkable pastel that hint at what was to come in the Dutch artist's career.

1 Welsh and Joosten, 1998, vol. 1, pp. 238–239.

137

Pablo Ruiz y Picasso
Spanish, 1881–1973

Horse and Coach
c. 1900

Ink on paper, $4\frac{1}{4} \times 6\frac{3}{4}$ in. (10.8 × 17.1 cm)
Signed lower right in pencil: "Picasso"
P.1976.2

Provenance: Mr. and Mrs. Harold P. Ullman, Los Angeles, gift 5 April 1976 to; Norton Simon Museum.

Technical Notes: The work is drawn on a sheet of very thin laid paper, which is slightly brittle. The paper is discolored to a light brown owing to exposure to light. Under magnification, the paper support is fibrous and shiny and may have inclusions of wood pulp. The ragged edge across the top, with small losses, indicates that it was torn out of a sketchbook and is most likely machine-made. The sketch is quickly drawn with ink, and the ink bleeds and sinks into the pulpy sheet. The medium is stable, with ink areas that are smudged and smeared from contact with a facing sheet in a notebook. In generally good condition, the paper is light struck and darkened throughout the sheet, with a lighter area around the perimeter where the mat shielded the drawing from light. There is surface soil at the bottom center edge and along the bottom left edge. The sketch is hinged to 2-ply board with two tiny hinges ($\frac{3}{8}$ inch) at the upper corners. The 2-ply backboard is taped to a decorative composite window mat. (SSB)

This rapidly executed little ink sketch of a horse, coach, and driver is lively and economical. It consists of about thirty-five distinct curved or straight lines, many of which do double duty: the sinuous line of the horse's reins also articulates its back; the short loop of the animal's harness establishes its shoulder; the curve of the horse's tail is the lower front end of the coach; the driver's torso is also the bench on which he sits. The drawing technique—schematic, abbreviated, and expressive—is that of an illustrator or caricaturist and is highly facile. It may have been partly inspired by the work of the mid-nineteenth-century French artist Constantin Guys or Henri de Toulouse-Lautrec. The latter's many sketches and lithographs of horses and riders from the 1880s and 1890s, including *Coach with Tandem Horses*,[1] exhibit a speed and virtuosity that are comparable to the qualities visible in *Horse and Coach*.

Pablo Picasso first came to know the works of Toulouse-Lautrec while still in Barcelona in the circle of the bohemian artists, writers, and anarchists who frequented the café Els Quatre Gats. It is possible that *Horse and Coach* was made at about this time, 1898–1899, but it was more likely made during the young artist's first trip to Paris in the late autumn and winter of 1900. Indeed, the coachman appears to wear a wrap over his shoulders, indicating cold weather. Moreover, the sheet on which the sketch was made must have been pulled from a small *carnet*, or sketchbook, the sort used by an artist who travels to a new place and wants to record his impressions quickly. The horse is trotting, the two spindly legs farthest from the picture plane are raised, the driver's whip is caught in midair, and the double loop of the forward right wheel of the coach looks as if it were moving. Picasso captured this motion in a sketch that took him no longer than the time taken by the coach to pass his line of sight.

Picasso's visit to Paris gave him the opportunity to gain firsthand knowledge of the previous generation of modernists who had challenged the authority of École instruction and the monopoly of the Salon-jury exhibition system. In addition to Toulouse-Lautrec, he admired the Nabi artists Édouard Vuillard, Pierre Bonnard, and Maurice Denis, as well as Paul Gauguin and Vincent van Gogh. *Horse and Coach* does not reveal these new infatuations, but it does expose something of the virtuosity required to assimilate the new art quickly. Indeed, the little drawing resembles no other by Picasso. Its authenticity, however, was attested by the artist himself in 1966, according to a letter in the museum files written by the artist's friend and longtime dealer Daniel-Henry Kahnweiler. The signature at lower right must have been added later. It is hard to imagine that any artist—even one as self-absorbed as Picasso—would have signed so small and modest a sketch until he sold it.

1 Dortu, 1971, vol. 6, no. D.4.372.

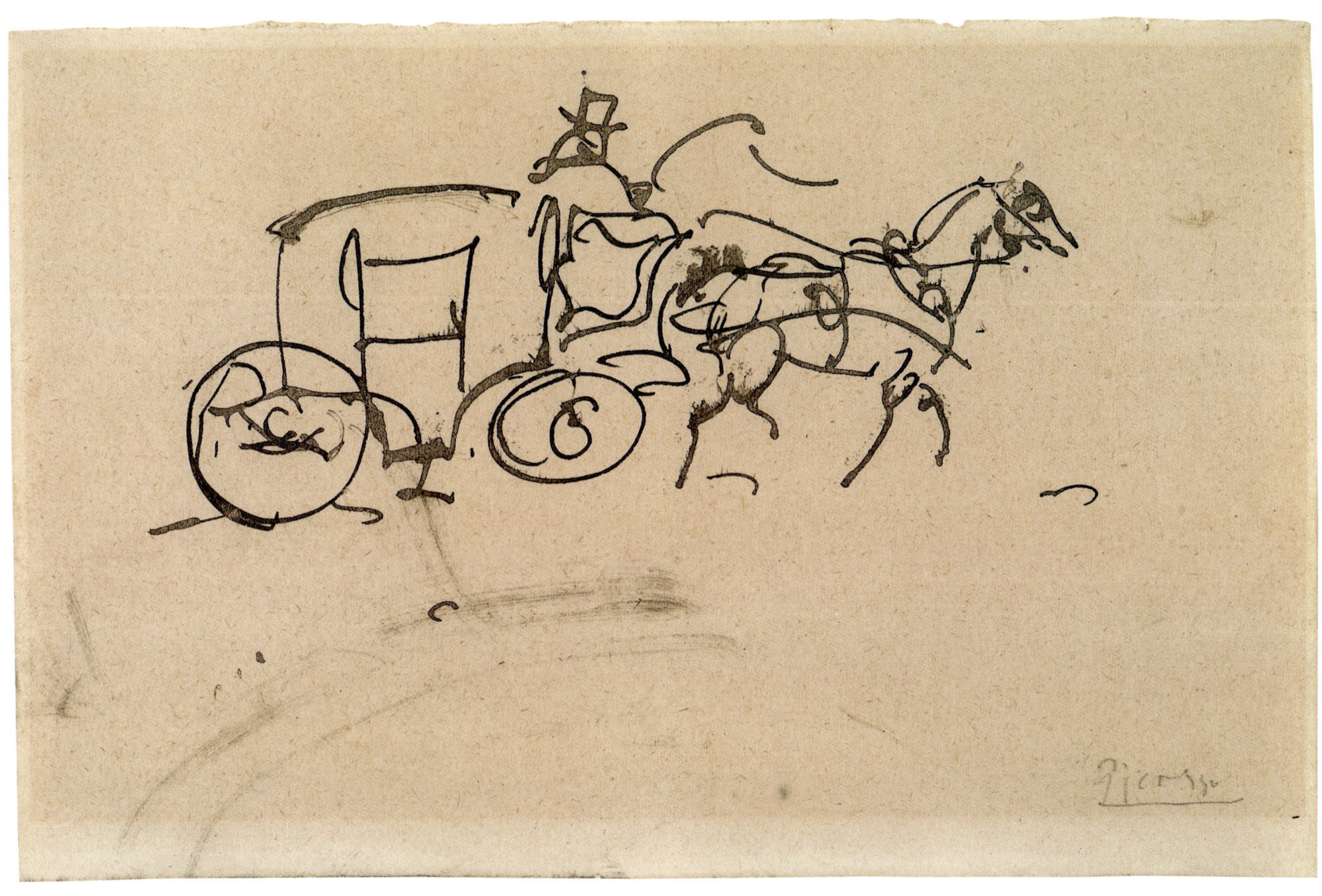

137

138

Pablo Ruiz y Picasso
Spanish, 1881–1973

The Moulin Rouge
1901

China ink on paper, $12\frac{3}{4} \times 19\frac{1}{2}$ in. (32.5 × 49.5 cm)
Signed in pencil lower right: Picasso
M.1979.34

Provenance: [Galerie Jacques Dubourg, Paris, by 1954]; [Galerie Daniel Malingue, Paris, sold 11 October 1979 to]; Norton Simon Art Foundation.

Exhibition: Paris, 1954b, no. 166.

References: Zervos, 1932–1978, vol. 21, no. 187; D. Chevalier, 1991, p. 16, ill.

Technical Notes: The work is drawn on a sheet of medium-weight, smooth laid paper with a deckled edge on the bottom. The sheet is planar and supple and is float-hinged at the top with two hinges to museum board. *The Moulin Rouge* is drawn in ink, with a brush. The drawing is made of a mixture of dark, fully inked strokes and expressive, thinly applied areas. The drawing is in very good condition. There is minor surface soil and a darkened $\frac{3}{4}$-inch band along the left edge of the sheet, caused by mat burn or exposure to light. In the upper left corner there is a small tear 1 inch from the left edge, and there is a pronounced crease at the lower left corner. (SSB)

This free and expressive ink and brush drawing depicts three people in a cabaret. At right, a young woman in a high-collared dress and exuberant feathered hat sits alone. She leans forward, smiles, rests her left elbow on a banister or wide ledge, and subtly beckons with her tapering left hand. A pair of cups and saucers, or possibly parfait glasses, lie on the ledge in front of her; the one at left may belong to her. At left, two large, half-length figures nearly fill their side of the drawing. They are separated from the woman at right by a vertical line that divides the paper almost in half. This line passes through the crossed hands behind the standing, bearded gentleman and becomes faint, branches into two, and fades away just before the deckled bottom edge of the paper. The seated woman in profile at left is the most conspicuous figure in the drawing. She wears a colossal, oblong hat that blocks our view of the nose and jaw of her companion and a ruffled collar or boa. Her hair cascades down her improbably long neck in thick, black, inky ringlets, and she holds a large glass or beer mug. Her face is spare, chiseled, and unyielding. The single visible eye is set high on the face, the nose is a narrow, vertical ledge, the lips are closed tightly together, and the chin is angular. The broad and busy cross-hatching at the bottom right of the figure may represent either a woven back to her chair or the checked trousers of the standing gentleman. In either case it anchors the entire composition.

The drawing suggests a modern narrative. The single woman at right is most likely a prostitute. She sits in the cheap seats of a cabaret, separated from the stage by a partition. Her exuberant hat, saucy smile, and soliciting gesture indicate that she is present both to enjoy the show and to find customers. The man and woman at the left are a couple. They may be married, or she may be a kept woman. (The casual thrust of her right elbow is slightly indecent.) Thus, the three figures together constitute a kind of satirical examination of relations between the sexes in places of urban amusement. The prostitute mocks the married or kept woman, while the latter tries hard not to see the former. The man in the picture is a mere spectator to the entire business.

Picasso's drawing is significant for several reasons. First, it represents a subject that was enormously important during the fin de siècle. The relations of the sexes, prostitution, femmes fatales, and devouring women were the subject of works by Edgar Degas, Jean-Louis Forain, Félix Vallotton, Paul Gauguin, Edvard Munch, and many others. (The drawing's present title, *The Moulin Rouge*, was bestowed on it in the 1960s. There is no reason to believe Picasso was intending to depict this large, famous music hall, and not one of the smaller *cafés chantants* such as Café des Ambassadeurs, Alcazar, Eden Concert, Eldorado, or any one of a number of others.) The theme of the relation or battle of the sexes would a little later be the starting point for Picasso's terrifying painting—and the starting point for Cubism—*Desmoiselles d'Avignon* (The Museum of Modern Art, New York). The seated woman at left in Picasso's drawing possesses an elongated, Egyptian eye, such as would be seen in *Desmoiselles* and other Cubist works that followed. In addition, her mouth and nostrils have begun their migration from the middle to the side of the face, a move that would be completed in later Cubist works.

page 514 Henri-Marie-Raymond de Toulouse-Lautrec, *Red-Headed Woman in the Garden of M. Foret* (detail of cat. no. 123)

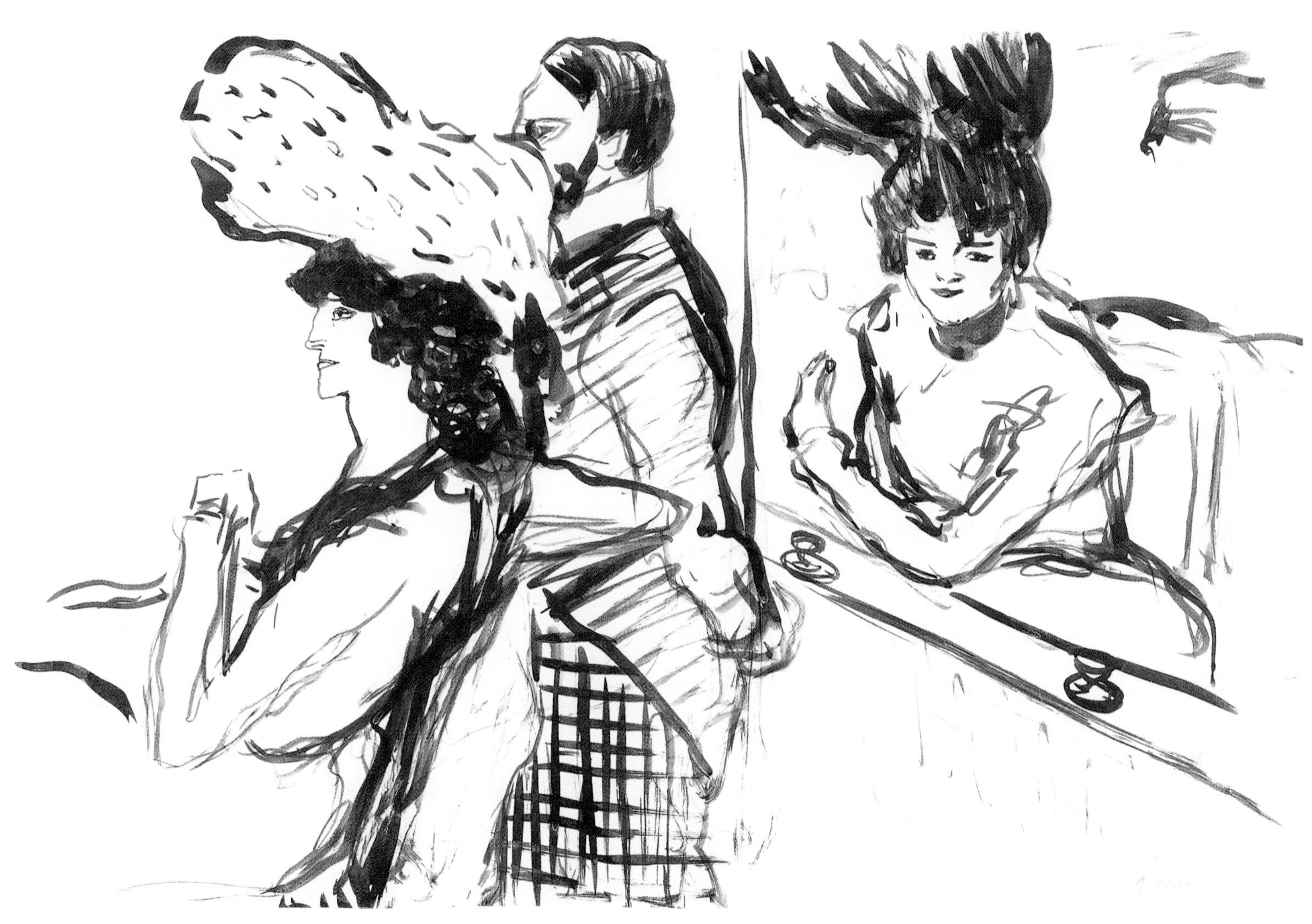

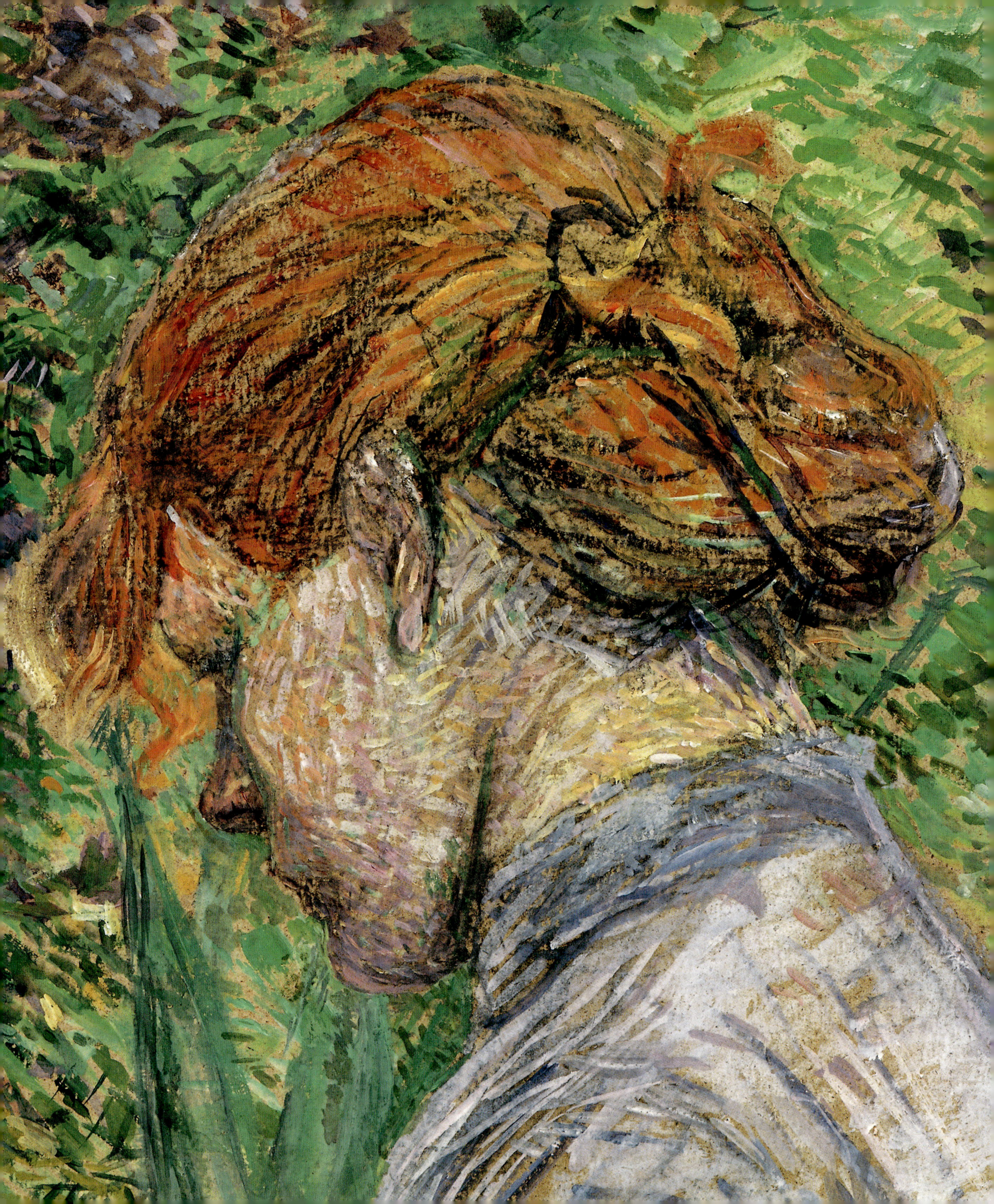

Artists' Letters

L.1

Sir Lawrence Alma-Tadema
Dutch, 1836–1912

Letter to William Lemaire & Co., Paris
12 June 1877

Ink on paper, $6\frac{1}{8} \times 3$ 15/16 in. (15.5×10 cm)
(A second sheet with graphite sketches, 4 3/4 × 3 7/16 in.
[12×8.7 cm] recto: rear view of a man with a hat, signed lower right: "Alma Thadema"; verso: architectural sketch)
M.1989.1.01a.L

Provenance: [William H. Schab Gallery, New York, sold February 1989 to]; Norton Simon Art Foundation.

Text:

12 Juin 1877
TOWNSHEND HOUSE,
NORTH GATE,
REGENTS PARK. N.W.

Messieurs
Je viens de recevoir votre envoi et je m'empresse de vous envoyer un chèque pour le montant de la facture que j'espère vous me retournerez acquitée.
Vous remerciant de votre exactitude, je vous prie d'agréer mes civilités empressées,
L. Alma-Tadema

Wm. Lemaire & Co.
33 Boulevard des Italiens, Paris

Translation:

12 June 1877
TOWNSHEND HOUSE,
NORTH GATE,
REGENTS PARK. N.W.

Dear Sirs
I have just received your letter and I am sending you right away a check to pay off the bill; I hope you will return it to me marked "paid."
I thank you for your punctuality, accept my good wishes.
L. Alma-Tadema

Wm. Lemaire & Co.
33 Boulevard des Italiens, Paris

L.2

Léon Bonnat
French, 1833–1922

Letter to an artist

Ink on paper, $6\frac{1}{8} \times 8$ in. (15.6×20.3 cm)
M.1989.1.02.L

Provenance: [William H. Schab Gallery, New York, sold February 1989 to]; Norton Simon Art Foundation.

Text:

Cher ami,
Vous me gâtez trop en m'envoyant ces merveilles que vous publiez de temps en temps. C'est de l'art pur et c'est parfait à tous égards.
Merci mille fois et tout à vous,
L. Bonnat

Translation:

Dear friend,
You spoil me too much in sending me these marvelous papers that you publish from time to time. This is pure art and perfect in all aspects.
A thousand thanks, yours truly,
L. Bonnat

L.3

Amédée-Charles-Henry de Noé, called Cham
French, 1818–1879

Invitation to an event for Pierre Véron
Ink on paper, $6\frac{5}{8} \times 8\frac{3}{8}$ in. (16.8×21.3 cm)
M.1989.1.04.L

Provenance: [William H. Schab Gallery, New York, sold February 1989 to]; Norton Simon Art Foundation.

Text:

Homme de tant d'Esprit!

Lundi 25 mars à 7 h nous fêtons la voix de Pierre Véron. Faites nous l'extrême plaisir d'être des notres. Oh oui ! Je vous en supplie. J'attends une bonne réponse.
Bien affectueusement,
Cham
Ce 19 mars

Translation:

Man of such Spirit!

On Monday, 25 March at 7 o'clock we will celebrate the voice of Pierre Véron. Give us the extreme pleasure of joining us. Oh yes! I beg you. I am waiting for a positive answer.
Most affectionately,
Cham
This 19 March

L.4

Jean-Baptiste-Camille Corot
French, 1796–1875

Letter to E. Brandois
26 April 1866

Ink on paper, sheet: $8\frac{3}{16} \times 10\frac{1}{2}$ in. (20.8×26.7 cm); envelope: $2\frac{7}{8} \times 4\frac{3}{8}$ in. (7.3×11.1 cm)
M.1989.1.5

Provenance: [William H. Schab Gallery, New York, sold February 1989 to]; Norton Simon Art Foundation.

Text:

Beauvais le 26 avril

Mon cher ami

J'avais l'intention d'aller vous voir avant de partir. Le temps m'a manqué. Je voulais savoir de vos nouvelles & vous prévenir que lorsque vous serez assez fort pour monter à l'atelier d'aller rue Paradis. Les tableaux Demidoff sont là maintenant.

En attendant le plaisir de vous serrer la main prochainement
Tout à vous
C. Corot

Souvenir pour votre frère heureux

Translation:

Beauvais, 26 April 1866

My dear friend,

I planned to go and visit you before I left. I did not have time. I wanted to know of your news and to know when you will be strong enough to go up to the studio on rue du Paradis. The Demidoff paintings are there now.

Awaiting the pleasure of shaking hands with you soon
Yours always,
C. Corot

Best wishes to your nice brother

L.5

Gustave Courbet
French, 1819–1877

Letter to M. Ilmoëton[?]
17 January 1870

Ink on paper, $8\frac{1}{4} \times 5\frac{3}{8}$ in. (21×13.7 cm)
M.1989.1.06

Provenance: [William H. Schab Gallery, New York, sold February 1989 to]; Norton Simon Art Foundation.

Reference: Chu, 1992, pp. 361–362, no. 70-1.

Text:

Ornans 17 janvier 1870

Mon cher Ilmoëton[?]

J'arrive d'un grand voyage en Allemagne, a mon arrivée j'ai eu le désespoir de perdre mon plus ancien ami Max Buchon le poète, et mon parent aussi—Je suis dans un tel état de marasme que je ne vous ai pas répondu. Cependant votre lettre est très aimable, et très polie.

Je vous donne toute permission comme vous le pensez bien, et quand au payement c'est à votre volonté. Il y a une chose qui m'inquiète, j'avais vendu le droit de reproduction photographique à Mr. Ledot ainé sous les Arcades Rivoli pour trois ans, c'était pendant l'exposition de ce tableau mais je crois qu'il y a plus de trois ans. Regardez dans un livret. Vous trouverez des photographies de deux grandeurs chez Michelez rue Jacob 50. Si ça ne vous suffit pas allez dans mon atelier et servez-vous de cette lettre vis à vis de mon concierge pour y entrer et travailler.

Tout à vous, cher ami, bien des choses à tous les amis.
G. Courbet

A bientôt la partie de billard. Je ne suis plus guère fort.

Translation:

Ornans, 17 January 1890

Dear Ilmoëton[?]

I just came back from a long trip to Germany. On my return I found myself in despair as I lost my oldest friend, Max Buchon, the poet, and my relative as well—I am in a state of depression which is why I did not answer you. However, your letter was very kind and polite.

Of course, I give you my permission, and regarding payment it's up to you.

There is one thing that worries me: I sold the reproduction rights for three years to the elder Mr. Ledot, of the Rivoli Arcades. It was during the exhibition of this painting, but I think, it has now been more than 3 years. Check the catalogue. You will find photos in two different sizes at Michelez's, 50 rue Jacob. If that is not sufficient, go to my studio and show this letter to my concierge to enter and work.

Yours ever, dear friend, relay my best to all our friends.
G. Courbet

See you soon for a billiard game. I am no longer very good.

L.6

George Cruikshank
English, 1792–1878

Letter to the editor of the London *Times*

Ink on paper, two sheets; page one: $8\frac{3}{4} \times 7\frac{1}{16}$ in. (22.2 × 17.9 cm); page two: $8\frac{7}{8} \times 7\frac{1}{16}$ in. (22.5 × 17.9 cm)
M.89.1.7

Provenance: [William H. Schab Gallery, New York, sold February 1989 to]; Norton Simon Art Foundation.

Text:

The Electric Telegraph
To the Editor of "The Times"

Sir:

Having the honor of being a friend of Mr. [Sir Charles] Wheatstone also feeling much gratified ~~by J. D.~~ with the letter of "J. D." & also your just and complimentary remarks in reference to his part in the discovery & introduction of the electric telegraph. I beg to be allowed to state that the discovery arose from the circumstance of Mr. Wheatstone having when first appointed lecturer at the "Kings College" 7 miles of wire in the lower part of that building—which abuts upon the river Thames—for the purpose of measuring the speed of lightning—or the electric current—and upon one occasion when explaining his experiments to me he said—"I intend one day if possible to lay some of this wire across the bed of the Thames & carrying it up to the top of the Tower on the other side—& so make signals"—This was I believe the first idea—or suggestion of a "submarine telegraph"—

We are also indebted to Mr. Wheatstone for his electric work for ~~about this same time when~~ long before this telegraph came before the public he also [was] explaining the machinery to me he said as it was possible that one party might be asleep at one end of the wire—he had so arranged the working that the first touch should ring a bell at the other end—even if thousands of miles apart! This it will be admitted is an important part of the discovery and therefore I am sure everyone will also feel that the man who has done such wonders for the public advantage world at large deserves the honor and rewards which "J.D." and yourself have suggested should be confirmed upon the old and highly esteemed friend of yr. ob. Ser.
George Cruikshank

L.7

Honoré Daumier
French, 1808–1879

30 January 1870

Ink on paper, $8\frac{3}{16} \times 5\frac{1}{4}$ in. (20.8 × 13.3 cm)
M 1989.1.08

Provenance: [William H. Schab Gallery, New York, sold February 1989 to]; Norton Simon Art Foundation.

Text:

30 janvier 70

Monsieur

Me voici rentré a Paris dont j'ai été absent tout l'été.

Je suis maintenant Monsieur tout a votre disposition. Quand j'aurai l'honneur de vous voir je vous dirai la cause de l'impardonnable retard de ma réponse a votre lettre du mois de juin.

En attendant, excusez-moi, Monsieur, et agréer l'expression de mes sentiments distingués.
H. Daumier

J'ai a votre disposition un portrait lithographié ou une photographie.

Translation:

30 January [18]70

Sir,

I have now returned to Paris, from whence I was away all summer.

I am now, Sir, entirely at your disposal. When I have the honor to see you I'll tell you the reason of my unforgivable delay in replying to your letter of June.

In the meantime, please accept my apology and my most heartfelt sentiments,
H. Daumier

I have at your disposal a lithographic portrait or a photograph.

L.8

Edgar Degas
French, 1834–1917

Letter to Durand-Ruel
Postmarked 30 March 1901

Ink on blue paper, $5\frac{1}{4} \times 4\frac{3}{8}$ in. (13.3 × 11.1 cm)
M.1973.8.1

Provenance: (Letter accompanied the pastel entitled *Répétition de Ballet*, purchased from Degas by Mrs. H. O. Havemeyer,* New York, which then went to); Adaline Havemeyer Frelinghuysen, New York; Georges J. Frelinghuysen (sale, Parke-Bernet, 14 April 1965, to); Norton Simon.

Text:

Cher Monsieur
Ayez la bonté de m'apporter demain dimanche dans l'après-midi
500 F
Remerciements
Degas

Translation:

Dear Sir,
Please be kind enough to bring me F 500 tomorrow (Sunday) in the afternoon.
With thanks,
Degas

*A note from Mrs. Havemeyer accompanies the letter: "Petit bleu sent by Degas to Durand Ruel. To reproduce in Chap. on Degas of my Memoirs. It belongs to Adaline Frelinghuysen. Be careful of it and return. L. W. Havemeyer, Aug. 1917"

L.9

Édouard Detaille
French, 1848–1912

Letter to Camille Paris
17 January 1895

Ink on paper, $6\frac{1}{8} \times 4\frac{3}{16}$ in. (15.6 × 10.6 cm)
M.1989.1.09a

Provenance: [William H. Schab Gallery, New York, sold February 1989 to]; Norton Simon Art Foundation.

Text:

Merci, mon cher Paris, pour votre sympathique témoignage et recevez l'expression de mes cordiaux sentiments,
Edouard Detaille

17 janvier 95 Monte Carlo

Translation:

Thank you, my dear Paris, for your expression of sympathy, and accept my warmest wishes.
Edouard Detaille

17 January 95 Monte Carlo

L.10

Édouard Detaille
French, 1848–1912

Letter to M. Hoskier

Ink on paper, $6\frac{1}{4} \times 9\frac{1}{16}$ in. (15.9 × 23 cm)
M.1989.1.09b

Provenance: [William H. Schab Gallery, New York, sold February 1989 to]; Norton Simon Art Foundation.

Text:

Le Havre

Mon Cher Monsieur Hoskier
Pardonnez-moi de ne pouvoir me joindre à tous vos amis pour vous apporter mes félicitations à l'occasion du mariage de Mademoiselle Hoskier, mais je suis en ce moment au Havre, appelé par un triste devoir de famille: je viens de perdre un de mes frères ainés qui habite cette ville depuis de longues années. Recevez mes bien amicales félicitations que je vous demande de faire agréer à tous les vôtres, et croyez à ma sincère affection.
Édouard Detaille

Translation:

Le Havre

My Dear Mr. Hoskier,
Please forgive me for not being able to join your friends to congratulate you on the wedding of Mademoiselle Hoskier, but I am in Le Havre at the moment because of a family obligation: I just lost one of my older brothers who lived in this town for many years. Accept my friendliest congratulations which I ask you to pass on to your family and be assured of my sincere affection.
Édouard Detaille

L.11

Édouard Detaille
French, 1848–1912

Letter to a gentleman
24 April 1911

Ink on paper, $6\frac{1}{4} \times 9\frac{1}{16}$ in. (15.9 × 23 cm)
M.1989.1.09c

Provenance: [William H. Schab Gallery, New York, sold February 1989 to]; Norton Simon Art Foundation.

Text:

Cher Monsieur

Je vous remercie bien vivement de l'envoi de votre ouvrage sur les affiches de recrutement. C'est tout a fait interessant et amusant et je vous exprime tous mes compliments pour ce travail qui vous fait grand honneur et qui fait aussi grand honneur à la sabretache.*

Je ne me doutais pas que j'avais pris part, sans le vouloir, à la confection d'une affiche. J'ai retrouvé sur celle qui a trait aux engagements pour la cavalerie, toute une série de cavaliers exactement copiés sur les dessins et aquarelles mais l'auteur ne s'est pas donné grand mal pour inventer : c'est bien plus commode—il a eu la pudeur de ne pas signer . . .

Croyez, cher ami, à mes sentiments de cordiale sympathie.
Édouard Detaille

24 avril 1911

Translation:

Dear Sir,

Thank you very much for sending me your work on the recruiting posters. It is interesting and funny, and all my compliments for this work that honors you and is also a compliment to the sabretache.*

I did not think that, without knowing it, I took part in the making of a poster. On the one that pertains to the cavalry engagements, I found a series of horsemen, exact copies of the drawings and watercolors. The author did not do much work to create it: it was easy—he had the decency not to sign it . . .
Cordially,
Édouard Detaille

24 April 1911

**sabretache* (nineteenth-century word): a leather satchel suspended on the left side of the body by long straps from the sword belt of a cavalry officer.

L.12

Narcisse-Virgile Diaz de la Peña
French, 1807–1876

Letter to the dealer Goupil

Ink on paper, $5\frac{5}{16} \times 4\frac{3}{16}$ in. (13.5 × 10.6 cm)
M.1989.1.10

Provenance: [William H. Schab Gallery, New York, sold February 1989 to]; Norton Simon Art Foundation.

Text:

Mon cher Goupil
Faites moi le plaisir de passer au no. 14 aujourd'hui samedi.
Bonne poignée de main.
N. Diaz

Translation:

My Dear Goupil,
Please drop by at number 14 today, Saturday.
With a friendly handshake.
N. Diaz

L.13

Jean-Louis Forain
French, 1852–1931

Letter to M. Rosati, editor of *Écho de Paris*
c. 1900

Ink on paper, $5\frac{3}{16} \times 4\frac{7}{16}$ in. (13.2 × 11.3 cm)
M.1989.1.11

Provenance: [William H. Schab Gallery, New York, sold February 1989 to]; Norton Simon Art Foundation.

Text:

Dimanche

Mon vieux Rosati,
~~Sans le sou~~
Veux-tu prendre la peine de faire composer: "un protégé du F.: André" au lieu de "L'Armée de Coblentz."
Bien à toi,
Forain
Exemple
Doux Pays
Un protégé du F.: André . . .
[sketch]
. . . au tableau d'avancements.

Translation:

Sunday

My Dear Old Friend Rosati,
~~Without the [sou]~~
Would you have the following printed: "a protégé of F.: André," instead of "The Coblentz Army."
Yours,
Forain
Example
Gentle Country
A protégé of F.: André . . .
[sketch]
. . . on the promotions board.

L.14

Paul Gauguin
French, 1848–1903

Letter to Camille Pissarro
1884

Ink on paper, 10 13/16 × 8 3/8 in. (27.5 × 21.3 cm)
M.89.1.12

Provenance: [William H. Schab Gallery, New York, sold February 1989 to]; Norton Simon Art Foundation.

Text:

[letterhead for Dillies & Cie, Roubaix, "Fabrique Spéciale de Toiles Imperméables & Impourrissables, P. Gauguin, Representant"]

Mon cher Pissarro,

Je viens de recevoir vos eaux fortes que mon ami Favre vient de m'envoyer avec la photographie groupe de votre famille. Très intéressante pour un amateur, ma femme est fort contente d'avoir vos enfants; au milieu de tous ces blonds scandinaves ils sont tout à fait comme des êtres venus du fond de l'Orient. La petite est adorable dans tous ses atours, moins réussi le petit Tiolo.

Vos eaux fortes sont très intéressantes surtout pour le dessin qui vous est là bien personnel et chose extraordinaire très rapproché des anciens. Et on dit que vous allez du sens opposé. La facture est moins curieuse, j'aurais aimé à en avoir une de l'ancien temps ou vous posiez des grains donnant au noir le ton froid que vous mettez en peinture dans les ombres. D'un autre côté une exécution souple ne fait pas mal.

Je viens d'aller chez quelques peintres danois jeunes ayant naturellement travaillé à Paris, tous copient ou de Nittis ou le grand Bastien-Lepage. Ils sont en train de faire suscription pour contribuer à un monument pour le grand homme. Qu'en dites vous! Kroyer m'a dit qu'il lui semblait que de Nittis et Lepage avaient atteint dans la perfection ce que les impressionistes avaient commencé.

Vous voyez que c'est partout la même chose et qu'on est toujours à côté de l'art. En somme ce serait bien amusant de voir si peu de peintres être dans la vérité, si soi même on n'en souffrait pas pécunièrement. Ah, mon cher Pissarro dans quel gachis je me suis fourré en ce moment. Pas d'argent et pas moyen d'en gagner d'ici 5 6 mois sur cette affaire. Quand à la peinture pas même 10 F. Je n'ose penser à l'avenir.

Et vous où en êtes vous j'espère que vous allez votre petit train train. Durand-Ruel se relève-t-il en dessous mais avec son académie de St-Luc notre patron bien aimé.

J'ai été chez le comte de Nolke que nous connaissons ici. Il a de la succcession paternelle une galerie fort belle de tableaux anciens Rembrandt Rubens Teniers, etc. . . . Dans un de ses salons il y a 2 immenses tapisseries admirables avec 2 vues de Venise admirables toiles de 100 environ je ne sais de qui. Les meubles sont dignes de figurer au Louvre et bien par terre et sur la table (une table ancienne très belle) on a mis un tapis de 40 f comme on les fait maintenant horrible naturellement. Vous voyez quel est le gout néant à notre époque chez des gens <u>nobles</u> <u>et</u> <u>très</u> <u>riches</u>. Il faudrait une bonne révolution pour balayer tout celà. Quand vous avez le temps écrivez-moi un petit mot; donnez-moi des nouvelles de Paris artistique et de toute votre famille.
Bien des choses à tout le monde
Votre tout dévoué
P. Gauguin

Translation:

[letterhead for Dillies & Co., Roubaix, "Special Manufacturers of Impermeable & Spoilproof Fabrics, P. Gauguin, Representative"]

My dear Pissarro,

I just received your etchings that my friend Favre sent me with your family's photographs. Very interesting for a connoisseur, my wife is very happy to have a picture of your children; among all these blond Scandinavians they are absolutely like beings from the depths of the Orient. The little girl is adorable all dressed up; less successful is little Tiolo.

Your etchings are very interesting, especially the drawing that has your personal touch and—an extraordinary thing—very close to your earlier ones. And they say you are moving in the opposite direction. The workmanship is less interesting; I would have rather seen something like the one you did some time ago when you were using dots that gave a cold tone to the dark shadows in your painting. On the other hand a free execution is not bad.

I just visited some Danish painters who have naturally worked in Paris; they all copy either de Nittis or the great Bastien-Lepage. They are raising money to contribute to a monument for the great man. What do you think! Kroyer told me that he thought de Nittis and Lepage had perfected what the Impressionists had started.

You see it's the same everywhere and one is always outside art. All in all it would be very amusing to see so few painters being in the way of truth—if one did not suffer financially from it. My dear Pissarro I am in such a mess right now. I don't have any money and no way to earn any for 5 or 6 months in this business. As for painting, not even 10 francs. I don't want to think about the future.

And what about you? I hope you are progressing slowly but surely. Is Durand-Ruel's business looking up with his Academy of St. Luke, our loved patron?

I visited Count Nolke whom we know here. He inherited from his father a beautiful gallery of old paintings by Rembrandt, Rubens, Teniers, etc. . . . In one of the rooms there are 2 large beautiful tapestries with 2 views of Venice, admirable canvases of about 100 [cm], I don't know by whom. The furniture deserves to be at the Louvre and on the floor and on the table (a very beautiful old table) was spread a tapestry of 40 francs which was very ugly, as they so often are these days. You see what nowadays is the bad taste of the <u>nobility</u> <u>and</u> <u>the</u> <u>very</u> <u>rich</u>. We need a revolution to sweep all this away. When you have time write me a little note and give me the news of the Paris art world and your whole family.

All the best to everyone.
Your devoted,
P. Gauguin

L.15

Paul Gauguin
French, 1848–1903

Letter to the lawyer Léonce Brault
1903

Ink on paper, 10 × $7\frac{15}{16}$ in. (25.4 × 20.2 cm)
M.89.1.13

Provenance: [William H. Schab Gallery, New York, sold February 1989 to]; Norton Simon Art Foundation.

Text:

Monsieur Brault

Nous avons reçu la visite de Piquenot administ. Je l'ai entrevu quelques instants.

Le capitaine Porlier nous a declaré que Mr Piquenot avait reçu l'ordre de faire une enquête sur les affaires de Tauata et qu'il en était empoisonné parce que disait-il il était arrivé à Taiohae après dejà l'execution dite à Taioae et qu'à Taiohae mal informé par le gendarme qui lui aurait dit que celà provenait d'un ordre verbal donné par le commandant de Zelée de la part du gouverneur etc. . . . un tas d'histoires. En fin de compte d'après son enquête ~~il vous~~ le gendarme de Tauata lui aurait montré un ordre du brigadier Charpillet, en tout et pour tout et dit qu'il avait donné des reçus sur papier blanc ce que Mr. Picquenot n'aurait pas eu le temps de vérifier car il lui aurait été prouvé que c'était faux, chose cependant qui avait une grande importance pour démontrer le mensonge du gendarme.

~~Quoiqu'il en soit~~ En outre Mr Porlier nous aurait dit que Mr. Picquenot aurait donné ordre de ne plus percevoir. Quoiqu'il en soit ~~n'ayant pas en mesure~~ n'étant pas à même de verifier la verité des paroles de Mr. Porlier je vous serai reconnaissant de vous informer du résultat de l'enquête faisant remarquer que Mr Picquenot se trouve en cette affaire presqu'aussi compromis que le gendarme et ne peut être tout a fait juge et partie.

Bien entendu je ne désire pas de mal à Mr Picquenot et si son enquête dit la verité on doit s'en contenter :

1. A savoir que : a-t-il ordonné la ~~cessation~~ non perception du ½ coprah récolté sur les terres :

2. Le gendarme a-t-il donné reçu (avec souche à l'appui imprimé) et donné de ce fait le compte exact des sommes perçues/contrôlé et au cas mauvais ce gendarme sera-t-il puni!

3. Le gendarme Tauata a-t-il fait voir quel était l'ordre qui le faisait agir et l'a-t-il soit affiché ou autrement signifié regulièrement aux indigènes

4. A-t-il ordonné le remboursement des sommes indûment perçues.

Je viens d'aller à Tauata pour m'assurer des faits et voici—
Le gendarme n'a rien changé à sa manière de faire. Ci-inclus une lettre qui prouve que le juge n'a été informé de rien puisqu'il a condamné sévèrement. ~~Ils ont voulu aller en appel et je vous prie de défendre ceux-là comme les autres car c'est vraiment indigne et méchant ce qui se passe à Tauata avec ce gendarme. Le capitaine Marchant ne ferait pas mieux que ces gendarmes et le juge. Autre chose qui est indigne ceux là n'osent pas aller en appel : le juge a condamné quelques indigènes pour avoir accepté du savon des navires baleiniers au lieu de l'argent pour leur travail.~~

Je vous enverrai par le prochain courrier tout un dossier pour causes indigènes à défendre en appel. Et moi-même peut-être aurai-je besoin de vos services car je suis en lutte avec la gendarmerie qui me menace de poursuites.

En tous cas je vous prie de terminer cette affaire de Tauata que vous avez si bien commencée: il ne s'agit pas de se faire jouer par Mr. Piquenot et il faut trace d'écritures regulières pour la perception faite par le gendarme.

Je certifie qu'il n'a jamais donné de reçu.
Paul Gauguin

Translation:

Mister Brault,

Administrator Picquenot visited us. I saw him for only a few moments.

Captain Porlier informed us that Mr. Picquenot had been ordered to investigate the situation at Tauata and that he was annoyed, he said, because he arrived in Taiohae after the execution had already taken place, and while in Taiohae he was misinformed by the policeman who told him that the verbal order came from the commander of Zelée on behalf of the governor, etc. . . . a long story. Finally, according to his investigation, the gendarme of Tauata showed him an order from Corporal Charpillet who told him that he gave some receipts on white paper to Mr. Picquenot who did not have time to verify them as he was told they were false. However, this would have been of great importance in proving the policeman's lie.

In addition Mr. Porlier told us that Mr. Picquenot was ordered to stop collecting. Nonetheless, being unable to verify the truth of Mr. Porlier's words, I would be grateful if you could check the result of the investigation, and would like to point out that Mr. Picquenot seems as compromised in this affair as the gendarme, and cannot be both the judge and the accuser.

Of course, I do not wish any harm to Mr. Picquenot and if his report tells the truth, we should be satisfied with it:

1. That is to say: was he given the order to stop collecting ½ of the copra crop from the land?

2. Did the policeman receive a batch of printed receipt proofs and did he give the exact breakdown of the perceived sums; and has he checked them? If not will the policeman be punished!

3. Has the Tauata policeman shown evidence of the order that gave him the authority to act and did he either post it or advise the natives?

4. Did he order reimbursement of the sums that were unduly collected?

I just came back from Tauata to verify the facts and—The policeman never changed his procedure. Enclosed is a letter proving that the judge was not informed of any of this, as he gave a heavy sentence.

With the next mail, I will send you a complete file of native causes in appeal. I may need your services because the police station is threatening to sue me.

In any case I ask you to close this Tauata affair that you started so well: you cannot be fooled by Mr. Picquenot and the policeman must present written proofs of sums collected on a regular basis.

I certify that he never gave any receipts.
Paul Gauguin

L.16

VINCENT VAN GOGH
Dutch, 1853–1890

Letter to the Ginoux family in Arles
c. 21 May 1890

Ink on paper, $8\frac{1}{2} \times 13\frac{15}{16}$ in. (21.6 × 35.4 cm)
M.89.1.64

PROVENANCE: [William H. Schab Gallery, New York, sold February 1989 to]; Norton Simon Art Foundation.

REFERENCE: Van Gogh, 1958, vol. 3, no. 640a.

TEXT:

Mes chers amis Ginoux, de suite je veux répondre la lettre de Mme Ginoux pour dire que j'ai été bien content d'avoir de vos nouvelles. Je regrette bien que M. Ginoux se soit blessé et aie tant souffert. Je vous prie faites faire l'emballage de mes affaires par quelqu'un pour que lui ne s'éreinte pas avec, je vous rembourserai volontiers de tous les frais que vous pourriez avoir, mais que lui ne se fatigue pas trop de peur que sa blessure ne s'ouvre. Mais ainsi j'y compte que vous expedierez samedi car j'attends après.

Oui, moi aussi j'ai bien regretté de ne pas pouvoir revenir à Arles pour prendre congé de vous tous, car vous savez bien que je m'étais attaché à gens et choses de chez vous d'une amitié sincère. Mais dans les derniers temps j'attrappais d'avantage la maladie des autres que de guérir la mienne. La société des autres malades m'influençait mal et enfin je n'y comprenais plus rien. Alors j'ai senti qu'il valait mieux essayer un changement et d'ailleurs le plaisir de revoir mon frère sa famille et les amis peintres jusqu'aujourd'hui m'a fait du bien et je me sens absolument calme et en état normal. Le médecin d'ici dit qu'il faut se jeter dans le travail en plein et ainsi se distraire. Celui la se connait bien en peinture et aime beaucoup la mienne il m'encourage fort et deux trois fois par semaine il vient passer quelques heures avec moi pour voir ce que je fais.

Ils ont deux fois écrit un article sur mes tableaux une fois dans un journal Parisien et l'autre fois à Bruxelles où j'avais exposé et maintenant dernièrement encore dans un journal de mon pays la Hollande et cela fait que beaucoup de gens ont été voir mes tableaux et que j'en ai vendu dans de meilleures conditions. Et ce n'est pas fini. Il est d'ailleurs certains que depuis que j'ai cessé de boire j'ai fait du meilleur travail qu'auparavant. Il y a toujours cela de gagné.

Mais je pense souvent à vous tous encore on ne peut pas comme on veut dans la vie là ou l'on se sent attaché le plus il faut partir. Mais les souvenirs restent et l'on se souvient— obscurement comme dans un miroir—des amis absents. Ainsi j'espère que l'expedition pourra se faire samedi. Voici encore l'adresse.

Vincent van Gogh, Chez Ravoux, place de la Mairie, Auvers sur Oise (Seine et Oise), Petite vitesse

Comme cela il ne saurait y avoir erreur. Et je vous remercie d'avance de votre peine mais que Ginoux prenne un homme pour faire l'emballage et ne s'ereinte pas. Je vous rembouserai les frais.

Vous souhaitant bonne santé et complète guerison. Salutations bien cordiales,
Vincent van Gogh

TRANSLATION:

My dear friends, I will reply to Mrs. Ginoux's letter without delay, to tell you that I am happy to have heard from you. I am very sorry to hear that Mr. Ginoux was injured and suffered much pain. I urge you to let somebody else pack my things, so that he need not wear himself out. I shall pay you back all the expenses that you incur, but I insist upon his not exerting himself too much lest the wound burst open again. In this way I count on your sending the things off Saturday, for I anxiously await them.

Yes, I too was very sorry that I could not return to Arles to say good-bye to you all, for you know well that I had become attached to the people and things of your town with a sincere affection. But lately I contracted the other patients' disease to such an extent that I could not be cured of mine. The company of the other patients had a bad influence on me, and in the end I was absolutely unable to comprehend anything, then I felt I had better try a change, and the pleasure of seeing my brother, his family, and my painter friends again has done me a lot of good, and I am feeling completely calm and normal. The doctor here says that I ought to throw myself into my work with all my strength, and so distract my mind.

This gentleman knows a good deal about painting, and he greatly likes mine. He encourages me very much, and two or three times a week he comes and visits me for a few hours to see what I am doing.

Twice they have written articles on my pictures. Once in a Paris newspaper, and the other time in a newspaper in Brussels, where I had an exhibition, and now, a very short time ago, there was an article in a paper of my native country, Holland, and the consequence was that many people went to look at my pictures and that I sold a few under the best terms. And this is not the end. Besides, it is certain that I have done better work since I stopped drinking, so much is gained.

But still I often think of you all. One cannot do what one wants in life. The more you feel attached to a spot, the more ruthlessly you are compelled to leave it, but the memories remain, and one remembers—as in a looking glass, darkly—one's absent friends. So I hope the shipment can be done on Saturday. Again, here is the address:

Vincent van Gogh, c/o Ravoux, place de la Mairie, Auvers-sur-Oise (Seine-et-Oise) Petite vitesse.

In this way there can be no mistakes. And I thank you in advance for your trouble, and mind that Ginoux hires a man to do the packing and does not exert himself; I shall repay your expenses.

Wishing you good health and complete recovery, cordially,
Vincent van Gogh

L.17

Jean-Jacques Henner
French, 1829–1905

Letter to a lady

Ink on paper, 5 1/16 × 8 in. (12.9 × 20.3 cm)
M.1989.1.15a

Provenance: [William H. Schab Gallery, New York, sold February 1989 to]; Norton Simon Art Foundation.

Text:

Chère Madame

Voulez-vous être bon pour moi, excusez moi pour lundi nous avons un diner pour une décoration remis deja plusieurs fois et qui vient d' être fixé à lundi. Je tiens beaucoup a y être et vous savez tout le plaisir que j'ai a venir chez vous. Je demande a renoncer au plaisir pour un devoir, j'en suis on ne peut plus contrarié.

Puis-je compter sur la bonne amitié de Chaplin et de vous pour m'excuser.
Votre [ami] devoué,
JJ Henner

Translation:

Dear Madame,

Please be kind enough to excuse me for Monday as we have a decoration dinner already postponed several times and now scheduled for Monday. I want to attend although you know the pleasure I have in coming to your place. I ask to relinquish the pleasure for a duty, one I cannot be more opposed to.

Can I count on the good friendship of Chaplin and you to excuse me?
Your devoted [friend],
JJ Henner

L.18

Jean-Jacques Henner
French, 1829–1905

Letter to the director of *L'Illustration*
31 March 1893

Ink on paper, 6 × 3 7/8 in. (15.2 × 9.8 cm)
M.1989.1.15b

Provenance: [William H. Schab Gallery, New York, sold February 1989 to]; Norton Simon Art Foundation.

Text:

Monsieur le Directeur
l'Illustration

Monsieur,

J'autorise M. Gaston Mayer à faire reproduire (d'après l'illustration) mon envoi au Salon de cette année dans les journaux de Chicago.
JJ Henner

Paris le 31 mars 1893

Translation:

The Director of *L'Illustration*

Dear Sir,

I authorize Mr. Gaston Mayer to reproduce (according to *L'Illustration*) my artwork for this year's Salon in the Chicago newspapers.
JJ Henner

Paris, 31 March 1893

L.19

Edouard Manet
French, 1832–1883

Letter to a gentleman
1 June (no year)

Ink on paper, 7 × 9 in. (17.8 × 22.9 cm)
M. 89.1.18

Provenance: [William H. Schab Gallery, New York, sold February 1989 to]; Norton Simon Art Foundation.

Text:

1er juin

Cher Monsieur,

J'ai en ce moment des fleurs qui pourraient peut-être vous plaire. Si vous aviez un moment vous seriez aimable de passer à l'atelier,
Amitiés
E. Manet

Translation:

1 June

Dear Sir,

I currently have some flowers that you might like. If you have a moment, please come by the studio.
Your friend,
E. Manet

L.20

Jean-François Millet
French, 1814–1875

Letter to the artist's brother Jean-Baptiste
24 July 1860

Ink on paper, $8\frac{1}{8} \times 5\frac{1}{4}$ in. (20.6 × 13.3 cm)
M.89.1.22

Provenance: [William H. Schab Gallery, New York, sold February 1989 to]; Norton Simon Art Foundation.

Text:

Mardi matin

Mon cher Jean
Sensier* m'a répondu qu'il a obtenu cent francs que tu peux prendre chez lui dès que tu voudras. Les choses que je dois faire faire sont commandées & je les aurai Lundi prochain dès le matin, ainsi tu te marierais ce jour la que je pourrais très bien être à ton mariage. Avertis-moi à temps du jour qui sera fixé.
Bonjour & bonne santé
Ton frère
J-F. Millet

Translation:

Tuesday morning

My dear Jean,
Sensier replied that he got one hundred francs that you can pick up at his place whenever you want. The things that I need to have done have been ordered and I will get them next Monday in the morning, therefore if you get married the same day I could certainly be there at your wedding. Let me know the time of day that you choose.
Good day & good health
Your brother
J-F. Millet

*Alfred Sensier (1815–1877) was a collector and friend of the Barbizon painters, who encouraged Millet and helped him to sell his paintings.

L.21

Camille Pissarro
French, 1830–1903

Letter to Claude Monet
7 December 1885

Ink on paper, $8\frac{1}{4} \times 5\frac{5}{16}$ in. (21 × 13.5 cm)
M.89.1.25

Provenance: [William H. Schab Gallery, New York, sold February 1989 to]; Norton Simon Art Foundation.

Text:

Paris 7 Dec 1885
Mon Cher Monet

On parle beaucoup d'exposition depuis quelque temps, de tout côté il en est question.

Je suis allé faire une visite à Mlle Cassatt, il y avait longtemps que je lui avais promis d'aller la voir sans parvenir à trouver le temps. Cloué ici sans le sou pour aller à Éragny, j'ai pu aller d'un côté d'autre.

Les premières paroles échangées ont été pour parler de l'exposition. Ne pourrions-nous, nous entendre à cet effet? Nous, Degas, Caillebotte, Guillaumin, Mme Berthe Morisot, Mlle Cassatt et deux ou trois autres, formeraient un excellent élément d'exposition, le difficile serait de s'entendre. Je crois qu'en principe il ne faut pas la faire à nous tout seul (c'est-à-dire l'élément Durand), il faut que l'exposition ait l'initiative des artistes eux mêmes et surtout le prouver clairement pur la composition.

Qu'en dites vous?

Ecrivez-moi à ~~Éragny~~ Paris car je compte partir mercredi si c'est possible.

Tachez que je reçoive votre lettre mercredi matin.
Votre bien dévoué
C. Pissarro

Rue des petites écuries 42

Translation:

Paris, 7 December 1885
My dear Monet,

All around us, for some time now, there's been talk of the exhibition.

I paid a visit to Mlle Cassatt. For a long time, I had promised to go and see her but had not found the time to do so. Stuck here without a cent to go to Éragny, I was nevertheless able to find a way to go.

Our first words were to talk about the exhibition. Can we reach an agreement among us about it? All of us—Degas, Caillebotte, Guillaumin, Mme Berthe Morisot, Mlle Cassatt, and two or three others—would form an excellent group for the exhibition, the more difficult problem would be to get along. In my opinion, we should not do it alone (that is to say Durand's part). The artists themselves should initiate the exhibition and the composition should clearly reflect it.

What do you think?

Please write to me in ~~Éragny~~ Paris, as I intend to leave Wednesday morning if it is possible.

Make sure that I receive your letter on Wednesday morning.

Your devoted friend,
C. Pissarro

Rue des Petites Ecuries 42

L.22

Camille Pissarro
French, 1830–1903

Fragment of a letter to Pissarro's niece, Esther; the first page(s) are missing.
c. 1890

Ink on paper, 8¼ × 5⅜ in. (21 × 13.7 cm)
M.89.1.26

Provenance: [William H. Schab Gallery, New York, sold February 1989 to]; Norton Simon Art Foundation.

Text:

. . . faites à la mécanique achetées tout faites, etc, etc. C'est navrant.—Tu vois par ce tableau peu enchanteur la grandeur du service que tu rendrais à ces deux garçons et à moi ma chère, un grand poid de moins sur la conscience!— J'irai certainement à Londres, aussitôt que possible.

Je te remercie bien des copies que tu t'aies donné le mal de faire, c'est ma fois très bien dans le caractère. Ce sont je vois des épreuves d'artistes, excepté ceux marqués A (qui veut dire aciéré) que l'on peut tirer à un grand nombre d'exemplaires, les autres sont très rares c'est tiré à 4, 10, 15 tout au plus.

Encore une fois merci, nous verrons.

Embrassez ma chère Alice et bien des choses à ton père. Grand-mère est aussi bien que possible pour son âge mais qu'elle est tracassière, Amélie a fort à faire à se faire écouter, c'est dur je t'assure.

Je t'embrasse,
Ton oncle affectionné
C. Pissarro

Lucien est arrivé hier, pour m'assister un peu. Il se joint à moi pour vous saluer tous.

J'oubliais dans ma lettre de te dire que l'une des grandes calamités de notre temps, surtout pour les choses de l'art qui demande ~~surtout~~ la sensation personnelle si fugitive, si capricieuse, c'était le système des concours; je vois par ta lettre qu'il y a des élus dans cette école, je vois Georges absolument privé de ses moyens, car il est capable de faire un profil pur comme quelqu'artiste des temps passés et aussi quelquefois aussi nul qu'un bébé. Cela tout simplement parce qu'il ne sait pas et qu'il n'a que des sensations.

Translation:

. . . mechanically processed, bought ready-made, etc. etc. It's a great pity.—This unattractive picture shows the great service that you are doing to these two boys and to me, my dear, and a big weight off my conscience!—I will definitely go to London, as soon as possible.

I thank you for the copies that you took the time to do; it is one of your [good] qualities. They are proofs by artists, except those marked "A" (that is to say, steel-faced [*aciéré*]) that can be reproduced many times, the others are very rare, they are copied only 4, 10, or 15 times at the most.

Again thank you, we'll see.

Please kiss my dear Alice and all the best to your father. Grandmother is as well as she can be for her age. She is worrisome, and Amélie has a hard time of it making herself heard; it is difficult I assure you.

I embrace you,
Your affectionate uncle
C. Pissarro,

Lucien arrived yesterday to help me a little. He also sends his greetings.

I forgot in my letter to tell you that one of the disasters of our time, especially for our art that requires so subjective, so fleeting, and so capricious a sensibility, is the entrance examination system; according to your letter there was favoritism in this school; I see Georges completely without means, because he is capable of drawing a pure profile like an artist from another era, and sometimes he is as inexperienced as a baby. It is simply because he does not know and only feels.

L.23

Camille Pissarro
French, 1830–1903

Letter to Georges Lecomte
28 April 1892

Ink on paper, 7⅛ × 9⅛ in. (18.1 × 23.2 cm)
M. 89.1.27

Provenance: [William H. Schab Gallery, New York, sold February 1989 to]; Norton Simon Art Foundation.

Text:

Éragny par Gisors (Eure)
28 av 1892

Mon Cher Lecomte

Vous seriez bien gentil de me faire savoir à quelle époque on jouera votre piece afin que je m'arrange en cas de voyage à Paris. J'ai lu dans *L'Illustration* que vous passeriez en mai??

Je n'ai aucune nouvelle de l'article de Geffroy dans *la Revue encyclopédique*, ni reçu rien de Mr. Roger Marx a qui j'ai fait remettre une épreuve de mon portrait et de Cézanne, savez-vous quelque chose?

Et la famille Luce? et les amis? que deviennent-ils; ici tout va à peu près, je buche, malheureusement le mauvais temps me désespère. Reçu des nouvelles de Lucien qui me prie de le rappeller à votre souvenir.

Vous devez être bien surmené par vos répétitions, mais aussi quel succès! J'espère que vous en aurez un bien grand, vous le méritez certes!

Bon courage mon cher ami, et à bientôt je l'espère

Sincèrement votre

C. Pissarro

TRANSLATION:

Éragny par Gisors (Eure)

28 April 1892

My dear Lecomte,

Please let me know when your play will open in which case I will come to Paris. I read in *L'Illustration* that it will appear in May??

I don't have any news regarding the article by Geffroy in the *Revue encyclopédique*, nor from Mr. Roger Marx to whom I forwarded a proof of my portrait and of Cézanne, do you know anything?

And the Luce family? And our friends how are they? Everything here is all right, I work hard; unfortunately, the bad weather is depressing. I received news from Lucien who asked me to send his wishes.

You must be under stress because of the rehearsals, but what a success! I hope it will be grand, you deserve it!

Courage, my dear friend, and I hope to see you soon.

Sincerely yours,

C. Pissarro

L.24

CAMILLE PISSARRO

French, 1830–1903

Letter to Pissarro's pharmacist

30 August 1892

Ink on paper, $7\frac{1}{8} \times 9\frac{1}{4}$ in. (18.1 × 23.5 cm)

M.89.1.28

PROVENANCE: [William H. Schab Gallery, New York, sold February 1989 to]; Norton Simon Art Foundation.

TEXT:

Éragny par Gisors

Eure

30 aout 92

Monsieur Deroles

Je vous prie de m'envoyer les médicaments suivants a Éragny

Cuprum—6 en gouttes

Grands tubes {Cuprum—18 en globules

{Vératrum—12 en globules (12)

Et à l'adresse suivante:

Mr. C. Pissarro chez Mr O Mirbeau aux Damps par Pont-de-l'Arche, Eure.

Les médicaments ci-après.

Camph. TM en gouttes

Vératrum 12—do.—(12)

Cuprum 18—do.—

Grands tubes {Vératrum 6 en globules

{Cuprum 18 en globules.

C. Pissarro

TRANSLATION:

Éragny par Gisors

Eure

30 August 1892

Mr. Deroles,

Please be so kind as to send me the following medications at Éragny

Cuprum—6 drops

Large tubes {Cuprum—18 globules

{Vératrum— 2 globules (12)

At the following address:

Mr. C. Pissaro c/o Mr. O. Mirbeau aux Damps par Pont de l'Arche, Eure

The following medications:

Camphor TM in drops

Vératrum 12—ditto (12)

Cuprum 18—ditto—

Large tubes {Vératrum 6 globules

{Cuprum 18 globules

C. Pissarro

L.25

CAMILLE PISSARRO

French, 1830–1903

Two drafts of an order for a gravestone for Pissarro's son Félix

1898

Ink on paper, $7 \times 4\frac{1}{2}$ in. (17.8 × 11.4 cm)

M.89.1.29

PROVENANCE: [William H. Schab Gallery, New York, sold February 1989 to]; Norton Simon Art Foundation.

TEXT (recto):

Monsieur

~~Selon l~~

Je vous donne la commande selon l'estimation que vous me faites pour l'érection d'une tombe ~~à la mémoire de mon fils~~ en pierre dure dit "Robin Hood Stone."

Text (verso):

Mr.

Je vous donne la commande d'une tombe en pierre dure dit Robin Hood Stone, selon le devis que vous me faites dans votre lettre du 6 juin 98—c'est à dire au prix 13 £ treize livres, avec l'engagement de vous conformer au dessin approuvé par les autorités du Cimetière de payer les frais d'érection de la dite tombe et a ~~garder~~ de la garder en bon état pendant 3 ans.

~~Pour les grav les lettres gravées et oscurceées au prix de quinze shillings par cent~~

~~Les letters, gravées, en "Lead Imperishable letters" à 5 cinq shillings et~~

Les lettres gravées en "lead imperishable" à 5 cinq shilling et six pence par douzaine de lettres.

Voici l'épitaphe:

à la mémoire de
notre fils regretté
Félix Pissarro
né à Pontoise le 24 juillet 1874
décédé à Kew Ri le 25 novembre 1897

Translation (recto):

Dear Sir,
~~According to the~~
This letter is to order a gravestone ~~in my son's memory~~ in hard stone called "Robin Hood Stone," as per your estimate.

Translation (verso):

Dear Sir,

This letter is to order a gravestone in hard stone called Robin Hood stone, as per your letter dated 6 June 1898, at an estimated price of £13 (thirteen pounds sterling), with your assurance to conform to the design preapproved by the cemetery authorities to pay the fees for the erection of said gravestone and to keep it in perfect condition for 3 years.

~~For the engraved and darkened letters priced at fifteen shillings for one hundred~~

~~The engraved letters in "imperishable lead" letters for 5 five shillings and~~

The engraved letters in "imperishable lead" at five shillings and six pence per dozen letters.

Here is the epitaph:

in memory of
our beloved son
Félix Pissarro
born in Pontoise on 24 July 1874
died in Kew, Richmond, on 25 November 1897

L.26

Camille Pissarro
French, 1830–1903

Letter to Mr. Dellerba
26 January 1899

Ink on paper, 7 × 8½ in. (17.8 × 21.6 cm)
M.89.1.30

Provenance: [William H. Schab Gallery, New York, sold February 1989 to]; Norton Simon Art Foundation.

Text:

Paris
204 Rue de Rivoli
26 janv. 99

Cher Monsieur.
Voici la liste des Tableaux actuellement dans mon atelier que j'estime au plus bas prix:

16 toiles de		10 ________	16,000
1	"	20 ________	1,200
5	"	25 ________	7,500
7	"	30 ________	14,000
14	"	8 —anciennes que j'estime à des prix un peu plus élevés	21,000
			69,700 [*sic*]

Recevez, Cher Monsieur, mes amicales salutations
C. Pissarro

à Mr. Dellerba
47 r. de Douai
Paris

nb: Vous pouvez m'assurer le chiffre de 60 mille fr.

Translation:

Paris
204 rue de Rivoli
26 Jan. 99

Dear Sir,
Following is the list of all the paintings currently in my workshop estimated at the lowest price:

16 Paintings of		10 ________	16,000
1	"	20 ________	1,200
5	"	25 ________	7,500
7	"	30 ________	14,000
14	"	8 —older works valued at slightly higher prices	21,000
			69,700 [*sic*]

With friendly greetings,
C. Pissarro

to Mr. Dellerba
47 r. de Douai
Paris

nb: Could you assure me of the sum of 60 thousand fr.

L.27

Camille Pissarro
French, 1830–1903

Letter to Pissarro's son Rodolphe
20 October 1900

Ink on paper, 7 × 8⅞ in. (17.8 × 22.5 cm)
M. 89.1.31

Provenance: [William H. Schab Gallery, New York, sold February 1989 to]; Norton Simon Art Foundation.

Text:

Éragny-Barincourt par Gisors, Eure
20 oct. 1900

Mon cher Rodolphe

En lisant l'Aurore ce matin j'apprends qu'il y a eu un accident au Métropolitain assez grave 32 personnes blessées,—gare là dessous, je crois qu'il serait sage de ne pas se presser à prendre cette voie de communication, car décidemment ils n'y ont pas encore la main, méfiez-vous! Je crois qu'Alfred ferait bien de s'abstenir.

Ta mère te prie d'aller place Dauphine et de prendre la mesure exacte longueur, hauteur et profondeur de l'espace qui se trouve sous le poël de la cuisine, elle en a besoin le plus tôt possible pour faire un coffre à charbon. Il faut que les mesures soient exacte. Si tu n'as pas un mètre il faut en acheter un, car j'en aurai besoin.

Bien des choses à Alfred de notre part.—ecris nous et dis moi si cela marche bien pour la nourriture.

J'ai fini mes deux toiles j'en ai une troisième toile de 15 presque fini et commencé d'autres, je serai donc prêt bientôt, mais il y a encore à faire à la maison.

Nous t'embrassons
Ton père aff.
C. Pissarro

Translation:

Éragny-Barincourt par Gisors, Eure
20 Oct. 1900

My dear Rodolphe,

While reading l'Aurore this morning, I learned that there was a serious accident in the Metro: 32 people were hurt—be careful in the underground. I think it would be wise not to hurry to take this means of transportation, because they don't have the experience yet, watch out! I think Alfred should refrain from taking it.

Your mother would like you to go to place Dauphine to take the exact measurement: length, height, and depth of the space underneath the kitchen stove.* She needs it as soon as possible to have a coal chest made. The measurements should be exact. If you do not have a yardstick buy one, I can use it.

All the best to Alfred from all of us. Write to us and let us know if everything is okay for the food.

I finished the two canvases. I have a third canvas of 15 almost finished and started others. I will be ready soon; there are still things to do at home.

We embrace you,
Your affectionate father
C. Pissarro

*Pissarro has included a sketch of the space he wants measured.

L.28

Pierre-Cécile Puvis de Chavannes
French, 1824–1898

Letter to a lady writer
16 February 1895

Ink on paper, 5½ × 3¾ in. (14 × 9.5 cm)
M.1989.1.32a

Provenance: [William H. Schab Gallery, New York, sold February 1989 to]; Norton Simon Art Foundation.

Text:

16 Février 95

Chère Madame

Je viens de tourner la dernière page de votre livre offert avec tant de gracieuse bonté, et si vivant—c'est une forte et ravissante croisade contre le chic et le snobisme—S'ils meurent par vous, je demande à tenir un des cordons du Poele.

Respecteusement.
Votre dévoué
P. Puvis de C

Translation:

16 February 95

Dear Madame,

I just turned the last page of your book that you gave me with such gracious kindness, and so full of life—it is a ravishing crusade against style and snobbery—If they die because of you, I ask to be one of the pallbearers.

Respectfully,
Your devoted friend,
P. Puvis de C.

L.29

Pierre-Cécile Puvis de Chavannes
French, 1824–1898

Letter to Mr. Perzugalli, a painter-glassmaker
30 March 1896

Ink on paper, 5½ × 4⅜ in. (14 × 11.1 cm)
M.1989.1.32b

Provenance: [William H. Schab Gallery, New York, sold February 1989 to]; Norton Simon Art Foundation.

Text:

Monsieur

Je suis tout à fait incompétent sur la question que vous me sou-mettez. Le mieux pour être renseigné serait que vous vouliez bien en écrire à Mr. Cazier president de la section des objets d'art.

Veuillez agréer l'expression de mes sentiments distingués

P. Puvis de Chavannes

30 mars 96

Translation:

Dear Sir,

I don't have the knowledge with which to answer the question that you are asking me. The best thing would be to send it to Mr. Cazier, president of the art objects section.

Please accept my most sincere greetings,

P. Puvis de Chavannes

30 March 96

L.30

Pierre-Joseph Redouté
Belgian, 1759–1840

Letter to a gentleman

Ink on paper, $8\frac{1}{8} \times 16$ in. (20.6×40.6 cm)
M.89.1.34

Provenance: [William H. Schab Gallery, New York, sold February 1989 to]; Norton Simon Art Foundation.

Text:

My lord,

Knowing your love for the arts, and the munificence with which you encourage them, I take the liberty of enclosing the prospectus of a work which I have just published, in the hope of obtaining your subscription.

I may perhaps be permitted to observe that I have already attached my name to several works such as the "Liliacées" and "L'iconographie des Roses"; all undertaken more with a view to the promotion of science than from any hope of personal emolument.

Should my work meet with a favourable reception, I shall esteem myself much your debtor; should you, on the other hand, decline subscribing, I still hope that you will excuse the step which I have taken, and in the meantime allow me to subscribe myself with great respect,

Your most obedient and humble Servant,

P. Redouté

6 rue de Seine / 6 St. Germain

L.31

Pierre-Auguste Renoir
French, 1841–1919

Letter to Paul Berard
10 February 1903

Ink on paper, $8\frac{1}{8} \times 10\frac{3}{8}$ in. (20.6×26.4 cm)
M.1989.1.35

Provenance: [William H. Schab Gallery, New York, sold February 1989 to]; Norton Simon Art Foundation.

Text:

Cher ami

J'ai quitté Paris comme une bombe pour fuire les pointes de feu ou les ponctions et me voici encore installé au Cannet. J'ai vraiment besoin d'un peu de tranquilité et comme il fait très beau j'espère toujours que de bonnes suées vont remplacer avantageusement les remèdes jusqu'à présent inutiles.

Ici ce n'est pas d'une folle gaité mais j'ai le grand air. Je ne sais si j'aurai le plaisir de vous voir cette année. Je ne vous y pousse pas malgré le contentement de vous voir, car si je n'avais pas ma peinture qui me fait passer le temps au bout de trois jours je désirerais revoir le nord. Je pense que vous continuez a vous porter admirablement et que rien ne cloche chez vous. J'espère du reste recevoir un peu de vos nouvelles quand vous aurez le temps.

Mille amitiés mon cher ami et bonne santé.

Renoir

Le Cannet, Alpes Maritimes
10 février 03

Translation:

My dear Friend

I rushed out of Paris to flee the line of fire as well as the punctures and here I am in Le Cannet. I really need some peace and quiet and because the weather is very nice I hope that a good sweat will work where the other remedies were unsuccessful.

It is not very joyful here but I have the outdoors. I don't know if I will see you this year. I do not press you in spite of the pleasure of seeing you, because if I did not do any painting which keeps me occupied, after 3 days I would want to go back north. I hope that your health is still very good and that everything is fine at your house. Moreover, I hope you will send me some news when you have a moment.

With much affection, dear friend, and best wishes for your health,

Renoir

Le Cannet, Alpes Maritimes
10 February [19]03

L.32

Auguste Rodin
French, 1840–1917

Letter to Rose Beuret

Ink on paper, $3\frac{1}{2} \times 4\frac{1}{2}$ in. (8.9 × 11.4 cm)
M.89.1.36

Provenance: [William H. Schab Gallery, New York, sold February 1989 to]; Norton Simon Art Foundation.

Text:

Ma Bonne petite Rose,
Ecris-moi toujours à Tours poste restante.
Ne t'ennuie pas et sois assez gentille pour te bien porter, tu sais que je pense à toi qui est si obeissante quand tu veux, et quand tu tiens à me faire plaisir. Je travaille et en ai encore pour quelque temps.
Je voudrais que tu prennes huit ou quinze jours chez Vivien ce qui te ferait du bien. Je t'envoi un bon baiser de vive amitié.
Ton ami véritable, Rodin

Translation:

My Good little Rose,
You can always write to me at general delivery, Tours.
Do not miss me and please stay well, you know that I think about you who is so obedient when you want and when you wish to please me. I am working and need more time.
I would like you to take eight or fifteen days at Vivien's, it will be good for you. I am sending you a friendly little kiss.
Your true friend, Rodin

L.33

Augustus Saint-Gaudens
American, 1840–1907

Letter to L. C. L. Jordan
26 February 1889

Ink on paper, $7\frac{15}{16} \times 4\frac{7}{8}$ in. (20.2 × 12.4 cm)
M.89.1.40

Provenance: [William H. Schab Gallery, New York, sold February 1989 to]; Norton Simon Art Foundation.

Text:

148 West 36th Street
Feb 26/89
Mr. L. C. L. Jordan

Dear Sir
I am extremely obliged to you for your courtesy in lending me the bust of Washington. Will you kindly give it to Louis when he calls for it and

Believe me
Yours very truly
Augustus St-Gaudens

L.34

Paul Signac
French, 1863–1935

Letter to a gentleman

Ink on paper, $8\frac{1}{2} \times 5\frac{3}{8}$ in. (21.6 × 13.7 cm)
M.1989.1.39.L

Provenance: [William H. Schab Gallery, New York, sold February 1989 to]; Norton Simon Art Foundation.

Text:

(letterhead for Société des Artistes Indépendants / Reconnue d'utilité publique / Siège social: 18, Rue Mazarine, Paris / Président: Paul Signac)

Cher Monsieur
Ce "crayon de couleurs"—vue d'Asnières—est bien de moi. Il doit dater de 1884 ou 1885. J'étais bien jeune! Mais il est tout de même gentil.
Bien à vous
P. Signac

Translation:

Dear Sir,
This colored drawing—View of Asnières—is definitely by me. It dates from 1884 or 1885. I was very young! But all the same it is nice.
Yours,
P. Signac

L.35

Thomas Sully
American, 1783–1872

Letter to Jonathan Miller
11 January 1869

Ink on paper, $5\frac{5}{8} \times 7\frac{9}{16}$ in. (14.3 × 19.2 cm)
M.89.1.41

Provenance: [William H. Schab Gallery, New York, sold February 1989 to]; Norton Simon Art Foundation.

Text:

Philadelphia Jan. 11, 1869
When Mr. Miller hears of the death of Thos. Sully will he call at his former residence, and Mr. Duane will show him the pictures (which are tied together by a string).
Respectfully
Thos. Sully

L.36

Joseph Mallord William Turner
English, 1775–1851

Letter to Charles Stokes
10 February 1843

Ink on paper, $7\frac{3}{16} \times 8\frac{7}{8}$ in. (18.3 × 22.5 cm)
M.89.1.42

Provenance: [William H. Schab Gallery, New York, sold February 1989 to]; Norton Simon Art Foundation.

Text:

Warren Street
Feb. 10th 43

Sir

Permit me to return you my most sincere Thanks for the loan of your admirable picture of Sir Francis Chanterey which I have now sent. I hope you will pardon me for having kept it so long. It is an excellent work of art, and Mr. A. Cunningham assures me, in his opinion more like, than any other picture. The plate is now printing, and I hope next week to be able to offer you a few proofs for your folio, which I trust you will honor me by the acceptance, and they may meet your approbations.

I am Dear Sir
Yours very truly & much obliged
Turner

Charles Stokes Esq.

Bibliography

Books and Articles

ADHÉMAR, 1954
Adhémar, Jean, *Honoré Daumier*, Paris, 1954.

ADHÉMAR, 1962
Adhémar, Jean, *Toulouse-Lautrec*, Paris, 1962.

ADLER AND GARB, 1987
Adler, Kathleen, and Tamar Garb, *Berthe Morisot*, Oxford, 1987.

ALAUZEN, 1969
Alauzen, André M., and Pierre Ripert, *Monticelli, sa vie et son oeuvre*, Paris, 1969.

ALEXANDRE, 1893
Alexandre, Arsène, "La Décoration de la mairie de Bagnolet," *Eclair*, 8 November 1893, p. 3.

ALEXANDRE, 1921
Alexandre, Arsène, *Claude Monet*, Paris, 1921.

ALEXANDRE, 1928
Alexandre, Arsène, *Daumier*, Paris, 1928.

ALEXANDRIAN, 1980
Alexandrian, Sarane, *Seurat*, New York, 1980.

ALEXIS, 1887
Alexis, Paul, "Catalogue de la collection Eugène Murer," *Le Cri du peuple*, 21 October 1887, n.p.

ALPATOV, 1961
Alpatov, Michel, "Corot à Venise: Une tableau du Musée Pouchkine á Moscou," *Art de France: revue annuelle de l'art ancien et moderne*, no. 1, (1961), pp. 169–175.

ALPERS, 1976
Alpers, Svetlana, "Describe or Narrate? A Problem in Realistic Representation," *New Literary History* 8, no. 1 (Autumn 1976), pp. 15–41.

ALPERS, 1988
Alpers, Svetlana, *Rembrandt's Enterprise: The Studio and the Market*, Chicago, 1988.

ALZARD, 1950
Alzard, Jean, *Ingres et l'ingrisme*, Paris, 1950.

AMERICAN ART NEWS, 1912
"Great Rousseau Sold," *American Art News* 10, no. 13 (6 January 1912).

LES AMIS DE GUSTAVE COURBET, 1955
Les Amis de Gustave Courbet, bulletin no. 15 (1955).

DE ANGELIS, 1974
de Angelis, R., *L'Opera pittorica completa di Goya*, Milan, 1974.

ANGOULVENT, 1933?
Angoulvent, Monique, *Berthe Morisot*, Paris, 1933?

ANNALES, 1812
Annales du musée et de l'école moderne des beaux-arts, Paris, 1812.

ANSIEAU, 1998
Ansieau, Joëlle, *Georges Lacombe, 1868–1916: Catalogue raisonné*, Paris, 1998.

ANTOINE, 1891
Antoine, Jules, "Critique d'art: Pavillion de la Ville de Paris. Exposition des artistes indépendants," *La Plume*, no. 49 (1 May 1891), pp. 156–157.

D'ARGENCOURT AND FOUCART, 1977
d'Argencourt, Louise, and J. Foucart, *Puvis de Chavannes*. [Exh. cat. Grand Palais, Paris.] Paris, 1977.

ARMSTRONG, 2002
Armstrong, Carol, *Manet/Manette*, New Haven, 2002.

ARNOLD, 1995
Arnold, Matthias, *Vincent van Gogh: Werk und Wirkung*, Munich, 1995.

ART DIGEST, 1937
"Manet, First Leader of Impressionism, Seen in Comprehensive Show," *Art Digest* 11, no. 12 (15 March 1937), p. 9.

ART INSTITUTE OF CHICAGO, 1923
Art Institute of Chicago, *Bulletin of the Art Institute of Chicago* 17, no. 9 (December 1923).

ART INSTITUTE OF CHICAGO, 1924
Art Institute of Chicago, "Studies for the Childhood of Saint Geneviève, Puvis de Chavannes," *Bulletin of the Art Institute of Chicago* 18 (January 1924), pp. 117–120.

ART INSTITUTE OF CHICAGO, 1925
Art Institute of Chicago, *A Guide to the Paintings in the Permanent Collection*, Chicago, 1925.

L'ARTISTE, 1841
"Salon de 1841, portraits, études, miniatures, fleurs et natures mortes," *L'Artiste*, 2nd series, vol. 7, 1841.

ART NEWS, 1924
"Chicago Institute Gets Mural Studies by Puvis de Chavannes," *Art News* 22, no. 26 (15 April 1924), p. 1.

ART NEWS, 1927
"The Stillman Collection in Coming Sale," *Art News* 25, no. 16 (22 January 1927), pp. 1, 10.

ART NEWS, 1932
"Great French Art Exhibit Now at Burlington House," *Art News* 30, no. 15 (9 January 1932), pp. 5, 8.

ART NEWS, 1933
"Manet and Renoir Figure Together in Loan Exhibition," *Art News* 32, no. 11 (16 December 1933), pp. 3, 11.

Arts Council of Great Britain, 1978
Arts Council of Great Britain, *Gustave Courbet, 1819–1877* [Exh. cat. Royal Academy of Arts, London.] London, 1978.

Artwork, 1930
Artwork 6, no. 23 (Autumn 1930), p. 180.

Astruc, 1859
Astruc, Zacharie, *Les 14 stations du Salon—1859—suivit d'un récit douloureaux*, Paris, 1859.

Aubrun, 1974
Aubrun, Marie-Madeleine, *Jules Dupré, 1811–1889, catalogue raisonné de l'oeuvre peint, dessiné et gravé*, Paris, 1974.

Auffret, 2004
Auffret, François, *Jongkind, 1819–1891, biographie illustrée*, Paris, 2004.

Aurier, 1892
Aurier, Albert, "Beaux-Arts: Les Symbolistes," *Revue encyclopédique* 2, 32 (1 April 1892).

Auzas, 1950
Auzas, P., *Peinture de Cézanne*, Paris, 1950.

Bacou, 1956
Bacou, Roseline, *Odilon Redon*, 2 vols., Geneva, 1956.

Bacou, 1964
Bacou, Roseline, "Décors d'appartements au temps des Nabis," *Art de France* 4 (1964), pp. 190–205.

Bade, 1992
Bade, Patrick, *Renoir*, London, 1992.

Bätschmann, 1998
Bätschmann, Oskar, "Les Portraits anonymes: La Transformation du tableau de genre," in *Corot, un artiste et son temps.* Actes des colloques organisés au musée du Louvre par le Service culturel les 1 et 2 mars 1996 à Paris, pp. 309–329, Paris, 1998.

Bailey, 1997
Bailey, Colin B., *Renoir's Portraits: Impressions of an Age.* [Exh. cat. National Gallery of Canada, Ottawa; The Art Institute of Chicago; Kimbell Art Museum, Fort Worth.] New Haven, 1997.

Bailly-Herzberg, 1980
Bailly-Herzberg, Janine, "Chronology," in *Camille Pissarro, 1830–1903*, pp. 59–65. [Exh. cat. Hayward Gallery, London; Grand Palais, Paris; Museum of Fine Arts, Boston.] London, 1980.

Bailly-Herzberg, 1980–1991
Bailly-Herzberg, Janine, *Correspondance de Camille Pissarro*, 5 vols., Paris, 1980–1991.

Bajou-Charpentreau, 1993
Bajou-Charpentreau, Valérie M., *Frédéric Bazille, 1841–1870*, Aix-en-Provence, 1993.

Bajou-Charpentreau, 1996
Bajou-Charpentreau, Valérie M., "Virgilio Narcisso Diaz de la Peña," in *The Dictionary of Art*, ed. Jane Turner, New York, 1996, vol. 8, pp. 859–860.

Bajou-Charpentreau, 1999
Bajou-Charpentreau, Valérie M., *Monsieur Ingres*, Paris, 1999.

Bareau, 1986
Bareau, Juliet Wilson, "Édouard Vuillard et les princes Bibesco," *Revue de l'art*, no. 74 (1986), pp. 37–46.

Barnes and de Mazia, 1939
Barnes, Albert, and Violette de Mazia, *The Art of Cézanne*, New York, 1939.

Barruel, 2005
Barruel, Thérèse, "Vers le mieux, une devise nabie?," *48/14 La revue du Musée d'Orsay*, 20 (Spring 2005), pp. 26–37.

Barzini and Mandel, 1971
Barzini, Luigi, and Gabriele Mandel, *L'Opera pittorica completa di Daumier*, Milan, 1971.

Bataille, G., 1929
Bataille, Georges, "Jean-Baptiste Corot (1796–1875): Compositions classiques," *Documents: Doctrines, archéologie, beaux-arts, ethnographie* 1, no. 2 (1929), pp. 84–92.

Bataille and Wildenstein, 1961
Bataille, Marie-Louise, and Georges Wildenstein, *Berthe Morisot. Catalogue des peintures, pastels et aquarelles*, Paris, 1961.

Baudelaire, 1975–1976
Baudelaire, Charles, *Oeuvres complètes*, 2 vols., Paris, 1975–1976.

Bazin, 1942
Bazin, Germain, *Corot*, Paris, 1942.

Bazin, 1947
Bazin, Germain, *L'Époque impressionniste avec notices biographiques et bibliographiques*, Paris, 1947 (2nd ed., Paris, 1953).

Bazin, 1989
Bazin, Germain, *Théodore Géricault. Étude critique, documents et catalogue raisonné*, 7 vols., Paris, 1989.

Beaumont, 1900
Beaumont, Charles de, "Jean-Louis Ducis, peintre," *Réunion de la Société des beaux-arts des départements* 24 (1900), pp. 520–547.

Bell, 1978
Bell, Clive, *The French Impressionists*, New York, 1978.

Bellier de la Chavignerie and Avray, 1882
Bellier de la Chavignerie, Émile, and Louis Avray, *Dictionnaire général des artistes de l'école française depuis l'origine des arts du dessin jusqu'à nos jours*, 2 vols., Paris, 1882.

Bénédite, Laran, and Gaston-Dreyfus, 1911
Bénédite, Léonce, Jean Laran, and Philippe Gaston-Dreyfus, *Courbet*, Paris, 1911.

Bénédite, Laran, and Gaston-Dreyfus, 1912
Bénédite, Léonce, Jean Laran, and Philippe Gaston-Dreyfus, *Gustave Courbet, with a Biographical and Critical Study*, London, 1912.

Bénézit, 1966
Bénézit, E., *Dictionnaire critique et documentaire des peintres, sculpteurs, dessinateurs et graveurs*, Paris, 1966.

Benjamin, 1989
Benjamin, Roger, "Recovering Authors: The Modern Copy, Copy Exhibitions and Matisse," *Art History* 12, no. 2 (June 1989), pp. 176–201.

Benjamin, 1993
Benjamin, Roger, "The Decorative Landscape, Fauvism, and the Arabesque of Observation," *Art Bulletin* 75, no. 2 (June 1993), pp. 295–316.

Berger, K., 1964
Berger, Klaus, *Odilon Redon: Phantasie und Farbe*, Cologne, 1964 (English ed., London, 1964).

Berger, R., 1986
Berger, R., *Art and Technology*, New York, 1986.

Berhaut, 1978
Berhaut, Marie, *Caillebotte: Sa Vie et son oeuvre*, 2nd ed., Paris, 1978.

Berhaut, 1994
Berhaut, Marie, *Gustave Caillebotte: Catalogue raisonné des peintures et pastels*, Paris, 1994.

Bernard, B., 1985
Bernard, Bruce, ed., *Vincent by Himself: A Selection of Van Gogh's Paintings and Drawings, Together with Extracts from His Letters*, Boston, 1985.

Bernard, B., 1986a
Bernard, Bruce, ed., *The Impressionist Revolution*, London, 1986.

Bernard, B., 1986b
Bernard, Bruce, *The Impressionists*, London, 1986.

Bernard, E., 1908
Bernard, Emile, "Erinnerungen an Paul Cézanne," *Kunst und Künstler* 6 (1908), pp. 421–429, 475–480, 521–527.

Bernard, T., 1930
Bernard, Tristan, "Jos Hessel," *La Renaissance* 13 (January 1930), pp. 20–22.

Bernheim de Villers, 1930
Bernheim de Villers, C., *Corot: Peintre de figures*, Paris, 1930.

Berr de Turique, n.d.
Berr de Turique, Marcelle, *Renoir*, Paris, n.d.

Berson, 1996
Berson, Ruth, ed., *The New Painting: Impressionism, 1874–1886: Documentation*, 2 vols., San Francisco, 1996.

Bertram, 1929
Bertram, Anthony, *The World's Masters: Cézanne, 1839–1906*, London, 1929.

de Beruete y Moret, 1917
de Beruete y Moret, Aureliano, *Goya: Composiciones y figuras*, 3 vols., Madrid, 1917.

de Beruete y Moret, 1922
de Beruete y Moret, Aureliano, *Goya as Portrait Painter*, Boston, 1922.

Bezombes, 1953
Bezombes, Roger, *L'Exotisme dans l'art et la pensée*, Paris, 1953.

Blanche, 1920
Blanche, Jacques-Émile, *Quatre-vingts ans de peinture libre, 1800–1885*, Paris, 1920.

Blanche, 1932
Blanche, Jacques-Émile, "Le XIXe siècle," *Gazette des beaux-arts* 7 (January 1932), pp. 77–96.

Bodelsen, 1968
Bodelsen, Merete, "Early Impressionists Sales, 1874–94 in the Light of Some Unpublished 'Procès-Verbaux,'" *Burlington Magazine* 110 (June 1968), pp. 330–349.

Boime, 1971
Boime, Albert, *The Academy and French Painting in the Nineteenth Century*, London, 1971.

Boime, 1980
Boime, Albert, *Thomas Couture and the Eclectic Vision*, London, 1980.

Boime, 2004
Boime, Albert, *Art in an Age of Counter-revolution, 1815–1848*, Chicago, 2004.

de Bona, 1900?
de Bona, Félix, [Blanche Besserve], *Une Famille de peintres, Horace Vernet et ses ancêtres*, Lille, 1900?

Bonafoux, 1986
Bonafoux, Pascal, *The Impressionists: Portraits and Confidences*, New York, 1986.

Bonafoux, 1994
Bonafoux, Pascal, *Bazille: Les Plaisirs et les jours*, Paris, 1994.

Bonnet, 1957
Bonnet, Paul, "Seurat et le néoimpression-nisme," *Le Crocodile* (Lyon), November–December 1957, pp. 6–22.

Bonnici, 1989
Bonnici, Claude-Jeanne, *Paul Guigou*, Aix-en-Provence, 1989.

Bortolatto, 1972
Bortolatto, Luigina Rossi, *L'Opera completa di Claude Monet*, Milan, 1972.

Boucher, 1979
Boucher, M. C., *Catalogue des dessins et peintures de Puvis de Chavannes*. [Exh. cat. Petit Palais, Paris.] Paris, 1979.

Bourgeois, 1928
Bourgeois, Stephan, *The Adolph Lewisohn Collection of Modern French Paintings and Sculptures, With an Essay on French Painting during the Nineteenth Century and Notes on Each Artist's Life and Works*, New York, 1928.

Boyer, 1978
Boyer, Patricia Eckert, ed., *The Nabis and the Parisian Avant-Garde*. [Exh. cat. Jane Voorhees Zimmerli Art Museum, Rutgers University, New Brunswick.] New Brunswick, N.J., 1978.

Boyle-Turner, 1988
Boyle-Turner, Caroline, *Paul Serusier, la technique, l'oeuvre*, Lausanne, 1988.

Brame and Lorenceau, 1991
Brame and Lorenceau, *Anquetin: La Passion d'être peintre*, Paris, 1991.

Bransten, 1944
Bransten, Ellen H., "The Significance of the Clown in Paintings by Daumier, Picasso and Rouault," *Pacific Art Review* 3 (1944), pp. 21–39.

Bredius, 1936
Bredius, Abraham, *The Paintings of Rembrandt*, Vienna, 1936.

Brenneman, 2001
Brenneman, David, *Monet: A View from the River*, Atlanta, 2001.

Bréon, 1988
Bréon, Emmanuel, ed., *Claude-Marie, Édouard et Guillaume Dubufe: Portraits d'un siècle d'élégance parisienne*. [Exh. cat. Délégation à l'Action Artistique de la Ville de Paris.] Paris, 1988.

Brettell, 1981
Brettell, Richard R., "Landscape by Édouard Vuillard is major addition to 19th-century French collection," *Bulletin of the Art Institute of Chicago* 75, no. 4 (October–December 1981), pp. 7–8.

Brettell, 1990
Brettell, Richard R., *Pissarro and Pontoise*, New Haven, 1990.

Brettell, 1996
Brettell, Richard R., "The River Seine: Subject and Symbol in Nineteenth-Century French Art and Literature," in *Impressionists on the Seine: A Celebration of Renoir's "Luncheon of the Boating Party,"* pp. 87–129, [Exh. cat. Phillips Collection, Washington, D.C.] Washington, D.C., 1996.

Brettell, 2002
Brettell, Richard R., et al., *Nineteenth- and Twentieth-Century European Drawings in the Robert Lehman Collection*, New York, 2002.

Brettell and Fonsmark, 2005
Brettell, Richard R., and Anne-Birgitte Fonsmark, *Gauguin and Impressionism*. [Exh. cat. Kimbell Art Museum, Fort Worth; Ordrupgaard, Copenhagen.], New Haven, 2005.

Brian, 1940
Brian, Doris, "Paris and London: Past Prospects," *Art News* 39, no. 5 (2 November 1940), pp. 6–7, 16.

Bricon, 1900
Bricon, Étienne, *Psychologie d'art. Les Maîtres de la fin du XIXe siècle*, Paris, 1900.

Brombert, 1996
Brombert, Beth Archer, *Édouard Manet, Rebel in a Frock Coat*, Chicago, 1996.

Brommer, 1981
Brommer, Gerald F., *Discovering Art History*, Worcester, Mass., 1981 (2nd ed., 1988).

Bryant, 1915
Bryant, L. M., *What Pictures to See in America*, New York, 1915.

Caby, 1968
Caby, Robert, "Le Joueur de guitare," *Bulletin de la Société d'études pour la connaissance d'Édouard Manet*, no. 3 (September 1968), pp. 5–7.

Cachin et al., 1983
Cachin, Françoise, et al., *Manet.* [Exh. cat. Galeries nationales du Grand Palais, Paris; Metropolitan Museum of Art, New York.] New York, 1983.

Cachin, et al., 1996
Cachin, Françoise, et al., *Cézanne.* [Exh. cat. Galeries nationales du Grand Palais, Paris; Tate Gallery, London; Museum of Art, Philadelphia.] New York, 1996.

Cachin, 2000
Cachin, Françoise, *Signac, catalogue raisonné de l'oeuvre peint*, Paris, 2000.

Cahen, 1900
Cahen, Gustave, *Eugène Boudin, sa vie et son oeuvre*, Paris, 1900.

Callen, 1978
Callen, Anthea, *Renoir*, London, 1978.

Callen, 2000
Callen, Anthea, *The Art of Impressionism: Painting Technique and the Making of Modernity*, New Haven, 2000.

Cariou, 1995
Cariou, André, *Les Peintres de Pont-Aven*, Rennes, 1995.

Carrà, 1967
Carrà, Massimo, "Gauguin e il gruppo di Pont-Aven," *L'arte moderna* 1, no. 6 (1967), pp. 201–240.

Cassou, 1953
Cassou, Jean, *Les Impressionnistes et leur époque*, Paris, 1953.

Castagnary, 1864
Castagnary, J.-A., *Les Libres propos*, Paris, 1864

Castagnary, 1882
Castagnary, J.-A., "Expositions des oeuvres de Gustave Courbet," in *Modern Art in Paris: Exhibitions of Realist Art*, ed. Theodore Reff, New York, 1981.

Ceán-Bermúdez, 1800
Ceán-Bermúdez, J. A., *Diccionario historico de los mas illustres profesores de las bellas artes en España*, Madrid, 1800.

Cézanne, 1912
Cézanne, Paul, *Paul Cézanne-Mappe. Fünfzehn Autotypen*, Munich, 1912.

Cézanne, 1937
Cézanne, Paul, *Cézanne*, Vienna, 1937.

Champa, 1973
Champa, Kermit S., *Studies in Early Impressionism*, New Haven, 1973.

Chamson, 1949
Chamson, André, *Renoir*, Lausanne, 1949.

Charensol, 1928
Charensol, Georges, "Les Expositions," *L'Art vivant*, 1 March 1928, pp. 188–190.

Chastel, 1946
Chastel, André, *Vuillard, 1868–1940*, Paris, 1946.

Chastel, 1954
Chastel, André, "Vuillard," *Art News Annual* 23 (1954), pp. 26–57, 180, 182, 184.

Chastel and Minervino, 1972
Chastel, André, and Fiorella Minervino, *L'Opera completa di Seurat*, Milan, 1972.

Chavance, 1926
Chavance, René, "Claude Monet," *Le Figaro artistique* [4?], no. 133 (16 December 1926), pp. 147–149.

Chennevières, 1885
Chennevières, Philippe de, *Les Décorations du Panthéon*, Paris, 1885.

Chennevières, 1979
Chennevières, Philippe de, *Souvenirs d'un directeur des beaux-arts*, Paris, 1979.

Chevalier, D., 1991
Chevalier, Denys, *Picasso: The Blue and Rose Periods*, New York, 1991.

Chevalier, L., 1973
Chevalier, Louis, *Laboring Classes and Dangerous Classes In Paris During the First Half of the Nineteenth Century*, Trans. Frank Jellinek, New York, 1973.

Chiego, 1974
Chiego, William Joseph, "The Influence of Carle and Horace Vernet on the Art of Théodore Géricault," Ph.D. dissertation, Case Western Reserve University, 1974.

Christensen, 1993
Christensen, Carol, "The Painting Materials and Technique of Paul Gauguin," *Conservation Research*, Studies in the History of Art, Monograph 41, Series II, National Gallery of Art, Washington, D.C., 1993.

Chu, 1992
Chu, Petra Ten-Doesschate, *Letters of Gustave Courbet*, Chicago, 1992.

Chu, 1993
Chu, Petra Ten-Doesschate, "Scatology and the Realist Aesthetic," *Art Journal* 52, no. 3 (Fall 1993), pp. 41–46.

Clairet, Montalant, and Rouart, 1997
Clairet, Alain, Delphine Montalant, and Yves Rouart, *Berthe Morisot, 1841–1895: Catalogue raisonné de l'oeuvre peint*, Montolivet, 1997.

Clark, 1973a
Clark, T. J., *Image of the People: Gustave Courbet and the 1848 Revolution*, London, 1973.

Clark, 1973b
Clark, T. J., *The Absolute Bourgeois: Artists and Politics in France, 1848–1851*, London, 1973.

Clarke, 1991
Clarke, Michael, *Corot and the Art of Landscape*, London, 1991.

Cleveland, 1982
Cleveland Museum of Art, *European Paintings of the 16th, 17th, and 18th Centuries: The Cleveland Museum of Art Catalogue of Paintings, Part Three*, Cleveland, 1982.

Cogeval, 1993
Cogeval, Guy, *Vuillard. Le Temps détourné*, Paris, 1993.

COGEVAL, 2003
Cogeval, Guy, et al., *Édouard Vuillard.* [Exh. cat. National Gallery of Art, Washington, D.C.; Museum of Fine Arts, Montreal; Galeries nationales du Grand Palais, Paris; Royal Academy of Arts, London.] New Haven, 2003.

COGNIAT, 1939
Cogniat, Raymond, *Cézanne,* Paris, 1939.

COGNIAT, 1974
Cogniat, Raymond, *Pissarro,* Paris, 1974.

LE CONSTITUTIONNEL, 1841
"Salon de 1841," *Le Constitutionnel,* 6 May 1841.

CONISBEE AND COUTAGNE, 2006
Conisbee, Philip, and Denis Coutagne, *Cézanne in Provence.* [Exh. cat. National Gallery of Art, Washington, D.C.; Musée Granet, Aix-en-Provence.] New Haven, 2006.

COOPER, 1946
Cooper, Douglas, *Georges Seurat: Une Baignade à Asnières,* London, 1946.

COPLANS, 1975
Coplans, John, "Diary of a Disaster," *Artforum* 13, no. 6 (February 1975) pp. 28–45.

COQUIOT, 1923
Coquiot, Gustave, *Vincent van Gogh,* Paris, 1923.

CORCORAN, 1903
Corcoran Gallery of Art, *Catalogue of the Corcoran Gallery of Art,* Washington, D.C., 1903.

CORCORAN, 1915
Corcoran Gallery of Art, *Catalogue of the Paintings in the Corcoran Gallery of Art,* Washington, D.C., 1915.

CORCORAN, 1939
Corcoran Gallery of Art, *Illustrated Handbook of Paintings, Sculpture and Other Art Objects,* Washington, D.C., 1939.

CORNINI, 1974
Cornini, A., *Egon Schiele's Portraits,* Berkeley, 1974.

COURAL, 1985
Coural, Natalie, "Recherches sur la collection Mortarieu au Musée Ingres à Montauban," *Bulletin du Musée Ingres,* nos. 55–56, (December 1985), pp. 13–38.

COURTHION, 1948
Courthion, Pierre, *Courbet raconté par lui-même et par ses amis,* Geneva, 1948.

COURTHION, 1953
Courthion, Pierre, *Manet raconté par lui-même et par ses amis,* Lausanne, 1953.

COURTHION, 1968
Courthion, Pierre, *Seurat,* New York, 1968.

COVEY, 1991
Covey, Herbert C., *Images of Older People in Western Art and Society,* New York, 1991.

CROMBIE, 1968
Crombie, Theodore, "London Galleries: Autumn Assortment," *Apollo* 88, no. 81 (November 1968), pp. 378–384.

CROSMAN, 1988
Crosman, C., *The Artist's Mother: Portraits and Homages,* New York, 1988.

CROUTIER, 1989
Croutier, Alev Lytle, *Harem: The World behind the Veil,* New York, 1989.

CZYMMEK, 2004
Czymmek, Götz, "Jongkind et les impressionnistes. Un précurseur inclassable," *Dossier de l'art,* no. 108 (June 2004), pp. 56–65.

DANIELS, 1977
Daniels, Jeffrey, "Old Masters on the Move," *Art and Artists* 11, no. 12 (March 1977), pp. 16–19.

DARRAGON, 1991
Darragon, Éric, *Manet,* Paris, 1991.

DAUBERVILLE AND DAUBERVILLE, 1965
Dauberville, Jean, and Henry Dauberville, *Bonnard: Catalogue raisonné de l'oeuvre peint, 1888–1905,* 4 vols., Paris, 1965.

DAULTE, 1950
Daulte, François, "Le Peinture de portrait," *Arts,* no. 266 (9 June 1950), pp. 1, 8.

DAULTE, 1952
Daulte, François, *Frédéric Bazille et son temps,* Geneva, 1952.

DAULTE, 1959
Daulte, François, *Alfred Sisley: Catalogue raisonné de l'oeuvre peint,* Lausanne, 1959.

DAULTE, 1960
Daulte, François, "Un provençal pur: Paul Guigou," *Connaissance des Arts,* no. 98 (April 1960), pp. 70–77.

DAULTE, 1967
Daulte, François, "Un Siècle d'art français dans les collections suisses, à l'Orangerie des Tuileries," *La Revue du Louvre et des musées de France* 17, no. 3 (1967), pp. 143–150.

DAULTE, 1970
Daulte, François, "Bazille: Son Oeuvre s'achève en 1870," *Connaissance des Arts,* no. 226 (December 1970), pp. 86–91.

DAULTE, 1971
Daulte, François, *Auguste Renoir: Catalogue raisonné de l'oeuvre peint,* Lausanne, 1971.

DAULTE, 1992
Daulte, François, *Frédéric Bazille et les débuts de l'impressionisme: Catalogue raisonné de l'oeuvre de peint,* Paris, 1992.

DAYOT, 1898
Dayot, Armand, *Les Vernet,* Paris, 1898.

DEGAND AND ROUART, 1958
Degand, Léon, and Denis Rouart, *Claude Monet,* Geneva, 1958.

DELABORDE, 1870
Delaborde, Henri, *Ingres. Sa Vie, ses travaux, sa doctrine,* Paris, 1870.

DELAGE, 1982
Delage, Roger, *Iconographie musicale Chabrier,* Paris, 1982.

DELANNOY, 1996
Delannoy, Agnès, *Symbolistes et Nabis, Maurice Denis et son temps,* Paris, 1996.

DELPLATO, 2002
DelPlato, Joan, *Multiple Wives, Multiple Pleasures: Representing the Harem, 1800–1875,* Cranbury, N.J., 2002.

DERI, 1919
Deri, Max, *Die Malerei im XIX. Jahrhundert: entwicklungsgeschichtliche Darstellung auf psychologisher Grundlage,* 2 vols., Berlin, 1919 (other eds., Berlin, 1920, 1923).

DESPARMET FITZ-GERALD, 1928–1950
Desparmet Fitz-Gerald, Xavière, *L'Oeuvre peint de Goya,* 2 vols., Paris, 1928–1950.

DESTREMAU, 1989
Destremau, Frédéric, *Les Années d'avant-garde de Louis Anquetin, "Apprentissage et Arrimage de la Modernité",* Maîtrise d'histoire de l'art, Université de Paris–I–Panthéon Sorbonne, Institut d'art et d'archéologie de Paris, Paris, 1989.

DEWHURST, 1904
Dewhurst, Wynford, *Impressionist Painting: Its Genesis and Development,* London, 1904.

Didier Aaron, 1987
Didier Aaron, Inc., *A Timeless Heritage: Masterworks of Painting for Today's Collector.* [Exh. cat. Didier Aaron, Inc., New York.] New York, 1987.

Distel, 1985
Distel, Anne, "Renoir's Collectors: The Pâtissier, the Priest and the Prince," in *Renoir*, pp. 19–29 [Exh. cat. Hayward Gallery, London, Galeries nationales du Grand Palais, Paris; Museum of Fine Arts, Boston.] London, 1985.

Distel, 1990
Distel, Anne, *Impressionism: The First Collectors*, New York, 1990.

Distel, 1991
Distel, Anne, *Seurat*, Chêne, 1991.

Doblado, 1822
Don Leucadio Doblado [Joseph Blanco White], *Letters from Spain*, London, 1822.

Dolan, 1990
Dolan, Thérèse, "Frédéric Bazille and the Goncourt Brothers' *Manette Salomon*," *Gazette des beaux-arts* 115, no. 1453 (February 1990), pp. 99–103.

Dorival, 1948
Dorival, Bernard, *Cézanne*, New York, 1948.

Dorn, 1990
Dorn, Roland, *Décoration Vincent van Goghs Werkreihe für das Gelbe Haus in Arles*, Zurich, 1990.

Dorn, Hille, and Kronjäger, 1994
Dorn, Roland, Karoline Hille, and Jochen Kronjäger, eds., *Stiftung und Sammlung Sally Falk*, Mannheim, 1994.

Dorn, 2000
Dorn, Roland, et al., *Van Gogh Face to Face: The Portraits.* [Exh. cat. Institute of Arts, Detroit; Museum of Fine Arts, Boston; Museum of Art, Philadelphia.] Detroit, 2000.

Dorra, 1994
Dorra, Henri, ed., *Symbolist Art Theories*, Berkeley, 1994.

Dortu, 1971
Dortu, M. G., *Toulouse-Lautrec et son oeuvre*, 6 vols., New York, 1971.

Drucker, 1944
Drucker, Michel, *Renoir*, Paris, 1944 (another ed., Paris, 1955).

Druick and Zegers, 2001
Druick, Douglas, and Peter Zegers, *Van Gogh and Gauguin: The Studio of the South.* [Exh. cat. Art Institute of Chicago; Rijksmuseum Vincent van Gogh, Amsterdam.] Chicago, 2001.

Dubosc, 1910
Dubosc, Georges, "Claude Monet au Havre," *Journal de Rouen*, 23 December 1910, p. 4.

Dubuisson, 1924
Dubuisson, A., *Richard Parkes Bonington: His Life and Work*, London, 1924.

Düchting, 2000
Düchting, Hajo, *Georges Seurat, 1859–1891: The Master of Pointillism*, Cologne, 2000.

Dugdale, 1965
Dugdale, James, "Vuillard the Decorator—I. First Phase, the 1890s," *Apollo* 81, no. 36 (February 1965), pp. 94–101.

Dujardin, 1888
Édouard Dujardin, "Aux XX et au Indépendants–Le cloisonisme," *La Revue Indépendante* 6 (March 1888), pp. 487–492.

Dumas and Cogeval, 1990
Dumas, Ann, and Guy Cogeval, *Vuillard.* [Exh. cat. Musée des Beaux-Arts, Lyon; Fondation Caixa de Pensions, Barcelona; Musée des Beaux-Arts, Nantes.] Paris, 1990.

Dumas, 1997
Dumas, Ann, *The Private Collection of Edgar Degas.* [Exh. cat. Metropolitan Museum of Art, New York.] New York, 1997.

Duret, 1902
Duret, Théodore, *Histoire d'Édouard Manet et son oeuvre. Avec un catalogue des peintures et des pastels*, Paris, 1902.

Duret, 1906
Duret, Théodore, *Histoire des peintres impressionnistes*, Paris, 1906.

Duret, 1910
Duret, Théodore, *Manet and the French Impressionists*, trans. J. E. Crawford Flitch, London, 1910.

Duret, 1923
Duret, Théodore, *Die Impressionisten*, Berlin, 1923.

Duret, 1926
Duret, Théodore, *Histoire d'Édouard Manet et son oeuvre. Avec un catalogue des peintures et des pastels*, 4th ed., Paris, 1926.

Duret, 1939
Duret, Théodore, *Histoire des peintres impressionnistes*, 4th ed., Paris, 1939.

Duret-Robert, 1978
Duret-Robert, François, "The Fluctuating Dollar Prices for Impressionist Paintings (1860s–1960s)," in *Impressionism in Perspective*, ed. Barbara Ehrlich White, pp. 97–104, Englewood Cliffs, N.J., 1978.

Dyrness, 2001
Dyrness, William, *Visual Faith: Art, Theology, and Worship in Dialogue*, Grand Rapids, Mich., 2001.

Easton, 1989
Easton, Elizabeth W., *The Intimate Interiors of Edouard Vuillard*, Washington, D.C., 1989.

Ecker, 1991
Ecker, Jürgen, *Anselm Feuerbach, Leben und Werk: Kritischer Katalog der Gemälde, Ölskizzen und Ölstudien*, Munich, 1991.

Édouard-Joseph, 1934
Édouard-Joseph, René, *Dictionnaire biographique des artistes contemporaines, 1910–1930*, 3 vols., Paris, 1934.

Eisenman, 1997
Eisenman, Stephen F., *Gauguin's Skirt*, London, 1997.

Eisenman, 2002
Eisenman, Stephen F., *Nineteenth Century Art: A Critical History*, London, 2002.

Eisenman, 2003
Eisenman, Stephen F. "Monet and the Autonomy of Painting," in *Monet: Atti del convegno*, ed. Marco Goldin, et al., pp. 139–144, Conegliano, 2003.

Eitner, 1959
Eitner, Lorenz, "The Sale of Gericault's Studio in 1824," *Gazette des beaux-arts* 53, no. 1081 (February 1959), pp. 115–126.

Eitner, 1971
Eitner, Lorenz, *Géricault* [exh. cat. Los Angeles County Museum of Art] Los Angeles, 1971.

Eitner, 2000
Eitner, Lorenz, *The Collections of the National Gallery of Art Systematic Catalogue. French Paintings of the Nineteenth Century. Part I: Before Impressionism*, Washington, D.C., 2000.

Elgar, 1958
Elgar, F., *Van Gogh*, New York, 1958.

Escholier, 1923
Escholier, Raymond, *Daumier, peintre et lithographe*, Paris, 1923.

Escholier, 1934
Escholier, Raymond, *Daumier*, Paris, 1934.

"Exposición Corot," 1971
"Noticias de Arte: Exposición Corot," *Goya* 103 (July–August 1971), pp. 59–63.

Exum, 1986
Exum, J. Cheryl, "The Mothers of Israel: The Patriarchal Narratives from a Feminist Perspective," *Bible Review* 2, no. 1 (Spring 1986), pp. 60–67.

Fagles, 1978
Fagles, R., *I, Vincent: Poems from the Pictures of Van Gogh*, Princeton, 1978.

Faille, 1927
Faille, J.-B. de la, *L'Époque française de van Gogh*, Paris, 1927.

Faille, 1928
Faille, J.-B. de la, *L'Oeuvre de Vincent van Gogh: Catalogue raisonné*, 4 vols., Paris, 1928.

Faille, 1939
Faille, J.-B. de la, *Vincent van Gogh*, Paris, 1939.

Faille, 1970
Faille, J.-B. de la, *The Works of Vincent van Gogh: His Paintings and Drawings*, Amsterdam, 1970.

Fanica, 1995
Fanica, Pierre-Olivier, *Charles Jacque, 1813–1894: Graveur original et peintre animalier*, Montigny-sur-Loing, 1995.

Fantin-Latour, 1911
Fantin-Latour, Victoria Dubourg, *Catalogue de l'oeuvre complet (1849–1904) de Fantin-Latour*, Paris, 1911 (repr. New York, 1969).

Farr, 1958
Farr, Dennis, *William Etty*, London, 1958.

Faunce, 1993
Faunce, Sarah, *Gustave Courbet*, New York, 1993.

Faunce and Nochlin, 1988
Faunce, Sarah, and Linda Nochlin, *Courbet Reconsidered*. [Exh. cat. Brooklyn Museum.] New Haven, 1988.

Faure, 1936
Faure, Élie, *Corot*, Paris, 1936.

Faxon, 1982
Faxon, Alicia Craig, *Jean-Louis Forain: A Catalogue Raisonné of the Prints*, New York, 1982.

Feilchenfeldt, 1988
Feilchenfeldt, Walter, *Vincent van Gogh and Paul Cassirer, Berlin: The Reception of Van Gogh in Germany from 1901–1914*, Zwolle, 1988.

Feilchenfeldt, 2006
Feilchenfeldt, Walter, *By Appointment Only: Cézanne, Van Gogh, and Some Secrets of Art Dealing*, London, 2006.

Fels, F., 1925
Fels, Florent, *Claude Monet*, Paris, 1925.

Fels, M., 1929
Fels, Marthe de, *La Vie de Claude Monet*, Paris, 1929.

Fère, 1868
Fère, Guyot de, "Ducis," *Nouvelle Biographie générale*, Paris, 1868, vol. 15.

Fernier, 1977
Fernier, Robert, *La Vie et l'oeuvre de Gustave Courbet: Catalogue raisonné, peintures, 1819–1865*, 2 vols., Lausanne, 1977.

Fleischmann, 1938
Fleischmann, Benno, *Honoré Daumier*, Vienna, 1938.

Florisoone, 1947
Florisoone, Michel, *Manet*, Monaco, 1947.

Fontainas, 1923
Fontainas, André, *La Peinture de Daumier*, Paris, 1923.

Fontainas, 1927
Fontainas, André, *Daumier*, Paris, 1927.

Forgione, 2005
Forgione, Nancy, "Everyday Life in Motion: The Art of Walking in Late-Nineteenth-Century Paris," *Art Bulletin* 87, no. 4 (December 2005), pp. 664–687.

Formes, 1931
Formes, no. 20 (December 1931).

Fosca, 1928
Fosca, François, "Corot chez P. Rosenberg: Paysages d'Italie et figures," *L'Amour de l'art* 8, no. 5 (May 1928), pp. 161–173.

Fosca, 1958
Fosca, François, *Corot: Sa Vie et son oeuvre*, Brussels, 1958.

Foucart, 1968
Foucart, Jacques, et al., *Ingres in Italia*. [Exh. cat. Villa Medici, Rome.] Rome, 1968.

Fouchet, 1974
Fouchet, Max-Pol, *Les Nus de Renoir*, Lausanne, 1974.

Frèches-Thory and Terrasse, 1991
Frèches-Thory, Claire, and Antoine Terrasse, *The Nabis: Bonnard, Vuillard, and Their Circle*, trans. Mary Pardoe, New York, 1991 (originally published as *Les Nabis*, Paris, 1990).

Frèches-Thory and Perucchi-Petri, 1993
Frèches-Thory, Claire, and Ursula Perucchi-Petri, *Nabis, 1888–1900*. [Exh. cat. Galeries nationales du Grand Palais, Paris; Kunsthaus, Zürich.] Paris, 1993.

Fried, 1990
Fried, Michael, *Courbet's Realism*, Chicago, 1990.

Friedländer, 1922
Friedländer, Max J., "Über Paul Cézanne," *Die Kunst für Alle* 37 (February 1922), pp. 137–145.

Fry, 1929
Fry, Roger, "Cézannes Udvikling," *Samleren* 6, no. 9 (1929), pp. 101–103, 113–119, 129–140.

Fuchs, 1927
Fuchs, Eduard, *Der Maler Daumier*, Munich, 1927.

Fuchs, 1930
Fuchs, Eduard, *Der Maler Daumier*, Munich, 1930.

Gachet, 1956
Gachet, Paul, *Le Docteur Gachet et Murer: Deux Amis des impressionnistes*, Paris, 1956.

Galeries nationales de Grand Palais, 1974
Galeries nationales de Grand Palais, *De David à Delacroix: La Peinture française de 1774 à 1830*. [Exh. cat. Grand Palais, Paris; Institute of Arts, Detroit; Metropolitan Museum of Art, New York.] Paris, 1974.

Galeries nationales du Petit Palais, 1967
Galeries nationales du Petit Palais, *Ingres.* [Exh. cat. Petit Palais, Paris.] Paris, 1967.

Gassier, 1971
Gassier, Pierre, with Juliet Wilson and François Lachenal, *The Life and Complete Work of Francisco Goya with a Catalogue Raisonné of the Paintings, Drawings and Engravings*, New York, 1971 (2nd ed., New York, 1981).

Gassier, 1973
Gassier, Pierre, *Francisco Goya Drawings: The Complete Albums*, New York, 1973.

Gaunt and Roe, 1943
Gaunt, William, and F. Gordon Roe, *Etty and the Nude*, Leigh-on-Sea, 1943.

Gaunt, 1952
Gaunt, William, *Renoir*, London, 1952.

Gaunt, 1982
Gaunt, William, *Renoir*, Oxford, 1982.

Gaussen, 2002
Gaussen, Frédéric, *Visites d'ateliers*, Paris, 2002.

Gauthier, 1950
Gauthier, Maximilien, *Daumier*, Paris, 1950.

Gautier, 1861
Gautier, Théophile, *Abcédaire du Salon de 1861*, Paris, 1861.

Gazette des beaux-arts, 1912
"Un Million pour un Rousseau" *Gazette des beaux-arts*, (18 January 1912).

Gazette des beaux-arts, 1938
"La Peinture française du XIX siècle en Suisse," *Gazette des beaux-arts*, 32 (1938).

Gedo, 1989
Gedo, John E., *Portraits of the Artist*, Hillsdale, N.J., 1989.

Geffroy, 1901
Geffroy, Gustave, *Daumier*, 1901.

Geffroy, 1922
Geffroy, Gustave, *Claude Monet, sa vie, son temps, son oeuvre*, Paris, 1922.

George, 1931
George, Waldemar, "The Twilight of a God," *Apollo* 14, no. 80 (August 1931), pp. 75–82.

George, 1939
George, Waldemar, "Guigou," *Beaux-Arts*, no. 336 (9 June 1939), p. 5.

Georges-Michel, 1945
Georges-Michel, Michel, *Les Grandes Époques de la peinture "moderne" de Delacroix à nos jours*, Paris, 1945.

Gimpel, 1927
Gimpel, René, "At Giverny with Claude Monet," trans. Alice M. Sharkey, *Art in America* 15, no. 4 (June 1927), pp. 168–174.

Gimpel, 1963
Gimpel, René, *Journal d'un collectionneur, marchand de tableaux*, Paris, 1963.

Glynn, 1973
Glynn, Eugene, "To Express . . . a Serious Sorrow," *The Print Collector's Newsletter* 4, no. 4 (September–October 1973), pp. 88–90.

van Gogh, n.d.
Vincent van Gogh, 40 photocollographies d'après ses tableaux et dessins, Amsterdam, n.d.

van Gogh, 1936
Letters to an Artist from Vincent van Gogh to Anton Ridder van Rappard, trans. R. van Mussel, New York, 1936.

van Gogh, 1958
van Gogh, Vincent, *The Complete Letters of Vincent van Gogh*, 3 vols., Greenwich, Conn., 1958.

Goldin, 2001
Goldin, Marco, *Monet: I Luoghi della pittura*, Conegliano, 2001.

Goldin, 2002
Goldin, Marco, *L'Impressionismo e l'età di Van Gogh*, Treviso, Casa dei Carreresi, 2002.

Goldwater, 1958
Goldwater, Robert, "Renoir at Wildenstein," *Art in America* 46, no. 1 (Spring 1958), pp. 60–62.

Gombrich, 1962
Gombrich, Ernst Hans, *Art and Illusion: A Study in the Psychology of Pictorial Representation*, London, 1962.

de Goncourt, 1885
de Goncourt, Edmond, *Journal, Mémoires*, 17 June 1885, in Hefting, 1975.

Gordon and Forge, 1983
Gordon, Robert, and Andrew Forge, *Monet*, New York, 1983.

Goteborg, 1968
Goteborg, Konstmuseum, *Emile Bernard: Malningar, akvareller, teckningar, grafik*, Goteborg, 1968.

Goulinat, 1925
Goulinat, J.-G., "Technique picturale: Le Métier des impressionnistes," *L'Art vivant*, 1 February 1925, pp. 22–23.

Gowing, 1956
Gowing, Lawrence, "Notes on the Development of Cézanne," *Burlington Magazine*, 98, no. 639 (June 1956), pp. 185–192.

Gowing, 1988
Gowing, Lawrence, *Cézanne: The Early Years, 1859–1872*, New York, 1988.

Graber, 1943
Graber, Hans, *Camille Pissarro, Alfred Sisley, Claude Monet nach eigenen und fremden Zeugnissen*, Basel, 1943.

Grappe, 1909
Grappe, Georges, *Claude Monet*, Paris, 1909.

Grappe, 1941
Grappe, Georges, *Monet*, Paris, 1941.

Green, 1990
Green, Nicholas, *The Spectacle of Nature: Landscape and Bourgeois Culture in Nineteenth-century France*, New York, 1990.

Grenier, 1990
Grenier, Catherine, *Seurat: Catalogo completo dei dipinti*, Florence, 1990.

Groom, 1990
Groom, Gloria, "Landscape as Decoration: Édouard Vuillard's Île-de-France Paintings for Adam Natanson," *Museum Studies* 16, no. 2 (1990), pp. 146–165.

Groom, 1993
Groom, Gloria, *Édouard Vuillard Painter-Decorator: Patrons and Projects, 1892–1912*, New Haven, 1993.

Groom, 1995
Groom, Gloria, "Acquisitions in Focus: The Art Institute of Chicago," *Apollo* 142, no. 406 (December 1995), pp. 59–61.

Groom, 2001
Groom, Gloria, *Beyond the Easel: Decorative Painting by Bonnard, Vuillard, Denis, and Roussel, 1890–1930*. [Exh. cat. Art Institute of Chicago; Metropolitan Museum of Art, New York.] Chicago, 2001.

Grossvogel, 2000
Grossvogel, Jill-Elyse, *Claude-Émile Schuffenecker, Catalogue Raisonné, Vol. 1*, San Francisco, 2000.

Grunchec, 1976
Grunchec, Philippe, "L'Inventaire posthume de Théodore Géricault (1791–1824)," *Bulletin de la Société de l'histoire de l'art français*, 1976, pp. 395–420.

Grunchec, 1982
Grunchec, Philippe, *Géricault: Dessins et acquarelles de chevaux*, Lausanne, 1982 (English ed., New York, 1984).

Grunchec and Thuillier, 1978
Grunchec, Philippe, and Jacques Thuillier, *L'Opera completa di Géricault*, Milan, 1978 (French ed., Paris, 1978).

Gudiol, 1971
Gudiol, José, *Goya, 1746–1828: Biography, Analytical Study and Catalogue of His Paintings*, trans. Kenneth Lyons, 4 vols., New York, 1971.

Guérif, 1943
Guérif, J., *À la recherche d'une esthétique protestante: Frédéric Bazille*, Aix-en-Provence, 1943.

Guffey, 2001
Guffey, Elizabeth E., *Drawing an Elusive Line: The Art of Pierre-Paul Prud'hon*, Cranbury, N.J., 2001.

Guicheteau, 1976
Guicheteau, Marcel, *Paul Sérusier*, Paris, 1976.

Guiffrey, 1924
Guiffrey, Jean, *L'Oeuvre de P.-P. Prud'hon*, Paris, 1924.

Guillin, 1990
Guillin, Anne, *Les Peintres et les Hauts-de-Seine*, Paris, 1990.

Hamel, 1910
Hamel, M., "Salon d'Automne," *Les Arts: revue mensuelle des musées, collections, expositions* 9, no. 107 (November 1910), pp. 4–18.

Hamilton, 1992
Hamilton, Vivien, *Boudin at Trouville*, Glasgow, 1992.

Hannema, 1955
Hannema, D., *Catalogue of the H. E. ten Cate Collection*, trans. G. Talma-Schilthuis and David Fletcher, 2 vols., Rotterdam, 1955.

Hanson, 1968
Hanson, Anne Coffin, "Manet's Subject Matter and a Source of Popular Imagery," *Museum Studies* 3 (1968), pp. 63–80.

Hanson, 1979
Hanson, Anne Coffin, *Manet and the Modern Tradition*, New Haven, 1979.

Harper, 1981
Harper, Paula Hays, *Daumier's Clowns: Les Saltimbanques et Les Parades; New Biographical and Political Functions for a Nineteenth Century Myth*, New York, 1981.

Harris and Nochlin, 1976
Harris, Anne Sutherland, and Linda Nochlin, *Women Artists: 1550–1950*. [Exh. cat. County Museum of Art, Los Angeles; University Art Museum, the University of Texas, Austin; Museum of Art, Carnegie Institute, Pittsburgh; Brooklyn Museum.] New York, 1976.

de Hauke, 1961
de Hauke, Cesar, *Seurat et son oeuvre*, Paris, 1961.

Havelaar, 1915
Havelaar, Just, "Vincent van Gogh," *Moderne Kunstwerken* 6 (1915).

Hazama, 1933
Hazama, I., *Courbet*, part 7, *Nouvelles Éditions selectionnées des grands peintres occidentaux*, Tokyo, 1933.

Hefting, 1975
Hefting, Victorine, *Jongkind: Sa Vie, son oeuvre, son époque*, Paris, 1975.

Held, 1980
Held, Julius S., *The Oil Sketches of Peter Paul Rubens: A Critical Catalogue*, 2 vols., Princeton, 1980.

Hellebranth, 1976
Hellebranth, Robert, *Charles-François Daubigny, 1817–1878*, Morges, 1976.

Herbert, 1959
Herbert, Robert L., "Seurat and Puvis de Chavannes," *Yale University Art Gallery Bulletin*, 25, no. 2 (October 1959), pp. 22–29.

Herbert, 1988
Herbert, Robert L., *Impressionism: Art, Leisure, and Parisian Society*, New Haven, 1988.

Herbert, 1991
Herbert, Robert L., et al., *Georges Seurat, 1859–1891*. [Exh. cat. Galeries nationales du Grand Palais, Paris; Metropolitan Museum of Art, New York.] New York, 1991.

Herding, 1991
Herding, *Courbet: To Venture Independence*, New Haven, 1991.

Hess, T., 1953
Hess, Thomas B., "Ingres," *Art News Annual*, 22 (1953), pp. 146–172, 176, 178, 180–182.

Hess, W., 1957
Hess, Walter, "Zum Bild des Menschen in der Kunst Cézannes," *Die Kunst und das schöne Heim, Monatsschrift für Malerei, Plastik, Graphik, Architektur und Wohnkultur* 55 (June 1957), pp. 335–339.

van Heugten, 1995
van Heugten, Sjraar, "Radiographic Images of Vincent van Gogh's Paintings in the Collection of the Van Gogh Museum," *Van Gogh Museum Journal*, 1995, pp. 62–85.

Hiatt, 1896
Hiatt, Charles, *Picture Posters: A Short History of the Illustrated Placard*, London, 1896.

Higonnet, 1992
Higonnet, Anne, *Berthe Morisot's Images of Women*, London, 1992.

Hodge, 2002
Hodge, Susie, *Claude Monet*, London, 2002.

Homburg, 1992
Homburg, Cornelia, "Affirming Modernity: van Gogh's *Arlésienne*," *Simiolus* 21, no. 3 (1992), pp. 127–138.

Homburg, 1996
Homburg, Cornelia, *The Copy Turns Original: Vincent van Gogh and a New Approach to Traditional Art Practice*, Amsterdam, 1996.

Horticq, 1928
Horticq, Louis, *Ingres, l'Oeuvre du maître*, Paris, 1928.

House, 1981
House, John, *Monet*, Oxford, 1981.

House, 1994
House, John, *Renoir, Master Impressionist*, Sydney, 1994.

Huguette Berès, 1990
Huguette Berès, *Au temps des Nabis*. [Exh. cat. Huguette Berès, Paris.] Paris, 1990.

Hulsker, 1970
Hulsker, Jan, *Dageboek van Van Gogh*, Amsterdam, 1970.

Hulsker, 1977
Hulsker, Jan, *Van Gogh en zijn weg*, Amsterdam, 1977 (English ed., *The Complete van Gogh: Paintings, Drawings, Sketches*, New York, 1980).

Hustin, 1893
Hustin, Arthur, *Les Artistes célèbres: Constant Troyon*, Paris, 1893.

Hutton, 1994
Hutton, J. G., *Neo-Impressionism and the Search for Solid Ground*, Baton Rouge, La., 1994.

Huyghe, 1937
Huyghe, René, ed., "Vincent van Gogh: sa vie et son oeuvre," *L'Amour de l'art*, April 1937, pp. 1–40.

Huyghe, 1969
Huyghe, René, *L'Art et le monde moderne*, 2 vols., Paris, 1969.

Isaacson, 1972
Isaacson, Joel, *Monet: Le Déjeuner sur l'herbe*, New York, 1972.

Isaacson, 1978
Isaacson, Joel, *Observation and Reflection: Claude Monet*, Oxford, 1978.

Ives, Stein, and Steiner, 1997
Ives, Colta, Susan Slyson Stein, and Julie A. Steiner, *The Private Collection of Edgar Degas: A Summary Catalogue*, New York, 1997.

Jamot and Wildenstein, 1932
Jamot, Paul, and Georges Wildenstein, *Manet*, 2 vols., Paris, 1932.

Jaworska, 1972
Jaworska, Wladyslawa, *Gauguin and the Pont-Aven School*, New York, 1972.

Jedlicka, 1947
Jedlicka, Gotthard, *Renoir*, Bern, 1947.

Jirat-Wasiutyński, 2001
Jirat-Wasiutyński, Vojtěch, "Van Gogh in the South: Antimodernism and Exoticism in the Arlesian Paintings," in *Antimodernism and Artistic Experience: Policing the Boundaries of Modernity*, ed. Lynda Jessup, pp. 177–191, Toronto, 2001.

Jirat-Wasiutyński and Newton, 2000
Jirat-Wasiutyński, Vojtěch, and H. Travers Newton Jr., *Technique and Meaning in the Paintings of Paul Gauguin*, Cambridge, 2000.

Johnson, 1979
Johnson, Ron, "Vincent van Gogh and the Vernacular: The Poet's Garden," *Arts Magazine* 53, no. 6 (February 1979), pp. 98–104.

Joly, 1966
Joly, G., "Au musée Galliéra, de Renoir à Chagall," *L'Aurore* 27 September 1966, p. 13.

Jourdain, 1948
Jourdain, Francis, *Lautrec*, Paris, 1948.

Jourdain, 1958
Jourdain, Francis, "Émile Bernard: le bon génie de Gauguin," *Connaissance des Arts*, no. 78 (August 1958), pp. 28–33.

Jouy and Jay, 1822
Jouy, Étienne de, and Antoine Jay, *Salon d'Horace Vernet, analyse historique et pittoresque des quarante-cinq tableaux*, Paris, 1822.

Joyant, 1926
Joyant, Maurice, *Henri de Toulouse-Lautrec, 1864–1901, peintre*, Paris, 1926.

Kahn, 1934
Kahn, Gustave, "Les Beaux-Arts. Exposition Camille Pissarro et ses fils," *Le Quotidien*, 3 December 1934, pp. 1–2.

Kennedy, 1987
Kennedy, Brian P., "Sir Alfred Chester Beatty and the NGI," *Irish Arts Review* 4, no. 1 (Spring 1987), pp. 41–54.

Kimbell Art Museum, 1972
Kimbell Art Museum, *Catalogue of the Collection*, Fort Worth, 1972.

Kinney, 1994
Kinney, Leila, "Fashion and Figuration in Modern Life Paintings," *Architecture, in Fashion*, Deborah Fausch et al., pp. 270–313, New York, 1994.

Klossowski, 1908
Klossowski, Erich, *Honoré Daumier*, Munich, 1908.

Klossowski, 1923
Klossowski, Erich, *Honoré Daumier*, 2nd ed., Munich, 1923.

Kostenevich, 1995
Kostenevich, Albert, *Hidden Treasures Revealed: Impressionist Masterpieces and Other Important French Paintings Preserved by the State Hermitage Museum St. Petersburg*, New York, 1995.

Kunst und Künstler, 1919
"Kunstausstellungen," *Kunst und Künstler* 17 (1919), pp. 203–204.

Kunstler, 1930
Kunstler, Charles, *Camille Pissarro*, Paris, 1930.

Lacambre, 1975
Lacambre, Jean, "Claude-Marie Dubufe," in *French Painting, 1774–1830: The Age of Revolution*, pp. 404–405. [Exh. cat. Grand Palais, Paris; Institute of Arts, Detroit; Metropolitan Museum of Art, New York.] Detroit, 1975.

Lafuente Ferrari, 1947
Lafuente Ferrari, Enrique, *Antecedentes, coincidiencias e influencias del arte de Goya*, Madrid, 1947.

Lambert, 1933
Lambert, Élie, "Manet et l'Espagne," *Gazette des beaux-arts* 9 (June 1933), pp. 369–382.

Lambinet, 2003
Musée Lambinet, *Versailles: Vie artistique, littéraire et mondaine, 1889–1939*, Paris, 2003.

Lamort de Gail, 1989
Lamort de Gail, Sylvie, *Paul Guigou: Catalogue raisonné*, 2 vols., Paris, 1989.

Lanöe-Villène, 1905
Lanöe-Villène, Georges, *Histoire de l'école française de paysage depuis Chintreuil jusqu'à 1900*, Nantes, 1905.

Lapauze, 1910
Lapauze, Henry, *Le Roman d'amour de M. Ingres*, Paris, 1910.

Lapauze, 1911
Lapauze, Henry, *Ingres, sa vie et son oeuvre (1780–1867) d'après des documents inédits*, Paris, 1911.

Laprade, 1935
Laprade, Jacques de, "Frédéric Bazille," *Beaux-Arts* 73, no. 117 (29 March 1935), pp. 1, 8.

Laprade, 1945
Laprade, Jacques de, *Georges Seurat*, Monaco, 1945.

Laprade, 1952
Laprade, Jacques de, *Seurat*, Paris, 1952.

Lassaigne, 1938
Lassaigne, Jacques, *Daumier*, trans. Eveline Byam Shaw, New York, 1938.

LASSAIGNE, 1939
Lassaigne, Jacques, *Toulouse Lautrec*, trans. Mary Chamot, Paris, 1939.

LATHOM, 1931
Lathom, Xenia, *Claude Monet*, New York, 1931.

LAVEISSIÈRE, 1997
Laveissière, Sylvain, *Pierre-Paul Prud'hon*, New York, 1997.

LECALDANO, 1977
Lecaldano, Paolo., *L'Opera pittorica completa di Van Gogh*, 2 vols., Milan, 1977.

LECOMTE, 1891
Lecomte, Georges, "Le Salon des Indépendants," *L'Art dans les deux mondes*, no. 19 (28 March 1891), p. 225.

LÉGER, 1929
Léger, Charles, *Courbet*, Paris, 1929.

LÉGER, 1930
Léger, Charles, *Claude Monet*, Paris, 1930.

LÉGER, 1948
Léger, Charles, *Courbet et son temps (lettres et documents inédits)*, Paris, 1948.

LEMOINE, 2002
Lemoine, Serge, ed., *Toward Modern Art: From Puvis de Chavannes to Matisse and Picasso*, New York, 2002.

LEMOISNE, 1946–1949
Lemoisne, Paul-André, *Degas et son oeuvre*, 4 vols., Paris, 1946–1949.

LEMONNIER, 1888
Lemonnier, Camille, *Les Peintres de la vie*, Paris, 1888.

LERMINA, 1884
J. Lermina, "Henri Rochefort," *Dictionnaire universel illustré biographique ... de la France contemporaine, etc.*, Paris, 1884.

LE ROUX, 1889
Le Roux, Hugues, "Silhouettes parisiennes: l'exposition de Claude Monet," *Gil Blas*, 11, no. 3393 (3 March 1889), pp. 1–2.

LETHÈVE, 1959
Lethève, Jacques, *Impressionnistes et symbolistes devant la presse*, Paris, 1959.

LEVINE, 1994
Levine, Steven Z., *Monet, Narcissus, and Self-Reflection: The Modernist Myth of Self*, Chicago, 1994.

VAN LINDERT AND VAN UITERT, 1990A
van Lindert, Juleke, and Evert van Uitert, *Een eigentijdse expressje*, Amsterdam, 1990.

VAN LINDERT AND VAN UITERT, 1990B
van Lindert, Juleke, and Evert van Uitert, *Vincent van Gogh en zijn portretten*, Amsterdam, 1990.

LINDON, 1958
Lindon, Raymond, "Étretat et les peintres," *Gazette des beaux-arts* 51, nos. 1072–1073 (May–June 1958), pp. 353–360.

LLOYD, 1979
Lloyd, Christopher, *Pissarro*, Oxford, 1979.

LLOYD, 1981
Lloyd, Christopher, *Camille Pissarro*, New York, 1981.

LONGHI AND MAYER, 1938
Longhi, Roberto, and August L. Mayer, eds., *Gli Antici Pintori spagnoli della collezione Contini-Bonacossi*, Rome, 1938.

LORD, 1939
Lord, Douglas, "Shorter Notices: Views of Paris—An Exhibition in New York," *Burlington Magazine* 74, no. 430 (January 1939), pp. 40–41.

LUCKHARDT AND SCHNEEDE, 2001
Luckhardt, Ulrich, and Uwe M. Schneede, *Private Schätze. Über das Sammeln von Kunst in Hamburg bis 1933*, Hamburg, 2001.

LURIE, 1970
Lurie, Ann Tzeutschler, "Goya: St. Ambrose," *Bulletin of the Cleveland Museum of Art* 57, no. 5 (May 1970), pp. 130–140.

LUTHI, 1974
Luthi, Jean-Jacques, *Émile Bernard, l'initiateur*, Paris, 1974.

LUTHI, 1976
Luthi, Jean-Jacques, *Émile Bernard: Chef de l'école de Pont-Aven*, Paris, 1976.

LUTHI, 1982
Luthi, Jean-Jacques, *Émile Bernard: Catalogue raisonné de l'oeuvre peint*, Paris, 1982.

MACCOLL, 1901
MacColl, Dugald Sutherland, *Nineteenth Century Art*, Glasgow, 1902 (list of works in Glasgow International Exhibition, 1901).

MAILLARD, 1967
Maillard, Robert, ed., *Dictionnaire universel de l'art et des artistes*, 3 vols., Paris, 1967.

MAISON, 1961
Maison, "Daumier's Paintings and Drawings," in *Daumier* [Exh. cat. Tate Gallery, London.] London, 1961.

MAISON, 1968
Maison, K. E., *Honoré Daumier, Catalogue Raisonné of Paintings, Watercolors and Drawings*, London, 1968.

MALINGUE, 1943
Malingue, Maurice, *Claude Monet*, Paris, 1943.

MANET, 1987
Manet, Julie, *Growing up with the Impressionists: The Diary of Julie Manet*, London, 1987.

MANSON, 1928
Manson, J. B., "A Century of French Painting," *Apollo* 8, no. 47 (November 1928), pp. 276–280.

MANTZ, 1865
Mantz, Paul, "Salon de 1865," *Gazette des beaux-arts* 19 (July 1865), pp. 5–42.

MANTZ, 1877
Mantz, Paul, "L'Exposition des peintres impressionnistes," *Le Temps*, 22 April 1877, p. 3.

MARANDEL, 1992
Marandel, Jean-Patrice, "Frédéric Bazille: The Lure of Exoticism," in *Frédéric Bazille: Prophet of Impressionism*, trans. John Goodman, pp. 67–75. [Exh. cat. Musée Fabre, Montpellier; Brooklyn Museum; Dixon Gallery and Gardens, Memphis.] Brooklyn, 1992.

MARTINI, 1978A
Martini, Alberto, *Monet*, New York, 1978.

MARTINI, 1978B
Martini, Alberto, *Renoir*, New York, 1978.

MATHEY, 1956
Mathey, François, *L'Impressionnisme*, Paris, 1956.

MATHEY, 1992
Mathey, François, *Les Impressionnistes et leur temps*, Paris, 1992.

MAUCLAIR, 1924
Mauclair, Camille, *Claude Monet*, Paris, 1924.

MAYER, 1923
Mayer, August L., *Francisco de Goya*, Munich, 1923.

MAYER, 1924
Mayer, August L., *Francisco de Goya*, London, 1924.

McCleery, 1974
McCleery, William, "A Businessman and Art Collector Talks of Art and Business," *University: A Princeton Quarterly*, no. 60 (Spring 1974), pp. 8–13, 27–28.

McMahon, 1937
McMahon, A. Philip, "Manet Fifty Years Later," *Parnassus* 9, no. 3 (March 1937), pp. 6–10 and 38–39.

Meier-Graefe, 1904
Meier-Graefe, Julius, *Entwicklungs-Geschichte der modernen Kunst*, 3 vols., Munich, 1904.

Meier-Graefe, 1910
Meier-Graefe, Julius, *Paul Cézanne*, Munich, 1910 (other eds., Munich, 1913, Munich, 1923, London, 1927).

Meier-Graefe, 1912a
Meier-Graefe, Julius, *Corot und Courbet*, Munich, 1912.

Meier-Graefe, 1912b
Meier-Graefe, Julius, *Edouard Manet*, Munich, 1912.

Meier-Graefe, 1918
Meier-Graefe, Julius, *Paul Cézanne und sein Kreis*, Munich, 1918 (3rd ed., Munich, 1922).

Meier-Graefe, 1921
Meier-Graefe, Julius, *Courbet*, Munich, 1921.

Meier-Graefe, 1929a
Meier-Graefe, Julius, *Renoir*, Leipzig, 1929.

Meier-Graefe, 1929b
Meier-Graefe, Julius, "Honoré Daumier—Fifty Years After," trans. J. Holroyd-Reece, *International Studio* 94, no. 388 (September 1929), pp. 20–25.

Meier-Graefe, 1930
Meier-Graefe, Julius, *Corot*, Berlin, 1930.

Mélikian and Wildenstein, 1967
Mélikian, Souren, and Daniel Wildenstein, "Manet, les vrais et les autres," *Réalités*, February 1967, pp. 70–77 (English ed., "That's Not a Manet—I painted It Myself!" no. 196 [March 1967], pp. 52–59).

Méras, 1967
Méras, Mathieu, "Ingres et le baron Vialètes de Mortarieu," in *Colloque Ingres, Les Actes du Colloque Ingres ont été édités par les Amis du Musée Ingres*, pp. 115–122, Montaubon, 1967.

Merlhès, Victor, 1989
Merlhès, Victor, *Paul Gauguin et Vincent van Gogh, 1887–1888: lettres retrouvées, sources ignorées*, Papeete, Tahiti, 1989.

Metropolitan Museum of Art, 1916
Metropolitan Museum of Art, "Notes: Loan of Paintings by Puvis de Chavannes," *Bulletin of the Metropolitan Museum of Art* 11, no. 6 (June 1916), pp. 134–135.

Michel and Laran, 1912
Michel, André and Jean Laran, *Puvis de Chavannes*, Philadelphia, 1912.

Michel, F.-B., 1992
Michel, François-Bernard, *Frédéric Bazille. Réflexions sur la peinture, la médicine, le paysage et le portrait*, Paris, 1992.

Michel, Prince of Greece, 1992
Michel, Prince of Greece, *Portrait et seduction*, Paris, 1992.

Minneapolis Institute of Arts, 1930
Minneapolis Institute of Arts, "A Sketch by Puvis de Chavannes," *Bulletin of the Minneapolis Institute of Arts* 19, no. 9 (1 March 1930), pp. 44–46.

Mireur, 1901–1912
Mireur, Hippolyte, *Dictionnaire des ventes d'art faites en France et à l'étranger pendant les XVIIIme et XIXme siècles*, 7 vols, Paris, 1901–1912.

Moffett, 1986
Moffett, Charles S., ed., *The New Painting: Impressionism, 1874–1886*. [Exh. cat. Fine Arts Museums of San Francisco; National Gallery of Art, Washington, D.C.] San Francisco, 1986.

Monet, 1957
Monet, Claude, "The Artist as a Young Man," *Art News Annual* 26 (1957) (Eng. trans. of artist's statement in Thiébault-Sisson's article, *Le Temps*, 1900), pp. 126–128, 196–199.

Monneret, 1978–1981
Monneret, Sophie, *L'Impressionnisme et son époque: Dictionnaire international illustré*, 4 vols., Paris, 1978–1981.

Monneret, 1989
Monneret, Sophie, *Renoir*, Paris, 1989.

Montreal, 1984
William Bouguereau, 1825–1905. [Exh. cat. Musée du Petit-Palais, Paris; Musée des Beaux-Arts, Montreal; The Wadsworth Atheneum, Hartford.] Montreal, 1984.

Moreau-Nélaton, 1906
Moreau-Nélaton, Étienne, "Catalogue manuscrit de l'oeuvre de Manet," Paris, 1906, Bibliothèque Nationale de France, Paris.

Moreau-Nélaton, 1924
Moreau-Nélaton, Étienne, *Corot raconté par lui-même*, Paris, 1924.

Moreau-Nélaton, 1926
Moreau-Nélaton, Étienne, *Manet raconté par lui-même*, 2 vols., Paris, 1926.

Mornand, 1957
Mornand, Pierre, *Émile Bernard et ses amis: van Gogh, Gauguin, Toulouse-Lautrec, Cézanne, Odilon Redon*, Geneva, 1957.

Moueix, 1969
Moueix, Jean-François, *Un Amateur d'art éclairé à Bordeaux: Gabriel Frizeau, 1870–1938*, 2 vols., Bordeaux, 1969.

Mount, 1966
Mount, Charles Merrill, *Monet*, New York, 1966.

Mullins, 1974
Mullins, Edwin, "A New Light: 100 Years On," *Daily Telegraph Magazine*, no. 483 (8 February 1974), pp. 32–38.

Munich, 1956
Vincent van Gogh, 1853–1890. [Exh. cat. Haus der Kunst, Munich.] Munich, 1956.

Murray, 1991
Murray, Gale B., *Toulouse-Lautrec: The Formative Years, 1878–1891*, Oxford, 1991.

Musée du Petit Palais, 1986
Musée du Petit Palais, *Le Triomphe des mairies: Grand Décors républicains à Paris, 1870–1914*. [Exh. cat. Musée du Petit Palais, Paris.] Paris, 1986.

Naef, 1977–1980
Naef, Hans, *Die Bildniszeichnungen von J.-A.-D. Ingres*, 5 vols., Bern, 1977–1980.

National Gallery of Scotland, 1986
National Gallery of Scotland, *Lighting up the Landscape: French Impressionism and Its Origins*. [Exh. cat. National Gallery of Scotland, Edinburgh.] Edinburgh, 1986.

NÉRET, 2001
Néret, Gilles, *Renoir: Painter of Happiness, 1841–1919*, London, 2001.

NEW YORK TIMES, 1937
"Le Mendiant, by Edouard Manet," *New York Times*, 14 March 1937.

NOCHLIN, 1967
Nochlin, Linda, "Gustave Courbet's *Meeting*: A Portrait of the Artist as a Wandering Jew," *Art Bulletin* 49 (1967).

NOCHLIN, 1971
Nochlin, Linda, *Realism*, New York, 1971.

NOVOTNY, 1937
Novotny, Fritz, *Paul Cézanne*, Vienna, 1937.

OAKLEY, 1980
Oakley, Lucy, *Pierre Auguste Renoir*, New York, 1980.

ORIENTI AND VENTURI, 1967
Orienti, Sandra, and Marcello Venturi, *L'Opera pittorica di Edouard Manet*, Milan, 1967 (Eng. ed. with Phoebe Pool, New York, 1967; French ed. with Denis Rouart, Paris, 1970).

ORIENTI AND PICON, 1970
Orienti, Sandra; and Gaëtan Picon, *L'Opera completa di Cézanne*, Milan, 1970 (French ed., Paris, 1975).

OSTINI, 1908
Ostini, Fritz von, "Die Frühjahrsausstellung der Münchener Secession," *Die Kunst für Alle* 17 (1 May 1908), pp. 337–350.

OULMONT, 1928
Oulmont, Charles, *Les Femmes peintres du XVIIIe siècle*, Paris, 1928.

PALMER, 1990
Palmer, Larry, "Van Gogh: A small but powerful commentary on the gathering of art," *International Fine Art Collector* 1, no. 1 (1990), pp. 72–75.

DU PASQUIER, STURM, AND JEAN-RICHARD, 1995
du Pasquier, Jacqueline, Fabienne Xavière Sturm, and Pierrette Jean-Richard, *L'âge d'or du petit portrait* [exh. cat., Musée des Arts Décoratifs, Bordeaux; Musée de l'Horlogerie, Geneva; Musée du Louvre, Paris] (Paris, 1995), pp. 188, 235.

PATIN, 2002
Patin, Sylvie, "Berthe Morisot et ses 'confrères les impressionnistes,'" in *Berthe Morisot, 1841–1895*, pp. 42–62. [Exh. cat., Palais des beaux-arts, Lille; Fondation Pierre Gianadda, Martigny.] Paris, 2002.

PATTERSON, 1973
Patterson, Jerry E., "The Appreciation of Renoir," *Art News* 72, no. 2 (February 1973), pp. 43–45.

PELLETAN, 1841
Pelletan, Eugène, "Salon de 1841," *La Presse*, 3 June 1841, pp. 1–2.

PERRUCHOT, 1958
Perruchot, Henri, "Renoir, peintre des femmes et des fleurs," *Le Jardin des arts*, no. 45 (July 1958), pp. 605–611.

PERUTZ, 1993
Perutz, Vivien, *Édouard Manet*, Lewisburg, Pa., 1993.

PETRIE, 1979
Petrie, Brian, *Claude Monet: The First of the Impressionists*, Oxford, 1979.

PFISTER, 1927
Pfister, Kurt, *Cézanne: Gestalt, Werk, Mythos*, Potsdam, 1927.

PHILADELPHIA, 1937
Philadelphia Museum of Art, *Daumier, 1808–1879*. [Exh. cat. Museum of Art, Philadelphia.] Philadelphia, 1937.

PHILLIPS, 1922
Phillips, Duncan, "Honoré Daumier," *Honoré Daumier, Appreciations of His Life and Works*, The Phillips Publications, no. 2, New York, 1922, pp. 13–35.

PHILLIPS, 1926
Phillips, Duncan, *A Collection in the Making*, New York, 1926.

PHILLIPS, 1931
Phillips, Duncan, *The Artist Sees Differently*, New York, 1931.

PICKVANCE, 1986
Pickvance, Ronald, *Van Gogh in Saint-Rémy and Auvers*, New York, 1986.

PIGALLE, 1865A
Pigalle, "Guigou," *L'Autographe au Salon et dans les ateliers*, no. 3 (13 May 1865), p. 28.

PIGALLE, 1865B
Pigalle, "Monet," *L'Autographe au Salon et dans les ateliers*, no. 9 (24 June 1865), p. 76.

PILLEMENT, 1930
Pillement, Georges, "À l'exposition de Pissarro," *La Revue française*, 16 March 1930, pp. 259–260.

PISSARRO, J., 1993
Pissarro, Joachim, *Camille Pissarro*, New York, 1993.

PISSARRO, J., 2005
Pissarro, Joachim, *Cézanne and Pissarro 1865–1885: Pioneering Modern Painting* [Exh. cat. The Museum of Modern Art, New York; Los Angeles County Museum of Art; Musée d'Orsay, Paris.] New York, 2005.

PISSARRO AND SNOLLAERTS, 2005
Pissarro, Joachim, and Claire Durand-Ruel Snollaerts, *Pissarro: Critical Catalogue of Paintings*, 3 vols., Milan, 2005.

PISSARRO AND VENTURI, 1939
Pissarro, Ludovic Rodo, and Lionello Venturi, *Camille Pissarro: Son Art—Son Oeuvre*, 2 vols., Paris, 1939.

PITMAN, 1998
Pitman, Dianne W., *Bazille: Purity, Pose, and Painting in the 1860s*, University Park, Pa., 1998.

PONCE ART MUSEUM, 1983
Ponce Art Museum, *Francisco Oller: A Realist-Impressionist*, Ponce, Puerto Rico, 1983.

PORRO, 1992
Porro, René, *Claude-Émile Schuffenecker, 1851–1934*, Combeau-Fontaine, 1992.

POULAIN, 1932
Poulain, Gaston, *Bazille et ses amis*, Paris, 1932.

PRATHER AND STUCKEY, 1987
Prather, Marla, and Charles Stuckey, eds., *Gauguin: A Retrospective*, New York, 1987.

PRICE, 1972
Price, Aimée Brown, "Puvis de Chavannes: A Study of the Easel Paintings and a Catalogue of the Painted Works," Ph.D. diss., Yale University, 1972.

PRICE, 1994
Price, Aimée Brown, *Pierre Puvis de Chavannes*. [Exh. cat. Van Gogh Museum, Amsterdam.] Amsterdam, 1994.

PRICE, 1995
Price, Aimée Brown, "Pierre Puvis de Chavannes: Saint Geneviève as a Child in Prayer," *Van Gogh Museum Journal*, 1995, pp. 118–133.

Privat, 1865
Privat, Gonzague, *Place aux jeunes! Causeries critiques sur le Salon de 1865*, Paris, 1865.

Przyblyski, 1995
Przyblyski, Jeannene M. "Le Parti Pris des Choses: French Still Life and Modern Painting, 1848–1976." Ph.D. diss., University of California, Berkeley, 1995.

Przyblyski, 1996
Przyblyski, Jeannene M., "Courbet, the Commune, and the Meanings of Still Life in 1871," *Art Journal* 55, no. 2 (Summer 1996), pp. 28–37.

Radius and Camesasca, 1968
Radius, Emilio, and Ettore Camesasca, *L'Opera completa di Ingres*, Milan, 1968.

Rapetti, 2005
Rapetti, Rodolphe, *Le Symbolisme*, Paris, 2005.

Raynal, 1936
Raynal, Maurice, *Cézanne,* New York, 1936.

Reclus, 1875–1894
Élisée Reclus, *L'Homme et la terre*, Paris 1875–1894, 19 vols.

Redon, 1960
Redon, Arï, *Lettres à Odilon Redon*, Paris, 1960.

Régamey, 1927
Régamey, Raymond, "La Formation de Claude Monet," *Gazette des beaux-arts* 15, (February 1927), pp. 65–84.

Reid, 1962
Reid, A. J. McNeill, "Courbet Paintings in Scotland," *Scottish Art Review* 8, no. 3 (1962), pp. 1–4, 33.

La Renaissance, 1923
"Edouard Jonas," *La Renaissance* 6 (June 1923), pp. 339–342.

Reuterswärd, 1948
Reuterswärd, Oscar, *Monet: En konstnärshistorik*, Stockholm, 1948.

Réveil, 1828–1834
Réveil, Étienne-Achille, *Musée de peinture et de sculpture, ou Recueil des principaux tableaux, statues et bas-reliefs des collections publiques et particulières de l'Europe. ...*, Paris, 1828–1834.

Rewald, 1937
Rewald, John, "Paysages de Paris de Corot à Utrillo," *La Renaissance* 20 (January 1937), pp. 6–32.

Rewald, 1939
Rewald, John, *Cézanne*, New York, 1939.

Rewald, 1943
Rewald, John, *Georges Seurat*, New York, 1943 (French ed., Paris, 1948).

Rewald, 1946
Rewald, John, *The History of Impressionism*, New York, 1946.

Rewald, 1948a
Rewald, John, *Paul Cézanne: A Biography*, New York, 1948.

Rewald, 1948b
Rewald, John, *Paul Cézanne*, trans. Margaret Liebman, London, 1948 (first published as *Cézanne et Zola*, Paris, 1936).

Rewald, 1950
Rewald, John, *The Ordeal of Paul Cézanne*, trans. Margaret Liebman, London, 1950.

Rewald, 1956
Rewald, John, "Quelques notes et documents sur Odilon Redon," *Gazette des beaux-arts* 48, no. 1054 (November 1956), pp. 81–124.

Rewald and Dorra, 1959
Rewald, John, and Henri Dorra, *Seurat: L'Oeuvre peint, biographie et catalogue critique*, Paris, 1959.

Rewald, 1961
Rewald, John, *The History of Impressionism*, rev. ed., New York, 1961.

Rewald, 1968
Rewald, John, *Cézanne: A Biography*, New York, 1968.

Rewald, 1973
Rewald, John, *The History of Impressionism*, 4th rev. ed., New York, 1973.

Rewald, 1974
Rewald, John, "The Impressionist Brush," *Metropolitan Museum of Art Bulletin* 32, no. 3 (1973–1974), pp. 2–56.

Rewald, 1986a
Rewald, John, *Cézanne: A Biography*, New York, 1986.

Rewald, 1986b
Rewald, John, "Some Notes and Documents on Odilon Redon," in *Studies in Post-Impressionism*, ed. Irene Gordon and Frances Weitzenhoffer, pp. 214–243, New York, 1986.

Rewald, 1990
Rewald, John, *Seurat: A Biography*, New York, 1990.

Rewald, 1996
Rewald, John, *The Paintings of Paul Cézanne: A Catalogue Raisonné*, 2 vols., New York, 1996.

Rey, J., 1982
Rey, Jean Dominique, *Berthe Morisot*, trans. Shirley Jennings, New York, 1982.

Rey, R., 1965
Rey, Robert, *Daumier*, New York, 1965.

Riat, 1906
Riat, Georges, *Gustave Courbet, peintre*, Paris, 1906.

Rich, 1957
Rich, Daniel Catton, "Homage to Claude Monet," *Art Institute of Chicago Quarterly* 51, no. 2 (1 April 1957), pp. 22–34.

Rich and Herbert, 1958
Rich, Daniel Catton and Robert L. Herbert, *Seurat, Paintings and Drawings.* [Exh. cat. Art Institute, Chicago; Museum of Modern Art, New York.] Chicago, 1958.

Rishel, 1983
Rishel, Joseph, ed., *Cézanne in Philadelphia Collections.* [Exh. cat. Museum of Art, Philadelphia.] Philadelphia, 1983.

Rivière, 1921
Rivière, Georges, *Renoir et ses amis*, Paris, 1921.

Rivière, 1923
Rivière, Georges Henri, *Le Maître Paul Cézanne,* Paris, 1923.

Rivière, 1933
Rivière, Georges, *Cézanne, le peintre solitaire,* Paris, 1933.

Robaut, 1905
Robaut, Alfred, *L'Oeuvre de Corot: Catalogue raisonné et illustré*, 4 vols., Paris, 1905.

Robaut, Carton
Robaut, Alfred, "Cartons Alfred Robaut. Notes, croquis, calques, photographies, estampes," 35 cartons, Cabinet des Estampes, Bibliothèque nationale de France, Paris, BN/CE S.N.R. On deposit at the Service d'étude et de documentation, Département des peintures, musée du Louvre, Paris.

Roberts, 1976
Roberts, Keith, "Current and Forthcoming

Exhibitions: London," *Burlington Magazine* 118, no. 885 (December 1976), pp. 874–879.

ROBINSON, 1975
Robinson, Jane, *Edward G. Robinson's World of Art*, New York, 1975.

ROBIQUET, 1948
Robiquet, Jean, *L'Impressionnisme vécu*, Paris, 1948.

ROGER-MARX, 1946
Roger-Marx, Claude, *Vuillard: His Life and Work*, London, 1946.

ROLAND, 1991
Roland, Henry, *Behind the Facade: Recollections of an Art Dealer*, London, 1991.

ROSENHAGEN, 1906
Rosenhagen, Hans, "Die XI. Ausstellung der Berliner Sezession. II. (Schluss)," *Die Kunst für Alle* 13 (1 July 1906), pp. 433–446.

ROSENTHAL, 1911
Rosenthal, Léon, *Daumier*, Paris, 1911.

DE ROTONCHAMP, 1925
de Rotonchamp, Jean, *Paul Gauguin, 1848–1903*, Paris, 1925.

ROUART AND WILDENSTEIN, 1975
Rouart, Denis, and Daniel Wildenstein, *Édouard Manet: Catalogue raisonné*, 2 vols., Lausanne and Paris, 1975.

RUBIN, 1994
Rubin, James H., *Manet's Silence and the Poetics of Bouquets*, London, 1994.

RUBIN, 2003
Rubin, James H., *Impressionist Cats and Dogs*, New Haven, 2003.

RUSSELL, 1971
Russell, John, *Édouard Vuillard, 1868–1940*, London, 1971.

RUUTZ-REES, 1880
Ruutz-Rees, Janet, *Horace Vernet*, London, 1880.

SACHS, K., 2000
Sachs, Katherine, "Chronology: Arles," in *Van Gogh Face to Face: The Portraits*, pp. 126–133. [Exh. cat. Institute of Arts, Detroit; Museum of Fine Arts, Bonton; Museum of Art, Philadelphia.] Detroit, 2000.

SACHS, M., 1939
Sachs, Maurice, *Honoré Daumier*, Paris, 1939.

SADLEIR, 1924
Sadleir, Michael, *Daumier, the Man and the Artist*, London, 1924.

DE SALAS, 1978
de Salas, Xavier, *Goya*, London, 1978.

SALOMON AND COGEVAL, 2003
Salomon, Antoine, and Guy Cogeval, *Vuillard: The Inexhaustible Glance: Critical Catalogue of Paintings and Pastels*, 3 vols., Milan, 2003.

SALOMON, 1967
Salomon, Jacques, *Projet pour la decoration d'une mairie*, n.p., 1967.

SÁNCHEZ CANTÓN, 1946
Sánchez Cantón, Francisco Javier, "Goya, pintor religioso," *Revista de ideas esteticas* 4, nos. 15–16 (July–December 1946), pp. 277–306.

SÁNCHEZ CANTÓN, 1951
Sánchez Cantón, Francisco Javier, *Vida y obras de Goya*, Madrid, 1951.

SÁNCHEZ DE RIVERA Y MOSET, 1943
Sánchez de Rivera y Moset, Daniel, *Goya: La Leyenda, la enfermedad y las pinturas religiosas*, Madrid, 1943.

SANTAMARINA, 1942
Santamarina, Antonio, "My Pleasure in Collecting," *Magazine of Art* 35, no. 2 (February 1942), pp. 52–57.

SARGEANT, 1952
Sargeant, Winthrop, "Cézanne, the Great Paintings of a Frustrated Recluse Changed the Whole Course of Modern Art," *Life* 32, no. 8 (25 February 1952), pp. 76–94.

SARRAUTE, 1948
Sarraute, Gabriel, *Catalogue de l'oeuvre de Frédéric Bazille*, Paris, 1948.

SAYRE, 1964
Sayre, Eleanor A., "Eight Books of Drawings by Goya—I," *Burlington Magazine*, 106, no. 730 (January 1964), pp. 19–31.

SCHAPIRO, 1973
Schapiro, Meyer, *Paul Cézanne*, Paris, 1973.

SCHAPIRO, 1978
Schapiro, Meyer, *Modern Art—19th and 20th Centuries, Selected Papers*, New York, 1978.

SCHAUB-KOCH, 1935
Schaub-Koch, Emile, *Psychanalyse d'un peintre moderne: Henri de Toulouse Lautrec*, Paris, 1935.

SCHEFFLER, 1931
Scheffler, Karl, "Die Sammlung Max Silberberg," *Kunst und Künstler* 30, no. 1 (October 1931), pp. 3–20.

SCHERJON AND DE GRUYTER, 1937
Scherjon, W., and J. de Gruyter, *Vincent van Gogh's Great Period: Arles, St. Rémy and Auvers-sur-Oise*, Amsterdam, 1937.

SCHILDT, 1946
Schildt, G., *Cézanne*, Stockholm, 1946.

SCHIRRMEISTER, 1982
Schirrmeister, Anne, *Camille Pissarro*, New York, 1982.

SCHIRRMEISTER, 1990
Schirrmeister, Anne, "La Dernière Mode: Berthe Morisot and Costume," in *Perspectives on Morisot*, ed. T. J. Edelstein, pp. 103–115, New York, 1990.

SCHLENOFF, 1956
Schlenoff, Norman, *Ingres, ses sources littéraires*, Paris, 1956.

SCHMIT, 1973
Schmit, Robert, *Eugène Boudin 1824–1898*, 3 vols., Paris, 1973.

SCHMIT AND SCHMIT, 1993
Schmit, Robert, and Manuel Schmit, *Stanislas Lépine, 1835–1892: Catalogue raisonné de l'oeuvre peint*, Paris, 1993.

SCHNEIDER, B., 1984
Schneider, Bruno F., *Renoir*, New York, 1984.

SCHNEIDER, C., 1985
Schneider, Cynthia P., "Renoir: Le Peintre de figures comme paysagiste," *Apollo* 122, no. 281 (July 1985), pp. 49–56.

SCHULMAN, 1995
Schulman, Michel, *Frédéric Bazille, 1841–1870: Catalogue raisonné. Peintures, dessins, pastels, aquarelles. Sa Vie, son oeuvre, sa correspondance*, Paris, 1995.

SCHULMAN, 1999
Schulman, Michel, *Théodore Rousseau, 1812–1867*, Paris, 1999.

SCHULZE, 1973
Schulze, Franz, "Some Lesser Known Aspects of Renoir's Art," *Art News* 72, no. 2 (February 1973), pp. 39–42.

SCHWEICHER, 1953
Schweicher, Curt, *Daumier*, Stuttgart, 1953.

SEGARD, 1914
Segard, Achille, *Peintres d'aujourd'hui: Les Decorateurs*, 3rd ed., Paris, 1914.

SEIBERLING, 1994
Seiberling, Grace, "Monet's Hauling a Boat,

Honfleur," *Porticus: Journal of the Memorial Art Gallery of the University of Rochester* 17–19 (1994–1996), pp. 38–43.

SEITZ, 1960
Seitz, William C., *Monet*, London, 1960.

SELZ, 1988
Selz, Jean, *La Vie et l'oeuvre de Camille Corot*, Paris, 1988.

SENSIER, 1872
Sensier, A., *Souvenirs sur Théodore Rousseau*, Paris, 1872.

SERRET AND FABIANI, 1971
Serret, Georges, and Dominique Fabiani, *Armand Guillaumin, 1841–1927: Catalogue raisonné de l'oeuvre peint*, Paris, 1971.

SÉRRULAZ, 1955
Sérrulaz, Maurice, *Camille Pissarro*, Arcueil, France, 1955.

SÉRUSIER, 1942
Sérusier, Paul, *ABC de la peinture suivi d'une étude sur la vie et l'oeuvre de Paul Sérusier par Maurice Denis*, Paris, 1942.

SETA, 1998
Seta, Cesare de, "Prima di Corot. Pittori e scrittori tra Roma e Napoli," in Corot, un artiste et son temps. Actes des colloques organisés au musée du Louvre par le Service culturel, les 1 et 2 mars 1996 à Paris, pp. 385–395, Paris, 1998.

SHACKELFORD, 2000
Shackelford, George, *Vincent van Gogh: The Painter and the Portrait*, New York, 2000.

SHEON, 1967
Sheon, Aaron, "Monticelli and Van Gogh," *Apollo* 85, no. 64 (June 1967), pp. 444–448.

SHIKES AND HARPER, 1980
Shikes, Ralph E., and Paula Harper, *Pissarro: His Life and Work*, New York, 1980.

SHIMADA, 1986
Shimada, Norio, *The Artists Who Left the Great Works*, Tokyo, 1986.

SHIMADA AND SAKAGAMI, 2001
Shimada, Norio and Keiko Sakagami, *Claude Monet, Volume 1, 1858–1880*, Tokyo, 2001.

SKEGGS, 1987
Skeggs, Douglas, *River of Light: Monet's Impressions of the Seine*, New York, 1987.

SOFFICI, 1921
Soffici, Ardengo, "Daumier Pittore," *Dedalo* 2 (November 1921), pp. 405–419.

SORIA, 1949
Soria, Martín Sebastián, "Las Miniaturas y retratos-miniaturas de Goya," *Cobalto* 49, no. 2 (1949), pp. 1[9]–4[12].

SOTH, 2000
Soth, Lauren, "Fantasy and Reality in the Hague Drawings," *Van Gogh Face to Face: The Portraits*, pp. 60–79. [Exh. cat. Institute of Arts, Detroit; Museum of Fine Arts, Bonton; Museum of Art, Philadelphia.] Detroit, 2000.

SOULLIÉ, 1900
Soullié, Louis, *Les Grands Peintres aux ventes publiques, I: Peintures, pastels, aquarelles, dessins de Constant Troyon*, Paris, 1900.

STEADMAN, 1972
Steadman, David W., "The Norton Simon Exhibition at Princeton," *Art Journal* 32, no. 1 (Fall 1972), pp. 34–40.

STEADMAN, 1973A
Steadman, David W., "A Major Resource for a Teaching Museum: Selections from the Norton Simon, Inc. Museum of Art," *Princeton Alumni Weekly*, 6 February 1973, pp. 8–13.

STEADMAN, 1973B
Steadman, David W., "The Landscape in Art," *University: A Princeton Quarterly*, no. 57 (Summer 1973), pp. 6–11.

STEADMAN, 1975
Steadman, David W., *The Graphic Art of Francisco Goya from the Norton Simon Foundation, the Norton Simon, Inc. Museum of Art and the Pomona College Collections.* [Exh. cat. Galleries of the Claremont Colleges, Claremont.] Claremont, Calif., 1975.

STEADMAN, 1976
Steadman, David W., "Painting in France, 1860–1940," *Connoisseur* 193, no. 777 (November 1976), pp. 220–231.

STEIN, A., 2003
Stein, Adolphe, et al., *Catalogue de l'oeuvre de Jongkind: Peintures, aquarelles, dessins et gravures*, Paris, 2003.

STEIN, S., 1986
Stein, Susan Alyson, ed., *Van Gogh: A Retrospective*, New York, 1986.

STERLING, 1934
Sterling, Charles, *Daumier, peintures, aquarelles, dessins.* [Exh. cat. Musée de l'Orangerie, Paris.] Paris, 1934.

STEVENS, 1990
Stevens, MaryAnne, et al., *Émile Bernard, 1868–1941: A Pioneer of Modern Art*, Zwolle, 1990.

STEVENS, 1992
Stevens, MaryAnne, ed., *Alfred Sisley.* [Exh. cat. Royal Academy of Arts, London; Musée d'Orsay, Paris; Walters Art Gallery, Baltimore.] New Haven, 1992.

STEVENSON, 1991
Stevenson, Lesley, *Renoir*, London, 1991.

STEVENSON, 1992
Stevenson, Lesley, *Manet*, New York, 1992.

STOLL, 1957A
Stoll, Robert Thomas, *Die französischen Impressionisten*, Zurich, 1957.

STOLL, 1957B
Stoll, Robert Thomas, *La Peinture impressionniste*, trans. Jean-Louis Cornuz, Lausanne, 1957.

STUCKEY, 1979
Stuckey, Charles F., *Toulouse-Lautrec: Paintings.* [Exh. cat. Art Institute, Chicago.] Chicago, 1979.

STUCKEY, 1985
Stuckey, Charles F., ed., *Monet: A Retrospective*, New York, 1985.

THE STUDIO, 1932
"A Modern Picture Collection," *The Studio* 104, no. 473 (August 1932), pp. 77–81.

SUGANA AND CAPRONI, 1969
Sugana, Gabriele M., and Giorgio Caproni, *L'Opera completa di Toulouse-Lautrec*, Milan, 1969.

SUGANA, 1972
Sugana, Gabriele M., *Tout l'Oeuvre peint de Gauguin*, Milan, 1972.

SULLIVAN, 1982
Sullivan, Edward J., *Goya and the Art of His Time.* [Exh. cat. Meadows Museum, Southern Methodist University, Dallas.] Dallas, 1982.

SUND, 1992
Sund, Judy, *True to Temperament: Van Gogh and French Naturalist Literature*, Cambridge, 1992.

SUND, 2002
Sund, Judy, *Van Gogh*, London, 2002.

SUTTON, D., 1976
Sutton, Denys, "Editorial: The Vase and the

Wash-Tub," *Apollo* 103, no. 170 (March 1976), pp. 166–171.

Sutton, P., 1986
Sutton, Peter, *A Guide to Dutch Art in America*, Grand Rapids, 1986.

Tabarant, 1924
Tabarant, Adolphe, *Pissarro*, Paris, 1924.

Tabarant, 1931
Tabarant, Adolphe, *Manet: Histoire catalographique*, Paris, 1931.

Tabarant, 1932a
Tabarant, Adolphe, *Manet*, Paris, 1932.

Tabarant, 1932b
Tabarant, Adolphe, "À propos de la Rétrospective de Manet à l'Orangerie," *La Renaissance* 15, nos. 7–9 (July–September 1932), pp. 136–141.

Tabarant, 1942
Tabarant, Adolphe, *La Vie artistique au temps de Baudelaire*, Paris, 1942.

Tabarant, 1947
Tabarant, Adolphe, *Manet et ses oeuvres*, [4th ed.] Paris, 1947.

Taillandier, 1967
Taillandier, Yvon, *Monet*, Paris, 1967.

Ternois, 1965
Ternois, Daniel, *Inventaire des collections publiques français*, vol. 11, *Montauban—Musée Ingres, Peintures, Ingres et son temps*, Paris, 1965.

Terrasse, 1970
Terrasse, Antoine, *Denis: intimités*, Lausanne, 1970.

Therond, 1987
Therond, R., "Cézanne: Le Solitaire farouche," *Les Grands Peintres* 6 (Spring 1987), pp. 3–10.

Thiébault-Sisson, 1900
Thiébault-Sisson, François, "Claude Monet: les années d'épreuves," *Le Temps*, 26 November 1900, p. 3.

Thomas, D., 1980
Thomas, David, *Renoir*, London, 1980.

Thomas, G., 2000
Thomas, Greg M., *Art and Ecology in Nineteenth-Century France: The Landscapes of Théodore Rousseau*, Princeton, 2000.

Thomson, B., 1988
Thomson, Belinda, *Vuillard*, Oxford, 1988.

Thomson and Howard, 1988
Thomson, Belinda, and Michael Howard, *Impressionism*, London, 1988.

Thomson, R., 1982
Thomson, Richard, "'Les Quat' Pattes': The Image of the Dog in Late Nineteenth-century French Art," *Art History* 5, no. 3 (September 1982), pp. 323–337.

Thomson, R., 1985
Thomson, Richard, *Seurat*, Oxford, 1985.

Thomson, R., 1990
Thomson, Richard, *Camille Pissarro: Impressionism, Landscape, and Rural Labour*, London, 1990.

Thomson, R., 1991
Thomson, Richard, *Toulouse-Lautrec*. [Exh. cat. Hayward Gallery, London; Galeries nationales du Grand Palais, Paris.] New Haven, 1991.

Thomson, R., 1994
Thomson, Richard, "Puvis de Chavannes. Amsterdam, Van Gogh Museum," *Burlington Magazine* 136, no. 1096 (July 1994), pp. 476–478.

The Times, 1899
"Ireland: Dublin, April 2," *The Times*, no. 35, 793 (3 April 1899), p. 5.

Tinterow and Conisbee, 1999
Tinterow, Gary, and Philip Conisbee, eds., *Portraits by Ingres: Image of an Epoch*. [Exh. cat. Metropolitan Museum of Art, New York.] New York, 1999.

Tinterow and Loyrette, 1994
Tinterow, Gary, and Henri Loyrette, *Origins of Impressionism*, New York, 1994.

Tinterow, Pantazzi, and Pomarède, 1996
Tinterow, Gary, Michael Pantazzi, and Vincent Pomarède, *Corot* [exh. cat., Galeries Nationales du Grand Palais, Paris; National Gallery of Canada, Ottawa; Metropolitan Museum of Art, New York] (New York, 1996).

Tokyo, 1996
Tokyo, Yasuda Kasai Museum of Art, *Concealed van Gogh: Radiographic Images of Vincent van Gogh's Paintings in the Collection of the Van Gogh Museum*, Tokyo, 1996.

Toussaint, 1975
Toussaint, Hélène, et al., *Hommage à Corot*. [Exh. cat. Musée de l'Orangerie, Paris.] Paris 1975.

Toussaint, 1977
Toussaint, Hélène, *Gustave Courbet, 1819–1877*. [Exh. cat. Galeries nationales d'exposition du Grand Palais, Paris; Royal Academy of Arts, London.] London, 1977.

Tralbaut, 1959
Tralbaut, Marc Edo, *Van Gogh, a Pictorial Biography*, New York, 1959.

Travis, 1995
Travis, David, "Navigating Nature with Gustave Caillebotte, Painter and Skipper," lecture for the Old Master's Society of the Art Institute of Chicago, 23 February 1995.

Treble, 1975
Treble, R., *Van Gogh and His Art*, London, 1975.

Trudzinski, 1987
Trudzinski, M., *Die italienischen und französischen Handzeichnungen im Kupferstichkabinett der Landesgalerie*, Hanover, 1987.

Tucker, 1995
Tucker, Paul Hayes, *Claude Monet: Life and Art*, New Haven, 1995.

Turner, 1996
Turner, Jane, ed., *The Dictionary of Art*, 34 vols., London, 1996.

Uhde-Bernays, 1929
Uhde-Bernays, Hermann, *Feuerbach Beschreibender Katalog seiner sämtlichen Gemälde*, Munich, 1929.

van Uitert, van Tilborgh, and van Heugten, 1990
van Uitert, Evert, Louis van Tilborgh, and Sjraar van Heugten, *Vincent van Gogh*. [Exh. cat. Rijksmuseum Vincent van Gogh, Amsterdam.] New York, 1990.

Vachon, 1900
Vachon, Marius, *William-Adolphe Bouguereau*, Paris, 1900.

Vanbeselaere, 1937
Vanbeselaere, W., *De Hollandische periode (1880–1885) in het werk van Vincent van Gogh*, Antwerp, 1937.

Vasari, 1912–1915
Vasari, Giorgio, *Lives of the Most Eminent*

Painters, Sculptors and Architects, trans. Gaston Du C. De Vere, London, 1912–1915.

Vatout and Quénot, 1826
Vatout, Jean, and J.-P. Quénot, *Notices historiques sur les tableaux de la Galerie de S.A.R. Monseigneur le Duc d'Orléans*, 4 vols., Paris, 1826.

Venturi, 1929
Venturi, Lionello, "Manet," *L'Arte* 32, no. 19 (1929), pp. 145–164.

Venturi, 1936
Venturi, Lionello, *Cézanne: Son art—Son oeuvre*, 2 vols., Paris, 1936.

Venturi, 1939
Venturi, Lionello, *Les archives de l'impressionnisme*, 2 vols., Paris, 1939.

Venturi, 1951
Venturi, Lionello, "Giunte a Cézanne," *Commentari*, January–March 1951, pp. 47–50.

Vigne, 1995
Vigne, Georges, *Ingres*, Paris, 1995.

Vincent, 1956
Vincent, Madeleine, *La Peinture des XIXe et XXe siècles*, Lyon, 1956.

Vollard, 1914
Vollard, Ambroise, *Paul Cézanne*, Paris, 1914.

Vollard, 1919
Vollard, Ambroise, *La Vie et l'oeuvre de Pierre-Auguste Renoir*, Paris, 1919.

Vollard, 1937
Vollard, Ambroise, *Souvenirs d'un marchand de tableaux*, Paris, 1937.

Wadley, 1987
Wadley, Nicholas, ed., *Renoir: A Retrospective*, New York, 1987.

Waldmann, 1913
Waldmann, Emil, "Leibl und die Franzosen," *Kunst und Künstler* 12 (October 1913), pp. 43–54.

Waldmann, 1923
Waldmann, Emil, *Edouard Manet*, Berlin, 1923.

Waldmann, 1927
Waldmann, Emil, *Die Kunst des Realismus und des Impressionismus*, Berlin, 1927.

Wallace, 1969
Wallace, R., *The World of van Gogh, 1853–1890*, New York, 1969.

Ward, 1996
Ward, Martha, *Pissarro, Neo-Impressionism, and the Spaces of the Avant-Garde*, Chicago, 1996.

Warnod, 1989
Warnod, Jeanine, *E. Vuillard*, New York, 1989.

Watson, 1926
Watson, Forbes, "American Collections: No. III—The Adolph Lewisohn Collection," *The Arts* 10, no. 1 (July 1926), pp. 15–48.

Wattenmaker, 1975
Wattenmaker, Richard J., *Puvis de Chavannes and the Modern Tradition.* [Exh. cat. Art Gallery of Ontario, Toronto.] Toronto, 1975.

Weisberg, 1978a
Weisberg, Gabriel P., "The Traditional Realism of François Bonvin," *Bulletin of the Cleveland Museum of Art* 65, no. 9 (November 1978), pp. 280–298.

Weisberg, 1978b
Weisberg, Gabriel P., *Images of Women: Printmakers in France from 1830 to 1930.* [Exh. cat. Utah Museum of Fine Arts, University of Utah, Salt Lake City.] Salt Lake City, 1978.

Weisblat, 1999
Weisblat, Leigh Bullard, "Paul Gauguin (1848–1903)," in *The Eye of Duncan Phillips: A Collection in the Making*, ed. Erika D. Passantino, New Haven, 1999, pp. 110–111.

Welsh and Joosten, 1998
Welsh, Robert P., and Joop M. Joosten, *Piet Mondrian: Catalogue Raisonné*, New York, 1998.

Welsh-Ovcharov, 1981
Welsh-Ovcharov, Bogomila, *Vincent van Gogh and the Birth of Cloisonism.* [Exh. cat. Art Gallery of Ontario, Toronto; Rijksmuseum Vincent van Gogh, Amsterdam.] Toronto, 1981.

Welsh-Ovcharov, 2001
Welsh-Ovcharov, Bogomila, "Paul Gauguin's Third Visit to Brittany: June 1889—November 1890," in *Gauguin's Nirvana: Painters at Le Pouldu 1889–90*, ed. Eric M. Zafran, pp. 14–59. [Exh. cat. Wadsworth Atheneum Museum of Art, Hartford.] New Haven, 2001.

Westheim, 1918
Westheim, Paul, "Erinnerung an eine Sammlung," *Das Kunstblatt* 2, no. 8 (August 1918), pp. 233–241.

Whelan, 1998
Whelan, Richard, *Impressionist Flowers: Art of the Bouquet*, Cobb, Calif., 1998.

Wheldon, 1975
Wheldon, Keith, *Renoir and His Art*, London, 1975.

White, 1984
White, Barbara Ehrlich, *Renoir: His Life, Art, and Letters*, New York, 1984.

Whiteley, 1996
Whiteley, Jon, "Claude-Marie Dubufe," in *The Dictionary of Art*, ed. Jane Turner, New York, 1996, vol. 9, pp. 331–332.

Wichmann, 1962
Wichmann, Siegfried, "Intimität des Dekors: Edouard Vuillard, ein Überwinder des Impressionismus," *Die Kunst und das schöne Heim, Monatsschrift für Malerei, Plastik, Graphik, Architektur und Wohnkultur* 60, no. 9 (June 1962), pp. 354–357.

Wildenstein, A., 1992
Wildenstein, Alec, *Odilon Redon: Catalogue raisonné de l'oeuvre peint et dessiné*, 4 vols., Paris, 1992.

Wildenstein & Co., 1947
Wildenstein & Co., *The Art and Life of Vincent van Gogh*, New York, 1947.

Wildenstein, D., 1967a
Wildenstein, Daniel, "Claude Monet," *Kindlers Malerei Lexikon*, Zurich, 1967, vol. 4, pp. 462–470.

Wildenstein, D., 1967b
Wildenstein, Daniel, *Monet. Impressions*, Lausanne, 1967.

Wildenstein, D., 1971
Wildenstein, Daniel, *Monet*, Milan, 1971.

Wildenstein, D., 1974–1991
Wildenstein, Daniel, *Claude Monet: Biographie et catalogue raisonné*, 5 vols., Lausanne, 1974–1991.

Wildenstein, D., 1999
Wildenstein, Daniel, *Monet, or the Triumph of Impressionism*, Cologne, 1999.

Wildenstein, G., 1932
Wildenstein, Georges, "Painting from America in the French Exhibition," *Fine Arts* 18, no. 2 (January 1932), pp. 22–26, 54.

WILDENSTEIN, G., 1956
Wildenstein, Georges, *Ingres*, London, 1956.

WILDENSTEIN, G., 1964
Wildenstein, Georges, *Gauguin*, Paris, 1964.

WILENSKI, 1931
Wilenski, R. H., *French Painting*, Boston, 1931.

WILLIAMS, 2003
Adam Williams Fine Art Ltd., *Jean Luc Baroni Ltd, Master Paintings and Sculpture*, New York, 2003.

WILLIS, 1973
Willis, Thomas, "Renoir on Renoir," *Chicago Tribune Magazine*, 28 January 1973, pp. 52–55.

WILSON, P., 1981
Wilson, Patricia Boyd, "Drawn Home Again," *The Christian Science Monitor*, 12 August 1981, p. 20.

WILSON, W., 1970
Wilson, William, "Two van Goghs for the Price of One," *Los Angeles Times*, 4 January 1970, p. 44.

WILSON, W., 1987
Wilson, William, "The Intense Life of Vincent van Gogh," *Los Angeles Times Calendar*, 15 February 1987, pp. 90–91.

WILSON-BAREAU, 1994
Wilson-Bareau, Juliet, *Goya: Truth and Fantasy; The Small Paintings*. [Exh. cat. Museo del Prado, Madrid; Royal Academy of Arts, London; Art Institute of Chicago.] New Haven, 1994.

WILSON-BAREAU, 2001
Wilson-Bareau, Juliet, *Goya: Drawings from His Private Albums*, London, 2001.

WINTERMUTE, 1989
Wintermute, Alan, *1789: French Art during the Revolution*. [Exh. cat. Colnaghi, New York.] New York, 1989.

WISE, 1975
Wise, Susan, ed., *Paintings by Monet*. [Exh. cat. Art Institute of Chicago.] Chicago, 1975.

WISSMAN, 1989
Wissman, Fronia E., "Corot's Salon Paintings: Sources from French Classicism to Contemporary Theater Design," 2 vols., Ph.D. diss., Yale University, 1989.

WITTMER, 1991
Wittmer, Pierre, *Caillebotte and His Garden at Yerres*, New York, 1991.

VAN DER WOLK, 1986
van der Wolk, Johannes, *De Schetsboeken van Vincent van Gogh*, Amsterdam, 1986.

WYKES-JOYCE, 1966
Wykes-Joyce, Max, "Fantin-Latour's Flowers," *Amateur Artist* 1, no. 4 (August 1966), pp. 12–15.

YOUNG, 1976
Young, Eric, "Spanish Paintings from the Gothic to Goya," *Connoisseur* 193, no. 777 (November 1976), pp. 176–185.

YOUNG, 1978
Young, Eric, *Francisco Goya*, London, 1978.

YRIARTE, 1876
Yriarte, Charles, "Le Salon de 1876," *Gazette des beaux-arts* 13 ([1] June 1876), pp. 689–729.

ZEISHO, 1921
Zeisho, Atzouji, *Paul Cézanne*, Tokyo, 1921.

ZERVOS, 1932–1978
Zervos, Christian, *Pablo Picasso*, 33 vols., Paris, 1932–1978.

ZIMMERMANN, A., 1986
Zimmermann, Antje, *Studien zum Figurenbild bei Corot*, Cologne, 1986.

ZIMMERMANN, M., 1991
Zimmermann, M., *Seuratsa and the Art Theory of His Time*, Antwerp, 1991.

ZOLA, 1974
Zola, Émile, *Le bon combat de Courbet aux Impressionnistes*, ed. Jean-Paul Bouillon, Paris, 1974.

ZURICH, 1935
Gustave Courbet. [Exh. cat. Kunsthaus, Zurich.] Zurich, 1935.

Exhibition Catalogues

ALBI, 1960
Albi, Musée Toulouse-Lautrec, *Exposition Édouard Vuillard (1868–1940): Peintures, aquarelles, dessins*, 11 July–25 September 1960. (Vuillard, cat. 131)

ALBI, 1963
Albi, Musée Toulouse-Lautrec, *Maurice Denis*, 28 June–29 September 1963. (Denis, cat. 135)

AMSTERDAM, 1905
Amsterdam, Stedelijk Museum, *Vincent van Gogh*, July–August 1905. (van Gogh, cats. 108, 110)

AMSTERDAM, 1928
Amsterdam, E. J. van Wisselingh & Co., *Cent Ans de peinture française: Exposition*, 16 April–5 May 1928. (Corot, cat. 20)

AMSTERDAM, 1932
Amsterdam, Kunsthandel Huinck en Scherjon, *Schilderijen door Vincent van Gogh, J. B. Jongkind, Floris Vester*, 1932. (van Gogh, cat. 106)

AMSTERDAM, 1938
Amsterdam, Stedelijk Museum, *Honderd Jaar Fransche Kunst*, 2 July–25 September 1938. (Manet, cat. 68)

AMSTERDAM, 1956
Amsterdam, E. J. van Wisselingh & Co., *Vincent van Gogh 1853–1890. Quelques oeuvres de l'époque 1881–1886 provenant de collections particulières Néerlandaises*, 20 February–17 March 1956. (van Gogh, cat. 107)

AMSTERDAM, 1963a
Amsterdam, E. J. van Wisselingh & Co., *Maîtres français XIXme siècle*, 22 April–7 June 1963. (Troyon, cat. 32)

AMSTERDAM, 1963b
Amsterdam, E. J. van Wisselingh & Co., *Maîtres français XIXme et XXme siècle*, 18 November–20 December 1963. (van Gogh, cat. 108)

AMSTERDAM, 1971
Amsterdam, E. J. van Wisselingh & Co., *Maîtres français XIXme et XXme siècle*, 3 May–4 June 1971. (Forain, cat. 101; van Gogh, cat. 107)

AMSTERDAM, 1994
Amsterdam, Van Gogh Museum, *Pierre Puvis de Chavannes*, 25 February–29 May 1994. (Puvis de Chavannes, cat. 58)

ANTWERP, 1952
Antwerp, Koninklijk Museum voor schone Kunsten, *De Arbeid in de Kunst, van Meunier tot Permeke*, 26 April–30 June 1952. (van Gogh, cat. 108)

BALTIMORE, 1936
Baltimore, The Baltimore Museum of Art, *C. Pissarro*, 1–30 November 1936. (Pissarro, cat. 63)

BASEL, 1917
Basel, Kunsthalle, *Peinture française*, 10 January–4 February 1917. (Pissarro, cat. 64)

Basel, 1921
Basel, Kunsthalle, *Exposition de peinture française*, 8 May–30 June 1921. (Corot, cat. 22)

Basel, 1949
Basel, Kunsthalle, *Édouard Vuillard (1868–1940), Charles Hug*, 26 March–1 May 1949. (Vuillard, cats. 131, 132)

Berkeley, 1970
Berkeley, University of California Art Museum, *Excellence: Art from the University Community*, 6 November 1970–9 January 1971. (Sisley, cat. 78; Cézanne, cat. 80; van Gogh, cat. 111)

Berlin, 1906
Berlin, Secession Ausstellungshaus, *Elfte Ausstellung der Berliner Secession*, Spring 1906. (Manet, cat. 68)

Berlin, 1909
Berlin, Paul Cassirer, [*Group Exhibition*], 17 November–12 December 1909. (Cézanne, cat. 82)

Berlin, 1914a
Berlin, Paul Cassirer, *Vincent van Gogh*, May–June 1914. (van Gogh, cat. 111)

Berlin, 1914b
Berlin, Secession Ausstellungshaus, *Erste Ausstellung der freien Secession*, 12 April–end September 1914. (Cézanne, cat. 82)

Bern, 1951
Bern, Kunsthalle, *Die Maler der Revue Blanche: Toulouse-Lautrec und die Nabis*, 21 March–22 April 1951. (Denis, cat. 135)

Bern, 1957
Bern, Kunstmuseum, *Camille Pissarro, 1830–1903*, 19 January–10 March 1957. (Pissarro, cat. 64)

Bern, 1962
Bern, Kunstmuseum, *Gustave Courbet*, 22 September–18 November 1962. (Courbet, cats. 41, 42, 47)

Besançon, 1952
Besançon, Musée des Beaux-Arts, *Exposition Gustave Courbet, 1819–1877*, 23 August–10 October 1952. (Courbet, cat. 41)

Birmingham, 1973
Birmingham, Alabama Museum of Art, *French Impressionism and Post-Impressionism*, 10–26 February 1973. (Monticelli, cat. 50)

Boston, 1915
Boston, Brooks Reed Gallery, *Tableaux Durand-Ruel*, November 1915 (traveled to Chicago, Auditorium Hotel, December 1915). (Monet, cat. 86)

Boston, 1935
Boston, Museum of Fine Arts, *Independent Painters of Nineteenth Century Paris*, 15 March–28 April 1935. (Manet, cat. 68)

Boston, 1962
Boston, Museum of Fine Arts, *Vincent van Gogh: Paintings, Watercolors, Drawings*, 22 March–29 April 1962. (van Gogh, cat. 109)

Bremen, 1965
Bremen, Kunsthalle, *Ker-Xavier Roussel, 1867–1944*, 1965. (Roussel, cat. 125)

Bremen, 1967
Bremen, Kunsthalle, *Emile Bernard: Gemälde, Handzeichnungen, Aquarelle, Druckgraphik*, 5 February–2 April 1967. (Bernard, cat. 127)

Bristol, 1968
Bristol, City Art Gallery, *From a Private Collection: A Special Exhibition for Museums Week*, 1968. (Courbet, cat. 43)

Brooklyn, 1956
Brooklyn Museum, *Religious Painting 15th–19th Century: An Exhibition of European Paintings from American Collections*, 2 October–13 November 1956. (Puvis, cat. 58)

Brussels, 1888
Brussels, *Vème Exposition des XX*, 6 February 1888. (Possibly Toulouse-Lautrec, cats. 122, 123)

Buenos Aires, 1933
Buenos Aires, Museo Nacional de Bellas Artes, *Escuela francesa siglos XIX y XX*, 20 October–5 November 1933. (Renoir, Cat. 92; Toulouse-Lautrec, cat. 122)

Buenos Aires, 1947
Buenos Aires, Galerie Wildenstein, *Renoir*, October 1947. (Renoir, cat. 92)

Buenos Aires, 1949
Buenos Aires, Museo Nacional de Bellas Artes, *La Pintura francesa de Manet a nuestros dias*, July 1949. (Toulouse-Lautrec, cat. 122)

Buenos Aires, 1950
Buenos Aires, Galeria Viau, *Degas et Lautrec*, 1950. (Toulouse-Lautrec, cat. 122)

Buenos Aires, 1962
Buenos Aires, Museo Nacional de Bellas Artes, *El Impresionismo frances en las colecciones Argentinas*, September–October 1962. (Renoir, cat. 92)

Buenos Aires, 1964
Buenos Aires, Instituto Torcuato, *Henri de Toulouse-Lautrec, di Tella 1864–1964*, 30 October–29 November 1964. (Toulouse-Lautrec, cat. 122)

Buffalo, 1930
Buffalo, Fine Arts Academy, *Twenty-fifth Anniversary of the Opening of the Albright Art Gallery*, 16 November–14 December 1930. (Manet, cat. 68)

Buffalo, 1932
Buffalo, Fine Arts Academy, Albright Art Gallery, *The Nineteenth Century: French Art in Retrospect*, 1–30 November 1932. (Toulouse-Lautrec, cat. 123)

Cedar Rapids, 1952
Cedar Rapids, Iowa, Coe College, *Centennial Exhibition*, 1952. (Corot, cat. 23)

Chapel Hill, 1978
Chapel Hill, University of North Carolina, William Hayes Ackland Memorial Art Center, *French Nineteenth Century Oil Sketches: David to Degas*, 5 March–16 April 1978. (Prud'hon, cat. 6)

Chicago, 1930
Chicago, Art Institute, *Loan Exhibition of Paintings, Drawings, Prints, and Posters*, 23 December 1930–18 January 1931. (Toulouse-Lautrec, cat. 123)

Chicago, 1933
Chicago, Arts Club, *Paintings by Claude Monet in Retrospect, 1868–1913*, 6–31 January 1933. (Monet, cat. 86)

Chicago, 1934
Chicago, Art Institute, *A Century of Progress*, 1 June–1 November 1934. (Corot, cat. 23)

Chicago, 1937
Chicago, Findlay Galleries, *Barbizon Exhibition*, 1937. (Corot, cat. 23)

Chicago, 1940
Chicago, Arts Club of Chicago, *Origins of Modern Art*, 2–30 April 1940. (Corot, cat. 23)

Chicago, 1960
Chicago, Art Institute, *Corot 1796–1875: An Exhibition of His Paintings and Graphic Works*, 6 October–13 November 1960. (Corot, cat. 23)

Chicago, 1969
Chicago, Art Institute, *Chicago Private Collectors*, July 1969. (Monet, cat. 86)

Chicago, 1973
Chicago, Art Institute, *Paintings by Renoir*, 3 February–1 April 1973. (Renoir, cat. 88)

Chicago, 1978
Chicago, Art Institute, *Frédéric Bazille and Early Impressionism*, 4 March–30 April 1978. (Bazille, cat. 87; Guigou, cat. 70)

Claremont, 1963
Claremont, Calif., Pomona College Gallery, *Muse or Ego: Salon and Independent Artists of the 1880s*, 17 April–12 May 1963. (Manet, cat. 67)

Cleveland, 1936
Cleveland, Museum of Art, *The Twentieth Anniversary Exhibition*, 26 June–4 October 1936. (van Gogh, cat. 110)

Cologne, 1912
Cologne, Städtische Ausstellungshalle, *Internationale Kunstausstellung des Sonderbundes westdeutscher Kunstfreunde und Künstler zu Köln*, 25 May–30 September 1912. (Cézanne, cats. 80, 82; van Gogh, cat. 110)

Cologne, 1978
Cologne, Galerie Abels, *Französische Landschaftsmaler 1850–1950*, 1978. (Trouillebert, cat. 62)

Copenhagen, 1922
Copenhagen, *Udstilling af aeldre og nyere hollandsk Malerkunst*, June 1922. (van Gogh, cat. 110)

Copenhagen, 1956
Copenhagen, Winkel & Magnussen, *Gauguin og Hans Venner*, June–July 1956. (Sérusier, cat. 120)

Dallas, 1961
Dallas, Museum for Contemporary Arts, *Impressionists and Their Forebears from Barbizon*, 9 March–2 April 1961. (Renoir, cat. 88)

Dayton, 1951
Dayton, Art Institute, *The City by the River and the Sea: Five Centuries of Skylines*, 18 April–3 June 1951. (Renoir, cat. 88)

Dayton, 1960
Dayton, Art Institute, *French Paintings, 1789–1929, from the Collection of Walter P. Chrysler, Jr.* 25 March–22 May 1960. (Bernard, cat. 129)

Des Moines, 1955
Des Moines, Art Center, *Communicating Art from Midwest Collections*, 1955. (Corot, cat. 23)

Detroit, 1954
Detroit, Institute of the Arts, *The Two Sides of the Medal: French Painting from Gérôme to Gauguin*, 1954. (Manet, cats. 68, 69; Renoir, cat. 88; Toulouse-Lautrec, cat. 124)

Dresden, 1914
Dresden, Galerie Ernst Arnold, *Ausstellung Französischer Malerei des XIX. Jahrhunderts*, April–May 1914. (Courbet, cat. 44)

Dresden, 1926
Dresden, Staatliche Kunstsammlungen, 1926. (van Gogh, cat. 111)

Dublin, 1899
Dublin, Leinster Lecture Hall, *Art Loan Exhibition*, 1–8 April 1899. (Manet, cat. 69)

Edinburgh, 1886
Edinburgh, *International Exhibition*, 1886. (Courbet, cat. 46)

Edinburgh, 1967
Edinburgh, Scottish Arts Council, *A Man of Influence: Alex Reid, 1854–1928*, Summer 1967. (Courbet, cat. 46)

Geneva, 1947
Geneva, Musée Rath, *172 oeuvres de Vincent van Gogh (1853–1890)*, 22 March–20 April 1947. (van Gogh, cat. 108)

Geneva, 1968
Geneva, Petit Palais, *L'Aube du XXe siècle de Renoir à Chagall*, 1968. (Lacombe, cat. 130)

Geneva, 1977
Geneva, Petit Palais, *Gustave Moreau et le symbolisme*, 1977. (Lacombe, cat. 130)

Glasgow, 1878
Glasgow, *Loan Exhibition in Aid of the Royal Infirmary*, 1878. (Courbet, cat. 46)

Glasgow, 1888
Glasgow, *International Exhibition*, 1888. (Courbet, cCat. 46)

Glasgow, 1901
Glasgow, *International Exhibition*, 1901. (Courbet, cat. 46)

Glasgow, 1930
Glasgow, Galerie Lefevre, *Nineteenth and Twentieth Century French Paintings*, October 1930. (Seurat, cat. 113)

Goteborg, 1968
Goteborg, Konstmuseum, *Emile Bernard: Må6lningar, akvareller, teckningar, grafik*, 13 December 1968–26 January 1969 (traveled to Lyngby, Sophienholm-Kunstmuseum, 2 February–30 March 1969; Stockholm, Thielska Galleriet, 5 April–15 August 1969). (Bernard, cat. 127)

The Hague, 1898
The Hague, Arts and Crafts Gallery, *Vincent van Gogh*, November 1898. (van Gogh, cat. 110)

The Hague, 1950
The Hague, Gemeentemuseum, *Verzameling H. P. Bremmer*, 9 March–23 April 1950. (van Gogh, cat. 106)

The Hague, 1957
The Hague, Gemeentemuseum, *Odilon Redon*, 3 May–23 June 1957, no. 178. (Redon, cat. 83)

Irvine, 1967
Irvine, University of California, *A Selection of Nineteenth and Twentieth Century Works from The Hunt Foods and Industries Museum of Art Collection*, 7–22 March 1967 (traveled to Davis, University of California, 3–28 April 1967; Riverside, University of California, 10–30 May 1967; San Diego, Fine Arts Gallery, 7 July–1 October 1967). (Daubigny, cat. 39)

La Tour de Peilz, 1950
La Tour de Peilz, Musée Jenisch, *Exposition Gustave Courbet*, 8 July–3 October 1950. (Courbet, cat. 41)

Lausanne, 1964
Lausanne, Palais de Beaulieu, *Chefs-d'oeuvre des collections suisses de Manet à Picasso*, 1964. (Manet, cat. 68)

Lexington, 1973
Lexington, University of Kentucky Art Gallery, *Academic Painting*, 21 October–11 November 1973. (Couture, cat. 37)

Liège, 1946
Liège, Musée des Beaux-Arts, *Vincent van Gogh*, October 1946. (van Gogh, cat. 108)

Lille, 1967
Lille, Palais des Beaux-Arts, *Emile Bernard, 1868–1941: Peintures, dessins, gravures*, 12 April–12 June 1967. (Bernard, cat. 127)

LIVERPOOL, 1933
Liverpool, Walker Art Gallery, *Fifty-ninth Autumn Exhibition*, 4 October–13 December 1933. (Manet, cat. 67)

LONDON, 1871
London, *Second Annual Exhibition in London of Pictures, The Contributions of The Society of French Artists*, 29 June 1871. (Dupre, cat. 34)

LONDON, 1872a
London, Durand-Ruel, *Third Exhibition of the Society of French Artists*, Spring 1872. (Manet, cat. 68)

LONDON, 1872b
London, 168 New Bond Street, W., *Fifth Exhibition of the Society of French Artists*, 1872. (Renoir, cat. 88)

LONDON, 1905
London, Grafton Galleries, *Masterpieces of French Art*, 1905. (Monet, cat. 86)

LONDON, 1930
London, Alex. Reid & Lefevre, *Renoir and the Post-Impressionists*, June–July 1930. (Seurat, cat. 113)

LONDON, 1932
London, Royal Academy of Arts, *Exhibition of French Art, 1200–1900*, 4 January–5 March 1932. (Daumier, cat. 31; Manet, cat. 67; Rousseau, cat. 35)

LONDON, 1934
London, Royal Academy, *British Art*, 6 January–10 March 1934. (Etty, cat. 13)

LONDON, 1935
London, Arthur Tooth & Sons Ltd., *"La Flèche d'Or": A Loan Exhibition of Pictures from Private Collections in Paris*, 8 May–1 June 1935. (Corot, cat. 20)

LONDON, 1936a
London, Arthur Tooth & Sons, *Selected Pictures by Claude Monet (1840–1926)*, 12 March–4 April 1936. (Monet, cats. 84, 86)

LONDON, 1936b
London, Adams Gallery, *Paintings by William Etty*, 20 May–20 June 1936. (Etty, cat. 13)

LONDON, 1936c
London, New Burlington Galleries, *Exhibition of Masters of French 19th Century Painting*, 1–31 October 1936. (Corot, cat. 20; Manet, cat. 69)

LONDON, 1937a
London, Arthur Tooth & Sons Ltd., *Selected Pictures by J. B. Jongkind, 1819–1891*, 18 March–10 April 1937. (Jongkind, cat. 49)

LONDON, 1937b
London, Wildenstein & Co., *Centenary Memorial Exhibition of John Constable R.A.*, 21 April–29 May 1937. (Etty, cat. 13)

LONDON, 1937c
London, Thos. Agnew & Sons, *Paintings and Drawings by Camille Pissarro*, November 1937. (Pissarro, cat. 64)

LONDON, 1939
London, Wildenstein and Co., *Homage to Paul Cézanne (1839–1906)*, July 1939. (Cézanne, cats. 79, 82)

LONDON, 1943
London, National Gallery, *Nineteenth Century French Paintings*, February–March 1943. (Cézanne, cat. 69)

LONDON, 1946
London, Lefevre Gallery, *Delacroix to Dufy: French Paintings of the 19th and 20th Centuries, in Aid of the Contemporary Art Society*, June–July 1946. (Cézanne, cat. 82)

LONDON, 1949
London, Arthur Tooth & Sons Ltd., *Anthology—Loan Exhibition of French Pictures from Private Collections in Aid of the Blind Children at Dorton House, Aylesbury*, 8–28 June 1949. (Jongkind, cat. 49)

LONDON, 1951
London, Arthur Tooth & Sons, Ltd., *Paris-Londres: A Collection of Pictures Recently Purchased in France*, 11 April–11 May 1951. (Sisley, cat. 78)

LONDON, 1952
London, Marlborough Fine Art Ltd., *Théodore Géricault, 1791–1824. Proceeds in Aid of the Tate Gallery's Rodin Group Appeal*, October–November 1952. (Gericault, cat. 18)

LONDON, 1953
London, Marlborough Gallery, *Gustave Courbet*, May–June 1953. (Courbet, cat. 41)

LONDON, 1954a
London, Tate Gallery, *The Pleydell-Bouverie Collection of Impressionist and Other Paintings, Lent by the Hon. Mrs. A. E. Pleydell-Bouverie*, 26 January–25 April 1954. (Sisley, cat. 78)

LONDON, 1954b
London, Wildenstein & Co., *Paris in the Nineties*, 1954. (Roussel, cat. 125)

LONDON, 1955
London, The Arts Council of Great Britain, *An Exhibition of Paintings by William Etty*, 1955. (Etty, cat. 13)

LONDON, 1963
London, Marlborough Fine Art, *A Great Period of French Painting: An Exhibition Held in Memory of the Late Miss Clariça Davidson*, June–July 1963. (Courbet, cat. 46)

LONDON, 1964
London, Wildenstein & Co., *Ker Xavier Roussel*, 1964. (Roussel, cat. 125)

LONDON, 1965
London, Hallsborough Gallery, *Exhibition: From Butinone to Chagall, Fine Paintings and Drawings of Six Centuries*, 12 May–23 July 1965. (Fantin-Latour, cat. 76)

LONDON, 1966a
London, Tate Gallery, *Gauguin and the Pont-Aven Group*, 7 January–13 February 1966 (traveled to Zurich, Kunsthaus, March–April 1966). (Bernard, cat. 127)

LONDON, 1966b
London, Lefevre Gallery, *XIX and XX Century French Paintings and Drawings*, November–December 1966. (van Gogh, cat. 108)

LONDON, 1967a
London, Arthur Tooth & Sons Ltd., *Paris-Londres: A Collection of Pictures Many Recently Acquired in France*, 31 May–24 June 1967. (Jongkind, cat. 49)

LONDON, 1967b
London, Lefevre Gallery, *XIX and XX Century French Paintings*, 16 November–22 December 1967. (Monticelli, cat. 51)

LONDON, 1968
London, Lefevre Gallery, *XIX and XX Century French Paintings*, 7 November–21 December 1968. (Courbet, cat. 46)

LONDON, 1969
London, Lefevre Gallery, *Claude Monet, the Early Years: From British Collections in Aid of the Police Dependants' Trust*, 8 May–7 June 1969. (Monet, cat. 84)

LONDON, 1973
London, Lefevre Gallery, *Important XIX and XX Century Paintings*, 1 November–22 December 1973. (Courbet, cat. 42)

London, 1978
London, Heim Gallery Ltd., *Forgotten French Art from the First to the Second Empire: Autumn Exhibition*, 23 November–22 December 1978. (Ducis, cat. 9; Abel de Pujol, cat. 12)

Los Angeles, 1940
Los Angeles, County Museum, *The Development of Impressionism*, 12 January–28 February 1940. (Pissarro, cat. 64)

Los Angeles, 1943
Los Angeles, Dalzell Hatfield Galleries, *Corot–Daumier*, 22 February–15 March 1943. (Corot, cat. 23)

Los Angeles, 1955
Los Angeles, County Museum, *Pierre-Auguste Renoir, 1841–1919: Paintings, Drawings, Prints and Sculpture*, 14 July–21 August 1955 (traveled to San Francisco, Museum of Art, 1 September–2 October 1955). (Renoir, cat. 88)

Los Angeles, 1956
Los Angeles, County Museum, *The Gladys Lloyd Robinson and Edward G. Robinson Collection: An Exhibition Lent through the Courtesy of the Trustees of the Collection Samuel Hurwitz, Orange, California and Edward G. Robinson*, 11 September–11 November 1956 (traveled to San Francisco, California Palace of the Legion of Honor, 30 November 1956–13 January 1957). (Vuillard, cat. 134)

Los Angeles, 1958
Los Angeles, County Museum, *Honoré Daumier*, 12 November–21 December 1958. (Daumier, cats. 30, 31)

Los Angeles, 1965
Los Angeles, County Museum of Art, *A Selection from the Mr. and Mrs. Norton Simon Collection Honoring the College Art Association*, 18 January–7 March 1965. (cats. 21, 30, 31, 40, 63, 67, 69, 81, 82, 89, 91, 99, 112, 124)

Los Angeles, 1967
Los Angeles, City National Bank (Pershing Square), *Selected Paintings from the Collection of Mr. and Mrs. William Goetz*, January 1967. (Monet, cat. 86)

Los Angeles, 1991
Los Angeles, County Museum of Art, *Monet to Matisse: French Art in Southern California Collections*, 1991. (Pissarro, cat. 65)

Los Angeles, 2006
Los Angeles, J. Paul Getty Museum, *Courbet and the Modern Landscape*, 21 February–14 May 2006 (traveled to Houston, Museum of Fine Arts, 18 June–10 September 2006; Baltimore, The Walters Art Museum, 15 October 2006–7 January 2007).(Courbet, cats. 43, 44; Los Angeles only)

Lyon, 1936
Lyon, Musée de Lyon, *Exposition Corot*, 24 May–28 June 1936. (Corot, cats. 22, 24)

Lyon, 1954
Lyon, Musée des Beaux-Arts, *Courbet. Exposition organisée sous l'égide du Syndicat d'initiative de Lyon*, 1954. (Courbet, cat. 41)

Madrid, 1900
Madrid, Ministerio de Instrucción Pública y Bellas Artes, *Obras de Goya*, May 1900. (Goya, cat. 4)

Madrid, 1993
Madrid, Museo del Prado, *Goya: Truth and Fantasy; The Small Paintings*, 18 November 1993–27 February 1994 (traveled to London, Royal Academy of Arts, 17 March–12 June 1994; Chicago, Art Institute, 16 July–16 October 1994). (Goya, cat. 4)

Malibu, 1996
Malibu, J. Paul Getty Museum, *Roger Fenton: The Orientalist Suite*, 16 July–6 October 1996. (Devéria, cat. 25)

Manchester, 1923
Manchester, Thomas Agnew and Sons, *Loan Exhibition of Masterpieces of French Art of the 19th Century in Aid of the Lord Mayor's Appeal for the Hospitals*, 1923. (Gauguin, cat. 99)

Manchester, 1934
Manchester, City Art Gallery, *British Art*, 5 April–26 May 1934. (Etty, cat. 13)

Mannheim, 1964
Mannheim, Städtische Kunsthalle, *Les Nabis et Leurs Amis*, 23 October 1963–6 January 1964. (Sérusier, cat. 120)

Milan, 1959
Milan, Palazzo Reale, *Édouard Vuillard*, October–November 1959. (Vuillard, cat. 131)

Milwaukee, 1957
Milwaukee, Art Institute, *Inaugural Exhibition: El Greco, Rembrandt, Goya, Cézanne, Van Gogh, Picasso*, 12 September–20 October 1957. (van Gogh, cat. 107)

Milwaukee, 1977
Milwaukee, Art Center, *Collecting the Masters*, 3 June–31 July 1977. (Manet, cat. 67)

Minneapolis, 1960
Minneapolis, Institute of the Arts, *Drawings, Paintings and Sculpture from Three Private Collections*, 13 July–14 August 1960. (van Gogh, cat. 106)

Minneapolis, 1962
Minneapolis, University of Minnesota Gallery, *The Nineteenth Century: 125 Master Drawings*, 1962. (van Gogh, cat. 106)

Minneapolis, 1968
Minneapolis, Institute of the Arts, *Selections from the Drawing Collection of David Daniels*, 1968 (traveled to Chicago, Art Institute; Kansas City, Nelson Gallery-Atkins Museum; Cambridge, Fogg Art Museum). (van Gogh, cat. 106)

Montauban, 1862
Montauban, Hôtel-de-Ville, *Exposition des beaux-arts*, May 1862. (Ingres, cat. 11)

Montpellier, 1927
Montpellier, Exposition internationale, *Rétrospective Bazille*, May–June 1927. (Bazille, cat. 67)

Montpellier, 1941
Montpellier, Musée Fabre, *Centenaire de Frédéric Bazille*, May–June 1941. (Bazille, cat. 67)

Montpellier, 1959
Montpellier, Musée Fabre, *Frédéric Bazille, Exposition organisée en l'honneur du XVIIme Congrés de l'association des pédiatres de langue française*, 13–31 October 1959. (Bazille, cat. 67)

Montreal, 1967
Montreal, Galerie Hervé, *A. Renoir*, May–June 1967. (Renoir, cat. 93)

Munich, 1908
Munich, *Secession*, 1908. (Vuillard, cat. 132)

Munich, 1930
Munich, Neue Pinakothek, *Sammlung Schloss Rohoncz*, 1930. (Pissarro, cat. 65)

Munich, 1956
Munich, Haus der Kunst, *Vincent van Gogh*, October–December 1956. (van Gogh, cat. 108)

Munich, 1966
Munich, Galleria del Levante, *Pont-Aven et les Nabis*, 8 November 1966–10 January 1967. (Bernard, cat. 127)

Munich, 1968
Munich, Haus der Kunst, *Édouard Vuillard, Xavier Roussel*, 16 March–12 May 1968 (traveled to Paris, Orangerie des Tuileries, 28 May–16 September 1968). (Roussel, cat. 125)

Newark, 1961
Newark, Museum, *Nineteenth Century Master Drawings*, 16 March–30 April 1961. (van Gogh, cat. 106)

New York, 1886
New York, American Art Galleries, *Works in Oil and Pastel by the Impressionists of Paris*, April 1886 (traveled to New York, National Academy of Design, May–June 1886). (Monet, cat. 86)

New York, 1894
New York, Durand-Ruel, *Paintings and Drawings by Puvis de Chavannes*, 1894. (Puvis de Chavannes, cat. 58)

New York, 1914
New York, Galerie Durand-Ruel, *Exhibition of Paintings by Renoir*, 7–21 February 1914. (Renoir, cat. 90)

New York, 1920a
New York, Colony Club, *A Selected Group of Modern French and American Paintings*, 26 March–4 April 1920. (Monet, cat. 86)

New York, 1920b
New York, Metropolitan Museum of Art, *Fiftieth Anniversary Exhibition*, 8 May–1 November 1920. (Rousseau, cat. 35)

New York, 1924
New York, [location unknown], *Les Trois Impressionnistes: Monet, Pissarro, Sisley*, 1924. (Monet, cat. 86)

New York, 1928a
New York, M. Knoedler & Co., *A Century of French Painting: Exhibition Organised for the Benefit of the French Hospital of New York*, 12 November– 8 December 1928. (Corot, cat. 20)

New York, 1928b
New York, Metropolitan Museum of Art, *Spanish Paintings from El Greco to Goya*, 1928. (Goya, cat. 5)

New York, 1930
New York, Museum of Modern Art, *Corot, Daumier: Eighth Loan Exhibition*, 16 October–23 November 1930. (Corot, cat. 23; Daumier, cat. 31)

New York, 1931a
New York, Museum of Modern Art, *Tenth Loan Exhibition: Lautréc–Redon*, 1 February–2 March 1931. (Toulouse-Lautrec, cat. 123)

New York, 1931b
New York, American Art Association, Anderson Galleries, *Exhibition of Important Paintings: Old and Modern Masters in the New York Art Market from the Collections of Leading New York Dealers*, 15 March–4 April 1931. (Monet, cat. 86)

New York, 1931c
New York, Knoedler Galleries, *The Landscape in French Painting: XIX–XX Centuries*, October–November 1931. (Rousseau, cat. 35)

New York, 1932a
New York, Metropolitan Museum of Art, *Taste of Today in Masterpieces of Painting*, 1932. (Daumier, cat. 31)

New York, 1932b
New York, C. W. Kraushaar Art Galleries, *Paintings*, 11 October–5 November 1932. (Pissarro, cat. 64)

New York, 1934a
New York, Durand-Ruel Galleries, *Exhibition of Important Paintings by Great French Masters of the Nineteenth Century, Organized by Paul Rosenberg and Durand-Ruel for the Benefit of the Children's Aid Society and the French Hospital of New York*, 12 February–10 March 1934. (Daumier, cat. 31)

New York, 1934b
New York, M. Knoedler & Co., *A Loan Exhibition of Paintings by Goya under the Patronage of His Excellency Señor Don Juan Francisco de Cárdenas, Spanish Ambassador*, 9–21 April 1934. (Goya, cat. 5)

New York, 1937a
New York, Wildenstein & Co., *Édouard Manet, 1832–1883: A Retrospective Loan Exhibition for the Benefit of the French Hospital and the Lisa Day Nursery*, 19 March–17 April 1937. (Manet, cat. 68)

New York, 1937b
New York, Jacques Seligmann & Co. Inc., *Exhibition of French Masters from Courbet to Seurat*, 22 March–17 April 1937. (Corot, cat. 23)

New York, 1938
New York, Wildenstein & Co., *Great Portraits from Impressionism to Modernism*, 1–29 March 1938. (van Gogh, cat. 110)

New York, 1939a
New York, M. Knoedler & Co., *Views of Paris*, 9–28 January 1939. (Renoir, cat. 88)

New York, 1939b
New York, C. W. Kraushaar Art Galleries, *A Collection of XIXth Century French Paintings*, 30 January–25 February 1939. (Pissarro, cat. 64)

New York, 1940a
New York, Durand-Ruel, *Paintings by Claude Monet*, 2–23 March 1940. (Monet, cat. 86)

New York, 1940b
New York, World's Fair, *Masterpieces of Art*, May–October 1940. (van Gogh, cat. 110)

New York, 1940c
New York, Durand-Ruel, *Paintings of Paris for the Benefit of the British War Relief Society*, 29 October–16 November, 1940. (Renoir, cat. 88)

New York, 1943a
New York, Wildenstein & Co., *A Loan Exhibition of Fashion in Headdress, 1450–1943, for the Benefit of New York Infirmary for Women and Children*, 27 April–27 May 1943. (Goya, cat. 5)

New York, 1943b
New York, Wildenstein & Co., *The Art and Life of Vincent van Gogh: Loan Exhibition in Aid of American and Dutch War Relief*, 6 October–7 November 1943. (van Gogh, cats. 111, 110)

New York, 1943c
New York, Knoedler Galleries, *Loan Exhibition of the Collection of Pictures of Erich Maria Remarque*, 18 October–13 November 1943. (Daumier, cat. 30)

New York, 1945a
New York, Wildenstein, *A Loan Exhibition of Paintings by Claude Monet for the Benefit of the Children of Giverny*, 11 April–12 May 1945. (Monet, cat. 86)

New York, 1945b
New York, Paul Rosenberg & Co., *Exhibition of French Paintings of the XIXth and XXth Centuries*, 26 November–22 December 1945. (Toulouse-Lautrec, cat. 124)

New York, 1946a
New York, Durand-Ruel Galleries, *Six 19th-Century French Artists*, 25 March–30 April 1946. (Pissarro, cat. 63)

New York, 1946b
New York, Wildenstein & Co., *Toulouse-Lautrec*, 23 October–23 November 1946. (Toulouse-Lautrec, cat. 123)

New York, 1947
New York, Paul Rosenberg & Co., *Great French Masters of the 19th century*, 1947. (Toulouse-Lautrec, cat. 124)

New York, 1950
New York, Wildenstein, *A Loan Exhibition of Renoir for the Benefit of the New York Infirmary*, 23 March–29 April 1950. (Renoir, cat. 88)

New York, 1953a
New York, Paul Rosenberg, *Collector's Choice*, 17 March–18 April 1953. (van Gogh, cat. 110)

New York, 1953b
New York, Residence of Jakob Goldschmidt (32 East 64th Street), *Collection of Mr. Jakob Goldschmidt, under the Auspices of the Greenwich House Music School Committee*, November 1953. (Pissarro, cat. 63)

New York, 1955
New York, Wildenstein & Co., *Van Gogh*, 24 March–30 April 1955. (van Gogh, cat. 110)

New York, 1956a
New York, Paul Rosenberg & Co., *Loan Exhibition of Paintings by Gustave Courbet (1819–1877)*, 16 January–11 February 1956. (Courbet, cat. 45)

New York, 1956b
New York, Museum of Modern Art, *Toulouse-Lautrec: Paintings, Drawings, Posters and Lithographs*, 20 March–6 May 1956. (Toulouse-Lautrec, cat. 124)

New York, 1956c
New York, Paul Rosenberg & Co., *Loan Exhibition of Paintings by J. B. C. Corot (1796–1875)*, 5 November–1 December 1956. (Corot, cat. 23)

New York, 1957
New York, Hirschl & Adler Galleries, *Emile Bernard at Pont-Aven (1886–1893)*, 20 February–23 March 1957. (Bernard, cat. 129)

New York, 1958
New York, Wildenstein, *Loan Exhibition: Renoir, for the Benefit of the Citizens' Committee for Children of New York City, Inc.*, 8 April–10 May 1958. (Renoir, cat. 88)

New York, 1959
New York, Wildenstein and Co., *Loan Exhibition: Cézanne, under the Patronage of Mrs. Dwight D. Eisenhower and His Excellency, Monsieur Hervé Alphand, the Ambassador of France to the United States, for the Benefit of the National Organization of Mentally Ill Children*, 5 November–5 December 1959. (Cézanne, cat. 79)

New York, 1963
New York, Wildenstein, *Birth of Impressionism*, 7 March–6 April 1963. (Rousseau, cat. 35)

New York, 1964a
New York, Wildenstein & Co., *Toulouse-Lautrec*, 7 February–14 March 1964. (Toulouse-Lautrec, cat. 123)

New York, 1964b
New York, Wildenstein and Co., *Vuillard: Loan Exhibition, under the Patronage of Monsieur Michel Legendre, Consul General of France in New York, and Monsieur Édouard Morot-Sir, Cultural Counselor to the French Embassy, for the Benefit of the Albert Einstein College of Medicine*, 16 October–21 November 1964. (Vuillard, cat. 132)

New York, 1965
New York, Wildenstein, *Loan Exhibition: Olympia's Progeny. . . . for the Benefit of the Association for Mentally Ill Children in Manhattan, Inc.*, 28 October–27 November 1965. (Renoir, cat. 88)

New York, 1966a
New York, M. Knoedler & Co., *Impressionist Treasures from Private Collections in New York for the Benefit of St. Luke's Hospital Center Building Fund*, 12–29 January 1966. (Renoir, cat. 88)

New York, 1966b
New York, Acquavella Galleries, *Flowers by Fantin-Latour: An Exhibition Organized for the Benefit of the Boys' Club of New York*, 2 November–3 December 1966. (Fantin-Latour, cat. 76)

New York, 1968a
New York, Hammer Galleries, *40th Anniversary Loan Exhibition, 1928–1968*, 7 November–7 December 1968. (Gauguin, cat. 99)

New York, 1968b
New York, Wildenstein and Co., *Gustave Caillebotte*, 1968. (Caillebotte, cat. 98)

New York, 1969
New York, Richard Feigen & Co., *Claude Monet. for the Benefit of the Metropolitan Museum of Art*, 15 October–15 November 1969. (Monet, cat. 86)

New York, 1972
New York, Wildenstein & Co., *Faces from the World of Impressionism and Post-Impressionism*, 2 November–9 December 1972. (van Gogh, cat. 110)

New York, 1974a
New York, Metropolitan Museum of Art, *Sixth International Exhibition presented by C.I.N.O.A., La Confédération Internationale des Négociants en Oeuvres d'Art/The International Confederation of Dealers in Works of Art*, 19 October 1974–5 January 1975. (Goya, cat. 4)

New York, 1974b
New York, Hirschl & Adler Galleries, *Quality: An Experience in Collecting*, 12 November–7 December 1974. (Bernard, cat. 129)

New York, 1975
New York, Wildenstein, *Nature as Scene: French Landscape Painting from Poussin to Bonnard*, 29 October–6 December 1975. (Rousseau, cat. 35)

New York, 1981
New York, Acquavella Galleries, Inc., *XIX & XX Century Master Paintings*, 30 October–30 November 1981. (Pissarro, cat. 64)

Northampton, 1934
Northampton, Mass., Smith College Museum of Art, *Exhibition of Portraits and Early Landscapes by J. B. C. Corot*, 12 November–9 December 1934. (Corot, cat. 23)

Norton, 1976
Norton, Mass., Wheaton College, Watson Gallery, *Process of Perfection*, 15 November–15 December 1976. (Seurat, cat. 113)

Oakland, 1969
Oakland, Calif., Oakland Museum, *Art Treasures in California: An Exhibition of Master Paintings from Museums and Public Collections in California*, 29 November–31 December 1969. (Bonnard, cat. 126)

Omaha, 1951
Omaha, Neb., Joslyn Memorial Art Museum, *The Beginnings of Modern Painting, France, 1800–1910*, 4 October–4 November 1951. (Corot, cat. 23)

Paris, 1812
Paris, *Salon*, 1812. (Ducis, cat. 9)

Paris, 1822
Paris, *Salon d'Horace Vernet . . . exposés chez lui*, 1822. (Vernet, cat. 14)

Paris, 1827
Paris, *Salon*, 1827. (Dubufe, cats. 15, 16)

Paris, 1839
Paris, *Salon*, 1839. (Corot, cat. 21)

Paris, 1841
Paris, Salon, 1841. (Couture, cat. 37)

Paris, 1850
Paris, Salon, 1850–1851. (Bougereau, cat. 59)

Paris, 1865a
Paris, Galerie Martinet, *Édouard Manet*, 1865. (Manet, cat. 67)

Paris, 1865b
Paris, *Salon*, 1865. (Guigou, cat. 70; Monet, cat. 84)

Paris, 1867
Paris, Rond-Point du pont de l'Alma, *Exposition des oeuvres de M. G. Courbet*, 1867. (Courbet, cat. 43)

Paris, 1873
Paris, *Salon*, 1873. (Couder, cat. 38)

Paris, 1875
Paris, École Nationale des Beaux-Arts, *Exposition de l'oeuvre de Corot*, May 1875. (Corot, cat. 24)

Paris, 1878
Paris, Galerie Durand-Ruel & Cie, *Exposition rétrospective de tableaux et dessins des maîtres modernes*, 1878. (Corot, cat. 24)

Paris, 1882
Paris, 251 rue Saint-Honoré, *7e Exposition des artistes indépendants*, March 1882. (Monet, cat. 86)

Paris, 1883a
Paris, Galerie Durand-Ruel, *Camille Pissarro*, 1–25 May 1883. (Pissarro, cat. 64)

Paris, 1883b
Paris, Galerie Georges Petit, *Cent chefs-d'oeuvre*, 1883. (Rousseau, cat. 35)

Paris, 1884
Paris, École nationale des Beaux-Arts, *Exposition des oeuvres d'Édouard Manet*, 6–28 January 1884 (Manet, cats. 67, 68)

Paris, 1885
Paris, Salle des États au Louvre, *Exposition de tableaux, statues, et objets d'art au profit de l'œuvre des orphelins d'Alsace-Lorraine*, 1885. (Manet, cat. 67)

Paris, 1886
Paris, Galerie Durand-Ruel & Cie, *Exposition de maîtres du siècle*, April–May 1886. (Corot, cat. 24)

Paris, 1887
Paris, Galerie Durand-Ruel, *Tableaux, pastels, et dessins par Puvis de Chavannes*, 1887. (Puvis de Chavannes, cat. 58)

Paris, 1889
Paris, Palais du Champ de Mars, Galerie des Beaux-Arts, *Exposition centennale de l'art français* (Exposition universelle), 1889. (Corot, Cat. 23; Puvis de Chavannes, cat. 58)

Paris, 1891
Paris, Société des artistes indépendants, *7me Exposition*, 20 March–27 April 1891. (Anquetin, cat. 117)

Paris, 1893
Paris, Galerie Georges Petit, *L'Exposition des portraits des écrivains et journalistes du siècle 1793–1893*, June 1893. (Courbet, cat. 47)

Paris, 1895a
Paris, Galerie La Bodinière, *Lépine*, January 1895. (Lépine, cat. 73)

Paris, 1895b
Paris, Palais Galliera, *Exposition organisée au profit du monument du centenaire de Corot*, May–June 1895. (Corot, cat. 23)

Paris, 1896
Paris, Galerie Durand-Ruel, *Berthe Morisot (Madame Eugène Manet) . . . Exposition de son oeuvre,* 5–21 March 1896. (Morisot, cat. 94)

Paris, 1897
Paris, Galerie Georges Petit, *Exposition A. Sisley*, February 1897. (Sisley, cat. 78)

Paris, 1899a
Paris, École des Beaux-Arts, *Exposition des oeuvres d'Eugène Boudin*, 9–30 January 1899. (Boudin, cat. 56)

Paris, 1899b
Paris, Galeries Durand-Ruel, *Tableaux et aquarelles de Jongkind*, 15 May–10 June 1899. (Jongkind, cat. 49)

Paris, 1901a
Paris, Bernheim-Jeune, *Vincent van Gogh*, 15–31 March 1901. (van Gogh, cats. 111, 112)

Paris, 1901b
Paris, École des Beaux-Arts, *Exposition Daumier*, May 1901. (Daumier, cat. 31)

Paris, 1904
Paris, Petit Palais, *Salon d'Automne*, 15 October–15 November 1904. (Puvis de Chavannes, cat. 57; Cézanne, cat. 82; Renoir, cats. 91, 92; Vuillard, cat. 132)

Paris, 1906
Paris, Galerie Georges Petit, *Trouillebert*, 16–31 December 1906. (Trouillebert, cat. 62)

Paris, 1908a
Paris, Galerie Georges Petit, *Daumier*, 1908. (Daumier, cat. 30)

Paris, 1908b
Paris, Galerie Bernheim-Jeune, *Retrospective Georges Seurat*, 14 December 1908–9 January 1909. (Seurat, cat. 114)

Paris, 1910a
Paris, Bernheim-Jeune, *D'après les maîtres*, 1910. (Redon, cat. 83)

Paris, 1910b
Paris, Galerie Georges Petit, *Exposition de chefs d'œuvre de l'école française: Vingt peintres du XIXe siècle . . . au profit de l'assistance aux Militaires coloniaux et légionnaires*, 2–31 May 1910. (Corot, cat. 21)

Paris, 1910c
Paris, Salon d'Automne, *Exposition rétrospective d'oeuvres de Frédéric Bazille*, 1 October–8 November 1910. (Bazille, cat. 87)

Paris, 1911
Paris, Galerie Bernheim-Jeune, *Vuillard*, 13–25 February 1911. (Vuillard, cat. 134)

Paris, 1912
Paris, Galerie Durand-Ruel, *Portraits par Renoir*, 5–20 June 1912. (Renoir, cat. 92)

Paris, 1913
Paris, Galerie Druet, 17–29 November 1913. (Sérusier, cat. 121)

Paris, 1914a
Paris, Galeries Paul Rosenberg, *Exposition d'oeuvres de Toulouse-Lautrec*, 20 January–3 February 1914. (Toulouse-Loutrec, cat. 124)

Paris, 1914b
Paris, Galerie Brunner, *Exposition rétrospective*

des peintres de Vénise (XVIIIe et XIXe siècles): Organisée au profit de l'oeuvre de bienfaisance la fraternité artistique sur l'initiative de la Revue l'art et les artistes, 18 May–20 June 1914. (Corot, cat. 20)

Paris, 1914c
Paris, Galerie Manzi Joyant, *Exposition rétrospective de l'oeuvre de H. de Toulouse-Lautrec (1864–1901)*, 15 June–11 July 1914. (Toulouse-Lautrec, cats. 123, 124)

Paris, 1917a
Paris, Galerie Georges Petit, *Exposition d'oeuvres d'Alfred Sisley*, 14 May–7 June 1917. (Sisley, cat. 78)

Paris, 1917b
Paris, Galerie Bernheim, *Courbet*, December 1917–January 1918. (Courbet, cat. 42)

Paris, 1919
Paris, Galerie Bernheim-Jeune, *Courbet*, 18–31 July 1919. (Courbet, Cat. 42)

Paris, 1920
Paris, Galerie Durand-Ruel, *Exposition Renoir*, 29 November–18 December 1920. (Renoir, cat. 92)

Paris, 1926
Paris, Hôtel des Négociants, *Explication des peintures, gravures, miniatures et autres ouvrages de femmes peintres du XVIIIe siècle*, 1926. (Bouliar, cat. 8)

Paris, 1927
Paris, Galerie Bernheim-Jeune, *Cinquante Renoir choisis parmi les nus, les fleurs, les enfants*, 28 February–25 March 1927. (Renoir, cat. 93; van Gogh, cat. 112)

Paris, 1928a
Paris, Galerie Durand-Ruel, *Tableaux par Camille Pissarro*, 27 February–10 March 1928. (Pissarro, cat. 64)

Paris, 1928b
Paris, Société des Amis du Musée du Luxembourg, *Portraits et figures de femmes: Ingres à Picasso*, 1–30 June 1928. (Anquetin, 117)

Paris, 1928c
Paris, Paul Rosenberg, *Exposition d'oeuvres de Camille J.-B. Corot (1796–1875): Figures et paysages d'Italie au profit de la Bibliothèque d'art et d'archéologie de l'Université de Paris*, 6 June–7 July 1928. (Corot, cats. 21, 22)

Paris, 1930
Paris, Musée de l'Orangerie, *Centenaire de la naissance de Camille Pissarro*, February–March 1930. (Pissarro, cats. 64, 66)

Paris, 1931
Paris, Musée des Arts Décoratifs, *Exposition H. de Toulouse-Lautrec*, 9 April–17 May 1931. (Toulouse-Lautrec, cat. 124)

Paris, 1932
Paris, Orangerie des Tuileries, *Manet: 1832–1883*, June–July 1932. (Manet, cat. 68)

Paris, 1934a
Paris, "Les expositions de "Beaux-Arts" et de "La Gazette des Beaux-Arts," *Gauguin: Ses Amis l'école de Pont-Aven et l'Académie Julian*, February–March 1934. (van Gogh, cat. 112)

Paris, 1934b
Paris, Petit Palais, *Odilon Redon*, February–March 1934, no. 32. (Redon, cat. 83)

Paris, 1934c
Paris, Musée des Arts Décoratifs, *Les Artistes français en Italie de Poussin à Renoir*. May–July 1934. (Corot, cat. 20)

Paris, 1934d
Paris, Musée de l'Orangerie, *Daumier, peintures, aquarelles, dessins*, 1934. (Daumier, cat. 31)

Paris, 1934e
Paris, Galerie Marcel Bernheim, *Pissarro et ses fils*, 30 November–13 December 1934. (Pissarro, cat. 66).

Paris, 1935a
Paris, Association des Étudiants Protestants, *Exposition Frédéric Bazille, 1841–1870*, 1935. (Bazille, cat. 87)

Paris, 1935b
Paris, Galerie Durand-Ruel, *Claude Monet de 1865 à 1888*, November– December 1935. (Monet, cat. 86)

Paris, 1936a
Paris, Paul Rosenberg, *Exposition Seurat (1859–1891)*, 3–29 February 1936. (Seurat, cat. 113)

Paris, 1936b
Paris, Bernheim-Jeune, *Cent ans de théâtre, music-hall et cirque, dix-neuvième siècle, organisée au profit de la Société des Amis du Louvre*, 25 May–13 July 1936. (Daumier, cat. 31)

Paris, 1936c
Paris, Musée de l'Orangerie, *Cézanne*, May–October 1936. (Cézanne, cat. 79)

Paris, 1936d
Paris, Paul Rosenberg, *Exposition "Le grand siècle": Organisée au profit de la Société des amis du Louvre*, 15 June–11 July 1936. (Corot, cat. 20)

Paris, 1936e
Paris, Musée de l'Orangerie, *Corot*, 1936. (Corot, cats. 22, 24)

Paris, 1937
Paris, *Exposition internationale de 1937, Groupe I, Classe III*, June–October 1937. (van Gogh, cat. 111)

Paris, 1938a
Paris, Musée des Arts Décoratifs, *E. Vuillard*, May–July 1938. (Vuillard, cat. 132)

Paris, 1938b
Paris, La Gazette des Beaux-Arts, *La Peinture française du XIX siècle en Suisse. Exposition organisée par La Gazette des Beaux-Arts, avec le concours du Kunsthaus Musée des Beaux-Arts de Zurich, au profit de la Société helvetique de Bienfaisance en France*, 3 May–31 July 1938. (Courbet, cat. 41)

Paris, 1938c
Paris, Galerie Bernheim-Jeune, *Exposition de Renoir, portraitiste (1841–1919) organisé au profit de la Société des amis du Louvre*, 10 June–27 July 1938. (Renoir, cat. 91)

Paris, 1939a
Paris, Paul Rosenberg, *Exposition Cézanne (1839–1906), organisée à l'occasion de son centenaire au profit de l'oeuvre de l'allitement maternel*, 21 February–1 April 1939. (Cézanne, cat. 82)

Paris, 1939b
Paris, Galerie Daber, *Guigou*, 2–24 June 1939. (Guigou, cat. 71)

Paris, 1943
Paris, Galerie Parvillée, *L'École de Pont-Aven et les Nabis*, 11 May–11 June 1943. (Vuillard, cat. 131)

Paris, 1944
Paris, Galerie Maratier, *K.-X. Roussel*, 1944. (Roussel, cat. 125)

Paris, 1946
Paris, Musée des Arts Décoratifs, *Les Goncourt et leur temps*, 1946. (Forain, cat. 102)

Paris, 1947
Paris, Musée de l'Orangerie, *Vincent van Gogh*, January–March 1947. (van Gogh, cat. 108)

Paris, 1948
Paris, Galerie Charpentier, *Vuillard*, 1948. (Vuillard, cat. 133)

Paris, 1949
Paris, Galerie Alfred Daber, *Courbet: Exposition du 130e anniversaire de sa naissance au profit des Amis de Gustave Courbet*, May–June 1949. (Courbet, cat. 45)

Paris, 1950a
Paris, Galerie André Weil, *Pissarro*, 1–27 June 1950. (Pissarro, cat. 66)

Paris, 1950b
Paris, Galerie Wildenstein, *Bazille. Exposition organisée au profit du Musée de Montpellier*, June–July 1950. (Bazille, cat. 87)

Paris, 1951
Paris, Galerie Charpentier, *Nature mortes françaises du XVIIe siècle à nos jours*, 1951, no. 166. (Redon, cat. 83)

Paris, 1952a
Paris, Galerie des Beaux-Arts, *Claude Monet*, 19 June–17 July 1952 (traveled to The Hague, Gemeentemuseum, 24 July–22 September 1952. (Monet, cat. 84)

Paris, 1952b
Paris, Bibliothèque nationale, *J.-L. Forain, peintre, dessinateur et graveur*, June–September 1952. (Forain, cat. 102)

Paris, 1953
Paris, Galerie Charpentier, *Figures nues d'école français*, 28 May–30 September 1953. (Renoir, cat. 93)

Paris, 1954a
Paris, Galerie Beaux-Arts, *Chefs-d'oeuvre de Renoir dans les collections particulières françaises. Exposition organisée au profit de la Ligue contre le Taudis*, 10–27 June 1954. (Renoir, cat. 93)

Paris, 1954b
Paris, Musée national d'Art Moderne, *Le Dessin de Toulouse-Lautrec aux cubistes*, 1954. (Picasso, cat. 138)

Paris, 1955a
Paris, Musée national d'Art Moderne, *Bonnard, Vuillard et les Nabis (1888–1903)*, 8 June–2 October 1955. (Roussel, cat. 125; Sérusier, cat. 120; Vuillard, cat. 131)

Paris, 1955b
Paris, Musée du Petit Palais, *Gustave Courbet*, 1955. (Courbet, cat. 41)

Paris, 1956
Paris, Galerie Durand-Ruel, *Exposition Camille Pissarro, organisée au profit de la Société des amis du Louvre*, 26 June–14 September 1956. (Pissarro, cat. 64)

Paris, 1957
Paris, Musée Jacquemart-André, *Seurat*, November–December 1957. (Seurat, cat. 114)

Paris, 1958
Paris, Musée national d'Art Moderne, *De l'impressionnisme à nos jours: Aquarelles, pastels, gouaches*, 27 June 1958. (Forain, cat. 102)

Paris, 1959a
Paris, Galerie Durand-Ruel, *Émile Bernard, époque de Pont-Aven, 1883–1893*, 24 April–15 May 1959. (Bernard, cat. 127)

Paris, 1959b
Paris, Musée du Petit Palais, *De Gericault à Matisse: Chefs d'oeuvre français des collections suisses*, March–May 1959. (Courbet, cat. 41)

Paris, 1959c
Paris, Galerie Durand-Ruel, *Exposition Claude Monet 1840–1926, organisée au profit de la Société des amis du Louvre*, 22 May–30 September 1959. (Monet, cat. 84)

Paris, 1960
Paris, Musée Jacquemart-André, *Vincent van Gogh*, February–March 1960. (van Gogh, cat. 108)

Paris, 1961
Paris, Musée Jacquemart-André, *Exposition Berthe Morisot*, 1961. (Morisot, cat. 94)

Paris, 1962a
Paris, Galerie Daber, *Peinture 1830–1940: oeuvres de Delacroix à Maillol*, May 1962. (Courbet, cat. 42)

Paris, 1962b
Paris, Galerie Durand-Ruel, *C. Pissarro, 1830–1903, exposition organisée au profit de la Société des amis du Louvre*, 29 May–28 September 1962. (Pissarro, cat. 64)

Paris, 1962c
Paris, Musée du Louvre, *Figures de Corot*, June–September 1962. (Corot, cat. 23)

Paris, 1964
Paris, Galerie Philippe Reichenbach, *Forain–peintures, aquarelles, pastels*, 10–27 June 1964. (Forain, cat. 104)

Paris, 1966a
Paris, *Les Indépendants à Belle Époque. Rétrospective, 1895–1901*, 25 March–17 April 1966. (Lacombe, cat. 130)

Paris, 1966b
Paris, Musée Galliera, *60 Maîtres de Montmartre à Montparnasse, de Renoir à Chagall*, 1966. (Lacombe, cat. 130)

Paris, 1967
Paris, Musée de l'Orangerie, *Chefs-d'oeuvre des collections suisses de Manet à Picasso*, 1967. (Manet, cat. 68)

Paris, 1968
Paris, Galerie Schmit, *Exposition Lépine*, 15 May–15 June 1968. (Lépine, cat. 74)

Paris, 1970
Paris, Orangerie des Tuileries, *Maurice Denis*, 3 June–31 August 1970. (Denis, cat. 135)

Paris, 1971
Paris, Galerie Schmit, *Exposition Corot, 1796–1875*, 12 May–12 June 1971. (Corot, cat. 22)

Paris, 1972
Paris, Galerie Schmit, *Les Impressionnistes et leurs précurseurs*, 17 May–17 June 1972. (Morisot, cat. 94)

Paris, 1977
Paris, Grand Palais, *Gustave Courbet*, 1 October 1977–2 January 1978 (traveled to London, Royal Academy of Arts, 19 January–19 March 1978). (Courbet, cat. 41)

Paris, 1978a
Paris, Galerie La Cave, *L'École de Pont-Aven*, April–June 1978. (Meyer de Haan, cat. 105; Roy, cat. 118)

Paris, 1978b
Paris, Musée Marmottan, *Jean-Louis Forain, 1852–1931*, May–June 1978. (Forain, cats. 102, 104)

Paris, 1996
Paris, Grand Palais, *Corot, 1796–1875*, 28 February–27 May 1996 (traveled to Ottawa, National Gallery of Canada, 21 June–22 September 1996; New York, Metropolitan Museum of Art, 22 October 1996–19 January 1997. (Corot, cats. 20, 22)

Philadelphia, 1933
Philadelphia, Pennsylvania Museum of Art, *Manet and Renoir*, 29 November 1933–1 January 1934. (Manet, cat. 68)

Philadelphia, 1946
Philadelphia, Museum of Art, *Corot, 1796–1875*, 11 May–16 June 1946. (Corot, cat. 23)

Philadelphia, 1955
Philadelphia, Museum of Art, *Toulouse-Lautrec*, 29 October–11 December 1955 (traveled to Chicago, Art Institute, 2 January–15 February 1956). (Toulouse-Lautrec, cat. 124)

Philadelphia, 1959
Philadelphia, Museum of Art, *Gustave Courbet*, 17 December 1959–14 February 1960, no. 43, ill. (traveled to Boston, Museum of Fine Arts, 26 February–14 April 1960). (Courbet, cats. 42, 45)

Philadelphia, 1960
Philadelphia, Museum of Art, *The Pitcairn Collection*, Summer 1960. (van Gogh, cat. 111)

Philadelphia, 1966
Philadelphia, Museum of Art, *Édouard Manet, 1832–1883*, 3 November–11 December 1966 (traveled to Chicago, Art Institute, 13 January–19 February 1967) (Manet, cats. 67, 68, 69)

Philadelphia, 1967
Philadelphia, Museum of Art, *The Frances Vogel Spitzer Collection*, Summer 1967. (Cézanne, cat. 79)

Philadelphia, 1969
Philadelphia, Museum of Art, *Recent Acquisitions by the Norton Simon, Inc. Museum of Art*, 24 January–August 1969. (Cézanne, cat. 79; Monticelli, cat. 51; Renoir, cats. 88, 93; Seurat, cat. 114; Sisley, cat. 78)

Pittsburgh, 1936
Pittsburgh, Carnegie Institute, *A Survey of French Painting*, 2 April–14 May 1936. (Corot, cat. 23)

Pittsburgh, 1978
Pittsburgh, Carnegie Institute, Museum of Art, *Monticelli: His Contemporaries, His Influence*, 27 October 1978–7 January 1979 (traveled to Toronto, Art Gallery of Ontario, 27 January–11 March 1979; Washington, D.C., Corcoran Gallery of Art, 21 April–27 May 1979; Amsterdam, Rijksmuseum Vincent van Gogh, 28 June–2 September 1979). (Monticelli, cats. 50, 52)

Pomona, 1950
Pomona, Calif., Los Angeles County Fair, *Masters of Art from 1790 to 1950*, 15 September–1 October 1950. (Corot, cat. 23; Courbet, cat. 44)

Pont-Aven, 1961
Pont-Aven, Hôtel de Ville, *Gauguin et ses amis. Exposition organisé par l'Association Paul Gauguin*, 8 August–14 September 1961. (Redon, cat. 83)

Pont-Aven, 1968
Pont-Aven, Hôtel de Ville, *Centenaire d'Émile Bernard*, June–September 1968. (Bernard, cat. 127)

Portland, 1956
Portland, Oregon, Portland Art Museum, *Paintings from the Collection of Walter P. Chrysler, Jr.*, 2 March–15 April 1956 (traveled to Seattle Art Museum, 27 April–27 May 1956; San Francisco, California Palace of the Legion of Honor, 12 June–11 July 1956; Los Angeles County Museum, 26 July–26 August 1956; Minneapolis Institute of Arts, 8 September–7 October 1956; City Art Museum of St. Louis, 19 October–18 November 1956; Kansas City, William Rockhill Nelson Gallery of Art, 30 November 1956–2 January 1957; Detroit Institute of Arts 18 January–17 February 1957; Boston, Museum of Fine Arts, 7 March–14 April 1957). (Vuillard, cat. 132)

Portland, 1968
Portland, Oregon, Portland Art Museum, *Recent Acquisitions by the Norton Simon, Inc. Museum of Art*, 12 November 1968–20 April 1969. (Signac, cat. 119)

Prague, 1923
Prague, Obecní Dům, *Výstava Francouzského umění XIX. a XX. Století*, May–June 1923. (Prud'hon, cat. 6)

Princeton, 1972
Princeton, University Art Museum, *Selections from the Norton Simon, Inc. Museum of Art*, 3 December 1972–17 July 1974. (cats. 25, 39, 49, 51, 58, 75, 79, 93, 95, 111, 114, 119)

Quimper, 1932
Quimper, Musée des Beaux-Arts, *Exposition Artistique de Quimper*, 1932. (Sérusier, cat. 121)

Rotterdam, 1904
Rotterdam, Kunstzalen Oldenzeel, *Vincent van Gogh*, 10 November–15 December 1904. (van Gogh, cats. 108, 110)

Rouen, 1896
Rouen, Hôtel du Dauphin et d'Espagne, *Magnifique collection d'impressionistes dont 30 toiles de Renoir*, May 1896 (organized by Murer and exhibited in his home). (Renoir, cat. 92)

St. Louis, 1931
St. Louis, City Art Museum, *Loan Exhibition of French Painting, 1800–1880*, January 1931. (Manet, cat. 68)

Salisbury, 1957
Salisbury (Southern Rhodesia), The Rhodes National Gallery, *Rembrandt to Picasso*, 16 July–1 September 1957. (Gericault, Cat. 18)

San Bernardino, 1980
San Bernardino, California State College, Art Gallery, *Symbolism: Europe and America at the End of the Nineteenth Century*, 27 April–10 June 1980. (Anquetin, cat. 116; Denis, cat. 135)

San Francisco, 1934
San Francisco, California Palace of the Legion of Honor, *French Painting from the Fifteenth Century to the Present Day*, 8 June–8 July 1934. (Manet, cat. 68)

San Francisco, 1938
San Francisco, Museum of Art, *Impressionism: Paintings by Monet, Pissarro, Renoir, Seurat, Sisley*, Summer 1938. (Pissarro, cat. 63)

San Francisco, 1959
San Francisco, California Palace of the Legion of Honor, *The Collection of Mr. and Mrs. William Goetz*, 18 April–31 May 1959. (Monet, cat. 86)

San Francisco, 1973
San Francisco, California Palace of the Legion of Honor, *Three Centuries of French Art: Selections from The Norton Simon, Inc. Museum of Art and The Norton Simon Foundation*, 3 May 1973–15 June 1976. (cats. 21, 22, 30, 31, 43, 44, 45, 46, 47, 53, 68, 69, 74, 76, 78, 80, 81, 85, 87, 88, 91, 99, 108, 112, 124, 126)

San Francisco, 1974
San Francisco, California Palace of the Legion of Honor, *Three Centuries of French Art: Selections from The Norton Simon, Inc. Museum of Art and The Norton Simon Foundation*, 19 October 1974–15 June 1976. (cats. 20, 25, 39,

40, 48, 49, 51, 56, 58, 70, 71, 73, 75, 79, 83, 84, 93, 95, 107, 111, 114, 119, 123, 132)

South Hadley, 1966
South Hadley, Mass., Mount Holyoke, Dwight Art Memorial, *The Legacy of David and Ingres to Nineteenth Century Art: A Loan Exhibition Organized by the Mount Holyoke Friends of Art to Honor the Inauguration of the Amy M. Sacker Memorial Lectureship*, 12 October–13 November 1966. (Puvis de Chavannes, cat. 58)

Springfield, 1935
Springfield, Museum of Fine Arts, *French Painting from Cézanne to the Present*, 7 December 1935–5 January 1936. (van Gogh, cat. 110)

Tokyo, 1927
Tokyo, Sankyo Building, *Exposition d'art français contemporain au Japon*, July 1927. (Sérusier, cat. 121)

Tokyo, 1936
Tokyo, Société nationale des Beaux-Arts, *Émile Bernard*, April 1936. (Bernard, cat. 127)

Tokyo, 1961
Tokyo, *L'Exposition d'art français au Japon*, 1961–1962. (Roussel, cat. 125)

Tokyo, 1984
Tokyo, Isetan Museum of Art, *Rétrospective Camille Pissarro*, 9 March–9 April 1984 (traveled to Fukuoka Art Museum 25 April–20 May 1984; Kyoto Municipal Museum of Art, 26 May–1 July 1984). (Pissarro, cat. 64)

Toledo, 1937
Toledo, Museum of Art, *Paintings by French Impressionists and Post-Impressionists*, 7 November–12 December 1937. (Manet, cat. 68)

Venice, 1954
Venice, XXVII Biennale Internazionale d'Arte, *Courbet*, 1954. (Courbet, cat. 41)

Vevey, 1954
Vevey, Musée Jénisch, *Paris 1900*, 1954. (Roussel, cat. 125)

Vienna, 1906
Vienna, Galerie H. O. Miethke, *Vincent van Gogh*, January 1906. (van Gogh, cat. 111)

Vienna, 1909
Vienna, Secession, *Der Internationalen Kunstschau Wien 1909*, May–October 1909. (van Gogh, cat. 111)

Vienna, 1925
Vienna, Secession, *Die führenden Meister der französischen Kunst im XIX Jahrhundert*, March–April 1925. (van Gogh, cat. 111)

Washington, 1959
Washington, D.C., National Gallery of Art, *Masterpieces of Impressionist and Post-Impressionist Painting*, 25 April–24 May 1959. (Renoir, cat. 88)

Washington, 1966
Washington D.C., National Gallery of Art, *French Paintings from the Collections of Mr. and Mrs. Paul Mellon and Mrs. Mellon Bruce*, 17 March–1 May 1966. (Toulouse-Lautrec, cat. 123)

Winterthur, 1953
Winterthur, Kunstmuseum, *Théodore Géricault, 1791–1824*, 30 August–8 November 1953. (Gericault, cat. 18)

York, 1949
York, City Art Gallery, *Etty Centenary*, 13 November–31 December 1949. (Etty, cat. 13)

Zurich, 1935
Zurich, Kunsthaus, *Gustave Courbet*, 15 December 1935–31 March 1936. (Courbet, cat. 41)

Photograph Acknowledgments

Amiens, Musée de Picardie: fig. 48b.
Amsterdam, Van Gogh Museum (Vincent van Gogh Foundation): figs. 52a, 106b, 107a, 108a, 109a, 110c, 111a.
Ann Arbor, The University of Michigan Museum of Art: fig. 36a.
Baltimore Museum of Art: fig. 45d.
Basel, Kunstmuseum: figs. 65a, 127b.
Berlin, Nationalgalerie, Staatliche Museen, Bildarchiv Preussischer Kulturbesitz / Art Resource, NY: fig. 88d.
Bordeaux, Musée des Beaux Arts, © M.B.A. de Bordeaux; Photo: Lysiane Gauthier: fig. 56b
Boston, Isabella Stewart Gardner Museum: fig. 84b.
Boston, Museum of Fine Arts: fig. 22a.
Brussels, Musées royaux d'Art et d'Histoire: fig. 58a.
University of Cambridge, Fitzwilliam Museum: fig. 79c.
Cambridge, Mass., Harvard University Art Museums, Fogg Art Museum: fig. 111b.
Chartres, Musée des Beaux-Arts: fig. 6b.
The Art Institute of Chicago: figs. 33a, 67e, 68a, 68b, 70a, 73a, 75b, 82b, 119a, 120b, 122b, 132a.
Chicago, Private collection: fig. 23
The Cleveland Museum of Art: fig. 3a.
Cologne, Wallraf-Richartz Museum: figs. 43a, 68f, 132d.
Copenhagen, Ny Carlsberg Glyptotek; Photo: Ole Haupt: figs. 68d, 78b; 99a.
Copenhagen, Ordrupgaard; Photo: Pernille Klemp: fig. 99c.
Dallas Museum of Art: fig. 35a.
Detroit Institute of Arts: fig. 41b.
Dublin, National Gallery of Ireland: fig. 5b.
Duluth, Tweed Museum of Art, University of Minnesota: fig. 36b.
Edinburgh, National Gallery of Scotland: figs. 70c, 85b.
Fontenay-Tresigny, France, Photo courtesy of the Comité Quignon: fig. 100a
Fort Worth, Kimbell Art Museum; Photo: Michael Bodycomb, 2001: fig. 84a.
Geneva, Petit Palais, Musée d'Art Moderne: fig. 130a.
The Hague, Gemeentemuseum: fig. 88c.
The Hague, Royal Cabinet of Paintings Mauritshuis: fig. 32a.
The Hague, Museum Mesdag: fig. 46a.
Hamburg, Kunsthalle, Kupferstichkabinett: fig. 1a.
Hartford, CT., Wadsworth Atheneum Museum of Art: figs. 31b, 116a.
Kansas City, The Nelson-Atkins Museum of Art: fig. 99b; Photo: E. G. Schempf; fig. 14.
Lawrence, Kansas, Spencer Museum of Art: fig. 118b.
Liverpool, National Museums and Galleries on Merseyside, Walker Art Gallery: f ig. 133a.
London, Christie's Images: figs. 80c, 86b
London, Courtauld Institute of Art Gallery, The Samuel Courtauld Trust: figs. 81c, 82c, 114c.
London, Courtauld Institute, Witt Library, Archives of Thos. Agnew & Sons, Ltd.: figs. 73b-c.
London, Lefevre Fine Art Ltd.: fig. 20a
London, The National Gallery: figs. 13b, 29a, 46b, 53b, 80b.
London, Tate Gallery, / Art Resource, NY: fig. 64e
London, Victoria & Albert Museum: figs. 13a, 85d.
Los Angeles, County Museum of Art: fig. 2.
Los Angeles, The J. Paul Getty Museum: figs. 19, 21a–b, 22, 110b.
Los Angeles, University of Southern California, Fisher Gallery: fig. 36d.
Lyon, Musée des Beaux-Arts; Photo: © Studio Basset: fig. 51b.
Madrid, Museo del Prado: figs. 1b, 1d, 4a, 4b, 68c, 68e, 68g–68i.
Madrid, Museo de la Real Academia de Bellas Artes de San Fernando: fig. 2b.
Madrid, Museo Romantico: fig. 3b.
Madrid, Private Collection: fig. 3c.
Madrid, Carmen Thyssen-Bornemisza Collection on loan at the Museo Thyssen-Bornemisza: figs. 34a, 129a.
Melbourne, National Gallery of Victoria: fig. 20c.
Merion, Penn., The Barnes Foundation™ All Rights Reserved: figs. 81b, 91a.
The Minneapolis Institute of Arts: figs. 53a, 81a.
Montauban, Musée Ingres: fig. 11a.
Montpellier, Musée Fabre: figs. 14b, 41c, 87c, 87d.
Moscow, Pushkin Museum of Fine Arts: fig. 20b.
Munich, Bayerisches Staatsgemäldesammlungen, Alte Pinakothek: fig. 109b.
Munich, Bayerisches Staatsgemäldesammlungen, Neue Pinakothek: fig. 70d.
New York, The Metropolitan Museum of Art: figs. 23a, 45e, 67f, 69c, 76a, 78a, 79a, 98a, 101c, 112a, 123b.
New York, Museum of Modern Art: figs. 114a, 131b.
New York, Private Collection: fig. 86a.
Oberlin, Allen Memorial Art Museum: fig. 88e.
Oslo, National Gallery of Norway: fig. 88b.
Ottawa, National Gallery of Canada: fig. 2a.
Otterlo, Coll. Kröller-Muller Museum: figs. 107b, 108c, 108d, 108e.
Oxford, Ashmolean Museum: fig. 63a.
Paris, Archives Vuillard: fig. 132c.
Paris, Coll. Federation Mutualiste Parisienne: fig. 102b.
Paris, Musée Carnavalet: fig. 8b.
Paris, Musée du Louvre: figs. 6a, 7a, 11b, 18b, 21c, 38a, 52b, 113a, 117a, 132b.
Paris, Musée National d'Art Moderne, Centre Georges Pompidou: fig. 127a.
Paris, Musée de l'Orangerie: fig. 80a.
Paris, Musée d'Orsay: figs. 41a, 44b, 45a, 67a, 69a, 69b, 79b, 82a, 92b, 96a, 97b, 101a, 101b, 102c, 114b.
Paris, Panthéon: fig. 57a.
Paris, Private Collection: fig. 48a.
Pasadena, Jennifer Jones Simon Art Trust; Photo: Antoni E. Dolinski: cat. 15–16, 36, 38, 72, 91, 97, 101, 115, 128–129; Photo: Ken McKnight: cat. 19; Photo: Eddie Verlangieri: cat. 13, 32, 37, 66, 90, 118, 121.
Pasadena, Norton Simon Art Foundation; Photo: Antoni E. Dolinski: cat. 1–2, 5–8, 12, 17, 23–25, 33, 39, 41–42, 44, 46, 49, 51–52, 56, 58–60, 63, 67, 69, 71, 75, 77–79, 81–83, 87, 93–96, 99, 103–104, 106,

110-114, 116–117, 119, 122, 125, 127, 130–131, 133, 135, 138, figs. 31c, 82d, 87b, 110d; Photo: Los Angeles County Museum of Art Conservation Center: figs. 23b–c, 59c; Photo: Eddie Verlangieri: cat. 10, 14, 30–31, 62, 64, 92, 100, 102, figs. 1c, 1e, 14c, 52c, 64d–64e.

Pasadena, Norton Simon Museum; Photo: Antoni E. Dolinski: cat. 54, 55, 65, 137; Photo: Eddie Verlangieri: cat. 18.

Pasadena, The Norton Simon Foundation; Photo: Antoni E. Dolinski: cat. 3, 4, 9, 11, 20–22, 28, 34, 35, 40, 43, 45, 47–48, 50, 53, 68, 70, 74, 76, 80, 84–86, 88–89, 98, 105, 107–109, 120, 123–124, 126, 132, 134, 136, fig. 86c; Photo: Los Angeles County Museum of Art Conservation Center: fig. 108b; Photo: Eddie Verlangieri: cat. 26–27, 29, 57, 61.

Philadelphia Museum of Art: figs. 57b, 67g.

Musée de Pontoise: fig. 64a.

Quimper, Musée des Beaux-Arts: fig. 105a.

Memorial Art Gallery of the University of Rochester; Photo: James Via: figs. 39a, 84d.

Rotterdam, Museum Boijmans van Beuningen: fig. 67c.

Rouen, Musée des Beaux-Arts: figs. 14a, 125c.

St. Louis Museum of Art: fig. 45c.

St. Petersburg, State Hermitage Museum: figs. 9a, 51a, 135a.

Saint-Tropez, Musée de L'Annonciade: fig. 131a.

Fine Arts Museums of San Francisco: fig. 8a.

Shelburne, Vermont, The Shelburne Museum: fig. 67b.

Tarrytown, NY, Lyndhurst: fig. 59a.

Toledo Museum of Art: fig. 42a.

Tulsa, The Philbrook Museum of Art: fig. 36c.

United Kingdom, Stapleton Collection: fig. 26a.

Versailles, Musée Lambinet: fig. 130c.

Châteaux de Versailles et de Trianon: fig. 47b.

Wake Forest University Print Collection; Photo: Martine Sherrill: fig. 25a

Washington, D.C., National Gallery of Art: figs. 5a, 23d, 44a, 59b, 67d, 86d, 87a, 97a, 104a, 124a.

Washington, D.C., The Phillips Collection: figs. 31a, 92c, 105b.

Williamstown, Sterling and Francine Clark Art Institute: figs. 85c, 95a.

Zurich, Foundation Collection, E. G. Bürhle: fig. 56a.

Zurich, Kunsthaus: fig. 84c.

Additional Acknowledgments

Alinari / Art Resource, NY: fig. 13b.

The Bridgeman Art Library International: figs. 26, 30, 1a, 3b, 13a, 20a, 26a, 63a, 84b, 135a.

Bridgeman-Giraudon, Art Resource / NY: figs. 8b, 11a, 102b, 125c.

Foto Marburg / Art Resource, NY: fig. 106a

Erich Lessing / Art Resource, NY: figs. 6a, 11b, 18b, 20b, 38a, 41a, 41c, 67a, 68h, 69a, 69b, 79b, 80a, 82a, 87d, 97b, 101b, 102c, 113a, 117a, 130a, 132d.

Réunion des Musées Nationaux / Art Resource, NY: figs. 7a, 14a, 21c, 44b, 45a, 47b, 52b, 87c, 96a, 101a, 114b, 127a, 132b.

Scala / Art Resource, NY: figs. 2b, 4b, 9a, 51a, 68d-e, 68g, 68i, 92b, 114a.

Index